PF	Present value of a one-time cash flow
PV	Present value
P/E	Price-to-earnings multiple
r	Rate of return on a security; for fixed-income securities, r may denote the rate of interest for a particular period
r_f	The risk-free rate of interest
r_M	The rate of return on the market portfolio
ROE	Return on equity, incremental economic earnings per dollar reinvested in the firm
S_p	Reward-to-volatility ratio of a portfolio, also called Sharpe's measure; the excess expected return divided by the standard deviation
S_t	Stock price at time t
t	Time
T_p	Treynor's measure for a portfolio, excess expected return divided by beta
U	Utility function
V	Intrinsic value of a firm, the present value of future dividends per share
X	Exercise price of an option
y	Yield to maturity
α	Rate of return beyond the value that would be forecast from the market's return and the systematic risk of the security
β	Systematic or market risk of a security
ρ_{ij}	Correlation coefficient between returns on securities i and j
σ	Standard deviation
σ^2	Variance
$\mathrm{Cov}(r_i, r_j)$	Covariance between returns on securities i and j

INVESTMENTS

THE IRWIN SERIES IN FINANCE

Stephen A. Ross
Sterling Professor of Economics and Finance
Yale University
Consulting Editor

FINANCIAL MANAGEMENT

Block and Hirt
Foundations of Financial Management
Seventh Edition

Brooks
PC Fingame: *The Financial Management Decision Game*
Version 2.0

Bruner
Case Studies in Finance: *Managing for Corporate Value Creation*
Second Edition

Fruhan, Kester, Mason, Piper, and Ruback
Case Problems in Finance
Tenth Edition

Harrington
Corporate Financial Analysis: *Decisions in a Global Environment*
Fourth Edition

Helfert
Techniques of Financial Analysis
Eighth Edition

Higgins
Analysis for Financial Management
Fourth Edition

Kallberg and Parkinson
Corporate Liquidity: *Management and Measurement*

Nunnally and Plath
Cases in Finance

Ross, Westerfield, and Jaffe
Corporate Finance
Third Edition

Ross, Westerfield, and Jordan
Essentials of Corporate Finance

Ross, Westerfield, and Jordan
Fundamentals of Corporate Finance
Third Edition

Schary
Cases in Financial Management

Stonehill and Eiteman
Finance: *An International Perspective*

White
Financial Analysis with an Electronic Calculator
Second Edition

INVESTMENTS

Bodie, Kane, and Marcus
Essentials of Investments
Second Edition

Bodie, Kane, and Marcus
Investments
Third Edition

Cohen, Zinbarg, and Zeikel
Investment Analysis and Portfolio Management
Fifth Edition

Hirt and Block
Fundamentals of Investment Management
Fifth Edition

Lorie, Dodd, and Kimpton
The Stock Market: *Theories and Evidence*
Second Edition

Morningstar, Inc. and Remaley
U.S. Equities OnFloppy
Annual Edition

Shimko
The Innovative Investor
Version 3.0

FINANCIAL INSTITUTIONS AND MARKETS

Rose
Commercial Bank Management: *Producing and Selling Financial Services*
Third Edition

Rose
Money and Capital Markets: *The Financial System in an Increasingly Global Economy*
Fifth Edition

Rose
Readings on Financial Institutions and Markets
1995–96 Edition

Rose and Kolari
Financial Institutions: *Understanding and Managing Financial Services*
Fifth Edition

Saunders
Financial Institutions Management: *A Modern Perspective*

REAL ESTATE

Berston
California Real Estate Principles
Seventh Edition

Berston
California Real Estate Practice
Sixth Edition

Brueggeman and Fisher
Real Estate Finance and Investments
Tenth Edition

Smith and Corgel
Real Estate Perspectives: *An Introduction to Real Estate*
Second Edition

FINANCIAL PLANNING AND INSURANCE

Allen, Melone, Rosenbloom, and VanDerhei
Pension Planning: *Pensions, Profit-Sharing, and Other Deferred Compensation Plans*
Seventh Edition

Crawford
Law and the Life Insurance Contract
Seventh Edition

Crawford
Life and Health Insurance Law
LOMA Edition

Hirsch and Donaldson
Casualty Claim Practice
Fifth Edition

Kapoor, Dlabay, and Hughes
Personal Finance
Fourth Edition

Kellison
Theory of Interest
Second Edition

Rokes
Human Relations in Handling Insurance Claims
Second Edition

INVESTMENTS

Third Edition

ZVI BODIE

Boston University

ALEX KANE

University of California, San Diego

ALAN J. MARCUS

Boston College

IRWIN

Chicago • Bogotá • Boston • Buenos Aires • Caracas
London • Madrid • Mexico City • Sydney • Toronto

To our families with love and gratitude.

IRWIN Concerned about Our Environment

In recognition of the fact that our company is a large end-user of fragile yet replenishable resources, we at IRWIN can assure you that every effort is made to meet or exceed Environmental Protection Agency (EPA) recommendations and requirements for a "greener" workplace.

To preserve these natural assets, a number of environmental policies, both companywide and department-specific, have been implemented. From the use of 50% recycled paper in our textbooks to the printing of promotional materials with recycled stock and soy inks to our office paper recycling program, we are committed to reducing waste and replacing environmentally unsafe products with safer alternatives.

Senior sponsoring editor: James M. Keefe
Developmental editor: Amy K. Winston
Project editors: Ethel Shiell/Amy E. Lund
Production supervisor: Laurie Kersch
Designers: Heidi J. Baughman/Ellen Pettengell
Cover illustration: J. W. Stewart
Art Studio: Weimer Graphics, Inc.
Assistant manager, graphics: Charlene R. Breeden
Compositor: Weimer Graphics, Inc.
Typeface: 10/12 Times Roman
Printer: R. R. Donnelley & Sons Company

Times Mirror
Higher Education Group

Library of Congress Cataloging-in-Publication Data

Bodie, Zvi.
Investments / Zvi Bodie, Alex Kane, Alan J. Marcus. — 3rd ed.
p. cm.
Includes bibliographical references and indexes.
ISBN 0–256–14638–1
1. Investments. 2. Portfolio management. I. Kane, Alex.
II. Marcus, Alan J. III. Title.
HG4521.B564 1986
332.63'2—dc20 95–23345

Printed in the United States of America
1 2 3 4 5 6 7 8 9 0 DO 2 1 0 9 8 7 6 5

About the Authors

Zvi Bodie
Boston University

Zvi Bodie is Professor of Finance at Boston University School of Management. He holds a Ph.D. from the Massachusetts Institute of Technology and has served as visiting professor at Harvard University and M.I.T. He currently serves as a member of the Global Financial System Group at Harvard University and of the Pension Research Council at the University of Pennsylvania. He has published widely on pension finance, the management of financial guarantees in both the private and public sector, and investment strategy in an inflationary environment. His edited volumes include *Pensions and the Economy: Sources, Uses and Limitations of Data; Pensions in the U.S. Economy; Issues in Pension Economics;* and *Financial Aspects of the U.S. Pension System.* His research on pensions has focused on the funding and investment policies of private pension plans and on public policies such as the provision of government pension insurance. He has consulted on pension policy for the U.S. Department of Labor, the State of Israel, and Bankers Trust Co.

Alex Kane
University of California, San Diego

Alex Kane is professor of finance and economics at the Graduate School of International Relations and Pacific Studies at the University of California, San Diego. He was Visiting Professor at the Faculty of Economics, University of Tokyo; Graduate School of Business, Harvard; Kennedy School of Government, Harvard; and Research Associate, National Bureau of Economic Research. An author of many articles in finance and management journals, Professor Kane's research is mainly in corporate finance, portfolio management, and capital markets, most recently in the measurement of market volatility and pricing of options. Professor Kane is the developer of the *International Simulation Laboratory (ISL)* for training and experimental research in executive decision making.

Alan J. Marcus

Boston College

Alan Marcus is Professor of Finance in the Wallace E. Carroll School of Management at Boston College. He received his Ph.D. in Economics from MIT in 1981. Professor Marcus recently has been a Visiting Professor at the Athens Laboratory of Business Administration and at MIT's Sloan School of Management and has served as a Research Associate at the National Bureau of Economic Research. He also is the director of the Chartered Financial Analysts Review Program at Boston College. Professor Marcus has published widely in the fields of capital markets and portfolio management, with an emphasis on applications of futures and options pricing models. His consulting work has ranged from new product development to provision of expert testimony in utility rate proceedings. He also spent two years at the Federal Home Loan Mortgage Corporation (Freddie Mac) where he developed models of mortgage pricing and credit risk.

Preface

In teaching and practice, the field of investments has experienced many changes over the last two decades. This is due in part to an abundance of newly designed securities, in part to the creation of new trading strategies that would have been impossible without concurrent advances in computer technology, and in part to rapid advances in the theory of investments that have come out of the academic community. In no other field, perhaps, is the transmission of theory to real-world practice as rapid as is now commonplace in the financial industry. These developments place new burdens on practitioners and teachers of investments far beyond what was required only a short while ago.

Investments is intended primarily as a textbook for courses in investment analysis. Our guiding principle has been to present the material in a framework that is organized by a central core of consistent fundamental principles. We make every attempt to strip away unnecessary mathematical and technical detail, and we have concentrated on providing the intuition that may guide students and practitioners as they confront new ideas and challenges in their professional lives.

Our primary goal is to present material of practical value, but all three of us are active researchers in the science of financial economics and find virtually all of the material in this book to be of great intellectual interest. Fortunately, we think, there is no contradiction in the field of investments between the pursuit of truth and the pursuit of money. Quite the opposite. The capital asset pricing model, the arbitrage pricing model, the efficient markets hypothesis, the option-pricing model, and the other centerpieces of modern financial research are as much intellectually satisfying subjects of scientific inquiry as they are of immense practical importance for the sophisticated investor.

Since 1983 we have participated in annual review programs for candidates from all over the world preparing for the Chartered Financial Analyst examinations. From its inception in 1963 the CFA program has come to symbolize high standards of professionalism in the investment community. The CFA curriculum represents the consensus of a committee of distinguished scholars and practitioners regarding the core of knowledge required by the investment professional.

This book has benefited from our continuing CFA experience in two ways. First, we have incorporated in the text much of the content of the readings and other study materials in the official CFA curriculum. As a result, the book includes some material not found in most other investments texts. Most notably, Part VIII presents material on portfolio management principles and techniques that stems largely from the CFA curriculum. Second, we have included questions from CFA examinations in the end-of-chapter problem sets throughout the book. The number of CFA questions has been greatly expanded in this edition.

Realistic Presentation of Modern Portfolio Theory

The exposition of modern portfolio theory in this text differs from its presentation in all other major investments texts in that we develop the basic model starting with a risk-free asset such as a bank certificate of deposit or a U.S. Treasury bill, and a single risky asset such as a common stock mutual fund.[1] Not until later do we add other risky assets. Other texts develop the model by first assuming that the investor has to choose from two risky assets; only later do they introduce the possibility of investing in a risk-free asset. Ultimately both approaches reach the same end point, which is a model in which there are many risky assets in addition to a risk-free asset.

We think our approach is better for two important reasons. First, it corresponds to the actual procedure that most individual investors follow. Typically, one starts with all of one's money invested in a bank account and only then considers how much to invest in something riskier that may offer the prospect of a higher expected return. The next logical step is to consider the addition of other risky assets such as real estate or gold, which requires determining whether the benefits of such increased diversification are worth the additional transaction costs involved in including them in one's portfolio.

The second advantage of our approach is that it vastly simplifies exposition of the mathematics for deriving the menu of risk-return combinations open to the investor. Portfolio optimization techniques are mathematically complex, ultimately requiring a computer. Anything that can help to simplify their presentation should thus be welcome. In short, we believe our approach is both more realistic and analytically simpler than the conventional one.

New in the Third Edition

The outline of this edition of *Investments* is essentially the same as in the second edition. Many of the major innovations relate to enhanced coverage of timely topics. What follows is a brief summary of the more important changes in this edition. In addition to the specific changes cited below, we direct the reader to the extensive additions to and changes in the boxed material containing timely readings from the financial press, including *The Wall Street Journal*, *Business Week*, and *The Economist*. We

[1]We define and discuss mutual funds in Chapter 3. For now it is sufficient to know that a common stock mutual fund is a diversified portfolio of stocks in which an investor can invest as much money as desired.

have also added to the collection of CFA problems presented with the problem sets at the end of each chapter.

Market Structure

We update our treatment of market microstructure with additional discussion of the competition between the NYSE and Nasdaq markets, and new coverage of the recent controversy over trading practices in the Nasdaq market. We also expand our coverage of international differences in market structure.

Risk and Return

We have updated our discussion of empirical evidence on the risk-return relationship; in particular, we have updated our treatment of the "anomalies" literature (for example, the book-to-market effect), with emphasis on the interpretation of these results.

Fixed-Income Markets

Chapter 13 on bond pricing has been reorganized and now contains more extensive coverage of different measures of bond yields and returns, for example, yield to call, realized compound yield, and so on. Chapter 15 on fixed-income portfolio management now contains coverage of fixed-income derivatives such as inverse floaters or stripped mortgage-backed securities that have been created through financial engineering.

Security Analysis

Chapter 16 on macroeconomic and industry analysis has been expanded to provide more coverage of international issues as well as greatly enhanced coverage of industry analysis, industry lifecycles, and industry structure. Chapter 17 on equity valuation analysis contains an expanded discussion of the interpretation of the price-earnings ratio. A discussion of comparability issues in financial statements across national boundaries has been added to Chapter 18 on Financial Statement Analysis.

Derivative Markets

An introduction to new exotic options has been added to Chapter 19. Chapter 22 now includes more material on the valuation of swaps and credit risk in swaps markets. (Interest-rate swaps as asset allocation tools also receive a new treatment in Chapter 15.)

Players and Strategies

An extensive discussion of the proposition that stocks are less risky in the long-run has been added as an appendix to Chapter 27. Also, please note that the material on

"Managing Investment Companies," formerly Chapter 29, is now included in the Instructor's Manual.

Recent Developments in Investments Research

We have introduced a new chapter (Chapter 29) that is devoted to a discussion of recent developments in investments research. This chapter introduces and summarizes innovative research that we believe may have important implications for practitioners in the not-too-distant future. In this edition, we focus on statistical modeling of stock market volatility, new research on the risk-return relationship, and an innovative approach to option pricing.

Pedagogical Features

This book contains several features designed to make it easy for the student to understand, absorb, and apply the concepts and techniques presented. Each chapter begins with an **overview,** which describes the material to be covered, and ends with a detailed **summary,** which recapitulates the main ideas presented.

Learning investments is in many ways like learning a new language. Before one can communicate, one must learn the basic vocabulary. To facilitate this process, all new terms are presented in **boldface** type the first time we use them, and at the end of each chapter there is a **Key Terms** section listing the most important new terms introduced in that chapter. A **Glossary** of all of the terms used appears at the end of the book.

Boxes containing short articles from business periodicals are included throughout the book. We think they enliven the text discussion with examples from the world of current events. The article in the Prologue from *Business Week* on the invasion of Wall Street by so-called rocket scientists is an example. We chose the boxed material on the basis of relevance, clarity of presentation, and consistency with good sense.

A unique feature of this book is the inclusion of **Concept Checks** in the body of the text. These self-test questions and problems enable the student to determine whether he or she has understood the preceding material and to reinforce that understanding. Detailed solutions to all these questions are provided in Appendix B at the end of the book.

These Concept Checks may be approached in a variety of ways. They may be skipped altogether in a first reading of the chapter with no loss in continuity. They can then be answered with any degree of diligence and application upon the second reading. Finally, they can serve as models for solving the end-of-chapter problems assigned by the instructor.

Each chapter also contains a list of **Selected Readings** that are annotated to guide the student toward useful sources of additional information in specific subject areas.

The **end-of-chapter problems** progress from the simple to the complex. We strongly believe that practice in solving problems is a critical part of learning investments, so we have provided lots of problems. Many are taken from CFA examinations and therefore represent the kinds of questions that professionals in the field believe are relevant to the "real world." These problems are identified by an icon in the text margin.

Ancillary Materials

The Innovative Investor

The Innovative Investor, by David Shimko, is now available in a DOS format, which uses Lotus 1-2-3 templates, and both Windows and DOS formats, which use Excel spreadsheets. This software is designed to provide students quick access to difficult financial calculations, in applications covering stocks, bonds, callables and convertibles, options, futures, asset allocation, and portfolio performance valuation. All spreadsheets come with comprehensive analysis and automatic graphing and printing capabilities. The "real-world" applications presented in The Innovative Investor are designed to enhance the student's understanding of the concepts and techniques presented in the text.

U.S. Equities on Floppy—Educational Version

U.S. Equities on Floppy is a fundamental database and analysis system of approximately 6,000 companies with common stock trading on the NYSE, AMEX, and Nasdaq National Market exchanges. This software can be used to solve selected end-of-chapter problems in Chapters 12, 16, 17, and 18. These problems are clearly identified with the U.S. Equities on Floppy icon. This software can be packaged with the textbook. For additional information, please contact your local Irwin representative.

Instructor's Manual

The Instructor's Manual, prepared by Linda J. Martin at Arizona State University, has been revised and improved in this edition. Each chapter includes a chapter overview, a review of learning objectives, an annotated chapter outline, and teaching tips and insights ("Perspectives"). In addition, the Instructor's Manual includes a total of 175 transparency masters that can be prepared as acetates for lecture use.

Test Bank

The Test Bank to accompany *Investments*, third edition, has been revised to increase both the quantity and level of difficulty of the multiple-choice questions. Short answer essay questions are also provided for each chapter to further test student comprehension and critical thinking abilities. The test bank is also available in computerized version. Test bank disks are available in DOS, Windows, and Macintosh-compatible formats.

Solutions Manual

The Solutions Manual includes a detailed solution to each end-of-chapter problem. This manual is available for packaging with the text. Please contact your local Irwin representative for further details on how to order the Solutions manual/textbook package.

Acknowledgments

The development of this book involved the efforts of many dedicated professionals. Almost 250 academic colleagues who teach investments responded to a detailed market survey in the spring of 1994. That input provided useful information about the focus and structure of the modern investments course and afforded a unique insight into the needs of both students and instructors of investments. We would like to thank each survey respondent again for providing us with such important information.

Throughout the development of this text, experienced instructors have provided critical feedback and suggestions for improvement. These individuals deserve a special thanks for their valuable insights and contributions. The following instructors played a vital role in the development of this and previous editions of *Investments*:

Scott Besley
University of Florida

John Binder
University of Illinois at Chicago

Anna Craig
Emory University

David C. Distad
University of California at Berkeley

Michael C. Ehrhardt
University of Tennessee at Knoxville

David Ellis
Texas A & M University

Jeremy Goh
Washington University

Mahmoud Haddad
Wayne State University

Robert G. Hansen
Dartmouth College

Joel Hasbrouck
New York University

Andrea Heuson
University of Miami

Shalom J. Hochman
University of Houston

A. James Ifflander
A. James Ifflander and Associates

Robert Jennings
Indiana University

Susan D. Jordan
University of Missouri at Columbia

G. Andrew Karolyi
Ohio State University

Josef Lakonishok
University of Illinois at Champaign/Urbana

Dennis Lasser
Binghamton University

Christopher K. Ma
Texas Tech University

Anil K. Makhija
University of Pittsburgh

Steven Mann
University of South Carolina

Deryl W. Martin
Tennessee Technical University

Jean Masson
University of Ottawa

Rick Meyer
University of South Florida

Don B. Panton
University of Texas at Arlington

Leonard Rosenthal
Bentley College

Eileen St. Pierre
University of Northern Colorado

Anthony Sanders
Ohio State University

John Settle
Portland State University

Edward C. Sims
Western Illinois University

Keith V. Smith
Purdue University

Patricia B. Smith
University of New Hampshire

Laura T. Starks
University of Texas

Jack Treynor
Treynor Capital Management

Charles A. Trzincka
SUNY Buffalo

Simon Wheatley
University of Chicago

James Williams
California State University at Northridge

Tony R. Wingler
University of North Carolina at Greensboro

Hsiu-Kwang Wu
University of Alabama

Thomas J. Zwirlein
University of Colorado at Colorado Springs

For granting us permission to include many of their examination questions in the text, we are grateful to the Institute of Chartered Financial Analysts.

Much credit is due also to the development and production team: our special thanks go to Jim Keefe, Senior Sponsoring Editor; Amy Winston, Developmental Editor; Ethel Shiell, Project Editor; and Laurie Kersch, Production Supervisor.

Finally, we thank Judy, Hava, and Sheryl, who contributed to the book with their support and understanding.

Zvi Bodie
Alex Kane
Alan J. Marcus

Contents in Brief

Contents

List of Boxes

INVESTMENTS

Part I

Introduction

Prologue

THIS IS A BOOK ABOUT INVESTING IN SECURITIES SUCH AS STOCKS, BONDS, OPTIONS, AND FUTURES CONTRACTS. It is intended to provide an understanding of how to analyze these securities, how to determine whether they are appropriate for inclusion in your **investment portfolio** (the set of securities you choose to hold), and how to buy and sell them.

We can usefully divide the process of investing, both in theory and in practice, into two parts: security analysis and portfolio management. **Security analysis** is the attempt to determine whether an individual security is correctly valued in the marketplace; that is, it is the search for mispriced securities. **Portfolio management** is the process of combining securities into a portfolio tailored to the investor's preferences and needs, monitoring that portfolio, and evaluating its performance. This book is intended to provide a thorough treatment of both parts of the investment process.

This book is designed first and foremost to impart knowledge of practical value to anyone interested in becoming an investment professional or a sophisticated private investor. It provides a lot of institutional detail, but of necessity it also contains a lot of theory. It is impossible to be a sophisticated investor or investment professional today without a sound basis in valuation theory, modern portfolio theory, and option pricing theory at the level presented in the following chapters.

THE MAIN THEMES OF INVESTMENTS

The Risk-Return Trade-off

One simple strategy for an investor to pursue is to keep all of his or her money invested in a bank account. This strategy has a number of advantages. It is safe, and it requires no expertise and little effort on the part of the investor.

However, if an investor is willing to consider the possibility of taking on some risk, there is the potential reward of higher expected returns. A considerable part of this book is devoted to exploring the nature of this **risk-return trade-off** and the principles of rational portfolio choice associated with it. The approach we present is known as **modern portfolio theory (MPT).**

The main organizing principle of MPT is **efficient diversification.** The basic idea is that any investor who is averse to risk, that is, who requires a higher expected return in order to increase exposure to risk, will be made better off by reorganizing the portfolio so as to increase its expected return without taking on additional risk.

In this book we devote considerable space to explaining the principles of efficient diversification and applying them to the issue of **asset allocation.** Asset allocation is the choice of how much to invest in each of the broad asset classes—stocks, bonds, cash, real estate, foreign securities, *derivative securities,*[1] gold, and possibly others—to achieve the best portfolio given the investor's objectives and constraints.

Active versus Passive Management

We define **passive management** as a strategy of holding a well-diversified portfolio of generic security types without attempting to outperform other investors through superior market forecasting or superior ability to find mispriced securities. Depending on the approach used to find the best portfolio mix, passive management can be quite sophisticated. Indeed, as we show in our exposition of the asset allocation decision, efficient diversification can be a rather complex process, requiring many inputs and the aid of a computer.

Active management can take two forms: market timing and security selection. The most popular kind of **market timing** is trying to time the stock market, increasing one's commitment to stocks when one is "bullish" (when one thinks the market will do relatively well), and moving out of stocks when one is "bearish." But market timing is potentially just as profitable in the markets for fixed-income securities, where the name of the game is forecasting interest rates. Successful market timing, whether in the market for stocks or for bonds, requires superior forecasting ability.

Security selection is the attempt to find mispriced securities and to improve one's risk-return trade-off by concentrating on such securities. Security selection can involve both buying those securities believed to be underpriced and selling those believed to be overpriced. Successful security selection requires the sacrifice of some amount of diversification.

A large body of empirical evidence supports a theory called the **efficient markets hypothesis (EMH),** which among other things says that active management of both types should not be expected to work for very long. The basic reasoning behind the EMH is that in a competitive financial environment successful trading strategies tend to "self- destruct." Bargains may exist for brief periods, but with so many talented high-

---

[1] Derivative securities include options and futures contracts. They are described briefly in Chapter 2 and then discussed in much greater detail in Part VI.

ly paid analysts scouring the markets for them, by the time you or I "discover" them, they are no longer bargains.

To be sure, there are some extremely successful investors, but according to the EMH one can account for some or all of them on the basis of luck rather than skill. And even if their success in the past derived from skill at finding some extraordinary bargains, the EMH would say their chances to continue to find more in the future are slight. Even the legendary Benjamin Graham,[2] the father of modern security analysis and the teacher of some of today's investment giants, has said that the job of finding true bargains has become difficult if not impossible in today's competitive environment. In part, this situation is testimony to the success Graham and his followers have had in teaching the principles of fundamental analysis.

Our view is that markets are nearly efficient. Nevertheless, even in this competitive environment profit opportunities may exist for especially diligent and creative investors. This idea motivates our treatment of active portfolio management in Part VII, which is a section unique to this textbook.

Equilibrium Pricing Relationships

A fascinating feature of financial markets, and one that is not at all apparent to the untrained observer, is that the prices of securities must often have a specific relationship to each other, because if the relationships are violated then market forces will come into play to restore them. Financial economists refer to these as *equilibrium pricing relationships,* and in this text we explain them in detail.

Perhaps the best known of these relationships are the following:

1. The security market line (expected return–beta) relationship.
2. The put-call parity relationship.
3. The Black-Scholes option pricing model.
4. The spot-futures parity relationship.
5. The international interest rate parity relationship.

These relationships are more than just intellectually pleasing theoretical constructs. In most cases, if they are violated the first investors to discover the violation have opportunities for large profits with little or no risk. For example, the recent practice of *index arbitrage* is primarily a systematic method of profiting from violations of equilibrium pricing relationships in the market for the Standard & Poor's 500 stock-index futures contract.

A well-trained investment professional must not only be aware of these equilibrium relationships, but also must understand why they exist and how to profit from any violation of them. We have tried to provide the basis for this knowledge throughout the book, as well as in the specific chapters in which these relationships are presented and explained.

[2] We will have much more to say about Graham and his ideas about investing in Chapter 18.

The Use of Options and Futures Contracts in Implementing Investment Strategy

In today's securities markets, there are a variety of ways sophisticated investors can tailor the set of possible investment outcomes to their specific knowledge or preferences regarding security returns. The emergence of markets for so-called derivative securities such as options and futures contracts has made it possible to implement strategies unheard of only a few short years ago. Perhaps in no other area of investments is the recent business school graduate at a greater advantage over the investment veteran who studied investments several years ago.

Probably the most well known of these strategies is *portfolio insurance.* There are a variety of ways an investor can combine stocks and/or bonds with derivative securities to eliminate the possibility of loss of principal while preserving much of the upside potential of an investment in the stock market. These securities and strategies are here to stay. The investment professional must understand and master them if he or she is to avoid technological obsolescence.

In our chapters on derivative securities we explain in some detail and with a minimum of mathematics the use of options and futures in implementing portfolio insurance and other investment strategies.

Text Organization

The text has nine parts, which are fairly independent and may be studied in a variety of sequences. Part I is introductory and contains much institutional material. Part II contains the core of modern portfolio theory as it relates to optimal portfolio selection. Part III contains the core of modern portfolio theory as it relates to the equilibrium structure of expected rates of return on risky assets. It builds on the material in Part II and therefore must be preceded by it.

Part IV, which is on the analysis and valuation of fixed-income securities, is the first of three parts on security valuation. Part V is devoted to equity securities. Part VI covers derivative assets such as options, futures contracts, and convertible securities.

Part VII is devoted to active portfolio management and performance measurement. It has as a prerequisite the material on MPT in Part II. Part VIII is about the process of portfolio management.

Other Features

A unique feature is the inclusion of self-test questions and problems within the following chapters. These Concept Checks are designed to provide the student with a means for determining whether he or she has understood the preceding material and for reinforcing that understanding. Detailed solutions to all Concept Checks are provided at the end of the book.

These in-chapter questions may be used in a variety of ways. They may be skipped altogether in a first reading of the chapter with no loss in continuity. They can then be done with any degree of diligence and intensity upon the second reading. Finally, they can serve as models for solving the end-of-chapter problems.

The end-of-chapter problems progress from the simple to the complex. We strongly believe that practice in solving problems is a critical part of learning investments, so we have provided many opportunities. Many are taken from past Chartered Financial Analyst examinations and therefore represent the kinds of questions that professionals in the field believe are relevant to the "real world." The *Study Guide,* which accompanies the text, provides many more practice problems with solutions.

The Investments Field and Career Opportunities

As with any other field of scientific inquiry, the theory of investments is constantly changing and, we believe, advancing. In that sense we too are always learning something new. What makes it especially exciting is that the lag between discovery and application in investments is extraordinarily short. For example, the Black-Scholes option pricing formula and the dynamic hedging strategy that is its mainspring were developed in 1973.[3] Just a few years later practitioners were busy applying it on the Chicago Board Options Exchange.

Far from being an exception, the example of the Black-Scholes formula has become the paradigm for the relationship between the academic and applied worlds in investments. Indeed, Fischer Black himself is an example of this development, moving from a professorship at MIT's Sloan School of Management to a partnership in the investment banking firm of Goldman Sachs.

We believe that the field of investments offers great opportunities for careers that are both fascinating and lucrative, but the competition is fierce. A mastery of the material in this text will, we hope, give you a competitive advantage.

Key Terms

Investment portfolio
Security analysis
Portfolio management
Risk-return trade-off
Modern portfolio theory
Efficient diversification
Asset allocation
Passive management
Active management
Market timing
Security selection
Efficient markets hypothesis

[3]See Fischer Black and M. Scholes, "The Pricing of Options and Corporate Liabilities," *Journal of Political Economy,* May–June 1973.

Rocket Scientists Are Revolutionizing Wall Street

Former Academics Are Pioneering Ways to Make More Money with Less Risk

Before coming to Wall Street in 1980, Henry Nicholas Hanson was a physicist at Brown University, where he researched the properties of helium at low temperatures. Now Hanson, a Salomon Brothers vice president, is one of Wall Street's leading authorities on stock-index futures.

Stanley Diller is a former economics professor. In the mid-1970s, at the age of 40, he started a bond research department at Goldman, Sachs & Co. Now at Bear Stearns & Co., Diller is said to earn at least $500,000 a year and tells his colleagues: "Never call me doctor. It would cut my salary by 75 percent."

Fischer Black, one of the nation's leading finance academics, left a tenured full professorship at Massachusetts Institute of Technology in early 1984 to become a vice president at Goldman Sachs. Black is internationally known for developing an option-pricing model that traders use to value stock options.

The three men represent Wall Street's new breed, known as the "rocket scientists" or "quants." These former academics, trained in mathematics, and the whiz kids, most from the physical sciences, who have come after them, are revolutionizing the stock and bond markets. They are the brains behind program trading—the controversial use of stock-index futures to lock in high risk-free yields. They have introduced a plethora of new financial products, including interest rate swaps, zero-coupon bonds, and new types of mortgage-backed securities. In the process, they've made hundreds of millions of dollars for the brokerage houses that employ them and for the firms' clients.

Fischer Black

Today the top firms employ more than 1,000 rocket scientists and usually pay them well over six figures. Indeed, the Wall Street whiz kids—just like top traders and salesmen—can become millionaires in only a few years. "There is no other way a technical guy is going to make that kind of money," says Diller.

Pigeonholed

The first rocket scientists on Wall Street were cut from a different mold. In the early 1970s they and their computer programs were used for back-office functions such as data processing to handle increased trading volume. Although they vastly increased the efficiency of the brokerage industry, they were pigeonholed by top management.

But by the end of that decade, as interest rates began fluctuating wildly and the deregulation of the financial markets was picking up steam, Wall Street houses turned to the quants in increasing numbers. The firms desperately needed ways to protect against the calamitous movements in bond prices that could wipe out their capital. To their horror, they found that the old way of hedging one bond against another of a different maturity was often producing big losses. Rocket scientists solved the problem using "'convexity," a tool from calculus that describes the behavior of bond prices when interest rates move violently. They also designed new hedges using options and futures contracts.

Now the quants are in the mainstream of virtually all activity in the markets. They helped develop the hottest game on Wall Street: program trading. To play, a brokerage house or institutional client usually buys stocks that make up an index, such as the Standard & Poor's 500-stock index, and simultaneously sells short a matching futures contract that generally commands a premium over the underlying stocks. Risk-free profits come because on expiration the value of the futures contract must equal the value of the stock index.

(Continued)

The trick is to buy as few stocks as possible, both to minimize transaction costs and to make sure that both sides of the trade are done at the same time. Yet the basket of securities must still track the entire index. For example, the rocket scientists showed the program traders how they can approximate the S&P 500 with 95 percent accuracy by buying only about half the stocks in the index.

The quants are also involved in other types of buy programs that have nothing to do with risk-free arbitrage. They are using their computers to decide when to buy as many as 2,000 different stocks at a time worth hundreds of millions of dollars. Doing such trades all at once saves transaction fees and reduces the risk that the market will change before the trade can be accomplished. "Clients call us, and we will commit to buy or sell an entire portfolio at a given price," says Arthur S. Estey, a vice president at Shearson Lehman Brothers and a former finance professor. Indecd, a good part of the 34-point rise in the Dow industrials on April 8 resulted from a $300 million buy program that was unrelated to arbitrage.

Nervous Clients

The whiz kids have also developed a kind of insurance that is being sold to portfolio managers. As the stock market has soared, nervous clients have sought to guard their gains. By selling short futures, big investors can protect themselves against general market declines and still stay invested in individual stocks. Such "insurance" has helped keep the stock market at high levels while reducing the level of risk to investors. "People don't have to use their capital to make major moves just to play the direction of the market," says Hugh A. Johnson, chief investment strategist with First Albany Corp.

The rocket scientists continue to streamline the bond markets. Even during periods of relative interest rate stability, bond managers incur risks if they don't protect themselves against an uptick in rates. But if they're not careful, the hedge they use can kill them. Since October, interest rates have fallen 3 percentage points. The typical hedge—usually the short sale of futures—created a big loss. The offsetting gain should have been in the bond itself.

But companies have the right to call bonds if interest rates fall steeply. Thus a bondholder who sells futures contracts short could find himself losing a fortune on the short sale without making anything on the bonds themselves. The quants were summoned, and they devised hedge programs that overcame the call problem. The quants' solution "is the talk of the town right now," says Dexter E. Senft, a managing director of First Boston Corp.

Senft, 33, has become a role model for the new Wall Street whiz kid. In 1983, he invented the collateralized mortgage obligation [CMO], a type of mortgage-backed security. Rather than keep him in a corner, First Boston rewarded him with the title and money of managing director. But no one argues that he is overpaid. The CMO market, starting from nothing three years ago, is approaching $35 billion.

Other phenomenally successful products of the quants include zero-coupon bonds, which are issued at a huge discount but pay no interest. Currently, there are over $200 billion worth of outstanding Treasury zeros alone. Interest rate swaps, which permit two companies to exchange fixed-rate debt for the floating-rate variety, is also a $200 billion business. Neither interest rate swaps nor zero coupon bonds even existed before 1981.

Direct Involvement

The rise of the older rocket scientists on Wall Street has inspired a whole new generation, many of whom have abandoned other careers. James Kennedy, head of Merrill Lynch & Co.'s Debt Strategy Group, went to medical school in New Zealand. A member of his team, John H. Carlson, is a meteorologist who, before coming to Merrill, sold long-range weather forecasts to commodity brokers.

James A. Tilley's Ph.D. thesis was titled *The Effects of Spin-Orbit Interactions in Itinerant Ferromagnets.* Now at Morgan Stanley & Co., Tilley helps insurance companies meet their policyholder obligations by matching those cash needs with the flows generated from investments. He exhibits the polish of the typical investment banker—not the dishevelment of the stereotyped technician.

(Continued)

More and more rocket scientists, like Tilley, are getting directly involved with corporate clients. Kennedy of Merrill Lynch recalls a client that had a series of payments totaling $45 million to make over 5 years and owned bonds whose cash flows precisely matched those obligations. Merrill's rocket scientists were asked whether there might be a less expensive way to do it. They constructed a new portfolio that would save the client $1 million. They also developed a solution that could save the company even more money if the client was willing to borrow money for a short period. The company did, and saved $3 million.

The successful Wall Street rocket scientists have learned to operate within time and budget constraints.

Some analytical problems, such as matching the cash flows of assets and liabilities, "if run to completion, would occupy the largest computer mainframes for weeks," says First Boston's Senft. "Rocket scientists get the computer to give answers that are close enough in a short time—like 15 minutes—to reduce the risk of a change in the market prices during the analysis."

The message that Wall Street wants rocket scientists is being heard on university campuses. From MIT to the University of California at Berkeley, big firms are actively courting students with advanced degrees in all scientific fields. Meanwhile, investment managers around the country are struggling to keep up with the latest techniques of the quants. "We make sure we make a quarterly pilgrimage to the esoteric pillars of money management," says Bruce P. Bedford, chairman of Flagship Financial Inc. in Dayton, Ohio. "Some of it is above our heads, yeah." But "that's where the action is."

Chapter 1
The Investment Environment

EVEN A CURSORY GLANCE AT *THE WALL STREET JOURNAL* REVEALS A BEWILDERING COLLECTION OF SECURITIES, MARKETS, AND FINANCIAL INSTITUTIONS. Although it may appear so, the financial environment is not chaotic: There is rhyme and reason behind the array of instruments and markets. The central message we want to convey in this chapter is that financial markets and institutions evolve in response to the desires, technologies, and regulatory constraints of the investors in the economy. In fact, we could *predict* the general shape of the investment environment (if not the design of particular securities) if we knew nothing more than these desires, technologies, and constraints).

This chapter provides a broad overview of the investment environment. We begin by examining the differences between financial assets and real assets. We proceed to the three broad sectors of the financial environment: households, businesses, and government. We see how many features of the investment environment are natural responses of profit-seeking firms and individuals to opportunities created by the demands of these sectors, and we examine the driving forces behind financial innovation. Next, we discuss recent trends in financial markets. Finally, we conclude with a discussion of the relationship between households and the business sector.

1.1 Real Assets versus Financial Assets

The material wealth of a society is determined ultimately by the productive capacity of its economy—the goods and services that can be provided to its members. This productive capacity is a function of the **real assets** of the economy: the land, buildings, knowledge, and machines that are used to produce goods and the workers whose skills are necessary to use those resources. Together, physical and "human" assets generate the entire spectrum of output produced and consumed by the society.

In contrast to such real assets are **financial assets** such as stocks or bonds. These assets, per se, do not represent a society's wealth. Shares of stock are no more than sheets of paper; they do not directly contribute to the productive capacity of the economy. Instead, financial assets contribute to the productive capacity of the economy *indirectly,* because they allow for separation of the ownership and management of the firm and facilitate the transfer of funds to enterprises with attractive investment opportunities. Financial assets certainly contribute to the wealth of the individuals or firms holding them. This is because financial assets are *claims* to the income generated by real assets or claims on income from the government.

When the real assets used by a firm ultimately generate income, the income is allocated to investors according to their ownership of the financial assets, or securities, issued by the firm. Bondholders, for example, are entitled to a flow of income based on the interest rate and par value of the bond. Equityholders or stockholders are entitled to any residual income after bondholders and other creditors are paid. In this way the values of financial assets are derived from and depend on the values of the underlying real assets of the firm.

Real assets are income-generating assets, whereas financial assets define the allocation of income or wealth among investors. Individuals can choose between consuming their current endowments of wealth today and investing for the future. When they invest for the future, they may choose to hold financial assets. The money a firm receives when it issues securities (sells them to investors) is used to purchase real assets. Ultimately, then, the returns on a financial asset come from the income produced by the real assets that are financed by the issuance of the security. In this way, it is useful to view financial assets as the means by which individuals hold their claims on real assets in well-developed economies. Most of us cannot personally own auto plants, but we can hold shares of General Motors or Ford, which provide us with income derived from the production of automobiles.

An operational distinction between real and financial assets involves the balance sheets of individuals and firms in the economy. Real assets appear only on the asset side of the balance sheet. In contrast, financial assets always appear on both sides of balance sheets. Your financial claim on a firm is an asset, but the firm's issuance of that claim is the firm's liability. When we aggregate over all balance sheets, financial assets will cancel out, leaving only the sum of real assets as the net wealth of the aggregate economy.

Another way of distinguishing between financial and real assets is to note that financial assets are created *and destroyed* in the ordinary course of doing business. For example, when a loan is paid off, both the creditor's claim (a financial asset) and the debtor's obligation (a financial liability) cease to exist. In contrast, real assets are destroyed only by accident or by wearing out over time.

The distinction between real and financial assets is apparent when we compare the composition of national wealth in the United States, presented in Table 1.1, with the financial assets and liabilities of U.S. households shown in Table 1.2. National wealth consists of structures, equipment, inventories of goods, and land. (It does not include the value of "human capital"—the value of the earnings potential of the work force.) In

Table 1.1 National Net Worth, 1993

Assets	$ Billion
Residential structures	$ 5,521
Plant and equipment	5,770
Inventories	1,118
Consumer durables	2,336
Land	4,279
Gold and SDRs	20
Net claims on foreigners	(633)
TOTAL	$18,411*

*Column sum may differ from total because of rounding errors.
Source: *Balance Sheets for the United States, 1945–93*, Washington D.C.: Board of the Federal Reserve System, September 1994.

Table 1.2 Balance Sheet of U.S. Households, 1993

Assets	$ Billion	% Total	Liabilities and Net Worth	$ Billion	% Total
Tangible assets					
Houses	$4,239	15.4%	Mortgages	$ 3,149	11.5%
Land	2,903	10.6	Consumer credit	867	3.2
Durables	2,336	8.5	Other loans	154	0.6
Other	493	1.8	Other	297	1.1
Total tangibles	9,970	36.3	Total liabilities	4,468	16.3
Financial assets					
Deposits	3,057	11.1			
Life insurance reserves	468	1.7			
Pension reserves	4,982	18.1			
Corporate equity	4,060	14.8			
Equity in noncorporate business	2,428	8.8			
Debt securities	1,502	5.5			
Other	1,028	3.7			
Total financial assets	17,525	63.7	Net worth	23,027	83.7
TOTAL	$21,167	100.0%		$27,495	100.0%

Source: *Balance Sheets for the United States,* 1945–93, Washington D.C.: Board of the Federal Reserve System, September 1994.

contrast, Table 1.2 includes financial assets such as bank accounts, corporate equity, bonds, and mortgages.

Persons in the United States tend to hold their financial claims in an indirect form. In fact, only about one-quarter of the adult U.S. population holds shares directly. The claims of most individuals on firms are mediated through institutions that hold shares on their behalf: institutional investors such as pension funds, insurance companies,

Table 1.3 Holdings of Corporate Equities in the United States, 1993

Sector	Share Ownership, $ Billions	% of Total
Private pension funds	$1,038.3	17.3%
State and local pension funds	481.1	8.0
Insurance companies	263.2	4.4
Mutual funds	637.1	10.6
Bank personal trusts	199.0	3.3
Foreign investors	326.9	5.4
Households and nonprofit organizations	3,022.5	50.3
Other	38.4	0.6
TOTAL	$6,006.5	100.0%

Source: *New York Stock Exchange Fact Book, 1994.*

mutual funds, and college endowments. Table 1.3 shows that today approximately half of all U.S. equity is held by institutional investors.

CONCEPT CHECK

Question 1. Are the following assets real or financial?*

a. Patents
b. Lease obligations
c. Customer goodwill
d. A college education
e. A $5 bill

1.2 CLIENTS OF THE FINANCIAL SYSTEM

We start our analysis with a broad view of the major clients that place demands on the financial system. By considering the needs of these clients, we can gain considerable insight into why organizations and institutions have evolved as they have.

We can classify the clientele of the investment environment into three groups: the household sector, the corporate sector, and the government sector. This trichotomy is not perfect; it excludes some organizations such as not-for-profit agencies and has difficulty with some hybrids such as unincorporated or family-run businesses. Nevertheless, from the standpoint of capital markets, the three-group classification is useful.

The Household Sector

Households constantly make economic decisions concerning such activities as work, job training, retirement planning, and savings versus consumption. We will take most of these decisions as being already made and focus on financial decisions specifically.

*Answers to all concept check questions can be found in Appendix B.

Essentially, we concern ourselves only with what financial assets households desire to hold.

Even this limited focus, however, leaves a broad range of issues to consider. Most households are potentially interested in a wide array of assets, and the assets that are attractive can vary considerably depending on the household's economic situation. Even a limited consideration of taxes and risk preferences can lead to widely varying asset demands, and this demand for variety is, as we shall see, a driving force behind financial innovation.

Taxes lead to varying asset demands because people in different tax brackets "transform" before-tax income to after-tax income at different rates. For example, high-tax-bracket investors naturally will seek tax-free securities, compared with low-tax-bracket investors who want primarily higher-yielding taxable securities. A desire to minimize taxes also leads to demand for securities that are exempt from state and local taxes. This, in turn, causes demand for portfolios that specialize in tax-exempt bonds of one particular state. In other words, differential tax status creates "tax clienteles" that in turn give rise to demand for a range of assets with a variety of tax implications. The demand of investors encourages entrepreneurs to offer such portfolios (for a fee, of course!).

Risk considerations also create demand for a diverse set of investment alternatives. At an obvious level, differences in risk tolerance create demand for assets with a variety of risk-return combinations. Individuals also have particular hedging requirements that contribute to diverse investment demands.

Consider, for example, a resident of New York City who plans to sell her house and retire to Miami, Florida, in 15 years. Such a plan seems feasible if real estate prices in the two cities do not diverge before her retirement. How can one hedge Miami real estate prices now, short of purchasing a home there immediately rather than at retirement? One way to hedge the risk is to purchase securities that will increase in value if Florida real estate becomes more expensive. This creates a hedging demand for an asset with a particular risk characteristic. Such demands lead profit-seeking financial corporations to supply the desired goods: observe Florida real estate investment trusts (REITs) that allow individuals to invest in securities whose performance is tied to Florida real estate prices. If Florida real estate becomes more expensive, the REIT will increase in value. The individual's loss as a potential purchaser of Florida real estate is offset by her gain as an investor in that real estate. This is only one example of how a myriad of risk-specific assets are demanded *and created* by agents in the financial environment.

Risk motives also lead to demand for ways that investors can easily diversify their portfolios and even out their risk exposure. We will see that these diversification motives inevitably give rise to mutual funds that offer small individual investors the ability to invest in a wide range of stocks, bonds, precious metals, and virtually all other financial instruments.

The Business Sector

Whereas household financial decisions are concerned with how to invest money, businesses typically need to raise money to finance their investments in real assets: plant, equipment, technological know-how, and so forth. Table 1.4 presents balance sheets of

Table 1.4 Balance Sheet of Nonfinancial U.S. Business, 1993*

Assets	$ Billion	% Total	Liabilities and Net Worth	$ Billion	% Total
Tangible assets			Liabilities		
Equipment and structures	$3,886	50.6%	Bonds and mortgages	$1,612	21.0%
Land	90	1.2	Bank loans	515	6.7
Inventories	989	12.9	Other loans	419	5.5
Total tangibles	4,965	64.6	Trade debt	727	9.5
			Other	626	8.1
			Total liabilities	3,900	50.8
Financial assets					
Deposits and cash	294	3.8			
Marketable securities	530	6.9			
Consumer credit	75	1.0			
Trade credit	873	11.4			
Other	944	12.3			
Total financial assets	2,716	35.4	Net worth	3,781	49.2
TOTAL	$7,681	100.0%		$7,681	100.0%

*Column sums may differ from total because of rounding error.
Source: *Balance Sheets for the United States, 1943–93*, Board of the Federal Reserve System, September 1994.

U.S. corporations as a whole. The heavy concentration on tangible assets is obvious. Broadly speaking, there are two ways for businesses to raise money—they can borrow it, either from banks or directly from households by issuing bonds, or they can "take in new partners" by issuing stocks, which are ownership shares in the firm.

Businesses issuing securities to the public have several objectives. First, they want to get the best price possible for their securities. Second, they want to market the issues to the public at the lowest possible cost. This has two implications. First, businesses might want to farm out the marketing of their securities to firms that specialize in such security issuance, because it is unlikely that any single firm is in the market often enough to justify a full-time security issuance division. Issue of securities requires immense effort. The security issue must be brought to the attention of the public. Buyers then must subscribe to the issue, and records of subscriptions and deposits must be kept. The allocation of the security to each buyer must be determined, and subscribers finally must exchange money for securities. These activities clearly call for specialists. The complexities of security issuance have been the catalyst for creation of an investment banking industry to cater to business demands. We will return to this industry shortly.

The second implication of the desire for low-cost security issuance is that most businesses will prefer to issue fairly simple securities that require the least extensive incremental analysis and, correspondingly, are the least expensive to arrange. Such a demand for simplicity or uniformity by business-sector security issuers is likely to be at odds with the household sector's demand for a wide variety of risk-specific securities. This mismatch of objectives gives rise to an industry of middlemen who act as intermediaries between the two sectors, specializing in transforming simple securities to complex issues that suit particular market niches.

Table 1.5 Financial Assets and Liabilities of the U.S. Government, 1994

Assets	$ Billion	% Total	Liabilities	$ Billion	% Total
Deposits, currency, gold	$ 94.8	19.9%	Currency	$ 25.3	0.7%
Mortgages	66.5	14.0	Government securities	3,395.4	88.9
Loans	138.2	29.0	Insurance and pension reserves	344.2	9.0
Other	176.3	37.1	Other	53.9	1.4
TOTAL	$475.8	100.0%	TOTAL	$3,818.8	100.0%

Source: Data from *Flow of Funds Accounts: Flows & Outstandings,* Board of Governors of the Federal Reserve System, 1994.

The Government Sector

Like businesses, governments often need to finance their expenditures by borrowing. Unlike businesses, governments cannot sell equity shares; they are restricted to borrowing to raise funds when tax revenues are not sufficient to cover expenditures. They also can print money, of course, but this source of funds is limited by its inflationary implications, and so most governments usually try to avoid excessive use of the printing press.

Governments have a special advantage in borrowing money because their taxing power makes them very creditworthy and, therefore, able to borrow at the lowest rates. The financial component of the federal government's balance sheet is presented in Table 1.5. Notice that the major liabilities are government securities, such as Treasury bonds or Treasury bills.

A second, special role of the government is in regulating the financial environment. Some government regulations are relatively innocuous. For example, the Securities and Exchange Commission is responsible for disclosure laws that are designed to enforce truthfulness in various financial transactions. Other regulations have been much more controversial.

One example is Regulation Q, which for decades put a ceiling on the interest rates that banks were allowed to pay to depositors, until it was repealed by the Depository Institutions Deregulation and Monetary Control Act of 1980. These ceilings were supposedly a response to widespread bank failures during the Great Depression. By curbing interest rates, the government hoped to limit further failures. The idea was that if banks could not pay high interest rates to compete for depositors, their profits and safety margins presumably would improve. The result was predictable: Instead of competing through interest rates, banks competed by offering "free" gifts for initiating deposits and by opening more numerous and convenient branch locations. Another result also was predictable: Bank competitors stepped in to fill the void created by Regulation Q. The great success of money market funds in the 1970s came in large part from depositors leaving banks that were prohibited from paying competitive rates. Indeed, much financial innovation may be viewed as responses to government tax and regulatory rules.

1.3 The Environment Responds to Clientele Demands

When enough clients demand and are willing to pay for a service, it is likely in a capitalistic economy that a profit-seeking supplier will find a way to provide and charge for that service. This is the mechanism that leads to the diversity of financial markets. Let us consider the market responses to the disparate demands of the three sectors.

Financial Intermediation

Recall that the financial problem facing households is how best to invest their funds. The relative smallness of most households makes direct investment intrinsically difficult. A small investor obviously cannot advertise in the local newspaper his or her willingness to lend money to businesses that need to finance investments. Instead, **financial intermediaries** such as banks, investment companies, insurance companies, or credit unions naturally evolve to bring the two sectors together. Financial intermediaries sell their own liabilities to raise funds that are used to purchase liabilities of other corporations.

For example, a bank raises funds by borrowing (taking in deposits) and lending that money to (purchasing the loans of) other borrowers. The spread between the rates paid to depositors and the rates charged to borrowers is the source of the bank's profit. In this way, lenders and borrowers do not need to contact each other directly. Instead, each goes to the bank, which acts as an intermediary between the two. The problem of matching lenders with borrowers is solved when each comes independently to the common intermediary. The convenience and cost savings the bank offers the borrowers and lenders allow it to profit from the spread between the rates on its loans and the rates on its deposits. In other words, the problem of coordination creates a market niche for the bank as intermediary. Profit opportunities alone dictate that banks will emerge in a trading economy.

Financial intermediaries are distinguished from other businesses in that both their assets and their liabilities are overwhelmingly financial. Table 1.6 shows that the balance sheets of financial institutions include very small amounts of tangible assets. Compare Table 1.6 with Table 1.4, the balance sheet of the nonfinancial corporate sector. The contrast arises precisely because intermediaries are middlemen, simply moving funds from one sector to another. In fact, from a bird's-eye view, this is the primary social function of such intermediaries, to channel household savings to the business sector.

Other examples of financial intermediaries are investment companies, insurance companies, and credit unions. All these firms offer similar advantages, in addition to playing a middleman role. First, by pooling the resources of many small investors, they are able to lend considerable sums to large borrowers. Second, by lending to many borrowers, intermediaries achieve significant diversification, meaning they can accept loans that individually might be risky. Third, intermediaries build expertise through the volume of business they do. One individual trying to borrow or lend directly would have much less specialized knowledge of how to structure and execute the transaction with another party.

Table 1.6 Balance Sheet of Financial Institutions, 1993*

Assets	$ Billion	% Total	Liabilities and Net Worth	$ Billion	% Total
Tangible assets			Liabilities		
Equipment and structures	$ 493	3.0%	Deposits	$ 3,518	21.2%
Land	116	.7	Mutual fund shares	1,429	8.6
Total tangibles	608	3.7	Life insurance reserves	457	2.8
			Pension reserves	4,650	28.1
			Money market securities	1,017	6.1
			Bonds and mortgages	1,409	8.5
			Other	2,777	16.7
			Total liabilities	15,258	92.1
Financial assets					
Deposits and cash	725	4.4			
Government securities	3,554	21.5			
Corporate bonds	1,860	11.2			
Mortgages	2,227	13.4			
Consumer credit	792	4.8			
Bank and other loans	1,611	9.7			
Corporate equity	3,193	19.3			
Other	1,989	12.0			
Total financial assets	15,951	96.3	Net worth	1,300	7.9
TOTAL	$16,559	100.0%		$16,559	100.0%

*Column sums may differ from total because of rounding error.
Source: *Balance Sheets for the United States, 1945–93,* Washington, D.C.: Board of the Federal Reserve System, September 1994.

Mutual funds, which pool together and manage the money of many investors, also arise out of the "smallness problem." Here, the problem is that most household portfolios are not large enough to be spread across a wide variety of securities. It is very expensive in terms of brokerage fees to purchase one or two shares of many different firms, and it clearly is more economical for stocks and bonds to be purchased and sold in large blocks. This observation reveals a profit opportunity that has been filled by mutual funds offered by many investment companies.

Mutual funds pool the limited funds of small investors into large amounts, thereby gaining the advantages of large-scale trading; investors are assigned a prorated share of the total funds according to the size of their investment. This system gives small investors advantages that they are willing to pay for via a management fee to the mutual fund operator. Mutual funds are logical extensions of an investment club or cooperative, in which individuals themselves team up and pool funds. The fund sets up shop as a firm that accepts the assets of many investors, acting as an investment agent on their behalf. Again, the advantages of specialization are sufficiently large that the fund can provide a valuable service and still charge enough for it to clear a handsome profit.

Investment companies also can design portfolios specifically for large investors with particular goals. In contrast, mutual funds are sold in the retail market, and their investment philosophies are differentiated mainly by strategies that are likely to attract a large number of clients. Some investment companies manage "commingled funds," in which the monies of different clients with similar goals are merged into a "mini-mutual fund," which is run according to the common preferences of those clients.

Economies of scale also explain the proliferation of analytic services available to investors. Newsletters, databases, and brokerage house research services all exploit the fact that the expense of collecting information is best borne by having a few agents engage in research to be sold to a large client base. This setup arises naturally. Investors clearly want information, but, with only small portfolios to manage, they do not find it economical to incur the expense of collecting it. Hence, a profit opportunity emerges: A firm can perform this service for many clients and charge for it.

Investment Banking

Just as economies of scale and specialization create profit opportunities for financial intermediaries, so too do these economies create niches for firms that perform specialized services for businesses. We said before that firms raise much of their capital by selling securities such as stocks and bonds to the public. Because these firms do not do so frequently, however, investment banking firms that specialize in such activities are able to offer their services at a cost below that of running an in-house security issuance division.

Investment bankers such as Merrill Lynch, Salomon Brothers, or Goldman, Sachs advise the issuing firm on the prices it can charge for the securities issued, market conditions, appropriate interest rates, and so forth. Ultimately, the investment banking firm handles the marketing of the security issue to the public.

Investment bankers also can help firms design securities with special desirable properties. As an example of this practice, consider a pharmaceutical company undertaking a risky R&D project for a new drug. It needs to raise money for research costs and realizes that if the research is successful it will need to build a new manufacturing plant requiring still more financing. To deal with this contingency, the investment banker might design a bond-with-warrant issue. (A *warrant* is a security giving its holder the option to purchase stock from the firm at a specified price up until the warrant's expiration date.) The bonds and warrants are issued, and the research commences. If the research is eventually successful, the stock price will increase, the warrantholders will find it advantageous to exercise their options to purchase additional shares, and as they purchase those shares, additional funds will flow to the firm precisely as they are needed to finance the new manufacturing plant. The design of the financing scheme lets the firm avoid two separate security offerings and saves the considerable costs of the second offering. The exercise of the warrants provides additional financing at no additional flotation costs.

Financial Innovation and Derivatives

The example of the pharmaceutical company illustrates one source of financial innovation. The company's need for initial and contingent financing led to a creative packaging of securities that met the particular needs of the firm. The investment diversity desired by households, however, is far greater than most businesses have a desire to satisfy. Most firms find it simpler to issue "plain vanilla" securities, leaving exotic variants to others who specialize in financial markets. This, of course, creates a profit opportunity for innovative security design and repackaging that investment bankers are only too happy to fill.

Consider the astonishing changes in the mortgage markets since 1970, when mortgage pass-through securities were first introduced by the Government National Mortgage Association (GNMA, or Ginnie Mae). These pass-throughs aggregate individual home mortgages into relatively homogenous pools. Each pool acts as backing for a GNMA **pass-through security**. GNMA securityholders receive the principal and interest payments made on the underlying mortgage pool. For example, the pool might total $100 million of 10 percent, 30-year conventional mortgages. The purchaser of the pool receives all monthly interest and principal payments made on the pool. The banks that originated the mortgages continue to service them, but no longer own the mortgage investments; these have been passed through to the GNMA securityholders.

Pass-through securities were a tremendous innovation in mortgage markets. The *securitization* of mortgages meant that mortgages could be traded just like other securities in national financial markets. Availability of funds no longer depended on local credit conditions; with mortgage pass-throughs trading in national markets, mortgage funds could flow from any region to wherever demand was greatest.

The next round of innovation came when it became apparent that investors might be interested in mortgage-backed securities with different effective times to maturity. Thus was born the *collateralized mortgage obligation,* or CMO. The CMO meets the demand for mortgage-backed securities with a range of maturities by dividing the overall pool into a series of classes called tranches. The so-called fast-pay tranche receives all the principal payments made on the entire mortgage pool until the total investment of the investors in the tranche is repaid. In the meantime, investors in the other tranches receive only interest on their investment. In this way, the fast-pay tranche is retired first and is the shortest-term mortgage-backed security. The next tranche then receives all of the principal payments until it is retired, and so on, until the slow-pay tranche, the longest-term class, finally receives payback of principal after all other tranches have been retired.

Although these securities are relatively complex, the message here is that security demand elicited a market response. The waves of product development in the last two decades are responses to perceived profit opportunities created by as-yet unsatisfied demands for securities with particular risk, return, tax, and timing attributes. As the investment banking industry becomes ever more sophisticated, security creation and customization become more routine. Most new securities are created by dismantling and rebundling more basic securities. For example, the CMO is a dismantling of a simpler mortgage-backed security into component tranches. A Wall Street joke asks how many investment bankers it takes to sell a light bulb. The answer is 100—one to break the bulb and 99 to sell off the individual fragments.

This discussion leads to the notion of primitive versus derivative securities. A **primitive security** offers returns based only on the status of the issuer. For example, bonds make stipulated interest payments depending only on the solvency of the issuing firm.

Dividends paid to stockholders depend as well on the board of directors' assessment of the firm's financial position. In contrast, **derivative securities** yield returns that depend on additional factors pertaining to the prices of other assets. For example, the payoff to stock options depends on the price of the underlying stock. In our mortgage examples the derivative mortgage-backed securities offer payouts that depend on the original mortgages, which are the primitive securities. Much of the innovation in security design may be viewed as the continual creation of new types of derivative securities from the available set of primitive securities.

Derivatives have become an integral part of the investment environment. One use of derivatives, perhaps the primary use, is to hedge risks. However, derivatives also can be used to take highly speculative positions. Moreover, when complex derivatives are misunderstood, firms that believe they are hedging might in fact be increasing their exposure to various sources of risk. This seemed to be the case in 1994 when several firms lost large sums on their derivatives positions. Among the more spectacular losses were those of Procter & Gamble, which took a $157 million pre-tax charge on two interest-rate-related derivative products, and Piper Jaffray Companies, a financial services firm which suffered a loss of $700 million in its fixed income portfolios, many of which were believed by clients to be very conservatively invested. Despite these losses, derivatives will continue to play an important role in portfolio management and the financial system. We will return to this topic later in the text. For the time being, however, we direct you to the primer on derivatives in the nearby box.

CONCEPT CHECK

Question 2. If you take out a car loan, is the loan a primitive security or a derivative security?

Question 3. Explain how a car loan from a bank creates both financial assets and financial liabilities.

Response to Taxation and Regulation

We have seen that much financial innovation and security creation may be viewed as a natural market response to unfulfilled investor needs. Another driving force behind innovation is the ongoing game played between governments and investors on taxation and regulation. Many financial innovations are direct responses to government attempts either to regulate or to tax investments of various sorts. We can illustrate this with several examples.

We have already noted how Regulation Q, which limited bank deposit interest rates, spurred the growth of the money market industry. It also was one reason for the birth of the Eurodollar market. Because Regulation Q did not apply to dollar-denominated time deposits in foreign accounts, many U.S. banks and foreign competitors established branches in Western Europe, where they could offer competitive rates outside the jurisdiction of U.S. regulators. The growth of the Eurodollar market was also the result of another U.S. regulation: reserve requirements. Foreign branches were exempt from such requirements and were thus better able to compete for deposits. Ironically, despite the fact that Regulation Q no longer exists, the Eurodollar market continues to thrive, thus complicating the lives of U.S. monetary policymakers.

Understanding the Complex World of Derivatives

What are derivatives anyway, and why are people saying such terrible things about them?

Some critics see the derivatives market as a multi-trillion-dollar house of cards composed of interlocking, highly leveraged transactions. They fear that the default of a single large player could stun the world financial system.

But others, including Federal Reserve Chairman Alan Greenspan, say the risk of such a meltdown is negligible. Proponents stress that the market's hazards are more than outweighed by the benefits derivatives provide in helping banks, corporations and investors manage their risks.

Because the science of derivatives is relatively new, there's no easy way to gauge the ultimate impact these instruments will have. There are now more than 1,200 different kinds of derivatives on the market, most of which require a computer program to figure out. Surveying this complex subject, dozens of derivatives experts offered these insights:

Q: What is the broadest definition of derivatives?

A: Derivatives are financial arrangements between two parties whose payments are based on, or "derived" from, the performance of some agreed-upon benchmark. Derivatives can be issued based on currencies, commodities, government or corporate debt, home mortgages, stocks, interest rates, or any combination.

Company stock options, for instance, allow employees and executives to profit from changes in a company's stock price without actually owning shares. Without knowing it, homeowners frequently use a type of privately traded "forward" contract when they apply for a mortgage and lock in a borrowing rate for their house closing, typically for as many as 60 days in the future.

Q: What are the most common forms of derivatives?

A: Derivatives come in two basic categories, option-type contracts and forward-type contracts. These may be exchange-listed, such as futures and stock options, or they may be privately traded.

Options give buyers the right, but not the obligation, to buy or sell an asset at a preset price over a specific period. The option's price is usually a small percentage of the underlying asset's value.

Forward-type contracts, which include forwards, futures and swaps, commit the buyer and the seller to trade a given asset at a set price on a future date. These

(Continued)

Another innovation attributable largely to tax avoidance motives is the long-term deep discount, or zero-coupon, bond. These bonds, often called *zeros,* pay little or no interest, instead providing returns to investors through a redemption price that is higher than the initial sales price. Corporations were allowed for tax purposes to impute an implied interest expense based on this built-in price appreciation. The government's technique for imputing tax-deductible interest expenses, however, proved to be too generous in the early years of the bonds' lives, so corporations issued these bonds widely to exploit the resulting tax benefit. Ultimately, the Treasury caught on, amended its interest imputation procedure, and the flow of new zeros dried up.

Meanwhile, however, the financial markets had discovered that zeros were useful ways to lock in a long-term investment return. When the supply of primitive zero-coupon bonds ended, financial innovators created derivative zeros by purchasing U.S. Treasury bonds, "stripping" off the coupons, and selling them separately as zeros.

are "price fixing" agreements that saddle the buyer with the same price risks as actually owning the asset. But normally, no money changes hands until the delivery date, when the contract is often settled in cash rather than by exchanging the asset.

Q: In business, what are they used for?

A: While derivatives can be powerful speculative instruments, businesses most often use them to hedge. For instance, companies often use forwards and exchange-listed futures to protect against fluctuations in currency or commodity prices, thereby helping to manage import and raw-materials costs. Options can serve a similar purpose; interest-rate options such as caps and floors help companies control financing costs in much the same way that caps on adjustable-rate mortgages do for homeowners.

Q: How do over-the-counter derivatives generally originate?

A: A derivatives dealer, generally a bank or securities firm, enters into a private contract with a corporation, investor or another dealer. The contract commits the dealer to provide a return linked to a desired interest rate, currency or other asset. For example, in an interest-rate swap, the dealer might receive a floating rate in return for paying a fixed rate.

Q: Why are derivatives potentially dangerous?

A: Because these contracts expose the two parties to market moves with little or no money actually changing hands, they involve leverage. And that leverage may be vastly increased by the terms of a particular contract. In the derivatives that hurt P&G, for instance, a given move in U.S. or German interest rates was multiplied 10 times or more.

When things go well, that leverage provides a big return, compared with the amount of capital at risk. But it also causes equally big losses when markets move the wrong way. Even companies that use derivatives to hedge, rather than speculate, may be at risk, since their operation would rarely produce perfectly offsetting gains.

Q: If they are so dangerous, why are so many businesses using derivatives?

A: They are among the cheapest and most readily available means at companies' disposal to buffer themselves against shocks in currency values, commodity prices and interest rates. Donald Nicoliasen, a Price Waterhouse expert on derivatives, says derivatives "are a new tool in everybody's bag to better manage business returns and risks."

Source: Lee Berton, "Understanding the Complex World of Derivative," *The Wall Street Journal,* June 14, 1994. Excerpted by permission of *The Wall Street Journal*

Another tax-induced innovation is the **dual fund.** Under U.S. tax law, capital gains are taxed at lower rates than dividends. The differential means high-tax-bracket investors prefer capital gains, whereas tax-exempt investors are happy to receive dividends. Entrepreneurs therefore created dual funds (the derivative asset) in which *income* and *capital* shares on a portfolio of stocks (the primitive assets) were sold separately. The income shareholders receive the dividends on the portfolio, plus their share of the initial value when the portfolio is cashed in. The capital shareholders receive their share of initial value plus any accumulated capital gains.

There are plenty of other examples. The Eurobond market came into existence as a response to changes in U.S. tax law. Financial futures markets were stimulated by abandonment in the early 1970s of the system of fixed exchange rates and by new federal regulations that overrode state laws treating some financial futures as gambling arrangements.

The general tendency is clear: Tax and regulatory pressures on the financial system very often lead to unanticipated financial innovations when profit-seeking investors make an end run around the government's restrictions. The constant game of regulatory catch-up sets off another flow of new innovations.

1.4 Markets and Market Structure

Just as securities and financial institutions come into existence as natural responses to investor demands, so too do markets evolve to meet needs. Consider what would happen if organized markets did not exist. Households that wanted to borrow would need to find others that wanted to lend. Inevitably, a meeting place for borrowers and lenders would be settled on, and that meeting place would evolve into a financial market. A pub in old London called Lloyd's launched the maritime insurance industry. A Manhattan curb on Wall Street became synonymous with the financial world.

We can differentiate four types of markets: direct search markets, brokered markets, dealer markets, and auction markets.

A **direct search market** is the least organized market. Here, buyers and sellers must seek each other out directly. One example of a transaction taking place in such a market would be the sale of a used refrigerator in which the seller advertises for buyers in a local newspaper. Such markets are characterized by sporadic participation and low-priced and nonstandard goods. It does not pay most people or firms to seek profits by specializing in such an environment.

The next level of organization is a **brokered market.** In markets where trading in a good is sufficiently active, brokers can find it profitable to offer search services to buyers and sellers. A good example is the real estate market, where economies of scale in searches for available homes and for prospective buyers make it worthwhile for participants to pay brokers to conduct the searches for them. Brokers in given markets develop specialized knowledge on valuing assets traded in that given market.

An important brokered investment market is the so-called **primary market,** where new issues of securities are offered to the public. In the primary market investment bankers act as brokers; they seek out investors to purchase securities directly from the issuing corporation.

Another brokered market is that for large **block transactions,** in which very large blocks of stock are bought or sold. These blocks are so large (technically more than 10,000 shares but usually much larger) that brokers or "block houses" often are engaged to search directly for other large traders, rather than bringing the trade directly to the stock exchange where relatively smaller investors trade.

When trading activity in a particular type of asset increases, **dealer markets** arise. Here, dealers specialize in various commodities, purchase assets for their own inventory, and sell goods for a profit from their inventory. Dealers, unlike brokers, trade assets for their own accounts. The dealer's profit margin is the "bid-asked" spread—the difference between the price at which the dealer buys for and sells from inventory. Dealer markets save traders on search costs because market participants can easily look up prices at which they can buy from or sell to dealers. Obviously, a fair amount of market activity is required before dealing in a market is an attractive source of income. The over-the-counter securities market is one example of a dealer market.

Trading among investors of already-issued securities is said to take place in **secondary markets.** Therefore, the over-the-counter market is one example of a secondary market. Trading in secondary markets does not affect the outstanding amount of securities; ownership is simply transferred from one investor to another.

The most integrated market is an **auction market,** in which all transactors in a good converge at one place to bid on or offer a good. The New York Stock Exchange (NYSE) is an example of an auction market. An advantage of auction markets over dealer markets is that one need not search to find the best price for a good. If all participants converge, they can arrive at mutually agreeable prices and, thus, save the bid-asked spread.

Continuous auction markets (as opposed to periodic auctions such as in the art world) require very heavy and frequent trading to cover the expense of maintaining the market. For this reason, the NYSE and other exchanges set up listing requirements, which limit the shares traded on the exchange to those of firms in which sufficient trading interest is likely to exist.

The organized stock exchanges are also secondary markets. They are organized for investors to trade existing securities among themselves.

CONCEPT CHECK

Question 4. Many assets trade in more than one type of market. In what types of markets do the following trade?

a. Used cars
b. Paintings
c. Rare coins

1.5 ONGOING TRENDS

Several important trends have changed the contemporary investment environment:

1. Globalization
2. Securitization
3. Credit enhancement
4. Financial engineering

Each is the logical consequence of the demand and supply forces that give rise to specialized markets and instruments.

Globalization

If a wider array of investment choices can improve welfare, why should we limit ourselves to purely domestic assets? **Globalization** requires efficient communication technology and the dismantling of regulatory constraints. These tendencies in worldwide investment environments have encouraged international investing in recent years.

U.S. investors commonly can take advantage of foreign investment opportunities in several ways: (1) purchase foreign securities using American Depositary Receipts (ADRs), which are domestically traded securities that represent claims to shares of foreign stocks; (2) purchase foreign securities that are offered in dollars; (3) buy mutual funds that invest internationally; and (4) buy derivative securities with payoffs that depend on prices in foreign security markets. Years ago, a U.S. investor who wished to hold a French stock had to engage in four transactions: (1) purchase French francs, (2) purchase the stock on the French Bourse, (3) sell the stock in France, and (4) sell the French francs for dollars. Today, the same investor can purchase ADRs of this stock.

Brokers who act as intermediaries for such transactions hold an inventory of stock from which they sell shares, denominated in U.S. dollars. Now, there is no more technical difference between investing in a French or a U.S. stock than there is in holding a Massachusetts-backed stock compared with a California-based stock. Of course, the investment implications may differ: The nearby box emphasizes that ADRs still expose investors to exchange rate risk.

Many foreign firms are so eager to lure U.S. investors that they will save these investors the expense of paying the higher commissions that are associated with the ADRs. Figure 1.1 shows a case in point. Cadbury Schweppes is a United Kingdom-based corporation that marketed its stock directly to U.S. investors in ADRs. Each ADR represents a claim to 10 shares of Cadbury Schweppes stock.

An example of how far globalization has progressed appears in Figure 1.2. Here, Walt Disney is selling debt claims denominated in European currency units (ECUs), an index of a basket of European currency values.

Securitization

Until recently, financial intermediaries served to channel funds from national capital markets to smaller local ones. **Securitization,** however, now allows borrowers to enter capital markets directly. In this procedure pools of loans typically are aggregated into pass-through securities, such as mortgage pool pass-throughs. Then, investors can invest in securities backed by those pools. The transformation of these pools into standardized securities enables issuers to deal in a volume large enough that they can bypass intermediaries. We have already discussed this phenomenon in the context of the securitization of the mortgage market. Today, about three-quarters of all conventional mortgages are securitized by government mortgage agencies.

Another example of securitization is the collateralized automobile receivable (CAR), a pass-through arrangement for car loans. Figure 1.3 (see page 30) shows an example of such a note. The loan originator passes the loan payments through to the holder of the CAR. Aside from mortgages, the biggest asset-backed securities are for credit card debt, car loans, home equity loans, and student loans.

Credit Enhancement

In the past, a corporation that was not in the best of financial conditions would be able to obtain loans only through commercial banks. The banks' credit departments scruti-

ADR Holders Feel Heat From Crisis in Mexico

NEW YORK—Surprise!

You might have been buying stocks like **Telefonos de Mexico** on the New York Stock Exchange with dollars and receiving your dividends in dollars. But you were never protected from either the risk that the stock might tumble or that the Mexican currency might collapse.

Investors who have been active buyers of foreign stocks through the purchase of American depositary receipts on U.S. exchanges are finding out the hard way that it's easy to buy them, but well nigh impossible to escape the risks—including the currency risk—foreign shares represent.

That's coming home with a vengeance in the case of Mexican ADRs, which had been popular vehicles for U.S. investors seeking to play what once was the darling of the emerging-markets crowd. With the peso losing 39% of its value since the crisis began on Dec. 20 through yesterday, four of the 10 worst-performing stocks on the New York Stock Exchange for the last quarter of 1994 were Mexican ADRs.

Double Whammy

ADRs are negotiable certificates or electronic entries that certify that the holder owns shares of a foreign company that are on deposit in the company's home market. Because they trade on U.S. exchanges and are priced in dollars they are a very convenient way for American investors to buy foreign shares. But their prices reflect not only the underlying value of the company in its home market, but also the relative value of the company's home-market currency against the dollar. In the worst case, both the stock price at home and the home currency could fall, as they have in the case of Mexican stocks, dealing U.S. holders of ADRs a double whammy.

Foreign companies like ADRs because they can be used to gain additional exposure for their stocks and, less frequently, to actually raise new capital in the U.S. The booming ADR growth for the past few years—a record 7.2 billion ADR shares were traded in the U.S. in 1994—has given American investors access to stocks in countries as disparate as Germany and Belize.

The tremendous growth in ADRs has meant big business for the U.S. exchanges, depositary institutions (usually banks) and brokerage firms that deal in ADRs. At the end of 1994, there were 1,397 depositary receipt programs in the U.S., according to Citicorp. Of the 254 new stocks listed on the Big Board in 1994, 52 were foreign companies, most of which used ADRs. The National Association of Securities Dealers has seven sales representatives scouring the globe to persuade foreign companies to list their shares in the U.S.

But Mexico's financial crisis, and the resulting losses to U.S. investors, is likely to slow the pace at which foreign companies come to U.S. markets, at least in the near term.

"We're cautious about Latin America in the short term," said Mark A. Bach, vice president and ADR global sales director at Citibank. "And the pace of activity from China has been slowing, and I don't see it increasing dramatically. But, in the long term, we still think the globalization of markets and the need for global capital raising won't go away."

Source: Dave Kansas, "ADR Holders Feel Heat From Crisis in Mexico," *The Wall Street Journal,* January 12, 1995. Excerpted by permission of

nized each customer. A business shopping around for a loan might be sized up simultaneously by several different banks.

Today, the credit-hungry corporation can arrange for **credit enhancement.** It engages an insurance company to put its credit behind the corporation's, for a fee. The firm can then float a bond of "enhanced" credit rating directly to the public.

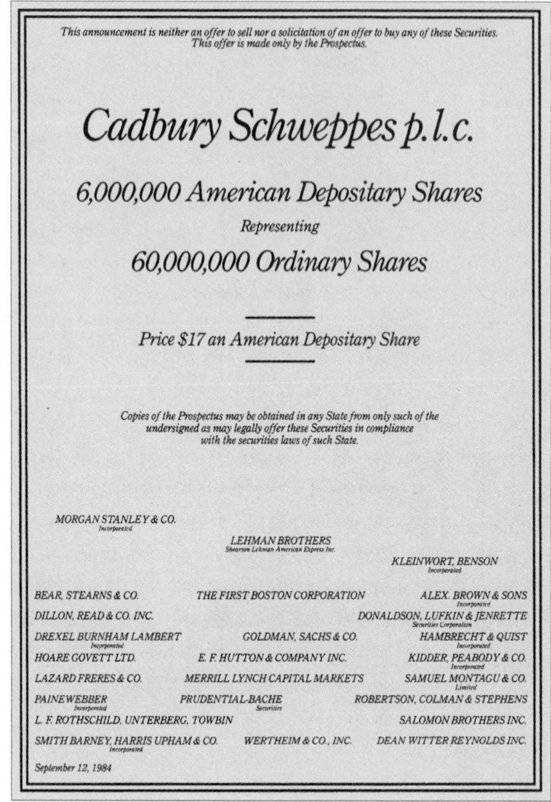

This announcement is neither an offer to sell nor a solicitation of an offer to buy any of these Securities. This offer is made only by the Prospectus.
Cadbury Schweppes p.l.c.
6,000,000 American Depositary Shares
Representing
60,000,000 Ordinary Shares
Price $17 an American Depositary Share
Copies of the Prospectus may be obtained in any State from only such of the undersigned as may legally offer these Securities in compliance with the securities laws of such State.
MORGAN STANLEY & CO. Incorporated
LEHMAN BROTHERS Shearson Lehman American Express Inc.
KLEINWORT, BENSON Incorporated
BEAR, STEARNS & CO.
THE FIRST BOSTON CORPORATION
ALEX. BROWN & SONS Incorporated
DILLON, READ & CO. INC.
DONALDSON, LUFKIN & JENRETTE Securities Corporation
DREXEL BURNHAM LAMBERT Incorporated
GOLDMAN, SACHS & CO.
HAMBRECHT & QUIST Incorporated
HOARE GOVETT LTD.
E. F. HUTTON & COMPANY INC.
KIDDER, PEABODY & CO. Incorporated
LAZARD FRERES & CO.
MERRILL LYNCH CAPITAL MARKETS
SAMUEL MONTAGU & CO. Limited
PAINEWEBBER Incorporated
PRUDENTIAL-BACHE Securities
ROBERTSON, COLMAN & STEPHENS
L. F. ROTHSCHILD, UNTERBERG, TOWBIN
SALOMON BROTHERS INC.
SMITH BARNEY, HARRIS UPHAM & CO. Incorporated
WERTHEIM & CO., INC.
DEAN WITTER REYNOLDS INC.
September 12, 1984

Figure 1.1
Globalization and American depositary receipts

Figure 1.4 (see page 31) shows an example of credit enhancement in a joint financial venture between the Rockefeller Group and Aetna Casualty and Surety. The Rockefeller Group is a privately held corporation and thus exempt from a large part of typical disclosure rules. It cannot issue publicly traded bonds at reasonably low yields without revealing information to the public that it wishes to keep private. Instead, it purchases Aetna's backing. Aetna can perform its own credit analysis, keeping the information revealed confidential.

Financial Engineering

Disparate investor demands elicit a supply of exotic securities. Creative security design often calls for **bundling** primitive and derivative securities into one composite security. One such example appears in Figure 1.5 (see page 32). The Chubb Corporation, with the aid of Goldman, Sachs, has combined three primitive securities—stocks, bonds, and preferred stock—into one hybrid security. Chubb is issuing preferred stock that is convertible into common stock, at the option of the holder, and exchangeable into con-

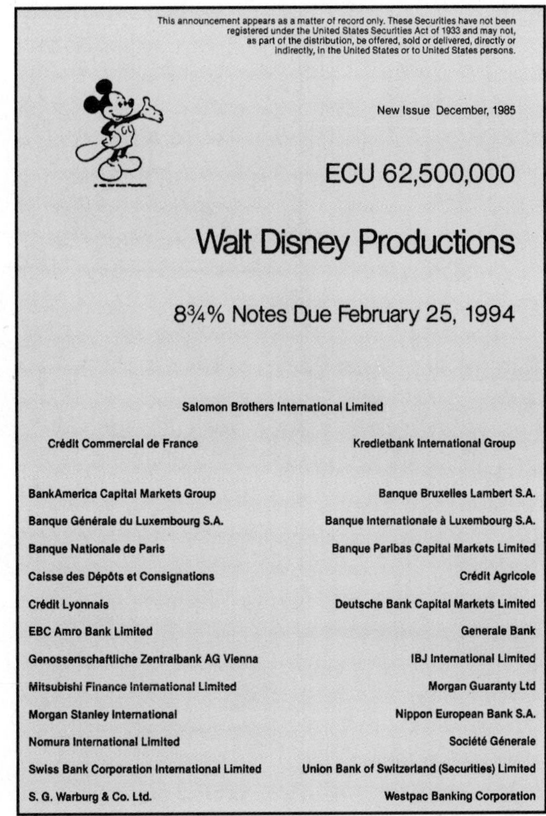

This announcement appears as a matter of record only. These Securities have not been registered under the United States Securities Act of 1933 and may not, as part of the distribution, be offered, sold or delivered, directly or indirectly, in the United States or to United States persons.

New Issue December, 1985

ECU 62,500,000

Walt Disney Productions

8¾% Notes Due February 25, 1994

Salomon Brothers International Limited

Crédit Commercial de France | Kredietbank International Group

BankAmerica Capital Markets Group	Banque Bruxelles Lambert S.A.
Banque Générale du Luxembourg S.A.	Banque Internationale à Luxembourg S.A.
Banque Nationale de Paris	Banque Paribas Capital Markets Limited
Caisse des Dépôts et Consignations	Crédit Agricole
Crédit Lyonnais	Deutsche Bank Capital Markets Limited
EBC Amro Bank Limited	Generale Bank
Genossenschaftliche Zentralbank AG Vienna	IBJ International Limited
Mitsubishi Finance International Limited	Morgan Guaranty Ltd
Morgan Stanley International	Nippon European Bank S.A.
Nomura International Limited	Société Génerale
Swiss Bank Corporation International Limited	Union Bank of Switzerland (Securities) Limited
S. G. Warburg & Co. Ltd.	Westpac Banking Corporation

Figure 1.2
Globalization: A debt issue denominated in European currency units

vertible bonds at the option of the firm. Hence, this security is a bundling of preferred stock with several options.

Quite often, creating a security that appears to be attractive requires **unbundling** of an asset. An example is given in Figure 1.6 (see page 33). There, a mortgage pass-through certificate is unbundled into two classes. Class 1 receives only principal payments from the mortgage pool, whereas class 2 receives only interest payments. Another example of unbundling was given in the discussion of financial innovation and CMOs in Section 1.3.

The process of bundling and unbundling is called **financial engineering,** which refers to the creation and design of securities with custom-tailored characteristics, often regarding exposures to various source of risk. Financial engineers view securities as bundles of (possibly risky) cash flows that may be carved up and rearranged according to the needs or desires of traders in the security markets. Many of the derivative securities we spoke of earlier in the chapter are products of financial engineering.

CONCEPT CHECK Question 5. How can tax motives contribute to the desire for unbundling?

Figure 1.3
Securitization of automobile loans

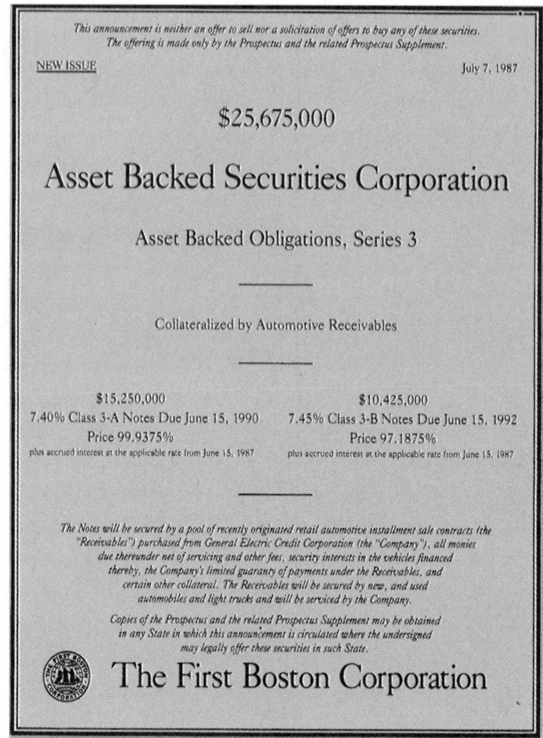

This announcement is neither an offer to sell nor a solicitation of offers to buy any of these securities.
The offering is made only by the Prospectus and the related Prospectus Supplement.

NEW ISSUE July 7, 1987

$25,675,000

Asset Backed Securities Corporation

Asset Backed Obligations, Series 3

Collateralized by Automotive Receivables

$15,250,000	$10,425,000
7.40% Class 3-A Notes Due June 15, 1990	7.45% Class 3-B Notes Due June 15, 1992
Price 99.9375%	Price 97.1875%
plus accrued interest at the applicable rate from June 15, 1987	plus accrued interest at the applicable rate from June 15, 1987

The Notes will be secured by a pool of recently originated retail automotive installment sale contracts (the "Receivables") purchased from General Electric Credit Corporation (the "Company"), all monies due thereunder net of servicing and other fees, security interests in the vehicles financed thereby, the Company's limited guaranty of payments under the Receivables, and certain other collateral. The Receivables will be secured by new, and used automobiles and light trucks and will be serviced by the Company.

Copies of the Prospectus and the related Prospectus Supplement may be obtained in any State in which this announcement is circulated where the undersigned may legally offer these securities in such State.

The First Boston Corporation

1.6 On the Relationship between Households and Businesses

Occasional waves of takeovers, particularly with the development of exotic defenses, bring to the surface public misgivings about "unproductive speculation" on Wall Street. Many see a need to curb such activities that purportedly divert funds from productive use and cause plant shutdowns and unemployment. An important related issue that may not come up in the public debate is the inherent conflict among households, the direct and indirect shareholders of businesses, and the professional managers who run them. This issue is an important feature of the investment environment.

The control structure of a typical, publicly traded firm is modeled on a democratic arrangement. Its main features are, in theory, as follows:

1. No one has to own shares. Willing investors buy shares, satisfied shareholders can buy more, and unsatisfied shareholders can unload the stock at any time.
2. Management has to disclose to the public a great deal of information, which is audited by independent experts.
3. Important decisions of management must be approved by voting in shareholder meetings.
4. In any election, the rule is one-share/one-vote; thus, shareholder voting power is proportional to the shareholder's stake in the corporation. Absentee shareholders can vote by proxy.

Figure 1.4
Aetna's credit enhancement of the Rockefeller Group's bond

Offering Circular

$100,000,000

Rockefeller Group International Finance N.V.

13¼% Notes Due 1989

Unconditionally Guaranteed as to Payment of Principal and Interest by

Rockefeller Group, Inc.

and under a Surety Bond Issued by

The Ætna Casualty and Surety Company

Issue Price 99¾%

Principal of, premium, if any, and interest on the Notes will be payable without deduction for, or on account of, United States or Netherlands Antilles withholding taxes, all as set forth herein. Interest will be payable annually on June 21, commencing in 1985.

The Notes will mature on June 21, 1989. The Notes are redeemable (i) as a whole or from time to time in part, on or after June 21, 1987 at a redemption price equal to 101¼% of the principal amount of the Notes if made prior to June 21, 1988 and 100½% of the principal amount of the Notes if made on or after June 21, 1988, plus, in each case, accrued interest to the date fixed for redemption, and (ii) as a whole at any time in the event of certain developments involving United States or Netherlands Antilles withholding taxes, at their principal amount plus accrued interest to the date fixed for redemption. See "Description of the Notes". The Notes may also be redeemed as a whole, at a redemption price equal to their principal amount plus accrued interest to the date fixed for redemption, at the option of The Ætna Casualty and Surety Company ("Ætna") upon the occurrence of certain events. See "Description of the Surety Bond".

The Notes will be unconditionally guaranteed as to the payment of principal, premium, if any, and interest and certain other amounts by Rockefeller Group, Inc. As a private corporation, Rockefeller Group, Inc., does not disclose financial information to the public. Accordingly, arrangements have been made for payments of principal of, premium, if any, and interest on, and certain other amounts with respect to, the Notes to be guaranteed under a Surety Bond issued by Ætna. See "Description of the Notes" and "Description of the Surety Bond".

Application has been made to list the Notes on the Luxembourg Stock Exchange.

The Notes have not been registered under the United States Securities Act of 1933 and may not be offered or sold, directly or indirectly, in the United States of America, or its territories or possessions or to citizens, nationals or residents thereof, except as set forth herein. See "Underwriting".

A temporary global Note without interest coupons in the amount of $100,000,000 will be delivered to a depositary in London for the account of participants in Euro-clear and CEDEL S.A. on or about June 21, 1984 and will be exchangeable for definitive Notes not earlier than 90 days after the completion of the distribution upon certification that such Notes are not beneficially owned by United States citizens, nationals or residents, as set forth herein. Interest on the Notes will not be payable until issuance of the definitive Notes. See "Description of the Notes—Denominaton and Transfer".

MORGAN GUARANTY LTD

AMRO INTERNATIONAL LIMITED — CHASE MANHATTAN LIMITED

CREDIT SUISSE FIRST BOSTON LIMITED — DEUTSCHE BANK AKTIENGESELLSCHAFT

DRESDNER BANK AKTIENGESELLSCHAFT — ENSKILDA SECURITIES SKANDINAVISKA ENSKILDA LIMITED

LEHMAN BROTHERS INTERNATIONAL SHEARSON LEHMAN/AMERICAN EXPRESS INC — SAMUEL MONTAGU & CO. LIMITED

ORION ROYAL BANK LIMITED — SOCIÉTÉ GÉNÉRALE

SOCIÉTÉ GÉNÉRALE DE BANQUE S.A. — SWISS BANK CORPORATION INTERNATIONAL LIMITED

UNION BANK OF SWITZERLAND (SECURITIES) LIMITED — S. G. WARBURG & CO. LTD.

May 25, 1984

5. Corporate management, from the president down, is subject to control by the board of directors led by the chairperson. Individual directors are elected by shareholders, who can unseat directors in any meeting. Shareholder meetings can be called by shareholders, as well as by management. One annual meeting is mandatory.

Given such a system, what can go wrong? If management is unsatisfactory, the board in principle will oust it. If the board members are not on their toes, shareholders will oust them. In the end, if all works as intended, the corporation will be run by management that executes the (aggregate) will of shareholders.

Management, however, can hurt shareholders in two ways. First, incompetent managers may be very expensive to shareholders (and to corporate employees, who also are stakeholders). Second, management's control of pecuniary rewards and other perquisites comes directly from the pockets of shareholders. This creates a conflict between management and shareholders, which is called the **agency problem.** A great deal of financial theory is dedicated to the analysis of this problem. Corporate executives are probably the best-compensated professionals in the nation, which is fine as long as the shareholders are happy. After all, competition itself should ensure that man-

Figure 1.5
Bundling creates a complex security

3,000,000 Shares

The Chubb Corporation

$4.25 Convertible Exchangeable Preferred Stock

(Stated Value $50 Per Share)

The $4.25 Convertible Exchangeable Preferred Stock (the "Preferred Stock"), $1.00 par value, of The Chubb Corporation (the "Corporation") offered hereby is convertible at the option of the holder at any time, unless previously redeemed, into Common Stock, $1.00 par value, of the Corporation (the "Common Stock") at the rate of .722 shares of Common Stock for each share of Preferred Stock (equivalent to a conversion price of $69.25 per share), subject to adjustment under certain conditions. On March 25, 1985, the last reported sale price of the Common Stock on the New York Stock Exchange was $57 1/4 per share.

The Preferred Stock also is exchangeable in whole at the sole option of the Corporation on any dividend payment date beginning April 15, 1988 for the Corporation's 8 1/2% Convertible Subordinated Debentures due April 15, 2010 (the "Debentures") at the rate of $50 principal amount of Debentures for each share of Preferred Stock. See "Description of Debentures".

The Preferred Stock is redeemable for cash at any time, in whole or in part, at the option of the Corporation at redemption prices declining to $50 on April 15, 1995, plus accrued and unpaid dividends to the redemption date. However, the Preferred Stock is not redeemable prior to April 15, 1988 unless the closing price of the Common Stock on the New York Stock Exchange shall have equaled or exceeded 140% of the then effective conversion price per share for at least 20 consecutive trading days ending within 5 days prior to the notice of redemption. Dividends on the Preferred Stock will be cumulative and are payable quarterly on January 15, April 15, July 15 and October 15. The initial dividend will be payable on July 15, 1985 and will accrue from the date of issuance. See "Description of Preferred Stock".

Application will be made to list the Preferred Stock on the New York Stock Exchange.

THESE SECURITIES HAVE NOT BEEN APPROVED OR DISAPPROVED BY THE SECURITIES AND EXCHANGE COMMISSION NOR HAS THE COMMISSION PASSED UPON THE ACCURACY OR ADEQUACY OF THIS PROSPECTUS. ANY REPRESENTATION TO THE CONTRARY IS A CRIMINAL OFFENSE.

	Initial Public Offering Price	Underwriting Discount	Proceeds to Corporation(1)
Per Share	$50.00	$1.375	$48.625
Total	$150,000,000	$4,125,000	$145,875,000

(1) Before deducting expenses payable by the Corporation estimated at $500,000.

The shares of Preferred Stock are offered severally by the Underwriters, as specified herein, subject to receipt and acceptance by them and subject to their right to reject any order in whole or in part. It is expected that certificates for the shares of Preferred Stock will be ready for delivery at the offices of Goldman, Sachs & Co., New York, New York on or about April 2, 1985.

Goldman, Sachs & Co.

The date of this Prospectus is March 26, 1985.

agerial resource compensation is allocated as efficiently as any production factor in the economy.

This is not a minor issue, because a lot of money is at stake. The mere size of modern corporations and the risk imposed by complex and changing environment and technology mean a large amount of wealth is endangered every day.

When we have large corporations and many diversified investors, however, control is very dispersed. In many cases even the largest shareholder holds less than 2% of the shares. Management, as a whole, through executive stock options and compensation shares, may become important shareholders. By and by, one finds that management controls the board, rather than vice versa.

What about proxy fights to wrest control of the firm from current management? Evidence shows that the cost of an average proxy fight is in the millions of dollars. Shareholders who attempt such a fight have to use their own funds. Management that defends against it uses corporate coffers in addition to already existing communication channels to shareholders at large. Little wonder that few such attempts are made. When they are, 75% fail. Dissidents win some seats on the board of directors in a majority of cases, but seldom enough to assume control of the company. Ousting the management of a large corporation is a modern-day version of David's battle with Goliath.

Figure 1.6 Unbundling of mortgages into principal- and interest-only securities

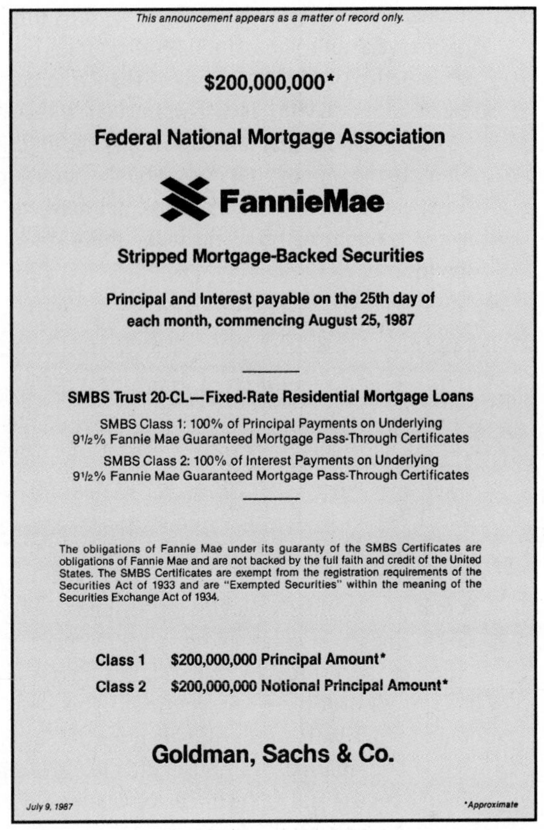
This announcement appears as a matter of record only.

$200,000,000*

Federal National Mortgage Association

FannieMae

Stripped Mortgage-Backed Securities

Principal and Interest payable on the 25th day of each month, commencing August 25, 1987

SMBS Trust 20-CL—Fixed-Rate Residential Mortgage Loans

SMBS Class 1: 100% of Principal Payments on Underlying 9½% Fannie Mae Guaranteed Mortgage Pass-Through Certificates

SMBS Class 2: 100% of Interest Payments on Underlying 9½% Fannie Mae Guaranteed Mortgage Pass-Through Certificates

The obligations of Fannie Mae under its guaranty of the SMBS Certificates are obligations of Fannie Mae and are not backed by the full faith and credit of the United States. The SMBS Certificates are exempt from the registration requirements of the Securities Act of 1933 and are "Exempted Securities" within the meaning of the Securities Exchange Act of 1934.

Class 1 $200,000,000 Principal Amount*

Class 2 $200,000,000 Notional Principal Amount*

Goldman, Sachs & Co.

July 9, 1987 *Approximate

In fact, shareholders' greatest protection is the hunger and might of other businesses. How does this sword of Damocles work? A bad management team, whether incompetent or excessively greedy, presumably causes the firm's shares to sell at a price that reflects its poor performance. Now imagine the management of one business observing another that is underperforming. All it has to do is acquire the underperforming business, fire current management, put in place their own (presumably better) people, and the stock price should reflect their expectations of improved performance. The acquiring firm might therefore be willing to bid up the price of shares of the target firm by as much as 50% to acquire it. In the process, the economy gets rid of one bad management team and becomes more efficient.

Just the threat of this mechanism ought to keep management on its toes. However, give management the ability to engage in expensive takeover defenses (at shareholder expense, of course), and their vulnerability is limited. The danger of antitakeover regulation that allows poor managers to protect their positions is clear.

What about the arguments that takeovers lead to shutdowns and unemployment, and that funds for takeovers are diverted from productive resources? A firm that takes over another one must believe that it can improve operations. If it pays a premium for the acquisition, the acquiring firm must believe it can create additional value to justify the purchase price. Potential efficiency gains might therefore be expected to be an impetus for mergers and acquisitions. Of course, one might argue that some acquisitions are motivated more by tax motives than true economic efficiency, but this seems more a reason to modify tax law than intrude in the market for corporate control.

The argument that takeover funds are diverted from productive uses is without merit. After all, the money that is paid by the acquirer to the target firm's shareholders does not disappear; it is reinvested in financial markets. In the end, the displacement of bad management ought to bring in, if anything, more investment funds in this newly created opportunity.

Summary

1. Real assets are used to produce the goods and services created by an economy. Financial assets are claims to the income generated by real assets. Securities are financial assets. Financial assets are part of an investor's wealth, but not part of national wealth. Instead, financial assets determine how the "national pie" is split up among investors.
2. The three sectors of the financial environment are households, businesses, and government. Households decide on investing their funds. Businesses and government, in contrast, typically need to raise funds.
3. The diverse tax and risk preferences of households create a demand for a wide variety of securities. In contrast, businesses typically find it more efficient to offer relatively uniform types of securities. This conflict gives rise to an industry that creates complex derivative securities from primitive ones.
4. The smallness of households leads to a market niche for financial intermediaries, mutual funds, and investment companies. Economies of scale and specialization are factors supporting the investment banking industry.
5. Four types of markets may be distinguished: direct search, brokered, dealer, and auction markets. Securities are sold in all but direct search markets.
6. Four recent trends in the financial environment are globalization, securitization, credit enhancement, and financial engineering.
7. Stockholders own the corporation and, in principle, can oust an unsatisfactory management team. In practice, ouster may be difficult because of the advantage that management has in proxy fights. The threat of takeover helps keep management doing its best for the firm.

Key Terms

Real assets
Financial assets
Financial intermediaries
Mutual funds
Investment bankers
Pass-through security
Primitive security
Block transactions
Dealer markets
Secondary market
Auction market
Globalization
Securitization
Credit enhancement

Derivative security
Dual fund
Direct search market
Brokered market
Primary market
Bundling
Unbundling
Financial engineering
Agency problem

Selected Readings

Excellent discussions of financial innovation may be found in:

Miller, Merton H. "Financial Innovation: The Last Twenty Years and the Next." *Journal of Financial and Quantitative Analysis* 21 (December 1986), pp. 459–71.

Miller, Merton H. "Financial Innovation: Achievements and Prospects." *Journal of Applied Corporate Finance* 4 (Winter 1992).

Several trends in the capital markets are discussed in:

Economic Report of the President, which is published annually.

Problems

1. Suppose you discover a treasure chest of $10 billion in cash.
   a. Is this a real or financial asset?
   b. Is society any richer for the discovery?
   c. Are you wealthier?
   d. Can you reconcile your answers to *(b)* and *(c)*? Is anyone worse off as a result of the discovery?
2. Lanni Products is a start-up computer software development firm. It currently owns computer equipment worth $30,000 and has cash on hand of $20,000 contributed by Lanni's owners. For each of the following transactions, identify the real and/or financial assets that trade hands. Are any financial assets created or destroyed in the transaction?
   a. Lanni takes out a bank loan. It receives $50,000 in cash and signs a note promising to pay back the loan over three years.
   b. Lanni uses the cash from the bank plus $20,000 of its own funds to finance the development of new financial planning software.
   c. Lanni sells the software product to Microsoft, which will market it to the public under the Microsoft name. Lanni accepts payment in the form of 1,500 shares of Microsoft stock.
   d. Lanni sells the shares of stock for $80 per share, and uses part of the proceeds to pay off the bank loan.
3. Reconsider Lanni Products from Problem 2.
   a. Prepare its balance sheet just after it gets the bank loan. What is the ratio of real assets to financial assets?
   b. Prepare the balance sheet after Lanni spends the $70,000 to develop the product. What is the ratio of real assets to financial assets?
   c. Prepare the balance sheet after it accepts payment of shares from Microsoft. What is the ratio of real assets to financial assets?

Figure 1.7
A gold-backed security

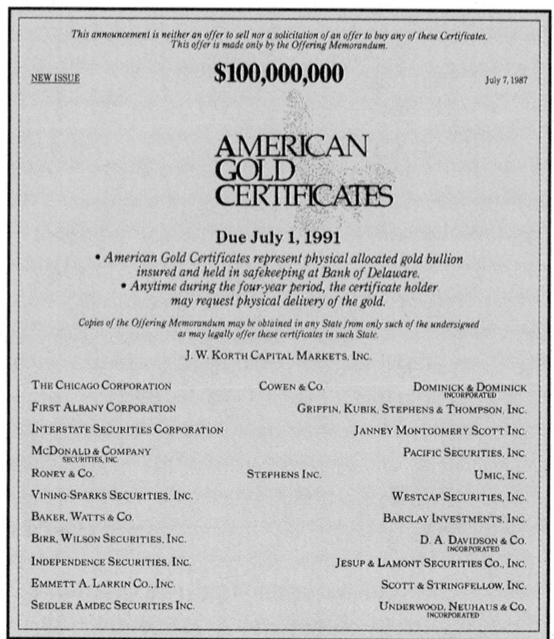

4. Examine the balance sheet of the financial sector. What is the ratio of tangible assets to total assets? What is the ratio for nonfinancial firms? Why should this difference be expected?
5. In the 1960s, the U.S. government instituted a 30% withholding tax on interest payments on bonds sold in the United States to overseas investors. (It has since been repealed.) What connection does this have to the contemporaneous growth of the huge Eurobond market, where U.S. firms issue dollar-denominated bonds overseas?
6. Consider Figure 1.7, which describes an issue of American gold certificates.
   a. Is this issue a primary or secondary market transaction?
   b. Are the certificates primitive or derivative assets?
   c. What market niche is filled by this offering?
7. Why would you expect securitization to take place only in highly developed capital markets?
8. Suppose that you are an executive of General Motors, and that a large share of your potential income is derived from year-end bonuses that depend on GM's annual profits.
   a. Would purchase of GM stock be an effective hedging strategy for the executive who is worried about the uncertainty surrounding her bonus?
   b. Would purchase of Toyota stock be an effective hedge strategy?

9. Consider again the GM executive in Problem 8. In light of the fact that the design of the annual bonus exposes the executive to risk that she would like to shed, why doesn't GM instead pay her a fixed salary that doesn't entail this uncertainty?
10. What is the relationship between securitization and the role of financial intermediaries in the economy? What happens to financial intermediaries as securitization progresses?
11. Many investors would like to invest part of their portfolios in real estate, but obviously cannot on their own purchase office buildings or strip malls. Explain how this situation creates a profit incentive for investment firms that can sponsor REITs (real estate investment trusts).
12. Financial engineering has been disparaged as nothing more than paper shuffling. Critics argue that resources that go to *rearranging* wealth (i.e., bundling and unbundling financial assets) might better be spent on *creating* wealth (i.e., creating real assets). Evaluate this criticism. Are there any benefits realized by creating an array of derivative securities from various primary securities?
13. Although we stated that real assets comprise the true productive capacity of an economy, it is hard to conceive of a modern economy without well-developed financial markets and security types. How would the productive capacity of the U.S. economy be affected if there were no markets in which one could trade financial assets?
14. Why does it make sense that the first futures markets introduced in 19th-century America were for trades in agricultural products? For example, why did we not see instead futures for goods such as paper or pencils?

Chapter 2
Markets and Instruments

THIS CHAPTER COVERS A RANGE OF FINANCIAL SECURITIES AND THE MARKETS IN WHICH THEY TRADE. Our goal is to introduce you to the features of various security types. This foundation will be necessary to understand the more analytic material that follows in later chapters.

We refer to the traditional classification of securities into money market instruments or capital market instruments. The **money market** includes short-term, marketable, liquid, low-risk debt securities. Money market instruments sometimes are called *cash equivalents* because of their safety and liquidity. **Capital markets,** in contrast, include longer-term and riskier securities. Securities in the capital market are much more diverse than those found within the money market. For this reason, we will subdivide the capital market into four segments. Accordingly, this chapter contains a discussion of five markets overall: the money market, longer-term fixed income capital markets, equity markets, and the two so-called derivative markets, options and futures markets.

2.1 THE MONEY MARKET

The money market is a subsector of the fixed-income market. It consists of very short-term debt securities that usually are highly marketable. Many of these securities trade in large denominations, and so are out of the reach of individual investors. Money market funds, however, are easily accessible to small investors. These mutual funds pool the resources of many investors and purchase a wide variety of money market securities on their behalf.

Figure 2.1 is a reprint of a money rates listing from *The Wall Street Journal*. It includes the various instruments of the money market that we will describe in detail. Table 2.1 lists outstanding volume in 1994 of the major instruments of the money market.

Figure 2.1

Rates on money market securities

Source: *The Wall Street Journal*, November 7, 1994. Reprinted by permission of *The Wall Street Journal*,

MONEY RATES

Friday, November 4, 1994

The key U.S. and foreign annual interest rates below are a guide to general levels but don't always represent actual transactions.

PRIME RATE: 7¾%. The base rate on corporate loans posted by at least 75% of the nation's 30 largest banks.

FEDERAL FUNDS: 4¾% high, 4⅜% low, 4½% near closing bid, 4⅝% offered. Reserves traded among commercial banks for overnight use in amounts of $1 million or more. Source: Prebon Yamane (U.S.A.) Inc.

DISCOUNT RATE: 4%. The charge on loans to depository institutions by the Federal Reserve Banks.

CALL MONEY: 6½%. The charge on loans to brokers on stock exchange collateral. Source: Dow Jones Telerate Inc.

COMMERCIAL PAPER placed directly by General Electric Capital Corp.: 5% 30 to 59 days; 5.48% 60 to 74 days; 5.50% 75 to 89 days; 5.53% 90 to 119 days; 5.60% 120 to 149 days; 5.65% 150 to 179 days; 5.75% 180 to 259 days; 5.97% 260 to 270 days.

COMMERCIAL PAPER: High-grade unsecured notes sold through dealers by major corporations: 5.11% 30 days; 5.62% 60 days; 5.68% 90 days.

CERTIFICATES OF DEPOSIT: 4.36% one month; 4.70% two months; 4.79% three months; 5.30% six months; 5.80% one year. Average of top rates paid by major New York banks on primary new issues of negotiable C.D.s, usually on amounts of $1 million and more. The minimum unit is $100,000. Typical rates in the secondary market: 5.09% one month; 5.66% three months; 5.96% six months.

BANKERS ACCEPTANCES: 5.07% 30 days; 5.53% 60 days; 5.56% 90 days; 5.62% 120 days; 5.72% 150 days; 5.81% 180 days. Offered rates of negotiable, bank-backed business credit instruments typically financing an import order.

LONDON LATE EURODOLLARS: 5 3/16% - 5 1/16% one month; 5 11/16% - 5 9/16% two months; 5¾% - 5⅝% three months; 5 13/16% - 5 11/16% four months; 5 15/16% - 5 13/16% five months; 6 1/16% - 5 15/16% six months.

LONDON INTERBANK OFFERED RATES (LIBOR): 5 3/16% one month; 5¾% three months; 6 1/16% six months; 6 11/16% one year. The average of interbank offered rates for dollar deposits in the London market based on quotations at five major banks. Effective rate for contracts entered into two days from date appearing at top of this column.

FOREIGN PRIME RATES: Canada 7%; Germany 5.20%; Japan 3%; Switzerland 7.50%; Britain 5.75%. These rate indications aren't directly comparable; lending practices vary widely by location.

TREASURY BILLS: Results of the Monday, October 31, 1994, auction of short-term U.S. government bills, sold at a discount from face value in units of $10,000 to $1 million: 5.07% 13 weeks; 5.51% 26 weeks.

FEDERAL HOME LOAN MORTGAGE CORP. (Freddie Mac): Posted yields on 30-year mortgage commitments. Delivery within 30 days 9.23%, 60 days 9.30%, standard conventional fixed-rate mortgages; 5.875%, 2% rate capped one-year adjustable rate mortgages. Source: Dow Jones Telerate Inc.

FEDERAL NATIONAL MORTGAGE ASSOCIATION (Fannie Mae): Posted yields on 30 year mortgage commitments (priced at par) for delivery within 30 days 9.22%, 60 days 9.30%, standard conventional fixed rate-mortgages; 7.60%, 6/2 rate capped one-year adjustable rate mortgages. Source: Dow Jones Telerate Inc.

MERRILL LYNCH READY ASSETS TRUST: 4.40%. Annualized average rate of return after expenses for the past 30 days; not a forecast of future returns.

Table 2.1 Components of the Money Market (December 1993)

	$ Billion
Overnight repurchase agreements	$ 84.7
Term repurchase agreements	95.3
Small-denomination time deposits*	783.5
Large-denomination time deposits†	331.5
Term Eurodollars	47.8
Short-term Treasury securities‡	322.3
Bankers' acceptances‡	16.2
Commercial paper‡	386.2

*Less than $100,000 denomination.
†More than $100,000 denomination.
‡November 1993.
Source: Data from *Economic Report of the President,* U.S. Government Printing Office, 1994.

Treasury Bills

U.S. *Treasury bills* are the most marketable of all money market instruments. T-bills represent the simplest form of borrowing: The government raises money by selling bills to the public. Investors buy the bills at a discount from the stated maturity value. At the bill's maturity, the holder receives from the government a payment equal to the face value of the bill. The difference between the purchase price and ultimate maturity value constitutes the investor's earnings.

T-bills with initial maturities of 91 days or 182 days are issued weekly. Offerings of 52-week bills are made monthly. Sales are conducted via auction, at which investors can submit competitive or noncompetitive bids. A competitive bid is an order for a given quantity of bills at a specific offered price. The order is filled only if the bid is high enough relative to other bids to be accepted. A noncompetitive bid is an unconditional offer to purchase bills at the average price of the successful competitive bids.

The Treasury rank-orders bids by offering price and accepts bids in order of descending price until the entire issue is absorbed by competitive and noncompetitive bids. Competitive bidders face two dangers: They may bid too high and overpay for the bills, or they may bid too low and be shut out of the auction. Noncompetitive bidders, by contrast, pay the average price for the issue, and all noncompetitive bids are accepted up to a maximum of $1 million per bid. In recent years noncompetitive bids have absorbed between 10% and 20% of the total auction.

Individuals can purchase T-bills directly at auction or on the secondary market from a government securities dealer. T-bills are highly liquid; that is, they are easily converted to cash and sold at low transaction cost and with not much price risk. Unlike most other money market instruments, which sell in minimum denominations of $100,000, T-bills sell in minimum denominations of only $10,000. The income earned on T-bills is exempt from all state and local taxes, another characteristic distinguishing them from other money market instruments.

Bank Discount Yields. T-bill yields are not quoted in the financial pages as effective annual rates of return. Instead, the **bank discount yield** is used. To illustrate this method, consider a $10,000 par value T-bill sold at $9,600 with a maturity of a half-year, or 182 days. With the bank discount method, the bill's discount from par value, which here equals $400, is "annualized" based on a 360-day year. The $400 discount is annualized as

$$\$400 \times (360/182) = \$791.21$$

The result is divided by the $10,000 par value to obtain a bank discount yield of 7.912% per year. Rather than report T-bill prices, the financial pages report these discount yields.

The bank discount yield is not an accurate measure of the effective annual rate of return. To see this, note that the half-year holding period return on the bill is 4.17%; the $9,600 investment provides $400 in earnings, and 400/9600 = .0417. The compound interest–annualized rate of return, or **effective annual yield**, is therefore

$$(1.0417)^2 - 1 = .0851$$
$$= 8.51\%$$

We can highlight the source of the discrepancy between the bank discount yield and effective annual yield by examining the bank discount formula:

$$r_{BD} = \frac{10{,}000 - P}{10{,}000} \times \frac{360}{n} \qquad (2.1)$$

where P is the bond price, n is the maturity of the bill in days, and r_{BD} is the bank discount yield. (Actually, because of the convention of *skip-day settlement*, n is reported

Figure 2.2

Treasury bill listings

Source: *The Wall Street Journal*, November 1, 1994. Reprinted by permission of *The Wall Street Journal*,

TREASURY BILLS

Maturity	Days to Mat.	Bid	Asked	Chg.	Ask Yld.
Nov 03 '94	1	4.25	4.15	−0.03	4.21
Nov 10 '94	8	4.40	4.30	−0.02	4.36
Nov 17 '94	15	4.40	4.30	....	4.37
Nov 25 '94	23	4.27	4.17	+0.02	4.24
Dec 01 '94	29	4.29	4.25	....	4.32
Dec 08 '94	36	4.49	4.47	+0.02	4.55
Dec 15 '94	43	4.60	4.58	+0.02	4.67
Dec 22 '94	50	4.74	4.70	+0.02	4.80
Dec 29 '94	57	4.57	4.53	+0.01	4.63
Jan 05 '95	64	4.81	4.79	−0.01	4.90
Jan 12 '95	71	4.89	4.87	+0.01	4.99
Jan 19 '95	78	4.98	4.96	+0.02	5.08
Jan 26 '95	**85**	**5.03**	**5.01**	**+0.02**	**5.14**
Feb 02 '95	92	5.05	5.03	+0.02	5.17
Feb 09 '95	99	5.09	5.07	+0.01	5.21
Feb 16 '95	106	5.11	5.09	....	5.24

TREASURY BILLS

Maturity	Days to Mat.	Bid	Asked	Chg.	Ask Yld.
Feb 23 '95	113	5.11	5.09	−0.01	5.24
Mar 02 '95	120	5.18	5.16	....	5.32
Mar 09 '95	127	5.20	5.18	....	5.35
Mar 16 '95	134	5.25	5.23	+0.01	5.41
Mar 23 '95	141	5.27	5.25	....	5.43
Mar 30 '95	148	5.29	5.27	....	5.46
Apr 06 '95	155	5.38	5.36	+0.01	5.56
Apr 13 '95	162	5.40	5.38	....	5.59
Apr 20 '95	169	5.44	5.42	+0.01	5.64
Apr 27 '95	**176**	**5.45**	**5.43**	**+0.01**	**5.66**
May 04 '95	183	5.49	5.47	....	5.70
Jun 01 '95	211	5.54	5.52	+0.01	5.76
Jun 29 '95	239	5.57	5.55	+0.01	5.80
Jul 27 '95	267	5.66	5.64	....	5.91
Aug 24 '95	295	5.71	5.69	+0.01	5.98
Sep 21 '95	323	5.73	5.71	+0.01	6.02
Oct 19 '95	351	5.81	5.79	....	6.13

as though the T-bill sale will not be consummated until two business days after the date on which the T-bill price is quoted. For example, Figure 2.2, which reports prices for October 31, 1994, shows only one day to maturity for the first bill despite the fact that three days remain until maturity.)

The bank discount formula thus takes the bill's discount from par as a fraction of par value and then annualizes by the factor $360/n$. There are three problems with this technique, and they all combine to reduce the bank discount yield compared with the effective annual yield. First, the bank discount yield is annualized using a 360-day year rather than a 365-day year. Second, the annualization technique uses simple interest rather than compound interest. Multiplication by $360/n$ does not account for the ability to earn interest on interest, which is the essence of compounding. Finally, the denominator in the first term in equation 2.1 is the par value, \$10,000, rather than the purchase price of the bill, P. We want an interest rate to tell us the income that we can earn per dollar invested, but dollars invested here are P, not \$10,000. Less than \$10,000 is required to purchase the bill.

Figure 2.2 shows Treasury bill listings from *The Wall Street Journal* for prices on October 31, 1994. The discount yield on the bill maturing on January 26, 1995 is 5.03% based on the bid price of the bond and 5.01% based on the asked price. (The bid price is the price at which a customer can sell the bill to a dealer in the security, whereas the asked price is the price at which the customer can buy a security from a dealer. The difference in bid and asked prices is a source of profit to the dealer.)

To determine the bill's true market price, we must solve equation 2.1 for P. Rearranging equation 2.1, we obtain

$$P = 10{,}000 \times [1 - r_{BD} \times (n/360)] \tag{2.2}$$

Equation 2.2 in effect first "deannualizes" the bank discount yield to obtain the actual proportional discount from par, then finds the fraction of par for which the bond sells (which is the expression in brackets), and finally multiplies the result by par value, or \$10,000. In the case at hand, $n = 85$ days for a January 26 maturity bond. The discount yield based on the asked price is 5.01% or .0501, so that the asked price of the bill is

$$\$10{,}000 \times [1 - .0501 \times (85/360)] = \$9{,}881.708$$

CONCEPT CHECK Question 1. Find the bid price of the preceding bill based on the bank discount yield at bid.

The "yield" column in Figure 2.2 is the **bond equivalent yield** of the T-bill. This is the bill's yield over its life, assuming that it is purchased for the asked price, and annualized using simple interest techniques. The bond equivalent yield (r_{BEY}) is expressed as

$$r_{BEY} = \frac{10{,}000 - P}{P} \times \frac{365}{n} \tag{2.3}$$

In equation 2.3 the holding period return of the bill is computed in the first term on the right-hand side as the price increase of the bill if held until maturity per dollar paid for the bill. The second term annualizes that yield. Note that the bond equivalent yield correctly uses the price of the bill in the denominator of the first term and uses a 365-day year in the second term to annualize. (In leap years, we use a 366-day year in equation 2.3.) It still, however, uses a simple interest procedure to annualize, also known as *annual percentage rate,* or APR, and so problems still remain in comparing yields on bills with different maturities. Nevertheless, yields on most securities with less than a year to maturity are annualized using a simple interest approach.

Thus, for our demonstration bill,

$$r_{BEY} = \frac{10{,}000 - 9{,}881.708}{9{,}881.708} \times \frac{365}{85} = .0514$$

or 5.14%, as reported in *The Wall Street Journal.*

A convenient formula relating the bond equivalent yield to the bank discount yield is

$$r_{BEY} = \frac{365 \times r_{BD}}{360 - (r_{BD} \times n)}$$

where r_{BD} is the discount yield. Here, $r_{BD} = .0501$, so that

$$r_{BEY} = \frac{365 \times .0501}{360 - (.0501 \times 85)} = .0514$$

as derived previously.

Finally, the effective annual yield on the bill based on the asked price, 9,881.708, is derived as follows: The bond's 85-day return equals (10,000 − 9,881.708)/9,881.708, or 1.197%. Annualizing this return, we obtain $(1.01197)^{365/85} = 1.0524$, implying an effective annual interest rate of 5.24%.

This example illustrates the general rule that the bank discount yield is less than the bond equivalent yield, which in turn is less than the compounded, or effective, annual yield.

Certificates of Deposit

A certificate of deposit, or CD, is a time deposit with a bank. Time deposits may not be withdrawn on demand. The bank pays interest and principal to the depositor only at the end of the fixed term of the CD. CDs issued in denominations greater than $100,000 are usually negotiable, however; that is, they can be sold to another investor if the owner needs to cash in the certificate before its maturity date. Short-term CDs are highly marketable, although the market significantly thins out for maturities of six months or more. CDs are treated as bank deposits by the Federal Deposit Insurance Corporation, so they are insured for up to $100,000 in the event of a bank insolvency.

Commercial Paper

Large, well-known companies often issue their own short-term unsecured debt notes rather than borrow directly from banks. These notes are called *commercial paper*. Very often, commercial paper is backed by a bank line of credit, which gives the borrower access to cash that can be used (if needed) to pay off the paper at maturity. Commercial paper maturities range up to 270 days; longer maturities would require registration with the Securities and Exchange Commission and so are almost never issued. Most often, commercial paper is issued with maturities of less than one or two months. Usually, it is issued in multiples of $100,000. Therefore, small investors can invest in commercial paper only indirectly, via money market mutual funds.

Commercial paper is considered to be a fairly safe asset, because a firm's condition presumably can be monitored and predicted over a term as short as one month. Many firms issue commercial paper intending to roll it over at maturity, that is, issue new paper to obtain the funds necessary to retire the old paper. If lenders become complacent about a firm's prospects and grant rollovers heedlessly, they can suffer big losses. When Penn Central defaulted in 1970, it had $82 million of commercial paper outstanding. However, the Penn Central episode was the only major default on commercial paper in the past 40 years. Largely because of the Penn Central default, almost all commercial paper today is rated for credit quality by one or more of the following rating agencies: Moody's Investor Services, Standard & Poor's Corporation, Fitch Investor Service, and/or Duff and Phelps.

Bankers' Acceptances

A *banker's acceptance* starts as an order to a bank by a bank's customer to pay a sum of money at a future date, typically within six months. At this stage, it is similar to a postdated check. When the bank endorses the order for payment as "accepted," it assumes responsibility for ultimate payment to the holder of the acceptance. At this point, the acceptance may be traded in secondary markets like any other claim on the bank. Bankers' acceptances are considered very safe assets because traders can substitute the bank's credit standing for their own. They are used widely in foreign trade where the creditworthiness of one trader is unknown to the trading partner. Acceptances sell at a discount from the face value of the payment order, just as T-bills sell at a discount from par value.

Eurodollars

Eurodollars are dollar-denominated deposits at foreign banks or foreign branches of American banks. By locating outside the United States, these banks escape regulation by the Federal Reserve Board. Despite the tag "Euro," these accounts need not be in European banks, although that is where the practice of accepting dollar-denominated deposits outside the United States began.

Most Eurodollar deposits are for large sums, and most are time deposits of less than six months' maturity. A variation on the Eurodollar time deposit is the Eurodollar certificate of deposit. A Eurodollar CD resembles a domestic bank CD except that it is the liability of a non-U.S. branch of a bank, typically a London branch. The advantage of Eurodollar CDs over Eurodollar time deposits is that the holder can sell the asset to realize its cash value before maturity. Eurodollar CDs are considered less liquid and riskier than domestic CDs, however, and thus offer higher yields. Firms also issue Eurodollar bonds, which are dollar-denominated bonds in Europe, although bonds are not a money market investment because of their long maturities.

Repos and Reverses

Dealers in government securities use *repurchase agreements*, also called "repos" or "RPs," as a form of short-term, usually overnight, borrowing. The dealer sells government securities to an investor on an overnight basis, with an agreement to buy back those securities the next day at a slightly higher price. The increase in the price is the overnight interest. The dealer thus takes out a one-day loan from the investor, and the securities serve as collateral.

A *term repo* is essentially an identical transaction, except that the term of the implicit loan can be 30 days or more. Repos are considered very safe in terms of credit risk because the loans are backed by the government securities. A *reverse repo* is the mirror image of a repo. Here, the dealer finds an investor holding government securities and buys them, agreeing to sell them back at a specified higher price on a future date.

The repo market was upset by several failures of government security dealers in 1985. In these cases the dealers had entered into the typical repo arrangements with investors, pledging government securities as collateral. The investors did not take physical possession of the securities as they could have under the purchase and resale arrangement. Some of the dealers, unfortunately, fraudulently pledged the same securities as collateral in different repos; when the dealers went under, the investors found that they could not collect the securities that they had "purchased" in the first phase of the repo transaction. In the wake of the scandal, repo rates for nonprimary dealers increased, whereas rates for some well-capitalized firms fell as investors became more sensitive to credit risk.[1] Investors can best protect themselves by taking delivery of the securities, either directly or through an agent such as a bank custodian.

[1]Stephen A. Lumpkin, "Repurchase and Reverse Repurchase Agreements," in T. Cook and T. Rowe (editors), *Instruments of the Money Market* (Richmond, Va.: Federal Reserve Bank of Richmond, 1986).

Federal Funds

Just as most of us maintain deposits at banks, banks maintain deposits of their own at a Federal Reserve bank. Each member bank of the Federal Reserve System, or "the Fed," is required to maintain a minimum balance in a reserve account with the Fed. The required balance depends on the total deposits of the bank's customers. Funds in the bank's reserve account are called *federal funds* or *fed funds*. At any time, some banks have more funds than required at the Fed. Other banks, primarily big banks in New York and other financial centers, tend to have a shortage of federal funds. In the federal funds market, banks with excess funds lend to those with a shortage. These loans, which are usually overnight transactions, are arranged at a rate of interest called the federal funds rate.

Although the fed funds market arose primarily as a way for banks to transfer balances to meet reserve requirements, today the market has evolved to the point that many large banks use federal funds in a straightforward way as one component of their total sources of funding. Therefore, the fed funds rate is simply the rate of interest on very short-term loans among financial institutions.

Brokers' Calls

Individuals who buy stocks on margin borrow part of the funds to pay for the stocks from their broker. The broker in turn may borrow the funds from a bank, agreeing to repay the bank immediately (on call) if the bank requests it. The rate paid on such loans is usually about 1% higher than the rate on short-term T-bills.

The LIBOR Market

The **London Interbank Offered Rate** (LIBOR) is the rate at which large banks in London are willing to lend money among themselves. This rate, which is quoted on dollar-denominated loans, has become the premier short-term interest rate quoted in the European money market, and it serves as a reference rate for a wide range of transactions. For example, a corporation might borrow at a floating rate equal to LIBOR plus 2%.

Yields on Money Market Instruments

Although most money market securities are of low risk, they are not risk-free. For example, as we noted earlier, the commercial paper market was rocked by the Penn Central bankruptcy, which precipitated a default on $82 million of commercial paper. Money market investors became more sensitive to creditworthiness after this episode, and the yield spread between low- and high-quality paper widened.

The securities of the money market do promise yields greater than those on default-free T-bills, at least in part because of greater relative riskiness. In addition, many investors require more liquidity; thus they will accept lower yields on securities such as T-bills that can be quickly and cheaply sold for cash. Figure 2.3 shows that bank CDs,

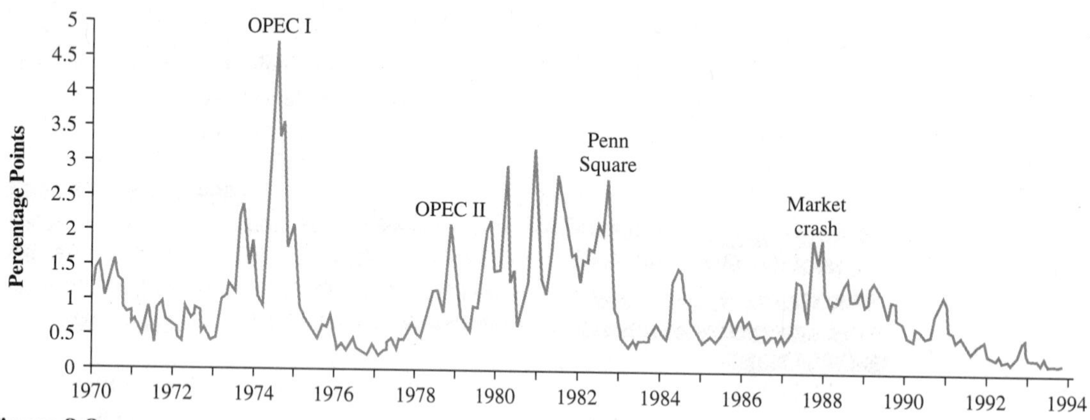

Figure 2.3
The spread between 3-month CD and Treasury bill rates

for example, consistently have paid a risk premium over T-bills. Moreover, that risk premium increased with economic crises such as the energy price shocks associated with the two OPEC disturbances, the failures of Continental Illinois and Penn Square banks, or the stock market crash in 1987.

2.2 The Fixed-Income Capital Market

The fixed-income capital market is composed of longer-term borrowing instruments than those that trade in the money market. This market includes Treasury notes and bonds, corporate bonds, municipal bonds, mortgage securities, and federal agency debt.

Treasury Notes and Bonds

The U.S. government borrows funds in large part by selling *Treasury notes* and *Treasury bonds*. T-note maturities range up to 10 years, whereas bonds are issued with maturities ranging from 10 to 30 years. Both are issued in denominations of $1,000 or more. Both make semiannual coupon payments that are set at an initial level that enables the government to sell the securities at or near par value. Aside from their differing maturities at issuance, the only major distinction between T-notes and T-bonds is that T-bonds may be callable during a given period, usually the last five years of the bond's life. The call provision gives the Treasury the right to repurchase the bond at par value. Although the Treasury hasn't issued these bonds since 1984, several previously issued callable bonds are still outstanding.

Figure 2.4 is an excerpt from a listing of Treasury issues in *The Wall Street Journal*. Note the bond (*arrow*) that matures in August 2000. The coupon income, or interest, paid by the bond is 8¾% of par value, meaning that a $1,000 face-value bond pays

Figure 2.4

Treasury bonds and notes

Source: *The Wall Street Journal*, 1994. Reprinted by permission of *The Wall Street Journal*, © 1994 Dow Jones & Company, Inc. All Rights Reserved Worldwide.

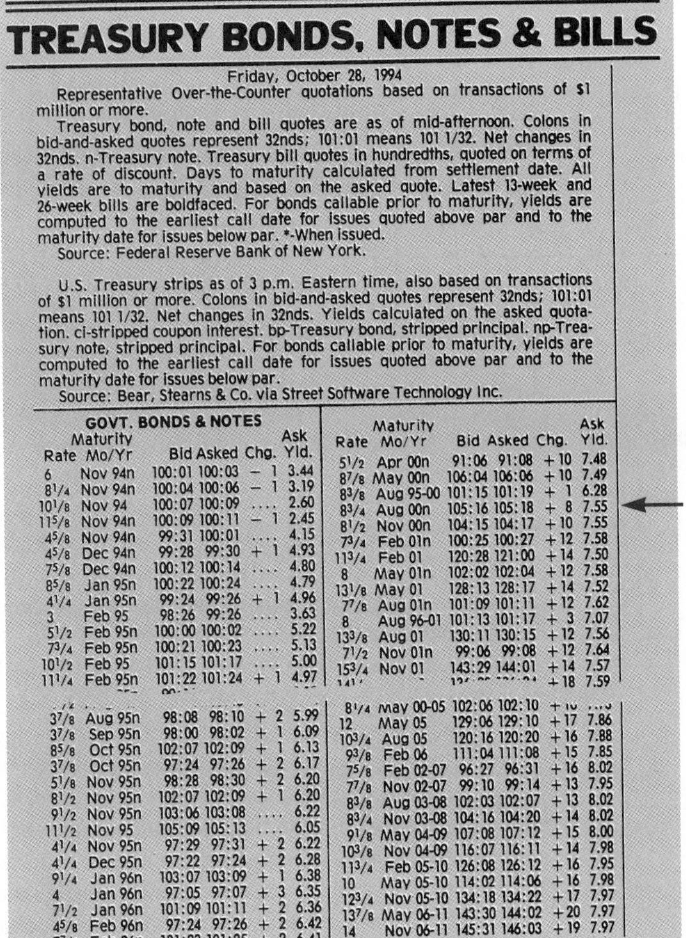

TREASURY BONDS, NOTES & BILLS

Friday, October 28, 1994

Representative Over-the-Counter quotations based on transactions of $1 million or more.

Treasury bond, note and bill quotes are as of mid-afternoon. Colons in bid-and-asked quotes represent 32nds; 101:01 means 101 1/32. Net changes in 32nds. n-Treasury note. Treasury bill quotes in hundredths, quoted on terms of a rate of discount. Days to maturity calculated from settlement date. All yields are to maturity and based on the asked quote. Latest 13-week and 26-week bills are boldfaced. For bonds callable prior to maturity, yields are computed to the earliest call date for issues quoted above par and to the maturity date for issues below par. *-When issued.

Source: Federal Reserve Bank of New York.

U.S. Treasury strips as of 3 p.m. Eastern time, also based on transactions of $1 million or more. Colons in bid-and-asked quotes represent 32nds; 101:01 means 101 1/32. Net changes in 32nds. Yields calculated on the asked quotation. ci-stripped coupon interest. bp-Treasury bond, stripped principal. np-Treasury note, stripped principal. For bonds callable prior to maturity, yields are computed to the earliest call date for issues quoted above par and to the maturity date for issues below par.

Source: Bear, Stearns & Co. via Street Software Technology Inc.

GOVT. BONDS & NOTES

Rate	Maturity Mo/Yr	Bid	Asked	Chg.	Ask Yld.
6	Nov 94n	100:01	100:03	− 1	3.44
8 1/4	Nov 94n	100:04	100:06	− 1	3.19
10 1/8	Nov 94	100:07	100:09	....	2.60
11 5/8	Nov 94n	100:09	100:11	− 1	2.45
4 5/8	Nov 94n	99:31	100:01	....	4.15
4 5/8	Dec 94n	99:28	99:30	+ 1	4.93
7 5/8	Dec 94n	100:12	100:14	....	4.80
8 5/8	Jan 95n	100:22	100:24	....	4.79
4 1/4	Jan 95n	99:24	99:26	+ 1	4.96
3	Feb 95	98:26	99:26	....	3.63
5 1/2	Feb 95n	100:00	100:02	....	5.22
7 3/4	Feb 95n	100:21	100:23	....	5.13
10 1/2	Feb 95	101:15	101:17	....	5.00
11 1/4	Feb 95n	101:22	101:24	+ 1	4.97
3 7/8	Aug 95n	98:08	98:10	+ 2	5.99
3 7/8	Sep 95n	98:00	98:02	+ 1	6.09
8 5/8	Oct 95n	102:07	102:09	+ 1	6.13
3 7/8	Oct 95n	97:24	97:26	+ 2	6.17
5 1/8	Nov 95n	98:28	98:30	+ 2	6.20
8 1/2	Nov 95n	102:07	102:09	+ 1	6.20
9 1/2	Nov 95n	103:06	103:08	....	6.22
11 1/2	Nov 95	105:09	105:13	....	6.05
4 1/4	Nov 95n	97:29	97:31	+ 2	6.22
4 1/4	Dec 95n	97:22	97:24	+ 2	6.28
9 1/4	Jan 96n	103:07	103:09	+ 1	6.38
4	Jan 96n	97:05	97:07	+ 3	6.35
7 1/2	Jan 96n	101:09	101:11	+ 2	6.36
4 5/8	Feb 96n	97:24	97:26	+ 2	6.42
7 7/8	Feb 96n	101:23	101:25	+ 2	6.41

Rate	Maturity Mo/Yr	Bid	Asked	Chg.	Ask Yld.
5 1/2	Apr 00n	91:06	91:08	+ 10	7.48
8 7/8	May 00n	106:04	106:06	+ 10	7.49
8 3/8	Aug 95-00	101:15	101:19	+ 1	6.28
8 3/4	Aug 00n	105:16	105:18	+ 8	7.55
8 1/2	Nov 00n	104:15	104:17	+ 10	7.55
7 3/4	Feb 01n	100:25	100:27	+ 12	7.58
11 3/4	Feb 01	120:28	121:00	+ 14	7.50
8	May 01n	102:02	102:04	+ 12	7.58
13 1/8	May 01	128:13	128:17	+ 14	7.52
7 7/8	Aug 01n	101:09	101:11	+ 12	7.62
8	Aug 96-01	101:13	101:17	+ 3	7.07
13 3/8	Aug 01	130:11	130:15	+ 12	7.56
7 1/2	Nov 01n	99:06	99:08	+ 12	7.64
15 3/4	Nov 01	143:29	144:01	+ 14	7.57
[illegible]	[illegible]	[illegible]	[illegible]	+ 18	7.59
8 1/4	May 00-05	102:06	102:10	[illegible]	[illegible]
12	May 05	129:06	129:10	+ 17	7.86
10 3/4	Aug 05	120:16	120:20	+ 16	7.88
9 3/8	Feb 06	111:04	111:08	+ 15	7.85
7 5/8	Feb 02-07	96:27	96:31	+ 16	8.02
7 7/8	Nov 02-07	99:10	99:14	+ 13	7.95
8 3/8	Aug 03-08	102:03	102:07	+ 13	8.02
8 3/4	Nov 03-08	104:16	104:20	+ 14	8.02
9 1/8	May 04-09	107:08	107:12	+ 15	8.00
10 3/8	Nov 04-09	116:07	116:11	+ 14	7.98
11 3/4	Feb 05-10	126:08	126:12	+ 16	7.95
10	May 05-10	114:02	114:06	+ 16	7.98
12 3/4	Nov 05-10	134:18	134:22	+ 17	7.97
13 7/8	May 06-11	143:30	144:02	+ 20	7.97
14	Nov 06-11	145:31	146:03	+ 19	7.97

$87.50 in annual interest in two semiannual installments of $43.75 each. The numbers to the right of the colon in the bid and asked prices represent units of $\frac{1}{32}$ of a point.

The bid price of the August 2000 bond is $105\frac{16}{32}$, or 105.50. The asked price is $105\frac{18}{32}$, or 105.5625. Although bonds are sold in denominations of $1,000 par value, the prices are quoted as a percentage of par value. Thus the bid price of 105.50 should be interpreted as 105.50% of par or $1,055 for the $1,000 par value bond. Similarly, the bond could be bought from a dealer for $1,055.625. The +8 bid change means the closing bid price on this day increased $\frac{8}{32}$ (as a percentage of par value) from the previous day's closing bid price. Finally, the yield to maturity on the bond based on the asked price is 7.55%.

The **yield to maturity** reported in the financial pages is calculated by determining the semiannual yield and then doubling it, rather than compounding it for two half-year periods. This use of a simple interest technique to annualize means that the yield is quoted on an annual percentage rate (APR) basis rather than as an effective annual yield. The APR method in this context is also called the *bond equivalent yield.*

You can pick out the callable bonds in Figure 2.4 because a range of years appears in the maturity-date column. These are the years during which the bond is callable. Yields on premium bonds (bonds selling above par value) are calculated as the yield to the first call date, whereas yields on discount bonds are calculated as the yield to maturity date.

CONCEPT CHECK

Question 2. Why does it make sense to calculate yields on discount bonds to maturity and yields on premium bonds to the first call date?

Federal Agency Debt

Some government agencies issue their own securities to finance their activities. These agencies usually are formed to channel credit to a particular sector of the economy that Congress believes might not receive adequate credit through normal private sources. Figure 2.5 reproduces listings of some of these securities from *The Wall Street Journal.* The majority of the debt is issued in support of farm credit and home mortgages.

The major mortgage-related agencies are the Federal Home Loan Bank (FHLB), the Federal National Mortgage Association (FNMA, or Fannie Mae), the Government National Mortgage Association (GNMA, or Ginnie Mae), and the Federal Home Loan Mortgage Corporation (FHLMC, or Freddie Mac). The FHLB borrows money by issuing securities and lends this money to savings and loan institutions to be lent in turn to individuals borrowing for home mortgages.

Freddie Mac and Ginnie Mae were organized to provide liquidity to the mortgage market. Until the pass-through securities sponsored by these agencies were established (see the discussion of mortgages and mortgage-backed securities later in this section), the lack of a secondary market in mortgages hampered the flow of investment funds into mortgages and made mortgage markets dependent on local, rather than national, credit availability.

The farm credit agencies consist of

1. The 12 district Banks for Cooperatives, which make seasonal loans to farm cooperatives.
2. The 12 Federal Land Banks, which make mortgage loans on farm properties.
3. The 12 Federal Intermediate Credit Banks, which provide short-term financing for production and marketing of crops and livestock.

Some of these agencies are government owned, and therefore can be viewed as branches of the U.S. government. Thus, their debt is fully free of default risk. Ginnie Mae is an example of a government-owned agency. Other agencies, such as the farm credit agencies, the Federal Home Loan Bank, Fannie Mae, and Freddie Mac, are merely federally *sponsored.*

Although the debt of federally sponsored agencies is not explicitly insured by the federal government, it is widely assumed that the government would step in with assis-

Figure 2.5
Government agency issues

Source: *The Wall Street Journal*, November 1, 1994. Reprinted by permission of *The Wall Street Journal*, © 1994 Dow Jones & Company, Inc. All Rights Reserved Worldwide.

GOVERNMENT AGENCY & SIMILAR ISSUES

Monday, October 31, 1994

Over-the-Counter mid-afternoon quotations based on large transactions, usually $1 million or more. Colons in bid-and-asked quotes represent 32nds; 101:01 means 101 1/32.

All yields are calculated to maturity, and based on the asked quote. * – Callable issue, maturity date shown. For issues callable prior to maturity, yields are computed to the earliest call date for issues quoted above par, or 100, and to the maturity date for issues below par.

Source: Bear, Stearns & Co. via Street Software Technology Inc.

FNMA Issues

Rate	Mat.	Bid	Asked	Yld.
9.25	11-94	100:03	100:05	2.12
5.50	12-94	100:00	100:02	4.92
9.00	1-95	100:21	100:23	5.02
11.95	1-95	101:06	101:08	5.08
11.50	2-95	101:15	101:17	5.64
8.85	3-95	101:01	101:03	5.64
11.70	5-95	103:00	103:02	5.63
11.15	6-95	102:28	102:30	6.14
4.75	8-95	98:25	98:27	6.24
10.50	9-95	103:14	103:18	6.15
8.80	11-95	102:14	102:18	6.17
10.60	11-95	104:06	104:10	6.17
9.20	1-96	103:08	103:14	6.14
7.00	2-96	100:22	100:28	6.26
9.35	2-96	103:18	103:24	6.23
8.50	6-96	102:11	102:17	6.80
8.75	6-96	102:23	102:29	6.80
8.00	7-96	101:22	101:28	6.80
7.90	8-96	101:19	101:25	6.81
8.15	8-96	102:00	102:06	6.81
7.70	9-96	101:10	101:16	6.82
8.63	9-96	102:29	103:03	6.81
7.05	10-96	100:04	100:10	6.87
8.45	10-96	102:22	102:28	6.86
6.90	11-96*	99:07	99:13	7.22
7.70	12-96	100:27	101:01	7.16
8.20	12-96	102:08	102:14	6.95
6.20	1-97*	97:14	97:20	7.39
7.60	1-97	100:22	100:28	7.15
7.05	3-97*	99:04	99:10	7.37
7.00	4-97*	98:31	99:05	7.38
6.75	4-97	98:30	99:04	7.14
9.20	6-97	104:23	104:29	7.10
8.95	7-97	104:09	104:15	7.09
8.80	7-97	103:30	104:04	7.10
9.55	9-97	105:27	106:01	7.17
5.70	9-97*	95:22	95:28	7.32
5.35	10-97*	94:16	94:22	7.39
6.05	10-97*	96:01	96:07	7.49
6.05	11-97	96:12	96:18	7.34
9.55	11-97	105:17	105:23	7.40
7.10	12-97*	99:01	99:07	7.38
8.60	12-97*	100:02	100:08	6.01
9.55	12-97	105:20	105:26	7.41
6.30	12-97*	97:00	97:06	7.32
6.05	1-98	96:00	96:06	7.41
8.65	2-98	103:10	103:16	7.42
8.20	3-98	101:22	101:28	7.55
5.30	3-98*	93:06	93:12	7.57
5.25	3-98	93:04	93:10	7.51
9.15	4-98	104:21	104:27	7.52
8.38	4-98*	100:01	100:07	7.89
8.15	5-98	101:30	102:04	7.45

Rate	Mat.	Bid	Asked	Yld.
6.80	1-03	92:06	92:14	8.08
6.40	3-03*	88:11	88:19	8.31
6.63	4-03*	89:20	89:28	8.32
6.45	6-03*	88:20	88:28	8.28
6.20	7-03*	87:14	87:22	8.21
6.25	8-03*	87:04	87:12	8.30
5.45	10-03	83:13	83:21	8.05
6.20	11-03*	87:01	87:09	8.22
5.80	12-03	85:14	85:22	8.05
6.40	1-04*	88:01	88:09	8.24
6.90	3-04*	90:22	90:30	8.31
6.85	4-04	91:30	92:06	8.05
7.60	4-04*	94:17	94:25	8.41
7.65	4-04*	94:27	95:03	8.41
7.55	6-04*	94:20	94:28	8.33
7.40	7-04	95:16	95:24	8.04
8.05	7-04*	97:01	97:09	8.46
7.70	8-04*	95:14	95:22	8.35
7.85	9-04*	96:09	96:17	8.37
8.25	10-04*	98:27	99:03	8.39
8.40	10-04*	99:27	100:03	8.39
0.00	7-14	18:04	18:12	8.80
10.35	12-15	120:00	120:08	8.30
8.20	3-16	97:13	97:21	8.44
8.95	2-18	106:02	106:10	8.33
8.10	8-19	97:05	97:13	8.35
0.00	10-19	11:31	12:07	8.61
9.65	8-20*	103:08	103:16	9.29
9.50	11-20*	104:15	104:23	9.03

Federal Home Loan Bank

Rate	Mat.	Bid	Asked	Yld.
4.75	11-94	99:31	100:01	4.17
5.89	11-94	100:01	100:03	4.31
8.20	11-94	100:06	100:08	4.13
8.05	12-94	100:12	100:14	4.97
5.45	1-95	100:00	100:02	5.10
8.40	1-95	100:21	100:23	5.13

Tennessee Valley Authority

Rate	Mat.	Bid	Asked	Yld.
4.38	3-96*	97:02	97:08	6.55
8.25	11-96	102:08	102:14	6.94
4.60	12-96*	95:09	95:15	6.93
6.00	1-97*	97:24	97:30	7.02
6.25	8-99*	95:02	95:10	7.44
7.63	9-99*	98:25	99:01	7.86
8.38	10-99	102:22	102:30	7.64
7.88	9-01*	98:26	99:02	8.05
7.45	10-01*	97:14	97:22	7.89
6.88	1-02*	93:30	94:06	7.95
6.88	8-02*	93:23	93:31	7.93
7.63	9-22*	89:25	90:01	8.57
7.75	12-22*	90:04	90:12	8.67
8.05	7-24*	93:25	94:01	8.61
8.63	11-29*	97:04	97:12	8.87
8.25	9-34*	93:02	93:10	8.86
8.25	4-42*	95:03	95:11	8.66
7.25	7-43	83:11	83:19	8.70
6.88	12-43*	79:12	79:20	8.67

GNMA Mtge. Issues

Rate	Mat.	Bid	Asked	a-Bond Yld.
6.00	30Yr	82:28	83:04	8.63
6.50	30Yr	86:12	86:20	8.59
7.00	30Yr	89:20	89:28	8.68
7.50	30Yr	92:28	93:04	8.74
8.00	30Yr	95:30	96:06	8.78
8.50	30Yr	98:26	99:02	8.81
9.00	30Yr	101:25	102:01	8.74
9.50	30Yr	104:20	104:28	8.57
10.00	30Yr	107:04	107:12	8.41
10.50	30Yr	108:20	108:28	8.48
11.00	30Yr	110:14	110:22	8.56
11.50	30Yr	111:13	111:21	8.76
12.00	30Yr	112:12	112:20	8.61

World Bank Bonds

Rate	Mat.	Bid	Asked	Yld.
11.63	12-94	100:15	100:17	6.84
8.63	10-95	101:26	101:30	6.40
[illegible]	[illegible]	[illegible]	[illegible]	[illegible]

Federal Farm Credit Bank

Rate	Mat.	Bid	Asked	Yld.
3.62	12-94	99:27	99:29	4.72
4.83	12-94	99:31	100:01	4.41
4.94	12-94	99:31	100:01	4.46
11.45	12-94	100:16	100:18	4.24
3.61	1-95	99:22	99:24	5.04
4.84	1-95	99:28	99:30	5.13
5.00	1-95	99:29	99:31	5.16
8.30	1-95	100:19	100:21	5.12
3.53	2-95	99:12	99:14	5.79
5.17	2-95	99:26	99:28	5.61
5.38	2-95	100:00	100:02	5.12
5.19	3-95	99:26	99:28	5.53
6.38	4-95	100:06	100:08	5.74
4.43	4-95	99:13	99:15	5.71
5.49	4-95	99:27	99:29	5.69
5.16	5-95	99:22	99:24	5.68
5.85	5-95	100:01	100:03	5.66
5.47	6-95	99:20	99:22	6.02
5.38	8-95	99:10	99:12	6.23
5.70	9-95	99:16	99:18	6.24
5.79	10-95	99:17	99:21	6.18
6.33	11-95	100:02	100:06	6.13
5.50	12-95	99:05	99:09	6.18
5.08	1-96	98:18	98:24	6.17
6.65	5-96	99:20	99:26	6.78
4.55	2-97*	94:11	94:17	7.22
5.12	3-97*	95:13	95:19	7.20
11.90	10-97	112:01	112:07	7.25
5.27	2-99*	91:09	91:17	7.64
5.79	3-99*	92:26	93:02	7.70
8.65	10-99	103:21	103:29	7.68
7.95	4-02*	97:16	97:24	8.36

Student Loan Marketing

Rate	Mat.	Bid	Asked	Yld.
8.55	2-95	100:20	100:22	5.61
5.28	2-95	99:26	99:28	5.70
7.63	3-95	100:20	100:22	5.64
9.50	9-97*	100:00	100:06	9.41
9.80	9-00*	101:31	102:07	7.14
7.00	12-02	93:11	93:19	8.09
0.00	5-14	16:01	16:09	9.51
0.00	10-22	9:04	9:12	8.66

Financing Corporation

Rate	Mat.	Bid	Asked	Yld.
10.70	10-17	123:17	123:25	8.35
9.80	11-17	114:15	114:23	8.35
9.40	2-18	110:14	110:22	8.35
9.80	4-18	114:17	114:25	8.35
10.00	5-18	116:19	116:27	8.35
10.35	8-18	120:07	120:15	8.35
9.65	11-18	113:04	113:12	8.35

tance if an agency neared default. Thus, these securities are considered extremely safe assets, and their yield spread above Treasury securities is quite small.

Municipal Bonds

Municipal bonds are issued by state and local governments. They are similar to Treasury and corporate bonds except that their interest income is exempt from federal income taxation. The interest income also is exempt from state and local taxation in the issuing state. Capital gains taxes, however, must be paid on "munis," when the bonds mature or if they are sold for more than the investor's purchase price.

Two types of municipal bonds may be distinguished. These are *general obligation* bonds, which are backed by the "full faith and credit"(i.e., the taxing power) of the issuer, and *revenue bonds*, which are issued to finance particular projects and are

Figure 2.6

Outstanding tax-exempt debt

Source: *Flow of Funds Accounts: Flows and Outstandings*, Washington, D.C.: Board of Governors of the Federal Reserve System, September 1994.

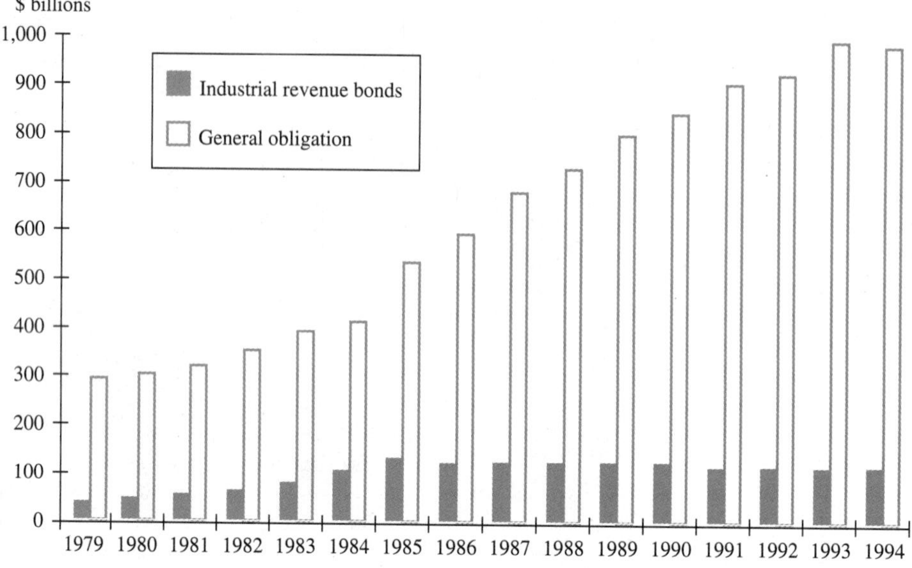

backed either by the revenues from that project or by the particular municipal agency operating the project. Typical issuers of revenue bonds are airports, hospitals, and turnpike or port authorities. Obviously, revenue bonds are riskier in terms of default than are general obligation bonds.

An *industrial developmental bond* is a revenue bond that is issued to finance commercial enterprises, such as the construction of a factory that can be operated by a private firm. In effect, these private-purpose bonds give the firm access to the municipality's ability to borrow at tax-exempt rates.

Like Treasury bonds, municipal bonds vary widely in maturity. A good deal of the debt issued is in the form of short-term *tax anticipation notes*, which raise funds to pay for expenses before actual collection of taxes. Other municipal debt is long term and used to fund large capital investments. Maturities range up to 30 years.

The key feature of municipal bonds is their tax-exempt status. Because investors pay neither federal nor state taxes on the interest proceeds, they are willing to accept lower yields on these securities. These lower yields represent a huge savings to state and local governments. Correspondingly, they constitute a huge drain of potential tax revenue from the federal government, and the government has shown some dismay over the explosive increase in use of industrial development bonds.

By the mid-1980s, Congress became concerned that these bonds were being used to take advantage of the tax-exempt feature of municipal bonds rather than as a source of funds for publicly desirable investments. The Tax Reform Act of 1986 placed new restrictions on the issuance of tax-exempt bonds. Since 1988, each state is allowed to issue mortgage revenue and private-purpose tax-exempt bonds only up to a limit of $50 per capita or $150 million, whichever is larger. In fact, the outstanding amount of industrial revenue bonds stopped growing after 1986, as evidenced in Figure 2.6.

Table 2.2 Equivalent Taxable Yields Corresponding to Various Tax-Exempt Yields

	Tax-Exempt Yield				
Marginal Tax Rate	**2%**	**4%**	**6%**	**8%**	**10%**
20%	2.5	5.0	7.5	10.0	12.5
30	2.9	5.7	8.6	11.4	14.3
40	3.3	6.7	10.0	13.3	16.7
50	4.0	8.0	12.0	16.0	20.0

An investor choosing between taxable and tax-exempt bonds must compare after-tax returns on each bond. An exact comparison requires a computation of after-tax rates of return that explicitly accounts for taxes on income and realized capital gains. In practice, there is a simpler rule of thumb. If we let t denote the investor's marginal tax bracket and r denote the total before-tax rate of return available on taxable bonds, then $r(1 - t)$ is the after-tax rate available on those securities. If this value exceeds the rate on municipal bonds, r_m, the investor does better holding the taxable bonds. Otherwise, the tax-exempt municipals provide higher after-tax returns.

One way to compare bonds is to determine the interest rate on taxable bonds that would be necessary to provide an after-tax return equal to that of municipals. To derive this value, we set after-tax yields equal, and solve for the **equivalent taxable yield** of the tax-exempt bond. This is the rate a taxable bond must offer to match the after-tax yield on the tax-free municipal.

$$r(1 - t) = r_m \tag{2.4}$$

or

$$r = r_m/(1 - t) \tag{2.5}$$

Thus, the equivalent taxable yield is simply the tax-free rate divided by $1 - t$. Table 2.2 presents equivalent taxable yields for several municipal yields and tax rates.

This table frequently appears in the marketing literature for tax-exempt mutual bond funds because it demonstrates to high tax-bracket investors that municipal bonds offer highly attractive equivalent taxable yields. Each entry is calculated from equation 2.5. If the equivalent taxable yield exceeds the actual yields offered on taxable bonds, the investor is better off after taxes holding municipal bonds. Notice that the equivalent taxable interest rate increases with the investor's tax bracket; the higher the bracket, the more valuable the tax-exempt feature of municipals. Thus, high tax-bracket investors tend to hold municipals.

We also can use equations 2.4 or 2.5 to find the tax bracket at which investors are indifferent between taxable and tax-exempt bonds. The cutoff tax bracket is given by solving equation 2.4 for the tax bracket at which after-tax yields are equal. Doing so, we find that

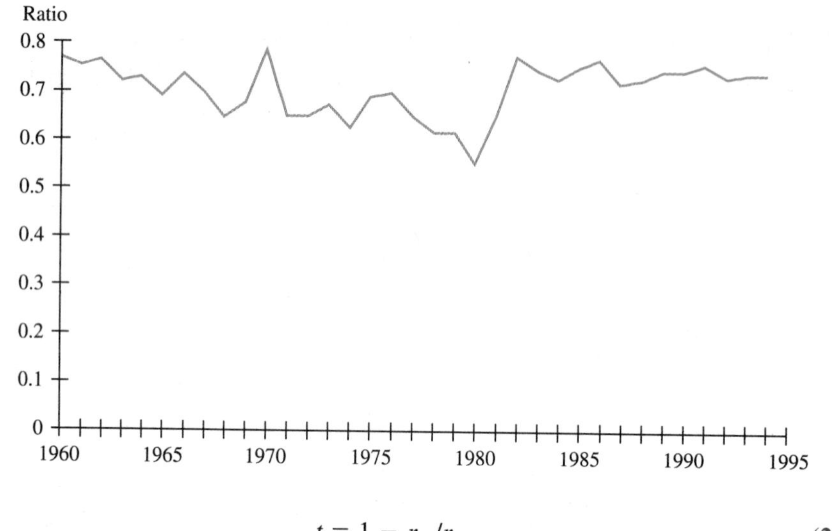

Figure 2.7
Ratio of yields on tax-exempt to taxable bonds, 1960–1994

Source: Data from *Moody's Municipal and Government Manual*, Moody's Investors Service, 1994.

$$t = 1 - r_m/r \quad (2.6)$$

Thus, the yield ratio r_m/r is a key determinant of the attractiveness of municipal bonds. The higher the yield ratio, the lower the cutoff tax bracket, and the more individuals will prefer to hold municipal debt. Figure 2.7 graphs the yield ratio since 1960. In recent years, the ratio has hovered at about .73, implying that investors in (federal plus local) tax brackets greater than 27% would derive greater after-tax yields from municipals. Note, however, that it is difficult to control precisely for differences in the risks of these bonds, so the cutoff tax bracket must be taken as approximate.

CONCEPT CHECK

Question 3. Suppose your tax bracket is 28%. Would you prefer to earn a 6% taxable return or a 4% tax-free return? What is the equivalent taxable yield of the 4% tax-free yield?

Corporate Bonds

Corporate bonds enable private firms to borrow money directly from the public. These bonds are similar in structure to Treasury issues—they typically pay semiannual coupons over their lives and return the face value to the bondholder at maturity. However, they differ most importantly from Treasury bonds in degree of risk. Default risk is a real consideration in the purchase of corporate bonds, and Chapter 13 discusses this issue in considerable detail. For now, we distinguish only among *secured bonds,* which have specific collateral backing them in the event of firm bankruptcy; unsecured bonds called *debentures,* which have no collateral; and *subordinated debentures,* which have a lower priority claim to the firm's assets in the event of bankruptcy.

Corporate bonds usually come with options attached. *Callable bonds* give the firm the option to repurchase the bond from the holder at a stipulated call price. *Convertible bonds* give the bondholder the option to convert each bond into a stipulated number of shares of stock. These options are treated in more detail in Chapter 13.

Figure 2.8
Corporate bond listings

Source: *The Wall Street Journal*, October 31, 1994. Reprinted by permission of the *The Wall Street Journal*,

NEW YORK EXCHANGE BONDS

Bonds	Cur Yld	Vol	Close	Net Chg.
v|ColuG 10¼99f	...	5	122⅛	+ 2¾
v|ColuG 9s93f	...	5	120	...
v|ColuG 10¼11f	...	10	128	...
CmwE 7⅝03J	8.4	1	91	− 1
CmwE 8¼07	8.8	2	94¼	− ½
CompUSA 9½00	11.6	311	82	+ ⅞
ConrPer 6¾01	cv	89	78¼	− ¼
ConrPer 6½02	cv	50	79¾	− ½
Consec 8⅛03	9.4	15	86⅞	+ ⅜
CnNG 5⅞98	6.3	10	93⅛	− 1⅞
ConNG 7¼15	cv	5	101	+ ¼
Cornl 7¾98	7.8	5	98⅞	− ⅜
CrayRs 6⅛11	cv	520	70¾	− 2¼
DataGn 01	cv	30	87⅞	+ 1⅝
Datpnt 8⅞06	cv	300	40⅜	+ ⅜
DelPw 6⅜97	6.6	6	97⅛	− ⅞
DetEd 6.4s98	6.8	86	94¾	− 1¼
duPnt dc6s01	6.7	294	89¼	+ ⅜
Eckerd 9¼04	9.6	153	96⅝	+ ⅝
EmbSuit 11s99	10.6	1	104	− ⅞
EBP 6¾06	cv	10	73	− 1
Enron 10¾98	10.4	20	103¾	+ 1¼
EthAln 8¾01	8.8	10	99⅜	− ¼
F&M 11½03	22.5	150	51	− ½
FairCp 13⅛06	14.6	20	90⅛	− 2⅜
FldNtl 09	...	15	33⅜	− 1⅞
Fldcst 6s12	cv	45	79	+ 2
FstRep 8½08	9.5	4	89⅞	+ 1⅝
GMA dc6s11	8.0	33	74¾	+ ⅜
GMA zr12	...	58	211⅞	+ 3⅝
GMA zr15	...	59	167	+ 2⅜
GMA 8¼16	9.0	165	91¾	+ ⅛
GMA 8⅜97	8.2	25	102⅛	+ ⅝
GnCorp 8s02	8.3	7	96¼	− ¾
GEICap 7⅞06	8.1	84	97	− ½
GHost 11½02	13.1	94	87⅞	+ ⅞
GHost 8s02	cv	4	75	...
Genrad 7¼11	cv	25	71½	...
GaGlf 15s00	14.5	148	103¼	− ¼
GaPw 6⅞02	7.5	20	92⅛	− ½
Gdrch 7s97	7.2	3	97	− 1½
GrnTrFn 10¼02	9.4	50	109½	+ 1½
Hallwd na13½09	...	149	35⅜	− 2⅞
Hallw na13½09C	...	7	40	+ 4
Hallwd 7s00	11.7	118	60	+ 1
HlthsoR 9½01	9.8	125	97	...
Hlttrst 10¾02	9.9	22	108⅝	+ ½
Hlttrst 8¾05	9.0	244	96¾	+ ¼
Hertz 6⅝00	7.1	15	93½	+ ⅜
HomeDp 4½97	cv	29	119	+ 1
HostM 9⅛00	9.3	20	98	+ ⅛
HostM 11¼05	11.2	350	100½	+ ⅛
HostM 10⅜11	10.3	103	100⅜	+ ½
ICN 12⅞98	12.7	10	101¾	+ ¼
IMC Glb 6¼01	cv	15	92½	+ ¾
IllBel 7⅝06	8.0	25	95⅜	+ ¼
v|Intlgc 11.99s96f		79	20	− 3

Quotations as of 4 p.m. Eastern Time
Friday, October 28, 1994

Volume $23,513,000

	Domestic Fri.	Domestic Thu.	All Issues Fri.	All Issues Thu.
Issues traded	342	352	345	356
Advances	182	141	185	142
Declines	101	145	101	147
Unchanged	59	66	59	67
New highs	1	3	1	3
New lows	35	47	35	47

SALES SINCE JANUARY 1
(000 omitted)

1994	1993	1992
$6,111,811	$8,320,880	$9,915,302

Dow Jones Bond Averages

−1993− High	−1993− Low	−1994− High	−1994− Low		−1994− Close	−1994− Chg.	−1994− %Yld	−1993− Close	−1993− Chg.
109.77	103.49	105.61	95.16	20 Bonds	95.21	+0.05	7.94	109.52	....
105.59	102.30	103.43	90.20	10 Utilities	90.20	−0.19	8.51	104.54	+ 0.01
114.51	104.58	107.93	98.76	10 Industrials	100.23	+0.30	7.36	114.50	− 0.01

Bonds	Cur Yld	Vol	Close	Net Chg.
MarO 7s02	7.8	100	90	...
Masco 5¼12	cv	95	83¾	− ¼
Mascotch 03	cv	56	66½	− ¾
Maxus 8½08	9.8	2	87	+ 1⅜
v|McCro 7½s94f	...	11	9⅞	− ⅝
v|McCro 7¾95f	...	1	11¾	+ 2
McDnl 9¾99	9.3	71	104½	...
McDnlDg 8⅝97	8.4	20	102⅜	− ⅛
McDnlDg 9¼02	8.9	52	103⅜	− ½
McDnlDg 9¾12	9.4	2	104	+ ⅛
McDnlDg 8¼00	8.2	10	100¼	− ¼
Mead 6¾12	cv	26	102¾	+ ¾
MichB 7¾11	8.3	11	93½	+ ¾
MichB 7s12	8.0	5	87	+ 1
MKT 5½33f	...	10	54	+ 1
MPac 5s45f	...	5	55¾	+ ⅜
Mobil 8⅜01	8.1	42	103½	+ 1⅛
NRut 8½98	8.3	5	102¼	...
NtEdu 6½11	cv	13	54¾	− ¼
NYTel 4⅝97	5.0	5	92½	− ⅜
NYTel 7½09	8.3	33	89⅞	+ ⅛
NYTel 7¾06	8.2	20	94⅜	+ ⅞
NYTel 7⅞17	8.8	116	90	+ ⅛
NYTel 7s25	8.8	15	80	− 1¼
NoPac 4s97st	4.3	3	94	+ 2
NorfW 4.85s15	6.5	1	75	+ 7

Bonds	Cur Yld	Vol	Close	Net Chg.
PierOn dc11½03	11.2	24	102⅝	...
Pier1 6⅞02	cv	2	92½	+ ½
PotEl 7s18	cv	40	94	− ¾
PSInd 7s02	7.7	2	91½	− ⅞
PSEG 8¾21	9.0	55	97	+ 1⅞
PSEG 7⅝00	7.8	10	98⅛	...
PSEG 7½23	8.9	10	83⅞	− 1¾
PSvEG 7s24	8.6	5	81¼	+ 2⅝
RJR 7⅜01	8.3	5	88¾	− ⅛
RJR Nb 10½98	10.0	9	105¼	+ ½
RJR Nb 8.3s99	8.6	138	96⅛	+ ⅛
RJR Nb 13½01	12.4	22	108⅝	+ 1
RJR Nb 8¾04	9.7	61	90⅝	+ ⅝
RJR Nb 8⅝02	9.5	189	91⅛	...
RJR Nb 7⅝03	9.1	78	84¼	...
RJR Nb 8s00	8.6	387	93	+ ⅛
RJR Nb 8¾05	9.8	403	89⅝	+ ½
RJR Nb 9¼13	10.5	372	88¼	+ ¼
Rallys 9⅞00	15.7	77	63	− ½
RalsP 9½16	9.2	17	103	...
RalsP 9s96	8.8	20	102⅜	− ⅝
RelGrp 9s00	9.8	60	92	+ ⅛
RelGrp 9¾03	10.9	190	89½	− ⅛
RepNY 8⅜07	8.4	20	100	...
Revl 10⅞10	11.5	12	94⅞	+ ⅝
Revl 9½99	10.2	140	93	+ ½

Figure 2.8 is a partial listing of corporate bond prices from *The Wall Street Journal*. The listings are similar to those for Treasury bonds. The highlighted Detroit Edison bond listed has a coupon rate of 6.4% and a maturity date of 1998. Its **current yield,** defined as annual coupon income divided by price, is 6.8%. (Note that current yield is a different measure from yield to maturity. The differences are explored in Chapter 13). A total of 86 bonds traded on this particular day. The closing price of the bond was 94¾% of par, or $947.50, which was lower than the previous day's close by 1¼% of par value.

Mortgages and Mortgage-Backed Securities

An investments text of 20 years ago probably would not include a section on mortgage loans, because investors could not invest in these loans. Now, because of the explosion in mortgage-backed securities, almost anyone can invest in a portfolio of mortgage loans, and these securities have become a major component of the fixed-income market.

Until the 1970s, almost all home mortgages were written for a long term (15- to 30-year maturity), with a fixed interest rate over the life of the loan, and with equal fixed monthly payments. These so-called conventional mortgages are still the most popular, but a diverse set of alternative mortgage designs has developed.

Fixed-rate mortgages have posed difficulties to lenders in years of increasing interest rates. Because banks and thrift institutions traditionally issued short-term liabilities (the deposits of their customers) and held long-term assets such as fixed-rate mortgages, they suffered losses when interest rates increased and the rates paid on deposits increased while mortgage income remained fixed.

The *adjustable-rate mortgage* was a response to this interest rate risk. These mortgages require the borrower to pay an interest rate that varies with some measure of the current market interest rate. For example, the interest rate might be set at 2 points above the current rate on one-year Treasury bills and might be adjusted once a year. Usually, the contract sets a limit, or cap, on the maximum size of an interest rate change within a year and over the life of the contract. The adjustable-rate contract shifts much of the risk of fluctuations in interest rates from the lender to the borrower.

Because of the shifting of interest rate risk to their customers, banks are willing to offer lower rates on adjustable-rate mortgages than on conventional fixed-rate mortgages. This proved to be a great inducement to borrowers during a period of high interest rates in the early 1980s. As interest rates fell, however, conventional mortgages appear to have regained popularity.

A *mortgage-backed security* is either an ownership claim in a pool of mortgages or an obligation that is secured by such a pool. These claims represent securitization of mortgage loans. Mortgage lenders originate loans and then sell packages of these loans in the secondary market. Specifically, they sell their claim to the cash inflows from the mortgages as those loans are paid off. The mortgage originator continues to service the loan, collecting principal and interest payments, and passes these payments along to the purchaser of the mortgage. For this reason, these mortgage-backed securities are called *pass-throughs*.

For example, suppose that ten 30-year mortgages, each with a principal value of $100,000, are grouped together into a million-dollar pool. If the mortgage rate is 10%, then the first month's payment for each loan would be $877.57, of which $833.33 would be interest and $44.24 would be principal repayment. The holder of the mortgage pool would receive a payment in the first month of $8,775.70, the total payments of all 10 of the mortgages in the pool.[2] In addition, if one of the mortgages happens to be paid off in any month, the holder of the pass-through security also receives that payment of

[2]Actually, the institution that services the loan and the pass-through agency that guarantees the loan each retain a portion of the monthly payment as a charge for their services. Thus, the interest rate received by the pass-through investor is a bit less than the interest rate paid by the borrower. For example, although the 10 homeowners together make total monthly payments of $8,775.70, the holder of the pass-through security may receive a total payment of only $8,740.

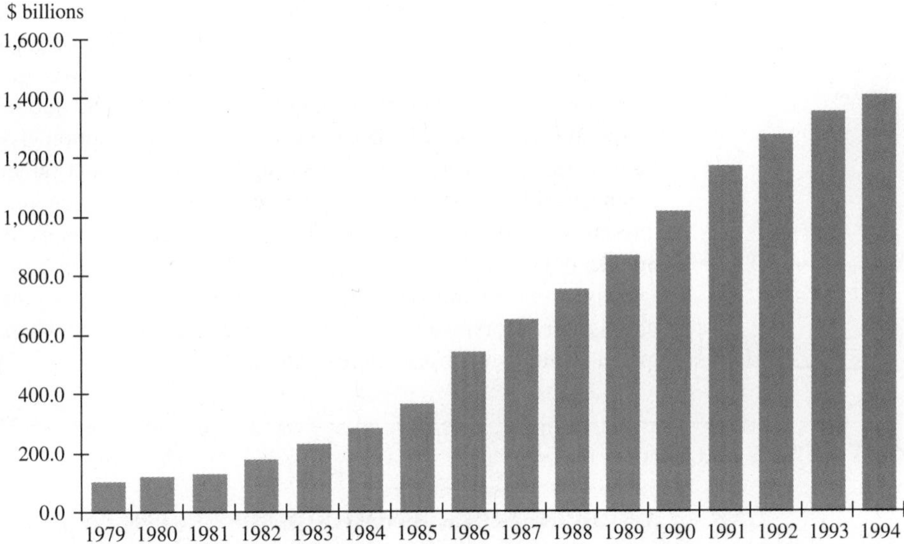

Figure 2.9
Mortgage-backed securities outstanding, 1979–1994

Source: *Flow of Funds Accounts: Flows and Outstandings,* Washington D.C.: Board of Governors of the Federal Reserve System, September 1994.

principal. In future months, of course, the pool will comprise a fewer number of loans, and the interest and principal payments will be lower. The prepaid mortgage in effect represents a partial retirement of the pass-through holder's investment.

Mortgage-backed pass-through securities were first introduced by the Government National Mortgage Association (GNMA, or Ginnie Mae) in 1970. GNMA pass-throughs carry a guarantee from the U.S. government that ensures timely payment of principal and interest, even if the borrower defaults on the mortgage. This guarantee increases the marketability of the pass-through. Thus, investors can buy or sell GNMA securities like any other bond.

Other mortgage pass-throughs have since become popular. These are sponsored by FNMA (Federal National Mortgage Association, or Fannie Mae) and FHLMC (Federal Home Loan Mortgage Corp., or Freddie Mac). As of the second quarter of 1994, roughly $1.41 trillion of mortgages were securitized into mortgage-backed securities. This makes the mortgage-backed securities market bigger than the $1.25 trillion corporate bond market and more than 40% as large as the $3.2 trillion market in Treasury securities. Figure 2.9 illustrates the explosive growth of mortgage-backed securities since 1970.

The success of mortgage-backed pass-throughs has encouraged introduction of pass-through securities backed by other assets. For example, the Student Loan Marketing Association (SLMA, or Sallie Mae) sponsors pass-throughs backed by loans originated under the Guaranteed Student Loan Program and by other loans granted under various federal programs for higher education.

Although pass-through securities often guarantee payment of interest and principal, they do not guarantee the rate of return. Holders of mortgage pass-throughs therefore can be severely disappointed in their returns in years when interest rates drop significantly. This is because homeowners usually have an option to prepay, or pay ahead of schedule, the remaining principal outstanding on their mortgages.

This right is essentially an option held by the borrower to "call back" the loan for the remaining principal balance, quite analogous to the option held by government or corporate issuers of callable bonds. The prepayment option gives the borrower the right to buy back the loan at the outstanding principal amount rather than at the present discounted value of the *scheduled* remaining payments. When interest rates fall, so that the present value of the scheduled mortgage payments increases, the borrower may choose to take out a new loan at today's lower interest rate and use the proceeds of the loan to prepay or retire the outstanding mortgage. This refinancing may disappoint pass-through investors, who are liable to "receive a call" just when they might have anticipated capital gains from interest rate declines.

2.3 Equity Securities

Common Stock as Ownership Shares

Common stocks, also known as *equity securities* or *equities*, represent ownership shares in a corporation. Each share of common stock entitles its owner to one vote on any matters of corporate governance that are put to a vote at the corporation's annual meeting and to a share in the financial benefits of ownership.[3]

The corporation is controlled by a board of directors elected by the shareholders. The board, which meets only a few times each year, selects managers who actually run the corporation on a day-to-day basis. Managers have the authority to make most business decisions without the board's specific approval. The board's mandate is to oversee the management to ensure that it acts in the best interests of shareholders.

The members of the board are elected at the annual meeting. Shareholders who do not attend the annual meeting can vote by *proxy,* empowering another party to vote in their name. Management usually solicits the proxies of shareholders and normally gets a vast majority of these proxy votes. Occasionally, however, a group of shareholders intent on unseating the current management or altering its policies will wage a proxy fight to gain the voting rights of shareholders not attending the annual meeting. Thus, although management usually has considerable discretion to run the firm as it sees fit—without daily oversight from the equityholders who actually own the firm—both oversight from the board and the possibility of a proxy fight serve as checks on that discretion.

Another related check on management's discretion is the possibility of a corporate takeover. In these episodes, an outside investor who believes that the firm is mismanaged will attempt to acquire the firm. Usually, this is accomplished with a *tender offer,* which is an offer made to purchase at a stipulated price, usually substantially above the current market price, some or all of the shares held by the current stockholders. If the

[3]A corporation sometimes issues two classes of common stock, one bearing the right to vote, the other not. Because of its restricted rights, the nonvoting stock might sell for a lower price.

tender is successful, the acquiring investor purchases enough shares to obtain control of the firm and can replace its management.

The common stock of most large corporations can be bought or sold freely on one or more stock exchanges. A corporation whose stock is not publicly traded is said to be closely held. In most closely held corporations, the owners of the firm also take an active role in its management. Therefore, takeovers are generally not an issue.

Thus, although there is substantial separation of the ownership and the control of large corporations, there are at least some implicit controls on management that tend to force it to act in the interests of the shareholders.

Characteristics of Common Stock

The two most important characteristics of common stock as an investment are its **residual claim** and **limited liability** features.

Residual claim means that stockholders are the last in line of all those who have a claim on the assets and income of the corporation. In a liquidation of the firm's assets the shareholders have a claim to what is left after all other claimants such as the tax authorities, employees, suppliers, bondholders, and other creditors have been paid. For a firm not in liquidation, shareholders have claim to the part of operating income left over after interest and taxes have been paid. Management can either pay this residual as cash dividends to shareholders or reinvest it in the business to increase the value of the shares.

Limited liability means that the most shareholders can lose in the event of failure of the corporation is their original investment. Unlike owners of unincorporated businesses, whose creditors can lay claim to the personal assets of the owner (house, car, furniture), corporate shareholders may at worst have worthless stock. They are not personally liable for the firm's obligations.

CONCEPT CHECK

Question 4.

a. If you buy 100 shares of IBM stock, to what are you entitled?

b. What is the most money you can make on this investment over the next year?

c. If you pay $50 per share, what is the most money you could lose over the year?

Stock Market Listings

Figure 2.10 is a partial listing from *The Wall Street Journal* of stocks traded on the New York Stock Exchange. The NYSE is one of several markets in which investors may buy or sell shares of stock. We will examine these markets in detail in Chapter 3.

To interpret the information provided for each traded stock, consider the listing for Baltimore Gas and Electric, BaltimrGE. The first two columns provide the highest and lowest price at which the stock has traded in the last 52 weeks, 26⅜ and 20½ respectively. The 1.52 figure means that dividend payout to its shareholders over the last quarter was $1.52 per share at an annual rate. This value corresponds to a dividend yield of 6.5%, meaning that the dividend paid per dollar of each share is .065. That is, BaltimrGE stock is selling at 23¼ (the last recorded or "close" price in the next-to-last

NEW YORK STOCK EXCHANGE COMPOSITE TRANSACTIONS

-B-B-B-

	52 Weeks Hi	52 Weeks Lo	Stock	Sym	Div	Yld %	PE	Vol 100s	Hi	Lo	Close	Net Chg
	38¾	31¾	BCE Inc g	BCE	2.68	...	...	1494	35⅛	34¾	35⅛	+ ⅜
	21¼	14⅜	BetHldg	BTV		...	23	124	16⅝	16⅝	16⅝	...
	9½	6	BET	BEP	.24e	3.6	...	37	6⅞	6¾	6¾	− ¼
	22⅞	17⅜	♣BJ Svc	BJS		...	26	783	20¼	19¼	20¼	+ 1⅛
s	16¾	7⅝	BMC	BMC	.02p	...	18	105	16½	16⅜	16⅜	...
	27⅝	19⅛	BP Prudhoe	BPT	1.48e	7.1	...	268	21¼	20⅞	20⅞	− ¼
	35⅞	29⅞	BRE Prop	BRE	2.40	7.8	15	104	30⅞	30½	30⅝	...
	4⅞	3½	BRT RltyTr	BRT		...	dd	83	4¼	4⅛	4⅛	...
	5½	3	Bairnco	BZ	.20	5.2	dd	87	4	3⅞	3⅞	...
	24	**17**	**BakrHughs**	**BHI**	**.46**	**2.2**	**32**	**25076**	**20⅞**	**20¼**	**20¾**	**+ 1⅜**
	19⅛	15⅞	BakrFentrs	BKF	2.24e	13.8	...	145	16¼	16	16¼	+ ¼
s	27½	21¼	BaldorElec	BEZ	.40	1.6	20	217	26⅜	25½	25⅝	− ¾
	31¼	24⅜	Ball Cp	BLL	.60	2.1	dd	435	28⅛	27¾	28	...
	18	8½	♣BallrdMed	BMP	.05i	.5	14	141	9⅞	9¾	9⅞	+ ⅛
	10⅛	6⅜	BallyEntmt	BLY		...	dd	1222	6⅞	6½	6¾	+ ⅛
	20½	12⅜	BaltimrBcp	BBB	.20	1.0	23	113	20⅜	20⅜	20⅜	...
→	26⅜	20½	BaltimrGE	BGE	1.52	6.5	13	1940	23¼	22¾	23¼	+ ½
	75½	56½	BaltimrGE pfB		4.50	7.8	...	1	58	58	58	+ 1½
s	38	26¾	BancOne	ONE	1.24b	4.3	9	13150	28⅞	27⅝	28⅞	+ 1
	29¾	25¼	BancoBilV pf		2.44	9.5	...	1216	26	25½	25⅝	− ¼
▼	26⅞	21¼	BancoBilV pfC		2.00	9.5	...	24	21	20¾	21	− ½
	26⅛	20¾	BancoBilV	BBV	1.23e	4.8	...	245	26	25⅝	25⅝	+ ⅛
	28⅝	24⅛	BancoBilV pfB		2.25	9.2	...	8	24½	24⅜	24½	+ ¼
	17	12	BanComercial	BPC	.34e	2.5	...	113	13¾	13⅝	13⅝	− ⅛
	52¾	34	BancoSantdr	STD	6.41e	15.8	...	252	40⅞	40⅜	40½	...
	1⅛	¾	Benguet	BE		...	...	34	⅞	13/16	⅞	+ 1/16
	19⅞	13¾	♣BergnBruns	BBC	.48	3.1	21	884	15⅝	15	15⅝	+ ½
▲	20000	15150	BerkHathwy	BRK		...	31	z43	20400	20000	20400	+ 500
	12½	9½	BrkshreRlty	BRI	.86	9.1	53	425	9¾	9½	9½	− ⅛
n	2¼	½	BrkshreRlty wt			...	...	19	⅝	⅝	⅝	...
	10¾	8	BerryPete	BRY	.40	4.2	dd	73	9¾	9½	9⅝	...
FD			BestBuyCap pf			...	...	13208	50⅜	50	50	...
s	41⅝	18¾	BestBuy	BBY		...	36	11505	37⅜	36⅞	37	− ½
	24¼	16⅛	BethSteel	BS	j	...	dd	4077	19	18½	18⅞	+ ½
	55⅝	50¼	BethSteel pf		5.00	9.4	...	34	53⅛	52⅞	53⅛	+ ½
	28¼	25⅜	BethSteel pfB		2.50	9.2	...	12	27¼	27⅛	27¼	...
	53⅝	40	BetzLab	BTL	1.44	2.9	24	693	49⅞	48½	49⅞	+ 1⅜
	16⅛	10¾	BeverlyEnt	BEV		...	19	2568	15⅛	14⅞	15	...
	67	52½	BeverlyEnt pf		2.75	4.5	...	99	61¾	61¼	61¼	+ ¼
	33⅝	26½	BIC Cp	BIC	.80	2.8	14	33	29	28½	29	+ ⅜
	37⅝	11¾	BiocraftLabs	BCL	.10	.6	77	244	17⅞	17½	17⅝	− ⅛
	8⅛	5¼	BioWhit	BWI		...	25	73	7¼	7⅛	7⅛	− ⅛
	32⅝	22½	♣BirmghamStl	BIR	.40	1.5	24	364	26¾	26	26¾	+ ¾
▲	24⅞	17	BlackDeck	BDK	.40	1.6	21	20196	25⅛	24⅝	24¾	+ ⅜
	24⅝	17⅞	BlackHills	BKH	1.32	6.5	12	74	20⅜	20	20⅜	+ ⅜
	10¾	7¾	BlackRockAdv	BAT	.73	9.0	...	60	8⅛	8	8⅛	...
	15⅝	13⅛	BlkrkCal2008	BFC	.86	6.4	...	145	13½	13⅜	13⅜	...
	15⅝	11⅞	BlkrkFla2008	BRF	.86	7.0	...	301	12¼	11⅞	12¼	+ ⅜
	8⅝	6⅛	BlackRockIncTr	BKT	.75	12.0	...	1000	6¼	6⅛	6¼	+ ⅛
	10⅞	8½	BlkrkMuni	BMT	.62	7.1	...	707	9	8¾	8¾	+ ⅛

Figure 2.10

Stock market listings

Source: *The Wall Street Journal,* October 31, 1994. Reprinted by permission of *The Wall Street Journal,*

column), so that the dividend yield is 1.52/23.25 = .0654, or 6.5%. The stock listings show that dividend yields vary widely among firms. It is important to recognize that high-dividend-yield stocks are not necessarily better investments than low-yield stocks. Total return to an investor comes from dividends and **capital gains,** or appreciation in the value of the stock. Low-dividend-yield firms presumably offer greater prospects for capital gains, or investors would not be willing to hold the low-yield firms in their portfolios.

The P/E ratio, or **price–earnings ratio,** is the ratio of the current stock price to last year's earnings. The P/E ratio tells us how much stock purchasers must pay per dollar of earnings that the firm generates for each share. The P/E ratio also varies widely across firms. Where the dividend yield and P/E ratio are not reported in Figure 2.10 the firms have zero dividends, or zero or negative earnings. We shall have much to say about P/E ratios in Chapter 17.

The sales column shows that 1,940 hundred shares of the stock were traded. Shares commonly are traded in round lots of 100 shares each. Investors who wish to trade in smaller "odd lots" generally must pay higher commissions to their stockbrokers. The highest price and lowest price per share at which the stock traded on that day were 23¼ and 22¾, respectively. The last, or closing, price of 23¼ was up ½ from the closing price of the previous day.

Preferred Stock

Preferred stock has features similar to both equity and debt. Like a bond, it promises to pay to its holder fixed dividends each year. In this sense preferred stock is similar to an infinite-maturity bond, that is, a perpetuity. It also resembles a bond in that it does not convey voting power regarding the management of the firm. Preferred stock is an equity investment, however, in the sense that failure to pay the dividend does not precipitate corporate bankruptcy. Instead, preferred dividends are usually *cumulative;* that is, unpaid dividends cumulate and must be paid in full before any dividends may be paid to holders of common stock.

Preferred stock also differs from bonds in terms of its tax treatment for the firm. Because preferred stock payments are treated as dividends rather than interest, they are not tax-deductible expenses for the firm. This disadvantage is somewhat offset by the fact that corporations may exclude 70% of dividends received from domestic corporations in the computation of their taxable income. Preferred stocks therefore make desirable fixed-income investments for some corporations. Even though they rank after bonds in the event of corporate bankruptcy, preferred stock often sells at lower yields than do corporate bonds. Presumably, this reflects the value of the dividend exclusion, because risk considerations alone indicate that preferred stock ought to offer higher yields than bonds. Individual investors, who cannot use the 70% exclusion, generally will find preferred stock yields unattractive relative to those on other available assets.

Preferred stock is issued in variations similar to those of corporate bonds. It may be callable by the issuing firm, in which case it is said to be *redeemable.* It also may be convertible into common stock at some specified conversion ratio. A relatively recent innovation in the market is adjustable rate preferred stock, which, similar to adjustable-rate mortgages, ties the dividend to current market interest rates.

2.4 Stock and Bond Market Indexes

Stock Market Indexes

The daily performance of the Dow Jones Industrial Average is a staple portion of the evening news report. Although the Dow is the best-known measure of the performance of the stock market, it is only one of several indicators. Other more broadly based indexes are computed and published daily. In addition, several indexes of bond market performance are widely available.

The ever-increasing role of international trade and investments has made indexes of foreign financial markets part of the general news. Thus, foreign stock exchange indexes such as the Nikkei Average of Tokyo and the Financial Times index of London are fast becoming household names.

Table 2.3 Data to Construct Stock Price Indexes

Stock	Initial Price	Final Price	Shares (Million)	Initial Value of Outstanding Stock ($ Million)	Final Value of Outstanding Stock ($ Million)
ABC	$ 25	$30	20	$500	$600
XYZ	100	90	1	100	90
TOTAL				$600	$690

Dow Jones Averages

The Dow Jones Industrial Average (DJIA) of 30 large, "blue-chip" corporations has been computed since 1896. Its long history probably accounts for its preeminence in the public mind. (The average covered only 20 stocks until 1928.)

Originally, the DJIA was calculated as the simple average of the stocks included in the index. Thus, if there were 30 stocks in the index, one would add up the value of the 30 stocks and divide by 30. The percentage change in the DJIA would then be the percentage change in the average price of the 30 shares.

This procedure means that the percentage change in the DJIA measures the return on a portfolio that invests one share in each of the 30 stocks in the index. The value of such a portfolio (holding one share of each stock in the index) is the sum of the 30 prices. Because the percentage change in the *average* of the 30 prices is the same as the percentage change in the *sum* of the 30 prices, the index and the portfolio have the same percentage change each day.

To illustrate, consider the data in Table 2.3 for a hypothetical two-stock version of the Dow Jones Average. Stock ABC sells initially at $25 a share, while XYZ sells for $100. Therefore, the initial value of the index would be (25 + 100)/2 = 62.5. The final share prices are $30 for stock ABC and $90 for XYZ, so the average falls by 2.5 to (30 + 90)/2 = 60. The 2.5 point drop in the index is a 4% decrease: 2.5/62.5 = .04. Similarly, a portfolio holding one share of each stock would have an initial value of $25 + $100 = $125 and a final value of $30 + $90 = $120, for an identical 4% decrease.

Because the Dow measures the return on a portfolio that holds one share of each stock, it is called a **price-weighted average.** The amount of money invested in each company represented in the portfolio is proportional to that company's share price.

Price-weighted averages give higher-priced shares more weight in determining performance of the index. For example, although ABC increased by 20%, while XYZ fell by only 10%, the index dropped in value. This is because the 20% increase in ABC represented a smaller price gain ($5 per share) than the 10% decrease in XYZ ($10 per share). The "Dow portfolio" has four times as much invested in XYZ as in ABC because XYZ's price is four times that of ABC. Therefore, XYZ dominates the average.

You might wonder why the DJIA is now (in early 1995) at a level of about 4200 if it is supposed to be the average price of the 30 stocks in the index. The DJIA no longer equals the average price of the 30 stocks because the averaging procedure is adjusted

Table 2.4 Data to Construct Stock Price Indexes After a Stock Split

Stock	Initial Price	Final Price	Shares (Million)	Initial Value of Outstanding Stock ($ Million)	Final Value of Outstanding Stock ($ Million)
ABC	$25	$30	20	$500	$600
XYZ	50	45	2	100	90
TOTAL				$600	$690

whenever a stock splits, pays a stock dividend of more than 10%, or when one company in the group of 30 industrial firms is replaced by another. When these events occur, the divisor used to compute the "average price" is adjusted so as to leave the index unaffected by the event.

For example, if XYZ were to split two for one and its share price to fall to $50, we would not want the average to fall, as that would incorrectly indicate a fall in the general level of market prices. Following a split, the divisor must be reduced to a value that leaves the average unaffected by the split. Table 2.4 illustrates this point. The initial share price of XYZ, which was $100 in Table 2.3, falls to $50 if the stock splits at the beginning of the period. Notice that the number of shares outstanding doubles, leaving the market value of the total shares unaffected. The divisor, d, which originally was 2.0 when the two-stock average was initiated, must be reset to a value that leaves the "average" unchanged. Because the sum of the postsplit stock prices is 75, while the presplit average price was 62.5, we calculate the new value of d by solving $75/d = 62.5$. The value of d, therefore, falls from its original value of 2.0 to $75/62.5 = 1.20$, and the initial value of the average is unaffected by the split: $75/1.20 = 62.5$.

At period-end, ABC will sell for $30, while XYZ will sell for $45, representing the same negative 10% return it was assumed to earn in Table 2.3. The new value of the price-weighted average is $(30 + 45)/1.20 = 62.5$. The index is unchanged, so the rate of return is zero, rather than the −4% return calculated before the split.

This return is greater than that calculated before the split. The relative weight of XYZ, which is the poorer-performing stock, is lower after the split because its price is lower; hence, the performance of the average improves. This example illustrates that the implicit weighting scheme of a price-weighted average is somewhat arbitrary, being determined by the prices rather than by the outstanding market values (price per share times number of shares) of the shares in the average.

Because the Dow Jones Averages are based on small numbers of firms, care must be taken to ensure that they are representative of the broad market. As a result, the composition of the average is changed every so often to reflect changes in the economy. The last change took place on May 6, 1991, when Walt Disney, J. P. Morgan, and Caterpillar were added to the index and Navistar, USX Corp., and Primerica were dropped. The changes increased the representation of the service sector in the index to reflect the growing role of that sector in the economy. The nearby box presents the history of the firms in the index since 1928. The fate of many companies once considered "the bluest of the blue chips" is striking evidence of the changes in the U.S. economy in the last 65 years.

In the same way that the divisor is updated for stock splits, if one firm is dropped from the average and another firm with a different price is added, the divisor has to be updated to leave the average unchanged by the substitution. By now, the divisor for the Dow Jones Industrial Average has fallen to a value of about .56.

CONCEPT CHECK

Question 5. Suppose XYZ in Table 2.3 increases in price to $110, while ABC falls to $20. Find the percentage change in the price-weighted average of these two stocks. Compare that to the percentage return of a portfolio that holds one share in each company.

Dow Jones & Company also computes a Transportation Average of 20 airline, trucking, and railroad stocks; a Public Utility Average of 15 electric and natural gas utilities; and a Composite Average combining the 65 firms of the three separate averages. Each is a price-weighted average, and thus overweights the performance of high-priced stocks.

Figure 2.11 reproduces some of the data reported on the Dow Jones Averages from *The Wall Street Journal* (which is owned by Dow Jones & Company). The bars show the range of values assumed by the average on each day. The cross-hatch indicates the closing value of the average.

Standard & Poor's Indexes

The Standard & Poor's Composite 500 (S&P 500) stock index represents an improvement over the Dow Jones Averages in two ways. First, it is a more broadly based index of 500 firms. Secondly, it is a **market-value-weighted index.** In the case of the firms XYZ and ABC discussed above, the S&P 500 would give ABC five times the weight given to XYZ because the market value of its outstanding equity is five times larger, $500 million versus $100 million.

The S&P 500 is computed by calculating the total market value of the 500 firms in the index and the total market value of those firms on the previous day of trading. The percentage increase in the total market value from one day to the next represents the increase in the index. The rate of return of the index equals the rate of return that would be earned by an investor holding a portfolio of all 500 firms in the index in proportion to their market values, except that the index does not reflect cash dividends paid by those firms.

To illustrate, look again at Table 2.3. If the initial level of a market value-weighted index of stocks ABC and XYZ were set equal to an arbitrarily chosen starting value such as 100, the index value at year-end would be 100(690/600) = 115. The increase in the index reflects the 15% return earned on a portfolio consisting of those two stocks held in proportion to outstanding market values.

Unlike the price-weighted index, the value-weighted index gives more weight to ABC. Whereas the price-weighted index fell because it was dominated by higher-price

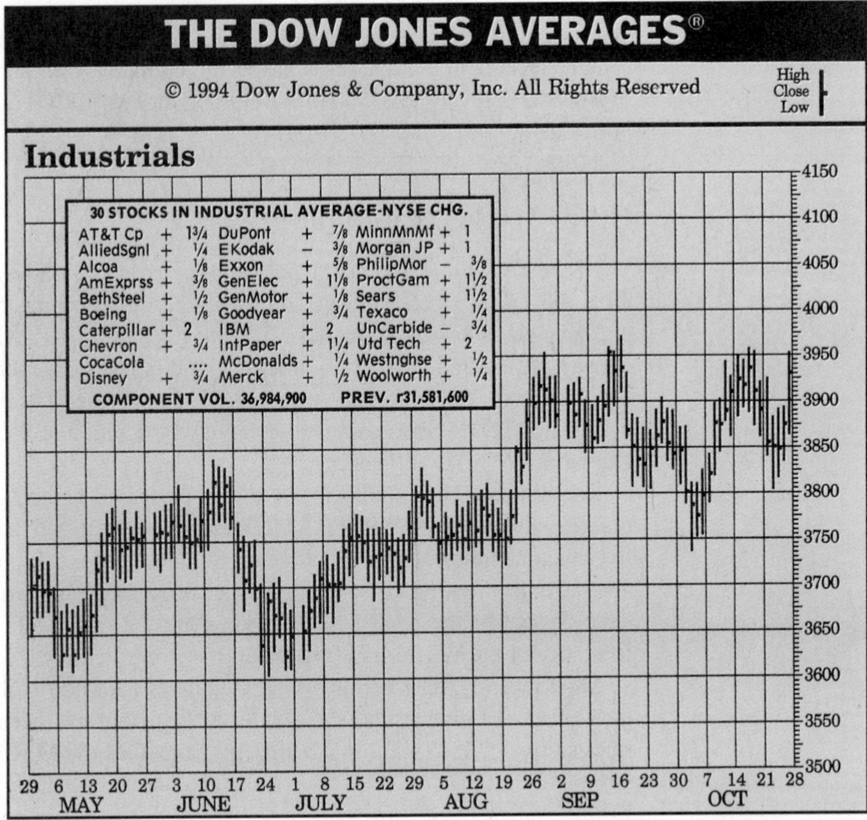

Figure 2.11
The Dow Jones Industrial Average

Source: Reprinted by permission of *The Wall Street Journal,* © 1994 Dow Jones & Company, Inc. All Rights Reserved Worldwide

XYZ, the value-weighted index rises because it gives more weight to ABC, the stock with the higher total market value.

Note also from Tables 2.3 and 2.4 that market value-weighted indexes are unaffected by stock splits. The total market value of the outstanding XYZ stock increases from \$100 million to \$110 million regardless of the stock split, thereby rendering the split irrelevant to the performance of the index.

A nice feature of both market value-weighted and price-weighted indexes is that they reflect the returns to buy-and-hold portfolio strategies. If one were to buy each share in the index in proportion to its outstanding market value, the value-weighted index would perfectly track capital gains on the underlying portfolio. Similarly, a price-weighted index tracks the returns on a portfolio comprised of equal shares of each firm.

Investors today can purchase shares in mutual funds that hold shares in proportion to their representation in the S&P 500. These **index funds** yield a return equal to that of the S&P 500 index and so provide a low-cost passive investment strategy for equity investors.

Standard & Poor's also publishes a 400-stock Industrial Index, a 20-stock Transportation Index, a 40-stock Utility Index, and a 40-stock Financial Index.

CONCEPT CHECK

Question 6. Reconsider companies XYZ and ABC from question 5. Calculate the percentage change in the market value-weighted index. Compare that to the rate of return of a portfolio that holds $500 of ABC stock for every $100 of XYZ stock (i.e., an index portfolio).

Other Market Value Indexes

The New York Stock Exchange publishes a market value-weighted composite index of all NYSE-listed stocks, in addition to subindexes for industrial, utility, transportation, and financial stocks. The American Stock Exchange, or AMEX, also computes a market value-weighted index of its stocks. These indexes are even more broadly based than the S&P 500. The National Association of Securities Dealers publishes an index of nearly 3,000 OTC firms using the National Association of Securities Dealers Automatic Quotations (NASDAQ) service.

The ultimate U.S. equity index so far computed is the Wilshire 5000 index of the market value of all NYSE and AMEX stocks plus actively traded OTC stocks. Despite its name, the index actually includes about 6,000 stocks. Figure 2.12 reproduces a *Wall Street Journal* listing of stock index performance. Vanguard offers a mutual fund to small investors, the Total Stock Market Portfolio, that enables them to match the performance of the Wilshire 5000 index.

More recently, market value-weighted indexes of non-U.S. stock markets have been developed and disseminated. A leader in this field has been Morgan Stanley Capital International (MSCI). Table 2.5 presents several of the MSCI indexes.

Equally Weighted Indexes. Market performance is sometimes measured by an equally weighted average of the returns of each stock in an index. Such an averaging technique, by placing equal weight on each return, corresponds to an implicit portfolio strategy that places equal dollar values on each stock. This is in contrast to both price weighting (which requires equal numbers of shares of each stock) and market value weighting (which requires investments in proportion to outstanding value).

Unlike price- or market-value-weighted indexes, equally weighted indexes do not correspond to buy-and-hold portfolio strategies. Suppose that you start with equal dollar investments in the two stocks of Table 2.3, ABC and XYZ. Because ABC increases in value by 20% over the year while XYZ decreases by 10%, your portfolio no longer is equally weighted. It is now more heavily invested in ABC. To reset the portfolio to equal weights, you would need to rebalance: either sell off some ABC stock and/or purchase more XYZ stock. Such rebalancing would be necessary to align the return on your portfolio with that on the equally weighted index.

The Value Line Index. The Dow Jones and market-value-weighted indexes all use arithmetic averaging: They all sum up either prices or market values and divide by a divisor. In contrast, the Value Line index is an equally weighted **geometric average** of the performance of about 1,700 firms. To compare geometric and arithmetic averages, suppose that three firms have returns on a trading day as follows:

Figure 2.12
Performance of stock indexes

Source: Reprinted by permission of *The Wall Street Journal,* ©1994 Dow Jones & Company, Inc. All Rights Reserved Worldwide.

STOCK MARKET DATA BANK **10/28/94**

MAJOR INDEXES

HIGH	LOW (†365 DAY)		CLOSE	NET CHG	% CHG	†365 DAY CHG	% CHG	FROM 12/31	% CHG
DOW JONES AVERAGES									
3978.36	3593.35	30 Industrials	3930.66	+ 55.51	+ 1.43	+ 250.07	+ 6.79	+ 176.57	+ 4.70
1862.29	1438.50	20 Transportation	1536.77	+ 41.45	+ 2.77	− 190.30	− 11.02	− 225.55	− 12.80
241.17	175.85	15 Utilities	181.65	+ 3.49	+ 1.96	− 59.12	− 24.55	− 47.65	− 20.78
1447.06	1255.54	65 Composite	1314.33	+ 24.74	+ 1.92	− 52.75	− 3.86	− 66.70	− 4.83
456.27	416.31	Equity Mkt. Index	446.88	+ 7.46	+ 1.70	+ 3.93	+ 0.89	+ 4.69	+ 1.06
NEW YORK STOCK EXCHANGE									
267.71	243.14	Composite	259.43	+ 3.86	+ 1.51	+ 0.05	+ 0.02	+ 0.35	+ 0.14
327.93	298.30	Industrials	327.56	+ 4.68	+ 1.45	+ 16.23	+ 5.21	+ 12.30	+ 3.90
241.72	199.04	Utilities	204.94	+ 3.20	+ 1.59	− 36.78	− 15.22	− 24.98	− 10.86
285.03	224.36	Transportation	236.17	+ 4.41	+ 1.90	− 25.33	− 9.69	− 34.31	− 12.68
224.90	200.49	Finance	205.76	+ 3.43	+ 1.70	− 16.38	− 7.37	− 11.06	− 5.10
STANDARD & POOR'S INDEXES									
482.00	438.92	500 Index	473.77	+ 7.92	+ 1.70	+ 5.94	+ 1.27	+ 7.32	+ 1.57
562.99	510.05	Industrials	562.99	+ 8.71	+ 1.57	+ 27.50	+ 5.14	+ 22.80	+ 4.22
453.63	348.57	Transportation	370.11	+ 7.79	+ 2.15	− 45.90	− 11.03	− 55.49	− 13.04
184.28	148.69	Utilities	153.39	+ 2.95	+ 1.96	− 30.89	− 16.76	− 19.19	− 11.12
46.94	41.39	Financials	43.90	+ 0.99	+ 2.31	− 1.22	− 2.70	− 0.37	− 0.84
184.79	162.44	400 MidCap	176.91	+ 2.87	+ 1.65	+ 1.00	+ 0.57	− 2.47	− 1.38
NASDAQ									
803.93	693.79	Composite	776.15	+ 8.68	+ 1.13	− 3.11	− 0.40	− 0.65	− 0.08
851.80	703.27	Industrials	787.33	+ 8.66	+ 1.11	− 10.02	− 1.26	− 18.51	− 2.30
949.10	858.96	Insurance	923.77	+ 10.39	+ 1.14	− 13.11	− 1.40	+ 3.18	+ 0.35
787.92	662.57	Banks	736.21	+ 1.00	+ 0.14	+ 30.17	+ 4.27	+ 46.78	+ 6.79
356.61	307.55	Nat. Mkt. Comp.	345.49	+ 3.91	+ 1.14	+ 1.23	+ 0.36	+ 1.88	+ 0.55
342.72	282.87	Nat. Mkt. Indus.	318.79	+ 3.50	+ 1.11	+ 0.26	+ 0.08	− 3.97	− 1.23
OTHERS									
487.89	422.67	Amex	458.16	+ 3.07	+ 0.67	− 23.28	− 4.84	− 18.99	− 3.98
305.87	273.73	Value-Line(geom.)	288.28	+ 3.41	+ 1.20	− 4.88	− 1.66	− 7.00	− 2.37
271.08	238.96	Russell 2000	255.00	+ 2.74	+ 1.09	− 4.18	− 1.61	− 3.59	− 1.39
4804.31	4373.58	Wilshire 5000	4679.38	+ 67.05	+ 1.45	+ 6.61	+ 0.14	+ 21.55	+ 0.46

†-Based on comparable trading day in preceding year.

Stock	Return
A	10%
B	−5%
C	20%

An equally weighted arithmetic average of these returns would be

$$[.10 + (-.05) + .20]/3 = .0833 = 8.33\%$$

In contrast, the geometric average, r_G, is computed as

$$1 + r_G = [(1 + .10)(1 - .05)(1 + .20)]^{1/3} = 1.0784$$

HOW THE 30 STOCKS IN THE DOW JONES INDUSTRIAL AVERAGE HAVE CHANGED SINCE OCTOBER 1, 1928

Year of change shown in ( ); * denotes name change, in some cases following a takeover or merger. To track changes in the components, begin in the column for 1928 and work across. For instance, American Sugar was replaced by Borden in 1930, which in turn was replaced by Du Pont in 1935.

Oct. 1, 1928	1929	1930s	1940s	1950s	1960s	1970s	1980s	May 8, 1991
Allied Chemical & Dye							Allied-Signal*('85)	Allied-Signal
Wright Aeronautical	Curtiss-Wright ('29)	Hudson Motor ('30) Coca-Cola ('32) National Steel ('35)		Aluminum Co. of America ('59)				Aluminum Co. of America
North American		Johns-Manville ('30)					Amer. Express ('82)	American Express
Victor Talking Machine	Natl Cash Register ('29)	IBM ('32) AT&T ('39)						AT&T
Bethlehem Steel								Bethlehem Steel
International Nickel						Inco Ltd.*('76)	Boeing ('87)	Boeing
International Harvester							Navistar*('86)	Caterpillar
Goodrich		Standard Oil (Calif) ('30)					Chevron*('84)	Chevron
Texas Gulf Sulphur		Intl. Shoe ('32) United Aircraft ('33) National Distillers ('34)		Owens-Illinois ('59)			Coca-Cola ('87)	Coca-Cola
U.S. Steel							USX Corp.*('86)	Walt Disney
American Sugar		Borden ('30) Du Pont ('35)						DuPont
American Tobacco (B)		Eastman Kodak ('30)						Eastman Kodak
Standard Oil (N.J.)						Exxon*('72)		Exxon
General Electric								General Electric
General Motors								General Motors
Atlantic Refining		Goodyear ('30)						Goodyear
Chrysler						IBM ('79)		IBM
Paramount Publix		Loew's ('32)		Intl. Paper ('56)				International Paper
General Railway Signal		Liggett & Myers ('30) Amer. Tobacco ('32)					McDonald's ('85)	McDonald's
Mack Trucks		Drug Inc. ('32) Corn Products ('33)		Swift & Co. ('59)		Esmark*('73) Merck ('79)		Merck
American Smelting				Anaconda ('59)		Minn. Mining ('76)		Minn. Mining
American Can							Primerica*('87)	J.P. Morgan
Postum Inc.	General Foods *('29)						Philip Morris ('85)	Philip Morris
Nash Motors		United Trans. ('30) Proctor &Gamble ('32)						Procter & Gamble
Sears Roebuck								Sears Roebuck
Texas Corp.				Texaco*('59)				Texaco
Union Carbide								Union Carbide
Radio Corp.		Nash Motors ('32) United Aircraft ('39)				United Tech.*('75)		United Technologies
Westinghouse Electric								Westinghouse Electric
Woolworth								Woolworth

Source: *The Wall Street Journal*, May 3, 1991. Reprinted by permission of *The Wall Street Journal*,

Table 2.5 Selected MSCI Stock Indexes

International Indexes	Special Areas	National Indexes	
The World Index	The World Index ex USA	Spain	Australia
North America	Kokusal Index (World ex Japan)	Sweden	Singapore/Malaysia
EAFE	EASEA Index (EAFE ex Japan)	Switzerland	Belgium
Europe 13	Pacific ex Japan	United Kingdom	Netherlands
Nordic Countries	The World Index ex The UK	Italy	Denmark
Pacific	EAFE ex The UK	Japan	Norway
Far East	Europe 13 ex The UK	Hong Kong	Canada
		New Zealand	Germany
		France	Austria
		United States	Finland

Source: Morgan Stanley Capital International Perspective III '90, Geneva, Switzerland.

for a geometric average of 7.84%. The general formula for the geometric average is

$$1 + r_G = [(1 + r_1)(1 + r_2) \ldots (1 + r_n)]^{1/n}$$

where r_i is the return on the ith security in the index.

Note that the geometric average is less than the arithmetic average. This is a general property; whenever there is variation in performance among the stocks in an index, the geometric average will be less than the arithmetic average.[4] For this reason the Value Line index provides a downward-biased measure of the rate of return that would be earned by an investor purchasing an equally weighted portfolio of all the stocks in the index. In fact, there is no portfolio strategy that results in a rate of return equal to that of a geometric index.

Foreign and International Stock Market Indexes

Development in financial markets worldwide includes the construction of indexes for these markets. The popular indexes are broader than the Dow Jones average and most are value weighted.

The most important are the Nikkei, FTSE (pronounced "footsie"), and DAX. The Nikkei 225 is a price-weighted average of the largest Tokyo Stock Exchange (TSE) stocks. The Nikkei 300 is a value-weighted index. FTSE is published by the *Financial Times* of London and is a value-weighted index of 100 of the largest London Stock Exchange corporations. The DAX index is the premier German stock index.

Figure 2.13 shows the list of foreign stock exchange indexes published by the *Financial Times.* Other indexes such as J.P. Morgan's (see Table 2.5) provide a rich picture of international indexes for professional investors.

[4] See Chapter 24 for more discussion of this issue.

Figure 2.13
Listing of foreign stock market indexes

Source: Reprinted by permission of *Financial Times* (of London) Dec. 13, 1993.

INDICES

Argentina	
General (29/12/77)	(u)
Australia	
All Ordinaries (1/1/80)	2084.9
All Mining (1/1/80)	948.1
Austria	
Credit Aktein (30/12/84)	422.22
Traded Index (2/1/91)	1095.75
Belgium	
BEL20 (1/1/91)	1428.78
Brazil	
Bovespa (29/12/83)	(u)
Canada	
Metals Mints♦(1976)	3497.71
Composite♦(1975)	4280.30
Portfolio§§ (4/1/83)	2054.58
Chile	
IPGA Gen (31/12/80)	(u)
Denmark	
CopenhagenSE (3/1/83)	362.52
Finland	
HEX General (28/12/90)	1550.0
France	
CAC General (31/12/81)	—
CAC 40 (31/12/87)	2196.13
Germany	
FAZ Aktien (31/12/58)	826.26
Commerzbank (1/12/63)	2365.3
DAX (30/12/87)	2161.13
Greece	
Athens SE (31/12/80)	912.43
Hong Kong	
Hang Seng (31/7/64)	10228.11
India	
BSE Sens (1979)	3401.9
Indonesia	
Jaicarta Comp. (10/8/82)	528.46
Ireland	
ISEQ Overall (4/1/88)	1822.93
Italy	
Banca Comm Ital (1972)	583.11
MIB General (4/1/93)	1281.0
Japan	
Nikkei 225 (16/5/49)	17237.43
Nikkei 300 (1/10/82)	270.32
Topix (4/1/68)	1456.71
2nd Section (4/1/68)	1874.41
Malaysia	
KLSE Comp. (4/4/86)	1075.85
Mexico	
IPC (Nov 1978)	(u)
Netherland	
CBS TttRtnGen (End 83)	407.6
CBS All Shr (End 83)	270.7
New Zealand	
Cap. 40 (1/7/86)	2103.97
Norway	
Oslo SE(Ind) (2/1/83)	886.24
Philippines	
Manila Comp (2/1/85)	2513.29
Portugal	
BTA (1977)	2566.8
Singapore	
SES All—S'pore (2/4/75)	580.46
South Africa	
JSE Gold (28/9/78)	2050.0 ♥
JSE Indl. (26/9/78)	5057.0 ♥
South Korea	
KoreaCmpEx (4/1/80)**	861.72
Spain	
Madrid SE (30/12/85)	306.05
Sweden	
AffarsvardnGen (1/2/37)	1350.6
Switzerland	
Swiss Bk Ind (31/12/58)	1248.73
SBC General (1/4/87)	976.40
Taiwan	
WeightedPr. (30/6/66)**	4644.03
Thailand	
Bangkok SET (30/4/75)	(c)
Turkey	
Istanbul Cmp. (Jan 1986)	17591.9
WORLD	
MS Capital Int (1/1/70)$	593.8*

Bond Market Indicators

Just as stock market indexes provide guidance concerning the performance of the overall stock market, several bond market indicators measure the performance of various categories of bonds. The three most well-known groups of indexes are those of Merrill Lynch, Lehman Brothers, and Salomon Brothers. Table 2.6 lists some of the indexes compiled by Lehman Brothers, as well as some characteristics of those indexes as of October 1994. The Lehman Brothers Government/Corporate Bond Index is perhaps the premier indicator of bond market performance.

The Lehman and Salomon Brothers indexes are computed monthly, and all measure total returns as the sum of capital gains plus interest income derived from the bonds during the month. Any intra-month cash distributions received from the bonds are

Table 2.6 Selected Lehman Brothers Bond Indexes, October 1994

	Number of Issues	Market Value ($ Billion)	Coupon	Yield	Maturity	Duration*
Aggregate	4,834	$3,996	7.50	7.82	8.82	5.06
Government/Corporate	4,115	2,794	7.48	7.60	9.29	5.09
Intermediate	2,789	2,035	6.98	7.32	4.13	3.35
Long-term	1,326	759	8.82	8.35	23.18	9.74
Governments	1,010	2,157	7.32	7.37	8.43	4.79
Intermediate	885	1,635	6.79	7.14	3.75	3.12
Long-term	125	522	9.00	8.10	23.12	10.02
Government Agencies	834	270	7.19	7.72	9.77	5.36
Intermediate	754	210	6.93	7.53	4.60	3.62
Long-term	80	59	8.12	8.40	28.10	11.52
Corporates	3,105	637	8.03	8.37	12.18	6.10
Intermediate	1,904	400	7.79	8.06	5.66	4.30
Long-term	1,201	237	8.43	8.90	23.17	9.13
Utilities	1,053	223	7.73	8.62	17.43	7.58
Intermediate	607	131	7.23	8.13	6.17	4.71
Long-term	446	92	8.10	8.94	25.72	9.69
Yankees	386	120	8.15	8.37	12.49	6.34
Asset-Backed	125	55	6.69	7.33	2.86	2.48
Credit cards	67	38	7.12	7.39	3.37	2.87
Autos	37	14	5.68	7.08	1.63	1.52
Home equity	21	3	6.00	7.76	2.22	1.94
Mortgages	594	1,147	7.59	8.38	7.98	5.13
GNMA	202	352	8.08	8.53	9.00	5.55
Freddie Mac	216	386	7.28	8.29	7.28	4.83
Fannie Mae	176	409	7.75	8.34	7.75	5.06

*Duration is defined and discussed in Chapter 15.
Source: Lehman Brothers.

assumed to be invested during the month at the T-bill rate. The Merrill Lynch indexes are computed daily.

The major problem with these indexes is that true rates of return on many bonds are difficult to compute because the infrequency with which the bonds trade make reliable up-to-date prices difficult to obtain. In practice, prices often must be estimated from bond valuation models. These "matrix" prices may differ substantially from true market values.

2.5 Derivative Markets

One of the most significant developments in financial markets in recent years has been the growth of futures and options markets. These instruments provide payoffs that depend on the values of other assets such as commodity prices, bond and stock prices, or market index values. For this reason these instruments sometimes are called **derivative assets,** or **contingent claims.** Their values derive from or are contingent on the values of other assets.

Options

A *call option* gives its holder the right to purchase an asset for a specified price, called the *exercise* or *strike price,* on or before a specified expiration date. For example, a July call option on IBM stock with an exercise price of $70 entitles its owner to purchase IBM stock for a price of $70 at any time up to and including the expiration date in July. Each option contract is for the purchase of 100 shares. However, quotations are made on a per-share basis. The holder of the call need not exercise the option; it will be profitable to exercise only if the market value of the asset that may be purchased exceeds the exercise price.

When the market price exceeds the exercise price, the option holder may "call away" the asset for the exercise price and reap a profit equal to the difference between the stock price and the exercise price. Otherwise, the option will be left unexercised. If not exercised before the expiration date of the contract, the option simply expires and no longer has value. Calls therefore provide greater profits when stock prices increase and thus represent bullish investment vehicles.

In contrast, a *put option* gives its holder the right to sell an asset for a specified exercise price on or before a specified expiration date. A July put on IBM with an exercise price of $70 thus entitles its owner to sell IBM stock to the put writer at a price of $70 at any time before expiration in July, even if the market price of IBM is lower than $70. Whereas profits on call options increase when the asset increases in value, profits on put options increase when the asset value falls. The put is exercised only if its holder can deliver an asset worth less than the exercise price in return for the exercise price.

Figure 2.14 presents stock option quotations from *The Wall Street Journal.* The highlighted options are for IBM. The repeated number under the name of the firm is the current price of IBM shares, $74½. The two columns to the right of IBM give the exercise price and expiration month of each option. Thus, we see that the paper reports data on call and put options on IBM with exercise prices ranging from $55 to $85 per share in $5 increments, and with expiration dates in January, April, November, and December. These exercise prices bracket the current price of IBM shares.

The next four columns provided trading volume and closing prices of each option. For example, 4,453 contracts traded on the November expiration call with an exercise price of $75. The last trade price was $1 5/16, meaning that an option to purchase one share of IBM at an exercise price of $75 sold for $1.3125. Each option *contract,* therefore, cost $131.25.

Notice that the prices of call options decrease as the exercise price increases. For example, the November maturity call with exercise price $80 costs only $¼. This makes sense, because the right to purchase a share at a higher exercise price is less valuable. Conversely, put prices increase with the exercise price. The right to sell a share of IBM at a price of $75 in November cost $1⅞ while the right to sell at $80 cost $5⅛.

Figure 2.14
Options market listings

Source: *The Wall Street Journal,* November 1, 1994. Reprinted by permission of *The Wall Street Journal,*

LISTED OPTIONS QUOTATIONS

Option/Strike	Exp.	Call Vol.	Call Last	Put Vol.	Put Last
				...	...
InstSy	10	Apr	27	3/16	...	...
IntgDv	25	Nov	71	4	565	5/16
28 3/8	25	Dec	...	...	40	15/16
28 3/8	30	Nov	111	7/8	100	2 3/8
28 3/8	30	Feb	32	2 13/16	25	4 1/8
28 3/8	30	May	41	4	5	5
IntgHS	35	Dec	25	5 7/8	...	...
Intel	50	Jan	15	13	35	5/16
62 1/8	55	Nov	176	7 1/2	23	1/8
62 1/8	55	Dec	2	8	30	7/16
62 1/8	55	Jan	50	9	50	5/8
62 1/8	55	Apr	35	10 3/8	...	...
62 1/8	60	Nov	1491	2 7/8	747	11/16
62 1/8	60	Dec	186	4 3/8	206	1 1/4
62 1/8	60	Jan	164	4 7/8	226	2
62 1/8	60	Apr	50	7	66	2 3/4
62 1/8	65	Nov	1780	9/16	84	3 1/4
62 1/8	65	Dec	825	1 3/8	230	3 3/4
62 1/8	65	Jan	431	2 1/4	52	4 3/8
62 1/8	65	Apr	66	4 1/8	5	5 1/8
62 1/8	70	Nov	105	1/16	...	...
62 1/8	70	Jan	199	15/16	...	...
62 1/8	70	Apr	53	2 5/16	...	...
62 1/8	72 1/2	Jan	102	5/8	...	...
Intelcm	15	Nov	56	3/4	...	...
IntelEl	15	Dec	119	1 1/2	...	...
IntNtk	5	Jan	75	1/2	75	1 1/2
IntrDig	5	Mar	320	7/16	...	...
Intrmag	17 1/2	Nov	100	3/8	...	...
I B M	55	Jan	130	20 1/2	...	...
74 1/2	60	Jan	274	15 5/8	171	3/16
74 1/2	60	Apr	5	16 3/8	61	1/2
74 1/2	65	Nov	20	9 1/2	137	1/16
74 1/2	65	Dec	230	10 3/8	...	...
74 1/2	65	Jan	136	11 1/4	493	1/2
74 1/2	65	Apr	8	12	60	1 1/16
74 1/2	70	Nov	572	4 3/4	1128	1/4
74 1/2	70	Dec	51	6 1/8	359	3/4
74 1/2	70	Jan	813	6 1/2	850	1 3/8
74 1/2	70	Apr	62	8 1/4	36	2 1/4
74 1/2	75	Nov	4453	1 5/16	2736	1 7/8
74 1/2	75	Dec	513	2 1/2	319	2 11/16
74 1/2	75	Jan	1423	3 1/2	711	3 3/8
74 1/2	75	Apr	194	5 1/4	82	4 1/2
74 1/2	80	Nov	800	1/4	30	5 1/8
74 1/2	80	Dec	614	7/8	3	5 5/8
74 1/2	80	Jan	639	1 5/8	117	6 1/8
74 1/2	80	Apr	136	3 1/8	34	7 1/8
74 1/2	85	Jan	216	11/16	50	10
74 1/2	85	Apr	61	1 15/16	...	...
InCble	35	Dec	66	7/16	...	...
IntFam	12 1/2	Nov	...	...	40	5/16
13 1/8	12 1/2	Dec	...	...	40	7/16
13 1/8	12 1/2	Feb	150	1 7/16	...	...
13 1/8	15	Nov	150	3/16	...	...
In Flv	45	Feb	35	1 11/16	...	...
IGame	17 1/2	Nov	115	1 9/16	71	3/8

Option/Strike	Exp.	Call Vol.	Call Last	Put Vol.	Put Last
39 3/8	35	Jan	23	5 1/4	342	9/16
39 3/8	35	Apr	...	...	362	1 1/8
39 3/8	40	Nov	270	3/4	62	1 5/16
39 3/8	40	Dec	291	1 1/4	50	2
39 3/8	40	Jan	213	2	145	2 5/16
39 3/8	40	Apr	53	3 1/8	5	3
39 3/8	45	Jan	50	1/2	...	...
39 3/8	45	Apr	83	1 1/4	25	6 1/2
MesaInc	5	Nov	70	1/4	...	...
Methnx	10	Jan	35	5 1/8	...	...
15	12 1/2	Nov	125	2 1/2	...	...
15	12 1/2	Apr	...	...	33	1 1/4
15	15	Nov	2531	3/4	39	3/4
15	15	Dec	107	1 1/4	10	1 3/16
15	15	Jan	243	1 5/8	14	1 5/8
15	15	Apr	70	2 3/4	10	2 1/4
15	17 1/2	Nov	172	3/16	...	...
15	17 1/2	Dec	26	1/2	...	...
15	17 1/2	Jan	235	7/8	...	...
15	17 1/2	Apr	258	1 3/4	...	...
15	20	Apr	45	1 3/16	20	5 5/8
MichNt	80	Nov	47	1 1/2	...	...
MicrAg	12 1/2	Nov	70	3/4	10	3/4
12 1/2	15	Feb	98	7/8	...	...
Mcrchp	40	Nov	...	...	40	3/16
46 7/8	45	Nov	63	3 1/4	4	1 15/16
46 7/8	45	Jan	160	6 3/8	...	...
MicrTc	30	Jan	14	10 1/2	110	9/16
39 5/8	35	Nov	111	5 1/8	707	7/16
39 5/8	35	Jan	91	6 7/8	19	1 1/2
39 5/8	40	Nov	1168	1 3/4	157	1 3/4
39 5/8	40	Dec	281	2 15/16	5	2 1/2
39 5/8	40	Jan	142	3 3/4	48	3 3/8
39 5/8	40	Apr	51	5 5/8	43	4 7/8
39 5/8	45	Nov	141	3/8	20	5 1/4
39 5/8	45	Dec	27	1 5/16	...	...
39 5/8	45	Jan	229	2	...	...
39 5/8	45	Apr	30	3 7/8	...	...
Microp	7 1/2	Feb	90	1 1/4	...	...
Micsft	40	Jan	32	23 1/2	...	...
63	45	Apr	30	19 5/8	...	...
63	50	Jan	11	14	301	1/4
63	50	Apr	2	13 5/8	30	9/16
63	55	Nov	243	8 1/8	237	1/16
63	55	Dec	25	9	20	5/16
63	55	Jan	110	9 1/2	302	5/8
63	55	Apr	158	11 1/8	50	1 1/4
63	57 1/2	Jan	249	7 1/2	4	1
63	60	Nov	783	3 1/2	656	7/16
63	60	Dec	101	4 1/2	996	1 1/8
63	60	Jan	460	5 1/2	67	1 1/2
63	60	Apr	186	7 1/4	24	2 1/2
63	65	Nov	1452	3/4	282	2 7/8
63	65	Dec	1186	1 5/8	85	2 3/4
63	65	Jan	1267	2 5/8	44	3 5/8
63	65	Apr	206	4 5/8	19	5
MidAtl	20	Dec	55	3 3/4	...	...
23 1/8	25	Nov	2	1/2	35	2 1/2
M M M	50	Jan	30	5 7/8		

CONCEPT CHECK Question 7. What would be the profit or loss per share of stock to an investor who bought the November maturity IBM call option with exercise price 70 if the stock price at the expiration of the option is 78? What about a purchaser of the put option with the same exercise price and maturity?

Futures Contracts

The *futures contract* calls for delivery of an asset or its cash value at a specified delivery or maturity date for an agreed-upon price, called the futures price, to be paid at contract maturity. The *long position* is held by the trader who commits to purchasing the

Figure 2.15
Financial futures listings

Source: *The Wall Street Journal,* Reprinted by permission of *The Wall Street Journal,* © 1994 Dow Jones & Company, Inc. All Rights Reserved Worldwide.

FUTURES PRICES

INDEX

	Open	High	Low	Settle	Chg	High	Low	Open Interest
S&P 500 INDEX (CME) $500 times index								
Dec	467.50	476.90	466.75	476.20	+ 9.00	487.10	438.85	224,300
Mr95	470.50	480.10	470.00	479.40	+ 9.00	484.10	441.45	12,922
June	479.25	483.70	473.90	483.25	+ 9.00	487.40	449.50	3,274
Sept	483.90	487.70	483.00	487.25	+ 9.00	487.70	462.00	591
Est vol 113,492; vol Thur 68,956; open int 241,087, +2,640.								
Indx prelim High 473.78; Low 465.80; Close 463.77 +7.92								
S&P MIDCAP 400 (CME) $500 times index								
Dec	175.20	178.60	175.20	178.15	+ 3.00	187.05	163.50	13,680
Est vol 1,531; vol Thur 608; open int 13,701, +140.								
The index: High 176.91; Low 174.04; Close 176.91 + +2.87								
NIKKEI 225 STOCK AVERAGE (CME)—$5 times index								
Dec	19840.	19980.	19840.	19955.	+ 75.0	21800.	17030.	25,122
Est vol 1,142; vol Thur 868; open int 25,128, −137.								
The index: High 19904.08; Low 19725.65; Close 19805.16 +8.80								
GSCI (CME)—$250 times nearby index								
Dec	181.90	182.20	181.10	181.70	− .10	187.20	176.20	5,832
Fb95	180.20	180.20	179.50	179.70	− .20	181.20	176.00	709
Est vol 1,293; vol Thur 1,581; open int 6,541, +979.								
The index: High 180.65; Low 179.15; Close 180.24 +.13								
MAJOR MARKET INDEX (CME)—$500 times index								
Nov	403.30	410.00	403.10	409.40	+ 5.60	411.20	389.60	3,890
Dec	403.45	410.60	403.46	409.85	+ 5.60	411.50	361.75	358
Est vol 455; vol Thur 225; open int 4,255, +70.								
The index: High 409.40; Low 403.13; Close 409.11 +5.74								
NYSE COMPOSITE INDEX (NYFE)—500 times index								
Dec	256.20	261.15	256.15	260.70	+ 4.30	264.50	244.15	3,920
Mr95	257.60	262.20	257.60	262.10	+ 4.30	264.60	248.50	204
Est vol 4,170; vol Thur na; open int na, na.								
The index: High 259.44; Low 255.56; Close 259.43 +3.86								
KR-CRB INDEX (NYFE)—500 times index								

commodity on the delivery date. The trader who takes the short position commits to delivering the commodity at contract maturity.

Figure 2.15 illustrates the listing of several stock index futures contracts as they appear in *The Wall Street Journal.* The top line in boldface type gives the contract name, the exchange on which the futures contract is traded in parentheses, and the contract size. Thus, the first contract listed is for the S&P 500 index, traded on the Chicago Mercantile Exchange (CME). Each contract calls for delivery of 500 times the value of the S&P 500 stock price index.

The next several rows detail price data for contracts expiring on various dates. The December 1994 maturity contract opened during the day at a futures price of 467.50 per unit of the index. (The last line of the entry shows that the S&P 500 index was at 463.77 at close of trading on the day of the listing.) The highest futures price during the day was 476.90, the lowest was 466.75, and the settlement price (a representative trading price during the last few minutes of trading) was 476.20. The settlement price increased by 9.00 from the previous trading day. The highest and lowest futures prices over the contract's life to date have been 487.10 and 438.85, respectively. Finally, open interest, or the number of outstanding contracts, was 224,300. Corresponding information is given for each maturity date.

The trader holding the long position profits from price increases. Suppose that at expiration the S&P 500 index is at 480. The long position trader who entered the contract at the futures price of 476.20 would pay the previously agreed-upon 476.20 for each unit of the index, which at contract maturity would be worth 480. Because each contract calls for delivery of 500 times the index, ignoring brokerage fees, the profit to the long position would equal 500 × (480 − 476.20) = $1,900. Conversely, the short position must deliver 500 times the value of the index for the previously agreed-upon futures price. The short position's loss equals the long position's profit.

The right to purchase the asset at an agreed-upon price, as opposed to the obligation, distinguishes call options from long positions in futures contracts. A futures contract *obliges* the long position to purchase the asset at the futures price; the call option, in contrast, *conveys the right* to purchase the asset at the exercise price. The purchase will be made only if it yields a profit.

Clearly, a holder of a call has a better position than does the holder of a long position on a futures contract with a futures price equal to the option's exercise price. This advantage, of course, comes only at a price. Call options must be purchased; futures contracts may be entered into without cost. The purchase price of an option is called the *premium.* It represents the compensation the holder of the call must pay for the ability to exercise the option only when it is profitable to do so. Similarly, the difference between a put option and a short futures position is the right, as opposed to the obligation, to sell an asset at an agreed-upon price.

Summary

1. Money market securities are very short-term debt obligations. They are usually highly marketable and have relatively low credit risk. Their low maturities and low credit risk ensure minimal capital gains or losses. These securities trade in large denominations, but may be purchased indirectly through money market funds.

2. Much of the U.S. government borrowing is in the form of Treasury bonds and notes. These are coupon-paying bonds usually issued at or near par value. Treasury bonds are similar in design to coupon-paying corporate bonds.

3. Municipal bonds are distinguished largely by their tax-exempt status. Interest payments (but not capital gains) on these securities are exempt from federal income taxes. The taxable equivalent yield offered by a municipal bond equals $r_m/(1 - t)$, where r_m is the municipal yield and t is the investor's tax bracket.

4. Mortgage pass-through securities are pools of mortgages sold in one package. Owners of pass-throughs receive all principal and interest payments made by the borrower. The bank that originally issued the mortgage merely services the mortgage, simply "passing through" the payments to the purchasers of the mortgage. A federal agency may guarantee the payment of interest and principal on mortgages pooled into these pass-through securities.

5. Common stock is an ownership share in a corporation. Each share entitles its owner to one vote on matters of corporate governance and to a prorated share of the dividends paid to shareholders. Stock, or equity, owners are the residual claimants on the income earned by the firm.

6. Preferred stock usually pays fixed dividends for the life of the firm; it is a perpetuity. A firm's failure to pay the dividend due on preferred stock, however, does not precipitate corporate bankruptcy. Instead, unpaid dividends simply cumulate. New varieties of preferred stock include convertible and adjustable-rate issues.

7. Many stock market indexes measure the performance of the overall market. The Dow Jones Averages, the oldest and best-known indicators, are price-weighted indexes. Today, many broad-based, market-value-weighted indexes are computed daily. These include the Standard & Poor's 500 Stock Index, the NYSE and AMEX indexes, the NASDAQ index, and the Wilshire 5000 Index. The Value Line index is a geometrically weighted average of about 1,700 firms.

8. A call option is a right to purchase an asset at a stipulated exercise price on or before a maturity date. A put option is the right to sell an asset at some exercise price. Calls increase in value while puts decrease in value as the value of the underlying asset increases.

9. A futures contract is an obligation to buy or sell an asset at a stipulated futures price on a maturity date. The long position, which commits to purchasing, gains if the asset value increases while the short position, which commits to purchasing, loses.

Key Terms

Money market
Capital markets
Bank discount yield
Effective annual yield
Bond equivalent yield
London Interbank Offered Rate
Yield to maturity
Equivalent taxable yield
Current yield
Residual claim
Limited liability
Capital gains
Price–earnings ratio
Price-weighted average
Market-value-weighted index
Index funds
Geometric average
Derivative assets
Contingent claims

Selected Readings

The standard reference to the securities, terminology, and organization of the money market is still:

Stigum, Marcia. *The Money Market.* Homewood, Ill.: Dow Jones-Irwin, 1983.

A good survey of a wide variety of financial markets and instruments is:

Logue, Dennis E. (editor). *The WG&L Handbook of Financial Markets.* Cincinnati, Ohio: Warren, Gorham & Lamont, 1995.

A survey textbook on capital markets, with emphasis on institutional features, and sections on the money market, as well as debt, equity, and derivative markets is:

Fabozzi, Frank J., and Franco Modigliani. *Capital Markets: Institutions and Instruments.* Englewood Cliffs, N.J.: Prentice Hall, 1992.

Problems

1. The following multiple-choice problems are based on questions that appeared in past CFA examinations.*

*Reprinted, with permission, from the 1986 *CFA Study Guide*. Copyright 1986, The Institute of Chartered Financial Analysts, Charlottesville, VA. All rights reserved.

a. Preferred stock
   i. Is actually a form of equity.
   ii. Pays dividends not fully taxable to U.S. corporations.
   iii. Is normally considered a fixed-income security.
   iv. All of the above.

b. Straight preferred stock yields usually are lower than yields on straight bonds of the same quality because of:
   i. Marketability.
   ii. Risk.
   iii. Taxation.
   iv. Call protection.

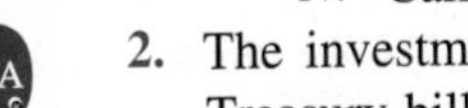

2. The investment manager of a corporate pension fund has purchased a U.S. Treasury bill with 180 days to maturity at a price of $9,600 per $10,000 face value. The manager has computed the bank discount yield at 8%.*
   a. Calculate the bond equivalent yield for the Treasury bill. Show calculations. (Ignore skip-day settlement.)
   b. Briefly state two reasons why a Treasury bill's bond equivalent yield is always different from the discount yield.

3. A bill has a bank discount yield of 6.81% based on the asked price, and 6.90% based on the bid price. The maturity of the bill (already accounting for skip-day settlement) is 60 days. Find the bid and asked prices of the bill.

4. Reconsider the T-bill of question 3. Calculate its bond equivalent yield and effective annual yield based on the ask price. Confirm that these yields exceed the discount yield.

5. Which security offers a higher effective annual yield?
   a. i. A three-month bill selling at $9,764.
   ii. A six-month bill selling at $9,539.
   b. Calculate the bank discount yield on each bill.

6. A Treasury bill with 90-day maturity sells at a bank discount yield of 3%.
   a. What is the price of the bill?
   b. What is the 90-day holding period return of the bill?
   c. What is the bond equivalent yield of the bill?
   d. What is the effective annual yield of the bill?

7. Find the after-tax return to a corporation that buys a share of preferred stock at $40, sells it at year-end at $40, and receives a $4 year-end dividend. The firm is in the 30% tax bracket.

8. Consider the three stocks in the following table. P_t represents price at time t, and Q_t represents shares outstanding at time t. Stock C splits two for one in the last period.

	P_0	Q_0	P_1	Q_1	P_2	Q_2
A	90	100	95	100	95	100
B	50	200	45	200	45	200
C	100	200	110	200	55	400

a. Calculate the rate of return on a price-weighted index of the three stocks for the first period ($t = 0$ to $t = 1$).

b. What must happen to the divisor for the price-weighted index in year 2?

c. Calculate the price-weighted index for the second period ($t = 1$ to $t = 2$).

9. Using the data in problem 8, calculate the first period rates of return on the following indexes of the three stocks:
   a. A market-value-weighted index.
   b. An equally weighted index.
   c. A geometric index.
10. An investor is in a 28% tax bracket. If corporate bonds offer 9% yields, what must municipals offer for the investor to prefer them to corporate bonds?
11. Short-term municipal bonds currently offer yields of 4%, while comparable taxable bonds pay 5%. Which gives you the higher after-tax yield if your tax bracket is:
    a. Zero.
    b. 10%.
    c. 20%.
    d. 30%.
12. Find the equivalent taxable yield of the municipal bond in the previous question for tax brackets of zero, 10%, 20%, and 30%.
13. Which security should sell at a greater price?
    a. A 10-year Treasury bond with a 9% coupon rate versus a 10-year T-bond with a 10% coupon.
    b. A three-month maturity call option with an exercise price of $40 versus a three-month call on the same stock with an exercise price of $35.
    c. A put option on a stock selling at $50, or a put option on another stock selling at $60 (all other relevant features of the stocks and options may be assumed to be identical).
    d. A three-month T-bill with a discount yield of 6.1% versus a three-month bill with a discount yield of 6.2%.
14. Why do call options with exercise prices greater than the price of the underlying stock sell for positive prices?
15. Both a call and a put currently are traded on stock XYZ; both have strike prices of $50 and maturities of six months. What will be the profit to an investor who buys the call for $4 in the following scenarios for stock prices in six months?
    a. $40.
    b. $45.
    c. $50.
    d. $55.
    e. $60.

    What will be the profit in each scenario to an investor who buys the put for $6?
16. Explain the difference between a put option and a short position in a futures contract.

17. Explain the difference between a call option and a long position in a futures contract.
18. What would you expect to happen to the spread between yields on commercial paper and Treasury bills if the economy were to enter a steep recession?
19. Examine the first 50 stocks listed in the stock market listings for NYSE stocks in your local newspaper. For how many of these stocks is the 52-week high price at least 50% greater than the 52-week low price? What do you conclude about the volatility of prices on individual stocks?

Chapter 3
How Securities Are Traded

THE FIRST TIME A SECURITY TRADES IS WHEN IT IS ISSUED. Therefore, we begin our examination of trading with a look at how securities are first marketed to the public by investment bankers, the midwives of securities. Then, we turn to the various exchanges where already-issued securities can be traded among investors. We examine the competition among the New York Stock Exchange, the American Stock Exchange, the regional exchanges, and the over-the-counter market for the patronage of security traders.

Next, we turn to the mechanics of trading in these various markets. We describe the role of the specialist in exchange markets and the dealer in over-the-counter markets. We also touch briefly on block trading and the SuperDot system of the NYSE for electronically routing orders to the floor of the exchange. We discuss the costs of trading and describe the recent debate between the NYSE and its competitors over which market provides the lowest-cost trading arena.

We then describe the essentials of specific transactions such as buying on margin and selling stock short and discuss relevant regulations governing security trading. We will see that some regulations, such as those governing insider trading, can be difficult to interpret in practice.

Finally, we discuss alternatives to trading securities directly by investing with investment companies such as mutual funds. We also detail the costs that may be incurred using this alternative.

3.1 How Firms Issue Securities

When firms need to raise capital they may choose to sell (or *float*) new securities. These new issues of stocks, bonds, or other securities typically are marketed to the public by investment bankers in what is called the **primary market.** Purchase and sale of already-issued securities among private investors takes place in the **secondary market.**

There are two types of primary market issues of common stock. *Initial public offerings,* or *IPOs,* are stocks issued by a formerly privately owned company selling stock to the public for the first time. *Seasoned new issues* are offered by companies that already have floated equity. A sale by IBM of new shares of stock, for example, would constitute a seasoned new issue.

In the case of bonds we also distinguish between two types of primary market issues: a *public offering,* which is an issue of bonds sold to the general investing public that can then be traded on the secondary market; and a *private placement,* which is an issue that is sold to a few institutional investors at most, and is generally held to maturity.

Investment Bankers and Underwriting

Public offerings of both stocks and bonds typically are marketed via an **underwriting** by investment bankers. In fact, more than one investment banker usually markets the securities. A lead firm forms an *underwriting syndicate* of other investment bankers to share the responsibility for the stock issue.

The bankers advise the firm regarding the terms on which it should attempt to sell the securities. A preliminary registration statement must be filed with the Securities and Exchange Commission (SEC) describing the issue and the prospects of the company. This *preliminary prospectus* is known as a *red herring* because of a statement printed in red that the company is not attempting to sell the security before the registration is approved. When the statement is finalized and approved by the SEC, it is called the **prospectus.** At this time the price at which the securities will be offered to the public is announced.

There are two methods of underwriting a securities issue. In a *firm commitment* underwriting arrangement the investment bankers purchase the securities from the issuing company and then resell them to the public. The issuing firm sells the securities to the underwriting syndicate for the public offering price less a spread that serves as compensation to the underwriters. In such an arrangement the underwriters assume the full risk that the shares cannot in fact be sold to the public at the stipulated offering price. Figure 3.1 depicts the relationship among the firm issuing the security, the underwriting syndicate, and the public.

An alternative to firm commitment is the *best-efforts* agreement. In this case the investment banker agrees to help the firm sell the issue to the public, but does not actually purchase the securities. The banker simply acts as an intermediary between the public and the firm and thus does not bear the risk of being unable to resell purchased securities at the offering price. The best-efforts procedure is more common for initial public offerings of common stock, for which the appropriate share price is less certain.

Corporations engage investment bankers either by negotiation or by competitive bidding. Negotiation is more common. Besides being compensated by the spread between the purchase price and the public offering price, an investment banker may receive shares of common stock or other securities of the firm. In the case of competitive bidding, a firm may announce its intent to issue securities and invite investment

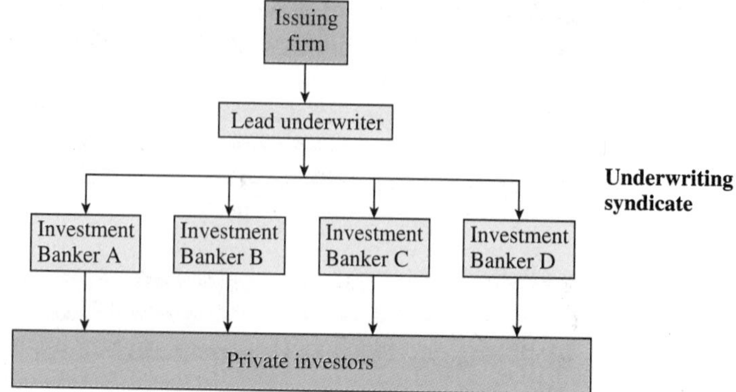

Figure 3.1
Relationship among a firm issuing securities, the underwriters, and the public

bankers to submit bids for the underwriting. Such a bidding process may reduce the cost of the issue; it might also bring fewer services from the investment banker. Many public utilities are required to solicit competitive bids from underwriters.

Shelf Registration

An important innovation in the method of issuing securities was introduced in 1982, when the SEC approved Rule 415, which allows firms to register securities and gradually sell them to the public for two years after the initial registration. Because the securities are already registered, they can be sold on short notice with little additional paperwork. In addition, they can be sold in small amounts without incurring substantial flotation costs. The securities are "on the shelf," ready to be issued, which has given rise to the term *shelf registration.*

Underpricing

Underwriters face a peculiar conflict of interest. On the one hand, acting in the best interest of the issuing firm, they should attempt to market securities to the public at the highest possible price, thereby maximizing the revenue realized from the offering. On the other hand, if they set the offering price higher than the public will pay, they will be unable to market the securities to customers. Underwriters left with unmarketable securities will be forced to sell them at a loss on the secondary market. Thus, the investment banker bears the price risk of an underwritten issue.

Underwriters, therefore, must balance their own interests against those of their clients. The lower the public offering price, the less capital the firm raises, but the greater the chance that the securities can be sold at that price. Also, the lower the price, the less effort needed to find investors to purchase the securities. If the offering is made at a low enough price, investors will beat down the doors of the underwriters to purchase the securities.

In fact, there is some evidence that IPOs of common stock often are underpriced compared with the price at which they could be marketed. Studies of IPO pricing in many countries consistently show that investors who purchased shares of an issue at the initial offering price and then resold the stock shortly after public trading began (usually a few days to a few weeks after the purchase) would have earned substantial abnormal returns.[1] For example, average abnormal returns on IPOs in the United States have been about 16%; in the United Kingdom, 11%; in Japan, 32%; in Germany, 21%; and in Canada, 9%.[2] A dramatic case of underpricing took place in 1993, when Boston Chicken stock was issued at $20 a share and jumped to $49 the first day of trading. Investors who bought at the issue price earned a one-day return of 149%. Such abnormal returns would indicate that stock is offered to the public at a price substantially below that which investors are willing to pay. Such underpricing means that IPOs commonly are oversubscribed; that is, there is demand from the public for more of the shares at the offering price than there are shares being offered.

3.2 WHERE SECURITIES ARE TRADED

Once securities are issued to the public, investors may trade them among themselves. Purchase and sale of already issued securities take place in the secondary markets, which consist of (1) national and local securities exchanges, (2) the over-the-counter market, and (3) direct trading between two parties.

The Secondary Markets

There are nine major **stock exchanges** in the United States. Two of these, the New York Stock Exchange (NYSE) and the American Stock Exchange (AMEX), are national in scope. The others are regional exchanges, which list firms located in a particular geographic area. There are also several exchanges for the trading of options and futures contracts, which we will discuss in the options and futures chapters.

An exchange provides a facility for its members to trade securities, and only members of the exchange may trade there. Therefore memberships, or *seats,* on the exchange are valuable assets. The majority of seats are *commission broker* seats, most of which are owned by the large full-service brokerage firms. The seat entitles the firm to place one of its brokers on the floor of the exchange where he or she can execute trades. The exchange member charges investors for executing trades on their behalf. The commissions that members can earn through this activity determine the market value of a seat. A seat on the NYSE has sold over the years for $4,000 in 1878, $35,000 in 1977, and as high as $1,150,000 in 1987 before falling considerably after that (see Table 3.1).

[1] Abnormal return measures the return on the investment net of the portion that can be attributed to general market movements. See the discussion of this concept in Chapter 12.

[2] Jay R. Ritter and Kathleen A. Weiss, "Going Public," *The New Palgrave Dictionary of Money and Finance,* 1992.

Table 3.1 Seat Prices on the NYSE

Year	High	Low	Year	High	Low
1875	$ 6,800	$ 4,300	1987	$1,150,000	$605,000
1905	85,000	72,000	1988	820,000	580,000
1935	140,000	65,000	1989	675,000	420,000
1965	250,000	190,000	1990	430,000	250,000
1975	138,000	55,000	1991	440,000	345,000
1980	275,000	175,000	1992	600,000	410,000
1985	480,000	310,000	1993	775,000	500,000
1986	600,000	455,000			

Source: New York Stock Exchange *Fact Book,* 1994.

The NYSE is by far the largest single exchange. The shares of approximately 2,300 firms trade there, and nearly 3,000 stock issues (common and preferred stock) are listed. Daily trading volume on the NYSE averaged 264.5 million shares in 1993. Table 3.2 shows the trading activity of securities listed on the various stock exchanges as of 1993.

From Table 3.2 you can see that the NYSE accounts for about 85% of the trading that takes place on stock exchanges. The AMEX also is national in scope, but it focuses more on listing smaller and younger firms than does the NYSE. Regional exchanges provide a market for trading shares of local firms that do not meet the listing requirements of the national exchanges. The national exchanges are willing to list a stock (allow trading in that stock on the exchange) only if the firm meets certain criteria of size and stability.

Table 3.3 gives the initial listing requirements for the NYSE. These requirements ensure that a firm is of significant trading interest before the NYSE will allocate facilities for it to be traded on the floor of the exchange. If a listed company suffers a decline and fails to meet the criteria in Table 3.3, it may be delisted from the exchange.

Regional exchanges also sponsor trading of some firms that are traded on national exchanges. This dual listing enables local brokerage firms to trade in shares of large firms without needing to purchase a membership on the NYSE.

The NYSE recently has lost market share to the regional exchanges and, far more dramatically, to the over-the-counter market. Today, approximately two-thirds of the trades in stocks listed on the NYSE are actually executed on the NYSE. In contrast, about 80% of the trades in NYSE-listed shares were executed on the exchange in the early 1980s. The loss is attributed to lower commissions charged on other exchanges, although the NYSE believes that a more inclusive treatment of trading costs would show that it is the most cost-effective trading arena. In any case, many of these non-NYSE trades were for relatively small transactions. The NYSE is still by far the preferred exchange for large traders, and its market share of exchange-listed companies (when measured in share volume rather than number of trades) is still a bit above 80%.

Table 3.2 Trading in Various Stock Markets, 1993

	Trading Volume during the Year (Billions of Shares)	Percentage of Total	Dollar Volume of Trading (Billions of Dollars)	Percentage of Total
Exchange trading				
New York	66.92	84.0%	$2,283.4	88.8%
American	4.58	5.7	56.7	2.2
Regional exchanges*	8.17	10.3	232.2	9.0
TOTAL	79.67	100.0%	$2,572.3	100.0%
Dealer market				
Nasdaq	66.54	100.0%	$1,350.1	100.0%

*Regional exchanges include the Boston, Cincinnati, Chicago, Pacific, and Philadelphia Stock Exchanges.
Source: 1994 Nasdaq *Fact Book and Company Directory.*

Table 3.3 Initial Listing Requirements for the NYSE

Pretax income in last year	$ 2,500,000
Average annual pretax income in previous two years	$ 2,000,000
Net tangible assets	$18,000,000
Market value of publicly held stock	$18,000,000
Shares publicly held	1,100,000
Number of holders of 100 shares or more	2,000

Source: Data from the New York Stock Exchange *Fact Book,* 1994.

The over-the-counter Nasdaq market has posed a bigger competitive challenge to the NYSE. Its share of trading volume in NYSE-listed firms increased from 2.5% in 1983 to 7.4% in 1993. Moreover, many large firms that would be eligible to list their shares on the NYSE now choose to list on Nasdaq. Some of the well-known firms currently trading on Nasdaq are Microsoft, Intel, Apple Computer, Sun Microsystems, and MCI Communications.[3] Total trading volume in over-the-counter stocks on the computerized Nasdaq system (described in detail shortly) has increased sixfold in the last decade, rising from about 50 million shares per day in 1984 to 300 million shares in 1994. Share volume on Nasdaq in the first half of 1994 actually surpassed that on the NYSE. However, because Nasdaq-listed firms tend to sell at lower prices, the dollar value of Nasdaq trades is still only about 60% that of NYSE trades.

Other new sources of competition to the NYSE come from abroad. For example, the London Stock Exchange is preferred by some traders because it offers greater anonymity. In addition, new restrictions introduced by the NYSE to limit price volatility in the wake of the market crash of 1987 are viewed by some traders as another reason to trade abroad. These so-called circuit breakers are discussed below.

[3] It should be noted, however, that some observers in 1994 believe that Nasdaq will be vulnerable to defections by these and other firms in the wake of the antitrust investigation against Nasdaq dealers, which is described later in the chapter.

Table 3.4 Partial Listing Requirements for the American Stock Exchange and Nasdaq

	AMEX Emerging Company Marketplace			
	Companies Not Now Traded on Nasdaq	Companies Presently Traded on Nasdaq	Usual AMEX Entry Standards	Nasdaq Entry Standards
Total assets	$4 million	$2 million	None	$4 million
Capital and surplus	$2 million	$1 million	$4 million	$2 million
Number of shares in public hands	250,000 shares	250,000 shares	500,000 shares	500,000 shares
Market value of shares	$2.5 million	$2.5 million	$3 million	$3 million
Price of stock	$3	$1	$3	$5
Pretax income	None	None	$750,000	$750,000

Source: AMEX and Nasdaq *Fact Books,* 1994.

In a bid to increase the number of firms it lists, the AMEX instituted in 1992 a set of less stringent listing standards for an "emerging company marketplace" of smaller firms. By the beginning of 1994, 22 firms were traded on the emerging company market. Shares of these newer and smaller firms traditionally have traded in the over-the-counter, or Nasdaq, market. Table 3.4 presents current AMEX listing requirements, the proposed emerging company standards, and the Nasdaq entry standards.

Although most common stocks are traded on the exchanges, most bonds and other fixed-income securities are not. Corporate bonds are traded both on the exchanges and over the counter, but all federal and municipal government bonds are traded only over the counter.

The Over-the-Counter Market

Roughly 35,000 issues are traded on the **over-the-counter** (OTC) **market** and any security may be traded there, but the OTC market is not a formal exchange. There are no membership requirements for trading, nor are there listing requirements for securities. In the OTC market thousands of brokers register with the SEC as dealers in OTC securities. Security dealers quote prices at which they are willing to buy or sell securities. A broker can execute a trade by contacting the dealer listing an attractive quote.

Before 1971, all OTC quotations of stock were recorded manually and published daily. The so-called *pink sheets* were the means by which dealers communicated their interest in trading at various prices. This was a cumbersome and inefficient technique, and published quotes were a full day out of date. In 1971 the National Association of Securities Dealers Automated Quotation system, or **NASDAQ,** began to offer immediate information on a computer-linked system of bid and asked prices for stocks offered by various dealers. The **bid price** is that at which a dealer is willing to purchase a security; the **asked price** is that at which the dealer will sell a security. The system allows a dealer who receives a buy or sell order from an investor to examine all current quotes, call the dealer with the best quote, and execute a trade. Securities of nearly 5,000 firms are quoted on the system, which is now called the Nasdaq Stock Market, and is no longer treated as an acronym. Nasdaq listing requirements are presented in Table 3.4.

Nasdaq has three levels of subscribers. The highest, Level 3, is for firms dealing, or "making markets," in OTC securities. These market makers maintain inventories of a security and continually stand ready to buy these shares from or sell them to the public at the quoted bid and asked price. They earn profits from the spread between the bid price and the asked price. Level 3 subscribers may enter the bid and asked prices at which they are willing to buy or sell stocks into the computer network and update these quotes as desired.

Level 2 subscribers receive all bid and asked quotes but cannot enter their own quotes. These subscribers tend to be brokerage firms that execute trades for clients but do not actively deal in the stocks for their own accounts. Brokers attempting to buy or sell shares call the market maker who has the best quote to execute a trade.

Level 1 subscribers receive only the median, or "representative," bid and asked prices on each stock. Level 1 subscribers are investors who are not actively buying and selling securities, yet the service provides them with general information.

For bonds, the over-the-counter market is a loosely organized network of dealers linked together by a computer quotation system. In practice, the corporate bond market often is quite "thin," in that there are few investors interested in trading a particular bond at any particular time. The bond market is therefore subject to a type of "liquidity risk," because it can be difficult to sell holdings quickly if the need arises.

The Third and Fourth Markets

The **third market** refers to trading of exchange-listed securities on the OTC market. Until the 1970s, members of the NYSE were required to execute all their trades of NYSE-listed securities on the exchange and to charge commissions according to a fixed schedule. This schedule was disadvantageous to large traders, who were prevented from realizing economies of scale on large trades. The restriction led brokerage firms that were not members of the NYSE, and so not bound by its rules, to establish trading in the OTC market on large NYSE-listed firms. These trades took place at lower commissions than would have been charged on the NYSE, and the third market grew dramatically until 1972 when the NYSE allowed negotiated commissions on orders exceeding $300,000. On May 1, 1975, frequently referred to as "May Day," commissions on all orders became negotiable.

The **fourth market** refers to direct trading between investors in exchange-listed securities without benefit of a broker. Large institutions that wish to avoid brokerage fees altogether may engage in direct trading. The fourth market has grown dramatically in recent years as big institutional investors have begun using electronic trading networks to step around brokers. Networks such as Instinet or Posit allow traders to trade stocks directly without ever going through a broker or an exchange. Posit allows for trades in both single stocks and stock portfolios. Both networks allow for much greater anonymity than exchange trading. On some days, Instinet accounts for up to 20% of the total volume of trading on Nasdaq-listed shares.

The National Market System

The Securities Act Amendments of 1975 directed the Securities and Exchange Commission to implement a national competitive securities market. Such a market would entail centralized reporting of transactions and a centralized quotation system, and would result in enhanced competition among market makers. In 1975 a "Consolidated Tape" began reporting trades on the NYSE, the AMEX, and the major regional exchanges, as well as on Nasdaq-listed stocks. In 1977 the Consolidated Quotations Service began providing on-line bid and asked quotes for NYSE securities also traded on various other exchanges. This enhances competition by allowing traders to find the best exchange for a desired trade. In 1978 the Intermarket Trading System was implemented to link seven exchanges by computer (NYSE, AMEX, Boston, Cincinnati, Midwest, Pacific, and Philadelphia). Brokers and market makers can thus display quotes on all markets and execute cross-market trades.

A central limit-order book would be the ultimate centralization of the marketplace. In such a system, orders from all exchanges would be listed centrally, and all traders could fill all orders.

Market Structure in Other Countries

The structure of security markets varies considerably from one country to another. A full cross-country comparison is far beyond the scope of this text. Therefore, we will instead briefly review the two biggest non-U.S. stock markets: The London and Tokyo exchanges. Figure 3.2 shows the volume of trading in major world markets.

The London Stock Exchange is conveniently located between the world's two largest financial markets, those of the United States and Japan. The trading day in London overlaps with Tokyo in the morning and with New York in the afternoon. Trading arrangements on the London Stock Exchange resemble those on Nasdaq. Competing dealers who wish to make a market in a stock enter bid and asked prices into the Stock Exchange Automated Quotations computer system. Market orders can then be matched against those quotes. However, negotiation among institutional traders results in more trades being executed "inside the published quotes" than is true of Nasdaq. As in the United States, security firms are allowed to act as both dealers and as brokerage firms, that is, both making a market in securities and executing trades for their clients.

The London Stock Exchange is attractive to some traders because it offers greater anonymity than U.S. markets, primarily because records of trades are not published for a period of time until after they are completed. Therefore, it is harder for market participants to observe or infer a trading program of another investor until after that investor has completed the program. This anonymity can be quite attractive to institutional traders that wish to buy or sell large quantities of stock over a period of time.

The Tokyo Stock Exchange (TSE) is the largest stock exchange in Japan, accounting for about 80% of total trading. There is no specialist system on the TSE. Instead, a *saitori* maintains a public limit order book, matches market and limit orders, and is obliged to follow certain actions to slow down price movements when simple match-

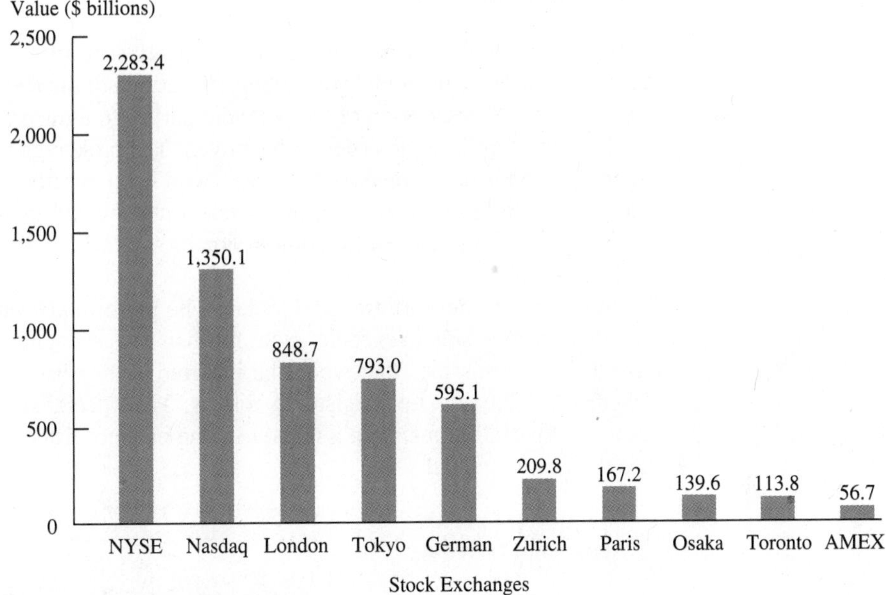

Figure 3.2
1993 dollar volume of equity trading in major world markets
Source: *1994 Nasdaq Fact Book and Company Directory.*

ing of orders would result in price changes greater than exchange-prescribed minimums. In their clerical role of matching orders *saitoris* are somewhat similar to specialists on the NYSE. However, *saitoris* do not trade for their own accounts, and therefore are quite different from either dealers or specialists in the United States.

Because the *saitori* performs an essentially clerical role, there are no market making services or liquidity provided to the market by dealers or specialists. The limit-order book is the primary provider of liquidity. In this regard, the TSE bears some resemblance to the fourth market in the United States, in which buyers and sellers trade directly via networks such as Instinet or Posit. On the TSE, however, if order imbalances would result in price movements across sequential trades that considered too extreme by the exchange, the *saitori* may temporarily halt trading and advertise the imbalance in the hope of attracting additional trading interest to the "weak" side of the market.

The TSE organizes stocks into two categories. The First Section consists of about 1,200 of the most actively traded stocks. The Second Section is for about 400 less actively trade stocks. Trading in the larger First Section stocks occurs on the floor of the exchange. The remaining securities in First Section and the Second Section trade electronically.

3.3 Trading on Exchanges

Most of the material in this section applies to all securities traded on exchanges. Some of it, however, applies just to stocks, and in such cases we use the terms *stocks* or *shares.*

The Participants

When an investor instructs a broker to buy or sell securities, a number of players must act to consummate the trade. We start our discussion of the mechanics of exchange trading with a brief description of the potential parties to a trade.

The investor places an order with a broker. The brokerage firm owning a seat on the exchange contacts its *commission broker,* who is on the floor of the exchange, to execute the order. *Floor brokers* are independent members of the exchange who own their own seats and handle work for commission brokers when those brokers have too many orders to handle.

Registered traders are frequent traders who perform no public function, but instead use their membership to execute trades for their own accounts. By trading directly, they avoid the commissions that would be incurred if they had to trade through a broker. There are relatively few registered traders. The **specialist** is central to the trading process. Specialists maintain a market in one or more listed securities. We will examine their role in detail shortly.

Types of Orders

Investors may issue several types of orders to their brokers. *Market orders* are simple buy or sell orders that are to be executed immediately at current market prices. In contrast, investors can issue *limit orders,* whereby they specify prices at which they are willing to buy or sell a security. If the stock falls below the limit on a limit-buy order, then the trade is to be executed. If stock XYZ is selling at $45, for example, a limit-buy order may instruct the broker to buy the stock if and when the share price falls below $43. Correspondingly, a limit-sell order instructs the broker to sell as soon as the stock price goes above the specified limit.

Stop-loss orders are similar to limit orders in that the trade is not to be executed unless the stock hits a price limit. In this case, however, the stock is to be sold if its price falls *below* a stipulated level. As the name suggests, the order lets the stock be sold to stop further losses from accumulating. Symmetrically, *stop-buy orders* specify that the stock should be bought when its price rises above a given limit. These trades often accompany short sales, and they are used to limit potential losses from the short position. Short sales are discussed in greater detail in Section 3.7. Figure 3.3 organizes these four types of trades in a simple matrix.

Orders also can be limited by a time period. Day orders, for example, expire at the close of the trading day. If it is not executed on that day, the order is canceled. *Open or good-till-canceled orders,* in contrast, remain in force for up to six months unless canceled by the customer. At the other extreme, *fill or kill* orders expire if the broker cannot fill them immediately.

Specialists and the Execution of Trades

A specialist "makes a market" in the shares of one or more firms. This task may require the specialist to act as either a broker or dealer. The specialist's role as a broker is sim-

Figure 3.3
Limit orders

		Condition: Price below the Limit	Condition: Price above the Limit
Action	Buy	Limit buy order	Stop buy order
Action	Sell	Stop loss order	Limit sell order

ply to execute the orders of other brokers. Specialists may also buy or sell shares of stock for their own portfolios. When no other broker can be found to take the other side of a trade, specialists will do so even if it means they must buy for or sell from their own accounts. The NYSE commissions these companies to perform this service and monitors their performance. In this role, specialists act as dealers in the stock.

Part of the specialist's job as a broker is simply mechanical. The specialist maintains a "book" listing all outstanding unexecuted limit orders entered by brokers on behalf of clients. (Actually, the book is now a computer console.) When limit orders can be executed at market prices, the specialist executes, or "crosses," the trade.

The specialist is required to use the highest outstanding offered purchase price and lowest outstanding offered selling price when matching trades. Therefore, the specialist system results in an auction market, meaning all buy and all sell orders come to one location, and the best orders "win" the trades. In this role, the specialist acts merely as a facilitator.

The more interesting function of the specialist is to maintain a "fair and orderly market" by acting as a dealer in the stock. In return for the exclusive right to make the market in a specific stock on the exchange, the specialist is required to maintain an orderly market by buying and selling shares from inventory. Specialists maintain their own portfolios of stock and quote bid and asked prices at which they are obligated to meet at least a limited amount of market orders. If market buy orders come in, specialists must sell shares from their own accounts at the asked price; if sell orders come in, they must stand willing to buy at the listed bid price.[4]

Ordinarily, however, in an active market specialists can cross buy and sell orders without their own direct participation. That is, the specialist's own inventory of securities need not be the primary means of order execution. Occasionally, however, the specialist's bid and asked prices will be better than those offered by any other market participant. Therefore, at any point the effective asked price in the market is the lower of either the specialist's asked price or the lowest of the unfilled limit-sell orders.

---

[4] Actually, the specialist's published price quotes are valid only for a given number of shares. If a buy or sell order is placed for more shares than the quotation size, the specialist has the right to revise the quote.

Similarly, the effective bid price is the highest of unfilled limit-buy orders or the specialist's bid. These procedures ensure that the specialist provides liquidity to the market.

By standing ready to trade at quoted bid and asked prices, the specialist is exposed somewhat to exploitation by other traders. Large traders with ready access to late-breaking news will trade with specialists only if the specialists' quoted prices are temporarily out of line with assessments based on the traders' (possibly superior) information. Specialists who cannot match the information resources of large traders will be at a disadvantage when their quoted prices offer profit opportunities to more informed traders.

You might wonder why specialists do not protect their interests by setting a low bid price and a high asked price. A specialist using that strategy would not suffer losses by maintaining a too-low asked price or a too-high bid price in a period of dramatic movements in the stock price. Specialists who offer a narrow spread between the bid and the asked prices have little leeway for error and must constantly monitor market conditions to avoid offering other investors advantageous terms.

There are two reasons why large bid-asked spreads are not viable options for the specialist. First, one source of the specialist's income is derived from frequent trading at the bid and asked prices, with the spread as the trading profit. A too-large spread would tend to discourage investors from trading, and the specialist's business would dry up. Another reason specialists cannot use large bid-ask spreads to protect their interests is that they are obligated to provide *price continuity* to the market.

To illustrate the principle of price continuity, suppose that the highest limit-buy order for a stock is $30 while the lower limit-sell order is at $32. When a market buy order comes in, it is matched to the best limit-sell at $32. A market sell order would be matched to the best limit-buy at $30. As market buys and sells come to the floor randomly, the stock price would fluctuate between $30 and $32. The exchange would consider this excessive volatility, and the specialist would be expected to step in with bid and/or asked prices in between these values to reduce the bid-asked spread to an acceptable level, such as $\frac{1}{4}$ or $\frac{1}{2}$ point.

Specialists earn income both from commissions for acting as brokers for orders and from the spread between the bid and asked prices at which they buy and sell securities. It also appears that specialists' access to their "book" of limit orders gives them unique knowledge about the probable direction of price movement over short periods of time. For example, suppose the specialist sees that a stock now selling for $45 has limit-buy orders for over 100,000 shares at prices ranging from $44.50 to $44.75. This latent buying demand provides a cushion of support, because it is unlikely that enough sell pressure could come in during the next few hours to cause the price to drop below $44.50. If there are very few limit-sell orders above $45, some transient buying demand could raise the price substantially. The specialist in such circumstances realizes that a position in the stock offers little downside risk and substantial upside potential. Such immediate access to the trading intentions of other market participants seems to allow a specialist to earn substantial profits on personal transactions.

The specialist system was subject to extraordinary pressure during the market crash of October 19, 1987, when stock prices fell about 25% on one day. In the face of overwhelming sell pressure, market makers were called upon to purchase huge amounts of

Table. 3.5 Block Transactions on the New York Stock Exchange

Year	Shares (Thousands)	Percentage of Reported Volume	Average Number of Block Transactions per Day
1965	48,262	3.1%	9
1970	450,908	15.4	68
1975	778,540	16.6	136
1980	3,311,132	29.2	528
1985	14,222,272	51.7	2,139
1990	19,681,849	49.6	3,333
1991	22,474,383	49.6	3,878
1992	26,069,383	50.7	4,468
1993	35,959,117	53.7	5,841

Source: Data from the New York Stock Exchange *Fact Book,* 1994.

stock. Specialists as a whole bought $486 million of stock on this single day.[5] However, as prices continued to fall, these market makers suffered large losses, thereby eliminating much of their net worth. This, in turn, made banks wary of lending additional funds to specialist firms and precluded further share purchases by those firms. Only assurances by the Federal Reserve to make ample credit available to the financial system reestablished banks' willingness to lend. Nevertheless, the stock market came close to a halt during the crash. Since the crash, the NYSE has sharply increased the capital requirements for its specialist firms.

Moreover, in the wake of the market collapse many specialists apparently decided not to sacrifice their own capital in a seemingly hopeless effort to shore up prices. Although specialists as a whole were net purchasers of stock, fully 30% of the specialists in a sample of large stocks were net sellers on October 19. These firms came under criticism for failing to live up to their mandate to attempt to support an orderly market.

Block Sales

Institutional investors frequently trade blocks of several thousand shares of stock. Table 3.5 shows that **block transactions** of over 10,000 shares now account for about half of all trading on the NYSE. Although a 10,000 share trade is considered commonplace today, large blocks often cannot be handled comfortably by specialists who do not wish to hold very large amounts of stock in their inventory. For example, the largest block transaction in terms of dollar value in 1993 was for $726 million of shares in Chevron.

In response to this problem, "block houses" have evolved to aid in the placement of block trades. Block houses are brokerage firms that help to find potential buyers or sellers of large block trades. Once a trader has been located, the block is sent to the exchange floor where the trade is executed by the specialist. If such traders cannot be identified, the block house might purchase all or part of a block sale for its own account. The broker then can resell the shares to the public.

[5] This discussion is based on the Brady Commission report. See the Selected Readings at the end of the chapter

The DOT System

A relatively recent innovation is the Designated Order Turnaround (DOT) system, and its technically improved successor, SuperDot. SuperDot enables exchange members to send orders directly to the specialist over computer lines. The largest market order that can be handled is 30,099 shares. In 1993, SuperDot processed an average of 231,000 orders per day, with an average execution time of 25 seconds.

SuperDot is especially useful to program traders. A **program trade** is a coordinated purchase or sale of an entire basket of stocks. Many trading strategies (such as index arbitrage, a topic we will study in Chapter 22) require that an entire portfolio of stocks be purchased or sold simultaneously in a coordinated program. SuperDot is the tool that enables the many trading orders to be sent out at once and executed almost simultaneously.

Approximately three-fourths of all orders are submitted through SuperDot. However, these tend to be smaller orders, and account for a lower percentage of total trading volume.

Settlement

As of June 1995, an order executed on the exchange must be settled within three working days. The purchaser must deliver the cash, and the seller must deliver the stock to the broker, who in turn delivers it to the buyer's broker. Transfer of the shares is made easier when the firm's clients keep their securities in *street name,* meaning that the broker holds the shares registered in the firm's own name on behalf of the client.

Settlement is simplified further by a clearinghouse. The trades of all exchange members are recorded each day, with members' transactions netted out, so that each member need only transfer or receive the net number of shares sold or bought that day. Each member settles only with the clearinghouse, instead of with each firm with whom trades were executed.

3.4 Trading on the OTC Market

On the exchanges all trading takes place through a specialist. Trades on the OTC market, however, are negotiated directly through dealers. Each dealer maintains an inventory of selected securities. Dealers sell from their inventories at asked prices and buy for them at bid prices.

An investor who wishes to purchase or sell shares engages a broker, who tries to locate the dealer offering the best deal on the security. This contrasts with exchange trading, where all buy or sell orders are negotiated through the specialist, who arranges for the best bids to get the trade. In the OTC market brokers must search the offers of dealers directly to find the best trading opportunity.

Because this system bypasses the specialist system, OTC trades do not require a centralized trading floor as do exchange-listed stocks. Dealers can be located anywhere, as long as they can communicate effectively with other buyers and sellers.

One disadvantage of the decentralized dealer market is that the investing public is vulnerable to *trading through,* which refers to the practice of dealers of trading with the public at their quoted bid or asked prices even if other customers have offered to trade at better prices. For example, a dealer who posts a \$20 bid and \$20 1/2 asked price for a stock may continue to fill market buy orders at this asked price and market sell orders at this bid price, even if there are limit orders by public customers "inside the spread," for example, limit orders to buy at \$20 1/8, or limit orders to sell at \$20 3/8. This practice harms the investor whose limit order is not filled (is "traded through"), as well as the investor whose market buy or sell order is not filled at the best available price.

Trading through on Nasdaq sometimes results from imperfect coordination among dealers. A limit order placed with one broker may not be seen by brokers for other traders because computer systems are not linked and only the broker's own bid and asked prices are posted on the Nasdaq system. In contrast, trading through is strictly forbidden on the NYSE or AMEX, where "price priority" requires that the specialist fill the best-priced order first. Moreover, because all traders in an exchange market must trade through the specialist, the exchange provides true *price discovery,* meaning that market prices reflects prices at which *all* participants at that moment are willing to trade. This is the advantage of a centralized auction market.

3.5 Trading Costs

Part of the cost of trading a security is obvious and explicit. Your broker must be paid a commission. Individuals may choose from two kinds of brokers: full-service or discount. Full-service brokers, who provide a variety of services, often are referred to as account executives or financial consultants. Besides carrying out the basic services of executing orders, holding securities for safekeeping, extending margin loans, and facilitating short sales, normally they provide information and advice relating to investment alternatives. Full-service brokers usually are supported by a research staff that issues analyses and forecasts of general economic, industry, and company conditions and often makes specific buy or sell recommendations. Some customers take the ultimate leap of faith and allow a full-service broker to make buy and sell decisions for them by establishing a *discretionary account.* This step requires an unusual degree of trust on the part of the customer, because an unscrupulous broker can "churn" an account, that is, trade securities excessively, in order to generate commissions.

Discount brokers, on the other hand, provide "no-frills" services. They buy and sell securities, hold them for safekeeping, offer margin loans, and facilitate short sales, and that is all. The only information they provide about the securities they handle consists of price quotations.

In recent years, discount brokerage services have become increasingly available. Today, many banks, thrift institutions, and mutual fund management companies offer such services to the investing public as part of a general trend toward the creation of one-stop financial "supermarkets." Table 3.6 presents commission charges quoted by several discount brokerage houses.

One important service that most brokers, both full-service and discount, offer their customers is an automatic cash management feature allowing cash generated from the sale of securities or from the receipt of dividends or interest to be almost immediately

Table 3.6 How Discount Brokerage Commissions Compare

Commission charges quoted by several discounters for buying or selling various amounts of a $26 stock and charges at two full-service firms. (Prices to nearest dollar.)

	Number of Shares Traded				
Brokerage Firm	**100**	**200**	**400**	**1,000**	**2,500**
Fidelity Investments					
Brokerage account	$51	$ 86	$106	$151	$216
FidelityPlus	48	82	100	143	206
Spartan Brokerage	44	44	52	94	192
Andrew Peck	50	56	72	90	140
Quick & Reilly	49	61	85	121	175
Charles Schwab	49	82	100	143	206
Waterhouse Securities	35	35	60	128	240
Jack White & Co.	48	71	89	132	210
York Securities	35	35	53	75	125
Merrill Lynch	80	132	228	418	728
Shearson Lehman	75	139	241	497	878

Note: Many firms offer additional discounts or rebates for active traders, with the amount linked to trading activity.
Source: *The Wall Street Journal,* March 6, 1991. Reprinted by permission of *The Wall Street Journal,* © 1991 Dow Jones & Company, Inc. All Rights Reserved Worldwide.

invested in a money market fund. This ensures that there will never be "idle" cash (uninvested cash) in the investor's account.

In addition to the explicit part of trading costs—the broker's commission—there is an implicit part—the dealer's **bid-asked spread.** Sometimes the broker is a dealer in the security being traded and will charge no commission, but will collect the fee entirely in the form of the bid-asked spread.

Another implicit cost of trading that some observers would distinguish is the price concession an investor may be forced to make for trading in any quantity that exceeds the quantity the dealer is willing to trade at the posted bid or asked price.

The commission for trading common stocks is generally around 2% of the value of the transaction, but it can vary significantly. Before 1975 the schedule of commissions was fixed, but in today's environment of negotiated commissions there is substantial flexibility. On some trades, full-service brokers will offer even lower commissions than will discount brokers. In general, it pays the investor to shop around.

Total trading costs consisting of the commission, the dealer bid-asked spread, and the price concession can be substantial. According to one study, the round-trip costs (costs of purchase and resale) of trading large blocks of stocks of small companies can be as high as 30%.[6]

[6] T. F. Loeb, "Trading Cost: The Critical Link Between Investment Information and Results," *Financial Analysts Journal,* May–June 1983.

However, in most cases costs of trades are far smaller. The commissions can be as low as 0.25% of the value of stocks traded for large transactions made through discount houses.

An ongoing controversy between the NYSE and its competitors is the extent to which better execution on the NYSE offsets the generally lower explicit costs of trading in other markets. Execution refers to the size of the effective bid-ask spread and the amount of price impact in a market. The NYSE believes that many investors focus too intently on the costs they can see, despite the fact that quality of execution can be a far more important determinant of total costs. When the specialist's spread is greater than an eighth of a point, roughly 35% of NYSE trades are executed at a price inside the quoted spread.[7] This can happen because floor brokers at the specialist's post can bid above or sell below the specialist's quote. In this way, two public orders cross without incurring the specialist's spread.

In contrast, in a dealer market such as Nasdaq, all trades go through the dealer, and all trades, therefore, are subject to a bid-ask spread. The client never sees the spread as an explicit cost, however. The price at which the trade is executed incorporates the dealer's spread, but this part of the trading cost is never reported to the investor. Similarly, regional markets are disadvantaged in terms of execution because their lower trading volume means that fewer brokers congregate at a specialist's post, resulting in a lower probability of two public orders crossing.

In October 1994, the Justice Department announced an investigation of the Nasdaq Stock Market regarding possible collusion among market makers to maintain spreads at artificially high levels. The probe derives from the observation that Nasdaq stocks rarely trade at bid-ask spreads of odd eighths, that is, $\frac{1}{8}$, $\frac{3}{8}$, $\frac{5}{8}$, or $\frac{7}{8}$. Even for the biggest and most active shares trading on Nasdaq, such as Apple Computer or Lotus Development, the vast majority of trades seem to be executed at quarter-point or half-point spreads. Cooperation among Nasdaq dealers to increase their profits by maintaining wide spreads would be a violation of antitrust laws. The investigation was ongoing as this book went to press.

A controversial practice is "paying for order flow." This entails paying a broker a rebate for directing the trade to a particular dealer rather than to the NYSE. By bringing the trade to a dealer instead of to the exchange, however, the broker eliminates the possibility that the trade could have been executed without incurring a spread. Moreover, a broker that is paid for order flow might direct a trade to a dealer that does not even offer the most competitive price. (Indeed, the fact that dealers can afford to pay for order flow suggests that they are able to lay off the trade at better prices elsewhere, and, therefore, that the broker also could have found a better price with some additional effort.)

Such practices raise serious ethical questions, because the broker's primary obligation is to obtain the best deal for the client. Payment for order flow might be justified if the rebate were passed along to the client either directly or through lower commissions. However, until a new SEC rule that requires brokerage firms to disclose payment

---

[7] John C. Coffee, Jr., "A Break or a Bribe? Undisclosed Rebates Benefit Brokers, Not Clients," *Barron's*, September 17, 1990.

for order flow goes into effect in 1995, brokers are not required to disclose such rebates unless the client submits a written request for such information.

3.6 Buying on Margin

Investors who purchase stocks on **margin** borrow part of the purchase price of the stock from their brokers. The brokers, in turn, borrow money from banks at the call money rate to finance these purchases, and charge their clients that rate plus a service charge for the loan. All securities purchased on margin must be left with the brokerage firm in street name, because the securities are used as collateral for the loan.

The Board of Governors of the Federal Reserve System sets limits on the extent to which stock purchases may be financed via margin loans. Currently, the maximum margin is 50%, meaning that at most 50% of the purchase price may be borrowed. In addition, the exchange or your broker may require a higher margin.

The percentage margin is defined as the ratio of the net worth, or "equity value" of the account to the market value of the securities. To demonstrate, suppose that the investor initially pays $6,000 toward the purchase of $10,000 worth of stock (100 shares at $100 per share), borrowing the remaining $4,000 from the broker. The account will have a balance sheet as follows:

Assets		Liabilities and Owner's Equity	
Value of stock	$10,000	Loan from broker	$4,000
		Equity	$6,000

The initial percentage margin is

$$\text{Margin} = \frac{\text{Equity}}{\text{Value of assets}} = \frac{6{,}000}{10{,}000} = .60.$$

If the stock's price declines to $70 per share, the account balance becomes:

Value of stock	$7,000	Loan from broker	$4,000
		Equity	$3,000

The equity in the account falls by the full decrease in the stock value, and the percentage margin is now $3,000/$7,000 = .43, or 43%.

If the stock value were to fall below $4,000, equity would become negative, meaning that the value of the stock is no longer sufficient collateral to cover the loan from the broker. To guard against this possibility, the broker sets a *maintenance margin.* If the percentage margin falls below the maintenance level, the broker will issue a *margin call* requiring the investor to add new cash or securities to the margin account. If the investor does not act, the broker may sell the securities from the account to pay off enough of the loan to restore the percentage margin to an acceptable level.

An example will show how the maintenance margin works. Suppose the maintenance margin is 30%. How far could the stock price fall before the investor would get a margin call? To answer this question requires some algebra.

Let P be the price of the stock. The value of the investor's 100 shares is then $100P$, and the equity in his or her account is $100P - \$4{,}000$. The percentage margin is therefore $(100P - \$4{,}000)/100P$. The price at which the percentage margin equals the maintenance margin of .3 is found by solving the equation:

$$\frac{100P - \$4{,}000}{100P} = .3$$

which implies that $P = \$57.14$. If the price of the stock were to fall below \$57.14 per share, the investor would get a margin call.

CONCEPT CHECK Question 1. If the maintenance margin in the example we have discussed were 40%, how far could the stock price fall before the investor would get a margin call?

Why do investors buy stocks (or bonds) on margin? They do so when they wish to invest an amount greater than their own money alone would allow. Thus, they can achieve greater upside potential, but they also expose themselves to greater downside risk.

To see how, let us suppose that an investor is bullish (optimistic) on IBM stock, which is currently selling at \$100 per share. The investor has \$10,000 to invest and expects IBM stock to go up in price by 30% during the next year. Ignoring any dividends, the expected rate of return would thus be 30% if the investor spent only \$10,000 to buy 100 shares.

But now let us assume that the investor also borrows another \$10,000 from the broker and invests it in IBM also. The total investment in IBM would thus be \$20,000 (for 200 shares). Assuming an interest rate on the margin loan of 9% per year, what will be the investor's rate of return now (again ignoring dividends) if IBM stock does go up 30% by year's end?

The 200 shares will be worth \$26,000. Paying off \$10,900 of principal and interest on the margin loan leaves \$15,100 (\$26,000 − \$10,900). The rate of return, therefore, will be

$$\frac{\$15{,}100 - \$10{,}000}{\$10{,}000} = 51\%$$

The investor has parlayed a 30% rise in the stock's price into a 51% rate of return on the \$10,000 investment.

Doing so, however, magnifies the downside risk. Suppose that instead of going up by 30% the price of IBM stock goes down by 30% to \$70 per share. In that case the 200 shares will be worth \$14,000, and the investor is left with \$3,100 after paying off the \$10,900 of principal and interest on the loan. The result is a disastrous rate of return:

$$\frac{\$3{,}100 - \$10{,}000}{\$10{,}000} = -69\%$$

Table 3.7 summarizes the possible results of these hypothetical transactions. Note that if there is no change in IBM's stock price, the investor loses 9%, the cost of the loan.

Table 3.7 Illustration of Buying Stock on Margin

Change in Stock Price	End of Year Value of Shares	Repayment of Principal and Interest	Investor's Rate of Return*
30% increase	$26,000	$10,900	51%
No change	20,000	10,900	−9%
30% decrease	14,000	10,900	−69%

*Assuming the investor buys $20,000 worth of stock by borrowing $10,000 at an interest rate of 9% per year.

CONCEPT CHECK

Question 2. Suppose that in the previous example the investor borrows only $5,000 at the same interest rate of 9% per year. What will be the rate of return if the price of IBM stock goes up by 30%? If it goes down by 30%? If it remains unchanged?

3.7 SHORT SALES

Normally, an investor would first buy a stock and later sell it. With a short sale, the order is reversed. First, you sell and then you buy the shares. In both cases, you begin and end with no shares.

A **short sale** allows investors to profit from a decline in a security's price. Instead of buying, an investor borrows a share of stock from a broker and sells it. Later, the short seller must purchase a share of the same stock in the market in order to replace the share that was borrowed. This is called *covering the short position.* Table 3.8 compares stock purchases to short sales.

The short seller anticipates the stock price will fall, and the share can be purchased at a lower price than it initially sold for; therefore, the short seller reaps a profit. Short sellers must not only replace the shares but also pay the lender of the security any dividends paid during the short sale.

In practice, the shares loaned out for a short sale are typically provided by the short seller's brokerage firm, which holds a wide variety of securities of its other investors in street name. The owner of the shares will not even know that the shares have been lent to the short seller. If the owner wishes to sell the shares, the brokerage firm will simply borrow shares from another investor. Therefore, the short sale may have an indefinite term. However, if the brokerage firm cannot locate new shares to replace the ones sold, the short seller will need to repay the loan immediately by purchasing shares in the market and turning them over to the brokerage house to close out the loan.

Exchange rules permit short sales only after an *uptick,* that is, only when the last recorded change in the stock price is positive. This rule apparently is meant to prevent waves of speculation against the stock. In other words, the votes of "no confidence" in the stock that short sales represent may be entered only after a price increase.

Finally, exchange rules require that proceeds from a short sale must be kept on account with the broker. The short seller, therefore, cannot invest these funds to generate income. In addition, short sellers are required to post margin (which is essentially

Table 3.8 Cash Flows from Purchasing versus Short Selling Shares of Stock

Purchase of Stock		
Time	**Action**	**Cash Flow**
0	Buy share	− Initial price
1	Receive dividend, sell share	Ending price + dividend

Profit = (Ending price + dividend) − Initial price

Note: A negative cash flow implies a cash outflow.

Short Sale of Stock		
Time	**Action**	**Cash Flow**
0	Borrow share; sell it	+ Initial price
1	Repay dividend and buy share to replace the share originally borrowed	− (Ending price + Dividend)

Profit = Initial price − (Ending price + dividend)

collateral) with the broker to ensure that the trader can cover any losses sustained should the stock price rise during the period of the short sale.[8]

To illustrate the actual mechanics of short selling, suppose that you are bearish (pessimistic) on IBM stock, and that its current market price is $100 per share. You tell your broker to sell short 1,000 shares. The broker borrows 1,000 shares either from another customer's account or from another broker.

The $100,000 cash proceeds from the short sale are credited to your account. Suppose the broker has a 50% margin requirement on short sales. This means that you must have other cash or securities in your account worth at least $50,000 that can serve as margin (that is, collateral) on the short sale. Let us suppose that you have $50,000 in Treasury bills. Your account with the broker after the short sale will then be:

Assets		Liabilities and Owner's Equity	
Cash	$100,000	Short position in IBM stock (1,000 shares owed)	$100,000
T-bills	$ 50,000	Equity	$ 50,000

Your initial percentage margin is the ratio of the equity in the account, $50,000, to the current value of the shares you have borrowed and eventually must return, $100,000:

$$\text{Percentage margin} = \frac{\text{Equity}}{\text{Value of stock owed}} = \frac{\$50{,}000}{\$100{,}000} = .50$$

[8] We should note that although we have been describing a short sale of a stock, bonds also may be sold short.

Suppose you are right, and IBM stock falls to $70 per share. You can now close out your position at a profit. To cover the short sale, you buy 1,000 shares to replace the ones you borrowed. Because the shares now sell for $70, the purchase costs only $70,000. Because your account was credited for $100,000 when the shares were borrowed and sold, your profit is $30,000: The profit equals the decline in the share price times the number of shares sold short. On the other hand, if the price of IBM stock goes up while you are short, you may get a margin call from your broker.

Let us suppose that the broker has a maintenance margin of 30% on short sales. This means that the equity in your account must be at least 30% of the value of your short position at all times. How far can the price of IBM stock go up before you get a margin call?

Let P be the price of IBM stock. Then the value of the shares you must return is $1{,}000P$, and the equity in your account is $150,000 − $1{,}000P$. Your short position margin ratio is therefore ($150,000 − $1{,}000P$)/$1{,}000P$. The critical value of P is thus

$$\frac{\text{Equity}}{\text{Value of shares owed}} = \frac{\$150{,}000 - 1{,}000P}{1{,}000P} = .3$$

which implies that $P = \$115.38$ per share. If IBM stock should rise above $115.38 per share, you will get a margin call, and you will either have to put up additional cash or cover your short position.

CONCEPT CHECK Question 3. If the short position maintenance margin in the preceding example were 40%, how far could the stock price rise before the investor would get a margin call?

3.8 REGULATION OF SECURITIES MARKETS

Government Regulation

Trading in securities markets in the United States is regulated under a myriad of laws. The two major laws are the Securities Act of 1933 and the Securities Exchange Act of 1934. The 1933 act requires full disclosure of relevant information relating to the issue of new securities. This is the act that requires registration of new securities and the issuance of a prospectus that details the financial prospects of the firm. The 1934 act established the Securities and Exchange Commission to administer the provisions of the 1933 act. It also extended the disclosure principle of the 1933 act by requiring firms with issued securities on secondary exchanges to periodically disclose relevant financial information.

SEC approval of a prospectus or financial report does not mean that it views the security as a good investment. The SEC cares only that the relevant facts are disclosed; investors make their own evaluations of the security's value. The 1934 act also empowered the SEC to register and regulate securities exchanges, OTC trading, brokers, and dealers. The act thus established the SEC as the administrative agency responsible for broad oversight of the securities markets. The SEC, however, shares oversight with other regulatory agencies. For example, the Commodity Futures Trading Commission

(CFTC) regulates trading in futures markets, whereas the Federal Reserve has broad responsibility for the health of the U.S. financial system. In this role the Fed sets margin requirements on stocks and stock options and regulates bank lending to securities markets participants.

The Securities Investor Protection Act of 1970 established the Securities Investor Protection Corporation (SIPC) to protect investors from losses if their brokerage firms fail. Just as the Federal Deposit Insurance Corporation provides federal protection to depositors against bank failure, the SIPC ensures that investors will receive securities held for their account in street name by the failed brokerage firm up to a limit of $500,000 per customer. The SIPC is financed by levying an "insurance premium" on its participating, or member, brokerage firms. It also may borrow money from the SEC if its own funds are insufficient to meet its obligations.

In addition to federal regulations, security trading is subject to state laws. The laws providing for state regulation of securities are known generally as *blue sky laws,* because they attempt to prevent the false promotion and sale of securities representing nothing more than blue sky. State laws to outlaw fraud in security sales were instituted before the Securities Act of 1933. Varying state laws were somewhat unified when many states adopted portions of the Uniform Securities Act, which was proposed in 1956.

Self-Regulation and Circuit Breakers

Much of the securities industry relies on self-regulation. The SEC delegates to secondary exchanges much of the responsibility for day-to-day oversight of trading. Similarly, the National Association of Securities Dealers oversees trading of OTC securities. The Institute of Chartered Financial Analysts' Code of Ethics and Professional Conduct sets out principles that govern the behavior of CFAs.

The market collapse of 1987 prompted several suggestions for regulatory change. Among these was a call for "circuit breakers" to slow or stop trading during periods of extreme volatility. In response, the NYSE has instituted the following rules:

Trading halts: When the Dow Jones Industrial Average declines by 250 points from its previous day's close, trading is halted for one hour. If the average falls by 400 points from its previous day's close, trading is halted for two hours.

Sidecars: If the S&P 500 futures contract falls by 12 points from its previous day's close, all program trades executed through SuperDot must sit unexecuted for 5 minutes. (In addition, a 12-point drop will trigger the Chicago Mercantile Exchange to halt trading in the S&P 500 futures contract for one hour.)

Collars: When the Dow moves 50 points in either direction from the previous day's close, Rule 80A of the NYSE requires that index arbitrage orders pass a "tick test." In a falling market, sell orders may be executed only at a plus tick or zero-plus tick, meaning that the trade may be done at a higher price than the last trade (a plus tick) or at the last price if the last recorded change in the stock price is positive (a zero-plus tick). The rule remains in effect for the rest of the day unless the Dow returns to within 25 points of the previous day's close.

The idea behind circuit breakers is that a temporary halt in trading during periods of very high volatility can help mitigate informational problems that might contribute to excessive price swings. For example, even if a trader is unaware of any specific adverse economic news, if he or she sees the market plummeting, he or she will suspect that there might be a good reason for the price drop and will become unwilling to buy shares. In fact, the trader might decide to sell shares to avoid losses. Thus, feedback from price swings to trading behavior can exacerbate market movements. Circuit breakers give participants a chance to assess market fundamentals while prices are temporarily frozen. In this way, they have a chance to decide whether price movements are warranted while the market is closed.

Of course, circuit breakers have no bearing on trading in non-U.S. markets. It is quite possible that they simply have induced those who engage in program trading to move their operations into foreign exchanges.

Insider Trading

One of the important restrictions on trading involves *insider trading.* It is illegal for anyone to transact in securities to profit from **inside information,** that is, private information held by officers, directors, or major stockholders that has not yet been divulged to the public. The difficulty is that the definition of *insiders* can be ambiguous. Although it is obvious that the chief financial officer of a firm is an insider, it is less clear whether the firm's biggest supplier can be considered an insider. However, the supplier may deduce the firm's near-term prospects from significant changes in orders. This gives the supplier a unique form of private information, yet the supplier does not necessarily qualify as an insider. These ambiguities plague security analysts, whose job is to uncover as much information as possible concerning the firm's expected prospects. The distinction between legal private information and illegal inside information can be fuzzy.

The SEC requires officers, directors, and major stockholders of all publicly held firms to report all of their transactions in their firm's stock. A compendium of insider trades is published monthly in the SEC's *Official Summary of Securities Transactions and Holdings.* The idea is to inform the public of any implicit votes of confidence or no confidence made by insiders.

Do insiders exploit their knowledge? The answer seems to be, to a limited degree, yes. Two forms of evidence support this conclusion. First, there is abundant evidence of "leakage" of useful information to some traders before any public announcement of that information. For example, share prices of firms announcing dividend increases (which the market interprets as good news concerning the firm's prospects) commonly increase in value a few days *before* the public announcement of the increase.[9] Clearly, some investors are acting on the good news before it is released to the public. Similarly, share prices tend to increase a few days before the public announcement of above-trend

[9] See, for example, J. Aharony and I. Swary, "Quarterly Dividend and Earnings Announcement and Stockholders' Return: An Empirical Analysis," *Journal of Finance* 35 (March 1980).

earnings growth.[10] At the same time, share prices still rise substantially on the day of the public release of good news, indicating that insiders, or their associates, have not fully bid up the price of the stock to the level commensurate with that news.

The second sort of evidence on insider trading is based on returns earned on trades by insiders. Researchers have examined the SEC's summary of insider trading to measure the performance of insiders. In one of the best known of these studies, Jaffee[11] examined the abnormal return on stock over the months following purchases or sales by insiders. For months in which insider purchasers of a stock exceeded insider sellers of the stock by three or more, the stocks had an abnormal return in the following eight months of about 5%. When insider sellers exceeded inside buyers, however, the stock tended to perform poorly.

An issue related to that of insiders trading on privileged information is the extent to which corporate insiders can be held accountable for *releasing* information to the market that then turns out to be incorrect. Firms routinely make public their estimates of future earnings. If those projections turn out to be wrong, the firms are vulnerable to being sued for damages, either by investors who claim to have bought shares based on overly optimistic forecasts, or by investors who claim to have sold shares based on overly pessimistic forecasts. These suits have become so common that the SEC is considering a change in the liability standards under which such suits can be pursued. The nearby box contains a discussion of this issue.

3.9 Mutual Funds and Other Investment Companies

As an alternative to investing in securities through a broker (or in addition to it), many individuals invest in mutual funds sponsored by investment companies. This section explains how these institutions work.

Mutual Funds

Mutual funds are firms that manage pools of other people's money. Individuals buy shares of mutual funds, and the funds invest the money in certain specified types of assets (e.g., common stocks, tax-exempt bonds, mortgages). The shares issued to the investors entitle them to a pro rata portion of the income generated by these assets.

Mutual funds perform several important functions for their shareholders:

1. *Record keeping and administration:* The funds prepare periodic status reports and reinvest dividends and interest.
2. *Diversification and divisibility:* By pooling their money, investment companies enable shareholders to hold fractional shares of many different securities. Funds can act as large investors even if any individual shareholder cannot.

[10] See, for example, George Foster, Chris Olsen, and Terry Shevlin, "Earnings Releases, Anomalies, and the Behavior of Security Returns," *The Accounting Review,* October 1984.

[11] Jeffrey F. Jaffee, "Special Information and Insider Trading," *Journal of Business* 47 (July 1974).

Now It's SEC vs. the Lawyers

"Lawyers Acknowledge Litigation Crisis."

Improbable as that headline may sound, that's exactly what's happening in Washington these days. For far too long, gun-slinging plaintiffs' lawyers have forestalled meaningful discussion, much less meaningful reform, of the crisis affecting the securities litigation system in America.

But the numbers tell an undeniable story—there is a crisis and it's getting worse. In 1989, cash settlements for securities class-action suits totaled an estimated $529 million. In 1993, settlements jumped nearly threefold to $1.4 billion. Those payments come right off the bottom line or out of the R&D budget, thus hampering U.S. competitiveness.

Recently, the Securities and Exchange Commission decided to stand up and be heard on this issue. In a "concept release" that carries symbolic significance far beyond its simple terms, the SEC announced this month that it has decided to re-examine the liability standards for companies that issue earnings projections and other forward-looking information to investors.

Under present law, the SEC encourages companies to provide forward-looking information—or, put another way, senior management's best estimate of where the company is heading. Unfortunately, one weak link exists in the chain of information between management and investors—"entrepreneurial" plaintiffs' lawyers. Never bashful about exploiting new opportunities, plaintiffs' attorneys have used class-action lawsuits as a means of making companies guarantors of any and all forward-looking statements. Pity the chief financial officer who estimates future earnings of "X" if, due to unforeseen events, the actual earnings come in at "X minus 1."

Job one at the SEC is the protection of investors. This is a duty at which the SEC has excelled for more than 60 years. Thanks in large part to the diligent efforts and professionalism of the SEC, a regulatory structure has evolved in the U.S. that has allowed the deepest and fairest markets in the world to develop.

Identifying the problem, however, is only half of the equation. Workable solutions must also be found. In my view, the model to follow in attempting to solve this litigation crisis already exists. The SEC should adopt a rule that provides a "safe harbor" patterned after the state corporate-law doctrine known as the "business judgment rule" to protect companies that provide good-faith projections to investors. Under this new rule, the SEC, and not private "get-rich-quick" litigation mills, would be responsible for policing companies that make material misstatements regarding forward-looking information.

The SEC knows that investors want full and fair disclosure, and has committed itself to making it safe for companies to provide such disclosure again. Under the business judgment rule, officers and directors would be protected from hindsight-based judicial review of shareholder antifraud claims, unless a plaintiff could establish a conflict, a lack of good faith, or a failure of honest and reasonable belief. The business judgment rule is based on the premise that it is the duty of the directors to run the corporation and that courts should not second-guess directors' good-faith business decisions.

No one should make the mistake of interpreting the SEC's action as an invitation to commit fraud. The SEC has the authority to bring actions against companies making false or misleading forward-looking statements and will continue to do so. While some may argue that the SEC does not have the resources to pursue every conceivable case in this area, that's precisely the point. Perhaps not every conceivable case needs to be brought in order to protect our markets. We should have a minimum threshold of improper conduct, which excludes good-faith mistakes, before the legal papers start to fly. Investors will clearly be the winners in the long run as the flow of communication between senior management and investors is enhanced.

These first steps by the SEC reflect a moment of some historic importance—the point at which the government moved from merely debating whether a litigation crisis exists in this country to grappling with solutions to the crisis. In sports terms, the pre-game warm-ups are now over, and the real ballgame has begun.

This article was written by J. Carter Beese, Jr., who is a member of the Securities and Exchange Commission.

Source: *The Wall Street Journal,* October 28, 1994. Excerpted by permission of *The Wall Street Journal,*

3. *Professional management:* Many, but not all, mutual funds have full-time staffs of security analysts and portfolio managers who attempt to achieve superior investment results for their shareholders.
4. *Lower transaction costs:* By trading large blocks of securities, investment companies can achieve substantial savings on brokerage fees and commissions.

There are two types of mutual funds: **closed-end funds** and **open-end funds.** Open-end funds stand ready to redeem or issue shares at their net asset value (NAV), which is the market value of all securities held divided by the number of shares outstanding. The number of shares outstanding of an open-end fund changes daily as investors buy new shares or redeem old shares. Closed-end funds do not redeem or issue shares at net asset value. Shares of closed-end funds are traded through brokers, as are other common stocks, and their price can therefore differ from NAV.

Figure 3.4 shows a listing of closed-end funds' NAVs and prices from *The Wall Street Journal.* The list of these "Publicly Traded Funds" appears weekly on Mondays. Note that in most cases the stock price is different from the NAV, and many are trading below NAV.[12]

Many investors consider closed-end fund shares selling at a discount to their NAV to be a true bargain. Even if the market price never rises to the level of NAV, the dividend yield on an investment in the fund would exceed the dividend yield on the same securities held outside of the fund. To see this, imagine a fund with an NAV of $10 per share and a market price of $9 that pays an annual dividend of $1 per share. Its dividend yield based on NAV is 10% per year, which is the yield obtainable by buying the securities directly. However, the dividend yield to someone buying shares in the fund at $9 would be 11.11% per year.

The market price of open-end funds, on the other hand, cannot fall below NAV because these funds redeem shares at NAV. The offer price will exceed NAV, however, if the fund carries a load. Shares of a **load fund** are sold by security brokers, many insurance brokers, and others. A load is in effect a sales commission, usually from 3% to 8.5% of NAV, which is paid to the seller.

Shares of a **no-load fund** are bought directly from the fund at NAV and carry no sales charge.[13] The investment performance of no-load funds does not differ systematically from that of load funds, so it would seem that an investor who buys into a load fund is simply paying the retail price for an equivalent item readily available wholesale.

At the end of 1993 there were 4,683 open-end mutual funds with assets of $1.83 trillion. Of these, 714 were money market funds (including tax-free money market funds) with assets of $459 billion. Table 3.9 gives a breakdown of the number of mutual funds and their assets by size and type of fund at the end of 1993.

---

[12] The divergence of the market price of a closed-end fund's shares from NAV constitutes a major puzzle, yet to be satisfactorily explained by finance theorists.

[13] No-load funds advertise in the financial pages of newspapers and usually have toll-free telephone numbers for prospective investors to call for information and application forms.

Figure 3.4
Closed-end mutual funds

Source: *The Wall Street Journal,* October 31, 1994. Reprinted by permission of *The Wall Street Journal,*

CLOSED END FUNDS

Friday, October 28, 1994

Closed-end funds sell a limited number of shares and invest the proceeds in securities. Unlike open-end funds, closed-ends generally do not buy their shares back from investors who wish to cash in their holdings. Instead, fund shares trade on a stock exchange. The following list, provided by Lipper Analytical Services, shows the exchange where each fund trades (A: American; C: Chicago; N: NYSE; O: Nasdaq; T: Toronto; z: does not trade on an exchange). The data also include the fund's most recent net asset value, its closing share price on the day NAV was calculated, and the percentage difference between the market price and the NAV (often called the premium or discount). For equity funds, the final column provides 52-week returns based on market prices plus dividends. For bond funds, the final column shows the past 12 months' income distributions as a percentage of the current market price. Footnotes appear after a fund's name. a: the NAV and market price are ex dividend. b: the NAV is fully diluted. c: NAV, market price and premium or discount are as of Thursday's close. d: NAV, market price and premium or discount are as of Wednesday's close. e: NAV assumes rights offering is fully subscribed. v: NAV is converted at the commercial Rand rate. y: NAV and market price are in Canadian dollars. All other footnotes refer to unusual circumstances; explanations for those that appear can be found at the bottom of this list. N/A signifies that the information is not available or not applicable.

Fund Name	Stock Exch	NAV	Market Price	Prem /Disc	52 week Market Return
General Equity Funds					
Adams Express	N	19.85	17 1/8	−13.7	−3.2
Baker Fentress	N	20.13	16 1/4	−19.3	−2.0
Bergstrom Cap	A	99.91	91 1/4	− 8.7	−5.1
Blue Chip Value	N	7.91	6 7/8	−13.1	−11.8
Central Secs	A	18.80	17 1/4	− 8.2	11.2
Charles Allmon	N	10.57	9 5/8	− 8.9	−0.2
Engex	A	10.67	7 3/8	−30.9	−38.5
Equus II	A	20.04	13	−35.1	17.7
Gabelli Equity	N	10.00	10 3/8	+ 3.8	−1.1
General American	N	24.26	20 7/8	−14.0	−6.0
Inefficient Mkt	A	12.24	9 3/4	−20.3	−9.3
Jundt Growth	N	15.46	14 1/8	− 8.6	5.9
Liberty All-Star	N	9.88	9 1/4	− 6.4	−5.5
Morgan FunShares -c	O	7.45	7	− 6.0	N/A
Morgan Gr Sm Cap	N	11.89	9 3/4	−18.0	−9.3
NAIC Growth -c	C	11.48	9 1/4	−19.4	−11.0
Royce Value	N	13.74	11 5/8	−15.4	−10.4
Salomon SBF -a	N	14.64	12 3/8	−15.5	2.5
Source Capital	N	39.64	40	+ 0.9	−6.9
Spectra	O	18.80	14 1/2	−22.9	4.3
Tri-Continental	N	26.93	22 5/8	−16.0	−0.6
Z-Seven	O	16.39	17	+ 3.7	−0.3
Zweig	N	10.42	10 3/8	− 0.4	−13.9

Management Companies and Mutual Fund Investment Policies

Management companies are firms that manage a family of mutual funds. They typically organize the funds and then collect a management fee for operating them. Some of the most well-known management companies are Fidelity, Dreyfus, and Vanguard. Each offers an array of open-end mutual funds with different investment policies.

Figure 3.5 shows a small part of the listings for mutual funds published every weekday in *The Wall Street Journal.* Below the boldface type that gives the name of the management company is the list of that company's "family" of funds. Immediately to the right of each fund's name is a code to its investment objective. *The Wall Street Journal*

Table 3.9 Classification of Mutual Funds (as of December 31, 1993)

Type of Fund	Number of Funds	Assets ($ Million)	% of Total
Common Stock			
Maximum capital gain	130	$ 36,766	2.0%
Small company growth	162	41,678	2.3
International equity	306	108,865	5.9
Long-term growth	531	206,940	11.2
Growth and income	303	186,333	10.1
Equity income	89	35,932	1.9
	1,521	$ 616,514	33.7%
Bond Funds			
Flexible income	59	$45,887	2.5%
Corporate bond	347	89,961	4.9
Corporate high yield	101	49,862	2.7
Government mortgage-backed	148	66,379	3.6
Government securities	348	118,548	6.4
Municipal bonds	283	115,870	6.3
Municipal high yield	45	30,526	1.7
Municipal single state	660	110,728	6.0
International bond	130	36,266	2.0
	2,121	$ 664,027	36.3%
Specialized			
Energy/natural resources	28	$ 2,209	0.1%
Financial services	11	1,728	0.0
Gold and precious metals	35	5,825	0.3
Health care	16	4,408	0.2
Other	31	2,304	0.1
Technology	21	3,567	0.2
Utilities	53	29,118	1.6
	195	$ 49,159	2.7%
Money Market			
Taxable	481	$ 364,132	19.7%
Tax-free	233	95,123	5.2
	714	$ 459,255	25.1%
Balanced	132	38,590	2.1
TOTAL	4,683	$1,827,545	100.0%

Column sums subject to rounding error.
Source: *Investment Companies 1994,* CDA/Wiesenberger Investment Companies Service, 1355 Piccard Dr., Rockville, MD 20850.

classifies each fund into one of 27 categories based on investment objective. For example, G&I denotes a growth and income fund. The price and NAV of the fund is given in the next two columns. No-load funds are the ones whose offer price equals NAV (for which NL is listed in the offer price column). The final columns report on the change in NAV from the previous day, and total fund returns over various investment periods. (The data presented in the last four columns differ on various days of the week.)

Figure 3.5
Listing of mutual fund quotations

Source: Reprinted by permission of *The Wall Street Journal*, © 1994 Dow Jones & Company, Inc. All Rights Reserved Worldwide.

MUTUAL FUND QUOTATIONS

	Inv. Obj.	NAV	Offer Price	NAV Chg.	Total Return YTD	Total Return 39 wks	Total Return 5 yrs	R
USGv p	MTG	4.70	4.95	...	−5.3	−6.1	+6.3	D
St Farm Fds:								
Balan	S&B	31.42	31.42	−0.04	+3.9	+0.2	+12.6	A
Gwth	GRO	23.03	23.03	−0.03	+4.7	+1.0	+11.1	B
Interm	BIN	9.77	9.77	−0.01	−1.1	−1.7	+6.9	C
Muni	GLM	7.88	7.88	...	−4.3	−5.2	+6.7	B
Stepstone Funds:								
Balan p	S&B	11.41	NL	−0.03	−1.8	−4.3	NS	..
BlChGrI	GRO	9.60	NL	−0.04	NS	NA	NS	..
GovSec	MTG	8.94	NL	−0.02	NS	NA	NS	..
GrEq p	GRO	14.17	NL	−0.10	−2.0	−5.5	NS	..
IntBd	BIN	9.64	NL	−0.01	−4.5	−5.8	NS	..
LtdMatGvA	BST	9.50	NL	−0.01	−1.1	−1.7	NS	..
VIMom	G&I	13.42	NL	−0.05	−0.8	−4.5	NS	..
Stratton Funds:								
Dividend	SEC	23.59	NL	−0.08	−13.4	−11.7	+5.9	D
Growth	G&I	20.14	NL	+0.01	+7.7	+4.7	+7.7	E
SmCap	SML	25.35	NL	−0.02	−3.4	−4.8	NS	..
Strong Funds:								
Advtg	BST	10.03	NL	...	+3.1	+2.5	+7.5	A
AmUtil	SEC	9.65	NL	−0.06	−1.5	−1.9	NS	..
AsiaPc	ITL	9.95	NL	−0.09	−0.4	NA	NS	..
CmStk	GRO	18.09	NL	−0.03	+2.0	−0.7	NS	..
Discov	CAP	16.78	NL	...	−4.4	−8.4	+14.7	A
GovSc	MTG	9.61	NL	−0.01	−4.5	−5.8	+8.5	A
Growth	GRO	11.45	NL	−0.03	+15.7	NA	NS	..
HiYlMu	HYM	9.23	NL	...	−2.8	−4.2	NS	..
Inco	BND	9.30	NL	−0.02	−3.2	−5.2	+5.4	E
InsMu	ISM	9.83	NL	+0.01	−10.5	−11.2	NS	..
Intl	ITL	14.09	NL	−0.07	+1.5	−5.2	NS	..
Invst	S&B	18.12	NL	−0.03	−1.9	−4.0	+7.9	D
MunBd	GLM	8.96	NL	+0.02	−8.2	−9.0	+6.7	B
Oppty	GRO	29.37	NL	−0.06	+6.1	+2.3	+12.5	A
ST Bd	BST	9.60	NL	...	−0.8	−1.8	+6.8	B
STMun	STM	9.73	NL	+0.01	−2.3	−3.1	NS	..
Total	G&I	23.83	NL	−0.06	−1.0	−5.7	+8.7	D
SummitHY	BHI	9.78	10.27	+0.01	NS	NS	NS	..
SunAmerica Fds:								
BalAsA p	S&B	14.65	15.54	−0.05	−0.5	−4.2	NS	..
BalAsB t	S&B	14.65	14.65	−0.05	−1.0	−4.6	+8.5	C
BlueChipB t	GRO	15.36	15.36	−0.05	−1.3	−5.0	+4.4	E
DivIncB t	BND	4.40	4.40	...	−6.6	−8.5	NS	..
FedScB t	MTG	9.65	9.65	−0.03	−3.3	−4.2	+5.5	E
GlbBalB	S&B	6.83	6.83	−0.03	NS	NS	NS	..
HiIncA p	BHI	7.05	7.40	...	−7.5	−9.5	+10.6	C
HiIncB t	BHI	7.06	7.06	...	−7.9	−9.4	NS	..
MidCapA p	GRO	13.78	14.62	−0.06	−5.0	−8.7	+7.7	D
SmlCoGrA p	SML	17.60	18.67	−0.04	+2.2	−2.2	+9.9	D
SmlCoGrB t	SML	17.46	17.46	−0.05	+1.6	−2.7	NS	..
TE InsA p	ISM	11.32	11.88	−0.01	−6.9	−7.8	+4.7	E
TE InsB	ISM	11.33	11.33	−0.01	−7.3	NA	NS	..
USGvA p	MTG	8.07	8.47	−0.01	−1.4	−2.0	NS	..
USGvB t	MTG	8.08	8.08	−0.01	−1.8	−2.4	+5.5	E
TARGET:								
InterBd	BIN	9.61	NL	−0.01	−2.6	−3.1	NS	..
IntlBd	WBD	9.93	NL	−0.01	NS	NS	NS	..
IntlEq	ITL	13.85	NL	−0.10	+5.8	−4.5	NS	..
LgCapGr	GRO	10.08	NL	...	+1.7	−0.1	NS	..
LgCapVal	G&I	10.45	NL	−0.03	+3.5	+1.2	NS	..
MtgBkd	MTG	9.48	NL	−0.02	−1.9	−2.5	NS	..
SmCapGr	SML	11.51	NL	−0.10	−3.0	−7.8	NS	..
SmCapVal	SML	11.57	NL	+0.04	−7.1	−8.9	NS	..
TotRetBd	BND	9.43	NL	−0.02	−4.8	−5.4	NS	..
TIFF Inv Pro:								
Bond	...	9.68	9.68	−0.02	NA	NA	NA	..
Emg Mkt	...	10.67	10.67	−0.06	NA	NA	NA	..
Intl Eq	...	10.43	10.43	−0.05	NA	NA	NA	..
US Eq	...	10.23	10.23	−0.02	NA	NA	NA	..
Templeton Group:								
AmerTr r	GRO	13.79	13.79	−0.01	+3.5	−2.2	NS	..
CapAcc	S&B	15.37	15.37	−0.02	+6.6	−2.1	NS	..
DevMkt p	ITL	14.71	15.61	−0.05	−3.2	−6.2	NS	..
Forgn p	ITL	9.27	9.84	−0.02	+4.4	−1.1	+12.4	A
GlInfra	WOR	10.34	10.97	−0.02	NS	NS	NS	..
GlbOp p	WOR	13.34	14.15	−0.05	+0.2	−5.8	NS	..
Grwth p	WOR	16.98	18.02	−0.04	+4.5	−1.8	+12.8	A
USLargeStk	G&I	5.18	NL	−0.02	+0.4	−2.6	NS	..
ValFrg	GRO	10.06	10.06	−0.01	+5.8	+4.0	+7.4	D
Vance Exchange:								
CapE	GRO	175.82	175.82	−0.49	+6.3	+2.9	+11.4	B
DBst	GRO	87.21	87.21	−0.30	0.0	−1.3	+8.3	D
Divrs	GRO	172.12	172.12	−0.44	−0.3	−2.3	+8.2	D
EBos	GRO	203.06	203.06	−0.61	−1.5	−3.4	+7.4	D
ExFd	GRO	258.91	258.91	−0.22	+4.2	+2.8	+9.6	C
FdEx	GRO	143.86	143.86	−0.25	−2.9	−5.1	+9.0	C
ScFid	GRO	126.15	126.15	−0.56	+1.0	−2.8	+7.2	E
Vanguard Group:								
AdmIT	BIN	9.42	NL	−0.03	−5.5	−6.5	NS	..
AdmLT	BND	8.98	NL	−0.05	−10.2	−11.9	NS	..
AdmST	BST	9.75	NL	−0.01	−0.4	−0.9	NS	..
AssetA	S&B	13.68	NL	−0.06	−3.9	−6.7	+8.9	C
Convrt	S&B	11.15	NL	−0.03	−3.6	−5.2	+10.2	A
EqInc	EQI	13.12	NL	−0.05	−0.8	−2.8	+7.2	D
Explr	SML	45.76	NL	−0.09	+1.4	−0.9	+12.8	C
Morg	GRO	11.90	NL	−0.04	−0.1	−2.8	+9.3	C
Prmcp	GRO	20.55	NL	−0.09	+12.0	+6.2	+13.9	A
Quant	G&I	15.90	NL	−0.05	0.0	−2.9	+10.3	B
STAR	S&B	13.23	NL	−0.02	+0.5	−2.1	+8.4	C
TxMCap	GRO	10.09	NL	−0.03	NS	NS	NS	..
TrIntl	ITL	32.77	NL	−0.18	+7.3	−0.7	+6.0	D
TrUS	G&I	29.74	NL	−0.15	−2.2	−7.1	+7.2	E
STTsry	BST	9.87	NL	−0.01	−0.6	−1.1	NS	..
STFed	BST	9.77	NL	−0.01	−1.0	−1.6	+6.9	B
STCorp	BST	10.38	NL	−0.01	−0.2	−0.8	+7.4	A
ITTsry	BIN	9.60	NL	−0.02	−5.5	−6.6	NS	..
GNMA	MTG	9.54	NL	−0.01	−2.5	−2.9	+7.5	A
ITCorp	BIN	8.94	NL	−0.02	−5.3	−6.1	NS	..
LTTsry	BND	8.90	NL	−0.04	−10.3	−11.8	+7.0	D
LTCorp	BND	7.92	NL	−0.03	−7.8	−9.3	+8.4	A
HYCorp	BHI	7.24	NL	...	−2.5	−4.6	+9.8	D
Prefd	BND	8.20	NL	...	−9.3	−10.4	+7.7	B
IdxTotB	BIN	9.15	NL	−0.01	−3.8	−4.9	+7.3	B
IdxSTB	BST	9.58	NL	−0.01	NS	NS	NS	..
IdxITB	BIN	9.17	NL	−0.02	NS	NS	NS	..
Idx Bal	S&B	10.52	NL	−0.02	−1.4	−3.6	NS	..
Idx 500	G&I	43.92	NL	−0.09	+1.9	−1.5	+9.8	B
IdxExt	MID	19.21	NL	−0.07	−0.4	−3.6	+9.7	E
IdxTot	GRO	11.61	NL	−0.03	+0.9	−2.4	NS	..
IdxGro	GRO	10.46	NL	...	+4.1	+1.7	NS	..
IdxVal	G&I	11.37	NL	−0.05	−0.5	−4.8	NS	..
IdxSmC	SML	15.58	NL	−0.06	−0.6	−4.5	+10.7	D
IdxEMkt	ITL	12.45	NL	−0.16	NS	NS	NS	..
IdxEur	ITL	12.35	NL	−0.02	+4.2	−1.3	NS	..
IdxPac	ITL	11.48	NL	−0.10	+13.3	+1.2	NS	..
IdxInst	G&I	44.35	NL	−0.09	+2.0	−1.4	NS	..
MuHY	HYM	9.55	NL	...	−8.7	−9.6	+7.1	B
MuInt	IDM	12.35	NL	...	−4.4	−5.2	+7.4	A
MuLtd	STM	10.39	NL	+0.01	−0.4	−1.0	+6.1	A
MuLong	GLM	9.72	NL	−0.01	−9.5	−10.1	+6.9	A
MuInIg	ISM	11.04	NL	−0.02	−9.4	−10.3	+6.6	A
MuSht	STM	15.36	NL	...	+1.3	+0.9	+4.9	E
CAInsIT	IDM	9.61	NL	−0.01	NS	NS	NS	..
CAInsLT	ISM	9.83	NL	...	−9.3	−10.1	+6.4	A
FL Ins	MFL	9.52	NL	−0.01	−9.2	−10.1	NS	..
NJIns	MNJ	10.31	NL	−0.01	−9.2	−10.0	+6.6	A
NYIns	ISM	9.63	NL	−0.01	−9.4	−10.1	+6.6	A
OHIns	MOH	10.19	NL	−0.01	−9.3	−10.3	NS	..
PAIns	MPA	9.98	NL	−0.01	−8.3	−9.2	+6.9	A
SPEnrg r	SEC	15.91	NL	−0.14	+6.2	−0.9	+9.9	B
SPGold r	SEC	13.91	NL	−0.05	+1.3	+1.0	+7.0	C
SPHlth r	SEC	38.05	NL	+0.02	+10.3	+5.9	+17.2	A
SPUtil	SEC	10.01	NL	−0.05	−9.1	−8.7	NS	..
USGro	GRO	15.56	NL	−0.01	+4.2	+0.7	+10.9	B
IntlGr	ITL	14.09	NL	...	+4.3	−1.6	+7.5	C
WellsI	S&B	17.28	NL	−0.05	−5.6	−6.9	+8.8	C
Wellfn	S&B	19.64	NL	−0.06	−0.8	−4.0	+8.8	C
Wndsr	G&I	14.13	NL	−0.08	+3.0	−3.0	+8.9	C
WndsII	G&I	17.08	NL	−0.02	+1.4	−2.1	+9.0	C
Venture Advisers:								
IncPl	BHI	4.86	5.10	...	+1.6	−0.3	+7.9	E
Muni t	HYM	8.88	8.88	...	+0.2	−0.2	+6.8	C
NY Ven	GRO	11.90	12.49	[illegible]	[illegible]	[illegible]	[illegible]	[illegible]

Figure 3.5 includes the Vanguard listings. Often the fund name describes its investment policy. For example, the GNMA fund invests in mortgage-backed securities, the municipal intermediate fund (MuInt) invests in intermediate term municipal bonds, and the high-yield bond fund (HYCorp) invests in large part in speculative grade or "junk" bonds with high yields. However, names of common stock funds often give little or no

clue as to their investment policies. Examples are Vanguard's Windsor fund or Wellington fund.

Wiesenberger's (an investment service company) manual *Investment Companies* classifies common stock funds as having the following objectives:

1. Maximum capital gain.
2. Growth.
3. Growth and income.
4. Income.
5. Income and security.

The objectives are "arranged in descending order of emphasis on capital appreciation and, consequently, in ascending order of the importance placed on current income and relative price stability."

Some funds are designed as candidates for an individual's whole investment portfolio. Wiesenberger's manual classifies such funds, which hold both equities and fixed-income securities, as *income* or *balanced funds.* Income funds "provide as liberal a current income from investments as possible," whereas balanced funds "minimize investment risks so far as this is possible without unduly sacrificing possibilities for long-term growth and current income."

Finally, an **index fund** tries to match the performance of a broad market index. For example, Vanguard Index Trust 500 Portfolio (Idx 500) is a no-load mutual fund that replicates the composition of the Standard & Poor's 500 stock index, thus providing a relatively low-cost way for small investors to pursue a passive common stock investment strategy. You can see that Vanguard offers more than a dozen index funds, including portfolios indexed to the bond market (Idx Tot B), the Wilshire 5000 Index (Idx Tot), the Russell 200 Index of small firms (Idx Sm C), as well as European and Pacific Basin indexed portfolios.

Costs of Trading Mutual Funds

Investors must consider not only the fund's stated investment policy, but also its management fees and other expenses. You should be aware of four general classes of fees.

Front-End Load. A front-end load is a commission or sales charge paid when you purchase the shares. These charges typically fall between 3% and 8.5% and are used to pay brokers to sell the fund. Low-load funds have loads that range from 1% to 3% of invested funds. No-load funds have no front-end sales charges. Loads effectively reduce the funds being invested. Each $1,000 invested in a fund with an 8.5% load results in a sales charge of $85, and a portfolio that starts at only $915. You need cumulative returns of 9.3% of your net investment (85/915 = .093) just to break even.

Back-End Load. A back-end load is a redemption or "exit" fee incurred when you sell your shares. Typically, funds that impose back-end loads start them at 5% or 6% and reduce them by 1 percentage point for every year the funds are left invested. Thus, an exit fee that starts at 6% would fall to 4% by the start of your third year.

Operating Expenses. Operating expenses refer to the costs incurred by the mutual fund in operating the portfolio, including administrative expenses and advisory fees paid to the investment manager. These expenses are usually expressed as a percent of total assets under management and may range from 0.2% to 2%.

12b-1 Charges. The Securities and Exchange Commission allows the manager of 12b-1 funds to use fund assets to pay for distribution costs such as advertising, promotional literature including annual reports and prospectuses, and commissions paid to brokers. These 12b-1 fees are named after the SEC rule that permits use of these plans. Some funds use 12b-1 charges instead of front-end loads to generate fees with which to pay brokers. 12b-1 charges (if any) must be added to operating expenses to obtain the true annual expense ratio of the fund. The SEC now requires that all funds publish a consolidated expense table that summarizes all relevant fees.

You can identify funds with various charges by the following letters placed after the fund name in the listing of mutual funds in the financial pages: *r* denotes redemption or exit fees (also called a deferred sales charge); *p* denotes 12b-1 fees; *t* denotes both redemption and 12b-1 fees. Finally, you can identify front-end fees because two prices will be listed. The offer price is what you must pay for a fund. The net asset value (NAV), which is the value per share of the assets held in the fund, is what you will receive if you sell your shares. The difference is the load. For example, consider Figure 3.5. The highlighted fund at the bottom left corner of Figure 3.5 has an offer price of $8.47 and an NAV of $8.07, implying a front-end load of 4.96%. In addition, the *p* indicates the presence of 12b-1 fees. Funds with no loads are identified by the abbreviation NL in the offering price column.

Fees can have a big effect on performance. Table 3.10 shows the cumulative value of three funds, all of which start with $10,000 and earn an annual 12% return on investment before fees. Fund A has total operating expenses of 0.5%, no load, and no 12b-1 charges. This might represent a low-cost producer like Vanguard. Fund B has no load but has 1% in management expenses and 0.5% in 12b-1 fees. This level of fees is perhaps slightly above average, but not unusual in the industry. Finally, fund C has 1% in management expenses, no 12b-1 charges, but assesses an 8% front-end load on purchases as well as reinvested dividends. We assume the dividend yield on the fund is 5%.

Note the substantial return advantage of low-cost fund A. Moreover, that differential is greater for longer investment horizons.

Although expenses can have a big impact on net investment performance, it is sometimes difficult for the investor in a mutual fund to measure those expenses accurately. This is because of the common practice of paying for some expenses in *soft dollars.* A portfolio manager earns soft dollar credits with a stockbroker by directing the fund's trades to that broker. Based on those credits, the broker will pay for some of the mutual fund's expenses, such as for databases, computer hardware, or stock-quotation systems. The soft dollar arrangement means that the stockbroker effectively returns part of the trading commission to the fund. The advantage to the mutual fund is that purchases made with soft dollars are not included in the fund's expenses, so the fund can advertise an unrealistically low expense ratio to the public. Although the firm may have paid

Table 3.10 Impact of Costs on Investment Performance

	Cumulative Proceeds (All Dividends Reinvested)		
	Fund A	Fund B	Fund C
Initial investment*	$10,000	$10,000	$ 9,200
5 years	17,234	16,474	15,225
10 years	29,669	27,141	25,196
15 years	51,183	44,713	41,698
20 years	88,206	73,662	69,006

*After front-end load, if any.

Notes

1. Fund A is no load with .5% expense ratio.
2. Fund B is no load with 1.5% expense ratio.
3. Fund C has an 8% load on purchase and reinvested dividends with a 1% expense ratio. The dividend yield on fund C is 5%. (Thus, the 8% load on reinvested dividends reduces net returns by .08 × 5% = 0.4%.)
4. Gross return on all funds is 12% per year before expenses.

the broker needlessly high commissions to obtain the soft dollar "rebate," trading costs also are not included in the fund's expenses. The impact of the higher trading commission shows up instead in net investment performance. Soft dollar arrangements make it difficult for investors to compare fund expenses, and have recently come under attack. The nearby box explores some of the issues.

Unit Investment Trusts

Unit investment trusts are pools of money invested in a portfolio that, in contrast to mutual funds, is fixed for the life of the fund. To form a unit trust, a sponsor, typically a brokerage firm, buys a set of securities and sells shares called *redeemable trust certificates* to investors at a premium above NAV. All income and repayments of principal are paid out by the fund's trustee (a bank or trust company) to the shareholders. Most unit trusts hold fixed-income securities and expire at their maturity. There is no active management of a unit trust by definition, because the portfolio composition is fixed.

Commingled Funds

Commingled funds are investment pools managed by banks and insurance companies for trust or retirement accounts that are too small to warrant managing on a separate basis. A commingled fund is similar in form to an open-end mutual fund. Instead of shares, though, the fund offers units that are bought and sold at net asset value. A bank or insurance company may offer an array of different commingled funds for trust or retirement accounts to choose from, for example, a money market fund, a bond fund, and a common stock fund.

Use of 'Soft Dollars' Makes a Hard Task For Investors Comparing Fund Costs

Savvy investors have learned that mutual funds with lean expenses can produce better returns. But can you find out what a fund's expenses really are?

Probably not, because fund managers can, and do, hide much of their actual costs by paying for research, computers, stock-quote systems and even phone calls and newspaper subscriptions with so-called soft dollars instead of cash.

It works like this: Say a fund manager needs a new laptop computer. Instead of buying the laptop and putting it down as a fund expense, the manager pays a slightly higher-than-necessary commission to a stockbroker—hence the term soft dollars—and the broker buys the laptop for him. Or, the fund manager might buy the computer himself and send the bill to the broker. In general, a fund's expenses cover management fees and general operating costs, but not commissions.

The more a fund manager can use soft dollars to pay expenses, the less expensive it appears that it is to run the fund—because soft dollars aren't included in calculating a fund's annual expenses. The consumer reading a prospectus is none the wiser.

Raising Trading Costs

Soft dollars can also result in higher trading costs for the fund. That can occur if a fund group's trading desk improperly steers stock and bond trades to certain soft-dollar brokers despite higher commissions charged by those brokers.

Despite their resemblance to kickbacks, soft dollars are legal in most instances. And they are nothing new. They originated way back when the Securities and Exchange Commission required brokerage firms to charge customers fixed commission rates. Soft dollars became a popular incentive for brokers to offer customers, and when the SEC deregulated commissions in 1975, it allowed the practice to continue.

But that may change. In August the SEC proposed new measures that would bring to light at least a small portion of soft-dollar use. And in September the agency's chairman, Arthur Levitt, denounced soft dollars in a speech, advising fund directors "to stay on top of issues" raised by their use.

The August proposal would require fund managers to include expenses such as custodial fees, printing and

Real Estate Investment Trusts (REITs)

A REIT is similar to a closed-end mutual fund. REITs invest in real estate or loans secured by real estate. Besides issuing shares, they raise capital by borrowing from banks and issuing bonds and mortgages. Most of them are highly leveraged (debt-financed), with a typical debt ratio of 70%.

There are two principal kinds of REITs. *Equity trusts* invest in real estate directly, whereas *mortgage trusts* invest primarily in mortgages and construction loans. REITs generally are established by banks, insurance companies, or mortgage companies, which then serve as investment managers to earn a fee.

REITs are exempt from taxes as long as at least 95% of their taxable income is distributed to shareholders. For shareholders, however, the dividends are taxable as personal income.

Summary

1. Firms issue securities to raise the capital necessary to finance their investments. Investment bankers market these securities to the public on the primary market. Invest-

legal fees in calculating a fund's expense ratio, fee table and current yield. But it wouldn't include such major expenses as research, software and databases.

Calls for Tougher Rules

Some regulators think the proposal should go further. One senior SEC official, who insisted on anonymity, calls the plan a "cowardly" attempt at reform, which would miss about 90% of soft-dollar business. "Funds know expenses are important and they all want to underreport," says the official. For consumers, "it's much more important over the long run to contain expenses than to chase winners," says the official, who estimates that, on average, soft-dollar use adds a hidden 5% to the annual cost of running a fund. And the cost of running a fund comes out of investors' pockets.

The limited disclosure proposed so far by the SEC is supported by many in the fund industry, including its biggest trade group, the Investment Company Institute. "Those who appear to have artificially low expense ratios will no longer be able to compete based on expense ratios that are lower than they should be," says Dan Maclean, general counsel at Dreyfus Mutual Funds in New York.

But the ICI, Dreyfus and many other fund groups don't want the SEC to force funds to tell how much research or research-related service they buy with soft dollars. It would be too difficult for a fund group to break up its research costs and allocate them to individual funds, they say. Research on a broad topic, such as the direction of interest rates, often influences the investment decisions of several funds in a group.

Informing the Investors

But Harold Bradley, head trader for Twentieth Century Mutual Funds, disagrees. "How will disclosure kill anything that is right and good for the shareholders? Wouldn't they like to know their money is being well-stewarded?" he asks.

Mr. Bradley says the SEC ought to lift the lid so consumers can see where their real dollars are going and what they are getting in return. The Twentieth Century group favors including soft-dollar expenses in calculating a fund's expense ratio and yield. "We're not saying put an end to the practice," says Mr. Bradley. "We're saying, let's put some rules in place."

Source: *The Wall Street Journal,* January 6, 1995. Excerpted by permission of *The Wall Street Journal,*

ment bankers generally act as underwriters who purchase the securities from the firm and resell them to the public at a markup. Before the securities may be sold to the public, the firm must publish an SEC-approved prospectus that provides information on the firm's prospects.

2. Issued securities are traded on the secondary market, that is, on organized stock exchanges, the over-the-counter market, or, for large traders, through direct negotiation. Only members of exchanges may trade on the exchange. Brokerage firms holding seats on the exchange sell their services to individuals, charging commissions for executing trades on their behalf. The NYSE and, to a lesser extent, the AMEX have fairly strict listing requirements. Regional exchanges provide listing opportunities for local firms that do not meet the requirements of the national exchanges.

3. Trading of common stocks in exchanges takes place through specialists. Specialists act to maintain an orderly market in the shares of one or more firms, maintaining "books" of limit-buy and limit-sell orders and matching trades at mutually acceptable prices. Specialists also will accept market orders by selling from or buying for their own inventory of stocks.

4. The over-the-counter market is not a formal exchange but an informal network of brokers and dealers who negotiate sales of securities. The Nasdaq system provides on-line computer quotes offered by dealers in the stock. When an individual wishes to purchase or sell a share, the broker can search the listing of offered bid and asked prices, call the dealer who has the best quote, and execute the trade.

5. Block transactions account for about half of trading volume. These trades often are too large to be handled readily by specialists, and thus block houses have developed that specialize in these transactions, identifying potential trading partners for their clients.

6. Buying on margin means borrowing money from a broker in order to buy more securities. By buying securities on margin, an investor magnifies both the upside potential and the downside risk. If the equity in a margin account falls below the required maintenance level, the investor will get a margin call from the broker.

7. Short selling is the practice of selling securities that the seller does not own. The short seller borrows the securities sold through a broker and may be required to cover the short position at any time on demand. The cash proceeds of a short sale are always kept in escrow by the broker, and the broker usually requires that the short seller deposit additional cash or securities to serve as margin (collateral) for the short sale.

8. Securities trading is regulated by the Securities and Exchange Commission, as well as by self-regulation of the exchanges. Many of the important regulations have to do with full disclosure of relevant information concerning the securities in question. Inside trading rules also prohibit traders from attempting to profit from insider information.

9. In addition to providing the basic services of executing buy and sell orders, holding securities for safekeeping, making margin loans, and facilitating short sales, full-service brokers offer investors information, advice, and even investment decisions. Discount brokers offer only the basic brokerage services but usually charge less.

10. Total trading costs consist of commissions, the dealer's bid-asked spread, and price concessions.

11. As an alternative to investing in securities through a broker, many individuals invest in mutual funds and other investment companies. Mutual funds free the individual from many of the administrative burdens of owning individual securities and offer the prospect of superior investment results. Mutual funds are classified according to whether they are open-end or closed-end, load or no-load, and by the type of securities in which they invest. REITs are specialized investment companies that invest in real estate and loans secured by real estate.

Key Terms

Primary market
Secondary market
Underwriting
Prospectus
Stock exchanges
Over-the-counter market
Block transactions
Program trades
Bid-asked spread
Margin
Short sale
Inside information

NASDAQ
Bid price
Asked price
Third market
Fourth market
Specialist
Closed-end fund
Open-end fund
Load fund
No-load fund
Index fund

Selected Readings

A good treatment of investment banking, including evidence on IPOs, is:
Smith, Clifford W. "Investment Banking and the Capital Acquisition Process." *Journal of Financial Economics* 15 (January–February 1986).

An overview of market organization is provided in:
Schwartz, Robert A. *Equity Markets: Structure, Trading, and Performance.* New York: Harper & Row, 1988.

The *Fact Books* of the NYSE, AMEX, and Nasdaq are published annually and contain extensive data on trading in the respective markets.

An "encyclopedia" of mutual funds with profiles on thousands of funds is:
Investment Companies, CDA Wiesenberger Investment Companies, Rockville, Maryland, 1994.

Problems

1. FBN, Inc. has just sold 100,000 shares in an initial public offering. The underwriter's explicit fees were $70,000. The offering price for the shares was $50, but immediately upon issue the share price jumped to $53.
   a. What is your best guess as to the total cost to FBN of the equity issue?
   b. Is the entire cost of the underwriting a source of profit to the underwriters?
2. Suppose that you sell short 100 shares of IBM, now selling at $70 per share.
   a. What is your maximum possible loss?
   b. What happens to the maximum loss if you simultaneously place a stop-buy order at $78?
3. An expiring put will be exercised and the stock will be sold if the stock price is below the exercise price. A stop-loss order causes a stock sale when the stock price falls below some limit. Compare and contrast the two strategies of purchasing put options versus issuing a stop-loss order.
4. Compare call options and stop-buy orders.
5. Here is some price information on Marriott:

	Bid	Asked
Marriott	37¼	38⅛

   You have placed a stop-loss order to sell at $38. What are you telling your broker? Given market prices, will your order be executed?
6. Do you think it is possible to replace market-making specialists by a fully automated computerized trade-matching system?

7. Consider the following limit-order book of a specialist. The last trade in the stock took place at a price of $50.

Limit-Buy Orders		Limit-Sell Orders	
Price ($)	**Shares**	**Price ($)**	**Shares**
49.75	500	50.25	100
49.50	800	51.50	100
49.25	500	54.75	300
49.00	200	58.25	100
48.50	600		

   a. If a market-buy order for 100 shares comes in, at what price will it be filled?
   b. At what price would the next market-buy order be filled?
   c. If you were the specialist, would you desire to increase or decrease your inventory of this stock?

8. What purpose does the Designated Order Turnaround system (SuperDot) serve on the New York Stock Exchange?
9. Who sets the bid and asked price for a stock traded over the counter? Would you expect the spread to be higher on actively or inactively traded stocks?
10. Consider the following data concerning the NYSE:

Year	Average Daily Trading Volume (Thousands of Shares)	Annual High Price of an Exchange Membership
1988	161,461	$820,000
1989	165,470	675,000
1990	156,777	430,000
1991	178,917	440,000
1992	202,266	600,000
1993	264,519	775,000

   a. What do you conclude about the short-run relationship between trading activity and the value of a seat?
   b. Based on these data, what do you think has happened over the last six years to the average commission charged to traders?

11. You are bullish on AT&T stock. The current market price is $50 per share, and you have $5,000 of your own to invest. You borrow an additional $5,000 from your broker at an interest rate of 8% per year and invest $10,000 in the stock.
   a. What will be your rate of return if the price of AT&T stock goes up by 10% during the next year? (Ignore the expected dividend.)
   b. How far does the price of AT&T stock have to fall for you to get a margin call if the maintenance margin is 30%?

12. You've borrowed $20,000 on margin to buy shares in Disney, which is now selling at $80 per share. Your account starts at the initial margin requirement of 50%. The maintenance margin is 35%. Two days later, the stock price falls to $75 per share.

a. Will you receive a margin call?
b. How low can the price of Disney shares fall before you receive a margin call?

13. You are bearish on AT&T stock and decide to sell short 100 shares at the current market price of $50 per share.
    a. How much in cash or securities must you put into your brokerage account if the broker's initial margin requirement is 50% of the value of the short position?
    b. How high can the price of the stock go before you get a margin call if the maintenance margin is 30% of the value of the short position?
14. On January 1, you sold short one round lot (i.e., 100 shares) of Zenith stock at $14 per share. On March 1, a dividend of $2 per share was paid. On April 1, you covered the short sale by buying the stock at a price of $9 per share. You paid 50 cents per share in commissions for each transaction. What is the value of your account on April 1?
15. Call one full-service broker and one discount broker and find out the transaction costs of implementing the following strategies:
    a. Buying 100 shares of IBM now and selling them six months from now.
    b. Investing an equivalent amount of six-month at-the-money call options (calls with strike price equal to the stock price) on IBM stock now and selling them six months from now.

The following questions are from past CFA examinations:

16. If you place a stop-loss order to sell 100 shares of stock at $55 when the current price is $62, how much will you receive for each share if the price drops to $50?*
    a. $50.
    b. $55.
    c. $54⅞.
    d. Cannot tell from the information given.

17. You wish to sell short 100 shares of XYZ Corporation stock. If the last two transactions were at 34⅛ followed by 34¼, you only can sell short on the next transaction at a price of*
    a. 34⅛ or higher.
    b. 34¼ or higher.
    c. 34¼ or lower.
    d. 34⅛ or lower.

18. Specialists on the New York Stock Exchange do all of the following *except:*
    a. Act as dealers for their own accounts.*
    b. Execute limit orders.
    c. Help provide liquidity to the marketplace.
    d. Act as odd-lot dealers.

Chapter 4
Concepts and Issues

THIS CHAPTER INTRODUCES SOME KEY CONCEPTS AND ISSUES THAT ARE CENTRAL TO INFORMED INVESTMENT DECISION MAKING. The material presented is basic to the development of the theory in subsequent parts of the book. We start with the determination of real and nominal interest rates and risk premiums on risky securities. Then we review the historical record of rates of return on bills, bonds, and stocks. Next we elaborate on the concept of risk, emphasizing inflation risk and the need to view risk in a portfolio context. We conclude by introducing the law of one price, which states that securities or combinations of securities will be priced so that no investor can make riskless arbitrage profits by trading them.

4.1 Determinants of the Level of Interest Rates

Interest rates and forecasts of their future values are among the most important inputs into an investment decision. For example, suppose you have $10,000 in a savings account. The bank pays you a variable interest rate tied to some short-term reference rate such as the 30-day Treasury bill rate. You have the option of moving some or all of your money into a longer-term certificate of deposit that offers a fixed rate over the term of the deposit.

Your decision depends critically on your outlook for interest rates. If you think rates will fall, you will want to lock in the current higher rates by investing in a relatively long-term CD. If you expect rates to rise, you will want to postpone committing any funds to long-term CDs.

Forecasting interest rates is one of the most notoriously difficult parts of applied macroeconomics. Nonetheless, we do have a good understanding of the fundamental factors that determine the level of interest rates:

1. The supply of funds from savers, primarily households.
2. The demand for funds from businesses to be used to finance physical investments in plant, equipment, and inventories (real assets or capital formation).
3. The government's net supply and/or demand for funds as modified by actions of the Federal Reserve Bank.

Before we elaborate on these forces and resultant interest rates, we need to distinguish real from nominal interest rates.

Real and Nominal Rates of Interest

Suppose exactly one year ago you deposited \$1,000 in a one-year time deposit guaranteeing a rate of interest of 10%. You are about to collect \$1,100 in cash.

If your \$100 return for real? That depends on what money can buy these days, relative to what you *could* buy a year ago. The consumer price index (CPI) measures purchasing power by averaging the prices of goods and services in the consumption basket of an average urban family of four. Although this basket may not represent your particular consumption plan, suppose for now that it does.

Suppose the rate of inflation (percent change in the CPI, denoted by i) for the last year amounted to $i = 6\%$. This tells you that the purchasing power of money is reduced by 6% a year. The value of each dollar depreciates by 6% a year in terms of the goods it can buy. Therefore, part of your interest earnings are offset by the reduction in the purchasing power of the dollars you will receive at the end of the year. With a 10% interest rate, after you net out the 6% reduction in the purchasing power of money, you are left with a net increase in purchasing power of about 4%. Thus, we need to distinguish between a **nominal interest rate**—the growth rate of your money—and a **real interest rate**—the growth rate of your purchasing power. If we call R the nominal rate, r the real rate, and i the inflation rate, then we conclude

$$r \approx R - i$$

In words, the real rate of interest is the nominal rate reduced by the loss of purchasing power resulting from inflation.

In fact, the exact relationship between the real and nominal interest rate is given by:

$$1 + r = \frac{1 + R}{1 + i}$$

This is because the growth factor of your purchasing power, $1 + r$, equals the growth factor of your money, $1 + R$, divided by the new price level, that is, $1 + i$ times its value in the previous period. The exact relationship can be rearranged to

$$r = \frac{R - i}{1 + i}$$

which shows that the approximation rule overstates the real rate by the factor $1 + i$.

For example, if the interest rate on a one-year CD is 8%, and you expect inflation to be 5% over the coming year, then using the approximation formula, you expect the real

Figure 4.1
Determination of the equilibrium real rate of interest

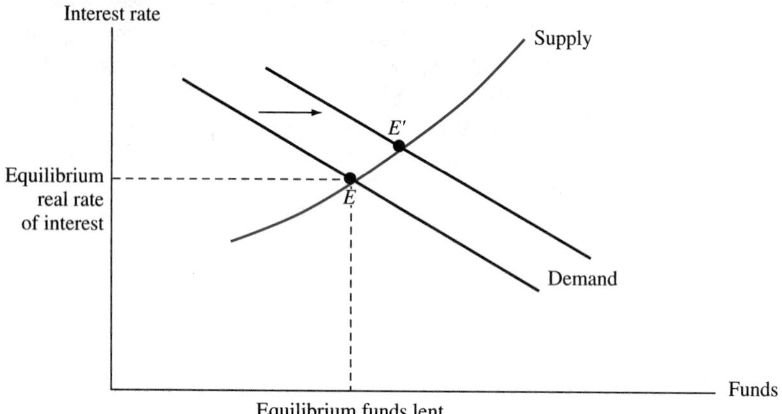

rate to be $r = 8\% - 5\% = 3\%$. Using the exact formula, the real rate is $r = \dfrac{.08 - .05}{1 + .05}$ $= .0286$, or 2.86%. Therefore, the approximation rule overstates the expected real rate by only 0.14% (14 basis points). The approximation rule is more exact for small inflation rates and is perfectly exact for continuously compounded rates. We discuss further details in the appendix to this chapter.

Before the decision to invest, you should realize that conventional certificates of deposit offer a guaranteed *nominal* rate of interest. Thus, you can only infer the expected real rate by subtracting your expectation of the rate of inflation.

It is always possible to calculate the real rate after the fact. The inflation rate is published by the Bureau of Labor Statistics (BLS). The future real rate, however, is unknown, and one has to rely on expectations. In other words, because future inflation is risky, the real rate of return is risky even if the nominal rate is risk free.

The Equilibrium Real Rate of Interest

Three basic factors—supply, demand, and government actions—determine the *real* interest rate. The nominal interest rate, which is the rate we actually observe, is the real rate plus the expected rate of inflation. So a fourth factor affecting the interest rate is the expected rate of inflation.

Although there are many different interest rates economywide (as many as there are types of securities), economists frequently talk as if there were a single representative rate. We can use this abstraction to gain some insights into determining the real rate of interest if we consider the supply and demand curves for funds.

Figure 4.1 shows a downward-sloping demand curve and an upward-sloping supply curve. On the horizontal axis, we measure the quantity of funds, and on the vertical axis, we measure the real rate of interest.

The supply curve slopes up from left to right because the higher the real interest rate, the greater the supply of household savings. The assumption is that at higher real interest rates households will choose to postpone some current consumption and set aside or invest more of their disposable income for future use.[1]

The demand curve slopes down from left to right because the lower the real interest rate, the more businesses will want to invest in physical capital. Assuming that businesses rank projects by the expected real return on invested capital, firms will undertake more projects the lower the real interest rate on the funds needed to finance those projects.

Equilibrium is at the point of intersection of the supply and demand curves, point E in Figure 4.1.

The government and the central bank (Federal Reserve) can shift these supply and demand curves either to the right or to the left through fiscal and monetary policies. For example, consider an increase in the government's budget deficit. This increases the government's borrowing demand and shifts the demand curve to the right, which causes the equilibrium real interest rate to rise to point E'. That is, a forecast that indicates higher than previously expected government borrowing increases expected future interest rates. The Fed can offset such a rise through an expansionary monetary policy, which will shift the supply curve to the right.

Thus, although the fundamental determinants of the real interest rate are the propensity of households to save and the expected productivity (or we could say profitability) of investment in physical capital, the real rate can be affected as well by government fiscal and monetary policies.

The Equilibrium Nominal Rate of Interest

We've seen that the real rate of return on an asset is approximately equal to the nominal rate minus the inflation rate. Because investors should be concerned with their real returns—the increase in their purchasing power—we would expect that as the inflation rate increases, investors will demand higher nominal rates of return on their investments. This higher rate is necessary to maintain the expected real return offered by an investment.

Irving Fisher (1930) argued that the nominal rate ought to increase one for one with increases in the expected inflation rate. If we use the notation $E(i)$ to denote the current expectation of the inflation rate that will prevail over the coming period, then we can state the so-called *Fisher equation* formally as:

$$R = r + E(i)$$

This relationship has been debated and empirically investigated. The equation implies that if real rates are reasonably stable, then increases in nominal rates ought to predict higher inflation rates. The results are mixed; although the data do not strongly support this relationship, nominal interest rates seem to predict inflation as well as alternative methods, in part because we are unable to forecast inflation well with any method.

[1] There is considerable disagreement among experts on the issue of whether household saving does go up in response to an increase in the real interest rate.

One reason it is difficult to determine the empirical validity of the Fisher hypothesis that changes in nominal rates predict changes in future inflation rates is that the real rate also changes unpredictably over time. Nominal interest rates can be viewed as the sum of the required real rate on nominally risk-free assets, plus a "noisy" forecast of inflation.

In Part IV, we discuss the relationship between short- and long-term interest rates. Longer rates incorporate forecasts for long-term inflation. For this reason alone, interest rates on bonds of different maturity may diverge. In addition, we will see that prices of longer-term bonds are more volatile than those of short-term bonds. This implies that expected returns on longer-term bonds may include a risk premium, so that the expected real rate offered by bonds of varying maturity also may vary.

CONCEPT CHECK

Question 1.

a. Suppose the real interest rate is 3% per year and the expected inflation rate is 8%. What is the nominal interest rate?

b. Suppose the expected inflation rate rises to 10%, but the real rate is unchanged. What happens to the nominal interest rate?

Bills and Inflation, 1953–1993

The Fisher equation predicts a close connection between inflation and the rate of return on T-bills. This is apparent in Figure 4.2, which plots both time series on the same set of axes. Both series tend to move together, which is consistent with our previous statement that expected inflation is a significant force determining the nominal rate of interest.

For a holding period of 30 days, the difference between actual and expected inflation is not large. The 30-day bill rate will adjust rapidly to changes in expected inflation induced by observed changes in actual inflation. It is not surprising that we see nominal rates on bills move roughly in tandem with inflation over time.

Taxes and the Real Rate of Interest

Tax liabilities are based on *nominal* income and the tax rate determined by the investor's tax bracket. Congress recognized the resultant "bracket creep" (when nominal income grows due to inflation and pushes taxpayers into higher brackets) and mandated index-linked tax brackets in the Tax Reform Act of 1986.

Index-linked tax brackets do not provide relief from the effect of inflation on the taxation of savings, however. Given a tax rate (t) and a nominal interest rate (R), the after-tax interest rate is $R(1 - t)$. The real, after-tax rate is approximately the after-tax nominal rate minus the inflation rate:

$$R(1 - t) - i = (r + i)(1 - t) - i = r(1 - t) - it$$

Thus, the after-tax real rate of return falls as the inflation rate rises. Investors suffer an inflation penalty equal to the tax rate times the inflation rate. If, for example, you are

Figure 4.2
Bills and inflation, 1953 to 1993

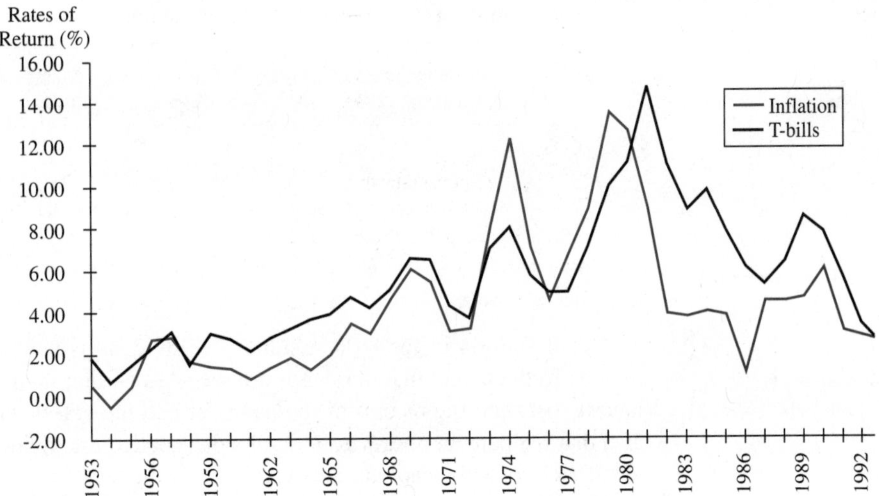

in a 30% tax bracket and your investments yield 12%, while inflation runs at the rate of 8%, then your before-tax real rate is 4%, and you *should*, in an inflation-protected tax system, net after taxes $4(1 - .3) = 2.8\%$. But the tax code does not recognize that the first 8% of your return is no more than compensation for inflation—not real income—and hence your tax includes an additional $8\% \times .3 = 2.4\%$, so that your after-tax real interest rate, at 0.4%, is almost wiped out.

4.2 Risk and Risk Premiums

Risk means uncertainty about future rates of return. We can quantify that uncertainty using probability distributions.

For example, suppose you are considering investing some of your money, now all invested in a bank account, in a stock market index fund. The price of a share in the fund is currently \$100, and your *time horizon* is one year. You expect the cash dividend during the year to be \$4, so your expected *dividend yield* (dividends earned per dollar invested) is 4%.

Your total holding-period return (HPR) will depend on the price you expect to prevail one year from now. Suppose your best guess is that it will be \$110 per share. Then your *capital gain* will be \$10 and your HPR 14%. The definition of the holding period return in this context is capital gain income plus dividend income per dollar invested in the stock at the start of the period:

$$\text{HPR} = \frac{\text{Ending price of a share} - \text{Beginning price} + \text{Cash dividend}}{\text{Beginning price}}$$

In our case we have:

$$\text{HPR} = \frac{\$110 - \$100 + \$4}{\$100} = .14, \text{ or } 14\%$$

Table 4.1 Probability Distribution of HPR on the Stock Market

State of the Economy	Probability	Ending Price	HPR
Boom	.25	$140	44%
Normal growth	.50	110	14
Recession	.25	80	−16

This definition of the HPR assumes the dividend is paid at the end of the holding period. To the extent that dividends are received earlier, the HPR ignores reinvestment income between the receipt of the payment and the end of the holding period. Recall also that the percent return from dividends is called the dividend yield, and so the dividend yield plus the capital gains yield equals the HPR.

There is considerable uncertainty about the price of a share a year from now, however, so you cannot be sure about your eventual HPR. We can try to quantify our beliefs about the state of the economy and the stock market, however, in terms of three possible scenarios with probabilities as presented in Table 4.1.

How can we evaluate this probability distribution? Throughout this book we will characterize probability distributions of rates of return in terms of their expected or mean return, $E(r)$, and their standard deviation, σ. The expected rate of return is a probability-weighted average of the rates of return in all scenarios. Calling $p(s)$ the probability of each scenario and $r(s)$ the HPR in each scenario, where scenarios are labeled or "indexed" by the variable s, we may write the expected return as:

$$E(r) = \sum_s p(s)r(s) \tag{4.1}$$

Applying this formula to the data in Table 4.1, we find that the expected rate of return on the index fund is:

$$E(r) = .25 \times 44\% + .5 \times 14\% + .25 \times (-16\%) = 14\%$$

The standard deviation of the rate of return (σ) is a measure of risk. It is defined as the square root of the variance, which in turn is defined as the expected value of the squared deviations from the expected return. The higher the volatility in outcomes, the higher will be the average value of these squared deviations. Therefore, variance and standard deviation measure the uncertainty of outcomes. Symbolically,

$$\sigma^2 = \sum_s p(s)\,[r(s) - E(r)]^2 \tag{4.2}$$

Therefore, in our example,

$$\sigma^2 = .25(44 - 14)^2 + .5(14 - 14)^2 + .25(-16 - 14)^2 = 450$$

and

$$\sigma = 21.21\%$$

Clearly, what would trouble potential investors in the index fund is the downside risk of a −16% rate of return, not the upside potential of a 44% rate of return. The standard deviation of the rate of return does not distinguish between these two; it treats both as deviations from the mean. As long as the probability distribution is more or less symmetric about the mean, σ is an adequate measure of risk. In the special case where we can assume that the probability distribution is normal—represented by the well-known bell-shaped curve—$E(r)$ and σ are perfectly adequate to characterize the distribution.

Getting back to the example, how much, if anything, should you invest in the index fund? First, you must ask how much of an expected reward is offered for the risk involved in investing money in stocks.

We measure the reward as the difference between the *expected* HPR on the index stock fund and the **risk-free rate,** that is, the rate you can earn by leaving money in risk-free assets such as T-bills, money market funds, or the bank. We call this difference the **risk premium** on common stocks. If the risk-free rate in the example is 6% per year, and the expected index fund return is 14%, then the risk premium on stocks is 8% per year. The difference between the *actual* rate of return on a risky asset and the risk-free rate is called **excess return.** Therefore, the risk premium is the expected excess return.

The degree to which investors are willing to commit funds to stocks depends on **risk aversion.** CFAs and financial analysts generally assume investors are risk averse in the sense that, if the risk premium were zero, people would not be willing to invest any money in stocks. In theory then, there must always be a positive risk premium on stocks in order to induce risk-averse investors to hold the existing supply of stocks instead of placing all their money in risk-free assets.

Although this sample scenario analysis illustrates the concepts behind the quantification of risk and return, you may still wonder how to get a more realistic estimate of $E(r)$ and σ for common stocks and other types of securities. Here history has insights to offer.

4.3 The Historical Record

Bills, Bonds, and Stocks, 1926–1993

The record of past rates of return is one possible source of information about risk premiums and standard deviations. We can estimate the historical risk premium by taking an average of the past excess returns, that is, differences between the HPRs on an asset class and the risk-free rate. Table 4.2 presents the annual HPRs on three asset classes for the period 1926–1993.

The fourth column shows the one-year HPR on a policy of "rolling over" 30-day Treasury bills as they mature. Because T-bill rates can change from month to month, the total rate of return on T-bills is riskless only for 30-day holding periods. The third column presents the annual HPR an investor would have earned by investing in U.S.

Table 4.2 Rates of Return, 1926–1993

Date	Stocks (%)	Long-Term Government Bonds (%)	Treasury Bills (%)	Inflation (%) (CPI)
1926	11.62%	7.77%	3.27%	−1.49%
1927	37.49	8.93	3.12	−2.08
1928	43.61	0.10	3.24	−0.97
1929	8.42	3.42	4.75	0.19
1930	−24.90	4.66	2.41	−6.03
1931	−43.34	−5.31	1.07	−9.52
1932	−8.19	16.84	0.96	−10.30
1933	53.99	−0.08	0.30	0.51
1934	−1.44	10.02	0.16	2.03
1935	47.67	4.98	0.17	2.99
1936	33.92	7.51	0.18	1.21
1937	−35.03	0.23	0.31	3.10
1938	31.12	5.53	−0.02	−2.78
1939	−0.41	5.94	0.02	−0.48
1940	−9.78	6.09	0.00	0.96
1941	−11.59	0.93	0.06	9.72
1942	20.34	3.22	0.27	9.29
1943	25.90	2.08	0.35	3.16
1944	19.75	2.81	0.33	2.11
1945	36.44	10.73	0.33	2.25
1946	−8.07	−0.10	0.35	18.17
1947	5.71	−2.63	0.50	9.01
1948	5.50	3.40	0.81	2.71
1949	18.79	6.45	1.10	−1.80
1950	31.71	0.06	1.20	5.79
1951	24.02	−3.94	1.49	5.87
1952	18.37	1.16	1.66	0.88
1953	−0.99	3.63	1.82	0.63
1954	52.62	7.19	0.86	−0.50
1955	31.56	−1.30	1.57	0.37
1956	6.56	−5.59	2.46	2.86
1957	−10.78	7.45	3.14	3.02
1958	43.36	−6.10	1.54	1.76
1959	11.96	−2.26	2.95	1.50
1960	−0.47	13.78	2.66	1.48
1961	26.89	0.97	2.13	0.67
1962	−8.73	6.89	2.73	1.22

Treasury bonds with 20-year maturities. The second column is the HPR on the Standard & Poor's Composite Index of common stocks, the value-weighted stock portfolio of 500 of the largest corporations in the United States. Finally, the last column gives the annual inflation rate as measured by the rate of change in the CPI.

At the bottom of each column are four descriptive statistics. The first is the arithmetic mean or average HPR. For bills, it is 3.73%; for bonds, 5.35%; and for common stock, 12.31%. These numbers imply an average excess return suggesting a risk pre-

Table 4.2 *(Continued)*

Date	Stocks (%)	Long-Term Government Bonds (%)	Treasury Bills (%)	Inflation (%) (CPI)
1963	22.80%	1.21%	3.12%	1.65%
1964	16.48	3.51	3.54	1.19
1965	12.45	0.71	3.93	1.92
1966	−10.06	3.65	4.76	3.35
1967	23.98	−9.19	4.21	3.04
1968	11.06	−0.26	5.21	4.72
1969	−8.50	−5.08	6.58	6.11
1970	4.01	12.10	6.53	5.49
1971	14.31	13.23	4.39	3.36
1972	18.98	5.68	3.84	3.41
1973	−14.66	−1.11	6.93	8.80
1974	−26.47	4.35	8.00	12.20
1975	37.20	9.19	5.80	7.01
1976	23.84	16.75	5.08	4.81
1977	−7.18	−0.67	5.12	6.77
1978	6.56	−1.16	7.18	9.03
1979	18.44	−1.22	10.38	13.31
1980	32.42	−3.95	11.24	12.40
1981	−4.91	1.85	14.71	8.94
1982	21.41	40.35	10.54	3.87
1983	22.51	0.68	8.80	3.80
1984	6.27	15.43	9.85	3.95
1985	32.16	30.97	7.72	3.77
1986	18.47	24.44	6.16	1.13
1987	5.23	−2.69	5.47	4.41
1988	16.81	9.67	6.35	4.42
1989	31.49	18.11	8.37	4.65
1990	−3.17	6.18	7.81	6.11
1991	30.55	19.30	5.60	3.06
1992	7.67	8.05	3.51	2.90
1993	9.99	18.24	2.90	2.75
Average	12.31	5.35	3.73	3.23
Standard deviation	20.46	8.67	3.32	4.64
Maximum	53.99	40.35	14.71	18.17
Minimum	−43.34	−9.19	−0.02	−10.30

Source: Data from the Center for Research of Security Prices, University of Chicago.

mium of 1.62% per year on bonds and 8.58% on stocks (the average excess return is the average HPR less the average risk-free rate of 3.73%).

The second statistic at the bottom of Table 4.2 is the standard deviation. The higher the standard deviation, the higher the variability of the HPR.

This standard deviation is based on historical data rather than forecasts of *future* scenarios as in equation 4.2. The formula for historical variance, however, is similar to equation 4.2:

Figure 4.3
Rates of return on stocks, bonds, and T-bills, 1926–1993

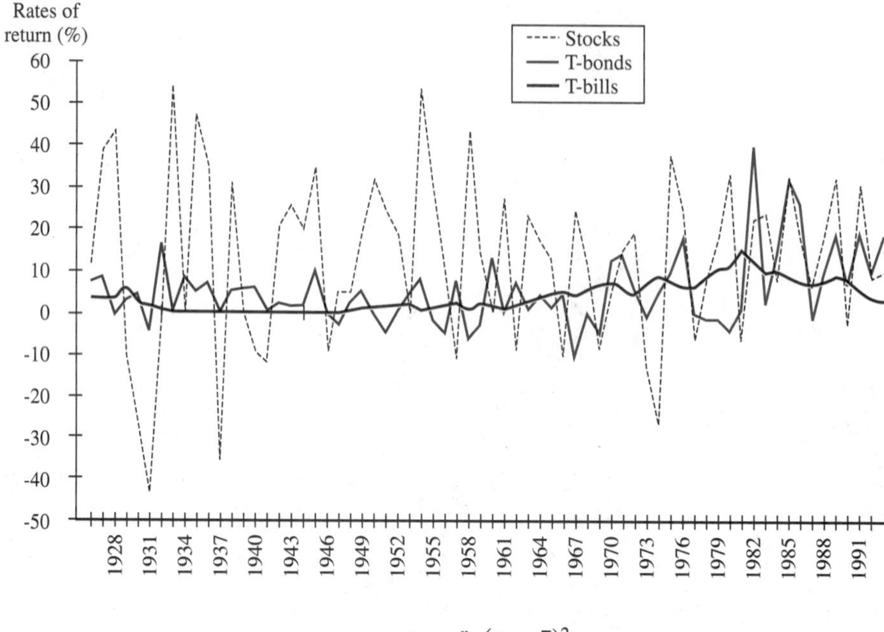

$$\sigma^2 = \frac{n}{n-1} \sum_{t=1}^{n} \frac{(r_t - \bar{r})^2}{n}$$

Here, each year's outcome (r_t) is taken as a possible scenario. [We multiply by $n/(n-1)$ to eliminate statistical bias in the estimate of variance.] Deviations are simply taken from the historical average, $\bar{r}$, instead of the expected value $E(r)$. Each historical outcome is taken as equally likely and given a "probability" of $1/n$.

Figure 4.3 gives a graphic representation of the relative variabilities of the annual HPR for the three different asset classes. We have plotted the three time series on the same set of axes, each in a different color. The graph shows very clearly that the annual HPR on stocks is the most variable series. The standard deviation of stock returns has been 20.46% compared to 8.67% for bonds and 3.32% for bills. Here is evidence of the risk-return trade-off that characterizes security markets: The markets with the highest average returns also are the most volatile.

The other summary measures at the end of Table 4.2 show the highest and lowest annual HPR (the range) for each asset over the 68-year period. The extent of this range is another measure of the relative riskiness of each asset class. It, too, confirms the ranking of stocks as the riskiest and bills as the least risky of the three asset classes.

An all-stock portfolio with a standard deviation of 20.46% would represent a very volatile investment. For example, if stock returns are normally distributed with a standard deviation of 20.46% and an expected rate of return of 12.31% (the historical average), in roughly one year out of three, returns will be less than −8.15% (12.31 − 20.46) or greater than 32.77% (12.31 + 20.46).

Figure 4.4 is a graph of the normal curve with mean 12.31% and standard deviation 20.46%. The graph shows the theoretical probability of rates of return within various ranges given these parameters.

Figure 4.4
The normal distribution

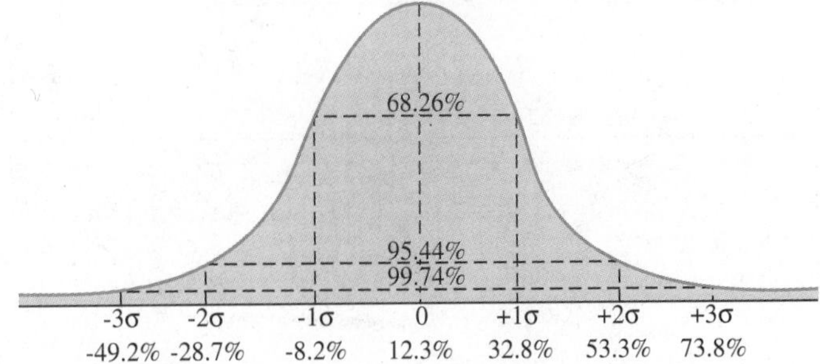

Figure 4.5
Frequency distributions of annual HPR

Source: Modified from *Stocks, Bonds, Bills and Inflation* [SBBI]: *1993 Yearbook* (Chicago: Ibbotson Associates).

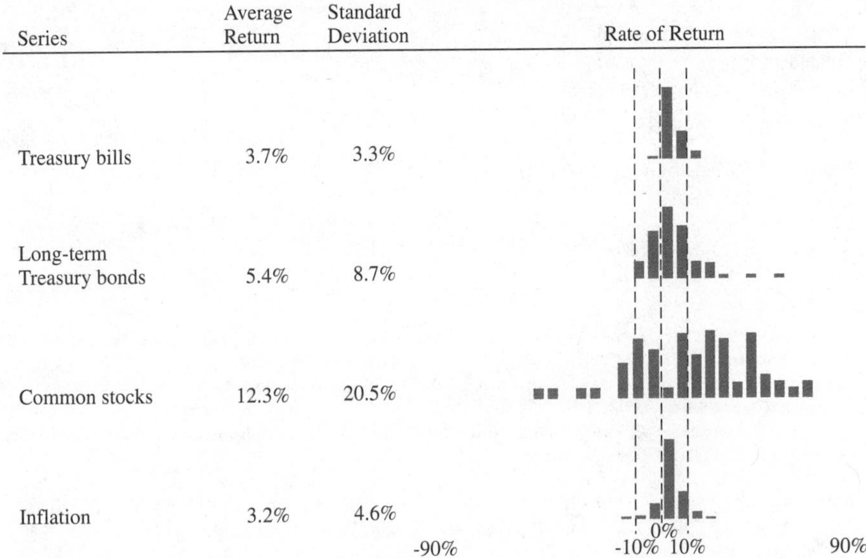

Series
Average Return
Standard Deviation
Rate of Return
Treasury bills 3.7% 3.3%
Long-term Treasury bonds 5.4% 8.7%
Common stocks 12.3% 20.5%
Inflation 3.2% 4.6%
-90%
-10% 0% 10%
90%

Figure 4.5 presents another view of the historical data, the actual frequency distribution of returns on various asset classes over the period 1926–1993. Again, the greater range of stock returns relative to bill or bond returns is obvious. Figure 4.5 also illustrates the risk-return trade-off in the security market. Common stocks, which are represented by the S&P 500 Index, have shown greater volatility of returns than bonds, but have offered higher average returns to investors. The nearby box presents a brief overview of the performance and risk characteristics of a wider range of assets.

We should stress that variability of HPR in the past can be an unreliable guide to risk, at least in the case of the risk-free asset. For an investor with a holding period of one year, for example, a one-year T-bill is a riskless investment, at least in terms of its nominal return, which is known with certainty. However, the standard deviation of the one-year T-bill rate estimated from historical data is not zero: This reflects variation in expected returns rather than fluctuations of actual returns around prior expectations.

INVESTING: WHAT TO BUY WHEN?

In making broad-scale investment decisions, investors may want to know how various types of investments have performed during booms, recessions, high inflation, and low inflation. The table shows how 10 asset categories performed during representative years since World War II. But history rarely repeats itself, so historical performance is only a rough guide to the figure.

	Average Annual Return on Investment*			
Investment	**Recession**	**Boom**	**High Inflation**	**Low Inflation**
Bonds (long-term government)	17%	4%	−1%	8%
Commodity index	1	−6	15	−5
Diamonds (1-carat investment grade)	−4	8	79	15
Gold† (bullion)	−8	−9	105	19
Private home	4	6	6	5
Real estate‡ (commercial)	9	13	18	6
Silver (bullion)	3	−6	94	4
Stocks (blue chip)	14	7	−3	21
Stocks (small growth-company)	17	14	7	12
Treasury bills (3-month)	6	5	7	3

*In most cases, figures are computed as follows: Recession—average of performance during calendar years 1946, 1975, and 1982; boom—average of 1951, 1965, and 1984; high inflation—average of 1947, 1974, and 1980; low inflation—average of 1955, 1961, and 1986.
†Gold figures are based only on data since 1971 and may be less reliable than others.
‡Commercial real estate figures are based only on data since 1978 and may be less reliable than others.
Source: Modified from *The Wall Street Journal,* November 13, 1987. Reprinted by permission of *The Wall Street Journal,* © 1987 Dow Jones & Company, Inc. All Rights Reserved Worldwide.
Sources: Commerce Dept.; Commodity Research Bureau; DeBeers Inc.; Diamond Registry; Dow Jones & Co.; Dun & Bradstreet; Handy & Harman; Ibbotson Associates; Charles Kroll (Diversified Investor's Forecast); Merrill Lynch; National Council of Real Estate Investment Fiduciaries; Frank B. Russell Co.; Shearson Lehman Bros.; T. Rowe Price New Horizons Fund.

Does the risk of the HPR on a financial asset reflect the risk of the cash flows from the real assets on which the financial assets are a claim? This is one of the most interesting and elusive questions in empirical finance. Ideally, the answer would be in the affirmative, reflecting prudent and competitive investment practices. So far, the evidence is inconclusive, as discussed in Chapter 12 on market efficiency.

The risk of cash flows of real assets reflects both *business risk* (profit fluctuations due to business conditions) and *financial risk* (increased profit fluctuations due to leverage). This reminds us that an all-stock portfolio represents claims on leveraged corporations. Most corporations carry some debt, the service of which is a fixed cost. Greater fixed cost makes profits riskier; thus, leverage increases equity risk.

CONCEPT CHECK Question 2. Compute the average excess return on stocks (over the T-bill rate) and its standard deviation for the years 1926–1934.

Table 4.3 Purchasing Power of $1,000 20 Years from Now and 20-Year Real Annualized HPR

Assumed Annual Rate of Inflation	Number of Dollars Required 20 Years from Now to Buy What $1 Buys Today	Purchasing Power of $1,000 to Be Received in 20 Years	Annualized Real HPR
4%	$2.19	$456.39	7.69%
6	3.21	311.80	5.66
8	4.66	214.55	3.70
10	6.73	148.64	1.82
12	9.65	103.67	

Purchasing price of bond is $103.7.
Nominal 20-year annualized HPR is 12% per year.
Purchasing power = $\$1{,}000/(1 + \text{inflation rate})^{20}$.
Real HPR, r, is computed from the following relationship:

$$r = (1 + R)/(1 + i) - 1$$
$$= 1.12/(1 + i) - 1$$

4.4 Real versus Nominal Risk

The distinction between the real and the nominal rate of return is crucial in making investment choices when investors are interested in the future purchasing power of their wealth. Thus, a U.S. Treasury bond that offers a "risk-free" *nominal* rate of return is not truly a risk-free investment—it does not guarantee the future purchasing power of its cash flow.

An example might be a bond that pays $1,000 on a date 20 years from now but nothing in the interim. Although some people see such a zero-coupon bond as a convenient way for individuals to lock in attractive, risk-free, long-term interest rates (particularly in IRA or Keogh[2] accounts), the evidence in Table 4.3 is rather discouraging about the value of $1,000 in 20 years in terms of today's purchasing power.

Suppose the price of the bond is $103.67, giving a nominal rate of return of 12% per year (since $103.67 \times 1.12^{20} = 1{,}000$). We can compute the real annualized HPR for each inflation rate.

A revealing comparison is at a 12% rate of inflation. At that rate, Table 4.3 shows that the purchasing power of the $1,000 to be received in 20 years would be $103.67, what was paid initially for the bond. The real HPR in these circumstances is zero. When the rate of inflation equals the nominal rate of interest, the price of goods increases just as fast as the money accumulated from the investment, and there is no growth in purchasing power.

At an inflation rate of only 4% per year, however, the purchasing power of $1,000 will be $456.39 in terms of today's prices; that is, the investment of $103.67 grows to a real value of $456.39, for a real 20-year annualized HPR of 7.69% per year.

---

[2] A tax shelter for self-employed individuals.

Again looking at Table 4.3, you can see that an investor expecting an inflation rate of 8% per year anticipates a real annualized HPR of 3.70%. If the actual rate of inflation turns out to be 10% per year, the resulting real HPR is only 1.82% per year. These differences show the important distinction between expected and actual inflation rates.

Even professional economic forecasters acknowledge that their inflation forecasts are hardly certain even for the next year, not to mention the next 20. When you look at an asset from the perspective of its future purchasing power, you can see that an asset that is riskless in nominal terms can be very risky in real terms.

CONCEPT CHECK Question 3. Suppose the rate of inflation turns out to be 13% per year. What will be the real annualized 20-year HPR on the nominally risk-free bond?

4.5 RISK IN A PORTFOLIO CONTEXT

The riskiness of a security cannot be judged in isolation from an investor's entire portfolio of assets. Sometimes, adding a seemingly risky asset to a portfolio actually reduces the risk of the portfolio as a whole. Investing in an asset in order to reduce the overall risk of a portfolio is called **hedging**.

The most direct example of hedging is an insurance contract, which is a legal arrangement transferring a specific risk from the insured to the insurer for a specified cost (the insurance premium). Suppose you own a \$100,000 house and have total net worth of \$300,000. There is a small possibility that your house will burn to the ground within the coming year. If it does, your net wealth will be reduced by \$100,000. If it does not, your wealth remains unchanged (independent of any income from this and other investments, which we shall ignore to simplify the example).

Say your probability assessment of the event "the house will burn to the ground during the coming year" is 0.002. Your expected loss ($0.002 \times \$100{,}000 = \$200$) is small in terms of your overall wealth. On the other hand, a fire would reduce your wealth by a full one-third.

An insurance contract to cover this risk might cost \$220, a price that exceeds the expected loss and thereby provides expected profit to the insurer. If we evaluate the payoff to the insurance contract in isolation, insurance looks like a risky security.

Not only is the expected profit of the policy negative (−\$20), and the expected rate of return negative ($-20/220 = -9.09\%$), but the risk also seems to be substantial. The standard deviation of the policy's payoff is identical to that of the uninsured house. You receive either \$100,000 (with probability 0.002) or nothing (with probability 0.998), a payoff structure that might remind you of a lottery.

Does this mean only risk lovers should purchase insurance? Clearly not. Instead, the example illustrates the fallacy of evaluating the risk of an asset (the insurance contract) separately from the other assets owned by the investor.

Consider the insured house as a *portfolio* that includes the insurance contract and the house.

Portfolio Component	Value if No Fire	Value if Fire
House	$100,000	0
Insurance contract	0	$100,000

The payoff of the entire portfolio, house plus policy, in the two outcomes is identical and equal to $100,000 because the house is insured for its precise value, and the insurance kicks in only when the value of the house goes to zero (in the event of a fire). Thus, the portfolio's overall risk has been reduced to zero.

The lesson of this example is that although people are concerned about the volatility of the value of their overall portfolios, they do *not* necessarily dislike volatility in individual components of their portfolios. This has important implications for the measurement of asset risk, the topic of Chapter 7. Most risk-averse people would invest in the "risky" insurance policy we describe, even with its negative expected HPR.

4.6 The Law of One Price and Arbitrage

One of the most fundamental concepts in investments is arbitrage, as you will see again and again throughout this book. **Arbitrage** is the act of buying an asset at once price and simultaneously selling it or its equivalent at a higher price.

If you can buy Kodak stock over the counter for $128.00 per share and sell it on the New York Stock Exchange for $128.50, you can make a risk-free arbitrage profit of 50 cents per share. Furthermore, by synchronizing the purchase and sale you might not have to tie up any of your own funds in the transaction. You can use the proceeds from the sale at $128.50 to finance the purchase at $128 and clear the 50 cents without investing any of your own money.

Pure arbitrage opportunities of this sort are understandably rare, because it takes the participation of only a few arbitrageurs (maybe only one) to eliminate the price differential. The increased demand for Kodak by arbitrageurs buying on the OTC market would tend to drive the price above $128, and the increased supply of Kodak on the NYSE would drive the price down, until the stock would reach a single price in both markets.

This is of course a simplified example of arbitrage and the activity of arbitrageurs. In practice, there are transaction costs to deal with, and often the arbitrage opportunity involves not one security but combinations of securities. We will see in later chapters that Kodak stock can be created synthetically, using Kodak options plus T-bills, and arbitrage considerations, therefore, dictate a pricing relationship that must hold among these securities.

Practitioners and academicians may often disagree about the right way to characterize equilibrium yield and price relationships, but almost everyone would agree that the *law of one price* holds almost all of the time in the securities markets. Stated simply, the law of one price is that equivalent securities or bundles of securities are priced so that risk-free arbitrage is not possible.

SUMMARY

1. The economy's equilibrium level of real interest rates depends on the willingness of households to save, as reflected in the supply curve of funds, and on the expected profitability of business investment in plant, equipment, and inventories, as reflected in the demand curve for funds. It depends also on government fiscal and monetary policy.

2. The nominal rate of interest is the equilibrium real rate plus the expected rates of inflation. In general, we can directly observe only nominal interest rates; from them, we must infer expected real rates, using inflation forecasts.

3. The equilibrium expected rate of return on any security is the sum of the equilibrium real rate of interest, the expected rate of inflation, and a security-specific risk premium.

4. Investors face a trade-off between risk and expected return. Historical data confirm our intuition that assets with low degrees of risk provide lower returns on average than do those of higher risk.

5. Assets with guaranteed nominal interest rates are risky in real terms because the future inflation rate is uncertain.

6. The riskiness of a security should always be viewed in the context of an investor's total portfolio of assets. Some securities, such as insurance contracts, that would seem quite risky in isolation actually help reduce the risk of an investor's overall portfolio.

7. The "law of one price" says two securities or groups of securities with the same payoff structure must sell for the same price. If two identical securities (or packages of securities) are selling in two markets at different prices, it should be profitable to buy the security in the low-priced market and sell it in the high-priced market simultaneously. In the process, arbitrageurs, who engage in this activity for a profit, drive up the price in the low-price market and drive down the price in the high-priced market, eliminating the price differential.

Key Terms

Nominal interest rate
Real interest rate
Risk-free rate
Risk premium
Excess return
Risk aversion
Hedging
Arbitrage

Selected Readings

The classic work of the determination of the level of interest rates is:

Fisher, Irving. *The Theory of Interest: As Determined by Impatience to Spend Income and Opportunity to Invest It.* New York: Augustus M. Kelley, Publishers, 1965, originally published in 1930.

The standard reference for historical returns on a variety of instruments, updated annually is:

Stocks, Bonds, Bills and Inflation: 1993 Yearbook. Chicago: Ibbotson Associates, Inc., 1994.

Problems

1. You have $5,000 to invest for the next year and are considering three alternatives:
   a. A money market fund with an average maturity of 30 days offering a current yield of 6% per year.
   b. A one-year savings deposit at a bank offering an interest rate of 7.5%.
   c. A 20-year U.S. Treasury bond offering a yield to maturity of 9% per year.
   What role does your forecast of future interest rates play in your decisions?
2. Use Figure 4.1 in the text to analyze the effect of the following on the level of real interest rates:
   a. Businesses become more optimistic about future demand for their products and decide to increase their capital spending.
   b. Households are induced to save more because of increased uncertainty about their future social security benefits.
   c. The Federal Reserve Board undertakes open market sales of U.S. Treasury securities in order to reduce the supply of money.
3. You are considering the choice between investing $50,000 in a conventional one-year bank CD offering an interest rate of 8% and a one-year "Inflation-Plus" CD offering 3% per year plus the rate of inflation.
   a. Which is the safer investment?
   b. Which offers the higher expected return?
   c. If you expect the rate of inflation to be 4% over the next year, which is the better investment? Why?
   d. If we observe a risk-free nominal interest rate of 8% per year and a risk-free real rate of 3%, can we infer that the market's expected rate of inflation is 5% per year?
4. Look at Table 4.1 in the text. Suppose you now revise your expectations regarding the stock market as follows:

State of the Economy	Probability	Ending Price	HPR
Boom	.3	$140	44%
Normal growth	.4	110	14
Recession	.3	80	−16

   Use equations 4.1 and 4.2 to compute the mean and standard deviation of the HPR on stocks. Compare your revised parameters with the ones in the text.
5. Derive the probability distribution of the one-year HPR on a 30-year U.S. Treasury bond with a 9% coupon if it is currently selling at par and the probability distribution of its yield to maturity a year from now is as follows:

State of the Economy	Probability	YTM
Boom	.25	12.0%
Normal growth	.50	9.0
Recession	.25	7.5

For simplicity, assume the entire 9% coupon is paid at the end of the year rather than every six months.

6. Using the historical risk premiums as your guide, what would be your estimate of the expected annual HPR on the S&P 500 stock portfolio if the current risk-free interest rate were 8%?
7. Compute the means and standard deviations of the annual HPR listed in Table 4.2 of the text using only the last 30 years, 1964–1993. How do these statistics compare with those computed from the data for the period 1926–1941? Which do you think are the most relevant statistics to use for projecting into the future?
8. During a period of severe inflation, a bond offered a nominal HPR of 80% per year. The inflation rate was 70% per year.
   a. What was the real HPR on the bond over the year?
   b. Compare this real HPR to the approximation $R = r + i$.
9. You own a house worth $250,000 and intend to insure it fully against fire for the next year. Suppose the probability of its burning to the ground during the year is 0.001 and that an insurance policy covering the full value costs $500. Consider the insurance policy as a security.
   a. What is its expected holding-period return?
   b. What is the standard deviation of its HPR?
   c. Is the policy a risky asset? Why?
10. Suppose that the inflation rate is expected to be 3% in the near future. Using the historical data provided in this chapter, what would be your predictions for:
   a. The T-bill rate?
   b. The expected rate of return on the stock market?
   c. The risk premium on the stock market?
11. The unification of Germany in 1990 led to forecasts of huge amounts of capital investment in what was formerly East Germany. Why would this development affect real interest rates?
12. Would anyone ever rationally invest in a stock if the expected total rate of return on the stock were less than the rate available on riskless T-bills? Relate your answer to the insurance example presented in the chapter.

13. Given $100,000 to invest, what is the expected risk premium in dollars of investing in equities versus risk-free T-bills (U.S. Treasury bills) based on the following table?*

Action	Probability	Expected Return
Invest in equities	.6	$50,000
	.4	−$30,000
Invest in risk-free T-bill	1.0	$ 5,000

   a. $13,000.
   b. $15,000.

*Reprinted, with permission, from the Level I 1992 *CFA Study Guide*. Copyright 1992, Association for Investment Management and Research, Charlottesville, VA. All rights reserved.

c. \$18,000.
d. \$20,000.

14. Based on the scenarios below, what is the expected return for a portfolio with the following return profile?*

	Market Condition		
	Bear	Normal	Bull
Probability	.2	.3	.5
Rate of return	−25%	10%	24%

a. 4%.
b. 10%.
c. 20%.
d. 25%.

Use the following expectations on Stocks X and Y to answer questions 15 through 17 (round to the nearest percent).

	Bear Market	Normal Market	Bull Market
Probability	0.2	0.5	0.3
Stock X	−20%	18%	50%
Stock Y	−15%	20%	10%

15. What is the expected return for Stocks X and Y?†

	Stock X	Stock Y
a.	18%	5%
b.	18%	12%
c.	20%	11%
d.	20%	10%

16. What is the standard deviation of returns on Stocks X and Y?†

	Stock X	Stock Y
a.	15%	26%
b.	20%	4%
c.	24%	13%
d.	28%	8%

17. Assume that of your \$10,000 portfolio, you invest \$9,000 in Stock X and \$1,000 in Stock Y. What is the expected return on your portfolio?†
a. 18%.
b. 19%.

c. 20%.
d. 23%.

Problems 18–19 represent a greater challenge. You may need to review the definitions of call and put options in Chapter 2.

18. You are faced with the probability distribution of the HPR on the stock market index fund given in Table 4.1 of the text. Suppose the price of a put option on a share of the index fund with exercise price of $110 and maturity of one year is $12.
    a. What is the probability distribution of the HPR on the put option?
    b. What is the probability distribution of the HPR on a portfolio consisting of one share of the index fund and a put option?
    c. In what sense does buying the put option constitute a purchase of insurance in this case?
19. Take as given the conditions described in the previous question, and suppose the risk-free interest rate is 6% per year. You are contemplating investing $107.55 in a one-year CD and simultaneously buying a call option on the stock market index fund with an exercise price of $110 and a maturity of one year. What is the probability distribution of your dollar return at the end of the year?

Appendix: Continuous Compounding

Suppose that your money earns interest at an annual nominal percentage rate (APR) of 6% per year compounded semiannually. What is your *effective* annual rate of return, accounting for compound interest?

We find the answer by first computing the per (compounding) period rate, 3% per half-year, and then computing the future value (FV) at the end of the year per dollar invested at the beginning of the year. In this example, we get

$$\text{FV} = (1.03)^2 = 1.0609$$

The effective annual rate (R_{EFF}) is just this number minus 1.0.

$$R_{\text{EFF}} = 1.0609 - 1 = .0609 = 6.09\% \text{ per year}$$

The general formula for the effective annual rate is:

$$R_{\text{EFF}} = \left(1 + \frac{\text{APR}}{n}\right)^n - 1$$

where APR is the annual percentage rate, and n the number of compounding periods per year. Table 4A.1 presents the effective annual rates corresponding to an annual percentage rate of 6% per year for different compounding frequencies.

As the compounding frequency increases, $(1 + \text{APR}/n)^n$ gets closer and closer to e^{APR} where e is the number 2.71828 (rounded off to the fifth decimal place). In our

Table 4A.1 Effective Annual Rates for APR of 6%

Compounding Frequency	n	R_{EFF} (%)
Annually	1	6.00000
Semiannually	2	6.09000
Quarterly	4	6.13636
Monthly	12	6.16778
Weekly	52	6.17998
Daily	365	6.18313

example, $e^{.06} = 1.0618365$. Therefore, if interest is continuously compounded, $R_{EFF} = .0618365$, or 6.18365% per year.

Using continuously compounded rates simplifies the algebraic relationship between real and nominal rates of return. To see how, let us compute the real rate of return first using annual compounding and then using continuous compounding. Assume the nominal interest rate is 6% per year compounded annually and the rate of inflation is 4% per year compounded annually. Using the relationship

$$\text{Real rate} = \frac{1 + \text{Nominal rate}}{1 + \text{Inflation rate}} - 1$$

$$r = \frac{(1 + R)}{(1 + i)} - 1 = \frac{R - i}{1 + i}$$

we find that the effective annual real rate is:

$$r = 1.06/1.04 - 1 = .01923 = 1.923\% \text{ per year}$$

With continuous compounding, the relationship becomes:

$$e^r = e^R / e^i = e^{R - i}$$

Taking the natural logarithm we get:

$$r = R - i$$

$$\text{Real rate} = \text{Nominal rate} - \text{Inflation rate}$$

all expressed as annual, continuously compounded percentage rates.

Thus, if we assume a nominal interest rate of 6% per year compounded continuously and an inflation rate of 4% per year compounded continuously, the real rate is 2% per year compounded continuously.

To pay a fair interest rate to a depositor, the compounding frequency must be at least equal to the frequency of deposits and withdrawals. Only when you compound at least as frequently as transactions in an account can you assure that each dollar will earn the full interest due for the exact duration it has been in the account. These days, on-line computing for deposits is common, so one expects the frequency of compounding to grow until the use of continuous or at least daily compounding becomes the norm.

Part II

Portfolio Theory

Chapter 5

Risk and Risk Aversion

THE INVESTMENT PROCESS CONSISTS OF TWO BROAD TASKS. One task is security and market analysis, by which we assess the risk and expected-return attributes of the entire set of possible investment vehicles. The second task is the formation of an optimal portfolio of assets. This task involves the determination of the best risk-return opportunities available from feasible investment portfolios and the choice of the best portfolio from the feasible set. We start our formal analysis of investments with this latter task, called *portfolio theory.* We return to the security analysis task in later chapters.

This chapter introduces three themes in portfolio theory, all centering on risk. The first is the basic tenet that investors avoid risk and demand a reward for engaging in risky investments. The reward is taken as a risk premium, an expected rate of return higher than that available on alternative risk-free investments.

The second theme allows us to summarize and quantify investors' personal trade-offs between portfolio risk and expected return. To do this we introduce the utility function, which assumes that investors can assign a welfare, or "utility," score to any investment portfolio depending on its risk and return.

Finally, the third fundamental principle is that we cannot evaluate the risk of an asset separate from the portfolio of which it is a part; that is, the proper way to measure the risk of an individual asset is to assess its impact on the volatility of the entire portfolio of investments. Taking this approach, we find that seemingly risky securities may be portfolio stabilizers and actually low-risk assets.

Appendix A to this chapter describes the theory and practice of measuring portfolio risk by the variance or standard deviation of returns. We discuss other potentially relevant characteristics of the probability distribution of portfolio returns, as well as the circumstances in which variance is sufficient to measure risk. Appendix B discusses the classical theory of risk aversion.

5.1 RISK AND RISK AVERSION

Risk with Simple Prospects

The presence of risk means that more than one outcome is possible. A *simple prospect* is an investment opportunity in which a certain initial wealth is placed at risk, and there are only two possible outcomes. For the sake of simplicity, it is useful to begin our analysis and elucidate some basic concepts using simple prospects.[1]

Take as an example initial wealth, W, of \$100,000, and assume two possible results. With a probability, $p = .6$, the favorable outcome will occur, leading to final wealth, $W_1 = \$150{,}000$. Otherwise, with probability $1 - p = .4$, a less favorable outcome, $W_2 = \$80{,}000$, will occur. We can represent the simple prospect using an event tree:

$$W = \$100{,}000 \quad \begin{cases} \xrightarrow{p\,=\,.6} & W_1 = \$150{,}000 \\ \xrightarrow[1-p\,=\,.4]{} & W_2 = \$80{,}000 \end{cases}$$

Suppose that an investor, Susan, is offered an investment portfolio with a payoff in one year that is described by such a simple prospect. How can she evaluate this portfolio?

First, she could try to summarize it using descriptive statistics. For instance, her mean or expected end-of-year wealth, denoted $E(W)$, is

$$\begin{aligned} E(W) &= pW_1 + (1-p)W_2 \\ &= .6 \times 150{,}000 + .4 \times 80{,}000 \\ &= \$122{,}000 \end{aligned}$$

The expected profit on the \$100,000 investment portfolio is \$22,000: 122,000 − 100,000. The variance, σ^2, of the portfolio's payoff is calculated as the expected value of the squared deviations of each possible outcome from the mean:

$$\begin{aligned} \sigma^2 &= p[W_1 - E(W)]^2 + (1-p)\,[W_2 - E(W)]^2 \\ &= .6\,(150{,}000 - 122{,}000)^2 + .4(80{,}000 - 122{,}000)^2 \\ &= 1{,}176{,}000{,}000 \end{aligned}$$

The standard deviation, σ, which is the square root of the variance, is therefore \$34,292.86.

Clearly, this is risky business: the standard deviation of the payoff is large, much larger than the expected profit of \$22,000. Whether the expected profit is large enough to justify such risk depends on the alternative portfolios.

Let us suppose Treasury bills are one alternative to Susan's risky portfolio. Suppose that at the time of the decision, a one-year T-bill offers a rate of return of 5%; \$100,000 can be invested to yield a sure profit of \$5,000. We can now draw Susan's decision tree.

---

[1] Chapters 5 through 7 rely on some basic results from elementary statistics. For a refresher, see the Quantitative Review in the Appendix at the end of the book.

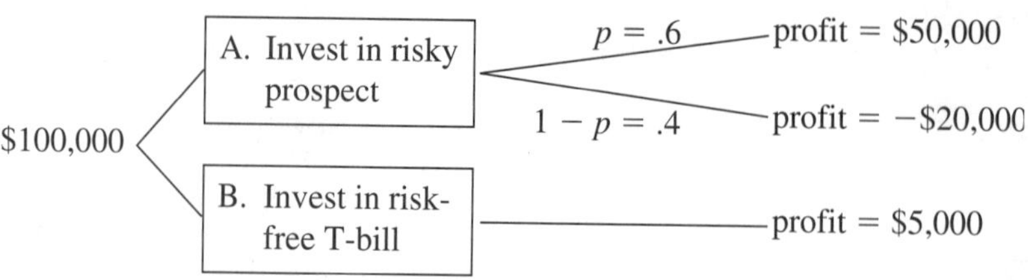

Earlier, we showed the expected profit on the prospect to be $22,000. Therefore the expected marginal, or incremental, profit of the risky portfolio over investing in safe T-bills is

$$\$22{,}000 - \$5{,}000 = \$17{,}000$$

meaning that one can earn a **risk premium** of $17,000 as compensation for the risk of the investment.

The question of whether a given risk premium provides adequate compensation for the investment's risk is age-old. Indeed, one of the central concerns of finance theory (and much of this text) is the measurement of risk and the determination of the risk premiums that investors can expect of risky assets in well-functioning capital markets.

CONCEPT CHECK Question 1. What is the risk premium of Susan's risky portfolio in terms of rate of return rather than dollars?

Risk, Speculation, and Gambling

One definition of *speculation* is "the assumption of considerable business risk in obtaining commensurate gain." Although this definition is fine linguistically, it is useless without first specifying what is meant by "commensurate gain" and "considerable risk."

By "commensurate gain" we mean a positive expected profit beyond the risk-free alternative. This is the risk premium. In our example, the dollar risk premium is the profit net of the alternative, which is the sure T-bill profit. The risk premium is the incremental expected gain from taking on the risk. By "considerable risk" we mean that the risk is sufficient to affect the decision. An individual might reject a prospect that has a positive risk premium because the added gain is insufficient to make up for the risk involved.

To gamble is "to bet or wager on an uncertain outcome." If you compare this definition to that of speculation, you will see that the central difference is the lack of "commensurate gain." Economically speaking, a gamble is the assumption of risk for no purpose but enjoyment of the risk itself, whereas speculation is undertaken in spite of the risk involved because one perceives a favorable risk-return trade-off. To turn a gamble into a speculative prospect requires an adequate risk premium for compensation of risk-averse investors for the risks that they bear. Hence, *risk aversion and speculation are not inconsistent.*

In some cases a gamble may appear to the participants as speculation. Suppose that two investors disagree sharply about the future exchange rate of the U.S. dollar against the British pound. They may choose to bet on the outcome. Suppose that Paul will pay Mary $100 if the value of £1 exceeds $1.70 one year from now, whereas Mary will pay Paul if the pound is worth less then $1.70. There are only two relevant outcomes: (1) the pound will exceed $1.70, or (2) it will fall below $1.70. If both Paul and Mary agree on the probabilities of the two possible outcomes, and if neither party anticipates a loss, it must be that they assign $p = .5$ to each outcome. In that case the expected profit to both is zero and each has entered one side of a gambling prospect.

What is more likely, however, is that the bet results from differences in the probabilities that Paul and Mary assign to the outcome. Mary assigns it $p > .5$, whereas Paul's assessment is $p < .5$. They perceive, subjectively, two different prospects. Economists call this case of differing beliefs "heterogeneous expectations." In such cases investors on each side of a financial position see themselves as speculating rather than gambling.

Both Paul and Mary should be asking, "Why is the other willing to invest in the side of a risky prospect that I believe offers a negative expected profit?" The ideal way to resolve heterogeneous beliefs is for Paul and Mary to "merge their information," that is, for each party to verify that he or she possesses all relevant information and processes the information properly. Of course, the acquisition of information and the extensive communication that is required to eliminate all heterogeneity in expectations is costly, and thus up to a point heterogeneous expectations cannot be taken as irrational. If, however, Paul and Mary enter such contracts frequently, they would recognize the information problem in one of two ways: Either they will realize that they are creating gambles when each wins half of the bets, or the consistent loser will admit that he or she has been betting on the basis of inferior forecasts.

CONCEPT CHECK

Question 2. Assume that dollar-denominated T-bills in the United States and pound-denominated bills in the United Kingdom offer equal yields to maturity. Both are short-term assets, and both are free of default risk. Neither offers investors a risk premium. However, a U.S. investor who holds U.K. bills is subject to exchange rate risk, because the pounds earned on the U.K. bills eventually will be exchanged for dollars at the future exchange rate. Is the U.S. investor engaging in speculation or gambling?

Risk Aversion and Utility Values

We have discussed risk with simple prospects and how risk premiums bear on speculation. A prospect that has a zero risk premium is called a *fair game.* Investors who are **risk averse** reject investment portfolios that are fair games or worse. Risk-averse investors are willing to consider only risk-free or speculative prospects. Loosely speaking, a risk-averse investor "penalizes" the expected rate of return of a risky portfolio by a certain percentage (or penalizes the expected profit by a dollar amount) to account for the risk involved. The greater the risk the investor perceives, the larger the penalty. One might wonder why we assume risk aversion as fundamental. We believe that most investors accept this view from simple introspection, but we discuss the question more fully in Appendix B of this chapter.

We can formalize this notion of a risk-penalty system. To do so, we will assume that each investor can assign a welfare, or **utility,** score to competing investment portfolios based on the expected return and risk of those portfolios. The utility score may be viewed as a means of ranking portfolios. Higher utility values are assigned to portfolios with more attractive risk-return profiles. Portfolios receive higher utility scores for higher expected returns and lower scores for higher volatility. Many particular "scoring" systems are legitimate. One reasonable function that is commonly employed by financial theorists assigns a portfolio with expected return $E(r)$ and variance of returns σ^2 the following utility score:

$$U = E(r) - .005\,A\sigma^2 \tag{5.1}$$

where U is the utility value and A is an index of the investor's aversion. (The factor of .005 is a scaling convention that allows us to express the expected return and standard deviation in equation 5.1 as percentages rather than decimals.)

Equation 5.1 is consistent with the notion that utility is enhanced by high expected returns and diminished by high risk. (Whether variance is an adequate measure of portfolio risk is discussed in Appendix A.) The extent to which variance lowers utility depends on A, the investor's degree of risk aversion. More risk-averse investors (who have the larger As) penalize risky investments more severely. Investors choosing among competing investment portfolios will select the one providing the highest utility level.

Notice in equation 5.1 that the utility provided by a risk-free portfolio is simply the rate of return on the portfolio, because there is no penalization for risk. This provides us with a convenient benchmark for evaluating portfolios. For example, recall Susan's investment problem, choosing between a portfolio with an expected return of 22% and a standard deviation $\sigma = 34\%$ and T-bills providing a risk-free return of 5%. Although the risk premium on the risky portfolio is large, 17%, the risk of the project is so great that Susan does not need to be very risk averse to choose the safe all-bills strategy. Even for $A = 3$, a moderate risk-aversion parameter, equation 5.1 shows the risky portfolio's utility value as $22 - .005 \times 3 \times 34^2 = 4.66\%$, which is slightly lower than the risk-free rate. In this case, Susan would reject the portfolio in favor of T-bills.

The downward adjustment of the expected return as a penalty for risk is $.005 \times 3 \times 34^2 = 17.34\%$. If Susan were less risk averse (more risk tolerant), for example with $A = 2$, she would adjust the expected rate of return downward by only 11.56%. In that case the utility level of the portfolio would be 10.44%, higher than the risk-free rate, leading her to accept the prospect.

CONCEPT CHECK Question 3. A portfolio has an expected rate of return of 20%, and standard deviation of 20%. Bills offer a sure rate of return of 7%. Which investment alternative will be chosen by an investor whose $A = 4$? What if $A = 8$?

Because we can compare utility values to the rate offered on risk-free investments when choosing between a risky portfolio and a safe one, we may interpret a portfolio's utility value as its "certainty equivalent" rate of return to an investor. That is, the

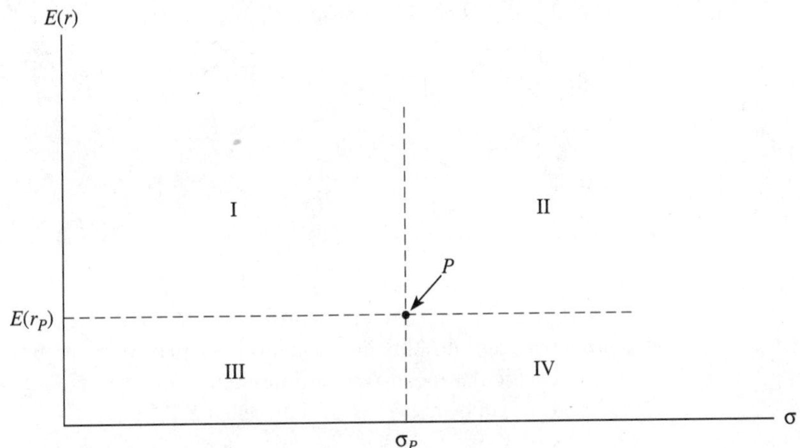

Figure 5.1
The Trade-off between risk and return of a potential investment portfolio

certainty equivalent rate of a portfolio is the rate that risk-free investments would need to offer with certainty to be considered as equally attractive as the risky portfolio.

Now we can say that a portfolio is desirable only if its certainty equivalent return exceeds that of the risk-free alternative. A sufficiently risk-averse investor may assign any risky portfolio, even one with a positive risk premium, a certainty equivalent rate of return that is below the risk-free rate, which will cause the investor to reject the portfolio. At the same time, a less risk-averse (more risk-tolerant) investor will assign the same portfolio a certainty equivalent rate that exceeds the risk-free rate and thus will prefer the portfolio to the risk-free alternative. If the risk premium is zero or negative to begin with, any downward adjustment to utility only makes the portfolio look worse. Its certainty equivalent rate will be below that of the risk-free alternative for all risk-averse investors.

In contrast to risk-averse investors, **risk-neutral** investors judge risky prospects solely by their expected rates of return. The level of risk is irrelevant to the risk-neutral investor, meaning that there is no penalization for risk. For this investor a portfolio's certainty equivalent rate is simply its expected rate of return.

A **risk lover** is willing to engage in fair games and gambles; this investor adjusts the expected return upward to take into account the "fun" of confronting the prospect's risk. Risk lovers will always take a fair game because their upward adjustment of utility for risk gives the fair game a certainty equivalent that exceeds the alternative of the risk-free investment.

We can depict the individual's trade-off between risk and return by plotting the characteristics of potential investment portfolios that the individual would view as equally attractive on a graph with axes measuring the expected value and standard deviation of portfolio returns. Figure 5.1 plots the characteristics of one portfolio.

Portfolio P, which has expected return $E(r_P)$ and standard deviation σ_P, is preferred by risk-averse investors to any portfolio in quadrant IV because it has an expected return equal to or greater than any portfolio in that quadrant and a standard deviation equal to or smaller than any portfolio in that quadrant. Conversely, any portfolio in

Table 5.1 Utility Values of Possible Portfolios

Expected Return, $E(r)$	Standard Deviation, σ	Utility = $E(r) - .005A\sigma^2$
10%	20.0%	$10 - .005 \times 4 \times 400 = 2$
15	25.5	$15 - .005 \times 4 \times 650 = 2$
20	30.0	$20 - .005 \times 4 \times 900 = 2$
25	33.9	$25 - .005 \times 4 \times 1{,}150 = 2$

quadrant I is preferable to portfolio *P* because its expected return is equal to or greater than *P*'s and its standard deviation is equal to or smaller than *P*'s.

This is the mean-standard deviation, or equivalently, **mean-variance (M-V) criterion.** It can be stated as: *A* dominates *B* if

$$E(r_A) \geq E(r_B)$$

and

$$\sigma_A \leq \sigma_B$$

and at least one inequality is strict (rules out the equality).

In the expected return–standard deviation graph the preferred direction is northwest, because in this direction we simultaneously increase the expected return *and* decrease the variance of the rate of return. This means that any portfolio that lies northwest of *P* is superior to *P*.

What can be said about portfolios in the quadrants II and III? Their desirability, compared with *P*, depends on the exact nature of the investor's risk aversion. Suppose an investor identifies all portfolios that are equally attractive as portfolio *P*. Starting at *P*, an increase in standard deviation lowers utility; it must be compensated for by an increase in expected return. Thus, point *Q* is equally desirable to this investor as *P*. Investors will be equally attracted to portfolios with high risk and high expected returns compared with other portfolios with lower risk but lower expected returns.

These equally preferred portfolios will lie on a curve in the mean–standard deviation graph that connects all portfolio points with the same utility value (Figure 5.2). This is called the **indifference curve.**

To determine some of the points that appear on the indifference curve, examine the utility values of several possible portfolios for an investor with $A = 4$, presented in Table 5.1. Note that each portfolio offers identical utility, because the high-return portfolios also have high risk. Although in practice the exact indifference curves of various investors cannot be known, this analysis can take us a long way in determining appropriate principles for portfolio selection strategy.

CONCEPT CHECK

Question 4.

a. How will the indifference curve of a less risk-averse investor compare to the indifference curve drawn in Figure 5.2?

b. Draw both indifference curves passing through point *P*.

Figure 5.2
The indifference curve

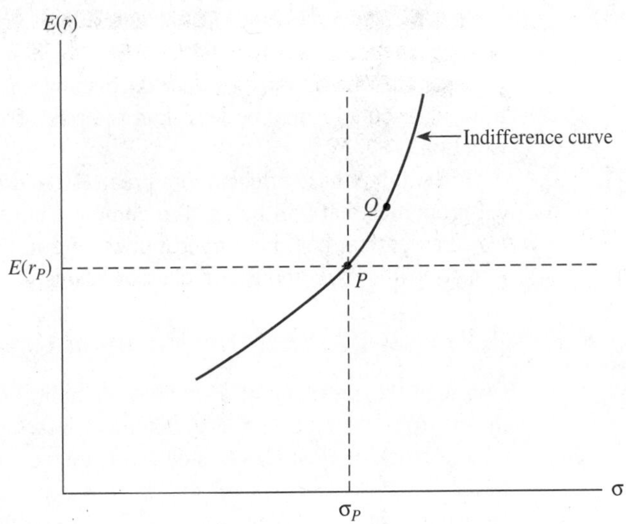

5.2 Portfolio Risk

Asset Risk versus Portfolio Risk

We have focused so far on the return and risk of an individual's overall investment portfolio. Such portfolios are composed of diverse types of assets. In addition to their direct investment in financial markets, investors have stakes in pension funds, life insurance policies with savings components, homes, and not least, the earning power of their skills (human capital).

We saw in Chapter 4 that, sometimes, adding a seemingly risky asset to a portfolio actually reduces the risk of the overall portfolio. The example we cited was that of a fire insurance policy. Although the policy viewed in isolation had a very uncertain and volatile payoff, it clearly was a portfolio risk-reducer because it provided a positive payoff precisely when another major part of the portfolio, the investor's house, fared poorly. Investing in an asset with a payoff pattern that offsets your exposure to a particular source of risk is called **hedging.**

Insurance contracts are obvious hedging vehicles. In many contexts financial markets offer similar, although perhaps less direct, hedging opportunities. For example, consider two firms, one producing suntan lotion, the other producing umbrellas. The shareholders of each firm face weather risk of an opposite nature. A rainy summer lowers the return on the suntan-lotion firm but raises it *on* the umbrella firm. Shares of the umbrella firm act as "weather insurance" for the suntan-lotion firm shareholders in precisely the same way that fire insurance policies insure houses. When the lotion firm does poorly (bad weather), the "insurance" asset (umbrella shares) provides a high payoff that offsets the loss.

Another means to control portfolio risk is **diversification,** by which we mean that investments are made in a wide variety of assets so that the exposure to the risk of any particular security is limited. By placing one's eggs in many baskets, overall portfolio risk actually may be less than the risk of any component security considered in isolation.

To examine these effects more precisely, and to lay a foundation for the mathematical properties that will be used in coming chapters, we will consider an example with less than perfect hedging opportunities, and in the process review the statistics underlying portfolio risk and return characteristics.

A Review of Portfolio Mathematics

Consider the problem of Humanex, a nonprofit organization deriving more of its income from the return on its endowment. Years ago, the founders of Best Candy willed a large block of Best Candy stock to Humanex with the provision that Humanex may never sell it. This block of shares now comprises 50% of Humanex's endowment. Humanex has free choice as to where to invest the remainder of its portfolio.[2]

The value of Best Candy stock is sensitive to the price of sugar. In years when the Caribbean sugar crop fails, the price of sugar rises significantly and Best Candy suffers considerable losses. We can describe the fortunes of Best Candy stock using the following scenario analysis:

	Normal Year for Sugar		Abnormal Year
	Bullish Stock Market	Bearish Stock Market	Sugar Crisis
Probability	.5	.3	.2
Rate of return	25%	10%	−25%

To summarize these three possible outcomes using conventional statistics, we review some of the key rules governing the properties of risky assets and portfolios.

Rule 1. The mean or **expected return** of an asset is a probability-weighted average of its return in all scenarios. Calling $Pr(s)$ the probability of scenario s and $r(s)$ the return in scenario s, we may write the expected return, $E(r)$, as

$$E(r) = \sum_s Pr(s)r(s) \tag{5.2}$$

Applying this formula to the case at hand, with three possible scenarios, we find that the expected rate of return of Best Candy's stock is

$$\begin{aligned} E(r_{\text{Best}}) &= .5 \times 25 + .3 \times 10 + .2(-25) \\ &= 10.5\% \end{aligned}$$

[2] The portfolio is admittedly unusual. We use this example only to illustrate the various strategies that might be used to control risk and to review some useful results from statistics.

Rule 2. The **variance** of an asset's returns is the expected value of the squared deviations from the expected return. Symbolically,

$$\sigma^2 = \sum_s Pr(s)[r(s) - E(r)]^2 \tag{5.3}$$

Therefore, in our example

$$\begin{aligned}\sigma^2_{\text{Best}} &= .5(25 - 10.5)^2 + .3(10 - 10.5)^2 + .2(-25 - 10.5)^2 \\ &= 357.25\end{aligned}$$

The **standard deviation** of Best's return, which is the square root of the variance, is $\sqrt{357.25} = 18.9\%$.

Humanex has 50% of its endowment in Best's stock. To reduce the risk of the overall portfolio, it could invest the remainder in T-bills, which yield a sure rate of return of 5%. To derive the return of the overall portfolio, we apply rule 3:

Rule 3. The rate of return on a portfolio is a weighted average of the rates of return of each asset comprising the portfolio, with portfolio proportions as weights. This implies that the *expected* rate of return on a portfolio is a weighted average of the *expected* rate of return on each component asset.

In this case, the portfolio proportions in each asset are .5, and the portfolio's expected rate of return is

$$\begin{aligned}E(r_{\text{Humanex}}) &= .5E(r_{\text{Best}}) + .5r_{\text{Bills}} \\ &= .5 \times 10.5 + .5 \times 5 \\ &= 7.75\%\end{aligned}$$

The standard deviation of the portfolio may be derived from the following:

Rule 4. When a risky asset is combined with a risk-free asset, the portfolio standard deviation equals the risky asset's standard deviation multiplied by the portfolio proportion invested in the asset.

In this case, the Humanex portfolio is 50% invested in Best stock and 50% invested in risk-free bills. Therefore

$$\begin{aligned}\sigma_{\text{Humanex}} &= .5\sigma_{\text{Best}} \\ &= .5 \times 18.9 \\ &= 9.45\%\end{aligned}$$

By reducing its exposure to the risk of Best by half, Humanex reduces its portfolio standard deviation by half. The cost of this risk reduction, however, is a reduction in expected return. The expected rate of return on Best stock is 10.5%. The expected return on the one-half T-bill portfolio is 7.75%. This makes the risk premiums over the 5% rate on risk-free bills 5.5% for Best stock and 2.75% for the half T-bill portfolio. By reducing the share of Best stock in the portfolio by one-half, Humanex reduces its portfolio risk premium by one-half, from 5.5% to 2.75%.

In an effort to improve the contribution of the endowment to the operating budget, Humanex's trustees hire Sally, a recent MBA, as a consultant. Investigating the sugar and candy industry, Sally discovers, not surprisingly, that during years of sugar crisis in the Caribbean basin, SugarKane, a big Hawaiian sugar company, reaps unusual profits and its stock price soars. A scenario analysis of SugarKane's stock looks like this:

	Normal Year for Sugar		Abnormal Year
	Bullish Stock Market	Bearish Stock Market	Sugar Crisis
Probability	.5	.3	.2
Rate of return	1%	–5%	35%

The expected rate of return on SugarKane's stock is 6%, and its standard deviation is 14.73%. Thus, SugarKane is almost as volatile as Best, yet its expected return is only a notch better than the T-bill rate. This cursory analysis makes SugarKane appear to be an unattractive investment. For Humanex, however, the stock holds great promise.

SugarKane offers excellent hedging potential for holders of Best stock because its return is highest precisely when Best's return is lowest—during a Caribbean sugar crisis. Consider Humanex's portfolio when it splits its investment evenly between Best and SugarKane. The rate of return for each scenario is the simple average of the rates on Best and SugarKane because the portfolio is split evenly between the two stocks (see rule 3).

	Normal Year for Sugar		Abnormal Year
	Bullish Stock Market	Bearish Stock Market	Sugar Crisis
Probability	.5	.3	.2
Rate of return	13.0%	2.5%	5.0%

The expected rate of return on Humanex's hedged portfolio is 8.25% with a standard deviation of 4.83%.

Sally now summarizes the reward and risk of the three alternatives:

Portfolio	Expected Return	Standard Deviation
All in Best Candy	10.50%	18.90%
Half in T-bills	7.575	9.45
Half in SugarKane	8.25	4.83

The numbers speak for themselves. The hedge portfolio including SugarKane clearly dominates the simple risk-reduction strategy of investing in safe T-bills. It has higher expected return *and* lower standard deviation than the one-half T-bill portfolio. The point is that, despite SugarKane's large standard deviation of return, it is a risk reducer for some investors—in this case, those holding Best stock.

The risk of the individual assets in the portfolio must be measured in the context of the effect of their return on overall portfolio variability. This example demonstrates that assets with returns that are inversely associated with the initial risky position are the most powerful risk reducers.

CONCEPT CHECK

Question 5. Suppose that the stock market offers an expected rate of return of 20%, with a standard deviation of 15%. Gold has an expected rate of return of 18%, with a standard deviation of 17%. In view of the market's higher expected return and lower uncertainty, will anyone choose to hold gold in a portfolio?

To quantify the hedging or diversification potential of an asset, we use the concepts of covariance and correlation. The **covariance** measures how much the returns on two risky assets move in tandem. A positive covariance means that asset returns move together. A negative covariance means that they vary inversely, as in the case of Best and SugarKane.

To measure covariance, we look at return "surprises" or deviations from expected value in each scenario. Consider the product of each stock's deviation from expected return in a particular scenario:

$$[r_{\text{Best}} - E(r_{\text{Best}})]\,[r_{\text{Kane}} - E(r_{\text{Kane}})]$$

This product will be positive if the returns of the two stocks move together across scenarios, that is, if both returns exceed their expectations or both fall short of those expectations in the scenario in question. On the other hand, if one stock's return exceeds its expected value when the other's falls short, the product will be negative. Thus, a good measure of how much the returns move together is the *expected value* of this product across all scenarios, which is defined as the covariance.

$$\text{Cov}(r_{\text{Best}}, r_{\text{Kane}}) = \sum_s Pr(s)\,[r_{\text{Best}}(s) - E(r_{\text{Best}})][r_{\text{Kane}}(s) - E(r_{\text{Kane}})] \tag{5.4}$$

In this example, with $E(r_{\text{Best}}) = 10.5\%$ and $E(r_{\text{Kane}}) = 6\%$, and with returns in each scenario summarized as follows, we compute the covariance by applying equation 5.4.

	Normal Year for Sugar		Abnormal Year
	Bullish Stock Market	Bearish Stock Market	Sugar Crisis
Probability	.5	.3	.2
Stock			
Best Candy	25%	10%	–25%
SugarKane	1%	–5%	35%

The covariance between the two stocks is

$$\begin{aligned}\text{Cov}(r_{\text{Best}}, r_{\text{Kane}}) &= .5(25 - 10.5)(1 - 6) \\ &\quad + .3(10 - 10.5)(-5 - 6) + .2(-25 - 10.5)(35 - 6) \\ &= -240.5\end{aligned}$$

The negative covariance confirms the hedging quality of SugarKane stock relative to Best Candy. SugarKane's returns move inversely with Best's.

An easier statistic to interpret than the covariance is the **correlation coefficient,** which scales the covariance to a value between −1 (perfect negative correlation) and

+1 (perfect positive correlation). The correlation coefficient between two variables equals their covariance divided by the product of the standard deviations. Denoting the correlation by the Greek letter ρ, we find that

$$\begin{aligned}\rho(\text{Best, SugarKane}) &= \frac{\text{Cov}[r_{\text{Best}}, r_{\text{SugarKane}}]}{\sigma_{\text{Best}}\sigma_{\text{SugarKane}}}\\ &= \frac{-240.5}{18.9 \times 14.73}\\ &= -.86\end{aligned}$$

This large negative correlation (close to −1) confirms the strong tendency of Best and SugarKane stocks to move inversely, or "out of phase" with one another.

The impact of the covariance of asset returns on portfolio risk is apparent in the following formula for portfolio variance.

Rule 5. When two risky assets with variances σ_1^2 and σ_2^2, respectively, are combined into a portfolio with portfolio weights w_1 and w_2, respectively, the portfolio variance σ_P^2 is given by

$$\sigma_P^2 = w_1^2\sigma_1^2 + w_2^2\sigma_2^2 + 2w_1w_2\text{Cov}(r_1,r_2).$$

In this example, with equal weights in Best and SugarKane, $w_1 = w_2 = .5$, and with $\sigma_{\text{Best}} = 18.9\%$, $\sigma_{\text{Kane}} = 14.73\%$, and $\text{Cov}(r_{\text{Best}}, r_{\text{Kane}}) = -240.5$, we find that

$$\sigma_P^2 = .5^2 \times 18.9^2 + .5^2 \times 14.73^2 + 2 \times .5 \times .5 \times (-240.5) = 23.3$$

or that $\sigma_P = \sqrt{23.3} = 4.83\%$, precisely the same answer for the standard deviation of the returns on the hedged portfolio that we derived earlier from the scenario analysis.

Rule 5 for portfolio variance highlights the effect of covariance on portfolio risk. A positive covariance increases portfolio variance, and a negative covariance acts to reduce portfolio variance. This makes sense because returns on negatively correlated assets tend to be offsetting, which stabilizes portfolio returns.

Basically, hedging involves the purchase of a risky asset that is negatively correlated with the existing portfolio. This negative correlation makes the volatility of the hedge asset a risk-reducing feature. A hedge strategy is a powerful alternative to the simple risk-reduction strategy of including a risk-free asset in the portfolio.

In later chapters we will see that, in a rational equilibrium, hedge assets must offer relatively low expected rates of return. The perfect hedge, an insurance contract, is by design perfectly negatively correlated with a specified risk. As one would expect in a "no free lunch" world, the insurance premium reduces the portfolio's expected rate of return.

CONCEPT CHECK Question 6. Suppose that the distribution of SugarKane stock is as follows:

Bullish Stock Market	Bearish Stock Market	Sugar Crisis
7%	−5%	20%

a. What would be its correlation with Best?
b. Is SugarKane stock a useful hedge asset now?
c. Calculate the portfolio rate of return in each scenario and the standard deviation of the portfolio from the scenario returns. Then evaluate σ_P using rule 5.
d. Are the two methods of computing portfolio standard deviations consistent?

SUMMARY

1. Speculation is the undertaking of a risky investment for its risk premium. The risk premium has to be large enough to compensate a risk-averse investor for the risk of the investment.

2. A fair game is a risky prospect that has a zero-risk premium. It will not be undertaken by a risk-averse investor.

3. Investors' preferences toward the expected return and volatility of a portfolio may be expressed by a utility function that is higher for higher expected returns and lower for higher portfolio variances. More risk-averse investors will apply greater penalties for risk. We can describe these preferences graphically using indifference curves.

4. The desirability of a risky portfolio to a risk-averse investor may be summarized by the certainty equivalent value of the portfolio. The certainty equivalent rate of return is a value that, if it is received with certainty, would yield the same utility as the risky portfolio.

5. Hedging is the purchase of a risky asset to reduce the risk of a portfolio. The negative correlation between the hedge asset and the initial portfolio turns the volatility of the hedge asset into a risk-*reducing* feature. When a hedge asset is perfectly negatively correlated with the initial portfolio, it serves as a perfect hedge and works like an insurance contract on the portfolio.

Key Terms

Risk premium
Risk averse
Utility
Certainty equivalent rate
Risk neutral
Risk lover
Mean-variance (M-V) criterion
Indifference curve
Hedging
Diversification
Expected return
Variance
Standard deviation
Covariance
Correlation coefficient

Selected Readings

A classic work on risk and risk aversion is:

Arrow, Kenneth, *Essays in the Theory of Risk Bearing.* Amsterdam: North Holland, 1971.

Some good statistics texts with business applications are:

Levy, Haim; and Moshe Ben-Horim. *Statistics: Decisions and Applications in Business and Economics.* New York: Random House, 1984.

Wonnacott, Thomas H., and Ronald J. Wonnacott. *Introductory Statistics for Business and Economics.* New York: Wiley, 1984.

Problems

1. Consider a risky portfolio. The end-of-year cash flow derived from the portfolio will be either \$50,000 or \$150,000 with equal probabilities of .5. The alternative risk-free investment in T-bills pays 5% per year.
   a. If you require a risk premium of 10%, how much will you be willing to pay for the portfolio?
   b. Suppose that the portfolio can be purchased for the amount you found in (*a*). What will be the expected rate of return on the portfolio?
   c. Now suppose that you require a risk premium of 15%. What is the price that you will be willing to pay?
   d. Comparing your answers to (*a*) and (*c*), what do you conclude about the relationship between the required risk premium on a portfolio and the price at which the portfolio will sell?
2. Consider a portfolio that offers an expected rate of return of 10% and a standard deviation of 15%. T-bills offer a risk-free 8% rate of return. What is the maximum level of risk aversion for which the risky portfolio is still preferred to bills?
3. Draw the indifference curve in the expected return–standard deviation plan corresponding to a utility level of 5% for an investor with a risk aversion coefficient of 3. (Hint: choose several possible standard deviations, ranging from 5% to 25% and find the expected rates of return providing a utility level of 5. Then plot the expected return–standard deviation points so derived.)
4. Now draw the indifference curve corresponding to a utility level of 4% for an investor with risk aversion coefficient $A = 4$. Comparing your answers to questions 3 and 4, what do you conclude?
5. Draw an indifference curve for a risk-neutral investor providing utility level 5%.
6. What must be true about the sign of the risk aversion coefficient, *A,* for a risk lover? Draw the indifference curve for a utility level of 5% for a risk lover.

Use the following data in answering questions 7, 8, and 9.

Utility Formula Data

Investment	Expected Return $E(r)$	Standard Deviation σ
1	12%	30%
2	15	50
3	21	16
4	24	21

$$U = E(r) - .005\,A\sigma^2 \text{ where } A = 4.$$

7. Based on the utility formula above, which investment would you select if you were risk averse?*

a. 1.
b. 2.
c. 3.
d. 4.

8. Based on the utility formula above, which investment would you select if you were risk neutral?*
a. 1.
b. 2.
c. 3.
d. 4.

9. The variable *(A)* in the utility formula represents the:*
a. investor's return requirement
b. investor's aversion to risk
c. certainty-equivalent rate of the portfolio
d. preference for one unit of return per four units of risk

Consider historical data showing that the average annual rate of return on the S&P 500 portfolio over the past 68 years has averaged about 8.5% more than the Treasury bill return and that the S&P 500 standard deviation has been about 21% per year. Assume these values are representative of investors' expectations for future performance and that the current T-bill rate is 6%. Use these values to answer questions 10 to 12.

10. Calculate the expected return and variance of portfolios invested in T-bills and the S&P 500 index with weights as follows:

W_{bills}	W_{index}
0	1.0
0.2	0.8
0.4	0.6
0.6	0.4
0.8	0.2
1.0	0

11. Calculate the utility levels of each portfolio of question 10 for an investor with $A = 3$. What do you conclude?

12. Repeat question 11 for an investor with $A = 5$. What do you conclude?

Reconsider the Best and SugarKane stock market hedging example in the text, but assume for questions 13 to 15 that the probability distribution of the rate of return on SugarKane stock is as follows:

	Bullish Stock Market	Bearish Stock Market	Sugar Crisis
Probability	.5	.3	.2
Rate of return	10%	−5%	20%

*Reprinted, with permission, from the Level I 1991 *CFA Study Guide.*

13. If Humanex's portfolio is half Best stock and half SugarKane, what are its expected return and standard deviation? Calculate the standard deviation from the portfolio returns in each scenario.
14. What is the covariance between Best and SugarKane?
15. Calculate the portfolio standard deviation using rule 5 and show that the result is consistent with your answer to question 13.

APPENDIX A: A DEFENSE OF MEAN-VARIANCE ANALYSIS

Describing Probability Distributions

The axiom of risk aversion needs little defense. So far, however, our treatment of risk has been limiting in that it took the variance (or, equivalently, the standard deviation) of portfolio returns as an adequate risk measure. In situations in which variance alone is not adequate to measure risk this assumption is potentially restrictive. Here, we provide some justification for mean-variance analysis.

The basic question is how one can best describe the uncertainty of portfolio rates of return. In principle, one could list all possible outcomes for the portfolio over a given period. If each outcome results in a payoff such as a dollar profit or rate of return, then this payoff value is the *random variable* in question. A list assigning a probability to all possible values of the random variable is called the probability distribution of the random variable.

The reward for holding a portfolio is typically measured by the expected rate of return across all possible scenarios, which equals

$$E(r) = \sum_{s=1}^{n} Pr(s)r_s$$

where $s = 1, \ldots, n$ are the possible outcomes or scenarios, r_s is the rate of return for outcome s, and $Pr(s)$ is the probability associated with it.

Actually, the expected value or mean is not the only candidate for the central value of a probability distribution. Other candidates are the median and the mode.

The median is defined as the outcome value that exceeds the outcome values for half the population and is exceeded by the other half. Whereas the expected rate of return is a weighted average of the outcomes, the weights being the probabilities, the median is based on the rank order of the outcomes and takes into account only the order of the outcome values rather than the values themselves.

The median differs significantly from the mean in cases where the expected value is dominated by extreme values. One example is the income (or wealth) distribution in a population. A relatively small number of households command a disproportionate share of total income (and wealth). The mean income is "pulled up" by these extreme values, which makes it nonrepresentative. The median is free of this effect, since it equals the income level that is exceeded by half the population, regardless of by how much.

Finally, a third candidate for the measure of central value is the mode, which is the most likely value of the distribution or the outcome with the highest probability. However, the expected value is by far the most widely used measure of central or average tendency.

We now turn to the characterization of the risk implied by the nature of the probability distribution of returns. In general, it is impossible to quantify risk by a single number. The idea is to describe the likelihood and magnitudes of "surprises" (deviations from the mean) with as small a set of statistics as is needed for accuracy. The easiest way to accomplish this is to answer a set of questions in order of their informational value and to stop at the point where additional questions would not affect our notion of the risk-return trade-off.

The first question is, "What is a typical deviation from the expected value?" A natural answer would be, "The expected deviation from the expected value is ______." Unfortunately, this answer is meaningless because it is necessarily zero: Positive deviations from the mean are offset exactly by negative deviations.

There are two ways of getting around this problem. The first is to use the expected *absolute* value of the deviation. This is known as MAD (mean absolute deviation), which is given by

$$\sum_{s=1}^{n} Pr(s) \times \text{Absolute Value}[r_s - E(r)]$$

The second is to use the expected *squared* deviation from the mean, which is simply the variance of the probability distribution:

$$\sigma^2 = \sum_{s=1}^{n} Pr(s)\,[r_s - E(r)]^2$$

Note that the unit of measurement of the variance is "percent squared." To return to our original units, we compute the standard deviation as the square root of the variance, which is measured in percentage terms, as is the expected value. The variance also is called the *second central moment* around the mean, with the expected return itself being the first moment.

Although the variance measures the average squared deviation from the expected value, it does not provide a full description of risk. To see why, consider the two probability distributions for rates of return on a portfolio, in Figure 5A.1.

A and *B* are probability distributions with identical expected values and variances. The graphs show that the variances are identical because probability distribution *B* is the mirror image of *A*.

What is the principal difference between *A* and *B*? *A* is characterized by more likely but small losses and less likely but extreme gains. This pattern is reversed in *B*. The difference is important. When we talk about risk, we really mean "*bad* surprises." The "bad surprises" in *A*, although they are more likely, are small (and limited) in magnitude. The "bad surprises" in *B* could be extreme, indeed unbounded. A risk-averse investor will prefer *A* to *B* on these grounds; hence, it is worthwhile to quantify this characteristic. The asymmetry of the distribution is called skewness, which we measure by the *third central moment,* given by

$$M^3 = \sum_{s=1}^{n} Pr(s)\,[r_s - E(r)]^3$$

Cubing the deviations from expected value preserves their signs, which allows us to distinguish good from bad surprises. Because this procedure gives greater weight to

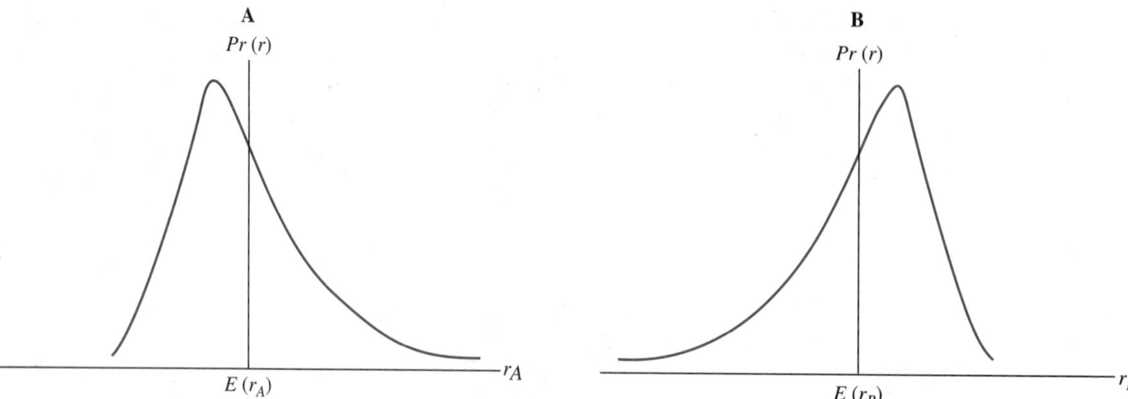

Figure 5A.1
Skewed probability distributions for rates of return on a portfolio

larger deviations, it causes the "long tail" of the distribution to dominate the measure of skewness. Thus the skewness of the distribution will be positive for a right-skewed distribution such as *A* and negative for a left-skewed distribution such as *B*. The asymmetry is a relevant characteristic, although it is not as important as the magnitude of the standard deviation.

To summarize, the first moment (expected value) represents the reward. The second and higher central moments characterize the uncertainty of the reward. All the even moments (variance, M_4, etc.) represent the likelihood of extreme values. Larger values for these moments indicate greater uncertainty. The odd moments (M_3, M_5, etc.) represent measures of asymmetry. Positive numbers are associated with positive skewness and hence are desirable.

We can characterize the risk aversion of any investor by the preference scheme that the investor assigns to the various moments of the distribution. In other words, we can write the utility value derived from the probability distribution as

$$U = E(r) - b_0\sigma^2 + b_1M_3 - b_2M_4 + b_3M_5 - \dots$$

where the importance of the terms lessens as we proceed to higher moments. Notice that the "good" (odd) moments have positive coefficients, whereas the "bad" (even) moments have minus signs in front of the coefficients.

How many moments are needed to describe the investor's assessment of the probability distribution adequately? Samuelson's "Fundamental Approximation Theorem of Portfolio Analysis in Terms of Means, Variances, and Higher Moments"[3] proves that in many important circumstances:

[3] Paul A. Samuelson, "The Fundamental Approximation Theorem of Portfolio Analysis in Terms of Means, Variances, and Higher Moments," *Review of Economic Studies* 37 (1970).

1. The importance of all moments beyond the variance is much smaller than that of the expected value and variance. In other words, disregarding moments higher than the variance will not affect portfolio choice.
2. The variance is as important as the mean to investor welfare.

Samuelson's proof is the major theoretical justification for mean-variance analysis. Under the conditions of this proof mean and variance are equally important, and we can overlook all other moments without harm.

The major assumption that Samuelson makes to arrive at this conclusion concerns the "compactness" of the distribution of stock returns. The distribution of the rate of return on a portfolio is said to be compact if the risk can be controlled by the investor. Practically speaking, we test for compactness of the distribution by posing a question: Will the risk of my position in the portfolio decline if I hold it for a shorter period, or will the risk approach zero if I hold the risky portfolio for only an instant? If the answer is yes, then the distribution is compact.

In general, compactness may be seen as being equivalent to continuity of stock prices. If stock prices do not take sudden jumps, then the uncertainty of stock returns over smaller and smaller time periods decreases. Under these circumstances investors who can rebalance their portfolios frequently will act so as to make higher moments of the stock return distribution so small as to be unimportant. It is not that skewness, for example, does not matter in principle. It is, instead, that the actions of investors in frequently revising their portfolios will limit higher moments to negligible levels.

Continuity or compactness is not, however, an innocuous assumption. Portfolio revisions entail transaction costs, meaning that rebalancing must of necessity be somewhat limited and that skewness and other higher moments cannot entirely be ignored. Compactness also rules out such phenomena as the major stock price jumps that occur in response to takeover attempts. It also rules out such dramatic events as the 25% one-day decline of the stock market on October 19, 1987. Except for these relatively unusual events, however, mean-variance analysis is adequate. In most cases, if the portfolio may be revised frequently, we need to worry about the mean and variance only.

Portfolio theory, for the most part, is built on the assumption that the conditions for mean-variance (or mean–standard deviation) analysis are satisfied. Accordingly, we typically ignore higher moments.

CONCEPT CHECK Question 5A.1. How does the simultaneous popularity of both lotteries and insurance policies confirm the notion that individuals prefer positive to negative skewness of portfolio returns?

Normal and Lognormal Distributions

Modern portfolio theory, for the most part, assumes that asset returns are normally distributed. This is a convenient assumption because the normal distribution can be described completely by its mean and variance, justifying mean-variance analysis. The argument has been that, even if individual asset returns are not exactly normal, the

Table 5A.1 Frequency Distribution of Rates of Return from a One-Year Investment in Randomly Selected Portfolios from NYSE-Listed Stocks

	$N = 1$		$N = 8$		$N = 32$		$N = 128$	
Statistic	**Observed**	**Normal**	**Observed**	**Normal**	**Observed**	**Normal**	**Observed**	**Normal**
Minimum	−71.1	NA	−12.4	NA	6.5	NA	16.4	NA
5th centile	−14.4	−39.2	8.1	4.6	17.4	16.7	22.7	22.6
20th centile	−.5	6.3	16.3	16.1	22.2	22.3	25.3	25.3
50th centile	19.6	28.2	26.4	28.2	27.8	28.2	28.1	28.2
70th centile	38.7	49.7	33.8	35.7	31.6	32.9	30.0	30.0
95th centile	96.3	95.6	54.3	51.8	40.9	39.9	34.1	33.8
Maximum	442.6	NA	136.7	NA	73.7	NA	43.1	NA
Mean	28.2	28.2	28.2	28.2	28.2	28.2	28.2	28.2
Standard deviation	41.0	41.0	14.4	14.4	7.1	7.1	3.4	3.4
Skewness (M_3)	255.4	0.0	88.7	0.0	44.5	0.0	17.7	0.0
Sample size	1,227	—	131,072	—	32,768	—	16,384	—

Source: Lawrence Fisher and James H. Lorie, "Some Studies of Variability of Returns on Investments in Common Stocks," *Journal of Business* 43 (April 1970).

distribution of returns of a large portfolio will resemble a normal distribution quite closely.

The data support this argument. Table 5A.1 shows summaries of the results of one-year investments in many portfolios selected randomly from NYSE stocks. The portfolios are listed in order of increasing degrees of diversification; that is, the numbers of stocks in each portfolio sample are 1, 8, 32, and 128. The percentiles of the distribution of returns for each portfolio are compared to what one would have expected from portfolios identical in mean and variance but drawn from a normal distribution.

Looking first at the single stock portfolio ($n = 1$), the departure of the return distribution from normality is significant. The mean of the sample is 28.2%, and the standard deviation is 41.0%. In the case of normal distribution with the same mean and standard deviation, we would expect the fifth percentile stock to lose 39.2%, but the fifth percentile stock actually lost 14.4%. In addition, although the normal distribution's mean coincides with its median, the actual sample median of the single stock was 19.6%, far below the sample mean of 28.2%.

In contrast, the returns of the 128-stock portfolios are virtually identical in distribution to the hypothetical normally distributed portfolio. The normal distribution therefore is a pretty good working assumption for well-diversified portfolios. How large a portfolio must be for this result to take hold depends on how far the distribution of the individual stocks is from normality. It appears that a portfolio typically must include at least 32 stocks for the one-year return to be close to normally distributed.

There remain theoretical objections to the assumption that individual stock returns are normally distributed. Given that a stock price cannot be negative, the normal distribution cannot be truly representative of the behavior of a holding period rate of return

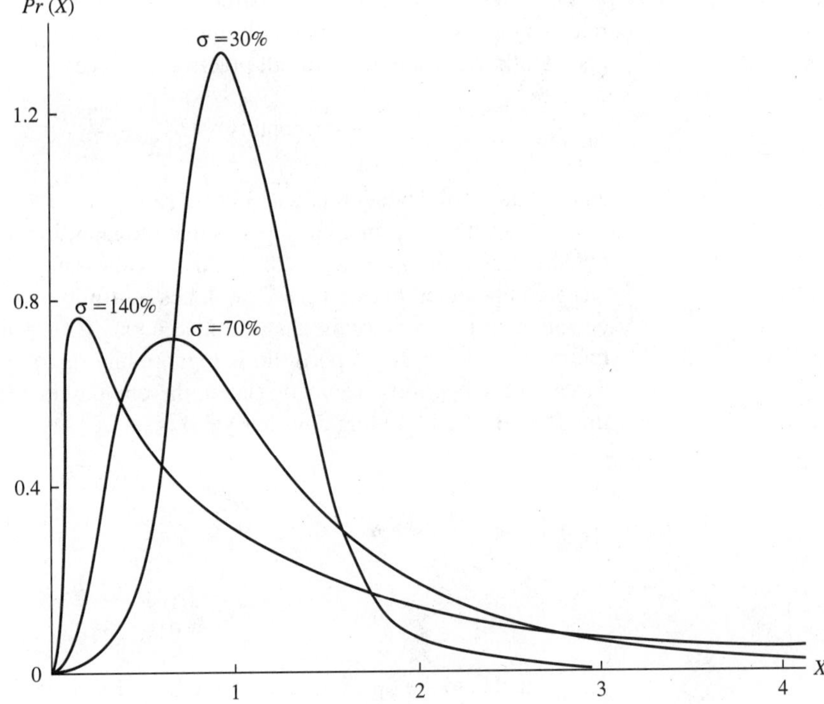

Figure 5A.2
The Lognormal distribution for three values of σ.
Source: J. Atchison and J. A. C. Brown, *The Lognormal Distribution* (New York: Cambridge University Press, 1976).

because it allows for any outcome, including the whole range of negative prices. Specifically, rates of return lower than -100% are theoretically impossible because they imply the possibility of negative security prices. The failure of the normal distribution to rule out such outcomes must be viewed as a shortcoming.

An alternative assumption is that the continuously compounded annual rate of return is normally distributed. If we call this rate r and we call the effective annual rate r_e, then the $r_e = e^r - 1$, and because e^r can never be negative, the smallest possible value for r_e is -1 or -100%. Thus, this assumption nicely rules out the troublesome possibility of negative prices while still conveying the advantages of working with normal distributions.

Under this assumption the distribution of r_e will be *lognormal.* This distribution is depicted in Figure 5A.2.

For *short* holding periods, that is, where t is small, the approximation of $r_e(t) = e^{rt} - 1$ by rt is quite accurate and the normal distribution provides a good approximation to the lognormal. With rt normally distributed, the effective annual return over short time periods may be taken as approximately normally distributed.

For short holding periods, therefore, the mean and standard deviation of the effective holding period returns are proportional to the mean and standard deviation of the annual, continuously compounded rate of return on the stock and to the time interval.

Therefore, if the standard deviation of the annual continuously compounded rate of return on a stock is 40% ($\sigma = .40$), then the variance of the holding period return for one month, for example, is for all practical purposes

$$\sigma^2(\text{monthly}) = \frac{\sigma^2}{12} = \frac{.16}{12} = .0133$$

and the standard deviation is $\sqrt{.0133} = .1155$.

To illustrate this principle, suppose that the Dow Jones Industrials went up one day by 30 points from 4,200 to 4,230. Is this a "large" move? Looking at annual, continuously compounded rates on the Dow Jones portfolio, we find that the annual standard deviation in post-war years has averaged about 16%. Under the assumption that the return on the Dow Jones portfolio is lognormally distributed and that returns between successive subperiods are uncorrelated, the one-day distribution has a standard deviation (based on 250 trading days per year) of

$$\begin{aligned}\sigma(\text{day}) &= \sigma(\text{year})\sqrt{1/250} \\ &= \frac{.16}{\sqrt{250}} \\ &= .0101 \\ &= 1.01\% \text{ per day}\end{aligned}$$

Applying this to the opening level of the Dow Jones on the trading day, 4,200, we find that the daily standard deviation of the Dow Jones index is 4,200 × .0101 = 42.4 points per day.

Because the daily rate on the Dow Jones portfolio is approximately normal, we know that in one day out of three, the Dow Jones will move by more than 1% either way. Thus, a move of 30 points is hardly an unusual event.

CONCEPT CHECK Question 5A.2. Look again at Table 5A.1. Are you surprised that the minimum rates of return are less negative for more diversified portfolios? Is your explanation consistent with the behavior of the sample's maximum rates of return?

Summary: Appendix A

1. The probability distribution of the rate of return can be characterized by its moments. The reward from taking the risk is measured by the first moment, which is the mean of the return distribution. Higher moments characterize the risk. Even moments provide information on the likelihood of extreme values, and odd moments provide information on the asymmetry of the distribution.
2. Investors' risk preferences can be characterized by their preferences for the various moments of the distribution. The fundamental approximation theorem shows that when portfolios are revised often enough, and prices are continuous, the desirability of a portfolio can be measured by its mean and variance alone.
3. The rates of return on well-diversified portfolios for holding periods that are not too long can be approximated by a normal distribution. For short holding periods (up to one month), the normal distribution is a good approximation for the lognormal.

Problem: Appendix A

1. The Smartstock investment consulting group prepared the following scenario analysis for the end-of-year dividend and stock price of Klink Inc., which is selling now at $12 per share:

		End-of-Year	
Scenario	**Probability**	**Dividend ($)**	**Price ($)**
1	.10	0	0
2	.20	0.25	2.00
3	.40	0.40	14.00
4	.25	0.60	20.00
5	.05	0.85	30.00

Compute the rate of return for each scenario and

a. The mean, median, and mode

b. The standard deviation and mean absolute deviation

c. The first moment, and the second and third moments around the mean. Is the probability distribution of Klink stock positively skewed?

APPENDIX B: RISK AVERSION AND EXPECTED UTILITY

We digress here to examine the rationale behind our contention that investors are risk averse. Recognition of risk aversion as central in investment decisions goes back at least to 1738. Daniel Bernoulli, one of a famous Swiss family of distinguished mathematicians, spent the years 1725 through 1733 in St. Petersburg, where he analyzed the following coin-toss game. To enter the game one pays an entry fee. Thereafter, a coin is tossed until the *first* head appears. The number of tails, denoted by n, that appears until the first head is tossed is used to compute the payoff, $\$R$, to the participant, as

$$R(n) = 2^n$$

The probability of no tails before the first head ($n = 0$) is $\frac{1}{2}$ and the corresponding payoff is $2^0 = \$1$. The probability of one tail and then heads ($n = 1$) is $\frac{1}{2} \times \frac{1}{2}$ with payoff $2^1 = \$2$, the probability of two tails and then heads ($n = 2$) is $\frac{1}{2} \times \frac{1}{2} \times \frac{1}{2}$, and so forth.

The following table illustrates the probabilities and payoffs for various outcomes:

Tails	Probability	Payoff = $\$R(n)$	Probability × Payoff
0	$\frac{1}{2}$	$1	$1/2
1	$\frac{1}{4}$	$2	$1/2
2	$\frac{1}{8}$	$4	$1/2
3	$\frac{1}{16}$	$8	$1/2
•	•	•	•
•	•	•	•
•	•	•	•
n	$(1/2)^{n+1}$	$\$2^n$	$1/2

The expected payoff is therefore

$$E(R) = \sum_{n=0}^{\infty} Pr(n)R(n)$$
$$= 1/2 + 1/2 + \ldots$$
$$= \infty$$

The evaluation of this game is called the "St. Petersburg Paradox." Although the expected payoff is infinite, participants obviously will be willing to purchase tickets to play the game only at a finite, and possibly quite modest, entry fee.

Bernoulli resolved the paradox by noting that investors do not assign the same value per dollar to all payoffs. Specifically, the greater their wealth, the less their "appreciation" for each extra dollar. We can make this insight mathematically precise by assigning a welfare or utility value to any level of investor wealth. Our utility function should increase as wealth is higher, but each extra dollar of wealth should increase utility by progressively smaller amounts.[4] (Modern economists would say that investors exhibit "decreasing marginal utility" from an additional payoff dollar.) One particular function that assigns a subjective value to the investor from a payoff of $\$R$, which has a smaller value per dollar the greater the payoff, is the function $\log(R)$. If this function measures utility values of wealth, the subjective utility value of the game is indeed finite.[5] The certain wealth level necessary to yield this utility value is \$2.38, because $\log(2.38) = .866$. Hence the certainty equivalent value of the risky payoff is \$2.38, which is the maximum amount that this investor will pay to play the game.

Von Neumann and Morgenstern adapted this approach to investment theory in a complete axiomatic system in 1946. Avoiding unnecessary technical detail, we restrict ourselves here to an intuitive exposition of the rationale for risk aversion.

Imagine two individuals who are identical twins, except that one of them is less fortunate than the other. Peter has only \$1,000 to his name while Paul has a net worth of \$200,000. How many hours of work would each twin be willing to offer to earn one extra dollar? It is likely that Peter (the poor twin) has more essential uses for the extra money than does Paul. Therefore, Peter will offer more hours. In other words, Peter derives a greater personal welfare or assigns a greater "utility" value to the 1,001st dollar than Paul does to the 200,001st. Figure 5B.1 depicts graphically the relationship between the wealth and the utility value of wealth that is consistent with this notion of decreasing marginal utility.

Individuals have different rates of decrease in their marginal utility of wealth. What is constant is the *principle* that per-dollar utility decreases with wealth. Functions that exhibit the property of decreasing per-unit value as the number of units grows are called

---

[4] This utility is similar in spirit to the one that assigns a satisfaction level to portfolios with given risk-and-return attributes. However, the utility function here refers not to investor's satisfaction with alternative portfolio choices but only to the subjective welfare they derive from different levels of wealth.

[5] If we substitute the "utility" value, $\log(R)$, for the dollar payoff, R, to obtain an expected utility value of the game (rather than expected dollar value), we have, calling $V(R)$ the expected utility.

$$V(R) = \sum_{n=0}^{\infty} Pr(n)\log[R(n)] = \sum_{n=0}^{\infty} (\tfrac{1}{2})^{n+1}\log(2^n) \approx 0.866$$

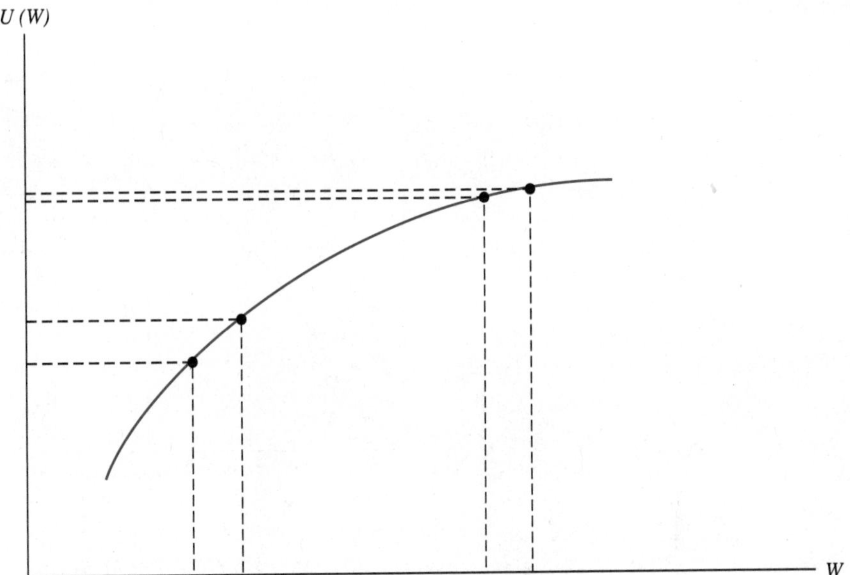

Figure 5B.1
Utility of wealth with a log utility function

concave. A simple example is the log function, familiar from high school mathematics. Of course, a log function will not fit all investors, but it is consistent with the risk aversion that we assume for all investors.

Now consider the following simple prospect:

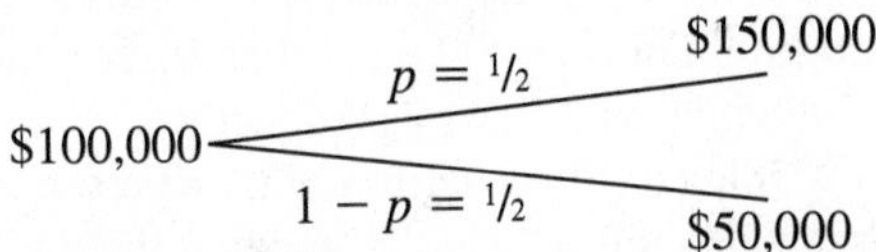

This is a fair game in that the expected profit is zero. Suppose, however, that the curve in Figure 5B.1 represents the investor's utility value of wealth, assuming a log utility function. Figure 5B.2 shows this curve with the numerical values marked.

Figure 5B.2 shows that the loss in utility from losing $50,000 exceeds the gain from winning $50,000. Consider the gain first. With probability $p = .5$, wealth goes from $100,000 to $150,000. Using the log utility function, utility goes from log(100,000) = 11.51 to log(150,000) = 11.92, the distance G on the graph. This gain is $G = 11.92 - 11.51 = .41$. In expected utility terms, then, the gain is $pG = .5 \times .41 = .21$.

Now consider the possibility of coming up on the short end of the prospect. In that case, wealth goes from $100,000 to $50,000. The loss in utility, the distance L on the graph, is $L = \log(100{,}000) - \log(50{,}000) = 11.51 - 10.82 = .69$. Thus, the loss in expected utility terms is $(1 - p)L = .5 \times .69 = .35$, which exceeds the gain in expected utility from the possibility of winning the game.

We compute the expected utility from the risky prospect:

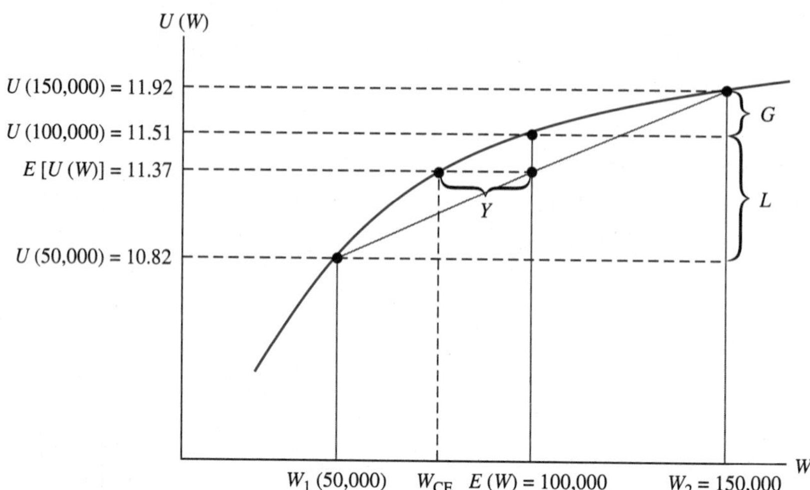

Figure 5B.2
Fair games and expected utility

$$
\begin{aligned}
E[U(W)] &= pU(W_1) + (1 - p)U(W_2) \\
&= \tfrac{1}{2}\log(50{,}000) + \tfrac{1}{2}\log(150{,}000) \\
&= 11.37
\end{aligned}
$$

If the prospect is rejected, the utility value of the (sure) \$100,000 is log(100,000) = 11.51, greater than that of the fair game (11.37). Hence, the risk-averse investor will reject the fair game.

Using a specific investor utility function (such as the log utility) allows us to compute the certainty equivalent value of the risky prospect to a given investor, Mary Smith. This is the amount that, if received with certainty, Mary would consider equally attractive as the risky prospect.

If log utility describes Mary's preferences toward wealth outcomes, then Figure 5B.2 can also tell us what is, for her, the dollar value of the prospect. We ask, "What sure level of wealth has a utility value of 11.37 (which equals the expected utility from the prospect)?" A horizontal line drawn at the level 11.37 intersects the utility curve at the level of wealth W_{CE}. This means that

$$\log(W_{CE}) = 11.37$$

which implies that

$$
\begin{aligned}
W_{CE} &= e^{11.37} \\
&= \$86{,}681.86
\end{aligned}
$$

W_{CE} is therefore the certainty equivalent of the prospect. The distance Y in Figure 5B.2 is the penalty, or the downward adjustment, to the expected profit that is attributable to the risk of the prospect.

$$
\begin{aligned}
Y &= E(W) - W_{CE} \\
&= \$100{,}000 - \$86{,}681.86 \\
&= \$13{,}318.13
\end{aligned}
$$

Smith views \$86,681.56 for certain as being equal in utility value as \$100,000 at risk. Therefore, she would be indifferent between the two.

CONCEPT CHECK

Question 5B.1. Suppose the utility function is $U(W) = \sqrt{W}$.

a. What is the utility level at wealth levels \$50,000 and \$150,000?

b. What is expected utility if p still equals .5?

c. What is the certainty equivalent of the risky prospect?

d. Does this utility function also display risk aversion?

e. Does this utility function display more or less risk aversion than the log utility function?

Does revealed behavior of investors demonstrate risk aversion? Looking at prices and past rates of return in financial markets, we can answer with a resounding "yes." With remarkable consistency, riskier bonds are sold at lower prices than are safer ones with otherwise similar characteristics. Riskier stocks also have provided higher average rates of return over long periods of time than less risky assets such as T-bills. For example, over the 1926 to 1993 period, the average rate of return on the S&P 500 portfolio exceeded the T-bill return by about 8.5% per year.

It is abundantly clear from financial data that the average, or representative, investor exhibits substantial risk aversion. For readers who recognize that financial assets are priced to compensate for risk by providing a risk premium and at the same time feel the urge for some gambling, we have a constructive recommendation: direct your gambling desire to investment in financial markets. As Von Neumann once said, "The stock market is a casino with the odds in your favor." A small risk-seeking investment may provide all the excitement you want with a positive expected return to boot!

Problems: Appendix B

1. Suppose that your wealth is \$250,000. You buy a \$200,000 house and invest the remainder in a risk-free asset paying an annual interest rate of 6%. There is a probability of .001 that your house will burn to the ground and its value be reduced to zero. With a log utility of end-of-year wealth, how much would you be willing to pay for insurance (at the beginning of the year)? (Assume that, if the house does not burn down, its end-of-year value still will be \$200,000.)
2. If the cost of insuring your house is \$1 per \$1,000 of value, what will be the certainty equivalent of your end-of-year wealth if you insure your house at:
   a. ½ its value.
   b. Its full value.
   c. 1½ times its value.

Chapter 6
Capital Allocation between the Risky Asset and the Risk-Free Asset

PORTFOLIO MANAGERS SEEK TO ACHIEVE THE BEST POSSIBLE TRADE-OFF BETWEEN RISK AND RETURN. A top-down analysis of their strategies starts with the broadest details about the exact makeup of the portfolio.

For example, the **capital allocation decision** is the choice of the proportion of the overall portfolio to place in safe but low-return money market securities versus risky but higher-return securities like stocks. The choice of the fraction of funds apportioned to risky investments is the first part of the investor's **asset allocation decision**, which describes the distribution of risky investments across broad asset classes like stocks, bonds, real estate, foreign assets, and so on. Finally, the **security selection decision** describes the choice of which particular securities to hold within each asset class.

The top-down analysis of portfolio construction has much to recommend it. Most institutional investors follow a top-down approach. Capital allocation and asset allocation decisions will be made at a high organizational level, with the choice of the specific securities to hold within each asset class delegated to particular portfolio managers. When investors partake in frequent capital or asset allocation revisions, they are called *market timers*. Individual investors typically follow a less-structured approach to money management, but they also typically give priority to broader allocation issues. For example, an individual's first decision is usually how much of his or her wealth must be left in a safe bank or money market account.

This chapter treats the broadest part of the asset allocation decision, capital allocation between risk-free assets versus the risky portion of the portfolio. We will take the composition of the risky portfolio as given and refer to it as "the" **risky asset**. In Chapter 7 we will examine how the composition of the risky portfolio may best be determined. For now, however, we start our "top-down journey" by asking how an investor decides how much to invest in the risky versus the risk-free asset.

This capital allocation problem may be solved in two stages. First, we determine the risk-return trade-off encountered when choosing between the risky and risk-free assets. Then, we show how risk aversion determines the optimal mix of the two assets. This analysis leads us to examine so-called passive strategies, which call for allocation of the portfolio between a (risk-free) money market fund and an index fund of common stocks.

6.1 Capital Allocation across Risky and Risk-Free Portfolios

History shows us that long-term bonds have been riskier investments than investments in Treasury bills, and that stock investments have been riskier still. On the other hand, the riskier investments have offered higher average returns. Investors, of course, do not make all-or-nothing choices from these investment classes. They can and do construct their portfolios using securities from all asset classes. Some of the portfolio may be in risk-free Treasury bills, and some in high-risk stocks.

The most straightforward way to control the risk of the portfolio is through the fraction of the portfolio invested in Treasury bills and other safe money market securities versus risky assets. This capital allocation decision is an example of an asset allocation choice—a choice among broad investment classes, rather than among the specific securities within each asset class. Most investment professionals consider asset allocation the most important part of portfolio construction. Consider this statement by John Bogle, the chairman of the Vanguard Group of Investment Companies:

> The most fundamental decision of investing is the allocation of your assets: How much should you own in stock, How much should you own in bonds? How much should you own in cash reserves? . . . That decision [has been shown to account] for an astonishing 94% of the differences in total returns achieved by institutionally managed pension funds . . . There is no reason to believe that the same relationship does not also hold true for individual investors.[1]

Therefore, we start our discussion of the risk-return trade-off available to investors by examining the most basic asset allocation choice: the choice of how much of the portfolio to place in risk-free money market securities versus in other risky asset classes.

We will denote the investor's portfolio of risky assets as P, and the risk-free asset as F. We will assume for the sake of illustration that the risky component of the investor's overall portfolio is comprised of two mutual funds: one invested in stocks and the other invested in long-term bonds. For now, we take the composition of the risky portfolio as given and focus only on the allocation between it and risk-free securities. In the next chapter, we turn to asset allocation and security selection across risky assets.

[1] John C. Bogle, *Bogle on Mutual Funds* (Burr Ridge, IL: Irwin Professional Publishing, 1994), p. 235.

When we shift wealth from the risky portfolio to the risk-free asset, we do not change the relative proportions of the various risky assets within the risky portfolio. Rather, we reduce the relative weight of the risky portfolio as a whole in favor of risk-free assets.

For example, assume that the total market value of an initial portfolio is \$300,000, of which \$90,000 is invested in the Ready Asset money market fund, a risk-free asset for practical purposes. The remaining \$210,000 is invested in risky equity securities—\$113,400 in IBM and \$96,600 in GM. The IBM and GM holding is "the" risky portfolio, 54% in IBM and 46% in GM:

$$\text{IBM:} \quad w_1 = \frac{113{,}400}{210{,}000} = .54$$

$$\text{GM:} \quad w_2 = \frac{96{,}600}{210{,}000} = .46$$

The weight of the risky portfolio, P, in the **complete portfolio**, including risk-free investments, is denoted by y:

$$y = \frac{210{,}000}{300{,}000} = .7 \text{ (risky assets)}$$

$$1 - y = \frac{90{,}000}{300{,}000} = .3 \text{ (risk-free assets)}$$

The weights of each stock in the complete portfolio are as follows:

$$\text{IBM:} \quad \frac{\$113{,}400}{\$300{,}000} = .378$$

$$\text{GM:} \quad \frac{\$96{,}600}{\$300{,}000} = .322$$

$$\text{Risky portfolio} \quad = .700$$

The risky portfolio is 70% of the complete portfolio.

Suppose that the owner of this portfolio wishes to decrease risk by reducing the allocation to the risky portfolio from $y = .7$ to $y = .56$. The risky portfolio would total only \$168,000 (.56 × \$300,000 = \$168,000), requiring the sale of \$42,000 of the original \$210,000 risky holdings, with the proceeds used to purchase more shares in Ready Asset (the money market fund). Total holdings in the risk-free asset will increase to \$300,000(1 − .56) = \$132,000), or the original holdings plus the new contribution to the money market fund:

$$\$90{,}000 + \$42{,}000 = \$132{,}000$$

The key point, however, is that we leave the proportions of each stock in the risky portfolio unchanged. Because the weights of IBM and GM in the risky portfolio are .54 and .46, respectively, we sell .54 × \$42,000 = \$22,680 of IBM and .46 × \$42,000 = \$19,320 of GM. After the sale, the proportions of each share in the risky portfolio are in fact unchanged:

$$\text{IBM:} \quad w_1 = \frac{113{,}400 - 22{,}680}{210{,}000 - 42{,}000} = .54$$

$$\text{GM:} \quad w_2 = \frac{96{,}000 - 19{,}320}{210{,}000 - 42{,}000} = .46$$

Rather than thinking of our risky holdings as IBM and GM stock separately, we may view our holdings as if they were in a single fund that holds IBM and GM in fixed proportions. In this sense we treat the risky fund as a single risky asset, that asset being a particular bundle of securities. As we shift in and out of safe assets, we simply alter our holdings of that bundle of securities commensurately.

Given this assumption, we can now turn to the desirability of reducing risk by changing the risky/risk-free asset mix, that is, reducing risk by decreasing the proportion y. As long as we do not alter the weights of each stock within the risky portfolio, the probability distribution of the rate of return on the risky portfolio remains unchanged by the asset reallocation. What will change is the probability distribution of the rate of return on the *complete* portfolio that consists of the risky asset and the risk-free asset.

CONCEPT CHECK Question 1. What will be the dollar value of your position in IBM, and its proportion in your overall portfolio, if you decide to hold 50% of your investment budget in Ready Asset?

6.2 THE RISK-FREE ASSET

By virtue of its power to tax and control the money supply, only the government can issue default-free bonds. Even the default-free guarantee by itself is not sufficient to make the bonds risk-free in real terms. The only risk-free asset in real terms would be a perfectly price-indexed bond. Moreover, a default-free perfectly indexed bond offers a guaranteed real rate to an investor only if the maturity of the bond is identical to the investor's desired holding period. Even indexed bonds are subject to interest rate risk, because real interest rates change unpredictably through time. When future real rates are uncertain, so is the future price of perfectly indexed bonds.

Nevertheless, it is common practice to view Treasury bills as "the" **risk-free asset**. Their short-term nature makes their values insensitive to interest rate fluctuations. Indeed, an investor can lock in a short-term nominal return by buying a bill and holding it to maturity. Moreover, the inflation uncertainty over the course of a few weeks, or even months, is negligible compared with the uncertainty of stock market returns.

In practice, most investors use a broader range of money market instruments as a risk-free asset. All the money market instruments are virtually free of interest rate risk because of their short maturities and are fairly safe in terms of default or credit risk.

Most money market funds hold, for the most part, three types of securities—Treasury bills, bank certificates of deposit (CDs), and commercial paper (CP)—differing slightly in their default risk. The yields to maturity on CDs and CP for identical

Figure 6.1
Spread between three-month CD and T-bill rates

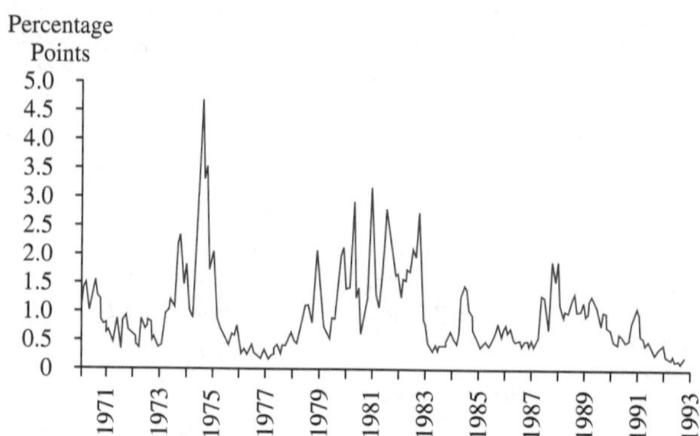

maturity, for example, are always somewhat higher than those of T-bills. The pattern of this yield spread for 90-day CDs is shown in Figure 6.1.

Money market funds have changed their relative holdings of these securities over time but, by and large, T-bills make up only about 15% of their portfolios. Nevertheless, the risk of such blue-chip short-term investments as CDs and CP is minuscule compared with that of most other assets such as long-term corporate bonds, common stocks, or real estate. Hence, we treat money market funds as the most easily accessible risk-free asset for most investors.

The notion of a risk-free asset seems straightforward, but nevertheless is the source of surprising amounts of confusion. Consider, for example, the nearby box, which touts the possibility of stock-marketlike returns without the risk. The article argues that long-term bonds can provide returns approximately three-quarters that of stocks with negligible risk. This analysis is faulty for several reasons.

First, the investment instruments suggested in the article are by no means risk free. Interest rate fluctuations impart uncertainty to the value of these securities at any time before their maturity dates. In fact, we saw in Figure 4.5 of Chapter 4 that the standard deviation of the rates of return on these long-term fixed-income securities has been about 8.7% per year.

Second, we have argued that the risk premium is properly viewed as an incremental rate of return above the risk-free rate. As the rates available on high-quality short-term instruments rise, so should the expected rate on riskier assets, if their risk premiums are to be preserved. When the article cites the long-term historical return on stocks as about 10%, and notes that fixed-income securities are now providing yields almost that high, it ignores the fact that the expected rate of return of the stock market might well have risen along with the rates available on these securities.

Finally, the article seems to imply that locking in a nominally risk-free rate for 5 or 10 years avoids risk. But, as Robert A. Clarfeld, who is quoted in the article, points out, a fixed nominal return leaves you exposed to opportunity-cost risk, because it is possible that available rates of return might continue to rise, leaving behind a portfolio with fixed payments.

Lock in Stock-Market Returns, While Avoiding the Risk

Are interest rates rising? Is inflation heating up? Are stocks riskier than bonds?

Who cares.

Bulls, bears and nervous Nellies can ignore the turmoil in the markets and lock in yields near 8%—and maybe higher—for the next five or 10 years.

How? By investing in municipal bonds, Treasury notes, zero-coupon Treasury bonds and even some bank certificates of deposit. Rising interest rates have pushed returns on these investments into the 8% range, tax-adjusted, as long as you don't touch the money early.

"It's an uncertain world, but by locking up an 8% return, you know pretty much what you're going to get at the end of the period," says Jim Floyd, senior analyst at Leuthold Group, an institutional-investment consulting group in Minneapolis.

What's more, that 8% return will probably be pretty close to how stocks will perform, with a sliver of the risk. Research by Leuthold suggests that although the long-term historical return on stocks is 10%, the return during the next decade is likely to be closer to 8%.

"If you can lock in 75% of the historical return of the stock market with zippo risk, what's stopping you?" asks James Wilson, a financial planner in Columbia, S.C.

Financial advisers caution, though, that you shouldn't overdo it. Although it may be prudent to anchor a portion of your holdings into a low-risk, fairly certain return, it's still wise to keep some money in the stock market.

"You want to participate in any upside should the market continue to perform," says Robert A. Clarfeld, a New York financial planner and accountant. He also cautions that inflation could heat up, eating up the value of an 8% return.

Safe Yields Now and Then

	Today	Beginning of 1994
Municipal bonds*	11.8%	10.3%
Treasury notes†	7.8	5.2
Treasury strips‡	8.1	7.0
Bank CDs§	7.7	5.4

*Taxable-equivalent yield on Bond Buyer municipal-bond index for investors in 36% federal tax bracket

†Five-year Treasury notes

‡Twenty-year zero-coupon Treasury bonds

§Highest-yield five-year bank certificate of deposit as quoted by BanxQuote Money Markets

Source: *The Wall Street Journal*, December 14, 1994. Excerpted by permission of *The Wall Street Journal*,

6.3 Portfolios of One Risky Asset and One Risk-Free Asset

In this section we examine the risk-return combinations available to investors. This is the "technological" part of asset allocation; it deals with only the opportunities available to investors given the features of the broad asset markets in which they can invest. In the next section we address the "personal" part of the problem—the specific individual's choice of the best risk-return combination from the set of feasible combinations.

Suppose that the investor has already decided on the composition of the optimal risky portfolio. The investment proportions in all the available risky assets are known. Now the final concern is with the proportion of the investment budget, y, to be allocated to the risky portfolio, P. The remaining proportion, $1 - y$, is to be invested in the risk-free asset, F.

Denote the risky rate of return by r_P and denote the expected rate of return on P by $E(r_P)$ and its standard deviation by σ_P. The rate of return on the risk-free asset is denoted as r_f. In the numerical example we assume that $E(r_P) = 15\%$, $\sigma_P = 22\%$, and that the risk-free rate is $r_f = 7\%$. Thus, the risk premium on the risky asset is $E(r_P) - r_f = 8\%$.

With a proportion, y, in the risky portfolio, and $1 - y$ in the risk-free asset, the rate of return on the *complete* portfolio, denoted C, is r_C where

$$r_C = yr_P + (1 - y)r_f$$

Taking the expectation of this portfolio's rate of return,

$$\begin{aligned} E(r_C) &= yE(r_P) + (1 - y)r_f \\ &= r_f + y[E(r_P) - r_f] \\ &= 7 + y(15 - 7) \end{aligned} \tag{6.1}$$

This result is easily interpreted. The base rate of return for any portfolio is the risk-free rate. In addition, the portfolio is *expected* to earn a risk premium that depends on the risk premium of the risky portfolio, $E(r_P) - r_f$, and the investor's exposure to the risky asset, denoted by y. Investors are assumed to be risk averse and thus unwilling to take on a risky position without a positive risk premium.

As we noted in Chapter 5, when we combine a risky asset and a risk-free asset in a portfolio, the standard deviation of that portfolio is the standard deviation of the risky asset multiplied by the weight of the risky asset in that portfolio. In our case, the complete portfolio consists of the risky asset and the risk- free asset. Because the standard deviation of the risky portfolio is $\sigma_P = 22\%$,

$$\begin{aligned} \sigma_C &= y\sigma_P \\ &= 22y \end{aligned} \tag{6.2}$$

which makes sense because the standard deviation of the portfolio is proportional to both the standard deviation of the risk asset and the proportion invested in it. In sum, the rate of return of the complete portfolio will have expected return $E(r_C) = r_f + y[E(r_P) - r_f] = 7 + 8y$ and standard deviation $\sigma_C = 22y$.

The next step is to plot the portfolio characteristics (as a function of y) in the expected return–standard deviation plane. This is done in Figure 6.2. The expected return–standard deviation combination for the risk-free asset, F, appears on the vertical axis because the standard deviation is zero. The risky asset, P, is plotted with a standard deviation, $\sigma_P = 22\%$ and expected return of 15%. If an investor chooses to invest solely in the risky asset, then $y = 1.0$, and the resulting portfolio is P. If the chosen position is $y = 0$, then $1 - y = 1.0$, and the resulting portfolio is the risk-free portfolio F.

What about the more interesting midrange portfolios where y lies between zero and 1? These portfolios will graph on the straight line connecting points F and P. The slope of that line is simply $[E(r_P) - r_f]/\sigma_P$ (or rise/run), in this case, 8/22.

The conclusion is straightforward. Increasing the fraction of the overall portfolio invested in the risky asset increases the expected return by the risk premium of equation 6.1, which is 8%. It also increases portfolio standard deviation according to equation 6.2 at the rate 22%. The extra return per extra risk is thus 8/22 = .36.

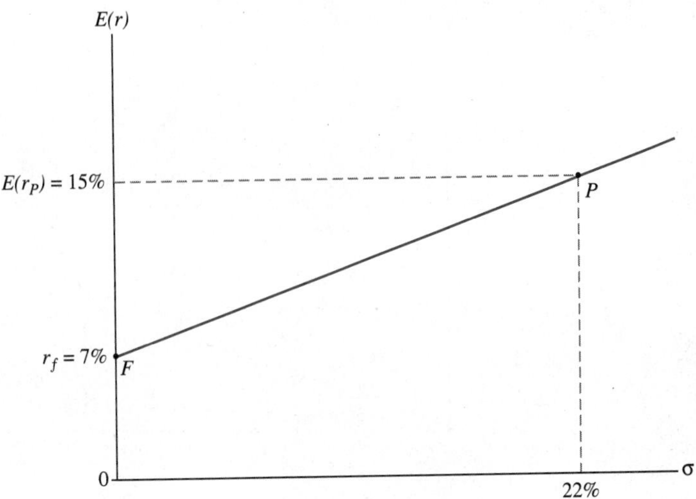

Figure 6.2
Expected return–standard deviation combinations

To derive the exact equation for the straight line between F and P, we rearrange equation 6.2 to find that $y = \sigma_C/\sigma_P$, and substitute for y in equation 6.1 to describe the expected return–standard deviation trade-off:

$$\begin{aligned} E[r_C(y)] &= r_f + y[E(r_P) - r_f] \\ &= r_f + \frac{\sigma_C}{\sigma_P}[E(r_P) - r_f] \\ &= 7 + \frac{8}{22}\sigma_C \end{aligned}$$

Thus, the expected return of the portfolio as a function of its standard deviation is a straight line, with intercept r_f and slope as follows:

$$\begin{aligned} S &= \frac{E(r_P) - r_f}{\sigma_P} \\ &= \frac{8}{22} \end{aligned}$$

Figure 6.3 graphs the *investment opportunity set*, which is the set of feasible expected return and standard deviation pairs of all portfolios resulting from different values of y. The graph is a straight line originating at r_f and going through the point labeled P.

This straight line is called the **capital allocation line** (CAL). It depicts all the risk-return combinations available to investors. The slope of the CAL, S, equals the increase in the expected return of the chosen portfolio per unit of additional standard deviation—in other words, the measure of extra return per extra risk. For this reason, the slope also is called the **reward-to-variability ratio.**

A portfolio equally divided between the risky asset and the risk-free asset, that is, where $y = .5$, will have an expected rate of return of $E(r_C) = 7 + .5 \times 8 = 11\%$, implying a risk premium of 4%, and a standard deviation of $\sigma_C = .5 \times 22 = 11\%$.

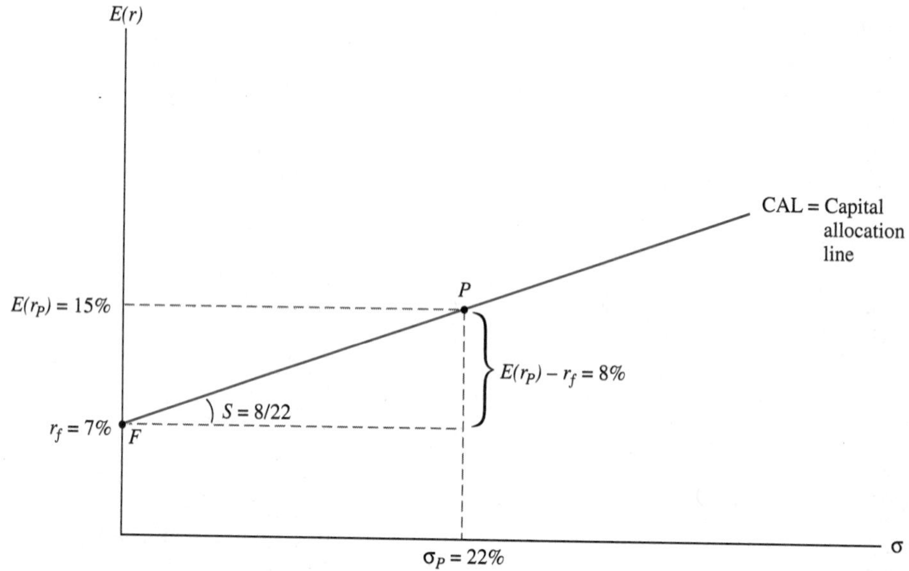

Figure 6.3
The investment opportunity set with a risky asset and a risk-free asset

It will plot on the line *FP* midway between *F* and *P*. The reward-to-variability ratio is $S = 8/22 = .36$.

CONCEPT CHECK Question 2. Can the reward-to-variability ratio, $S = [E(r_C - r_f]/\sigma_C$, of any combination of the risky asset and the risk-free asset be different from the ratio for the risky asset taken alone, $[E(r_P) - r_f]/\sigma_P$, which in this case is .36?

What about points on the line to the right of portfolio *P* in the investment opportunity set? If investors can borrow at the (risk-free) rate of $r_f = 7\%$, they can construct portfolios that may be plotted on the CAL to the right of *P*.

Suppose the investment budget is $300,000 and our investor borrows an additional $120,000, investing the total available funds in the risky asset. This is a *leveraged* position in the risky asset; it is financed in part by borrowing. In that case

$$y = \frac{420{,}000}{300{,}000} = 1.4$$

and $1 - y = 1 - 1.4 = -.4$, reflecting a short position in the risk-free asset, which is a borrowing position. Rather than lending at a 7% interest rate, the investor borrows at 7%. The distribution of the portfolio rate of return still exhibits the same reward-to-variability ratio:

$$E(r_C) = 7\% + (1.4 \times 8\%) = 18.2\%$$
$$\sigma_C = 1.45 \times 22\% = 30.8\%$$
$$S = \frac{E(r_C) - r_f}{\sigma_C} = \frac{18.2 - 7}{30.8} = .36$$

Figure 6.4
The opportunity set with differential borrowing and lending rates

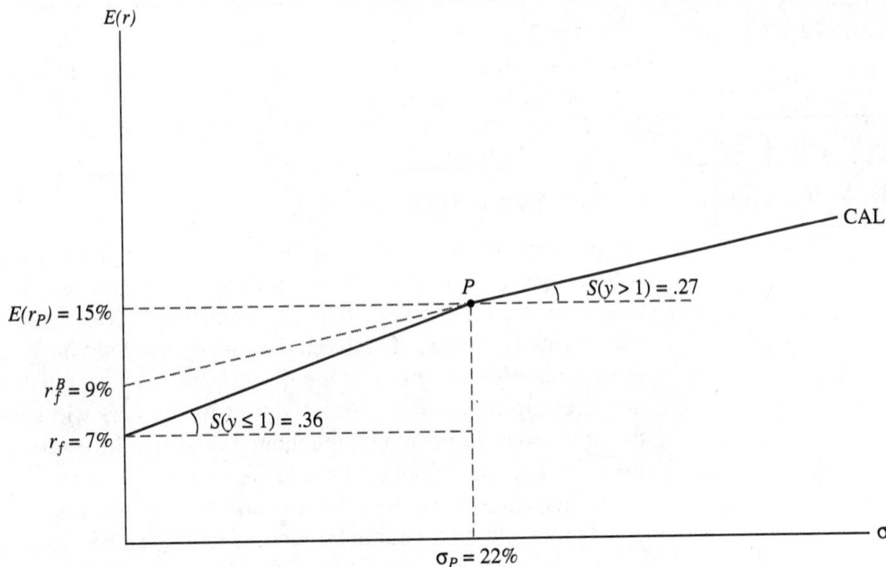

As one might expect, the leveraged portfolio has a higher standard deviation than does an unleveraged position in the risky asset.

Of course, nongovernment investors cannot borrow at the risk-free rate. The risk of a borrower's default causes lenders to demand higher interest rates on loans. Therefore, the nongovernment investor's borrowing cost will exceed the lending rate of $r_f = 7\%$. Suppose that the borrowing rate is $r_f^B = 9\%$. Then, in the borrowing range the reward-to-variability ratio, the slope of the CAL, will be $[E(r_P) - r_f^B]/\sigma_P = 6/22 = .27$. The CAL will, therefore, be "kinked" at point *P*, as shown in Figure 6.4. To the left of *P* the investor is lending at 7%, and the slope of the CAL is .36. To the right of *P*, where $y > 1$, the investor is borrowing to finance extra investments in the risky asset, and the slope is .27.

In practice, borrowing to invest in the risky portfolio is easy and straightforward if you have a margin account with a broker. All you have to do is tell your broker that you want to buy "on margin." Margin purchases may not exceed 50% of the purchase value. Therefore, if your net worth in the account is \$300,000, the broker is allowed to lend you up to \$300,000 to purchase additional stock.[2] You would then have \$600,000 on the asset side of your account and \$300,000 on the liability side, resulting in $y = 2.0$.

[2] Margin purchases require the investor to maintain the securities in a margin account with the broker. If the value of the securities declines below a "maintenance margin," a "margin call" is sent out, requiring a deposit to bring the net worth of the account up to the appropriate level. If the margin call is not met, regulations mandate that some or all of the securities be sold by the broker and the proceeds used to reestablish the required margin. See Chapter 3, Section 3.6, for further discussion.

CONCEPT CHECK Question 3. Suppose that there is a shift upward in the expected rate of return on the risky asset, from 15% to 17%. If all other parameters remain unchanged, what will be the slope of the CAL for $y \leq 1$ and $y > 1$?

6.4 RISK TOLERANCE AND ASSET ALLOCATION

We have shown how to develop the CAL, the graph of all feasible risk-return combinations available from different asset allocation choices. The investor confronting the CAL now must choose one optimal combination from the set of feasible choices. This choice entails a trade-off between risk and return. Individual investor differences in risk aversion imply that, given an identical opportunity set (as described by a risk-free rate and a reward-to-variability ratio), different investors will choose different positions in the risky asset. In particular, the more risk-averse investors will choose to hold less of the risky asset and more of the risk-free asset.

In Chapter 5 we showed that the utility an investor derives from a portfolio with a given probability distribution of rates of return can be described by the expected return and variance of the portfolio rate of return. Specifically, we developed the following representation:

$$U = E(r) - .005A\sigma^2$$

where A is the coefficient of risk aversion. We interpret this expression to say that the utility from a portfolio increases as the expected rate of return increases, and it decreases when the variance increases. The relative magnitude of these changes is governed by the coefficient of risk aversion A. For risk-neutral investors, $A = 0$. Higher levels of risk aversion are reflected in larger values for A.

An investor who faces a risk-free rate, r_f, and a risky portfolio with expected return $E(r_P)$ and standard deviation σ_P will find that, for any choice of y, the expected return of the complete portfolio is given by equation 6.1, part of which we repeat here:

$$E(r_C) = r_f + y[E(r_P) - r_f]$$

From equation 6.2, the variance of the overall portfolio is

$$\sigma_C^2 = y^2\sigma_P^2$$

The investor attempts to maximize his or her utility level, U, by choosing the best allocation to the risky asset, y. Typically, we write this problem as follows:

$$\max_y U = E(r_C) - .005A\sigma_C^2 = r_f + y[E(r_P) - r_f] - .005Ay^2\sigma_P^2$$

where A is the coefficient of risk aversion.

Students of calculus will remember that the maximization problem is solved by setting the derivative of this expression to zero. Doing so and solving for y yields the optimal position for risk-averse investors in the risky asset, y^*, as follows[3]:

[3] The derivative with respect to y equals $E(r_P) - r_f - .01yA\sigma_P^2$. Setting this expression equal to zero and solving for y yields equation 6.3.

$$y^* = \frac{E(r_P) - r_f}{.01A\sigma_P^2} \tag{6.3}$$

This solution shows that the optimal position in the risky asset is, as one would expect, *inversely* proportional to the level of risk aversion and the level of risk, as measured by the variance, and directly proportional to the risk premium offered by the risky asset.

Going back to our numerical example [$r_f = 7\%$, $E(r_P) = 15\%$, and $\sigma_P = 22\%$], the optimal solution for an investor with a coefficient of risk aversion, $A = 4$, is

$$y^* = \frac{15 - 7}{.01 \times 4 \times 22^2} = .41$$

In other words, this particular investor will invest 41% of the investment budget in the risky asset and 59% in the risk-free asset.

With 41% invested in the risky portfolio, the rate of return of the complete portfolio will have an expected return and standard deviation as follows:

$$\begin{aligned} E(r_C) &= 7 + .41 \times (15 - 7) \\ &= 10.28\% \\ \sigma_C &= .41 \times 22 \\ &= 9.02\% \end{aligned}$$

The risk premium of the complete portfolio is $E(r_C) - r_f = 3.28\%$, which is obtained by taking on a portfolio with a standard deviation of 9.02%. Notice that 3.28/9.02 = .36, which is the reward-to-variability ratio assumed for this problem.

A graphical way of presenting this decision problem is to use indifference curve analysis. Recall from Chapter 5 that the indifference curve is a graph in the expected return–standard deviation plane of all points that result in a given level of utility. The curve then displays the investor's required trade-off between expected return and standard deviation.

For example, suppose that the initial portfolio under consideration is the risky asset itself, $y = 1$. The dark-blue curve in Figure 6.5 represents the indifference curve for an investor with a degree of risk aversion, $A = 4$, that passes through the risky asset with $E(r_P) = 15\%$ and $\sigma_P = 22\%$. The light-blue curve, by contrast, shows an indifference curve going through P with a smaller degree of risk aversion, $A = 2$. The light indifference curve is flatter, that is, the more risk-tolerant (less risk-averse) investor requires a smaller increase in expected return to compensate for a given increase in standard deviation. The intercept of the indifference curve with the vertical axis is the *certainty equivalent* of the risky portfolio's expected rate of return because it gives a risk-free return with the same utility as the risky portfolio. Notice in Figure 6.5 that the less risk-averse investor (with $A = 2$) has a higher certainty equivalent for a risky portfolio such as P than the more risk-averse investor ($A = 4$).

Indifference curves can be drawn for many benchmark portfolios, representing various levels of utility. Figure 6.6 shows this set of indifference curves.

To show how to use indifference curve analysis to determine the choice of the optimal portfolio for a specific CAL, Figure 6.7 superimposes the graphs of the indifference curves on the graph of the investment opportunity set, the CAL.

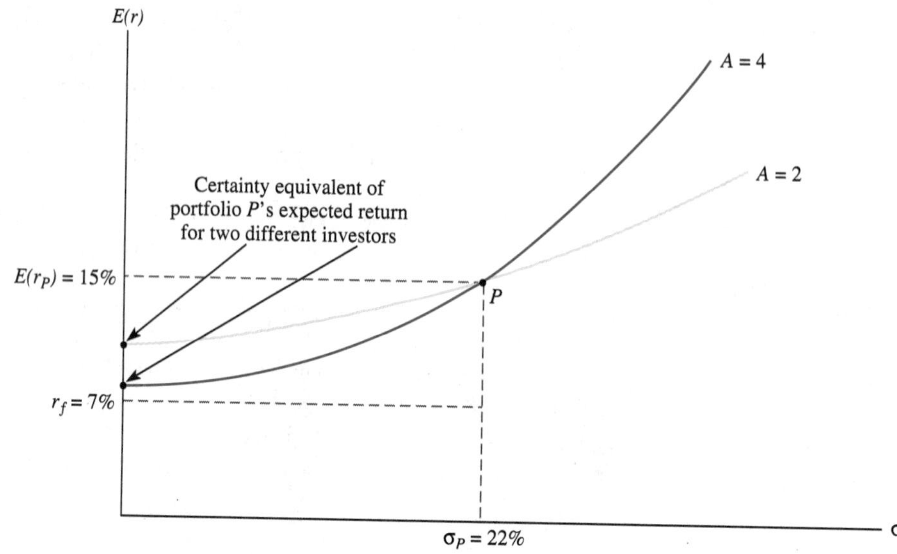

Figure 6.5
Two indifference curves through a risky asset

The investor seeks the position with the highest feasible level of utility, represented by the highest possible indifference curve that touches the investment opportunity set. This is the indifference curve tangent to the CAL.

This optimal overall portfolio is represented by point C on the investment opportunity set. Such a graphical approach yields the same solution as the algebraic approach:

$$E(r_C) = 10.28\%$$

and

$$\sigma_C = 9.02\%$$

which yields $y^* = .41$.

In summary, the asset allocation process can be broken down into two steps: (1) determine the CAL, and (2) find the point of highest utility along that line.

CONCEPT CHECK

Question 4.

a. If an investor's coefficient of risk aversion is $A = 3$, how does the optimal asset mix change? What are the new $E(r_C)$ and σ_C?

b. Suppose that the borrowing rate, $r_f^B = 9\%$, is greater than the lending rate, $r_f = 7\%$. Show, graphically, how the optimal portfolio choice of some investors will be affected by the higher borrowing rate. Which investors will *not* be affected by the borrowing rate?

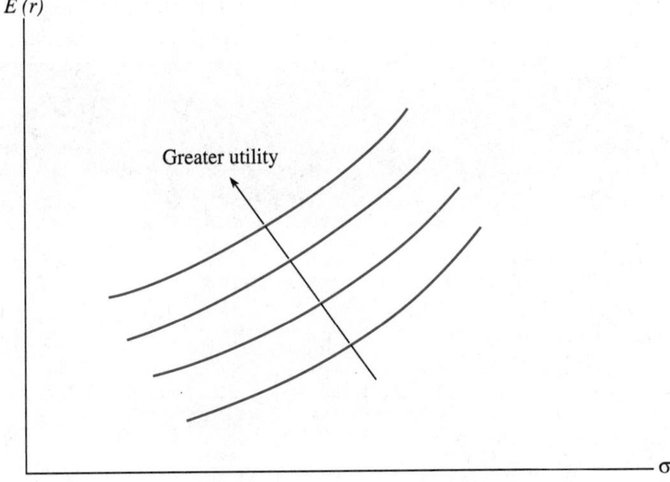

Figure 6.6
A set of indifference curves

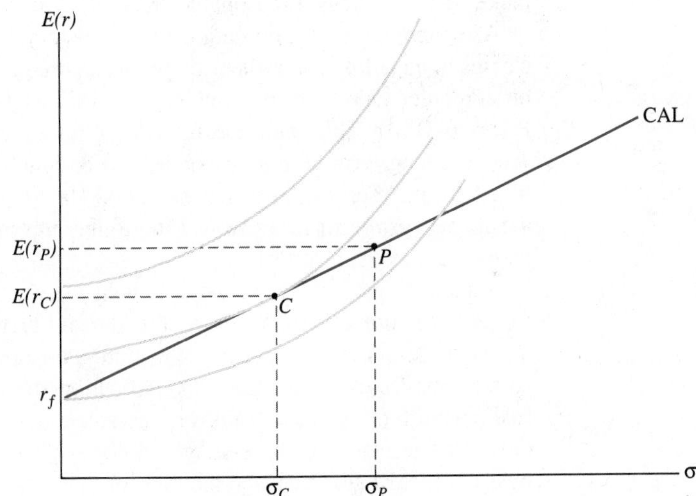

Figure 6.7
The graphical solution to the portfolio decision

6.5 Passive Strategies: The Capital Market Line

The CAL is derived with the risk-free and "the" risky portfolio P. Determination of the assets to include in risky portfolio P may result from a passive or an active strategy. A **passive strategy** describes a portfolio decision that avoids *any* direct or indirect security analysis.[4] At first blush, a passive strategy would appear to be naive. As will

[4] By "indirect security analysis" we mean the delegation of that responsibility to an intermediary such as a professional money manager.

Table 6.1 Average Rates of Return and Standard Deviations for Common Stocks and One-Month Bills, and the Risk Premium over Bills of Common Stock

	Common Stocks		One-Month Bills		Risk Premium of Common Stocks over Bills	
	Mean	S.D.	Mean	S.D.	Mean	S.D.
1926–1942	8.0	29.7	1.2	1.6	6.8	29.8
1943–1959	18.4	17.1	1.3	.9	17.1	17.4
1960–1976	8.4	17.4	4.7	1.7	3.7	18.3
1977–1993	14.4	13.2	7.8	3.0	6.6	13.3
1926–1993	12.3	20.5	3.7	3.3	8.6	20.9

become apparent, however, forces of supply and demand in large capital markets may make such a strategy a reasonable choice for many investors.

A comprehensive compilation of the history of rates of return on different asset classes in the 20th century is available on an ongoing basis.[5] The data also are available on computer tape from the University of Chicago's Center for Research in Security Prices (CRSP). This database includes rates of return on 30-day T-bills, long-term T-bonds, long-term corporate bonds, and common stocks. The CRSP tapes provide a monthly rate of return series for the period 1926 to the present and, for common stocks, a daily rate of return series from 1963 to the present. We can use these data to develop various passive strategies.

A natural candidate for a passively held risky asset would be a well-diversified portfolio of common stocks. We have already said that a passive strategy requires that we devote no resources to acquiring information on any individual stock or group of stocks, so we must follow a "neutral" diversification strategy. One way is to select a diversified portfolio of stocks that mirrors the value of the corporate sector of the U.S. economy. This results in a value-weighted portfolio in which, for example, the proportion invested in GM stock will be the ratio of GM's total market value to the market value of all listed stocks.

The most popular value-weighted index of U.S. stocks is the Standard & Poor's composite index of the 500 largest capitalization corporations (S&P 500). (Before March 1957 it consisted of 90 of the largest stocks.) Table 6.1 shows the historical record of this portfolio.

The last pair of columns shows the average risk premium over T-bills and the standard deviation of the common stock portfolio. The risk premium of 8.6% and standard deviation of 20.9% over the entire period are similar to the figures we assumed for the risky portfolio we used as an example in Section 6.4.

[5] R. G. Ibbotson and R. A. Sinquefield, *Stocks, Bonds, Bills, and Inflation* (SBBI), Updated in *SBBI 1994 Yearbook* (Chicago: Ibbotson Associates, 1995).

We call the capital allocation line provided by one-month T-bills and a broad index of common stocks the **capital market line** (CML). A passive strategy generates an investment opportunity set that is represented by the CML.

How reasonable is it for an investor to pursue a passive strategy? Of course, we cannot answer such a question without comparing the strategy to the costs and benefits accruing to an active portfolio strategy. Some thoughts are relevant at this point, however.

First, the alternative active strategy is not free. Whether you choose to invest the time and cost to acquire the information needed to generate an optimal active portfolio of risky assets, or whether you delegate the task to a professional who will charge a fee, construction of an active portfolio is more expensive than a passive one. The passive portfolio requires only small commissions on purchases of T-bills (or zero commissions if you purchase bills directly from the government) and management fees to a mutual fund company that offers a market index fund to the public. Vanguard, for example, operates the Index Trust 500 Portfolio that mimics the S&P 500 index. It purchases shares of the firms constituting the S&P 500 in proportion to the market values of the outstanding equity of each firm, and therefore essentially replicates the S&P 500 index. The fund thus duplicates the performance of this market index. It has one of the lowest operating expenses (as a percentage of assets) of all mutual stock funds precisely because it requires minimal managerial effort.

A second reason to pursue a passive strategy is the free-rider benefit. If there are many active, knowledgeable investors who quickly bid up prices of undervalued assets and force down prices of overvalued assets (by selling), we have to conclude that at any time most assets will be fairly priced. Therefore, a well-diversified portfolio of common stock will be a reasonably fair buy, and the passive strategy may not be inferior to that of the average active investor. (We will explain this assumption and provide a more comprehensive analysis of the relative success of passive strategies in later chapters.) Indeed, the nearby box shows that passive index funds have become quite popular investments in the last few years.

To summarize, however, a passive strategy involves investment in two passive portfolios: virtually risk-free short-term T-bills (or, alternatively, a money market fund), and a fund of common stocks that mimics a broad market index. The capital allocation line representing such a strategy is called the *capital market line*. Historically, based on 1926 to 1993 data, the passive risky portfolio offered an average risk premium of 8.6% and a standard deviation of 20.9%, resulting in a reward-to-variability ratio of .41. Passive investors allocate their investment budgets among instruments according to their degree of risk aversion.

We can use our analysis to deduce a typical investor's risk-aversion parameter. In 1993, the total market value of the S&P 500 stocks was about four times as large as the market value of all outstanding T-bills of less than six months' maturity. If we ignore all other assets (e.g., long-term bonds and real estate), and pretend that all investors followed a passive strategy, then the average investor's position in the risky asset (the S&P 500) was

$$y = \frac{4}{1+4} = .8$$

MORE WAYS TO WIN IN INDEX FUNDS

This may be the decade of the equity index fund. Once the exclusive preserve of institutional investors who wanted to match the performance of the stock market, such funds in increasing numbers now vie for the dollars of individuals. Since 1991, three important new stock indexes and dozens of index funds have appeared; according to Lipper Analytical Services, the retail segment of the business currently represents some $16 billion in assets.

Investing in index funds makes Mr. Spock-like sense. Pick any other kind of stock fund: The odds are less than fifty–fifty that it will beat the market over time, given the market's natural efficiency. Factor in the fund's administrative expenses, transaction costs, and perhaps a sales load. What is your chance of making money now?

Index funds, by contrast, win by being modest. They strive merely to replicate the stock market's performance, as judged by everyday Wall Street measures such as Standard & Poor's 500-stock index or the Russell 2000 index of small stocks. Each fund maintains a portfolio that closely matches the composition of its index; costs stay low because managers don't run up transaction expenses in trying to beat the market. And returns? Take a look at the oldest index fund available to individuals, the Vanguard Index Trust 500. Launched in 1976 and modeled on the S&P 500, the fund has returned 15.7% per year over the past decade. That's just under the 16.2% average annual return of the index itself—and far ahead of the 13.1% annual compound return for the typical growth and income fund.

The most popular index funds are those that match the S&P 500; they number in the dozens. Before leaping into one, however, consider that while the S&P 500 index represents about 70% of all publicly traded equity capital in the U.S., it is strongly influenced by the performance of the big guys, including struggling behemoths like IBM and Sears Roebuck.

Investors who don't want to miss out on the surges in small stocks, yet seek to diversify broadly, should peg their money to the Wilshire 5000. It actually represents some 6,000 stocks, including the S&P 500. Vanguard's Total Stock Market portfolio tracks the index, which beat the S&P 500 with a 9% return in 1992.

Equity Index Funds	Assets In Millions	Total Return 1992	Total Return 1987–92
Peoples S&P MidCap Index Fund Matches S&P MidCap 400	$ 55.8	11.9%	N.A.*
Vanguard 500 Portfolio Matches S&P 500	$6,872.4	18.2%	106.5%
Vanguard Total Stock Market Portfolio Matches Wilshire 5000	$ 299.0	8.9%	106.2%†
Vanguard Small Cap Stock Fund Matches Russell 2000	$ 293.7	18.2%	40.5%‡
Colonial International Equity Index Trust Matches EAFE	$ 7.1	−11.6%	5.3%

*Fund began in 6/91.
†Fund began in 4/92. Performance results are calculated from Vanguard's Extended Market Portfolio and 500 Portfolio.
‡Since 12/89.
Source: Lipper Analytical Services.

Source: Susan E. Kuhn, "More Ways to Win in Index Funds," *Fortune*, February 22, 1993, p. 27.

What degree of risk aversion must investors have for this portfolio to be optimal?

Assuming that the average investor uses the historical average risk premium (8.6%) and standard deviation (20.9%) to forecast future return and standard deviation, and noting that the weight in the risky portfolio was .80, we can work out the average investor's risk tolerance as follows:

$$y^* = \frac{E(r_M) - r_f}{.01 \times A\sigma_M^2}$$
$$= .8$$
$$= \frac{8.6}{.01 \times A \times 20.9^2}$$

which implies a coefficient of risk aversion of

$$A = \frac{8.6}{.01 \times .8 \times 20.9^2} = 2.46$$

This is, of course, mere speculation. We have assumed without basis that the average 1993 investor held the naive view that historical average rates of return and standard deviations are the best estimates of expected rates of return and risk, looking to the future. To the extent that in 1993 the average investor took advantage of contemporary information in addition to simple historical data, our estimate of $A = 2.46$ would be an unjustified inference. Nevertheless, a broad range of studies, taking into account the full range of available assets, places the degree of risk aversion for the representative investor in the range of 2.0 to 4.0.[6]

CONCEPT CHECK

Question 5. Suppose that expectations about the S&P 500 index and the T-bill rate are the same as they were in 1993, but you find that today a greater proportion is invested in T-bills than in 1993. What can you conclude about the change in risk tolerance over the years since 1993?

SUMMARY

1. Shifting funds from the risky portfolio to the risk-free asset is the simplest way to reduce risk. Other methods involve diversification of the risky portfolio and hedging. We take up these methods in later chapters.
2. T-bills provide a perfectly risk-free asset in nominal terms only. Nevertheless, the standard deviation of real rates on short-term T-bills is small compared to that of other assets such as long-term bonds and common stocks, so for the purpose of our analysis we consider T-bills as the risk-free asset. Money market funds hold, in addition to T-bills, short-term relatively safe obligations such as CP and CDs. These entail some default risk, but again the additional risk is small relative to most other risky assets. For convenience, we often refer to money market funds as risk-free assets.
3. An investor's risky portfolio (the risky asset) can be characterized by its reward-to-variability ratio, $S = [E(r_P) - r_f]/\sigma_P$. This ratio is also the slope of the CAL, the line that, when graphed, goes from the risk-free asset through the risky asset. All combinations of the risky asset and the risk-free asset lie on this line. Other things equal, an investor would prefer a steeper-sloping CAL, because that means higher expected return for any level of risk. If the borrowing rate is greater than the lending rate, the CAL will be "kinked" at the point of the risky asset.

---

[6] See, for example, I. Friend and M. Blume, "The Demand for Risky Assets," *American Economic Review* 64 (1974) or S. J. Grossman and R. J. Shiller, "The Determinants of the Variability of Stock Market Prices," *American Economic Review* 71 (1981).

4. The investor's degree of risk aversion is characterized by the slope of his or her indifference curve. Indifference curves show, at any level of expected return and risk, the required risk premium for taking on one additional percentage of standard deviation. More risk-averse investors have steeper indifference curves; that is, they require a greater risk premium for taking on more risk.

5. The optimal position, y^*, in the risky asset, is proportional to the risk premium and inversely proportional to the variance and degree of risk aversion:

$$y^* = \frac{E(r_P) - r_f}{.01A\sigma_P^2}$$

Graphically, this portfolio represents the point at which the indifference curve is tangent to the CAL.

6. A passive investment strategy disregards security analysis, targeting instead the risk-free asset and a broad portfolio of risky assets such as the S&P 500 stock portfolio. If in 1993 investors took the mean historical return and standard deviation of the S&P 500 as proxies for its expected return and standard deviation, then the market values of outstanding T-bills and the S&P 500 stocks would imply a degree of risk aversion of about $A = 2.46$ for the average investor. This is in line with other studies, which estimate typical risk aversion in the range of 2.0 through 4.0.

Key Terms

Capital allocation decision
Asset allocation decision
Security selection decision
Risky asset
Complete portfolio
Risk-free asset
Capital allocation line
Reward-to-variability ratio
Passive strategy
Capital market line

Selected Readings

The classic article describing the asset allocation choice, whereby investors choose the optimal fraction of their wealth to place in risk-free assets, is:

Tobin, James. "Liquidity Preference as Behavior Towards Risk." *Review of Economic Studies* 25 (February 1958).

Practitioner-oriented approaches to asset allocation may be found in:

Maginn, John L., and Donald L. Tuttle. *Managing Investment Portfolios: A Dynamic Process.* 2nd ed. New York: Warren, Gorham, & Lamont, 1990.

Problems

You manage a risky portfolio with an expected rate of return of 17% and a standard deviation of 27%. The T-bill rate is 7%.

1. Your client chooses to invest 70% of a portfolio in your fund and 30% in a T-bill money market fund. What is the expected value and standard deviation of the rate of return on your client's portfolio?

2. Suppose that your risky portfolio includes the following investments in the given proportions:

   Stock A: 27%
   Stock B: 33%
   Stock C: 40%

   What are the investment proportions of your client's overall portfolio, including the position in T-bills?
3. What is the reward-to-variability ratio (S) of your risky portfolio? Your client's?
4. Draw the CAL of your portfolio on an expected return–standard deviation diagram. What is the slope of the CAL? Show the position of your client on your fund's CAL.
5. Suppose that your client decides to invest in your portfolio a proportion y of the total investment budget so that the overall portfolio will have an expected rate of return of 15%.
   a. What is the proportion y?
   b. What are your client's investment proportions in your three stocks and the T-bill fund?
   c. What is the standard deviation of the rate of return on your client's portfolio?
6. Suppose that your client prefers to invest in your fund a proportion y that maximizes the expected return on the overall portfolio subject to the constraint that the overall portfolio's standard deviation will not exceed 20%.
   a. What is the investment proportion, y?
   b. What is the expected rate of return on the overall portfolio?
7. Your client's degree of risk aversion is $A = 3.5$.
   a. What proportion, y, of the total investment should be invested in your fund?
   b. What is the expected value and standard deviation of the rate of return on your client's optimized portfolio?

You estimate that a passive portfolio, that is, one invested in a risky portfolio that mimics the S&P 500 stock index, yields an expected rate of return of 13% with a standard deviation of 25%.

8. Draw the CML and your funds' CAL on an expected return–standard deviation diagram.
   a. What is the slope of the CML?
   b. Characterize in one short paragraph the advantage of your fund over the passive fund.
9. Your client ponders whether to switch the 70% that is invested in your fund to the passive portfolio.
   a. Explain to your client the disadvantage of the switch.
   b. Show your client the maximum fee you could charge (as a percentage of the investment in your fund deducted at the end of the year) that would still leave the client at least as well off investing in your fund as in the passive

one. (Hint: The fee will lower the slope of your client's CAL by reducing the expected return net of the fee.)

10. Consider the client in question 7 with $A = 3.5$
    a. If the client chose to invest in the passive portfolio, what proportion, y, would be selected?
    b. What fee (percentage of the investment in your fund, deducted at the end of the year) can you charge to make the client indifferent between your fund and the passive strategy?
11. Look at the data in Table 6.1 on the average risk premium of the S&P 500 over T-bills, and the standard deviation of that risk premium. Suppose that the S&P 500 is your risky portfolio.
    a. If your risk-aversion coefficient is 4 and you believe that the entire 1926–1993 period is representative of future expected performance, what fraction of your portfolio should be allocated to T-bills and what fraction to equity?
    b. What if you believe that the 1977–1993 period is representative?
    c. What do you conclude upon comparing your answers to (*a*) and (*b*)?
12. What do you think would happen to the expected return on stocks if investors perceived higher volatility in the equity market? Relate your answer to equation 6.3.
13. Consider the following information about the risky portfolio that you manage, and a risk-free asset: $E(r_P) = 11\%$, $\sigma_P = 15\%$, $r_f = 5\%$.
    a. Your client wants to invest a proportion of her total investment budget in your risky fund to provide an expected rate of return on her overall or complete portfolio equal to 8 percent. What proportion should she invest in the risky portfolio, P, and what proportion in the risk-free asset?
    b. What will be the standard deviation of the rate of return on her portfolio?
    c. Your other client wants the highest return possible subject to the constraint that you limit his standard deviation to be no more than 12%. Which client is more risk averse?

14. The change from a straight to a kinked capital allocation line is a result of the:*
    a. Reward-to-variability ratio increasing.
    b. Borrowing rate exceeding the lending rate.
    c. Investors risk tolerance decreasing.
    d. Increase in the portfolio proportion of the risk-free asset.

*Reprinted, with permission, from the Level I 1991 *CFA Study Guide*.

Problems 15–18 are more advanced. Suppose that the borrowing rate that your client faces is 9%. Continue to assume that the S&P 500 Index has an expected return of 13% and standard deviation of 25%.

15. Draw a diagram of the CML your client faces with the borrowing constraints. Superimpose on it two sets of indifference curves, one for a client who will choose to borrow, and one who will invest in both the index fund and a money market fund.

16. What is the range of risk aversion for which the client will neither borrow nor lend, that is, for which $y = 1$?

17. Solve problems 15 and 16 for a client who uses your fund rather than an index fund.

18. Amend your solution to problem 10(*b*) for clients in the risk-aversion range that you found in problem 16.

19. You manage an equity fund with an expected risk premium of 10% and an expected standard deviation of 14%. The rate on Treasury bills is 6%. Your client chooses to invest $60,000 of her portfolio in your equity fund and $40,000 in a T-bill money market fund. What is the expected return and standard deviation of return on your client's portfolio?*

	Expected Return	Standard Deviation of Return
a.	8.4%	8.4%
b.	8.4%	14.0%
c.	12.0%	8.4%
d.	12.0%	14.0%

20. What is the reward-to-variability ratio for the *equity fund* in question 19?*

a. 0.29.
b. 1.00.
c. 1.19.
d. 1.91.

*Reprinted, with permission, from the Level I 1993 *CFA Study Guide*.

Chapter 7

Optimal Risky Portfolios

IN CHAPTER 6 WE DISCUSSED THE CAPITAL ALLOCATION DECISION. That decision governs how an investor chooses between risk-free assets and "the" optimal portfolio of risky assets. This chapter explains how to construct that optimal risky portfolio.

We begin at the simplest level, with a discussion of how diversification can reduce the variability of portfolio returns. After establishing this basic point, we examine efficient diversification strategies at the asset allocation and security selection levels. We start with a simple, restricted example of asset allocation that excludes the risk-free asset. To that effect we use two risky mutual funds: a long-term bond fund and a stock fund. With this example we investigate the relationship between investment proportions and the resulting portfolio expected return and standard deviation. We then add a risk-free asset, for example, T-bills, to the menu of assets and determine the optimal asset allocation. We do so by combining the principles of optimal allocation between risky assets and risk-free assets (from Chapter 6) with the risky portfolio construction methodology.

Moving from asset allocation to security selection we first generalize our discussion of restricted asset allocation (with only two risky assets) to a universe of many risky securities. This generalization relies on the celebrated Markowitz portfolio selection model,[1] which identifies the set of efficient stock portfolios from the available universe of securities. Proceeding to capital allocation, we show how the best attainable capital allocation line emerges from the Markowitz algorithm. We pause to explain why portfolio optimization is often conducted in two stages, asset allocation and security selection, and discuss the potential inefficiency that may result from separating the asset allocation decision from security selection.

[1] Harry Markowitz, *Portfolio Selection: Efficient Diversification of Investments* (New York: John Wiley and Sons, 1959).

Finally, in the last two appendices, we examine common fallacies regarding the power of diversification in the contexts of the insurance principle and the notion of time diversification.

7.1 Diversification and Portfolio Risk

Suppose that your risky portfolio is composed of only one stock, Digital Equipment Corporation. What would be the sources of risk to this "portfolio?" You might think of two broad sources of uncertainty. First, there is the risk that comes from conditions in the general economy, such as the business cycle, the inflation rate, interest rates, and exchange rates. None of these macroeconomic factors can be predicted with certainty, and all affect the rate of return that Digital stock eventually will provide. In addition to these macroeconomic factors there are firm-specific influences, such as Digital's success in research and development, and personnel changes. These factors affect Digital without noticeably affecting other firms in the economy.

Now consider a naive **diversification** strategy, in which you include additional securities in your risky portfolio. For example, suppose that you place half of your risky portfolio in Exxon, leaving the other half in Digital. What should happen to portfolio risk? To the extent that the firm-specific influences on the two stocks differ, we should reduce portfolio risk. For example, when oil prices fall, hurting Exxon, computer prices might rise, helping Digital. The two effects are offsetting, and stabilize portfolio return.

But why end diversification at only two stocks? If we diversify into many more securities, we continue to spread out our exposure to firm-specific factors, and portfolio volatility should continue to fall. Ultimately, however, even if we include a large number of risky securities in our portfolio, we cannot avoid risk altogether. To the extent that virtually all securities are affected by the common macroeconomic factors, we cannot eliminate our exposure to these risk sources. For example, if all stocks are affected by the business cycle, we cannot avoid exposure to business cycle risk no matter how many stocks we hold.

When all risk is firm-specific, as in Figure 7.1**A,** diversification can reduce risk to arbitrarily low levels. The reason is that with all risk sources independent, and with the portfolio spread across many securities, the exposure to any particular source of risk is reduced to a negligible level. This is just an application of the well-known law of averages. The reduction of risk to very low levels in the case of independent risk sources is sometimes called the **insurance principle,** because of the common belief that an insurance company depends on the risk reduction achieved through diversification when it writes many policies insuring against many independent sources of risk, each policy being a small part of the company's overall portfolio. (See Appendix B to this chapter for a discussion of the insurance principle.)

When common sources of risk affect all firms, however, even extensive diversification cannot eliminate risk. In Figure 7.1**B,** portfolio standard deviation falls as the number of securities increases, but it cannot be reduced to zero.[2] The risk that remains even

[2] The interested reader can find a more rigorous demonstration of these points in Appendix A. That discussion, however, relies on tools developed later in this chapter.

Figure 7.1

Portfolio risk as a function of the number of stocks in the portfolio

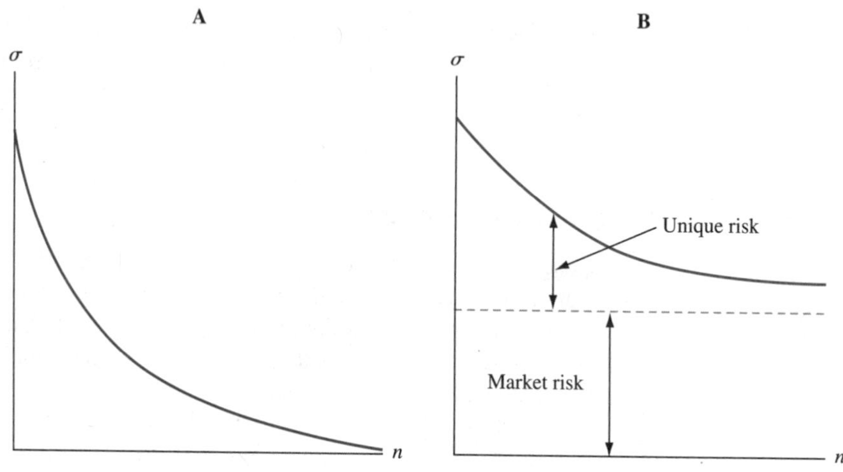

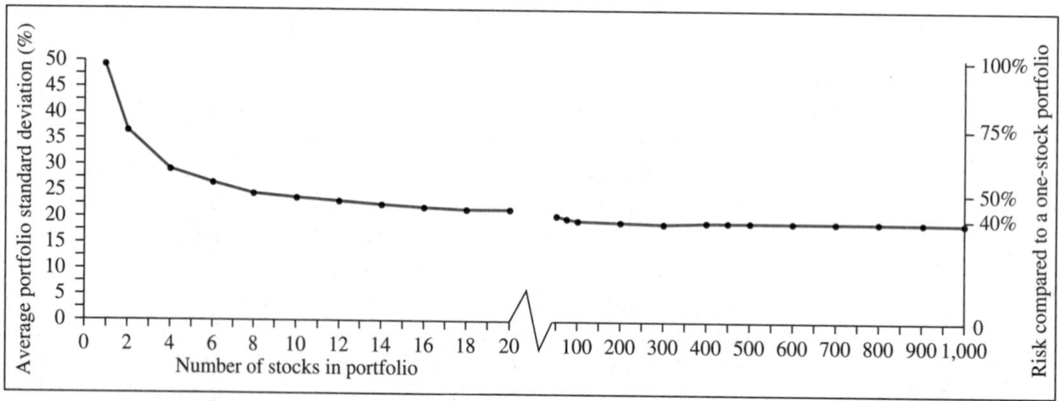

Figure 7.2

Portfolio diversification. The average standard deviation of returns of portfolios composed of only one stock was 49.2%. The average portfolio risk fell rapidly as the number of stocks included in the portfolio increased. In the limit, portfolio risk could be reduced to only 19.2%.

Source: Elton and Gruber, *Modern Portfolio Theory and Investment Analysis,* 2nd ed. (New York: John Wiley and Sons, 1989), p. 35; adapted by Meir Statman, "How Many Stocks Make a Diversified Portfolio," *Journal of Financial and Quantitative Analysis* 22 (September 1987).

after extensive diversification is called **market risk,** risk that is attributable to marketwide risk sources. Such risk is also called **systematic risk,** or **nondiversifiable risk.** In contrast, the risk that *can* be eliminated by diversification is called **unique risk, firm-specific risk, nonsystematic risk,** or **diversifiable risk.**

This analysis is borne out by empirical studies. Figure 7.2 shows the effect of portfolio diversification, using data on NYSE stocks.[3] The figure shows the average standard deviation of equally weighted portfolios constructed by selecting stocks at random

[3]Meir Statman, "How Many Stocks Make a Diversified Portfolio," *Journal of Financial and Quantitative Analysis* 22 (September 1987).

Table 7.1 Descriptive Statistics for Two Mutual Funds

	Debt		Equity
Expected return, $E(r)$	8%		13%
Standard deviation, σ	12%		20%
Covariance, $\text{Cov}(r_D, r_E)$		72	
Correlation coefficient, ρ_{DE}		.30	

as a function of the number of stocks in the portfolio. On average, portfolio risk does fall with diversification, but the power of diversification to reduce risk is limited by systematic or common sources of risk.

7.2 Portfolios of Two Risky Assets

In the last section we analyzed naive diversification, examining the risk of equally weighted portfolios of several securities. It is time now to study efficient diversification, whereby we construct risky portfolios to provide the lowest possible risk for any given level of expected return.

Constructing the optimal risky portfolio is a complicated statistical task. The *principles* we follow, however, are the same as those used to construct a portfolio from two risky assets only. We will analyze this easier process first and then backtrack a bit to see how we can generalize the technique to more realistic cases.

Assume for this purpose that an investor is limited to two assets. To benefit from diversification, our investor chooses for the first asset shares in a mutual fund that maintains a broad portfolio of long-term debt securities (D), and chooses for the second asset shares in a mutual fund that specializes in equities (E). The parameters of the joint probability distribution of returns is shown in Table 7.1.

A proportion denoted by w_D is invested in the bond fund, and the remainder, $1 - w_D$, denoted w_E, is invested in the stock fund. The rate of return on this portfolio will be

$$r_p = w_D r_D + w_E r_E$$

where r_p stands for the rate of return on the portfolio, r_D the rate of return on the debt fund, and r_E the rate of return on the equity fund.

As we noted in Chapter 5, the expected rate of return on the portfolio is a weighted average of expected returns on the component securities with portfolio proportions as weights:

$$E(r_p) = w_D E(r_D) + w_E E(r_E) \tag{7.1}$$

The variance of the two-asset portfolio (Rule 5 of Chapter 5) is

$$\sigma_p^2 = w_D^2 \sigma_D^2 + w_E^2 \sigma_E^2 + 2 w_D w_E \text{Cov}(r_D, r_E) \tag{7.2}$$

The first observation is that the variance of the portfolio, unlike the expected return, is *not* a weighted average of the individual asset variances. To understand the formula

Table 7.2 Bordered Covariance Matrix

	Covariances	
Portfolio Weights	w_D	w_E
w_D	σ_D^2	$\text{Cov}(r_D,r_E)$
w_E	$\text{Cov}(r_E,r_D)$	σ_E^2

for the portfolio variance more clearly, recall that the covariance of a variable with itself (in this case the variable is the uncertain rate of return) is the variance of that variable; that is

$$\begin{aligned}\text{Cov}\,(r_D,r_D) &= \sum_{\text{scenarios}} \Pr(\text{scenario})[r_D - E(r_D)][r_D - E(r_D)] \\ &= \sum_{\text{scenarios}} \Pr(\text{scenario})[r_D - E(r_D)]^2 \\ &= \sigma_D^2\end{aligned}$$

Therefore, another way to write the variance of the portfolio is as follows:

$$\sigma_p^2 = w_D w_D \text{Cov}(r_D,r_D) + w_E w_E \text{Cov}(r_E,r_E) + 2w_D w_E \text{Cov}(r_D,r_E)$$

In words, the variance of the portfolio is a weighted sum of covariances, where each weight is the product of the portfolio proportions of the pair of assets in the covariance term.

Why do we double the covariance between the two *different* assets in the last term of equation 7.2? This should become clear in the covariance matrix, Table 7.2, which is bordered by the portfolio weights.

The diagonal (from top left to bottom right) of the covariance matrix is made up of the asset variances. The off-diagonal elements are the covariances. Note that

$$\text{Cov}(r_D,r_E) = \text{Cov}(r_E,r_D)$$

so that the matrix is symmetric. To compute the portfolio variance, we sum over each term in the matrix, first multiplying it by the product of the portfolio proportions from the corresponding row and column. Thus, we have *one* term for each asset variance but twice the term for each covariance pair, because each covariance appears twice.

CONCEPT CHECK

Question 1.

a. Confirm that this simple rule for computing portfolio variance from the covariance matrix is consistent with equation 7.2

b. Consider a portfolio of three funds, *X, Y, Z*, with weights w_X, w_Y, and w_Z. Show that the portfolio variance is

$$w_X^2\sigma_X^2 + w_Y^2\sigma_Y^2 + w_Z^2\sigma_Z^2 + 2w_X w_Y \text{Cov}(r_X,r_Y) + 2w_X w_Z \text{Cov}(r_X,r_Z) + 2w_Y w_Z \text{Cov}(r_Y,r_Z)$$

As we discussed in Chapter 5, the portfolio variance is reduced if the covariance term is negative. This is the case in the use of hedge assets. It is important to recognize that even if the covariance term is positive, the portfolio standard deviation still is less than the weighted average of the individual security standard deviations, unless the two securities are perfectly positively correlated.

To see this, recall from Chapter 5, equation 5.5, that the covariance can be written as

$$\text{Cov}(r_D, r_E) = \rho_{DE}\sigma_D\sigma_E$$

Substituting into equation 7.2, we can rewrite the variance and standard deviation of the portfolio as

$$\sigma_p^2 = w_D^2\sigma_D^2 + w_E^2\sigma_E^2 + 2w_Dw_E\sigma_D\sigma_E\rho_{DE} \tag{7.3}$$

$$\sigma_p = \sqrt{\sigma_p^2} \tag{7.4}$$

You can see from this information that the covariance term adds the most to the portfolio variance when the correlation coefficient, ρ_{DE}, is highest, that is, when it equals 1—as it would in the case of perfect positive correlation. In this case the right-hand side of equation 7.3 is a perfect square, so it may be rewritten as follows:

$$\sigma_p^2 = (w_D\sigma_D + w_E\sigma_E)^2$$

or

$$\sigma_p = w_D\sigma_D + w_E\sigma_E$$

In other words, the standard deviation of the portfolio in the case of perfect positive correlation is just the weighted average of the component standard deviations. In all other cases the correlation coefficient is less than 1, making the portfolio standard deviation *less* than the weighted average of the component standard deviations.

We know already from Chapter 5 that a hedge asset reduces the portfolio variance. This algebraic exercise adds the additional insight that the standard deviation of a portfolio of assets is less than the weighted average of the component security standard deviations, even when the assets are positively correlated. Because the portfolio expected return is always the weighted average of its component expected returns, whereas its standard deviation is less than the weighted average of the component standard deviations, *portfolios of less than perfectly correlated assets always offer better risk–return opportunities than the individual component securities on their own.* The less correlation between the assets, the greater the gain in efficiency.

How low can portfolio standard deviation be? The lowest possible value of the correlation coefficient is −1, representing perfect negative correlation, in which case the portfolio variance is as follows[4]:

$$\sigma_p^2 = (w_D\sigma_D - w_E\sigma_E)^2$$

and the portfolio standard deviation is

[4]This expression also can be derived from equation 7.3. When $\rho_{DE} = -1$, equation 7.3 is a perfect square that can be factored as shown.

$$\sigma_p = \text{Absolute value } (w_D\sigma_D - w_E\sigma_E)$$

When $\rho = -1$, the investor has the opportunity of creating a perfectly hedged position. If the portfolio proportions are chosen as

$$w_D = \frac{\sigma_E}{\sigma_D + \sigma_E}$$

$$w_E = \frac{\sigma_D}{\sigma_D + \sigma_E} = 1 - w_D$$

the standard deviation of the portfolio will equal zero.[5]

Let us apply this analysis to the data of the bond and stock funds as presented in Table 7.1. Using these data, the formulas for the expected return, variance, and standard deviation of the portfolio are

$$E(r_p) = 8w_D + 13w_E \tag{7.5}$$

$$\sigma_p^2 = 12^2 w_D^2 + 20^2 w_E^2 + 2 \times 72 w_D w_E \tag{7.6}$$

$$\sigma_p = \sqrt{\sigma_P^2}$$

Now we are ready to experiment with different portfolio proportions to observe the effect on portfolio expected return and variance. Suppose we change the proportion invested in bonds. The effect on the portfolio's expected return is plotted in Figure 7.3. When the proportion invested in bonds varies from zero to 1 (so that the proportion in stock varies from 1 to zero), the portfolio expected return goes from 13% (the stock fund's expected return) to 8% (the expected return on bonds).

What happens to the right of this region, when $w_D > 1$ and $w_E < 0$? In this case portfolio strategy would be to sell the equity fund short and invest the proceeds of the short sale in the debt fund. This will decrease the expected return of the portfolio. For example, when $w_D = 2$ and $w_E = -1$, expected portfolio return falls to 3% [$2 \times 8 + (-1) \times 13$]. At this point the value of the bond fund in the portfolio is twice the net worth of the account. This extreme position is financed in part by short selling stocks equal in value to the portfolio's net worth.

The reverse happens when $w_D < 0$ and $w_E > 1$. This strategy calls for selling the bond fund short and using the proceeds to finance additional purchases of the equity fund.

Of course, varying investment proportions also has an effect on portfolio standard deviation. Table 7.3 presents portfolio standard deviations for different portfolio weights calculated from equations 7.3 and 7.4 for the assumed value of the correlation coefficient, .30, as well as for other values of ρ. Figure 7.4 shows the relationship between standard deviation and portfolio weights. Look first at the curve for $\rho_{DE} = .30$. The graph shows that as the portfolio weight in the equity fund increases from zero to 1, portfolio standard deviation first falls with the initial diversification from bonds into stocks, but then rises again as the portfolio becomes heavily concentrated in stocks, and

[5] It is possible to drive portfolio variance to zero with perfectly positively correlated assets as well, but this would require short sales.

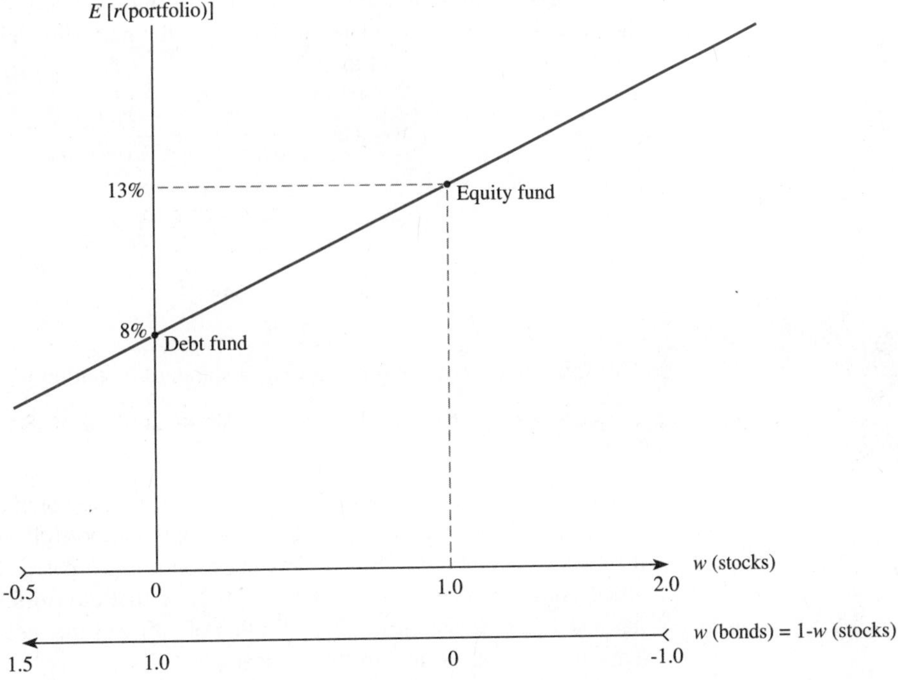

Figure 7.3 Portfolio expected return as a function of investment proportions

Table 7.3 Portfolio Standard Deviation as a Function of Investment Proportions

		Portfolio Standard Deviation for Given Correlation			
W_D	W_E	$\rho = -1$	$\rho = 0$	$\rho = 0.3$	$\rho = 1$
0	1.00	20.00%	20.00%	20.00%	20.00%
0.25	0.75	12.00	15.30	16.16	18.00
0.50	0.50	4.00	11.66	13.11	16.00
0.75	0.25	4.00	10.30	11.53	14.00
1.00	0	12.00	12.00	12.00	12.00
minimum σ_p		0.00	10.29	11.45	—
W_D at min σ_p		0.63	0.74	0.82	—

again is undiversified. This pattern will generally hold as long as the correlation coefficient between the funds is not too high. For a pair of assets with a large positive correlation of returns, the portfolio standard deviation will increase monotonically from the low-risk asset to the high-risk asset. Even in this case, however, there is a positive (if small) value of diversification.

What is the minimum level to which portfolio standard deviation can be held? For the parameter values stipulated in Table 7.1, the portfolio weights that solve this minimization problem turn out to be[6]:

$$\begin{aligned} w_{\text{Min}}(D) &= \frac{\sigma_E^2 - \text{Cov}(r_D, r_E)}{\sigma_D^2 + \sigma_E^2 - 2\text{Cov}(r_D, r_E)} \\ &= \frac{20^2 - 72}{12^2 + 20^2 - 2 \times 72} \\ &= .82 \\ w_{\text{Min}}(E) &= 1 - .82 \\ &= .18 \end{aligned} \tag{7.7}$$

This minimum variance portfolio has a standard deviation of

$$\begin{aligned} \sigma_{\text{Min}}(P) &= [.82^2 \times 12^2 + .18^2 \times 20^2 + 2 \times .82 \times .18 \times 72]^{1/2} \\ &= 11.45\% \end{aligned}$$

as indicated in the next-to-last line of Table 7.3 for the column $\rho = .30$.

The solid blue line in Figure 7.4 represents the portfolio standard deviation when $\rho = .30$ as a function of the investment proportions. It passes through the two undiversified portfolios of $w_D = 1$ and $w_E = 1$. Note that the **minimum-variance portfolio** has a standard deviation smaller than that of either of the individual component assets. This highlights the effect of diversification.

The other three lines in Figure 7.4 show how portfolio risk varies for other values of the correlation coefficient, holding the variances of each asset constant. These lines plot the values in the other three columns of Table 7.3.

The straight line connecting the undiversified portfolios of all bonds or all stocks, $w_D = 1$ or $w_E = 1$, demonstrates portfolio standard deviation with perfect positive correlation, $\rho = 1$. In this case there is no advantage from diversification, and the portfolio standard deviation is the simple weighted average of the component asset standard deviations.

The dotted curve below the $\rho = .30$ curve depicts portfolio risk for the case of uncorrelated assets, $\rho = 0$. With lower correlation between the two assets, diversification is more effective and portfolio risk is lower (at least when both assets are held in positive amounts). The minimum portfolio standard deviation when $\rho = 0$ is 10.29% (see Table 7.3), again lower than the standard deviation of either asset.

Finally, the upside-down triangular broken line illustrates the perfect hedge potential when the two assets are perfectly negatively correlated ($\rho = -1$). In this case the solution for the minimum-variance portfolio is

---

[6] This solution uses the minimization techniques of elementary calculus. Write out the expression for portfolio variance from equation 7.2, substitute $1 - w_D$ for w_E, differentiate the result with respect to w_D, set the derivative equal to zero, and solve for w_D. Alternatively, with a computer spreadsheet, you can obtain an accurate solution by generating a fine grid for Table 17.3 and observing the minimum.

Figure 7.4
Portfolio standard deviation as a function of investment proportions

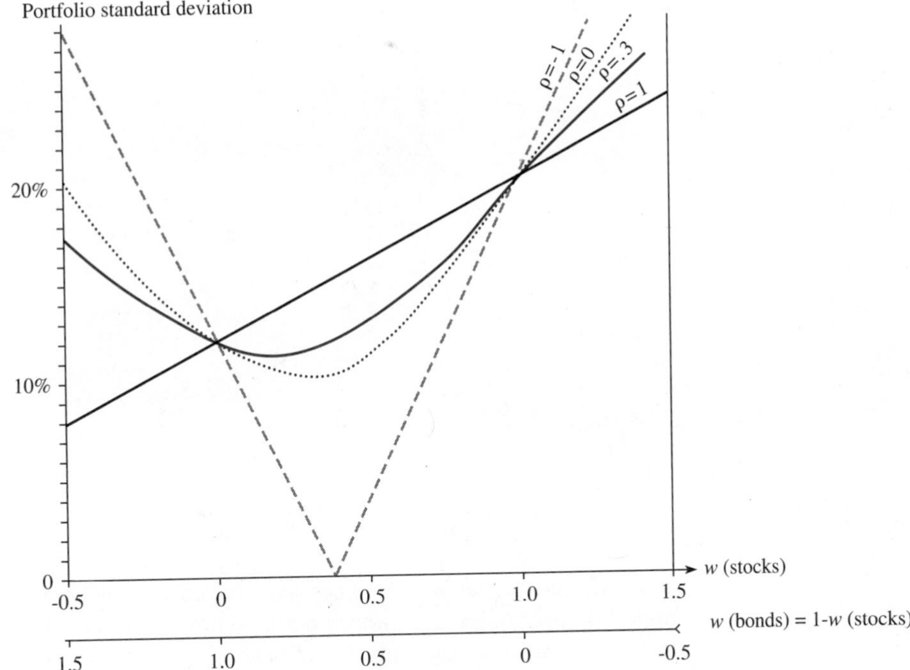

$$w_{\text{Min}}(D;\rho = -1) = \frac{\sigma_E}{\sigma_D + \sigma_E} = \frac{20}{12 + 20} = .625$$
$$w_{\text{Min}}(E;\rho = -1) = 1 - .625 = .375$$

and the portfolio variance (and standard deviation) is zero.

We can combine Figures 7.3 and 7.4 to demonstrate the relationship between the portfolio's level of risk (standard deviation) and the expected rate of return on that portfolio—given the parameters of the available assets. This is done in Figure 7.5. For any pair of investment proportions, w_D, w_E, we read the expected return from Figure 7.3 and the standard deviation from Figure 7.4. The resulting pairs of portfolio expected return and standard deviation are tabulated in Table 7.4 and plotted in Figure 7.5.

The solid blue line in Figure 7.5 shows the **portfolio opportunity set** for $\rho = .30$. We call it the portfolio opportunity set because it shows the combination of expected return and standard deviation of all the portfolios that can be constructed from the two available assets. The broken and dotted lines show the portfolio opportunity set for other values of the correlation coefficient. The line farthest to the right, which is the straight line connecting the undiversified portfolios, shows that there is no benefit from diversification when the correlation between the two assets is perfectly positive ($\rho = 1$). The opportunity set is not "pushed" to the northwest. The dotted line to the left of the solid blue curve shows that there is greater benefit from diversification when the correlation coefficient is zero than when it is positive.

Table 7.4 Portfolio Expected Returns and Standard Deviations with Various Correlation Coefficients

			Portfolio Standard Deviation for Given Correlation			
w_D	w_E	$E(r_p)$	$\rho = -1$	$\rho = 0$	$\rho = 0.3$	$\rho = 1$
0	1.00	13.00	20.00%	20.00%	20.00%	20.00%
0.25	0.75	11.75	12.00	15.30	16.16	18.00
0.50	0.50	10.50	4.00	11.66	13.11	16.00
0.75	0.25	9.25	4.00	10.30	11.53	14.00
1.00	0	8.00	12.00	12.00	12.00	12.00
			Minimum Variance Portfolio			
$w_D(\min)$			0.630	0.74	0.82	—
$E(r_p)$			9.875	9.32	8.90	—
σ_p			0.000	10.29	11.45	—

Finally, the broken $\rho = -1$ lines show the effect of perfect negative correlation. The portfolio opportunity set is linear, but now it offers a perfect hedging opportunity and the maximum advantage from diversification.

To summarize, although the expected rate of return of any portfolio is simply the weighted average of the asset expected returns, this is not true of the portfolio standard deviation. Potential benefits from diversification arise when correlation is less than perfectly positive. The lower the correlation coefficient, the greater the potential benefit of diversification. In the extreme case of perfect negative correlation, we have a perfect hedging opportunity and can construct a zero-variance portfolio.

Suppose now that an investor wishes to select the optimal portfolio from the opportunity set. The best portfolio will depend on risk aversion. Portfolios to the northeast in Figure 7.5 provide higher rates of return, but impose greater risk. The best trade-off among these choices is a matter of personal preference. Investors with greater risk aversion will prefer portfolios to the southwest, with lower expected return, but lower risk.[7]

CONCEPT CHECK Question 2. Compute and draw the portfolio opportunity set for the debt and equity funds when the correlation coefficient between them is $\rho = .25$.

[7] Given a level of risk aversion, one can determine the portfolio that provides the highest level of utility. Recall from Chapter 6 that we were able to describe the utility provided by a portfolio as a function of its expected return, $E(r_p)$, and its variance, σ_p^2, according to the relationship $U = E(r_p) - .005A\sigma_p^2$. The portfolio mean and variance are determined by the portfolio weights in the two funds, w_E and w_D, according to equations 7.1 and 7.2. Using those equations, one can show using elementary calculus that the optimal investment proportions in the two funds are:

$$w_D = \frac{E(r_D) - E(r_E) + .01A(\sigma_D^2 - \sigma_D\sigma_E\rho_{DE})}{.01A(\sigma_D^2 + \sigma_E^2 - 2\sigma_D\sigma_E\rho_{DE})}$$

$$w_E = 1 - w_D$$

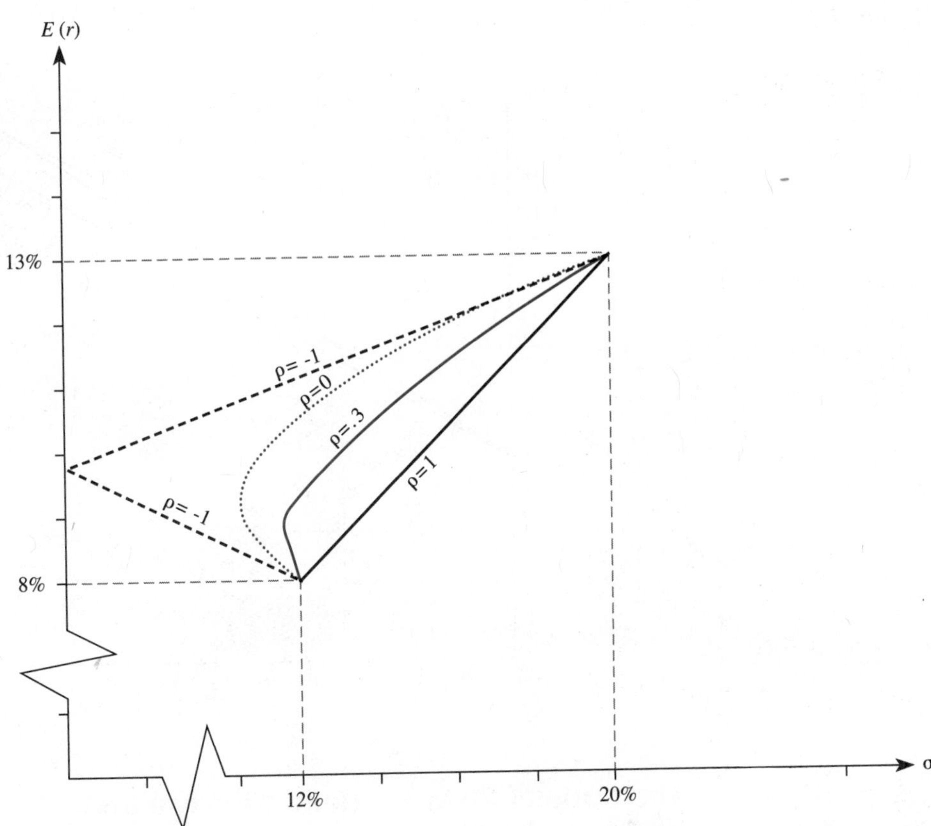

Figure 7.5
Portfolio expected return as a function of standard deviation

7.3 Asset Allocation with Stocks, Bonds, and Bills

In the previous chapter we examined the simplest asset allocation decision, that involving the choice of how much of the portfolio to leave in risk-free money market securities versus in a risky portfolio. We simply assumed that the risky portfolio was comprised of a stock and bond fund in given proportions. Of course, investors need to decide on the proportion of their portfolios to allocate to the stock versus the bond market. This, too, is an asset allocation decision. As the nearby box emphasizes, most investment professionals recognize that "the really critical decision is how to divvy up your money among stocks, bonds and supersafe investments such as Treasury bills."

In the last section, we derived the properties of portfolios formed by mixing two risky assets. Given this background, we now reintroduce the choice of the third, risk-free portfolio. This will allow us to complete the basic problem of asset allocation across the three key asset classes: stocks, bonds, and risk-free money market securities. Once you understand this case, it will be easy to see how portfolios of many risky securities might best be constructed.

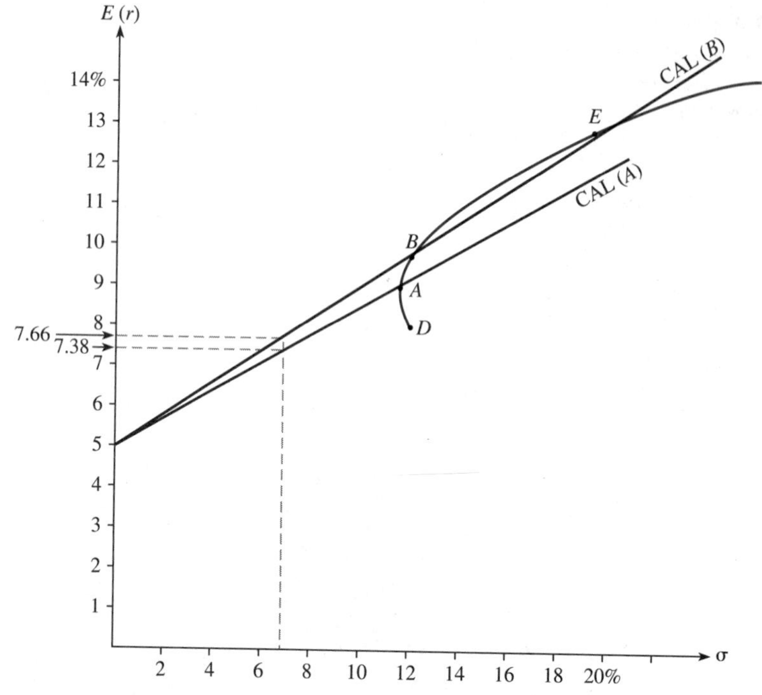

Figure 7.6 The opportunity set of the debt and equity funds and two feasible CALs.

The Optimal Risky Portfolio with Two Risky Assets and a Risk-Free Asset

What if our risky assets are still confined to the bond and stock funds, but now we can also invest in risk-free T-bills yielding 5%? We start with a graphical solution. Figure 7.6 shows the opportunity set generated from the joint probability distribution of the bond and stock funds, using the data from Table 7.1.

Two possible capital allocation lines (CALs) are drawn from the risk-free rate ($r_f =$ 5%) to two feasible portfolios. The first possible CAL is drawn through the minimum-variance portfolio A, which is invested 82% in bonds and 18% in stocks (equation 7.7). Portfolio A's expected return is $E(r_A) = 8.90\%$, and its standard deviation is $\sigma_A =$ 11.45%. With a T-bill rate of $r_f = 5\%$, the **reward-to-variability ratio,** which is the slope of the CAL combining T-bills and the minimum-variance portfolios, is

$$S_A = \frac{E(r_A) - r_f}{\sigma_A}$$

$$= \frac{8.9 - 5}{11.45} = .34$$

Now consider the CAL that uses portfolio B instead of A. Portfolio B invests 70% in bonds and 30% in stocks. Its expected return is 9.5% (giving it a risk premium of 4.5%), and its standard deviation is 11.70%. Thus, the reward-to- variability ratio on the CAL that is generated using Portfolio B is

Recipe for Successful Investing: First, Mix Assets Well

First things first.

If you want dazzling investment results, don't start your day foraging for hot stocks and stellar mutual funds. Instead, say investment advisers, the really critical decision is how to divvy up your money among stocks, bonds, and supersafe investments such as Treasury bills.

In Wall Street lingo, this mix of investments is called your asset allocation. "The asset-allocation choice is the first and most important decision," says William Droms, a finance professor at Georgetown University. "How much you have in [the stock market] really drives your results."

"You cannot get [stock market] returns from a bond portfolio, no matter how good your security selection is or how good the bond managers you use," says William John Mikus, a managing director of Financial Design, a Los Angeles investment adviser.

For proof, Mr. Mikus cites studies such as the 1991 analysis done by Gary Brinson, Brian Singer and Gilbert Beebower. That study, which looked at the 10-year results for 82 large pension plans, found that a plan's asset-allocation policy explained 91.5% of the return earned.

Designing a Portfolio

Because your asset mix is so important, some mutual fund companies now offer free services to help investors design their portfolios.

Gerald Perritt, editor of the Mutual Fund Letter, a Chicago newsletter, says you should vary your mix of assets depending on how long you plan to invest. The further you are from your investment goal, the more you should have in stocks. The closer you get, the more you should lean toward bonds and money-market instruments, such as Treasury bills. Bonds and money-market instruments may generate lower returns than stocks. But for those who need money in the near future, conservative investments make more sense, because there's less chance of suffering a devastating short-term loss.

Summarizing Your Assets

"One of the most important things people can do is summarize all their assets on one piece of paper and figure out their asset allocation," says Mr. Pond.

Once you've settled on a mix of stocks and bonds, you should seek to maintain the target percentages, says Mr. Pond. To do that, he advises figuring out your asset allocation once every six months. Because of a stock-market plunge, you could find that stocks are now a far smaller part of your portfolio than you envisaged. At such a time, you should put more into stocks and lighten up on bonds.

When devising portfolios, some investment advisers consider gold and real estate in addition to the usual trio of stocks, bonds and money-market instruments. Gold and real estate give "you a hedge against hyperinflation," says Mr. Droms. "But real estate is better than gold, because you'll get better long-run returns."

Source: Jonathan Clements, "Recipe for Successful Investing: First, Mix Assets Well," *The Wall Street Journal,* October 6, 1993. Reprinted by permission of *The Wall Street Journal,*

$$S_B = \frac{9.5 - 5}{11.7} = .38$$

which is higher than the reward-to-variability ratio of the CAL that we obtained using the minimum-variance portfolio and T-bills.

If the CAL that uses Portfolio B has a better reward- to-variability ratio than the CAL that uses Portfolio A, then for any level of risk (standard deviation) that an investor is willing to bear, the expected return is higher with Portfolio B. Figure 7.6 reflects this in showing that the CAL for Portfolio B is above the CAL for Portfolio A. In this sense, Portfolio B dominates Portfolio A.

In fact, the difference between the reward-to-variability ratios is

$$S_B - S_A = .04$$

This means we get four extra basis points expected return with CAL_B for each percentage point increase in standard deviation.

Look at Figure 7.6 again. If we are willing to bear a standard deviation of $\sigma_p = 7\%$, we can achieve a 7.38% expected return with the CAL of Portfolio A:

$$\begin{aligned} E(r_p)(\text{CAL}_A; \sigma_p = 7\%) &= r_f + 7S_A \\ &= 5 + 7 \times .34 = 7.38\% \end{aligned}$$

With the CAL of Portfolio B, we get expected return of 7.66%:

$$\begin{aligned} E(r_p)(\text{CAL}_B; \sigma_p = 7\%) &= r_f + 7S_B \\ &= 5 + 7 \times .38 = 7.66\% \end{aligned}$$

This is a difference of $.04 \times 7 = .28\%$, or 28 basis points.

But why stop at Portfolio B? We can continue to ratchet the CAL upward until it ultimately reaches the point of tangency with the investment opportunity set. This must yield the CAL with the highest feasible reward-to-variability ratio. Therefore the tangency portfolio, P, drawn in Figure 7.7, is the optimal risky portfolio to mix with T-bills. We can read the expected return and standard deviation of Portfolio P from the graph in Figure 7.7.

$$\begin{aligned} E(r_P) &= 11\% \\ \sigma_P &= 14.2\% \end{aligned}$$

In practice, we obtain the solution to this problem with a computer program. We can describe the process briefly, however.

The objective is to find the weights w_D, w_E that result in the highest slope of the CAL (i.e., the weights that result in the risky portfolio with the highest reward-to-variability ratio). Therefore, the objective is to maximize the slope of the CAL for any possible portfolio, p. Thus, our *objective function* is the slope that we have called S_p:

$$S_p = \frac{E(r_p) - r_f}{\sigma_p}$$

For the portfolio with two risky assets, the expected return and standard deviation of Portfolio p are

$$\begin{aligned} E(r_p) &= w_D E(r_D) + w_E E(r_E) \\ &= 8w_D + 13w_E \\ \sigma_p &= [w_D^2\sigma_D^2 + w_E^2\sigma_E^2 + 2w_D w_E \text{Cov}(r_D, r_E)]^{1/2} \\ &= [144w_D^2 + 400w_E^2 + 2 \times 72 w_D w_E]^{1/2} \end{aligned}$$

When we maximize the objective function, S_p, we have to satisfy the constraint that the portfolio weights sum to one (100%), that is, $w_D + w_E = 1$. Therefore, we solve a mathematical problem formally written as

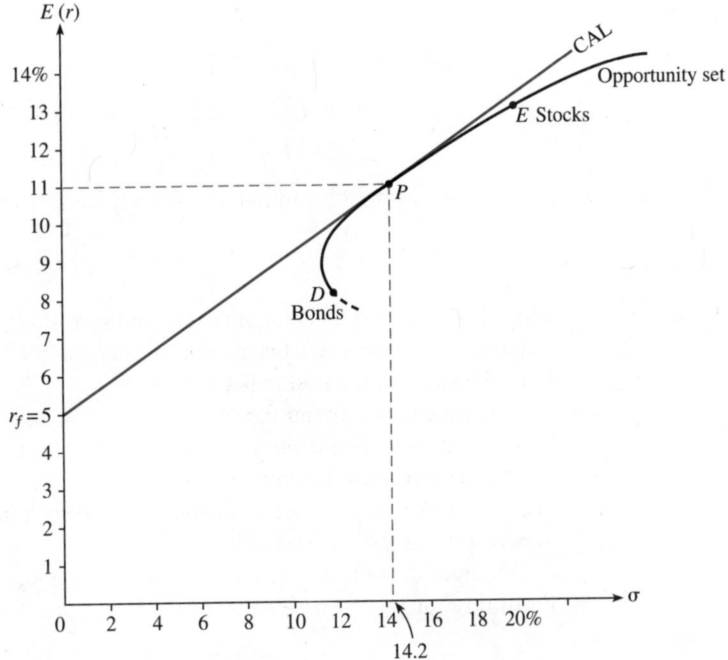

Figure 7.7
The opportunity set of the debt and equity funds with the optimal CAL and the optimal risky portfolio

$$\operatorname*{Max}_{w_i} S_p = \frac{E(r_p) - r_f}{\sigma_p}$$

Subject to $\Sigma w_i = 1$. This is a standard problem in calculus.

In the case of two risky assets, the solution for the weights of the **optimal risky portfolio,** *P*, can be shown to be as follows[8]:

$$w_D = \frac{[E(r_D) - r_f]\sigma_E^2 - [E(r_E) - r_f]\text{Cov}(r_D,r_E)}{[E(r_D) - r_f]\sigma_E^2 + [E(r_E) - r_f]\sigma_D^2 - [E(r_D) - r_f + E(r_E) - r_f]\text{Cov}(r_D,r_E)}$$
$$w_E = 1 - w_D \tag{7.8}$$

Substituting our data, the solution is

$$w_D = \frac{(8-5)\,400 - (13-5)\,72}{(8-5)\,400 + (13-5)\,144 - (8-5+13-5)\,72}$$
$$= .40$$
$$w_E = 1 - .4$$
$$= .6$$

The expected return of this optimal risky portfolio is 11%:

---

[8] The solution procedure is as follows. Substitute for $E(r_p)$ from equation 7.1 and for σ_p from equation 7.2. Substitute $1 - w_D$ for w_E. Differentiate the resulting expression for S_p with respect to w_D, set the derivative equal to zero, and solve for w_D.

$$E(r_P) = .4 \times 8 + .6 \times 13$$

The standard deviation is 14.2%:

$$\sigma_P = (.4^2 \times 144 + .6^2 \times 400 + 2 \times .4 \times .6 \times 72)^{1/2}$$
$$= 14.2\%$$

The CAL using this optimal portfolio has a slope of

$$S_P = \frac{11 - 5}{14.2} = .42$$

which is the reward-to-variability ratio of Portfolio P. Notice that this slope exceeds the slope of any of the other feasible portfolios that we have considered, as it must if it is to be the slope of the best feasible CAL.

In Chapter 6 we found the optimal *complete* portfolio given an optimal risky Portfolio and the CAL generated by a combination of this portfolio and T-bills. Now that we have constructed the optimal risky portfolio, P, we can use the individual investor's degree of risk aversion, A, to calculate the optimal proportion of the complete portfolio to invest in the risky component.

An investor with a coefficient of risk aversion, $A = 4$, would take a position in Portfolio P of

$$y = \frac{E(r_P) - r_f}{.01 \times A\sigma_P^2} \tag{7.9}$$

$$= \frac{11 - 5}{.01 \times 4 \times 14.2^2} = .7439$$

Thus, the investor will invest 74.39% of his or her wealth in Portfolio P and 25.61% in T-bills. Portfolio P consists of 40% in bonds, so the percentage of wealth in bonds will be $yw_D = .4 \times .7439 = .2976$, or 29.76%. Similarly, the investment in stocks will be $yw_E = .6 \times .7439 = .4463$, or 44.63%. The graphical solution of this asset allocation problem is presented in Figures 7.8 and 7.9.

Once we have reached this point, generalizing to the case of many risky assets is straightforward. Before we move on, let us briefly summarize the steps we followed to arrive at the complete portfolio.

1. Specify the return characteristics of all securities (expected returns, variances, covariances).
2. Establish the risky portfolio:
   a. Calculate the optimal risky portfolio, P (equation 7.8).
   b. Calculate the properties of Portfolio P using the weights determined in step (*a*) and equations 7.1 and 7.2.
3. Allocate funds between the risky portfolio and the risk-free asset:
   a. Calculate the fraction of the complete portfolio allocated to portfolio P (the risky portfolio) and to T-bills (the risk-free asset) (equation 7.9).
   b. Calculate the share of the complete portfolio invested in each asset and in T-bills.

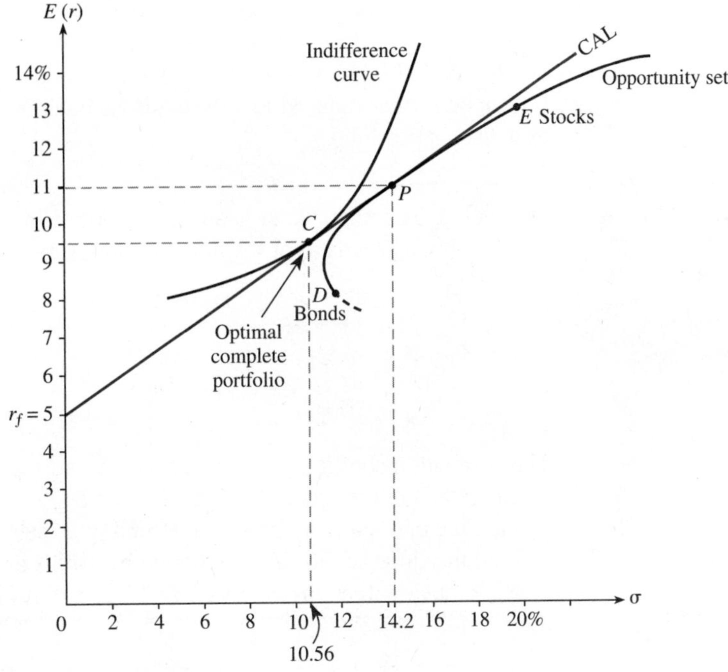

Figure 7.8
Determination of the optimal overall portfolio

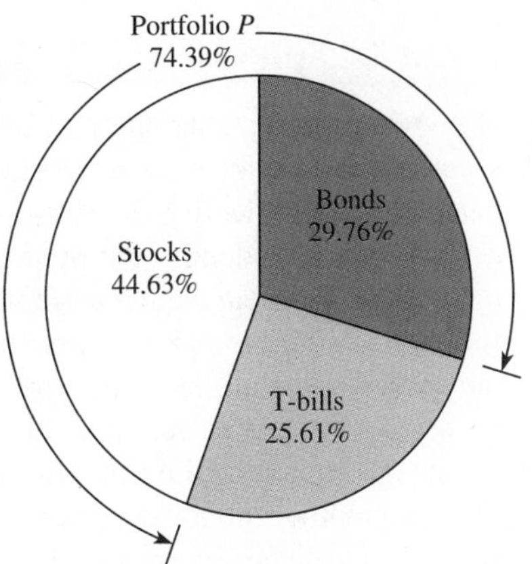

Figure 7.9
The proportions of the optimal overall portfolio

Before moving on, recall that the two assets in the asset allocation problem are already diversified portfolios. The diversification *within* each of these portfolios must be credited for a good deal of the risk reduction compared to undiversified single securities. For example, the standard deviation of the rate of return on an average stock is about 50% (see Figure 7.2). In contrast, the standard deviation of our hypothetical stock-index fund is only 20%, about equal to the historical standard deviation of the S&P 500 portfolio. This is evidence of the importance of diversification within the asset class.

Asset allocation between bonds and stocks contributed incrementally to the improvement in the reward-to-variability ratio of the complete portfolio. The CAL with stocks, bonds, and bills (Figure 7.7) shows that the standard deviation of the complete portfolio can be further reduced to 18% while maintaining the same expected return of 13% as the stock portfolio.

CONCEPT CHECK

Question 3. The universe of available securities includes two risky stock funds, *A* and *B*, and T-bills. The data for the universe are as follows:

	Expected Return	Standard Deviation
A	10%	20%
B	30	60
T-bills	5	0

The correlation coefficient between funds *A* and *B* is −.2.

a. Draw the opportunity set of Funds *A* and *B*.
b. Find the optimal risky portfolio, *P*, and its expected return and standard deviation.
c. Find the slope of the CAL supported by T-bills and Portfolio *P*.
d. How much will an investor with A 5 5 invest in Funds A and B, and in T-bills?

7.4 THE MARKOWITZ PORTFOLIO SELECTION MODEL

Security Selection

Now we can generalize the portfolio construction problem to the case of many risky securities and a risk-free asset. As in the two risky assets example, the problem has three parts. First, we identify the risk–return combinations available from the set of risky assets. Next, we identify the optimal portfolio of risky assets by finding the portfolio weights that result in the steepest CAL. Finally, we choose an appropriate complete portfolio by mixing the risk-free asset with the optimal risky portfolio. Before describing the process in detail, let us first present an overview.

The first step is to determine the risk–return opportunities available to the investor. These are summarized by the **minimum-variance frontier** of risky assets. This frontier is a graph of the lowest possible portfolio variance that can be attained for a given portfolio expected return. Given the set of data for expected returns, variances, and covariances, we can calculate the minimum-variance portfolio (or equivalently, minimum standard deviation portfolio) for any targeted expected return. Performing such a calculation for many such expected return targets results in a pairing between expected returns and minimum-risk portfolios that offer those expected returns. The plot of these expected return–standard deviation pairs is presented in Figure 7.10.

Notice that all the individual assets lie to the right inside the frontier, at least when we allow short sales in the construction of risky portfolios.[9] This tells us that risky port-

[9] When short sales are prohibited, single securities may lie on the frontier. For example, the security with the highest expected return must lie on the frontier, as the security represents the *only* way that one can obtain a return that high, and so it must

Figure 7.10
The minimum-variance frontier of risky assets

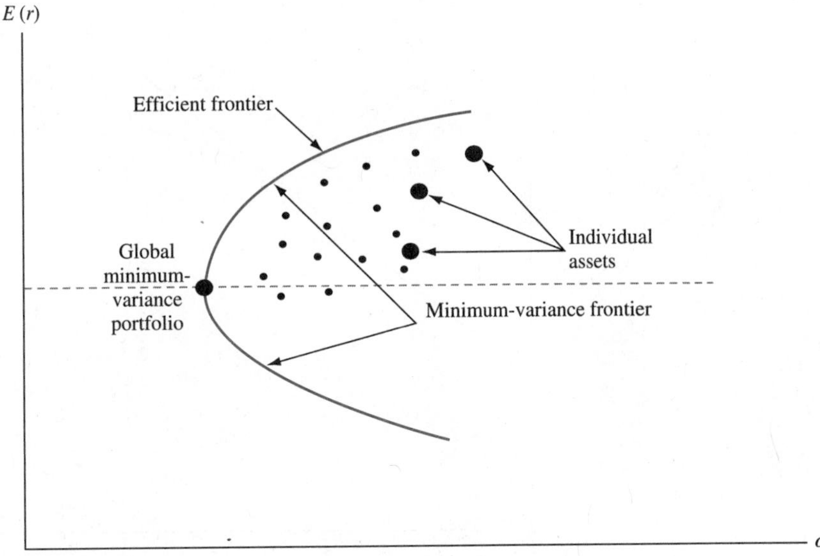

folios constituted of only a single asset are inefficient. Diversifying investments leads to portfolios with higher expected returns and lower standard deviations.

All the portfolios that lie on the minimum-variance frontier from the global minimum-variance portfolio and upward, provide the best risk–return combinations and thus are candidates for the optimal portfolio. The part of the frontier that lies above the global minimum-variance portfolio, therefore, is called the **efficient frontier.** For any portfolio on the lower portion of the minimum-variance frontier, there is a portfolio with the same standard deviation and a greater expected return positioned directly above it. Hence, the bottom part of the minimum-variance frontier is inefficient.

The second part of the optimization plan involves the risk-free asset. As before, we search for the capital allocation line with the highest reward-to-variability ratio (that is, the steepest slope) as shown in Figure 7.11.

The CAL that is supported by the optimal portfolio, *P*, is, as before, the one that is tangent to the efficient frontier. This CAL dominates all alternative feasible lines (the broken lines that are drawn through the frontier). Portfolio *P*, therefore, is the optimal risky portfolio.

Finally, in the last part of the problem the individual investor chooses the appropriate mix between the optimal risky portfolio *P* and T-bills, exactly as in Figure 7.8.

Now let us consider each part of the portfolio construction problem in more detail. In the first part of the problem, risk-return analysis, the portfolio manager needs, as inputs, a set of estimates for the expected returns of each security and a set of estimates for the covariance matrix. (In Part V on security analysis we will examine the security

also be the minimum-variance way to obtain that return. When short sales are feasible, however, portfolios can be constructed that offer the same expected return and lower variance. These portfolios typically will have short positions in low-expected-return securities.

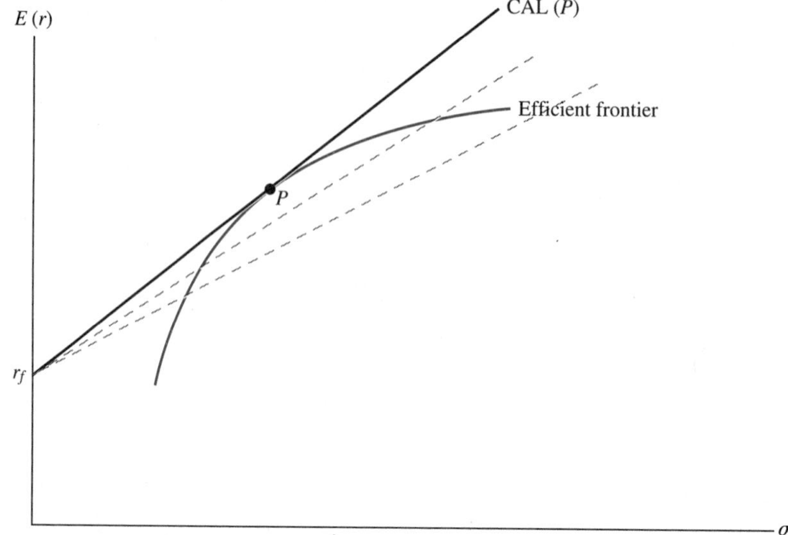

Figure 7.11
The efficient frontier of risky assets with the optimal CAL

valuation techniques and methods of financial analysis that analysts use. For now, we will assume that analysts already have spent the time and resources to prepare the inputs.)

Suppose that the horizon of the portfolio plan is one year. Therefore, all estimates pertain to a one-year holding period return. Our security analysts cover n securities. As of now, time zero, we observed these security prices: $P_1^0, \ldots P_n^0$. The analysts derive estimates for each security's expected rate of return by forecasting end-of-year (time 1) prices: $E(P_1^1), \ldots, E(P_n^1)$, and the expected dividends for the period: $E(D_1), \ldots, E(D_n)$. The set of expected rates of return is then computed from

$$E(r_i) = \frac{E(P_i^1) + E(D_i) - P_i^0}{P_i^0}$$

The covariances among the rates of return on the analyzed securities (the covariance matrix) usually are estimated from historical data. Another method is to use a scenario analysis of possible returns from all securities instead of, or as a supplement to, historical analysis.

The portfolio manager is now armed with the n estimates of $E(r_i)$ and the $n \times n$ estimates in the covariance matrix in which the n diagonal elements are estimates of the variances, σ_i^2, and the $n^2 - n = n(n - 1)$ off-diagonal elements are the estimates of the covariances between each pair of asset returns. (You can verify this from Table 7.2 for the case $n = 2$.) We know that each covariance appears twice in this table, so actually we have $n(n - 1)/2$ different covariances estimates. If our portfolio management unit covers 50 securities, our security analysts need to deliver 50 estimates of expected returns, 50 estimates of variances, and $50 \times 49/2 = 1{,}225$ different estimates of covariances. This is a daunting task! (We show later how the number of required estimates can be reduced substantially.)

Figure 7.12
The efficient portfolio set

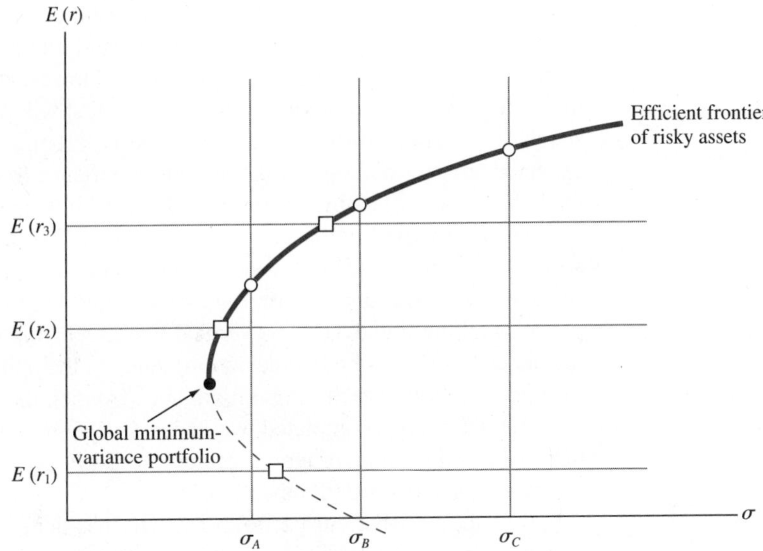

Once these estimates are compiled, the expected return and variance of any risky portfolio with weights in each security, w_i, can be calculated from the following formulas[10]:

$$E(r_p) = \sum_{i=1}^{n} w_i E(r_i) \tag{7.10}$$

$$\sigma_p^2 = \sum_{i=1}^{n} w_i^2 \sigma_i^2 + \sum_{\substack{i=1 \\ i \neq j}}^{n} \sum_{j=1}^{n} w_i w_j \text{Cov}(r_i, r_j) \tag{7.11}$$

We mentioned earlier that the idea of diversification is age-old. The phrase "don't put all your eggs in one basket" existed long before modern finance theory. It was not until 1952, however, that Harry Markowitz published a formal model of portfolio selection embodying diversification principles, thereby paving the way for his 1990 Nobel prize for economics. His model is precisely step one of portfolio management: the identification of the efficient set of portfolios, or, as it is often called, the *efficient frontier of risky assets.*

The principal idea behind the frontier set of risky portfolios is that, for any risk level, we are interested only in that portfolio with the highest expected return. Alternatively, the frontier is the set of portfolios that minimize the variance for any target expected return.

Indeed, the two methods of computing the efficient set of risky portfolios are equivalent. To see this, consider the graphical representation of these procedures. Figure 7.12 shows the minimum-variance frontier.

---

[10] Equation 7.11 follows from our discussion in Section 7.2 on using the bordered covariance matrix to obtain each term in the formula for the variance of a portfolio.

The points marked by rectangles are the result of a variance-minimization program. We first draw the constraint, that is, a horizontal line at the level of required expected return. We then look for the portfolio with the lowest standard deviation that plots on this horizontal line—we look for the portfolio that will plot farthest to the left (smallest standard deviation) on that line. When we repeat this for various levels of required expected returns, the shape of the minimum-variance frontier emerges. We then discard the bottom (dotted) half of the frontier, because it is inefficient.

In the alternative approach, we draw a vertical line that represents the standard deviation constraint. We then consider all portfolios that plot on this line (have the same standard deviation) and choose the one with the highest expected return, that is, that portfolio falling highest on this vertical line. Repeating this procedure for various vertical lines (levels of standard deviation) gives us the points marked by circles that trace the upper portion of the minimum-variance frontier, the efficient frontier.

When this step is completed, we have a list of efficient portfolios, because the solution to the optimization program includes the portfolio proportions, w_i, and the expected return, $E(r_p)$, and standard deviation, σ_p.

Let us restate what our portfolio manager has done so far. The estimates generated by the analysts were transformed into a set of expected rates of return and a covariance matrix. This group of estimates we shall call the **input list.** This input list is then fed into the optimization program.

Before we proceed to the second step of choosing the optimal risky portfolio from the frontier set, let us consider a practical point. Some clients may be subject to additional constraints. For example, many institutions are prohibited from taking short positions in any asset. For these clients the portfolio manager will add to the program constraints that rule out negative (short) positions in the search for efficient portfolios. In this special case it is possible that single assets may be, in and of themselves, efficient risky portfolios. For example, the asset with the highest expected return will be a frontier portfolio because, without the opportunity of short sales, the only way to obtain that rate of return is to hold the asset as one's entire risky portfolio.

Short-sale restrictions are by no means the only such constraints. For example, some clients may want to assure a minimal level of expected dividend yield from the optimal portfolio. In this case the input list will be expanded to include a set of expected dividend yields $d_1, \ldots, d_n$ and the optimization program will include an additional constraint that ensures that the expected dividend yield of the portfolio will equal or exceed the desired level, d.

Portfolio managers can tailor the efficient set to conform to any desire of the client. Of course, any constraint carries a price tag in the sense that an efficient frontier constructed subject to extra constraints will offer a reward-to-variability ratio inferior to that of a less constrained one. The client should be made aware of this cost and should carefully consider constraints that are not mandated by law.

Another type of constraint is aimed at ruling out investments in industries or countries considered ethically or politically undesirable. This is referred to as *socially responsible investing,* which entails a cost in the form of a lower risk premium on the resultant constrained, optimal portfolio. This cost can be justifiably seen as contribution to the underlying cause, albeit not a tax-deductible one.

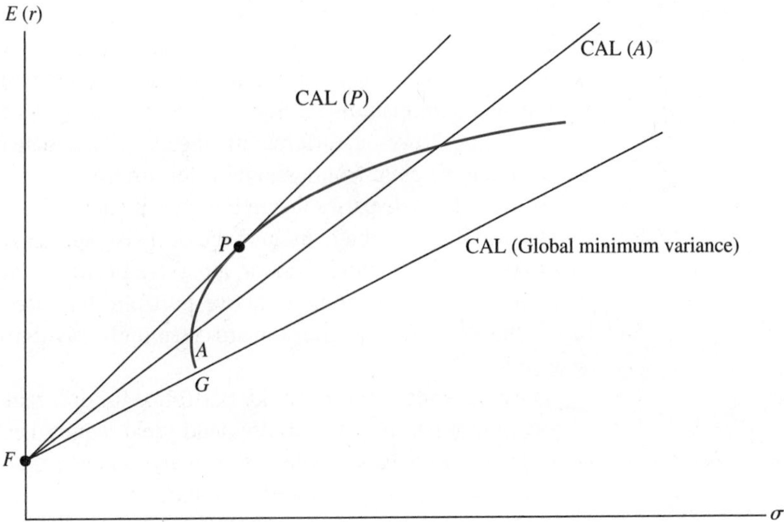

Figure 7.13
Capital allocation lines with various portfolios from the efficient set

Capital Allocation and the Separation Property

We are now ready to proceed to step two. This step introduces the risk-free asset. Figure 7.13 shows the efficient frontier plus three CALs representing various portfolios from the efficient set. As before, we ratchet up the CAL by selecting different portfolios until we reach Portfolio *P*, which is the tangency point of a line from *F* to the efficient frontier. Portfolio *P* maximizes the reward-to-variability ratio, the slope of the line from *F* to portfolios on the efficient frontier. At this point our portfolio manager is done. Portfolio *P* is the optimal risky portfolio for the manager's clients. This is a good time to ponder our results and their implementation.

The most striking conclusion is that a portfolio manager will offer the same risky portfolio, *P*, to all clients regardless of their degree of risk aversion.[11] The degree of risk aversion of the client comes into play only in the selection of the desired point on the CAL. Thus the only difference between clients' choices is that the more risk-averse client will invest more in the risk-free asset and less in the optimal risky portfolio, *P*, than will a less risk-averse client. However, both will use Portfolio *P* as their optimal risky investment vehicle.

This result is called a **separation property;** it tells us that the portfolio choice problem may be separated into two independent tasks. The first task, determination of the optimal risky portfolio, *P*, is purely technical. Given the manager's input list, the best risky portfolio is the same for all clients, regardless of risk aversion. The second task, however, allocation of the complete portfolio to T-bills versus the risky portfolio, depends on personal preference. Here the client is the decision maker.

[11] Clients who impose special restrictions (constraints) on the manager, such as dividend yield, will obtain another optimal portfolio. Any constraint that is added to an optimization problem leads, in general, to a different and less desirable optimum compared to an unconstrained program.

The crucial point is that the optimal portfolio P that the manager offers is the same for all clients. This result makes professional management more efficient and hence less costly. One management firm can serve any number of clients with relatively small incremental administrative costs.

In practice, however, different managers will estimate different input lists, thus deriving different efficient frontiers, and offer different "optimal" portfolios to their clients. The source of the disparity lies in the security analysis. It is worth mentioning here that the rule of GIGO (garbage in–garbage out) also applies to security analysis. If the quality of the security analysis is poor, a passive portfolio such as a market index fund will result in a better CAL than an active portfolio that uses low-quality security analysis to tilt the portfolio weights toward seemingly favorable (i.e., seemingly mispriced) securities.

As we have seen, optimal risky portfolios for different clients also may vary because of portfolio constraints such as dividend-yield requirements, tax considerations, or other client preferences. Nevertheless, this analysis suggests that only a very limited number of portfolios may be sufficient to serve the demands of a wide range of investors. This is the theoretical basis of the mutual fund industry.

The (computerized) optimization technique is the easiest part of the portfolio construction problem. The real arena of competition among portfolio managers is in sophisticated security analysis.

CONCEPT CHECK

Question 4. Suppose that two portfolio managers who work for competing investment management houses each employ a group of security analysts to prepare the input list for the Markowitz algorithm. When all is completed, it turns out that the efficient frontier obtained by portfolio manager A dominates that of manager B. By domination we mean that A's optimal risky portfolio lies northwest of B's. Hence, given a choice, investors will always prefer the risky portfolio that lies on the CAL of A.

a. What should be made of this outcome?

b. Should it be attributed to better security analysis by A's analysts?

c. Could it be that A's computer program is superior?

d. If you were advising clients (and had an advance glimpse at the efficient frontiers of various managers), would you tell them to periodically switch their money around to the manager with the most northwesterly portfolio?

Asset Allocation and Security Selection

As we have seen, the theories of security selection and asset allocation are identical. Both activities call for the construction of an efficient frontier, and the choice of a particular portfolio from along that frontier. The determination of the optimal combination of securities proceeds in the same manner as the analysis of the optimal combination of asset classes. Why, then, do we (and the investment community) distinguish between asset allocation and security selection?

Three factors are at work. First, as a result of greater need and ability to save (for college educations, recreation, longer life in retirement, health care needs, etc.), the demand for sophisticated investment management has increased enormously. Second, the growing spectrum of financial markets and financial instruments has put sophisticated investment beyond the capacity of most amateur investors. Finally, there are strong economic returns to scale in investment management. The end result is that the size of a competitive investment company has grown with the industry, and efficiency in organization has become an important issue.

A large investment company is likely to invest both in domestic and international markets and in a broad set of asset classes, each of which requires specialized expertise. Hence, the management of each asset-class portfolio needs to be decentralized, and it becomes impossible to simultaneously optimize the entire organization's risky portfolio in one stage, although this would be prescribed as optimal on *theoretical* grounds.

The practice is therefore to optimize the security selection of each asset-class portfolio independently. At the same time, top management continually updates the asset allocation of the organization, adjusting the investment budget of each asset-class portfolio. When changed frequently in response to intensive forecasting activity, these reallocations are called *market timing*. The shortcoming of this two-step approach to portfolio construction, versus the theory-based one-step optimization, is the failure to exploit the covariance of the individual securities in one asset-class portfolio with the individual securities in the other asset classes. Only the covariance matrix of the securities within each asset-class portfolio can be used. However, this loss might be small because of the depth of diversification of each portfolio and the extra layer of diversification at the asset allocation level.

7.5 Optimal Portfolios with Restrictions on the Risk-Free Asset

The availability of a risk-free asset greatly simplifies the portfolio decision. When all investors can borrow and lend at that risk-free rate, we are led to a *unique* optimal risky portfolio that is appropriate for all investors given a common input list. This portfolio maximizes the reward-to-variability ratio. All investors use the same risky portfolio and differ only in the proportion they invest in it and in the risk-free asset.

What if a risk-free asset is not available? Although T-bills are risk-free assets in nominal terms, their real returns are uncertain. Without a risk-free asset, there is no tangency portfolio that is best for all investors. In this case investors have to choose a portfolio from the efficient frontier of risky assets redrawn in Figure 7.14.

Each investor will now choose the optimal risky portfolio by superimposing a particular set of indifference curves on the efficient frontier, as Figure 7.14 shows. The optimal portfolio, *P*, for the investor whose risk aversion is represented by the set of indifference curves in Figure 7.14 is tangent to the highest attainable indifference curve.

Investors who are more risk averse than the one represented in Figure 7.14 would have steeper indifference curves, meaning that the tangency portfolio will be of smaller standard deviation and expected return than Portfolio *P*, such as Portfolio *Q*. Conversely, investors who are more risk tolerant than the one represented in Figure 7.14 would be characterized by flatter indifference curves, resulting in a tangency portfolio of higher expected return and standard deviation than Portfolio *P*, such as Portfolio *S*. The common feature of all these rational investors is that they choose portfolios on the efficient frontier; that is, they choose mean-variance efficient portfolios.

Figure 7.14
Portfolio selection without a risk-free asset

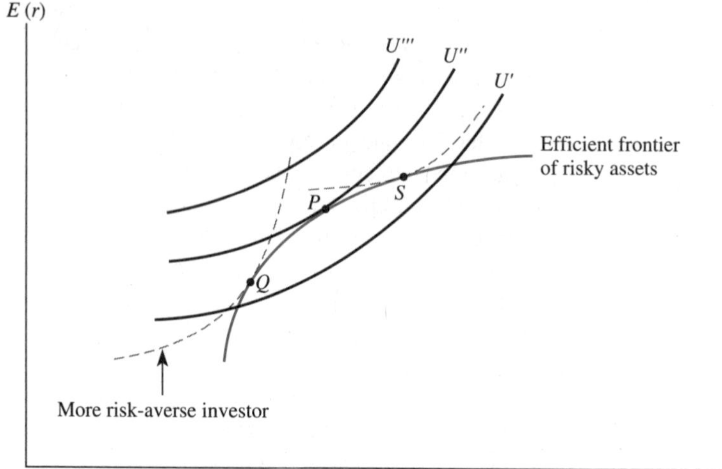

Even if virtually risk-free lending opportunities are available, many investors do face borrowing restrictions. They may be unable to borrow altogether, or, more realistically, they may face a borrowing rate that is significantly greater than the lending rate. Let us first consider investors who can lend without risk, but are prohibited from borrowing.

When a risk-free investment is available, but an investor can take only positive positions in it (he or she can lend at r_f, but cannot borrow), a CAL exists but is limited to the line *FP* as in Figure 7.15.

Any investors whose preferences are represented by indifference curves with tangency portfolios on the portion *FP* of the CAL, such as Portfolio *A*, are unaffected by the borrowing restriction. For such investors the borrowing restriction is a nonbinding constraint, because they are net *lenders,* lending some of their money at rate r_f.

Aggressive or more risk-tolerant investors, who *would* choose Portfolio *B* in the absence of the borrowing restriction, are affected, however. For them, the borrowing restriction is a binding constraint. Such investors will be driven to portfolios on the efficient frontier, such as Portfolio *Q*, which have higher expected return and standard deviation than does Portfolio *P* (but less than the unavailable Portfolio *B*). Portfolios such as *Q*, which are on the efficient frontier of risky assets, represent a zero investment in the risk-free asset.

Finally, we consider a more realistic case, that of feasible borrowing, but at a higher rate than r_f. An individual who borrows to invest in a risky portfolio will have to pay an interest rate higher than the T-bill rate. The lender will require a premium commensurate with the probability of default. For example, the call money rate charged by brokers on margin accounts is higher than the T-bill rate.

Investors who face a borrowing rate greater than the lending rate confront a three-part CAL such as in Figure 7.16. CAL_1, which is relevant in the range FP_1, represents the efficient portfolio set for defensive (risk-averse) investors. These investors invest part of their funds in T-bills at rate r_f. They find that the tangency Portfolio is P_1, and they choose a complete portfolio such as Portfolio *A* in Figure 7.17.

Figure 7.15
Portfolio selection with risk-free lending only

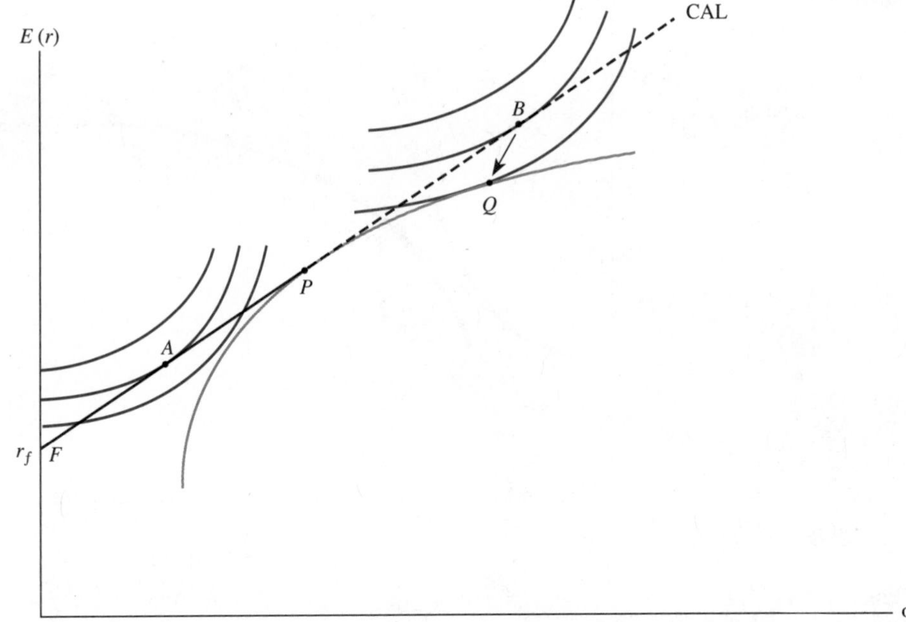

Figure 7.16
The investment opportunity set with differential rates for borrowing and lending

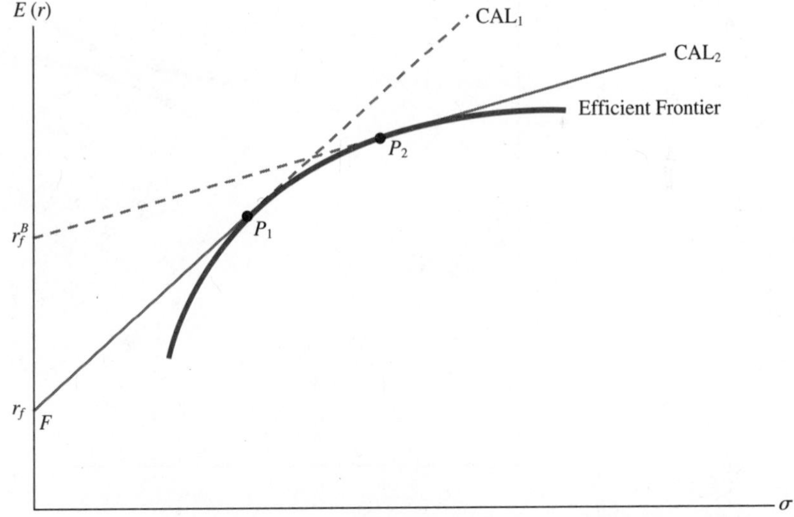

CAL$_2$, which is relevant in a range to the right of Portfolio P_2, represents the efficient portfolio set for more aggressive, or risk-tolerant, investors. This line starts at the borrowing rate, r_f^B, but it is unavailable in the range $r_f^B P_2$, because *lending* (investing in T-bills) is available only at the risk-free rate r_f, which is less than r_f^B.

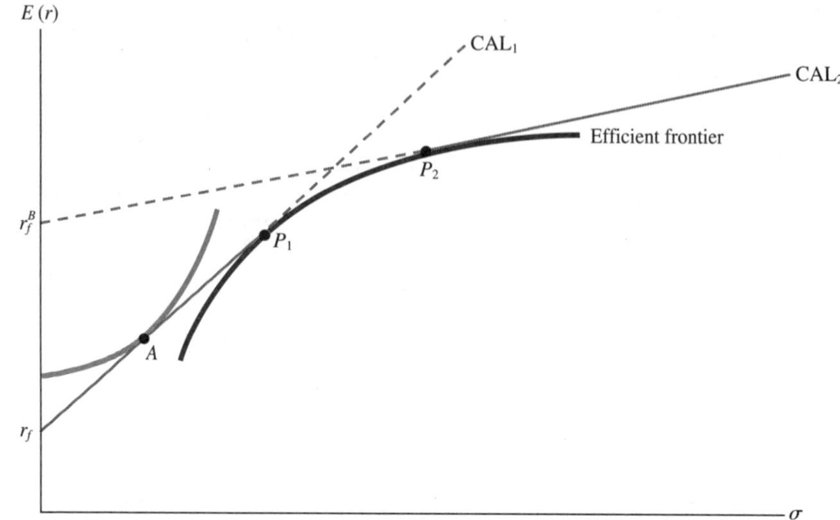

Figure 7.17
The optimal portfolio of defensive investors with differential borrowing and lending rates

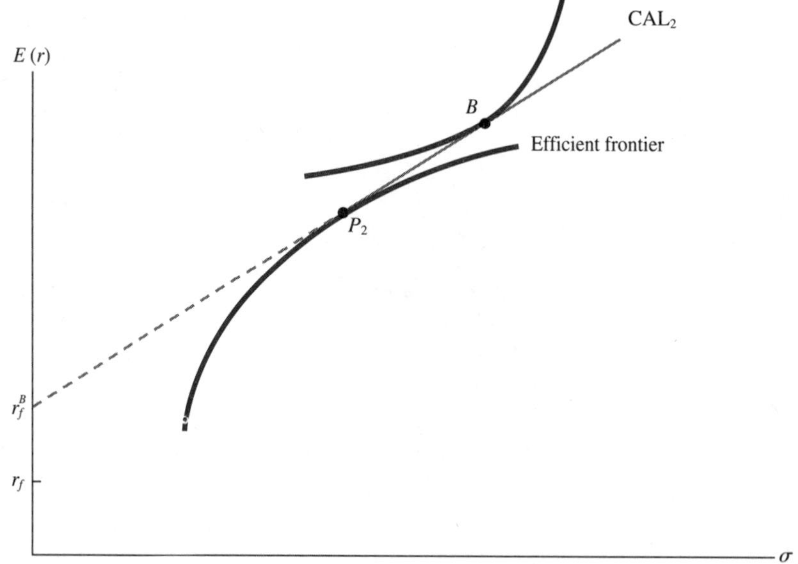

Figure 7.18
The optimal portfolio of aggressive investors with differential borrowing and lending rates

Investors who are willing to *borrow* at the higher rate, r_f^B, to invest in an optimal risky portfolio will choose Portfolio P_2 as their risky investment vehicle. Such a case is described in Figure 7.18, which superimposes a relatively risk-tolerant investor's indifference curve on CAL_2 of Figure 7.16. The investor with the indifference curve in Figure 7.18 chooses Portfolio P_2 as the optimal risky portfolio and borrows to invest in it, arriving at the overall Portfolio *B*.

Figure 7.19
The optimal portfolio of moderately risk-tolerant investors with differential borrowing and lending rates

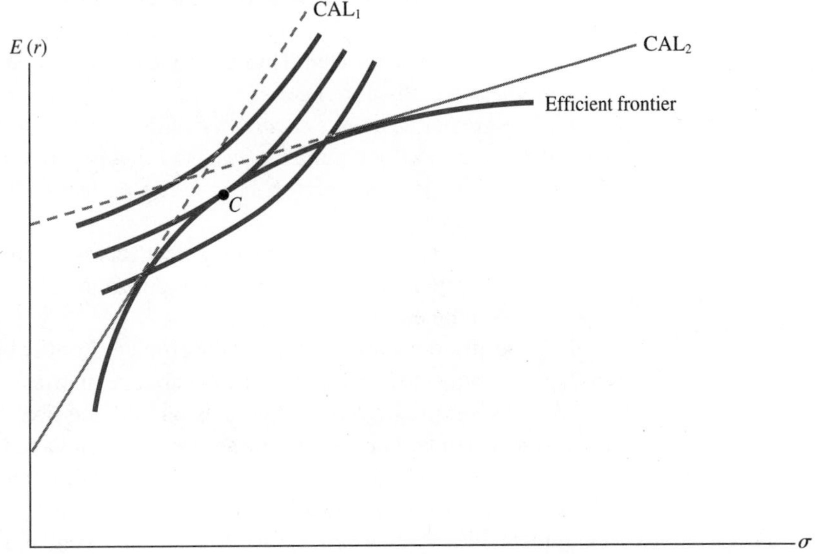

Investors in the middle range, neither defensive enough to invest in T-bills nor aggressive enough to borrow, choose a risky portfolio from the efficient frontier in the range P_1P_2. This case is described in Figure 7.19. The indifference curve representing the investor in Figure 7.19 leads to a tangency portfolio on the efficient frontier, Portfolio *C*.

CONCEPT CHECK

Question 5. With differential lending and borrowing rates, only investors with about average degrees of risk aversion will choose a portfolio in the range P_1P_2 in Figure 7.17. Other investors will choose a portfolio on CAL_1 if they are more risk averse, or on CAL_2 if they are more risk tolerant.

a. Does this mean that investors with average risk aversion are more dependent on the quality of the forecasts that generate the efficient frontier?

b. Describe the trade-off between expected return and standard deviation for portfolios between P_1 and P_2 in Figure 7.17 compared with portfolios on CAL_2 beyond P_2.

SUMMARY

1. The expected return of a portfolio is the weighted average of the component asset expected returns with the investment proportions as weights.

2. The variance of a portfolio is the weighted sum of the elements of the covariance matrix with the product of the investment proportions as weights. Thus, the variance of each asset is weighted by the square of its investment proportion. Each covariance of any pair of assets appears twice in the covariance matrix and, thus, the portfolio variance includes twice each covariance weighted by the product of the investment proportions in each of the two assets.

3. Even if the covariances are positive, the portfolio standard deviation is less than the weighted average of the component standard deviations, as long as the assets are not perfectly positively correlated. Thus portfolio diversification is of value as long as assets are less than perfectly correlated.

4. The greater an asset's *covariance* with the other assets in the portfolio, the more it contributes to portfolio variance. An asset that is perfectly negatively correlated with a portfolio can serve as a perfect hedge. The perfect hedge asset can reduce the portfolio variance to zero.

5. The efficient frontier is the graphical representation of a set of portfolios that maximize expected return for each level of portfolio risk. Rational investors will choose a portfolio on the efficient frontier.

6. A portfolio manager identifies the efficient frontier by first establishing estimates for the asset expected returns and the covariance matrix. This input list is then fed into an optimization program that reports as outputs the investment proportions, expected returns, and standard deviations of the portfolios on the efficient frontier.

7. In general, portfolio managers will arrive at different efficient portfolios because of difference in methods and quality of security analysis. Managers compete on the quality of their security analysis relative to their management fees.

8. If a risk-free asset is available and input lists are identical, all investors will choose the same portfolio on the efficient frontier of risky assets: the portfolio tangent to the CAL. All investors with identical input lists will hold an identical risky portfolio, differing only in how much each allocates to this optimal portfolio and to the risk-free asset. This result is characterized as the separation principle of portfolio construction.

9. When a risk-free asset is not available, each investor chooses a risky portfolio on the efficient frontier. If a risk-free asset is available but borrowing is restricted, only aggressive investors will be affected. They will choose portfolios on the efficient frontier according to their degree of risk tolerance.

Key Terms

Diversification
Insurance principle
Market risk
Systematic risk
Nondiversifiable risk
Unique risk
Firm-specific risk
Nonsystematic risk
Diversifiable risk
Minimum-variance portfolio
Portfolio opportunity set
Reward-to-variability ratio
Optimal risky portfolio
Minimum-variance frontier
Efficient frontier
Input list
Separation property

Selected Readings

Two frequently cited papers on the impact of diversification on portfolio risk are:

Evans, John L.; and Stephen H. Archer. "Diversification and the Reduction of Dispersion: An Empirical Analysis." *Journal of Finance,* December 1968.

Wagner, W. H.; and S. C. Lau. "The Effect of Diversification on Risk." *Financial Analysts Journal,* November–December 1971.

The seminal works on portfolio selection are:

Markowitz, Harry M. "Portfolio Selection." *Journal of Finance,* March 1952.

Markowitz, Harry M. *Portfolio Selection: Efficient Diversification of Investments.* New York: John Wiley & Sons, 1959.

Also see:

Samuelson, Paul A. "Risk & Uncertainty: A Fallacy of Large Numbers." *Scientia* 98 (1963).

Problems

The following data apply to Questions 1 through 8:

A pension fund manager is considering three mutual funds. The first is a stock fund, the second is a long-term government and corporate bond fund, and the third is a T-bill money market fund that yields a rate of 9%. The probability distribution of the risky funds is as follows:

	Expected Return	Standard Deviation
Stock fund (*S*)	22%	32%
Bond fund (*B*)	13	23

The correlation between the fund returns is .15.

1. What are the investment proportions of the minimum-variance portfolio of the two risky funds, and what is the expected value and standard deviation of its rate of return?
2. Tabulate and draw the investment opportunity set of the two risky funds. Use investment proportions for the stock funds of zero to 100% in increments of 20%.
3. Draw a tangent from the risk-free rate to the opportunity set. What does your graph show for the expected return and standard deviation of the optimal portfolio?
4. Solve numerically for the proportions of each asset, and for the expected return and standard deviation of the optimal risky portfolio.
5. What is the reward-to-variability ratio of the best feasible CAL?
6. You require that your portfolio yield an expected return of 15%, and that it be efficient on the best feasible CAL.
   a. What is the standard deviation of your portfolio?
   b. What is the proportion invested in the T-bill fund and each of the two risky funds?
7. If you were to use only the two risky funds, and still require an expected return of 15%, what must be the investment proportions of your portfolio? Compare its standard deviation to that of the optimized portfolio in Question 6. What do you conclude?
8. Suppose that you face the same opportunity set, but you cannot borrow. You wish to construct a portfolio with an expected return of 29%. What are the appropriate portfolio proportions and the resulting standard deviations? What reduction in standard deviation could you attain if you were allowed to borrow at the risk-free rate?

9. Stocks offer an expected rate of return of 18%, with a standard deviation of 22%. Gold offers an expected return of 10% with a standard deviation of 30%.
   a. In light of the apparent inferiority of gold with respect to both mean return and volatility, would anyone hold gold? If so, demonstrate graphically why one would do so.
   b. Given the data above, reanswer Question (*a*) with the additional assumption that the correlation coefficient between gold and stocks equals 1. Draw a graph illustrating why one would or would not hold gold in one's portfolio. Could this set of assumptions for expected returns, standard deviations, and correlation represent an equilibrium for the security market?
10. Suppose that there are many stock in the market and that the characteristics of Stocks *A* and *B* are given as follows:

Stock	Expected Return	Standard Deviation
A	10%	5%
B	15	10
	Correlation = −1	

   Suppose that it is possible to borrow at the risk-free rate, r_f. What must be the value of the risk-free rate? (Hint: Think about constructing a risk-free portfolio from Stocks A and B.)
11. Assume that expected returns and standard deviations for all securities (including the risk-free rate for borrowing and lending) are known. In this case all investors will have the same optimal risky portfolio. (True or false?)
12. The standard deviation of the portfolio is always equal to the weighted average of the standard deviations of the assets in the portfolio. (True or false?)
13. Suppose you have a project that has a .7 chance of doubling your investment in a year and a .3 chance of halving your investment in a year. What is the standard deviation of the rate of return on this investment?
14. Suppose that you have $1 million and the following two opportunities from which to construct a portfolio:
   a. Risk-free asset earning 12% per year.
   b. Risky asset earning 30% per year with a standard deviation of 40%.
   If you construct a portfolio with a standard deviation of 30 percent, what will be the rate of return?

The following data apply to questions 15 through 17.*

Hennessy & Associates manages a $30 million equity portfolio for the multimanager Wilstead Pension Fund. Jason Jones, financial vice president of Wilstead, noted that Hennessy had rather consistently achieved the best record among the Wilstead's six equity managers. Performance of the Hennessy portfolio had been clearly superior to that of the S&P 500 in four of the past five years. In the one less favorable year, the shortfall was trivial.

---

*Reprinted, with permission, from the Level III 1982 *CFA Study Guide*.

Hennessy is a "bottom-up" manager. The firm largely avoids any attempt to "time the market." It also focuses on selection of individual stocks, rather than the weighting of favored industries.

There is no apparent conformity of style among the six equity managers. The five managers, other than Hennessy, manage portfolios aggregating $250 million made up of more than 150 individual issues.

Jones is convinced that Hennessy is able to apply superior skill to stock selection, but the favorable returns are limited by the high degree of diversification in the portfolio. Over the years, the portfolio generally held 40–50 stocks, with about 2% to 3% of total funds committed to each issue. The reason Hennessy seemed to do well most years was because the firm was able to identify each year 10 or 12 issues which registered particularly large gains.

Based on this overview, Jones outlined the following plan to the Wilstead pension committee:

> Let's tell Hennessy to limit the portfolio to no more than 20 stocks. Hennessy will double the commitments to the stocks that it really favors, and eliminate the remainder. Except for this one new restriction, Hennessy should be free to manage the portfolio exactly as before.

All the members of the pension committee generally supported Jones's proposal because all agreed that Hennessy had seemed to demonstrate superior skill in selecting stocks. Yet, the proposal was a considerable departure from previous practice, and several committee members raised questions. Respond to each of the following questions.

15. *a.* Will the limitations of 20 stocks likely increase or decrease the risk of the portfolio? Explain.*

b. Is there any way Hennessy could reduce the number of issues from 40 to 20 without significantly affecting risk? Explain.

16. One committee member was particularly enthusiastic concerning Jones's proposal. He suggested that Hennessy's performance might benefit further from reduction in the number of issues to 10. If the reduction to 20 could be expected to be advantageous, explain why reduction to 10 might be less likely to be advantageous. (Assume that Wilstead will evaluate the Hennessy portfolio independently of the other portfolios in the fund.)*

17. Another committee member suggested that, rather than evaluate each managed portfolio independently of other portfolios, it might be better to consider the effects of a change in the Hennessy portfolio on the total fund. Explain how this broader point of view could affect the committee decision to limit the holdings in the Hennessy portfolio to either 10 or 20 issues.*

The following data are for problems 18 through 20.

The correlation coefficients between pairs of stocks is as follows: $Corr(A,B) = .85$; $Corr(A,C) = .60$; $Corr(A,D) = .45$. Each stock has an expected return of 8% and a standard deviation of 20%.

---

*Reprinted, with permission, from the Level III 1982 *CFA Study Guide*.

18. If your entire portfolio is now composed of Stock *A* and you can add some of only one stock to your portfolio, would you choose (explain your choice):
    a. *B*.
    b. *C*.
    c. *D*.
    d. Need more data.
19. Would the answer to Question 18 change for more risk-averse or risk-tolerant investors? Explain.
20. Suppose that in addition to investing in one more stock you can invest in T-bills as well. Would you change your answers to Questions 18 and 19 if the T-bill rate is 8%?

21. Which one of the following portfolios cannot lie on the efficient frontier as described by Markowitz?*

	Portfolio	Expected Return (%)	Standard Deviation(%)
a.	*W*	15	36
b.	*X*	12	15
c.	*Z*	5	7
d.	*Y*	9	21

22. Which statement about portfolio diversification is correct?*
    a. Proper diversification can reduce or eliminate systematic risk.
    b. Diversification reduces the portfolio's expected return because it reduces a portfolio's total risk.
    c. As more securities are added to a portfolio, total risk typically would be expected to fall at a decreasing rate.
    d. The risk-reducing benefits of diversification do not occur meaningfully until at least 30 individual securities are included in the portfolio.

Appendix A: The Power of Diversification

Section 7.1 introduced the concept of diversification and the limits to the benefits of diversification resulting from systematic risk. Given the tools we have developed, we can reconsider this intuition more rigorously and at the same time sharpen our insight regarding the power of diversification.

Recall from equation 7.11 that the general formula for the variance of a portfolio is

$$\sigma_p^2 = \sum_{i=1}^{n} w_i^2 \sigma_i^2 + \sum_{\substack{j=1 \\ j \neq i}}^{n} \sum_{i=1}^{n} w_i w_j \text{Cov}(r_i, r_j) \tag{7A.1}$$

Consider now the naive diversification strategy in which an equally weighted portfolio is constructed, meaning that $w_i = 1/n$ for each security. In this case equation 7A.1 may be rewritten as follows:

*Reprinted, with permission, from the Level I 1993 *CFA Study Guide*.

$$\sigma_p^2 = \frac{1}{n} \sum_{i=1}^{n} \frac{1}{n} \sigma_i^2 + \sum_{\substack{j=1 \\ j \neq i}}^{n} \sum_{i=1}^{n} \frac{1}{n^2} \text{Cov}(r_i, r_j) \tag{7A.2}$$

Note that there are n variance terms and $n(n - 1)$ covariance terms in equation 7A.2.

If we define the average variance and average covariance of the securities as

$$\bar{\sigma}^2 = \frac{1}{n} \sum_{i=1}^{n} \sigma_i^2$$

$$\overline{\text{Cov}} = \frac{1}{n(n-1)} \sum_{\substack{i=1 \\ j \neq i}}^{n} \sum_{j=1}^{n} \text{Cov}(r_i, r_j)$$

we can express portfolio variance as

$$\sigma_p^2 = \frac{1}{n} \bar{\sigma}^2 + \frac{n-1}{n} \overline{\text{Cov}} \tag{7A.3}$$

Now examine the effect of diversification. When the average covariance among security returns is zero, as it is when all risk is firm-specific, portfolio variance can be driven to zero. We see this from equation 7A.3: The second term on the right-hand side will be zero in this scenario, while the first term approaches zero as n becomes larger. Hence, when security returns are uncorrelated, the power of diversification to limit portfolio risk is unlimited.

However, the more important case is the one in which economywide risk factors impart positive correlation among stock returns. In this case, as the portfolio becomes more highly diversified (n increases) portfolio variance remains positive. Although firm-specific risk, represented by the first term in equation 7A.3, is still diversified away, the second term simply approaches $\overline{\text{Cov}}$ as n becomes greater. [Note that $(n - 1)/n = 1 - 1/n$, which approaches 1 for large n.] Thus, the irreducible risk of a diversified portfolio depends on the covariance of the returns of the component securities, which in turn is a function of the importance of systematic factors in the economy.

To see further the fundamental relationship between systematic risk and security correlations, suppose for simplicity that all securities have a common standard deviation, σ, and all security pairs have a common correlation coefficient ρ. Then the covariance between all pairs of securities is $\rho\sigma^2$, and equation 7A.3 becomes

$$\sigma_p^2 = \frac{1}{n} \sigma^2 + \frac{n-1}{n} \rho\sigma^2 \tag{7A.4}$$

The effect of correlation is now explicit. When $\rho = 0$, we again obtain the insurance principle, where portfolio variance approaches zero as n becomes greater. For $\rho > 0$, however, portfolio variance remains positive. In fact, for $\rho = 1$, portfolio variance equals σ^2 regardless of n, demonstrating that diversification is of no benefit: in the case of perfect correlation, all risk is systematic. More generally, as n becomes greater, equation 7A.4 shows that systematic risk becomes $\rho\sigma^2$.

Table 7A.1 presents portfolio standard deviation as we include ever greater numbers of securities in the portfolio for two cases: $\rho = 0$ and $\rho = .40$. The table takes σ to be 50%. As one would expect, portfolio risk is greater when $\rho = .40$. More surprising, perhaps, is that portfolio risk diminishes far less rapidly as n increases in the positive correlation case. The correlation among security returns limits the power of diversification.

Table 7A.1 Risk Reduction of Equally Weighted Portfolios in Correlated and Uncorrelated Universes

		$\rho = 0$		$\rho = .4$	
Universe Size n	**Optimal Portfolio Proportion $1/n$ (%)**	**Standard Deviation (%)**	**Reduction in σ**	**Standard Deviation (%)**	**Reduction in σ**
1	100	50.00	14.64	50.00	8.17
2	50	35.36		41.83	
5	20	22.36	1.95	36.06	.70
6	16.67	20.41		35.36	
10	10	15.81	.73	33.91	.20
11	9.09	15.08		33.71	
20	55	11.18	.27	32.79	.06
21	4.76	10.91		32.73	
100	1	5.00	.02	31.86	.00
101	.99	4.98		31.86	

Note that, for a 100-security portfolio, the standard deviation is 5% in the uncorrelated case—still significant when we consider the potential of zero standard deviation. For $\rho = .40$, the standard deviation is high, 31.86%, yet it is very close to undiversifiable systematic risk in the infinite-sized universe, $\sqrt{\rho\sigma^2} = \sqrt{.4 \times 50^2} = 31.62$ percent. At this point, further diversification is of little value.

We also gain an important insight from this exercise. When we hold diversified portfolios, the contribution to portfolio risk of a particular security will depend on the *covariance* of that security's return with those of other securities, and *not* on the security's variance. As we shall see in Chapter 8, this implies that fair risk premiums also should depend on covariances rather than total variability of returns.

CONCEPT CHECK

Question 7A.1 Suppose that the universe of available risky securities consists of a large number of stocks, identically distributed with $E(r) = 15\%$, $\sigma = 60\%$, and a common correlation coefficient of $\rho = .5$.

a. What is the expected return and standard deviation of an equally weighted risky portfolio of 25 stocks?

b. What is the smallest number of stocks necessary to generate an efficient portfolio with a standard deviation equal to or smaller than 43%?

c. What is the systematic risk in this universe?

d. If T-bills are available and yield 10%, what is the slope of the CAL?

APPENDIX B: THE INSURANCE PRINCIPLE: RISK-SHARING VERSUS RISK-POOLING

Mean-variance analysis has taken a strong hold among investment professionals, and insight into the mechanics of efficient diversification has become quite widespread. Common misconceptions or fallacies about diversification still persist, however, and we will try to put some to rest.

It is commonly believed that a large portfolio of independent insurance policies is a necessary and sufficient condition for an insurance company to shed its risk. The fact is that a multitude of independent insurance policies is neither necessary nor sufficient for a sound insurance portfolio. Actually, an individual insurer who would not insure a single policy also would be unwilling to insure a large portfolio of independent policies.

Consider Paul Samuelson's (1963) story. He once offered a colleague 2-to-1 odds on a $1,000 bet on the toss of a coin. His colleague refused, saying, "I won't bet because I would feel the $1,000 loss more than the $2,000 gain. But I'll take you on if you promise to let me make a hundred such bets."

Samuelson's colleague, as many others, might have explained his position, not quite correctly, that "One toss is not enough to make it reasonably sure that the law of averages will turn out in my favor. But with a hundred tosses of a coin, the law of averages will make it a darn good bet."

Another way to rationalize this argument is to think in terms of rates of return. In each bet you put up $1,000 and then get back $3,000 with a probability of one half, or zero with a probability of one half. The probability distribution of the rate of return is 200% with $p = \frac{1}{2}$ and -100% with $p = \frac{1}{2}$.

The bets are all independent and identical and therefore the expected return is $E(r) = \frac{1}{2}(200) + \frac{1}{2}(-100) = 50\%$, regardless of the number of bets. The standard deviation of the rate of return on the portfolio of independent bets is[12]

$$\sigma(n) = \frac{\sigma}{\sqrt{n}}$$

where σ is the standard deviation of a single bet:

$$\begin{aligned}\sigma &= [\tfrac{1}{2}(200 - 50)^2 + \tfrac{1}{2}(-100 - 50)^2]^{1/2} \\ &= 150\%\end{aligned}$$

The rate of return on a sequence of bets, in other words, has a smaller standard deviation than that of a single bet. By increasing the number of bets we can reduce the standard deviation of the rate of return to any desired level. It seems at first glance that Samuelson's colleague was correct. But he was not.

The fallacy of the argument lies in the use of a rate of return criterion to choose from portfolios *that are not equal in size*. Although the portfolio is equally weighted across bets, each extra bet increases the scale of the investment by $1,000. Recall from your corporate finance class that when choosing among mutually exclusive projects you cannot use the internal rate of return (IRR) as your decision criterion when the projects are of different sizes. You have to use the net present value (NPV) rule.

[12] This follows from equation 7.11, setting $w_i = 1/n$ and all covariances equal to zero because of the independence of the bets.

Consider the dollar profit (as opposed to rate of return) distribution of a single bet:

$$E(R) = \tfrac{1}{2} \times 2{,}000 + \tfrac{1}{2} \times (-1{,}000)$$
$$= \$500$$
$$\sigma_R = [\tfrac{1}{2}(2{,}000 - 500)^2 + \tfrac{1}{2}(-1{,}000 - 500)^2]^{1/2}$$
$$= \$1{,}500$$

These are independent bets where the total profit from n bets is the sum of the profits from the single bets. Therefore, with n bets

$$E[R(n)] = \$500n$$
$$\text{Variance}\,(\sum_{i=1}^{n} R_i) = n\sigma_R^2$$
$$\sigma_R(n) = \sqrt{n\sigma_R^2}$$
$$= \sigma_R\sqrt{n}$$

so that the standard deviation of the dollar return *increases* by a factor equal to the square root of the number of bets, n, in contrast to the standard deviation of the rate of return, which *decreases* by a factor of the square root of n.

As further evidence, consider the standard coin-tossing game. Whether one flips a fair coin 10 times or 1,000 times, the expected percentage of heads flipped is 50%. One expects the actual proportion of heads in a typical running of the 1,000-toss experiment to be closer to 50% than in the 10-toss experiment. This is the law of averages.

But the actual number of heads will typically depart from its expected value by a greater amount in the 1,000-toss experiment. For example, 504 heads is close to 50% and is 4 more than the expected number. To exceed the expected number of heads by 4 in the 10-toss game would require 9 out of 10 heads, which is a much more extreme departure from the mean. In the many-toss case, there is more volatility of the *number* of heads and less volatility of the *percentage* of heads. This is the same when an insurance company takes on more policies: The *dollar* variance of its portfolio increases while the *rate of return* variance falls.

The lesson is this: Rate of return analysis is appropriate when considering mutually exclusive portfolios of equal size, which is what we did in all the examples so far. We applied a fixed investment budget, and we investigated only the consequences of varying investment proportions in various assets. But if an insurance company takes on more and more insurance policies, it is increasing portfolio dollar investments. The analysis called for in that case must be cast in terms of dollar profits, in much the same way that NPV is called for instead of IRR when we compare different-sized projects. This is why risk-pooling (i.e., accumulating independent risky prospects) does not act to eliminate risk.

Samuelson's colleague should have counteroffered: "Let's make 1,000 bets, each with your \$2 against my \$1." Then he would be holding a portfolio of fixed size, equal to \$1,000, which is diversified into 1,000 identical independent prospects. This would make the insurance principle work.

Another way for Samuelson's colleague to get around the riskiness of this tempting bet is to share the large bets with friends. Consider a firm engaging in 1,000 of Paul Samuelson's bets. In each bet the firm puts up \$1,000 and receives \$3,000 or nothing as before. Each bet is too large for you. Yet if you hold a 1/1,000 share of the firm, your position is exactly the same as if you were to make 1,000 small bets of \$2 against \$1. A 1/1,000 share of a \$1,000 bet is equivalent to a \$1 bet. Holding a small share of many large bets essentially allows you to replace a stake in one large bet with a diversified portfolio of manageable bets.

How does this apply to insurance companies? Investors can purchase insurance company shares in the stock market, so they can choose to hold as small a position in the overall risk as they please. No matter how great the risk of the policies, a large group of individual small investors will agree to bear the risk if the expected rate of return exceeds the risk-free rate. Thus, it is the sharing of risk among many shareholders that makes the insurance industry tick.

Appendix C: The Fallacy of Time Diversification

The insurance story just discussed illustrates a misuse of rate of return analysis, specifically the mistake of comparing portfolios of different sizes. A more insidious version of this error often appears under the guise of "time diversification."

Consider the case of Mr. Frier, who has \$100,000. He is trying to figure out the appropriate allocation of this fund between risk-free T-bills that yield 10% and a risky portfolio that yields an annual rate of return with $E(r_p) = 15\%$ and $\sigma_p = 30\%$.

Mr. Frier took a course in finance in his youth. He likes quantitative models, and after careful introspection determines that his degree of risk aversion, A, is 4. Consequently, he calculates that his optimal allocation to the risky portfolio is

$$\begin{aligned} y &= \frac{E(r_p) - r_f}{.01 \times A\sigma_p^2} = \frac{15 - 10}{.01 \times 4 \times 30^2} \\ &= .14 \end{aligned}$$

that is, a 14% investment (\$14,000) in the risky portfolio.

With this strategy, Mr. Frier calculates his complete portfolio expected return and standard deviation by

$$\begin{aligned} E(r_C) &= r_f + y[E(r_p) - r_f] \\ &= 10.70\% \\ \sigma_C &= y\sigma_p \\ &= 4.20\% \end{aligned}$$

At this point, Mr. Frier gets cold feet because this fund is intended to provide the mainstay of his retirement wealth. He plans to retire in five years, and any mistake will be burdensome.

Mr. Frier calls Ms. Mavin, a highly recommended financial advisor. Ms. Mavin explains that indeed the time factor is all important. She cites academic research showing that asset rates of return over successive holding periods are independent. Therefore, she argues, returns in good years and bad years will tend to cancel out over the five-year period. Consequently, the average portfolio rate of return over the investment period will be less risky than would appear from the standard deviation of a single-year portfolio return. Because returns in each year are independent, Ms. Mavin tells Mr. Frier that a five-year investment is equivalent to a portfolio of five equally weighted

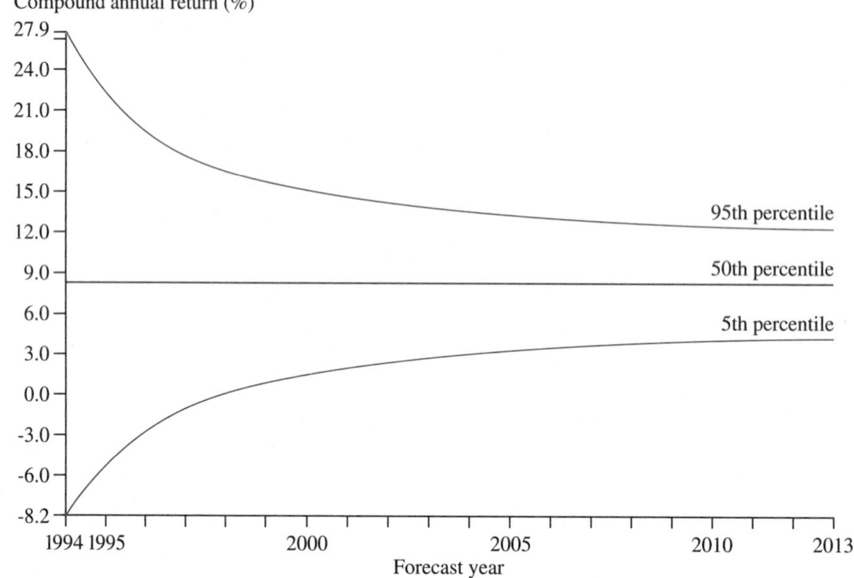

Figure 7C.1
Simulated return distributions for the period 1994–2013. Geometric average annual rates.

Source: *Stocks, Bonds, Bills, and Inflation: 1994 Yearbook* (Chicago: Ibbotson Associates, Inc., 1994).

independent assets. With such a portfolio, the (five-year) holding period return has a mean of

$$E[r_p(5)] = 15\% \text{ per year}$$

and standard deviation of[13]

$$\begin{aligned}\sigma_p(5) &= \frac{30}{\sqrt{5}} \\ &= 13.42\% \text{ per year}\end{aligned}$$

Mr. Frier is relieved. He believes that the effective standard deviation has fallen from 30% to 13.42%, and that the reward-to-variability ratio is much better than his first assessment.

Is Mr. Frier's newfound sense of security warranted? Specifically, is Ms. Mavin's time diversification really a risk-reducer? It is true that the standard deviation of the annualized *rate* of return over five years really is only 13.42% as Mavin claims, compared with the 30% one-year standard deviation. But what about the volatility of Mr. Frier's total retirement fund? With a standard deviation of the five-year average return of 13.42%, a one-standard-deviation disappointment in Mr. Frier's average return over the five-year period will affect final wealth by a factor of $(1 - .1342)^5 = .487$, meaning that final wealth will be less than one half of its expected value. This is a larger impact than the 30% one-year swing.

[13] The calculation for standard deviation is only approximate, because it assumes that the five- year return is the sum of each of the five one-year returns, and this formulation ignores compounding. The error is small, however, and does not affect the point we want to make.

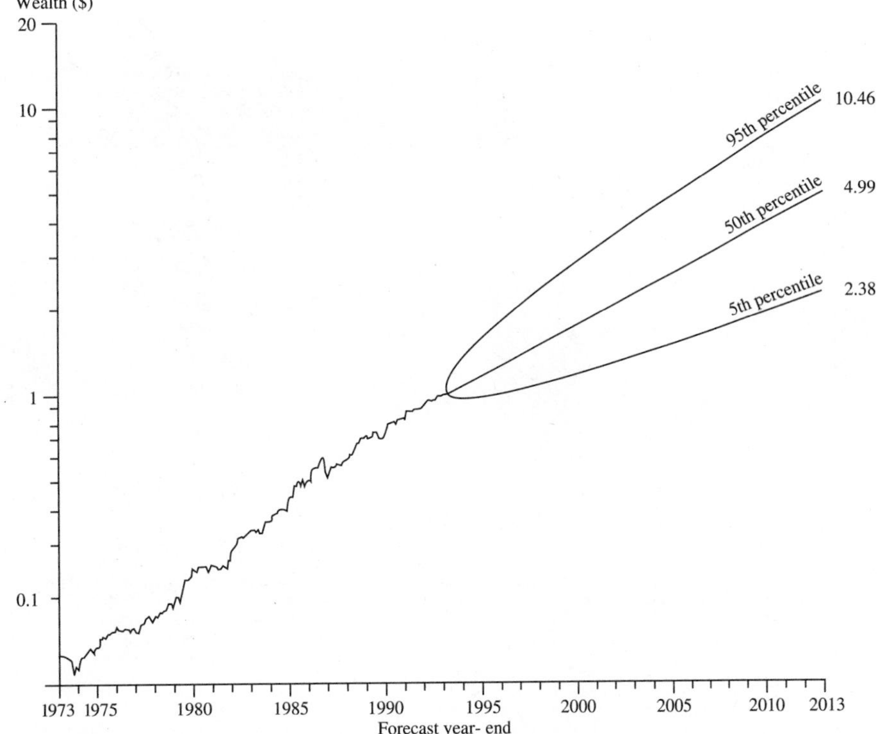

Figure 7C.2

Dollar returns on common stocks. Simulated distributions of nominal wealth index for the period 1994–2013 (year-end 1993 equals 1.00)

Source: *Stocks, Bonds, Bills, and Inflation: 1994 Yearbook* (Chicago: Ibbotson Associates, Inc., 1994).

Ms. Mavin is wrong: Time diversification does not reduce risk. Although it is true that the *per year* average rate of return has a smaller standard deviation for a longer time horizon, it also is true that the uncertainty compounds over a greater number of years. Unfortunately, this latter effect dominates in the sense that the *total return* becomes more uncertain the longer the investment horizon.

Figures 7C.1 and 7C.2 show the fallacy of time diversification. They represent simulated returns to a stock investment and show the range of possible outcomes. Although the confidence band around the expected rate of return on the investment narrows with investment life, the dollar confidence band widens.

Again, the coin-toss analogy is helpful. Think of each year's investment return as one flip of the coin. After many years, the average number of heads approaches 50%, but the possible deviation of total heads from one-half the number of flips still will be growing.

The lesson is, once again, that one should not use rate of return analysis to compare portfolios of different size. Investing for more than one holding period means that the amount of risk is growing. This is analogous to an insurer taking on more insurance policies. The fact that these policies are independent does not offset the effect of placing more funds at risk. Focus on the standard deviation of the rate of return should never obscure the more proper emphasis on the possible dollar values of a portfolio strategy.

Part III

Equilibrium in Capital Markets

Chapter 8
The Capital Asset Pricing Model

THE CAPITAL ASSET PRICING MODEL, ALMOST ALWAYS REFERRED TO AS THE CAPM, IS A CENTERPIECE OF MODERN FINANCIAL ECONOMICS. The model gives us a precise prediction of the relationship that we should observe between the risk of an asset and its expected return. This relationship serves two vital functions. First, it provides a benchmark rate of return for evaluating possible investments. For example, if we are analyzing securities, we might be interested in whether the expected return we forecast for a stock is more or less than its "fair" return given its risk. Second, the model helps us to make an educated guess as to the expected return on assets that have not yet been traded in the marketplace. For example, how do we price an initial public offering of stock? How will a major new investment project affect the return investors require on a company's stock? Although the CAPM does not fully withstand empirical tests, it is widely used because of the insight it offers and because its accuracy suffices for many important applications.

In this chapter we start with the basic version of the CAPM. We also show how the simple version may be extended without losing the insight and applicability of the model.

8.1 The Capital Asset Pricing Model

The capital asset pricing model is a set of predictions concerning equilibrium expected returns on risky assets. We intend to explain it in one short chapter but do not expect this to be easy going. Harry Markowitz laid down the foundation of modern portfolio management in 1952. The CAPM was developed 12 years later in articles by William

Sharpe,[1] John Lintner,[2] and Jan Mossin.[3] The time for this gestation indicates that the leap from Markowitz's portfolio selection model to the CAPM is not trivial.

We will approach the CAPM by posing the question "what if," where the "if" part refers to a simplified world. Positing an admittedly unrealistic world allows a relatively easy leap to the "then" part. Once we accomplish this, we can add complexity to the hypothesized environment one step at a time and see how the conclusions must be amended. This process allows us to derive a reasonably realistic and comprehensible model.

We can summarize the simplifying assumptions that lead to the basic version of the CAPM in the following list. The thrust of these assumptions is that we try to ensure that individuals are as alike as possible, with the notable exceptions of initial wealth and risk tolerance. We will see that conformity of investor behavior vastly simplifies our analysis.

1. There are many investors, each with an endowment (wealth) that is small compared to the total endowment of all investors. Investors are price-takers, in that they act as though security prices are unaffected by their own trades. This is the usual perfect competition assumption of microeconomics.
2. All investors plan for one identical holding period. This behavior sometimes is said to be myopic (short-sighted) in that it ignores everything that might happen after the end of the single-period horizon. Myopic behavior is, in general, suboptimal.
3. Investments are limited to a universe of publicly traded financial assets, such as stocks and bonds, and to risk-free borrowing or lending arrangements. This assumption rules out investment in nontraded assets such as in education (human capital), private enterprises, and governmentally funded assets such as town halls and international airports. It is assumed also that investors may borrow or lend any amount at a fixed, risk-free rate.
4. Investors pay no taxes on returns and no transaction costs (commissions and service charges) on trades in securities. In reality, of course, we know that investors are in different tax brackets and that this may govern the type of assets in which they invest. For example, tax implications may differ depending on whether the income is from interest, dividends, or capital gains. Furthermore, trading is costly, and commissions and fees depend on the size of the trade and the good standing of the individual investor.
5. All investors are rational mean-variance optimizers, meaning that they all use the Markowitz portfolio selection model.
6. All investors analyze securities in the same way and share the same economic view of the world. The result is identical estimates of the probability distribution of future cash flows from investing in the available securities; that is, for any set of security prices, they all derive the same input list to feed into the

[1] William Sharpe, "Capital Asset Prices: A Theory of Market Equilibrium," *Journal of Finance,* September 1964.
[2] John Lintner, "The Valuation of Risk Assets and the Selection of Risky Investments in Stock Portfolios and Capital Budgets," *Review of Economics and Statistics,* February 1965.
[3] Jan Mossin, "Equilibrium in a Capital Asset Market," *Econometrica,* October 1966.

Markowitz model. Given a set of security prices and the risk-free interest rate, all investors use the same expected returns and covariance matrix of security returns to generate the efficient frontier and the unique optimal risky portfolio. This assumption is often referred to as **homogeneous expectations** or beliefs.

These assumptions represent the "if" of our "what if" analysis. Obviously, they ignore many real-world complexities. With these assumptions, however, we can gain some powerful insights into the nature of equilibrium in security markets.

We can summarize the equilibrium that will prevail in this hypothetical world of securities and investors briefly. The rest of the chapter explains and elaborates on these implications.

1. All investors will choose to hold a portfolio of risky assets in proportions that duplicate representation of the assets in the **market portfolio** (*M*), which includes all traded assets. For simplicity, we often shall refer to all risky assets as stocks. The proportion of each stock in the market portfolio equals the market value of the stock (price per share multiplied by the number of shares outstanding) divided by the total market value of all stocks.
2. Not only will the market portfolio be on the efficient frontier, but it also will be the tangency portfolio to the optimal capital allocation line (CAL) derived by each and every investor. As a result, the capital market line (CML), the line from the risk-free rate through the market portfolio, *M*, is also the best attainable capital allocation line. All investors hold *M* as their optimal risky portfolio, differing only in the amount invested in it versus in the risk-free asset.
3. The risk premium on the market portfolio will be proportional to its risk and the degree of risk aversion of the representative investor. Mathematically,

$$E(r_M) - r_f = \overline{A}\sigma_M^2 \times .01$$

where σ_M^2 is the variance of the market portfolio and $\overline{A}$ is the average degree of risk aversion across investors. Note that because *M* is the optimal portfolio, which is efficiently diversified across all stocks, σ_M^2 is the systematic risk of this universe.
4. The risk premium on *individual* assets will be proportional to the risk premium on the market portfolio, *M*, and the *beta coefficient* of the security, relative to the market portfolio. We will see that beta measures the extent to which returns on the stock and the market move together. Formally, beta is defined as

$$\beta_i = \frac{\text{Cov}(r_i, r_M)}{\sigma_M^2}$$

and we can write

$$\begin{aligned} E(r_i) - r_f &= \frac{\text{Cov}(r_i, r_M)}{\sigma_M^2}[E(r_M) - r_f] \\ &= \beta_i [E(r_M) - r_f] \end{aligned}$$

We will elaborate on these results and their implications shortly.

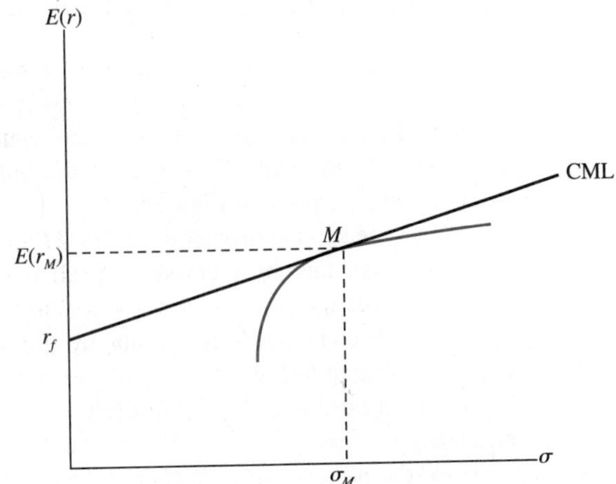

Figure 8.1
The efficient frontier and the capital market line

Why Do All Investors Hold the Market Portfolio?

Given the assumptions of the previous section, it is easy to see that all investors will desire to hold identical risky portfolios. If all investors use identical Markowitz analysis (Assumption 5) applied to the same universe of securities (Assumption 3) for the same time horizon (Assumption 2) and use the same input list (Assumption 6), they all must arrive at the same determination of the optimal risky portfolio, the portfolio on the efficient frontier identified by the tangency line from T-bills to that frontier, as in Figure 8.1. This implies that if the weight of GM stock, for example, in each common risky portfolio is 1%, then when we sum over all investors' portfolios to obtain the aggregate market portfolio, GM also will comprise 1% of the market portfolio. The same principle applies to the proportion of any stock in each investor's risky portfolio. As a result, the optimal risky portfolio of all investors is simply a share of the market portfolio, which we label *M* in Figure 8.1.

Now suppose that the optimal portfolio of our investors does not include the stock of some company, such as Delta Airlines. When all investors avoid Delta stock, the demand is zero, and Delta's price takes a free fall. As Delta stock gets progressively cheaper, it becomes ever more attractive an investment and all other stocks look (relatively) less attractive. Ultimately, Delta reaches a price where it is attractive enough to include in the optimal stock portfolio.

Such a price adjustment process guarantees that all stocks will be included in the optimal portfolio. It shows that *all* assets have to be included in the market portfolio. The only issue is the price at which investors will be willing to include a stock in their optimal risky portfolio.

This may seem a roundabout way to derive a simple result: If all investors hold an identical risky portfolio, this portfolio has to be *M,* the market portfolio. Our intention, however, is to demonstrate a connection between this result and its underpinnings, the equilibrating process that is fundamental to security market operation.

The Passive Strategy Is Efficient

In Chapter 6 we defined the CML (capital market line) as the CAL (capital allocation line) that is constructed from either a money market account or T-bills and the market portfolio. Perhaps now you can fully appreciate why the CML is an interesting CAL. In the simple world of the CAPM, M is the optimal tangency portfolio on the efficient frontier. This is shown in Figure 8.1

In this scenario the market portfolio, M, that all investors hold is based on the common input list, thereby incorporating all relevant information about the universe of securities. This means an investor can skip the trouble of doing specific analysis and obtain an efficient portfolio simply by holding the market portfolio. (Of course, if everyone were to follow this strategy, no one would perform security analysis, and this result would no longer hold. We discuss this issue in depth in Chapter 12 on market efficiency.)

Thus, the passive strategy of investing in a market index portfolio is efficient. For this reason, we sometimes call this result a **mutual fund theorem.** The mutual fund theorem is another incarnation of the separation property discussed in Chapter 7. Assuming that all investors choose to hold a market index mutual fund, we can separate portfolio selection into two components—a technological problem, creation of mutual funds by professional managers—and a personal problem that depends on an investor's risk aversion, allocation of the *complete* portfolio between the mutual fund and risk-free assets.

Of course, in reality different investment managers do create risky portfolios that differ from the market index. We attribute this in part to the use of different input lists in the formation of the optimal risky portfolio. Nevertheless, the significance of the mutual fund theorem is that a passive investor may view the market index as a reasonable first approximation of an efficient risky portfolio.

CONCEPT CHECK Question 1. If there are only a few investors who perform security analysis, and all others hold the market portfolio M, would the CML still be the efficient CAL for investors who do not engage in security analysis? Why or why not?

The Risk Premium of the Market Portfolio

In Chapter 6 we discussed how individual investors go about deciding how much to invest in the risky portfolio. Returning now to the decision of how much to invest in portfolio M versus in the risk-free asset, what can we deduce about the equilibrium risk premium of portfolio M?

We asserted earlier that the equilibrium risk premium on the market portfolio, $E(r_M) - r_f$, will be proportional to the average degree of risk aversion of the investor population and the risk of the market portfolio, σ_M^2. Now we can explain this result.

Recall that each individual investor chooses a proportion, y, allocated to the optimal portfolio M, such that

$$y = \frac{E(r_M) - r_f}{.01 \times A\sigma_M^2} \tag{8.1}$$

In the simplified CAPM economy risk-free investments involve borrowing and lending among investors. Any borrowing position must be offset by the lending position of the creditor. This means that net borrowing and lending across all investors must be zero, and in consequence the average position in the risky portfolio is 100% or $\overline{y} = 1$. Setting $y = 1$ in equation 8.1 and rearranging, we find that the risk premium on the market portfolio is related to its variance by the average degree of risk aversion.

$$E(r_M) - r_f = .01 \times \overline{A}\sigma_M^2 \tag{8.2}$$

CONCEPT CHECK

Question 2. Data from the period 1926 to 1993 for the S&P 500 index yield the following statistics: Average excess return, 8.6%; standard deviation, 20.5%.

a. To the extent that these averages approximated investor expectations for the period, what must have been the average coefficient of risk aversion?

b. If the coefficient of risk aversion were actually 3.5, what risk premium would have been consistent with the market's historical standard deviation?

Expected Returns on Individual Securities

The CAPM is built on the insight that the appropriate risk premium on an asset will be determined by its contribution to the risk of investors' overall portfolios. Portfolio risk is what matters to investors and is what governs the risk premiums they demand.

Remember that all investors use the same input list, that is, the same estimates of expected returns, variances, and covariances. We saw in Chapter 7 that these covariances can be arranged in a covariance matrix, so that the entry in the fifth row and third column, for example, would be the covariance between the rates of return on the fifth and third securities. Each diagonal entry of the matrix is the covariance of one security's return with itself, which is simply the variance of that security. We will consider the construction of the input list a bit later. For now, however, we take it as given.

Suppose, for example, that we want to gauge the portfolio risk of GM stock. We measure the contribution to the risk of the overall portfolio from holding GM stock by its covariance with the market portfolio. To see why this is so, let us look again at the way the variance of the market portfolio is calculated. To calculate the variance of the market portfolio, we use the covariance matrix bordered by market portfolio weights, as discussed in Chapter 7. We highlight GM in this depiction of the *n* stocks in the market portfolio.

Portfolio Weights	w_1	w_2	...	w_{GM}	...	w_n
w_1	$\text{Cov}(r_1,r_1)$	$\text{Cov}(r_1,r_2)$	...	$\text{Cov}(r_1,r_{GM})$	...	$\text{Cov}(r_1,r_n)$
w_2	$\text{Cov}(r_2,r_1)$	$\text{Cov}(r_2,r_2)$	...	$\text{Cov}(r_2,r_{GM})$	...	$\text{Cov}(r_2,r_n)$
•	•	•		•		•
•	•	•		•		•
•	•	•		•		•
w_{GM}	$\text{Cov}(r_{GM},r_1)$		...	$\text{Cov}(r_{GM},r_{GM})$	...	$\text{Cov}(r_{GM},r_n)$
•	•	•		•		•
•	•	•		•		•
w_n	$\text{Cov}(r_n,r_1)$	$\text{Cov}(r_n,r_2)$	...	$\text{Cov}(r_n,r_{GM})$	...	$\text{Cov}(r_n,r_n)$

Recall that we calculate the variance of the portfolio by summing over all the elements of the covariance matrix, first multiplying each element by the portfolio weights from the row and the column. The contribution of one stock to portfolio variance therefore can be expressed as the sum of all the covariance terms in the row corresponding to the stock where each covariance is multiplied by both the portfolio weight from its row and the weight from its column.[4]

For example, the contribution of GM's stock to the variance of the market portfolio is

$$w_{GM}[w_1 \text{Cov}(r_1, r_{GM}) + w_2 \text{Cov}(r_2, r_{GM}) + \ldots + w_{GM} \text{Cov}(r_{GM}, r_{GM}) + \ldots w_n \text{Cov}(r_n, r_{GM})] \tag{8.3}$$

Equation 8.3 provides a clue about the respective roles of variance and covariance in determining asset risk. It shows us that, when there are many stocks in the economy, there will be many more covariance terms than variance terms. Consequently, the covariance of a particular stock with all other stocks might be expected to have more to do with that stock's contribution to total portfolio risk than does its own variance. We may summarize the terms in brackets in equation 8.3 simply as the covariance of GM with the market portfolio. In other words, we can best measure the stock's contribution to the risk of the market portfolio by its covariance with that portfolio:

$$\text{GM's contribution to variance} = w_{GM} \text{Cov}(r_{GM}, r_M)$$

This should not surprise us. For example, if the covariance between GM and the rest of the market is negative, then GM makes a "negative contribution" to portfolio risk: By providing returns that move inversely with the rest of the market, GM stabilizes the return on the overall portfolio. If the covariance is positive, GM makes a positive contribution to overall portfolio risk because its returns amplify swings in the rest of the portfolio.

To prove this more rigorously, note that the rate of return on the market portfolio may be written as

$$r_M = \sum_{k=1}^{n} w_k r_k$$

Therefore, the covariance of the return on GM with the market portfolio is

$$\text{Cov}(r_{GM}, r_M) = \text{Cov}(r_{GM}, \sum_{k=1}^{n} w_k r_k) = \sum_{k=1}^{n} w_k \text{Cov}(r_{GM}, r_k) \tag{8.4}$$

Comparing the last term of equation 8.4 to the term in brackets in equation 8.3, we can see that the covariance of GM with the market portfolio is indeed proportional to the contribution of GM to the variance of the market portfolio.

---

[4] An alternative and equally valid approach would be to measure GM's contribution to market variance as the sum of the elements in the row *and* the column corresponding to GM. In this case, GM's contribution would be twice the sum in equation 8.3. The approach that we take in the text allocates contributions to portfolio risk among securities in a convenient manner in that the sum of the contributions of each stock equals the total portfolio variance, whereas the alternative measure of contribution would sum to twice the portfolio variance. This results from a type of double-counting, because adding both the rows and the columns for each stock would result in each entry in the matrix being added twice.

Having measured the contribution of GM stock to market variance, we may determine the appropriate risk premium for GM. We note first that the market portfolio has a risk premium of $E(r_M) - r_f$ and a variance of σ_M^2, for a reward-to-risk ratio of

$$\frac{E(r_M) - r_f}{\sigma_M^2} \tag{8.5}$$

This ratio often is called the **market price of risk,**[5] because it quantifies the extra return that investors demand to bear portfolio risk. The ratio of risk premium to variance tells us how much extra return must be earned per unit of portfolio risk.

Consider the average investor who is now invested 100% in the market portfolio and suppose he were to increase his position in the market portfolio by a tiny fraction, δ, financed by borrowing at the risk-free rate. Think of the new portfolio as a combination of three assets: the original position in the market with return r_M, plus a short (negative) position of size δ in the risk-free asset that will return $-\delta r_f$, plus a long position of size δ in the market that will return δr_M. The portfolio rate of return will be $r_M + \delta(r_M - r_f)$. Taking expectations and comparing with the original expected return, $E(r_M)$, the incremental expected rate of return will be

$$\Delta E(r) = \delta[E(r_M) - r_f]$$

To measure the impact of the portfolio shift on risk, we compute the new value of the portfolio variance. The new portfolio has a weight of $(1 + \delta)$ in the market and $-\delta$ in the risk-free asset. Therefore, the variance of the adjusted portfolio is

$$\sigma^2 = (1 + \delta)^2\sigma_M^2 = (1 + 2\delta + \delta^2)\sigma_M^2 = \sigma_M^2 + (2\delta + \delta^2)\,\sigma_M^2$$

However, if δ is very small, then δ^2 will be negligible compared to 2δ, so we may ignore this term.[6] Therefore, the variance of the adjusted portfolio is $\sigma_M^2 + 2\delta\sigma_M^2$, and portfolio variance has increased by

$$\Delta\sigma^2 = 2\delta\sigma_M^2$$

Summarizing these results, the trade-off between the *incremental risk premium* and *incremental risk*, referred to as the *marginal price of risk,* is given by the ratio

$$\frac{\Delta E(r)}{\Delta\sigma^2} = \frac{E(r_M) - r_f}{2\sigma_M^2}$$

and equals one-half the market price of risk of equation 8.5.

---

[5] We open ourselves to ambiguity in using this term, because the market portfolios' reward-to-variability ratio

$$\frac{E(r_M) - r_f}{\sigma_M}$$

sometimes is referred to as the market price of risk. Note that since the appropriate risk measure of GM is its covariance with the market portfolio (its contribution to the variance of the market portfolio), this risk is measured in percent squared. Accordingly, the price of this risk, $[E(r_M) - r_f]/\sigma^2$, is defined as the percentage of expected return per percent square of variance.

[6] For example, if δ is 1% (.01 of wealth), then its square is .0001 of wealth, one-hundredth of the original value. The term $\delta^2\sigma_M^2$ will be smaller than $2\delta\sigma_M^2$ by an order of magnitude.

Now suppose that, instead, investors were to invest the increment δ in GM stock, also financed by borrowing at the risk-free rate. The increase in mean excess return is

$$\Delta E(r) = \delta[E(r_{\text{GM}}) - r_f]$$

This portfolio has a weight of 1.0 in the market, δ in GM, and $-\delta$ in the risk-free asset. Its variance is $\sigma_M^2 + 2\delta\text{Cov}(r_M,r_{\text{GM}}) + \delta^2\,\sigma_{\text{GM}}^2$

The increase in variance here includes the variance of the incremental position in GM *plus* twice its covariance with the market:

$$\Delta\sigma^2 = \delta^2\,\sigma_{\text{GM}}^2 + 2\delta\text{Cov}(r_{\text{GM}},r_M)$$

Dropping the negligible term involving δ^2, the *marginal price of risk* of GM is

$$\frac{\Delta E(r)}{\Delta\sigma^2} = \frac{E(r_{\text{GM}}) - r_f}{2\text{Cov}(r_{\text{GM}},r_M)}$$

In equilibrium, the marginal price of risk of GM stock must equal that of the market portfolio. Otherwise, if the marginal price of risk of GM is greater than the market's, investors can increase their portfolio *average* price of risk by increasing the weight of GM in their portfolio. Until the price of GM stock rises relative to the market, investors will keep buying GM stock. The process will continue until stock prices adjust so that marginal price of risk of GM equals that of the market. The same process, in reverse, will equalize marginal prices of risk when GM's initial marginal price of risk is less than that of the market portfolio. Equating the marginal price of risk of GM's stock to that of the market results in a relationship between the risk premium of GM and that of the market.

$$\frac{E(r_{\text{GM}}) - r_f}{2\text{Cov}(r_{\text{GM}},r_M)} = \frac{E(r_M) - r_f}{2\sigma_M^2}$$

To determine the fair risk premium of GM stock, we rearrange slightly to obtain

$$E(r_{\text{GM}}) - r_f = \frac{\text{Cov}(r_{\text{GM}},r_M)}{\sigma_M^2}\,[E(r_M) - r_f] \tag{8.6}$$

The term $\text{Cov}(r_{\text{GM}},r_M)/\sigma_M^2$ measures the contribution of GM stock to the variance of the market portfolio as a fraction of the total variance of the market portfolio and is called **beta** and denoted by β. Using this measure, we can restate equation 8.6 as

$$E(r_{\text{GM}}) = r_f + \beta_{\text{GM}}[E(r_M) - r_f] \tag{8.7}$$

This **expected return–beta relationship** is the most familiar expression of the CAPM to practitioners. We will have a lot more to say about the expected return–beta relationship shortly.

We see now why the assumptions that made individuals act similarly are so useful. If everyone holds an identical risky portfolio, then everyone will find that the beta of each asset with the market portfolio equals the asset's beta with his or her own risky portfolio. Hence, everyone will agree on the appropriate risk premium for each asset.

Does the fact that few real-life investors actually hold the market portfolio imply that the CAPM is of no practical importance? Not necessarily. Recall from Chapter 7 that reasonably well-diversified portfolios shed firm-specific risk and are left with only systematic or market risk. Even if one does not hold the precise market portfolio, a well-diversified portfolio will be so very highly correlated with the market that a stock's beta relative to the market will still be a useful risk measure.

In fact, several authors have shown that modified versions of the CAPM will hold true even if we consider differences among individuals leading them to hold different portfolios. For example, Brennan[7] examined the impact of differences in investors' personal tax rates on market equilibrium, and Mayers[8] looked at the impact of nontraded assets such as human capital (earning power). Both found that although the market portfolio is no longer each investor's optimal risky portfolio, the expected return–beta relationship should still hold in a somewhat modified form.

If the expected return–beta relationship holds for any individual asset, it must hold for any combination of assets. Suppose that some portfolio P has weight w_k for stock k, where k takes on values $1, \ldots, n$. Writing out the CAPM equation 8.7 for each stock, and multiplying each equation by the weight of the stock in the portfolio, we obtain these equations, one for each stock:

$$\begin{array}{rcl} w_1E(r_1) &=& w_1r_f + w_1\beta_1[E(r_M) - r_f] \\ +\ w_2E(r_2) &=& w_2r_f + w_2\beta_2[E(r_M) - r_f] \\ +\quad \ldots &=& \ldots \\ +\ w_nE(r_n) &=& w_nr_f + w_n\beta_n[E(r_M) - r_f] \\ \hline E(r_P) &=& r_f + \beta_P[E(r_M) - r_f] \end{array}$$

Summing each column shows that the CAPM holds for the overall portfolio because $E(r_P) = \sum_k w_kE(r_k)$ is the expected return on the portfolio, and $\beta_P = \sum_k w_k\beta_k$ is the portfolio beta. Incidentally, this result has to be true for the market portfolio itself,

$$E(r_M) = r_f + \beta_M[E(r_M) - r_f]$$

Indeed, this is a tautology because $\beta_M = 1$, as we can verify by demonstrating that

$$\beta_M = \frac{\text{Cov}(r_M, r_M)}{\sigma_M^2} = \frac{\sigma_M^2}{\sigma_M^2}$$

This also establishes 1 as the weighted average value of beta across all assets. If the market beta is 1, and the market is a portfolio of all assets in the economy, the weighted average beta of all assets must be 1. Hence, betas greater than 1 are considered aggressive in that investment in high-beta stocks entails above-average sensitivity to market swings. Betas below 1 can be described as defensive.

A word of caution: We are all accustomed to hearing that well-managed firms will provide high rates of return. We agree this is true if one measures the *firm's* return on investments in plant and equipment. The CAPM, however, predicts returns on investments in the *securities* of the firm.

---

[7] Michael J. Brennan, "Taxes, Market Valuation, and Corporate Finance Policy," *National Tax Journal,* December 1973.

[8] David Mayers, "Nonmarketable Assets and Capital Market Equilibrium Under Uncertainty," in *Studies in the Theory of Capital Markets,* ed. M. C. Jensen (New York: Praeger, 1972).

Let us say that everyone knows a firm is well run. Its stock price will therefore be bid up, and consequently returns to stockholders who buy at those high prices will not be excessive. Security prices, in other words, reflect public information about a firm's prospects, but only the risk of the company (as measured by beta in the context of the CAPM) should affect expected returns. In a rational market investors receive high expected returns only if they are willing to bear risk.

CONCEPT CHECK Question 3. Suppose that the risk premium on the market portfolio is estimated at 8% with a standard deviation of 22%. What is the risk premium on a portfolio invested 25% in GM and 75% in Ford, if they have betas of 1.10 and 1.25, respectively?

The Security Market Line

We can view the expected return–beta relationship as a reward-risk equation. The beta of a security is the appropriate measure of its risk because beta is proportional to the risk that the security contributes to the optimal risky portfolio.

Risk-averse investors measure the risk of the optimal risky portfolio by its variance. In this world we would expect the reward, or the risk premium on individual assets, to depend on the risk that an individual asset contributes to the portfolio. The beta of a stock measures the stock's contribution to the variance of the market portfolio. Hence we expect, for any asset or portfolio, the required risk premium to be a function of beta. The CAPM confirms this intuition, stating further that the security's risk premium is directly proportional to both the beta and the risk premium of the market portfolio; that is, the risk premium equals $\beta[E(r_M) - r_f]$.

The expected return–beta relationship can be portrayed graphically as the **security market line (SML)** in Figure 8.2. Because the market beta is 1, the slope is the risk premium of the market portfolio. At the point where $\beta = 1$ on the horizontal axis (which is the market portfolio's beta) we can read off the vertical axis the expected return on the market portfolio.

It is useful to compare the security market line to the capital market line. The CML graphs the risk premiums of efficient portfolios (i.e., portfolios composed of the market and the risk-free asset) as a function of portfolio standard deviation. This is appropriate because standard deviation is a valid measure of risk for efficiently diversified portfolios that are candidates for an investor's overall portfolio. The SML, in contrast, graphs *individual asset* risk premiums as a function of asset risk. The relevant measure of risk for individual assets held as parts of well-diversified portfolios is not the asset's standard deviation or variance; it is, instead, the contribution of the asset to the portfolio variance, which we measure by the asset's beta. The SML is valid for both efficient portfolios and individual assets.

The security market line provides a benchmark for the evaluation of investment performance. Given the risk of an investment, as measured by its beta, the SML provides the required rate of return from that investment to compensate investors for risk, as well as the time value of money.

Because the security market line is the graphic representation of the expected return–beta relationship, "fairly priced" assets plot exactly on the SML; that is, their

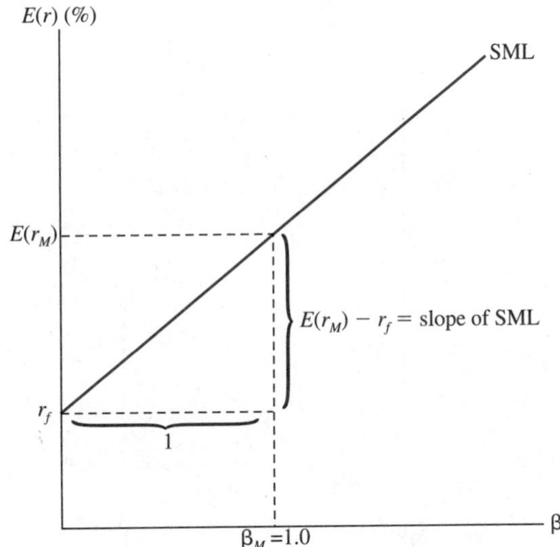

Figure 8.2
The security market line

expected returns are commensurate with their risk. Given the assumptions we made at the start of this section, all securities must lie on the SML in market equilibrium. Nevertheless, we see here how the CAPM may be of use in the money-management industry. Suppose that the SML relation is used as a benchmark to assess the fair expected return on a risky asset. Then security analysis is performed to calculate the return actually expected. (Notice that we depart here from the simple CAPM world in that some investors now apply their own unique analysis to derive an "input list" that may differ from their competitors'.) If a stock is perceived to be a good buy, or underpriced, it will provide an expected return in excess of the fair return stipulated by the SML. Underpriced stocks therefore plot above the SML: Given their betas, their expected returns are greater than dictated by the CAPM. Overpriced stocks plot below the SML.

The difference between the fair and actually expected rates of return on a stock is called the stock's **alpha,** denoted α. For example, if the market return is expected to be 14%, a stock has a beta of 1.2, and the T-bill rate is 6%, the SML would predict an expected return on the stock of 6 + 1.2 (14 − 6) = 15.6%. If one believed the stock would provide a return of 17%, the implied alpha would be 1.4% (see Figure 8.3).

The CAPM is also useful in capital budgeting decisions. For a firm considering a new project, the CAPM can provide the *required rate of return* that the project needs to yield, based on its beta, to be acceptable to investors. Managers can use the CAPM to obtain this cutoff internal rate of return (IRR) or "hurdle rate" for the project.

Yet another use of the CAPM is in utility rate-making cases. In this case the issue is the rate of return that a regulated utility should be allowed to earn on its investment in plant and equipment. Suppose that the equityholders have invested $100 million in the firm and that the beta of the equity is 0.6. If the T-bill rate is 6% and the market risk premium is 8%, then the fair profits to the firm would be assessed as 6 + .6(8) = 10.8%

Figure 8.3
The SML and a positive-alpha stock

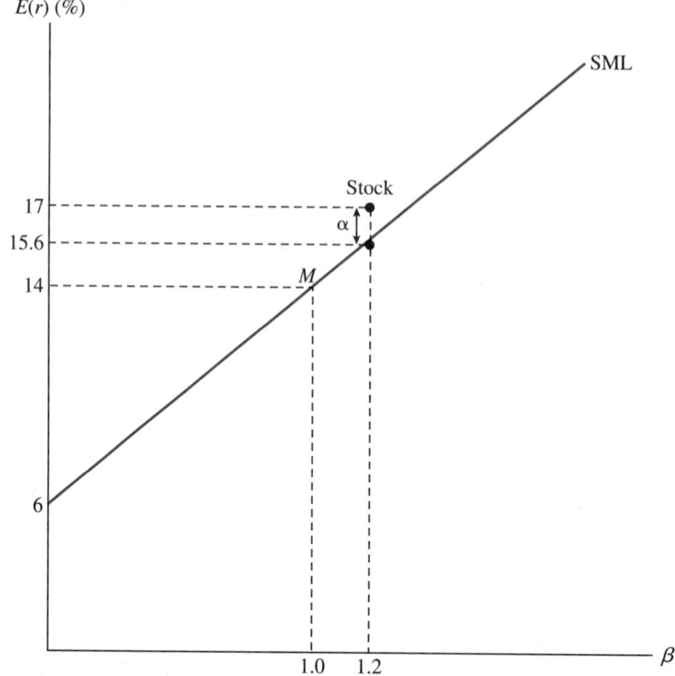

of the \$100 million investment, or \$10.8 million. The firm would be allowed to set prices at a level expected to generate these profits.

CONCEPT CHECK

Question 4. Stock XYZ has an expected return of 12% and risk of $\beta = 1$. Stock ABC has expected return of 13% and $\beta = 1.5$. The market's expected return is 11%, and $r_f = 5\%$.

a. According to the CAPM, which stock is a better buy?
b. What is the alpha of each stock? Plot the SML and each stock's risk-return point on one graph. Show the alphas graphically.

Question 5. The risk-free rate is 8% and the expected return on the market portfolio is 16%. A firm considers a project that is expected to have a beta of 1.3.

a. What is the required rate of return on the project?
b. If the expected IRR of the project is 19%, should it be accepted?

8.2 EXTENSIONS OF THE CAPM

The assumptions that allowed Sharpe to derive the simple version of the CAPM are admittedly unrealistic. Financial economists have been at work ever since the CAPM was devised to extend the model to more realistic scenarios.

There are two classes of extensions to the simple version of the CAPM. The first attempts to relax the assumptions that we outlined at the outset of the chapter. The second acknowledges the fact that investors worry about sources of risk other than the uncertain value of their securities, such as unexpected changes in relative prices of consumer goods. This idea involves the introduction of additional risk factors besides security returns, and we will discuss it further in Chapters 10 and 25.

The CAPM with Restricted Borrowing: The Zero-Beta Model

The CAPM is predicated on the assumption that all investors share an identical input list that they feed into the Markowitz algorithm. Thus, all investors agree on the location of the efficient (minimum-variance) frontier, where each portfolio has the lowest variance among all feasible portfolios at a target expected rate of return. When all investors can borrow and lend at the safe rate, r_f, all agree on the optimal tangency portfolio and choose to hold a share of the market portfolio.

When there are constraints on risk-free lending and/or borrowing, we will see that the market portfolio is no longer the common optimal portfolio for all investors. One "restriction" on risk-free borrowing and lending is that in a strict sense, once we account for inflation uncertainty, there is no truly risk-free asset in the U.S. economy. Only Treasury securities are entirely free of default risk, but these are nominal obligations, meaning that their real values are exposed to price level risk. In this sense there is no risk-free asset in the economy. Other restrictions have to do with differences in the rates at which investors can borrow and lend.

When investors no longer can borrow or lend at a common risk-free rate, they may choose risky portfolios from the entire set of efficient frontier portfolios according to how much risk they choose to bear. The market is no longer the common optimal portfolio. In fact, with investors choosing different portfolios, it is no longer obvious whether the market portfolio, which is the aggregate of all investors' portfolios, will even be on the efficient frontier. If the market portfolio is no longer mean-variance efficient, then the expected return–beta relationship of the CAPM will no longer characterize market equilibrium.

An equilibrium expected return–beta relationship in the case of restricted risk-free investments has been developed by Fischer Black.[9] Black's model is fairly difficult and requires a good deal of facility with mathematics. Therefore, we will satisfy ourselves with a sketch of Black's argument and spend more time with its implications.

Black's model of the CAPM in the absence of a risk-free asset rests on the three following properties of mean-variance efficient portfolios:

1. Any portfolio constructed by combining efficient portfolios is itself on the efficient frontier.
2. Every portfolio on the efficient frontier has a "companion" portfolio on the bottom half (the inefficient part) of the minimum-variance frontier with which it is uncorrelated. Because the portfolios are uncorrelated, the companion portfolio is referred to as the **zero-beta portfolio** of the efficient portfolio.

   The expected return of an efficient portfolio's zero-beta companion portfolio can be derived by the following graphical procedure. From any efficient

[9] Fischer Black, "Capital Market Equilibrium with Restricted Borrowing," *Journal of Business*, July 1972.

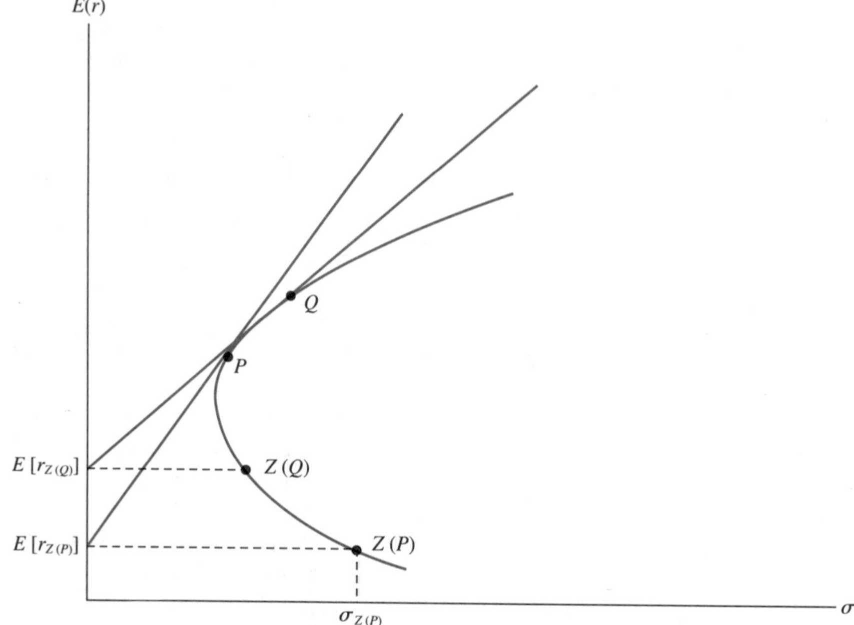

Figure 8.4 Efficient portfolios and their zero-beta companions

portfolio such as P in Figure 8.4 draw a tangency line to the vertical axis. The intercept will be the expected return on portfolio P's zero-beta companion portfolio, denoted $Z(P)$. The horizontal line from the intercept to the minimum-variance frontier identifies the standard deviation of the zero-beta portfolio. Notice in Figure 8.4 that different efficient portfolios such as P and Q have different zero-beta companions.

These tangency lines are helpful constructs only. They do *not* signify that one can invest in portfolios with expected return–standard deviation pairs along the line. That would be possible only by mixing a risk-free asset with the tangency portfolio. In this case, however, we assume that risk-free assets are not available to investors.

3. The expected return of any asset can be expressed as an exact, linear function of the expected return on any two frontier portfolios. Consider, for example, the minimum-variance frontier portfolios P and Q. Black showed that the expected return on any asset i can be expressed as

$$E(r_i) = E(r_Q) + [E(r_P) - E(r_Q)]\frac{\text{Cov}(r_i,r_P) - \text{Cov}(r_P,r_Q)}{\sigma_P^2 - \text{Cov}(r_P,r_Q)} \tag{8.8}$$

Note that Property 3 has nothing to do with market equilibrium. It is a purely mathematical property relating frontier portfolios and individual securities.

Given these three properties, it is easy to derive Black's model. The assumption of homogeneous expectations assures us that all investors use the same input list and compute the same minimum-variance frontier. Each investor will invest in an efficient port-

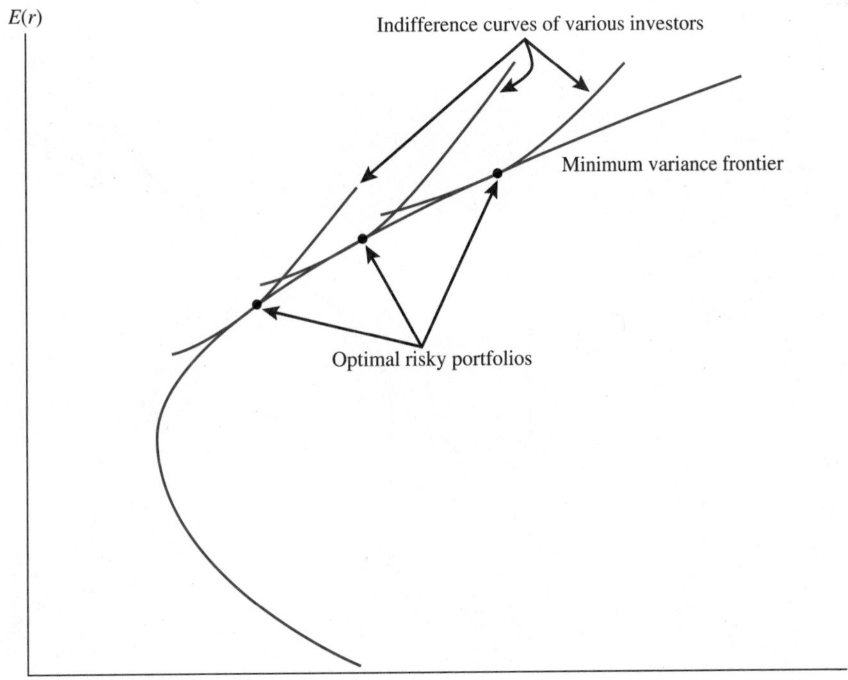

Figure 8.5
Portfolio selection with no risk-free assets

folio according to his or her degree of risk aversion, as in Figure 8.5. Therefore, the market portfolio, which is just the aggregate of all investors' portfolios, is a combination of efficient portfolios, and by Property 1, must itself be an efficient portfolio.

Next, recall equation 8.8 from Property 3. Instead of using the arbitrarily chosen frontier portfolios *P* and *Q* in the equation, let us instead use as our two frontier portfolios the market portfolio, *M,* and its zero-beta companion *Z(M).* This is a convenient pairing of portfolios because their mutual covariance is zero, causing equation 8.8 to simplify. Specifically, because $\text{Cov}[r_M, r_{Z(M)}] = 0$, the expected return of any asset *i,* using *M* and *Z(M)* as the benchmark frontier portfolios, can be expressed as

$$E(r_i) = E[r_{Z(M)}] + E[r_M - r_{Z(M)}] \frac{\text{Cov}(r_i, r_M)}{\sigma_M^2} \tag{8.9}$$

where *P* from equation 8.8 has been replaced by *M* and *Q* has been replaced by *Z(M).* Note that this is a variant of the simple CAPM, in which r_f simply has been replaced with $E[r_{Z(M)}]$.

Although Black derived this variant of the CAPM for the case in which no risk-free asset exists, the approach we have taken can be applied to many related scenarios. For example, consider an economy in which investors can lend at the risk-free rate (can buy T-bills, for example) but cannot borrow funds to invest. We first explored portfolio selection for this situation in Section 7.5. Now we can explore market equilibrium.

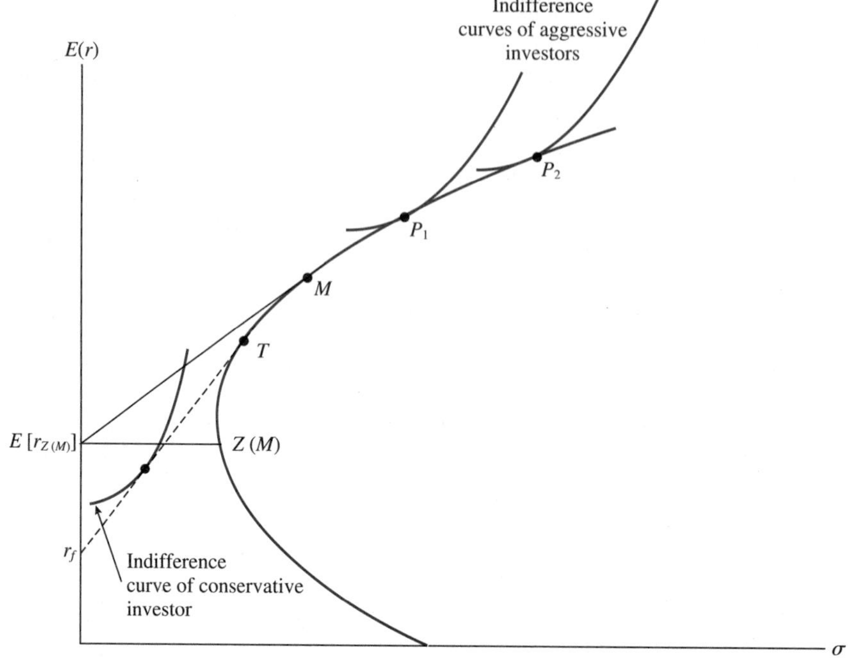

Figure 8.6
Capital market equilibrium with risk-free lending but no risk-free borrowing

Figure 8.6 shows that relatively conservative (risk-averse) investors will select the tangency portfolio, *T,* as their optimal risky portfolio and mix *T* with the safe asset. Relatively aggressive investors will choose efficient portfolios like P_1 or P_2. The market portfolio, *M,* will be a combination of these portfolios, all of which are efficient, meaning that the market also will be an efficient portfolio. Therefore, the zero-beta version of the CAPM will apply in this situation as well.

A more realistic scenario is one in which the investor can lend at the risk-free rate, r_f, and can borrow at a higher rate, r_f^B. This case was considered in Chapter 7. The same arguments that we have just employed can also be used to establish the zero-beta CAPM in this situation. Problem 18 at the end of this chapter asks you to fill in the details of the argument for this situation.

CONCEPT CHECK Question 6. Suppose that the zero-beta portfolio exhibits returns that are, on average, greater than the rate on T-bills. Is this fact relevant to the question of the validity of the CAPM?

Lifetime Consumption: The CAPM with Dynamic Programming

One of the restrictive assumptions for the simple version of the CAPM is that investors are myopic—they plan for one common holding period. Investors actually may be concerned with a lifetime consumption plan and a possible desire to leave a bequest to children. Consumption plans that are feasible for them depend on current wealth and future rates of return on the investment portfolio. These investors will want to rebalance their portfolios as often as required by changes in wealth.

However, Eugene Fama[10] showed that, even if we extend our analysis to a multiperiod setting, the single-period CAPM still may be appropriate. The key assumptions that Fama used to replace myopic planning horizons are that investor preferences are unchanging over time and the risk-free interest rate and probability distribution of security returns do not change unpredictably over time. Of course, this latter assumption is also unrealistic. However, the extension to the CAPM engendered by considering random changes to the so-called "investment opportunity set" must wait until Chapter 25.

8.3 The CAPM and Liquidity: A Theory of Illiquidity Premiums

Liquidity refers to the cost and ease with which an asset can be converted into cash, that is, sold. Traders have long recognized the importance of liquidity, and some evidence suggests that illiquidity can reduce market prices substantially. For example, one study[11] finds that market discounts on closely held (and therefore nontraded) firms can exceed 30%. It also reports on an unusual class of stocks that was issued with a provision that prohibited public trading for two to three years, which traded at a discount of about 30%. Interestingly, such a discount is similar to the three-year risk premium on an average stock, which has been between 8% and 9% per year. This suggests that premiums for illiquidity can be roughly of the same magnitude as risk premiums, and may deserve a comparable amount of attention.

A rigorous treatment of the value of liquidity was developed by Amihud and Mendelson.[12] We believe that liquidity will become an important part of standard valuation, and therefore present here a simplified version of their model.

Recall Assumption 4 of the CAPM, that all trading is costless. In reality, no security is perfectly liquid, in that all trades involve some transaction cost. Investors prefer more liquid assets with lower transaction costs, so it should not surprise us to find that (all else equal) relatively illiquid assets trade at lower prices, or equivalently, that the expected rate of return on illiquid assets must be higher. Therefore, an **illiquidity premium** must be impounded into the price of each asset. The impact of liquidity will depend on both the distribution of transaction costs across assets as well as the distribution of investors across investment horizons. We will use very simplified distributions to illustrate the effect of liquidity on equilibrium expected returns. However, you will see that these simplifications are expositional only, and that the predicted effect of liquidity on equilibrium returns is quite general.

---

[10] Eugene F. Fama, "Multiperiod Consumption-Investment Decisions," *American Economic Review* 60 (1970).

[11] Shannon P. Pratt, *Valuing a Business: The Analysis of Closely Held Companies,* 2nd ed. (Homewood, Ill.: Dow Jones–Irwin), 1989.

[12] Yakov Amihud and Haim Mendelson, "Asset Pricing and the Bid-Ask Spread," *Journal of Financial Economics* 17 (1986), pp. 223–49.

We will start with the simplest case, in which we can ignore systematic risk. Imagine, therefore, a world with a very large number of uncorrelated securities. Because the securities are uncorrelated, highly diversified portfolios of these securities will have standard deviations nearly equal to zero. Therefore, the diversified market portfolio will be virtually as safe as the risk-free asset and yield an expected return equal to the risk-free rate. Moreover, the covariance between any pair of securities also is zero, implying that the beta of any security with the diversified market portfolio is zero. Therefore, according to the CAPM, all assets should have expected rates of return equal to that of the risk-free asset, which we will take to be T-bills.

Assume that investors know in advance for how long they intend to hold their portfolios, and suppose that there are n types of investors, grouped by investment horizon. Type 1 investors intend to liquidate their portfolios in one period, Type 2 investors in two periods, and so on, until the longest-horizon investors (Type n) intend to hold their portfolios for n periods.

Because we are now dealing with a multiperiod model, we should be careful in our comparison with the single-period CAPM. However, we've seen that Fama's work (see footnote 10) implies that even if investors have multiperiod investment horizons, the simple expected return–beta relationship of the CAPM still might describe equilibrium security returns. To stay as close as possible to Fama's assumptions, we will assume that as investors liquidate their portfolios, just enough investors of each type enter the market to take the place of those who depart. Thus, in each period, there is identical demand for securities, as Fama required. However, even with these assumptions, the presence of trading costs *in conjunction with* differing investment horizons will require an adaptation of the CAPM.

We start with a simple structure of transaction costs as well, assuming that there are only two classes of securities: liquid and illiquid. These types of securities differ in their liquidation cost, the cost of selling the security at the end of the investment horizon. The liquidation cost of a class L (more liquid) stock to an investor with a horizon of h years (a type h investor) will reduce the per-period rate of return by $c_L/h\%$. For example, if the combination of commissions and the bid-ask spread on a security resulted in a liquidation cost of 10%, then the per-period rate of return for an investor who holds the stock for five years would be reduced by approximately 2% per year, whereas the return on a 10-year investment would fall by only 1% per year.[13] Class I (illiquid) assets have higher liquidation costs that reduce the per-period return by c_I/H%, where c_I is greater than c_L. Therefore, if you intend to hold a class L security for h periods, your expected rate of return *net* of transaction costs is $E(r_L) - c_L/h$. There is no liquidation cost on T-bills.

The following table presents the expected rates of return investors would realize from the risk-free asset and class L and class I stock portfolios *assuming* that the simple CAPM is correct and all securities have an expected rate of return of r.

[13] This simple structure of liquidation costs allows us to derive a correspondingly simple solution for the effect of liquidity on expected returns. Amihud and Mendelson used a more general formulation, but then needed to rely on complex and more difficult-to-interpret mathematical programming. All that matters for the qualitative results below, however, is that illiquidity costs be less onerous to longer-term investors.

Asset:	Risk-Free	Class L	Class I
Gross rate of return:	r	r	r
One-period liquidation cost:	0	c_L	c_I
Investor Type		**Net Rate of Return**	
1	r	$r - c_L$	$r - c_I$
2	r	$r - c_L/2$	$r - c_I/2$
. . .	. . .	. . .	. . .
n	r	$r - c_L/n$	$r - c_I/n$

These net rates of return are inconsistent with a market in equilibrium, because with equal gross rates of return of r, all investors would prefer to invest in zero-transaction-cost T-bills. As a result, both class L and class I stock prices must fall, causing their expected rates of return to rise until investors are willing to hold these shares.

Suppose, therefore, that each gross return is higher by some fraction of liquidation cost. Specifically, assume that the gross expected rate of return on class L stocks is $r + xc_L$ and that of class I stocks is $r + yc_I$, where x and y are smaller than 1. (These fractions must be less than 1, or else diversified stock portfolios would dominate the risk-free asset in term of net returns.) The *net* rate of return on class L stocks to an investor with a horizon of h will be $(r + xc_L) - c_L/h = r + c_L(x - 1/h)$. In general, the rates of return to investors will be:

Asset:	Risk-Free	Class L	Class I
Gross rate of return:	r	$r + xc_L$	$r + r + yc_I$
One-period liquidation cost:	0	c_L	c_I
Investor Type		**Net Rate of Return**	
1	r	$r + c_L(x - 1)$	$r + c_I/(y - 1)$
2	r	$r + c_L(x - 1/2)$	$r + c_I/(y - 1/2)$
. . .	. . .	. . .	. . .
n	r	$r + c_L(x - 1/n)$	$r + c_I/(y - 1/n)$

Notice that the liquidation cost has a greater impact on per-period returns for shorter-term investors. This is because the cost is amortized over fewer periods. As the horizon becomes very large, the per-period impact of the transaction cost approaches zero and the net rate of return approaches the gross rate.

Figure 8.7 graphs the net rate of return on the three asset classes for investors of differing horizons. The more illiquid stock has the lowest net rate of return for very short investment horizons because of its large liquidation costs. However, in equilibrium, the stock must be priced at a level that offers a rate of return high enough to induce some investors to hold it, implying that its gross rate of return must be higher than that of the more liquid stock. Therefore, for long enough investment horizons, the net return on class I stocks will exceed that on class L stocks.

Both stock classes underperform T-bills for very short investment horizons, because the transactions costs then have the largest per-period impact. Ultimately, however,

Figure 8.7
Net returns as a function of investment horizon

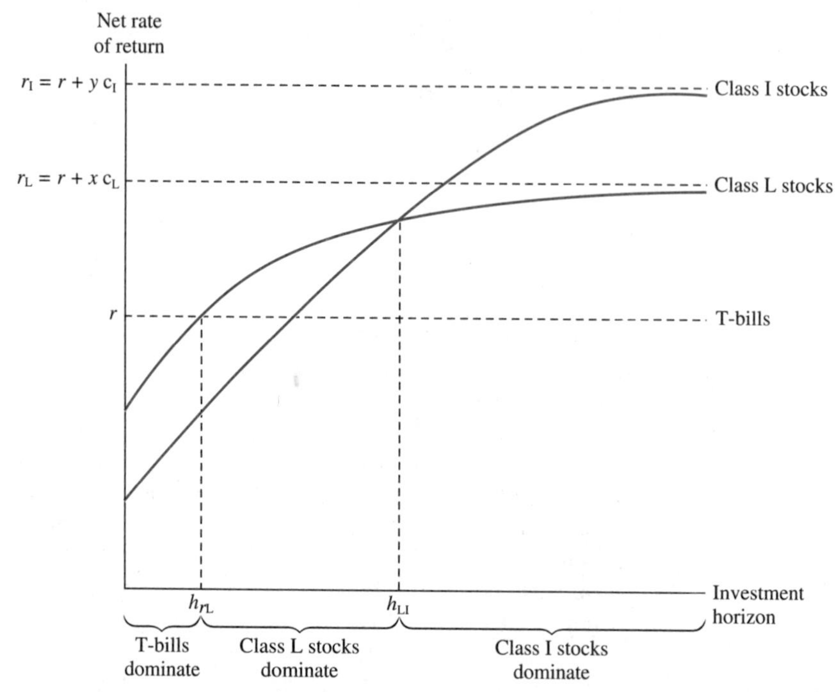

because the *gross* rate of return of stocks exceeds r, for a sufficiently long investment horizon, the more liquid stocks in class L will dominate bills. The threshold horizon can be read from Figure 8.7 as H_{rL}. Anyone with a horizon that exceeds H_{rL} will prefer class L stocks to T-bills. Those with horizons below H_{rL} will choose bills. For even longer horizons, because c_I exceeds c_L, the net rate of return on relatively illiquid class I stocks will exceed that on class L stocks. Therefore, investors with horizons greater than H_{LI} will specialize in the most illiquid stocks with the highest gross rate of return. These investors are harmed least by the effect of trading costs.

Now we can determine equilibrium illiquidity premiums. For the marginal investor with horizon H_{LI}, the *net* return from class I and L stocks is the same. Therefore,

$$r + c_L(x - 1/h_{LI}) = r + c_I(y - 1/h_{LI})$$

We can use this equation to solve for the relationship between x and y as follows:

$$y = \frac{1}{h_{LI}} + \frac{c_L}{c_I}\left(x - \frac{1}{h_{LI}}\right)$$

The expected gross return on illiquid stocks is then

$$r_I = r + c_L y = r + \frac{c_I}{h_{LI}} + c_L\left(x - \frac{1}{h_{LI}}\right) = r + c_L x + \frac{1}{h_{LI}}(c_I - c_L) \tag{8.10}$$

Recalling that the expected gross return on class L stocks is $r_L = r + c_L x$, we conclude that the illiquidity premium of class I versus class L stocks is

$$r_I - r_L = \frac{1}{h_{LI}}(c_I - c_L) \tag{8.11}$$

Similarly, we can derive the liquidity premium of class L stocks over T-bills. Here, the marginal investor who is indifferent between bills and class L stocks will have investment horizon h_{rL}, and a net rate of return just equal to r. Therefore, $r + c_L(x - 1/h_{rL}) = r$, implying that $x = 1/h_{rL}$, and the liquidity premium of class L stocks must be $xc_L = c_L/h_{rL}$. Therefore,

$$r_L - r = \frac{1}{h_{rL}} c_L \tag{8.12}$$

There are two lessons to be learned from this analysis. First, as predicted, equilibrium expected rates of return are bid up to compensate for transaction costs, as demonstrated by equations 8.11 and 8.12. Second, the illiquidity premium is *not* a linear function of transaction costs. In fact, the incremental illiquidity premium steadily declines as transaction costs increase. To see that this is so, suppose that c_L is 1% and $c_I - c_L$ is also 1%. Therefore, the transaction cost increases by 1% as you move out of bills into the more liquid stock class, and by another 1% as you move into the illiquid stock class. Equation 8.12 shows that the illiquidity premium of class L stocks over no-transaction-cost bills is then $1/h_{rL}$, and equation 8.11 shows that the illiquidity premium of class I over class L stocks is $1/h_{LI}$. But h_{LI} exceeds $1/h_{rL}$ (see Figure 8.7), so we conclude that the incremental effect of illiquidity declines as we move into ever more illiquid assets.

The reason for this last result is simple. Recall that investors will self-select into different asset classes, with longer-term investors holding assets with the highest gross return, but that are the most illiquid. For these investors, the effect of illiquidity is less costly because trading costs can be amortized over a longer horizon. Therefore, as these costs increase, the investment horizon associated with the holders of these assets also increases, which mitigates the impact on the required gross rate of return.

The distribution of investors will also affect the illiquidity premium. If many traders invest for a particular horizon, then the illiquidity premium will rise less rapidly around that horizon. Figure 8.8 illustrates this result. The curve labeled I corresponds to a relatively even distribution of investors across investment horizons. The curve labeled II, which flattens rapidly around the investment horizon h^*, would arise in a case where many investors have horizons of approximately h^*.

CONCEPT CHECK

Question 7. Consider a very illiquid asset class of stocks, class V, with $c_V < c_I$. Use a graph like Figure 8.7 to convince yourself that there is an investment horizon, h_{IV}, for which an investor would be indifferent between stocks in illiquidity classes I and V. Analogously to equation 8.11, in equilibrium, the differential in gross returns must be

$$r_V - r_I = \frac{1}{h_{IV}}(c_V - c_I) < r_I - r_L < r_L - r$$

Our analysis so far has focused on the case of uncorrelated assets, allowing us to ignore issues of systematic risk. This special case turns out to be easy to generalize. If we were to allow for correlation among assets due to common systematic risk factors,

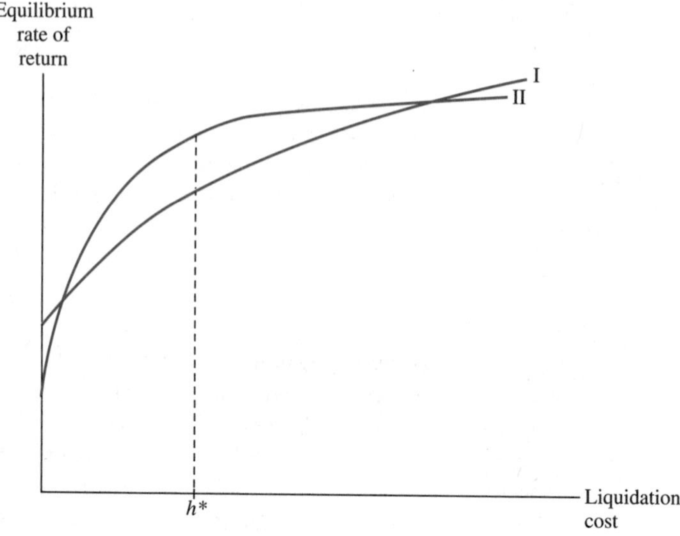

Figure 8.8
Rates of return as a function of liquidation cost for two populations with different distributions of investors across investment horizons

we would find that the illiquidity premium is simply additive to the risk premium of the usual CAPM.[14] Therefore, we can generalize the CAPM expected return–beta relationship to include a liquidity effect as follows:

$$E(r_i) - r_f = \beta_i[E(r_M) - r_f] + f(c_i)$$

where $f(c_i)$ is a function of trading costs that measures the effect of the illiquidity premium given the trading costs of security *i*. We have seen that $f(c_i)$ is increasing in c_i but at a decreasing rate. The usual CAPM equation is modified because each investor's optimal portfolio is now affected by liquidation cost as well as risk-return considerations.

The model can be generalized in other ways as well. For example, even if investors do not know their investment horizon for certain, as long as investors do not perceive a connection between unexpected needs to liquidate investments and security returns, the implications of the model are essentially unchanged, with expected horizons replacing actual horizons in equations 8.11 and 8.12.

Amihud and Mendelson provided a considerable amount of empirical evidence that liquidity has a substantial impact on gross stock returns. We will defer our discussion of most of that evidence until Chapter 11. However, for a preview of the quantitative significance of the illiquidity effect, examine Figure 8.9, which is derived from their study. It shows that average monthly returns over the 1961–1980 period rose from

[14] The only assumption necessary to obtain this result is that for each level of beta, there are many securities within that risk class, with a variety of transaction costs. (This is essentially the same assumption used by Modigliani and Miller in their famous capital structure irrelevance proposition.) Thus, our earlier analysis could be applied within each risk class, resulting in an illiquidity premium that simply adds on to the systematic risk premium.

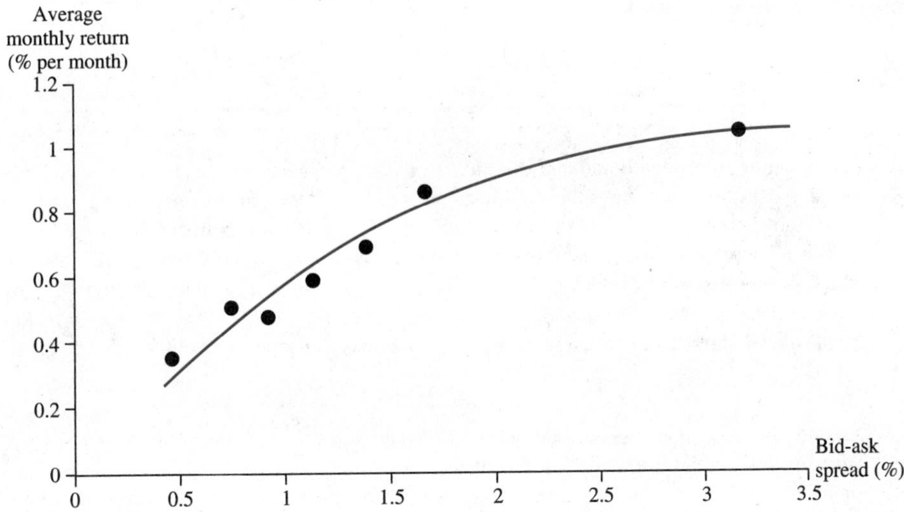

Figure 8.9
The relationship between illiquidity and average returns
Source: Derived from Yakov Amihud and Haim Mendelson, "Asset Pricing and the Bid-Ask Spread," *Journal of Financial Economics* 17 (1986), pp. 223–49.

0.35% for the group of stocks with the lowest bid-ask spread (the most liquid stocks) to 1.024% for the highest-spread stocks. This is an annualized differential of about 8%, nearly equal to the historical average risk premium on the S&P 500 index! Moreover, as their model predicts, the effect of the spread on average monthly returns is nonlinear, with a curve that flattens out as spreads increase. The nearby box from *The Wall Street Journal* also provides a discussion of liquidity effects.

SUMMARY

1. The CAPM assumes that investors are single-period planners who agree on a common input list from security analysis and seek mean-variance optimal portfolios.
2. The CAPM assumes that security markets are ideal in the sense that:
   a. They are large, and investors are price-takers.
   b. There are no taxes or transaction costs.
   c. All risky assets are publicly traded.
   d. Investors can borrow and lend any amount at a fixed risk-free rate.
3. With these assumptions, all investors hold identical risky portfolios. The CAPM holds that in equilibrium the market portfolio is the unique mean-variance efficient tangency portfolio. Thus, a passive strategy is efficient.
4. The CAPM market portfolio is a value-weighted portfolio. Each security is held in a proportion equal to its market value divided by the total market value of all securities.
5. If the market portfolio is efficient and the average investor neither borrows nor lends, then the risk premium on the market portfolio is proportional to its variance, σ_M^2, and to the average coefficient of risk aversion across investors A:

$$E(r_M) - r_f = .01 \times \overline{A}\sigma_M^2$$

Stock Investors Pay High Price for Liquidity

Given a choice between liquid and illiquid stocks, most investors, to the extent they think of it at all, opt for issues they know are easy to get in and out of.

But for long-term investors who don't trade often—which includes most individuals—that may be unnecessarily expensive. Recent studies of the performance of listed stocks show that, on average, less-liquid issues generate substantially higher returns—as much as several percentage points a year at the extremes.

"Liquidity is a valuable item that must be, and is, paid for even if it's not used," says Steven Wunch, a vice president at Kidder, Peabody & Co. In terms of investment strategy, he adds, "It only makes sense that if you don't need it or use it, don't pay for it."

Illiquidity Payoff

Among the academic studies that have attempted to quantify this illiquidity payoff is a recent work by two finance professors, Yakov Amihud of New York University and Tel Aviv University, and Haim Mendelson of the University of Rochester. Their study looks at New York Stock Exchange issues over the 1961–1980 period and defines liquidity in terms of bid-asked spreads as a percentage of overall share price.

Market makers use spreads in quoting stocks to define the difference between the price they'll bid to take stock off an investor's hands and the price they'll offer to sell stock to any willing buyer. The bid price is always somewhat lower because of the risk to the broker of tying up precious capital to hold stock in inventory until it can be resold.

If a stock is relatively illiquid, which means there's not a ready flow of orders from customers clamoring to buy it, there's more of a chance the broker will lose money on the trade. To hedge this risk, market makers demand an even bigger discount to service potential sellers, and the spread will widen further.

The study by Profs. Amihud and Mendelson shows that liquidity spreads—measured as a percentage discount from the stock's total price—ranged from less than 0.1 percent, for widely held International Business Machines Corp., to as much as 4 percent to 5 percent. The widest-spread group was dominated by smaller, low-priced stocks.

The study found that, overall, the least-liquid stocks averaged an 8.5 percent-a-year higher return than the most-liquid stocks over the 20-year period. On average, a one percentage point increase in the spread was associated with a 2.5 percent higher annual return for New York Stock Exchange stocks. The relationship held after results were adjusted for size and other risk factors.

An extension of the study of Big Board stocks done at *The Wall Street Journal's* request, produced similar findings. It showed that for the 1980–85 period, a one percentage-point-wider spread was associated with an extra average annual gain of 2.4 percent. Meanwhile, the least-liquid stocks outperformed the most-liquid stocks by almost six percentage points a year.

Cost of Trading

Since the cost of the spread is incurred each time the stock is traded, illiquid stocks can quickly become prohibitively expensive for investors who trade frequently. On the other hand, small, long-term investors needn't worry so much about spreads, since they can amortize them over a longer period.

In terms of investment strategy, this suggests "that the small investor should tailor the types of stocks he or she buys to his expected holding period," Prof. Mendelson says. If the investor expects to sell within three months, he says, it's better to pay up for liquidity and get the lowest spread. If the investor plans to hold the stock for a year or more, it makes sense to aim at stocks with spreads of 3 percent or more to capture the extra return.

Source: Barbara Donnelly, *The Wall Street Journal,* April 28, 1987, p. 37.

6. The CAPM implies that the risk premium on any individual asset or portfolio is the product of the risk premium on the market portfolio and the beta coefficient:

$$E(r) - r_f = \beta[E(r_M) - r_f]$$

where the beta coefficient is the covariance of the asset with the market portfolio as a fraction of the variance of the market portfolio

$$\beta = \frac{\text{Cov}(r, r_M)}{\sigma_M^2}$$

7. When risk-free investments are restricted but all other CAPM assumptions hold, then the simple version of the CAPM is replaced by its zero-beta version. Accordingly, the risk-free rate in the expected return–beta relationship is replaced by the zero-beta portfolio's expected return rate of return:

$$E(r_i) = E[r_{Z(M)}] + \beta_i E[r_M - r_{Z(M)}]$$

8. The simple version of the CAPM assumes that investors are myopic. When investors are assumed to be concerned with lifetime consumption and bequest plans, but investors' tastes and security return distributions are stable over time, the market portfolio remains efficient and the simple version of the expected return–beta relationship holds.

9. Liquidity costs can be incorporated into the CAPM relationship. When there is a large number of assets with any combination of beta and liquidity cost c_i, the expected return is bid up to reflect this undesired property according to:

$$E(r_i) - r_f = \beta_i[E(r_M) - r_f] + f(c_i)$$

Key Terms

Homogeneous expectations
Market portfolio
Mutual fund theorem
Market price of risk
Beta
Expected return–beta relationship
Security market line
Alpha
Zero-beta portfolio
Liquidity
Illiquidity premium

Selected Readings

A good introduction to the intuition of the CAPM is:

Malkiel, Burton G. *A Random Walk Down Wall Street.* New York: W. W. Norton, 1990.

The four articles that established the CAPM are:

Sharpe, William. "Capital Asset Prices: A Theory of Market Equilibrium." *Journal of Finance,* September 1964.

Lintner, John. "The Valuation of Risk Assets and the Selection of Risky Investments in Stock Portfolios and Capital Budgets." *Review of Economics and Statistics,* February 1965.

Mossin, Jan. "Equilibrium in a Capital Asset Market." *Econometrica.* October 1966.

Treynor, Jack. "Towards a Theory of Market Value of Risky Assets." Unpublished manuscript, 1961.

A review of the simple CAPM and its variants is contained in:

Jensen, Michael C. "The Foundation and Current State of Capital Market Theory." In Jensen, Michael C., ed. *Studies in the Theory of Capital Markets.* New York: Praeger Publishers, 1972.

The zero-beta version of the CAPM appeared in:

Black, Fischer. "Capital Market Equilibrium with Restricted Borrowing." *Journal of Business,* July 1972.

Excellent practitioner-oriented discussions of the CAPM are:

Mullins, David. "Does the Capital Asset Pricing Model Work?" *Harvard Business Review,* January/February 1982.

Rosenberg, Barr; and Andrew Rudd. "The Corporate Uses of Beta." In Stern, J. M.; and D. H. Chew, Jr., eds., *The Revolution in Corporate Finance.* New York: Basil Blackwell, 1986.

A good discussion of liquidity, asset prices, and financial policy can be found in:

Amihud Yakov; and Haim Mendelson. "Liquidity, Asset Prices and Financial Policy." *Financial Analysts Journal,* November–December 1991.

Problems

1. What is the beta of a portfolio with $E(r_p) = 20\%$, if $r_f = 5\%$ and $E(r_M) = 15\%$?
2. The market price of a security is \$40. Its expected rate of return is 13%. The risk-free rate is 7% and the market risk premium is 8%. What will be the market price of the security if its covariance with the market portfolio doubles (and all other variables remain unchanged)? Assume that the stock is expected to pay a constant dividend in perpetuity.
3. You are a consultant to a large manufacturing corporation that is considering a project with the following net after-tax cash flows (in millions of dollars):

Years from Now	After-Tax Cash Flow
0	−20
1–9	10
10	20

The project's beta is 1.7. Assuming that $r_f = 9\%$ and $E(r_M) = 19\%$, what is the net present value of the project? What is the highest possible beta estimate for the project before its NPV becomes negative?

4. Are the following true or false?
   a. Stocks with a beta of zero offer an expected rate of return of zero.
   b. The CAPM implies that investors require a higher return to hold highly volatile securities.
   c. You can construct a portfolio with beta of 0.75 by investing 0.75 of the investment budget in bills and the remainder in the market portfolio.
5. Consider the following table, which gives a security analyst's expected return on two stocks for two particular market returns:

Market Return	Aggressive Stock	Defensive Stock
5%	2%	3.5%
20	32	14

a. What are the betas of the two stocks?
b. What is the expected rate of return on each stock if the market return is equally likely to be 5% or 20%?
c. If the T-bill rate is 8% and the market return is equally likely to be 5% or 20%, draw the SML for this economy.
d. Plot the two securities on the SML graph. What are the alphas of each?
e. What hurdle rate should be used by the management of the aggressive firm for a project with the risk characteristics of the defensive firm's stock?

If the simple CAPM is valid, which of the following situations in Problems 6 to 12 are possible? Explain. Consider each situation independently.

6.

Portfolio	Expected Return	Beta
A	20	1.4
B	25	1.2

7.

Portfolio	Expected Return	Standard Deviation
A	30	35
B	40	25

8.

Portfolio	Expected Return	Standard Deviation
Risk-free	10	0
Market	18	24
A	16	12

9.

Portfolio	Expected Return	Standard Deviation
Risk-free	10	0
Market	18	24
A	20	22

10.

Portfolio	Expected Return	Beta
Risk-free	10	0
Market	18	1.0
A	16	1.5

11.

Portfolio	Expected Return	Beta
Risk-free	10	0
Market	18	1.0
A	16	.9

12.

Portfolio	Expected Return	Standard Deviation
Risk-free	10	0
Market	18	24
A	16	22

In Problems 13 to 15 assume that the risk-free rate of interest is 8% and the expected rate of return on the market is 18%.

13. A share of stock sells for $100 today. It will pay a dividend of $9 per share at the end of the year. Its beta is 1. What do investors expect the stock to sell for at the end of the year?
14. I am buying a firm with an expected cash flow of $1,000 but am unsure of its risk. If I think the beta of the firm is zero, when in fact the beta is really 1, how much *more* will I offer for the firm than it is truly worth?
15. A stock has an expected rate of return of 6%. What is its beta?
16. Two investment advisors are comparing performance. One averaged a 19% rate of return and the other a 16% rate of return. However, the beta of the first investor was 1.5, whereas that of the second was 1.
    a. Can you tell which investor was a better predictor of individual stocks (aside from the issue of general movements in the market)?
    b. If the T-bill rate were 6% and the market return during the period were 14%, which investor would be the superior stock selector?
    c. What if the T-bill rate were 3% and the market return were 15%?
17. In 1994 the rate of return on short-term government securities (perceived to be risk-free) was about 4%. Suppose the expected rate of return required by the market for a portfolio with a beta measure of 1 is 12%. According to the capital asset pricing model (security market line):
    a. What is the expected rate of return on the market portfolio?
    b. What would be the expected rate of return on a stock with $\beta = 0$?
    c. Suppose you consider buying a share of stock at $40. The stock is expected to pay $3 dividends next year and you expect it to sell then for $41. The stock risk has been evaluated by $\beta = -.5$. Is the stock overpriced or underpriced?
18. Suppose that you can invest risk-free at rate r_f but can borrow only at a higher rate, r_f^B. This case was considered in Section 7.5.
    a. Draw a minimum-variance frontier. Show on the graph the risky portfolio that will be selected by defensive investors. Show the portfolio that will be selected by aggressive investors.
    b. What portfolios will be selected by investors who neither borrow nor lend?
    c. Where will the market portfolio lie on the efficient frontier?
    d. Will the zero-beta CAPM be valid in this scenario? Explain. Show graphically the expected return on the zero-beta portfolio.
19. Consider an economy with two classes of investors. Tax-exempt investors can borrow or lend at the safe rate, r_f. Taxed investors pay tax rate t on all interest

income, so their net-of-tax safe interest rate is $r_f(1 - t)$. Show that the zero-beta CAPM will apply to this economy and that $(1 - t)r_f < E[r_{Z(M)}] < r_f$.

20. Suppose that borrowing is restricted so that the zero-beta version of the CAPM holds. The expected return on the market portfolio is 17%, and on the zero-beta portfolio it is 8%. What is the expected return on a portfolio with a beta of 0.6?

21. The security market line depicts:*

a. A security's expected return as a function of its systematic risk.
b. The market portfolio as the optimal portfolio of risky securities.
c. The relationship between a security's return and the return on an index.
d. The complete portfolio as a combination of the market portfolio and the risk-free asset.

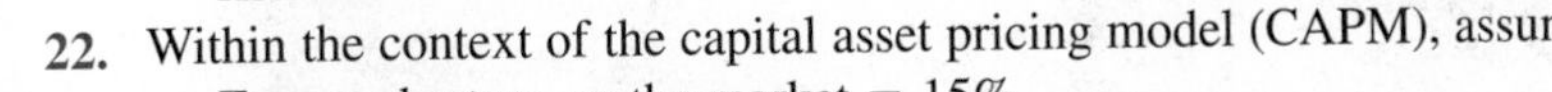

22. Within the context of the capital asset pricing model (CAPM), assume:*

- Expected return on the market = 15%.
- Risk-free rate = 8%.
- Expected rate of return on XYZ security = 17%.
- Beta of XYZ security = 1.25.

Which one of the following is correct?

a. XYZ is overpriced.
b. XYZ is fairly priced.
c. XYZ's alpha is −0.25%.
d. XYZ's alpha is 0.25%.

23. What is the expected return of a zero-beta security?*

a. Market rate of return.
b. Zero rate of return.
c. Negative rate of return.
d. Risk-free rate of return.

24. Briefly explain whether investors should expect a higher return from holding Portfolio A versus Portfolio B under capital asset pricing theory (CAPM). Assume that both portfolios are fully diversified.*

	Portfolio A	Portfolio B
Systematic risk (beta)	1.0	1.0
Specific risk for each individual security	High	Low

*Reprinted, with permission, from the Level I 1993 *CFA Study Guide.*

Chapter 9
Index Models

CHAPTER 7 INTRODUCED THE MARKOWITZ PORTFOLIO SELECTION MODEL, WHICH SHOWS HOW TO OBTAIN THE MAXIMUM RETURN POSSIBLE FOR ANY LEVEL OF PORTFOLIO RISK. Implementation of the Markowitz portfolio selection model, however, requires a huge number of estimates of covariances between all pairs of available securities. Moreover, these estimates have to be fed into a mathematical optimization program that requires vast computer capacity to perform the necessary calculations for large portfolios. Because the data requirements and computer capacity called for in the full-blown Markowitz procedure are overwhelming, we must search for a strategy that reduces the necessary compilation and processing of data. We will introduce in this chapter a simplifying assumption that at once eases our computational burden and offers significant new insights into the nature of systematic risk versus firm-specific risk. This abstraction is the notion of an "index model," specifying the process by which security returns are generated. Our discussion of the index model also will introduce the concept of factor models of security returns, a concept at the heart of contemporary investment theory and its applications.

9.1 A Single-Index Security Market

Systematic Risk versus Firm-Specific Risk

The success of a portfolio selection rule depends on the quality of the input list, that is, the estimates of expected security returns and the covariance matrix. In the long run, efficient portfolios will beat portfolios with less reliable input lists and consequently inferior reward-to-risk trade-offs.

Suppose your security analysts can thoroughly analyze 50 stocks. This means that your input list will include the following:

$$\begin{aligned} n &= \quad 50 \text{ estimates of expected returns} \\ n &= \quad 50 \text{ estimates of variances} \\ (n^2 - n)/2 &= \underline{1{,}225} \text{ estimates of covariances} \\ & \quad\; 1{,}325 \text{ estimates} \end{aligned}$$

This is a formidable task, particularly in light of the fact that a 50-security portfolio is relatively small. Doubling n to 100 will nearly quadruple the number of estimates to 5,150. If $n = 1{,}600$, roughly the number of NYSE stocks, we need nearly 1.3 *million* estimates.

Covariances between security returns tend to be positive because the same economic forces affect the fortunes of many firms. Some examples of common economic factors are business cycles, inflation, money-supply changes, technological changes, and prices of raw materials. All these (interrelated) factors affect almost all firms. Thus, unexpected changes in these variables cause, simultaneously, unexpected changes in the rates of return on the entire stock market.

Suppose that we group all these economic factors and any other relevant common factors into one macroeconomic indicator and assume that it moves the security market as a whole. We further assume that, beyond this common effect, all remaining uncertainty in stock returns is firm specific; that is, there is no other source of correlation between securities. Firm-specific events would include new inventions, deaths of key employees, and other factors that affect the fortune of the individual firm without affecting the broad economy in a measurable way.

We can summarize the distinction between macroeconomic and firm-specific factors by writing the return, r_i, realized on any security during some holding period as

$$r_i = E(r_i) + m_i + e_i \tag{9.1}$$

where $E(r_i)$ is the expected return on the security as of the beginning of the holding period, m_i is the impact of unanticipated macro events on the security's return during the period, and e_i is the impact of unanticipated firm-specific events. Both m_i and e_i have zero expected values because each represents the impact of unanticipated events, which by definition must average out to zero.

We can gain further insight by recognizing that different firms have different sensitivities to macroeconomic events. Thus, if we denote the unanticipated components of the macro factor by F, and denote the responsiveness of security i to macroevents by the Greek letter beta, β_i, then the macro component of the rate of return on security i is $m_i = \beta_i F$, and then equation 9.1 becomes[1]

$$r_i = E(r_i) + \beta_i F + e_i \tag{9.2}$$

[1] You may wonder why we choose the notation β for the responsiveness coefficient, because β already has been defined in Chapter 8 in the context of the CAPM. The choice is deliberate, however. Our reason will be obvious shortly.

Equation 9.2 is known as a **factor model** for stock returns. It is easy to imagine that a more realistic decomposition of security returns would require more than one factor in equation 9.2. We treat this issue in Chapter 10. For now, let us examine the easy case with only one macro factor.

Of course, a factor model is of little use without specifying a way to measure the factor that is posited to affect security returns. One reasonable approach is to assert that the rate of return on a broad index of securities such as the S&P 500 is a valid proxy for the common macro factor. This approach leads to an equation similar to the factor model, which is called a **single-index model** because it uses the market index to proxy for the common or systematic factor.

According to the index model, we can separate the actual or realized rate of return on a security into macro (systematic) and micro (firm-specific) components in a manner similar to that in equation 9.2. We write the rate of return on each security as a sum of three components:

	Symbol
1. The stock's expected return if the market is neutral, that is, if the market's excess return, $r_M - r_f$, is zero	α_i
2. The component of return due to movements in the overall market; β_i is the security's responsiveness to market movements	$\beta_i(r_M - r_f)$
3. The unexpected component due to unexpected events that are relevant only to this security (firm specific)	e_i

The holding period excess rate of return on the stock, which measures the stock's relative performance, then can be stated as

$$r_i - r_f = \alpha_i + \beta_i(r_M - r_f) + e_i$$

Let us denote security excess returns over the risk-free rate using capital *R*, and so rewrite this equation as

$$r_i = \alpha_i + \beta_i R_M + e_i \qquad (9.3)$$

We write the index model in terms of excess returns over r_f rather than in terms of total returns because the level of the stock market return represents the state of the macro economy only to the extent that it exceeds or falls short of the rate of return on risk-free T-bills. For example, in the 1950s, when T-bills were yielding only a 1% or 2% rate of return, a return of 8% or 9% on the stock market would be considered good news. In contrast, in the early 1980s, when bills were yielding over 10%, that same 8% or 9% stock market return would signal disappointing macroeconomic news.[2]

Equation 9.3 says that each security therefore has two sources of risk: *market or "systematic" risk*, attributable to its sensitivity to macroeconomic factors as reflected

[2] In practice, however, a "modified" index model is often used that is similar to equation 9.3 except that it uses total rather than excess returns. This practice is most common when daily data are used. In this case the rate of return on bills is on the order of only about 0.02% per day, so total and excess returns are almost indistinguishable.

in R_M, and *firm-specific* risk, as reflected in e. If we denote the variance of the excess return on the market, R_M, as σ_M^2, then we can break the variance of the rate of return on each stock into two components:

	Symbol
1. The variance attributable to the uncertainty of the common macroeconomic factors	$\beta_i^2\sigma_M^2$
2. The variance attributable to firm-specific uncertainty	$\sigma^2(e_i)$

The covariance between R_M and e_i is zero because e_i is defined as firm specific, that is, independent of movements in the market. Hence, calling σ_i^2 the variance of the rate of return on security i, we find that

$$\sigma_i^2 = \beta_i^2\sigma_M^2 + \sigma^2(e_i)$$

The covariance between the excess rates of return on two sticks, for example, R_i and R_j, derives only from the common factor, R_M, because e_i and e_j are each firm specific and therefore presumed to be uncorrelated. Hence, the covariance between two stocks is

$$\text{Cov}(R_i,R_j) = \text{Cov}(\beta_i R_M,\beta_j R_M) = \beta_i\beta_j\sigma_M^2 \tag{9.4}$$

These calculations show that if we have

n estimates of the expected excess returns, $E(R_i)$
n estimates of the sensitivity coefficients, β_i
n estimates of the firm-specific variances, $\sigma^2(e_i)$
1 estimate for the variance of the (common) macroeconomic factor, σ_M^2,

then these $(3n + 1)$ estimates will enable us to prepare the input list for this single-index security universe. Thus, for a 50-security portfolio we will need 151 estimates rather than 1,325, and for a 100-security portfolio we will need only 301 estimates rather than 5,150.

It is easy to see why the index model is such a useful abstraction. For large universes of securities the data estimates required for the Markowitz procedure are only a small fraction of what otherwise would be needed.

Another advantage is less obvious but equally important. The index model abstraction is crucial for specialization of effort in security analysis. If a covariance term had to be calculated directly for each security pair, then security analysts could not specialize by industry. For example, if one group were to specialize in the computer industry and another in the auto industry, who would have the common background to estimate the covariance *between* IBM and GM? Neither group would have the deep understanding of other industries necessary to make an informed judgment of comovements among industries. In contrast, the index model suggests a simple way to compute covariances. Covariances among securities are due to the influence of the single common factor, represented by the market index return, and can be easily estimated using equation 9.4.

The simplification derived from the index model assumption is, however, not without cost. The "cost" of the model lies in the restrictions it places on the structure of asset return uncertainty. The classification of uncertainty into a simple dichotomy—macro versus micro risk—oversimplifies sources of real-world uncertainty and misses some important sources of dependence in stock returns. For example, this dichotomy rules out industry events, events that may affect many firms within an industry without substantially affecting the broad macro economy.

Statistical analysis shows that relative to a single index, the firm-specific components of some firms are correlated. Examples are the nonmarket components of stocks in a single industry, such as computer stocks or auto stocks. At the same time, statistical significance does not always correspond to economic significance. Economically speaking, the question that is more relevant to the assumption of a single-index model is whether portfolios constructed using covariances that are estimated on the basis of the single-factor or single-index assumption are significantly different from, and less efficient than, portfolios constructed using covariances that are estimated directly for each pair of stocks. We explore this issue further in Part VII on active portfolio management.

CONCEPT CHECK

Question 1. Suppose that the index model for stocks A and B is estimated with the following results:

$$\begin{aligned} R_A &= 1.0\% + .9R_M + e_A \\ R_B &= -2.0\% + 1.1R_M + e_B \\ \sigma_M &= 20\% \\ \sigma(e_A) &= 30\% \\ \sigma(e_B) &= 10\% \end{aligned}$$

Find the standard deviation of each stock and the covariance between them.

Estimating the Index Model

Equation 9.3 also suggests how we might go about actually measuring market and firm-specific risk. Suppose that we observe the excess return on the market index and a specific asset over a number of holding periods. We use as an example monthly excess returns on the S&P 500 index and GM stock for a one-year period. We can summarize the results for a sample period in a **scatter diagram**, as illustrated in Figure 9.1.

The horizontal axis in Figure 9.1 measures the excess return (over the risk-free rate) on the market index, whereas the vertical axis measures the excess return on the asset in question (GM stock in our example). A pair of excess returns (one for the market index, one for GM stock) over a holding period constitutes one point on this scatter diagram. The points are numbered 1 through 12, representing excess returns for the S&P 500 and GM for each month from January through December. The single-index model states that the relationship between the excess returns on GM and the S&P 500 is given by

$$R_{GMt} = \alpha_{GM} + \beta_{GM}R_{Mt} + e_{GMt}$$

Figure 9.1
Characteristic line for GM

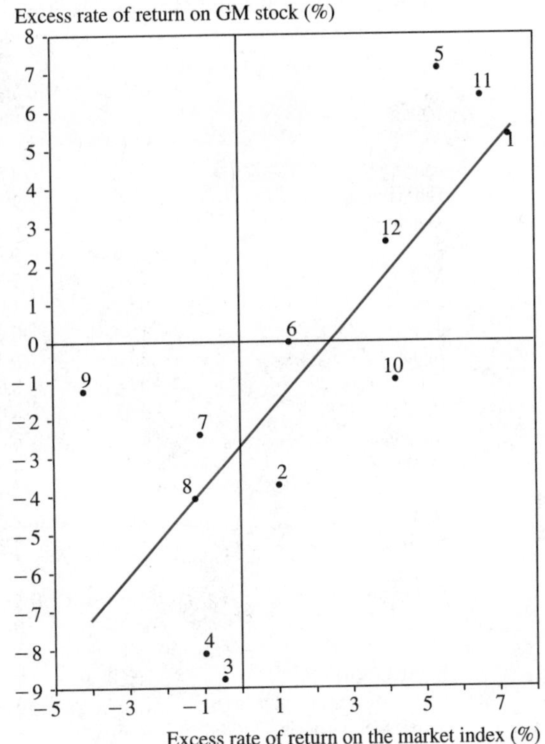

Note the resemblance of this relationship to a **regression equation.**

In a single-variable linear regression equation, the dependent variable plots around a straight line with an intercept α and a slope β. The deviations from the line, e_t, are assumed to be mutually independent and independent of the right-hand variable. Because these assumptions are identical to those of the index model we can look at the index model as a regression model. The sensitivity of GM to the market, measured by β_{GM}, is the slope of the regression line. The intercept of the regression line is α (which represents the average firm-specific return), and deviations of particular observations from the regression line are denoted e. These **residuals** are the differences between the actual stock return and the return that would be predicted from the regression equation describing the usual relationship between the stock and the market; therefore, they measure the impact of firm-specific events during the particular month. The parameters of interest, α, β, and Var(e), can be estimated using standard regression techniques.

Estimating the regression equation of the single-index model gives us the **security characteristic line** (SCL), which is plotted in Figure 9.1. (The regression results and raw data appear in Table 9.1.) The SCL is a plot of the typical excess return on a security over the risk-free rate as a function of the excess return on the market.

This sample of holding period returns is, of course, too small to yield reliable statistics. We use it only for demonstration. For this sample period we find that the beta coef-

Table 9.1 Characteristic Line for GM Stock

Month	GM Return	Market Return	Monthly T-Bill Rate	Excess GM Return	Excess Market Return
January	6.06	7.89	0.65	5.41	7.24
February	−2.86	1.51	0.58	−3.44	0.93
March	−8.18	0.23	0.62	−8.79	−0.38
April	−7.36	−0.29	0.72	−8.08	−1.01
May	7.76	5.58	0.66	7.10	4.92
June	0.52	1.73	0.55	−0.03	1.18
July	−1.74	−0.21	0.62	−2.36	−0.83
August	−3.00	−0.36	0.55	−3.55	−0.91
September	−0.56	−3.58	0.60	−1.16	−4.18
October	−0.37	4.62	0.65	−1.02	3.97
November	6.93	6.85	0.61	6.32	6.25
December	3.08	4.55	0.65	2.43	3.90
Mean	0.02	2.38	0.62	−0.60	1.75
Std Dev	4.97	3.33	0.05	4.97	3.32

Regression Results	$r_{GM} - r_f = \alpha + \beta(r_M - r_f)$	
	α	β
Estimated coefficient	−2.590	1.1357
Standard error of estimate	(1.547)	(0.309)

Variance of residuals = 12.601
Standard deviation of residuals = 3.550
R-SQR = 0.575

ficient of GM stock, as estimated by the slope of the regression line, is 1.1357, and that the intercept for this SCL is −2.59% per month.

For each month, our estimate of the residual, e, which is the deviation of GM's excess return from the prediction of the SCL, equals

$$\text{Deviation} = \text{actual} - \text{predicted return}$$
$$e_{GMt} = R_{GMt} - (\beta_{GM}R_{Mt} + \alpha_{GM})$$

These residuals are estimates of the monthly unexpected *firm-specific* component of the rate of return on GM stock. Hence, we can estimate the firm-specific variance by[3]

$$\sigma^2(e_{GM}) = \frac{1}{10}\sum_{t=1}^{12} e_t^2 = 12.60$$

Therefore, the standard deviation of the firm-specific component of GM's return, $\sigma(e_{GM})$, equals 3.55% per month.

[3] Because the mean of e_t is zero, e_t^2 is the squared deviation from its mean. The average value of e_t^2 is therefore the estimate of the variance of the firm-specific component. We divide the sum of squared residuals by the degrees of freedom of the regression, $n - 2 = 12 - 2 = 10$, to obtain an unbiased estimate of $\sigma^2(e)$.

The Index Model and Diversification

The index model, which was first suggested by Sharpe,[4] also offers insight into portfolio diversification. Suppose that we choose an equally weighted portfolio of n securities. The excess rate of return on each security is given by

$$R_i = \alpha_i + \beta_i R_M + e_i$$

Similarly, we can write the excess return on the portfolio of stocks as

$$R_P = \alpha_P + \beta_P R_M + e_P \tag{9.5}$$

We now show that, as the number of stocks included in this portfolio increases, the part of the portfolio risk attributable to nonmarket factors becomes ever smaller. This part of the risk is diversified away. In contrast, the market risk remains, regardless of the number of firms combined into the portfolio.

To understand these results, note that the excess rate of return on this equally weighted portfolio, for which $w_i = 1/n$, is

$$\begin{aligned} R_P &= \sum_{i=1}^{n} w_i R_i = \frac{1}{n}\sum_{i=1}^{n} R_i = \frac{1}{n}\sum_{i=1}^{n}(\alpha_i + \beta_i R_M + e_i) \\ &= \frac{1}{n}\sum_{i=1}^{n}\alpha_i + \left(\frac{1}{n}\sum_{i=1}^{n}\beta_i\right) R_M + \frac{1}{n}\sum_{i=1}^{n} e_i \end{aligned} \tag{9.6}$$

Comparing equations 9.5 and 9.6, we see that the portfolio has a sensitivity to the market given by

$$\beta_P = \frac{1}{n}\sum_{i=1}^{n}\beta_i$$

(which is the average of the individual β_is), and has a nonmarket return component of a constant (intercept)

$$\frac{1}{n}\sum_{i=1}^{n}\alpha_i$$

(which is the average of the individual alphas), plus the zero mean variable

$$e_P = \frac{1}{n}\sum_{i=1}^{n} e_i$$

which is the average of the firm-specific components. Hence, the portfolio's variance is

$$\sigma_P^2 = \beta_P^2\sigma_M^2 + \sigma^2(e_P) \tag{9.7}$$

The systematic risk component of the portfolio variance, which we defined as the part that depends on marketwide movements, is $\beta_P^2\,\sigma_M^2$ and depends on the average of the sensitivity coefficients of the individual securities. This part of the risk depends on portfolio beta and σ_M^2 and will persist regardless of the extent of portfolio diversification. No matter how many stocks are held, their common exposure to the market will be reflected in portfolio systematic risk.[5]

---

[4] William F. Sharpe, "A Simplified Model of Portfolio Analysis," *Management Science*, January 1963.

[5] Of course, one can construct a portfolio with zero systematic risk by mixing negative β and positive β assets. The point of our discussion is that the vast majority of securities have a positive β, implying that well-diversified portfolios with small holdings in large numbers of assets will indeed have positive systematic risk.

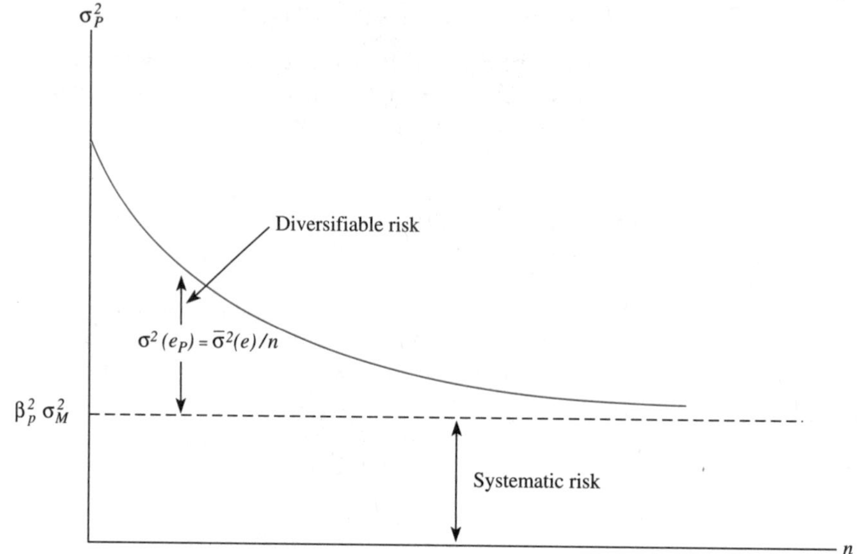

Figure 9.2
The variance of a portfolio with risk coefficient β in the single-factor economy

In contrast, the nonsystematic component of the portfolio variance is $\sigma^2(e_P)$ and is attributable to firm-specific components, e_i. Because these e_is are independent, and all have zero expected value, the law of averages can be applied to conclude that as more and more stocks are added to the portfolio, the firm-specific components tend to cancel out, resulting in ever-smaller nonmarket risk. Such risk is thus termed *diversifiable*. To see this more rigorously, examine the formula for the variance of the equally weighted "portfolio" of firm-specific components. Because the e_is are uncorrelated,

$$\sigma^2(e_P) = \sum_{i=1}^{n}\left(\frac{1}{n}\right)^2\sigma^2(e_i) = \frac{1}{n}\overline{\sigma}^2(e)$$

where $\overline{\sigma}^2(e)$ is the average of the firm-specific variances. Because this average is independent of n, when n gets large, $\sigma^2(e_P)$ becomes negligible.

To summarize, as diversification increases, the total variance of a portfolio approaches the systematic variance, defined as the variance of the market factor multiplied by the square of the portfolio sensitivity coefficient, β_P. This is shown in Figure 9.2.

Figure 9.2 shows that as more and more securities are combined into a portfolio, the portfolio variance decreases because of the diversification of firm-specific risk. However, the power of diversification is limited. Even for very large n, part of the risk remains because of the exposure of virtually all assets to the common, or market, factor. Therefore, this systematic risk is said to be nondiversifiable.

This analysis is borne out by empirical evidence. We saw the effect of portfolio diversification on portfolio standard deviations in Figure 7.2. These empirical results are similar to the theoretical graph presented here in Figure 9.2.

CONCEPT CHECK Question 2. Reconsider the two stocks in Concept Check 1. Suppose we form an equally weighted portfolio of A and B. What will be the nonsystematic standard deviation of that portfolio?

9.2 THE CAPM AND THE INDEX MODEL

Actual Returns versus Expected Returns

The CAPM is an elegant model. The question is whether it has real-world value—whether its implications are borne out by experience. Chapter 11 provides a range of empirical evidence on this point, but for now we will focus briefly on a more basic issue: Is the CAPM testable even in principle?

For starters, one central prediction of the CAPM is that the market portfolio is a mean-variance efficient portfolio. Consider that the CAPM treats all traded risky assets. To test the efficiency of the CAPM market portfolio, we would need to construct a value-weighted portfolio of a huge size and test its efficiency. So far, this task has not been feasible. An even more difficult problem, however, is that the CAPM implies relationships among *expected* returns, whereas all we can observe are actual or realized holding period returns, and these need not equal prior expectations. Even supposing we could construct a portfolio to represent the CAPM market portfolio satisfactorily, how would we test its mean-variance efficiency? We would have to show that the reward-to-variability ratio of the market portfolio is higher than that of any other portfolio. However, this reward-to-variability ratio is set in terms of expectations, and we have no way to observe these expectations directly.

The problem of measuring expectations haunts us as well when we try to establish the validity of the second central set of CAPM predictions, the expected return–beta relationship. This relationship is also defined in terms of expected returns $E(r_i)$ and $E(r_M)$:

$$E(r_i) = r_f + \beta_i [E(r_M) - r_f] \tag{9.8}$$

The upshot is that, as elegant and insightful as the CAPM is, we must make additional assumptions to make it implementable and testable.

The Index Model and Realized Returns

We have said that the CAPM is a statement about ex ante or expected returns, whereas in practice all anyone can observe directly are ex post or realized returns. To make the leap from expected to realized returns, we can employ the index model, which we will use in excess return form as

$$R_i = \alpha_i + \beta_i R_M + e_i \tag{9.9}$$

We saw in Section 9.1 how to apply standard regression analysis to estimate equation 9.9 using observable realized returns over some sample period. Let us now see how this framework for statistically decomposing actual stock returns meshes with the CAPM.

We start by deriving the covariance between the returns on stock i and the market index. By definition, the firm-specific or nonsystematic component is independent of the marketwide or systematic component, that is, $\text{Cov}(R_M, e_i) = 0$. From this relationship, it follows that the covariance of the excess rate of return on security i with that of the market index is

$$\begin{aligned}\text{Cov}(R_i, R_M) &= \text{Cov}(\beta_i R_M + e_i, R_M)\\ &= \beta_i \text{Cov}(R_M, R_M) + \text{Cov}(e_i, R_M)\\ &= \beta_i \sigma_M^2\end{aligned}$$

Note that we can drop α_i from the covariance terms because α_i is a constant and thus has zero covariance with all variables.

Because $\text{Cov}(R_i, R_M) = \beta_i \sigma_M^2$ the sensitivity coefficient, β_i, in equation 9.9, which is the slope of the regression line representing the index model, equals

$$\beta_i = \frac{\text{Cov}(R_i, R_M)}{\sigma_M^2}$$

The index model beta coefficient turns out to be the same beta as that of the CAPM expected return–beta relationship, except that we replace the (theoretical) market portfolio of the CAPM with the well-specified and observable market index.

CONCEPT CHECK

Question 3. The data below are drawn from a three-stock financial market that satisfies the single-index model.

Stock	Capitalization	Beta	Mean Excess Return	Standard Deviation
A	$3,000	1.0	10%	40%
B	$1,940	.2	2	30
C	$1,360	1.7	17	50

The single factor in this economy is perfectly correlated with the value-weighted index of the stock market. The standard deviation of the market index portfolio is 25%.

a. What is the mean excess return of the index portfolio?
b. What is the covariance between stock *A* and the index?
c. Break down the variance of stock *B* into its systematic and firm-specific components.

The Index Model and the Expected Return–Beta Relationship

Recall that the CAPM expected return–beta relationship is, for any asset i and the (theoretical) market portfolio,

$$E(r_i) - r_f = \beta_i[E(r_M) - r_f]$$

where $\beta_i = \text{Cov}(R_i, R_M)/\sigma_M^2$. This is a statement about the mean of expected excess return of assets relative to the mean excess return of the (theoretical) market portfolio.

If the index M in equation 9.9 represents the true market portfolio, we can take the expectation of each side of the equation to show that the index model specification is

$$E(r_i) - r_f = \alpha_i + \beta_i[E(r_M) - r_f]$$

A comparison of the index model relationship to the CAPM expected return–beta relationship (equation 9.8) shows that the CAPM predicts that α_i must be zero for all assets. The alpha of a stock is its expected return in excess of (or below) the fair expected return as predicted by the CAPM. If the stock is fairly priced, its alpha must be zero.

We emphasize again that this is a statement about *expected* returns on a security. After the fact, of course, some securities will do better or worse than expected and will have returns higher or lower than predicted by the CAPM relationship; that is, they will exhibit positive or negative alphas over a sample period. But this superior or inferior performance could not have been forecast in advance.

Therefore, if we estimate the index model for several firms, using equation 9.9 as a regression equation, we should find that the ex post or realized alphas (the regression intercepts) for the firms in our sample center around zero. If the initial expectation for alpha were zero, as many firms would be expected to have a positive as a negative alpha for some sample period. The CAPM states that the *expected* value of alpha is zero for all securities, whereas the index model representation of the CAPM holds that the *realized* value of alpha should average out to zero for a sample of historical observed returns. Just as important, the sample alphas should be unpredictable, that is, independent from one sample period to the next.

Some interesting evidence on this property was compiled by Michael Jensen,[6] who examined the alphas realized by mutual funds over the 10-year period 1955 to 1964. Figure 9.3 shows the frequency distribution of these alphas, which do indeed seem to be distributed around zero.

There is yet another applicable variation on the intuition of the index model, the **market model**. Formally, the market model states that the return "surprise" of any security is proportional to the return surprise of the market, plus a firm-specific surprise:

$$r_i - E(r_i) = \beta_i[r_M - E(r_M)] + e_i$$

This equation divides returns into firm-specific and systematic components somewhat differently from the index model. If the CAPM is valid, however, you can see that, substituting for $E(r_i)$ from equation 9.8, the market model equation becomes identical to the index model we have just presented. For this reason the terms "index model" and "market model" are sometimes used interchangeably.

CONCEPT CHECK

Question 4. Can you sort out the nuances of the following maze of models?

a. CAPM
b. Single-factor model
c. Single-index model
d. Market model

---

[6] Michael C. Jensen, "The Performance of Mutual Funds in the Period 1945–1964," *Journal of Finance* 23 (May 1968).

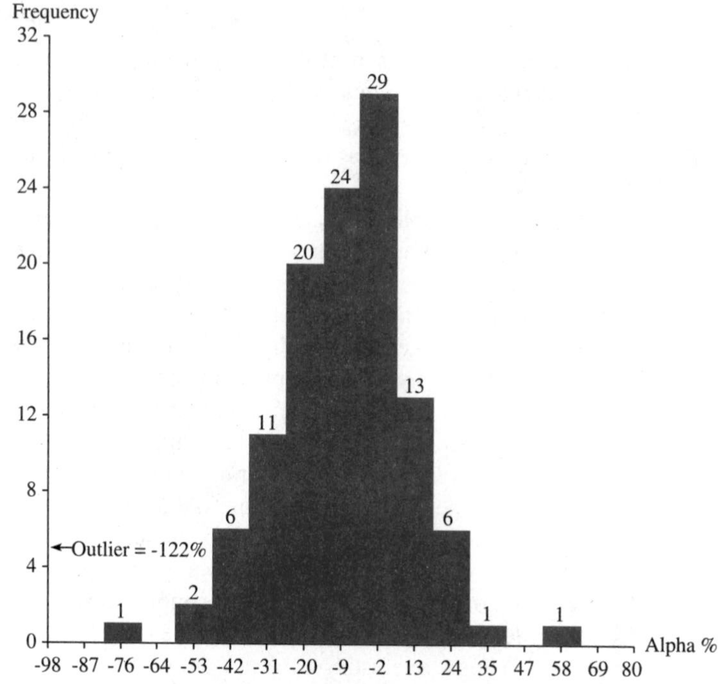

Figure 9.3
Frequency distribution of alphas
Source: Michael C. Jensen, "The Performance of Mutual Funds in the Period 1945–1964," *Journal of Finance* 23 (May 1968).

9.3 The Industry Version of the Index Model

Nor surprisingly, the index model has attracted the attention of practitioners. To the extent that it is approximately valid, it provides a convenient benchmark for security analysis.

A modern practitioner using the CAPM who has no special information about a security, or insight that is unavailable to the general public, will conclude that the security is "properly" priced. By "properly" priced, the analyst means that the expected return on the security is fair, given its risk, and therefore plots on the security market line. For instance, if one has no private information about GM's stock, then one should expect

$$E(r_{GM}) = r_f + \beta_{GM}[E(r_M) - r_f]$$

A portfolio manager who has a forecast for the market index, $E(r_M)$, and observes the risk-free T-bill rate, r_f, can use the model to determine the benchmark expected return for any stock. The beta coefficient, the market risk, σ_M^2, and the firm-specific risk, $\sigma^2(e)$, can be estimated from historical SCLs, that is, from regressions of security excess returns on market index excess returns.

There are many sources for such regression results. One widely used source is Research Computer Services Department of Merrill Lynch, Pierce, Fenner and Smith, Inc., which publishes a monthly *Security Risk Evaluation* book, commonly called the "beta book."

Security Risk Evaluation uses the S&P 500 index as the proxy for the market portfolio. It relies on the 60 most recent monthly observations to calculate regression parameters. Merrill Lunch and most services[7] use total returns, rather than excess returns (deviations from T-bill rates), in the regressions. In this way they estimate a variant of our index model, which is

$$r = a + br_M + e^* \tag{9.10}$$

instead of

$$r - r_f = \alpha + \beta(r_M - r_f) + e \tag{9.11}$$

To see the effect of this departure, we can rewrite equation 9.11 as

$$r = r_f + \alpha + \beta r_M - \beta r_f + e = \alpha + r_f(1 - \beta) + \beta r_M + e \tag{9.12}$$

Comparing equations 9.10 and 9.12, you can see that if r_f is constant over the sample period both equations have the same independent variable, r_M, and residual, e. Therefore, the slope coefficient will be the same in the two regressions.[8]

However, the intercept that Merrill Lynch calls alpha is really, using the parameters of the CAPM, an estimate of $\alpha + r_f(1 - \beta)$. The apparent justification for this procedure is that, on a monthly basis, $r_f(1 - \beta)$ is small and is apt to be swamped by the volatility of actual stock returns. But it is worth noting that for $\beta \neq 1$, the regression intercept in equation 9.10 will not equal the CAPM alpha as it does when excess returns are used as in equation 9.11.

Another way the Merrill Lynch procedure departs from the index model is in its use of percentage of changes in price instead of total rates of return. This means that the index model variant of Merrill Lynch ignores the dividend component of stock returns.

Table 9.2 illustrates a page from the beta book showing the estimates for GM. The fourth column, Close Price, shows the stock price at the end of the sample period. The next two columns show the beta and alpha coefficients. Remember that Merrill Lynch's alpha is actually $\alpha + r_f(1 - \beta)$.

The next column, *R*-SQR, shows the square of the correlation between r_i and r_M. The *R*-square statistic, which is sometimes called the *coefficient of determination*, gives the fraction of the variance of the dependent variable (the return on the stock) that is explained by movements in the independent variable (the return on the S&P 500 index). Recall from Section 9.1 that the part of the total variance of the rate of return on an asset, σ^2, that is explained by market returns is the systematic variance, $\beta^2\sigma_M^2$. Hence, the *R*-square is systematic variance over total variance, which tells us what fraction of a firm's volatility is attributable to market movements:

$$R\text{-square} = \frac{\beta^2\sigma_M^2}{\sigma^2}$$

[7] Value Line is another common source of security betas. Value Line uses weekly rather than monthly data and uses the New York Stock Exchange index instead of the S&P 500 as the market proxy.

[8] Actually, r_f does vary over time and so should not be grouped casually with the constant term in the regression. However, variations in r_f are tiny compared with the swings in the market return. The actual volatility in the T-bill rate has only a small impact on the estimated value of β.

Table 9.2 Market Sensitivity Statistics

Ticker Symbol	Security Name	June 1994 Close Price	Beta	Alpha	*R*-SQR	RESID STD DEV-*N*	Standard Error Beta	Standard Error Alpha	Adjusted Beta	Number of Observations
GBND	General Binding Corp	18.375	0.52	−0.06	0.02	10.52	0.37	1.38	0.68	60
GBDC	General Bldrs Corp	0.930	0.58	−1.03	0.00	17.38	0.62	2.28	0.72	60
GNCMA	General Communication Inc Class A	3.750	1.54	0.82	0.12	14.42	0.51	1.89	1.36	60
GCCC	General Computer Corp	8.375	0.93	1.67	0.06	12.43	0.44	1.63	0.95	60
GDC	General Datacomm Inds Inc	16.125	2.25	2.31	0.16	18.32	0.65	2.40	1.83	60
GD	General Dynamics Corp	40.875	0.54	0.63	0.03	9.02	0.32	1.18	0.69	60
GE	General Elec Co	46.625	1.21	0.39	0.61	3.53	0.13	0.46	1.14	60
JOB	General Employment Enterpris	4.063	0.91	1.20	0.01	20.50	0.73	2.69	0.94	60
GMCC	General Magnaplate Corp	4.500	0.97	0.00	0.04	14.18	0.50	1.86	0.98	60
GMW	General Microwave Corp	8.000	0.95	0.16	0.12	8.83	0.31	1.16	0.97	60
GIS	General MLS Inc	54.625	1.01	0.42	0.37	4.82	0.17	0.63	1.01	60
GM	General MTRS Corp	50.250	0.80	0.14	0.11	7.78	0.28	1.02	0.87	60 ←
GPU	General Pub Utils Cp	26.250	0.52	0.20	0.20	3.69	0.13	0.48	0.68	60
GRN	General RE Corp	108.875	1.07	0.42	0.31	5.75	0.20	0.75	1.05	60
GSX	General SIGNAL Corp	33.000	0.86	−0.01	0.22	5.85	0.21	0.77	0.91	60

Source: Modified from *Security Risk Evaluation*, Research Computer Services Department of Merrill Lynch, Pierce, Fenner and Smith, Inc. pp. 9–17. Based on S&P 500 index, using straight regression..

The firm-specific variance, $\sigma^2(e)$, is the part of the asset variance that is unexplained by the market index. Therefore, because

$$\sigma^2 = \beta^2\sigma_M^2 + \sigma^2(e)$$

the coefficient of determination also may be expressed as

$$R\text{-square} = 1 - \frac{\sigma^2(e)}{\sigma^2} \tag{9.13}$$

Accordingly, the column following *R*-SQR reports the standard deviation of the nonsystematic component, $\sigma(e)$, calling it RESID STD DEV-*N*, in reference to the fact that the *e*s are estimated by the regression residuals. This variable is an estimate of firm-specific risk.

The following two columns appear under the heading of Standard Error. These are statistics that allow us to test the significance of the regression coefficients. The standard error of an estimate is the standard deviation of the possible estimation error of the coefficient, which is a measure of the precision of the estimate. A rule of thumb is that if an estimated coefficient is less than twice its standard error, we cannot reject the hypothesis that the true coefficient is zero. The ratio of the coefficient to its standard error is the *t*-statistic that you may have studied in statistics. A *t*-statistic greater than 2 is the traditional cutoff for statistical significance. The two columns of the standard error of the estimated beta and alpha allow us a quick check on the statistical significance to these estimates.

The next-to-last column is called Adjusted Beta. The motivation for adjusting beta estimates is the observation that, on average, the beta coefficients of stocks seem to move toward 1 over time. One explanation for this phenomenon is intuitive. A business enterprise usually is established to produce a specific product or service, and a new firm may be more unconventional than an older one in many ways, from technology to management style. As it grows, however, a firm diversifies, first expanding to similar products and later to more diverse operations. As the firm becomes more conventional, it starts to resemble the rest of the economy even more. Thus, its beta coefficient will tend to change in the direction of 1.

Another explanation for this phenomenon is statistical. We know that the average beta over all securities is 1. Thus, before estimating the beta of a security our guess would be that it is 1. When we estimate this beta coefficient over a particular sample period, we sustain some unknown sampling error of the estimated beta. The greater the difference between our beta estimate and 1, the greater is the chance that we incurred a large estimation error and that, when we estimate this same beta in a subsequent sample period, the new estimate will be closer to 1.

The sample estimate of the beta coefficient is the best guess for the sample period. Given that beta has a tendency to evolve toward 1, however, a forecast of the future beta coefficient should adjust the sample estimate in that direction.

Merrill Lynch adjusts beta estimates in a simple way. They take the sample estimate of beta and average it with 1, using the weights of two-thirds and one-third:

$$\text{Adjusted beta} = \tfrac{2}{3}\ \text{sample beta} + \tfrac{1}{3}(1)$$

Finally, the last column shows the number of observations, which is 60 months, unless the stock is newly listed and fewer observations are available.

For the 60 months ending in June 1994, GM's beta was estimated at .80. Note that the adjusted beta for GM is .87, taking it a third of the way toward 1.

The sample period regression alpha is .14. Because GM's beta is less than 1, we know that this means that the index model alpha estimate is somewhat smaller. As we did in equation 9.11, we have to subtract $(1 - \beta)r_f$ from the regression alpha to obtain the index model alpha. Even so, the standard error of the alpha estimate is 1.02. The estimate of alpha is far less than twice its standard error. Consequently, we cannot reject the hypothesis that the true alpha is zero.

CONCEPT CHECK Question 5. What was GM's CAPM alpha per month during the period covered by the Merrill Lynch regression if during this period the average monthly rate of return on T-bills was 0.6%?

Most importantly, these alpha estimates are ex post (after the fact) measures. They do not mean that anyone could have forecasted these alpha values ex ante (before the fact). In fact, the name of the game in security analysis is to forecast alpha values ahead of time. A well-constructed portfolio that includes long positions in future positive alpha stocks and short positions in future negative alpha stocks will outperform the market index. They key term here is "well constructed," meaning that the portfolio has to balance concentration on high alpha stocks with the need for risk-reducing diversification. The beta and residual variance estimates from the index model regression make it possible to achieve this goal. (We examine this technique in more detail in Part VII on active portfolio management.)

Note that GM's RESID STD DEV-*N* is 7.78% per month and its *R*-SQR is .11. This tells us that $\sigma^2_{GM}(e) = 7.78^2 = 60.53$ and, because $R\text{-SQR} = 1 - \sigma^2(e)/\sigma^2$, we can solve for the estimate of GM's total standard deviation by rearranging equation 9.12 as follows:

$$\sigma_{GM} = \left[\frac{\sigma_{GM}(e)}{1 - R^2}\right]^{1/2} = \left(\frac{60.53}{.89}\right)^{1/2} = 8.25\% \text{ per month}$$

This is GM's monthly standard deviation for the sample period. Therefore, the annualized standard deviation for that period was $8.25\sqrt{12} = 28.58\%$.

In the absence of special information concerning GM, if our forecast for the market index is 14% and T-bills pay 6%, we learn from the Merrill Lynch beta book that the CAPM forecast for the rate of return on GM stock is

$$\begin{aligned} E(r_{GM}) &= r_f + \text{adjusted beta} \times [E(r_M) - r_f] \\ &= 6 + .80\,(14 - 6) \\ &= 12.40\% \end{aligned}$$

9.4 Predicting Betas

We saw in the previous section that betas estimated from past data may not be the best estimates of future betas: Betas seem to drift toward 1 over time. This suggests that we might want a forecasting model for beta.

One simple approach would be to collect data on beta in different periods and then estimate a regression equation:

$$\text{Current beta} = a + b\,(\text{Past beta}) \qquad \textbf{(9.14)}$$

Given estimates of *a* and *b*, we would then forecast future betas using the rule

$$\text{Forecast beta} = a + b\,(\text{Current beta})$$

There is no reason, however, to limit ourselves to such simple forecasting rules. Why not also investigate the predictive power of other financial variables in forecasting beta? For example, if we believe that firm size and debt ratios are two determinants of beta, we might specify an expanded version of equation 9.14 and estimate

$$\begin{aligned} \text{Current beta} &= \alpha \\ &\quad + b_1\,(\text{Past beta}) \\ &\quad + b_2\,(\text{Firm size}) \\ &\quad + b_3\,(\text{Debt ratio}) \end{aligned}$$

Now we would use estimates of α and b_1 through b_3 to forecast future betas.

Such an approach was followed by Rosenberg and Guy,[9] who found the following variables to help predict betas:

Table 9.3 Industry Betas and Adjustment Factors

Industry	Beta	Adjustment Factor
Agriculture	0.99	−.140
Drugs and medicine	1.14	−.099
Telephone	0.75	−.288
Energy utilities	0.60	−.237
Gold	0.36	−.827
Construction	1.27	.062
Air transport	1.80	.348
Trucking	1.31	.098
Consumer durables	1.44	.132

1. Variance of earnings.
2. Variance of cash flow.
3. Growth in earnings per share.
4. Market capitalization (firm size).
5. Dividend yield.
6. Debt to asset ratio.

Rosenberg and Guy also found that even after controlling for a firm's financial characteristics, industry group helps to predict beta. For example, they found that the beta values of gold mining companies are on average 0.827 lower than would be predicted based on financial characteristics alone. This should not be surprising; the −0.827 "adjustment factor" for the gold industry reflects the fact that gold values are inversely related to market returns.

Table 9.3 presents beta estimates and adjustment factors for a subset of firms in the Rosenberg and Guy study.

CONCEPT CHECK Question 6. Compare the first five and last four industries in Table 9.3. What characteristic seems to determine whether the adjustment factor is positive or negative?

SUMMARY

1. A single-factor model of the economy classifies sources of uncertainty as systematic (macroeconomic) factors or firm-specific (microeconomic) factors. The index model assumes that the macro factor can be represented by a broad index of stock returns.

2. The single-index model drastically reduces the necessary inputs into the Markowitz portfolio selection procedure. It also aids in specialization of labor in security analysis.

3. If the index model specification is valid, then the systematic risk of a portfolio or asset equals $\beta^2\sigma_M^2$ and the covariance between two assets equals $\beta_i \beta_j \sigma_M^2$.

[9] Barr Rosenberg and J. Guy, "Prediction of Beta from Investment Fundamentals, Parts 1 and 2," *Financial Analysts Journal*, May–June and July–August 1976.

4. The index model is estimated by applying regression analysis to excess rates of return. The slope of the regression curve is the beta of an asset, whereas the intercept is the asset's alpha during the sample period. The regression line is also called the *security characteristic line*. The regression beta is equivalent to the CAPM beta, except that the regression uses actual returns and the CAPM is specified in terms of expected returns. The CAPM predicts that the average value of alphas measured by the index model regression will be zero.

5. Practitioners routinely estimate the index model using total rather than excess rates of return. This makes their estimate of alpha equal to $\alpha + r_f(1 - \beta)$.

6. Betas show a tendency to evolve toward 1 over time. Beta forecasting rules attempt to predict this drift. Moreover, other financial variables can be used to help forecast betas.

Key Terms

Factor model
Single-index model
Scatter diagram
Regression equation
Residuals
Security characteristic line
Market model

Selected Readings

The seminal paper relating the index model to the portfolio selection problem is:

Sharpe, William F. "A Simplified Model of Portfolio Analysis." *Management Science*, January 1963.

Papers on the tendency of betas to drift over time are:

Blume, Marshall. "Betas and Their Regression Tendencies." *Journal of Finance* 10 (June 1975).
Klemkosky. R. C.; and J. D. Martin. "The Adjustment of Beta Forecasts." *Journal of Finance* 10 (September 1975).
Vasicek, O. "A Note on Using Cross-Sectional Information in Bayesian Estimation of Security Betas." *Journal of Finance* 8 (December 1973).

Papers on the relation between beta and firm characteristics are:

Rosenberg, Barr; and J. Guy. "Predictions of Beta from Investment Fundamentals." *Financial Analysts Journal* 32 (May–June 1976).
Robichek, A. A.; and R. A. Cohn. "The Economic Determinants of Systematic Risk." *Journal of Finance*, May 1974.

Problems

1. A portfolio management organization analyzes 75 stocks and constructs a mean-variance efficient portfolio that is constrained to these 75.
   a. How many estimates of expected returns, variances, and covariances are needed to optimize this portfolio?
   b. If one could safely assume that stock market returns closely resemble a single-index structure, how many estimates would be needed?
2. The following are estimates for two of the stocks in question 1.

Stock	Expected Return	Beta	Firm-Specific Standard Deviation
A	14	0.6	32
B	25	1.3	37

The market index has a standard deviation of 26%.

a. What is the standard deviation of stocks *A* and *B*?

b. Suppose that we were to construct a portfolio with proportions:

Stock *A*:	0.33	
Stock *B*:	0.38	
T-bills:	0.29	($r_f = 9\%$)

Compute the expected return, standard deviation, beta, and nonsystematic standard deviation of the portfolio.

3. Consider the following two regression lines for stocks *A* and *B* in the following figure.

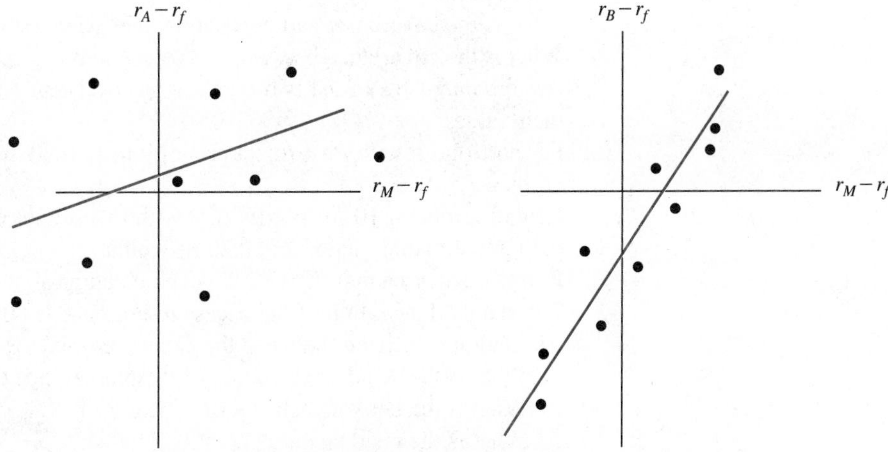

a. Which stock has higher firm-specific risk?

b. Which stock has greater systematic (market) risk?

c. Which stock has higher *R*-square?

d. Which stock has higher alpha?

e. Which stock has higher correlation with the market?

4. Consider the two (excess return) index model regression results for *A* and *B*:

$R_A = 1\% + 1.2R_M$
R-SQR = .576
RESID STD DEV-*N* = 10.3%
$R_B = -2\% + .8R_M$
R-SQR = .436
RESID STD DEV-*N* = 9.1%

a. Which stock has more firm-specific risk?

b. Which has greater market risk?

c. For which stock does market movement explain a greater fraction of return variability?

d. Which stock had an average return in excess of that predicted by the CAPM?

e. If r_f were constant at 6% and the regression had been run using total rather than excess returns, what would have been the regression intercept for stock *A*?

Use the following data for problems 5 through 11. Suppose that the index model for stocks *A* and *B* is estimated with the following results:

$$R_A = 2\% + .65R_M + e_A$$
$$R_B = 4\% + 1.10R_M + e_B$$
$$\sigma_M = 25\%;\ R\text{-SQR}_A = .15;\ R\text{-SQR}_B = .30$$

5. What is the standard deviation of each stock?
6. Break down the variance of each stock to the systematic and firm-specific components.
7. What is the covariance and correlation coefficient between two stocks?
8. What is the covariance between each stock and the market index?
9. Are the intercepts of the two regressions consistent with the CAPM? Interpret their values.
10. For portfolio *P* with investment proportions of 0.60 in *A* and 0.40 in *B*, rework problems 5, 6, and 8.
11. Rework problem 10 for portfolio *Q* with investment proportions of 0.50 in *P*, 0.30 in the market index, and 0.20 in T-bills.
12. In a two stock capital market, the capitalization of stock *A* is twice that of *B*. The standard deviation of the excess return on *A* is 30% and on *B* is 50%. The correlation coefficient between the excess returns is 0.7.
    a. What is the standard deviation of the market index portfolio?
    b. What is the beta of each stock?
    c. What is the residual variance of each stock?
    d. If the index model holds and stock *A* is expected to earn 11% in excess of the risk-free rate, what must be the risk premium on the market portfolio?
13. A stock recently has been estimated to have a beta of 1.24:
    a. What will Merrill Lynch compute as the "adjusted beta" of this stock?
    b. Suppose that you estimate the following regression describing the evolution of beta over time:

$$\beta_t = 0.3 + 0.7\beta_{t-1}$$

    What would be your predicted beta for next year?

14. When the annualized quarterly percentage rates of return for a stock market index were regressed against the returns for KM and WMT stocks over the period 1971 to 1980 in an ordinary least squares regression, the following results were obtained:

---

*Reprinted, with permission, from the Level I 1982 *CFA Study Guide*.

Statistic	KM	WMT
Alpha	−3.68%	13.96%
Beta	0.69	0.97
R-square	0.25	0.22
Residual standard deviation	13.02%	21.45%

Explain what these regression results tell the analyst about risk-and-return relationships for each stock over the 1971 to 1980 period. Comment on their implications for future risk-and-return relationships, assuming both stocks were included in a diversified common stock portfolio, especially in view of the following data obtained from two large brokerage houses in late December 1981:

Brokerage House	Beta of KM	Beta of WMT
A	.80	1.45
B	.75	1.20

where *A*'s betas are calculated on weekly price change data over the preceding 52 weeks and *B*'s betas are calculated on monthly price change data over the preceding 60 months.

15. Based on current dividend yields and expected growth rates, the expected rates of return on stocks *A* and *B* are 11% and 14%, respectively. The beta of stock *A* is 0.8, while that of stock *B* is 1.5. The T-bill rate is currently 6%, while the expected rate of return on the S&P 500 index is 12%. The standard deviation of stock *A* is 10% annually, while that of stock *B* is 11%.

a. If you currently hold a well-diversified portfolio, would you choose to add either of these stocks to your holdings?

b. If instead you could invest only in bills plus only one of these stocks, which stock would you choose? Explain your answer using either a graph or a quantitative measure of the attractiveness of the stocks.

16. Assume the correlation coefficient between Baker Fund and the S&P 500 Stock Index is 0.70. What percentage of Baker Fund's total risk is specific (i.e., nonsystematic)?*

a. 35%.

b. 49%.

c. 51%.

d. 70%.

17. The correlation between the Charlottesville International Fund and the EAFE Index is 1.0. The expected return on the EAFE Index is 11%, the expected return on Charlottesville International Fund is 9%, and the risk-free return in EAFE countries is 3%. Based on this analysis, the implied beta of Charlottesville International is:*

a. Negative.

b. 0.75.

c. 0.82.

d. 1.00.

*Reprinted, with permission, from the Level I 1993 *CFA Study Guide.*

Chapter 10
Arbitrage Pricing Theory

THE EXPLOITATION OF SECURITY MISPRICING IN SUCH A WAY THAT RISK-FREE ECONOMIC PROFITS MAY BE EARNED IS CALLED ARBITRAGE. It involves the simultaneous purchase and sale of equivalent securities in order to profit from discrepancies in their price relationship, and so it is an extension of the law of one price. The concept of arbitrage is central to the theory of capital markets. This chapter discusses the nature, and illustrates the use, of arbitrage. We show how to identify arbitrage opportunities and why investors will take as large a position as they can in arbitrage portfolios.

Perhaps the most basic principle of capital market theory is that equilibrium market prices are rational in that they rule out (risk-free) arbitrage opportunities. Pricing relationships that guarantee the absence of arbitrage possibilities are extremely powerful. If actual security prices allow for arbitrage, the result will be strong pressure on security prices to restore equilibrium. Only a few investors need be aware of arbitrage opportunities to bring about a large volume of trades, and these trades will bring prices back into balance.

The CAPM of the last two chapters gave us the security market line, a relationship between expected return and risk as measured by beta. The model discussed in this chapter, called the Arbitrage Pricing Theory, or APT, also stipulates a relationship between expected return and risk, but it uses different assumptions and techniques. We explore this relationship using well-diversified portfolios, showing that these portfolios are priced to satisfy the CAPM expected return–beta relationship. Because all well-diversified portfolios have to satisfy that relationship, we show that all individual securities almost certainly satisfy this same relationship. This reasoning allows the derivation of an SML relationship that avoids reliance on the unobservable, theoretical market portfolio that is central to the CAPM. Next, we show how the simple single-factor APT (just like the CAPM) can easily be generalized to a richer multifactor version. Finally, we discuss the similarities and differences between the APT and the CAPM and the index model.

10.1 Arbitrage: Profits and Opportunities

An arbitrage opportunity arises when an investor can construct a **zero investment portfolio** that will yield a *sure* profit. (The emphasis is on sure, i.e., risk-free.) A zero investment portfolio means that the investor need not use any of his or her own money. Obviously, to be able to construct a zero investment portfolio one has to be able to sell short at least one asset and use the proceeds to purchase (go long on) one or more assets. Borrowing may be considered a short position in the risk-free asset. Even a small investor using short positions in this fashion can take a large dollar position in such a portfolio.

An obvious case of an arbitrage opportunity arises when the law of one price is violated, as discussed in Chapter 4. When an asset is trading at different prices in two markets (and the price differential exceeds transaction costs), a simultaneous trade in the two markets can produce a sure profit (the net price differential) without any investment. One simply sells short the asset in the high-priced market and buys it in the low-priced market. The net proceeds are positive, and there is no risk because the long and short positions offset each other.

In modern markets with electronic communications and instantaneous execution, arbitrage opportunities have become rare but not extinct. The same technology that enables the market to absorb new information quickly also enables fast operators to make large profits by trading huge volumes at the instant that an arbitrage opportunity appears. This is the essence of index arbitrage, to be discussed in Part VI and Chapter 22.

From the simple case of a violation of the law of one price, let us proceed to a less obvious (yet just as profitable) arbitrage opportunity. Imagine that four stocks are traded in an economy with only four distinct, possible scenarios. The rates of return of the four stocks for each inflation-interest rate scenario appear in Table 10.1. The current prices of the stocks and rate of return statistics are shown in Table 10.2.

Eyeballing the rate of return data, there seems no clue to any arbitrage opportunity lurking in this set of investments. The expected returns, standard deviations, and correlations do not reveal any particular abnormality.

Consider, however, an equally weighted portfolio of the first three stocks (Apex, Bull, and Crush), and contrast its possible future rates of return with those of the fourth stock, Dreck. These returns are derived from Table 10.1 and summarized in the table directly below Table 10.2.

Table 10.1 Rate of Return Projections

	High Real Interest Rates		Low Real Interest Rates	
	High Inflation	**Low Inflation**	**High Inflation**	**Low Inflation**
Probability:	.25	.25	.25	.25
Stock				
Apex *(A)*	–20	20	40	60
Bull *(B)*	0	70	30	–20
Crush *(C)*	90	–20	–10	70
Dreck *(D)*	15	23	15	36

Table 10.2 Rate of Return Statistics

				Correlation Matrix			
Stock	**Current Price**	**Expected Return**	**Standard Deviation (%)**	**A**	**B**	**C**	**D**
A	$10	25	29.58%	1.00	–0.15	–0.29	0.68
B	10	20	33.91	–0.15	1.00	–0.87	–0.38
C	10	32.5	48.15	–0.29	–0.87	1.00	0.22
D	10	22.25	8.58	0.68	–0.38	0.22	1.00

	High Real Interest Rates		Low Real Interest Rates	
	Inflation Rate		Inflation Rate	
	High	**Low**	**High**	**Low**
Equally weighted portfolio (*A*, *B*, and *C*)	23.33	23.33	20.00	36.67
Dreck	15.00	23.00	15.00	36.00

This analysis reveals that in all scenarios the equally weighted portfolio will outperform Dreck. The rate of return statistics of the two alternatives are

	Mean	**Standard Deviation**	**Correlation**
Three-stock portfolio	25.83	6.40	0.94
Dreck	22.25	8.58	

The two investments are not perfectly correlated; that is, they are not perfect substitutes, meaning there is no violation of the law of one price here. Nevertheless, the equally weighted portfolio will fare better under *any* circumstances; thus any investor, no matter how risk averse, can take advantage of this perfect dominance. All that is required is for the investor to take a short position in Dreck and use the proceeds to purchase the equally weighted portfolio.[1] Let us see how it would work.

Suppose that we sell short 300,000 shares of Dreck and use the $3 million proceeds to buy 100,000 shares each of Apex, Bull, and Crush. The dollar profits in each of the four scenarios will be as follows:

		High Real Interest Rates		Low Real Interest Rates	
		Inflation Rate		Inflation Rate	
Stock	**Dollar Investment**	**High**	**Low**	**High**	**Low**
Apex	$ 1,000,000	$–200,000	$ 200,000	$ 400,000	$ 600,000
Bull	1,000,000	0	700,000	300,000	–200,000
Crush	1,000,000	900,000	–200,000	–100,000	700,000
Dreck	–3,000,000	–450,000	–690,000	–450,000	–1,080,000
Portfolio	0	$ 250,000	$ 10,000	$ 150,000	$ 20,000

The first column verifies that the net investment in our portfolio is zero. Yet this portfolio yields a positive profit according to any scenario. This is a money machine. Investors will want to take an infinite position in such a portfolio because larger positions entail no risk of losses, yet yield ever-growing profits. Theoretically, even a single investor would take such large positions that the market would react to the buying and selling pressure: the price of Dreck has to come down and/or the prices of Apex, Bull, and Crush have to go up. The arbitrage opportunity will be eliminated.

CONCEPT CHECK

Question 1. Suppose that Dreck's price starts falling without any change in its per-share dollar payoffs. How far must the price fall before arbitrage between Dreck and the equally weighted portfolio is no longer possible? (Hint: What happens to the amount of the equally weighted portfolio that can be purchased with the proceeds of the short sale as Dreck's price falls?)

The idea that equilibrium market prices ought to be rational in the sense that prices will move to rule out arbitrage opportunities is perhaps the most fundamental concept in capital market theory. Violation of this restriction would indicate the grossest form of market irrationality.

The critical property of a risk-free arbitrage portfolio is that any investor, regardless of risk aversion or wealth, will want to take an infinite position in it so that profits will be driven to an infinite level. Because those large positions will force prices up or down until the opportunity vanishes, we can derive restrictions on security prices that satisfy the condition that no arbitrage opportunities are left in the marketplace.

[1] Short selling is discussed in Chapter 3.

There is an important difference between (risk-free) arbitrage and risk-versus-return dominance arguments in support of equilibrium price relationships. A dominance argument holds that when an equilibrium price relationship is violated, many investors will make portfolio changes. Each individual investor will make a limited change, though, depending on his or her degree of risk aversion. Aggregation of these limited portfolio changes over many investors is required to create a large volume of buying and selling, which in turn restores equilibrium prices. When arbitrage opportunities exist, by contrast, each investor wants to take as large a position as possible; hence, it will not take many investors to bring about the price pressures necessary to restore equilibrium. For this reason, implications for prices derived from no-arbitrage arguments are stronger than implications derived from a risk-versus-return dominance argument.

The CAPM is an example of a dominance argument. The CAPM argues that all investors hold mean-variance efficient portfolios. If a security (or a bundle of securities) is mispriced, then investors will tilt their portfolios toward the underpriced and away from the overpriced securities. The resulting pressure on equilibrium prices results from many investors shifting their portfolios, each by a relatively small dollar amount. The assumption that a sufficiently large number of investors are mean-variance sensitive is critical, whereas the essence of the no-arbitrage condition is that even relatively few investors are enough to identify an arbitrage opportunity and then mobilize large dollar amounts to take advantage of it. Pressure on prices can result from only a few arbitrageurs.

Practitioners often use the terms "arbitrage" and "arbitrageurs" in ways other than our strict definition. "Arbitrageur" often is used to refer to a professional searching for mispriced securities in specific areas such as merger-target stocks, rather than to one who seeks strict (risk-free) arbitrage opportunities in the sense that no loss is possible. The search for mispriced securities rather than the more restrictive search for sure bets sometimes is called **risk arbitrage** to distinguish it from pure arbitrage.

To leap ahead, in Part VI we discuss "derivative" securities such as futures and options, where market values are completely determined by the prices of other securities or portfolios. For example, a call option on a stock has a value at maturity that is fully determined by the price of the stock. For such securities, strict arbitrage is a practical possibility, and the condition of no-arbitrage leads to exact pricing. In the case of stocks and other "primitive" securities (whose values are not determined strictly by a single asset or bundle of assets), no-arbitrage conditions must be obtained by appealing to diversification arguments.

10.2 Well-Diversified Portfolios and the APT

Stephen Ross developed the **Arbitrage Pricing Theory** (APT) in 1976.[2] As with our analysis of the CAPM, we begin with the simple version of his model, which assumes that only one systematic factor affects security returns. However, the usual discussion

[2] Stephen A. Ross, "Return, Risk and Arbitrage," in I. Friend and J. Bicksler, eds., *Risk and Return in Finance* (Cambridge, Mass.: Ballinger, 1976).

of the APT is concerned with the multifactor case, and we treat this richer model in Section 10.5.

Ross starts by examining a single-factor model similar in spirit to the market model introduced in Chapter 9. As in that model, uncertainty in asset returns has two sources: a common or macroeconomic factor, and a firm-specific or microeconomic cause. In the factor model the common factor is assumed to have zero expected value, and it is meant to measure new information concerning the macroeconomy. New information has, by definition, zero expected value. There is no need, however, to assume that the factor can be proxied by the return on a market index portfolio.

If we call F the deviation of the common factor from its expected value, β_i the sensitivity of firm i to that factor, and e_i the firm-specific disturbance, the factor model states that the actual return on firm i will equal its expected return plus a (zero expected value) random amount attributable to unanticipated economywide events, plus another (zero expected value) random amount attributable to firm-specific events.

Formally,

$$r_i = E(r_i) + \beta_i F + e_i$$

where $E(r_i)$ is the expected return on stock i. All the nonsystematic returns, the e_is, are uncorrelated among themselves and uncorrelated with the factor, F.

To make the factor model more concrete, consider an example. Suppose that the macro factor, F, is taken to be the unexpected percentage change in GNP, and that the consensus is that GNP will increase by 4% this year. Suppose also that a stock's β value is 1.2. If GNP increases by only 3%, then the value of F would be –1%, representing a 1% disappointment in actual growth versus expected growth. Given the stock's beta value, this disappointment would translate into a return on the stock that is 1.2% lower than previously expected. This macro surprise together with the firm-specific disturbance, e_i, determine the total departure of the stock's return from its originally expected value.

Well-Diversified Portfolios

Now we look at the risk of a portfolio of stocks. We first show that if a portfolio is well diversified, its firm-specific or nonfactor risk can be diversified away. Only factor (or systematic) risk remains. If we construct an n-stock portfolio with weights, w_i, $\Sigma\, w_i = 1$, then the rate of return on this portfolio is as follows:

$$r_P = E(r_P) + \beta_P F + e_P \qquad \textbf{(10.1)}$$

where

$$\beta_P = \Sigma w_i \beta_i$$

is the weighted average of the β_i of the n securities. The portfolio nonsystematic component (which is uncorrelated with F) is

$$e_P = \Sigma w_i e_i$$

which also is a weighted average, in this case of the e_i of each of the n securities.

We can divide the variance of this portfolio into systematic and nonsystematic sources, as we saw in Chapter 9. The portfolio variance is

$$\sigma_P^2 = \beta_P^2\sigma_F^2 + \sigma^2(e_P)$$

where σ_F^2 is the variance of the factor F, and $\sigma^2(e_P)$ is the nonsystematic risk of the portfolio, which is given by

$$\sigma^2(e_P) = \text{Variance}(\Sigma w_i e_i) = \Sigma w_i^2\sigma^2(e_i)$$

Note that in deriving the nonsystematic variance of the portfolio, we depend on the fact that the firm-specific e_is are uncorrelated and hence that the variance of the "portfolio" of nonsystematic e_is is the weighted sum of the individual nonsystematic variances (with the square of the investment proportions as weights).

If the portfolio were equally weighted, $w_i = 1/n$, then the nonsystematic variance would be

$$\sigma^2\left(e_i; w_i = \frac{1}{n}\right) = \Sigma\left(\frac{1}{n}\right)^2\sigma^2(e_i) = \frac{1}{n}\Sigma\frac{\sigma^2(e_i)}{n} = \frac{1}{n}\,\overline{\sigma}^2(e_i)$$

In this case, we divide the average nonsystematic variance, $\overline{\sigma}^2(e_i)$, by n, so that when the portfolio gets large (in the sense that n is large and the portfolio remains equally weighted across all n stocks), the nonsystematic variance approaches zero.

CONCEPT CHECK Question 2. What will be the nonsystematic standard deviation of the equally weighted portfolio if the average value of $\sigma^2(e_i)$ equals 30%, and (*a*) $n = 10$, (*b*) $n = 100$, (*c*) $n = 1{,}000$, and (*d*) $n = 10{,}000$? What do you conclude about the nonsystematic risk of large, diversified portfolios?

The set of portfolios for which the nonsystematic variance approaches zero as n gets large consists of more portfolios than just the equally weighted portfolio. Any portfolio for which each w_i becomes consistently smaller as n gets large (specifically, where each w_i^2 approaches zero as n gets large) will satisfy the condition that the portfolio nonsystematic risk will approach zero as n gets large.

In fact, this property motivates us to define a **well-diversified portfolio** as one that is diversified over a large enough number of securities with proportions, w_i, each small enough that for practical purposes the nonsystematic variance, $\sigma^2(e_P)$, is negligible. Because the expected value of e_P is zero, if its variance also is zero, we can conclude that any realized value of e_P will be virtually zero. Rewriting equation 10.1, we conclude that for a well-diversified portfolio for all practical purposes

$$r_P = E(r_P) + \beta_P F$$

and

$$\sigma_P^2 = \beta_P^2\sigma_F^2; \quad \sigma_P = \beta_P\sigma_F$$

Large (mostly institutional) investors hold portfolios of hundreds and even thousands of securities; thus, the concept of well-diversified portfolios clearly is operational in contemporary financial markets. Well-diversified portfolios, however, are not necessarily equally weighted.

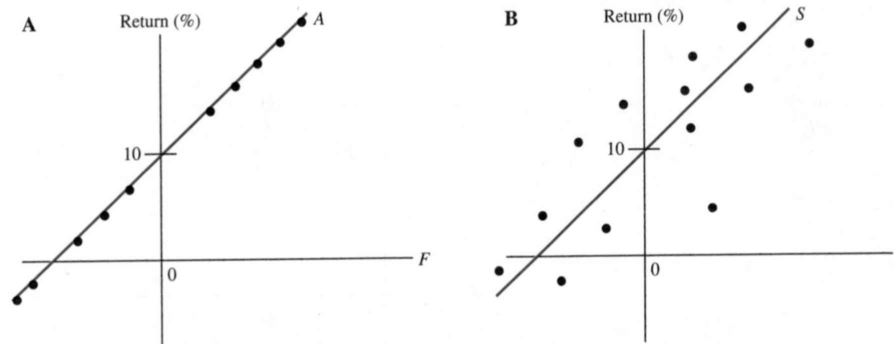

Figure 10.1
Returns as a function of the systematic factor.
A, Well-diversified Portfolio *A*.
B, Single stock *(S)*

As an illustration, consider a portfolio of 1,000 stocks. Let our position in the first stock be w%. Let the position in the second stock be $2w$%, the position in the third $3w$%, and so on. In this way our largest position (in the thousandth stock) is $1{,}000w$%. Can this portfolio possibly be well diversified, considering the fact that the largest position is 1,000 times the smallest position? Surprisingly, the answer is yes.

To see this, let us determine the largest weight in any one stock, in this case, the thousandth stock. The sum of the positions in all stocks must be 100%; therefore

$$w + 2w + \ldots + 1{,}000w = 100$$

Solving for w, we find that

$$w = 0.0002\%$$
$$1{,}000w = 0.2\%$$

Our *largest* position amounts to only 0.2 of 1%. And this is very far from an equally weighted portfolio. Yet, for practical purposes this still is a well-diversified portfolio.

Betas and Expected Returns

Because nonfactor risk can be diversified away, only factor risk commands a risk premium in market equilibrium. Nonsystematic risk across firms cancels out in well-diversified portfolios, so that only the systematic risk of a portfolio of securities can be related to its expected returns.

The solid line in Figure 10.1**A** plots the return of a well-diversified Portfolio *A* with $\beta_A = 1$ for various realizations of the systematic factor. The expected return of Portfolio *A* is 10%: this is where the solid line crosses the vertical axis. At this point the systematic factor is zero, implying no macro surprises. If the macro factor is positive, the portfolio's return exceeds its expected value; if it is negative, the portfolio's return falls short of its mean. The return on the portfolio is therefore

$$E(r_A) + \beta_A F = 10\% + 1.0 \times F$$

Compare Figure 10.1**A** with Figure 10.1**B**, which is a similar graph for a single stock (S) with $\beta_s = 1$. The undiversified stock is subject to nonsystematic risk, which is seen

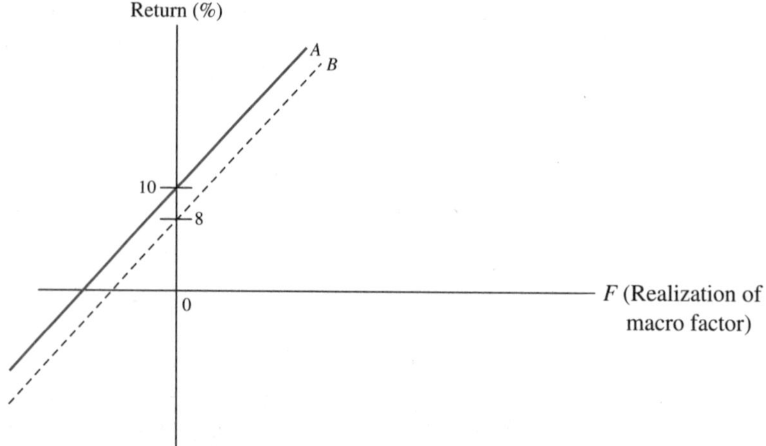

Figure 10.2
Returns as a function of the systematic factor: An arbitrage opportunity

in a scatter of points around the line. The well-diversified portfolio's return, in contrast, is determined completely by the systematic factor.

Now consider Figure 10.2, where the dashed line plots the return on another well-diversified portfolio, Portfolio *B*, with an expected return of 8% and β_B also equal to 1.0. Could Portfolios *A* and *B* coexist with the return pattern depicted? Clearly not: No matter what the systematic factor turns out to be, Portfolio *A* outperforms Portfolio *B*, leading to an arbitrage opportunity.

If you sell short \$1 million of *B* and buy \$1 million of *A*, a zero net investment strategy, your return would be \$20,000, as follows:

$(.10 + 1.0 \times F) \times \$1$ million	(from long position in *A*)
$-(.08 + 1.0 \times F) \times \$1$ million	(from short position in *B*)
$.02 \times \$1$ million $= \$20,000$	(net proceeds)

You make a risk-free profit because the factor risk cancels out across the long and short positions. Moreover, the strategy requires zero net investment. You should pursue it on an infinitely large scale until the return discrepancy between the two portfolios disappears. Portfolios with equal betas must have equal expected returns in market equilibrium, or arbitrage opportunities exist.

What about portfolios with different betas? We show now that their risk premiums must be proportional to beta. To see why, consider Figure 10.3. Suppose that the risk-free rate is 4% and that well-diversified portfolio *C*, with a beta of 0.5, has an expected return of 6%. Portfolio *C* plots below the line from the risk-free asset to Portfolio *A*. Consider, therefore, a new portfolio, *D*, composed of half of Portfolio *A* and half of the risk-free asset. Portfolio *D*'s beta will be $(\frac{1}{2} \times 0 + \frac{1}{2} \times 1.0) = 0.5$, and its expected return will be $(\frac{1}{2} \times 4 + \frac{1}{2} \times 10) = 7\%$. Now Portfolio *D* has an equal beta but a greater expected return than does Portfolio *C*. From our analysis in the previous paragraph we know that this constitutes an arbitrage opportunity.

Figure 10.3
An arbitrage opportunity

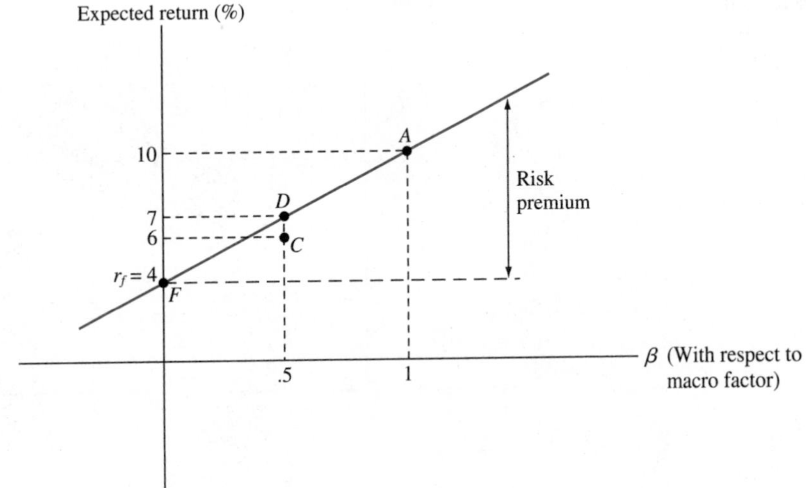

We conclude that, to preclude arbitrage opportunities, the expected return on all well-diversified portfolios must lie on the straight line from the risk-free asset in Figure 10.3. The equation of this line will dictate the expected return on all well-diversified portfolios.

Notice in Figure 10.3 that risk premiums are indeed proportional to portfolio betas. The risk premium is depicted by the vertical arrow, which measures the distance between the risk-free rate and the expected return on the portfolio. The risk premium is zero for $\beta = 0$, and rises in direct proportion to β.

Concept Check

Question 3. Suppose that Portfolio E is well diversified with a beta of $\frac{2}{3}$ and expected return of 9%. Would an arbitrage opportunity exist? If so, what would be the arbitrage opportunity?

The Security Market Line

Now consider the market portfolio as a well-diversified portfolio, and let us measure the systematic factor as the unexpected return on the market portfolio. The beta of the market portfolio is 1, since that is the beta of the market portfolio on itself. Because the market portfolio is on the line in Figure 10.3, we can use it to determine the equation describing the line. As Figure 10.4 shows, the intercept is r_f, and the slope is $E(r_M) - r_f$[rise $= E(r_M) - r_f$; run $= 1$], implying that the equation of the line is

$$E(r_P) = r_f + [E(r_M) - r_f]\beta_P \tag{10.2}$$

Hence, Figures 10.3 and 10.4 are identical to the SML relation of the CAPM.

We have used the no-arbitrage condition to obtain an expected return–beta relationship identical to that of the CAPM, without the restrictive assumptions of the CAPM. This suggests that despite its restrictive assumptions the main conclusion of the CAPM,

Figure 10.4
The security market line

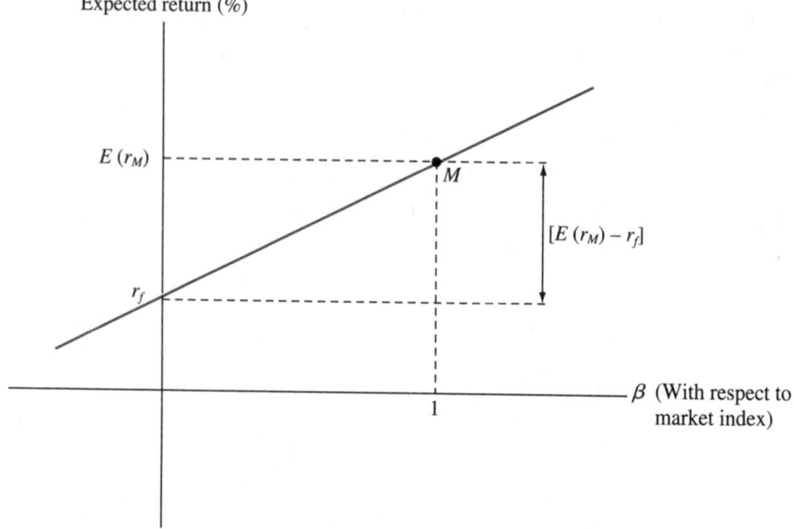

namely, the SML expected return–beta relationship, is likely to be at least approximately valid.

It is worth noting that in contrast to the CAPM the APT does not require that the benchmark portfolio in the SML relationship be the true market portfolio. Any well-diversified portfolio lying on the SML of Figure 10.3 may serve as the benchmark portfolio. For example, one might define the benchmark portfolio as the well-diversified portfolio most highly correlated with whatever systematic factor is thought to affect stock returns. Accordingly, the APT has more flexibility than does the CAPM because problems associated with an unobservable market portfolio are not a concern.

In addition, the APT provides further justification for use of the index model in the practical implementation of the SML relationship. Even if the index portfolio is not a precise proxy for the true market portfolio, which is a cause of considerable concern in the context of the CAPM, we now know that if the index portfolio is sufficiently well diversified, the SML relationship should still hold true according to the APT.

So far we have demonstrated the APT relationship for well-diversified portfolios only. The CAPM expected return–beta relationship applies to single assets, as well as to portfolios. In the next section we generalize the APT result one step further.

10.3 Individual Assets and the APT

We have demonstrated that, if arbitrage opportunities using well-diversified portfolios are to be ruled out, each portfolio's expected excess return must be proportional to its beta. For any two well-diversified portfolios P and Q, this can be written as

$$\frac{E(r_P) - r_f}{\beta_P} = \frac{E(r_Q) - r_f}{\beta_Q} \tag{10.3}$$

The question is whether this relationship tells us anything about the expected rates of return on the component stocks. The answer is that if this relationship is to be satisfied by all well-diversified portfolios, it almost surely must be satisfied by all individual securities, although the proof of this proposition is somewhat difficult. We note at the outset that, intuitively, we must prove simply that nonsystematic risk does not matter for security returns. The expected return–beta relationship that holds for well-diversified portfolios must also hold for individual securities.

First, we show that if individual securities satisfy equation 10.3, so will all portfolios. If for any two stocks, i and j, the same relationship holds exactly, that is,

$$\frac{E(r_i) - r_f}{\beta_i} = \frac{E(r_j) - r_f}{\beta_j} = K$$

where K is a constant for all securities, then by cross-multiplying, we can write, for any security, i,

$$E(r_i) = r_f + \beta_i K$$

Therefore, for any portfolio P with security weights w_i we have

$$E(r_P) = \Sigma w_i E(r_i) = r_f \Sigma w_i + K\Sigma w_i \beta_i$$

Because $\Sigma w_i = 1$ and $\beta_P = \Sigma w_i \beta_i$, we have

$$E(r_P) = r_f + \beta_P K$$

Thus, for all portfolios,

$$\frac{E(r_P) - r_f}{\beta_P} = K$$

and because all portfolios have the same K,

$$\frac{E(r_P) - r_f}{\beta_P} = \frac{E(r_Q) - r_f}{\beta_Q}$$

In other words, if the expected return–beta relationship holds for all single assets, then it will hold for *all* portfolios, well diversified or not.

CONCEPT CHECK

Question 4. Confirm the property expressed in equation 10.3 with a simple numerical example. Suppose that Portfolio P has an expected return of 10%, and β of 0.5, whereas Portfolio Q has an expected return of 15% and β of 1. The risk-free rate, r_f, is 5%.

a. Find K for these portfolios, and confirm that they are equal.

b. Find K for an equally weighted portfolio of P and Q, and show that it equals K for each individual security.

Now we show that it also is necessary that all securities satisfy the condition. To avoid extensive mathematics, we will satisfy ourselves with a less rigorous argument.

Suppose that the expected return–beta relationship is violated for all single assets. Now create a pair of well-diversified portfolios from these assets. What are the chances that, in spite of the fact that for any two single assets this relationship,

$$\frac{E(r_i) - r_f}{\beta_i} = \frac{E(r_j) - r_f}{\beta_j}$$

does not hold, the relationship *will* hold for the well-diversified portfolios as follows:

$$\frac{E(r_P) - r_f}{\beta_P} = \frac{E(r_Q) - r_f}{\beta_Q}$$

The chances are small, but it is possible that the relationships among the single securities are violated in offsetting ways so that somehow it holds for the pair of well-diversified portfolios.

Now construct yet another well-diversified portfolio. What are the chances that the violation of the relationships for single securities are such that the third portfolio also will fulfill the no-arbitrage expected return–beta relationship? Obviously, the chances are smaller still, but the relationship is possible. Continue with a fourth well-diversified portfolio, and so on. If the no-arbitrage expected return–beta relationship has to hold for infinitely many different, well-diversified portfolios, it must be virtually certain that the relationship holds for all individual securities.

We use the term "virtually certain" advisedly because we must distinguish this conclusion from the statement that all securities surely fulfill this relationship. The reason we cannot make the latter statement has to do with a property of well-diversified portfolios.

Recall that for a portfolio to qualify as well diversified it has to have very small positions in all securities. If, for example, only one security violates the expected return–beta relationship, then the effect of this violation for a well-diversified portfolio will be too small to be of importance for any practical purpose, and meaningful arbitrage opportunities will not arise. But if many securities violate the expected return–beta relationship, the relationship will no longer hold for well-diversified portfolios, and arbitrage opportunities will be available.

Consequently, we conclude that imposing the no-arbitrage condition on a single-factor security market implies maintenance of the expected return–beta relationship for all well-diversified portfolios and for all but, possibly, a *small* number of individual securities.

The APT serves many of the same functions as the CAPM. It gives us a benchmark for fair rates of return that can be used for capital budgeting, security evaluation, or investment performance evaluation. Moreover, the APT highlights the crucial distinction between nondiversifiable risk (factor risk) that requires a reward in the form of a risk premium and diversifiable risk that does not.

10.4 THE APT AND THE CAPM

The APT is an extremely appealing model. It depends on the assumption that a rational equilibrium in capital markets precludes arbitrage opportunities. A violation of the APT's pricing relationships will cause extremely strong pressure to restore them even if only a limited number of investors become aware of the disequilibrium.

Furthermore, the APT yields an expected return–beta relationship using a well-diversified portfolio that practically can be constructed from a large number of securities. In contrast, the CAPM is derived assuming an inherently unobservable "market" portfolio.

In spite of these appealing differences, the APT does not fully dominate the CAPM. The CAPM provides an unequivocal statement on the expected return–beta relationship for all assets, whereas the APT implies that this relationship holds for all but perhaps a small number of securities. This is an important difference, yet it is fruitless to pursue because the CAPM is not a readily testable model in the first place. A more productive comparison is between the APT and the index model.

Recall that the index model relies on the assumptions of the CAPM with additional assumptions that: (1) A specified market index is virtually perfectly correlated with the (unobservable) theoretical market portfolio; and (2) the probability distribution of stock returns is stationary, so that sample period returns can provide valid estimates of expected returns and variances.

The implication of the index model is that the market index portfolio is efficient and that the expected return–beta relationship holds for all assets. The assumption that the probability distribution of the security returns is stationary and the observability of the index make it possible to test the efficiency of the index and the expected return–beta relationship. The arguments leading from the assumptions to these implications rely on mean-variance efficiency; that is, if any security violates the expected beta relationship, then all investors (each relatively small) will tilt their portfolios so that their combined overall pressure on prices will restore an equilibrium that satisfies the relationship.

In contrast, the APT uses a single-factor security market assumption and arbitrage arguments to obtain the expected return–beta relationship for well-diversified portfolios. Because it focuses on the no-arbitrage condition, without the further assumptions of the market or index model, the APT cannot rule out a violation of the expected return–beta relationship for any particular asset. For this, we need the CAPM assumptions and its dominance arguments.

10.5 A Multifactor APT

We have assumed all along that there is only one systematic factor affecting stock returns. This simplifying assumption is in fact too simplistic. It is easy to think of several factors that might affect stock returns: business cycles, interest rate fluctuations, inflation rates, oil prices, and so on. Presumably, exposure to any of these factors will affect a stock's perceived riskiness and appropriate expected rate of return. We can use a multifactor version of the APT to accommodate these multiple sources of risk.

Suppose that we generalize the factor model expressed in equation 10.1 to a two-factor model:

$$r_i = E(r_i) + \beta_{i1}F_1 + \beta_{i2}F_2 + e_i \qquad (10.4)$$

Factor 1 might be, for example, departures of GNP growth from expectations, and factor 2 might be unanticipated inflation. Each factor has a zero expected value because each measures the surprise in the systematic variable rather than the level of the variable. Similarly, the firm-specific component of unexpected return, e_i, also has zero expected value. Extending such a two-factor model to any number of factors is straightforward.

Establishing a multifactor APT proceeds along lines very similar to those we followed in the simple one-factor case. First, we introduce the concept of a **factor portfolio,** which is a well-diversified portfolio constructed to have a beta of 1 on one of the factors and a beta of 0 on any other factor. This is an easy restriction to satisfy, because we have a large number of securities to choose from, and a relatively small number of factors. Factor portfolios will serve as the benchmark portfolios for a multifactor generalization of the security market line relationship.

Suppose that the two factor portfolios, called Portfolios 1 and 2, have expected returns $E(r_1) = 10\%$ and $E(r_2) = 12\%$. Suppose further that the risk-free rate is 4%. The risk premium on the first factor portfolio becomes $10\% - 4\% = 6\%$, whereas that on the second factor portfolio is $12\% - 4\% = 8\%$.

Now consider an arbitrary well-diversified portfolio, Portfolio *A*, with beta on the first factor, $\beta_{A1} = 0.5$, and beta on the second factor, $\beta_{A2} = 0.75$. The multifactor APT states that the overall risk premium on this portfolio must equal the sum of the risk premiums required as compensation to investors for each source of systematic risk. The risk premium attributable to risk factor 1 should be the portfolio's exposure to factor 1, β_{A1}, multiplied by the risk premium earned on the first factor portfolio, $E(r_1) - r_f$. Therefore, the portion of Portfolio *A*'s risk premium that is compensation for its exposure to the first factor is $\beta_{A1}[E(r_1) - r_f] = .5\,(10\% - 4\%) = 3\%$, whereas the risk premium attributable to risk factor 2 is $\beta_{A2}[E(r_2) - r_f] = .75(12\% - 4\%) = 6\%$. The total risk premium on the portfolio should be $3 + 6 = 9\%$. Therefore, the total return on the portfolio should be 13%:

4%	Risk-free rate
+3	Risk premium for exposure to factor 1
+6	Risk premium for exposure to factor 2
13%	Total expected return

To see why the expected return on the portfolio must be 13%, consider the following argument. Suppose that the expected return on Portfolio *A* were 12% rather than 13%. This return would give rise to an arbitrage opportunity. Form a portfolio from the factor portfolios with the same betas as Portfolio *A*. This requires weights of 0.5 on the first factor portfolio, 0.75 on the second factor portfolio, and −0.25 on the risk-free asset. This portfolio has exactly the same factor betas as Portfolio *A:* It has a beta of 0.5 on the first factor because of its 0.5 weight on the first factor portfolio, and a beta of 0.75 on the second factor.

However, in contrast to Portfolio *A*, which has a 12% expected return, this portfolio's expected return is $(0.5 \times 10) + (0.75 \times 12) - (0.25 \times 4) = 13\%$. A long position in this portfolio and a short position in Portfolio *A* would yield an arbitrage profit. The total return per dollar long or short in each position would be

$$\begin{array}{rl} 13\% + 0.5F_1 + 0.75F_2 & \text{(long position in factor portfolios)} \\ -\ (12\% + 0.5F_1 + 0.75F_2) & \text{(short position in Portfolio } A\text{)} \\ \hline 1\% & \end{array}$$

for a positive and risk-free return on a zero net investment position.

To generalize this argument, note that the factor exposure of any portfolio, P, is given by its betas, β_{P1} and β_{P2}. A competing portfolio formed from factor portfolios with weights β_{P1} in the first factor portfolio, β_{P2} in the second factor portfolio, and $1 - \beta_{P1} - \beta_{P2}$ in T-bills will have betas equal to those of Portfolio P, and expected return of

$$\begin{aligned} E(r_P) &= \beta_{P1}E(r_1) + \beta_{P2}E(r_2) + (1 - \beta_{P1} - \beta_{P2})r_f \\ &= r_f + \beta_{P1}[E(r_1) - r_f] + \beta_{P2}[E(r_2) - r_f] \end{aligned} \quad \textbf{(10.5)}$$

Hence, any well-diversified portfolio with betas β_{P1} and β_{P2} must have the return given in equation 10.5 if arbitrage opportunities are to be precluded. If you compare equations 10.2 and 10.5, you will see that equation 10.5 is simply a generalization of the one-factor SML.

Finally, the extension of the multifactor SML of equation 10.5 to individual assets is precisely the same as for the one-factor APT. Equation 10.5 cannot be satisfied by every well-diversified portfolio unless it is satisfied by virtually every security taken individually. This establishes a multifactor version of the APT. Hence, the fair rate of return on any stock with $\beta_1 = 0.5$ and $\beta_2 = 0.75$ is 13%. Equation 10.5 thus represents the multifactor SML for an economy with multiple sources of risk.

CONCEPT CHECK Question 5. Find the fair rate of return on a security with $\beta_1 = 0.2$ and $\beta_2 = 1.4$.

One shortcoming of the multifactor APT is that it gives no guidance concerning the determination of the risk premiums on the factor portfolios. In contrast, the CAPM implies that the risk premium on the market is determined by the market's variance and the average degree of risk aversion across investors. As it turns out, the CAPM also has a multifactor generalization, sometimes called the *consumer service model*, to be discussed in Chapter 25. This model provides some guidance concerning the risk premiums on the factor portfolios. Moreover, recent theoretical research has demonstrated that one may estimate an expected return–beta relationship even if the true factors or factor portfolios cannot be identified. This issue is treated in the papers by Reisman and Shanken cited in the selected readings at the end of this chapter.

SUMMARY

1. A (risk-free) arbitrage opportunity arises when two or more security prices enable investors to construct a zero net investment portfolio that will yield a sure profit.

2. Rational investors will want to take infinitely large positions in arbitrage portfolios regardless of their degree of risk aversion.

3. The presence of arbitrage opportunities and the resulting large volume of trades will create pressure on security prices. This pressure will continue until prices reach levels that preclude arbitrage. Only a few investors need to become aware of arbitrage opportunities to trigger this process because of the large volume of trades in which they will engage.

4. When securities are priced so that there are no risk-free arbitrage opportunities, we say that they satisfy the no-arbitrage condition. Price relationships that satisfy the no-arbitrage condition are important because we expect them to hold in real-world markets.

5. Portfolios are called "well-diversified" if they include a large number of securities and the investment proportion in each is sufficiently small. The proportion of a security in a well-diversified portfolio is small enough so that for all practical purposes a reasonable change in that security's rate of return will have a negligible effect on the portfolio's rate of return.

6. In a single-factor security market, all well-diversified portfolios have to satisfy the expected return–beta relationship of the security market line to satisfy the no-arbitrage condition.

7. If all well-diversified portfolios satisfy the expected return–beta relationship, then all but a small number of securities also must satisfy this relationship.

8. The assumption of a single-factor security market made in the simple version of the APT, together with the no-arbitrage condition, implies the same expected return–beta relationship as does the CAPM, yet it does not require the restrictive assumptions of the CAPM and its (unobservable) market portfolio. The price of this generality is that the APT does not guarantee this relationship for all securities at all times.

9. A multifactor APT generalizes the single-factor model to accommodate several sources of systematic risk.

Key Terms

Arbitrage
Zero investment portfolio
Risk arbitrage
Arbitrage Pricing Theory
Well-diversified portfolio
Factor portfolio

Selected Readings

Stephen Ross developed the arbitrage pricing theory in two articles:

Ross, S. A. "Return, Risk and Arbitrage." *Risk and Return in Finance*. Eds. I. Friend and J. Bicksler. Cambridge, Mass.: Ballinger, 1976.

Ross, S. A. "Arbitrage Theory of Capital Asset Pricing." *Journal of Economic Theory*, December 1976.

Articles exploring the factors that influence common stock returns are:

Bower, D. A.; R. S. Bower; and D. E. Logue. "Arbitrage Pricing and Utility Stock Returns." *Journal of Finance*, September 1984.

Chen, N. F.; R. Roll; and S. Ross. "Economic Forces and the Stock Market: Testing the APT and Alternative Asset Pricing Theories." *Journal of Business*, July 1986.

Sharpe, W. "Factors in New York Stock Exchange Security Returns, 1931–1979." *Journal of Portfolio Management*, Summer 1982.

Articles exploring the requirement from reference portfolios necessary to test the expected return–beta relationship are:

Reisman, H. "Reference Variables, Factor Structure, and the Approximate Multibeta Representation." *Journal of Finance*, September 1992.
Shanken, J. "Multivariate Proxies and Asset Pricing Relations: Living with the Roll Critique." *Journal of Financial Economics*, March 1987.

Problems

1. Suppose that two factors have been identified for the U.S. economy: the growth rate of industrial production, IP, and the inflation rate, IR. IP is expected to be 4%, and IR 6%. A stock with a beta of 1 on IP and 0.4 on IR currently is expected to provide a rate of return of 14%. If industrial production actually grows by 5%, while the inflation rate turns out to be 7%, what is your revised estimate of the expected rate of return on the stock?
2. Suppose that there are two independent economic factors, F_1 and F_2. The risk-free rate is 7%, and all stocks have independent firm-specific components with a standard deviation of 50%. The following are well-diversified portfolios:

Portfolio	Beta on F_1	Beta on F_2	Expected Return
A	1.8	2.1	40
B	2.0	-0.5	10

What is the expected return–beta relationship in this economy?

3. Consider the following data for a one-factor economy. All portfolios are well diversified.

Portfolio	$E(r)$	Beta
A	10%	1
F	4%	0

Suppose that another portfolio, Portfolio *E*, is well diversified with a beta of ⅔ and expected return of 9%. Would an arbitrage opportunity exist? If so, what would be the arbitrage strategy?

4. The following is a scenario for three stocks constructed by the security analysts of Pf Inc.

		Scenario Rate of Return (%)		
Stock	Price ($)	Recession	Average	Boom
A	10	−15	20	30
B	15	25	10	−10
C	50	12	15	12

a. Construct an arbitrage portfolio using these stocks.
b. How might these prices change when equilibrium is restored? Give an example where a change in Stock *C*'s price is sufficient to restore equilibrium, assuming that the dollar payoffs to Stock C remain the same.

5. Assume that both Portfolios A and B are well diversified, that $E(r_A) = 14\%$, and $E(r_B) = 14.8\%$. If the economy has only one factor, and $\beta_A = 1$, whereas $\beta_B = 1.1$, what must be the risk-free rate?
6. Assume that stock market returns have the market index as a common factor, and that all stocks in the economy have a beta of 1 on the market index. Firm-specific returns all have a standard deviation of 30%.

   Suppose that an analyst studies 20 stocks, and finds that one-half have an alpha of 3%, and the other half an alpha of − 3%. Suppose the analyst buys $1 million of an equally weighted portfolio of the positive alpha stocks, and shorts $1 million of an equally weighted portfolio of the negative alpha stocks.
   a. What is the expected profit (in dollars) and standard deviation of the analyst's profit?
   b. How does your answer change if the analyst examines 50 stocks instead of 20 stocks? 100 stocks?
7. Assume that security returns are generated by the single-index model.

$$R_i = \alpha_i + \beta_i R_M + e_i$$

   where R_i is the excess return for security i, and R_M is the market's excess return. Suppose also that there are three securities A, B, and C characterized by the following data:

Security	β_i	$E(R_i)$	$\sigma^2(e_i)$
A	.8	10%	5%
B	1.0	12	1
C	1.2	14	10

   a. If $\sigma_M^2 = 4\%$, calculate the variance of returns of Securities A, B, and C.
   b. Now assume that there are an infinite number of assets with return characteristics identical to those of A, B, and C respectively. If one forms a well-diversified portfolio of type A securities, what will be the mean and variance of the portfolio's excess returns? What about portfolios composed only of type B or C stocks?
   c. Is there an arbitrage opportunity in this market? What is it? Analyze the opportunity graphically.
8. The SML relationship states that the expected risk premium on a security in a one-factor model must be directly proportional to the security's beta. Suppose that this were not the case. For example, suppose that expected return rises more than proportionately with beta as in the figure below.
   a. How could you construct an arbitrage portfolio? (Hint: Consider combinations of Portfolios A and B, and compare the resultant portfolio to C.)
   b. We will see in Chapter 11 that some researchers have examined the relationship between average return on diversified portfolios and the β and β^2 of those portfolios. What should they have discovered about the effect of β^2 on portfolio return?

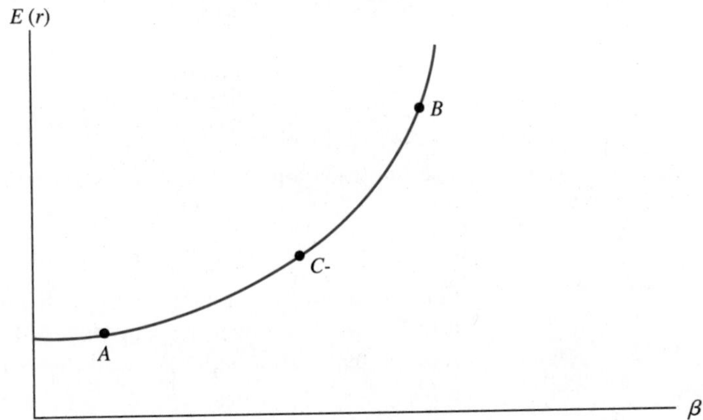

9. If the APT is to be a useful theory, the number of systematic factors in the economy must be small. Why?
10. The APT itself does not provide guidance concerning the factors that one might expect to determine risk premiums. How should researchers decide which factors to investigate? Why, for example, is industrial production a reasonable factor to test for a risk premium?
11. Consider the following multifactor (APT) model of security returns for a particular stock.

Factor	Factor Beta	Factor Risk Premium
Inflation	1.2	6%
Industrial production	0.5	8
Oil prices	0.3	3

a. If T-bills currently offer a 6% yield, find the expected rate of return on this stock if the market views the stock as fairly priced.

b. Suppose that the market expected the values for the three macro factors given in Column 1 below, but that the actual values turn out as given in Column 2. Calculate the revised expectations for the rate of return on the stock once the "surprises" become known.

Factor	Expected Rate of Change	Actual Rate of Change
Inflation	5%	4%
Industrial production	3	6
Oil prices	2	0

12. Suppose that the market can be described by the following three sources of systematic risk with associated risk premiums.

Factor	Risk Premium
Industrial production (*I*)	6%
Interest rates (*R*)	2
Consumer confidence (*C*)	4

The return on a particular stock is generated according to the following equation

$$r = 15\% + 1.0I + .5R + .75C + e$$

Find the equilibrium rate of return on this stock using the APT. The T-bill rate is 6%. Is the stock over- or underpriced? Explain.

13. Assume that both *X* and *Y* are well-diversified portfolios and the risk-free rate is 8%.

Portfolio	Expected Return	Beta
X	16%	1.00
Y	12%	0.25

In this situation you would conclude that Portfolios *X* and *Y*:
a. Are in equilibrium.
b. Offer an arbitrage opportunity.
c. Are both underpriced.
d. Are both fairly priced.

14. According to the theory of arbitrage:*
a. High-beta stocks are consistently overpriced.
b. Low-beta stocks are consistently overpriced.
c. Positive alpha stocks will quickly disappear.
d. Rational investors will arbitrage consistent with their risk tolerance.

15. A zero-investment portfolio with a positive alpha could arise if:*
a. The expected return of the portfolio equals zero.
b. The capital market line is tangent to the opportunity set.
c. The law of one price remains unviolated.
d. A risk-free arbitrage opportunity exists.

16. The Arbitrage Pricing Theory (APT) differs from the Capital Asset Pricing Model (CAPM) because the APT:*
a. Places more emphasis on market risk.
b. Minimizes the importance of diversification.
c. Recognizes multiple unsystematic risk factors.
d. Recognizes multiple systematic risk factors.

17. An investor will take as large a position as possible when an equilibrium price relationship is violated. This is an example of:*
a. A dominance argument.
b. The mean-variance efficient frontier.

c. A risk-free arbitrage.
d. The Capital Asset Pricing Model.

18. A zero-investment portfolio arises when:*
a. An investor has only downside risk.
b. The law of prices remains unviolated.
c. The opportunity set is not tangent to the capital allocation line.
d. A risk-free arbitrage opportunity exists.

Chapter 11

Empirical Evidence on Security Returns

BEFORE WE DISCUSS WHAT SORT OF EVIDENCE SUPPORTS THE IMPLICATIONS OF THE CAPM AND APT, WE MUST NOTE THAT THESE IMPLICATIONS ALREADY HAVE BEEN ACCEPTED IN WIDELY VARYING APPLICATIONS. Consider the following:

1. Many professional portfolio managers use the expected return–beta relationship of security returns. Furthermore, many firms rate the performance of portfolio managers according to the reward-to-variability ratios they maintain and the average rates of return they realize relative to the SML.
2. Regulatory commissions use the expected return–beta relationship along with forecasts of the market index return as one factor in determining the cost of capital for regulated firms.
3. Court rulings on torts cases sometimes use the expected return–beta relationship to determine discount rates to evaluate claims of lost future income.
4. Many firms use the SML to obtain a benchmark hurdle rate for capital budgeting decisions.

These practices show that the financial community has passed a favorable judgment on the CAPM and the APT, if only implicitly.

In this chapter we consider the evidence along more explicit and rigorous lines. The first part of the chapter presents the methodology that has been deployed in testing the single-factor CAPM and APT and assesses the results. The second part of the chapter provides an overview of current efforts to establish the validity of the multifactor versions of the CAPM and APT. Finally, we briefly report on current effort to model the volatility of stock returns, and their contribution to tests of the validity of the CAPM/APT.

Why lump together empirical works on the CAPM and APT? The CAPM is a theoretical construct that predicts *expected* rates of return on assets, relative to a market portfolio of all risky assets. It is difficult to test these predictions empirically because both expected returns and the exact market portfolio are unobservable (see Chapter 9). To overcome this difficulty, a single-factor or multifactor capital market usually is postulated, where a broad-based market index portfolio (such as the S&P 500) is assumed to represent the factor, or one of the factors. Furthermore, to obtain more reliable statistics, most tests have been conducted with the rates of return on well-diversified portfolios rather than on individual securities. For both of these reasons tests that have been directed at the CAPM actually have been more suitable to establish the validity of the APT. We will see that it is more important to distinguish the empirical work on the basis of the factor structure that is assumed or estimated than to distinguish between tests of the CAPM and the APT.

11.1 The Index Model and the Single-Factor APT

The Expected Return–Beta Relationship

Recall that if the expected return–beta relationship holds with respect to an observable ex ante efficient index, M, the expected rate of return on any security i is

$$E(r_i) = r_f + \beta_i[E(r_M) - r_f] \tag{11.1}$$

where β_i is defined as $\text{Cov}(r_i, r_M)/\sigma_M^2$.

This is the most commonly tested implication of the CAPM. Early simple tests followed three basic steps: establishing sample data, estimating the SCL (security characteristic line), and estimating the SML (security market line).

Setting Up the Sample Data. Determine a sample period of, for example, 60 monthly holding periods (five years). For each of the 60 holding periods collect the rates of return on 100 stocks, a market portfolio proxy (the S&P 500), and the one-month (risk-free) T-bills. Your data thus consist of

r_{it} $\quad i = 1, \ldots, 100$, and $t = 1, \ldots, 60$:
Returns on the 100 stocks over the 60-month sample period.
r_{Mt} $\quad$ Returns on the S&P 500 index over the sample period.
r_{ft} $\quad$ Risk-free rate each month.

This constitutes a table of $102 \times 60 = 6{,}120$ rates of return.

Estimating the SCL. View equation 11.1 as a security characteristic line (SCL), as in Chapter 9. For each stock, i, you estimate the beta coefficient as the slope of a **first-pass regression** equation. (The terminology *first-pass* regression is due to the fact that the estimated coefficients will be used as input into a **second-pass regression**.)

$$r_{it} - r_{ft} = a_i + b_i(r_{Mt} - r_{ft}) + e_{it}$$

You will use the following statistics in later analysis:

$\overline{r_i - r_f}$ = Sample averages (over the 60 observations) of the excess return on each of the 100 stocks
b_i = Sample estimates of the beta coefficients of each of the 100 stocks
$\overline{r_M - r_f}$ = Sample average of the excess return of the market index
$\sigma^2(e_i)$ = Estimates of the variance of the residuals for each of the 100 stocks

The sample average excess returns on each stock and the market portfolio are taken as estimates of expected excess returns, and the values of b_i are estimates of the true beta coefficients for the 100 stocks during the sample period. The $\sigma^2(e_i)$ estimates the nonsystematic risk of each of the 100 stocks.

CONCEPT CHECK

Question 1.

a. How many regressions estimates of the SCL do we have from the sample?
b. How many observations are there in each of the regressions?
c. To satisfy the CAPM, what should be the intercept in each of these regressions?

Estimating the SML. Now view equation 11.1 as a security market line (SML) with 100 observations for the stocks in your sample. You can estimate γ_0 and γ_1 in the following second-pass regression equation with b_i from the first pass as the independent variable:

$$\overline{r_i - r_f} = \gamma_0 + \gamma_1 b_i \qquad i = 1, \ldots, 100 \tag{11.2}$$

Compare equations 11.1 and 11.2; you should conclude that if the CAPM is valid, then γ_0 and γ_1 must satisfy

$$\gamma_0 = 0 \qquad \gamma_1 = \overline{r_M - r_f}$$

In fact, however, you can go a step further and argue that the key property of the expected return–beta relationship described by the SML is that the expected excess return on securities is determined *only* by the systematic risk (as measured by beta) and should be independent of the nonsystematic risk, as measured by the variance of the residuals, $\sigma^2(e_i)$, which also were estimated from the first-pass regression. These estimates can be added as a variable in equation 11.2 of an expanded SML that now looks like this:

$$\overline{r_i - r_f} = \gamma_0 + \gamma_1 b_i + \gamma_2 \sigma^2(e_i) \tag{11.3}$$

This *second-pass* regression is estimated with the hypotheses:

$$\gamma_0 = 0 \qquad \gamma_1 = \overline{r_M - r_f} \qquad \gamma_2 = 0$$

To the disappointment of early researchers, tests following this pattern consistently failed to support the index model and the results from such a test (first conducted by

John Lintner[1] and later replicated by Merton Miller and Myron Scholes[2]) using annual data on 631 NYSE stocks for 10 years, 1954 to 1963, are (with returns expressed as decimals rather than percentages)

Coefficient:	$\gamma_0 = .127$	$\gamma_1 = .042$	$\gamma_2 = .310$
Standard error:	.006	.006	.026
Sample average:		$\overline{r_M - r_f} = .165$	

Such results are totally inconsistent with the CAPM. First, the estimated SML is "too flat"; that is, the γ_1 coefficient is too small. The slope should be $\overline{r_M - r_f} = .165$ (16.5% per year), but it is estimated at only 0.42. The difference, .122, is about 20 times the standard error of the estimate, .006, which means that the measured slope of the SML is lower than it should be by a statistically significant margin. At the same time, the intercept of the estimated SML, γ_0, which is hypothesized to be zero, in fact equals .127, which is more than 20 times its standard error of .006.

CONCEPT CHECK

Question 2.

a. What is the implication of the empirical SML being "too flat"?

b. Do high- or low-beta stocks tend to outperform the predictions of the CAPM?

Second, and more damaging to the CAPM, is that nonsystematic risk seems to predict expected excess returns. The coefficient of the variable that measures nonsystematic risk, $\sigma^2(e_i)$, is .310, more than 10 times its standard error of .026.

There are, however, two principal flaws in these tests. The first is that statistical variation in stock returns introduces **measurement error** into the beta estimates, the *b* coefficients from the first-pass regressions. Using these estimates in place of the true beta coefficients in the estimation of the second-pass regression for the SML biases the estimates in the direction that we have observed: The measurement errors in the beta coefficients will lead to an estimate of the SML that is too flat and that has a positive (rather than zero) intercept.

The second problem results from the fact that the variance of the residuals is correlated with the beta coefficients of stocks. Stocks that have high betas tend also to have high nonsystematic risk. Add this effect to the measurement problem, and the coefficient of nonsystematic risk, γ_2, in the second-pass regression will be upward biased.

Indeed, a well-controlled simulation test by Miller and Scholes confirms these arguments. In this test a random number generator simulated rates of return with covariances similar to observed ones. The average returns were made to agree exactly with the CAPM expected return–beta relationship. Miller and Scholes then used these randomly generated rates of return in the tests we have described as if they were observed

[1] John Lintner, "Security Prices, Risk and Maximal Gains from Diversification," *Journal of Finance* 20 (December 1965)

[2] Merton H. Miller and Myron Scholes, "Rate of Return in Relation to Risk: A Reexamination of Some Recent Findings," in *Studies in the Theory of Capital Markets,* Michael C. Jensen, ed. (New York: Praeger Publishers, 1972).

from a sample of stock returns. The results of this "simulated" test were virtually identical to those reached using real data, despite the fact that the simulated returns were *constructed* to obey the SML, that is, the true γ coefficients were $\gamma_0 = 0$, $\gamma_1 = .165 = \overline{r_M - r_f}$, and $\gamma_2 = 0$.

This postmortem of the early test gets us back to square one. We can explain away the disappointing test results, but we have no positive results to support the CAPM-APT implications.

The next wave of tests was designed to overcome the measurement error problem that led to biased estimates of the SML. The innovation in these tests was to use portfolios rather than individual securities. Combining securities into portfolios diversifies away most of the firm-specific part of returns, thereby enhancing the precision of the estimates of beta and the expected rate of return of the portfolio of securities. This mitigates the statistical problems that arise from measurement error in the beta estimates.

Obviously, however, combining stocks into portfolios reduces the number of observations left for the second-pass regression. For example, suppose that we wish to group 100 stocks into portfolios of 20 stocks each. If the assumption of a single-factor market is reasonably accurate, then the residuals of the 20 stocks in each portfolio will be practically uncorrelated and, hence, the variance of the portfolio residual will be about 1/20th the residual variance of the average stock. Thus, the portfolio beta in the first-pass regression will be estimated with far better accuracy. However, now consider the second-pass regression. With individual securities we had 100 observations to estimate the second-pass coefficients. With portfolios of 20 stocks each we are left with only five observations for the second-pass regression.

To get the best of this trade-off, we need to construct portfolios with the largest possible dispersion of beta coefficients. Other things being equal, a sample yields more accurate regression estimates the more widely spaced are the observations of the independent variables. Consider the first-pass regressions where we estimate the SCL, that is, the relationship between the excess return on each stock and the market's excess return. If we have a sample with a great dispersion of market returns, we have a better shot at accurately estimating the effect of a change in the market return on the return of the stock. In our case, however, we have no control over the range of the market returns. But we can control the range of the independent variable of the second-pass regression, the portfolio betas. Rather than allocate 20 stocks to each portfolio randomly, we can rank portfolios by betas. Portfolio 1 will include the 20 highest-beta stocks and Portfolio 5 the 20 lowest-beta stocks. In that case a set of portfolios with small nonsystematic components, e_P, and widely spaced betas will yield reasonably powerful tests of the SML.

A study by Black, Jensen, and Scholes[3] (BJS) pioneered this method. The researchers used an elaborate method to design the sample portfolios and estimate their betas. To illustrate, let us assume that the data set consists of 500 stocks over a long sample period. We would split the sample period into three subperiods:

[3] Fischer Black, Michael C. Jensen, and Myron Scholes, "The Capital Asset Pricing Model: Some Empirical Tests," in *Studies in the Theory of Capital Markets,* Michael C. Jensen, ed. (New York: Praeger Publishers, 1972).

Overall Sample Period of 500 Stock Returns

Subperiod I: Preparing the Sample Portfolios	Subperiod II: First-Pass Regression	Subperiod III: Second-Pass Regression
Estimate *individual* stock betas and order them from highest to lowest beta. Form equally weighted portfolios of 50 stocks each, resulting in 10 portfolios from highest to lowest beta. This is a preparatory step for the first-pass regression.	Reestimate the betas of the 10 portfolios. These estimates will be used as the true betas for the SML estimates. The errors in measuring these betas are independent of the errors in the betas used to form the portfolios. This is the first-pass regression.	Use the average excess returns on the 10 portfolios from this period as estimates of the expected excess returns to regress on the betas from the previous subperiod. This is the second-pass regression.

The BJS study uses all available NYSE stock returns over the period 1931 to 1965. The number of available stocks increased from 582 in 1931 to 1,094 in 1965. The available stocks are allocated to 10 portfolios; thus, portfolio size varies over the period from 58 to 110 stocks. The size and diversification of these portfolios reduces measurement error considerably.

Summary statistics for the 10 portfolios appear in Table 11.1. The betas of the 10 portfolios for the entire period (420 months) are shown in the first line of the table. They range from .4992 to 1.5614 and are fairly evenly spaced. The next two lines show the intercepts (denoted by α) of the SCL for each portfolio. These values are small, and the ratios of these values to their standard errors [the *t*-statistics, $t(\alpha)$] are less than 2.0 for 9 out of the 10 portfolios. The pattern of these alpha values, however, begins to tell the story of the test results. The alphas are negative for high-beta portfolios ($\beta > 1$) and positive for low-beta portfolios ($\beta < 1$). This is a clue that, contrary to what the SML would imply, lower beta portfolios earned consistently better risk-adjusted returns than higher beta portfolios.

The next two lines in Table 11.1 show the correlation coefficients of the portfolio returns with the market index, $\rho(R_P,R_M)$, and the serial correlation of the nonsystematic component, e, of the portfolios between successive periods, $\rho(e_t,e_{t-1})$. The large size and corresponding diversification of the portfolios is such that we expect returns to be highly correlated with the market index. Indeed, the correlation coefficients range from .8981 to .9915. The nonsystematic components are not highly (auto) correlated from period to period: $\rho(e_t,e_{t-1})$ ranges from $-.1248$ to .1294.

From the last three lines of the table we note first that most of the risk of the 10 portfolios is systematic. The first of these lines shows the standard deviation of the residuals, our estimate of nonsystematic risk, $\sigma(e)$. The bottom line shows the standard deviation of the excess rate of return, σ. For the highest-beta portfolio the monthly standard deviation was 14.45% per month, of which 3.93% is nonsystematic. For the lowest-beta portfolio the standard deviation of the excess return was 4.95% per month, of which 2.18% is nonsystematic.

The next-to-last line in the table shows the average monthly excess returns for the 10 portfolios and the market (NYSE) index. The market index excess return averages 1.42% per month, and the average excess returns for the 10 portfolios range from .91% to 2.13% per month. As we should expect from the CAPM, the portfolios with betas

Table 11.1 Summary of Statistics for Time Series Tests (January 1931–December 1965)

	Portfolio Number										
Item*	**1**	**2**	**3**	**4**	**5**	**6**	**7**	**8**	**9**	**10**	R_M
β	1.5614	1.3838	1.2483	1.1625	1.0572	0.9229	0.8531	0.7534	0.6291	0.4992	1.0000
$\hat{\alpha} \bullet 10^2$	−0.0829	−0.1938	−0.0649	−0.0167	−0.0543	0.0593	0.0462	0.0812	0.1968	0.2012	
$t(\alpha)$	−0.4274	−1.9935	−0.7597	−0.2468	−0.8869	0.7878	0.7050	1.1837	2.3126	1.8684	
$\rho(\bar{R}, \bar{R}_M)$	0.9625	0.9875	0.9882	0.9914	0.9915	0.9833	0.9851	0.9793	0.9560	0.8981	
$\rho(\bar{e}_t, \bar{e}_{t-1})$	0.0549	−0.0638	0.0366	0.0073	−0.0708	−0.1248	0.1294	0.1041	0.0444	0.0992	
$\sigma(\bar{e})$	0.0393	0.0197	0.0173	0.0137	0.0124	0.0152	0.0133	0.0139	0.0172	0.0218	
$\bar{R}$	0.0213	0.0177	0.0171	0.0163	0.0145	0.0137	0.0126	0.0115	0.0109	0.0091	0.0142
σ	0.1445	0.1248	0.1126	0.1045	0.0950	0.0836	0.0772	0.0685	0.0586	0.0495	0.0891

*$\bar{R}$ = Average monthly excess returns, σ = Standard deviation of the monthly excess returns, ρ = Correlation coefficient.
Sample size for each regression, 420.
Note: Returns are expressed as decimals rather than percentages.
Source: Modified from Fischer Black, Michael C. Jensen, and Myron Scholes, "The Capital Asset Pricing Model: Some Empirical Tests," in *Studies in the Theory of Capital Markets,* Michael C. Jensen, ed. (New York: Praeger Publishers, 1972).

lower than 1 earned less than the market index, and the portfolios with betas higher than 1 earned more.

Figure 11.1 shows the second-pass regression estimate of the SML for the entire period. The upper left-hand corner of Figure 11.1 reveals the disappointing result for the CAPM hypothesis. The intercept of the estimated SML, the γ_0 coefficient, is 0.359% per month with a standard error of only 0.055% (its t-statistic is 6.53), so that the intercept, which is hypothesized by the CAPM to be zero, is positive and statistically significant.

The slope of the SML is 1.08. The CAPM hypothesis is that this slope, γ_1, should equal the expected excess return on the market index. For the sample period the market index averaged 1.42% per month. The difference, $\gamma_1 - (r_M - r_f)$, for this sample is thus −0.34% per month. The estimate SML is too flat again. The standard error of the estimate of γ_1 is 0.052%, so the difference (0.34%) is 6.54 times the standard error. Thus, the results are inconsistent with the CAPM hypothesis for γ_1.

Breaking the analysis into subperiods, BJS found no better results. Figure 11.2 shows the estimated SMLs for four subperiods. The intercepts are positive and statistically significant in three out of the four subperiods. Even worse, in the 1957 to 1965 subperiod the slope of the SML has the wrong sign.

At this point, BJS bring up the possibility that perhaps the sample results may verify the zero-beta version of the CAPM. Recall from Chapter 8 that when borrowing is restricted the CAPM expected return–beta relationship must be amended. As it turns out, all that is called for in moving to the zero-beta version of the CAPM is replacing the risk-free rate with the expected rate of return on the zero-beta portfolio (i.e., the minimum-variance portfolio uncorrelated with the market portfolio).

The representation of the CAPM expected return–beta relationship with a restriction on the risk-free investment (the zero-beta CAPM) is:

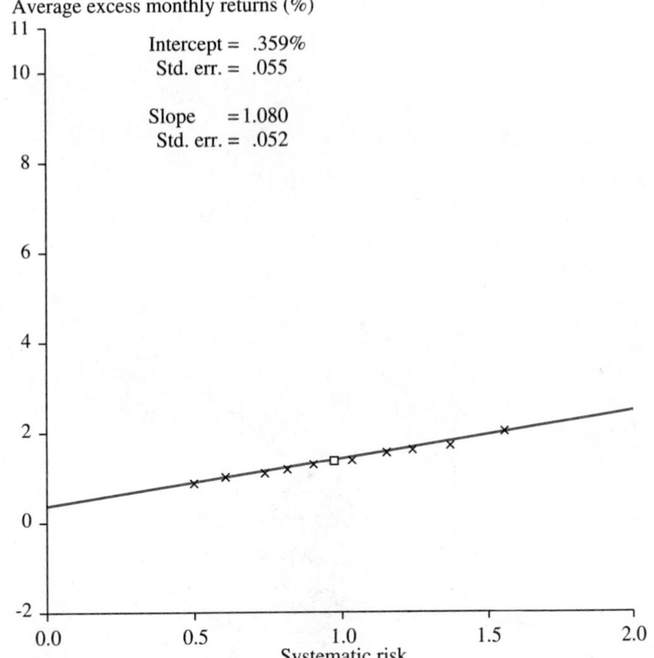

Figure 11.1

The second-pass regression estimate of the security market line

Source: Fischer Black, Michael C. Jensen, and Myron Scholes, "The Capital Asset Pricing Model: Some Empirical Tests," in *Studies in the Theory of Capital Markets,* Michael C. Jensen, ed. (New York: Praeger Publishers, 1972). Copyright © 1972 by Praeger Publishers, Inc. Reprinted with permission.

$$E(r_i) - E(r_{Z(M)}) = \beta_i[E(r_M) - E(r_{Z(M)})] \tag{11.4}$$

where $r_{Z(M)}$ is the rate of return on the zero-beta portfolio.

If we shift $E(r_{Z(M)})$ to the right-hand side and subtract the risk-free rate from both sides, equation 11.4 takes this form:

$$E(r_i) - r_f = E(r_{Z(M)}) - r_f + \beta_i[E(r_M) - E(r_{Z(M)})] \tag{11.5}$$

If we were to test this version of the CAPM, we would hypothesize that

$$\gamma_0 = E(r_{Z(M)}) - r_f$$
$$\gamma_1 = E(r_M) - E(r_{Z(M)})$$

To conduct their test, BJS needed to estimate returns on the zero-beta portfolio from the available data. To obtain these rates, they rearranged equation 11.5 and concluded that the actual rate of return on any stock in period t (as opposed to the expected return) would be described by

$$r_{it} = r_{Zt}(1 - \beta_i) + r_{Mt}\beta_i + e_{it} \tag{11.6}$$

Using the previously estimated beta coefficient, the zero-beta rate is *estimated* from the return of each stock by

$$r_Z = (r_{it} - \beta r_{Mt})/(1 - \beta_i) \tag{11.7}$$

Figure 11.2

The estimated security market lines for four subperiods

Source: Fischer Black, Michael C. Jensen, and Myron Scholes, "The Capital Asset Pricing Model: Some Empirical Tests," in *Studies in the Theory of Capital Markets,* Michael C. Jensen, ed. (New York: Praeger Publishers, 1972). Copyright © 1972 by Praeger Publishers, Inc. Reprinted with permission.

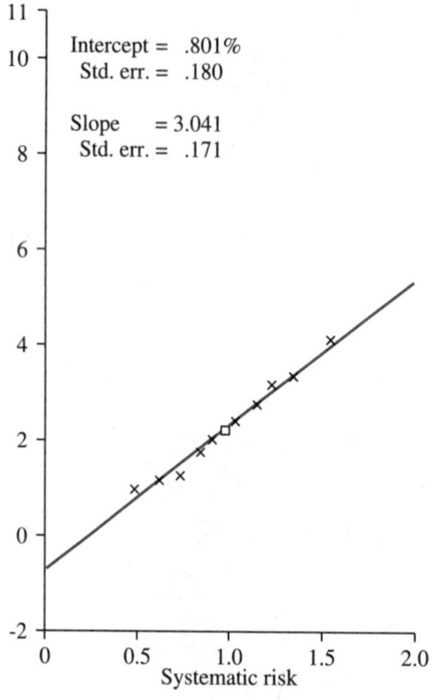

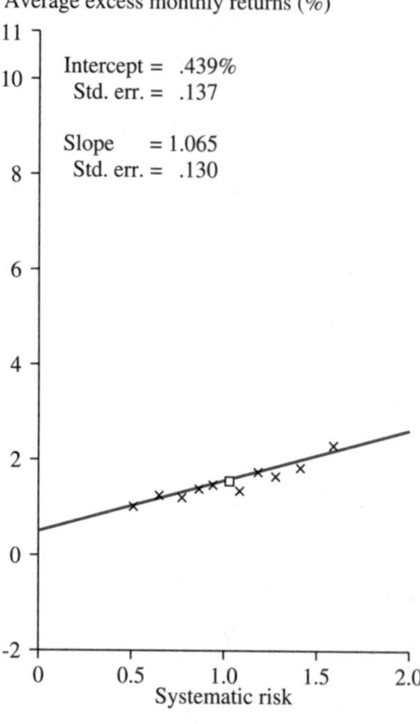

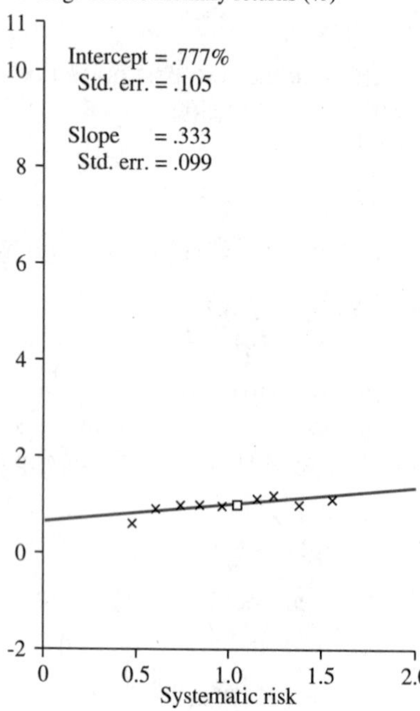

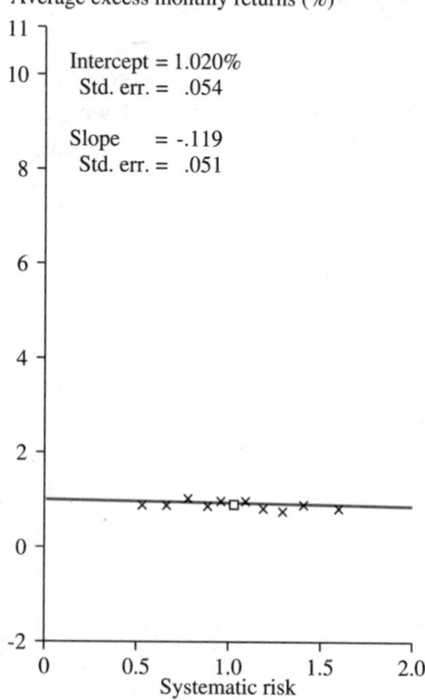

Note that the rate of return on each stock provides one estimate of the zero-beta rate. BJS use a statistically efficient technique to average these estimates across stocks and thus obtain, for each period, an efficient estimate of the zero-beta rate.

Using the time series of the estimated zero-beta rates for each subperiod, in conjunction with the market and individual stock returns, BJS examined the validity of the zero-beta version of the CAPM. Their major conclusions were:

1. The average return of the zero-beta portfolio is significantly greater than the risk-free rate.
2. The excess rate of return on the zero-beta portfolio explains some of the deviation of the results from the simple version of the CAPM, yet the regression estimates are not fully consistent with the zero-beta version of the CAPM either.

The fact that the average return on the zero-beta portfolio exceeds the risk-free rate is consistent with the restricted borrowing models of the CAPM presented in Chapter 8. It also is consistent with BJS's finding that the empirical SML is flatter than predicted by the simple CAPM.

CONCEPT CHECK

Question 3. What should be the average return on the zero-beta portfolio in the BJS test according to the zero-beta version of the CAPM?

BJS tested the SML equation directly with negative results, with and without restrictions on risk-free lending and borrowing. They did not concern themselves with other specific implications of the CAPM, such as that expected returns are independent of nonsystematic risk or that the relationship between expected returns and beta is linear.

Fama and MacBeth[4] used the BJS methodology to verify that the observed relationship between average excess returns and beta is indeed linear and that nonsystematic risk does not explain average excess returns. Using 20 portfolios constructed according to the BJS methodology, Fama and MacBeth expanded the estimation of the SML equation to include the square of the beta coefficient (to test for linearity of the relationship between returns and betas) and the estimated standard deviation of the residual (to test for the explanatory power of nonsystematic risk). For a sequence of many subperiods they estimated for each subperiod, the equation

$$r_i = \gamma_0 + \gamma_1\beta_i + \gamma_2\beta_i^2 + \gamma_3\sigma(e_i)$$

The term γ_2 measures potential nonlinearity of return, and γ_3 measures the explanatory power of nonsystematic risk, $\sigma(e_i)$. The Fama–MacBeth results show that the beta relationship is in fact linear (γ_2 is not significantly different from zero) and that nonsystematic risk does not explain average returns (γ_3 also is insignificant). At the same time, however, the authors reported that the SMLs, in general, remain too flat and have a positive significant intercept.

[4] Eugene Fama and James MacBeth, "Risk, Return, and Equilibrium: Empirical Tests," *Journal of Political Economy* 81 (March 1973)

We can summarize these conclusions:

1. The insights that are supported by the single-factor CAPM and APT are as follows:
   a. Expected rates of return are linear and increase with beta, the measure of systematic risk.
   b. Expected rates of return are not affected by nonsystematic risk.
2. The single-variable expected return–beta relationship predicted by either the risk-free rate or the zero-beta version of the CAPM is not fully consistent with empirical observation.

Thus, although the CAPM seems *qualitatively* correct, in that β matters and $\sigma(e_i)$ does not, empirical tests do not validate its *quantitative* predictions.

CONCEPT CHECK Question 4. What would you conclude if you performed the Fama and MacBeth tests and found that the coefficients on β^2 and $\sigma(e)$ were positive?

The Efficiency of the Market Index—Roll's Critique

In 1977, while researchers were improving test methodology in an effort to conclusively endorse or reject the validity of the CAPM, Richard Roll[5] threw a monkey wrench into their machinery. In the now-classic "Roll's Critique" he argued not only that the tests of the expected return–beta relationship are invalid, but also that it is doubtful that the CAPM can ever be tested.

Roll's critique included the following observations:

1. There is a single testable hypothesis associated with the CAPM: The market portfolio is mean-variance efficient.
2. All the other implications of the model, the best-known being the linear relation between expected return and beta, follow from the market portfolio's efficiency and therefore are not independently testable. There is an "if and only if" relation between the expected return–beta relationship and the efficiency of the market portfolio.
3. In any sample of observations of individual returns there will be an infinite number of ex post mean-variance efficient portfolios using the sample period returns and covariances (as opposed to the ex ante expected returns and covariances). Sample betas calculated between each such portfolio and individual assets will be exactly linearly related to sample mean returns. In other words, if betas are calculated against such portfolios, they will satisfy the SML relation exactly whether or not the true market portfolio is mean-variance efficient in an ex ante sense.

[5] Richard Roll, "A Critique of the Asset Pricing Theory's Tests: Part I: On Past and Potential Testability of the Theory," *Journal of Financial Economics* 4 (1977).

4. The CAPM is not testable unless we know the exact composition of the true market portfolio and use it in the tests. This implies that the theory is not testable unless *all* individual assets are included in the sample.
5. Using a proxy such as the S&P 500 for the market portfolio is subject to two difficulties. First, the proxy itself might be mean-variance efficient even when the true market portfolio is not. Conversely, the proxy may turn out to be inefficient, but obviously this alone implies nothing about the true market portfolio's efficiency. Furthermore, most reasonable market proxies will be very highly correlated with each other and with the true market whether or not they are mean-variance efficient. Such a high degree of correlation will make it seem that the exact composition of the market portfolio is unimportant, whereas the use of different proxies can lead to quite different conclusions. This problem is referred to as **benchmark error,** because it refers to the use of an incorrect benchmark (market proxy) portfolio in the tests of the theory.

Roll's criticism requires us to think in terms of two contexts and three portfolios. The contexts are as follows:

1. Ex ante expectations of rates of return and covariances.
2. Ex post (sample) averages of rates of return and estimates of covariances.

Clearly, the ex post (realized) rates of returns are random, and their measured averages and covariances are not necessarily equal to those that were expected ex ante.

Next, Roll argued that we have to worry about three types of portfolios:

1. The true (unobservable) market portfolio.
2. The portfolio that happens to be ex post efficient for a given sample of realized returns.
3. The portfolio that is chosen as the proxy for the market portfolio and is used to conduct the test.

Roll argued that the third portfolio, the market proxy, will be highly correlated with the first two portfolios. Because we do not know the exact composition of the true market portfolio, even if the data seem to support the expected return–beta relationship, we cannot tell whether this is (a) because we have tested the tautology that the ex post efficient portfolio (2) is indeed efficient, and therefore the expected return–beta relationship appears valid, or (b) that our index portfolio is in fact close enough to the unobservable market portfolio (1), and that *this* is the reason for the empirical finding of an expected return–beta relationship. Conversely, if we find that the results indicate that the expected return–beta relationship does not hold, we cannot tell whether the tests do not confirm the theory, or, instead, that the choice of the proxy for the market portfolio is inadequate.

Roll's critique was a serious blow to the CAPM. Indeed, it led to a now famous article in *Institutional Investor* called "Is Beta Dead?" However, the problems in testing the CAPM should not obscure the value of the model. The nearby box presents what we believe is a reasonably balanced view of the controversy.

BETA IS DEAD! LONG LIVE BETA!

Introduction

The philosophy of natural science as expounded by Karl Popper prescribes a logicoempiricist methodology for invalidating new theoretical models of the observed world, such as those hypothesized in the applied investment field by Harry Markowitz and Bill Sharpe. Their particular paradigm-shift has resulted in a plethora of theoretical investment models, including the Capital Asset Pricing Model (CAPM). Recent papers by Richard Roll, however, have suggested that the CAPM may not be susceptible to invalidation by such methodological tests.

The above paragraph shows quite clearly that it is, in fact, possible to do several things at once. Several imposing names are dropped, lots of long words are used, and a relatively simple statement is made utterly confusing—all in the same paragraph. The next Guinness Book of Records will surely have a new entry in this category, awarded to the author of the 1980 *Institutional Investor (I.I.)* article entitled "Is Beta Dead?," who managed to keep up this kind of thing for seven pages, thereby utterly confusing hundreds of investment managers.

About Theories

Modern Portfolio Theory (MPT) developed from the work done by Harry Markowitz in 1952 on Portfolio Selection. In essence, it is based on the single observation that the proper task of the investment manager is not simply to maximize expected return, but to do so at an acceptable level of risk. If this were not so, portfolios would consist solely of managers' favorite stocks, instead of combining different stocks which, although all not equally attractive when considered individually, together offer the maximum expected return for a given level of risk.

This observation itself was not new. The originality of Markowitz's contribution lay in showing how investment risk could be measured and, hence, how mathematics could be used to select the best possible portfolio from all the different combinations of a chosen list of stocks.

There have been many refinements of the theory since. What is now commonly referred to as MPT is no longer a single theory, but several different theories or models, together with their applications. These models may be grouped into three main categories: versions of the Market Model, versions of the Capital Asset Pricing Model (CAPM), and versions of the Efficient Market Hypothesis (EMH).

The most common misconception about MPT is that these three theoretical constructs are all part of the same one and that, therefore, they stand or fall together. While some of the applications depend on two or more of the models, the individual models themselves do not depend heavily on each other. It is thus quite possible that one could be "wrong" while the others were "right."

It is, in any case, a mistake to think in terms of theories being "right" or "wrong" absolutely. All theories are "wrong" in that sense, including, for example, Einstein's Theory of Relativity.

Karl Popper (see first sentence) is a philosopher of science who has pointed out that, even if a particular theory were "right," you could never actually prove it. All you can ever hope to do is prove that it is wrong. If you have a new theory, you keep testing it in as many different ways as possible to see if it doesn't work. As long as it works fairly well, you can assume that it might be right, but you will never know for sure. A good theory is generally reckoned to be one that works quite well most of the time.

Newton's theory about the way planets and stars move was considered to be a good theory for several hundred years. Then some smart engineer invented an extra-powerful telescope with a very accurate scale, and a bored astronomer who had nothing else to do one evening noticed that the orbit of Mercury, the smallest planet around these parts, wasn't quite where it should be. Suddenly, Newton's theory wasn't so hot any more, and we all had to wait a few more years for Einstein to come along and say, "Well it's nearly right, but if you put in this extra wrinkle here . . . ," and so invent Relativity.

(Continued)

Unfortunately for Einstein, smart engineers and bored astronomers are two a penny these days, even allowing for inflation, and they've already noticed one or two places where his theory is a tiny bit out.

Newton's theory is still taught in schools, and is widely used in many different applications. To give a somewhat gruesome example, it is used for ranging artillery fire. The theory may not be exactly right, but it is certainly right enough to kill people. On the other hand, Einstein's theory was used to plot the flight of the Apollo spacecraft because Newton's theory wasn't good enough to provide the rigorous degree of accuracy required.

This point about a theory being useful without needing to be right was also made about the CAPM in the *I.I.* article mentioned earlier. In that article, Barr Rosenberg was quoted as saying, "While the model is false, it's not very false." All models are false in this sense; what matters is how false they are, and to what extent this affects their application.

Much Ado about Nothing Very Much

Presumably, you may say, the *Institutional Investor* article on the demise of beta was supposed to be about something—but what exactly? The story the article was based on is actually more than five years old, and is quite simple.

In 1977 Richard Roll, the noted professor at U.C.L.A., published the first of a series of academic papers showing that there is a bit of a problem with the CAPM. The problem has to do with something else Karl Popper said about theories: namely, that any new theory that someone thinks up should not be given the time of day unless it can be tested.

In the Middle Ages any young priest who wanted to get ahead would think up a new theory about how many angels could balance on the head of a pin. Karl Popper would have said that they were all wasting their time, since there was no way of testing their theories.

What Richard Roll did was to point out that the CAPM can't be tested either. His reason was that to test it you first need to get hold of "the market," and that can't be done. A lot of so-called testing had already been done using "market proxies" such as the S&P 500. Roll pointed out, quite correctly, that using different proxies gave you different answers; and that, in any case, a proxy was merely a proxy and not what we were supposed to be testing.

The problem with using a proxy is that it is not the efficient market portfolio one would like it to be, but is an inefficient portfolio (i.e., one containing diversifiable risk), representing a subset of the market. Roll showed that one of the mathematical consequences of this was likely to be consistent errors in the betas.

It is worth pointing out that nearly everyone now agrees with this just as everyone agrees that the CAPM is clearly not true. These errors are fundamentally different from the random errors that arise from the fact that betas are estimated statistically, rather than measured directly. We might also note, en passant, that the gentlemen with calculators continue to work out Discounted Present Values, and that stocks still tend to go up and down together. The validity of EMH and the Market Model, meanwhile, remains unaffected by this controversy over CAPM.

The crucial point is this: beta is supposed to measure the market-related risk of a stock or portfolio. By using the S&P 500 index as a market proxy, we are going to get betas that actually measure S&P 500-related risk. What we were hoping to do is to separate the total risk of a stock into its diversifiable and non-diversifiable components. By using a proxy that is itself an inefficient portfolio, we run the risk of not separating the total risk into the correct proportions. The S&P 500-related beta could be bigger or smaller than the "real" beta.

The "furious controversy" that the *I.I.* article described is about how important these consistent errors in the betas are. If they are small (and there are good, though complex, reasons why this is likely to be the case), then we do not have much of a problem. If they are large, then we will have to be rather careful in those applications in which it is likely to matter.

No doubt the "furious controversy" will continue to rage in academic circles for some time yet, and when the dust settles it may well turn out that the current version of the CAPM belongs in the same basket as theories about angels and pins. More than likely, though, academics will have thought up a different version of the CAPM that can be tested. And when some subtle variant of the present CAPM is finally vindicated, it is a fairly

(Continued)

safe bet that beta will remain (though possibly in a different manifestation) the reigning measure of investment risk.

Is beta dead? One way to answer the question is to calculate (or buy) a few, and then watch what happens as the market goes up and down. The question then becomes fairly simple: do portfolios of high (or medium, or low) beta stocks exaggerate (or match, or dampen) market swings? Answer: yes.

The fact of the matter is that betas do work, more or less well depending mostly on how sensible we've been in calculating them. All betas are relative to one or another market proxy. According to Einstein, everything else is relative too, so this should not be too much of a problem. Naturally something's beta will change if it is measured against different market indices. It will also change if it is measured against hemlines, which many experienced market men believe to be a very reliable market proxy. The point is that is has to be measured against something, and it is therefore up to the user to decide which market proxy is most appropriate.

We know that these theories are not perfectly "right," but we also know that they are not too "wrong." Using MPT can provide valuable information on the risks incurred in different investment strategies. In short, while the model is false, it's not very false, and even a model that is a bit false is a great deal better than no model at all.

Source: Jason MacQueen in Joel M. Stern and Donald H. Chew, eds., *The Revolution in Corporate Finance* (Oxford, England: Basil Blackwell, 1986). Originally published in *Chase Financial Quarterly,* Chase Manhattan Bank, New York. Reprinted with permission.

With Roll's critique of the BJS and Fama–MacBeth methodology in mind, let us reassess the test results so far and consider what alternative tests might make sense. BJS used an equally weighted portfolio of all NYSE stocks as their proxy for the market portfolio. Because this portfolio included between 582 and 1,094 stocks throughout the sample period, there is no question that their market proxy was a well-diversified portfolio. The 10 test portfolios were equally weighted portfolios of between 58 and 110 stocks, also fairly well diversified. Perhaps we can view the BJS test really as a test of the APT, which applies only to well-diversified portfolios. As tests of the CAPM, however, Roll showed that the procedures are objectionable. Roll's critique tells us that all we can say about the BJS and Fama–MacBeth tests is that they, at best, constitute an attempt to verify a zero-beta version of the APT but provide no evidence about the CAPM.

Another inference we can draw from Roll's critique is that one way to test the CAPM is to test the efficiency of a market proxy. If we were to verify empirically that a legitimate market proxy is *the* efficient portfolio, we could endorse the CAPM's validity.

This is an important, albeit confusing, point. To relate it to first principles, we need first to distinguish portfolio mean-variance efficiency from informational efficiency. The concept of informational efficiency relates to the question of whether an asset or portfolio is "fairly priced." By "fairly" we mean that the price reflects all available information. For example, does the price of Digital Equipment stock reflect all available information about the earning potential of the corporation that arises from its current and expected future business plans? Chapter 12 is devoted to this concept and to the empirical issue of whether capital markets are informationally efficient.

The question of the informational efficiency of capital markets cannot be divorced from the question of mean-variance efficiency of asset portfolios, however. A central assumption of the simple CAPM is that all investors deduce the same input list from security analysis and hence construct identical efficient frontiers. Under these circumstances trade leads to the mean-variance efficiency of the market portfolio. However, this means that all investors use the same information when analyzing each asset. Therefore, according to CAPM hypothesis, all assets are informationally efficiently priced.

It is possible that capital markets are *informationally* efficient, but at the same time the CAPM is not valid and the market is not a *mean-variance* efficient portfolio. Roll, in addition to providing us with his now classic critique, realized this point and came up with a positive conclusion: Studies of the performance of professionally managed portfolios that were intended to test informational efficiency also may serve as indirect tests of the CAPM. If these tests lead to the conclusion that a market proxy portfolio consistently beats all professionally managed portfolios (on a risk-adjusted basis), then we may conclude that the market proxy is mean-variance efficient and the CAPM is valid. Conversely, if a professionally managed portfolio consistently outperforms the market proxy, then either the proxy is inadequate or the CAPM is invalid.

The motivation for comparing the performance of professional portfolio managers against the market proxy portfolio is simple. Professional managers are the best qualified to choose efficient portfolios, because they spend considerable resources on selecting and revising portfolios. Yet the CAPM predicts that all their efforts will fail, that one portfolio (the market portfolio) will outperform them all. If we find that, indeed, professional managers fail to beat the market proxy, the CAPM prediction is upheld. On the other hand, if professional managers can beat the proxy, we would have to conclude that the market proxy is inadequate and/or that the CAPM must be rejected.

The evidence on the performance of professional managers relative to a market proxy is strong. Sharpe[6] pioneered this line of investigation by studying the reward-to-variability ratio of 34 mutual funds. He concluded:

> We have shown that performance can be evaluated with a simple yet theoretically meaningful measure that considers both average return and risk. This measure precludes the "discovery" of differences in performance due solely to differences in objectives (e.g., the high average returns typically obtained by funds that consciously hold risky portfolios). However, even when performance is measured in this manner there are differences among funds; and such differences do not appear to be entirely transitory. To a major extent they can be explained by differences in expense ratios, lending support to the view that the capital market is highly efficient and that good managers concentrate on evaluating risk and providing diversification, spending little effort (and money) on the search for incorrectly priced securities. However, past performance per se also explains some of the differences. Further work is required before the significance of this result can be properly evaluated. But the burden of the proof may reasonably be placed on those who argue the traditional view—that the search for securities whose prices diverge from their intrinsic value is worth the expense required.

Sharpe recorded the annual rate of return that investors realized from 34 mutual funds over the 10-year period 1954 to 1963. He then measured the reward-to-variability ratio for each fund, dividing the average rate of return by the standard deviation of

[6] William Sharpe, "Mutual Fund Performance," *Journal of Business, Supplement on Security Prices* 39 (January 1966).

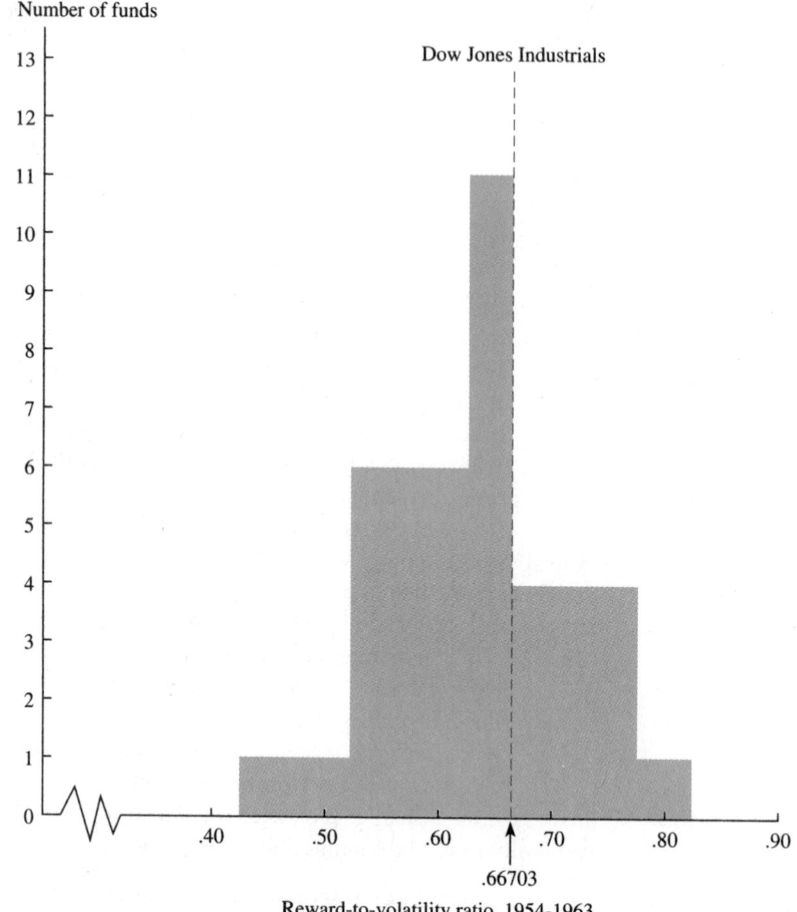

Figure 11.3
Mutual fund performance compared with the Dow Jones Industrials, 1954 to 1963

Source: William Sharpe, "Mutual Fund Performance," *Journal of Business Supplement on Security Prices* 39 (January 1966); published by the University of Chicago.

Industrial portfolio. The results are graphed in Figure 11.3. The figure shows that only 11 out of the 34 funds outperformed the Dow Jones Industrial portfolio, which is itself far from a satisfactory proxy for the theoretically efficient market portfolio.

Today, the picture is similar. Studies following Sharpe's investigated more funds, used shorter intervals (months instead of years) to estimate variables, and, most important, included a more reasonable proxy for the market portfolio, such as the S&P 500 or the NYSE index.

One example is a study by McDonald[7] that uses 123 mutual fund monthly returns over the 10-year period 1960 to 1969. The proxy for the market portfolio is the equally weighted portfolio of all NYSE stocks. Results of this study appear in Table 11.2, which

[7] John G. McDonald, "Objectives and Performance of Mutual Funds, 1960–1969," *Journal of Financial and Quantitative Analysis* 9 (June 1974).

Table 11.2 Systematic Risk and Performance

Systematic Risk			Performance Measures			
Risk Decile	Beta Range	Mean Beta	Monthly Excess Return (%)	Sharpe* Measure	Treynor† Measure	Jensen‡ Measure
10	1.22–1.46	1.34	.755	.122	.563	.128
9	1.09–1.21	1.14	.672	.130	.590	.144
8	1.02–1.07	1.04	.476	.107	.458	−.003
7	0.97–1.02	.99	.454	.110	.458	−.003
6	0.92–0.96	.94	.458	.112	.487	.023
5	0.88–0.92	.90	.520	.120	.578	.103
4	0.82–0.87	.84	.442	.118	.526	.055
3	0.73–0.81	.77	.461	.128	.599	.105
2	0.65–0.72	.69	.291	.091	.420	−.028
1	0.00–0.64	.49	.213	.078	.435	−.014
Sample means		.92	.477	.112	.518	.051
Market-based portfolios		—	—	.133	.510	0

*Reward-to-variability ratio: mean excess return divided by the standard deviation of fund return.

†Reward-to-systematic risk ratio: mean excess return divided by beta.

‡Alpha: estimated constant from least-squares regression of fund excess returns on market excess returns.

Source: Modified from John G. McDonald, "Objectives and Performance of Mutual Funds, 1960–1969," *Journal of Financial and Quantitative Analysis* 9 (June 1974).

shows the average reward-to-variability measure and other performance measures for each decile of the sample of funds ranked by systematic risk (beta). The bottom line in the table shows the reward-to-variability ratio for the market proxy. None of the deciles (with 12 to 13 funds in each decile) had a better reward-to-variability ratio than the proxy. The 123-fund average ratio for the period was .112, while the proxy's was .133.

Table 11.3 shows a breakdown by fund objective, from "maximum capital gain" to "income." Again, no category, on average, outperformed the proxy. In all, 84 funds out of 123 were outperformed by the NYSE equally weighted portfolio. These are typical results from studies of this nature, and so is McDonald's conclusion: "For the mutual funds as a whole, the data clearly show neither significantly 'superior' nor 'inferior' performance over the decade 1960–1969."

In the end, however, the question "How many managers beat the market portfolio over a given period?" is not very informative. First, we must be convinced that each of these managers shows a *statistically significant* superior performance (after adjusting for risk). Second, we must recognize that if a large number of managers are sampled, some are expected to succeed simply by the law of large numbers.

One way to account for the sampling problem is to subject managers' records to a test of persistence. Suppose you observe a sample of 100 managers over a period, and split them in two groups of superior and inferior performers. Then you observe the same managers over the next period, and split them again. The hypothesis is that, on average,

Table 11.3 Objectives and Performance

	Risk		Performance Measures			
Objective of Fund	Systematic Risk (Beta)	Total Variability (S.D.)	Mean Monthly Excess Return (%)	Sharpe* Measure	Treynor† Measure	Jensen‡ Measure
Maximum capital gain	1.22	5.90	.693	.117	.568	.122
Growth	1.01	4.57	.565	.124	.560	.099
Growth-income	0.90	3.93	.476	.121	.529	.058
Income-growth	0.86	3.80	.398	.105	.463	.004
Balanced	0.68	3.05	.214	.070	.314	−.099
Income	0.55	2.67	.252	.094	.458	−.002
Sample means	0.92	4.17	.477	.112	.518	.051
Market-based portfolios	—	—	—	.133	.510	0
Stock market index	1.00	3.83	.510	.133	.510	0
Bond market index §	0.18	1.42	.093	.065	.516	Not available

* Reward-to-variability ratio: mean excess return divided by the standard deviation of fund return.
†Reward to-systematic volatility ratio: mean excess return divided by beta.
‡Alpha: estimated constant from least-squares regression of fund excess returns on market excess returns (Jensen's delta).
§ Proxy measure based on arithmetic means of results for Keystone B-1 and B-4 funds, with returns adjusted for .042% per month average management fee.
Source: Modified from John G. McDonald, "Objectives and Performance of Mutual Funds, 1960–1969," *Journal of Financial and Quantitative Analysis* 9 (June 1974).

success or failure of managers does not persist across time periods. Usually, however, a researcher obtains data on managers for a certain period. The sample is first divided into two subperiods, and then managers are ranked in each period. For example, one study[8] reported the following results:

	1979–1981 Winners	1979–1981 Losers	Total
1976–1978 winners	44	19	63
1976–1978 losers	19	44	63
TOTAL	63	63	126

These results (which are repeated for more subperiods with similar statistics) indicate statistically significant persistence, suggesting that some managers may be consistently outperforming the market portfolio. As it turns out, however, this method, too, contains severe pitfalls.

Brown, Goetzmann, Ibbotson, and Ross[9] reported that the problems with studies of this type are twofold. First, they include only managers whose records are available for

[8] D. Hendricks, J. Patel, and R. Zeckhouser, "Hot Hands in Mutual Funds: The Persistence of Performance, 1974–1988," working paper, John F. Kennedy School of Government, Harvard University, 1991.
[9] Stephen J. Brown, William Goetzmann, Roger B. Ibbotson, and Stephen A. Ross, "Survivorship Bias in Performance Studies," working paper, Yale University, April 2, 1992.

both subperiods and exclude managers that dropped out after the first subperiod. Some of these managers may have been replaced because their performance was poor. Using simulation, the study showed that if only 5% of the lowest-ranking managers get cut off after the first subperiod, results of the remaining sample may show strong persistence even if managers' success is uncorrelated from one period to the next.

A further complication arises from the possibility that managers may be using similar styles, and hence their portfolios rates of return are correlated, period by period, although each of the returns may be uncorrelated from one period to the next. Such correlation may induce seeming persistence even when no manager is cut off after the first subperiod. When the lowest-ranking managers are cut off, such correlation exacerbates the survivorship bias.

11.2 Multiple Factors in Security Returns

Research into the multifactor nature of security returns is yet inconclusive. Identifying the factors and investigating the risk premiums of securities as a function of their factor loadings (betas) present greater statistical difficulties.

Two lines of inquiry have been pursued. In the first, researchers analyze security returns statistically to discern the significant factors and to construct portfolios that are highly correlated with those factors. They then estimate the average returns on these portfolios to determine whether these factors command risk premiums.

The second approach is to prespecify likely economic factors and identify portfolios that are highly correlated with these factors. The risk premiums on these portfolios are then estimated from sample average returns.

Identifying Factors from Security Returns

In exploratory factor analysis the exact number of factors is not known. Typically, a model with no factors is first fit to the data. This model assumes that asset returns are mutually uncorrelated. The goodness-of-fit measure from the model serves as a base value to express the total variability in returns. The researcher then fits a succession of factor models with increasing numbers of factors, comparing the goodness-of-fit measures of the various models. As each additional factor is added, a large improvement in the goodness-of-fit measures suggests that this is an important underlying factor that should be included. A small improvement in the fit suggests that the additional factor may have no real significance.

Factor analysis involving a large number of securities is a difficult task. In one of the most comprehensive studies to date, Lehman and Modest[10] used 750 NYSE and AMEX stocks to identify the factors. They concluded that, although the test results "may be interpreted as very weak evidence in favor of a ten factor model," the tests actually

[10] Bruce Lehman and David Modest, "The Empirical Foundation of the Arbitrage Pricing Theory," *Journal of Financial Economics* 21 (1988), pp. 213–54.

"provide very little information regarding the number of factors which underlie the APT. As the analysis suggests, the tests have little power to discriminate among models with different numbers of factors."

Paralleling the difficulty in identifying the factor structure from security returns, it has been difficult to demonstrate significant risk premiums on the **factor portfolios** that are constructed from this analysis. Although results may not be strong enough to disprove the hypothesis that the factor portfolios have insignificant risk premiums, the tests have little power to reject the hypothesis even when it is false. Reinganum and Conway[11] developed evidence that the large number of factors identified by factor analysis techniques may be a statistical fluke. Their work used a cross-validation technique to confirm the explanatory power of factor portfolios that are generated by factor analysis.

The cross-validation method splits the sample period rates of return into two subsamples of odd- and even-date rates of return. Factor analysis is used to identify factor portfolios from the odd-date subsample security returns. The rates of return from the even-date subsample are then used to test the explanatory power of these factor portfolios.

Suppose that the odd-date subsample produces 10 factor portfolios. We now compute the rates of return on the 10 portfolios for all the even dates. Let us assume that the first of the portfolios is the market index portfolio, r_M. Denote the other nine factor portfolio returns by $r_{P2}, \ldots, r_{P10}$. Next, we estimate 10 regression equations for all the stocks ($i = 1, \ldots, n$) using all the even-date returns ($t = 2, 4, 6, \ldots$) in the sample.

$$(1) \quad r_{it} = r_{ft} + \beta_{iM}(r_{Mt} - r_{ft}) + e_{i1t}$$

$$(2) \quad r_{it} = r_{ft} + \beta_{iM}(r_{Mt} - r_{ft}) + \beta_{iP2}(r_{P2t} - r_{ft}) + e_{i2t}$$

.

.

.

$$(10) \quad r_{it} = r_{ft} + \beta_{iM}(r_{Mt} - r_{ft}) + \beta_{iP2}(r_{P2t} - r_{ft}) + \beta_{iP3}(r_{P3t} - r_{ft}) + \ldots \beta_{iP10}(r_{P10t} - r_{ft}) + e_{i10t}$$

For each of the 10 regressions we estimate the variance of the residual $\sigma^2(e_{ikt})$, $k = 1, \ldots, 10$. The cross-validation test requires each additional factor portfolio to reduce the residual variance significantly.

The 10 first-pass factor portfolios appear in an order determined by their significance in the factor analysis of the odd-date subsample. In the second-pass (even-date) cross-validation test, Reinganum and Conway found that, of the 10, only one factor portfolio (the market index) remained significant, whereas just one other was borderline significant in explaining the variability of the residuals. The results demonstrate the statistical difficulties in identifying the factors that drive stock returns.

By design, these factor analysis tests are in the spirit of the APT rather than the mul-

[11] Marc Reinganum and Dolores Conway, "Cross Validation Tests of the APT," *Journal of Business and Economic Statistics* 6 (January 1988.)

By design, these factor analysis tests are in the spirit of the APT rather than the multifactor CAPM (explained in Chapter 25). The portfolios that researchers identify statistically as factor portfolios are not constructed with regard to any economic meaning, and the chance that any of them can be identified as an obvious hedge for some prespecified risk to future consumption is small.

Tests of Multifactor Equilibrium Models with Prespecified Factor Portfolios

The other avenue to test the multifactor equilibrium CAPM or APT is to choose portfolios that are designed to account for macroeconomic factors or to hedge specific risks and to test the multifactor model with these portfolios.

A full-blown test of the multifactor equilibrium model, with prespecified factors and hedge portfolios, is as yet unavailable. A test of this hypothesis requires three stages:

1. Specification of risk factors.
2. Identification of hedge portfolios.
3. Test of the explanatory power and risk premiums of the hedge portfolios.

A step in this direction was made by Chen, Roll, and Ross,[12] who hypothesized several possible variables that might proxy for systematic factors:

1. MP = Monthly growth rate in industrial production.
2. DEI = Changes in expected inflation measured by changes in short-term (T- bill) interest rates.
3. UI = Unexpected inflation defined as the difference between actual and expected inflation.
4. UPR = Unexpected changes in borne risk premiums measured by the difference between the returns on corporate Baa bonds and long-term government bonds.
5. UTS = Unexpected changes in the term premium measured by the difference between the returns on long- and short-term government bonds.

With the identification of these potential economic factors, Chen, Roll, and Ross skipped the procedure of identifying factor portfolios (the portfolios that have the highest correlation with the factors). Instead, by using the factors themselves, they implicitly assumed that factor portfolios exist that are perfectly correlated with the factors. The factors are now used in a test similar to that of Fama–MacBeth.

A critical part of the methodology is the grouping of stocks into portfolios. Recall that in the single-factor tests portfolios were constructed to span a wide range of betas to enhance the power of the test. In a multifactor framework the efficient criterion for grouping is less obvious. Chen, Roll, and Ross chose to group the sample stocks into 20 portfolios by size (market value of outstanding equity), a variable that is known to

---

[12] Nai-Fu Chen, Richard Roll, and Stephen Ross, "Economic Forces and the Stock Market," *Journal of Business* 59 (1986).

They first used five years of monthly data to estimate the factor betas of the 20 portfolios in a first-pass regression. This is accomplished by estimating the following regressions for each portfolio:

$$r = a + \beta_M r_M + \beta_{MP} MP + \beta_{DEI} DEI + \beta_{UI} UI + \beta_{URS} URS + \beta_{UTS} UTS + e$$

where M stands for the stock market index. Chen, Roll, and Ross used as the market index both the value-weighted NYSE index (VWNY) and the equally weighted NYSE index (EWNY).

Using the 20 sets of first-pass estimates of factor betas as the independent variables, they now estimated the second-pass regression (with 20 observations, one for each portfolio):

$$r = \gamma_0 + \gamma_M \beta_M + \gamma_{MP} \beta_{MP} + \gamma_{DEI} \beta_{DEI} + \gamma_{UI} \beta_{UI} + \gamma_{URS} \beta_{URS} + \gamma_{UTS} \beta_{UTS} + e$$

where the gammas become estimates of the risk premiums on the factors.

Chen, Roll, and Ross ran this second-pass regression for every month of their sample period, reestimating the first-pass factor betas once every 12 months. They ran the second-pass tests in four variations. First (Table 11.4, parts A and B), they excluded the market index altogether and used two alternative measures of industrial production (*YP* based on annual growth of industrial production and *MP* based on monthly growth). Finding that *MP* is a more effective measure, they next included the two versions of the market index, *EWNY* and *VWNY*, one at a time (Table 11.4, parts C and D). The estimated risk premiums (the values for the parameters, γ) were averaged over all the second-pass regressions corresponding to each subperiod listed in Table 11.4.

Note in Table 11.4, parts C and D, that the two market indexes *EWNY* (equally weighted index of NYSE) and *VWNY* (the value-weighted NYSE index) are not significant (their t-statistics of 1.218 and −0.633 are less than 2 for the overall sample period and for each subperiod). Note also that the *VWNY* factor has the wrong sign in that it seems to imply a negative market-risk premium. Industrial production (*MP*), the risk premium on bonds (*UPR*), and unanticipated inflation (*UI*) are the factors that appear to have significant explanatory power.

These results must be treated as only preliminary in this line of inquiry, but they indicate that it may be possible to hedge some economic factors that affect future consumption risk with appropriate portfolios. A CAPM or APT multifactor equilibrium expected return–beta relationship may one day supersede the now widely used single-factor model.

It is very difficult to identify the portfolios that serve to hedge common sources of risk to future consumption opportunities. The two lines of research explore the data in search of such portfolios. Factor analysis techniques indicate the portfolios that may be providing hedge services. Researchers can then try to figure out what the source of risk is and how important it is. The second line of research attempts to guess the identity of economic variables that are correlated with consumption risk and determine whether they indeed explain rates of return.

CONCEPT CHECK

Question 5. Compare the strategy of prespecifying the risk factor (as in Chen, Roll, and Ross's work) with that of exploratory factor analysis.

Table 11.4 Economic Variables and Pricing (percent per month × 10), Multivariate Approach

A	Years	*YP*	*MP*	*DEI*	*UI*	*UPR*	*UTS*	Constant
	1958–84	4.341	13.984	−.111	−.672	7.941	−5.8	4.112
		(.538)	(3.727)	(−1.499)	(−2.052)	(2.807)	(−1.844)	(1.334)
	1958–67	.417	15.760	.014	−.133	5.584	.535	4.868
		(.032)	(2.270)	(.191)	(−.259)	(1.923)	(.240)	(1.156)
	1968–77	1.819	15.645	−.264	−1.420	14.352	−14.329	−2.544
		(.145)	(2.504)	(−3.397)	(−3.470)	(3.161)	(−2.672)	(−.464)
	1978–84	13.549	8.937	−.070	−.373	2.150	−2.941	12.541
		(.774)	(1.602)	(−.289)	(−.442)	(.279)	(−.327)	(1.911)

B	Years	*MP*	*DEI*	*UI*	*UPR*	*UTS*	Constant
	1958–84	13.589	−.125	−6.29	7.205	−5.211	4.124
		(3.561)	(−1.640)	(−1.979)	(2.590)	(−1.690)	(1.361)
	1958–67	13.155	.006	−.191	5.560	−.008	4.989
		(1.897)	(.092)	(−.382)	(1.935)	(−.004)	(1.271)
	1968–77	16.966	−.245	−1.353	12.717	−13.142	−1.889
		(2.638)	(−3.215)	(−3.320)	(2.852)	(−2.554)	(−.334)
	1978–84	9.383	−.140	−.221	1.679	−1.312	11.477
		(1.588)	(−.552)	(−.274)	(.221)	(−.149)	(1.747)

C	Years	*EWNY*	*MP*	*DEI*	*UI*	*UPR*	*UTS*	Constant
	1958–84	5.021	14.009	−.128	.848	.130	−5.017	6.409
		(1.218)	(3.774)	(−1.666)	(−2.541)	(2.855)	(−1.576)	(1.848)
	1958–67	6.575	14.936	−.005	−.279	5.747	−.146	7.349
		(1.199)	(2.336)	(−.060)	(−.558)	(2.070)	(−.067)	(1.591)
	1968–77	2.334	17.593	−.248	−1.501	12.512	−9.904	3.542
		(.283)	(2.715)	(−3.039)	(−3.366)	(2.758)	(−2.015)	(.558)
	1978–84	6.638	7.563	−.132	−.729	5.273	−4.993	9.164
		(.906)	(1.253)	(−.529)	(−.847)	(.663)	(−.520)	(1.245)

D	Years	*VWNY*	*MP*	*DEI*	*UI*	*UPR*	*UTS*	Constant
	1958–84	−2.403	11.756	−.123	.795	8.274	−5.905	10.713
		(−.633)	(3.054)	(−1.600)	(−2.376)	(2.972)	(−1.879)	(2.755)
	1958–67	1.359	12.394	.005	−.209	5.204	−.086	9.527
		(.277)	(1.789)	(.064)	(−.415)	(1.815)	(−.040)	(1.984)
	1968–77	−5.269	13.466	−.255	−1.421	12.897	−11.708	8.582
		(−.717)	(2.038)	(−3.237)	(−3.106)	(2.955)	(−2.299)	(1.167)
	1978–84	−3.683	8.402	−.116	.739	6.056	−5.928	15.452
		(−.491)	(1.432)	(−.458)	(−.869)	(.782)	(−.644)	(1.867)

VWNY = Return on the value-weighted NYSE index; *EWNY* = Return on the equally weighted NYSE index; *MP* = Monthly growth rate in industrial production; *DEI* = Change in expected inflation; *UI* = Unanticipated inflation; *UPR* = Unanticipated change in the risk premium (Baa and under return—long-term government bond return); *UTS* = Unanticipated change in the term structure (long-term government bond return—Treasury-bill rate); and *YP* = Yearly growth rate in industrial production. Note that *t*-statistics are in parentheses.

Source: Modified from Nai-Fu Chen, Richard Roll, and Stephen Ross, "Economic Forces and the Stock Market," *Journal of Business* 59 (1986); published by the University of Chicago.

11.3 Time-Varying Volatility and the State of Tests of Capital Asset Pricing

In 1976, Fischer Black proposed to model the time-varying nature of asset-return volatility.[13] He suggested that such a model should include three effects. One is that the volatility depends on the stock price. (Generally, an increase in the stock price means a decrease in volatility.) A second is that the volatility tends to return to a long-term average. Finally, there are random changes in volatility. Although the idea was well received and widely cited, little was accomplished for quite a while.

In 1982 Robert F. Engle published a study[14] of U.K. inflation rates that measured their time-varying volatility. His model, named ARCH (autoregressive conditional heteroskedasticity), is based on the idea that a natural way to update a variance forecast is to average it with the most recent squared "surprise" (i.e., the deviation of the rate of return from its mean). ARCH introduced a statistically efficient algorithm to do just that.

This methodology caught fire in empirical research. A survey conducted[15] in May 1990 listed over 250 papers that employ ARCH in financial models. Moreover, an algorithm has been developed[16] to perform a joint estimation of the time series variances and the relationship between the mean and variance of returns (ARCH-M). By applying this technique to an array of assets, tests that relate mean asset returns to covariances can be devised.

Examination of the state of the empirical evidence on security returns reveals four facts. First, direct tests of either a single or multifactor CAPM have rejected the expected return–beta relationship. At the same time, there is no solid evidence that professional managers can persistently outperform well-diversified portfolios by exploiting the failure of security returns to price some factors or, conversely, by exploiting diversifiable risk factors.

Second, there is ample evidence that past security returns exhibit statistical "anomalies" or apparent profitable trading rules that could have been exploited by portfolio managers to produce abnormal rates of return. (More on this in Chapter 12 on market efficiency.) Such evidence is a reflection of the noted failure of the CAPM, which predicts that security alphas must average zero. Those who take this view must expect a more general theory to better explain asset returns.

Third, tests of extensions of the CAPM (that relax one or more of the simplifying assumptions) usually show that asset returns do indeed conform to the prediction of the modified model. One such example is the case of dividends and taxes.[17] A careful study

[13] Fischer Black, "Studies in Stock Price Volatility Changes," *Proceedings of the 1976 Business Meeting of the Business and Economic Statistics Sections, American Statistical Association,* pp. 177–81.

[14] Robert F. Engle, "Autoregressive Conditional Heteroskedasticity with Estimates of the Variance of U.K. Inflation," *Econometrica* 50 (1982), pp. 987–1008.

[15] Tim Bollerslev, Ray Y. Chou, Narayanan Jayaraman, and Kenneth F. Kroner, "ARCH Modeling in Finance: A Selective Review of the Theory and Empirical Evidence, with Suggestions for Future Research," *Journal of Econometrics* 48 (July/August 1992).

[16] Tim Bollerslev, Robert F. Engle, and Jeffrey M. Woolridge, "A Capital Asset Pricing Model with Time-Varying Covariances," *Journal of Political Economy* 96 (1989), pp. 116–31.

[17] Robert H. Litzenberger and Krishna Ramaswamy, "The Effects of Dividends on Common Stock Prices, Tax Effects or Information Effects," *Journal of Finance* 37 (1982).

of the joint effect of dividend yield and taxes shows that there is a positive but nonlinear association between common stock returns and dividend yields. Taxes drive investors in high tax brackets to tilt their portfolios toward lower-dividend-yield stocks, creating a dividend-clientele effect. The resultant relationship between dividend yield and expected returns violates the simple CAPM.

A more interesting example is the issue of liquidity. A study of the effect of liquidity on asset returns[18] shows that liquidity accounts for much of the puzzling effect of firm size on asset returns (see Chapter 12). Thus, one view of the state of empirical research is that the anomalies we now observe are associated with some extensions of the CAPM. Observers of this school pin their hopes on improved specifications of tests of the CAPM.

Finally, there is still a long way to go in accurate estimation of time-varying volatility (and the covariance structure) of asset returns, and in the incorporation of these estimates in the prediction of security returns.

SUMMARY

1. Although the single-factor expected return–beta relationship has not yet been confirmed by scientific standards, its use is already commonplace in economic life.
2. Early tests of the single-factor CAPM rejected the SML, finding that nonsystematic risk did explain average security returns.
3. Later tests controlling for the measurement error in beta found that nonsystematic risk does not explain portfolio returns but also that the estimated SML is too flat compared with what the CAPM would predict.
4. Roll's critique implied that the usual CAPM test is a test only of the mean-variance efficiency of a prespecified market proxy and therefore that tests of the linearity of the expected return–beta relationship do not bear on the validity of the model.
5. Tests of the mean-variance efficiency of professionally managed portfolios against the benchmark of a prespecified market index conform with Roll's critique in that they provide evidence of the efficiency of the prespecific market index.
6. Empirical evidence suggests that most professionally managed portfolios are outperformed by market indices, which lends weight to acceptance of the efficiency of those indexes and hence the CAPM.
7. Factor analysis of security returns suggests that more than one factor may be necessary for a valid expected return–beta relationship. This technique, however, does not identify the economic factors behind the factor portfolios.
8. Work on prespecified economic factors is ongoing. Preliminary results suggest that factors such as unanticipated inflation do play a role in the expected return–beta relationship of security returns.
9. Volatility of stock returns is constantly changing. Empirical evidence on stock returns must account for this phenomenon. Contemporary researchers use the variations of the ARCH-M algorithm to estimate the level of volatility and its effect on mean returns.

[18] Y. Amihud and H. Mendelson, "Asset Pricing and the Bid-Ask Spread," *Journal of Financial Economics* 17 (1986), pp. 223–49.

Key Terms

First-pass regression
Second-pass regression
Measurement error
Benchmark error
Factor portfolios

Selected Readings

The key readings concerning tests of the CAPM are still:

Black, Fischer; Michael C. Jensen; and Myron Scholes. "The Capital Asset Pricing Model: Some Empirical Tests." In *Studies in the Theory of Capital Markets.* Jensen, Michael D., ed. New York: Praeger Publishers, 1972.

Fama, Eugene; and James MacBeth. "Risk, Return, and Equilibrium: Empirical Tests." *Journal of Political Economy* 81 (1973), pp. 607–36.

Roll, Richard. "A Critique of the Asset Pricing Theory's Tests." *Journal of Financial Economics* 4 (1977).

A test of the model using more recent econometric tools is:

Gibbons, Michael. "Multivariate Tests of Financial Models." *Journal of Financial Economics* 10 (1982).

The factor analysis approach to testing multivariate models is treated in:

Roll, Richard; and Stephen Ross. "An Empirical Investigation of the Arbitrage Pricing Theory." *Journal of Finance* 20 (1980).

Lehman, Bruce; and David Modest. "The Empirical Foundation of the Arbitrage Pricing Theory." *Journal of Financial Economics* 21 (1988).

A good paper that tests the APT with prespecified factors is:

Chen, Nai-Fu; Richard Roll; and Stephen A. Ross. "Economic Forces and the Stock Market." *Journal of Business* 59 (1986).

Problems

The following annual excess rates of return were obtained for six portfolios and a market index portfolio:

Portfolios

Year	Market Index	A	B	C	D	E	F
1	26.4	38.1	32.6	23.6	15.2	11.9	38.0
2	17.9	21.9	20.2	17.6	14.6	11.8	19.8
3	13.4	13.4	15.1	13.0	13.2	9.0	14.4
4	10.6	9.8	10.4	11.4	12.1	11.0	9.7

1. Perform the first-pass regressions as did Black, Jensen, and Scholes, and tabulate the summary statistics as in Table 11.1.
2. Specify the hypotheses for a test of the second-pass regression for the SML.
3. Perform the second-pass SML regression by regressing the average excess return of each portfolio on its beta.
4. Summarize your test results and compare them to the reported results in the text.

5. Group the six portfolios into three, maximizing the dispersion of the betas of the three resultant portfolios. Repeat the test and explain any changes in the results.
6. Explain Roll's critique as it applies to the tests performed in Problems 1 to 5.
7. Compare the mean-variance efficiency of the six portfolios and the market index. Does the comparison support the CAPM?

Suppose that, in addition to the market factor that has been considered in Problems 1 to 7, a second factor is considered. The values of this factor for years 1 to 4 were as follows:

Year	Factor Value (%)
1	13
2	17
3	−21
4	27

8. Perform the first-pass regressions as did Chen, Roll, and Ross and tabulate the relevant summary statistics. (Hint: use a multivariable regression as in a standard spreadsheet package. Estimate the betas of the six portfolios on the two factors.)
9. Specify the hypothesis for a test of a second-pass regression for the multidimensional SML.
10. Do the data suggest a two-factor economy?
11. Can you identify a factor portfolio for the second factor?
12. CFA Richard Roll, in an article on using the capital asset pricing model (CAPM) to evaluate portfolio performance, indicated that it may not be possible to evaluate portfolio management ability if there is an error in the benchmark used.*
    a. In evaluating portfolio performance, describe the general procedure, with emphasis on the benchmark employed.
    b. Explain what Roll meant by the benchmark error and identify the specific problem with this benchmark.
    c. Draw a graph that shows how a portfolio that has been judged as superior relative to a "measured" security market line (SML) can be inferior relative to the "true" SML.
    d. Assume that you are informed that a given portfolio manager has been evaluated as superior when compared to the Dow Jones Industrial Average, the S&P 500, and the NYSE Composite Index. Explain whether this consensus would make you feel more comfortable regarding the portfolio manager's true ability.
    e. Although conceding the possible problem with benchmark errors as set forth by Roll, some contend this does not mean the CAPM is incorrect, but only that there is a measurement problem when implementing the theory. Others contend that because of benchmark errors the whole technique should be scrapped. Take and defend one of these positions.

*Reprinted, with permission, from the *CFA Study Guide*. Association for Investment Management and Research, Charlottesville, VA.

Chapter 12

Market Efficiency

ONE OF THE EARLY APPLICATIONS OF COMPUTERS IN ECONOMICS IN THE 1950S WAS TO ANALYZE ECONOMIC TIME SERIES. Business cycle theorists felt that tracing the evolution of several economic variables over time would clarify and predict the progress of the economy through boom and bust periods. A natural candidate for analysis was the behavior of stock market prices over time. Assuming that stock prices reflect the prospects of the firm, recurrent patterns of peaks and troughs in economic performance ought to show up in those prices.

Maurice Kendall examined this proposition in 1953.[1] He found to his great surprise that he could identify *no* predictable patterns in stock prices. Prices seemed to evolve randomly. They were as likely to go up as they were to go down on any particular day, regardless of past performance. The data provided no way to predict price movements.

At first blush, Kendall's results were disturbing to some financial economists. They seemed to imply that the stock market is dominated by erratic market psychology, or "animal spirits"—that it follows no logical rules. In short, the results appeared to confirm the irrationality of the market. On further reflection, however, economists came to reverse their interpretation of Kendall's study.

It soon became apparent that random price movements indicated a well-functioning or efficient market, not an irrational one. In this chapter we will explore the reasoning behind what may seem a surprising conclusion. We show how competition among analysts leads naturally to market efficiency, and we examine the implications of the efficient market hypothesis for investment policy. We also consider empirical evidence that supports and contradicts the notion of market efficiency.

---

[1] Maurice Kendall, "The Analysis of Economic Time Series, Part I: Prices," *Journal of the Royal Statistical Society* 96 (1953).

12.1 Random Walks and the Efficient Market Hypothesis

Suppose Kendall had discovered that stock prices are predictable. What a gold mine this would have been for investors! If they could use Kendall's equations to predict stock prices, investors would reap unending profits simply by purchasing stocks that the computer model implied were about to increase in price and by selling those stocks about to fall in price.

A moment's reflection should be enough to convince yourself that this situation could not persist for long. For example, suppose that the model predicts with great confidence that XYZ stock price, currently at $100 per share, will rise dramatically in three days to $110. What would all investors with access to the model's prediction do today? Obviously, they would place a great wave of immediate buy orders to cash in on the prospective increase in stock price. No one holding XYZ, however, would be willing to sell. The net effect would be an *immediate* jump in the stock price to $110. The forecast of a future price increase will lead instead to an immediate price increase. In other words, the stock price will immediately reflect the "good news" implicit in the model's forecast.

This simple example illustrates why Kendall's attempt to find recurrent patterns in stock price movements was doomed to failure. A forecast about favorable *future* performance leads instead to favorable *current* performance, as market participants all try to get in on the action before the price jump.

More generally, one might say that any information that could be used to predict stock performance must already be reflected in stock prices. As soon as there is any information indicating that a stock is underpriced and therefore offers a profit opportunity, investors flock to buy the stock and immediately bid up its price to a fair level, where only ordinary rates of return can be expected. These "ordinary rates" are simply rates of return commensurate with the risk of the stock.

However, if prices are bid immediately to fair levels, given all available information, it must be that they increase or decrease only in response to new information. New information, by definition, must be unpredictable; if it could be predicted, then the prediction would be part of today's information. Thus, stock prices that change in response to new (unpredictable) information also must move unpredictably.

This is the essence of the argument that stock prices should follow a **random walk**, that is, that price changes should be random and unpredictable.[2] Far from a proof of market irrationality, randomly evolving stock prices are the necessary consequence of intelligent investors competing to discover relevant information on which to buy or sell stocks before the rest of the market becomes aware of that information.

Don't confuse randomness in price *changes* with irrationality in the *level* of prices. If prices are determined rationally, then only new information will cause them to

[2] Actually, we are being a little loose with terminology here. Strictly speaking, we should characterize stock prices as following a submartingale, meaning that the expected change in the price can be positive, presumably as compensation for the time value of money and systematic risk. Moreover, the expected return may change over time as risk factors change. A random walk is more restrictive in that it constrains successive stock returns to be independent *and* identically distributed. Nevertheless, the term "random walk" is commonly used in the looser sense that price changes are essentially unpredictable. We will follow this convention.

change. Therefore, a random walk would be the natural result of prices that always reflect all current knowledge. Indeed, if stock price movements were predictable, that would be damning evidence of stock market inefficiency, because the ability to predict prices would indicate that all available information was not already reflected in stock prices. Therefore, the notion that stocks already reflect all available information is referred to as the **efficient market hypothesis** (EMH).[3]

Competition as the Source of Efficiency

Why should we expect stock prices to reflect "all available information"? After all, if you are willing to spend time and money on gathering information, it might seem reasonable that you could turn up something that has been overlooked by the rest of the investment community. When information is costly to uncover and analyze, one would expect investment analysis calling for such expenditures to result in an increased expected return.

This point has been stressed by Grossman and Stiglitz.[4] They argued that investors will have an incentive to spend time and resources to analyze and uncover new information only if such activity is likely to generate higher investment returns. Thus, in market equilibrium, efficient information-gathering activity should be fruitful. Although we would not, therefore, go so far as to say that you absolutely cannot come up with new information, it still makes sense to consider the competition.

Consider an investment management fund currently managing a $5 billion portfolio. Suppose that the fund manager can devise a research program that could increase the portfolio rate of return by 1/10 th of 1% per year, a seemingly modest amount. This program would increase the dollar return to the portfolio by $5 billion × .001, or $5 million. Therefore, the fund would be willing to spend up to $5 million per year on research to increase stock returns by a mere 1/10th of 1% per year. With such large rewards for such small increases in investment performance, it should not be surprising that professional portfolio managers are willing to spend large sums on industry analysts, computer support, and research effort, and therefore that price changes are, generally speaking, difficult to predict.

With so many well-backed analysts willing to spend considerable resources on research, there will not be many easy pickings in the market. Moreover, the incremental rates of return on research activity are likely to be so small that only managers of the largest portfolios will find them worth pursuing.

Although it may not literally be true that "all" relevant information will be uncovered, it is virtually certain that there are many investigators hot on the trail of most leads

[3] Market efficiency should not be confused with the idea of efficient portfolios introduced in Chapter 7. An informationally efficient *market* is one in which information is rapidly disseminated and reflected in prices. An efficient *portfolio* is one with the highest expected return for a given level of risk.

[4] Sanford J. Grossman and Joseph E. Stiglitz, "On the Impossibility of Informationally Efficient Markets," *American Economic Review* 70 (June 1980).

that may improve investment performance. Competition among these many well-backed, highly paid, aggressive analysts ensures that, as a general rule, stock prices ought to reflect available information regarding their proper levels.

Versions of the Efficient Market Hypothesis

It is common to distinguish among three versions of the EMH: the weak, semistrong, and strong forms of the hypothesis. These versions differ by their notions of what is meant by the term "all available information."

The **weak-form** hypothesis asserts that stock prices already reflect all information that can be derived by examining market trading data such as the history of past prices, trading volume, or short interest. This version of the hypothesis implies that trend analysis is fruitless. Past stock price data are publicly available and virtually costless to obtain. The weak-form hypothesis holds that if such data ever conveyed reliable signals about future performance, all investors would have learned already to exploit the signals. Ultimately, the signals lose their value as they become widely known because a buy signal, for instance, would result in an immediate price increase.

The **semistrong-form** hypothesis states that all publicly available information regarding the prospects of a firm must be reflected already in the stock price. Such information includes, in addition to past prices, fundamental data on the firm's product line, quality of management, balance sheet composition, patents held, earning forecasts, and accounting practices. Again, if any investor has access to such information from publicly available sources, one would expect it to be reflected in stock prices.

Finally, the **strong-form** version of the efficient market hypothesis states that stock prices reflect all information relevant to the firm, even including information available only to company insiders. This version of the hypothesis is quite extreme. Few would argue with the proposition that corporate officers have access to pertinent information long enough before public release to enable them to profit from trading on that information. Indeed, much of the activity of the Securities and Exchange Commission is directed toward preventing insiders from profiting by exploiting their privileged situation. Rule 10b-5 of the Security Exchange Act of 1934 sets limits on trading by corporate officers, directors, and substantial owners, requiring them to report trades to the SEC. These insiders, their relatives, and any associates who trade on information supplied by insiders are considered in violation of the law.

Defining insider trading is not always easy, however. After all, stock analysts are in the business of uncovering information not already widely known to market participants. As we saw in Chapter 3, the distinction between private and inside information is sometimes murky.

CONCEPT CHECK

Question 1. If the weak form of the efficient market hypothesis is valid, must the strong form also hold? Conversely, does strong-form efficiency imply weak-form efficiency?

12.2 Implications of the EMH for Investment Policy

Technical Analysis

Technical analysis is essentially the search for recurrent and predictable patterns in stock prices. Although technicians recognize the value of information regarding future economic prospects of the firm, they believe that such information is not necessary for a successful trading strategy. This is because whatever the fundamental reason for a change in stock price, if the stock price responds slowly enough, the analyst will be able to identify a trend that can be exploited during the adjustment period. The key to successful technical analysis is a sluggish response of stock prices to fundamental supply-and-demand factors. This prerequisite, of course, is diametrically opposed to the notion of an efficient market.

Technical analysts are sometimes called *chartists* because they study records or charts of past stock prices, hoping to find patterns they can exploit to make a profit. Figure 12.1 shows some of the types of patterns a chartist might hope to identify. The chartist may draw lines connecting the high and low prices for the day to examine any trends in the prices (Figure 12.1, **A**). The cross-bars indicate closing prices. This is called a search for "momentum." More complex patterns, such as the "breakaway" (Figure 12.1, **B**) or "head and shoulders" (Figure 12.1, **C**), are also believed to convey clear buy or sell signals. The head and shoulders is named for its rough resemblance to a portrait of a head with surrounding shoulders. Once the right shoulder is penetrated (known as piercing the neckline) chartists believe the stock is on the verge of a major decline in price.

The **Dow theory**, named after its creator Charles Dow (who established *The Wall Street Journal*), is the grandfather of most technical analysis. The aim of the Dow theory is to identify long-term trends in stock market prices. The two indicators used are the Dow Jones Industrial Average (DJIA) and the Dow Jones Transportation Average (DJTA). The DJIA is the key indicator of underlying trends, while the DJTA usually serves as a check to confirm or reject that signal.

The Dow theory posits three forces simultaneously affecting stock prices:

1. The *primary trend* is the long-term movement of prices, lasting from several months to several years.
2. *Secondary or intermediate* trends are caused by short-term deviations of prices from the underlying trend line. These deviations are eliminated via *corrections* when prices revert back to trend values.
3. *Tertiary or minor trends* are daily fluctuations of little importance.

Figure 12.2 represents these three components of stock price movements. In this figure, the primary trend is upward, but intermediate trends result in short-lived market declines lasting a few weeks. The intraday minor trends have no long-run impact on price.

Figure 12.3 depicts the course of the DJIA during 1988, a year that seems to provide a good example of price patterns consistent with Dow theory. The primary trend is upward, as evidenced by the fact that each market peak is higher than the previous peak

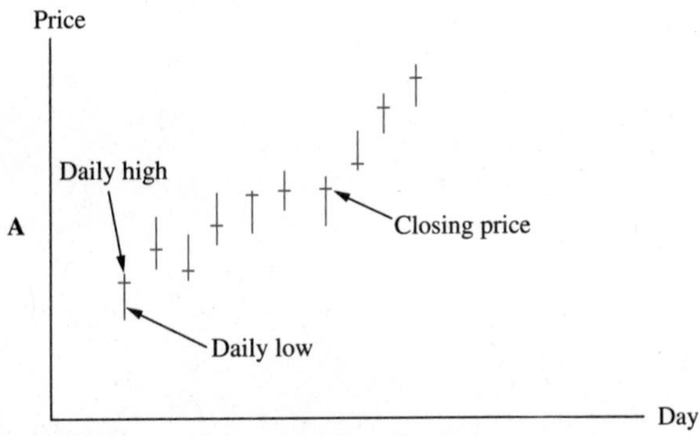

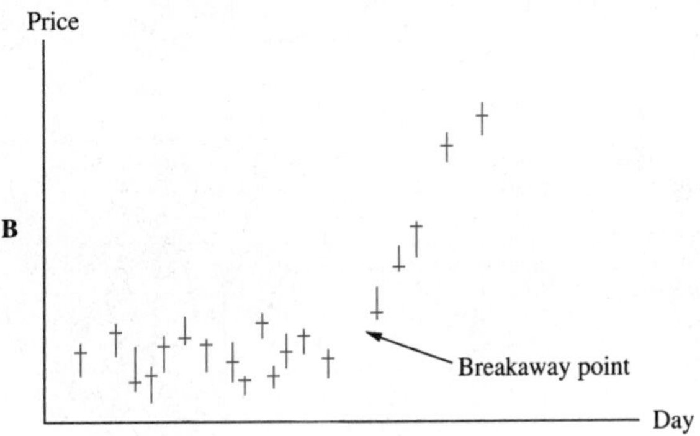

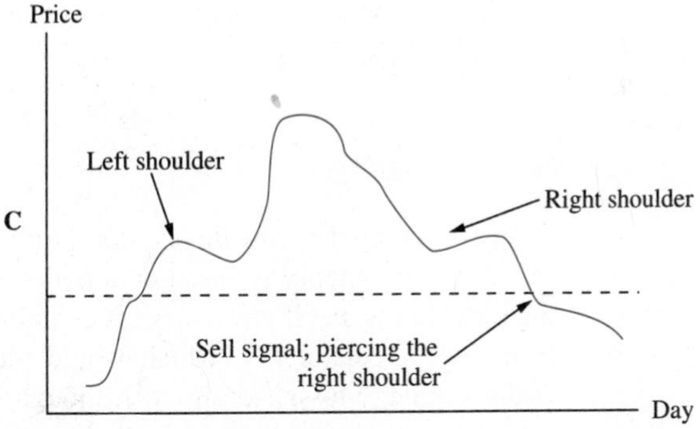

Figure 12.1
Technical analysis. **A**, Momentum (upward). **B**, Breakaway. **C**, Head and shoulders

(point **F** versus **D** versus **B**). Similarly, each low is higher than the previous low (**E** versus **C** versus **A**). This pattern of upward-moving "tops" and "bottoms" is one of the key ways to identify the underlying primary trend. Notice in Figure 12.3 that, despite the upward primary trend, intermediate trends still can lead to short periods of declining prices (points **B** through **C**, or **D** through **E**).

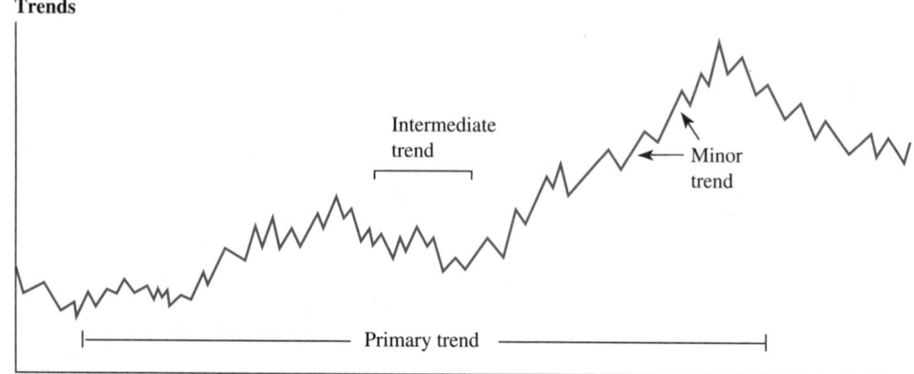

Figure 12.2
Dow theory trends
Source: Melanie F. Bowman and Thom Hartle, "Dow Theory," *Technical Analysis of Stocks and Commodities*, September 1990, p. 690.

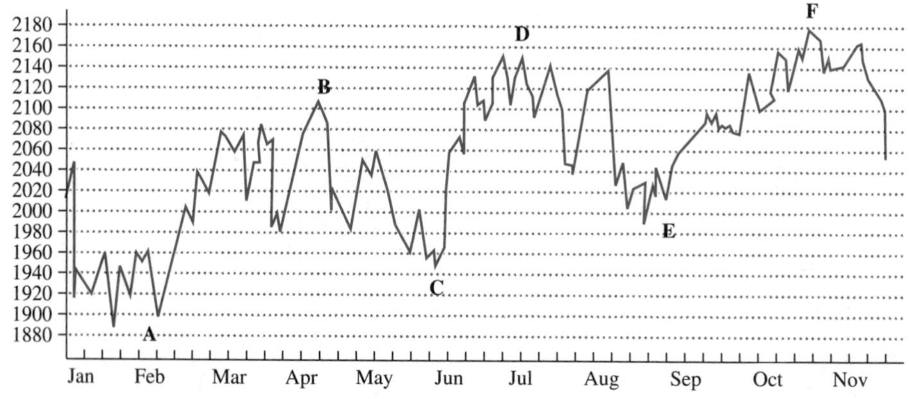

Figure 12.3
Dow Jones Industrial Average in 1988
Source: Melanie F. Bowman and Thom Hartle, "Dow Theory," *Technical Analysis of Stocks and Commodities*, September 1990, p. 690.

In evaluating the Dow theory, don't forget the lessons of the efficient market hypothesis. The Dow theory is based on a notion of predictably recurring price patterns. Yet, the EMH holds that if any pattern is exploitable, many investors would attempt to profit from such predictability, which would ultimately move stock prices and cause the trading strategy to self-destruct. Although Figure 12.3 certainly appears to describe a classic upward primary trend, one always must wonder whether we can see that trend only *after* the fact. Recognizing patterns as they emerge is far more difficult.

Recent variations on the Dow theory are the Elliott wave theory and the theory of Kondratieff waves. Like the Dow theory, the idea behind Elliott waves is that stock prices can be described by a set of wave patterns. Long-term and short-term wave cycles are superimposed and result in a complicated pattern of price movements, but by interpreting the cycles, one can, according to the theory, predict broad movements. Similarly, Kondratieff waves are named after a Russian economist who asserted that the macroeconomy (and thus the stock market) moves in broad waves lasting between 48 and 60 years. The Kondratieff waves are therefore analogous to Dow's primary trend, although of far longer duration. Kondratieff's assertion is hard to evaluate empirically, however, because cycles that last about 50 years provide only two full data points per century, which is hardly enough data to test the predictive power of the theory.

Other chartist techniques involve moving averages. In one version of this approach average prices over the past several months are taken as indicators of the "true value" of the stock. If the stock price is above this value, it may be expected to fall. In another version the moving average is taken as indicative of long-run trends. If the trend has been downward and if the current stock price is below the moving average, then a subsequent increase in the stock price above the moving average line (a "breakthrough") might signal a reversal of the downward trend.

Another technique is called the *relative strength* approach. The chartist compares stock performance over a recent period to performance of the market or other stocks in the same industry. A simple version of relative strength takes the ratio of the stock price to a market indicator such as the S&P 500 index. If the ratio increases over time, the stock is said to exhibit relative strength because its price performance is better than that of the broad market. Such strength presumably may continue for a long enough period of time to offer profit opportunities.

One of the most commonly heard components of technical analysis is the notion of **resistance levels** or **support levels**. These values are said to be price levels above which it is difficult for stock prices to rise, or below which it is unlikely for them to fall, and they are believed to be levels determined by market psychology.

Consider, for example, stock XYZ, which traded for several months at a price of $72, and then declined to $65. If the stock eventually begins to increase in price, $72 is considered a resistance level (according to this theory) because investors who bought originally at $72 will be anxious to sell their shares as soon as they can break even on their investment. Therefore, at prices near $72 a wave of selling pressure would exist. Such activity imparts a type of "memory" to the market that allows past price history to influence current stock prospects.

Technical analysts also focus on the volume of trading. The idea is that a price fall accompanied by heavy trading volume signals a more bearish market than if volume were smaller, because the price decline is taken as representing broader-based selling pressure. For example, the trin statistic ("trin" stands for trading index) equals

$$\text{Trin} = \frac{\text{Volume declining/Number declining}}{\text{Volume advancing/Number advancing}}$$

Therefore, trin is the ratio of average volume in declining issues to average volume in advancing issues. Ratios above 1.0 are considered bearish because the falling stocks would then have higher average volume than the advancing stocks, indicating net selling pressure. *The Wall Street Journal* reports trin every day in the market diary section, as in Figure 12.4

Note, however, for every buyer, there must be a seller of stock. Rising volume in a rising market should not necessarily indicate a larger imbalance of buyers versus sellers. For example, a trin statistic above 1.0, which is considered bearish, could equally well be interpreted as indicating that there is more *buying* activity in declining issues.

Figure 12.4

Market diary

Source: *The Wall Street Journal*, October 11, 1994. Reprinted by permission of *The Wall Street Journal*, © 1994 Dow Jones & Company, Inc. All Rights Reserved Worldwide.

DIARIES

NYSE	MON	FRI	WK AGO
Issues traded	2,829	2,855	2,859
Advances	1,414	1,245	841
Declines	731	946	1,351
Unchanged	684	664	667
New highs	30	23	41
New lows	74	151	74
zAdv vol (000)	142,394	159,595	99,489
zDecl vol (000)	47,098	85,032	135,861
zTotal vol (000)	213,112	284,225	269,112
Closing tick[1]	+197	+20	−22
Closing Arms[2] (trin)	.65	.68	.85
zBlock trades	5,324	6,413	5,991

[1]The net difference of the number of stocks closing higher than their previous trade from those closing lower, NYSE trading only.
[2]A comparison of the number of advancing and declining issues with the volume of shares rising and falling. Generally, a trin of less than 1.00 indicates buying demand; above 1.00 indicates selling pressure.
z-NYSE or Amex only.

The efficient market hypothesis implies that technical analysis is without merit. The past history of prices and trading volume is publicly available at minimal cost. Therefore, any information that was ever available from analyzing past prices has already been reflected in stock prices. As investors compete to exploit their common knowledge of a stock's price history, they necessarily drive stock prices to levels where expected rates of return are exactly commensurate with risk. At those levels one cannot expect abnormal returns.

As an example of how this process works, consider what would happen if the market believed that a level of $72 truly were a resistance level for stock XYZ. No one would be willing to purchase the stock at a price of $71.50, because it would have almost no room to increase in price, but ample room to fall. However, if no one would buy it at $71.50, then $71.50 would become a resistance level. But then, using a similar analysis, no one would buy it at $71, or $70, and so on. The notion of a resistance level is a logical conundrum. Its simple resolution is the recognition that if the stock is ever to sell at $71.50, investors *must* believe that the price can as easily increase as fall. The fact that investors are willing to purchase the stock at $71.50 is evidence of their belief that they can earn a fair expected rate of return at that price.

Concept Check

Question 2. If everyone in the market believes in resistance levels, why do these beliefs not become self-fulfilling prophecies?

An interesting question is whether a technical rule that seems to work will continue to work in the future once it becomes widely recognized. A clever analyst may occasionally uncover a profitable trading rule, but the real test of efficient markets is whether the rule itself becomes reflected in stock prices once its value is discovered.

Suppose, for example, that the Dow theory predicts an upward primary trend. If the theory is widely accepted, it follows that many investors will attempt to buy stocks immediately in anticipation of the price increase; the effect would be to bid up prices sharply and immediately rather than at the gradual, long-lived pace initially expected. The Dow theory's predicted trend would be replaced by a sharp jump in prices. It is in this sense that price patterns ought to be *self-destructing*. Once a useful technical rule (or price pattern) is discovered, it ought to be invalidated once the mass of traders attempt to exploit it.

Thus, the market dynamic is one of a continual search for profitable trading rules, followed by destruction by overuse of those rules found to be successful, followed by more search for yet-undiscovered rules.

Fundamental Analysis

Fundamental analysis uses earnings and dividend prospects of the firm, expectations of future interest rates, and risk evaluation of the firm to determine proper stock prices. Ultimately, it represents an attempt to determine the present discounted value of all the payments a stockholder will receive from each share of stock. If that value exceeds the stock price, the fundamental analyst would recommend purchasing the stock.

Fundamental analysts usually start with a study of past earnings and an examination of company balance sheets. They supplement this analysis with further detailed economic analysis, ordinarily including an evaluation of the quality of the firm's management, the firm's standing within its industry, and the prospects for the industry as a whole. The hope is to attain insight into future performance of the firm that is not yet recognized by the rest of the market. Chapters 16 through 18 provide a detailed discussion of the types of analyses that underlie fundamental analysis.

Once again, the efficient market hypothesis predicts that *most* fundamental analysis also is doomed to failure. If the analyst relies on publicly available earnings and industry information, his or her evaluation of the firm's prospects is not likely to be significantly more accurate than those of rival analysts. There are many well-informed, well-financed firms conducting such market research, and in the face of such competition it will be difficult to uncover data not also available to other analysts. Only analysts with a unique insight will be rewarded.

Fundamental analysis is much more difficult than merely identifying well-run firms with good prospects. Discovery of good firms does an investor no good in and of itself if the rest of the market also knows those firms are good. If the knowledge is already public, the investor will be forced to pay a high price for those firms and will not realize a superior rate of return.

The trick is not to identify firms that are good, but to find firms that are *better* than everyone else's estimate. Similarly, poorly run firms can be great bargains if they are not quite as bad as their stock prices suggest.

This is why fundamental analysis is difficult. It is not enough to do a good analysis of a firm; you can make money only if your analysis is better than that of your competitors because the market price is expected already to reflect all commonly available information.

Active versus Passive Portfolio Management

By now it is apparent that casual efforts to pick stocks are not likely to pay off. Competition among investors ensures that any easily implemented stock evaluation technique will be used widely enough so that any insights derived will be reflected in stock prices. Only serious, time-consuming, and expensive techniques are likely to generate the *differential* insight necessary to generate trading profits.

Moreover, these techniques are economically feasible only for managers of large portfolios. If you have only $100,000 to invest, even a 1% per year improvement in performance generates only $1,000 per year, hardly enough to justify herculean efforts. The billion-dollar manager, however, reaps extra income of $10 million annually from the same 1% increment.

If small investors are not in a favored position to conduct active portfolio management, what are their choices? The small investor probably is better off investing in mutual funds. By pooling resources in this way, small investors can gain from economies of size.

More difficult decisions remain, though. Can investors be sure that even large mutual funds have the ability or resources to uncover mispriced stocks? Furthermore, will any mispricing be sufficiently large to repay the costs entailed in active portfolio management?

Proponents of the efficient market hypothesis believe that active management is largely wasted effort and unlikely to justify the expenses incurred. Therefore, they advocate a **passive investment strategy** that makes no attempt to outsmart the market. A passive strategy aims only at establishing a well-diversified portfolio of securities without attempting to find under- or overvalued stocks. Passive management is usually characterized by a buy-and-hold strategy. Because the efficient market theory indicates that stock prices are at fair levels, given all available information, it makes no sense to buy and sell securities frequently, which generates large brokerage fees without increasing expected performance.

One common strategy for passive management is to create an **index fund**, which is a fund designed to replicate the performance of a broad-based index of stocks. For example, in 1976 the Vanguard Group of mutual funds introduced a mutual fund called the Index 500 Portfolio that holds stocks in direct proportion to their weight in the Standard & Poor's 500 stock price index. The performance of the Index 500 fund therefore replicates the performance of the S&P 500. Investors in this fund obtain broad diversification with relatively low management fees. The fees can be kept to a minimum because Vanguard does not need to pay analysts to assess stock prospects and does not incur transaction costs from high portfolio turnover. Indeed, while the typical annual charge for an actively managed fund is over 1% of assets, Vanguard charges a bit less than 0.2% for the Index 500 Portfolio.

Indexing has grown in appeal considerably since 1976. Vanguard's Index 500 Portfolio had approximately $8 billion in assets in early 1994, placing it among the 10 largest mutual funds. Both Fidelity and Dreyfus recently initiated S&P 500 index funds. Moreover, over $400 billion is now invested by institutional investors in indexed stock portfolios, most of which are pegged to the S&P 500. Many institutional investors now hold indexed bond portfolios as well as indexed stock portfolios. These portfolios aim to replicate the features of well-known bond indexes such as the Lehman or Salomon Brothers indexes.

A hybrid strategy also is fairly common, where the fund maintains a *passive core*, which is an indexed position, and augments that position with one or more actively managed portfolios.

As indexing has grown in popularity, however, some observers have come to criticize the strategy. They argue that because managers of indexed portfolios hold every stock in a given index, they do not exercise independent judgment as to the attractiveness of each particular security in that index. This, they argue, is a breach of the manager's fiduciary responsibility to invest only in securities viewed as attractive for the investor. The nearby box provides a discussion of this recent controversy. The "anomalies" referred to are discussed in detail later in the chapter.

CONCEPT CHECK

Question 3. What would happen to market efficiency if *all* investors attempted to follow a passive strategy?

The Role of Portfolio Management in an Efficient Market

If the market is efficient, why not throw darts at *The Wall Street Journal* instead of trying rationally to choose a stock portfolio? This is a tempting conclusion to draw from the notion that security prices are fairly set, but it is far too facile. There is a role for rational portfolio management, even in perfectly efficient markets.

You have learned that a basic principle in portfolio selection is diversification. Even if all stocks are priced fairly, each still poses firm-specific risk that can be eliminated through diversification. Therefore, rational security selection, even in an efficient market, calls for the selection of a well-diversified portfolio providing the systematic risk level that the investor wants.

Rational investment policy also requires that tax considerations be reflected in security choice. High-tax-bracket investors generally will not want the same securities that low-bracket investors find favorable. At an obvious level high-bracket investors find it advantageous to buy tax-exempt municipal bonds despite their relatively low pretax yields, whereas those same bonds are unattractive to low-tax-bracket investors. At a more subtle level high-bracket investors might want to tilt their portfolios in the direction of capital gains as opposed to dividend or interest income, because the option to defer the realization of capital gain income is more valuable the higher the current tax bracket. Hence, these investors may prefer stocks that yield low dividends yet offer greater expected capital gain income. They also will be more attracted to investment opportunities for which returns are sensitive to tax benefits, such as real estate ventures.

A third argument for rational portfolio management relates to the particular risk profile of the investor. For example, a General Motors executive whose annual bonus depends on GM's profits generally should not invest additional amounts in auto stocks. To the extent that his or her compensation already depends on GM's well-being, the executive is already overinvested in GM and should not exacerbate the lack of diversification.

American Pension Funds: Indexing Fingered

The rise of indexation is the most influential recent innovation in American money management. How inconvenient if some of the country's fund managers could be sued for using it.

Until the mid-1970s, most fund managers spent their time searching for undervalued equities in the hope that such stocks would subsequently soar, allowing the fund to outperform the market. Indexing—buying a portfolio of shares to mimic a stock-market index—can, by definition, never beat the market. Nevertheless, neither could "active" investors seem to do so consistently. So indexing caught on dramatically. In 1993 some $430 billion of American pension-fund money—a quarter of the total that pension funds held in equities that year—was indexed.

With so much indexing going on, most fund managers have not given a second thought to the possibility that they might be liable in court for using it. Yet Calpers, the huge pension fund for Californian public employees, thinks they might be. In a new study,* its general counsel argues that many index-fund managers—though not Calpers, despite the 80% of its equity funds that are indexed—risk falling foul of the law.

The problem, says Calpers, is that most indexers do not bother to monitor the performance of the individual companies whose shares they own. Their only concern is to keep their portfolio in line with the stock market benchmark. But such a strategy may lead managers to buy shares unwittingly in a firm that subsequently goes bust. Had they paid attention to the individual firm, rather than merely to its place in an index, they might have been able to force the firm's management to change its ways before disaster struck. Their lack of interest in the running of the firm, says Calpers, may breach the golden rule of fund management—the need to be a "prudent" investor. And that in turn might lead to lawsuits from disgruntled investors.

Why are indexers so cavalier? Indexing is based on the theory of efficient markets. This states that, because stock prices reflect all available information, investors cannot beat the market by picking individual stocks unless they are lucky. They would be wiser to reduce their risks by holding a diversified portfolio—ideally the market index. In a couple of test cases, American courts have accepted the theory, and agreed that indexing was prudent.

Now, however, as Calpers points out, efficient-market theory is under attack. Academics have uncovered scores of apparent market [anomalies], such as fairly predictable patterns of price movements. And the few, mostly big, index-fund managers that actively monitor the companies they own, reckon they have been able to improve the performance of some of those firms. Calpers, for instance, screens its indexed portfolio for the worst performers, then pays a visit to their managements.

The Calpers study says all this means that, in future, courts may not accept the "efficient-market" justification for passive indexing. Unless managers of index funds start to take a more active interest in the performance of the firms they invest in, they might find lawyers taking an active interest in the funds themselves.

*"An Ounce of Prevention: meeting the fiduciary duty to monitor an index fund through relationship investing," Calpers, March 1994.

Investors of varying ages also might warrant different portfolio policies with regard to risk bearing. For example, older investors who are essentially living off savings might choose to avoid long-term bonds whose market values fluctuate dramatically with changes in interest rates (discussed in Part IV). Because these investors are living off accumulated savings, they require conservation of principal. In contrast, younger investors might be more inclined toward long-term bonds. The steady flow of income over long periods of time that is locked in with long-term bonds can be more important than preservation of principal to those with long life expectancies.

In conclusion, there is a role for portfolio management even in an efficient market. Investors' optimal positions will vary according to factors such as age, tax bracket, risk aversion, and employment. The role of the portfolio manager in an efficient market is to tailor the portfolio to these needs, rather than to beat the market.

Book Values versus Market Values

A somewhat common belief is the notion that book values are intrinsically more trustworthy than are market values. Many firms, for example, are reluctant to issue additional stock when the market price of outstanding equity is lower than the book value of those shares. Issue under these circumstances is said to cause dilution of the original stockholders' ownership claim.

Perhaps this faith in book values derives from their stability. Although market values fluctuate daily, book values remain the same day in and day out. The stability of book values actually is a misleading virtue. Market prices fluctuate for a good reason: They move in response to new information about the economic prospects of the firm. The stability of book values in the face of new information is testament to their essential unreliability.

As an example of how book values can go wrong, imagine what would happen to the price of Exxon stock if the price of oil were to double overnight. The stock price would increase for the very good reason that Exxon's assets are now far more valuable. Yet the book value of Exxon's assets would remain unchanged. Its stability in the face of changing conditions clearly shows it is not a guide to true value.

12.3 Event Studies

The notion of informationally efficient markets leads to a powerful research methodology. If security prices reflect all currently available information, then price changes must reflect new information. Therefore, it seems that one should be able to measure the importance of an event of interest by examining price changes during the period in which the event occurs.

An **event study** describes a technique of empirical financial research that enables an observer to assess the impact of a particular event on a firm's stock price. A stock market analyst might want to study the impact of dividend changes on stock prices, for example. An event study would quantify the relationship between dividend changes and stock returns. Using the results of such a study together with a superior means of predicting dividend changes, the analyst could in principle earn superior trading profits.

Analyzing the impact of an announced change in dividends is more difficult than it might at first appear. On any particular day stock prices respond to a wide range of economic news such as updated forecasts for GDP, inflation rates, interest rates, or corporate profitability. Isolating the part of a stock price movement that is attributable to a dividend announcement is not a trivial exercise.

The statistical approach that researchers commonly use to measure the impact of a particular information release, such as the announcement of a dividend change, is a marriage of efficient market theory with the index model discussed in Chapter 9. We want to measure the unexpected return that results from an event. This is the difference between the actual stock return and the return that might have been expected given the performance of the market. This expected return can be calculated using the index model.

Recall that the index model holds that stock returns are determined by a market factor and a firm-specific factor. The stock return, r_t, during a given period, t, would be expressed mathematically as

$$r_t = a + br_{Mt} + e_t \tag{12.1}$$

where r_{Mt} is the market's rate of return during the period and e_t is the part of a security's return resulting from firm-specific events. The parameter b measures sensitivity to the market return, and a is the average rate of return the stock would realize in a period with a zero market return.[5] Equation 12.1 therefore provides a decomposition of r_t into market and firm-specific factors. The firm-specific return may be interpreted as the unexpected return that results from the event.

Determination of the firm-specific return in a given period requires that we obtain an estimate of the term e_t. Therefore, we rewrite equation 12.1:

$$e_t = r_t - (a + br_{Mt}) \tag{12.2}$$

Equation 12.2 has a simple interpretation: To determine the firm-specific component of a stock's return, subtract the return that the stock ordinarily would earn for a given level of market performance from the actual rate of return on the stock. The residual, e_t, is the stock's return over and above what one would predict based on broad market movements in that period, given the stock's sensitivity to the market.

For example, suppose that the analyst has estimated that $a = .5\%$ and $b = .8$. On a day that the market goes up by 1%, you would predict from equation 12.1 that the stock should rise by an expected value of $.5\% + .8 \times 1\% = 1.3\%$. If the stock actually rises by 2%, the analyst would infer that firm-specific news that day caused an additional stock return of $2\% - 1.3\% = .7$ percent. We sometimes refer to the term e_t in equation 12.2 as the **abnormal return**—the return beyond what would be predicted from market movements alone.

The general strategy in event studies is to estimate the abnormal return around the date that new information about a stock is released to the market and attribute the abnormal stock performance to the new information. The first step in the study is to estimate parameters a and b for each security in the study. These typically are calculated using index model regressions as described in Chapter 9 in a period before that in

[5] We know from Chapter 9, Section 9.3, that the CAPM implies that the intercept a in equation 12.1 should equal $r_f(1 - \beta)$. Nevertheless, it is customary to estimate the intercept in this equation empirically rather than imposing the CAPM value. One justification for this practice is that empirically fitted security market lines seem flatter than predicted by the CAPM (see Chapter 11) which would make the intercept implied by the CAPM too small.

which the event occurs. The prior period is used for estimation so that the impact of the event will not affect the estimates of the parameters. Next, the information release dates for each firm are recorded. For example, in a study of the impact of merger attempts on the stock prices of target firms, the announcement date is the date on which the public is informed that a merger is to be attempted. Finally, the abnormal returns of each firm surrounding the announcement date are computed, and the statistical significance and magnitude of the typical abnormal return is assessed to determine the impact of the newly released information.

One concern that complicates event studies arises from *leakage* of information. Leakage occurs when information regarding a relevant event is released to a small group of investors before official public release. In this case the stock price might start to increase (in the case of a "good news" announcement) days or weeks before the official announcement date. Any abnormal return on the announcement date is then a poor indicator of the total impact of the information release. A better indicator would be the **cumulative abnormal return**, which is simply the sum of all abnormal returns over the time period of interest. The cumulative abnormal return thus captures the total firm-specific stock movement for an entire period when the market might be responding to new information.

Figure 12.5 presents the results from a fairly typical event study. The authors of this study were interested in leakage of information before merger announcements and constructed a sample of 194 firms that were targets of takeover attempts. In most takeovers, stockholders of the acquired firms sell their shares to the acquirer at substantial premiums over market value. Announcement of a takeover attempt is good news for shareholders of the target firm and therefore should cause stock prices to jump.

Figure 12.5 confirms the good-news nature of the announcements. On the announcement day, called day 0, the average cumulative abnormal return (CAR) for the sample of takeover candidates increases substantially, indicating a large and positive abnormal return on the announcement date. Notice that immediately after the announcement date the CAR no longer increases or decreases significantly. This is in accord with the efficient market hypothesis. Once the new information became public, the stock prices jumped almost immediately in response to the good news. With prices once again fairly set, reflecting the effect of the new information, further abnormal returns on any particular day are equally likely to be positive or negative. In fact, for a sample of many firms, the average abnormal return will be extremely close to zero, and thus the CAR will show neither upward nor downward drift. This is precisely the pattern shown in Figure 12.5.

The lack of drift in CAR after the public announcement date is perhaps the clearest evidence of an efficient market impounding information into stock prices. This pattern is commonly observed. For example, Figure 12.6 presents results from an event study on dividend announcements. As expected, the firms announcing dividend increases enjoy positive abnormal returns, whereas those with dividend decreases suffer negative abnormal returns. In both cases, however, once the information is made public the stock price seems to adjust fully, with CARs exhibiting neither upward nor downward drift.

The pattern of returns for the days preceding the public announcement date yields some interesting evidence about efficient markets and information leakage. If insider

Figure 12.5

Cumulative abnormal returns before takeover attempts: Target companies

Source: Arthur Keown and John Pinkerton, "Merger Announcements and Insider Trading Activity," *Journal of Finance* 36 (September 1981).

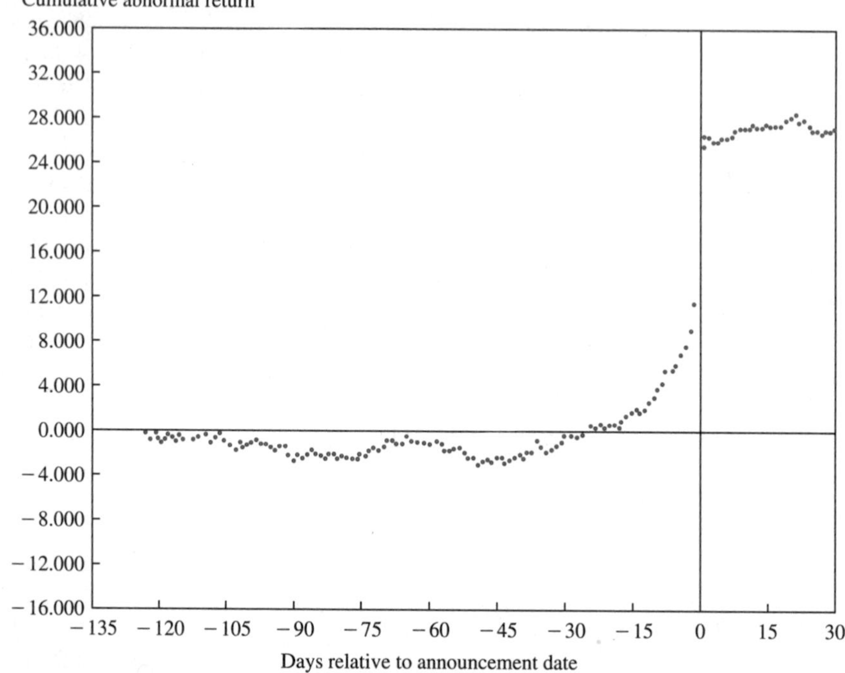

trading rules were perfectly obeyed and perfectly enforced, stock prices should show no abnormal returns on days before the public release of relevant news, because no special firm-specific information would be available to the market before public announcement. Instead, we should observe a clean jump in the stock price only on the announcement day. In fact, Figure 12.5 shows that the prices of the takeover targets clearly start an upward drift 30 days before the public announcement. There are two possible interpretations of this pattern. One is that information is leaking to some market participants who then purchase the stocks before the public announcement. At least some abuse of insider trading rules is occurring.

Another interpretation is that in the days before a takeover attempt the public becomes suspicious of the attempt as it observes someone buying large blocks of stock. As acquisition intentions become more evident, the probability of an attempted merger is gradually revised upward so that we see a gradual increase in CARs. Although this interpretation is certainly a valid possibility, evidence of leakage appears almost universally in event studies, even in cases where the public's access to information is not gradual. For example, the CARs associated with the dividend announcement presented in Figure 12.6 also exhibit leakage. It appears as if insider trading violations do occur.

Actually, the SEC itself can take some comfort from patterns such as that in Figures 12.5 and 12.6. If insider trading rules were widely and flagrantly violated, we would expect to see abnormal returns earlier than they appear in these results. For example, in the case of mergers, the CAR would turn positive as soon as acquiring firms decided on their takeover targets, because insiders would start trading immediately. By the time of

Figure 12.6
Cumulative abnormal returns surrounding dividend announcements
Source: J. Aharony and I. Swary, "Quarterly Dividend and Earnings Announcements and Stockholders' Return: An Empirical Analysis," *Journal of Finance* 35 (March 1980), pp. 1–12.

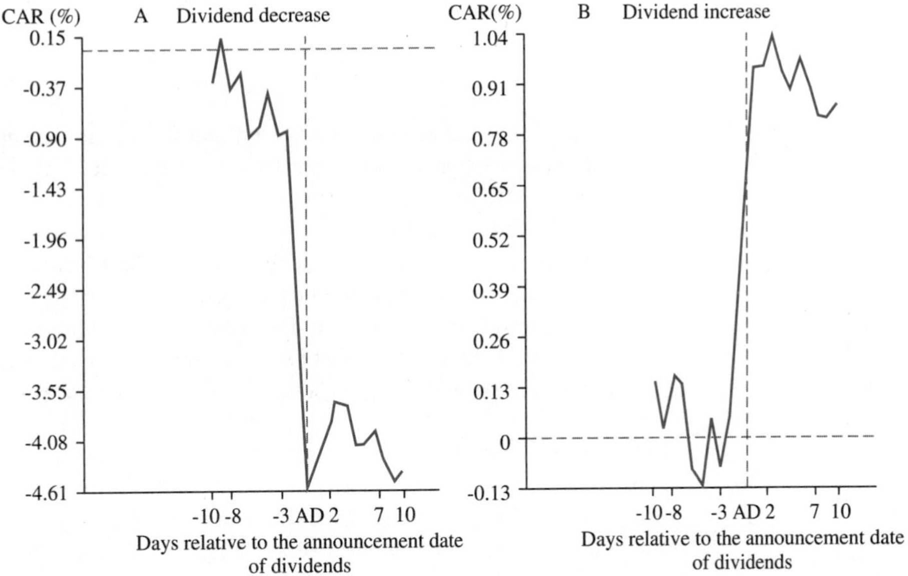

the public announcement, the insiders would have bid up the stock prices of target firms to levels reflecting the merger attempt, and the abnormal returns on the actual public announcement date would be close to zero. The dramatic increase in the CAR that we see on the announcement date indicates that a good deal of these announcements are indeed news to the market and that stock prices did not already reflect complete knowledge about the takeovers. It would appear, therefore, that SEC enforcement does have a substantial effect on restricting insider trading, even if some amount of it still persists.

Event study methodology has become a widely accepted tool to measure the economic impact of a wide range of events. For example, the SEC regularly uses event studies to measure illicit gains captured by traders who may have violated insider trading or other securities laws.[6] Event studies are also used in fraud cases, where the courts must assess damages caused by a fraudulent activity. As an example of the technique, suppose that a company with a market value of $100 million suffers an abnormal return of −6% on the day that news of a fraudulent activity surfaces. One might then infer that the damages sustained from the fraud were $6 million, because the value of the firm (after adjusting for general market movements) fell by 6% of $100 million when investors became aware of the news and reassessed the value of the stock.

CONCEPT CHECK

Question 4. Suppose that we see negative abnormal returns (declining CARs) after an announcement date. Is this a violation of efficient markets?

---

[6] For a review of SEC applications of this technique, see Mark Mitchell and Jeffry Netter, "The Role of Financial Economics in Securities Fraud Cases: Applications at the Securities and Exchange Commission," School of Business Administration, The University of Michigan, working paper No. 93-25, October 1993.

12.4 Are Markets Efficient?

The Issues

Not surprisingly, the efficient market hypothesis does not exactly arouse enthusiasm in the community of professional portfolio managers. It implies that a great deal of the activity of portfolio managers—the search for undervalued securities—is at best wasted effort, and quite probably harmful to clients because it costs money and leads to imperfectly diversified portfolios. Consequently, the EMH has never been widely accepted on Wall Street, and debate continues today on the degree to which security analysis can improve investment performance. Before discussing empirical tests of the hypothesis, we want to note three factors that together imply that the debate probably never will be settled: the *magnitude issue*, the *selection bias issue*, and the *lucky event issue*.

The Magnitude Issue. Consider an investment manager overseeing a $2 billion portfolio. If she can improve performance by only 1/10th of 1% per year, that effort will be worth .001 × $2 billion = $2 million annually. This manager clearly would be worth her salary! Yet can we, as observers, statistically measure her contribution? Probably not: a 1/10th of 1% contribution would be swamped by the yearly volatility of the market. Remember, the annual standard deviation of the well-diversified S&P 500 index has been more than 20% per year. Against these fluctuations a small increase in performance would be hard to detect. Nevertheless, $2 million remains an extremely valuable improvement in performance.

All might agree that stock prices are very close to fair values, and that only managers of large portfolios can earn enough trading profits to make the exploitation of minor mispricing worth the effort. According to this view, the actions of intelligent investment managers are the driving force behind the constant evolution of market prices to fair levels. Rather than ask the qualitative question "Are markets efficient?" we ought instead to ask a more quantitative question: "How efficient are markets?"

The Selection Bias Issue. Suppose that you discover an investment scheme that could really make money. You have two choices: either publish your technique in *The Wall Street Journal* to win fleeting fame, or keep your technique secret and use it to earn millions of dollars. Most investors would choose the latter option, which presents us with a conundrum. Only investors who find that an investment scheme cannot generate abnormal returns will be willing to report their findings to the whole world. Hence, opponents of the efficient markets view of the world always can use evidence that various techniques do not provide investment rewards as proof that the techniques that do work simply are not being reported to the public. This is a problem in *selection bias*; the outcomes we are able to observe have been preselected in favor of failed attempts. Therefore, we cannot fairly evaluate the true ability of portfolio managers to generate winning stock market strategies.

The Lucky Event Issue. In virtually any month it seems we read an article about some investor or investment company with a fantastic investment performance over the recent past. Surely the superior records of such investors disprove the efficient market hypothesis.

Yet this conclusion is far from obvious. As an analogy to the investment game, consider a contest to flip the most number of heads out of 50 trials using a fair coin. The expected outcome for any person is, of course, 50% heads and 50% tails. If 10,000 people, however, compete in this contest, it would not be surprising if at least one or two contestants flipped more than 75% heads. In fact, elementary statistics tells us that the expected number of contestants flipping 75% or more heads would be two. It would be silly, though, to crown these people the "head-flipping champions of the world." Obviously, they are simply the contestants who happened to get lucky on the day of the event. (See the nearby box.)

The analogy to efficient markets is clear. Under the hypothesis that any stock is fairly priced given all available information, any bet on a stock is simply a coin toss. There is equal likelihood of winning or losing the bet. However, if many investors using a variety of schemes make fair bets, statistically speaking, *some* of those investors will be lucky and win a great majority of the bets. For every big winner, there may be many big losers, but we never hear of these managers. The winners, though, turn up in *The Wall Street Journal* as the latest stock market gurus; then they can make a fortune publishing market newsletters.

Our point is that after the fact there will have been at least one successful investment scheme. A doubter will call the results luck, the successful investor will call it skill. The proper test would be to see whether the successful investors can repeat their performance in another period, yet this approach is rarely taken.

With these caveats in mind, we turn now to some of the empirical tests of the efficient market hypothesis.

CONCEPT CHECK

Question 5. Fidelity's Magellan Fund managed by Peter Lynch outperformed the S&P 500 in 11 of the 13 years that Lynch managed the fund, resulting in an average annual return more than 10% better than that of the Index. Is this performance sufficient to dissuade you from a belief in efficient markets? If not, would *any* performance record be sufficient to dissuade you?

Tests of Predictability in Stock Market Returns

Returns over Short Horizons. Early tests of efficient market were tests of the weak form. Could speculators find trends in past prices that would enable them to earn abnormal profits? This is essentially a test of the efficacy of technical analysis.

The already cited work of Kendall and of Roberts,[7] both of whom analyzed the possible existence of patterns in stock prices, suggest that such patterns are not to be found. Fama[8] later analyzed "runs" of stock prices to see whether the stock market exhibits "momentum" that can be exploited. (A run is a sequence of consecutive price increases

---

[7] Harry Roberts, "Stock Market 'Patterns' and Financial Analysis: Methodological Suggestions," *Journal of Finance* 14 (March 1959).

[8] Eugene Fama, "The Behavior of Stock Market Prices," *Journal of Business* 38 (January 1965).

How to Guarantee a Successful Market Newsletter

Suppose you want to make your fortune publishing a market newsletter. You need first to convince potential subscribers that you have talent worth paying for. Ah, but what if you have no talent? The solution is simple: start eight newsletters.

In year 1, let four of your newsletters predict an up-market and four a down-market. In year 2, let half of the originally optimistic group of newsletters continue to predict an up-market and the other half a down-market. Do the same for the originally pessimistic group. Continue in this manner to obtain the pattern of predictions in the table that follows (U = prediction of an up-market, D = prediction of a down-market).

After three years, no matter what has happened to the market, one of the newsletters would have had a prefect prediction record. This is because after three years there are $2^3 = 8$ outcomes for the market, and we have covered all eight possibilities with the eight newsletters. Now, we simply slough off the seven unsuccessful newsletters, and market the eighth newsletter based on its perfect track record. If we want to establish a newsletter with a perfect track record over a four-year period, we need $2^4 = 16$ newsletters. A five-year period requires 32 newsletters, and so on.

After the fact, the one newsletter that was always right will attract attention for your uncanny foresight and investors will rush to pay large fees for its advice. Your fortune is made, and you have never even researched the market!

WARNING: This scheme is illegal! The point, however, is that with hundreds of market newsletters, you can find one that has stumbled onto an apparently remarkable string of successful predictions without any real degree of skill. After the fact, *someone's* prediction history can seem to imply great forecasting skill. This person is the one we will read about in *The Wall Street Journal*; the others will be forgotten.

Newsletter Predictions

Year	1	2	3	4	5	6	7	8
1	U	U	U	U	D	D	D	D
2	U	U	D	D	U	U	D	D
3	U	D	U	D	U	D	U	D

or decreases.) For example, if the last three changes in daily stock prices were positive, could we be more confident that the next move also would be up?

Fama classified daily stock price movements of each of the 30 Dow Jones industrial stocks as positive, zero, or negative in order to test persistence of runs. He found that neither positive nor negative returns persisted to an extent that could contradict the efficient market hypothesis. Although there was some evidence of runs over very short time intervals (less than one day), the tendency for runs to persist was so slight that any attempt to exploit them would generate trading costs in excess of the expected abnormal returns.

Fama's results indicate weak serial correlation in stock market returns. Serial correlation refers to the tendency for stock returns to be related to past returns. Positive serial correlation means that positive returns tend to follow positive returns (a momentum type of property). Negative serial correlation means that positive returns tend to be followed by negative returns (a reversal or "correction" property).

Using more powerful statistical tools, more recent tests have confirmed Fama's results. Both Conrad and Kaul[9] and Lo and MacKinlay[10] examine weekly returns of NYSE stocks and find positive serial correlation over short horizons. However, as in Fama's study, the correlation coefficients of weekly returns tend to be fairly small, at least for large stocks for which price data are the most reliably up-to-date. Thus, while these studies demonstrate weak price trends over short periods, the evidence does not clearly suggest the existence of trading opportunities.

A more sophisticated version of trend analysis is a **filter rule**. A filter technique gives a rule for buying or selling a stock depending on past price movements. One rule, for example, might be: "Buy if the last two trades each resulted in a stock price increase." A more conventional one might be: "Buy a security if its price increased by 1%, and hold it until its price falls by more than 1% from the subsequent high." Alexander[11] and Fama and Blume[12] found that such filter rules generally could not generate trading profits.

The conclusion of the majority of weak-form tests using short-horizon returns is that the efficient market hypothesis is validated by stock market data. To be fair, however, one should note the criticism of efficient market skeptics, who argue that any filter rule or trend analysis that can be tested statistically is overly mechanical and cannot capture the finesse with which human investors can detect subtle but exploitable patterns in past prices.

Returns over Long Horizons. Although studies of short-horizon returns have detected minor positive serial correlation in stock market prices, more recent tests[13] of long-horizon returns (i.e., returns over multiyear periods) have found suggestions of pronounced negative long-term serial correlation. The latter result has given rise to a "fads hypothesis," which asserts that stock prices might overreact to relevant news. Such overreaction leads to positive serial correlation (momentum) over short time horizons. Subsequent correction of the overreaction leads to poor performance following good performance and vice versa. The corrections mean that a run of positive returns eventually will tend to be followed by negative returns, leading to negative serial correlation over longer horizons. These episodes of apparent overshooting followed by correction give stock prices the appearance of fluctuating around their fair values, and suggest that market prices exhibit excessive volatility compared to intrinsic value.[14]

---

[9] Jennifer Conrad and Gautam Kaul, "Time-Variation in Expected Returns," *Journal of Business* 61 (October 1988), pp. 409–25.

[10] Andrew W. Lo and A. Craig MacKinlay, "Stock Market Prices Do Not Follow Random Walks: Evidence from a Simple Specification Test," *Review of Financial Studies* 1 (1988), pp. 41–66.

[11] Sidney Alexander, "Price Movements in Speculative Markets: Trends or Random Walks. No. 2," in Paul Cootner (ed.), *The Random Character of Stock Market Prices* (Cambridge, Mass.: MIT Press, 1964).

[12] Eugene Fama and Marshall Blume, "Filter Rules and Stock Market Trading Profits," *Journal of Business* 39 (Supplement January 1966).

[13] Eugene F. Fama and Kenneth R. French, "Permanent and Temporary Components of Stock Prices," *Journal of Political Economy* 96 (April 1988), pp. 246–73; James Poterba and Lawrence Summers, "Mean Reversion in Stock Prices: Evidence and Implications, *Journal of Financial Economics* 22 (October 1988), pp. 27–59.

[14] The fads debate started as a controversy over excess volatility. See Robert J. Shiller, "Do Stock Prices Move Too Much to Be Justified by Subsequent Changes in Dividends?" *American Economic Review* 71 (June 1971), pp. 421–36. However, it is now apparent that excess volatility and fads are essentially different ways of describing the same phenomenon. For a discussion of this issue, see John H. Cochrane, "Volatility Tests and Efficient Markets: A Review Essay," National Bureau of Economic Research Working Paper No. 3591, January 1991.

These long-horizon results are dramatic, but the studies offer far from conclusive evidence regarding efficient markets. First, the study results need not be interpreted as evidence for stock market fads. An alternative interpretation of these results holds that they indicate only that market risk premiums vary over time. The response of market prices to variation in the risk premium can lead one to incorrectly infer the presence of mean reversion and excess volatility in prices. For example, when the risk premium and the required return on the market rises, stock prices will fall. When the market then rises (on average) at this higher rate of return, the data convey the impression of a stock price recovery. The impression of overshooting and correction is in fact no more than a rational response of market prices to changes in discount rates.

Second, these studies suffer from statistical problems. Because they rely on returns measured over long time periods, these tests of necessity are based on few observations of long-horizon returns. Moreover, it appears that much of the statistical support for mean reversion in stock market prices derives from returns during the Great Depression. Other periods do not provide strong support for the fads hypothesis.[15]

Predictors of Broad Market Returns. Several studies have documented the ability of easily observed variables to predict market returns. For example, Fama and French[16] showed that the return on the aggregate stock market tends to be higher when the dividend/price ratio, the dividend yield, is high. Campbell and Shiller[17] found that the earnings yield can predict market returns. Keim and Stambaugh[18] showed that bond market data such as the spread between yields on high- and low-grade corporate bonds also help predict broad market returns.

Again, the interpretation of these results is difficult. On the one hand, they may imply that stock returns can be predicted, in violation of the efficient market hypothesis. More probably, however, these variables are proxying for variation in the market risk premium. For example, given a level of dividends or earnings, stock prices will be lower and dividend and earnings yields will be higher when the risk premium (and therefore the expected market return) is higher. Thus, a high dividend or earnings yield will be associated with higher market returns. This does not indicate a violation of market efficiency. The predictability of market returns is due to predictability in the risk premium, not in risk-adjusted abnormal returns.

Fama and French[19] showed that the yield spread between high- and low-grade bonds has greater predictive power for returns on low-grade bonds than for returns on high-grade bonds, and greater predictive power for stock returns than for bond returns, sug-

---

[15] Myung J. Kim, Charles R. Nelson, and Richard Startz, "Mean Reversion in Stock Prices? A Reappraisal of the Empirical Evidence," National Bureau of Economic Research Working Paper No. 2795, December 1988.

[16] Eugene F. Fama and Kenneth R. French, "Dividend Yields and Expected Stock Returns," *Journal of Financial Economics* 22 (October 1988), pp. 3–25.

[17] John Y. Campbell and Robert Shiller, "Stock Prices, Earnings and Expected Dividends," *Journal of Finance* 43 (July 1988), pp. 661–76.

[18] Donald B. Keim and Robert F. Stambaugh, "Predicting Returns in the Stock and Bond Markets," *Journal of Financial Economics* 17 (1986), pp. 357–90.

[19] Eugene F. Fama and Kenneth R. French, "Business Conditions and Expected Returns on Stocks and Bonds," *Journal of Financial Economics* 25 (November 1989), pp. 3–22.

gesting that the predictability in returns is in fact a risk premium rather than evidence of market inefficiency. Similarly, the fact that the dividend yield on stocks helps to predict bond market returns suggests that the yield captures a risk premium common to both markets rather than mispricing in the equity market.

Portfolio Strategies and Market Anomalies

Fundamental analysis calls on a much wider range of information to create portfolios than does technical analysis, and tests of the value of fundamental analysis are thus correspondingly more difficult to evaluate. They have, however, revealed a number of so-called anomalies, that is, evidence that seems inconsistent with the efficient market hypothesis. We will review several such anomalies in the following pages.

We must note before starting that one major problem with these tests is that most require risk adjustments to portfolio performance and most tests use the CAPM to make the risk adjustments. We know that although beta seems to be a relevant descriptor of stock risk, the empirically measured quantitative trade-off between risk as measured by beta and expected return differs from the predictions of the CAPM. If we use the CAPM to adjust portfolio returns for risk, we run the risk that inappropriate adjustments will lead to the conclusion that various portfolio strategies can generate superior returns, when in fact it simply is the risk adjustment procedure that has failed.

Another way to put this is to note that tests of risk-adjusted returns are *joint tests* of the efficient market hypothesis *and* the risk adjustment procedure. If it appears that a portfolio strategy can generate superior returns, we must then choose between rejecting the EMH or rejecting the risk adjustment technique. Usually, the risk adjustment technique is based on more questionable assumptions than is the EMH; by opting to reject the procedure, we are left with no conclusion about market efficiency.

An example of this issue is the discovery by Basu[20] that portfolios of low price/earnings ratio stocks have higher returns than do high P/E portfolios. The **P/E effect** holds up even if returns are adjusted for portfolio beta. Is this a confirmation that the market systematically misprices stocks according to P/E ratio? This would be an extremely surprising and, to us, disturbing conclusion, because analysis of P/E ratios is such a simple procedure. Although it may be possible to earn superior returns using hard work and much insight, it hardly seems possible that such a simplistic technique is enough to generate abnormal returns. One possible interpretation of these results is that the model of capital market equilibrium is at fault in that the returns are not properly adjusted for risk.

This makes sense, because if two firms have the same expected earnings, then the riskier stock will sell at a lower price and lower P/E ratio. Because of its higher risk, the low P/E stock also will have higher expected returns. Therefore, unless the CAPM beta fully adjusts for risk, P/E will act as a useful additional descriptor of risk, and will

---

[20] Sanjoy Basu, "The investment Performance of Common Stocks in Relation to Their Price-Earnings Ratios: A Test of the Efficient Market Hypothesis," *Journal of Finance* 32 (June 1977), pp. 663–82; and "The Relationship between Earnings Yield, Market Value, and Return for NYSE Common Stocks: Further Evidence," *Journal of Financial Economics* 12 (June 1983).

be associated with abnormal returns if the CAPM is used to establish benchmark performance.

The Small-Firm Effect. One of the most important anomalies with respect to the efficient market hypothesis is the so-called size, or **small-firm effect**, originally documented by Banz.[21] Banz found that both total and risk-adjusted rates of return tend to fall with increases in the relative size of the firm, as measured by the market value of the firm's outstanding equity. Dividing all NYSE stocks into five quintiles according to firm size, Banz found that the average annual return of firms in the smallest-size quintile was 19.8% greater than the average return of firms in the largest-size quintile.

This is a huge premium; imagine earning a premium of this size on a billion-dollar portfolio. Yet it is remarkable that following a simple (even simplistic) rule such as "invest in low capitalization stocks" should enable an investor to earn excess returns. After all, any investor can measure firm size at little cost. One would not expect such minimal effort to yield such large rewards.

Later studies (Keim,[22] Reinganum,[23] and Blume and Stambaugh[24]) showed that the small-firm effect occurs virtually entirely in January, in fact, in the first two weeks of January. The size effect is in fact a "small-firm-in-January" effect.

Figure 12.7 illustrates the January effect. Keim ranked firms in order of increasing size as measured by market value of equity and then divided them into 10 portfolios grouped by the size of each firm. In each month of the year, he calculated the difference in the average excess return of firms in the smallest-firm portfolio and largest-firm portfolio. The average monthly differences over the years 1963 to 1979 appear in Figure 12.7. January clearly stands out as an exceptional month for small firms, with an average small-firm premium of .714% per day.

The results for the first five trading days in January are even more compelling. The difference in excess returns between the smallest-firm and largest-firm portfolios for the first five trading days of the year are as follows:

Trading Day	Differential Excess Return (Average for 1963–1979)
1	3.20
2	1.68
3	1.25
4	1.14
5	0.89
TOTAL	**8.16**

The total differential return is an amazing 8.16% over only five trading days.

[21] Rolf Banz, "The Relationship between Return and Market Value of Common Stocks," *Journal of Financial Economics* 9 (March 1981).

[22] Donald B. Keim, "Size Related Anomalies and Stock Return Seasonality: Further Empirical Evidence," *Journal of Financial Economics* 12 (June 1983).

[23] Marc R. Reinganum, "The Anomalous Stock Market Behavior of Small Firms in January: Empirical Tests for Tax-Loss Effects," *Journal of Financial Economics* 12 (June 1983).

[24] Marshall E. Blume and Robert F. Stambaugh, "Biases in Computed Returns: An Application to the Size Effect," *Journal of Finance Economics*, 1983.

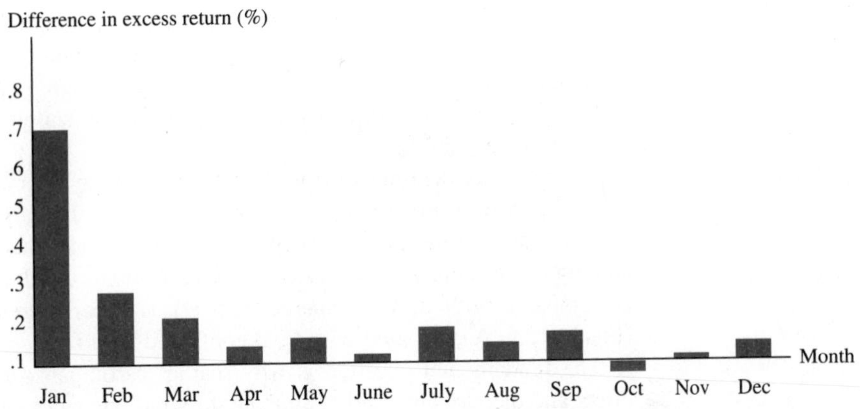

FIGURE 12.7
Average difference between daily excess returns (in percentages) of lowest-firm-size and highest-firm-size deciles for each month between 1963 and 1979.

Source: Data from Donald B. Keim, "Size Related Anomalies and Stock Return Seasonality: Further Empirical Evidence," *Journal of Financial Economics* 12 (June 1983).

Some researchers believe that the January effect is tied to tax-loss selling at the end of the year. The hypothesis is that many people sell stocks that have declined in price during the previous months to realize their capital losses before the end of the tax year. Such investors do not put the proceeds from these sales back into the stock market until after the turn of the year. At that point the rush of demand for stock places an upward pressure on prices that results in the January effect. Indeed, Ritter[25] showed that the ratio of stock purchases to sales of individual investors reaches an annual low at the end of December and an annual high at the beginning of January.

The January effect is said to show up most dramatically for the smallest firms because the small-firm group includes, as an empirical matter, stocks with the greatest variability of prices during the year. The group therefore includes a relatively large number of firms that have declined sufficiently to induce tax-loss selling.

From a theoretical standpoint, this theory has substantial flaws. First, if the positive January effect is a manifestation of buying pressure, it should be matched by a symmetric negative December effect when the tax-loss incentives induce selling pressure. Second, the predictable January effect flies in the face of efficient market theory. If investors who do not already hold these firms know that January will bring abnormal returns to the small-firm group, they should rush to purchase stock in December to capture those returns. This would push buying pressure from January to December. Rational investors should not "allow" such predictable abnormal January returns to persist. However, small firms outperform large ones in January in every year of Keim's study, 1963 to 1979.

Despite these theoretical objections, some empirical evidence supports the belief that the January effect is connected to tax-loss selling. For example, Reinganum found that, within size class, firms that had declined more severely in price had larger January returns. This pattern is illustrated in Figure 12.8. Reinganum divided firms into

25 Jay R. Ritter, "The Buying and Selling Behavior of Individual Investors at the Turn of the Year," *Journal of Finance* 43 (July 1988), pp. 701–17.

quartiles based on the extent to which stock prices had declined during the year. Big price declines would be expected to generate big January returns if these firms tend to be unloaded in December and enjoy demand pressure in January. The figure shows that the lowest quartile (biggest tax loss) portfolios within each size group show the greatest January effect.

A size effect continues to persist, however, even after adjusting for taxes. Small firms that rose in price continue to show abnormal January returns (Figure 12.8, **B**), whereas large firms that declined in price show no special January effect. Hence, although taxes appear to be associated with the abnormal January returns (Figure 12.8, **A** compared with **B**, **C** compared with **D**), size per se remains a factor in January (Figure 12.8, **A** compared with **C**, **B** compared with **D**).

The fundamental question is why market participants do not exploit the January effect and thereby ultimately eliminate it by bidding stock prices to appropriate levels. One possible explanation lies in segmentation of the market into two groups: institutional investors who invest primarily in large firms, and individual investors who invest disproportionately in smaller-sized firms. According to this view, managers of large institutional portfolios are the moving force behind efficient markets. It is professionals who seek out profit opportunities and bid prices to their appropriate levels. Institutional investors do not seem to buy at the small-sized end of the market, perhaps because of limits on allowed portfolio positions, so the small-firm anomaly persists without the force of their participation.

CONCEPT CHECK

Question 6. Does this market segmentation theory get the efficient market hypothesis off the hook, or are there still market mechanisms that in theory ought to act to eliminate the small-firm anomaly?

The Neglected-Firm Effect and Liquidity Effects. Arbel and Strebel[26] gave another interpretation of the small-firm-in-January effect. Because small firms tend to be neglected by large institutional traders, information about smaller firms is less available. This information deficiency makes smaller firms riskier investments that command higher returns. "Brand-name" firms, after all, are subject to considerable monitoring from institutional investors that assures high-quality information, and presumably investors do not purchase "generic" stocks without the prospect of greater returns.

As evidence for the **neglected-firm effect,** Arbel[27] measured the information deficiency of firms using the coefficient of variation of analysts' forecasts of earnings. (The coefficient of variation is the ratio of standard deviation to mean and measures the dispersion of forecasts. It is a "noise-to-signal" ratio.) The correlation coefficient between the coefficient of variation and total return was .676, quite high, and statistically significant. In a related test Arbel divided firms into highly researched, moderately researched, and neglected groups based on the number of institutions holding the stock. Table 12.1 shows that the January effect was largest for the neglected firms.

---

[26] Avner Arbel and Paul J Strebel, "Pay Attention to Neglected Firms," *Journal of Portfolio Management*, Winter 1983.
[27] Avner Arbel, "Generic Stocks: An Old Product in a New Package," *Journal of Portfolio Management*, Summer 1985.

FIGURE 12.8

Average daily returns in January for securities in the upper quartile and bottom quartile of the tax-loss selling distribution by market value of portfolio

Source: Marc R. Reinganum, "The Anomalous Stock Market Behavior of Small Firms in January: Empirical Tests for Tax-Loss Effects," *Journal of Financial Economics* 12 (June 1983).

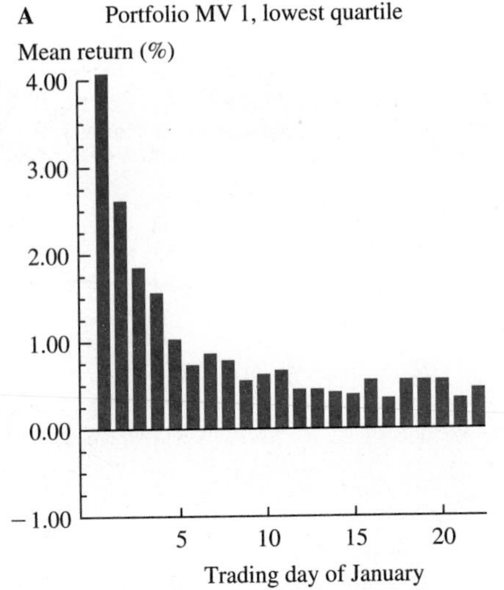

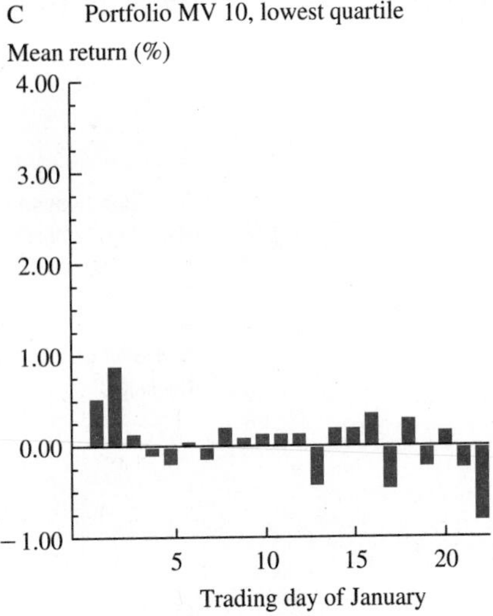

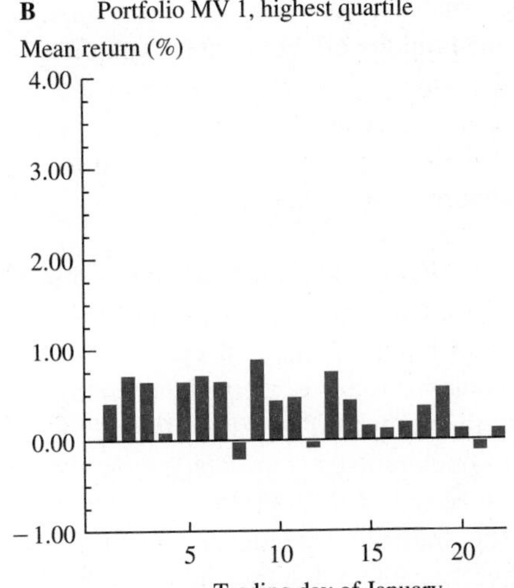

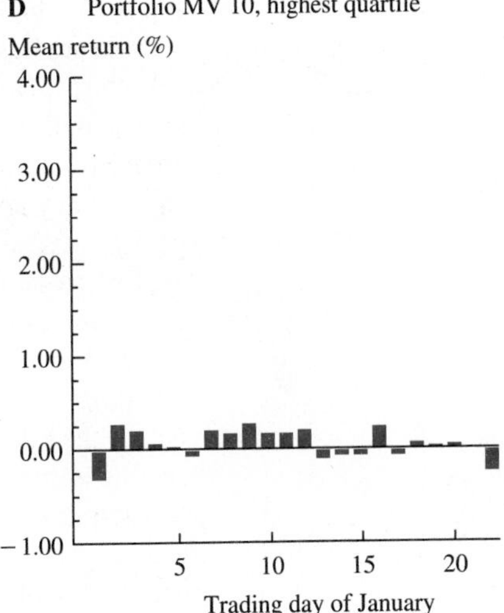

Work by Amihud and Mendelson[28] on the effect of liquidity on stock returns might be related to both the small-firm and neglected-firm effects. They argue that investors will demand a rate-of-return premium to invest in less liquid stocks that entail higher trading costs. (See Chapter 8 for more details.) Indeed, spreads for the least liquid

[28] Yakov Amihud and Haim Mendelson, "Asset Pricing and the Bid-Ask Spread," *Journal of Financial Economics* 17 (December 1986), pp. 223–50; and "Liquidity, Asset Prices, and Financial Policy," *Financial Analysts Journal* 47 (November/December 1991), pp. 56–66.

Table 12.1 January Effect by Degree of Neglect (1971–1980)

	Average January Return (%)	Average January Return Minus Average Return during Rest of Year (%)	Average January Return after Adjusting for Systematic Risk (%)
S&P 500 Companies			
Highly researched	2.48	1.63	−1.44
Moderately researched	4.95	4.19	1.69
Neglected	7.62	6.87	5.03
Non-S&P 500 Companies			
Neglected	11.32	10.72	7.71

Source: Avner Arbel, "Generic Stocks: An Old Product in a New Package," *Journal of Portfolio Management*, Summer 1985.

stocks easily can be more than 5% of stock value. In accord with their hypothesis, Amihud and Mendelson showed that these stocks show a strong tendency to exhibit abnormally high risk-adjusted rates of return. Because small and less-analyzed stocks as a rule are less liquid, the liquidity effect might be a partial explanation of their abnormal returns. However, this theory does not explain why the abnormal returns of small firms should be concentrated in January. In any case, exploiting these effects can be more difficult than it would appear. The high trading costs on small stocks can easily wipe out any apparent abnormal profit opportunity.

Market-to-Book Ratios. Fama and French and Reinganum[29] showed that a powerful predictor of returns across securities is the ratio of the market value of the firm's equity to the book value of equity. Fama and French stratified firms into 10 groups according to market-to-book ratios and examined the average monthly rate of return of each of the 10 groups during the period July 1963 through December 1990. The decile with the lowest market-to-book ratio had an average monthly return of 1.65%, while the highest-ratio decile averaged only 0.72% per month. Figure 12.9 shows the pattern of returns across deciles. The dramatic dependence of returns on market-to-book ratio is independent of beta, suggesting either that low market-to-book ratio firms are relatively underpriced, or that the market-to-book ratio is serving as a proxy for a risk factor that affects equilibrium expected returns.

In fact, Fama and French found that after controlling for the size and market-to-book effects, beta seemed to have no power to explain average security returns. This was a severe blow to modern portfolio theory and its implication that a security's systematic risk should determine its risk premium, and led many to ask, "Is beta dead again?" (See the box in Chapter 11 for a discussion of beta's "first death.")

[29] Eugene F. Fama and Kenneth R. French, "The Cross Section of Expected Stock Returns," *Journal of Finance* 47 (1992), pp. 427–65; Marc R. Reinganum, "The Anatomy of a Stock Market Winner," *Financial Analysts Journal*, March–April 1988, pp. 272–84.

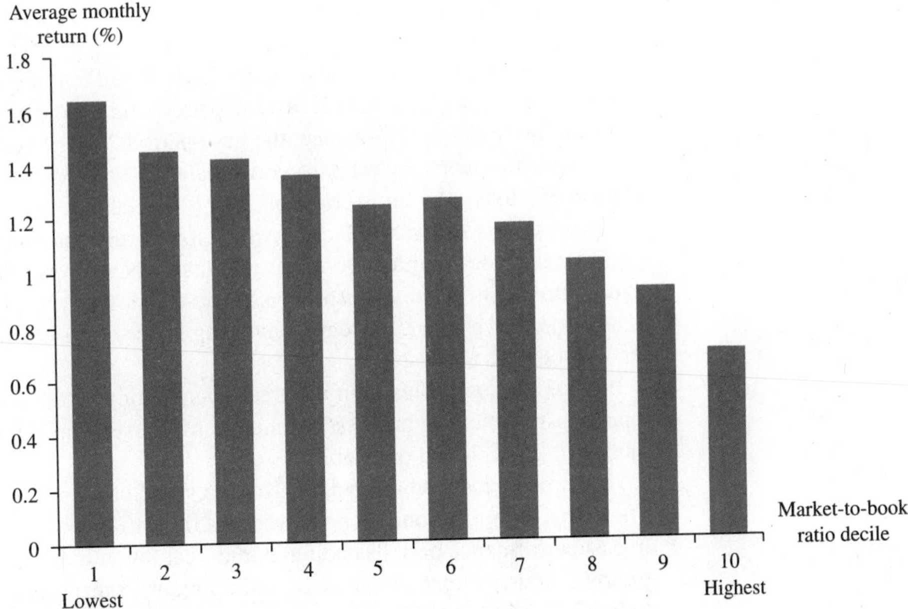

Figure 12.9
Average rate of return as a function of the ratio of market value to book value

Beta seems to have many lives, however. In a recent study, Kothari, Shanken, and Sloan[30] found that securities with high beta values do in fact have higher average returns when betas are estimated using annual rather than monthly returns. Moreover, their study revealed a market-to-book effect that is attenuated compared to the results in Fama and French and is furthermore inconsistent across different samples of securities. Although these results do not disprove a market-to-book effect, Kothari, Shanken, and Sloan concluded that the empirical case for the importance of this ratio may be weaker than the Fama–French study would suggest.

Reversals. We considered above the possibility that the aggregate stock market overreacts to economic news. Several studies have examined the overreaction hypothesis using returns on individual stocks. De Bondt and Thaler,[31] Jegadeesh,[32] Lehmann,[33] and Chopra, Lakonishok, and Ritter[34] all found strong tendencies for poorly performing stocks in one time period to experience sizable reversals over the subsequent

30 S. P. Kothari, Jay Shanken, and Richard G. Sloan, "Another Look at the Cross-Section of Expected Stock Returns," *Journal of Finance* 50 (March 1995), 185–224.
31 Werner F. M. DeBondt, and Richard Thaler, "Does the Stock Market Overreact?" *Journal of Finance* 40 (1985), pp. 793–805.
32 Narasimhan Jegadeesh, "Evidence of Predictable Behavior of Security Returns," *Journal of Finance* 45 (September 1990), pp. 881–98.
33 Bruce Lehmann, "Fads, Martingales and Market Efficiency," *Quarterly Journal of Economics* 105 (February 1990), pp. 1–28.
34 Navin Chopra, Josef Lakonishok, and Jay R. Ritter, "Measuring Abnormal Performance: Do Stocks Overreact?" *Journal of Financial Economics* 31 (1992), pp. 235–68.

period, while the best-performing stocks in a given period tend to follow with poor performance in the following period.

For example, the DeBondt and Thaler study found that if one were to rank order the performance of stocks over a five-year period and then group stocks into portfolios based on investment performance, the base-period "loser" portfolio (defined as the 35 stocks with the worst investment performance) outperformed the "winner" portfolio (the top 35 stocks) by an average of 25% (cumulative return) in the following three-year period. This **reversal effect**, in which losers rebound and winners fade back, suggests that the stock market overreacts to relevant news. After the overreaction is recognized, extreme investment performance is reversed. This phenomenon would imply that a *contrarian* investment strategy—investing in recent losers and avoiding recent winners—should be profitable.

It would be hard to explain apparent overreaction in the cross-section of stocks by appealing to time-varying risk premiums. Moreover, these returns seem pronounced enough to be exploited profitably.

However, a recent study by Ball, Kothari, and Shanken[35] suggested that the reversal effect may be an illusion. They showed that if portfolios are formed by grouping based on past performance periods ending in mid-year rather than in December (a variation in grouping strategy that ought to be unimportant), the reversal effect is substantially diminished. Moreover, the reversal effect seems to be concentrated in very low-priced stocks (e.g., prices of less than $1 per share), for which a bid-ask spread of even $1/8 can have a profound impact on measured return, and for which a liquidity effect may explain high average returns.[36] Finally, the *risk-adjusted* return of the contrarian strategy actually turns out to be statistically indistinguishable from zero, suggesting that the reversal effect is not an unexploited profit opportunity.

The reversal effect also seems to be dependent on the time horizon of the investment. DeBondt and Thaler found reversals over long (multi-year) horizons, and the Jegadeesh and Lehmann studies documented reversals over short horizons of a month or less. However, in an investigation of intermediate horizon stock price behavior (using 3 to 12-month holding periods), Jegadeesh and Titman[37] found that stocks exhibit a momentum property in which good or bad recent performance continues. This of course is the opposite of a reversal phenomenon.

Risk Premiums or Anomalies?

The small firm, market-to-book, and reversal effects are currently among the most puzzling phenomena in empirical finance. There are several interpretations of these effects. First note that to some extent, these three phenomena may be related. The feature that

[35] Ray Ball, S. P. Kothari, and Jan Shanken, "Problems in Measuring Portfolio Performance: An Application to Contrarian Investment Strategies," *Journal of Financial Economics* 37 (1995).

[36] This may explain why the choice of year-end versus mid-year grouping has such a significant impact on the results. Other studies have shown that close-of-year prices on the loser stocks are more likely to be quoted at the bid price. As a result, their initial prices are on average understated, and performance in the follow-up period is correspondingly overstated.

[37] Narasimhan Jegadeesh and Sheridan Titman, "Returns to Buying Winners and Selling Losers: Implications for Stock Market Efficiency," *Journal of Finance* 48 (March 1993), 65–91.

small firms, low market-to-book firms, and recent "losers" seem to have in common is a stock price that has fallen considerably in recent months or years. Indeed, a firm can become a small firm, or a low market-to-book firm by suffering a sharp drop in price. These groups therefore may contain a relatively high proportion of distressed firms that have suffered recent difficulties.

Fama and French[38] argue that these effects can be explained as manifestations of risk premiums. Using an arbitrage pricing type of model they show that stocks with higher "betas" (also known as factor loadings) on size or market-to-book factors have higher average returns; they interpret these returns as evidence of a risk premium associated with the factor. While size or market-to-book ratios per se are obviously not risk factors, they perhaps might act as proxies for more fundamental determinants of risk. Fama and French argue that these phenomena may therefore be consistent with a rational market in which expected returns are consistent with risk.

The opposite interpretation is offered by Lakonishok, Shleifer, and Vishney[39] who argue that these phenomena are evidence of inefficient markets, more specifically, of systematic errors in the forecasts of stock analysts. They believe that analysts extrapolate past performance too far into the future, and therefore overprice firms with recent good performance and underprice firms with recent poor performance. Ultimately, when market participants recognize their errors, prices reverse. This explanation is obviously consistent with the reversal effect, and also to a degree, consistent with the small firm and market-to-book effects because firms with sharp price drops may tend to be small or have low market-to-book ratios.

Daniel and Titman[40] attempt to test whether these effects can in fact be explained as risk premia. They first classify firms according to size and market-to-book ratio, and then further stratify portfolios based on the betas of each stock on size and market-to-book factors. They find that once size and market-to-book ratio are held fixed, the betas on these factors do not add any additional information about expected returns. They conclude that the characteristics per se, and not the betas on the size or market-to-book factors influence returns. This result is inconsistent with the Fama-French interpretation that the high returns on these portfolios may reflect risk premia.

The Daniel and Titman results do not *necessarily* imply irrational markets. As noted, it might be that these characteristics per se measure a distressed condition that itself commands a return premium. Moreover, as we have noted, a good part of these apparently abnormal returns may be reflective of an illiquidity premium since small and low-priced firms tend to have bigger bid-ask spreads. Nevertheless, a compelling explanation of these results has yet to be devised.

The Day-of-the-Week Effect. The small-firm-in-January effect is one example of seasonality in stock market returns, a recurrent pattern of turn-of-the-year abnormal returns. Another recurrent pattern, and in some ways an even odder one, is the

---

[38] Fama, Eugene F. and Kenneth R. French, "Common Risk Factors in the Returns on Stocks and Bonds," *Journal of Financial Economics* 33 (1993), 3–56.

[39] Lakonishok, Josef, Andrei Shleifer, and Robert W. Vishney, "Contrarian Investment, Extrapolation, and Risk," *Journal of Finance* 50 (1995), forthcoming.

[40] Daniel, Kent and Sheridan Titman, "Evidence of the Characteristics of Cross Sectional Variation in Stock Returns," working paper, Boston College, 1995.

weekend effect, documented by French[41] and Gibbons and Hess.[42] These researchers studied the pattern of stock returns from close of trading on Friday afternoon to close on Monday, to determine whether the three-day return spanning the weekend would be three times the typical return on a weekday. This was to be a test of whether the market operates on calendar time or trading time.

Much to their surprise, the typical Friday-to-Monday return was not larger than that of other weekdays—in fact, it was negative! Following is the mean return of the S&P 500 portfolio for each day of the week over the period July 1962 through December 1978. The Monday return is based on closing price Friday to closing price Monday, the Tuesday return is based on Monday closing to Tuesday closing, and so on:

	Monday	Tuesday	Wednesday	Thursday	Friday
Mean return:	−.134%	.002%	.096%	.028%	.084%

The negative Monday effect is extremely large. On an annualized basis, assuming 250 trading days a year, the return is −33.5% (−.134% × 250).

The weekend effect poses a problem for efficient market theorists. In frictionless markets one would expect this recurrent pattern to be "arbitraged away." Specifically, investors would sell stocks short late Friday afternoon, and repurchase them on Monday afternoon at an expected lower price, thereby capturing an abnormal return. The selling on Friday would drive prices down on Friday to a fair level in the sense that the Friday–Monday return would be expected to be positive and commensurate with the risk of the stock market.

In practice of course, such arbitrage activity would not pay. The magnitude of the weekend effect is not nearly large enough to offset the transaction costs involved in short selling and repurchasing the stocks. Hence, market frictions prevent the direct elimination of the weekend effect. Nevertheless, the effect should not be observed in efficient markets, even in the absence of direct arbitrage. If there is a predictable weekend effect, one would expect investors to shy away from purchases on Fridays, delaying them until Monday instead. Conversely, sales of stock originally scheduled for Monday optimally would be pushed up to the preceding Friday. This reshuffling of buying and selling would be enough to increase buy relative to sell pressure on Mondays to the point where the weekend effect would be dissipated. The persistence of the effect seems to indicate that investors have not paid attention to the predictable price pattern.

Inside Information. It would not be surprising if insiders were able to make superior profits trading in their firm's stock. The ability of insiders to trade profitably in their own stock has been documented in studies by Jaffe,[43] Seyhun,[44] Givoly and Palmon,[45]

[41] Kenneth French, "Stock Returns and the Weekend Effect," *Journal of Financial Economics* 8 (March 1980).
[42] Michael Gibbons, and Patrick Hess, "Day of the Week Effects and Asset Returns," *Journal of Business* 54 (October 1981).
[43] Jeffrey F. Jaffe, "Special Information and Insider Trading," *Journal of Business* 47 (July 1974).
[44] H. Nejat Seyhun, "Insiders' Profits, Costs of Trading and Market Efficiency," *Journal of Financial Economics* 16 (1986).

and others. Jaffe's was one of the earlier studies that documented the tendency for stock prices to rise after insiders intensively bought shares and to fall after intensive insider sales.

Can other investors benefit by following insiders' trades? The Securities and Exchange Commission requires all insiders to register their trading activity. The SEC publishes these trades in an *Official Summary of Insider Trading*. Once the *Official Summary* is published, the knowledge of the trades becomes public information. At that point, if markets are efficient, fully and immediately processing the information released in the *Official Summary* of trading, an investor should no longer be able to profit from following the pattern of those trades.

A study by Seyhun, which carefully tracked the public release dates of the *Official Summary*, found that following insider transactions would be to no avail. Although there is some tendency for stock prices to increase even after the *Official Summary* reports insider buying, the abnormal returns are not of sufficient magnitude to overcome transaction costs.

The Value Line Enigma. The Value Line Investment Survey is an investment advisory service that ranks securities on a timeliness scale of one (best buy) to five (sell). Ranks are based on relative earnings and price performance across securities, price momentum, quarterly earnings momentum, and a measure of unexpected earnings in the most recent quarter.

Several studies have examined the predictive value of the Value Line recommendations. Black[46] found that Portfolio 1 (the "buy" portfolio) had a risk-adjusted excess rate of return of 10%, whereas Portfolio 5 (the "sell" portfolio) had an abnormal return of −10%. These results imply a fantastic potential value to the Value Line forecasts. Copeland and Mayers[47] performed a similar study using a more sophisticated risk-adjustment technique, and found that the difference in the risk-adjusted performance of Portfolios 1 and 5 was much smaller; Portfolio 1 earned an abnormal six-month rate of return of 1.52%, whereas Portfolio 5 earned an abnormal return of −2.97%. Even this smaller difference, however, seems to be a substantial deviation from the prediction of the efficient market hypothesis.

Given Value Line's apparent success in predicting stock performance, we would expect that changes in Value Line's timeliness rankings would result in abnormal returns for affected stocks. This seems to be the case. Stickel[48] showed that Value Line rerankings generally are followed by abnormal stock returns in the expected direction. Interestingly enough, smaller firms tend to respond with greater sensitivity to rerankings. This pattern is consistent with the neglected-firm effect in that the

---

45 Dan Givoly and Dan Palmon, "Insider Trading and Exploitation of Inside Information: Some Empirical Evidence," *Journal of Business* 58 (1985).

46 Fischer Black, "Yes, Virginia, There is Hope: Test of the Value Line Ranking System," Graduate School of Business, University of Chicago, 1971.

47 Thomas E. Copeland, and David Mayers, "The Value Line Enigma (1965–1978): A Case Study of Performance Evaluation Issues," *Journal of Financial Economics* 11 (November 1982).

48 Scott E. Stickel, "The Effect of Value Line Investment Survey Rank Changes on Common Stock Prices," *Journal of Financial Economics* 14 (1985).

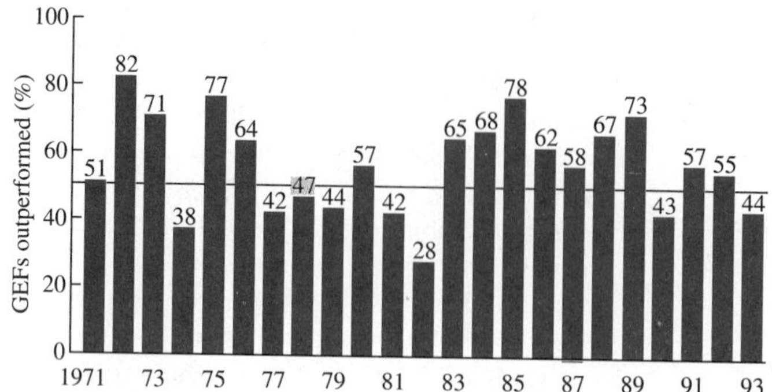

Figure 12.10 General equity funds outperformed by the Wilshire 5000 (1972–93)

Source: John C. Bogle, *Bogle on Mutual Funds: New Perspective for the Intelligent Investor* (New York: Irwin Professional Publishing), 1994.

information contained in a reranking carries greater weight for firms that are less intensively monitored.

The Market Crash of October 1987. The market crash of October 1987 seems to be a glaring counterexample to the efficient market hypothesis. If prices reflect market fundamentals, then defenders of the EMH must look for news on October 19 consistent with the 23% one-day decline in stock prices. Yet no events of such importance seem to have transpired on that date. The fantastic price swing is hard to reconcile with market fundamentals.

CONCEPT CHECK Question 7. Some say that continued worry concerning the U.S. trade deficit brought down the market on October 19. Is this explanation consistent with EMH?

Mutual Fund Performance. We have documented some of the apparent chinks in the armor of efficient market proponents. Ultimately, however, the issue of market efficiency boils down to whether skilled investors can make consistent abnormal trading profits. The best test is simply to look at the performance of market professionals to see if their performance is superior to that of a passive index fund that buys and holds the market.

Casual evidence does not support claims that professionally managed portfolios can consistently beat the market. In the decade ended in 1993, less than 30% of equity fund managers outperformed the Wilshire 5000 Index. Figure 12.10 shows year by year the percentage of mutual fund managers whose performance was inferior to the Wilshire 5000. Figure 12.11 shows the cumulative return of the Wilshire 5000 over these two decades compared to both the average general equity fund and the median equity pension fund. The annualized return of the Wilshire 5000 was 12.0% versus about 10.85% for the managed funds. The 1.15 percentage point margin is substantial. Even after accounting for a typical expense ratio for an index fund of .25% per year, a Wilshire 5000 index fund would have outperformed the typical actively managed equity fund by almost 1 percentage point per year.

Figure 12.11

Total stock market versus average general equity mutual fund and average equity pension fund—cumulative returns (1971–93)

Source: John C. Bogle, *Bogle on Mutual Funds: New Perspective for the Intelligent Investor* (New York: Irwin Professional Publishing), 1994.

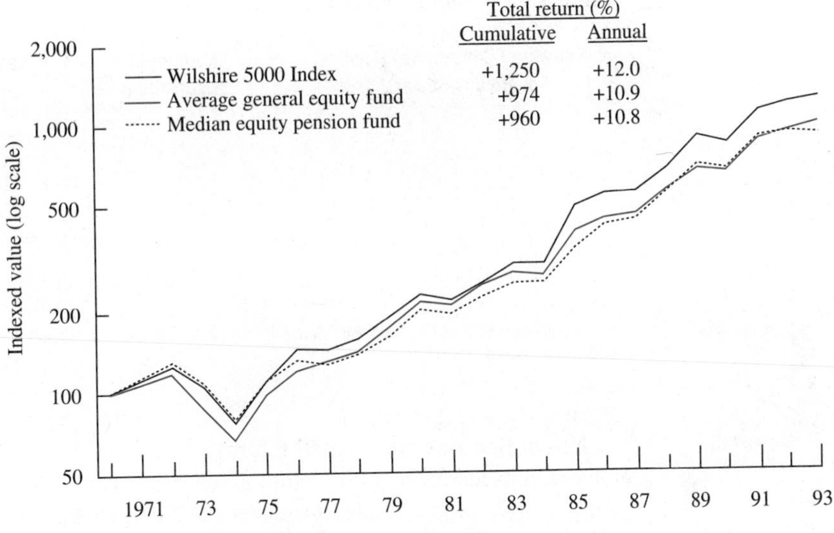

Figure 12.12

Bond funds versus Lehman Bond Index—cumulative returns (1983–92)

Source: John C. Bogle, *Bogle on Mutual Funds: New Perspective for the Intelligent Investor* (New York: Irwin Professional Publishing), 1994.

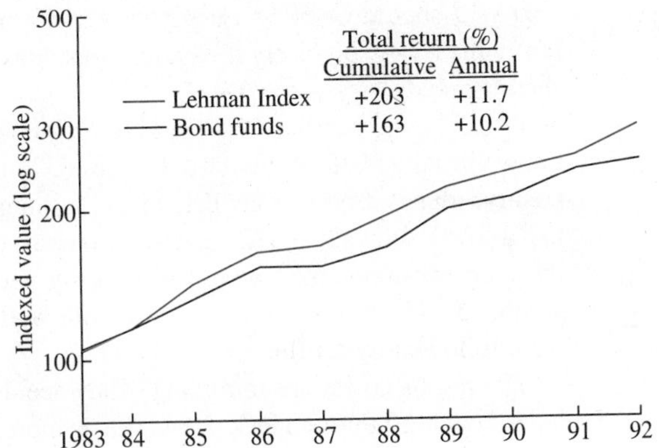

A similar pattern emerges for bonds. Figure 12.12 shows that the Lehman Brothers Bond Index outperformed the typical managed bond fund by about 1.5 percentage points per year in the decade ending in 1992.

Of course, one might argue that there are good managers and bad managers, and that the good managers can, in fact, consistently outperform the index. The real test of this notion is to see whether managers with good performance in a given year can repeat that performance in a following year. In other words, is the abnormal performance due to luck or skill? Jensen[49] performed such a test using 10 years of data on 115 mutual funds, a total of 1,150 annual observations.

[49] Michael C. Jensen, "Risk, the Pricing of Capital Assets, and the Evaluation of Investment Portfolios," *Journal of Business* 42 (April 1969).

Table 12.2 Mutual Fund Performance

Number of Consecutive Positive Alphas So Far	Number of Observations	Cases in Which the Next Alpha Is Positive (%)
1	574	50.4
2	312	52.0
3	161	53.4
4	79	55.8
5	41	46.4
6	17	35.3

Source: Michael C. Jensen, "Risk, the Pricing of Capital Assets, and the Evaluation of Investment Portfolios," *Journal of Business* 42 (April 1969).

Jensen first risk-adjusted all returns using the CAPM to obtain portfolio alphas, or returns in excess of required return given risk. Then he tested to see whether managers with positive alphas tended to repeat their performance in later years. If markets are efficient, and abnormal performance is due solely to the luck of the draw, the probability of following superior performance in a given year with superior performance the next year should be 50%: Each year's abnormal return is essentially like the toss of a fair coin. This is precisely the pattern that Jensen found. Table 12.2 is reproduced from Jensen's study.

In row 1, we see that 574 positive alphas were observed out of the 1,150 observations, virtually 50% on the nose. Of these 574 positive alphas, 50.4% were followed by positive alphas. So far, it appears that obtaining a positive alpha is pure luck, like a coin toss. Row 2 shows that 312 cases of two consecutive positive alphas were observed. Of these observations, 52% were followed by yet another positive alpha. Continuing, we see that 53.4% of three-in-a-row were followed by a fourth, and 55.8% of four-in-a-row were followed by a fifth.

The results so far are intriguing. They seem to suggest that most positive alphas are indeed obtained through luck. However, as more and more stringent filters are applied, the remaining managers show greater tendency to follow good performance with more good performance. This might suggest that there are a few, rare, superior managers who can consistently beat the market. However, at this point, the pattern collapses. Only 46.4% of the five-in-a-row group repeats the superior performance. Yet the sample size for this group is too small to make statistically precise inferences about the population of managers.

The ultimate interpretation of these results is thus to some extent a matter of faith. However, it seems clear that it is not wise to invest with an actively managed fund chosen at random. The average alpha of all funds was slightly negative even *before* subtracting all the costs of management.

A more recent study performed by Frank Russell Company, reported in *The Wall Street Journal*, examined the consistency of performance of more than 100 equity managers. The question posed is whether managers that performed well in one period tend to perform well in subsequent periods. In other words, is performance consistent across time? To answer this question, the sample of managers were ranked according to total

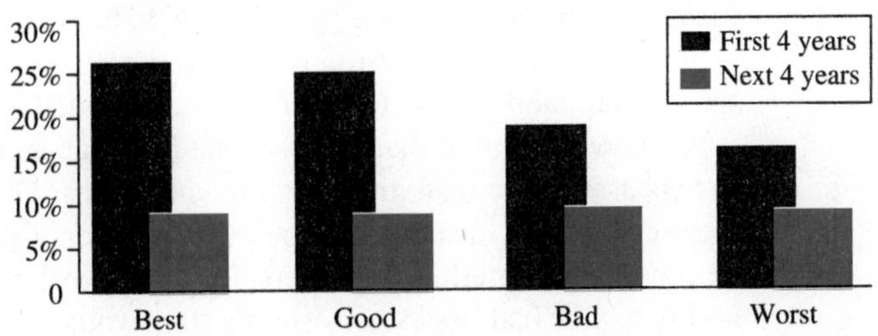

Figure 12.13 Performance consistency of equity managers

return in the 1983–1986 period. The managers were assigned to one of four groups based on their base-period performance. Then the performance of each group was computed in the 1987–1990 period. Figure 12.13 shows that the best performers in the 1983–1986 base period performed no better in 1987–1990 than the worst performers in the base period. The implication is that past performance has little predictive power concerning future performance. A similar conclusion was reached in an earlier study by Dunn and Theisen.[50]

More recent studies of the performance of mutual funds have reached mixed conclusions. Ippolito[51] examined returns of 143 mutual funds over the 1965–1984 period, and found that returns net of expenses and fees (but not net of loads) provided an average alpha across funds of 0.83%. On the other hand, the performance of most funds was not statistically significantly different from that of a purely passive strategy. The alphas of 127 funds were statistically indistinguishable from zero. Four funds had alphas significantly negative and 12 had significantly positive alphas.

In contrast, Brinson, Hood, and Beebower[52] found that portfolio returns of 91 pension plans were harmed by attempts at active management. They compared actual returns to a benchmark computed by assuming plan managers had held indexed portfolios for the bond and stock sectors of their portfolios and had maintained constant weights across market sectors. They concluded that deviations from indexed positions within each market reduced average returns by 0.36%, and that attempts to time the relative performance of fixed income versus equity markets reduced average returns by 0.66%.

Grinblatt and Titman[53] found evidence of abnormal returns and persistence of performance using five-year investment returns, but such persistence does not seem strong enough to be useful in forming investment strategies. Hendricks, Patel, and Zeckhauser[54] also documented some evidence of persistence. They found that invest-

[50] Patricia Dunn, and Rolf D. Theisen, "How Consistently Do Active Managers Win?" *Journal of Portfolio Management* 9 (Summer 1983).

[51] Richard A. Ippolito, "Efficiency with Costly Information: A Study of Mutual Fund Performance, 1965–1984," *Quarterly Journal of Economics* 104 (February 1989), pp. 1–24.

[52] Gary P. Brinson, L. Randolph Hood, and Gilbert L. Beebower, "Determinants of Portfolio Performance," *Financial Analysts Journal* 42 (July/August 1986), pp. 39–44.

[53] Mark Grinblatt and Sheridan Titman, "Mutual Fund Performance: An Analysis of Quarterly Portfolio Holdings, *Journal of Business* 62 (1989), pp. 393–416.

[54] Darryll Hendricks, Jayendu Patel, and Richard Zeckhauser, "Hot Hands in Mutual Funds: Short-Run Persistence of Relative Performance, 1974–1988," *Journal of Finance* 43 (March 1993), pp. 93–130.

ment performance in a base period tends to be predictive of performance over the next year, but no longer. Interestingly, poor performers in their study continued to underperform significantly while top performers continued to outperform but less dramatically.

Carhart[55] reported that much of the persistence in mutual fund performance is due to expenses rather than gross investment returns. This last point is important; although there can be no consistently superior performers in a fully efficient market, there *can* be consistently inferior performers. Repeated weak performance would not be due to an ability to pick bad stocks consistently (that would be impossible in an efficient market!) but could result from a consistently high expense ratio and consistently high portfolio turnover with the resulting trading costs. In this regard, it is interesting that Hendricks, Patel, and Zeckhauser also reported that the strongest consistency was found among the weakest performers. Nevertheless, even allowing for expenses, some amount of performance persistence seems to be due to differences in investment strategy. Carhart found, however, that the evidence of persistence is concentrated at the two extremes. This suggests that there may be a small group of exceptional managers who can with some consistency outperform a passive strategy, but that for the majority of managers, over- or underperformance in any period is largely a matter of chance.

In contrast to the extensive studies of equity fund managers, there have been very few studies on the performance of bond fund managers. In a recent paper, however, Blake, Elton, and Gruber[56] examined the performance of fixed-income mutual funds. They found that, on average, bond funds underperform passive fixed income indexes by an amount roughly equal to expenses, and that there is no evidence that past performance can predict future performance. Their evidence is consistent with the hypothesis that bond managers operate in an efficient market in which performance before expenses is only as good as that of a passive index.

Thus, the evidence on the risk-adjusted performance of professional managers is mixed at best. We conclude that the performance of professional managers is broadly consistent with market efficiency. The amounts by which professional managers as a group beat or are beaten by the market fall within the margin of statistical uncertainty. In any event, it is quite clear that performance superior to passive strategies is far from routine. Studies show either that most managers cannot outperform passive strategies, or that if there is a margin of superiority, it is small.

On the other hand, a small number of investment superstars—Peter Lynch (formerly of Fidelity's Magellan Fund), Warren Buffet (of Berkshire Hathaway), John Templeton (of Templeton Funds), and John Neff (of Vanguard's Windsor Fund) among them—have compiled career records that show a consistency of superior performance hard to reconcile with absolutely efficient markets. Nobel prize winner Paul Samuelson[57] reviewed this investment hall of fame but pointed out that the records of the vast majority of professional money managers offer convincing evidence that there are no easy strategies to guarantee success in the securities markets.

---

[55] Mark M. Carhart, "Persistence in Mutual Fund Performance Re-examined," University of Chicago, mimeo, 1992 and "On Persistence in Mutual Fund Performance," University of Chicago, mimeo, 1994.

[56] Christopher R. Blake, Edwin J. Elton, and Martin J. Gruber, "The Performance of Bond Mutual Funds," *Journal of Business* 66 (July 1993), pp. 371–404.

[57] Paul Samuelson, "The Judgment of Economic Science on Rational Portfolio Management," *Journal of Portfolio Management* 16 (Fall 1989), pp. 4–12.

So, Are Markets Efficient?

There is a telling joke about two economists walking down the street. They spot a $20 bill on the sidewalk. One starts to pick it up, but the other one says, "Don't bother; if the bill were real someone would have picked it up already."

The lesson is clear. An overly doctrinaire belief in efficient markets can paralyze the investor and make it appear that no research effort can be justified. This extreme view is probably unwarranted. There are enough anomalies in the empirical evidence to justify the search for underpriced securities that clearly goes on.

The bulk of the evidence, however, suggests that any supposedly superior investment strategy should be taken with many grains of salt. The market is competitive *enough* that only differentially superior information or insight will earn money; the easy pickings have been picked. In the end it is likely that the margin of superiority that any professional manager can add is so slight that the statistician will not easily be able to detect it.

We conclude that markets are very efficient, but that rewards to the especially diligent, intelligent, or creative may in fact be waiting.

Summary

1. Statistical research has shown that stock prices seem to follow a random walk with no discernible predictable patterns that investors can exploit. Such findings are now taken to be evidence of market efficiency, that is, of evidence that market prices reflect all currently available information. Only new information will move stock prices, and this information is equally likely to be good news or bad news.

2. Market participants distinguish among three forms of the efficient market hypothesis. The weak form asserts that all information to be derived from past stock prices already is reflected in stock prices. The semistrong form claims that all publicly available information is already reflected. The strong form, which generally is acknowledged to be extreme, asserts that all information, including insider information, is reflected in prices.

3. Technical analysis focuses on stock price patterns and on proxies for buy or sell pressure in the market. Fundamental analysis focuses on the determinants of the underlying value of the firm, such as current profitability and growth prospects. Because both types of analysis are based on public information, neither should generate excess profits if markets are operating efficiently.

4. Proponents of the efficient market hypothesis often advocate passive as opposed to active investment strategies. The policy of passive investors is to buy and hold a broad-based market index. They expend resources neither on market research nor on frequent purchase and sale of stocks. Passive strategies may be tailored to meet individual investor requirements.

5. Event studies are used to evaluate the economic impact of events of interest, using abnormal stock returns. Such studies usually show that there is some leakage of inside information to some market participants before the public announcement date. Therefore, insiders do seem to be able to exploit their access to information to at least a limited extent.

6. Empirical studies of technical analysis do not support the hypothesis that such analysis can generate superior trading profits. Only very short-term filters seem to offer any hope for profits, yet these are extremely expensive in terms of trading costs.

7. Several anomalies regarding fundamental analysis have been uncovered. These include the P/E effect, the small-firm-in-January effect, the neglected-firm effect, the weekend effect, the reversal effect, and the market-to-book effect. Whether these anomalies represent market inefficiency or poorly understood risk premia is still a matter of debate.

8. By and large, the performance record of professionally managed funds lends little credence to claims that professionals can consistently beat the market.

Key Terms

Random walk
Efficient market hypothesis
Weak-form EMH
Semistrong-form EMH
Strong-form EMH
Technical analysis
Dow theory
Resistance levels
Support levels
Fundamental analysis
Passive investment strategy
Index fund
Event study
Abnormal return
Cumulative abnormal return
Filter rule
P/E effect
Small-firm effect
Neglected-firm effect
Reversal effect
Weekend effect

Selected Readings

One of the best treatments of the efficient market hypothesis is:

Malkiel, Burton G. *A Random Walk Down Wall Street.* New York: W.W. Norton & Co., 1990. This paperback book provides an entertaining and insightful treatment of the ideas presented in this chapter as well as fascinating historical examples of securities markets in action.

A more rigorous introduction to the theoretical underpinnings of the EMH, as well as a review of early empirical work, may be found in:

Fama, Eugene F. "Efficient Capital Markets: A Review of Theory and Empirical Work." *Journal of Finance* 25 (May 1970).

A more recent survey is:

Fama, Eugene F. "Efficient Capital Markets: II." *Journal of Finance* 46 (December 1991).

Problems

1. If markets are efficient, what should be the correlation coefficient between stock returns for two nonoverlapping time periods?
2. Which of the following most appears to contradict the proposition that the stock market is *weakly* efficient? Explain.
   a. Over 25% of mutual funds outperform the market on average.
   b. Insiders earn abnormal trading profits.
   c. Every January, the stock market earns above-normal returns.

3. Suppose that, after conducting an analysis of past stock prices, you come up with the following observations. Which would appear to *contradict* the *weak* form of the efficient market hypothesis? Explain.
   a. The average rate of return is significantly greater than zero.
   b. The correlation between the return during a given week and the return during the following week is zero.
   c. One could have made superior returns by buying stock after a 10% rise in price and selling after a 10% fall.
   d. One could have made higher than average capital gains by holding stock with low dividend yields.
4. Which of the following statements are true if the efficient market hypothesis holds?
   a. It implies that future events can be forecast with perfect accuracy.
   b. It implies that prices reflect all available information.
   c. It implies that security prices change for no discernible reason.
   d. It implies that prices do not fluctuate.
5. Which of the following observations would provide evidence *against* the *semi-strong form* of the efficient market theory? Explain.
   a. Mutual fund managers do not on average make superior returns.
   b. You cannot make superior profits by buying (or selling) stocks after the announcement of an abnormal rise in dividends.
   c. Low P/E stocks tend to have positive abnormal returns.
   d. In any year approximately 50% of pension funds outperform the market.

Questions 6–10 are taken from past CFA exams.*

6. The semistrong form of the efficient market hypothesis asserts that stock prices:
   a. Fully reflect all historical price information.
   b. Fully reflect all publicly available information.
   c. Fully reflect all relevant information including insider information.
   d. May be predictable.
7. Assume that a company announces an unexpectedly large cash dividend to its shareholders. In an efficient market *without* information leakage, one might expect:
   a. An abnormal price change at the announcement.
   b. An abnormal price increase before the announcement.
   c. An abnormal price decrease after the announcement.
   d. No abnormal price change before or after the announcement.
8. Which *one* of the following would provide evidence *against* the semistrong form of the efficient market theory?
   a. About 50% of pension funds outperform the market in any year.
   b. All investors have learned to exploit signals about future performance.
   c. Trend analysis is worthless in determining stock prices.
   d. Low P/E stocks tend to have positive abnormal returns over the long run.
9. According to the efficient market hypothesis:

*Reprinted, with permission, from the Level I 1993 *CFA Study Guide*. Copyright 1993, Association for Investment Management and Research, Charlottesville, VA. All rights reserved.

a. High-beta stocks are consistently overpriced.
b. Low-beta stocks are consistently overpriced.
c. Positive alphas on stocks will quickly disappear.
d. Negative alpha stocks consistently yield low returns for arbitrageurs.

10. A "random walk" occurs when:
    a. Stock price changes are random but predictable.
    b. Stock prices respond slowly to both new and old information.
    c. Future price changes are uncorrelated with past price changes.
    d. Past information is useful in predicting future prices.
11. A successful firm like Wal-Mart has consistently generated large profits for years. Is this a violation of the EMH?
12. Suppose you find that prices of stocks before large dividend increases show on average consistently positive abnormal returns. Is this a violation of the EMH?
13. "If the business cycle is predictable, and a stock has a positive beta, the stock's returns also must be predictable." Respond.
14. Which of the following phenomena would be either consistent with or a violation of the efficient market hypothesis? Explain briefly.
    a. Nearly half of all professionally managed mutual funds are able to outperform the S&P 500 in a typical year.
    b. Money managers that outperform the market (on a risk-adjusted basis) in one year are likely to outperform in the following year.
    c. Stock prices tend to be predictably more volatile in January than in other months.
    d. Stock prices of companies that announce increased earnings in January tend to outperform the market in February.
    e. Stocks that perform well in one week perform poorly in the following week.
15. "If all securities are fairly priced, all must offer equal market rates of return." Comment.
16. An index model regression applied to past monthly returns in General Motors' stock price produces the following estimates, which are believed to be stable over time:

    $$r_{\text{GM}} = 0.10\% + 1.1 r_M$$

    If the market index subsequently rises by 8% and General Motors' stock price rises by 7%, what is the abnormal change in General Motors' stock price?
17. The monthly rate of return on T-bills is 1%. The market went up this month by 1.5%. In addition, AmbChaser, Inc., which has an equity beta of 2, surprisingly just won a lawsuit that awards it $1 million immediately.
    a. If the original value of AmbChaser equity were $100 million, what would you guess was the rate of return of its stock this month?
    b. What is your answer to (*a*) if the market had expected AmbChaser to win $2 million?
18. In a recent closely contested lawsuit, Apex sued Bpex for patent infringement. The jury came back today with its decision. The rate of return on Apex was $r_A = 3.1\%$. The rate of return on Bpex was only $r_B = 2.5\%$. The market today responded to very encouraging news about the unemployment rate, and $r_M =$

3%. The historical relationship between returns on these stocks and the market portfolio has been estimated from index model regressions as:

$$\text{Apex: } r_A = 0.2\% + 1.4r_M$$
$$\text{Bpex: } r_B = -0.1\% + 0.6r_M$$

Based on these data, which company do you think won the lawsuit?

19. Investors *expect* the market rate of return in the coming year to be 12%. The T-bill rate is 4%. Changing Fortunes Industries' stock has a beta of 0.5. The market value of its outstanding equity is $100 million.

a. What is your best guess currently as to the expected rate of return on Changing Fortunes' stock? You believe that the stock is fairly priced.

b. If the market return in the coming year actually turns out to be 10%, what is your best guess as to the rate of return that will be earned on Changing Fortunes' stock?

c. Suppose now that Changing Fortunes, wins a major lawsuit during the year. The settlement is $5 million. Changing Fortunes' stock return during the year turns out to be 10%. What is your best guess as to the settlement the market previously *expected* Changing Fortunes to receive from the lawsuit? (Continue to assume that the market return in the year turned out to be 10%.) The magnitude of the lawsuit is the only unexpected firm-specific event during the year.

20. Dollar-cost averaging means that you buy equal dollar amounts of a stock every period, for example, $500 per month. The strategy is based on the idea that when the stock price is low, your fixed monthly purchase will buy more shares, and when the price is high, fewer shares. Averaging over time, you will end up buying more shares when the stock is cheaper and fewer when it is relatively expensive. Therefore, by design, you will exhibit good market timing. Evaluate this strategy.

21. Steady Growth Industries has never missed a dividend payment in its 94-year history. Does this make it more attractive to you as a possible purchase for your stock portfolio?

22. We know that the market should respond positively to good news, and that good-news events such as the coming end of a recession can be predicted with at least some accuracy. Why, then, can we not predict that the market will go up as the economy recovers?

23. If prices are as likely to increase as decrease, why do investors earn positive returns from the market on average?

24. You know that firm XYZ is very poorly run. On a scale of 1 (worst) to 10 (best), you would give it a score of 3. The market consensus evaluation is that the management score is only 2. Should you buy or sell the stock?

25. Examine the accompanying figure,[58] which presents cumulative abnormal returns both before and after dates on which insiders buy or sell shares in their

[58] From Nejat H. Seyhun, "Insiders, Profits, Costs of Trading and Market Efficiency," *Journal of Financial Economics* 16 (1986).

firms. How do you interpret this figure? What are we to make of the pattern of CARs before and after the event date?

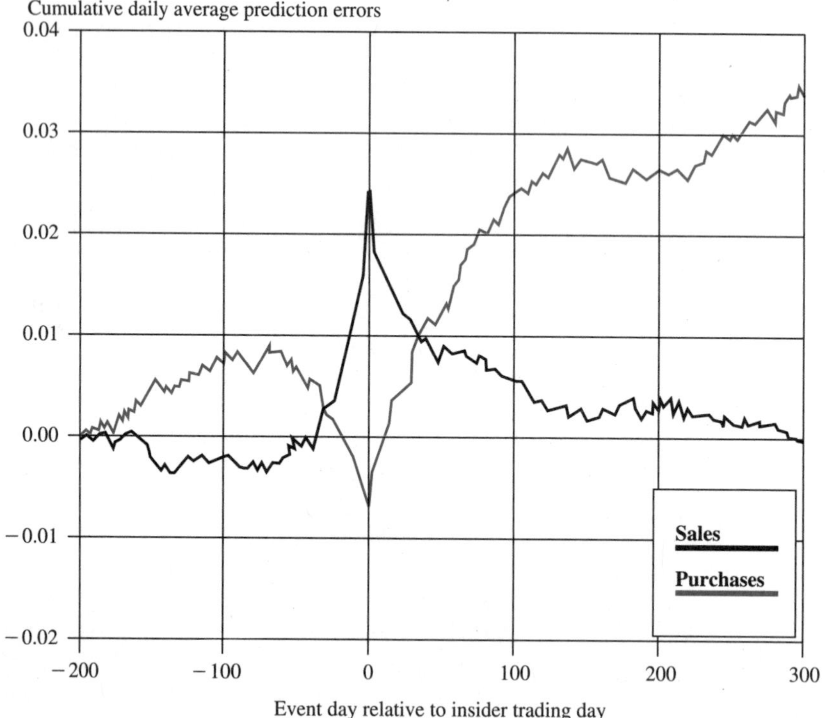

26. Suppose that during a certain week the Fed announces a new monetary growth policy, Congress surprisingly passes legislation restricting imports of foreign automobiles, and Ford comes out with a new car model that it believes will increase profits substantially. How might you go about measuring the market's assessment of Ford's new model?
27. Good News, Inc. just announced an increase in its annual earnings, yet its stock price fell. Is there a rational explanation for this phenomenon?
28. Some authors contend that professional managers are incapable of outperforming the market. Others come to an opposite conclusion. Compare and contrast the assumptions about the stock market that support (1) passive portfolio management, and (2) active portfolio management.

The following information should be used in solving problems 29 and 30:

As director of research for a medium-sized investment firm, Jeff Cheney was concerned about the mediocre investment results experienced by the firm in recent years. He met with his two senior equity analysts to consider alternatives to the stock selection techniques employed in the past.

One of the analysts suggested that the current literature has examined the relationship between price/earnings ratios (P/E) and securities returns. A number of studies had concluded that high P/E stocks tended to have higher betas and lower risk-adjusted returns than stocks with low P/E ratios.

The analyst also referred to recent studies analyzing the relationship between security returns and company size as measured by equity capitalization. The studies concluded that when compared to the S&P 500 Index, small-capitalization stocks tended to provide above-average risk-adjusted returns, whereas large-capitalization stocks tended to provide below-average risk-adjusted returns. It was further noted that little correlation was found to exist between a company's P/E ratio and the size of its equity capitalization.

Jeff's firm has employed a strategy of complete diversification and the use of beta as a measure of portfolio risk. He and his analysts were intrigued as to how these recent studies might be applied to their stock selection techniques and thereby improve their performance. Given the results of the studies indicated above:

29. Explain how the results of these studies might be used in the stock selection and portfolio management process. Briefly discuss the effects on the objectives of diversification and on the measurement of portfolio risk.

30. List the reasons and briefly discuss why this firm might *not* want to adopt a new strategy based on these studies in place of their current strategy of complete diversification and the use of beta as a measure of portfolio risk.

31. You are a portfolio manager meeting a client. During the conversation that followed your formal review of her account, your client asked the following question:

> My grandson, who is studying investments, tells me that one of the best ways to make money in the stock market is to buy the stocks of small-capitalization firms on a Monday morning late in December and to sell the stocks one month later. What is he talking about?

a. Identify the apparent market anomalies that would justify the proposed strategy.

b. *Explain* why you believe such a strategy might or might not work in the future.

32. Use data from U.S. Equities OnFloppy to rank firms based on one of these criteria:

a. Market to book ratio (ratio of stock price to book value per share).

b. Price-earnings ratio.

c. Market capitalization (size).

d. Institutional holdings.

e. A criterion that interests you.

Divide firms into 10 groups based on their ranking for the criterion you choose, and calculate the average rate of return of the firms in each group. Do you confirm or reject any of the anomalies cited in this chapter? Can you uncover a new anomaly? *Note:* For your test to be valid, you must form your portfolios based on criteria observed at the *beginning* of the period when you form the stock groups. (Why?)

33. Use U.S. Equities OnFloppy to calculate the average beta of the firms in each group in Question 32. Use this value, the T-bill rate, and a reasonable estimate of the market risk premium to calculate the risk-adjusted abnormal return of each group. Does the anomaly remain even after risk adjusting?

34. Now form stock groups that use more than one criterion simultaneously. For example, form a portfolio of stocks that are both in the lowest quartile of price-earnings ratios and in the lowest quartile of market-to-book ratio. Does selecting portfolios based on more than one characteristic improve the ability to form portfolios with abnormal returns?

Part IV

Fixed-Income Securities

Chapter 13
Bond Prices and Yields

IN THE PREVIOUS CHAPTERS ON RISK AND RETURN RELATIONSHIPS, WE HAVE TREATED SECURITIES AT A HIGH LEVEL OF ABSTRACTION. We have assumed implicitly that a prior, detailed analysis of each security already has been performed, and that its risk and return features have been assessed.

We turn now to specific analyses of particular security markets. We examine valuation principles, determinants of risk and return, and portfolio strategies commonly used within and across the various markets.

We begin by analyzing **fixed-income securities.** A fixed-income security is a claim on a specified periodic stream of income. Fixed-income securities have the advantage of being relatively easy to understand because the level of payments is fixed in advance. Risk considerations are minimal as long as the issuer of the security is sufficiently creditworthy. That makes these securities a convenient starting point for our analysis of the universe of potential investment vehicles.

The bond is the basic fixed-income security, and this chapter reviews the principles of bond pricing. We show how bond prices are set in accordance with market interest rates, and why bond prices change with those rates. After examining the Treasury bond market, where default risk may be ignored, we move to the corporate bond sector. Here, we look at the determinants of credit risk and the default premium built into bond yields. We examine the impact of call and convertibility provisions on prices and yields. Finally, we discuss certain tax rules that apply to fixed income investments, and show how to calculate after-tax returns.

13.1 Bond Characteristics

A **bond** is a borrowing arrangement in which the borrower issues (sells) an IOU to the investor. The arrangement obligates the issuer to make specified payments to the bondholder on specified dates. A typical *coupon bond* obligates the issuer to make semiannual payments of interest, called coupon payments, to the bondholder for the life of the bond, and then to pay in addition the bond's **par value** (equivalently, **face value**) at the bond's maturity date. The **coupon rate** of the bond is the coupon payment divided by the bond's par value.

To illustrate, a bond with par value of $1,000 and coupon rate of 8% might be sold to a buyer for $1,000. The bondholder is then entitled to a payment of 8% of $1,000, or $80 per year, for the stated life of the bond, say 30 years. The $80 payment typically comes in two semiannual installments of $40 each. At the end of the 30-year life of the bond, the issuer also pays the $1,000 par value to the bondholder.

Bonds usually are issued with coupon rates set high enough to induce investors to pay par value to buy the bond. Sometimes, however, **zero-coupon bonds** are issued that make no coupon payments. In this case, investors receive par value at the maturity date, but receive no interest payments until then: The bond has a coupon rate of zero. These bonds are issued at prices considerably below par value, and the investor's return comes solely from the difference between issue price and the payment of par value at maturity. We will return to these bonds below.

Treasury Bonds and Notes

Figure 13.1 is an excerpt from the listing of Treasury issues in *The Wall Street Journal*. Treasury note maturities range up to 10 years, whereas Treasury bonds are issued with maturities ranging from 10 to 30 years. Both are issued in denominations of $1,000 or more. Both make semiannual coupon payments. Aside from their differing maturities at issue date, the only major distinction between T-notes and T-bonds is that in the past, some T-bonds were *callable* for a given period, usually during the last five years of the bond's life. The call provision gives the Treasury the right to repurchase the bond at par value during the call period. The Treasury no longer issues callable bonds, but several previously issued bonds still are outstanding.

The callable bonds are easily identified in Figure 13.1 because a range of years appears in the maturity date column. The first date is the time at which the bond is first callable. The second date is the maturity date of the bond. The bond may be called by the Treasury at any coupon date in the call period, but must be retired by the maturity date.

The highlighted bond in Figure 13.1 matures in November 1997. Its coupon rate is $7\frac{3}{8}$%. Par value is $1,000; thus, the bond pays interest of $73.75 per year in two semiannual payments of $36.875. Payments are made in November and May of each year. The bid and ask prices[1] are quoted in points plus fractions of $\frac{1}{32}$ of a point (the

[1] Recall that the bid price is the price at which you can sell the bond to a dealer. The ask price, which is slightly higher, is the price at which you can buy the bond from a dealer.

Figure 13.1
Listing of treasury issues

Source: *The Wall Street Journal,* November 16, 1994. Reprinted by permission of *The Wall Street Journal,* © 1994 Dow Jones & Company, Inc. All Rights Reserved Worldwide.

TREASURY BONDS, NOTES & BILLS

Tuesday, November 15, 1994

Representative Over-the-Counter quotations based on transactions of $1 million or more.

Treasury bond, note and bill quotes are as of mid-afternoon. Colons in bid-and-asked quotes represent 32nds; 101:01 means 101 1/32. Net changes in 32nds. n-Treasury note. Treasury bill quotes in hundredths, quoted on terms of a rate of discount. Days to maturity calculated from settlement date. All yields are to maturity and based on the asked quote. Latest 13-week and 26-week bills are boldfaced. For bonds callable prior to maturity, yields are computed to the earliest call date for issues quoted above par and to the maturity date for issues below par. *-When issued.

Source: Federal Reserve Bank of New York.

U.S. Treasury strips as of 3 p.m. Eastern time, also based on transactions of $1 million or more. Colons in bid-and-asked quotes represent 32nds; 101:01 means 101 1/32. Net changes in 32nds. Yields calculated on the asked quotation. ci-stripped coupon interest. bp-Treasury bond, stripped principal. np-Treasury note, stripped principal. For bonds callable prior to maturity, yields are computed to the earliest call date for issues quoted above par and to the maturity date for issues below par.

Source: Bear, Stearns & Co. via Street Software Technology Inc.

GOVT. BONDS & NOTES

Rate	Maturity Mo/Yr	Bid	Asked	Chg.	Ask Yld.
4 5/8	Nov 94n	99:31	100:01	....	3.67
4 5/8	Dec 94n	99:28	99:30	+ 1	5.06
7 5/8	Dec 94n	100:07	100:09	....	5.11
8 5/8	Jan 95n	100:16	100:18	....	4.94
4 1/4	Jan 95n	99:23	99:25	....	5.27
3	Feb 95	99:00	100:00	+ 1	2.98
5 1/2	Feb 95n	99:31	100:01	....	5.30
7 3/4	Feb 95n	100:16	100:18	− 1	5.31
10 1/2	Feb 95	101:05	101:07	− 1	5.31
11 1/4	Feb 95n	101:12	101:14	− 1	5.15
3 7/8	Feb 95n	99:16	99:18	....	5.39
3 7/8	Mar 95n	99:09	99:11	− 1	5.67
8 3/8	Apr 95n	100:31	101:01	− 1	5.75
3 7/8	Apr 95n	99:02	99:04	− 1	5.85
5 7/8	May 95n	99:30	100:00	....	5.87
11 1/2	Nov 95	104:25	104:29	− 1	6.33
4 1/4	Nov 95n	97:21	97:23	− 2	6.56
4 1/4	Dec 95n	97:14	97:16	− 2	6.60
9 1/4	Jan 96n	102:26	102:28	− 1	6.64
4	Jan 96n	96:29	96:31	− 2	6.66
7 1/2	Jan 96n	100:29	100:31	− 1	6.65
4 5/8	Feb 96n	97:15	97:17	− 2	6.72
7 7/8	Feb 96n	101:10	101:12	− 1	6.71
8 7/8	Feb 96n	102:15	102:17	− 3	6.72
4 5/8	Feb 96n	97:13	97:15	− 2	6.71
7 1/2	Feb 96n	100:28	100:30	− 2	6.73
5 1/8	Mar 96n	97:27	97:29	− 2	6.75
7 3/4	Mar 96n	101:07	101:09	− 2	6.75
9 3/8	Apr 96n	103:11	103:13	− 3	6.80
5 1/2	Apr 96n	98:05	98:07	− 2	6.81
7 5/8	Apr 96n	101:02	101:04	− 2	6.80
4 1/4	May 96n	96:10	96:12	− 2	6.84
7 3/8	May 96n	100:22	100:24	− 2	6.84
5 7/8	May 96n	98:17	98:19	− 2	6.86
7 5/8	May 96n	101:02	101:04	− 2	6.84
6	Jun 96n	98:19	98:21	− 3	6.89
7 7/8	Jun 96n	101:14	101:16	− 3	6.88
7 7/8	Jul 96n	101:14	101:16	− 2	6.90
6 1/8	Jul 96n	98:21	98:23	− 2	6.93
7 7/8	Jul 96n	101:14	101:16	− 2	6.93
4 3/8	Aug 96n	95:24	95:26	− 2	6.96
6 1/4	Aug 96n	98:23	98:25	− 2	6.99
7 1/4	Aug 96n	100:12	100:14	− 2	6.99
6 1/2	Sep 96n	99:03	99:05	− 2	6.99
7	Sep 96n	99:31	100:01	− 2	6.98
8	Oct 96n	101:20	101:22	− 3	7.04
6 7/8	Oct 96n	99:20	99:22	− 2	7.05
4 3/8	Nov 96n	94:30	95:00	− 3	7.11
7 1/4	Nov 96n	100:09	100:11	− 2	7.06
6 1/2	Nov 96n	98:27	98:29	− 3	7.09
6 1/8	Dec 96n	98:04	98:06	− 3	7.06
8	Jan 97n	101:20	101:22	− 3	7.14
6 1/4	Jan 97n	98:04	98:06	− 3	7.15
4 3/4	Feb 97n	94:31	95:01	− 2	7.18
6 3/4	Feb 97n	99:00	99:02	− 3	7.20
6 7/8	Mar 97n	99:08	99:10	− 3	7.20
8 1/2	Apr 97n	102:22	102:24	− 3	7.24
6 7/8	Apr 97n	99:04	99:06	− 3	7.24
6 1/2	May 97n	98:07	98:09	− 3	7.27
8 1/2	May 97n	102:22	102:24	− 4	7.27
6 3/4	May 97n	98:23	98:25	− 4	7.28
6 3/8	Jun 97n	97:29	97:31	− 2	7.24
8 1/2	Jul 97n	102:26	102:28	− 2	7.29
5 1/2	Jul 97n	95:19	95:21	− 2	7.30
6 1/2	Aug 97n	97:29	97:31	− 2	7.33
8 5/8	Aug 97n	103:04	103:06	− 3	7.32
5 5/8	Aug 97n	95:22	95:24	− 2	7.34
5 1/2	Sep 97n	95:07	95:09	− 3	7.35
8 3/4	Oct 97n	103:15	103:17	− 3	7.38
5 3/4	Oct 97n	95:22	95:24	− 2	7.38
7 3/8	Nov 97n	99:29	99:31	− 3	7.39
8 7/8	Nov 97n	103:27	103:29	− 3	7.40
6	Nov 97n	96:05	96:07	− 3	7.41
6	Dec 97n	96:02	96:04	− 2	7.41
7 7/8	Jan 98n	101:04	101:06	− 2	7.45
8 3/4	Aug 00n	104:22	104:24	+ 2	7.71
8 1/2	Nov 00n	103:22	103:24	+ 4	7.71
7 3/4	Feb 01n	100:02	100:04	....	7.72
11 3/4	Feb 01	119:20	119:24	....	7.71
8	May 01n	101:10	101:12	+ 3	7.73
13 1/8	May 01	127:11	127:15	+ 3	7.68
7 7/8	Aug 01n	100:19	100:21	+ 5	7.75
8	Aug 96-01	100:28	101:00	− 2	7.38
13 3/8	Aug 01	129:07	129:11	+ 2	7.71
7 1/2	Nov 01n	98:16	98:18	+ 3	7.77
15 3/4	Nov 01	142:23	142:27	+ 1	7.71
14 1/4	Feb 02	135:15	135:19	+ 2	7.74
7 1/2	May 02n	98:11	98:13	+ 4	7.78
6 3/8	Aug 02n	91:20	91:22	+ 6	7.83
11 5/8	Nov 02	122:04	122:08	+ 4	7.83
6 1/4	Feb 02n	90:11	90:13	+ 7	7.85
8 3/8	Aug 03-08	101:18	101:22	+ 5	8.10
8 3/4	Nov 03-08	104:00	104:04	+ 5	8.10
9 1/8	May 04-09	106:27	106:31	+ 7	8.06
10 3/8	Nov 04-09	115:22	115:26	+ 8	8.04
11 3/4	Feb 05-10	125:21	125:25	+ 9	8.01
10	May 05-10	113:15	113:19	+ 8	8.06
12 3/4	Nov 05-10	133:29	134:01	+ 9	8.03
13 7/8	May 06-11	143:00	143:04	+ 8	8.05
14	Nov 06-11	145:04	145:08	+ 8	8.05
10 3/8	Nov 07-12	117:23	117:27	+ 9	8.13
12	Aug 08-13	131:17	131:21	+ 9	8.13
13 1/4	May 09-14	143:01	143:05	+ 8	8.13
12 1/2	Aug 09-14	137:00	137:04	+ 9	8.13
11 3/4	Nov 09-14	131:01	131:05	+ 9	8.12
11 1/4	Feb 15	130:14	130:16	+17	8.15
10 5/8	Aug 15	124:14	124:16	+18	8.16
9 7/8	Nov 15	117:00	117:02	+17	8.16
9 1/4	Feb 16	110:23	110:25	+12	8.17
7 1/4	May 16	90:27	90:29	+14	8.15
7 1/2	Nov 16	93:07	93:09	+15	8.16
8 3/4	May 17	105:25	105:27	+16	8.18
8 7/8	Aug 17	107:02	107:04	+16	8.18
9 1/8	May 18	109:23	109:25	+15	8.18
9	Nov 18	108:17	108:19	+17	8.18
8 7/8	Feb 19	107:07	107:09	+17	8.18
8 1/8	Aug 19	99:13	99:15	+14	8.18
8 1/2	Feb 20	103:12	103:14	+17	8.18
8 3/4	May 20	106:02	106:04	+16	8.17
8 3/4	Aug 20	106:03	106:05	+16	8.17
7 7/8	Feb 21	96:24	96:26	+14	8.17
8 1/8	May 21	99:16	99:18	+15	8.17
8 1/8	Aug 21	99:18	99:20	+15	8.16
8	Nov 21	98:09	98:11	+15	8.15
7 1/4	Aug 22	90:10	90:12	+15	8.13
7 5/8	Nov 22	94:16	94:18	+16	8.12
7 1/8	Feb 23	89:02	89:04	+14	8.11
6 1/4	Aug 23	79:17	79:19	+15	8.09
7 1/2	Nov 24	93:27	93:29	+14	8.04

U.S. TREASURY STRIPS

Mat.	Type	Bid	Asked	Chg.	Ask Yld.
Feb 95	ci	98:22	98:22	....	5.46
Feb 95	np	98:21	98:21	....	5.51
May 95	ci	97:05	97:05	+ 1	5.92
May 95	np	97:03	97:04	+ 1	6.00
Aug 95	ci	95:19	95:20	− 1	6.11
Aug 95	np	95:16	95:17	− 1	6.25
Nov 95	ci	93:28	93:28	− 2	6.44
Nov 95	np	93:25	93:26	− 2	6.52
Feb 96	ci	92:04	92:05	− 1	6.66
Feb 96	np	92:02	92:03	− 2	6.74
May 96	ci	90:13	90:14	− 1	6.84
May 96	np	90:12	90:13	− 1	6.86
Aug 96	ci	88:28	88:30	− 1	6.84
Nov 96	ci	87:01	87:03	− 2	7.06
Nov 96	np	86:31	87:00	− 2	7.10
Feb 97	ci	85:10	85:12	− 1	7.17
May 97	ci	83:19	83:21	− 1	7.29
Feb 03	np	52:22	52:26	+ 5	7.90
May 03	ci	51:11	51:15	+ 5	7.97
Aug 03	ci	50:09	50:13	+ 5	7.99
Aug 03	np	50:17	50:22	+ 5	7.93
Nov 03	ci	49:08	49:12	+ 5	8.00
Feb 04	ci	48:07	48:11	+ 5	8.02
Feb 04	np	48:18	48:22	+ 5	7.94
May 04	ci	47:07	47:11	+ 5	8.03
May 04	np	47:16	47:20	+ 5	7.97
Aug 04	ci	46:07	46:11	+ 5	8.05
Aug 04	np	46:19	46:23	+ 5	7.96
Nov 04	ci	45:08	45:12	+ 5	8.06
Nov 04	bp	45:21	45:25	+ 6	7.97
Feb 05	ci	44:10	44:14	+ 6	8.08
May 05	ci	43:12	43:16	+ 6	8.09
May 05	bp	43:11	43:15	+ 6	8.10
Aug 05	ci	42:14	42:18	+ 6	8.11
Aug 05	bp	42:15	42:19	+ 6	8.10
Nov 05	ci	41:17	41:22	+ 6	8.12
Feb 06	ci	40:22	40:26	+ 6	8.13
Feb 06	bp	41:05	41:09	+ 6	8.02
May 06	ci	39:26	39:31	+ 6	8.14
Aug 06	ci	39:00	39:05	+ 6	8.15
Nov 06	ci	38:06	38:10	+ 6	8.16
Feb 07	ci	37:11	37:15	+ 6	8.18
May 07	ci	36:19	36:23	+ 6	8.18
Aug 07	ci	35:25	35:30	+ 6	8.20
Nov 07	ci	35:00	35:05	+ 6	8.21
Feb 08	ci	34:09	34:13	+ 6	8.22
May 08	ci	33:17	33:21	+ 6	8.23
Aug 08	ci	32:26	32:30	+ 6	8.24
Nov 08	ci	32:04	32:08	+ 6	8.25
Feb 09	ci	31:14	31:18	+ 6	8.26
May 09	ci	30:24	30:28	+ 6	8.27
Aug 09	ci	30:03	30:07	+ 6	8.28
Nov 09	ci	29:14	29:18	+ 6	8.29
Nov 09	bp	29:06	29:10	+ 6	8.35
Feb 10	ci	29:24	29:29	+ 6	8.30
Nov 14	ci	19:11	19:14	+ 7	8.36
Feb 15	ci	18:31	19:02	+ 7	8.35
Feb 15	bp	19:01	19:05	+ 7	8.33
May 15	ci	18:18	18:22	+ 7	8.35
Aug 15	ci	18:06	18:10	+ 7	8.35
Aug 15	bp	18:09	18:12	+ 7	8.33
Nov 15	ci	17:27	17:30	+ 7	8.35
Nov 15	bp	17:29	18:00	+ 7	8.33
Feb 16	ci	17:15	17:18	+ 7	8.35
Feb 16	bp	17:17	17:21	+ 7	8.33
May 16	ci	17:04	17:07	+ 7	8.35
May 16	bp	17:15	17:18	+ 7	8.25
Aug 16	ci	16:24	16:28	+ 7	8.35
Nov 16	ci	16:14	16:17	+ 7	8.35
Nov 16	bp	16:22	16:25	+ 7	8.28
Feb 17	ci	16:03	16:07	+ 7	8.35
May 17	ci	15:25	15:28	+ 7	8.35
May 17	bp	15:28	15:31	+ 7	8.32
Aug 17	ci	15:15	15:18	+ 7	8.35
Aug 17	bp	15:17	15:21	+ 7	8.32
Nov 17	ci	15:05	15:08	+ 7	8.34
Feb 18	ci	14:27	14:31	+ 7	8.34
May 18	ci	14:18	14:21	+ 7	8.34
May 18	bp	14:20	14:24	+ 7	8.32
Aug 18	ci	14:08	14:11	+ 7	8.34
Nov 18	ci	14:00	14:03	+ 7	8.34
Nov 18	bp	14:02	14:05	+ 7	8.32
Feb 19	ci	13:23	13:26	+ 7	8.33
Feb 19	bp	13:26	13:29	+ 7	8.31
May 19	ci	13:15	13:18	+ 7	8.33
Aug 19	ci	13:06	13:09	+ 7	8.33
Aug 19	bp	13:11	13:14	+ 7	8.28
Nov 19	ci	12:30	13:01	+ 7	8.32
Feb 20	ci	12:22	12:25	+ 7	8.31
Feb 20	bp	12:26	12:29	+ 7	8.28
May 20	ci	12:14	12:17	+ 7	8.31
May 20	bp	12:18	12:21	+ 8	8.27
Aug 20	ci	12:07	12:10	+ 7	8.30
Aug 20	bp	12:11	12:14	+ 7	8.26
Nov 20	ci	12:01	12:03	+ 7	8.29
Feb 21	ci	11:26	11:29	+ 7	8.28
Feb 21	bp	11:30	12:01	+ 7	8.24
May 21	ci	11:20	11:22	+ 7	8.26
May 21	bp	11:23	11:26	+ 7	8.22
Aug 21	ci	11:15	11:18	+ 7	8.23
Aug 21	bp	11:19	11:22	+ 7	8.19
Nov 21	ci	11:10	11:13	+ 7	8.20
Nov 21	bp	11:14	11:17	+ 7	8.16
Feb 22	ci	11:05	11:07	+ 7	8.19
May 22	ci	11:00	11:03	+ 7	8.16
Aug 22	ci	10:29	11:00	+ 7	8.12
Aug 22	bp	11:01	11:03	+ 7	8.08
Nov 22	ci	10:24	10:27	+ 7	8.09
Nov 22	bp	10:27	10:29	+ 7	8.07
Feb 23	ci	10:22	10:24	+ 7	8.05
Feb 23	bp	10:24	10:26	+ 7	8.03
May 23	ci	10:15	10:18	+ 6	8.05
Aug 23	ci	10:11	10:14	+ 7	8.02
Aug 23	bp	10:15	10:18	+ 7	7.98
[illegible]	[illegible]	[illegible]	[illegible]	[illegible]	[illegible]

numbers after the colons are the fractions of a point). Although bonds are sold in denominations of $1,000 par value, the prices are quoted as a percentage of par value. Therefore, the bid price of the bond is 99:29 = 99 $^{29}/_{32}$ = 99.90625% of par value or $999.0625, whereas the ask price is 99$^{31}/_{32}$% of par, or $999.6875.

The last column, labeled "Ask Yld," is the yield to maturity on the bond based on the ask price. The yield to maturity is a measure of the average rate of return to an investor who purchases the bond for the ask price and holds it until its maturity date. We will have much to say about yield to maturity below.

Accrued Interest and Quoted Bond Prices. The bond prices that you see quoted in the financial pages are not actually the prices that investors pay for the bond. This is because the quoted price does not include the interest that accrues between coupon payment dates.

If a bond is purchased between coupon payments, the buyer must pay the seller for accrued interest, the prorated share of the upcoming semiannual coupon. For example, if 40 days have passed since the last coupon payment, and there are 182 days in the semiannual coupon period, the seller is entitled to a payment of accrued interest of 40/182 of the semiannual coupon. The sale, or *invoice price*, of the bond would equal the stated price plus the accrued interest.

To illustrate, suppose that the coupon rate is 8%. Then the semiannual coupon payment is $40. Because 40 days have passed since the last coupon payment, the accrued interest on the bond is $40 × (40/182) = $8.79. If the quoted price of the bond is $990, then the invoice price will be $990 + $8.79 = $998.79.

The practice of quoting bond prices net of accrued interest explains why the price of a maturing bond is listed at $1,000 rather than $1,000 plus one coupon payment. A purchaser of an 8% coupon bond one day before the bond's maturity would receive $1,040 on the following day and so should be willing to pay a total price of $1,040 for the bond. In fact, $40 of that total payment constitutes the accrued interest for the preceding half-year period. The bond price is quoted net of accrued interest in the financial pages and thus appears as $1,000.

Corporate Bonds

Like the government, corporations borrow money by issuing bonds. Figure 13.2 is a sample of corporate bond listings in *The Wall Street Journal*. The data presented here differ only slightly from U.S. Treasury bond listings. For example, the highlighted Mobil bond pays a coupon rate of 8% and matures in 2032. Unlike Treasury bonds, corporate bonds trade in increments of 1/8 point. Mobil's *current yield* is 8.2%, which is simply the annual coupon payment divided by the bond price ($80/$970). Note that current yield measures only the annual interest income the bondholder receives as a percentage of the price paid for the bond. It ignores the fact that an investor who buys the bond for $970 will be able to redeem it for $1,000 on the maturity date. Prospective price appreciation or depreciation does not enter the computation of the current yield. The trading volume column shows that 53 bonds traded on that day. The change from yesterday's closing price is given in the last column. Like government

Figure 13.2
Listing of corporate bonds

Source: *The Wall Street Journal,* November 9, 1994. Reprinted by permission of *The Wall Street Journal,*

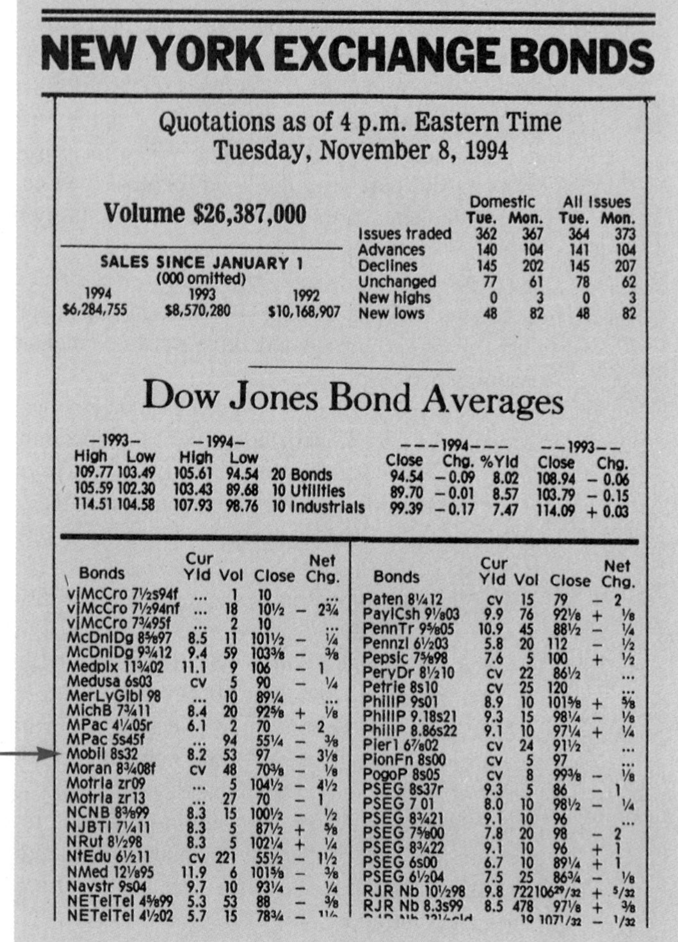

NEW YORK EXCHANGE BONDS

Quotations as of 4 p.m. Eastern Time
Tuesday, November 8, 1994

Volume $26,387,000

SALES SINCE JANUARY 1
(000 omitted)

1994	1993	1992
$6,284,755	$8,570,280	$10,168,907

	Domestic Tue.	Domestic Mon.	All Issues Tue.	All Issues Mon.
Issues traded	362	367	364	373
Advances	140	104	141	104
Declines	145	202	145	207
Unchanged	77	61	78	62
New highs	0	3	0	3
New lows	48	82	48	82

Dow Jones Bond Averages

−1993− High	−1993− Low	−1994− High	−1994− Low		−1994− Close	−1994− Chg.	−1994− %Yld	−1993− Close	−1993− Chg.
109.77	103.49	105.61	94.54	20 Bonds	94.54	−0.09	8.02	108.94	− 0.06
105.59	102.30	103.43	89.68	10 Utilities	89.70	−0.01	8.57	103.79	− 0.15
114.51	104.58	107.93	98.76	10 Industrials	99.39	−0.17	7.47	114.09	+ 0.03

Bonds	Cur Yld	Vol	Close	Net Chg.
vjMcCro 7½s94f	...	1	10	...
vjMcCro 7½94nf	...	18	10½	− 2¾
vjMcCro 7¾95f	...	2	10	...
McDnlDg 8⅝97	8.5	11	101½	− ¼
McDnlDg 9¾12	9.4	59	103⅜	− ⅜
Medplx 11¾02	11.1	9	106	− 1
Medusa 6s03	cv	5	90	− ¼
MerLyGlbl 98	...	10	89¼	...
MichB 7¾11	8.4	20	92⅝	+ ⅛
MPac 4¼05r	6.1	2	70	− 2
MPac 5s45f	...	94	55¼	− ⅜
Mobil 8s32	8.2	53	97	− 3⅛
Moran 8¾08f	cv	48	70⅜	− ⅛
Motrla zr09	...	5	104½	− 4½
Motrla zr13	...	27	70	− 1
NCNB 8⅜99	8.3	15	100½	− ½
NJBTl 7¼11	8.3	5	87½	+ ⅝
NRut 8½98	8.3	5	102¼	+ ¼
NtEdu 6½11	cv	221	55½	− 1½
NMed 12⅛95	11.9	6	101⅝	− ⅜
Navstr 9s04	9.7	10	93¼	− ¼
NETelTel 4⅝99	5.3	53	88	− ⅜
NETelTel 4½02	5.7	15	78¾	− [illegible]

Bonds	Cur Yld	Vol	Close	Net Chg.
Paten 8¼12	cv	15	79	− 2
PaylCsh 9⅛03	9.9	76	92⅛	+ ⅛
PennTr 9⅝05	10.9	45	88½	− ¼
Pennzl 6½03	5.8	20	112	− ½
Pepsic 7⅝98	7.6	5	100	+ ½
PeryDr 8½10	cv	22	86½	...
Petrie 8s10	cv	25	120	...
PhilIP 9s01	8.9	10	101⅝	+ ⅝
PhilIP 9.18s21	9.3	15	98¼	− ⅛
PhilIP 8.86s22	9.1	10	97¼	+ ¼
Pier1 6⅞02	cv	24	91½	...
PionFn 8s00	cv	5	97	...
PogoP 8s05	cv	8	99⅜	− ⅛
PSEG 8s37r	9.3	5	86	− 1
PSEG 7 01	8.0	10	98½	− ¼
PSEG 8¾21	9.1	10	96	...
PSEG 7⅝00	7.8	20	98	− 2
PSEG 8¾22	9.1	10	96	+ 1
PSEG 6s00	6.7	10	89¼	+ 1
PSEG 6½04	7.5	25	86¾	− ⅛
RJR Nb 10½98	9.8	722	106 29/32	+ 5/32
RJR Nb 8.3s99	8.5	478	97⅛	+ ⅜
[illegible]		19	107 1/32	− 1/32

bonds, corporate bonds sell in units of $1,000 par value but are quoted as a percentage of par value.

Although the bonds listed in Figure 13.2 trade on a formal exchange operated by the New York Stock Exchange, most bonds are traded over the counter in a loosely organized network of bond dealers linked by a computer quotation system. (See Chapter 3 for a comparison of exchange versus OTC trading.) In practice, the bond market can be quite "thin," in that there are few investors interested in trading a particular bond at any particular time. Figure 13.2 shows that trading volume of many bonds on the New York exchange is quite low. On any day, it could be difficult to find a buyer or seller for a particular issue, which introduces some "liquidity risk" into the bond market. It may be difficult to sell bond holdings quickly if the need arises.

Bonds issued in the United States today are *registered*, meaning that the issuing firm keeps records of the owner of the bond and can mail interest checks to the owner.

Registration of bonds is helpful to tax authorities in the enforcement of tax collection. *Bearer bonds* are those traded without any record of ownership. The investor's physical possession of the bond certificate is the only evidence of ownership. These are now rare in the United States, but less rare in Europe.

Call Provisions on Corporate Bonds. Although we have seen that the Treasury no longer issues callable bonds, most corporate bonds are issued with call provisions. The call provision allows the issuer to repurchase the bond at a specified *call price* before the maturity date. For example, if a company issues a bond with a high coupon rate when market interest rates are high, and interest rates later fall, the firm might like to retire the high-coupon debt and issue new bonds at a lower coupon rate to reduce interest payments. This is calling *refunding*.

The call price of a bond is commonly set at an initial level near par value plus one annual coupon payment. The call price falls as time passes, gradually approaching par value.

Callable bonds typically come with a period of call protection, an initial time during which the bonds are not callable. Such bonds are referred to as *deferred* callable bonds.

The option to call the bond is valuable to the firm, allowing it to buy back the bonds and refinance at lower interest rates when market rates fall. Of course, the firm's benefit is the bondholder's burden. Holders of called bonds forfeit their bonds for the call price, thereby giving up the prospect of an attractive rate of interest on their original investment. To compensate investors for this risk, callable bonds are issued with higher coupons and promised yields to maturity than noncallable bonds.

CONCEPT CHECK

Question 1. Suppose that General Motors issues two bonds with identical coupon rates and maturity dates. One bond is callable, however, whereas the other is not. Which bond will sell at a higher price?

Convertible Bonds. **Convertible bonds** give bondholders an option to exchange each bond for a specified number of shares of common stock of the firm. The *conversion ratio* gives the number of shares for which each bond may be exchanged. To see the value of this right, suppose a convertible bond that is issued at par value of $1,000 is convertible into 40 shares of a firm's stock. The current stock price is $20 per share, so the option to convert is not profitable now. Should the stock price later rise to $30, however, each bond may be converted profitably into $1,200 worth of stock. The *market conversion value* is the current value of the shares for which the bonds may be exchanged. At the $20 stock price, for example, the bond's conversion value is $800. The *conversion premium* is the excess of the bond value over its conversion value. If the bond were selling currently for $950, its premium would be $150.

Convertible bonds give their holders the ability to share in price appreciation of the company's stock. Again, this benefit comes at a price; convertible bonds offer lower coupon rates and stated or promised yields to maturity than do nonconvertible bonds. At the same time, the actual return on the convertible bond may exceed the stated yield to maturity if the option to convert becomes profitable.

We discuss convertible and callable bonds further in Chapter 19.

Puttable Bonds. A relatively new development is the **put bond** or extendable bond. Although the callable bond gives the issuer the option to extend or retire the bond at the call date, the put bond gives this option to the bondholder. If the bond's coupon rate exceeds current market yields, for instance, the bondholder will choose to extend the bond's life. If the bond's coupon rate is too low, it will be optimal not to extend; the bondholder instead reclaims principal, which can be invested at current yields.

Floating-Rate Bonds. **Floating-rate bonds** make interest payments that are tied to some measure of current market rates. For example, the rate might be adjusted annually to the current T-bill rate plus 2%. If the one-year T-bill rate at the adjustment date is 4%, the bond's coupon rate over the next year would then be 6%. This arrangement means that the bond always pays approximately current market rates.

The major risk involved in floaters has to do with changing credit conditions. The yield spread is fixed over the life of the security, which may be many years. If the financial health of the firm deteriorates, then a greater yield premium would be required than is offered by the security. In this case, the price of the bond would fall. Although the coupon rate on floaters adjusts to changes in the general level of market interest rates, it does not adjust to changes in the financial condition of the firm.

Preferred Stock

Although preferred stock strictly speaking is considered to be equity, it often is included in the fixed-income universe. This is because, like bonds, preferred stock promises to pay a specified stream of dividends. However, unlike bonds, the failure to pay the promised dividend does not result in corporate bankruptcy. Instead, the dividends owed simply cumulate, and the common stockholders may not receive any dividends until the preferred stockholders have been paid in full. In the event of bankruptcy, the claim of preferred stockholders to the firm's assets have lower priority than those of bondholders, but higher priority than those of common stockholders.

Most preferred stock pays a fixed dividend. Therefore, it is in effect a perpetuity, providing a level cash flow indefinitely. In the last few years, however, adjustable or floating rate preferred stock has become popular. Floating rate preferred stock is much like floating rate bonds. The dividend rate is linked to a measure of current market interest rates and is adjusted at regular intervals.

Other Issuers

There are, of course, several issuers of bonds in addition to the Treasury and private corporations. For example, state and local governments issue municipal bonds. The outstanding feature of these is that interest payments are tax free. We examined municipal bonds and the value of the tax exemption in Chapter 2.

Government agencies such as the Federal Home Loan Bank Board, the Farm Credit agencies, and the mortgage pass-through agencies Ginnie Mae, Fannie Mae, and Freddie Mac, also issue considerable amounts of bonds. These too were reviewed in Chapter 2.

Finally, several foreign issuers market dollar-denominated bonds in the United States.

13.2 Default Risk

Although bonds generally *promise* a fixed flow of income, that income stream is not riskless unless the investor can be sure the issuer will not default on the obligation. While U.S. government bonds may be treated as free of default risk, this is not true of corporate bonds. If the company goes bankrupt, the bondholders will not receive all the payments they have been promised. Therefore, the actual payments on these bonds are uncertain, for they depend to some degree on the ultimate financial status of the firm.

Bond default risk is measured by Moody's Investor Services and Standard & Poor's Corporation, both of which provide financial information on firms as well as quality ratings of large corporate and municipal bond issues. Both firms assign letter grades to the bonds of corporations and municipalities to reflect their assessment of the safety of the bond issue. The top rating is AAA (Standard & Poor's) or Aaa (Moody's). Moody's modifies each rating class with a 1, 2, or 3 suffix (e.g., Aaa1, Aaa2, Aaa3) to provide a finer gradation of ratings. S&P uses a + or − modification.

Those rated BBB or above (S&P) or Baa and above (Moody's) are considered **investment grade bonds,** whereas lower-rated bonds are classified as **speculative grade or junk bonds.** Certain regulated institutional investors such as insurance companies have not always been allowed to invest in speculative grade bonds.

Figure 13.3 provides the definitions of each bond rating classification.

Junk Bonds

Junk bonds, also known as *high-yield bonds*, are nothing more than speculative grade (low-rated or unrated) bonds. Before 1977, almost all junk bonds were "fallen angels," that is, bonds issued by firms that originally had investment grade ratings but that had since been downgraded. In 1977, however, firms began to issue "original-issue junk."

Much of the credit for this innovation is given to Drexel Burnham Lambert, and especially its trader, Michael Milken. Drexel had long enjoyed a niche as a junk bond trader and had established a network of potential investors in junk bonds. Its reasoning for marketing original-issue junk, so-called emerging credits, lay in the belief that default rates on these bonds did not justify the large yield spreads commonly exhibited in the marketplace. Firms not able to muster an investment grade rating were happy to have Drexel (and other investment bankers) market their bonds directly to the public, as this opened up a new source of financing. Junk issues were a lower-cost financing alternative than borrowing from banks.

High-yield bonds gained considerable notoriety in the 1980s when they were used as financing vehicles in leveraged buyouts and hostile takeover attempts. High-yield bonds also were extremely popular with investors. Although such bonds constituted only 3.7% of the corporate bond market in 1977, they accounted for 23% of the market by 1987.

Figure 13.3
Definitions of each bond rating class

Source: Stephen A. Ross and Randolph W. Westerfield, *Corporate Finance* (St. Louis: Times Mirror/Mosby College Publishing, 1988). Data from various editions of *Standard & Poor's Bond Guide* and *Moody's Bond Guide*.

Bond Ratings

	Very High Quality	High Quality	Speculative	Very Poor
Standard & Poor's	AAA AA	A BBB	BB B	CCC D
Moody's	Aaa Aa	A Baa	Ba B	Caa C

At times both Moody's and Standard & Poor's have used adjustments to these ratings. S&P uses plus and minus signs: A+ is the strongest A Rating and A− the weakest. Moody's uses a 1, 2, or 3 designation—with 1 indicating the strongest.

Moody's	S&P	
Aaa	AAA	Debt rated Aaa and AAA has the highest rating. Capacity to pay interest and principal is extremely strong.
Aa	AA	Debt rated Aa and AA has a very strong capacity to pay interest and repay principal. Together with the highest rating, this group comprises the high-grade bond class.
A	A	Debt rated A has a strong capacity to pay interest and repay principal, although it is somewhat more susceptible to the adverse effects of changes in circumstances and economic conditions than debt in higher rated categories.
Baa	BBB	Debt rated Baa and BBB is regarded as having an adequate capacity to pay interest and repay principal. Whereas it normally exhibits adequate protection parameters, adverse economic conditions or changing circumstances are more likely to lead to a weakened capacity to pay interest and repay principal for debt in this category than in higher rated categories. These bonds are medium grade obligations.
Ba B Caa Ca	BB B CCC CC	Debt rated in these categories is regarded, on balance, as predominantly speculative with respect to capacity to pay interest and repay principal in accordance with the terms of the obligation. BB and Ba indicate the lowest degree of speculation, and CC and Ca the highest degree of speculation. Although such debt will likely have some quality and protective characteristics, these are outweighed by large uncertainties or major risk exposures to adverse conditions. Some issues may be in default.
C	C	This rating is reserved for income bonds on which no interest is being paid.
D	D	Debt rated D is in default, and payment of interest and/or repayment of principal is in arrears.

Shortly thereafter, however, the junk bond market suffered. The legal difficulties of Drexel and Michael Milken in connection with Wall Street's insider trading scandals of the late 1980s tainted the junk bond market. Drexel agreed to pay $650 million in fines and plead guilty to six felony charges to avoid racketeering charges. Milken was indicted on racketeering and security fraud charges, resigned from Drexel, and eventually agreed in a plea bargain to plead guilty to six felony charges and to pay $600 million in fines. Moreover, as the high-yield bond market tumbled in late 1989, Drexel suffered large losses in its own billion-dollar portfolio of junk bonds. In February 1990, Drexel filed for bankruptcy.

At the height of Drexel's difficulties, the high-yield bond market nearly dried up. New issues of high-yield bonds fell from $24 billion in 1989 to less than $1 billion in 1990, and prices on these issues fell so severely that their yields exceeded Treasury yields by about 7.5 percentage points, the largest margin in history. Since then, the market has rebounded. New issues in 1993 were a record-breaking $55 billion. However, it is worth noting that the average credit quality of high-yield debt issued in 1993 was higher than the average quality in the boom years of the 1980s.

Determinants of Bond Safety

Bond rating agencies base their quality ratings largely on an analysis of the level and trend of some of the issuer's financial ratios. The key ratios used to evaluate safety are:

1. *Coverage ratios*—Ratios of company earnings to fixed costs. For example, the *times-interest-earned ratio* is the ratio of earnings before interest payments and taxes to interest obligations. The *fixed-charge coverage ratio* adds lease payments and sinking fund payments to interest obligations to arrive at the ratio of earnings to all fixed cash obligations. Low or falling coverage ratios signal possible cash flow difficulties.
2. *Leverage ratio*—Debt to equity ratio. A too-high leverage ratio indicates excessive indebtedness, signaling the possibility the firm will be unable to earn enough to satisfy the obligations on its bonds.
3. *Liquidity ratios*—The two common liquidity ratios are the *current ratio* (current assets/current liabilities) and the *quick ratio* (current assets excluding inventories/current liabilities). These ratios measure the firm's ability to pay bills coming due with cash currently being collected.
4. *Profitability ratios*—Measures of rates of return on assets or equity. Profitability ratios are indicators of a firm's overall financial health. The *return on assets* (earnings before interest and taxes divided by total assets) is the most popular of these measures. Firms with higher return on assets should be better able to raise money in security markets because they offer prospects for better returns on the firm's investments.
5. *Cash flow to debt ratio*—This is the ratio of total cash flow to outstanding debt.

Standard & Poor's has computed three-year median values of selected ratios for firms in several rating classes, which we present in Table 13.1. Of course, ratios must be evaluated in the context of industry standards, and analysts differ in the weights they place on particular ratios. Nevertheless, Table 13.1 demonstrates the tendency of ratios to improve along with the firm's rating class.

In fact, the heavy dependence of bond ratings on publicly available financial data is evidence of an interesting phenomenon. You might think that an increase or decrease in bond rating would cause substantial bond price gains or losses, but this is not the case. Weinstein[2] found that bond prices move in *anticipation* of rating changes, which is evidence that investors themselves track the financial status of bond issuers. This is consistent with an efficient market. Rating changes actually largely confirm a change in

[2] Mark I. Weinstein, "The Effect of a Rating Change Announcement on Bond Price," *Journal of Financial Economics*, December 1977.

Table 13.1 Rating Classes and Median Financial Ratios, 1991–1993

Rating Category	Fixed-Charge Coverage Ratio	Cash Flow to Total Debt	Return on Capital (%)	Long-Term Debt to Capital (%)
AAA	6.34	0.49	24.2	11.7
AA	4.48	0.32	18.4	19.1
A	2.93	0.17	13.5	29.4
BBB	1.82	0.04	9.7	39.6
BB	1.33	0.01	9.1	51.1
B	0.78	(0.02)	6.3	61.8

Source: Standard & Poor's *Debt Rating Guide*, 1994. Reprinted by permission of Standard & Poor's Ratings Group.

status that has been reflected in security prices already. Holthausen and Leftwich,[3] however, found that bond rating downgrades (but not upgrades) are associated with abnormal returns in the stock of the affected company.

Many studies have tested whether financial ratios can in fact be used to predict default risk. One of the best-known series of tests has been conducted by Edward Altman, who has used discriminant analysis to predict bankruptcy. With this technique a firm is assigned a score based on its financial characteristics. If its score exceeds a cutoff value, the firm is deemed creditworthy. A score below the cutoff value indicates significant bankruptcy risk in the near future.

To illustrate the technique, suppose that we were to collect data on the return on equity (ROE) and coverage ratios of a sample of firms, and then keep records of any corporate bankruptcies. In Figure 13.4 we plot the ROE and coverage ratios for each firm using X for firms that eventually went bankrupt and O for those that remained solvent. Clearly, the X and O firms show different patterns of data, with the solvent firms typically showing higher values for the two ratios.

The discriminant analysis determines the equation of the line that best separates the X and O observations. Suppose that the equation of the line is $.75 = .9 \times \text{ROE} + .4 \times \text{Coverage}$. Each firm is assigned a "Z-score" equal to $.9 \times \text{ROE} + .4 \times \text{Coverage}$ using the firm's ROE and coverage ratios. If the Z-score exceeds .75, the firm plots above the line and is considered a safe bet; Z-scores below .75 foretell financial difficulty.

Altman[4] found the following equation to best separate failing and nonfailing firms:

$$Z = 3.3\frac{\text{EBIT}}{\text{Total assets}} + 99.9\frac{\text{Sales}}{\text{Assets}} + .6\frac{\text{Market value of equity}}{\text{Book value of debt}} + 1.4\frac{\text{Retained earnings}}{\text{Total assets}} + 1.2\frac{\text{Working capital}}{\text{Total assets}}$$

[3] Robert W. Holthausen and Richard E. Leftwich, "The Effect of Bond Rating Changes on Common Stock Prices," *Journal of Financial Economics* 17 (September 1986).

[4] Edward I. Altman, "Financial Ratios, Discriminant Analysis, and the Prediction of Corporate Bankruptcy," *Journal of Finance* 23 (September 1968).

Figure 13.4
Discriminant analysis

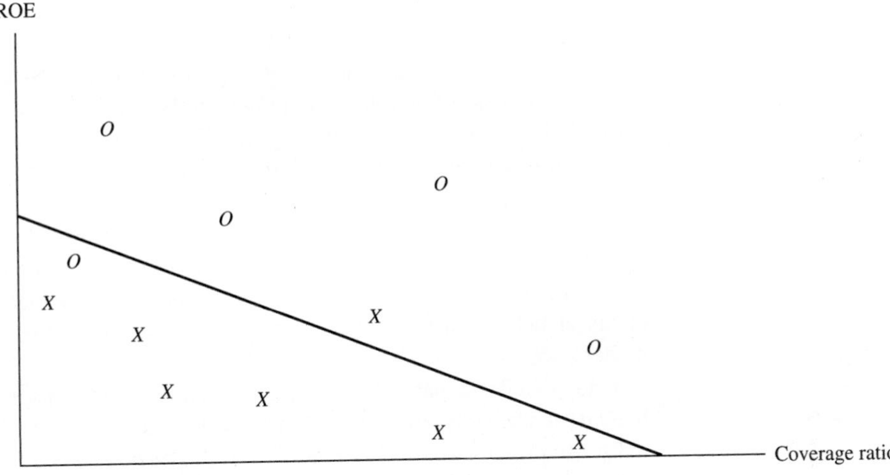

CONCEPT CHECK Question 2. Suppose we add a new variable equal to current liabilities/current assets to Altman's equation. Would you expect this variable to receive a positive or negative coefficient?

Bond Indentures

A bond is issued with an **indenture,** which is the contract between the issuer and the bondholder. Part of the indenture is a set of restrictions on the firm issuing the bond to protect the rights of the bondholders. Such restrictions include provisions relating to collateral, sinking funds, dividend policy, and further borrowing. The issuing firm agrees to these so-called *protective covenants* in order to market its bonds to investors concerned about the safety of the bond issue.

Sinking Funds. Bonds call for the payment of par value at the end of the bond's life. This payment constitutes a large cash commitment for the issuer. To help ensure the commitment does not create a cash flow crisis, the firm agrees to establish a **sinking fund** to spread the payment burden over several years. The fund may operate in one of two ways:

1. The firm may repurchase a fraction of the outstanding bonds in the open market each year.
2. The firm may purchase a fraction of the outstanding bonds at a special call price associated with the sinking fund provision. The firm has an option to purchase the bonds at either the market price or the sinking fund price, whichever is lower. To allocate the burden of the sinking fund call fairly among bondholders, the bonds chosen for the call are selected at random based on serial number.[5]

[5] Although it is uncommon, the sinking fund provision also may call for periodic payments to a trustee, with the payments invested so that the accumulated sum can be used for retirement of the entire issue at maturity.

The sinking fund call differs from a conventional bond call in two important ways. First, the firm can repurchase only a limited fraction of the bond issue at the sinking fund call price. At best, some indentures allow firms to use a *doubling option*, which allows repurchase of double the required number of bonds at the sinking fund call price. Second, the sinking fund call price generally is lower than the call price established by other call provisions in the indenture. The sinking fund call price usually is set at the bond's par value.

Although sinking funds ostensibly protect bondholders by making principal repayment more likely, they can hurt the investor. If interest rates fall and bond prices rise, firms will benefit from the sinking fund provision that enables them to repurchase their bonds at below-market prices. In these circumstances, the firm's gain is the bondholder's loss.

One bond issue that does not require a sinking fund is a *serial bond* issue. In a serial bond issue, the firm sells bonds with staggered maturity dates. As bonds mature sequentially, the principal repayment burden for the firm is spread over time just as it is with a sinking fund. Serial bonds do not include call provisions.

Subordination of Further Debt. One of the factors determining bond safety is total outstanding debt of the issuer. If you bought a bond today, you would be understandably distressed to see the firm tripling its outstanding debt tomorrow. Your bond would be of lower quality than it appeared when you bought it. To prevent firms from harming bondholders in this manner, **subordination clauses** restrict the amount of additional borrowing. Additional debt might be required to be subordinated in priority to existing debt; that is, in the event of bankruptcy, *subordinated* or *junior* debtholders will not be paid unless and until the prior senior debt is fully paid off. For this reason, subordination is sometimes called a "me-first rule," meaning the senior (earlier) bondholders are to be paid first in the event of bankruptcy.

Dividend Restrictions. Covenants also limit firms in the amount of dividends they are allowed to pay. These limitations protect the bondholders because they force the firm to retain assets rather than paying them out to stockholders. A typical restriction disallows payments of dividends if cumulative dividends paid since the firm's inception exceed cumulative net income plus proceeds from sales of stock.

Collateral. Some bonds are issued with specific collateral behind them. **Collateral** can take several forms, but it represents a particular asset of the firm that the bondholders receive if the firm defaults on the bond. If the collateral is property, the bond is called a *mortgage bond.* If the collateral takes the form of other securities held by the firm, the bond is a *collateral trust bond.* In the case of equipment, the bond is known as an *equipment obligation bond.* This last form of collateral is used most commonly by firms such as railroads, where the equipment is fairly standard and can be easily sold to another firm should the firm default and the bondholders acquire the collateral.

Because of the specific collateral that backs them, collaterized bonds generally are considered the safest variety of corporate bonds. General **debenture** bonds by contrast do not provide for specific collateral; they are *unsecured* bonds. The bondholder relies solely on the general earning power of the firm for the bond's safety. If the firm

Figure 13.5

Callable bond issued by Mobil

Source: *Moody's Industrial Manual*, Moody's Investor Services, 1994.

& Mobil Corp. debenture 8s, due 2032:
Rating — Aa2

AUTH — $250,000,000.
OUTSTG — Dec. 31, 1993, $250,000,000.
DATED — Oct. 30, 1991.
INTEREST — F&A 12.
TRUSTEE — Chemical Bank.
DENOMINATION — Fully registered, $1,000 and integral multiples thereof. Transferable and exchangeable without service charge.
CALLABLE — As a whole or in part, at any time, on or after Aug. 12, 2002, at the option of Co. on at least 30 but not more than 60 days' notice to each Aug. 11 as follows:

2003	105.007	2004	104.756	2005	104.506
2006	104.256	2007	104.005	2008	103.755
2009	103.505	2010	103.254	2011	103.004
2012	102.754	2013	102.503	2014	102.253
2015	102.003	2016	101.752	2017	101.502
2018	101.252	2019	101.001	2020	100.751
2021	100.501	2022	100.250		

and thereafter at 100 plus accrued interest.
SECURITY — Not secured. Ranks equally with all other unsecured and unsubordinated indebtedness of Co. Co. nor any Affiliate will not incurr any indebtedness; provided that Co. will not create as sucurity for any indebtedness for borrowed money, any mortgage, pledge, security interest or lien on any stock or indebtedness is directly owned by Co., without effectively providing that the debt securities shall be secured equally and ratably with such indebtedness, so long as such indebtedness shall be so secured.
INDENTURE MODIFICATION — Indenture may be modified, except as provided with, consent of 66⅔% of debs. outstg.
RIGHTS ON DEFAULT — Trustee, or 25% of debs. outstg., may declare principal dua nad payable (30 days' grace for payment of interest).
LISTED — On New York Stock Exchange.
PURPOSE — Proceeds used for general corporate purposes.
OFFERED — ($250,000,000) at 99.51 plus accrued interest (proceeds to Co., 99.11) on Aug. 5, 1992 thru Merrill Lynch & Co., Donaldson, Lufkin & Jenerette Securities Corp., PaineWebber Inc., Prudential Securities Inc., Smith Barney, Harris Upham & Co. Inc. and associates.

defaults, debenture owners become general creditors of the firm. Because they are safer, collateralized bonds generally offer lower yields than general debentures.

Figure 13.5 shows the terms of a bond issued by Mobil as described in *Moody's Industrial Manual*. (This is the bond highlighted in Figure 13.2.) The terms of the bond are typical and illustrate many of the indenture provisions we have mentioned. The bond is registered and listed on the NYSE. Although it was issued in 1991, it is not callable until 2002. Although the call price started at 105.007% of par value, it falls gradually until it reaches par after 2020.

13.3 Bond Pricing

Review of the Present Value Relationship

Because a bond's coupon payments and principal repayment all occur months or years in the future, the price an investor would be willing to pay for a claim to those payments depends on the value of dollars to be received in the future compared to dollars in hand today. The *present value* of a claim to a dollar to be paid in the future is the market price at which that claim would sell if it were traded in the securities market.

We know that the present value of a dollar to be received in the future is less than one dollar. The time spent waiting to receive the dollar imposes an opportunity cost on the investor—if the money is not in hand today, it cannot be invested to start generating income immediately. Denoting the current market interest rate by r, the present value of a dollar to be receive n years from now is $1/(1 + r)^n$.

To see why this is so, consider an example in which the interest rate is 5%, $r = .05$. According to the present value rule, the value of $1 to be received in 10 years would be $1/(1.05)^{10} = \$.614$. A little over 61 cents is the amount that would be paid in the marketplace for a claim to a payment of $1 in 10 years. This is because a person investing today at the going 5% rate of interest realizes that only $.614 needs to be set aside now in order to provide a final value of $1 in 10 years, as $\$.614 \times 1.05^{10} = \$1.00$. The present value formula tells us exactly how much an investor should be willing to pay for a claim to a future cash flow. This value will be the current price of the claim.

We simplify for now by assuming there is one interest rate that is appropriate for discounting cash flows of any maturity, but we can relax this assumption easily. In practice, there may be different discount rates for cash flows accruing in different periods. For the time being, however, we ignore this refinement.

Bond Pricing

To value a security, we discount its expected cash flows by the appropriate discount rate. The cash flows from a bond consist of coupon payments until the maturity date plus the final payment of par value. Therefore

$$\text{Bond value} = \text{Present value of coupons} + \text{present value of par value}$$

If we call the maturity date T and call the interest rate r, the bond value can be written as

$$\text{Bond value} = \sum_{t=1}^{T} \frac{\text{Coupon}}{(1 + r)^t} + \frac{\text{Par value}}{(1 + r)^T} \qquad \textbf{(13.1)}$$

The summation sign in equation 13.1 directs us to add the present value of each coupon payment; each coupon is discounted based on the time until it will be paid. The first term on the right-hand side of equation 13.1 is the present value of an annuity. The second term is the present value of a single amount, the final payment of the bond's par value.

An Example: Bond Pricing. We discussed earlier an 8% coupon, 30-year maturity bond with par value of $1,000 paying 60 semiannual coupon payments of $40 each. Suppose that the interest rate is 8% annually, or 4% per six-month period. Then the value of the bond can be written as

$$\text{Price} = \sum_{t=1}^{60} \frac{\$40}{(1.04)^t} + \frac{\$1{,}000}{(1.04)^{60}} \qquad \textbf{(13.2)}$$

Figure 13.6
The inverse relationship between bond prices and yields

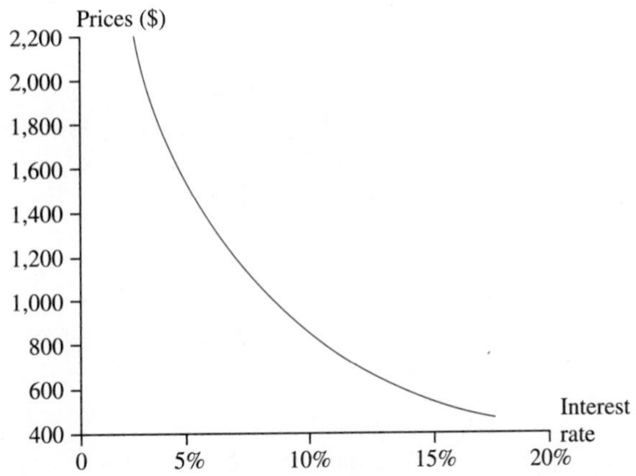

For notational simplicity, we can write equation 13.2 as

$$\text{Price} = \$40 \times \text{PA}(4\%, 60) + \$1{,}000 \times \text{PF}(4\%, 60)$$

where PA(4%, 60) represents the present value of an annuity of $1 when the interest rate is 4% and the annuity lasts for 60 six-month periods, and PF(4%, 60) is the present value of a single payment of $1 to be received in 60 periods.

It is easy to confirm that the present value of the bond's 60 semiannual coupon payments of $40 each is $904.94, whereas the $1,000 final payment of par value has a present value of $95.06, for a total bond value of $1,000. You can perform these calculations on any financial calculator or use a set of present value tables.

In this example, the coupon rate equals yield to maturity, and the bond price equals par value. If the interest rate were not equal to the bond's coupon rate, the bond would not sell at par value. For example, if the interest rate were to rise to 10% (5% per six months), the bond's price would fall by $189.29 to $810.71, as follows

$$\begin{aligned} &\$40 \times \text{PA}(5\%, 60) + \$1{,}000 \times \text{PF}(5\%, 60) \\ &= \$757.17 + \$53.54 \\ &= \$810.71 \end{aligned}$$

At a higher interest rate, the present value of the payments to be received by the bondholder is lower. Therefore, the bond price will fall as market interest rates rise. This illustrates a crucial general rule in bond valuation. When interest rates rise, bond prices must fall because the present value of the bond's payments are obtained by discounting at a higher interest rate.

Figure 13.6 shows the price of the 30-year, 8% coupon bond for a range of interest rates. The negative slope illustrates the inverse relationship between prices and yields. Note also from the figure (and from Table 13.2) that the shape of the curve implies that an increase in the interest rate results in a price decline that is smaller than the price gain resulting from a decrease of equal magnitude in the interest rate. This property of bond prices is called *convexity* because of the convex shape of the bond price curve. This curvature reflects the fact that progressive increases in the interest rate result in

Table 13.2 Bond Prices at Different Interest Rates (8% coupon bond, coupons paid semiannually)

	Bond Price at Given Market Interest Rate				
Time to Maturity	**4%**	**6%**	**8%**	**10%**	**12%**
1 year	1,038.83	1,029.13	1,000.00	981.41	963.33
10 years	1,327.03	1,148.77	1,000.00	875.35	770.60
20 years	1,547.11	1,231.15	1,000.00	828.41	699.07
30 years	1,695.22	1,276.76	1,000.00	810.71	676.77

progressively smaller reductions in the bond price.[6] Therefore, the price curve becomes flatter at higher interest rates.

CONCEPT CHECK

Question 3. Calculate the price of the bond for a market interest rate of 3% per half year. Compare the capital gains for the interest rate decline to the losses incurred when the rate increases to 5%.

Corporate bonds typically are issued at par value. This means that the underwriters of the bond issue (the firms that market the bonds to the public for the issuing corporation) must choose a coupon rate that very closely approximates market yields. In a primary issue of bonds, the underwriters attempt to sell the newly issued bonds directly to their customers. If the coupon rate is inadequate, investors will not pay par value for the bonds.

After the bonds are issued, bondholders may buy or sell bonds in secondary markets, such as the one operated by the New York Stock Exchange or the over-the-counter market, where most bonds trade. In these secondary markets, bond prices move in accordance with market forces. The bond prices fluctuate inversely with the market interest rate.

The inverse relationship between price and yield is a central feature of fixed-income securities. Interest rate fluctuations represent the main source of risk in the fixed-income market, and we devote considerable attention in Chapter 15 to assessing the sensitivity of bond prices to market yields. For now, however, it is sufficient to highlight one key factor that determines that sensitivity, namely, the maturity of the bond.

A general rule in evaluating bond price risk is that, keeping all other factors the same, the longer the maturity of the bond, the greater the sensitivity of price to fluctuations in the interest rate. For example, consider Table 13.2, which presents the price of an 8% coupon bond at different market yields and times to maturity. For any departure of the interest rate from 8% (the rate at which the bond sells at par value), the change in the bond price is smaller for shorter times to maturity.

[6] The progressively smaller impact of interest rate increases results from the fact that at higher rates the bond is worth less. Therefore, an additional increase in rates operates on a smaller initial base, resulting in a smaller price reduction.

This makes sense. If you buy the bond at par with an 8% coupon rate, and market rates subsequently rise, then you suffer a loss: You have tied up your money earning 8% when alternative investments offer higher returns. This is reflected in a capital loss on the bond—a fall in its market price. The longer the period for which your money is tied up, the greater the loss, and correspondingly the greater the drop in the bond price. In Table 13.2, the row for one-year maturity bonds shows little price sensitivity—that is, with only one year's earnings at stake, changes in interest rates are not too threatening. But for 30-year maturity bonds, interest rate swings have a large impact on bond prices.

This is why short-term Treasury securities such as T-bills are considered to be the safest. They are free not only of default risk, but also largely of price risk attributable to interest rate volatility.

13.4 BOND YIELDS

We have noted that the current yield of a bond measures only the cash income provided by the bond as a percentage of bond price and ignores any prospective capital gains or losses. We would like a measure of rate of return that accounts for both current income as well as the price increase or decrease over the bond's life. The yield to maturity is the standard measure of the total rate of return of the bond over its life. However, it is far from a perfect measure, and we will explore several variations of this statistic.

Yield to Maturity

In practice, an investor considering the purchase of a bond is not quoted a promised rate of return. Instead, the investor must use the bond price, maturity date, and coupon payments to infer the return offered by the bond over its life. The **yield to maturity** (YTM) is a measure of the average rate of return that will be earned on a bond if it is bought now and held until maturity. To calculate the yield to maturity, we solve the bond price equation for the interest rate given the bond's price.

For example, suppose an 8% coupon, 30-year bond is selling at $1,276.76. What average rate of return would be earned by an investor purchasing the bond at this price? To answer this question, we find the interest rate at which the present value of the remaining bond payments equals the bond price. This is the rate that is consistent with the observed price of the bond. Therefore, we solve for r in the following equation.

$$\$1{,}276.76 = \sum_{t=1}^{60} \frac{\$40}{(1+r)^t} + \frac{\$1{,}000}{(1+r)^{60}}$$

or, equivalently

$$1{,}276.76 = 40 \times \text{PA}(r, 60) + 1{,}000 \times \text{PF}(r, 60)$$

These equations have only one unknown variable, the interest rate, r. You can use a financial calculator to confirm that the solution to the equation is $r = .03$, or 3% per half year.[7] This is considered the bond's yield to maturity, as the bond would be fairly

[7] Without a financial calculator, you still could solve the equation, but you would need to use a trial-and-error approach.

priced at $1,276.76 if the fair market rate of return on the bond over its entire life were 3% per half year.

The financial press reports yields on an annualized basis, however, and annualizes the bond's semiannual yield using simple interest techniques, resulting in an annual percentage rate or APR. Yields annualized using simple interest are also called "bond equivalent yields." Therefore, the semiannual yield would be doubled and reported in the newspaper as a bond equivalent yield of 6%. The *effective* annual yield of the bond, however, accounts for compound interest. If one earns 3% interest every six months, then after one year, each dollar invested grows with interest to $\$1 \times (1.03)^2 = 1.0609$, and the effective annual interest rate on the bond is 6.09%.

The bond's yield to maturity is the internal rate of return on an investment in the bond. The yield to maturity can be interpreted as the compound rate of return over the life of the bond under the assumption that all bond coupons can be reinvested at an interest rate equal to the bond's yield to maturity. Yield to maturity is widely accepted as a proxy for average return.

Yield to maturity is different from the *current yield* of a bond, which is the bond's annual coupon payment divided by the bond price. For example, for the 8%, 30-year bond currently selling at $1,276.76, the current yield would be $80/$1,276.76 = .0627, or 6.27% per year. In contrast, recall that the effective annual yield to maturity is 6.09%. For this bond, which is selling at a premium over par value ($1,276 rather than $1,000), the coupon rate (8%) exceeds the current yield (6.27%), which exceeds the yield to maturity (6.09%). The coupon rate exceeds current yield because the coupon rate divides the coupon payments by par value ($1,000) rather than by the bond price ($1,276). In turn, the current yield exceeds yield to maturity because the yield to maturity accounts for the built-in capital loss on the bond; the bond bought today for $1,276 will eventually fall in value to $1,000 at maturity.

CONCEPT CHECK Question 4. What will be the relationship among coupon rate, current yield, and yield to maturity for bonds selling at discounts from par?

Yield to Call

Yield to maturity is calculated on the assumption that the bond will be held until maturity. What if the bond is callable, however, and may be retired prior to the maturity date? How should we measure average rate of return for bonds subject to a call provision?

Figure 13.7 illustrates the risk of call to the bondholder. The colored line is the value at various market interest rates of a "straight" (i.e., noncallable) bond with par value $1,000, an 8% coupon rate, and a 30-year time to maturity. If interest rates fall, the bond price, which equals the present value of the promised payments, can rise substantially.

Now consider a bond that has the same coupon rate and maturity date but is callable at 110% of par value, or $1,100. When interest rates fall, the present value of the bond's *scheduled* payments rises, but the call provision allows the issuer to repurchase the bond at the call price. If the call price is less than the present value of the scheduled payments, the issuer can call the bond at the expense of the bondholder.

The black line in Figure 13.7 is the value of the callable bond. At high interest rates, the risk of call is negligible, and the values of the straight and callable bonds converge.

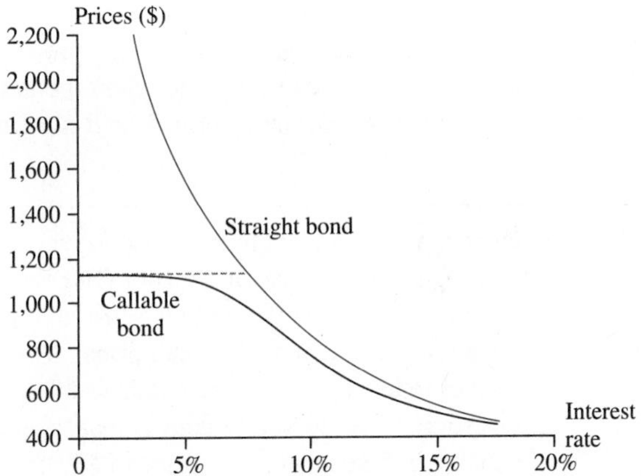

Figure 13.7
Bond prices: Callable and straight debt

At lower rates, however, the values of the bonds begin to diverge, with the difference reflecting the value of the firm's option to reclaim the callable bond at the call price. At very low rates, the bond is called, and its value is simply the call price, $1,100.

This analysis suggests that bond market analysts might be more interested in a bond's yield to call rather than yield to maturity if the bond is especially vulnerable to being called. The yield to call is calculated just like the yield to maturity except that the time until call replaces time until maturity, and the call price replaces the par value.

For example, suppose the 8% coupon, 30-year maturity bond sells for $1,150 and is callable in 10 years at a call price of $1,100. Its yield to maturity and yield to call would be calculated using the following inputs:

	Yield to Call	Yield to Maturity
Coupon payment	$40	$40
Number of semiannual periods	20 periods	60 periods
Final payment	$1,100	$1,000
Price	$1,150	$1,150

The yield to call is then 6.64%, whereas yield to maturity is 6.82%.

We have noted that most callable bonds are issued with an initial period of call protection. In addition, an implicit form of call protection operates for bonds selling at deep discounts from their call prices. Even if interest rates fall a bit, deep-discount bonds still will sell below the call price and thus will not be subject to a call.

Premium bonds that might be selling near their call prices, however, are especially apt to be called if rates fall further. If interest rates fall, a callable premium bond is likely to provide a lower return than could be earned on a discount bond whose potential price appreciation is not limited by the likelihood of a call. Investors in premium bonds often are more interested in the bond's yield to call rather than yield to maturity as a consequence, because it may appear to them that the bond will be retired at the call date.

In fact, the yield reported for callable Treasury bonds in the financial pages of the newspaper (see Figure 13.1) is the yield to *call* for premium bonds and the yield to *maturity* for discount bonds. This is because the call price on Treasury issues is simply par value. If the bond is selling at a premium, it is likely that the Treasury will find it advantageous to call the bond when it enters the call period. If the bond is selling at a discount from par, the Treasury will not find it advantageous to exercise its option to call.

CONCEPT CHECK

Question 5. The yield to maturity on two 10-year maturity bonds currently is 7%. Each bond has a call price of $1,100. One bond has a coupon rate of 6%, the other 8%. Assume for simplicity that bonds are called as soon as the present value of their remaining payments exceeds their call price. What will be the capital gain on each bond if the market interest rate suddenly falls to 6%?

Question 6. A 20-year maturity 9% coupon bond paying coupons semiannually is callable in 5 years at a call price of $1,050. The bond currently sells at a yield to maturity of 8%. What is the yield to call?

Yield to Maturity and Default Risk

Because corporate bonds are subject to default risk, we must distinguish between the bond's promised yield to maturity and its expected yield. The promised or stated yield will be realized only if the firm meets the obligations of the bond issue. Therefore, the stated yield is the *maximum possible* yield to maturity of the bond. The expected yield to maturity must take into account the possibility of a default.

For example, in August 1993, Wang Laboratories, Inc., was in bankruptcy proceedings, and its bonds due in 2009 were selling at about 35% of par value, resulting in a yield to maturity of over 26%. Investors did not really expect these bonds to provide a 26% rate of return. They recognized that bondholders were very unlikely to receive all the payments promised in the bond contract, and that the yield based on *expected* cash flows was far less than the yield based on *promised* cash flows.

To illustrate the difference between expected and promised yield to maturity, suppose a firm issued a 9% coupon bond 20 years ago. The bond now has 10 years left until its maturity date but the firm is having financial difficulties. Investors believe that the firm will be able to make good on the remaining interest payments, but that at the maturity date, the firm will be forced into bankruptcy, and bondholders will receive only 70% of par value. The bond is selling at $750.

Yield to maturity (YTM) would then be calculated using the following inputs:

	Expected YTM	Stated YTM
Coupon payment	$45	$45
Number of semiannual periods	20 periods	20 periods
Final payment	$700	$1,000
Price	$750	$750

The yield to maturity based on promised payments is 13.7%. Based on the expected payment of $700 at maturity, however, the yield to maturity would be only 11.6%. The stated yield to maturity is greater than the yield investors actually expect to receive.

Figure 13.8 Yields on long-term bonds

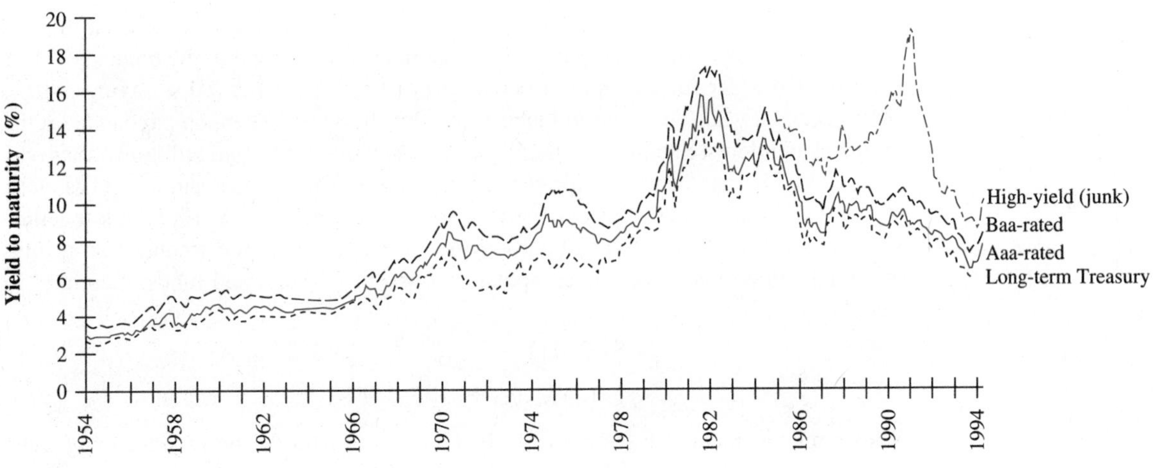

CONCEPT CHECK Question 7. What is the expected yield to maturity if the firm is in even worse condition and investors expect a final payment of only $600?

To compensate for the possibility of default, corporate bonds must offer a **default premium.** The default premium is the difference between the promised yield on a corporate bond and the yield of an otherwise-identical government bond that is riskless in terms of default. If the firm remains solvent and actually pays the investor all of the promised cash flows, the investor will realize a higher yield to maturity than would be realized from the government bond. If, however, the firm goes bankrupt, the corporate bond is likely to provide a lower return than the government bond. The corporate bond has the potential for both better and worse performance than the default-free Treasury bond. In other words, it is riskier.

The pattern of default premiums offered on risky bonds is sometimes called the *risk structure of interest rates*. The greater the default risk, the higher the default premium. Figure 13.8 shows yield to maturity of bonds of different risk classes since 1954 and yields on junk bonds since 1986. You can see here clear evidence of default-risk premiums on promised yields.

One particular manner in which yield spreads seem to vary over time is related to the business cycle. Yield spreads tend to be wider when the economy is in a recession. Apparently, investors perceive a higher probability of bankruptcy when the economy is faltering, even holding bond ratings constant. They require a commensurately higher default premium. This is sometimes termed a *flight to quality*, meaning that investors move their funds into safer bonds unless they can obtain larger premiums on lower-rated securities.

Realized Compound Yield versus Yield to Maturity

We have noted that yield to maturity will equal the rate of return realized over the life of the bond if all coupons are reinvested at an interest rate equal to the bond's yield to maturity. Consider for example, a two-year bond selling at par value paying a 10% coupon once a year. The yield to maturity is 10%. If the $100 coupon payment is reinvested at an interest rate of 10%, the $1,000 investment in the bond will grow after two years to $1,210, as illustrated in Figure 13.9, Panel **A**. The coupon paid in the first year is reinvested and grows with interest to a second-year value of $110, which together with the second coupon payment and payment of par value in the second year, results in a total value of $1,210. The compound growth rate of invested funds, therefore, is calculated from

$$\$1{,}000\,(1 + y_{\text{realized}})^2 = \$1{,}210$$
$$y_{\text{realized}} = .10 = 10\%$$

With a reinvestment rate equal to the 10% yield to maturity, the *realized* compound yield equals yield to maturity.

But what if the reinvestment rate is not 10%? If the coupon can be invested at more than 10%, funds will grow to more than $1,210, and the realized compound return will exceed 10%. If the reinvestment rate is less than 10%, so will be the realized compound return.

Suppose for example that the interest rate at which the coupon can be invested equals 8%. The following calculations are illustrated in Panel **B** of Figure 13.9.

Future value of first coupon payment with interest earnings	$100 × 1.08 = $ 108
Cash payment in second year (final coupon plus par value)	$1,100
Total value of investment with reinvested coupons	$1,208

The realized compound yield is computed by calculating the compound rate of growth of invested funds, assuming that all coupon payments are reinvested. The investor purchased the bond for par at $1,000, and this investment grew to $1,208.

$$\$1{,}000\,(1 + y_{\text{realized}})^2 = \$1{,}208$$
$$y_{\text{realized}} = .0991 = 9.91\%$$

This example highlights the problem with conventional yield to maturity when reinvestment rates can change over time. Conventional yield to maturity will not equal realized compound return. However, in an economy with future interest rate uncertainty, the rates at which interim coupons will be reinvested are not yet known. Therefore, although realized compound yield can be computed *after* the investment period ends, it cannot be computed in advance without a forecast of future reinvestment rates. This reduces much of the attraction of the realized yield measure.

Yield to Maturity versus Holding Period Return

You should not confuse the rate of return on a bond over any particular holding period with the bond's yield to maturity. The yield to maturity is defined as the single discount

Figure 13.9
Growth of invested funds

A. Reinvestment rate = 10%

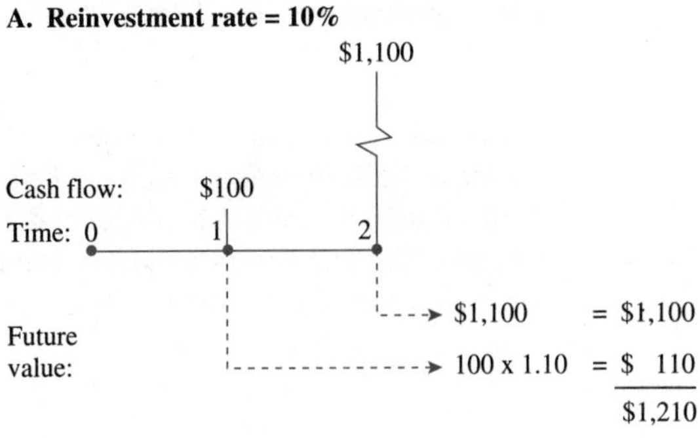

B. Reinvestment rate = 8%

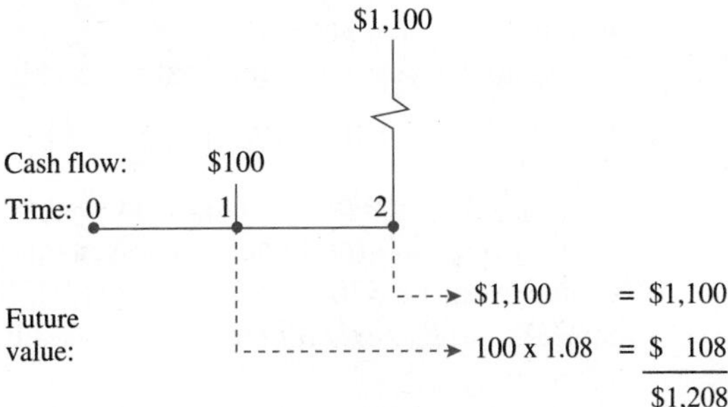

rate at which the present value of the payments provided by the bond equals its price. The yield to maturity is a measure of the average rate of return over the bond's life if it is held until maturity. In contrast, the holding period return equals income earned over a period (including capital gains or losses) as a percentage of the bond price at the start of the period. The holding period return can be calculated for any holding period based on the income generated over that period.

For example, if a 30-year bond paying an annual coupon of $80 is purchased for $1,000, its yield to maturity is 8%. If the bond price increases to $1,050 by year end, its yield to maturity will fall below 8% (the bond is now selling above par value, so yield to maturity must be less than the 8% coupon rate), but the holding period return for the year is greater than 8%:

$$\text{Holding period return} = \frac{\$80 + (\$1,050 - \$1,000)}{\$1,000} = .13, \text{ or } 13\%$$

13.5 Bond Prices over Time

As we noted earlier, a bond will sell at par value when its coupon rate equals the market interest rate. In these circumstances, the investor receives fair compensation for the time value of money in the form of the recurring interest payments. No further capital gain is necessary to provide fair compensation.

When the coupon rate is lower than the market interest rate, the coupon payments alone will not provide investors as high a return as they could earn elsewhere in the market. To receive a fair return on such an investment, investors also need to earn price appreciation on their bonds. The bonds, therefore, would have to sell below par value to provide a "built-in" capital gain on the investment.

To illustrate this point, suppose a bond was issued several years ago when the interest rate was 7%. The bond's annual coupon rate was thus set at 7%. (We will suppose for simplicity that the bond pays its coupon annually.) Now, with three years left in the bond's life, the interest rate is 8% per year. The bond's fair market price is the present value of the remaining annual coupons plus payment of par value. That present value is

$$\$70 \times \text{PA}(8\%, 3) + \$1{,}000 \times \text{PF}(8\%, 3) = \$974.23$$

which is less than par value.

In another year, after the next coupon is paid, the bond would sell at

$$\$70 \times \text{PA}\ (8\%, 2) + \$1{,}000 \times \text{PF}(8\%, 2) = \$982.17$$

thereby yielding a capital gain over the year of $7.94. If an investor had purchased the bond at $974.23, the total return over the year would equal the coupon payment plus capital gain, or $70 + $7.94 = $77.94. This represents a rate of return of $77.94/$974.23, or 8%, exactly the current rate of return available elsewhere in the market.

CONCEPT CHECK Question 8. What will the bond price be in yet another year, when only one year remains until maturity? What is the rate of return to an investor who purchases the bond at $982.17 and sells it one year hence?

When bond prices are set according to the present value formula, any discount from par value provides an anticipated capital gain that will augment a below-market coupon rate just sufficiently to provide a fair total rate of return. Conversely, if the coupon rate exceeds the market interest rate, the interest income by itself is greater than that available elsewhere in the market. Investors will bid up the price of these bonds above their par values. As the bonds approach maturity, they will fall in value because fewer of these above-market coupon payments remain. The resulting capital losses offset the large coupon payments so that the bondholder again receives only a fair rate of return.

Question 8 at the end of the chapter asks you to work through the case of the high coupon bond. Figure 13.10 traces out the price paths of high and low coupon bonds (net of accrued interest) as time to maturity approaches. The low coupon bond enjoys capital gains, whereas the high coupon bond suffers capital losses.

We use these examples to show that each bond offers investors the same total rate of return. Although the capital gain versus income components differ, the price of each bond is set to provide competitive rates, as we should expect in well-functioning capital markets. Security returns all should be comparable on an after-tax risk-adjusted basis. If they are not, investors will try to sell low-return securities, thereby driving down the prices until the total return at the now-lower price is competitive with other

Figure 13.10
Price paths of coupon bonds

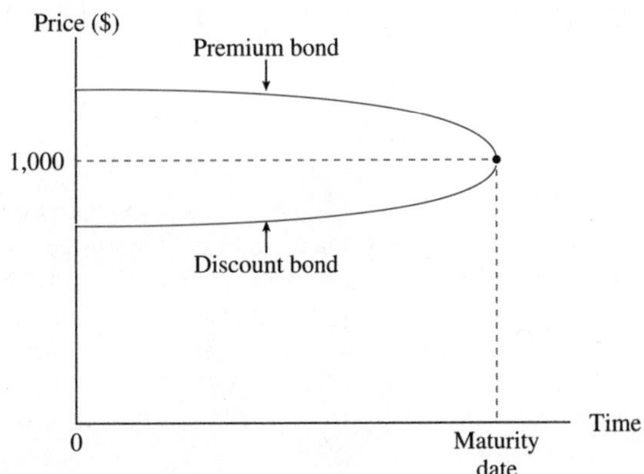

securities. Prices should continue to adjust until all securities are fairly priced in that expected returns are appropriate (given necessary risk and tax adjustments).

Zero-Coupon Bonds

Original issue discount bonds are less common than coupon bonds issued at par. These are bonds that are issued intentionally with low coupon rates that cause the bond to sell at a discount from par value. An extreme example of this type of bond is the *zero-coupon bond*, which carries no coupons and must provide all its return in the form of price appreciation. Zeros provide only one cash flow to their owners, and that is on the maturity date of the bond.

U.S. Treasury bills are examples of short-term zero-coupon instruments. The Treasury issues or sells a bill for some amount less than $10,000, agreeing to repay $10,000 at the bill's maturity. All of the investor's return comes in the form of price appreciation over time.

Longer-term zero-coupon bonds are commonly created synthetically. Several investment banking firms buy coupon-paying Treasury bonds and sell rights to single payments backed by the bonds. These bonds are said to be *stripped* of coupons, and so are called *Treasury strips*. (See Figure 13.1 to see the listing of these bonds in *The Wall Street Journal*.) They often have colorful names such as CATS (certificates of accrual on Treasury securities, issued by Salomon Brothers) or TIGRs (Treasury investment growth receipts, issued by Merrill Lynch). The single payments are, in essence, zero-coupon bonds collateralized by the original Treasury securities and so are virtually free of default risk (see the nearby box).

What should happen to prices of zeros as time passes? On their maturity dates, zeros must sell for par value. Before maturity, however, they should sell at discounts from par, because of the time value of money. As time passes, price should approach par value. In fact, if the interest rate is constant a zero's price will increase at exactly the rate of interest.

To illustrate this property, consider a zero with 30 years until maturity, and suppose the market interest rate is 10% per year. The price of the bond today will be

LYONs and TIGRs, No Bears, Oh, My! LYONs and TIGRs, No . . .

Blame it all on Merrill Lynch & Co.

The firm's TIGRs—Treasury investment growth receipts—were successful enough to spawn a slew of imitators. Salomon Brothers Inc. soon followed with CATS, or certificates of accrual on Treasury securities. Now, more than animals are running amok on Wall Street.

How About a Test Drive?

Salomon is selling securities backed by auto loans called CARs, or certificates of automobile receivables. Drexel Burnham Lambert Inc. calls its version of the same thing FASTBACs, or first automotive short-term bonds and certificates.

One type of securities can be bought, depending on the firm, as STARS or short-term auction-rate stock; DARTS or Dutch-auction-rate transferable securities; MAPS, market-auction preferred stock; AMPS, auction-market preferred stock; and CAMPS, cumulative auction-market preferred stock.

Shearson Lehman Brothers Inc. recently tagged a floating-rate mortgage-backed security with one of Wall Street's most popular words: FIRSTS, or floating-interest-rate short-term securities.

Merrill Lynch, knowing no boundaries, added COLTS, or continuously offered long-term securities, and OPOSSMS, options to purchase or sell specific mortgage-backed securities. Salomon bolstered its line-up with HOMES, or homeowner-mortgage Euro securities, and CARDs, certificates for amortizing revolving debts, backed by credit-card receivables.

A Salomon spokeswoman gives one explanation for the practice: "Names without acronyms can be tongue-twisting and hard to remember." A Merrill official offers another: "It's one-upmanship."

Some officials say the trend has gotten out of hand. Wesley Jones, head of product development at First Boston Corp., says if an acronym "sounds like an animal, it won't describe what you've got."

ZCCBs and SLOBs

Likewise, by the time a name has been massaged to produce an acronym, it may tell little of the product. For example, Merrill Lynch offers LYONs, or liquid-yield option notes; these are really zero-coupon convertible bonds, but calling them ZCCBs wouldn't sound nearly as good for these companions of TIGRs.

Of course, the uncontrived names of some securities actually form acronyms, but these rarely make useful marketing tools. First Boston, for instance, once underwrote an offering of secured-lease obligation bonds. It used the full name.

From *The Wall Street Journal*, February 18, 1987.

$\$1{,}000/(1.10)^{30} = \$57.31$. Next year, with only 29 years until maturity, the price will be $\$1{,}000/(1.10)^{29} = \$63.04$, a 10% increase over its previous-year value. Because the par value of the bond is now discounted for one fewer year, its price has increased by the one-year discount factor.

Figure 13.11 presents the price path of a 10-year zero-coupon bond until its maturity date for an annual market interest rate of 10%. The bond prices rise exponentially, not linearly, until its maturity.

After-Tax Returns

The tax authorities recognize that the "built-in" price appreciation on original issue discount (OID) bonds such as zero-coupon bonds represents an implicit interest payment

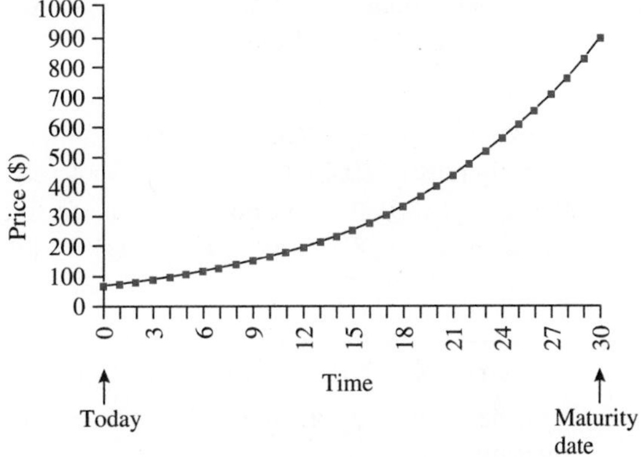

Figure 13.11
The price of a 30-year zero-coupon bond over time. Price equals $1000/(1.10)^T$ where T is time until maturity

to the holder of the security. The IRS, therefore, calculates a price appreciation schedule to impute taxable interest income for the built-in appreciation during a tax year, even if the asset is not sold or does not mature until a future year. Any additional gains or losses that arise from changes in market interest rates are treated as capital gains or losses if the OID bond is sold during the tax year.

Let's consider an example. If the interest rate originally is 10%, the 30-year zero would be issued at a price of $\$1,000/(1.10)^{30} = \$57.31$. The following year, the IRS calculates what the bond price would be if the yield remains at 10%. This is $\$1,000/(1.10)^{29} = \$63.04$. Therefore, the IRS imputes interest income of $\$63.04 - \$57.31 = \$5.73$. This amount is subject to tax. Notice that the imputed interest income is based on a "constant yield method" that ignores any changes in market interest rates.

If interest rates actually fall, let's say to 9.9%, the bond price actually will be $\$1,000/(1.099)^{29} = \$64.72$. If the bond is sold, then the difference between \$64.72 and \$63.04 will be treated as capital gains income and taxed at the capital gains tax rate. If the bond is not sold, then the price difference is an unrealized capital gain and does not result in taxes in that year. In either case, the investor must pay taxes on the \$5.73 of imputed interest at the rate on ordinary income.

The same reasoning is applied to the taxation of other original issue discount bonds, even if they are not zero-coupon bonds. Consider as an example, a 30-year maturity bond that is issued with a coupon rate of 4% and a yield to maturity of 8%. For simplicity, we will assume that the bond pays coupons once annually. Because of the low coupon rate, the bond will be issued at a price far below par value, specifically at a price of \$549.69. If the bond's yield to maturity remains at 8%, then its price in one year will rise to \$553.66. (Confirm this for yourself.) This provides a pre-tax holding period return of exactly 8%:

$$\text{HPR} = \frac{\$40 + (\$553.66 - \$549.69)}{\$549.69} = .08$$

The increase in the bond price based on a constant yield, however, is treated as interest income, so the investor is required to pay taxes on imputed interest income of $\$553.66 - \$549.69 = \$3.97$. If the bond's yield actually changes during the year, the difference between the bond's price and the "constant-yield value" of $553.66 would be treated as capital gains income if the bond is sold.

CONCEPT CHECK

Question 9. Suppose that the yield to maturity of the 4% coupon, 30-year maturity bond actually falls to 7% by the end of the first year, and that the investor sells the bond after the first year. If the investor's tax rate on interest income is 36% and the tax rate on capital gains is 28%, what is the investor's after-tax rate of return?

SUMMARY

1. Fixed-income securities are distinguished by their promise to pay a fixed or specified stream of income to their holders. The coupon bond is a typical fixed-income security.

2. Treasury notes and bonds have original maturities greater than one year. They are issued at or near par value, with their prices quoted net of accrued interest. T-bonds may be callable during their last five years of life.

3. When bonds are subject to potential default, the stated yield to maturity is the maximum possible yield to maturity that can be realized by the bondholder. In the event of default, however, that promised yield will not be realized. To compensate bond investors for default risk, bonds must offer default premiums, that is, promised yields in excess of those offered by default-free government securities. If the firm remains healthy, its bonds will provide higher returns than government bonds. Otherwise the returns may be lower.

4. Bond safety is often measured using financial ratio analysis. Bond indentures are another safeguard to protect the claims of bondholders. Common indentures specify sinking fund requirements, collateralization of the loan, dividend restrictions, and subordination of future debt.

5. Callable bonds should offer higher promised yields to maturity to compensate investors for the fact that they will not realize full capital gains should the interest rate fall and the bonds be called away from them at the stipulated call price. Bonds often are issued with a period of call protection. In addition, discount bonds selling significantly below their call price offer implicit call protection.

6. Put bonds give the bondholder rather than the issuer the option to terminate or extend the life of the bond.

7. Convertible bonds may be exchanged, at the bondholder's discretion, for a specified number of shares of stock. Convertible bondholders "pay" for this option by accepting a lower coupon rate on the security.

8. Floating-rate bonds pay a fixed premium over a reference short-term interest rate. Risk is limited because the rate paid is tied to current market conditions.

9. The yield to maturity is the single interest rate that equates the present value of a security's cash flows to its price. Bond prices and yields are inversely related. For premium bonds, the coupon rate is greater than the current yield, which is greater than the yield to maturity. The order of these inequalities is reversed for discount bonds.

10. The yield to maturity is often interpreted as an estimate of the average rate of return to an investor who purchases a bond and holds it until maturity. This interpreta-

tion is subject to error, however. Related measures are yield to call, realized compound yield, and expected (versus promised) yield to maturity.

11. Prices of zero-coupon bonds rise exponentially over time, providing a rate of appreciation equal to the interest rate. The IRS treats this price appreciation as imputed taxable interest income to the investor.

Key Terms

Fixed-income securities
Bond
Par value
Face value
Coupon rate
Zero-coupon bonds
Convertible bonds
Put bond
Floating-rate bonds
Investment grade bonds
Speculative grade or junk bonds
Indenture
Sinking fund
Subordination clauses
Collateral
Debenture
Yield to maturity
Default premium

Selected Readings

A comprehensive treatment of pricing issues related to fixed-income securities is given in:

Fabozzi, Frank J. *Bond Markets, Analysis, and Strategies,* 2nd edition. Englewood Cliffs, N.J.: Prentice Hall, 1993.

Surveys of fixed-income instruments and investment characteristics are contained in:

Fabozzi, Frank J.; T. Dessa Fabozzi; and Irving M. Pollack. *The Handbook of Fixed Income Securities.* Homewood, Ill.: Business One Irwin, 1991.

Stigum, Marcia; and Frank J. Fabozzi. *The Dow-Jones Guide to Bond and Money Market Investments.* Homewood, Ill.: Dow Jones–Irwin, 1987.

Problems

1. Which security has a higher *effective* annual interest rate?
   a. A three-month T-bill selling at $97,645.
   b. A coupon bond selling at par and paying a 10% coupon semiannually.
2. Treasury bonds paying an 8% coupon rate with *semiannual* payments currently sell at par value. What coupon rate would they have to pay in order to sell at par if they paid their coupons *annually*?
3. Two bonds have identical times to maturity and coupon rates. One is callable at 105, the other at 110. Which should have the higher yield to maturity? Why?
4. Consider a bond with a 10% coupon and with yield to maturity = 8%. If the bond's yield to maturity remains constant, then in one year, will the bond price be higher, lower, or unchanged? Why?
5. Consider an 8% coupon bond selling for $953.10 with three years until maturity making *annual* coupon payments. The interest rates in the next three years will be, with certainty, $r_1 = 8\%$, $r_2 = 10\%$, and $r_3 = 12\%$. Calculate the yield to maturity and realized compound yield of the bond.

6. In June 1982, when the yield to maturity (YTM) on long-term bonds was about 14%, many observers were projecting an eventual decline in these rates. It was not unusual to hear of customers urging portfolio managers to "lock in" these high rates by buying some new issues with these high coupons. You recognize that it is not possible to really lock in such returns for coupon bonds because of the potential reinvestment rate problem if rates decline. Assuming the following expectations for a five-year bond bought at par, compute the total realized compound yield (without taxes) for the bond below.*

   Coupon: 14% (assume annual interest payments at end of each year).
   Maturity: Five years.
   One-year reinvestment rates during:
   Year 2, 3: 10%.
   Year 4, 5: 8%.

7. Assume you have a one-year investment horizon and are trying to choose among three bonds. All have the same degree of default risk and mature in 10 years. The first is a zero-coupon bond that pays $1,000 at maturity. The second has an 8% coupon rate and pays the $80 coupon once per year. The third has a 10% coupon rate and pays the $100 coupon once per year.
   a. If all three bonds are now priced to yield 8% to maturity, what are their prices?
   b. If you expect their yields to maturity to be 8% at the beginning of next year, what will their prices be then? What is your before-tax holding period return on each bond? If your tax bracket is 30 percent on ordinary income and 20 percent on capital gains income, what will your after-tax rate of return be on each?
   c. Recalculate your answer to (*b*) under the assumption that you expect the yields to maturity on each bond to be 7% at the beginning of next year.
8. Consider a bond paying a coupon rate of 10% per year semiannually when the market interest rate is only 4% per half year. The bond has three years until maturity.
   a. Find the bond's price today and six months from now after the next coupon is paid.
   b. What is the total rate of return on the bond?
9. A newly-issued bond pays its coupons once annually. Its coupon rate is 5%, its maturity is 20 years, and its yield to maturity is 8%.
   a. Find the holding period return for a one-year investment period if the bond is selling at a yield to maturity of 7% by the end of the year.
   b. If you sell the bond after one year, what taxes will you owe if the tax rate on interest income is 40% and the tax rate on capital gains income is 30%? The bond is subject to original-issue discount tax treatment.
   c. What is the after-tax holding period return on the bond?
   d. Find the realized compound yield *before taxes* for a 2-year holding period, assuming that (1) you sell the bond after 2 years, (2) the bond yield is 7%

*Reprinted, with permission, from the *CFA Study Guide*. The Institute of Chartered Financial Analysts, Charlottesville, VA.

at the end of the second year, and (3) the coupon can be reinvested for one year at a 3% interest rate.

e. Use the tax rates in part *b* to compute the *after-tax* 2-year realized compound yield. Remember to take account of OID tax rules.

10. A bond with a coupon rate of 7% makes semiannual coupon payments on January 15 and July 15 of each year. *The Wall Street Journal* reports the ask price for the bond on January 30 at 100:02. What is the invoice price of the bond? The coupon period has 182 days.
11. A bond has a current yield of 9% and a yield to maturity of 10%. Is the bond selling above or below par value? Explain.
12. Is the coupon rate of the bond in question 11 more or less than 9%?
13. A newly issued 20-year maturity, zero-coupon bond is issued with a yield to maturity of 8% and face value $1,000. Find the imputed interest income in the first, second, and last year of the bond's life.
14. A newly issued 10-year maturity, 4% coupon bond making *annual* coupon payments is sold to the public at a price of $800. What will be an investor's taxable income from the bond over the coming year? The bond will not be sold at the end of the year. The bond is treated as an original issue discount bond.
15. A 30-year maturity, 8% coupon bond paying coupons semiannually is callable in five years at a call price of $1,100. The bond currently sells at a yield to maturity of 7% (3.5% per half-year).
    a. What is the yield to call?
    b. What is the yield to call if the call price is only $1,050?
    c. What is the yield to call if the call price is $1,100, but the bond can be called in two years instead of five years?
16. A 10-year bond of a firm in severe financial distress has a coupon rate of 14% and sells for $900. The firm is currently renegotiating the debt, and it appears that the lenders will allow the firm to reduce coupon payments on the bond to one-half the originally contracted amount. The firm can handle these lower payments. What is the stated and expected yield to maturity of the bonds? The bond makes its coupon payments annually.
17. A two-year bond with par value $1,000 making annual coupon payments of $100 is priced at $1,000. What is the yield to maturity of the bond? What will be the realized compound yield to maturity if the one year interest rate next year turns out to be (a) 8%, (b) 10%, (c) 12%?
18. The stated yield to maturity and realized compound yield to maturity of a (default-free) zero-coupon bond will always be equal. Why?
19. Suppose that today's date is April 15. A bond with a 10% coupon paid semiannually every January 15 and July 15 is listed in *The Wall Street Journal* as selling at an ask price of 101:04. If you buy the bond from a dealer today, what price will you pay for it?

20. Assume that in 1988 two firms, PG and CLX, were concurrently to undertake private debt placements with the following contractual details:*

---

*Reprinted, with permission, from the Level I 1993 *CFA Study Guide*.

	PG	CLX
Issue size	$1 billion	$100 million
Issue price	100	100
Maturity	1993*	2003
Coupon	10%	11%
Collateral	First mortgage	Unsecured
First call date	1998	1995
Call price	111	106
Sinking fund—beginning	nil	1993
—amount	nil	$5 million/year

*Extendable at the option of the holder for an additional 10 years (to 2003) with no change in coupon rate.

Ignoring credit quality, identify four features of these issues that might account for the lower coupon on the PG debt. Explain.

21. A large forest products manufacturer has outstanding two Baa-rated, $150 million par amount, intermediate-term debt issues:

	10.10% Notes	Floating-Rate Notes
Maturity	1995	1992
Issue date	6-12-85	9-27-84
Callable (beginning on)	6-15-91	10-01-89
Callable at	100	100
Sinking fund	None	None
Current coupon	10.10%	9.9%
Coupon changes	Fixed	Every 6 months
Rate adjusts to	—	1% above 6-month T-bill rate
Range since issued	—	12.9%–8.3%
Current price	73 3/8	97
Current yield	13.77%	10.3%
Yield to maturity	15.87%	—
Price range since issue	100–72	102–93

Given these data:

a. State the minimum coupon rate of interest at which the firm could sell a fixed-rate issue at par due in 1995. Assume the same indenture provisions as the 10.10% notes and disregard any tax considerations.

b. Give two reasons why the floating-rate notes are not selling at par.

c. State and justify whether the risk of call is high, moderate, or low for the fixed-rate issue.

d. Assuming a decline in interest rates is anticipated, identify and justify which issue would be most appropriate for an actively managed bond portfolio where total return is the primary objective.

e. Explain why yield to maturity is not valid for the floating-rate note.

22. You have the following information about a convertible bond issue:*

*Reprinted, with permission, from the *CFA Study Guide*. The Institute of Chartered Financial Analysts, Charlottesville, VA.

Burroughs Corp.
$7^1/_4$% Due 8/1/2010

Agency rating (Moody's/S&P)	A3/A−
Conversion ratio	12.882
Market price of convertible	$102.00
Market price of common stock	$ 66.00
Dividend per share—common	$ 2.60
Call price (first call—8/1/1990)	$106.00
Estimated floor price	$ 66.50

Using this information, calculate the following values and show calculations.

a. Market conversion value.
b. Conversion premium per common share.
c. Current yield—convertible.
d. Dividend yield—common.

23. As the portfolio manager for a large pension fund, you are offered the following bonds:*

	Coupon	Maturity	Price	Call Price	Yield to Maturity
Edgar Corp. (new issue)	14.00%	2002	$101 3/4	$114	13.75%
Edgar Corp. (new issue)	6.00	2002	48 1/8	103	13.60

Assuming you expect a decline in interest rates over the next three years, identify which of the bonds you would select. Justify your answer.†

24. *a.* In terms of option theory, explain the impact on the offering yield of adding a call feature to a proposed bond issue.
b. Explain the impact on the bond's expected life of adding a call feature to a proposed bond issue.
c. Describe *one* advantage and *one* disadvantage of including callable bonds in a portfolio.

25. Philip Morris may issue a 10-year maturity fixed-income security, which might include a sinking-fund provision and either refunding or call protection.‡
a. Describe a sinking-fund provision.
b. Explain the impact of a sinking-fund provision on:
i. The expected average life of the proposed security.
ii. Total principal and interest payments over the life of the proposed security.
c. From the investor's point of view, explain the rationale for demanding a sinking-fund provision.

26. The multiple-choice problems following are based on questions that appeared in past CFA examinations.*

* Reprinted, with permission, from the Level I 1986 *CFA Study Guide*. Copyright 1986, The Institute of Chartered Financial Analysts, Charlottesville, VA. All rights reserved.

† Reprinted, with permission, from the Level II 1993 *CFA Study Guide*. Copyright 1993, Association for Investment Management and Research, Charlottesville, VA. All rights reserved.

‡ Reprinted, with permission, from the Level I 1992 *CFA Study Guide*. Copyright 1992, Association for Investment Management and Research, Charlottesville, VA. All rights reserved.

a. Which bond probably has the highest credit quality?
   i. Sumter, South Carolina, Water and Sewer Revenue Bond.
   ii. Riley County, Kansas, General Obligation Bond.
   iii. University of Kansas Medical Center Refunding Revenue Bonds (insured by American Municipal Bond Assurance Corporation).
   iv. Euless, Texas, General Obligation Bond (refunded and secured by the U.S. government in escrow to maturity).

b. The spread between Treasury and BAA corporate bond yields widens when:
   i. Interest rates are low.
   ii. There is economic uncertainty.
   iii. There is a "flight from quality."
   iv. All of the above.

c. The market risk of an AAA-rated preferred stock relative to an AAA-rated bond is:
   i. Lower.
   ii. Higher.
   iii. Equal.
   iv. Unknown.

d. A bond with a call feature:
   i. Is attractive because the immediate receipt of principal plus premium produces a high return.
   ii. Is more apt to be called when interest rates are high because the interest saving will be greater.
   iii. Will usually have a higher yield than a similar noncallable bond.
   iv. None of the above.

e. The yield to maturity on a bond is:
   i. Below the coupon rate when the bond sells at a discount, and above the coupon rate when the bond sells at a premium.
   ii. The discount rate that will set the present value of the payments equal to the bond price.
   iii. The current yield plus the average annual capital gain rate.
   iv. Based on the assumption that any payments received are reinvested at the coupon rate.

f. A particular bond has a yield to maturity on an APR basis of 12.00% but makes equal quarterly payments. What is the effective annual yield to maturity?
   i. 11.45%.
   ii. 12.00%.
   iii. 12.55%.
   iv. 37.35%.

g. In which *one* of the following cases is the bond selling at a discount?
   i. Coupon rate is greater than current yield, which is greater than yield to maturity.
   ii. Coupon rate, current yield, and yield to maturity are all the same.

iii. Coupon rate is less than current yield, which is less than yield to maturity.
iv. Coupon rate is less than current yield, which is greater than yield to maturity.

h. Consider a five-year bond with a 10% coupon that has a present yield to maturity of 8%. If interest rates remain constant, one year from now the price of this bond will be:

i. Higher.
ii. Lower.
iii. The same.
iv. Par.

i. A revenue bond is distinguished from a general obligation bond in that revenue bonds:

i. Are issued by counties, special districts, cities, towns, and state-controlled authorities, whereas general obligation bonds are only issued by the states themselves.
ii. Are typically secured by limited taxing power, whereas general obligation bonds are secured by unlimited taxing power.
iii. Are issued to finance specific projects and are secured by the revenues of the project being financed.
iv. Have first claim to any revenue increase of the tax authority issuing the bonds.

j. Serial obligation bonds differ from *most* other bonds because:

i. They are secured by the assets and taxing power of the issuer.
ii. Their par value is usually well below $1,000.
iii. Their term to maturity is usually very long (30 years or more).
iv. They possess multiple maturity dates.

k. Which *one* of the following is *not* an advantage of convertible bonds for the investor?

i. The yield on the convertible will typically be higher than the yield on the underlying common stock.
ii. The convertible bond will likely participate in a major upward move in the price of the underlying common stock.
iii. Convertible bonds are typically secured by specific assets of the issuing company.
iv. Investors normally may convert to the underlying common stock.

l. The call feature of a bond means the:

i. Investor can call for payment on demand.
ii. Investor can only call if the firm defaults on an interest payment.
iii. Issuer can call the bond issue before the maturity date.
iv. Issuer can call the issue during the first three years.

m. The annual interest paid on a bond relative to its prevailing market price is called its:

i. Promised yield.

ii. Yield to maturity.
iii. Coupon rate.
iv. Current yield.

n. Which *one* of the following statements about convertible bonds is *false*?
i. The yield on the convertible will typically be higher than the yield on the underlying common stock.
ii. The convertible bond will likely participate in a major upward movement in the price of the underlying common stock.
iii. Convertible bonds are typically secured by specific assets of the issuing company.
iv. A convertible bond can be valued as a straight bond with an attached option.

o. All else being equal, which *one* of the following bonds *most likely* would sell at the highest yield?
i. Callable debenture.
ii. Puttable mortgage bond.
iii. Callable mortgage bond.
iv. Puttable debentures.

p. Yields on nonconvertible preferred stock usually are lower than yields on bonds of the same company because of differences in:
i. Marketability.
ii. Risk.
iii. Taxation.
iv. Call protection.

q. The yield to maturity on a bond is:
i. Below the coupon rate when the bond sells at a discount and above the coupon rate when the bond sells at a premium.
ii. The interest rate that makes the present value of the payments equal to the bond price.
iii. Based on the assumption that all future payments received are reinvested at the coupon rate.
iv. Based on the assumption that all future payments received are reinvested at future market rates.

Chapter 14
The Term Structure of Interest Rates

IN CHAPTER 13 WE ASSUMED FOR THE SAKE OF SIMPLICITY THAT THE SAME CONSTANT INTEREST RATE IS USED TO DISCOUNT CASH FLOWS OF ANY MATURITY. In the real world this is rarely the case. We have seen, for example, that in late 1994 short-term bonds and notes carried yields to maturity only slightly higher than 5% while the longest-term bonds offered yields above 8%. At the time when these bond prices were quoted, anyway, the longer-term securities had higher yields. This, in fact, is a common empirical pattern.

In this chapter we explore the pattern of interest rates for different-term assets. We attempt to identify the factors that account for that pattern and determine what information may be derived from an analysis of the so-called **term structure of interest rates,** the structure of interest rates for discounting cash flows of different maturities.

14.1 THE TERM STRUCTURE UNDER CERTAINTY

What do you conclude from the observation that longer-term bonds offer higher yields to maturity? One possibility is that longer-term bonds are riskier and that the higher yields are evidence of a risk premium that compensates for interest rate risk. Another possibility is that investors expect interest rates to rise and that the higher average yields on long-term bonds reflect the anticipation of high interest rates in the latter years of the bond's life. We will start our analysis of these possibilities with the easiest case: a world with no uncertainty where investors already know the path of future interest rates.

Bond Pricing

The interest rate for a given time interval is called the **short interest rate** for that period. Suppose that all participants in the bond market are convinced that the short rates for the next four years will follow the pattern in Table 14.1

Table 14.1 Interest Rates on One-Year Bonds in Coming Years

Year	Interest Rate
0 (Today)	8%
1	10
2	11
3	11

Of course, market participants cannot look up such a sequence of short rates in *The Wall Street Journal.* All they observe there are prices and yields of bonds of various maturities. Nevertheless, we can think of the short-rate sequence of Table 14.1 as the series of interest rates that investors keep in the back of their minds when they evaluate the prices of different bonds. Given this pattern of rates, what prices might we observe on various maturity bonds? To keep the algebra simple, for now we will treat only a zero-coupon bond.

A bond paying \$1,000 in one year would sell today for \$1,000/1.08 = \$925.93. Similarly, a two-year maturity bond would sell today at price

$$P = \frac{\$1{,}000}{(1.08)(1.10)} = \$841.75 \quad \textbf{(14.1)}$$

This is the present value of the future \$1,000 cash flow, because \$841.75 would need to be set aside now to provide a \$1,000 payment in two years. After one year, the \$841.75 set aside would grow to \$841.75(1.08) = \$909.09 and after the second year to \$909.09(1.10) = \$1,000.

In general we may write the present value of \$1 to be received after n periods as

$$\text{PV of \$1 in } n \text{ periods} = \frac{1}{(1 + r_1)(1 + r_2) \dots (1 + r_n)}$$

where r_i is the one-year interest rate that will prevail in year i. Continuing in this manner, we find the values of the three- and four-year bonds as shown in the middle column of Table 14.2.

From the bond prices we can calculate the yield to maturity on each bond. Recall that the yield is the *single* interest rate that equates the present value of the bond's payments to the bond's price. Although interest rates may vary over time, the yield to maturity is calculated as one "average" rate that is applied to discount all of the bond's payments. For example, the yield on the two-year zero-coupon bond, which we will call y_2, is the interest rate that satisfies

$$841.75 = 1{,}000/(1 + y_2)^2 \quad \textbf{(14.2)}$$

which we solve for $y_2 = .08995$. We repeat the process for the two other bonds, with results as reported in the table. For example, we find y_3 by solving

Table 14.2 Prices and Yields of Zero-Coupon Bonds

Time to Maturity	Price	Yield to Maturity
1	$925.93	8.000%
2	841.75	8.995
3	758.33	9.660
4	683.18	9.993

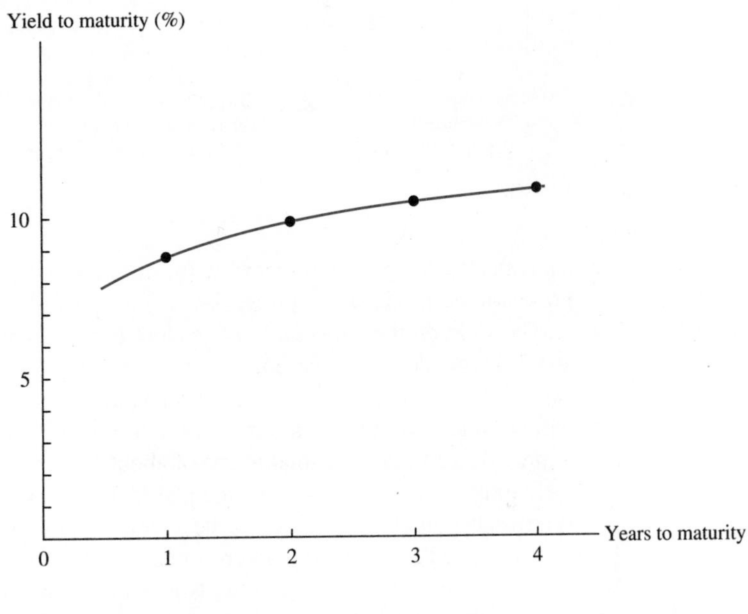

Figure 14.1
Yield curve

$$758.33 = 1{,}000/(1 + y_3)^3$$

Now we can make a graph of the yield to maturity on the four bonds as a function of time to maturity. This graph, which is called the **yield curve,** appears in Figure 14.1.

While the yield curve in Figure 14.1 rises smoothly, a wide range of curves may be observed in practice. Figure 14.2 presents three such curves. Panel **A** is the yield curve from November 1994, which is upward sloping. Panel **B** is a hump-shaped curve, first rising and then falling. The yield curve in Panel **C** is essentially flat.

The yield to maturity on zero-coupon bonds is sometimes called the **spot rate** that prevails today for a period corresponding to the maturity of the zero. The yield curve, or equivalently, the last column of Table 14.2, thus presents the spot rates for four maturities. Note that the spot rates or yields do *not* equal the one-year interest rates for each year.

To emphasize the difference between the sequence of *short* rates for each future year, and *spot* rates for different maturity dates, examine Figure 14.3. The first line of data presents the short rate for each annual period. The lower lines present the spot rates or

Figure 14.2
Treasury yield curves

Source: Various editions of *The Wall Street Journal*. Reprinted by permission of *The Wall Street Journal*, © 1989, 1994 Dow Jones & Company, Inc. All Rights Reserved Worldwide.

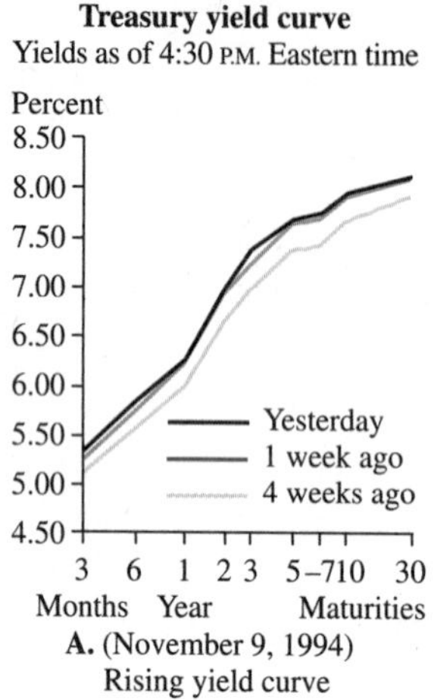

A. (November 9, 1994)
Rising yield curve

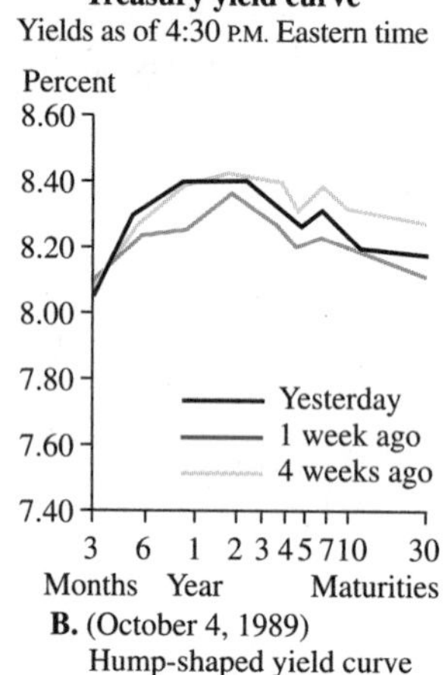

B. (October 4, 1989)
Hump-shaped yield curve

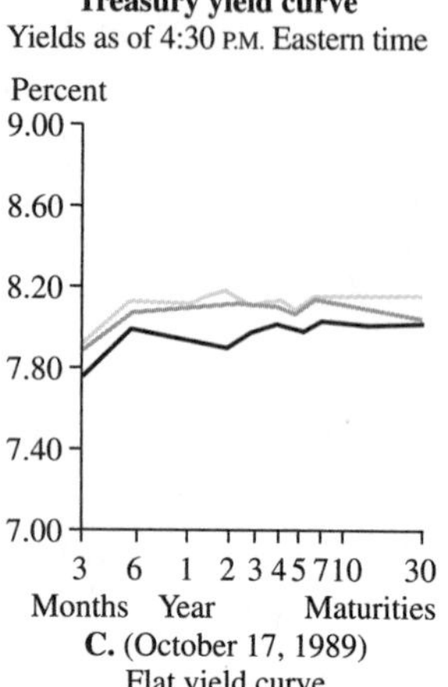

C. (October 17, 1989)
Flat yield curve

equivalently, the yields to maturity, for different holding periods that extend from the present to each relevant maturity date.

The yield on the two-year bond is close to the average of the short rates for years 1 and 2. This makes sense because if interest rates of 8% and 10% will prevail in the next two years, then (ignoring compound interest) a sequence of two one-year investments will provide a cumulative return of 18%. Therefore, we would expect a two-year bond to provide a competitive total return of about 18%, which translates into an annualized yield to maturity of 9%, just about equal to the 8.995% yield we derived in Table 14.2. Because the yield is a measure of the average return over the life of the bond, it should be determined by the market interest rates available in both years 1 and 2.

In fact, we can be more precise. Notice that equations 14.1 and 14.2 each relate the two-year bond's price to appropriate interest rates. Combining equations 14.1 and 14.2, we find

$$841.75 = \frac{1{,}000}{(1.08)(1.10)} = \frac{1{,}000}{(1 + y_2)^2}$$

so that

$$(1 + y_2)^2 = (1.08)(1.10)$$

and

$$1 + y_2 = [(1.08)(1.10)]^{1/2} = 1.08995$$

Similarly,

$$1 + y_3 = [(1 + r_1)(1 + r_2)(1 + r_3)]^{1/3}$$

and

$$1 + y_4 = [(1 + r_1)(1 + r_2)(1 + r_3)(1 + r_4)]^{1/4} \tag{14.3}$$

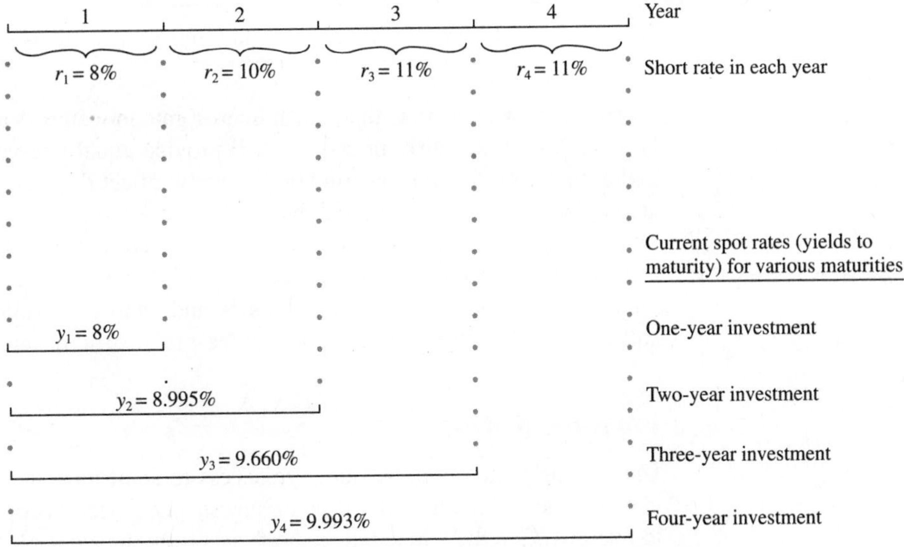

Figure 14.3
Short rates versus spot rates

and so on. Thus, the yields are in fact averages of the interest rates in each period. However, because of compound interest, the relationship is not an arithmetic average but a geometric one.

Holding-Period Returns

What is the rate of return on each of the four bonds in Table 14.2 over a one-year holding period? You might think at first that higher-yielding bonds would provide higher one-year rates of return, but this is not the case. In our simple world with no uncertainty all bonds must offer identical rates of return over any holding period. Otherwise, at least one bond would be dominated by the others in the sense that it would offer a lower rate of return than would combinations of other bonds; no one would be willing to hold the bond, and its price would fall. In fact, despite their different yields to maturity, each bond will provide a rate of return over the coming year equal to this year's short interest rate.

To confirm this point, we can compute the rates of return on each bond. The one-year bond is bought today for \$925.93 and matures in one year to its par value of \$1,000. Because the bond pays no coupon, total income is \$1,000 − \$925.93 = \$74.07, and the rate of return is \$74.07/\$925.93 = .08 or 8 percent. The two-year bond is bought today for \$841.75. Next year the interest rate will be 10%, and the bond will have one year left until maturity. It will sell for \$1,000/1.10 = \$909.09. Thus, the *holding-period return* is (\$909.09 − \$841.75)/\$841.75 = .08, again implying an 8% rate of return. Similarly, the three-year bond will be purchased for \$758.33 and will be sold at year-end for \$1,000/(1.10)(1.11) = \$819.00, for a rate of return (\$819.00 − \$758.33)/\$758.33 = .08, again, an 8% return.

CONCEPT CHECK Question 1. Confirm that the return on the four-year bond also will be 8%.

Therefore we conclude that, when interest rate movements are known with certainty, if all bonds are fairly priced, all will provide equal one-year rates of return. The higher yields on the longer-term bonds merely reflect the fact that future interest rates are higher than current rates, and that the longer bonds are still alive during the higher-rate period. Owners of the short-term bonds receive lower yields to maturity, but they can reinvest or "roll over" their proceeds for higher yields in later years when rates are higher. In the end, both long-term bonds and short-term rollover strategies provide equal returns over the holding period, at least in a world of interest rate certainty.

Forward Rates

Unfortunately, investors do not have access to short-term interest rate quotations for coming years. What they do have are newspaper quotations of bond prices and yields to maturity. Can they infer future short rates from the available data?

Suppose we are interested in the interest rate that will prevail during year 3, and we have access only to the data reported in Table 14.2. We start by comparing two alternatives, illustrated in Figure 14.4.

1. Invest in a three-year zero-coupon bond.
2. Invest in a two-year zero-coupon bond. After two years reinvest the proceeds in a one-year bond.

Assuming an investment of \$100, under strategy 1, with a yield to maturity of 9.660% on three-year zero-coupon bonds, our investment would grow to $\$100(1.0966)^3 = \$131.87$. Under strategy 2, the \$100 investment in the two-year bond would grow after two years to $\$100(1.08995)^2 = \$118.80$. Then in the third year it would grow by an additional factor of $1 + r_3$.

In a world of certainty both of these strategies must yield exactly the same final payoff. If strategy 1 were to dominate strategy 2, no one would hold two-year bonds; their prices would fall and their yields would rise. Likewise if strategy 2 dominated strategy 1, no one would hold three-year bonds. Therefore, we can conclude that $\$131.87 = \$118.80(1 + r_3)$, which implies that $(1 + r_3) = 1.11$, or $r_3 = 11\%$. This is in fact the rate that will prevail in year 3, as Table 14.1 indicates. Thus, our method of obtaining the third-period interest rate does provide the correct solution in the certainty case.

More generally, the comparison of the two strategies establishes that the return on a three-year bond equals that on a two-year bond and rollover strategy:

$$100(1 + y_3)^3 = 100(1 + y_2)^2(1 + r_3)$$

so that $1 + r_3 = (1 + y_3)^3/(1 + y_2)^2$. Generalizing, for the certainty case, a simple rule for inferring a future short interest rate from the yield curve of zero-coupon bonds is to use the following formula:

$$(1 + r_n) = (1 + y_n)^n/(1 + y_{n-1})^{n-1} \qquad \textbf{(14.4)}$$

Figure 14.4
Two three-year investment programs

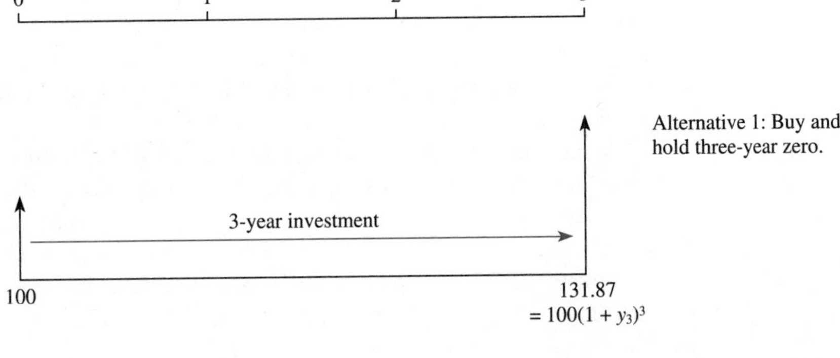

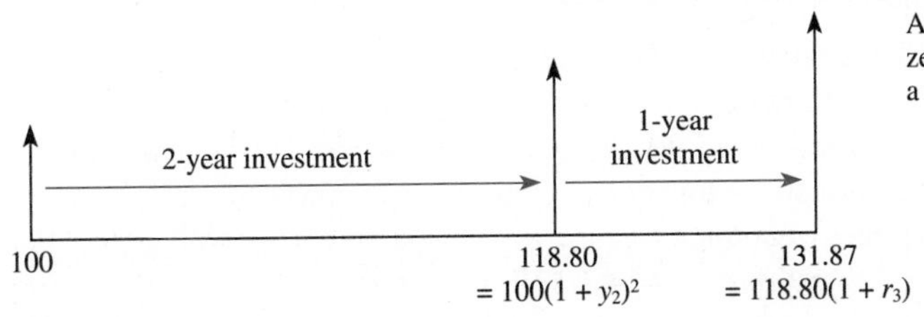

where n denotes the period in question and y_n is the yield to maturity of a zero-coupon bond with an n-period maturity.

Equation 14.4 has a simple interpretation. The numerator on the right-hand side is the total growth factor of an investment in an n-year zero held until maturity. Similarly, the denominator is the growth factor of an investment in an $(n - 1)$-year zero. Because the former investment lasts for one more year than the latter, the difference in these growth factors must be the rate of return available in year n when the $(n - 1)$-year zero can be rolled over into a one-year investment.

Of course, when future interest rates are uncertain, as they are in reality, there is no meaning to inferring "the" future short rate. No one knows today what the future interest rate will be. At best, we can speculate as to its expected value and associated uncertainty. Nevertheless, it still is common to use equation 14.4 to investigate the implications of the yield curve for future interest rates. In recognition of the fact that future interest rates are uncertain, we call the interest rate that we infer in this matter the **forward interest rate** rather than the *future short rate,* because it need not be the interest rate that actually will prevail at the future date.

If the forward rate for period n is f_n, we then define f_n by the equation

$$1 + f_n = (1 + y_n)^n/(1 + y_{n-1})^{n-1}$$

Equivalently, we may rewrite the equation as

$$(1 + y_n)^n = (1 + y_{n-1})^{n-1}(1 + f_n) \qquad \textbf{(14.5)}$$

In this formulation, the forward rate is *defined* as the "break-even" interest rate that equates the return on an n-period zero-coupon bond to that of a $(n-1)$- period zero-coupon bond rolled over into a one-year bond in year n. The actual total returns on the two n-year strategies will be equal if the spot interest rate in year n turns out to equal f_n.

We emphasize that the interest rate that actually will prevail in the future need not equal the forward rate, which is calculated from today's data. Indeed, it is not even necessarily the case that the forward rate equals the expected value of the future short interest rate. This is an issue that we address in much detail shortly. For now, however, we note that forward rates do equal future short rates in the special case of interest rate certainty.

14.2 MEASURING THE TERM STRUCTURE

Thus far we have focused on default-free zero-coupon bonds. These bonds are easiest to analyze because their maturity is given by their single payment. In practice, however, the great majority of bonds pay coupons, and most available data pertain to coupon bonds, so we must develop a general approach to calculate spot and forward rates from prices of coupon bonds.

Equations 14.4 and 14.5 for the determination of the forward rate from available yields apply only to zero-coupon bonds. They were derived by equating the returns to competing investment strategies that both used zeros. If coupon bonds had been used in those strategies, we would have had to deal with the issue of coupons paid and reinvested during the investment period, which complicates the analysis.

A further complication arises from the fact that bonds with different coupon rates can have different yields even if their maturities are equal. For example, consider two bonds, each with a two-year time to maturity and annual coupon payments. Bond A has a 3% coupon; bond B a 12% coupon. Using the interest rates of Table 14.1, we see that bond A will sell for

$$\frac{\$30}{1.08} + \frac{\$1,030}{(1.08)(1.10)} = \$894.78$$

At this price its yield to maturity is 8.98%. Bond B will sell for

$$\frac{\$120}{1.08} + \frac{\$1,120}{(1.08)(1.10)} = \$1,053.87$$

at which price its yield to maturity is 8.94%. Because bond B makes a greater share of its payments in the first year when the interest rate is lower, its yield to maturity is slightly lower. Because bonds with the same maturity can have different yields, we conclude that a single yield curve relating yields and times to maturity cannot be appropriate for all bonds.

The solution to this ambiguity is to perform all of our analysis using the yield curve for zero-coupon bonds, sometimes called the *pure yield curve*. Our goal, therefore, is to calculate the pure yield curve even if we have to use data on more common coupon-paying bonds.

The trick we use to infer the yield curve from data on coupon bonds is to treat each coupon payment as a separate "mini" zero-coupon bond. A coupon bond then becomes just a "portfolio" of many zeros. Indeed, we saw in the previous chapter that most zero-coupon bonds are created by stripping coupon payments from coupon bonds and repackaging the separate payments from many bonds into portfolios with common maturity dates. By determining the price of each of these "zeros" we can calculate the yield to that maturity date for a single-payment security and thereby construct the pure yield curve.

As a simple example of this technique, suppose that we observe an 8% coupon bond making semiannual payments with one year until maturity, selling at $986.10, and a 10% coupon bond, also with a year until maturity, selling at $1,004.78. To infer the short rates for the next two six-month periods, we first attempt to find the present value of each coupon payment taken individually, that is, treated as a mini zero-coupon bond. Call d_1 the present value of $1 to be received in half a year, and d_2 the present value of a dollar to be received in one year. (The d stands for discounted values; therefore, $d_1 = 1/(1 + r_1)$, where r_1 is the short rate for the first six-month period.) Then our two bonds must satisfy the simultaneous equations

$$986.10 = d_1 \times 40 + d_2 \times 1{,}040$$
$$1004.78 = d_1 \times 50 + d_2 \times 1{,}050$$

In each equation the bond's price is set equal to the discounted value of all of its remaining cash flows. Solving these equations we find that $d_1 = .95694$ and $d_2 = .91137$. Thus, if r_1 is the short rate for the first six-month period, then $d_1 = 1/(1 + r_1) = .95694$, so that $r_1 = .045$, and $d_2 = 1/[(1 + r_1)(1 + f_2)] = 1/[(1.045)(1 + f_2)] = .91137$, so that $f_2 = .05$. Thus, the two short rates are shown to be 4.5% for the first half-year period and 5% for the second.

CONCEPT CHECK

Question 2. A T-bill with six-month maturity and $10,000 face value sells for $9,700. A one-year maturity T-bond paying semiannual coupons of $40 sells for $1,000. Find the current six-month short rate, and the forward rate for the following six-month period.

When we analyze many bonds, such an inference procedure is more difficult, in part because of the greater number of bonds and time periods, but also because not all bonds give rise to identical estimates for the discounted value of a future $1 payment. In other words, there seem to be apparent error terms in the pricing relationship.[1] Nevertheless, treating these errors as random aberrations, we can use a statistical approach to infer the pattern of forward rates embedded in the yield curve.

To see how the statistical procedure would operate, suppose that we observe many coupon bonds, indexed by i, selling at prices P_i. The coupon and/or principal payment (the cash flow) of bond i at time t is denoted CF_{it}, and the present value of a $1 pay-

[1]We will consider later some of the reasons for the appearance of these error terms.

ment at time t, which is the implied price of a zero-coupon bond that we are trying to determine, is denoted d_t. Then for each bond we may write the following:

$$
\begin{aligned}
P_1 &= d_1\text{CF}_{11} + d_2\text{CF}_{12} + d_3\text{CF}_{13} + \ldots + e_1 \\
P_2 &= d_1\text{CF}_{21} + d_2\text{CF}_{22} + d_3\text{CF}_{23} + \ldots + e_2 \\
P_3 &= d_1\text{CF}_{31} + d_2\text{CF}_{32} + d_3\text{CF}_{33} + \ldots + e_3 \\
&\quad\vdots \qquad\qquad\qquad\qquad\qquad\qquad\qquad\quad \vdots \\
P_n &= d_1\text{CF}_{n1} + d_2\text{CF}_{n2} + d_3\text{CF}_{n3} + \ldots + e_n
\end{aligned}
\tag{14.6}
$$

Each line of equation system 14.6 equates the price of the bond to the sum of its cash flows, discounted according to time until payment. The last term in each equation, e_i, represents the error term that accounts for the deviations of a bond's price from the prediction of the equation.

Students of statistics will recognize that equation 14.6 is a simple system of equations that can be estimated by regression analysis. The dependent variables are the bond prices, the independent variables are the cash flows, and the coefficients d_t are to be estimated from the observed data.[2] The estimates of d_t are our inferences of the present value of $1 to be paid at time t. The pattern of d_t for various times to payment is called the *discount function*, because it gives the discounted value of $1 as a function of time until payment. From the discount function, which is equivalent to a list of zero-coupon bond prices for various maturity dates, we can calculate the yields on pure zero-coupon bonds. We would use Treasury securities in this procedure to avoid complications arising from default risk.

Before leaving the issue of the measurement of the yield curve, it is worth pausing briefly to discuss the error terms. Why is it that all bond prices do not conform exactly to a common discount function that sets price equal to present value? Two reasons relate to factors not accounted for in the regression analysis of equation 14.6: taxes and options associated with the bond.

Taxes affect bond prices because investors care about their after-tax return on investment. Therefore, the coupon payments should be treated as net of taxes. Similarly, if a bond is not selling at par value, the IRS may impute a "built-in" interest payment by amortizing the difference between the price and the par value of the bond. These considerations are difficult to capture in a mathematical formulation because different individuals are in different tax brackets, meaning that the net-of-tax cash flows from a given bond depend on the identity of the owner. Moreover, the specification of equation 14.6 implicitly assumes that the bond is held until maturity: it discounts *all* the bond's coupon and principal payments. This, of course, ignores the investor's option to sell the bond before maturity and so to realize a different stream of income from that described by equation 14.6. Moreover, it ignores the investor's ability to engage in *tax-timing options*. For example, an investor whose tax bracket is expected to change over time may benefit by realizing capital gains during the period when the tax rate is the lowest.

[2]In practice, variations of regression analysis called "splining techniques" are usually used to estimate the coefficients. This method was first suggested by McCulloch in the following two articles: J. Huston McCulloch, "Measuring the Term Structure of Interest Rates," *Journal of Business* 44 (January 1971); and "The Tax Adjusted Yield Curve," *Journal of Finance* 30 (June 1975).

Another feature affecting bond pricing is the call provision. First, if the bond is callable, how do we know whether to include in equation 14.6 coupon payments in years following the first call date? Similarly, the date of the principal repayment becomes uncertain. More important, one must realize that the issuer of the callable bond will exercise the option to call only when it is profitable to do so. Conversely, the call provision is a transfer of value away from the bondholder who has "sold" the option to call to the bond issuer. The call feature therefore will affect the bond's price, and introduce further error terms in the simple specification of equation 14.6.

Finally, we must recognize that the yield curve is based on price quotes that often are somewhat inaccurate. Price quotes used in the financial press may be stale (i.e., out of date), even if only by a few hours. Moreover, they may not represent prices at which dealers actually are willing to trade.

14.3 Interest Rate Uncertainty and Forward Rates

Let us turn now to the more difficult analysis of the term structure when future interest rates are uncertain. We have argued so far that, in a certain world, different investment strategies with common terminal dates must provide equal rates of return. For example, two consecutive one-year investments in zeros would need to offer the same total return as an equal-sized investment in a two-year zero. Therefore, under certainty,

$$(1 + r_1)(1 + r_2) = (1 + y_2)^2$$

What can we say when r_2 is not known today?

For example, referring once again to Table 14.1, suppose that today's rate, $r_1 = 8\%$, and that the expected rate next year is $E(r_2) = 10\%$. If bonds were priced based only on the expected value of the interest rate, then a one-year zero would sell for \$1,000/1.08 = \$925.93, and a two-year zero would sell for \$1,000/[(1.08)(1.10)] = \$841.75, just as in Table 14.2.

But now consider a short-term investor who wishes to invest only for one year. She can purchase the one-year zero and lock in a riskless 8% return because she knows that at the end of the year, the bond will be worth its maturity value of \$1,000. She also can purchase the two-year zero. Its *expected* rate of return also is 8%: Next year, the bond will have one year to maturity, and we expect that the one-year interest rate will be 10%, implying a price of \$909.09 and a holding-period return of 8%. But the rate of return on the two-year bond is risky. If next year's interest rate turns out to be above expectations, that is, greater than 10%, the bond price will be below \$909.09, and conversely if r_2 turns out to be less than 10%, the bond price will exceed \$909.09. Why should this short-term investor buy the risky two-year bond when its expected return is 8%, no better than that of the risk-free one-year bond? Clearly, she would not hold the two-year bond unless it offered an expected rate of return greater than the riskless 8% return available on the competing one-year bond. This requires that the two-year bond sell at a price lower than the \$841.75 value we derived when we ignored risk.

Suppose, for example, that most investors have short-term horizons and are willing to hold the two-year bond only if its price falls to \$819. At this price, the expected holding-period return on the two-year bond is 11% (because 909.09/819 = 1.11). The risk premium of the two-year bond, therefore, is 3%; it offers an expected rate of return of 11% versus the 8% risk-free return on the one-year bond. At this risk premium, investors are willing to bear the price risk associated with interest rate uncertainty.

In this environment, the forward rate, f_2, no longer equals the expected short rate, $E(r_2)$. Although we have assumed that $E(r_2) = 10\%$, it is easy to confirm that $f_2 = 13\%$. The yield to maturity on the two-year zeros selling at \$819 is 10.5%, and

$$1 + f_2 = \frac{(1 + y_2)^2}{1 + y_1} + \frac{1.105^2}{1.08} = 1.13$$

This result—that the forward rate exceeds the expected short rate—should not surprise us. We defined the forward rate as the interest rate that would need to prevail in the second year to make the long- and short-term investments equally attractive, ignoring risk. When we account for risk, it is clear that short-term investors will shy away from the long-term bond unless it offers an expected return greater than that offered by the one-year bond. Another way of putting this is to say that investors will require a risk premium to hold the longer-term bond. The risk-averse investor would be willing to hold the long-term bond only if $E(r_2)$ is less than the break-even value, f_2, because the lower the expectation of r_2 the greater the anticipated return on the long-term bond.

Therefore, if most individuals are short-term investors, bonds must have prices that make f_2 greater than $E(r_2)$. The forward rate will embody a premium compared with the expected future short-interest rate. This **liquidity premium** compensates short-term investors for the uncertainty about the price at which they will be able to sell their long-term bonds at the end of the year.[3]

CONCEPT CHECK

Question 3. Suppose that the required liquidity premium for the short-term investor is 1%. What must $E(r_2)$ be if f_2 is 10%?

Perhaps surprisingly, we also can imagine scenarios in which long-term bonds can be perceived by investors to be *safer* than short-term bonds. To see how, we now consider a "long-term" investor, who wishes to invest for a full two-year period. Suppose that the investor can purchase a two-year \$1,000 par value zero-coupon bond for \$841.75 and lock in a guaranteed yield to maturity of $y_2 = 9\%$. Alternatively, the investor can roll over two one-year investments. In this case an investment of 841.75 would grow in two years to $841.75 \times (1.08)(1 + r_2)$, which is an uncertain amount today because r_2 is not yet known. The break-even year-2 interest rate is, once again, the forward rate, 10%, because the forward rate is defined as the rate that equates the terminal value of the two investment strategies.

The expected value of the payoff of the rollover strategy is $841.75(1.08)\,[1 + E(r_2)]$. If $E(r_2)$ equals the forward rate, f_2, then the expected value of the payoff from the rollover strategy will equal the *known* payoff from the two-year maturity bond strategy.

Is this a reasonable presumption? Once again, it is only if the investor does not care about the uncertainty surrounding the final value of the rollover strategy. Whenever that

[3] *Liquidity* refers to the ability to sell an asset easily at a predictable price. Because long-term bonds have greater price risk, they are considered less liquid in this context and thus must offer a premium.

risk is important, the long-term investor will not be willing to engage in the rollover strategy unless its expected return exceeds that of the two-year bond. In this case the investor would require that

$$(1.08)[1 + E(r_2)] > (1.09)^2 = (1.08)(1 + f_2)$$

which implies that $E(r_2)$ exceeds f_2. The investor would require that the expected period 2 interest rate exceed the break-even value of 10%, which is the forward rate.

Therefore, if all investors were long-term investors, no one would be willing to hold short-term bonds unless those bonds offered a reward for bearing interest rate risk. In this situation bond prices would be set at levels such that rolling over short bonds resulted in greater expected return than holding long bonds. This would cause the forward rate to be less than the expected future spot rate.

For example, suppose that in fact $E(r_2) = 11\%$. The liquidity premium therefore is negative: $f_2 - E(r_2) = 10\% - 11\% = -1\%$. This is exactly opposite from the conclusion that we drew in the first case of the short-term investor. Clearly, whether forward rates will equal expected future short rates depends on investors' readiness to bear interest rate risk, as well as their willingness to hold bonds that do not correspond to their investment horizons.

14.4 Theories of the Term Structure

The Expectations Hypothesis

The simplest theory of the term structure is the **expectations hypothesis.** A common version of this hypothesis states that the forward rate equals the market consensus expectation of the future short interest rate; in other words, that $f_2 = E(r_2)$, and that liquidity premiums are zero. Because $f_2 = E(r_2)$, we may relate yields on long-term bonds to expectations of future interest rates. In addition, we can use the forward rates derived from the yield curve to infer market expectations of future short rates. For example, with $(1 + y_2)^2 = (1 + r_1)(1 + f_2)$ from equation 14.5, we may also write that $(1 + y_2)^2 = (1 + r_1)[1 + E(r_2)]$ if the expectations hypothesis is correct. The yield to maturity would thus be determined solely by current and expected future one-period interest rates. An upward-sloping yield curve would be clear evidence that investors anticipate increases in interest rates.

Concept Check Question 4. If the expectations hypothesis is valid, what can we conclude about the premiums necessary to induce investors to hold bonds of different maturities from their investment horizons?

Liquidity Preference

We noted in our discussion of the long- and short-term investors that short-term investors will be unwilling to hold long-term bonds unless the forward rate exceeds the expected short interest rate, $f_2 > E(r_2)$, whereas long-term investors will be unwilling to hold short bonds unless $E(r_2)$ exceeds f_2. In other words, both groups of investors require a premium to induce them to hold bonds with maturities different from their investment horizons. Advocates of the **liquidity preference theory** of the term structure believe that short-term investors dominate the market so that, generally speaking, the forward rate exceeds the expected short rate. The excess of f_2 over $E(r_2)$, the liquidity premium, is predicted to be positive.

CONCEPT CHECK Question 5. The liquidity premium hypothesis also holds that *issuers* of bonds prefer to issue long-term bonds. How would this preference contribute to a positive liquidity premium?

To illustrate the differing implications of these theories for the term structure of interest rates, consider a situation in which the short interest rate is expected to be constant indefinitely. Suppose that $r_1 = 10\%$ and that $E(r_2) = 10\%$, $E(r_3) = 10\%$, and so on. Under the expectations hypothesis the two-year yield to maturity could be derived from the following:

$$\begin{aligned}(1 + y_2)^2 &= (1 + r_1)[1 + E(r_2)]\\ &= (1.10)(1.10)\end{aligned}$$

so that y_2 equals 10%. Similarly, yields on all-maturity bonds would equal 10%.

In contrast, under the liquidity preference theory f_2 would exceed $E(r_2)$. For sake of illustration, suppose that f_2 is 11%, implying a 1% liquidity premium. Then, for two-year bonds:

$$\begin{aligned}(1 + y_2)^2 &= (1 + r_1)(1 + f_2)\\ &= (1.10)(1.11) = 1.221\end{aligned}$$

implying that $1 + y_2 = 1.105$. Similarly, if f_3 also equals 11%, then the yield on three-year bonds would be determined by

$$\begin{aligned}(1 + y_3)^3 &= (1 + r_1)(1 + f_2)(1 + f_3)\\ &= (1.10)(1.11)(1.11) = 1.35531\end{aligned}$$

implying that $1 + y_3 = 1.1067$. The plot of the yield curve in this situation would be given as in Figure 14.5, **A**. Such an upward-sloping yield curve is commonly observed in practice.

If interest rates are expected to change over time, then the liquidity premium may be overlaid on the path of expected spot rates to determine the forward interest rate. Then the yield to maturity for each date will be an average of the single-period forward rates. Several such possibilities for increasing and declining interest rates appear in Figure 14.5 **B** to **D**.

Market Segmentation and Preferred Habitat Theories

Both the liquidity premium and expectations hypothesis of the term structure implicitly view bonds of different maturities as potential substitutes for each other. An investor considering holding bonds of one maturity possibly can be lured instead into holding

Figure 14.5

Yield Curves. **A**, Constant expected short rate. Liquidity premium of 1%. Result is a rising yield curve. **B**, Declining expected short rates. Increasing liquidity premiums. Result is a rising yield curve despite falling expected interest rates

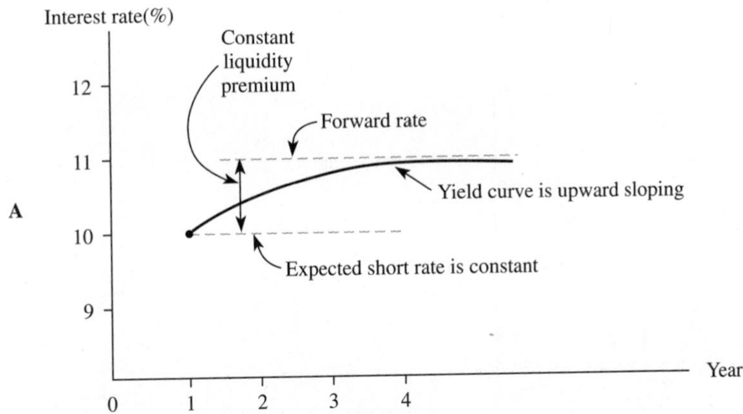

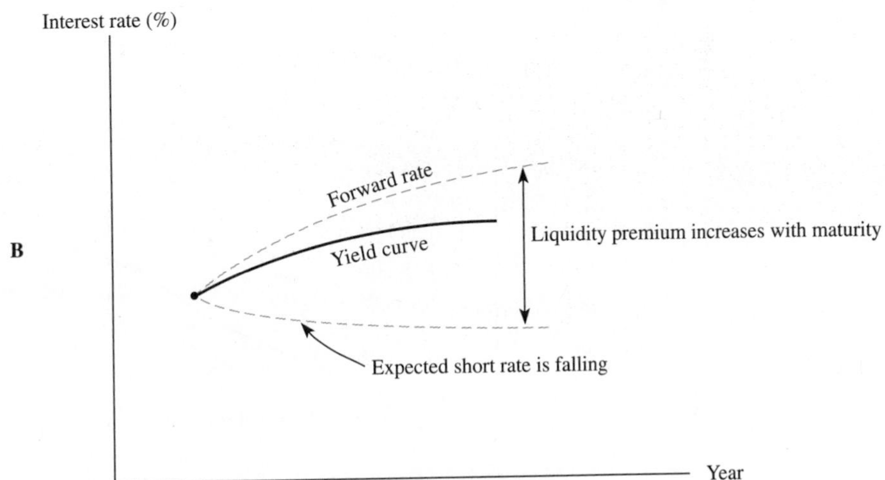

bonds of another maturity by the prospect of earning a risk premium. In this sense markets for bonds of all maturities are inextricably linked, and yields on short and long bonds are determined jointly in market equilibrium. Forward rates cannot differ from expected short rates by more than a fair liquidity premium, or else investors will reallocate their fixed-income portfolios to exploit what they perceive as abnormal profit opportunities elsewhere.

In contrast, the **market segmentation theory** holds that long- and short-maturity bonds are traded in essentially distinct or segmented markets, each of which finds its own equilibrium independently. The activities of long-term borrowers and lenders determine rates on long-term bonds. Similarly, short-term traders set short rates independently of long-term expectations. The term structure of interest rates, in this view, is determined by the equilibrium rates set in the various maturity markets.

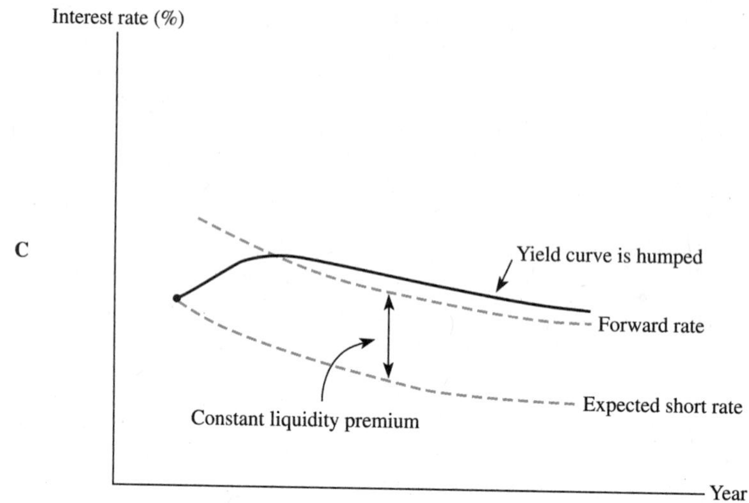

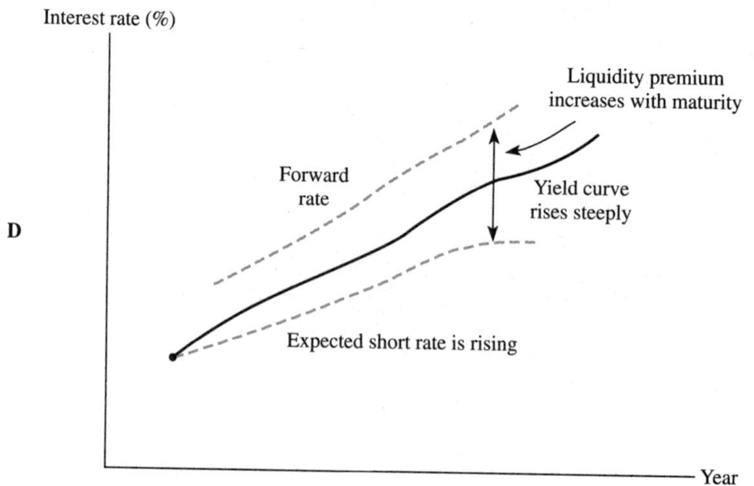

Figure 14.5
(Concluded)
C, Declining expected short rates. Constant liquidity premiums. Result is a hump-shaped yield curve.
D, Increasing expected short rates. Increasing liquidity premiums. Result is a sharply increasing yield curve

This view of the market is not common today. Both borrowers and lenders seem to compare long and short rates, as well as expectations of future rates, before deciding whether to borrow or lend long- or short-term. That they make these comparisons, and are willing to move into a particular maturity if it seems sufficiently profitable to do so, means that all-maturity bonds compete with each other for investors' attention, which implies that the rate on a bond of any given maturity is determined with an eye toward rates on competing bonds. This view of the market is called the **preferred habitat theory:** Investors prefer specific maturity ranges but can be induced to switch if premiums are sufficient. Markets are not so segmented that an appropriate premium cannot attract an investor who prefers one bond maturity to consider a different one.

14.5 Interpreting the Term Structure

We have seen that under certainty, 1 plus the yield to maturity on a zero-coupon bond is simply the geometric average of 1 plus the future short rates that will prevail over the life of the bond. This is the meaning of equation 14.3, which we repeat here:

$$1 + y_n = [(1 + r_1)(1 + r_2) \ldots (1 + r_n)]^{1/n}$$

When future rates are uncertain, we modify equation 14.3 by replacing future short rates with forward rates:

$$1 + y_n = [(1 + r_1)(1 + f_2)(1 + f_3) \ldots (1 + f_n)]^{1/n} \qquad (14.7)$$

Thus, there is a direct relationship between yields on various maturity bonds and forward interest rates. This relationship is the source of the information that can be gleaned from an analysis of the yield curve.

First, we ask what factors can account for a rising yield curve. Mathematically, if the yield curve is rising, f_{n+1} must exceed y_n. In words, the yield curve is upward sloping at any maturity date, *n*, for which the forward rate for the coming period is greater than the yield at that maturity. This rule follows from the notion of the yield to maturity as an average (albeit a geometric average) of forward rates.

If the yield curve is to rise as one moves to longer maturities, it must be the case that extension to a longer maturity results in the inclusion of a "new" forward rate that is higher than the average of the previously observed rates. This is analogous to the observation that if a new student's test score is to increase the class average, that student's score must exceed the class's average without her score. To raise the yield to maturity, an above-average forward rate must be added to the other rates in the averaging computation.

For example, if the yield to maturity on three-year bonds is 9%, then the yield on four-year bonds will satisfy the following equation:

$$(1 + y_4)^4 = (1.09)^3(1 + f_4)$$

If $f_4 = .09$, then y_4 also will equal .09. (Confirm this!) If f_4 is greater than 9%, y_4 will exceed 9%, and the yield curve will slope upward.

Concept Check

Question 6. Look back at Tables 14.1 and 14.2. Show that y_4 would exceed y_3 if and only if the interest rate for period four had been greater than 9.66%, which was the yield to maturity on the three-year bond, y_3.

Given that an upward-sloping yield curve is always associated with a forward rate higher than the spot, or current, yield, we need to ask next what can account for that higher forward rate. Unfortunately, there always are two possible answers to this question. Recall that the forward rate can be related to the expected future short rate according to this equation:

$$f_n = E(r_n) + \text{Liquidity premium}$$

where the liquidity premium might be necessary to induce investors to hold bonds of maturities that do not correspond to their preferred investment horizons.

By the way, the liquidity premium need not be positive, although that is the position generally taken by advocates of the liquidity premium hypothesis. We showed previously that if most investors have long-term horizons, the liquidity premium could be negative.

In any case, the equation shows that there are two reasons that the forward rate could be high. Either investors expect rising interest rates, meaning that $E(r_n)$ is high, or they require a large premium for holding longer-term bonds. Although it is tempting to infer from a rising yield curve that investors believe that interest rates will eventually increase, this is not a valid inference. Indeed, Figure 14.5, **A**, provides a simple counterexample to this line of reasoning. There, the spot rate is expected to stay at 10% forever. Yet there is a constant 1% liquidity premium so that all forward rates are 11%. The result is that the yield curve continually rises, starting at a level of 10% for one-year bonds, but eventually approaching 11% for long-term bonds as more and more forward rates at 11% are averaged into the yields to maturity.

Therefore, although it is true that expectations of increases in future interest rates can result in a rising yield curve, the converse is not true: A rising yield curve does not in and of itself imply expectations of higher future interest rates. This is the heart of the difficulty in drawing conclusions from the yield curve. The effects of possible liquidity premiums confound any simple attempt to extract expectations from the term structure. But estimating the market's expectations is a crucial task, because only by comparing your own expectations to those reflected in market prices can you determine whether you are relatively bullish or bearish on interest rates.

One very rough approach to deriving expected future spot rates is to assume that liquidity premiums are constant. An estimate of that premium can be subtracted from the forward rate to obtain the market's expected interest rate. For example, again making use of the example plotted in Figure 14.5, **A**, the researcher would estimate from historical data that a typical liquidity premium in this economy is 1%. After calculating the forward rate from the yield curve to be 11%, the expectation of the future spot rate would be determined to be 10%.

This approach has little to recommend it for two reasons. First, it is next to impossible to obtain precise estimates of a liquidity premium. The general approach to doing so would be to compare forward rates and eventually realized future short rates and to calculate the average difference between the two. However, the deviations between the two values can be quite large and unpredictable because of unanticipated economic events that affect the realized short rate. The data do not contain enough information to calculate a reliable estimate of the expected premium. Second, there is no reason to believe that the liquidity premium should be constant. Figure 14.6 shows the rate of return variability of prices of long-term Treasury bonds since 1971. Interest rate risk fluctuated dramatically during the period. So might we expect risk premiums on various maturity bonds to fluctuate, and empirical evidence suggests that term premiums do in fact fluctuate over time.[4] Still, as the accompanying box indicates, very steep

---

[4] See, for example, Richard Startz, "Do Forecast Errors or Term Premia Really Make the Difference between Long and Short Rates?" *Journal of Financial Economics* 10 (1982).

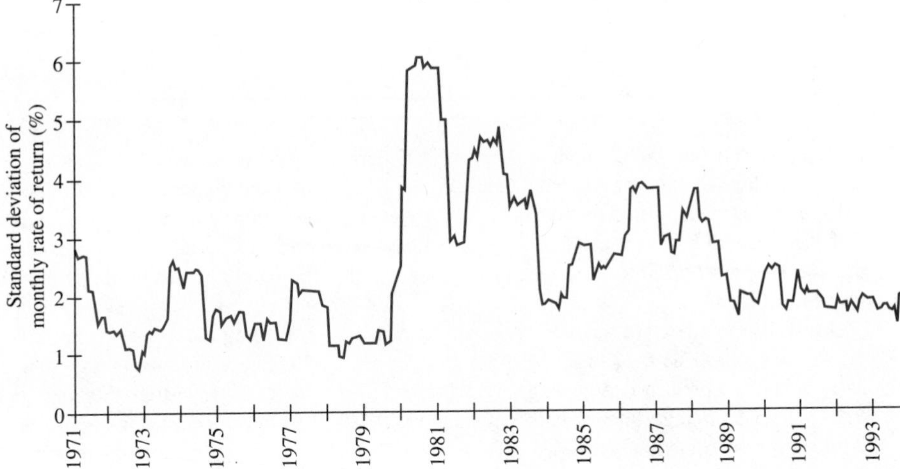

Figure 14.6
Price volatility of long-term Treasury bonds, 1971–1994

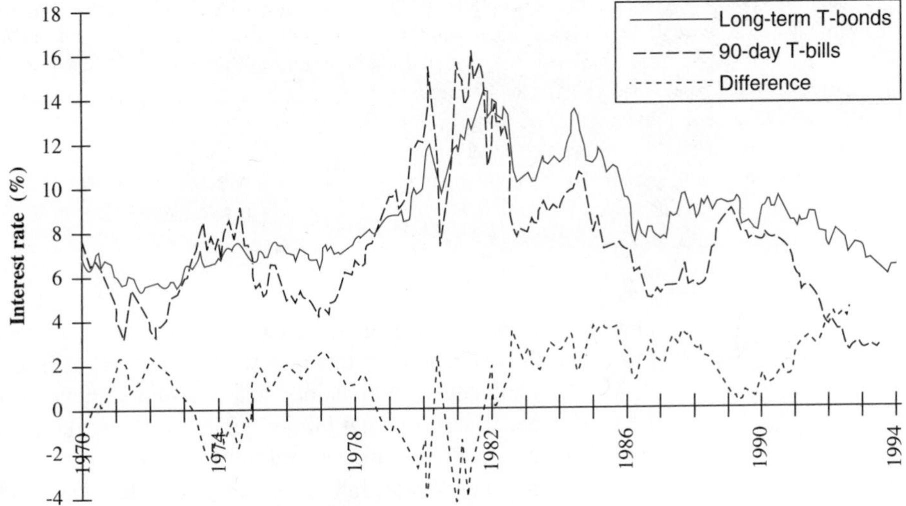

Figure 14.7
Yields on long-term versus 90-day Treasury securities: term spread, 1970–1994

yield curves are interpreted by many market professionals as warning signs of impending rate increases.

The usually observed upward slope of the yield curve, especially for short maturities, is the empirical basis for the liquidity premium doctrine that long-term bonds offer a positive liquidity premium. In the face of this empirical regularity, perhaps it is valid to interpret a downward-sloping yield curve as evidence that interest rates are expected to decline. If **term premiums,** the spread between yields on long- and short-term bonds, generally are positive, then anticipated declines in rates could account for a downward-sloping yield curve.

Figure 14.7 presents a history of yields on 90-day Treasury bills and long-term Treasury bonds. Yields on the longer-term bonds *generally* (roughly two-thirds of the

SHAPELY CURVES

For the seventh time in 12 months, America's Federal Reserve increased interest rates on February 1st. The half-point rise, which lifted the federal funds rate to 6% and the discount rate to 5.25%, had been widely expected. The question now, however, is whether it will prove to be the last.

Most economists are predicting a slowdown in growth this year. The question is whether it will come early enough to prevent overheating, and so relieve the Fed of the need to raise interest rates more aggressively. Although most economists are still forecasting a "soft landing" (in which annual growth conveniently slows to 2.5%, and stays there), a small but growing number now expect the economy to remain robust in early 1995; the eventual slowdown will therefore be much sharper.

The latter group of economists has become mesmerised by the shape of the yield curve—the graph that plots yields on securities of different maturities. In the past, the shape of this curve (more precisely, the gap in yields between long- and short-term bonds) has proved to be a good leading indicator of economic activity.

Why should this be? In normal times, investors demand higher yields on longer-dated bonds to compensate them for the greater risk, but the required premium varies according to their expectations of growth, inflation and thus the future path of interest rates. For example, the yield curve sloped steeply upwards in 1992–93, reflecting the market's expectation that future growth—and hence inflation and short-term interest rates—would increase. Investors therefore demanded a bigger premium on securities with a long maturity.

By contrast, when the Fed lifts short-term interest rates in order to dampen growth, the gap between long- and short-term bond yields usually narrows in a pincer movement. While yields on shorter-term bonds are pulled up by rising short-term interest rates, those on long-term bonds fall as inflationary expectations ease. If the Fed continues to tighten policy, short-term rates eventually rise above long-term rates and the yield curve becomes "inverted". Because investors expect weaker growth in future, and hence lower interest rates, they will accept lower rates on long-term bonds.

(Continued)

time) exceed those on the bills, meaning that the yield curve generally slopes upward. Moreover, the exceptions to this rule seem to precede episodes of falling short rates, which if anticipated, would induce a downward-sloping yield curve. For example, 1980–82 were years in which 90-day yields exceeded long-term yields. These years preceded a drastic drop in the general level of rates.

Why might interest rates fall? There are two factors to consider: the real rate and the inflation premium. Recall that the nominal interest rate is composed of the real rate plus a factor to compensate for the effect of inflation:

$$1 + \text{Nominal rate} = (1 + \text{Real rate})(1 + \text{Inflation rate})$$

or approximately,

$$\text{Nominal rate} \approx \text{Real rate} + \text{Inflation rate}$$

Therefore, an expected change in interest rates can be due to changes in either expected real rates or expected inflation rates. Usually, it is important to distinguish between these two possibilities because the economic environments associated with them may vary substantially. High real rates may indicate a rapidly expanding economy, high budget deficits, and tight monetary policy. Although high inflation rates also can arise out

A Fatal Inversion

As a forecasting tool, the yield curve has impressive credentials: it has become inverted 12–18 months before every recession during the past 40 years, and only once over that period has there been a false alarm, when an inversion of the curve was not followed by a recession. That was in 1965–66, when heavy government spending during the Vietnam war helped to avert a full recession, and growth merely slowed.

So what is the curve signalling now? Since late 1992, the gap between ten-year and three-year Treasury bonds has narrowed from 200 basis points (one-hundredths of one percent) to only 25 points (see chart), the smallest gap since the 1990 recession. On past experience, this signals a sharp slowdown in 1995–96 but not, as yet, a recession.

The Fed is playing a tough game: it must weigh up future inflationary risks against the danger of pushing the economy into recession. The snag is that monetary policy is not a science: there are long lags of around 18 months before changes in interest rates affect economic activity, and the extent of their impact is unclear. Alan Greenspan, the Fed's chairman, cannot, except by luck, bring the rate of growth exactly in line with the economy's productive potential. The best he can do to avoid a recession is to prevent serious overheating.

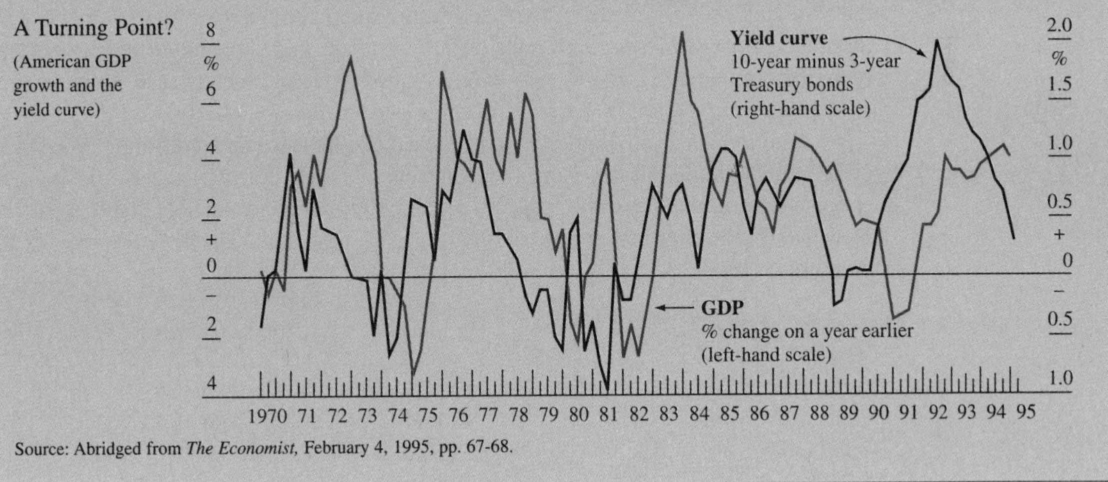

Source: Abridged from *The Economist,* February 4, 1995, pp. 67-68.

of a rapidly expanding economy, inflation also may be caused by rapid expansion of the money supply or supply-side shocks to the economy such as interruptions in oil supplies. These factors have very different implications for investments. Even if we conclude from an analysis of the yield curve that rates will fall, we need to analyze the macroeconomic factors that might cause such a decline.

SUMMARY

1. The term structure of interest rates refers to the interest rates for various terms to maturity embodied in the prices of default-free zero-coupon bonds.

2. In a world of certainty all investments must provide equal total returns for any investment period. Short-term holding-period returns on all bonds would be equal in a risk-free economy, and all equal to the rate available on short-term bonds. Similarly, total returns from rolling over short-term bonds over longer periods would equal the total return available from long-maturity bonds.

3. A pure yield curve could be plotted easily from a complete set of zero-coupon bonds. In practice, however, most bonds carry coupons, payable at different future times, so that yield-curve estimates usually must be inferred from prices of coupon bonds. Measurement of the term structure is complicated by tax issues such as tax timing options and the different tax brackets of different investors.

4. The forward rate of interest is the break-even future interest rate that would equate the total return from a rollover strategy to that of a longer-term zero-coupon bond. It is defined by the equation

$$(1 + y_n)^n(1 + f_{n+1}) = (1 + y_{n+1})^{n+1}$$

where n is a given number of periods from today. This equation can be used to show that yields to maturity and forward rates are related by the equation

$$(1 + y_n)^n = (1 + r_1)(1 + f_2)(1 + f_3) \ldots (1 + f_n)$$

5. A common version of the expectations hypothesis holds that forward interest rates are unbiased estimates of expected future interest rates. However, there are good reasons to believe that forward rates differ from expected short rates because of a risk premium known as a *liquidity premium*. A liquidity premium can cause the yield curve to slope upward even if no increase in short rates is anticipated.

6. The existence of liquidity premiums makes it extremely difficult to infer expected future interest rates from the yield curve. Such an inference would be made easier if we could assume the liquidity premium remained reasonably stable over time. However, both empirical and theoretical insights cast doubt on the constancy of that premium.

Key Terms

Term structure of interest rates
Short interest rate
Yield curve
Spot rate
Forward interest rate
Liquidity premium
Expectations hypothesis
Liquidity preference theory
Market segmentation theory
Preferred habitat theory
Term premiums

Selected Readings

A detailed presentation of yield-curve analytics and relationships among spot rates, yields to maturity, and realized compound yields is contained in:

Homer, Sidney, and Martin Liebowitz. *Inside the Yield Book: New Tools for Bond Market Strategy*. Englewood Cliffs, N.J.: Prentice Hall, 1972.

A discussion of the various versions of the expectations hypothesis is:

Cox, John, Jonathan Ingersoll, and Stephen Ross. "A Reexamination of Traditional Hypotheses about the Term Structure of Interest Rates." *Journal of Finance* 36 (September 1981).

Evidence on liquidity premiums may be found in:

Fama, Eugene. "The Information in the Term Structure." *Journal of Financial Economics* 13 (1984).

Mankiw, N. Gregory. "The Term Structure of Interest Rates Revisited." *Brookings Papers on Economic Activity* 61 (1986).

Problems in the measurement of the yield curve are treated in:

McCulloch, J. Houston. "The Tax-Adjusted Yield Curve." *Journal of Finance* 30 (June 1975).

Problems

1. *a.* Briefly explain why bonds of different maturities have different yields in terms of the (1) expectations, (2) liquidity, and (3) segmentation hypotheses.
   b. Briefly describe the implications of each of the three hypotheses when the yield curve is (1) upward sloping, and (2) downward sloping.*

2. Which one of the following is false?*
   a. The liquidity preference hypothesis indicates that, all things being equal, longer maturities will have a higher yield.
   b. The basic conclusion of the expectations hypothesis is that the long-term rate is equal to the anticipated short-term rate.
   c. The expectations hypothesis indicates a flat yield curve if anticipated future short-term rates are equal to current short-term rates.
   d. The segmentation hypothesis contends that borrowers and lenders are constrained to particular segments of the yield curve.
3. Under the expectations hypothesis, if the yield curve is upward sloping, the market must expect an increase in short-term interest rates. True/false/uncertain? Why?
4. Under the liquidity preference theory, if inflation is expected to be falling over the next few years, long-term interest rates will be higher than short-term rates. True/false/uncertain? Why?
5. The following is a list of prices for zero-coupon bonds of various maturities. Calculate the yields to maturity of each bond and the implied sequence of forward rates.

Maturity (Years)	Price of Bond($)
1	943.40
2	898.47
3	847.62
4	792.16

6. Assuming that the expectations hypothesis is valid, compute the expected price path of the four-year bond in Problem 5 as time passes. What is the rate of return of the bond in each year? Show that the expected return equals the forward rate for each year.

7. The following table shows yields to maturity of U.S. Treasury securities as of January 1, 1993:*

Term to Maturity (in years)	Yield to Maturity
1	3.50%
2	4.50
3	5.00
4	5.50
5	6.00
10	6.60

a. Based on the data in the table, calculate the implied forward one-year rate of interest at January 1, 1996.

b. Describe the conditions under which the calculated forward rate would be an unbiased estimate of the one-year spot rate of interest at January 1, 1996.

Assume that one year earlier, at January 1, 1992, the prevailing term structure for U.S. Treasury securities was such that the implied forward one-year rate of interest at January 1, 1996, was significantly higher than the corresponding rate implied by the term structure at January 1, 1993.

c. On the basis of the pure expectations theory of the term structure, briefly discuss *two* factors that could account for such a decline in the implied forward rate.

8. Would you expect the yield on a callable bond to lie above or below a yield curve fitted from noncallable bonds?

9. The current yield curve for default-free zero-coupon bonds is as follows:

Maturity (Years)	YTM
1	10%
2	11
3	12

a. What are the implied one-year forward rates?

b. Assume that the pure expectations hypothesis of the term structure is correct. If market expectations are accurate, what will the pure yield curve, that is, the yields to maturity on one- and two-year zero coupon bonds, be next year?

c. If you purchased a two-year zero coupon bond now, what is the expected total rate of return over the next year? If it were a three-year zero coupon bond? (Hint: Compute the current and expected future prices.) Ignore taxes.

d. What should be the current price of a three-year maturity bond with a 12% coupon rate paid annually? If you purchased it at that price, what would your total expected rate of return be over the next year (coupon plus price change)? Ignore taxes.

10. The term structure for zero-coupon bonds is currently:

Maturity (Years)	YTM
1	4%
2	5
3	6

Next year at this time, *you* expect it to be:

Maturity (Years)	YTM
1	5%
2	6
3	7

a. What do *you* expect the rate of return to be over the coming year on a three-year zero-coupon bond?
b. Under the expectations theory, what yields to maturity does *the market* expect to observe on one- and two-year zeros next year? Is the market's expectation of the return on the three-year bond more or less than yours?

11. The yield to maturity on one-year zero-coupon bonds is currently 7%; the YTM on two-year zeros is 8%. The Treasury plans to issue a two-year maturity *coupon* bond, paying coupons once per year with a coupon rate of 9%. The face value of the bond is $100.
a. At what price will the bond sell?
b. What will the yield to maturity on the bond be?
c. If the expectations theory of the yield curve is correct, what is the market expectation of the price that the bond will sell for next year?
d. Recalculate your answer to (*c*) if you believe in the liquidity preference theory and you believe that the liquidity premium is 1%.

12. Below is a list of prices for zero-coupon bonds of various maturities.

Maturity (Years)	Price of $1,000 Par Bond (Zero Coupon)
1	943.40
2	873.52
3	816.37

a. An 8.5% coupon $1,000 par bond pays an annual coupon and will mature in three years. What should the yield to maturity on the bond be?
b. If at the end of the first year the yield curve flattens out at 8%, what will be the one-year holding-period return on the coupon bond?

13. Prices of zero-coupon bonds reveal the following pattern of forward rates:

Year	Forward Rate
1	5%
2	7
3	8

In addition to the zero-coupon bond, investors also may purchase a three-year bond making annual payments of $60 with par value $1,000.
a. What is the price of the coupon bond?
b. What is the yield to maturity of the coupon bond?
c. Under the expectations hypothesis, what is the expected realized compound yield of the coupon bond?

d. If you forecast that the yield curve in one year will be flat at 7%, what is your forecast for the expected rate of return on the coupon bond for the one-year holding period?

14. You observe the following term structure:

	Effective Annual YTM
1-year zero-coupon bond	6.1%
2-year zero-coupon bond	6.2
3-year zero-coupon bond	6.3
4-year zero-coupon bond	6.4

a. If you believe that the term structure next year will be the same as today's, will the one-year or the four-year zeros provide a greater expected one-year return?

b. What if you believe in the expectations hypothesis?

15. U.S. Treasuries represent a significant holding in many pension portfolios. You decide to analyze the yield curve for U.S. Treasury Notes.*

a. Using the data in the table below, calculate the five-year spot and forward rates assuming annual compounding. Show your calculations.

U.S. Treasury Note Yield Curve Data

Years to Maturity	Par Coupon Yield-to- Maturity	Calculated Spot Rates	Calculated Forward Rates
1	5.00	5.00	5.00
2	5.20	5.21	5.42
3	6.00	6.05	7.75
4	7.00	7.16	10.56
5	7.00	—	—

b. Define and describe each of the following three concepts:

- Yield to maturity.
- Spot rate.
- Forward rate.

Explain how these *three* concepts are related.

You are considering the purchase of a zero-coupon U.S. Treasury Note with four years to maturity.

c. Based on the above yield curve analysis, calculate both the expected yield to maturity and the price for the security. Show your calculations.

16. The yield to maturity (YTM) on one-year-maturity zero-coupon bonds is 5% and the YTM on two-year-maturity zero-coupon bonds is 6%. The yield to

*Reprinted, with permission, from the Level II 1993 *CFA Study Guide.*

maturity on two-year-maturity coupon bonds with coupon rates of 12% (paid annually) is 5.8%. What arbitrage opportunity is available for an investment banking firm? What is the profit on the activity?

17. Suppose that a one-year zero-coupon bond with face value $100 currently sells at $94.34, while a two-year zero sells at $84.99. You are considering the purchase of a two-year maturity bond making *annual* coupon payments. The face value of the bond is $100, and the coupon rate is 12% per year.
    a. What is the yield to maturity of the two-year zero? The two-year coupon bond?
    b. What is the forward rate for the second year?
    c. If the expectations hypothesis is accepted, what are (1) the expected price of the coupon bond at the end of the first year and (2) the expected holding period return on the coupon bond over the first year?
    d. Will the expected rate of return be higher or lower if you accept the liquidity preference hypothesis?

Chapter 15
Fixed-Income Portfolio Management

IN THIS CHAPTER WE TURN TO VARIOUS STRATEGIES THAT FIXED-INCOME PORTFOLIO MANAGERS CAN PURSUE, MAKING A DISTINCTION BETWEEN PASSIVE AND ACTIVE STRATEGIES. A *passive investment strategy* takes market prices of securities as fairly set. Rather than attempting to beat the market by exploiting superior information or insight, passive managers act to maintain an appropriate risk/return balance given market opportunities. One special case of passive management is an immunization strategy that attempts to insulate or immunize the portfolio from interest rate risk.

An *active investment strategy* attempts to achieve returns more than commensurate with risk borne. In the context of fixed-income management this style of management can take two forms. Active managers either use interest rate forecasts to predict movements in the entire fixed-income market, or they employ some form of intramarket analysis to identify particular sectors of the fixed-income market or particular bonds that are relatively mispriced.

We start our discussion with an analysis of the sensitivity of bond prices to interest rate fluctuations. The concept of duration, which measures interest rate sensitivity, is basic to formulating both active and passive fixed-income strategies. We turn next to passive strategies and show how duration-matching strategies can be used to immunize the holding-period return of a fixed-income portfolio from interest rate risk. Finally, we explore a variety of active strategies, including intramarket analysis, interest rate forecasting, and interest rate swaps.

15.1 INTEREST RATE RISK

We have seen already that an inverse relationship exists between bond prices and yields, and we know that interest rates can fluctuate substantially. As interest rates rise

Table 15.1 Prices of 8% Coupon Bond (coupons paid semiannually)

Yield to Maturity (APR)	$T = 1$ Year	$T = 10$ Years	$T = 20$ Years
8%	1,000.00	1,000.00	1,000.00
9%	990.64	934.96	907.99
Change in price (%)*	0.94%	6.50%	9.20%

*Equals value of bond at a 9% yield to maturity divided by value of bond at (the original) 8% yield, minus 1.

and fall, bondholders experience capital losses and gains. These gains or losses make fixed-income investments risky, even if the coupon and principal payments are guaranteed, as in the case of Treasury obligations.

Why do bond prices respond to interest rate fluctuations? Remember that in a competitive market all securities must offer investors fair expected rates of return. If a bond is issued with an 8% coupon when competitive yields are 8%, then it will sell at par value. If the market rate rises to 9%, however, who would purchase an 8% coupon bond at par value? The bond price must fall until its expected return increases to the competitive level of 9%. Conversely, if the market rate falls to 7%, the 8% coupon on the bond is attractive compared to yields on alternative investments. In response, investors eager for that return would bid the bond price above its par value until the total rate of return falls to the market rate.

Interest Rate Sensitivity

It is easy to confirm with numerical examples that prices of long-term bonds generally are more sensitive to interest rate movements than are those of short-term bonds. Consider Table 15.1, which gives bond prices for 8% semiannual coupon bonds at different yields to maturity and times to maturity, T. [The interest rates are expressed as annual percentage rates (APRs), meaning that the true six-month yield is doubled to obtain the stated annual yield.]

The shortest-term bond falls in value by less than 1% when the interest rate increases from 8% to 9%. The 10-year bond falls by 6.5%, and the 20-year bond by over 9%. Longer-term bonds are more sensitive to interest rate increases because higher interest rates have a greater impact on more distant future payments. The one-year bond, for example, is so close to maturity that the present value of the remaining payments is hardly affected at all by the increase in the interest rate. As payments become progressively more distant, however, the effect of discounting at a higher rate becomes progressively more telling, and prices are affected much more by the increase in the interest rate.

Let us now look at a similar example using a zero-coupon bond rather than the 8% coupon bond. The results are shown in Table 15.2. Notice that for each maturity, the price of the zero-coupon bond falls by a greater proportional amount than the price of the 8% coupon bond. Because we know that long-term bonds are more sensitive to

Table 15.2 Prices of Zero-Coupon Bond (semiannual compounding)

Yield to Maturity (APR)	T = 1 Year	T = 10 Years	T = 20 Years
8%	924.56	456.39	208.29
9%	915.73	414.64	171.93
Change in price (%)*	0.96%	9.15%	17.46%

*Equals value of bond at a 9% yield to maturity divided by value of bond at (the original) 8% yield, minus 1.

interest rate movements than are short-term bonds, this observation suggests that in some sense a zero-coupon bond represents a longer-term bond than an equal-time-to-maturity coupon bond. In fact, this insight about effective maturity is a useful one that we can make mathematically precise.

To start, note that the times to maturity of the two bonds in this example are not perfect measures of the long- or short-term nature of the bonds. The 20-year 8% bond makes many coupon payments, most of which come years before the bond's maturity date. Each of these payments may be considered to have its own "maturity date," and the effective maturity of the bond is therefore some sort of average of the maturities of *all* the cash flows paid out by the bond. The zero-coupon bond, by contrast, makes only one payment at maturity. Its time to maturity is, therefore, a well-defined concept.

Duration

To deal with the ambiguity of the "maturity" of a bond making many payments, we need a measure of the average maturity of the bond's promised cash flows to serve as a useful summary statistic of the effective maturity of the bond. We would like also to use the measure as a guide to the sensitivity of a bond to interest rate changes, because we have noted that price sensitivity tends to increase with time to maturity.

Frederick Macaulay[1] termed the effective maturity concept the **duration** of the bond, and suggested that duration be computed as the weighted average of the times to each coupon or principal payment made by the bond. He recommended that the weight associated with each payment time be related to the "importance" of that payment to the value of the bond; specifically, that the weight applied to each payment time be the proportion of the total value of the bond accounted for by that payment. This proportion is just the present value of the payment divided by the bond price.

Therefore the weight, denoted w_t, associated with the cash flow made at time t (CF_t) would be

$$w_t = \frac{CF_t/(1+y)^t}{\text{Bond price}}$$

[1] Frederick Macaulay, *Some Theoretical Problems Suggested by the Movements of Interest Rates, Bond Yields, and Stock Prices in the United States since 1856* (New York: National Bureau of Economic Research, 1938).

Table 15.3 Calculating the Duration of Two Bonds

	(1) Time until Payment (in Years)	(2) Payment	(3) Payment Discounted at 5% Semiannually	(4) Weight*	(5) Column 1 Multiplied by Column 4
Bond A					
8% bond	.5	$ 40	$ 38.095	.0395	.0198
	1.0	40	36.281	.0376	.0376
	1.5	40	34.553	.0358	.0537
	2.0	1,040	855.611	.8871	1.7742
Sum:			$964.540	1.0000	1.8853
Bond B					
Zero-coupon bond	.5–1.5	$ 0	$ 0	0	0
	2.0	1,000	822.70	1.0	2
Sum:			$822.70	1.0	2

*Weight = Present value of each payment (column 3) divided by the bond price, $964.54 for bond A and $822.70 for bond B.

where y is the bond's yield to maturity. The numerator on the right-hand side of this equation is the present value of the cash flow occurring at time t while the denominator is the value of all the payments forthcoming from the bond. These weights sum to 1.0 because the sum of the cash flows discounted at the yield to maturity equals the bond price.

Using these values to calculate the weighted average of the times until the receipt of each of the bond's payments, we obtain Macaulay's duration formula:

$$D = \sum_{t=1}^{T} t \times w_t \tag{15.1}$$

As an example of the application of equation 15.1, we derive in Table 15.3 the durations of an 8% coupon and zero-coupon bond, each with two years to maturity. We assume that the yield to maturity on each bond is 10%, or 5% per half-year.

The numbers in column (5) are the products of time to payment and payment weight. Each of these products corresponds to one of the terms in equation (15.1). According to that equation, we can calculate the duration of each bond by adding the numbers in column (5).

The duration of the zero-coupon bond is exactly equal to its time to maturity, two years. This makes sense, because with only one payment, the average time until payment must be the bond's maturity. In contrast, the two-year coupon bond has a shorter duration of 1.8853 years.

Duration is a key concept in fixed-income portfolio management for at least three reasons. First, it is a simple summary statistic of the effective average maturity of the portfolio. Second, it turns out to be an essential tool in immunizing portfolios from interest rate risk. We will explore this application in section 15.2. Third, duration is a measure of the interest rate sensitivity of a portfolio, which we will explore here.

We have already noted that long-term bonds are more sensitive to interest rate movements than are short-term bonds. The duration measure enables us to quantify this relationship. Specifically, it can be shown that when interest rates change, the proportional change in a bond's price can be related to the change in its yield to maturity, y, according to the rule:

$$\frac{\Delta P}{P} = -D \times \left[\frac{\Delta(1+y)}{1+y}\right] \tag{15.2}$$

The proportional price change equals the proportional change in 1 plus the bond's yield times the bond's duration. Therefore, bond price volatility is proportional to the bond's duration, and duration becomes a natural measure of interest rate exposure.[2]

Practitioners commonly use equation (15.2) in a slightly different form. They define "modified duration" as $D^* = D/(1 + y)$, note that $\Delta(1 + y) = \Delta y$, and rewrite (15.2) as

$$\Delta P/P = -D^*\Delta y \tag{15.2'}$$

The percentage change in bond price is just the product of modified duration and the change in the bond's yield to maturity. Because the percentage change in the bond price is proportional to modified duration, modified duration is a natural measure of the bond's exposure to changes in interest rates.

To confirm the relationship between duration and the sensitivity of bond price to interest rate changes, let's compare the price sensitivity of the two-year coupon bond in Table 15.3, which has a duration of 1.8853 years, to the sensitivity of a zero-coupon bond with maturity *and* duration of 1.8853 years. Both should have equal price sensitivity if duration is a useful measure of interest rate exposure.

The coupon bond sells for $964.5405 at the initial semiannual interest rate of 5%. If the bond's semiannual yield increases by 1 basis point (1/100 of a percent) to 5.01%, its price will fall to $964.1942, a percentage decline of .0359%. The zero-coupon bond has a maturity of $1.8853 \times 2 = 3.7706$ half-year periods. (Because we use a half-year interest rate of 5%, we also need to define duration in terms of a number of half-year periods to maintain consistency of units.) At the initial half-year interest rate of 5%, it sells at a price of $831.9623 ($\$1{,}000/1.05^{3.7706}$). Its price falls to $831.6636 ($\$1{,}000/1.0501^{3.7706}$) when the interest rate increases, for an identical .0359 percent capital loss. We conclude, therefore, that equal-duration assets are in fact equally sensitive to interest rate movements.

---

[2] Actually, equation 15.2 is only approximately valid for large changes in the bond's yield. The approximation becomes exact as one considers smaller, or localized, changes in yields. Students of calculus will recognize that modified duration is proportional to the derivative of the bond's price with respect to changes in the bond's yield:

$$D^* = \frac{1}{P}\frac{dP}{dy}$$

As such, it gives a measure of the slope of the bond price curve only in the neighborhood of the current price.

Figure 15.1
Bond duration versus bond maturity

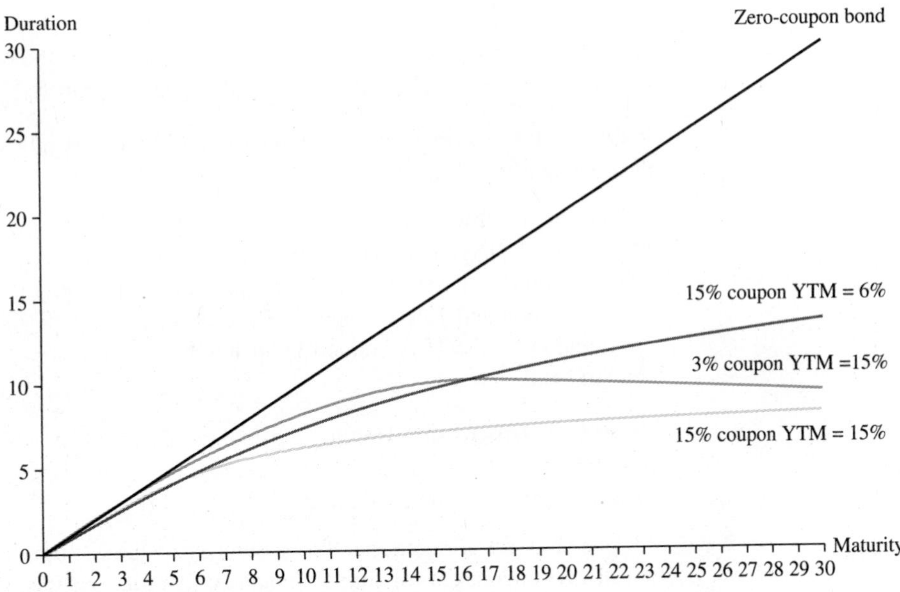

Incidentally, this example confirms the validity of equation 15.2. Note that the equation predicts that the proportional price change of the two bonds should have been 3.7706 × .0001/1.05 = .000359, or .0359%, exactly as we found from direct computation.

CONCEPT CHECK

Question 1.

a. Calculate as in Table 15.3 the price and duration of a two-year maturity, 9% coupon bond making annual coupon payments when the market interest rate is 10%.

b. Now suppose the interest rate increases to 10.05%. Calculate the new value of the bond, and the percentage change in the bond's price.

c. Calculate the percentage change in the bond's price predicted by the duration formula in equations 15.2 or 15.2′. Compare this value to your answer for *(b)*.

What Determines Duration?

The sensitivity of a bond's price to changes in market interest rates is influenced by three key factors: time to maturity, coupon rate, and yield to maturity. These determinants of price sensitivity are important to fixed-income portfolio management. Therefore, we summarize some of the important relationships in the following eight rules. These rules are also illustrated in Figure 15.1, which contains plots of durations of bonds of various coupon rates, yields to maturity, and times to maturity.

We have already established:

Rule 1 for Duration. The duration of a zero-coupon bond equals its time to maturity.

We have also seen that the two-year coupon bond has a lower duration than the two-year zero because coupons early in the bond's life lower the bond's weighted average time until payments. This illustrates another general property:

Rule 2 for Duration. Holding maturity constant, a bond's duration is higher when the coupon rate is lower.

This rule is attributable to the impact of early coupon payments on the average maturity of a bond's payments. The higher these coupons, the more they reduce the weighted average maturity of the payments. Compare the plots in Figure 15.1 of the durations of the 3% coupon and 15% coupon bonds, each with identical yields of 15%. The plot of the duration of the 15% coupon bond lies below the corresponding plot for the 3% coupon bond.

Rule 3 for Duration. Holding the coupon rate constant, a bond's duration generally increases with its time to maturity. Duration always increases with maturity for bonds selling at par or at a premium to par.

This property of duration is fairly intuitive. What is surprising is that duration need not always increase with time to maturity. It turns out that for some deep discount bonds, duration may fall with increases in maturity. However, for virtually all traded bonds it is safe to assume that duration increases with maturity.

Notice in Figure 15.1 that for the zero-coupon bond, maturity and duration are equal. However, for coupon bonds duration increases by less than a year with a year's increase in maturity. The slope of the duration graph is less than one.

Although long-maturity bonds generally will be high-duration bonds, duration is a better measure of the long-term nature of the bond because it also accounts for coupon payments. Time to maturity is an adequate statistic only when the bond pays no coupons; then, maturity and duration are equal.

Notice also in Figure 15.1 that the two 15% coupon bonds have different durations when they sell at different yields to maturity. The lower-yield bond has greater duration. This makes sense, because at lower yields the more distant payments made by the bond have relatively greater present values and account for a greater share of the bond's total value. Thus, in the weighted-average calculation of duration the distant payments receive greater weights, which results in a higher duration measure. This establishes rule 4:

Rule 4 for Duration. Holding other factors constant, the duration of a coupon bond is higher when the bond's yield to maturity is lower.

Rule 4 applies to coupon bonds. For zeros, of course, duration equals time to maturity, regardless of the yield to maturity.

Finally, we develop some algebraic rules for the duration of securities of special interest. These rules are derived from and consistent with the formula for duration given in equation 15.1 but may be easier to use for long-term bonds.

Rule 5 for Duration. The duration of a level perpetuity is $(1 + y)/y$. For example, at a 10% yield, the duration of a perpetuity that pays $100 once a year forever will equal $1.10/.10 = 11$ years, but at an 8% yield it will equal $1.08/.08 = 13.5$ years.

Rule 5 makes it obvious that maturity and duration can differ substantially. The maturity of the perpetuity is infinite, whereas the duration of the instrument at a 10% yield is only 11 years. The present-value-weighted cash flows early on in the life of the perpetuity dominate the computation of duration.

Notice from Figure 15.1 that as their maturities become ever longer, the durations of the two coupon bonds with yields of 15% both converge to the duration of the perpetuity with the same yield, 7.67 years.

CONCEPT CHECK Question 2. Show that the duration of the perpetuity increases as the interest rate decreases in accordance with rule 4.

Rule 6 for Duration. The duration of a level annuity is equal to the following:

$$\frac{1+y}{y} - \frac{T}{(1+y)^T - 1}$$

where T is the number of payments and y is the annuity's yield per payment period. For example, a 10-year annual annuity with a yield of 8% will have duration

$$\frac{1.08}{.08} - \frac{10}{1.08^{10} - 1} = 4.87 \text{ years}$$

Rule 7 for Duration. The duration of a coupon bond equals the following:

$$\frac{1+y}{y} - \frac{(1+y) + T(c-y)}{c[(1+y)^T - 1] + y}$$

where c is the coupon rate per payment period, T is the number of payment periods, and y is the bond's yield per payment period. For example, a 10% coupon bond with 20 years until maturity, paying coupons semiannually, would have a 5% semiannual coupon and 40 payment periods. If the yield to maturity were 4% per half-year period, the bond's duration would be

$$\frac{1.04}{.04} - \frac{1.04 + 40(.05 - .04)}{.05[1.04^{40} - 1] + .04} = 19.74 \text{ half-years} = 9.87 \text{ years}$$

This calculation reminds us again of the importance of maintaining consistency between the time units of the payment period and interest rate. When the bond pays a coupon semiannually, we must use the effective semiannual interest rate and semiannual coupon rate in all calculations. This unit of time (one half-year) is then carried into the duration measure, when we calculate duration to be 19.74 half-year periods.

Rule 8 for Duration. For coupon bonds selling at par value, rule 7 simplifies to the following formula for duration:

$$\frac{1+y}{y}\left[1 - \frac{1}{(1+y)^T}\right]$$

Durations can vary widely among traded bonds. Table 15.4 presents durations computed from rule 7 for several bonds all assumed to pay semiannual coupons and to yield 4% per half-year. Notice that duration decreases as coupon rates increase, and

Table 15.4 Bond Durations (in years) (initial bond yield = 8% APR)

	Coupon Rates (per Year)			
Years to Maturity	**6%**	**8%**	**10%**	**12%**
1	.985	.980	.976	.972
5	4.361	4.218	4.095	3.990
10	7.454	7.067	6.772	6.541
20	10.922	10.292	9.870	9.568
Infinite (perpetuity)	13.000	13.000	13.000	13.000

generally increases with time to maturity. According to Table 15.4 and equation 15.2, if the interest rate were to increase from 8% to 8.1%, the 6% coupon 20-year bond would fall in value by about 1.01% (10.922 × .1%/1.08), whereas the 10% coupon 1-year bond would fall by only 0.090%. Notice also from Table 15.4 that duration is independent of coupon rate only for the perpetual bond.

15.2 Passive Bond Management

Passive managers take bond prices as fairly set and seek to control only the risk of their fixed-income portfolio. Two broad classes of passive management are pursued in the fixed-income market. The first is an indexing strategy that attempts to replicate the performance of a given bond index. The second broad class of passive strategies are known as immunization techniques and are used widely by financial institutions such as insurance companies and pension funds. These are designed to shield the overall financial status of the institution from exposure to interest rate fluctuations.

Although both indexing and immunization strategies are alike in that they accept market prices as correctly set, they are very different in terms of risk exposure. A bond-index portfolio will have the same risk-reward profile as the bond market index to which it is tied. In contrast, immunization strategies seek to establish a virtually zero-risk profile, in which interest rate movements have no impact on the value of the firm. We will discuss both types of strategies in this section.

Bond-Index Funds

In principle, bond market indexing is similar to stock market indexing. The idea is to create a portfolio that mirrors the composition of an index that measures the broad market. In the U.S. equity market, for example, the S&P 500 is the most commonly used index for stock index funds, and these funds simply buy shares of each firm in the S&P 500 in proportion to the market value of outstanding equity. A similar strategy is used for bond-index funds, but as we shall see shortly, several modifications are required because of difficulties unique to the bond market and its indexes.

Table 15.5 The U.S. Fixed-Income Market, 1994

Sector	Size ($ billions)	Percentage of Market
Treasury	$3,368	41.0%
Federal agency	600	7.3
Corporate	1,255	15.3
Tax-exempt*	1,083	13.2
Mortgage-backed	1,416	17.2
Asset-backed	502	6.1
TOTAL	8,224	100.0

*Includes private purpose tax-exempt debt.
Source: *Flow of Funds Accounts, Flows and Outstandings*, Board of Governors of the Federal Reserve System, Second Quarter, 1994.

Table 15.6 Profile of Bond Indexes

	Lehman Brothers	Merrill Lynch	Salomon Brothers
Number of issues	Over 6,500	Over 5,000	Over 5,000
Maturity of included bonds	≥ 1 year	≥ 1 year	≥ 1 year
Excluded issues	Junk bonds Convertibles Flower bonds Floating rate	Junk bonds Convertibles Flower bonds	Junk bonds Convertibles Floating rate bonds
Weighting	Market value	Market value	Market value
Reinvestment of intramonth cash flows	No	Yes (in specific bond)	Yes (at one-month T-bill rate)
Daily availability	Yes	Yes	Yes

Source: Frank K. Reilly, G. Wenchi Kao, and David J. Wright, "Alternative Bond Market Indexes," *Financial Analysts Journal* (May–June 1992), pp. 44–58.

There are three major indexes of the broad bond market: the Salomon Brothers Broad Investment Grade (BIG) index, the Lehman Brothers Aggregate Index, and the Merrill Lynch Domestic Master Index. All three are market-value-weighted indexes of total returns and are computed daily. All three include government, corporate, mortgage-backed, and Yankee bonds in their universes. (Yankee bonds are dollar-denominated, SEC-registered bonds of foreign issuers sold in the United States.) All three indexes include only bonds with maturities greater than one year. As time passes, and the maturity of a bond falls below one year, the bond is dropped from the index. Table 15.5 presents a breakdown of the fixed-income market in 1994, and Table 15.6 presents some summary statistics pertaining to each index.

The first problem that arises in the formation of a bond index is apparent from Table 15.6. Each of these indexes includes more than 5,000 securities, making it quite

Figure 15.2
Stratification of bonds into cells

Term to Maturity \ Sector	Treasury	Agency	Mortgage-Backed	Industrial	Finance	Utility	Yankee
< 1 year	12.1%						
1–3 years	5.4%						
3–5 years			4.1%				
5–7 years							
7–10 years		0.1%					
10–15 years							
15–30 years			9.2%			3.4%	
30+ years							

difficult to purchase each security in the index in proportion to its market value. Moreover, many bonds are very thinly traded, meaning that identifying their owners and purchasing the securities at a fair market price can be difficult.

Bond-index funds also present more difficult rebalancing problems than do stock-index funds. Bonds are continually dropped from the index as their maturities fall below one year. Moreover, as new bonds are issued, they are added to the index. Therefore, in contrast to equity indexes, the securities used to compute bond indexes constantly change. As they do, the manager must update or rebalance the portfolio to ensure a close match between the composition of the portfolio and the bonds included in the index. The fact that bonds generate considerable interest income that must be reinvested further complicates the job of the index fund manager.

In practice, it is deemed infeasible to precisely replicate the broad bond indexes. Instead, a stratified sampling or *cellular* approach is often pursued. Figure 15.2 illustrates the idea behind the cellular approach. First, the bond market is stratified into several subclasses. Figure 15.2 shows a simple two-way breakdown by maturity and issuer, but in practice, other criteria such as the bond's coupon rate or the credit risk of the issuer also would be used to form cells. Bonds falling within each cell are then considered reasonably homogeneous. Next, the percentages of the entire universe (i.e., the bonds included in the index that is to be matched) falling within each cell are computed and reported, as we have done for a few cells in Figure 15.2. Finally, the portfolio manager establishes a bond portfolio with representation for each cell that matches the representation of that cell in the bond universe. In this way, the characteristics of the portfolio in terms of maturity, coupon rate, credit risk, industrial representation, and so on will match the characteristics of the index, and the performance of the portfolio likewise should match the index.

How well does this cellular method track the broad bond indexes? One way to measure the results is to calculate the average absolute value of the *tracking error* between the portfolio and the index. The tracking error in any month is the difference in the performance of the portfolio and the index. A Salomon Brothers study[3] found that a $100 million index fund could track the BIG index with average absolute tracking error of only 4 basis points per month. Not surprisingly, the Corporate subindex, which has the greatest diversity of bonds, was subject to the greatest monthly tracking error, 16 basis points, whereas the government bond subindex could be tracked far more closely, with average absolute error of only 2 basis points per month. Of course, tracking error will also be a function of the size of the index fund. A billion dollar fund should track the index more closely than a $100 million fund since the larger size of the portfolio allows a finer breakdown into smaller and more homogenous cells.

Roughly $100 billion of pension fund assets were invested in bond-index portfolios in 1994. These pension plans typically hire index managers and give them portfolios of over $100 million to manage. Smaller investors can index using mutual funds. For example, Fidelity offers a fund for investors with a minimum of $100,000 to invest. Vanguard's Bond Fund, which is pegged to the BIG index, is designed for small investors ($2,500 minimum).

Immunization

In contrast to indexing strategies, many institutions try to insulate their portfolios from interest rate risk altogether. Generally, there are two ways of viewing this risk, depending on the circumstances of the particular investor. Some institutions, such as banks, are concerned with protecting the current net worth or net market value of the firm against interest rate fluctuations. Other investors, such as pension funds, may face an obligation to make payments after a given number of years. These investors are more concerned with protecting the future values of their portfolios.

What is common to the bank and the pension fund, however, is interest rate risk. The net worth of the firm or the ability to meet future obligations fluctuates with interest rates. These institutions presumably might be interested in methods to control that risk. We will see that, by properly adjusting the maturity structure of their portfolios, these institutions can shed their interest rate risk. **Immunization** techniques refer to strategies used by such investors to shield their overall financial status from exposure to interest rate fluctuations.

Net Worth Immunization

Many banks and thrift institutions have a natural mismatch between asset and liability maturity structures. Bank liabilities are primarily the deposits owed to customers, most of which are very short-term in nature and, consequently, of low duration. Bank assets by contrast are composed largely of outstanding commercial and consumer loans or mortgages. These assets are of longer duration than are deposits, and their values are correspondingly more sensitive to interest rate fluctuations. In periods when interest rates increase unexpectedly, banks can suffer serious decreases in net worth—their assets fall in value by more than their liabilities.

---

[3] Reported in Sharmin Mossavar-Rahmani, *Bond Index Funds* (Chicago: Probus Publishing Company, 1991).

Flannery and James[4] have shown that prices of bank stock do in fact tend to fall when interest rates rise. In another study, Kopcke and Woglom[5] found that when measured by market values, total liabilities exceeded total assets for some savings banks in Connecticut in several years during the 1970s, a period following significant increases in interest rates. Had these banks been required to carry their assets at market value on their balance sheets, they would have been declared insolvent. Clearly, banks are subject to interest rate risk.

The watchword in bank portfolio strategy has become asset and liability management. Techniques called *gap management* were developed to limit the "gap" between asset and liability durations. Adjustable rate mortgages are one way to reduce the duration of bank asset portfolios. Unlike conventional mortgages, adjustable rate mortgages do not fall in value when market interest rates rise, because the rates they pay are tied to an index of the current market rate. Even if the indexing is imperfect or entails lags, indexing greatly diminishes sensitivity to interest rate fluctuations. On the other side of the balance sheet, the introduction of bank certificates of deposit with fixed terms to maturity serves to lengthen the duration of bank liabilities, also reducing the duration gap.

One way to view gap management is that the bank is attempting to equate the durations of assets and liabilities to effectively immunize its overall position from interest rate movements. Because bank assets and liabilities are roughly equal in size, if their durations also are equal, any change in interest rates will affect the values of assets and liabilities equally. Interest rates would have no effect on net worth, in other words. Therefore, net worth immunization requires a portfolio duration of zero. This will result if assets and liabilities are equal in both magnitude and duration.

CONCEPT CHECK

Question 3. If assets and liabilities are not equal, then immunization requires that $D_A A = D_L L$ where D denotes duration and A and L denote assets and liabilities, respectively. Explain why the simpler condition $D_A = D_L$ is no longer valid in this case.

Target Date Immunization

Pension funds are different from banks. They think more in terms of future commitments than current net worth. Pension funds have an obligation to provide workers with a flow of income upon their retirement, and they must have sufficient funds available to meet these commitments. As interest rates fluctuate, both the value of the assets held by the fund and the rate at which those assets generate income fluctuate. The pension fund manager, therefore, may want to protect or "immunize" the future accumulated value of the fund at some target date against interest rate movements.

Pension funds are not alone in this concern. Any institution with a future fixed obligation might consider immunization a reasonable risk management policy. Insurance

[4] Mark J. Flannery and Christopher M. James, "The Effect of Interest Rate Changes on the Common Stock Returns of Financial Institutions," *Journal of Finance* 39 (September 1984).

[5] Richard W. Kopcke and Geoffrey R. H. Woglom, "Regulation Q and Savings Bank Solvency—The Connecticut Experience," *The Regulation of Financial Institutions*, Federal Reserve Bank of Boston Conference Series, No. 21, 1979.

companies, for example, also pursue immunization strategies. Indeed, the notion of immunization was introduced by F. M. Redington,[6] an actuary for a life insurance company. The idea behind immunization is that duration-matched assets and liabilities let the asset portfolio meet the firm's obligations despite interest rate movements. Consider, for example, an insurance company that issues a guaranteed investment contract, or GIC, for $10,000. (Essentially, GICs are zero-coupon bonds issued by the insurance company to its customers. They are popular products for individuals' retirement-saving accounts.) If the GIC has a five-year maturity and a guaranteed interest rate of 8%, the insurance company is obligated to pay $\$10{,}000 \times (1.08)^5 = \$14{,}693.28$ in five years.

Suppose that the insurance company chooses to fund its obligation with $10,000 of 8% *annual* coupon bonds, selling at par value, with six years to maturity. As long as the market interest rate stays at 8%, the company has fully funded the obligation, as the present value of the obligation exactly equals the value of the bonds.

Table 15.7**A** shows that if interest rates remain at 8%, the accumulated funds from the bond will grow to exactly the $14,693.28 obligation. Over the five-year period, the year-end coupon income of $800 is reinvested at the prevailing 8% market interest rate. At the end of the period, the bonds can be sold for $10,000; they still will sell at par value because the coupon rate still equals the market interest rate. Total income after five years from reinvested coupons and the sale of the bond is precisely $14,693.28.

If interest rates change, however, two offsetting influences will affect the ability of the fund to grow to the targeted value of $14,693.28. If interest rates rise, the fund will suffer a capital loss, impairing its ability to satisfy the obligation. The bonds will be worth less in five years than if interest rates had remained at 8%. However, at a higher interest rate, reinvested coupons will grow at a faster rate, offsetting the capital loss. In other words, fixed-income investors face two offsetting types of interest rate risk: *price risk* and *reinvestment rate risk.* Increases in interest rates cause capital losses but at the same time increase the rate at which reinvested income will grow. If the portfolio duration is chosen appropriately, these two effects will cancel out exactly. When the portfolio duration is set equal to the investor's horizon date, the accumulated value of the investment fund at the horizon date will be unaffected by interest rate fluctuations. *For a horizon equal to the portfolio's duration, price risk and reinvestment risk exactly cancel out.*

In the example we are discussing, the duration of the six-year maturity bonds used to fund the GIC is five years. You can confirm this using rule 8. Because the fully funded plan has equal duration for its assets and liabilities, the insurance company should be immunized against interest rate fluctuations. To confirm that this is the case, let us now investigate whether the bond can generate enough income to pay off the obligation five years from now regardless of interest rate movements.

Tables 15.7**B** and **C** consider two possible interest rate scenarios: Rates either fall to 7% or increase to 9%. In both cases, the annual coupon payments from the bond are reinvested at the new interest rate, which is assumed to change before the first coupon payment, and the bond is sold in year 5 to help satisfy the obligation of the GIC.

[6] F. M. Redington, "Review of the Principle of Life-Office Valuations," *Journal of the Institute of Actuaries* 78 (1952).

Table 15.7 Terminal Value of a Bond Portfolio after Five Years (all proceeds reinvested)

Payment Number	Years Remaining until Obligation	Accumulated Value of Invested Payment		
A. Rates Remain at 8%				
1	4	$800 \times (1.08)^4$	=	1,088.39
2	3	$800 \times (1.08)^3$	=	1,007.77
3	2	$800 \times (1.08)^2$	=	933.12
4	1	$800 \times (1.08)^1$	=	864.00
5	0	$800 \times (1.08)^0$	=	800.00
Sale of bond	0	10,800/1.08	=	10,000.00
				14,693.28
B. Rates Fall to 7%				
1	4	$800 \times (1.07)^4$	=	1,048.64
2	3	$800 \times (1.07)^3$	=	980.03
3	2	$800 \times (1.07)^2$	=	915.92
4	1	$800 \times (1.07)^1$	=	856.00
5	0	$800 \times (1.07)^0$	=	800.00
Sale of bond	0	10,800/1.07	=	10,093.46
				14,694.05
C. Rates Increase to 9%				
1	4	$800 \times (1.09)^4$	=	1,129.27
2	3	$800 \times (1.09)^3$	=	1,036.02
3	2	$800 \times (1.09)^2$	=	950.48
4	1	$800 \times (1.09)^1$	=	872.00
5	0	$800 \times (1.09)^0$	=	800.00
Sale of bond	0	10,800/1.09	=	9,908.26
				14,696.02

Note: The sale price of the bond portfolio equals the portfolio's final payment ($10,800) divided by $1 + r$, because the time to maturity of the bonds will be one year at the time of sale.

Table 15.7**B** shows that if interest rates fall to 7%, the total funds will accumulate to $14,694.05, providing a small surplus of $.77. If rates increase to 9% as in Table 15.7**C**, the fund accumulates to $14,696.02, providing a small surplus of $2.74.

Several points are worth highlighting. First, duration matching balances the difference between the accumulated value of the coupon payments (reinvestment rate risk) and the sale value of the bond (price risk). That is, when interest rates fall, the coupons grow less than in the base case, but the gain on the sale of the bond offsets this. When interest rates rise, the resale value of the bond falls, but the coupons more than make up for this loss because they are reinvested at the higher rate. Figure 15.3 illustrates this case. The solid curve traces out the accumulated value of the bonds if interest rates

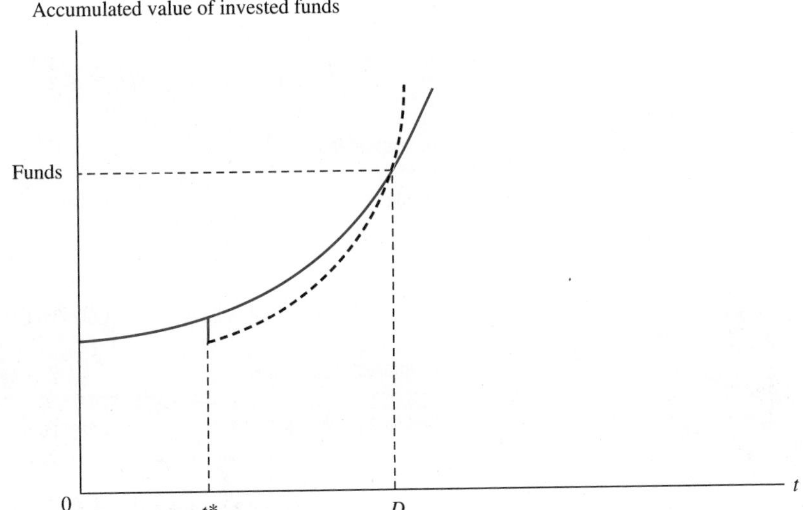

Figure 15.3
Growth of invested funds. The solid blue curve represents the growth of portfolio value at the original interest rate. If interest rates increase at time t^* the portfolio value initially falls but increases thereafter at the faster rate represented by the broken gray curve. At time D (duration) the curves cross.

remain at 8%. The dashed curve shows that value if interest rates happen to increase. The initial impact is a capital loss, but this loss eventually is offset by the now-faster growth rate of reinvested funds. At the five-year horizon date, the two effects just cancel, leaving the company able to satisfy its obligation with the accumulated proceeds from the bond.

We can also analyze immunization in terms of present as opposed to future values. Table 15.8**A** shows the initial balance sheet for the insurance company's GIC account. Both assets and the obligation have market values of $10,000, so that the plan is just fully funded. Tables 15.8**B** and **C** show that whether the interest rate increases or decreases, the value of the bonds funding the GIC and the present value of the company's obligation change by virtually identical amounts. Regardless of the interest rate change, the plan remains fully funded, with the surplus in Table 15.8**B** and **C** just about zero. The duration-matching strategy has ensured that both assets and liabilities react equally to interest rate fluctuations.

Figure 15.4 is a graph of the present values of the bond and the single-payment obligation as a function of the interest rate. At the current rate of 8%, the values are equal, and the obligation is fully funded by the bond. Moreover, the two present value curves are tangent at $y = 8\%$. As interest rates change, the change in value of both the asset and the obligation is equal, so the obligation remains fully funded. For greater changes in the interest rate, however, the present value curves diverge. This reflects the fact that the fund actually shows a small surplus at market interest rates other than 8%.

Why is there any surplus in the fund? After all, we claimed that a duration-matched asset and liability mix would result in indifference to interest rate shifts. Actually, such a claim is valid only for *small* changes in the interest rate, because as bond yields change, so too does duration. (Recall rule 4 for duration and footnote 2.) In our

Table 15.8 Market Value Balance Sheet

Assets		Liabilities	
A. Interest Rate = 8%			
Bonds	$10,000	Obligation	$10,000
B. Interest Rate = 7%			
Bonds	$10,476.65	Obligation	$10,476.11
C. Interest Rate = 9%			
Bonds	$ 9,551.41	Obligation	$9,549.62

Notes:

$$\text{Value of bonds} = 800\ PA(r, 6) + 10{,}000\ PF(r, 6)$$

$$\text{Value of obligation} = \frac{14{,}693.28}{(1 + r)^5} = 14{,}693.28\ PF(r,5)$$

example, although the duration of the bond is indeed equal to 5 years at a yield to maturity of 8%; it rises to 5.02 years when its yield falls to 7% and drops to 4.97 years at $y = 9\%$; that is, the bond and the obligation were not duration-matched *across* the interest rate shift, so that the position was not fully immunized.

This example highlights the importance of **rebalancing** immunized portfolios. As interest rates and asset durations change, a manager must rebalance the portfolio of fixed-income assets continually to realign its duration with the duration of the obligation. Moreover, even if interest rates do not change, asset durations *will* change solely because of the passage of time. Recall from Figure 15.1 that duration generally decreases less rapidly than does maturity. Thus, even if an obligation is immunized at the outset, as time passes the durations of the asset and liability will fall at different rates. Without portfolio rebalancing, durations will become unmatched and the goals of immunization will not be realized. Obviously, immunization is a passive strategy only in the sense that it does not involve attempts to identify undervalued securities. Immunization managers still actively update and monitor their positions.

As another example of the need for rebalancing, consider a portfolio manager facing an obligation of $19,487 in seven years, which, at a current market interest rate of 10%, has a present value of $10,000. Right now, suppose that the manager wishes to immunize the obligation by holding only three-year zero-coupon bonds and perpetuities paying annual coupons. (Our focus on zeros and perpetuities helps keep the algebra simple.) At current interest rates, the perpetuities have a duration of 1.10/.10 = 11 years. The duration of zero is simply three years.

For assets with equal yields, the duration of a portfolio is the weighted average of the durations of the assets comprising the portfolio. To achieve the desired portfolio duration of seven years, the manager would have to choose appropriate values for the

Figure 15.4
Immunization

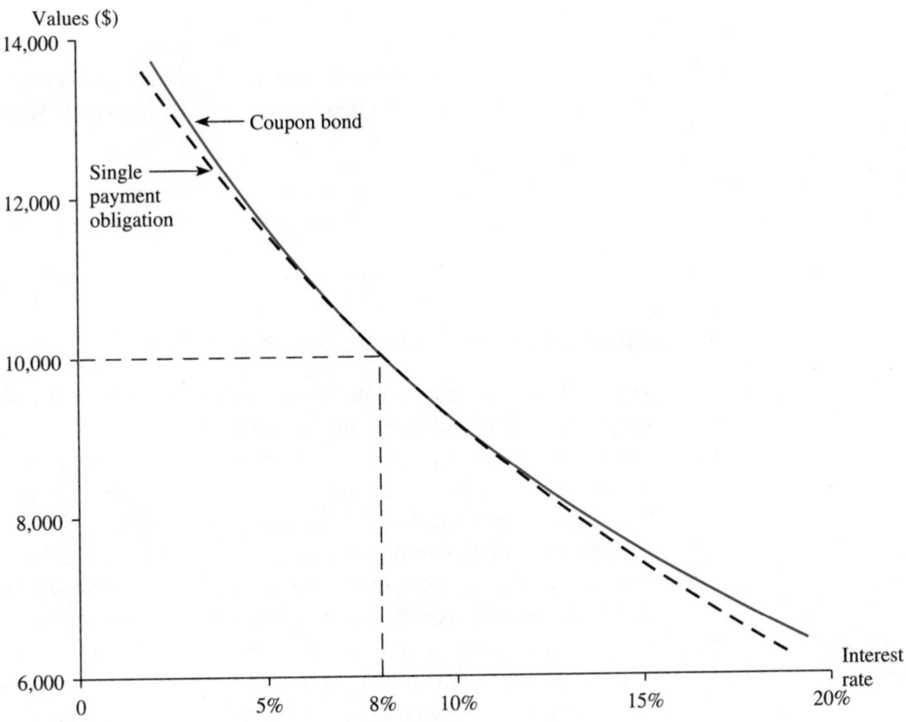

weights of the zero and the perpetuity in the overall portfolio. Call w the zero's weight and $(1 - w)$ the perpetuity's weight. Then w must be chosen to satisfy the equation

$$w \times 3 \text{ years} + (1 - w) \times 11 \text{ years} = 7 \text{ years}$$

which implies that $w = \frac{1}{2}$. The manager invests $5,000 in the zero-coupon bond and $5,000 in the perpetuity, providing annual coupon payments of $500 per year indefinitely. The portfolio duration is then seven years, and the position is immunized.

Next year, even if interest rates do not change, rebalancing will be necessary. The present value of the obligation has grown to $11,000, because it is one year closer to maturity. The manager's funds also have grown to $11,000: The zero-coupon bonds have increased in value from $5,000 to $5,500 with the passage of time, while the perpetuity has paid its annual $500 coupon and still is worth $5,000. However, the portfolio weights must be changed. The zero-coupon bond now will have duration of 2 years, while the perpetuity remains at 11 years. The obligation is now due in 6 years. The weights must now satisfy the equation

$$w \times 2 + (1 - w) \times 11 = 6$$

which implies that $w = \frac{5}{9}$. Now, the manager must invest a total of $\$11,000 \times \frac{5}{9} = \$6,111.11$ in the zero. This requires that the entire $500 coupon payment be invested in the zero and that an additional $111.11 of the perpetuity be sold and invested in the zero in order to maintain an immunized position.

Of course, rebalancing of the portfolio entails transaction costs as assets are bought or sold, so one cannot rebalance continuously. In practice, an appropriate compromise must be established between the desire for perfect immunization, which requires continual rebalancing, and the need to control trading costs, which dictates less frequent rebalancing.

CONCEPT CHECK

Question 4. What would be the immunizing weights in the second year if the interest rate had fallen to 8%?

Cash Flow Matching and Dedication

The problems associated with immunization seem to have a simple solution. Why not simply buy a zero-coupon bond that provides a payment in an amount exactly sufficient to cover the projected cash outlay? If we follow the principle of **cash flow matching** we automatically immunize the portfolio from interest rate movement because the cash flow from the bond and the obligation exactly offset each other.

Cash flow matching on a multiperiod basis is referred to as a **dedication strategy.** In this case, the manager selects either zero-coupon or coupon bonds that provide total cash flows in each period that match a series of obligations. The advantage of dedication is that it is a once-and-for-all approach to eliminating interest rate risk. Once the cash flows are matched, there is no need for rebalancing. The dedicated portfolio provides the cash necessary to pay the firm's liabilities regardless of the eventual path of interest rates.

Cash flow matching is not more widely pursued probably because of the constraints that it imposes on bond selection. Immunization-dedication strategies are appealing to firms that do not wish to bet on general movements in interest rates, but these firms may want to immunize using bonds that they perceive are undervalued. Cash flow matching, however, places so many more constraints on the bond selection process that it can be impossible to pursue a dedication strategy using only "underpriced" bonds. Firms looking for underpriced bonds give up exact and easy dedication for the possibility of achieving superior returns from the bond portfolio.

Sometimes, cash flow matching is not possible. To cash-flow-match for a pension fund that is obligated to pay out a perpetual flow of income to current and future retirees, the pension fund would need to purchase fixed-income securities with maturities ranging up to hundreds of years. Such securities do not exist, making exact dedication infeasible. Immunization is easy, however. If the interest rate is 8%, for example, the duration for the pension fund obligation is 1.08/.08 = 13.5 years (see rule 5 above). Therefore, the fund can immunize its obligation by purchasing zero-coupon bonds with a maturity of 13.5 years and a market value equal to that of the pension liabilities.

CONCEPT CHECK

Question 5. How would an increase in trading costs affect the attractiveness of dedication versus immunization?

Other Problems with Conventional Immunization

If you look back at the definition of duration in equation 15.1, you note that it uses the bond's yield to maturity to calculate the weight applied to the time until each coupon payment. Given this definition and limitations on the proper use of yield to maturity, it is perhaps not surprising that this notion of duration is strictly valid only for a flat yield curve for which all payments are discounted at a common interest rate.

If the yield curve is not flat, then the definition of duration must be modified and $CF_t/(1 + y)^t$ replaced with the present value of CF_t, where the present value of each cash flow is calculated by discounting with the appropriate interest rate from the yield curve corresponding to the date of the *particular* cash flow, instead of by discounting with the *bond's* yield to maturity. Moreover, even with this modification, duration matching will immunize portfolios only for parallel shifts in the yield curve. Clearly, this sort of restriction is unrealistic. As a result, much work has been devoted to generalizing the notion of duration. Multifactor duration models have been developed to allow for tilts and other distortions in the shape of the yield curve, in addition to shifts in its level. (We refer to some of this work in the suggested readings at the end of this chapter.) However, it does not appear that the added complexity of such models pays off in terms of substantially greater effectiveness.[7]

Finally, immunization can be an inappropriate goal in an inflationary environment. Immunization is essentially a nominal notion and makes sense only for nominal liabilities. It makes no sense to immunize a projected obligation that will grow with the price level using nominal assets such as bonds. For example, if your child will attend college in 15 years and if the annual cost of tuition is expected to be $15,000 at that time, immunizing your portfolio at a locked-in terminal value of $15,000 is not necessarily a risk-reducing strategy. The tuition obligation will vary with the realized inflation rate, whereas the asset portfolio's final value will not. In the end, the tuition obligation will not necessarily be matched by the value of the portfolio.

On this note, it is worth pointing out that immunization is a goal that may well be inappropriate for many investors who would find a zero-risk portfolio strategy unduly conservative. Full immunization is a fairly extreme position for a portfolio manager to pursue.

15.3 Active Bond Management

Sources of Potential Profit

Broadly speaking, there are two sources of potential value in active bond management. The first is interest rate forecasting, which tries to anticipate movements across the entire spectrum of the fixed-income market. If interest rate declines are anticipated, managers will increase portfolio duration (and vice versa). The second source of

[7] G. O. Bierwag, G. C. Kaufman, and A. Toevs, eds., *Innovations in Bond Portfolio Management: Duration Analysis and Immunization* (Greenwich, Conn.: JAI Press, 1983).

potential profit is identification of relative mispricing within the fixed-income market. An analyst, for example, might believe that the default premium on one particular bond is unnecessarily large and therefore that the bond is underpriced.

These techniques will generate abnormal returns only if the analyst's information or insight is superior to that of the market. You cannot profit from knowledge that rates are about to fall if everyone else in the market is aware of this. In that case the anticipated decreases in interest rates already are built into bond prices in the sense that long-duration bonds are already selling at higher prices that reflect the anticipated fall in future short rates. If the analyst does not have information before the market does, it will be too late to act on that information—prices will have responded already to the news. You know this from our discussion of market efficiency.

For now we simply repeat that valuable information is differential information. In this context it is worth nothing that interest rate forecasters have a notoriously poor track record. If you consider this record, you will approach attempts to time the bond market with caution.

Homer and Liebowitz[8] have coined a popular taxonomy of active bond portfolio strategies. They characterize portfolio rebalancing activities as one of four types of *bond swaps*. In the first two swaps the investor typically believes that the yield relationship between bonds or sectors is only temporarily out of alignment. When the aberration is eliminated, gains can be realized on the underpriced bond. The period of realignment is called the *workout period.*

1. The **substitution swap** is an exchange of one bond for a nearly identical substitute. The substituted bonds should be of essentially equal coupon, maturity, quality, call features, sinking fund provisions, and so on. This swap would be motivated by a belief that the market has temporarily mispriced the two bonds, and that the discrepancy between the prices of the bonds represents a profit opportunity.

   An example of a substitution swap would be a sale of a 20-year maturity, 9% coupon Ford Motor Company bond callable after 5 years at $1,050 that is priced to provide a yield to maturity of 9.05%, coupled with a purchase of a 9% coupon Chrysler bond with the same call provisions and time to maturity that yields 9.15%. If the bonds have about the same credit rating, there is no apparent reason for the Chrysler bonds to provide a higher yield. Therefore, the higher yield actually available in the market makes the Chrysler bond seem relatively attractive. Of course, the equality of credit risk is an important condition. If the Chrysler bond is in fact riskier, then its higher yield does not represent a bargain.

2. The **intermarket spread swap** is pursued when an investor believes that the yield spread between two sectors of the bond market is temporarily out of line. For example, if the current spread between corporate and government bonds is considered too wide and is expected to narrow, the investor will shift from gov-

[8] Sidney Homer and Martin L. Liebowitz, *Inside the Yield Book: New Tools for Bond Market Strategy* (Englewood Cliffs, N.J.: Prentice Hall, 1972).

ernment bonds into corporate bonds. If the yield spread does in fact narrow, corporates will outperform governments. For example, if the yield spread between 20-year Treasury bonds and 20-year Baa-rated corporate bonds is now 3%, and the historical spread has been only 2%, an investor might consider selling holdings of Treasury bonds and replacing them with corporates. If the yield spread eventually narrows, the Baa-rated corporate bonds will outperform the Treasuries.

Of course, the investor must consider carefully whether there is a good reason that the yield spread seems out of alignment. For example, the default premium on corporate bonds might have increased because the market is expecting a severe recession. In this case, the wider spread would not represent attractive pricing of corporates relative to Treasuries, but would simply be an adjustment for a perceived increase in credit risk.

3. The **rate anticipation swap** is pegged to interest rate forecasting. In this case if investors believe that rates will fall, they will swap into bonds of longer duration. Conversely, when rates are expected to rise, they will swap into shorter duration bonds. For example, the investor might sell a 5-year maturity Treasury bond, replacing it with a 25-year maturity Treasury bond. The new bond has the same lack of credit risk as the old one, but has longer duration.

4. The **pure yield pickup swap** is pursued not in response to perceived mispricing, but as a means of increasing return by holding higher-yield bonds. This must be viewed as an attempt to earn an expected term premium in higher-yield bonds. The investor is willing to bear the interest rate risk that this strategy entails.

   A yield pickup swap can be illustrated using the Treasury bond listings in Table 14.1 from the last chapter. You can see from that table that a Treasury note maturing in one year yields 5%, whereas one maturing in 30 years yields over 8%. The investor who swaps the shorter-term bond for the longer one will earn a higher rate of return as long as the yield curve does not shift up during the holding period. Of course if it does, the longer-duration bond will suffer a greater capital loss.

We can add a fifth swap, called a **tax swap,** to this list. This simply refers to a swap to exploit some tax advantage. For example, an investor may swap from one bond that has decreased in price to another if realization of capital losses is advantageous for tax purposes.

Investors and analysts commonly use this classification of strategies, at least implicitly. For example, consider these quotations from a Merrill Lynch Fixed-Income Strategy booklet.[9]

> Projected returns at alternative settings of the funds rate strongly favors ownership of short-term notes. At almost every [projected] setting of the [federal]funds rate, returns from both

[9] Reprinted from *Fixed Income Strategy* by permission of Merrill Lynch, Pierce, Fenner & Smith Incorporated © Copyright 1986.

10-year notes and 30-year bonds would be negative . . . In a rising interest rate environment, where yields rise by 35 basis points for two-year notes and 25 basis points for three-year notes, the two-year is projected to outperform by approximately 50 basis points [page 10].

This analysis is motivated by rate anticipation, which follows from Merrill's overall macroeconomic analysis. Given Merrill's belief in rising rates, it recommends short asset durations.

Following this general analysis comes a sector-oriented intermarket spread analysis that expresses Merrill's view that yield relationships across two fixed-income submarkets are temporarily out of line. The history of 1982 to 1984 leads Merrill to believe that corporate yields will fall relative to Treasury yields, making corporates attractive relative to Treasuries:

> Corporate/Treasury yield ratios are unusually high for both intermediate- and long-term securities. These ratios are now [April 1986] almost as high as those that emerged late in 1982, following a sharp drop in bond yields. The respective yield ratios for new-issue and long-term AA utilities and AA industrials were 1.17 and 1.13 at the end of this past quarter, compared with 1.22 and 1.15 in December 1982. By mid-1983, these ratios had declined to 1.10 and 1.08, respectively. By July 1984, they had declined further, to 1.08 and 1.05. Yield ratios for intermediate corporates display a similar pattern. This record suggests that corporate/Treasury yield ratios are likely to fall in the months ahead if, as we expect, the Treasury yield curve steepens [page 16].

Finally, we see an example of a yield pickup recommendation:

> Although the slope of the corporate yield curve is 30 to 50 basis points steeper than that of the Treasury curve, it has flattened by approximately the same degree. Thus any steepening in the Treasury curve would probably spark a similar response in corporates, hurting the long corporate market much more than the short and intermediate coupons. Consequently, the 2- to 10-year maturity sector performs far better in the total return simulations [than longer-term issues]. Moreover, since this is the steepest area of the yield curve, it offers investors the opportunity to capture more than 90 percent of the yield on long bonds while owning 10-year rather than 30-year maturities [page 17].

Horizon Analysis

One form of interest rate forecasting is called **horizon analysis.** The analyst using this approach selects a particular holding period and predicts the yield curve at the end of that period. Given a bond's time to maturity at the end of the holding period, its yield can be read from the predicted yield curve and its end-of-period price calculated. Then the analyst adds the coupon income and prospective capital gain of the bond to obtain the total return on the bond over the holding period.

For example, suppose that a 20-year maturity 10% coupon bond currently yields 9% and sells at $1,092.01. An analyst with a five-year time horizon would be concerned about the bond's price and the value of reinvested coupons five years hence. At that time the bond will have a 15-year maturity, so the analyst will predict the yield on 15-year maturity bonds at the end of the 5-year period to determine the bond's expected price. Suppose that the yield is expected to be 8%. Then the bond's end-of-period price will be (assuming 30 semiannual coupon payments):

$$50 \times PA(4\%,30) + 1{,}000 \times PF(4\%,30) = \$1{,}172.92$$

The capital gain on the bond therefore will be $80.91.

Meanwhile, the coupons paid by the bond will be reinvested over the five-year period. The analyst must predict a reinvestment rate at which the invested coupons can earn interest. Suppose that the assumed rate is 4% per six-month period. If all coupon payments are reinvested at this rate, the value of the 10 semiannual coupon payments with accumulated interest at the end of the five years will be $600.31. (This amount can be solved for as the future value of a $50 annuity after 10 periods with per period interest of 4%.) The total return provided by the bond over the five-year period will be $80.91 + $600.31 = $681.22 for a total five-year holding-period return of $681.22/ $1,092.01 = .624, or 62.4%.

The analyst repeats this procedure for many bonds and selects the ones promising superior holding-period returns for the portfolio.

CONCEPT CHECK

Question 6. Consider a 30-year 8% coupon bond currently selling at $896.81. The analyst believes that in five years the yield on 25-year bonds will be 8.5%. Should she purchase the 20-year bond just discussed or the 30-year bond today?

A particular version of horizon analysis is called **riding the yield curve,** which is a popular strategy among managers of short-term money market securities. If the yield curve is upward sloping *and* if it is projected that the curve will not shift during the investment horizon, then as bond maturities fall with the passage of time, their yields also will fall as they "ride" the yield curve toward the lower yields of shorter-term bonds. The decrease in yields will contribute to capital gains on the bonds.

To illustrate, suppose that the current yield curve is represented by Figure 15.5. For simplicity, we will express all interest rates as effective rates per quarter. A money manager might buy a nine-month bill currently priced to yield 1.5% per quarter, selling at $100/(1.015)^3 = 95.63$. *If* the yield on the bill were to remain unchanged over the quarter, then in three months, the bill would sell for $100/(1.015)^2 = 97.07$, providing a holding-period return precisely equal to the 1.5% yield to maturity.

However, remember that in three months, the bill will have a maturity of only six months. *If* the yield curve at the end of the quarter is unchanged from today, then the yield on the bill will fall from 1.5% to 1.25% per quarter. As time passes, the bill's maturity falls and its yield rides down the curve, as illustrated in Figure 15.5. Therefore, the bill will provide a holding-period rate of return greater than its original 1.5% yield. Specifically, in three months the bill will be priced at $100/(1.0125)^2 = 97.55$, therefore providing a rate of return of 2.0% $[(97.55 - 95.63)/95.63]$. Moreover, the longer-term asset will provide a higher rate of return than would the shorter-term one. For example, the three-month bill in Figure 15.5 will mature at the end of the holding period, and provide a riskless rate of return of 0.75%.

Thus, when the yield curve is upward sloping, and the horizon analysis projects an unchanged yield curve, longer-maturity assets will provide greater expected rates of return than shorter-term assets and the expected holding-period rate of return on the

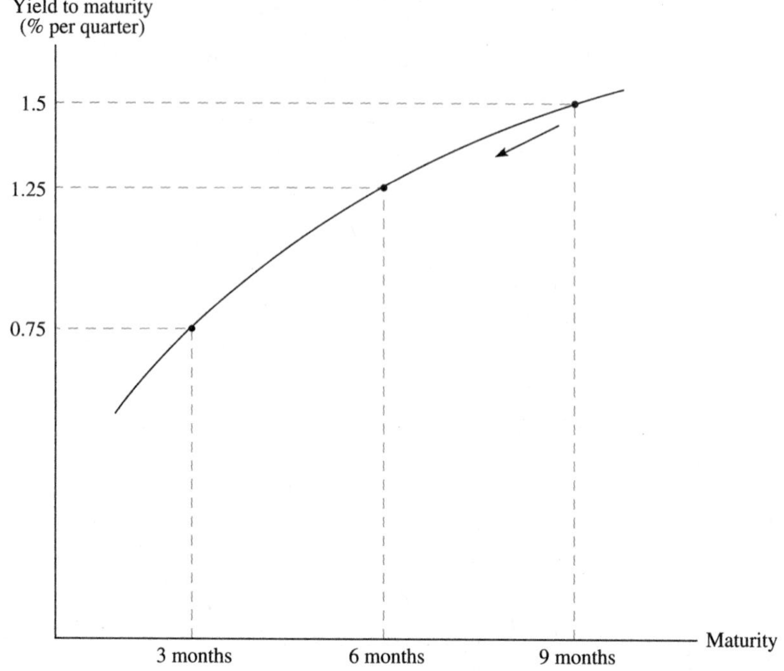

Figure 15.5
Riding the yield curve. As time passes and the bond's maturity decreases, its yield to maturity will fall *assuming* the yield curve is unchanged

fixed-income security will exceed its yield to maturity. Of course, you should always be skeptical of an apparent free lunch. Although extending maturity may increase the expected rate of return, that improvement may come at the price of additional risk. This, in fact, is the trade-off the portfolio manager is accepting if the yield curve is sloping upward because of a liquidity premium. The higher expected returns on the longer-term assets are no more than risk premiums.

The danger of riding the yield curve is that the yield curve will in fact rise over time. Indeed, according to the expectations hypothesis, an upward-sloping curve is evidence that market participants expect interest rates to be rising over time.

Contingent Immunization

Contingent immunization is a mixed passive-active strategy suggested by Liebowitz and Weinberger.[10] To illustrate, suppose that interest rates currently are 10% and that a manager's portfolio is worth $10 million right now. At current rates the manager could lock in, via conventional immunization techniques, a future portfolio value of $12.1 million after two years. Now suppose that the manager wishes to pursue active management but is willing to risk losses only to the extent that the terminal value of the portfolio would not drop lower than $11 million. Because only $9.09 million ($11 mil-

[10] Martin L. Liebowitz and Alfred Weinberger, "Contingent Immunization—Part I: Risk Control Procedures," *Financial Analysts Journal* 38 (November–December 1982).

lion/1.10^2) is required to achieve this minimum acceptable terminal value, and the portfolio currently is worth \$10 million, the manager can afford to risk some losses at the outset and might start off with an active strategy rather than immediately immunizing.

The key is to calculate the funds required to lock in via immunization a future value of \$11 million at current rates. If T denotes the time left until the horizon date, and r is the market interest rate at any particular time, then the value of the fund necessary to guarantee an ability to reach the minimum acceptable terminal value is \$11 million/$(1 + r)^T$, because this size portfolio, if immunized, will grow risk-free to \$11 million by the horizon date. This value becomes the trigger point: if and when the actual portfolio value dips to the trigger point, active management will cease. *Contingent* upon reaching the trigger, an immunization strategy is initiated instead, guaranteeing that the minimal acceptable performance can be realized.

Figure 15.6 illustrates two possible outcomes in a contingent immunization strategy. In Figure 15.6**A**, the portfolio falls in value and hits the trigger at time t^*. At that point, immunization is pursued and the portfolio rises smoothly to the \$11 million terminal value. In Figure 15.6**B**, the portfolio does well, never reaches the trigger point, and is worth more than \$11 million at the horizon date.

CONCEPT CHECK

Question 7. What would be the trigger point with a three-year horizon, an interest rate of 12%, and a minimum acceptable terminal value of \$10 million?

An Example of a Fixed-Income Investment Strategy

To demonstrate a reasonable active fixed-income portfolio strategy, we might consider the policies of Sanford Bernstein & Co., as presented in a speech by its manager of fixed-income investments, Francis Trainer. The company believes that big bets on general marketwide interest movements are unwise. Instead, it concentrates on exploiting numerous instances of perceived *relative* minor pricing misalignments *within* the fixed-income sector. The firm takes as a risk benchmark the Lehman Brothers Government/Corporate Bond Index, which contains a vast majority of publicly traded bonds with maturity greater than one year. The index is seen as a passive or neutral position from which any deviation for the portfolio must be justified by active analysis. Bernstein considers a neutral portfolio duration to be equal to that of the index, which was four and a half years on the date of Trainer's speech.

The firm is willing to make some bets on interest rate movements, but only to a limited degree. As Francis Trainer puts it in his speech:

> If we set duration of our portfolios at a level equal to the Index and never allow them to vary, this would imply that we are perpetually neutral on the direction of interest rates. However, as those of you who have followed our economic forecasts are aware, this is rarely the case. We believe the utilization of these forecasts will add value and, therefore, we incorporate our economic forecast into the bond management process by altering the durations of our portfolios.
>
> However, in order to prevent fixed-income performance from being dominated by the accuracy of just a single aspect of our research effort, we limit the degree to which we are willing to alter our interest rate exposure. Under the vast majority of circumstances, we will not permit the

Figure 15.6 Contingent immunization

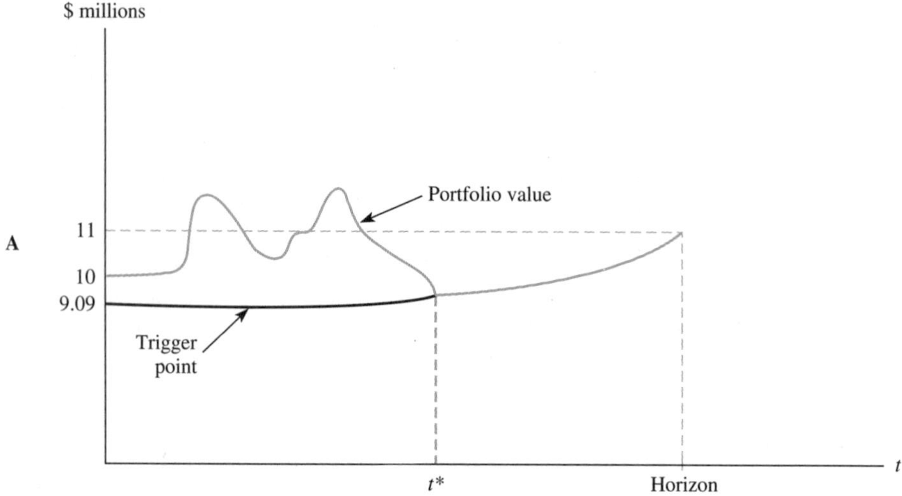

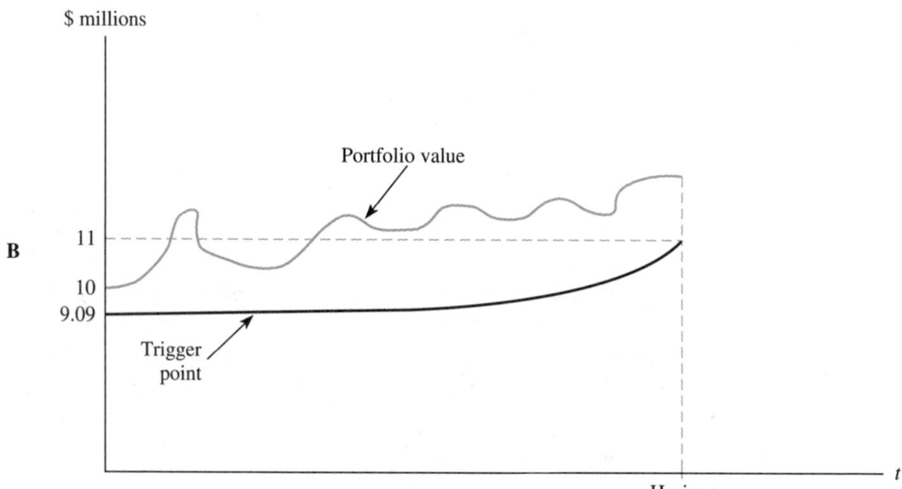

duration of our portfolios to differ from that of the Shearson Lehman Index [now the Lehman Brothers Index] by more than one year [page 4].

The company expends most of its effort in exploiting perceived numerous but minor inefficiencies in bond prices that result from lack of attention from its competitors. Its analysts follow about 1,000 securities, attempting to "identify specific securities that are attractive or unattractive as well as identify trends in the richness or cheapness of industries and sectors [p. 6]." These two activities would be characterized as substitution swaps and intermarket spread swaps in the Homer/Liebowitz scheme.

Sanford Bernstein & Co. realizes that market opportunities will arise, if at all, only in sectors of the bond market that present the least competition from other analysts. For this reason it tends to avoid recently issued bonds because "most of the attention that is focused on the bond market is concentrated on those securities that have been recently issued [p.7]." Similarly, it tends to focus on relatively more complicated bond issues in the belief that extensive research efforts give the firm a comparative advantage in that sector. Finally, the company does not take unnecessary risks. If there do not appear to be enough seemingly attractive bonds, remaining funds are placed in Treasury securities as a "neutral" parking space until new opportunities are identified.

To summarize the key features of Bernstein & Co.'s strategy, we can make the following observations:

1. The firm has a respect for market prices. It believes that usually only minor mispricing can be detected. It works to gain meaningful abnormal returns by combining numerous *small* profit opportunities, not by hoping for success of one big bet.
2. The firm recognizes that to have value its information cannot already be reflected in market prices. It maintains a large research staff and focuses on market niches that appear to be neglected by others.
3. It avoids dependence on forecasting interest rate movements, recognizing that such movements are extremely hard to predict, and that attempts to time the market easily can wipe out all its profits from intramarket analysis.

15.4 Interest Rate Swaps

Interest rate swaps have emerged recently as a major fixed-income tool. An interest rate swap is a contract between two parties to exchange a series of cash flows similar to those that would result if the parties instead were to exchange equal dollar values of different types of bonds. Swaps arose originally as a means of managing interest rate risk. The volume of swaps has increased from virtually zero in 1980 to over $3 trillion by 1993. (Interest rate swaps do not have anything to do with the Homer/Leibowitz bond swap taxonomy set out earlier.)

To illustrate how swaps work, consider the manager of a large portfolio that currently includes $100 million dollars par value of long-term bonds paying an average coupon rate of 7%. The manager believes that interest rates are about to rise. As a result, he would like to sell the bonds and replace them with either short-term or floating rate issues. However, it would be exceedingly expensive in terms of transaction costs to replace the portfolio every time the forecast for interest rates is updated. A cheaper and more flexible way to modify the portfolio is for the managers to "swap" the $7 million a year in interest income the portfolio currently generates for an amount of money that is tied to the short-term interest rate. That way, if rates do rise, so will the portfolio's interest income.

A swap dealer might advertise its willingness to exchange or "swap" a cash flow based on the six-month LIBOR rate for one based on a fixed rate of 7%. (The LIBOR, or London Interbank Offer Rate, is the interest rate at which banks borrow from each other in the Eurodollar market. It is the most commonly used short-term interest rate in the swap market.) The portfolio manager would then enter into a swap agreement with the dealer to *pay* 7% on "notional principal" of \$100 million and *receive* payment of the LIBOR rate on that amount of notional principal.[11] In other words, the manager swaps a payment of .07 × \$100 million for a payment of LIBOR × \$100 million. The manager's *net* cash flow from the swap agreement is therefore (LIBOR −.07) × \$100 million.

Note that the swap arrangement does not mean that a loan has been made. The participants have agreed only to exchange a fixed cash flow for a variable one.

Now consider the net cash flow to the manager's portfolio in three interest rate scenarios:

	LIBOR rate		
	6.5%	7.0%	7.5%
Interest income from bond portfolio (= 7% of \$100 million bond portfolio)	\$7,000,000	\$7,000,000	\$7,000,000
Cash flow from swap [= (LIBOR −7%) × notional principal of \$100 million]	(500,000)	0	500,000
TOTAL (= LIBOR ×\$100 million)	\$6,500,000	\$7,000,000	\$7,500,000

Notice that the total income on the overall position—bonds plus swap agreement—is now equal to the LIBOR rate in each scenario times \$100 million. The manager has, in effect, converted a fixed-rate bond portfolio into a synthetic floating-rate portfolio.

You can see now that swaps can be immensely useful for firms in a variety of applications. For example, a corporation that has issued fixed-rate debt can convert it into synthetic floating-rate debt by entering a swap to receive a fixed interest rate (offsetting its fixed-rate coupon obligation) and pay a floating rate. Or, a bank that pays current market interest rates to its depositors might enter a swap to receive a floating rate and pay a fixed rate on some amount of notional principal. This swap position, added to its floating rate deposit liability, would result in a net liability of a fixed stream of cash. The bank might then be able to invest in long-term fixed-rate loans without encountering interest rate risk.

What about the swap dealer? Why is the dealer, which is typically a financial intermediary such as a bank, willing to take on the opposite side of the swaps desired by these participants?

Consider a dealer who takes on one side of a swap, let's say paying LIBOR and receiving a fixed rate. The dealer will search for another trader in the swap market who wishes to receive a fixed rate and pay LIBOR. When the two swaps are combined, the dealer's position is effectively neutral on interest rates, paying LIBOR on one swap, and receiving it on another. Similarly, the dealer pays a fixed rate on one swap and receives it on another. The dealer becomes little more than an intermediary, funneling

[11] The participants to the swap do not loan each other money. They agree only to exchange a fixed cash flow for a variable cash flow that depends on the short-term interest rate. This is why the principal is described as *notional*. The notional principal is simply a way to describe the size of the swap agreement. In this example, the parties to the swap exchange a 7% fixed rate for the LIBOR rate; the difference between LIBOR and 7% is multiplied by notional principal to determine the cash flow exchanged by the parties.

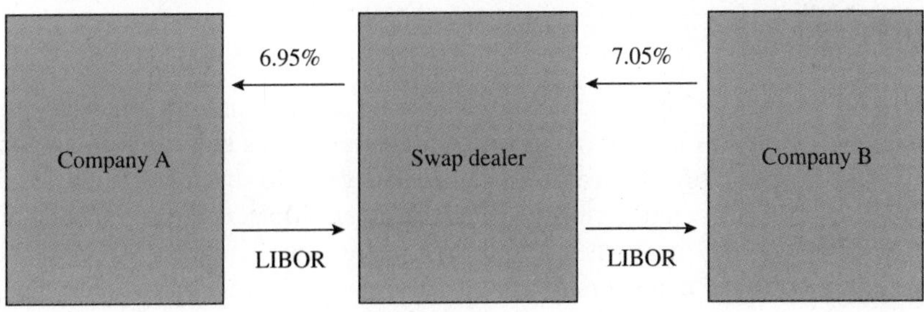

Figure 15.7
Interest rate swap. Company B pays a fixed rate of 7.05% to the swap dealer in return for LIBOR. Company A receives 6.95% from the dealer in return for LIBOR. The swap dealer realizes a cash flow each period equal to .1% of notional principal.

payments from one party to the other.[12] The dealer finds this activity profitable because he or she will charge a bid-ask spread on the transaction. This is illustrated in Figure 15.7. The bid-ask spread in the example illustrated in Figure 15.7 is .1% of notional principal each year.

CONCEPT CHECK

Question 8. A pension fund holds a portfolio of money market securities that the manager believes are paying excellent yields compared to other comparable-risk short-term securities. However, the manager believes that interest rates are about to fall. What type of swap will allow the fund to continue to hold its portfolio of short-term securities while at the same time benefiting from a decline in rates?

One might ask why firms go to the trouble of arranging swaps. For example, why wouldn't a corporation originally borrow short-term instead of borrowing long and entering a swap? In the early years of the swap market the answer seemed to lie in systematic differences in the perceived credit ratings in different markets. Participants in these markets claimed that European banks placed more weight than did U.S. banks on a firm's size, name recognition, and product line compared with its credit rating. Thus, it could have paid for a firm that wanted to borrow long-term to instead borrow short-term in the United States and swap into long-term obligations with a European trading partner. The practice exploited a type of market inefficiency—specifically, differences in credit assessments across national markets. Now, however, these inefficiencies seem to have been arbitraged away. Swaps simply provide a means to restructure balance sheets and manage risk very quickly with low transaction costs. We return to the role of swaps in risk management in Chapter 22.

Swaps create an interesting problem for financial statement analysis. Firms are not required to disclose interest rate swaps in corporate financial statements unless they have a "material impact" on the firm, and even then they appear only in the footnotes. Therefore, the firm's true net obligations may be quite different from its apparent or present debt structure.

[12] Actually, things are a bit more complicated. The dealer is more than just an intermediary because he or she bears the credit risk that one or the other of the parties to the swap might default on the obligation. Referring to Figure 15.7, if firm A defaults on its obligation, for example, the swap dealer still must maintain its commitment to firm B. In this sense, the dealer does more than simply pass through cash flows to the other swap participants.

15.5 Financial Engineering and Interest-Rate Derivatives

New financial instruments created through financial engineering can have highly unusual risk and return characteristics that offer both opportunities and challenges for fixed income portfolio managers. To illustrate the possibilities opened up by financial engineering, consider the inverse floater, which is a bond that pays a *lower* coupon payment when a reference interest rate rises. For example, an inverse floater may pay a coupon rate equal to 10% *minus* the rate on one-year Treasury bills. Therefore, if the T-bill rate is 4%, the bond will pay interest income equal to 10% − 4% = 6% of par value. You can see that such a bond will have an interest rate sensitivity much greater than that of a fixed-rate bond with comparable maturity. If the T-bill rate rises, say to 7%, the inverse floater's coupon payments fall to 3% of par value; in addition, as other interest rates rise along with the T-bill rate, the bond price falls as well for the usual reason that future cash flows are discounted at higher rates. Therefore, there is a dual impact on value and these securities perform especially poorly when interest rates rise. Conversely, inverse floaters perform especially well when rates fall: coupon payments rise, even as the discount rate falls.

While firms do not commonly issue inverse floaters, they may be created synthetically by allocating the cash flows from a fixed rate security into two *derivative* securities. An investment banking firm can buy a bond issue and carve the original security into a floating rate note and an inverse floater. The floater will receive interest payments that rise when the T-bill rate rises; the inverse floater will receive interest payments that fall when the T-bill rate rises. The sum of the interest payments due to the two classes of securities is fixed and equal to the interest from the original bond, the primary asset.

As a concrete example, consider a $100 million par value, 20-year maturity bond with a coupon rate of 8%. The bond issue therefore pays total interest of $8 million annually. An investment banking firm might arrange to use the cash flows from the underlying bond to support issues of a floating rate note and an inverse floater.[13] The floating rate notes might be issued with aggregate par value of $60 million and a coupon level equal to the T-bill rate plus one percent. If the T-bill rate currently is 6%, therefore, the coupon rate on the floater would be 7% and total interest payments would be .07 × $60 million = $4.2 million. This leaves $8 million − $4.2 million = $3.8 million available to pay interest on the interest floater. The coupon rate on the inverse floater might be set at 18.5% − 1.5 × (T-bill rate), which at the current T-bill rate equals 9.5%. Therefore, the coupon income flowing to the inverse floater is 9.5% of $40 million, or $3.8 million, which just absorbs the remaining interest flowing from the original bond.

Now suppose that in one year, the T-bill rate has increased by 1%. The coupon rate on the floater increases to 8%, while the coupon rate on the inverse floater falls to 18.5% − 1.5 × 7% = 8%. Again, total interest paid on the two derivative securities sums to $8 million: .08 × $60 million + .08 × $40 million = $8 million. However, the

[13] In practice, inverse floaters are often engineered from mortgage-backed securities, rather than conventional bonds. While the prepayment risk of the underlying mortgage pool presents another complication, the general structure of these bonds is similar to the one described here.

value of the inverse floater falls precipitously: Not only are market interest rates higher (which makes the present value of any future cash flow lower), but the coupon rate on the bond has fallen from 9.5% to 8%.[14] Therefore, the inverse floater will have extreme interest-rate sensitivity. When rates fall, its performance will be spectacular, but when rates rise, its performance will be disastrous.

The inverse floater is an example of an interest-rate derivative product created by financial engineering in which the cash flows from the original bond are unbundled and reallocated to the floater and inverse floater. Because of the impact of interest rates on its coupon rate, the inverse floater will have a very large effective duration,[15] in fact much longer than the maturity of the bond. This property can be useful to investors who wish to immunize very long duration liabilities; it is also obviously useful to investors who wish to speculate on decreases in interest rates.

Investors who speculated on interest rate declines were served well by inverse floaters in 1992 and 1993. For example, Piper Jaffray, a large mutual fund company, sponsored one of the best performing government bond mutual funds in these years. Part of that performance was due to its positions in inverse floaters. When rates increased rapidly in 1994, however, the fund suffered losses estimated at about $700 million. Unfortunately, this experience was replicated by many other investors.

Inverse floaters are not the only financially-engineered products with dramatic dependence on interest rates. In Chapters 1 and 2, we introduced you to derivative securities created by allocating the cash flows from mortgage-backed securities into various CMO (collateralized mortgage obligation) tranches. Some of the more popular mortgage derivative products are interest-only and principal-only strips. The interest-only (IO) strip gets all the interest payments from the mortgage pool and the principal-only (PO) strip gets all the principal payments. Both of these mortgage strips have extreme and interesting interest rate exposures. In both cases, the sensitivity is due to the effect of mortgage prepayments on the cash flows accruing to the securityholder.

PO securities, like inverse floaters, exhibit very long effective durations, that is, their values are very sensitive to interest rate fluctuations. When interest rates fall and mortgage holders prepay their mortgages, PO holders receive their principal payments much earlier than initially anticipated. Therefore, the payments are discounted for fewer years than expected and have much higher present value. Hence, PO strips perform extremely well when rates fall. Conversely, interest rate increases slow mortgage prepayments and reduce the value of PO strips. Investors who speculated on rate decreases in the early 1990s, tended to hold POs along with inverse floaters. These securities performed well when rates fell through 1993, but resulted in large losses in 1994 when interest rates rose dramatically.

---

[14] If the T-bill rate increases beyond 12.33%, the formula for the inverse floater's coupon would call for a negative coupon rate. However, in practice, the inverse floater provides that the coupon rate may never fall below zero. This floor on the coupon rate of the inverse floater necessitates a ceiling on the coupon rate of the floater. The total interest paid by the two securities is constrained to equal the interest provided by the underlying bond.

[15] Strictly speaking, the Macaulay duration (that is, the weighted average of the times until payment of each cash flow) of an inverse floater is not well defined, since the cash flows accruing from the bond are not fixed, but instead vary with the level of interest rates. The *effective* duration of a security therefore does not have the interpretation of an average maturity; it is defined instead as the percentage change in the price of a security given a one percentage point increase in yield. Therefore, effective duration, like Macaulay duration, measures interest-rate sensitivity.

The prices of interest only strips, on the other hand, fall when interest rates fall. This is because mortgage prepayments abruptly end the flow of interest payments accruing to IO securityholders. Because rising rates discourage prepayments, they increase the value of IO strips. Thus IOs have effective *negative* durations. They are good investments for an investor who wishes to bet on an increase in rates, or can be useful for hedging the value of a conventional fixed-income portfolio.

There are still other ways to make highly sensitive bets on the direction of interest rates. Some of these are custom-designed swaps in which the cash flow paid by one party to the swap varies dramatically with the level of some reference interest rate. Such swaps made news in 1994 when Procter & Gamble lost more than $100 million in an interest-rate swap that obligated it to make payments that exploded when interest rates increased. In the wake of its losses, P&G sued Bankers Trust, which sold it the swap, claiming that it was misled about the risks of the swap.

Interest rate derivatives are not necessarily bad, or even dangerous, investments. The dramatic sensitivity of their prices to interest rate fluctuations can be useful for hedging as well as for speculation. They can be potent risk management as well as risk-increasing tools. One Wall Street observer has compared them to power tools: When used well by a trained expert, they can serve a valuable function, but in untrained hands, they can lead to severe damage.

SUMMARY

1. Even default-free bonds such as Treasury issues are subject to interest rate risk. Longer-term bonds generally are more sensitive to interest rate shifts than are short-term bonds. A measure of the average life of a bond is Macaulay's duration, defined as the weighted average of the times until each payment made by the security, with weights proportional to the present value of the payment.

2. Duration is a direct measure of the sensitivity of a bond's price to a change in its yield. The proportional change in a bond's price equals the negative of duration multiplied by the proportional change in $1 + y$.

3. Immunization strategies are characteristic of passive fixed-income portfolio management. Such strategies attempt to render the individual or firm immune from movements in interest rates. This may take the form of immunizing net worth or, instead, immunizing the future accumulated value of a fixed-income portfolio.

4. Immunization of a fully funded plan is accomplished by matching the durations of assets and liabilities. To maintain an immunized position as time passes and interest rates change, the portfolio must be periodically rebalanced. Classic immunization also depends on parallel shifts in a flat yield curve. Given that this assumption is unrealistic, immunization generally will be less than complete. To mitigate the problem, multifactor duration models can be used to allow for variation in the shape of the yield curve.

5. A more direct form of immunization is dedication, or cash flow matching. If a portfolio is perfectly matched in cash flow with projected liabilities, rebalancing will be unnecessary.

6. Active bond management consists of interest rate forecasting techniques and intermarket spread analysis. One popular taxonomy classifies active strategies as sub-

stitution swaps, intermarket spread swaps, rate anticipation swaps, or pure yield pickup swaps.

7. Horizon analysis is a type of interest rate forecasting. In this procedure the analyst forecasts the position of the yield curve at the end of some holding period, and from that yield curve predicts corresponding bond prices. Bonds then can be ranked according to expected total returns (coupon plus capital gain) over the holding period.

8. Interest rate swaps are major recent developments in the fixed-income market. In these arrangements parties trade the cash flows of different securities without actually exchanging any securities directly. This is a useful tool to manage the duration of a portfolio. It also has been used by corporations to borrow at advantageous interest rates in foreign credit markets that are viewed as more hospitable than are domestic credit markets.

9. Financial engineering has created many new fixed-income derivative assets with novel risk characteristics.

Key Terms

Duration
Immunization
Rebalancing
Cash flow matching
Dedication strategy
Substitution swap
Intermarket spread swap
Rate anticipation swap
Pure yield pickup swap
Tax swap
Horizon analysis
Riding the yield curve
Contingent immunization
Interest rate swaps

Selected Readings

Duration and immunization are analyzed in a very extensive literature. Good treatments are:

Bierwag, G. O. *Duration Analysis*. Cambridge, Mass.: Ballinger Publishing Company, 1987.

Weil, Roman. "Macaulay's Duration: An Appreciation." *Journal of Business* 46 (October 1973).

Useful general references to techniques of fixed-income portfolio management may be found in a book of readings used by the Institute of Chartered Financial Analysts:

Fong, H. Gifford. "Portfolio Construction: Fixed Income." In John L. Maginn and Donald L. Tuttle (eds.), *Managing Investment Portfolios: A Dynamic Process*. 2nd ed. Boston: Warren, Gorham & Lamont, 1990.

Active bond management strategies are discussed in:

Fabozzi, Frank J. *Bond Markets, Analysis and Strategies*. 2nd ed. Englewood Cliffs, N.J.: Prentice Hall, 1993.

Bond indexing is treated in:

Mossavar-Rahmani, Sharmin. *Bond Index Funds*. Chicago: Probus Publishing Co., 1991.

For a detailed analysis of swaps see:

Brown, Keith C., and Donald J. Smith. *Interest Rate and Currency Swaps: A Tutorial*. Charlottesville, N.C.: Institute of Chartered Financial Analysts, 1995.

Problems

1. A nine-year bond has a yield of 10% and a duration of 7.194 years. If the market yield changes by 50 basis points, what is the percentage change in the bond's price?
2. Find the duration of a 6% coupon bond making *annual* coupon payments if it has three years until maturity and has a yield to maturity of 6%. What is the duration if the yield to maturity of 10%?
3. Find the duration of the bond in Problem 2 if the coupons are paid semiannually.
4. Rank the durations of the following pairs of bonds:
   a. Bond *A* is an 8% coupon bond, with a 20-year time to maturity selling at par value. Bond *B* is an 8% coupon bond, with a 20-year maturity time selling below par value.
   b. Bond *A* is a 20-year noncallable coupon bond with a coupon rate of 8%, selling at par. Bond *B* is a 20-year callable bond with a coupon rate of 9%, also selling at par.
5. An insurance company must make payments to a customer of $10 million in one year and $4 million in five years. The yield curve is flat at 10%.
   a. If it wants to fully fund and immunize its obligation to this customer with a *single* issue of a zero-coupon bond, what maturity bond must it purchase?
   b. What must be the face value and market value of that zero-coupon bond?

6. Rank the following bonds in order of descending duration:*

Bond	Coupon (%)	Time to Maturity (Years)	Yield to Maturity (%)
A	15	20	10%
B	15	15	10
C	0	20	10
D	8	20	10
E	15	15	15

7. Long-term Treasury bonds currently are selling at yields to maturity of nearly 8%. You expect interest rates to fall. The rest of the market thinks that they will remain unchanged over the coming year. In each question, choose the bond that will provide the higher holding-period return over the next year if you are correct. *Briefly* explain your answer.
   a. i. A Baa-rated bond with coupon rate 8% and time to maturity 20 years.
   ii. An Aaa-rated bond with coupon rate of 8% and time to maturity 20 years.
   b. i. An A-rated bond with coupon rate 4% and maturity 20 years, callable at 105.
   ii. An A-rated bond with coupon rate 8% and maturity 20 years, callable at 105.
   c. i. A 6% coupon noncallable T-bond with maturity 20 years and YTM = 8%.
   ii. A 9% coupon noncallable T-bond with maturity 20 years and YTM = 8%.

*Reprinted, with permission, from the *CFA Study Guide*. Association for Investment Management and Research, Charlottesville, VA.

8. Currently, the term structure is as follows: One-year bonds yield 7%, two-year bonds yield 8%, three-year bonds and greater maturity bonds all yield 9%. An investor is choosing between one-, two-, and three-year maturity bonds all paying *annual* coupons of 8%, once a year. Which bond should you buy if you strongly believe that at year-end the yield curve would be flat at 9%?

9. Philip Morris has issued bonds that pay semiannually with the following characteristics:*

Coupon	Yield-to-Maturity	Maturity	Macaulay Duration
8%	8%	15 years	10 years

   a. Calculate modified duration using the information above.
   b. Explain why modified duration is a better measure than maturity when calculating the bond's sensitivity to changes in interest rates.
   c. Identify the direction of change in modified duration if:
      i. The coupon of the bond were 4%, not 8%.
      ii. The maturity of the bond were 7 years, not 15 years.

10. You will be paying $10,000 a year in tuition expenses at the end of the next two years. Bonds currently yield 8%.
   a. What is the present value and duration of your obligation?
   b. What maturity zero-coupon bond would immunize your obligation?
   c. Suppose you buy a zero-coupon bond with value and duration equal to your obligation. Now suppose that rates immediately increase to 9%. What happens to your net position, that is, to the difference between the value of the bond and that of your tuition obligation? What if rates fall to 7%?

11. What type of interest rate swap would be appropriate for a corporation holding long-term assets that it funded with floating-rate bonds?

12. A corporation has issued a $10 million issue of floating rate bonds on which it pays an interest rate 1% over the LIBOR rate. The bonds are selling at par value. The firm is worried that rates are about to rise, and it would like to lock in a fixed interest rate on its borrowings. The firm sees that dealers in the swap market are offering swaps of LIBOR for 7%. What interest rate swap will convert the firm's interest obligation into one resembling a synthetic fixed-rate loan? What interest rate will it pay on that synthetic fixed-rate loan?

13. Pension funds pay lifetime annuities to recipients. If a firm will remain in business indefinitely, the pension obligation will resemble a perpetuity. Suppose, therefore, that you are managing a pension fund with obligations to make per petual payments of $2 million per year to beneficiaries. The yield to maturity on all bonds is 16%.
   a. If the duration of 5-year maturity bonds with coupon rates of 12% (paid annually) is 4 years and the duration of 20-year maturity bonds with coupon rates of 6% (paid annually) is 11 years, how much of each of these coupon bonds (in market value) will you want to hold to both fully fund and immunize your obligation?
   b. What will be the par value of your holdings in the 20-year coupon bond?

---

*Reprinted, with permission, from the Level I 1993 *CFA Study Guide*. Copyright 1993, Association for Investment Management and Research, Charlottesville, VA. All rights reserved.

14. You are managing a portfolio of $1 million. Your target duration is 10 years, and you can choose from two bonds: a zero-coupon bond with maturity of 5 years, and a perpetuity, each currently yielding 5%.
    a. How much of each bond will you hold in your portfolio?
    b. How will these fractions change *next year* if target duration is now nine years?
15. My pension plan will pay me $10,000 once a year for a 10-year period. The first payment will come in exactly five years. The pension fund wants to immunize its position.
    a. What is the duration of its obligation to me? The current interest rate is 10% per year.
    b. If the plan uses 5-year and 20-year zero-coupon bonds to construct the immunized position, how much money ought to be placed in each bond? What will be the *face value* of the holdings in each zero?

16. The ability to *immunize* a bond portfolio is very desirable for bond portfolio managers in some instances.*
    a. Discuss the components of interest rate risk—that is, assuming a change in interest rates over time, explain the two risks faced by the holder of a bond.
    b. Define immunization and discuss why a bond manager would immunize his portfolio.
    c. Explain why a duration-matching strategy is a superior technique to a maturity-matching strategy for the minimization of interest rate risk.
    d. Explain in specific terms how you would use a zero-coupon bond to immunize a bond portfolio. Discuss why a zero-coupon bond is an ideal instrument in this regard.
    e. Explain how contingent immunization, another bond portfolio management technique, differs from classical immunization. Discuss why a bond portfolio manager would engage in contingent immunization.

17. You are the manager for the bond portfolio of a pension fund. The policies of the fund allow for the use of active strategies in managing the bond portfolio.
    It appears that the economic cycle is beginning to mature, inflation is expected to accelerate, and in an effort to contain the economic expansion, central bank policy is moving toward constraint. For each of the situations below, *state* which one of the two bonds you would prefer. *Briefly justify* your answer in each case.
    a. Government of Canada (Canadian pay) 10% due in 1998 and priced at 98.75 to yield 10.50% to maturity.
    or
    Government of Canada (Canadian pay) 10% due in 2009 and priced at 91.75 to yield 11.19% to maturity.
    b. Texas Power and Light Co., 7½ due in 2002, rated AAA, and priced at 85 to yield 10.02% to maturity.
    or

*Reprinted, with permission, from the *CFA Study Guide*. Association for Investment Management and Research, Charlottesville, VA.

Arizona Public Service Co. 7.45 due in 2002, rated A−, and priced at 75 to yield 12.05% to maturity.

c. Commonwealth Edison $2\frac{3}{4}$ due in 1999, rated Baa, and priced at 61 to yield 12.2% to maturity.

or

Commonwealth Edison $15\frac{3}{8}$ due in 2000, rated Baa, and priced at 114.40 to yield 12.2% to maturity.

d. Shell Oil Co. $8\frac{1}{2}$ sinking fund debentures due in 2015, rated AAA (sinking fund begins 9/95 at par), and priced at 68 to yield 12.91% to maturity.

or

Warner-Lambert $8\frac{7}{8}$ sinking fund debentures due in 2015, rated AAA (sinking fund begins 4/99 at par), and priced at 74 to yield 12.31% to maturity.

e. Bank of Montreal (Canadian pay) 8% Certificates of Deposit due in 1996, rated AAA, and priced at 100 to yield 8% to maturity.

or

Bank of Montreal (Canadian pay) Floating Rate Note due in 2001, rated AAA. Coupon currently set at 7.1% and priced at 100 (coupon adjusted semiannually to .5% above the three-month Government of Canada Treasury bill rate).

18. Active bond management, as contrasted with a passive buy and hold strategy, has gained increased acceptance as investors have attempted to maximize the total return on bond portfolios under their management. The following bond swaps could have been made in recent years as investors attempted to increase the total return on their portfolio. From the information presented below, identify the reason(s) investors may have made each swap.

Action			Call	Price	YTM (%)
a.	Sell	Baa1 Electric Pwr. 1st mtg. $10\frac{5}{8}$% due 2000	108.24	$95\frac{5}{8}$	11.71
	Buy	Baa1 Electric Pwr. 1st mtg. $6\frac{3}{8}$% due 2001	105.20	$79\frac{1}{8}$	11.39
b.	Sell	Aaa Phone Co. notes $8\frac{1}{2}$% due 2001	101.50	$90\frac{1}{8}$	10.02
	Buy	U.S. Treasury notes $9\frac{1}{2}$% due 2001	NC	97.15	9.78
c.	Sell	Aa1 Apex Bank zero coupon due 2002	NC	$35\frac{1}{4}$	10.51
	Buy	Aa1 Apex Bank float rate notes due 2019	103.90	$90\frac{1}{4}$	—
d.	Sell	A1 Commonwealth Oil & Gas 1st mtg. $7\frac{1}{2}$% due 2007	105.75	72	11.09
	Buy	U.S. Treasury bond $7\frac{1}{2}$% due 2015	NC	80.60	9.40
e.	Sell	A1 Z mart convertible deb. 3% due 2009	103.90	$62\frac{3}{4}$	6.92
	Buy	A2 Lucky Ducks deb. $7\frac{3}{4}$% due 2015	109.86	65	12.43

19. Your client is concerned about the apparent inconsistency between the following two statements.*

- Short-term interest rates are more volatile than are long-term rates.
- The rates of return of long-term bonds are more volatile than are returns on short-term securities.

Discuss why these two statements are not necessarily inconsistent.

---

*Reprinted, with permission, from the *CFA Study Guide*. Association for Investment Management and Research, Charlottesville, VA.

20. A fixed-income portfolio manager is unwilling to realize a rate of return of less than 3% annually over a 5-year investment period on a portfolio currently valued at $1 million. Three years later, the interest rate is 8%. What is the trigger point of the portfolio at this time, that is, how low can the value of the portfolio fall before the manager will be forced to immunize to be assured of achieving the minimum acceptable return?
21. A 30-year maturity bond has a 7% coupon rate, paid annually. It sells today for $867.42. A 20-year maturity bond has 6.5% coupon rate, also paid annually. It sells today for $879.50. A bond market analyst forecasts that in 5 years, 25-year maturity bonds will sell at yields to maturity of 8% and 15-year maturity bonds will sell at yields of 7.5%. Because the yield curve is upward sloping, the analyst believes that coupons will be invested in short-term securities at a rate of 6%. Which bond offers the higher expected rate of return over the 5-year period?

22. Your firm, TMP, is to be interviewed as a possible manager for the $100 million indexed fixed-income portfolio being considered by the investment committee of a large endowment fund. Because the committee has not yet decided which of three indexes to use as their benchmark portfolio, the interview will focus on this issue. Information regarding each of the three indexes to be discussed is presented in the table below. By way of background, TMP is told that the committee has adopted an aggressive overall investment policy with a long-term horizon and an above-average risk tolerance.*

	Sector Mix Information		
	Index 1	**Index 2**	**Index 3**
U.S. Treasuries	50%	50%	80%
U.S. agencies	10	10	10
Corporates:			
Investment grade	10	10	5
Below-investment grade	5	5	0
Residential mortgages	20	25	5
Yankee bonds	5	0	0
Total	100%	100%	100%
Index modified duration	5.0	8.0	8.0
Index yield to maturity	7.50%	8.05%	8.00%

Both the level and the volatility of interest rates have been declining for the past several years. The committee believes these trends are unlikely to continue, and is seeking insight as to how the indexed portfolio might perform under a variety of alternative interest-rate scenarios. Two such scenarios are:

i. A cycle over which interest rates generally decline, but are accompanied by generally rising volatility;

*Reprinted, with permission, from the Level III *CFA Study Guide*.

ii. A cycle over which interest rates are generally flat from beginning to end, but in which volatility is high throughout.

a. Using only the data from the table, rank the three indexes in order of relative attractiveness under each of the two scenarios above, and justify your rankings by citing the factors that support your conclusions.

b. Recommend and justify one index to the committee for use as its benchmark portfolio. Take into account your answer to Problem *a* above and the information which you have been provided about the committee's investment policy.

c. Assume that the committee has selected an index to use as its benchmark and that TMP has been hired to construct and manage the indexed portfolio. Explain the practical problems associated with construction of an indexed fixed-income portfolio. Identify and briefly discuss two methods of such construction, including in your discussion one strength and one weakness of each method.

23. As part of your analysis of debt issued by Monticello Corporation, you are asked to evaluate two specific bond issues, shown in the table below.*

a. Using the duration and yield information in the table, compare the price and yield behavior of the two bonds under each of the following two scenarios:

- *Scenario 1*—Strong economic recovery with rising inflation expectations.
- *Scenario 2*—Economic recession with reduced inflation expectations.

b. Using the information in the table, calculate the projected price change for Bond B if the yield-to-maturity for this bond falls by 75 basis points.

c. Describe the shortcoming of analyzing Bond A strictly to call or to maturity.

Monticello Corporation Bond Information

	Bond A (Callable)	**Bond B (Noncallable)**
Maturity	2002	2002
Coupon	11.50%	7.25%
Current price	125.75	100.00
Yield-to-maturity	7.70%	7.25%
Modified duration to maturity	6.20	6.80
Call date	1996	—
Call price	105	—
Yield to call	5.10%	—
Modified duration to call	3.10	—

*Reprinted, with permission, from the Level II 1992 *CFA Study Guide*.

Part V

Security Analysis

Chapter 16
Macroeconomic and Industry Analysis

TO DETERMINE A PROPER PRICE FOR A FIRM'S STOCK, THE SECURITY ANALYST MUST FORECAST THE DIVIDEND AND EARNINGS THAT CAN BE EXPECTED FROM THE FIRM. Because the prospects of the firm are tied to those of the broader economy, however, valuation analyses must consider the business environment in which the firm operates. For some firms, macroeconomic and industry circumstances might have a greater influence on profits than the firm's relative performance within its industry.

It often makes sense to do a "top down" analysis of a firm's prospects. One starts with the broad economic environment, examining the state of the aggregate economy and even the international economy. From there, one considers the implications of the outside environment on the industry in which the firm operates. Finally, the firm's position within the industry is examined.

This chapter treats the broad-based aspects of fundamental analysis—macroeconomic and industry analysis. The two chapters following cover firm-specific analysis. We begin with a discussion of international factors relevant to firm performance, and move on to an overview of the significance of the key variables usually used to summarize the state of the macroeconomy. We then discuss government macroeconomic policy. We conclude the analysis of the macro environment with a discussion of business cycles. Finally, we move to industry analysis, treating issues concerning the sensitivity of the firm to the business cycle, the typical life cycle of an industry, and strategic issues that affect industry performance.

16.1 THE GLOBAL ECONOMY

A top-down analysis of a firm's prospects must start with the global economy. The international economy might affect a firm's export prospects, the price competition it faces from foreign competitors, or the profits it makes on investments abroad.

Table 16.1 Economic Performance in Selected Emerging Markets

		Stock Market Return in 1994	
	Growth in Real GDP, 1994	In Local Currency	In $ Terms
China	+10.4	− 22.2	−46.5
Hong Kong	+ 5.4	− 34.0	−34.1
India	+ 4.2	+ 16.5	+15.6
Indonesia	+ 6.5	− 19.8	−23.1
Malaysia	+ 8.9	− 24.0	−19.7
Philippines	+ 4.5	− 12.2	− 4.4
Singapore	+10.2	− 7.4	+ 2.1
South Korea	+ 8.1	+ 17.0	+19.9
Taiwan	+ 6.1	+ 17.4	+17.9
Thailand	+ 8.2	− 19.5	−18.4
Argentina	+ 4.5	− 19.8	−20.6
Brazil	+ 6.0	+993.4	+49.7
Chile	+ 3.9	+ 40.0	+44.8
Mexico	+ 4.5	− 12.5	−48.7
Venezuela	− 5.5	+ 35.9	−16.4
Greece	+ 1.1	− 7.8	− 4.7
Israel	+ 5.1	− 31.2	−33.6
Portugal	− 1.4	+ 10.6	+22.4
South Africa	+ 1.3	+ 19.3	+23.1
Turkey	− 8.6	+ 26.1	−54.6
Czech Republic	+ 1.2	− 31.9	−26.9
Hungary	+ 1.0	+ 16.5	+ 2.4
Poland	+ 4.3	− 36.0	−43.9
Russia	−16.0	—	—

Source: *The Economist,* January 7, 1995.

Certainly, despite the fact that the economies of most countries are linked in a global macroeconomy, there is considerable variation in the economic performance across countries at any time. Consider, for example, Table 16.1, which presents data on several so-called "emerging" economies. The table documents striking variation in growth rates of economic output in 1994. For example, while the Chinese economy grew by 10.4% in 1994, Russian output fell by 16%. Similarly, there was considerable variation in stock market returns in these countries in 1994, ranging from a 54.6% loss in Turkey to a 49.7% gain in Brazil.

These data illustrate that the national economic environment can be a crucial determinant of industry performance. It is far harder for businesses to succeed in a contracting economy than in an expanding one.

In addition, the global environment presents political risks of far greater magnitude than is typically encountered in U.S.-based investments. For example, when Turkish president Turgut Ozal died in April 1992, the Istanbul stock market fell by 10.5% in one day. Similarly, the Hong Kong stock market has been extremely sensitive to political developments concerning the transfer of governance to China. In 1992 and 1993, the

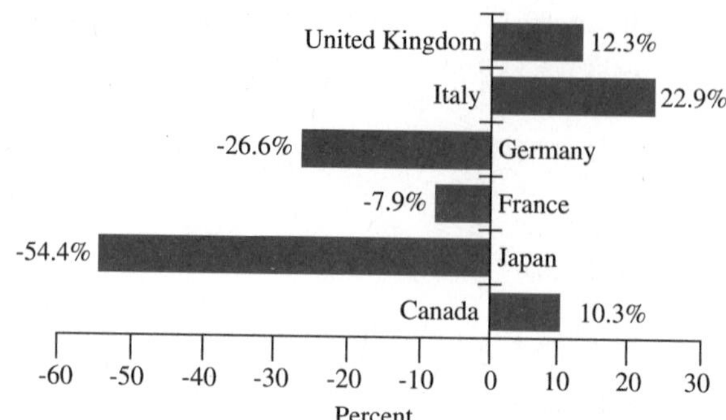

Figure 16.1 Change in real exchange rate: Dollar versus major currencies, 1983–1993

Mexican stock market responded dramatically to changing assessments regarding the prospects of passage of the North American Free Trade Agreement by the U.S. Congress. The presence of these political considerations adds a dimension of risk to foreign investments beyond the purely economic.

Of course, political developments can be positive as well. For example, the end of apartheid in South Africa and the resultant end of the economic embargo portend great growth for that economy. Similarly, peace agreements in the Middle East might result in rapid economic growth of the regional economies. These political developments (and the bumps along the way) offer significant opportunities to make or lose money.

Other political issues that are less sensational but still extremely important to economic growth and investment returns include issues of protectionism and trade policy, the free flow of capital, and the status of a nation's work force.

One obvious factor that affects the international competitiveness of a country's industries is the exchange rate between that country's currency and other currencies. The **exchange rate** is the rate at which domestic currency can be converted into foreign currency. For example, in late 1994, it took about 100 Japanese yen to purchase one U.S. dollar. We would say that the exchange rate is ¥100 per dollar, or equivalently, $.01 per yen.

As exchange rates fluctuate, the dollar value of goods priced in foreign currency similarly fluctuates. For example, in 1980, the dollar–yen exchange rate was about $.0045 per yen. Because the exchange rate today is $.01 per yen, a U.S. citizen would need more than twice as many dollars in 1994 to buy a product selling for ¥10,000 as would have been required in 1980. If the Japanese producer were to maintain a fixed yen price for its product, the price expressed in U.S. dollars would more than double. This would make Japanese products more expensive to U.S. consumers, however, and result in lost sales. Obviously, appreciation of the yen creates a problem for Japanese producers like automakers that must compete with U.S. producers.

Figure 16.1 shows the change in the purchasing power of the U.S. dollar relative to the purchasing power of the currencies of several major industrial countries in the decade ending in 1993. The ratio of purchasing powers is called the "real" or inflation-adjusted exchange rate. The change in the real exchange rate measures how much more or less expensive foreign goods have become to U.S. citizens, accounting for both exchange rate fluctuations and inflation differentials across countries. A positive value in Figure 16.1 means that the dollar has gained purchasing power relative to another currency; a negative number indicates a depreciating dollar. Therefore, the figure shows that goods priced in terms of the German or Japanese currencies have become far more expensive to U.S. consumers in the last decade but that goods priced in the U.K. or Canadian currencies have become cheaper. Conversely, goods priced in dollars have become more affordable to Japanese consumers, but more expensive to U.K. consumers.

16.2 THE DOMESTIC MACROECONOMY

The macroeconomy is the environment in which all firms operate. The importance of the macroeconomy in determining investment performance is illustrated in Figure 16.2, which compares the level of the S&P 500 stock price index to estimates of earnings per share of the S&P 500 companies. Stock prices commonly trade at between 8 to 12 times earnings, so the top boundary of the shaded area is drawn at estimated earnings times 12, and the bottom boundary is drawn at estimated earnings times 8. Given "normal" price-to-earnings ratios, we would expect the S&P 500 index to fall within these boundaries. Although the earnings-multiplier rule clearly is not perfect, it also seems clear that the level of the broad market and aggregate earnings do trend together. Thus, the first step in forecasting the performance of the broad market is to assess the status of the economy as a whole.

The ability to forecast the macroeconomy can translate into spectacular investment performance. But it is not enough to forecast the macroeconomy well. One must forecast it *better* than your competitors to earn abnormal profits.

In this section, we will review some of the key economic statistics used to describe the state of the macroeconomy. Some of these key variables are:

Gross Domestic Product. **Gross domestic product,** or GDP, is the measure of the economy's total production of goods and services. Rapidly growing GDP indicates an expanding economy with ample opportunity for a firm to increase sales. Another popular measure of the economy's output is *industrial production*. This statistic provides a measure of economic activity more narrowly focused on the manufacturing side of the economy.

Employment. The **unemployment rate** is the percentage of the total labor force (i.e., those who are either working or actively seeking employment) yet to find work. The unemployment rate measures the extent to which the economy is operating at full capacity. The unemployment rate is a factor related to workers only, but further insight into the strength of the economy can be gleaned from the unemployment rate for other factors of production. Analysts also look at the factory *capacity utilization rate*, which is the ratio of actual output from factories to potential output.

Inflation. **Inflation** is the rate at which the general level of prices is rising. High rates of inflation often are associated with "overheated" economies, that is, economies where the demand for goods and services is outstripping productive capacity, which leads to upward pressure on prices. Most governments walk a fine line in their economic policies. They hope to stimulate their economies enough to maintain nearly full

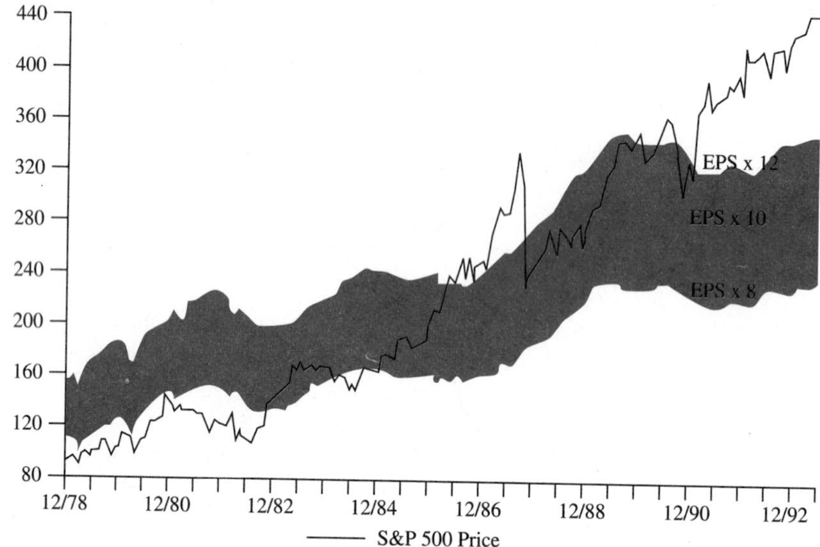

Figure 16.2 S&P 500 index versus earnings per share estimate

employment, but not so much as to bring on inflationary pressures. The perceived trade-off between inflation and unemployment is at the heart of many macroeconomic policy disputes. There is considerable room for disagreement as to the relative costs of these policies as well as the economy's relative vulnerability to these pressures at any particular time.

Interest Rates. High interest rates reduce the present value of future cash flows, thereby reducing the attractiveness of investment opportunities. For this reason, real interest rates are key determinants of business investment expenditures. Demand for housing and high-priced consumer durables such as automobiles, which are commonly financed, also is highly sensitive to interest rates because interest rates affect interest payments. (In Chapter 4, Section 4.1, we examined the determinants of interest rates.)

Budget Deficit. The **budget deficit** of the federal government is the difference between government spending and revenues. Any budgetary shortfall must be offset by government borrowing. Large amounts of government borrowing can force up interest rates by increasing the total demand for credit in the economy. Economists generally believe excessive government borrowing will "crowd out" private borrowing and investing by forcing up interest rates and choking off business investment.

Sentiment. Consumers' and producers' optimism or pessimism concerning the economy are important determinants of economic performance. If consumers have confidence in their future income levels, for example, they will be more willing to spend on big-ticket items. Similarly, businesses will increase production and inventory levels if they anticipate higher demand for their products. In this way, beliefs influence how much consumption and investment will be pursued and affect the aggregate demand for goods and services.

CONCEPT CHECK

Question 1. Consider an economy where the dominant industry is automobile production for domestic consumption as well as export. Now suppose the auto market is hurt by an increase in the length of time people use their cars before replacing them. Describe the probable effects of this change on (*a*) GDP, (*b*) unemployment, (*c*) the government budget deficit, and (*d*) interest rates.

16.3 DEMAND AND SUPPLY SHOCKS

A useful way to organize your analysis of the factors that might influence the macroeconomy is to classify any impact as a supply or demand shock. A **demand shock** is an event that affects the demand for goods and services in the economy. Examples of positive demand shocks are reductions in tax rates, increases in the money supply, increases in government spending, or increases in foreign export demand. A **supply shock** is an event that influences production capacity and costs. Examples of supply shocks are changes in the price of imported oil; freezes, floods, or droughts that might destroy large quantities of agricultural crops; changes in the educational level of an economy's work force; or changes in the wage rates at which the labor force is willing to work.

Demand shocks are usually characterized by aggregate output moving in the same direction as interest rates and inflation. For example, a big increase in government spending will tend to stimulate the economy and increase GDP. It also might increase interest rates by increasing the demand for borrowed funds by the government as well as by businesses that might desire to borrow to finance new ventures. Finally, it could increase the inflation rate if the demand for goods and services is raised to a level at or beyond the total productive capacity of the economy.

Supply shocks are usually characterized by aggregate output moving in the opposite direction of inflation and interest rates. For example, a big increase in the price of imported oil will be inflationary because costs of production will rise, which eventually will lead to increases in prices of finished goods. The increase in inflation rates over the near term can lead to higher nominal interest rates. Against this background, aggregate output will be falling. With raw materials more expensive, the productive capacity of the economy is reduced, as is the ability of individuals to purchase goods at now-higher prices. GDP, therefore, tends to fall.

How can we relate this framework to investment analysis? You want to identify the industries that will be most helped or hurt in any macroeconomic scenario you envision. For example, if you forecast a tightening of the money supply, you might want to avoid industries such as automobile producers that might be hurt by the likely increase in interest rates. We caution you again that these forecasts are no easy task. Macroeconomic predictions are notoriously unreliable. And again, you must be aware that in all likelihood your forecast will be made using only publicly available information. Any investment advantage you have will be a result only of better analysis—not better information.

An example of investment advice pegged to forecasts of the macroeconomy is given in the nearby box. The analyst notes the widespread belief that interest rates will be

Buys among Out-of-Favor Consumer Cyclicals

With the Federal Reserve pushing interest rates higher, many cyclical consumer stocks have been slipping this year. Despite an upbeat consumer mood and rising sales trends, consumer-related groups such as autos, home furnishings and appliances have underperformed the S&P 500 index. As the accompanying chart indicates, most of the consumer cyclicals' share price advance since the beginning of 1993 has been erased.

Despite the strong earnings gains, many investors believe that producers of "big ticket" durable goods will see profit margins shrink as high interest rates and a sluggish economy stymie sales growth over the next nine to 12 months. While we would agree that the pace of real GDP growth will ease significantly by mid-1995 to an annual rate of 1% to 2% from 3%–4% currently, we don't anticipate the kind of wrenching downturn that would produce a slump in profits. We foresee long-term interest rates peaking by the second quarter of 1995, allowing the economy to achieve a soft landing before regaining speed again later in 1995 and into 1996.

Under these conditions, consumer disposable incomes and job growth should continue to advance at a moderate pace throughout 1995. We expect consumer spending for durable goods such as autos and appliances to climb about 4%, compared with the more than 8% rise we see this year.

With our expectation that interest rates will ease in the second half of 1995 and that the economy will grow at a 1%–2% annual rate, we believe that many consumer goods producers will post healthy, if somewhat smaller, earnings gains next year and into 1996. For example, we expect the Big Three automakers' profits to rise 20% or more next year on a 7% increase in sales. Similarly, major appliance makers such as MAYTAG and WHIRLPOOL are likely to see unit sales continue to grow and 1995 profits climb 15% to 20%. Neither industry is likely to witness a cyclical earnings peak before 1996.

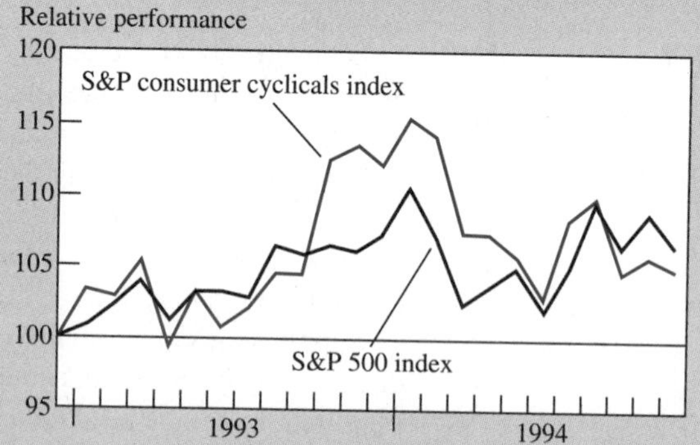

Source: *The Outlook,* Standard & Poor's Corp., November 30, 1994.

pushed higher by the Federal Reserve and, as a result, that the macroeconomy will slow. The analyst does not dispute this view qualitatively, but believes that the market consensus view is too pessimistic—that interest rates will peak sooner than generally expected and that growth, therefore, will be better than generally forecast. Because this view of the economy is comparatively bullish, the analyst recommends investments in industries that will be most sensitive to better-than-expected macroeconomic performance. These are industries that produce big-ticket consumer goods such as appliances and automobiles. Note that the basis of the analyst's recommendation is not a belief that the economy will be exceedingly strong in an absolute sense; rather, it is that that the economy will be stronger than it is expected to be by other investors. The analyst recognizes that the basis for an investment should be the forecast for the industry relative to the forecast implicitly built into security prices.

16.4 Federal Government Policy

As the previous section would suggest, the government has two broad classes of macroeconomic tools—those that affect the demand for goods and services and those that affect the supply. For most of postwar history, demand-side policy has been of primary interest. The focus has been on government spending, tax levels, and monetary policy. Since the 1980s, however, increasing attention has been focused on supply-side economics. Broadly interpreted, supply-side concerns have to do with enhancing the productive capacity of the economy, rather than increasing the demand for the goods and services the economy can produce. In practice, supply-side economists have focused on the appropriateness of the incentives to work, innovate, and take risks that result from our system of taxation. However, issues such as national policies on education, infrastructure (such as communication and transportation systems), and research and development also are properly regarded as part of supply-side macroeconomic policy.

Fiscal Policy

Fiscal policy refers to the government's spending and tax actions and is part of "demand-side management." Fiscal policy is probably the most direct way either to stimulate or to slow the economy. Decreases in government spending directly deflate the demand for goods and services. Similarly, increases in tax rates immediately siphon income from consumers and result in fairly rapid decreases in consumption.

Ironically, although fiscal policy has the most immediate impact on the economy, the formulation and implementation of such policy is usually painfully slow and involved. This is because fiscal policy requires enormous amounts of compromise between the executive and legislative branches. Tax and spending policy must be initiated and voted on by Congress, which requires considerable political negotiations, and any legislation passed must be signed by the president, requiring more negotiation. Thus, although the impact of fiscal policy is relatively immediate, its formulation is so cumbersome that fiscal policy cannot in practice be used to fine-tune the economy.

Moreover, much of government spending, such as that for Medicare or social security, is nondiscretionary, meaning that it is determined by formula rather than policy and cannot be changed in response to economic conditions. This places even more rigidity into the formulation of fiscal policy.

A common way to summarize the net impact of government fiscal policy is to look at the government's budget deficit or surplus, which is simply the difference between revenues and expenditures. A large deficit means the government is spending considerably more than it is taking in by way of taxes. The net effect is to increase the demand for goods (via spending) by more than it reduces the demand for goods (via taxes), therefore, stimulating the economy.

Monetary Policy

Monetary policy refers to the manipulation of the money supply to affect the macroeconomy and is the other main leg of demand-side policy. Monetary policy works largely through its impact on interest rates. Increases in the money supply lower short-term interest rates, ultimately encouraging investment and consumption demand. Over longer periods, however, most economists believe a higher money supply leads only to a higher price level and does not have a permanent effect on economic activity. Thus, the monetary authorities face a difficult balancing act. Expansionary monetary policy probably will lower interest rates and thereby stimulate investment and some consumption demand in the short run, but these circumstances ultimately will lead only to higher prices. The stimulation/inflation trade-off is implicit in all debate over proper monetary policy.

Fiscal policy is cumbersome to implement but has a fairly direct impact on the economy, whereas monetary policy is easily formulated and implemented but has a less direct impact. Monetary policy is determined by the Board of Governors of the Federal Reserve System. Board members are appointed by the president for 14-year terms and are reasonably insulated from political pressure. The board is small enough, and often sufficiently dominated by its chairperson, that policy can be formulated and modulated relatively easily.

Implementation of monetary policy also is quite direct. The most widely used tool is the open market operation, in which the Fed buys or sells bonds for its own account. When the Fed buys securities, it simply "writes a check," thereby increasing the money supply. (Unlike us, the Fed can pay for the securities without drawing down funds at a bank account.) Conversely, when the Fed sells a security, the money paid for it leaves the money supply. Open market operations occur daily, allowing the Fed to fine-tune its monetary policy.

Other tools at the Fed's disposal are the discount rate, which is the interest rate it charges banks on short-term loans, and the reserve requirement, which is the fraction of deposits that banks must hold as cash on hand or as deposits with the Fed. Reductions in the discount rate signal a more expansionary monetary policy. Lowering reserve requirements allows banks to make more loans with each dollar of deposits and stimulates the economy by increasing the effective money supply.

Monetary policy affects the economy in a more roundabout way than fiscal policy. Whereas fiscal policy directly stimulates or dampens the economy, monetary policy works largely through its impact on interest rates. Increases in the money supply lower interest rates, which stimulate investment demand. As the quantity of money in the economy increases, investors will find that their portfolios of assets include too much money. They will rebalance their portfolios by buying securities such as bonds, forcing bond prices up and interest rates down. In the longer run, individuals may increase their holdings of stocks as well and ultimately buy real assets, which stimulates consumption demand directly. The ultimate effect of monetary policy on investment and consumption demand, however, is less immediate than that of fiscal policy.

CONCEPT CHECK

Question 2. Suppose the government wants to stimulate the economy without increasing interest rates. What combination of fiscal and monetary policy might accomplish this goal?

Supply-Side Policies

Fiscal and monetary policy are demand-oriented tools that affect the economy by stimulating the total demand for goods and services. The implicit belief is that the economy will not by itself arrive at a full employment equilibrium, and that macroeconomic policy can push the economy toward this goal. In contrast, supply-side policies treat the issue of the productive capacity of the economy. The goal is to create an environment in which workers and owners of capital have the maximum incentive and ability to produce and develop goods.

Supply-side economists also pay considerable attention to tax policy. Whereas demand siders look at the effect of taxes on consumption demand, supply siders focus on incentives and marginal tax rates. They argue that lowering tax rates will elicit more investment and improve incentives to work, thereby enhancing economic growth. Some go so far as to claim that reductions in tax rates can lead to increases in tax revenues because the lower tax rates will cause the economy and the revenue tax base to grow by more than the tax rate is reduced.

CONCEPT CHECK Question 3. Large tax cuts in the 1980s were followed by rapid growth in GDP. How would demand-side and supply-side economists differ in their interpretations of this phenomenon?

16.5 BUSINESS CYCLES

We've looked at the tools the government uses to fine-tune the economy, attempting to maintain low unemployment and low inflation. Despite these efforts, economies repeatedly seem to pass through good and bad times. One determinant of the broad asset allocation decision of many analysts is a forecast of whether the macroeconomy is improving or deteriorating. A forecast that differs from the market consensus can have a major impact on investment strategy.

The Business Cycle

The economy recurrently experiences periods of expansion and contraction, although the length and depth of those cycles can be irregular. This recurring pattern of recession and recovery is called the **business cycle.** Figure 16.3 presents graphs of several measures of production and output for the years 1965–1993. The production series all show clear variation around a generally rising trend. The bottom graph of capacity utilization also evidences a clear cyclical (although irregular) pattern.

The transition points across cycles are called peaks and troughs, labeled P and T at the top of the graph. A **peak** is the transition from the end of an expansion to the start of a contraction. A **trough** occurs at the bottom of a recession just as the economy enters a recovery. The shaded areas in Figure 16.3 all represent periods of recession. The National Bureau of Economic Research (NBER) is the official designator of peak and trough points.

Figure 16.3 Cyclical indicators

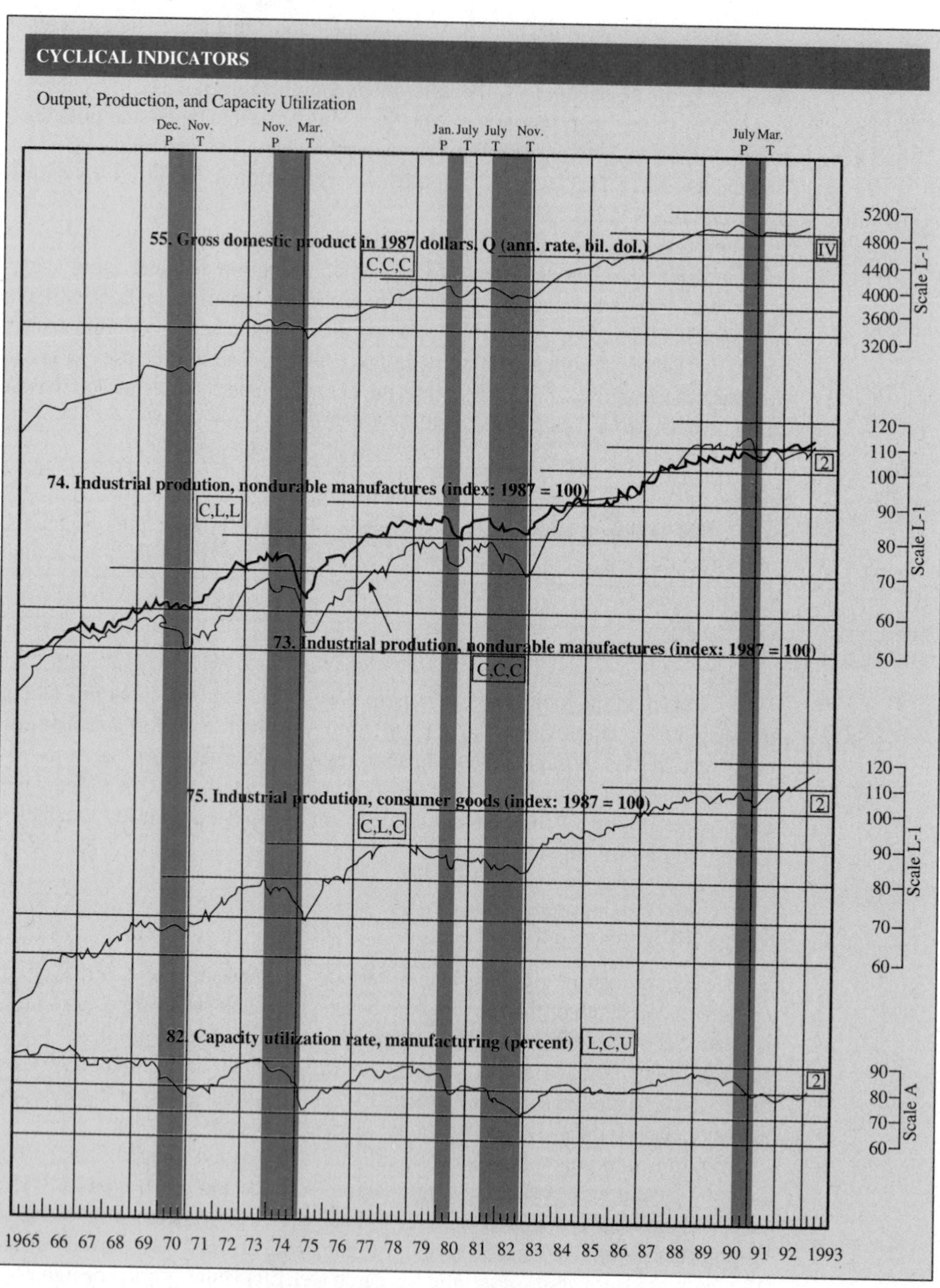

Source: *Survey of Current Business*, U.S. Department of Commerce, March 1993.

As the economy passes through different stages of the business cycle, the relative performance of different industry groups might be expected to vary. For example, at a trough, just before the economy begins to recover from a recession, one would expect that **cyclical industries,** those with above-average sensitivity to the state of the economy, would tend to outperform other industries. Examples of cyclical industries are producers of durable goods such as automobiles or washing machines. Because purchases of these goods can be deferred during a recession, sales are particularly sensitive to macroeconomic conditions. Other cyclical industries are producers of capital goods, that is, goods used by other firms to produce their own products. When demand is slack, few companies will be expanding and purchasing capital goods. Therefore, the capital goods industry bears the brunt of a slowdown, but does well in an expansion.

In contrast to cyclical firms, **defensive industries** have little sensitivity to the business cycle. These are industries that produce goods for which sales and profits are least sensitive to the state of the economy. Defensive industries include food producers and processors, pharmaceutical firms, and public utilities. These industries will outperform others when the economy enters a recession.

The cyclical/defensive classification corresponds well to the notion of systematic or market risk introduced in our discussion of portfolio theory. Firms in cyclical industries will have high-beta stocks, performing best when economic news is positive, but performing worst when news is bad. Conversely, defensive firms will have low betas and performance that is relatively unaffected by overall market conditions.

Unfortunately, it is not so easy to determine when the economy is passing through a peak or a trough. It if were, choosing between cyclical and defensive industries would be easy. As we know from our discussion of efficient markets, however, attractive investment choices will rarely be obvious. It usually is not apparent that a recession or expansion has started or ended until several months after the fact. With hindsight, the transitions from expansion to recession and back might be apparent, but it is often quite difficult to say whether the economy is heating up or slowing down at any moment.

Economic Indicators

Given the cyclical nature of the business cycle, it is not surprising that to some extent the cycle can be predicted. The NBER has developed a set of cyclical indicators to help forecast, measure, and interpret short-term fluctuations in economic activity. **Leading economic indicators** are those economic series that tend to rise or fall in advance of the rest of the economy. Coincident and lagging indicators, as their names suggest, move in tandem with or somewhat after the broad economy.

Eleven series are grouped into a widely followed composite index of leading economic indicators. Similarly, four coincident and seven lagging indicators form separate indexes. The composition of these indexes appears in Table 16.2.

Figure 16.4 graphs these three series over the period 1956–1993. The numbers on the charts near the turning points of each series indicate the length of the lead time or lag time (in months) from the turning point to the designated peak or trough of the

Table 16.2 Indexes of Economic Indicators

A. Leading Indicators

1. Average weekly hours of production workers (manufacturing)
2. Average weekly initial claims for unemployment insurance
3. Manufacturers' new orders (consumer goods and materials industries)
4. Vendor performance—slower deliveries diffusion index
5. Contracts and orders for plant and equipment
6. New private housing units authorized by local building permits
7. Change in manufacturers' unfilled orders (durable goods industries)
8. Change in sensitive materials prices
9. Stock prices, 500 common stocks
10. Money supply (M2)
11. Index of consumer expectations

B. Coincident Indicators

1. Employees on nonagricultural payrolls
2. Personal income less transfer payments
3. Industrial production
4. Manufacturing and trade sales

C. Lagging Indicators

1. Average duration of unemployment
2. Ratio of trade inventories to sales
3. Change in index of labor cost per unit of output
4. Average prime rate charged by banks
5. Commercial and industrial loans outstanding
6. Ratio of consumer installment credit outstanding to personal income
7. Change in consumer price index for services

Source: *Survey of Current Business,* U.S. Department of Commerce, March 1993.

corresponding business cycle. Although the index of leading indicators consistently turns before the rest of the economy, the lead time is somewhat erratic. Moreover, the lead time for peaks is consistently longer than that for troughs.

The stock market price index is a leading indicator. This is as it should be, as stock prices are forward-looking predictors of future profitability. Unfortunately, this makes the series of leading indicators much less useful for investment policy—by the time the series predicts an upturn, the market has already made its move. Although the business cycle may be somewhat predictable, the stock market may not be. This is just one more manifestation of the efficient market hypothesis.

The money supply is another leading indicator. This makes sense in light of our earlier discussion concerning the lags surrounding the effects of monetary policy on the economy. An expansionary monetary policy can be observed fairly quickly, but it might not affect the economy for several months. Therefore, today's monetary policy might well predict future economic activity.

Figure 16.4 Indexes of leading, coincident, and lagging indicators

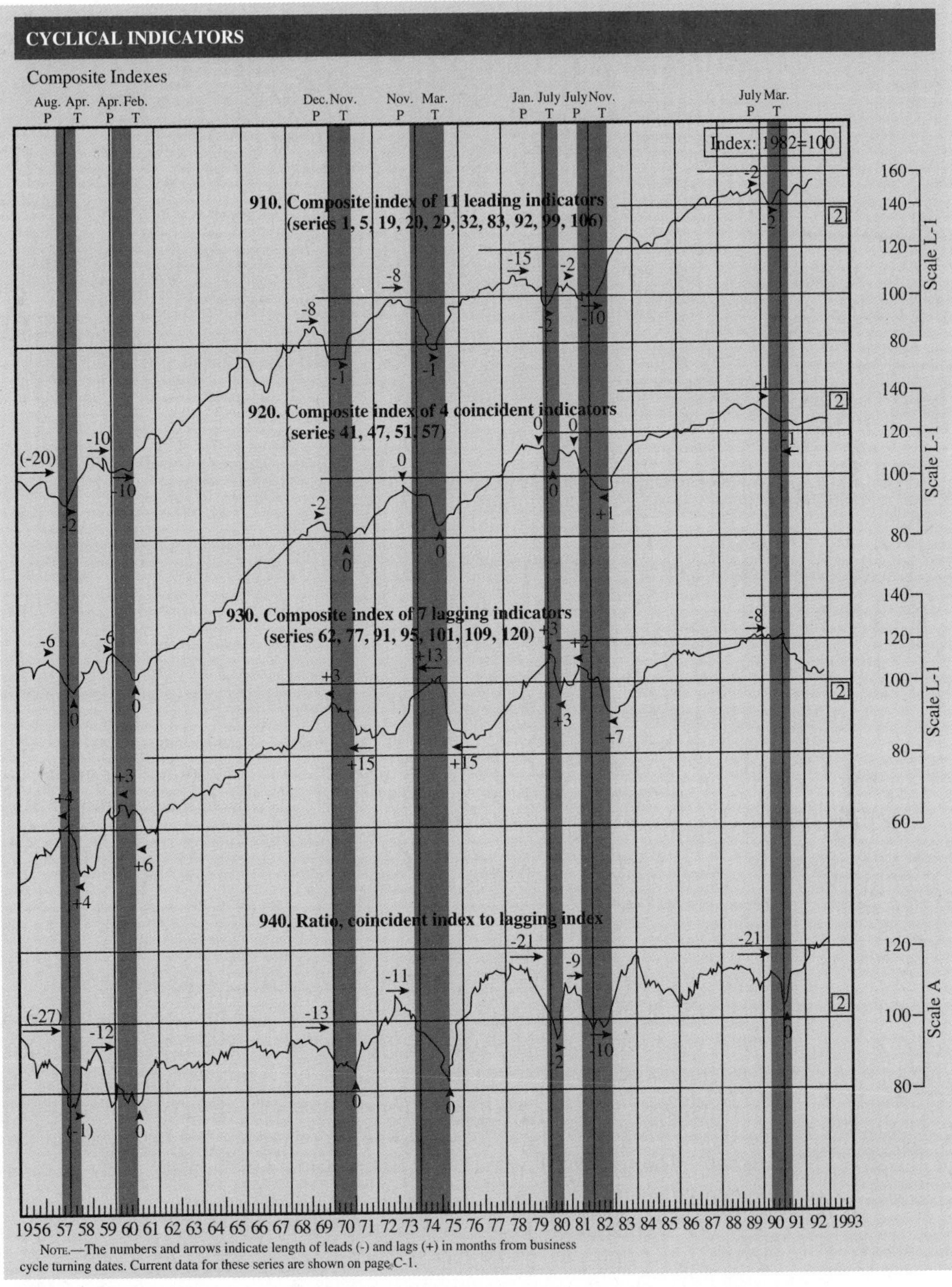

Source: *Survey of Current Business*, U.S. Department of Commerce, March 1993.

Figure 16.5 Earnings estimates in several industries

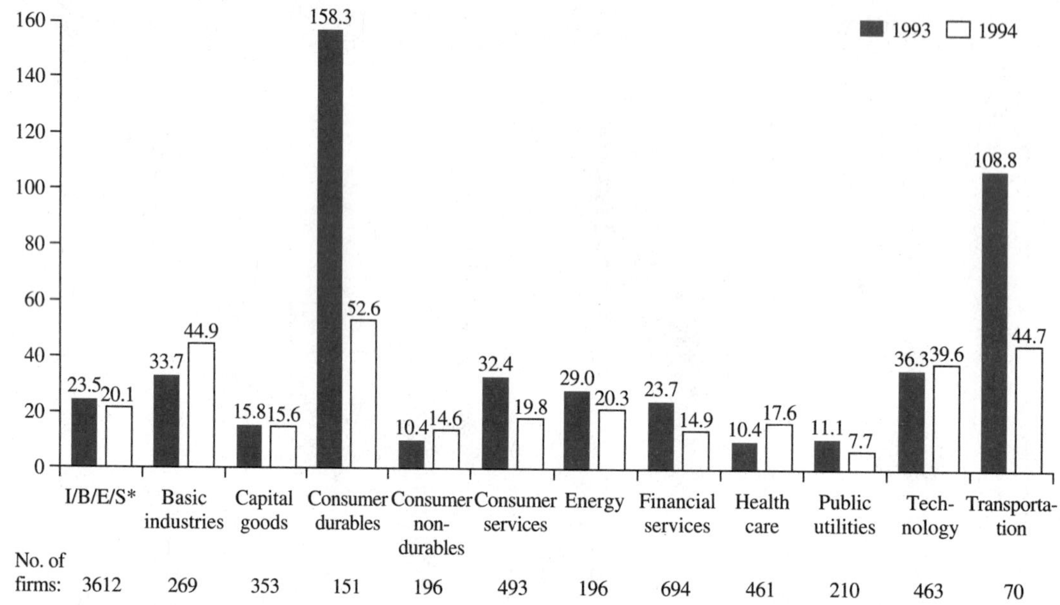

*Institutional Brokers Estimate System

Source: *U.S. Comments,* May 28, 1993. Institutional Brokers Estimate System (I/B/E/S).

Other leading indicators focus directly on decisions made today that will affect production in the near future. For example, manufacturers' new orders for goods, contracts and orders for plant and equipment, and housing starts all signal a coming expansion in the economy.

16.6 Industry Analysis

Industry analysis is important for the same reason that macroeconomic analysis is. Just as it is difficult for an industry to perform well when the macroeconomy is ailing, it is unusual for a firm in a troubled industry to perform well. Similarly, just as we have seen that economic performance can vary widely across countries, performance also can vary widely across industries. Figure 16.5 illustrates the dispersion of industry performance. It shows projected growth in earnings per share in 1994 for several major industry groups. The forecasts, which come from a survey of industry analysts, range from 7.7% for public utilities to 52.6% for consumer durables.

Industry groups show even more dispersion in their stock market performance. Figure 16.6 illustrates the performance of the 10 best- and 10 worst-performing industries in 1994. The spread in performance is remarkable, ranging from a 33.9% return for the drug-retailing industry to a 32.6% loss in the home construction industry.

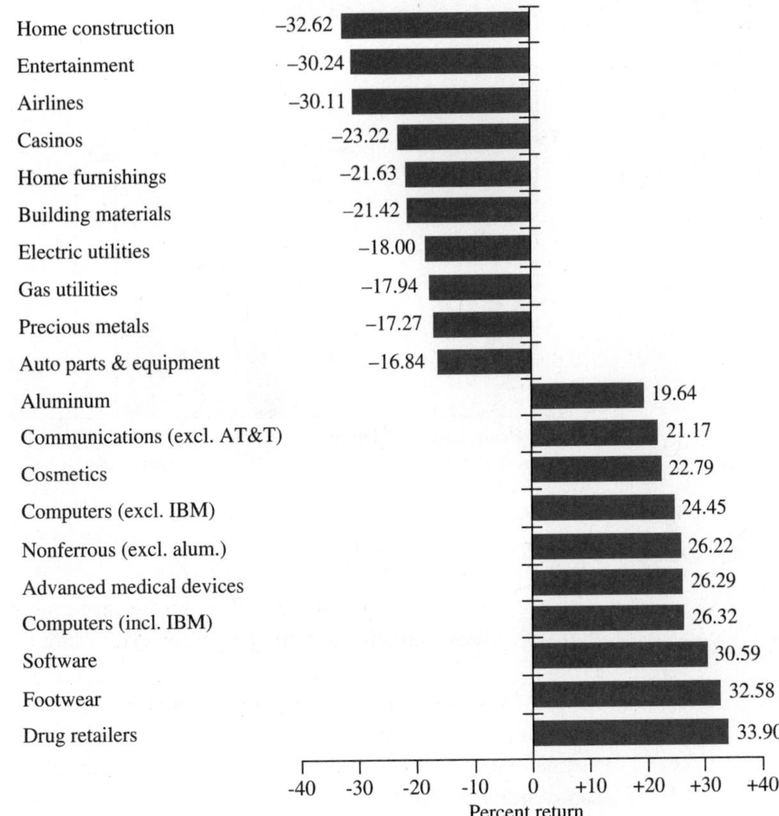

Figure 16.6
Industry stock price performance, 1994

Source: *The Wall Street Journal*, January 3, 1995. © 1995 Dow Jones & Company, Inc. All Rights Reserved Worldwide.

Defining an Industry

Although we know what we mean by an "industry," it can be difficult in practice to decide where to draw the line between one industry and another. Consider for example, the health care industry. Figure 16.5 shows that the forecast for 1994 growth in industry earnings per share was 17.6%. But the health care "industry" contains firms with widely differing products and prospects. Figure 16.7 breaks down the industry into six subgroups. The forecasted performance on these more narrowly defined groups differs widely, suggesting that they are not members of a homogeneous industry. Similarly, most of these subgroups in Figure 16.7 could be divided into even smaller and more homogeneous groups.

A useful way to define industry groups in practice is given by *Standard Industry Classification* or **SIC codes.** These are codes assigned by the U.S. government for the purpose of grouping firms for statistical analysis. The first two digits of the SIC codes denote very broad industry classifications. For example, the SIC codes assigned to any type of building contractor all start with 15. The third and fourth digits define the industry grouping more narrowly. For example, codes starting with 152 denote *residential* building contractors, and group 1521 contains *single-family* building contractors. Firms

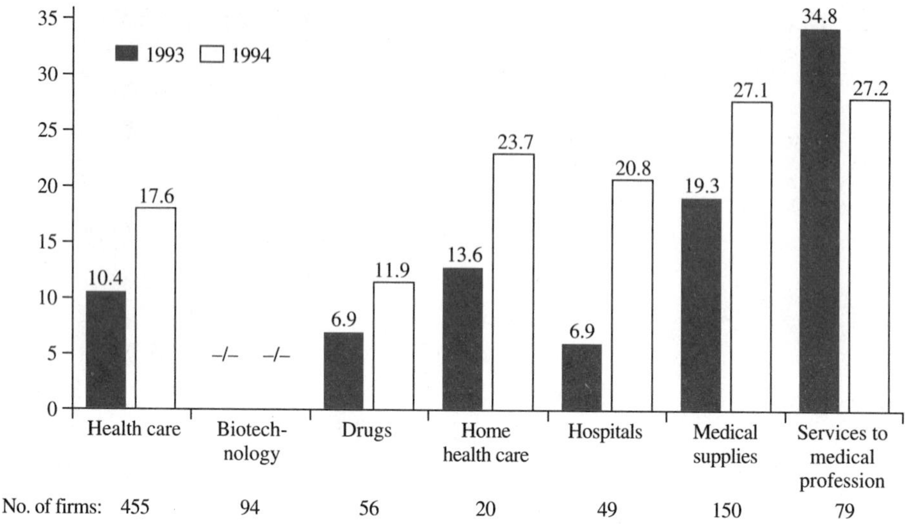

Figure 16.7
Earnings estimates for health care industries

with the same four-digit SIC code, therefore, are commonly taken to be in the same industry. Many statistics are computed for even more narrowly defined five-digit SIC groups.

SIC industry classifications are not perfect. For example, both J.C. Penney and Neiman Marcus are in group 5311, Department Stores. Yet the former is a high-volume "value" store, whereas the latter is a high-margin elite retailer. Are they really in the same industry? Still, SIC classifications are a tremendous aid in conducting industry analysis since they provide a means of focusing on very broad or fairly narrowly defined groups of firms.

Several other industry classifications are provided by other analysts, for example, Standard & Poor's reports on the performance of about 100 industry groups. S&P computes stock price indexes for each group, which is useful in assessing past investment performance. The *Value Line Investment Survey* reports on the conditions and prospects of about 1,700 firms, grouped into about 90 industries. Value Line's analysts prepare forecasts of the performance of industry groups as well as of each firm.

Sensitivity to the Business Cycle

Once the analyst forecasts the state of the macroeconomy, it is necessary to determine the implication of that forecast for specific industries. Not all industries are equally sensitive to the business cycle. For example, consider Figure 16.8, which is a graph of automobile production and shipments of cigarettes, both scaled so that 1963 has a value of 100.

Clearly, the cigarette industry is virtually independent of the business cycle. Demand for cigarettes does not seem affected by the state of the macroeconomy in any meaningful way. This is not surprising. Cigarette consumption is determined largely by habit and is a small enough part of most budgets that it will not be given up in hard times.

Figure 16.8
Industry cyclicality

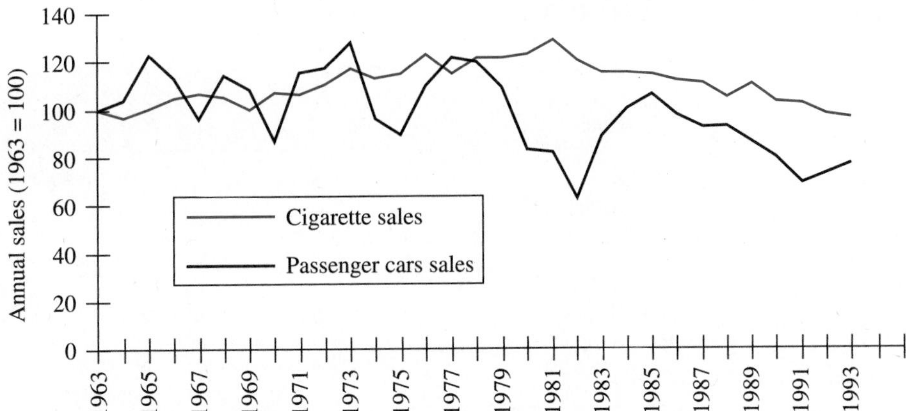

Source: Passenger car sales: *Ward's Automobile Yearbook,* 1994. Cigarette sales: Department of Alcohol, Tobacco, and Firearms Statistical Releases.

Auto production, by contrast, is highly volatile. In recessions, consumers can try to prolong the lives of their cars until their income is higher. For example, the worst year for auto production, according to Figure 16.8, was 1982. This was also a year of deep recession, with the unemployment rate at 9.5%.

Three factors will determine the sensitivity of a firm's earnings to the business cycle. First is the sensitivity of sales. Necessities will show little sensitivity to business conditions. Examples of industries in this group are food, drugs, and medical services. Other industries with low sensitivity are those for which income is not a crucial determinant of demand. As we noted, tobacco products are examples of this type of industry. Another industry in this group is movies, because consumers tend to substitute movies for more expensive sources of entertainment when income levels are low. In contrast, firms in industries such as machine tools, steel, autos, and transportation are highly sensitive to the state of the economy.

The second factor determining business cycle sensitivity is operating leverage, which refers to the division between fixed and variable costs. (Fixed costs are those the firm incurs regardless of its production levels. Variable costs are those that rise or fall as the firm produces more or less product.) Firms with greater amounts of variable as opposed to fixed costs will be less sensitive to business conditions. This is because in economic downturns, these firms can reduce costs as output falls in response to falling sales. Profits for firms with high fixed costs will swing more widely with sales because costs do not move to offset revenue variability. Firms with high fixed costs are said to have high operating leverage, as small swings in business conditions can have large impacts on profitability.

An example might help illustrate this concept. Consider two firms operating in the same industry with identical revenues in all phases of the business cycle: recession, normal, and expansion. Firm A has short-term leases on most of its equipment and can reduce its lease expenditures when production slackens. It has fixed costs of $5 million and variable costs of $1 per unit of output. Firm B has long-term leases on most of its

Table 16.3 Operating Leverage

Scenario:	Recession		Normal		Expansion	
Firm:	A	B	A	B	A	B
Sales (million units)	5	5	6	6	7	7
Price per unit	\$ 2	\$ 2	\$ 2	\$ 2	\$ 2	\$ 2
Revenue (\$ million)	10	10	12	12	14	14
Fixed Costs (\$ million)	5	8	5	8	5	8
Variable costs (\$ million)	5	2.5	6	3	7	3.5
Total costs (\$ million)	\$10	\$10.5	\$11	\$11	\$12	\$11.5
Profits	\$ 0	\$(0.5)	\$ 1	\$ 1	\$ 2	\$ 2.5

equipment and must make lease payments regardless of economic conditions. Its fixed costs are higher, \$8 million, but its variable costs are only \$.50 per unit. Table 16.3 shows that Firm A will do better in recessions than Firm B, but not as well in expansions. A's costs move in conjunction with its revenues to help performance in downturns and impede performance in upturns.

The third factor influencing business cycle sensitivity is financial leverage, which is the use of borrowing. Interest payments on debt must be paid regardless of sales. They are fixed costs that also increase the sensitivity of profits to business conditions. (We will have more to say about financial leverage in Chapter 18.)

Investors should not always prefer industries with lower sensitivity to the business cycle. Firms in sensitive industries will have high-beta stocks and are riskier. But while they swing lower in downturns, they also swing higher in upturns. As always, the issue you need to address is whether the expected return on the investment is fair compensation for the risks borne.

CONCEPT CHECK Question 4. What will be profits in the three scenarios for Firm C with fixed costs of \$2 million and variable costs of \$1.50 per unit? What are your conclusions regarding operating leverage and business risk?

Industry Life Cycles

Examine the biotechnology industry and you will find many firms with high rates of investment, high rates of return on investment, and low dividend payout rates. Do the same for the electric utility industry and you will find lower rates of return, lower investment rates, and higher dividend payout rates. Why should this be?

The biotech industry is still new. Recently, available technologies have created opportunities for highly profitable investment of resources. New products are protected

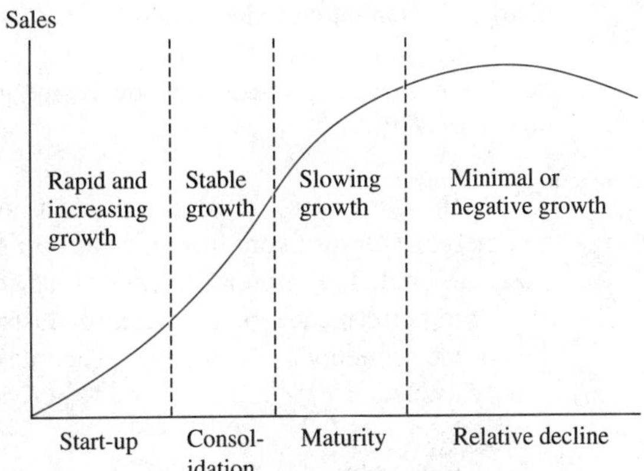

Figure 16.9
The industry life cycle

by patents, and profit margins are high. With such lucrative investment opportunities, firms find it advantageous to put all profits back into the firm. The companies grow rapidly on average.

Eventually, however, growth must slow. The high profit rates will induce new firms to enter the industry. Increasing competition will hold down prices and profit margins. New technologies become proven and more predictable, risk levels fall, and entry becomes even easier. As internal investment opportunities become less attractive, a lower fraction of profits are reinvested in the firm. Cash dividends increase.

Ultimately, in a mature industry, we observe "cash cows," firms with stable dividends and cash flows and little risk. Growth rates might be similar to that of the overall economy. Industries in early states of their life cycles offer high-risk/high-potential-return investments. Mature industries offer lower-risk, lower-return combinations.

This analysis suggests that a typical **industry life cycle** might be described by four stages: a start-up stage, characterized by extremely rapid growth; a consolidation stage, characterized by growth that is less rapid but still faster than that of the general economy; a maturity state, characterized by growth no faster than the general economy; and a stage of relative decline, in which the industry grows less rapidly than the rest of the economy, or actually shrinks. This industry life cycle is illustrated in Figure 16.9. Let us turn to an elaboration of each of these stages.

Start-Up Stage. The early stages of an industry are often characterized by a new technology or product such as VCRs or personal computers in the 1980s, or bioengineering in the 1990s. At this stage, it is difficult to predict which firms will emerge as industry leaders. Some firms will turn out to be wildly successful, and others will fail altogether. Therefore, there is considerable risk in selecting one particular firm within the industry.

At the industry level, however, sales and earnings will grow at an extremely rapid rate, because the new product has not yet saturated its market. For example, in 1980 very few households had VCRs. The potential market for the product therefore was the entire set of television-watching households. In contrast to this situation, consider the market for a mature product like refrigerators. Almost all households in the U.S. already have refrigerators, so the market for this good is primarily comprised of households replacing old refrigerators. Obviously, the growth rate in this market will be far less than for VCRs.

Consolidation Stage. After a product becomes established, industry leaders begin to emerge. The survivors from the start-up stage are more stable, and market share is easier to predict. Therefore, the performance of the surviving firms will more closely track the performance of the overall industry. The industry still grows faster than the rest of the economy as the product penetrates the marketplace and becomes more commonly used.

Maturity Stage. At this point, the product has reached its full potential for use by consumers. Further growth might merely track growth in the general economy. The product has become far more standardized, and producers are forced to compete to a greater extent on the basis of price. This leads to narrower profit margins and further pressure on profits. Firms at this stage sometimes are characterized as "cash cows," firms with reasonably stable cash flow but offering little opportunity for profitable expansion. The cash flow is best "milked from" rather than reinvested in the company.

Relative Decline. In this stage, the industry might grow at less than the rate of the overall economy, or might even shrink. This could be due to obsolescence of the product, competition from new products, or competition from new low-cost suppliers.

At which stage in the life cycle are investments in an industry most attractive? Conventional wisdom is that investors should seek firms in high-growth industries. This recipe for success is simplistic, however. If the security prices already reflect the likelihood for high growth, then it is too late to make money from that knowledge. Moreover, high growth and fat profits encourage competition from other producers. The exploitation of profit opportunities brings about new sources of supply that eventually reduce prices, profits, investment returns, and finally growth. This is the dynamic behind the progression from one stage of the industry life cycle to another. The famous portfolio manager Peter Lynch makes this point in *One Up on Wall Street*. He says that

> Many people prefer to invest in a high-growth industry, where there's a lot of sound and fury. Not me. I prefer to invest in a low-growth industry . . . In a low-growth industry, especially one that's boring and upsets people [such as funeral homes or the oil-drum retrieval business], there's no problem with competition. You don't have to protect your flanks from potential rivals . . . and this gives you the leeway to continue to grow [page 131].

In fact, Lynch uses an industry classification system in a very similar spirit to the life-cycle approach we have described. He places firms in the following six groups:

Slow Growers. Large and aging companies that will grow only slightly faster than the broad economy. These firms have matured from their earlier fast-growth phase. They usually have steady cash flow and pay a generous dividend, indicating that the firm is generating more cash than can be profitably reinvested in the firm.

Stalwarts. Large, well-known firms like Coca-Cola, Hershey's, or Colgate-Palmolive. They grow faster than the slow growers, but are not in the very rapid growth start-up stage. They also tend to be in noncyclical industries that are relatively unaffected by recessions.

Fast Growers. Small and aggressive new firms with annual growth rates in the neighborhood of 20% to 25%. Company growth can be due to broad industry growth or to an increase in market share in a more mature industry.

Cyclicals. These are firms with sales and profits that regularly expand and contract along with the business cycle. Examples are auto companies (see Figure 16.8 again), steel companies, or the construction industry.

Turnarounds. These are firms that are in bankruptcy or soon might be. If they can recover from what might appear to be imminent disaster, they can offer tremendous investment returns. A good example of this type of firm would be Chrysler in 1982, when it required a government guarantee on its debt to avoid bankruptcy. The stock price rose fifteenfold in the next five years.

Asset Plays. These are firms that have valuable assets not currently reflected in the stock price. For example, a company may own or be located on valuable real estate that is worth as much or more than the company's business enterprises. Sometimes the hidden asset can be tax-loss carryforwards. Other times the assets may be intangible. For example, a cable company might have a valuable list of cable subscribers. These assets do not immediately generate cash flow, and so may be more easily overlooked by other analysts attempting to value the firm.

Industry Structure and Performance

The maturation of an industry involves regular changes in the firm's competitive environment. As a final topic, we examine the relationship between industry structure, competitive strategy, and profitability. Michael Porter[1] has highlighted these five determinants of competition: threat of entry from new competitors, rivalry between existing competitors, price pressure from substitute products, bargaining power of buyers, and bargaining power of suppliers.

Threat of Entry. New entrants to an industry put pressure on price and profits. Even if a firm has not yet entered an industry, the potential for it to do so places pressure on prices, because high prices and profit margins will encourage entry by new competitors. Therefore, barriers to entry can be a key determinant of industry profitability. Barriers can take many forms. For example, existing firms may already have secure distribution channels for its products based on long-standing relationships with customers or suppliers that would be costly for a new entrant to duplicate. Brand loyalty also makes it

[1] Michael Porter, *Competitive Advantage: Creating and Sustaining Superior Performance* (New York: Free Press, 1985).

difficult for new entrants to penetrate a market, and gives firms more pricing discretion. Proprietary knowledge or patent protection also may give firms advantages in serving a market. Finally, an existing firm's experience in a market may give it cost advantages due to the learning that takes place over time.

Rivalry between Existing Competitors. When there are several competitors in an industry, there will generally be more price competition and lower profit margins as competitors seek to expand their share of the market. Slow industry growth contributes to this competition, because expansion must come at the expense of a rival's market share. High fixed costs also create pressure to reduce prices, because fixed costs put greater pressure on firms to operate near full capacity. Industries producing relatively homogeneous goods are also subject to considerable price pressure, because firms cannot compete on the basis of product differentiation.

Pressure from Substitute Products. Substitute products means that the industry faces competition from firms in related industries. For example, sugar producers compete with corn syrup producers. Wool producers compete with synthetic fiber producers. The availability of substitutes limits the prices that can be charged to customers.

Bargaining Power of Buyers. If a buyer purchases a large fraction of an industry's output, it will have considerable bargaining power and can demand price concessions. For example, auto producers can put pressure on suppliers of auto parts. This reduces the profitability of the auto parts industry.

Bargaining Power of Suppliers. If a supplier of a key input has monopolistic control over the product, it can demand higher prices for the good and squeeze profits out of the industry. One special case of this issue pertains to organized labor as a supplier of a key input to the production process. Labor unions engage in collective bargaining to increase the wages paid to workers. When the labor market is highly unionized, a significant share of the potential profits in the industry can be captured by the work force.

The key factor determining the bargaining power of suppliers is the availability of substitute products. If substitutes are available, the supplier has little clout and cannot extract higher prices.

An Example

The nearby box is excerpted from a macroeconomic and industry analysis in *The Wall Street Journal* that illustrates many of the concepts discussed in this chapter. The article focuses on attractive industry sectors in the last quarter of 1993. International considerations cited include the difficulties faced by Japanese companies arising from the appreciation of the yen compared to the dollar. This contributes to optimism concerning the U.S. computer chip industry, auto industry, and heavy machinery industry, for which much competition comes from Japanese producers.

The macroeconomic environment cited in the article includes continued moderation of interest and inflation rates associated with low economic growth. This environment

Stock-Pickers Offer Ways to Pierce Gloom

Pick your stocks carefully in the fourth quarter.

Investment strategists are forecasting that the overall market will flag during the quarter but gains are possible in technology-related groups such as semiconductors and telecommunications, both of which were top performers in the third quarter. Watch out for gold and basic materials such as aluminum and chemicals, the strategists also warn.

Further strong gains in economically sensitive stocks, which have led the market for most of the year, are far from assured, the analysts say. That's because many large industrial companies are feeling the increasing weight of the global economic slowdown. The worldwide malaise is offsetting whatever gains the U.S. economy is eking out, the analysts say.

"The cyclical story is starting to get long in the tooth for investors," says Joseph Battipaglia, chief investment strategist at Gruntal & Co.

Mr. Battipaglia predicts the Dow Jones Industrial Average will slide 5% to 7% from the 3600 level during the quarter. But investors can buck that trend by jumping into semiconductor stocks, Mr. Battipaglia says. He points out that U.S. chip makers are making strong headway in competition with Japanese manufacturers, which are suffering from a strong yen and a poor domestic economy.

In a related sector, telecommunications stocks are the favorites of many strategists. The fight for Paramount only adds luster to the group, analysts say. The possibility of future marriages is focusing attention on telecommunications companies and probably will enhance stock prices, they add.

"The alliances and relationships are getting much bigger than anyone imagined," says Mr. Battipaglia. "It means these stocks are likely to be relatively strong performers."

Some analysts, who are expecting interest rates to continue falling, see potential gains in stock groups linked to lower rates. Richard Hoffman, chief investment strategist at Cowen & Co., sees long-term rates heading toward 5.5% as inflation remains subdued. As a result, he predicts continued strong performances in the fourth quarter among home builders, building materials concerns, big banks, insurance companies and brokerage firms. All of those groups turned in sparkling performances during the past quarter. He also believes the utilities sector offers some promise. "The interest rate play is still available," says Mr. Hoffman.

Japan's economic difficulties benefit not only U.S. technology companies but auto makers and heavy machinery concerns, Mr. Hoffman says. "These groups have been in primary bull markets, and this will continue in the fourth quarter," he predicts.

Precious metals, which took a stunning dive during the third quarter after soaring for much of the year, may be headed for still more trouble, Mr. Hoffman predicts. He says gold will remain under pressure because inflation will be subdued and a fresh round of global currency instability isn't likely.

Source: Abridged from Steven E. Levingston, "Stock-Pickers Offer Ways to Pierce Gloom," *The Wall Street Journal,* October 1, 1993, p. C23.

leads to recommendations for investments in interest-rate sensitive industries such as banks and insurance companies but against investments in large industrial companies that "are feeling the increasing weight of the global slowdown."

Finally, some industry-specific considerations affect the investment recommendations. For example, the growing trend for strategic alliances and relationships in the telecommunications industry are thought to bode well for future performance.

Summary

1. Macroeconomic policy aims to maintain the economy near full employment without aggravating inflationary pressures. The proper trade-off between these two goals is a source of ongoing debate.

2. The traditional tools of macropolicy are government spending and tax collection, which comprise fiscal policy, and manipulation of the money supply via monetary policy. Expansionary fiscal policy can stimulate the economy and increase GDP but tends to increase interest rates. Expansionary monetary policy works by lowering interest rates.

3. The business cycle is the economy's recurring pattern of expansions and recessions. Leading economic indicators can be used to anticipate the evolution of the business cycle because their values tend to change before those of other key economic variables.

4. Industries differ in their sensitivity to the business cycle. More sensitive industries tend to be those producing high-priced durable goods for which the consumer has considerable discretion as to the timing of purchase. Examples are automobiles or consumer durables. Other sensitive industries are those that produce capital equipment for other firms. Operating leverage and financial leverage increase sensitivity to the business cycle.

Key Terms

Exchange rate
Gross domestic product
Unemployment rate
Inflation
Budget deficit
Demand shock
Supply shock
Fiscal policy
Monetary policy
Peak
Trough
Cyclical industries
Defensive industries
Business cycle
Leading economic indicators
SIC codes
Industry life cycle

Selected Readings

Overviews of the macroeconomy appear regularly in several business periodicals. Try, for example:

Business Week, Financial World, Fortune, or *Forbes*

More formal evaluations of the economy appear annually in:

The Economic Report of the President and weekly in the *Survey of Current Business.*

Problems

1. What monetary and fiscal policies might be prescribed for an economy in a deep recession?
2. Unlike other investors, you believe the Fed is going to dramatically loosen monetary policy. What would be your recommendations about investments in the following industries?

a. Gold mining.
b. Construction.

3. If you believe the U.S. dollar will depreciate more dramatically than do other investors, what will be your stance on investments in the U.S. auto producers?
4. According to supply-side economists, what will be the long-run impact on prices of a reduction in income tax rates?
5. Consider two firms producing videocassette recorders. One uses a highly automated robotics process, whereas the other uses human workers on an assembly line and pays overtime when there is heavy production demand.
   a. Which firm will have higher profits in a recession? In a boom?
   b. Which firm's stock will have a higher beta?
6. Here are four industries and four forecasts for the macroeconomy. Choose the industry that you would expect to perform best in each scenario.
   Industries: Housing construction, health care, gold mining, steel production.
   Economic Forecasts
   Deep recession: Falling inflation, falling interest rates, falling GDP.
   Superheated economy: Rapidly rising GDP, increasing inflation and interest rates.
   Healthy expansion: Rising GDP, mild inflation, low unemployment.
   Stagflation: Falling GDP, high inflation.
7. In which stage of the industry life cycle would you place the following industries? (Warning: There is often considerable room for disagreement concerning the "correct" answers to this question.)
   a. Oil well equipment. D
   b. Computer hardware. m
   c. Computer software. c
   d. Genetic engineering.
   e. Railroads. D
8. For each pair of firms, choose the one that you think would be more sensitive to the business cycle.
   a. General Autos or General Pharmaceuticals.
   b. Friendly Airlines or Happy Cinemas.
9. Choose an industry and identify the factors that will determine its performance in the next three years. What is your forecast for performance in that time period?
10. Why do you think the index of consumer expectations is a useful leading indicator of the macroeconomy? (See Table 16.2.)
11. Why do you think the change in the index of labor cost per unit of output is a useful lagging indicator of the macroeconomy? (See Table 16.2.)
12. You have $5,000 to invest for the next year and are considering three alternatives:
    a. A money market fund with an average maturity of 30 days offering a current yield of 6% per year.
    b. A one-year savings deposit at a bank offering an interest rate of 7.5%.
    c. A 20-year U.S. Treasury bond offering a yield to maturity of 9% per year.

What role does your forecast of future interest rates play in your decisions?

13. Universal Auto is a large multinational corporation headquartered in the United States. For segment reporting purposes, the company is engaged in two businesses: production of motor vehicles and information processing services.

The motor vehicle business is by far the larger of Universal's two segments. It consists mainly of domestic United States passenger car production, but also includes small truck manufacturing operations in the United States and passenger car production in other countries. this segment of Universal has had weak operating results for the past several years, including a large loss in 1992. Although the company does not reveal the operating results of its domestic passenger car segments, that part of Universal's business is generally believed to be primarily responsible for the weak performance of its motor vehicle segment.

Idata, the information processing services segment of Universal, was started by Universal about 15 years ago. This business has shown strong, steady growth that has been entirely internal; no acquisitions have been made.

An excerpt from a research report on Universal prepared by Paul Adams, a CFA candidate, states: . . . Based on our assumption that Universal will be able to increase prices significantly on U.S. passenger cars in 1993, we project a multibillion dollar profit improvement . . .*

a. Discuss the concept of an industrial life cycle by describing each of its four phases.

b. Identify where each of Universal's two primary businesses—passenger cars and information processing—is in such a cycle.

c. Discuss how product pricing should differ between Universal's two businesses, based on the location of each in the industrial life cycle.

14. Adam's research report (see Problem 13) continued as follows: "With a business recovery already underway, the expected profit surge should lead to a much higher price for Universal Auto stock. We strongly recommend purchase."*

a. Discuss the business cycle approach to investment timing. (Your answer should describe actions to be taken on both stocks and bonds at different points over a typical business cycle.)

b. Assuming Adam's assertion is correct (that a business recovery is already underway), evaluate the timeliness of his recommendation to purchase Universal Auto, a cyclical stock, based on the business cycle approach to investment timing.

15. General Weedkillers dominates the chemical weed control market with its patented product Weed-ex. The patent is about to expire, however. What are your forecasts for changes in the industry? Specifically, what will happen to industry prices, sales, the profit prospects of General Weedkillers, and the profit prospects of its competitors? What stage of the industry life cycle do you think is relevant for the analysis of this market?

---

*Reprinted, with permission, from the Level II 1993 *CFA Study Guide*. Copyright 1993, Association for Investment Management and Research, Charlottesville, VA. All rights reserved.

16. The following questions appeared on recent CFA Examinations.
    a. Which one of the following statements *best* expresses the central idea of countercyclical fiscal policy?
    (1) Planned government deficits are appropriate during economic booms, and planned surpluses are appropriate during economic recessions.
    (2) The balanced budget approach is the proper criterion for determining annual budget policy.
    (3) Actual deficits should equal actual surpluses during a period of deflation.
    (4) Government deficits are planned during economic recessions, and surpluses are utilized to restrain inflationary booms.

    b. The supply-side view stresses that:
    (1) Aggregate demand is the major determinant of real output and aggregate employment.
    (2) An increase in government expenditures and tax rates will cause real income to rise.
    (3) Tax rates are a major determinant of real output and aggregate employment.
    (4) Expansionary monetary policy will cause real output to expand without causing the rate of inflation to accelerate.

    c. Which one of the following propositions would a strong proponent of supply-side economics be most likely to stress?
    (1) Higher marginal tax rates will lead to a reduction in the size of the budget deficit and lower interest rates, because they expand government revenues.
    (2) Higher marginal tax rates promote economic inefficiency and thereby retard aggregate output, because they encourage investors to undertake low-productivity projects with substantial tax-shelter benefits.
    (3) Income redistribution payments will exert little impact on real aggregate supply, because they do not consume resources directly.
    (4) A tax reduction will increase the disposable income of households. Thus, the primary impact of a tax reduction on aggregate supply will stem from the influence of the tax change on the size of the budget deficit or surplus.

    d. Which one of the following series is *not* included in the index of leading economic indicators?
    (1) New building permits; private housing units.
    (2) Net business formation.
    (3) Stock prices.
    (4) Inventories on hand.

    e. How would an economist who believes in crowding out complete the following sentence? "The increase in the budget deficit causes real interest rates to rise, and therefore private spending and investment
    (1) Increase."
    (2) Stay the same."

(3) Decrease."

(4) Initially increase but eventually will decrease."

f. If the central monetary authorities want to reduce the supply of money to slow the rate of inflation, the central bank should:

(1) Sell government bonds, which will reduce the money supply; this will cause interest rates to rise and aggregate demand to fall.

(2) Buy government bonds, which will reduce the money supply; this will cause interest rates to rise and aggregate demand to fall.

(3) Decrease the discount rate, which will lower the market rate of interest; this will cause both costs and prices to fall.

(4) Increase taxes, which will reduce costs and cause prices to fall.

17. The corporate life-cycle theory predicts that firms with ample investment opportunities will maintain high investment rates, while more mature industries in which attractive investment opportunities are scarce will have higher dividend payout rates. Use U.S. Equities OnFloppy to test this prediction. Compare the dividend payout rates for a sample of industries. For example, consider electric utilities versus telecommunications equipment; tobacco versus home health care; etc. Comment on your findings.

Chapter 17
Equity Valuation Models

YOU SAW IN OUR DISCUSSION OF MARKET EFFICIENCY THAT FINDING UNDERVALUED SECURITIES IS HARDLY EASY. At the same time, there are enough chinks in the armor of the efficient market hypothesis that the search for such securities should not be dismissed out of hand. Moreover, it is the ongoing search for mispriced securities that maintains a nearly efficient market. Even infrequent discoveries of minor mispricing justify the salary of a stock market analyst.

This chapter describes the ways stock market analysts try to uncover mispriced securities. The models presented are those used by **fundamental analysts,** those analysts who use information concerning the current and prospective profitability of a company to assess its fair market value. Fundamental analysts are different from **technical analysts,** who essentially use trend analysis and measures of market conditions to uncover trading opportunities.

We start with a discussion of alternative measures of the value of a company. From there, we progress to quantitative tools called *dividend discount models* that security analysts commonly use to measure the value of a firm as an ongoing concern. Next, we turn to price/earnings, or P/E, ratios, explaining why they are of such interest to analysts but also highlighting some of their shortcomings. We explain how P/E ratios are tied to dividend valuation models and, more generally, to the growth prospects of the firm.

17.1 BALANCE SHEET VALUATION METHODS

A common valuation measure is **book value,** which is the net worth of a company as shown on the balance sheet. Table 17.1 gives the balance sheet totals for IBM to illustrate how to calculate book value per share.

Table 17.1 IBM Balance Sheet, December 31, 1993 ($ million)

Assets	Liabilities and Owners' Equity	
$81,113	Liabilities	$61,375
	Common equity	$19,738
	573.2 million shares outstanding	

The book value of IBM stock on December 31, 1993, was $34.43 per share ($19,738 million divided by 573.2 million shares). On that same date, IBM stock had a market price of $56.50. Would it be fair to say IBM stock was overpriced?

The book value is the result of applying a set of arbitrary accounting rules to spread the acquisition cost of assets over a specified number of years, whereas the market price of a stock takes account of the firm's value as a going concern. In other words, the market price reflects the present value of its expected future cash flows. It would be unusual if the market price of IBM stock were exactly equal to its book value.

Can book value represent a "floor" for the stock's price, below which level the market price can never fall? Although IBM's book value per share on December 31, 1993, was less than its market price, other evidence disproves this notion. On the same date, Digital Equipment Corp. stock had a book value of $36.19 per share and a market price of $34.25. Clearly, book value cannot always be a floor for the stock's price.

A better measure of a floor for the stock price is the **liquidation value** per share of the firm. This represents the amount of money that could be realized by breaking up the firm, selling its assets, repaying its debt, and distributing the remainder to the shareholders. The reasoning behind this concept is that if the market price of equity drops below the liquidation value of the firm, the firm becomes attractive as a takeover target. A corporate raider would find it profitable to buy enough shares to gain control and then actually to liquidate, because the liquidation value exceeds the value of the business as a going concern.

Another balance sheet concept that is of interest in valuing a firm is the **replacement cost** of its assets less its liabilities. Some analysts believe the market value of the firm cannot get too far above its replacement cost because, if it did, competitors would try to replicate the firm. The competitive pressure of other similar firms entering the same industry would drive down the market value of all firms until they come into equality with replacement cost.

This idea is popular among economists, and the ratio of market price to replacement cost is known as **Tobin's *q*,** after the Nobel-prize-winning economist James Tobin. In the long run, according to this view, the ratio of market price to replacement cost will tend toward 1, but the evidence is that this ratio can differ significantly from 1 for very long periods of time.

Although focusing on the balance sheet can give some useful information about a firm's liquidation value or its replacement cost, the analyst must usually turn to expected future cash flows for a better estimate of the firm's value as a going concern. We now examine the quantitative models that analysts use to value common stock in terms of the future earnings and dividends the firm will yield.

17.2 Intrinsic Value versus Market Price

The most popular model for assessing the value of a firm as a going concern takes off from the observation that an investor in stock expects a return consisting of cash dividends and capital gains or losses. We begin by assuming a one-year holding period and supposing that ABC stock has an expected dividend per share, $E(D_1)$, of \$4, the current price of a share, P_0, is \$48, and the expected price at the end of a year, $E(P_1)$, is \$52.

The holding-period return the investor expects is $E(D_1)$ plus the expected price appreciation, $E(P_1) - P_0$, all divided by the current price P_0:

$$\begin{aligned} \text{Expected HPR} &= E(r) \\ &= \frac{E(D_1) + [E(P_1) - P_0]}{P_0} \\ &= \frac{4 + (52 - 48)}{48} = .167 = 16.7\% \end{aligned}$$

Note that $E(\,)$ denotes an expected future value. Thus, $E(P_1)$ represents the expectation today of the stock price one year from now. $E(r)$ is referred to as the stock's expected holding-period return. It is the sum of the expected dividend yield, $E(D_1)/P_0$, and the expected rate of price appreciation, the capital gains yield, $[E(P_1) - P_0]/P_0$.

But what is the investor's *required* rate of return on the stock? From the CAPM we know that the required rate, k, is equal to $r_f + \beta[E(r_M - r_f]$. Suppose $r_f = 6\%$, $\beta = 1.2$, and $E(r_M) - r_f = 5\%$. Then then value of k is

$$k = 6\% + 1.2 \times 5\% = 12\%$$

The rate of return the investor expects exceeds the required rate based on ABC's risk by a margin of 4.7%. Naturally, the investor will want to include more of ABC stock in the portfolio than a passive strategy would indicate.

Another way to see this is to compare the intrinsic value of a share of stock to its market price. The **intrinsic value,** denoted V_0, of a share of stock is defined as the present value of all cash payments to the investor in the stock, including dividends as well as the proceeds from the ultimate sale of the stock, discounted at the appropriate risk-adjusted interest rate, k. Whenever the intrinsic value, or the investor's own estimate of what the stock is really worth, exceeds the market price, the stock is considered undervalued and a good investment. In the case of ABC, using a one-year investment horizon and a forecast that the stock can be sold at the end of the year at price $P_1 =$ \$52, the intrinsic value is

$$V_0 = \frac{E(D_1) + E(P_1)}{1 + k} = \frac{\$4 + \$52}{1.12} = \$50$$

Because intrinsic value, \$50, exceeds current price, \$48, we conclude the stock is undervalued in the market. We again conclude investors will want to buy more ABC than they would following a passive strategy.

If the intrinsic value turns out to be lower than the current market price, investors should buy less of it than under the passive strategy. It might even pay to go short on ABC stock as we discussed in Chapter 3.

In market equilibrium, the current market price will reflect the intrinsic value estimates of all market participants. This means the individual investor whose V_0 estimate differs from the market price, P_0, in effect must disagree with some or all of the market consensus estimates of $E(D_1)$, $E(P_1)$, or k. A common term for the market consensus value of the required rate of return, k, is the **market capitalization rate,** which we use often throughout this chapter.

CONCEPT CHECK

Question 1. You expect the price of IBX stock to be \$59.77 per share a year from now. Its current market price is \$50, and you expect it to pay a dividend one year from now of \$2.15 per share.

a. What is the stock's expected dividend yield, rate of price appreciation, and holding-period return?

b. If the stock has a beta of 1.15, the risk-free rate is 6% per year, and the expected rate of return on the market portfolio is 14% per year, what is the required rate of return on IBX stock?

c. What is the intrinsic value of IBX stock, and how does it compare to the current market price?

17.3 DIVIDEND DISCOUNT MODELS

Consider an investor who buys a share of Steady State Electronics stock, planning to hold it for one year. The intrinsic value of the share is the present value of the dividend to be received at the end of the first year, D_1, and the expected sales price, P_1. We will henceforth use the simpler notation P_1 instead of $E(P_1)$ to avoid clutter. Keep in mind, though, that future prices and dividends are unknown, and we are dealing with expected values, not certain values. We've already established

$$V_0 = \frac{D_1 + P_1}{1 + k} \tag{17.1}$$

Although this year's dividends are fairly predictable given a company's history, you might ask how we can estimate P_1, the year-end price. According to equation 17.1, V_1 (the year-end intrinsic value) will be

$$V_1 = \frac{D_2 + P_2}{1 + k}$$

If we assume the stock will be selling for its intrinsic value next year, then $V_1 = P_1$, and we can substitute this value for P_1 into equation 17.1 to find

$$V_0 = \frac{D_1}{1 + k} + \frac{D_2 + P_2}{(1 + k)^2}$$

This equation may be interpreted as the present value of dividends plus sales price for a two-year holding period. Of course, now we need to come up with a forecast of P_2. Continuing in the same way, we can replace P_2 by $(D_3 + P_3)/(1 + k)$, which relates

P_0 to the value of dividends plus the expected sales price for a three-year holding period.

More generally, for a holding period of H years, we can write the stock value as the present value of dividends over the H years, plus the ultimate sale price, P_H.

$$V_0 = \frac{D_1}{1+k} + \frac{D_2}{(1+k)^2} + \cdots + \frac{D_H + P_H}{(1+k)^H} \qquad (17.2)$$

Note the similarity between this formula and the bond valuation formula developed in Chapter 13. Each relates price to the present value of a stream of payments (coupons in the case of bonds, dividends in the case of stocks) and a final payment (the face value of the bond, or the sales price of the stock). The key differences in the case of stocks are the uncertainty of dividends, the lack of a fixed maturity date, and the unknown sales price at the horizon date. Indeed, one can continue to substitute for price indefinitely to conclude.

$$V_0 = \frac{D_1}{1+k} + \frac{D_2}{(1+k)^2} + \frac{D_3}{(1+k)^3} + \cdots \qquad (17.3)$$

Equation 17.3 states that the stock price should equal the present value of all expected future dividends into perpetuity. This formula is called the **dividend discount model (DDM)** of stock prices.

It is tempting, but incorrect, to conclude from equation 17.3 that the DDM focuses exclusively on dividends and ignores capital gains as a motive for investing in stock. Indeed, we assume explicitly in equation 17.1 that capital gains (as reflected in the expected sales price, P_1) are part of the stock's value. At the same time, the price at which you can sell a stock in the future depends on dividend forecasts at that time.

The reason only dividends appear in equation 17.3 is not that investors ignore capital gains. It is instead that those capital gains will be determined by dividend forecasts at the time the stock is sold. That is why in equation 17.2 we can write the stock price as the present value of dividends plus sales price for *any* horizon date. P_H is the present value at time H of all dividends expected to be paid after the horizon date. That value is then discounted back to today, time 0. The DDM asserts that stock prices are determined ultimately by the cash flows accruing to stockholders, and those are dividends.[1]

The Constant Growth DDM

Equation 17.3 as it stands is still not very useful in valuing a stock because it requires dividend forecasts for every year into the indefinite future. To make the DDM practical, we need to introduce some simplifying assumptions. A useful and common first pass at the problem is to assume that dividends are trending upward at a stable growth rate that we will call g. Then if $g = .05$, and the most recently paid dividend was $D_0 =$ 3.81, expected future dividends are

---

[1] If investors never expected a dividend to be paid, then this model implies that the stock would have no value. To reconcile the fact that nondividend-paying stocks do have a market value with this model, one must assume that investors expect that some day it may pay out some cash, even if only a liquidating dividend.

$$D_1 = D_0(1+g) = 3.81 \times 1.05 = 4.00$$
$$D_2 = D_0(1+g)^2 = 3.81 \times (1.05)^2 = 4.20$$
$$D_3 = D_0(1+g)^3 = 3.81 \times (1.05)^3 = 4.41 \text{ etc.}$$

Using these dividend forecasts in equation 17.3, we solve for intrinsic value as

$$V_0 = \frac{D_0(1+g)}{1+k} + \frac{D_0(1+g)^2}{(1+k)^2} + \frac{D_0(1+g)^3}{(1+k)^3} + \cdots$$

This equation can be simplified to[2]

$$V_0 = \frac{D_0(1+g)}{k-g} = \frac{D_1}{k-g} \quad \textbf{(17.4)}$$

Note in equation 17.4 that we divide D_1 (not D_0) by $k - g$ to calculate intrinsic value. If the market capitalization rate for Steady State is 12%, now we can use equation 17.4 to show that the intrinsic value of a share of Steady State stock is

$$\frac{\$4.00}{.12 - .05} = \$57.14$$

Equation 17.4 is called the **constant growth DDM** or the Gordon model, after Myron J. Gordon, who popularized the model. It should remind you of the formula for the present value of a perpetuity. If dividends were expected not to grow, then the dividend stream would be a simple perpetuity, and the valuation formula would be[3] $V_0 = D_1/k$. Equation 17.4 is a generalization of the perpetuity formula to cover the case of a *growing* perpetuity. As g increases (for a given value of D_1), the stock price also rises.

The constant growth DDM is valid only when g is less than k. If dividends were expected to grow forever at a rate faster than k, the value of the stock would be infinite. If an analyst derives an estimate of g that is greater than k, that growth rate must be

---

[2] Proof that the intrinsic value, V_0, of a stream of cash dividends growing at a constant rate, g, is equal to $\frac{D_1}{k-g}$:
By definition,

$$V_0 = \frac{D_1}{1+k} + \frac{D_1(1+g)}{(1+k)^2} + \frac{D_1(1+g)^2}{(1+k)^3} + \cdots \quad \text{(a)}$$

Multiplying through by $(1 + k)/(1 + g)$, we obtain

$$\frac{(1+k)}{(1+g)} V_0 = \frac{D_1}{(1+g)} + \frac{D_1}{(1+k)} + \frac{D_1(1+g)}{(1+k)^2} + \cdots \quad \text{(b)}$$

Subtracting equation a from equation b, we find that

$$\frac{(1+k)}{(1+g)} V_0 - V_0 = \frac{D_1}{(1+g)}$$

which implies

$$\frac{(k-g)V_0}{(1+g)} = \frac{D_1}{(1+g)}$$
$$V_0 = \frac{D_1}{k-g}$$

[3] Recall from introductory finance that the present value of a $1 per year perpetuity is $1/k$. For example, if $k = 10\%$, the value of the perpetuity is $1/.10 = $10. Notice that if $g = 0$ in equation 17.4, the constant growth DDM formula is the same as the perpetuity formula.

unsustainable in the long run. The appropriate valuation model to use in this case is a multistage DDM such as that discussed below.

The constant growth DDM is so widely used by stock market analysts that it is worth exploring some of its implications and limitations. The constant growth rate DDM implies that a stock's value will be greater:

1. The larger its expected dividend per share.
2. The lower the market capitalization rate, k.
3. The higher the expected growth rate of dividends.

Another implication of the constant growth model is that the stock price is expected to grow at the same rate as dividends. To see this, suppose Steady State stock is selling at its intrinsic value of \$57.14, so that $V_0 = P_0$. Then,

$$P_0 = \frac{D_1}{k - g}$$

Note that price is proportional to dividends. Therefore, next year, when the dividends paid to Steady State stockholders are expected to be higher by $g = 5\%$, price also should increase by 5%. To confirm this, note

$$D_2 = \$4(1.05) = \$4.20$$
$$P_1 = D_2/(k - g) = \$4.20/(.12 - .05) = \$60.00$$

which is 5% higher than the current price of \$57.14. To generalize,

$$P_1 = \frac{D_2}{k - g} = \frac{D_1(1 + g)}{k - g} = \frac{D_1}{k - g}(1 + g)$$
$$= P_0(1 + g)$$

Therefore, the DDM implies that in the case of constant growth of dividends, the rate of price appreciation in any year will equal that constant growth rate, g. Note that for a stock whose market price equals its intrinsic value ($V_0 = P_0$) the expected holding-period return will be

$$E(r) = \text{Dividend yield} + \text{Capital gains yield} \tag{17.5}$$
$$= \frac{D_1}{P_0} + \frac{P_1 - P_0}{P_0} = \frac{D_1}{P_0} + g$$

This formula offers a means to infer the market capitalization rate of a stock, for if the stock is selling at its intrinsic value, then $E(r) = k$, implying that $k = D_1/P_0 + g$. By observing the dividend yield, D_1/P_0, and estimating the growth rate of dividends, we can compute k. This equation is also known as the *discounted cash flow (DCF) formula*.

This is an approach often used in rate hearings for regulated public utilities. The regulatory agency responsible for approving utility pricing decisions is mandated to allow the firms to charge just enough to cover costs plus a "fair" profit, that is, one that allows a competitive return on the investment the firm has made in its productive capacity. In turn, that return is taken to be the expected return investors require on the stock of the firm. The $D_1/P_0 + g$ formula provides a means to infer that required return.

CONCEPT CHECK

Question 2.

a. IBX's stock dividend at the end of this year is expected to be \$2.15, and it is expected to grow at 11.2% per year forever. If the required rate of return on IBX stock is 15.2% per year, what is its intrinsic value?

b. If IBX's current market price is equal to this intrinsic value, what is next year's expected price?

c. If an investor were to buy IBX stock now and sell it after receiving the \$2.15 dividend a year from now, what is the expected capital gain (i.e., price appreciation) in percentage terms? What is the dividend yield, and what would be the holding-period return?

Convergence of Price to Intrinsic Value

Now suppose that the current market price of ABC stock is only \$48 per share and, therefore, that the stock now is undervalued by \$2 per share. In this case the expected rate of price appreciation depends on an additional assumption about whether the discrepancy between the intrinsic value and the market price will disappear, and if so, when.

One fairly common assumption is that the discrepancy will never disappear and that the market price will continue to grow at rate g forever. This implies that the discrepancy between intrinsic value and market price also will grow at the same rate. In our example:

Now	Next Year
$V_0 = \$50$	$V_1 = \$50 \times 1.04 = \$52$
$P_0 = \$48$	$P_1 = \$48 \times 1.04 = \$49.92$
$V_0 - P_0 = \$2$	$V_1 - P_1 = \$2 \times 1.04 = \$2.08$

Under this assumption the expected HPR will exceed the required rate, because the dividend yield is higher than it would be if P_0 were equal to V_0. In our example the dividend yield would be 8.33% instead of 8% so that the expected HPR would be $12^1/_3\%$ rather than 12%.

$$E(r) = \frac{D_1}{P_0} + g = \frac{\$4}{\$48} + .04 = .0833 + .04 = .1233$$

An investor who identifies this undervalued stock can get an expected dividend that exceeds the required yield by 33 basis points. This excess return is earned each year, and the market price never catches up to intrinsic value.

A second possible assumption is that the gap between market price and intrinsic value will disappear by the end of the year. In that case we would have $P_1 = V_1 = \$52$, and

$$E(r) = \frac{D_1}{P_0} + \frac{P_1 - P_0}{P_0} = \frac{4}{48} + \frac{52 - 48}{48} = .0833 + .0833 = .1667$$

The assumption of complete catch-up to intrinsic value produces a much larger one-year HPR. In future years the stock is expected to generate only fair rates of return.

Many stock analysts assume that a stock's price will approach its intrinsic value gradually over time—for example, over a five-year period. This puts their expected one-year HPR somewhere between the bounds of $12^1/_3\%$ and $16^2/_3\%$.

Stock Prices and Investment Opportunities

Consider two companies, Cash Cow, Inc., and Growth Prospects, each with expected earnings in the coming year of \$5 per share. Both companies could in principle pay out all of these earnings as dividends, maintaining a perpetual dividend flow of \$5 per share. If the market capitalization rate were $k = 12.5\%$, both companies would then be valued at $D_1/k = \$5/.125 = \$40$ per share. Neither firm would grow in value, because with all earnings paid out as dividends, and no earnings reinvested in the firm, both companies' capital stock and earnings capacity would remain unchanged over time; earnings and dividends would not grow.

Actually, we are referring here to earnings net of the funds necessary to maintain the productivity of the firm's capital, that is, earnings net of "economic depreciation." In other words, the earnings figure should be interpreted as the maximum amount of money the firm could pay out each year in perpetuity without depleting its productive capacity. For this reason, the net earnings number may be quite different from the accounting earnings figure that the firm reports in its financial statements. (We explore this further in the next chapter.)

Now suppose one of the firms, Growth Prospects, engages in projects that generate a return on investment of 15%, which is greater than the required rate of return, $k = 12.5\%$. It would be foolish for such a company to pay out all of its earnings as dividends. If Growth Prospects retains or plows back some of its earnings into its highly profitable projects, it can earn a 15% rate of return for its shareholders, whereas if it pays out all earnings as dividends, it forgoes the projects, leaving shareholders to invest the dividends in other opportunities at a fair market rate of only 12.5%. Suppose, therefore, that Growth Prospects lowers its **dividend payout ratio** (the fraction of earnings paid out as dividends) from 100% to 40%, maintaining a **plowback ratio** (the fraction of earnings reinvested in the firm) at 60%. The plowback ratio is also referred to as the **earnings retention ratio.**

The dividend of the company, therefore, will be \$2 (40% of \$5 earnings) instead of \$5. Will share price fall? No—it will rise! Although dividends initially fall under the earnings reinvestment policy, subsequent growth in the assets of the firm because of reinvested profits will generate growth in future dividends, which will be reflected in today's share price.

Figure 17.1 illustrates the dividend streams generated by Growth Prospects under two dividend policies. A low investment rate plan allows the firm to pay higher initial dividends, but results in a lower dividend growth rate. Eventually, a high reinvestment rate plan will provide higher dividends. If the dividend growth generated by the reinvested earnings is high enough, the stock will be worth more under the high reinvestment strategy.

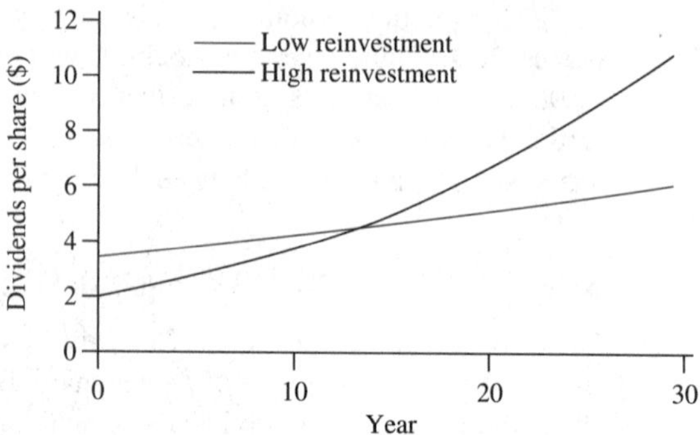

Figure 17.1
Dividend growth for two earnings reinvestment policies

How much growth will be generated? Suppose Growth Prospects starts with plant and equipment of \$100 million and is all equity financed. With a return on investment or equity (ROE) of 15%, total earnings are ROE × \$100 million = .15 × \$100 million = \$15 million. There are 3 million shares of stock outstanding, so earnings per share are \$5, as posited above. If 60% of the \$15 million in this year's earnings is reinvested, then the value of the firm's capital stock will increase by 0.60 × \$15 million = \$9 million, or by 9%. The percentage increase in the capital stock is the rate at which income was generated (ROE) times the plowback ratio (the fraction of earnings reinvested in more capital), which we will denote as b.

Now endowed with 9% more capital, the company earns 9% more income, and pays out 9% higher dividends. The growth rate of the dividends, therefore, is

$$g = \text{ROE} \times b = .15 \times .60 = .09$$

If the stock price equals its intrinsic value, it should sell at

$$P_0 = \frac{D_1}{k - g} = \frac{\$2}{.125 - .09} = \$57.14$$

When Growth Prospects pursued a no-growth policy and paid out all earnings as dividends, the stock price was only \$40. When it reduced current dividends and plowed funds back into the company, the growth rate increased enough to cause the stock price to increase.

The difference between the no-growth price of \$40 and the actual price of \$57.14 can be ascribed to the present value of the company's excellent investment opportunities. One way to think of the company's value is to describe its stock price as the sum of the no-growth value (the value of current earnings per share, E_1, in perpetuity) plus the present value of these growth opportunities, which we will denote as PVGO. In terms of the example we have been following, PVGO = 17.14:

$$\text{Price} = \text{No-growth value per share} + \text{PVGO} \qquad \textbf{(17.6)}$$

$$P_0 = \frac{E_1}{k} + \text{PVGO}$$

$$57.14 = 40 + 17.14$$

It is important to recognize that growth per se is not what investors desire. Growth enhances company value only if it is achieved by investment in projects with attractive profit opportunities (i.e., with ROE > k). To see why, let's now consider Growth Prospects's unfortunate sister company, Cash Cow, Inc. Cash Cow's ROE is only 12.5%, just equal to the required rate of return, k. The NPV of its investment opportunities is zero. We've seen that following a zero-growth strategy with $b = 0$ and $g = 0$, the value of Cash Cow will be $E_1/k = \$5/.125 = \$40$ per share. Now suppose Cash Cow chooses a plowback ratio of $b = .60$, the same as Growth Prospects's plowback. Then g would increase to

$$g = \text{ROE} \times b$$
$$= .125 \times 0.60 = 0.075$$

but the stock price is still

$$P_0 = \frac{D_1}{k - g} = \frac{\$2}{.125 - .075} = \$40$$

no different from the no-growth strategy.

In the case of Cash Cow, the dividend reduction used to free funds for reinvestment in the firm generates only enough growth to maintain the stock price at the current level. This is as it should be: If the firm's projects yield only what investors can earn on their own, shareholders cannot be made better off by a high reinvestment rate policy. This demonstrates that "growth" is not the same as growth opportunities. To justify reinvestment, the firm must engage in projects with better prospective returns than those shareholders can find elsewhere. Notice also that the PVGO of Cash Cow is zero: $\text{PVGO} = P_0 - E_1/k = 40 - 40 = 0$. With ROE $= k$, there is no advantage to plowing funds back into the firm; this shows up as PVGO of zero. In fact, this is why firms with considerable cash flow, but limited investment prospects are called "cash cows." The cash these firms generate is best taken out of or "milked from" the firm.

CONCEPT CHECK

Question 3. Calculate the price of a firm with a plowback ratio of 0.60 if its ROE is 20%. Current earnings, E_1, will be \$5 per share, and $k = 12.5\%$. Find the PVGO for this firm. Why is PVGO so high?

Question 4. Takeover Target is run by entrenched and incompetent management that insists on reinvesting 60% of its earnings in projects that provide an ROE of 10%, despite the fact that the firm's capitalization rate is $k = 15\%$. The firm's year-end dividend will be \$2 per share, paid out of earnings of \$5 per share. At what price will the stock sell? What is the present value of growth opportunities? Why would such a firm be a target for a takeover by another firm?

Life Cycles and Multistage Growth Models

As useful as the constant growth DDM formula is, you need to remember that it is based on a simplifying assumption, namely, that the dividend growth rate will be constant forever. In fact, firms typically pass through life cycles with very different dividend profiles in different phases. In early years, there are ample opportunities for

Table 17.2 Financial Ratios in Two Industries

	Return on Assets (%)	Payout Ratio (%)	Growth Rate 1994–97 (%)
Semiconductors			
Analog Devices	13.0	0.0	22.1
Cirrus Logic	14.5	0.0	15.5
Intel	19.0	11.0	2.4
Micron Technologies	13.5	5.0	10.7
Motorola	11.5	19.0	9.5
National Semiconductor	13.0	16.5	6.3
Novellus	14.0	0.0	13.4
Teradyne	9.5	0.0	4.0
Texas Instruments	12.0	27.0	4.6
Average	13.3	8.7	9.8
Electric Utilities			
Boston Edison	8.0	75.0	3.3
Central Maine Power	7.5	77.0	1.3
Central Vermont	9.0	79.0	4.6
Commonwealth Energy	7.5	77.0	2.0
Consolidated Edison	8.0	76.0	2.0
Eastern Utilities	8.0	65.0	5.1
Long Island Lighting	6.0	78.0	4.2
New England Electric	7.5	79.0	2.6
Northeastern Utilities	7.0	82.0	0.0
Average	7.6	76.4	2.8

Source: Value Line Investment Survey, 1993.

profitable reinvestment in the company. Payout ratios are low, and growth is correspondingly rapid. In later years, the firm matures, production capacity is sufficient to meet market demand, competitors enter the market, and attractive opportunities for reinvestment may become harder to find. In this mature phase, the firm may choose to increase the dividend payout ratio, rather than retain earnings. The dividend level increases, but thereafter grows at a slower rate because of fewer growth opportunities.

Table 17.2 demonstrates this profile. It gives Value Line's forecasts of return on assets, dividend payout ratio, and three-year growth rate in earnings per share of a sample of the firms included in the semiconductor industry versus those in the northeast region electric utility group. (We compare return on assets rather than return on equity because the latter is affected by leverage, which tends to be far greater in the electric utility industry than in the semiconductor industry. Return on assets measures operating income per dollar of total assets, regardless of whether the source of the capital supplied is debt or equity. We will return to this issue in the next chapter.)

The semiconductor firms as a group have had attractive investment opportunities. The average return on assets of these firms is forecast to be 13.3%, and the firms have responded with quite high plowback ratios. Many of these firms pay no dividends at all. The high return on assets and high plowback result in rapid growth. The average growth rate of earnings per share in this group is projected at 9.8%.

In contrast, the electric utilities are more representative of mature firms. Their return on assets is lower, 7.6%; dividend payout is higher, 76.4%; and average growth is lower, 2.8%.

To value companies with temporarily high growth, analysts use a multistage version of the dividend discount model. Dividends in the early high-growth period are forecast and their combined present value calculated. Then, once the firm is projected to settle down to a steady growth phase, the constant growth DDM is applied to value the remaining stream of dividends.

We can illustrate this with a real-life example. Figure 17.2 is a Value Line Investment Survey report on Motorola, a designer and manufacturer of electronic equipment and components. Some of the relevant information in mid-1993 is highlighted.

Motorola's beta appears at the circled A, the recent stock price at the B, the per share dividend payments at the C, the ROE (referred to as percent earned on net worth) at the D, and the dividend payout ratio (referred to as percent of all dividends to net profits) at the E. The rows ending at C, D, and E are historical time series. The bold-faced italicized entries under 1994 are estimates for that year. Similarly, the entries in the far right column (labeled 96–98) are forecasts for some time between 1996 and 1998, which we will take to be 1997.

Note that while dividends were \$.54 per share in 1994, dividends forecast for 1997 are \$.90; hence, Value Line forecasts rapid short-term growth in dividends, nearly 20% per year. If we use linear interpolation between 1994 and 1997, we obtain dividend forecasts as follows:

1994	\$.54
1995	\$.66
1996	\$.78
1997	\$.90

Now let us assume the dividend growth rate levels off in 1997. What is a good guess for that steady-state growth rate? Value Line forecasts a dividend payout ratio of 0.18 and an ROE of 14.0%, implying that long-term growth will be

$$g = \text{ROE} \times b = 14\% \times (1 - .18) = 11.5\%$$

Our estimate of Motorola's intrinsic value using an investment horizon of 1997 is therefore obtained from equation 17.2, which we restate here

$$V_{1993} = \frac{D_{1994}}{(1+k)} + \frac{D_{1995}}{(1+k)^2} + \frac{D_{1996}}{(1+k)^3} + \frac{D_{1997} + P_{1997}}{(1+k)^4}$$

$$= \frac{.54}{(1+k)} + \frac{.66}{(1+k)^2} + \frac{.78}{(1+k)^3} + \frac{.90 + P_{1997}}{(1+k)^4}$$

Here, P_{1997} represents the forecasted price at which we can sell our shares of Motorola at the end of 1997, when dividends enter their constant growth phase. That price, according to the constant growth DDM, should be

Figure 17.2 Value Line Investment Survey report on Motorola

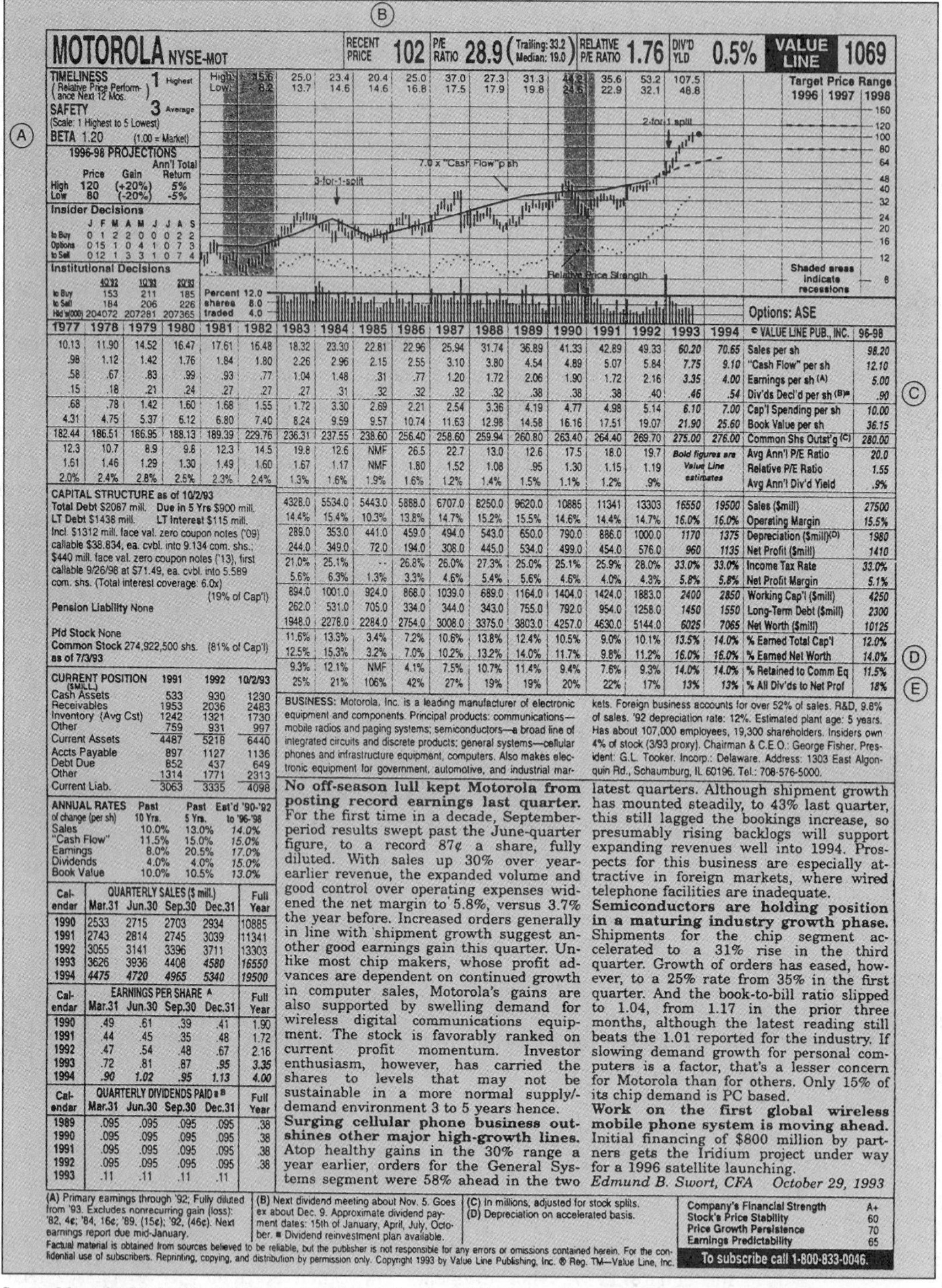

MOTOROLA NYSE-MOT | RECENT PRICE 102 | P/E RATIO 28.9 (Trailing: 33.2 Median: 19.0) | RELATIVE P/E RATIO 1.76 | DIV'D YLD 0.5% | VALUE LINE 1069

TIMELINESS 1 Highest (Relative Price Performance Next 12 Mos.)
SAFETY 3 Average (Scale: 1 Highest to 5 Lowest)
BETA 1.20 (1.00 = Market)

1996-98 PROJECTIONS	Price	Gain	Ann'l Total Return
High	120	(+20%)	5%
Low	80	(-20%)	-5%

Insider Decisions	J	F	M	A	M	J	J	A	S
to Buy	0	1	2	2	0	0	0	2	2
Options	0	15	1	0	4	1	0	7	3
to Sell	0	12	1	3	3	1	0	7	4

Institutional Decisions	4Q'92	1Q'93	2Q'93
to Buy	153	211	185
to Sell	184	206	226
Hld's(000)	204072	207281	207365

High: 15.6 25.0 23.4 20.4 25.0 37.0 27.3 31.3 44.2 35.6 53.2 107.5
Low: 8.2 13.7 14.6 14.6 16.8 17.5 17.9 19.8 24.5 22.9 32.1 48.8

Target Price Range 1996 | 1997 | 1998

3-for-1-split
7.0 x "Cash Flow" p sh
2-for-1 split
Relative Price Strength
Percent shares traded 12.0 8.0 4.0
Shaded areas indicate recessions
Options: ASE

1977	1978	1979	1980	1981	1982	1983	1984	1985	1986	1987	1988	1989	1990	1991	1992	1993	1994	© VALUE LINE PUB., INC.	96-98
10.13	11.90	14.52	16.47	17.61	16.48	18.32	23.30	22.81	22.96	25.94	31.74	36.89	41.33	42.89	49.33	*60.20*	*70.65*	Sales per sh	*98.20*
.98	1.12	1.42	1.76	1.84	1.80	2.26	2.96	2.15	2.55	3.10	3.80	4.54	4.89	5.07	5.84	*7.75*	*9.10*	"Cash Flow" per sh	*12.10*
.58	.67	.83	.99	.93	.77	1.04	1.48	.31	.77	1.20	1.72	2.06	1.90	1.72	2.16	*3.35*	*4.00*	Earnings per sh (A)	*5.00*
.15	.18	.21	.24	.27	.27	.27	.31	.32	.32	.32	.32	.38	.38	.38	.40	*.46*	*.54*	Div'ds Decl'd per sh (B)■	*.90*
.68	.78	1.42	1.60	1.68	1.55	1.72	3.30	2.69	2.21	2.54	3.36	4.19	4.77	4.98	5.14	*6.10*	*7.00*	Cap'l Spending per sh	*10.00*
4.31	4.75	5.37	6.12	6.80	7.40	8.24	9.59	9.57	10.74	11.63	12.98	14.58	16.16	17.51	19.07	*21.90*	*25.60*	Book Value per sh	*36.15*
182.44	186.51	186.95	188.13	189.39	229.76	236.31	237.55	238.60	256.40	258.60	259.94	260.80	263.40	264.40	269.70	*275.00*	*276.00*	Common Shs Outst'g (C)	*280.00*
12.3	10.7	8.9	9.8	12.3	14.5	19.8	12.6	NMF	26.5	22.7	13.0	12.6	17.5	18.0	19.7	*Bold figures are*		Avg Ann'l P/E Ratio	*20.0*
1.61	1.46	1.29	1.30	1.49	1.60	1.67	1.17	NMF	1.80	1.52	1.08	.95	1.30	1.15	1.19	*Value Line*		Relative P/E Ratio	*1.55*
2.0%	2.4%	2.8%	2.5%	2.3%	2.4%	1.3%	1.6%	1.9%	1.6%	1.2%	1.4%	1.5%	1.1%	1.2%	.9%	*estimates*		Avg Ann'l Div'd Yield	*.9%*

1983	1984	1985	1986	1987	1988	1989	1990	1991	1992	1993	1994		96-98
4328.0	5534.0	5443.0	5888.0	6707.0	8250.0	9620.0	10885	11341	13303	*16550*	*19500*	Sales ($mill)	*27500*
14.4%	15.4%	10.3%	13.8%	14.7%	15.2%	15.5%	14.6%	14.4%	14.7%	*16.0%*	*16.0%*	Operating Margin	*15.5%*
289.0	353.0	441.0	459.0	494.0	543.0	650.0	790.0	886.0	1000.0	*1170*	*1375*	Depreciation ($mill)(D)	*1980*
244.0	349.0	72.0	194.0	308.0	445.0	534.0	499.0	454.0	576.0	*960*	*1135*	Net Profit ($mill)	*1410*
21.0%	25.1%	--	26.8%	26.0%	27.3%	25.0%	25.1%	25.9%	28.0%	*33.0%*	*33.0%*	Income Tax Rate	*33.0%*
5.6%	6.3%	1.3%	3.3%	4.6%	5.4%	5.6%	4.6%	4.0%	4.3%	*5.8%*	*5.8%*	Net Profit Margin	*5.1%*
894.0	1001.0	924.0	868.0	1039.0	689.0	1164.0	1404.0	1424.0	1883.0	*2400*	*2850*	Working Cap'l ($mill)	*4250*
262.0	531.0	705.0	334.0	344.0	343.0	755.0	792.0	954.0	1258.0	*1450*	*1550*	Long-Term Debt ($mill)	*2300*
1948.0	2278.0	2284.0	2754.0	3008.0	3375.0	3803.0	4257.0	4630.0	5144.0	*6025*	*7065*	Net Worth ($mill)	*10125*
11.6%	13.3%	3.4%	7.2%	10.6%	13.8%	12.4%	10.5%	9.0%	10.1%	*13.5%*	*14.0%*	% Earned Total Cap'l	*12.0%*
12.5%	15.3%	3.2%	7.0%	10.2%	13.2%	14.0%	11.7%	9.8%	11.2%	*16.0%*	*16.0%*	% Earned Net Worth	*14.0%*
9.3%	12.1%	NMF	4.1%	7.5%	10.7%	11.4%	9.4%	7.6%	9.3%	*14.0%*	*14.0%*	% Retained to Comm Eq	*11.5%*
25%	21%	106%	42%	27%	19%	19%	20%	22%	17%	*13%*	*13%*	% All Div'ds to Net Prof	*18%*

CAPITAL STRUCTURE as of 10/2/93
Total Debt $2087 mill. Due in 5 Yrs $900 mill.
LT Debt $1438 mill. LT Interest $115 mill.
Incl. $1312 mill. face val. zero coupon notes ('09) callable $38.834, ea. cvbl. into 9.134 com. shs.; $440 mill. face val. zero coupon notes ('13), first callable 9/26/98 at $71.49, ea. cvbl. into 5.589 com. shs. (Total interest coverage: 6.0x) (19% of Cap'l)

Pension Liability None

Pfd Stock None
Common Stock 274,922,500 shs. (81% of Cap'l) as of 7/3/93

CURRENT POSITION ($MILL.)	1991	1992	10/2/93
Cash Assets	533	930	1230
Receivables	1953	2036	2483
Inventory (Avg Cst)	1242	1321	1730
Other	759	931	997
Current Assets	4487	5218	6440
Accts Payable	897	1127	1136
Debt Due	852	437	649
Other	1314	1771	2313
Current Liab.	3063	3335	4098

ANNUAL RATES of change (per sh)	Past 10 Yrs.	Past 5 Yrs.	Est'd '90-'92 to '96-'98
Sales	10.0%	13.0%	*14.0%*
"Cash Flow"	11.5%	15.0%	*15.0%*
Earnings	8.0%	20.5%	*17.0%*
Dividends	4.0%	4.0%	*15.0%*
Book Value	10.0%	10.5%	*13.0%*

Calendar	QUARTERLY SALES ($ mill.) Mar.31	Jun.30	Sep.30	Dec.31	Full Year
1990	2533	2715	2703	2934	10885
1991	2743	2814	2745	3039	11341
1992	3055	3141	3396	3711	13303
1993	3626	3936	4408	*4580*	*16550*
1994	*4475*	*4720*	*4965*	*5340*	*19500*

Calendar	EARNINGS PER SHARE A Mar.31	Jun.30	Sep.30	Dec.31	Full Year
1990	.49	.61	.39	.41	1.90
1991	.44	.45	.35	.48	1.72
1992	.47	.54	.48	.67	2.16
1993	.72	.81	.87	*.95*	*3.35*
1994	*.90*	*1.02*	*.95*	*1.13*	*4.00*

Calendar	QUARTERLY DIVIDENDS PAID ■ B Mar.31	Jun.30	Sep.30	Dec.31	Full Year
1989	.095	.095	.095	.095	.38
1990	.095	.095	.095	.095	.38
1991	.095	.095	.095	.095	.38
1992	.095	.095	.095	.095	.38
1993	.11	.11	.11	.11	

BUSINESS: Motorola, Inc. is a leading manufacturer of electronic equipment and components. Principal products: communications—mobile radios and paging systems; semiconductors—a broad line of integrated circuits and discrete products; general systems—cellular phones and infrastructure equipment, computers. Also makes electronic equipment for government, automotive, and industrial markets. Foreign business accounts for over 52% of sales. R&D, 9.8% of sales. '92 depreciation rate: 12%. Estimated plant age: 5 years. Has about 107,000 employees, 19,300 shareholders. Insiders own 4% of stock (3/93 proxy). Chairman & C.E.O.: George Fisher. President: G.L. Tooker. Incorp.: Delaware. Address: 1303 East Algonquin Rd., Schaumburg, IL 60196. Tel.: 708-576-5000.

No off-season lull kept Motorola from posting record earnings last quarter. For the first time in a decade, September-period results swept past the June-quarter figure, to a record 87¢ a share, fully diluted. With sales up 30% over year-earlier revenue, the expanded volume and good control over operating expenses widened the net margin to 5.8%, versus 3.7% the year before. Increased orders generally in line with shipment growth suggest another good earnings gain this quarter. Unlike most chip makers, whose profit advances are dependent on continued growth in computer sales, Motorola's gains are also supported by swelling demand for wireless digital communications equipment. The stock is favorably ranked on current profit momentum. Investor enthusiasm, however, has carried the shares to levels that may not be sustainable in a more normal supply/-demand environment 3 to 5 years hence.

Surging cellular phone business outshines other major high-growth lines. Atop healthy gains in the 30% range a year earlier, orders for the General Systems segment were 58% ahead in the two latest quarters. Although shipment growth has mounted steadily, to 43% last quarter, this still lagged the bookings increase, so presumably rising backlogs will support expanding revenues well into 1994. Prospects for this business are especially attractive in foreign markets, where wired telephone facilities are inadequate.

Semiconductors are holding position in a maturing industry growth phase. Shipments for the chip segment accelerated to a 31% rise in the third quarter. Growth of orders has eased, however, to a 25% rate from 35% in the first quarter. And the book-to-bill ratio slipped to 1.04, from 1.17 in the prior three months, although the latest reading still beats the 1.01 reported for the industry. If slowing demand growth for personal computers is a factor, that's a lesser concern for Motorola than for others. Only 15% of its chip demand is PC based.

Work on the first global wireless mobile phone system is moving ahead. Initial financing of $800 million by partners gets the Iridium project under way for a 1996 satellite launching.

Edmund B. Swort, CFA October 29, 1993

(A) Primary earnings through '92; Fully diluted from '93. Excludes nonrecurring gain (loss): '82, 4¢; '84, 16¢; '89, (15¢); '92, (46¢). Next earnings report due mid-January.
(B) Next dividend meeting about Nov. 5. Goes ex about Dec. 9. Approximate dividend payment dates: 15th of January, April, July, October. ■ Dividend reinvestment plan available.
(C) In millions, adjusted for stock splits.
(D) Depreciation on accelerated basis.

Company's Financial Strength	A+
Stock's Price Stability	60
Price Growth Persistence	70
Earnings Predictability	65

Source: Motorola, October 29, 1993. Copyright 1995 by Value Line Publishing, Inc. Reprinted by permission. All Rights Reserved.

$$P_{1997} = \frac{D_{1998}}{k - g} = \frac{D_{1997}(1 + g)}{k - g} = \frac{.90(1.115)}{k - .115}$$

The only variable remaining to be determined in order to calculate intrinsic value is the market capitalization rate, k.

One way to obtain k is from the CAPM. Observe from the Value Line data that Motorola's beta is 1.20. The risk-free rate in 1993 was about 3%. Suppose that the market risk premium were forecast at 7.75%.[4] This would imply that the forecast for the market return was

$$\text{Risk-free rate} + \text{market risk premium} = 3\% + 7.75\% = 10.75\%$$

Therefore, we can solve for the market capitalization rate for Motorola as

$$\begin{aligned} k &= r_f + \beta[E(r_M) - r_f] \\ &= 3\% + 1.2[10.75\% - 3\%] \\ &= 12.3\% \end{aligned}$$

Our guess for the stock price in 1997 is thus

$$P_{1997} = \frac{\$.90(1.115)}{.123 - .115} = \$125.44$$

and today's estimate of intrinsic value is

$$V_{1993} = \frac{.54}{(1.123)} + \frac{.66}{(1.123)^2} + \frac{.78}{(1.123)^3} + \frac{.90 + 125.44}{(1.123)^4} = \$80.99$$

We know from the Value Line report that Motorola's actual price was \$102 (at the circled B). Our intrinsic value analysis indicates Motorola was overpriced. Should we sell our holdings of Motorola or even sell Motorola short?

Perhaps. But before betting the farm, stop to consider how firm our estimate is. We've had to guess at dividends in the near future, the ultimate growth rate of those dividends, and the appropriate discount rate. Moreover, we've assumed Motorola will follow a relatively simple two-stage growth process. In practice, the growth of dividends can follow more complicated patterns. Even small errors in these approximations could upset a conclusion.

For example, suppose that we have underestimated Motorola's growth prospects and that the actual growth rate in the post-1997 period will be 11.8% rather than 11.5%, a change of only 0.3 percentage points. Using the higher growth rate in the dividend discount model would result in an intrinsic value in 1993 of \$128.65, which actually is greater than the stock price. Our conclusion regarding intrinsic value versus price is reversed.

This exercise shows that finding bargains is not as easy as it seems. Although the DDM is easy to apply, establishing its inputs is more of a challenge. This should not be

---

[4] The historical risk premium on the market portfolio has been closer to 8.5%. However, stock analysts in 1993 were relatively pessimistic about market performance over the short term. Although the historical risk premium is a guide as to the typical risk premium one might expect from the market, there is no reason that the risk premium cannot vary somewhat from period to period.

surprising. In even a moderately efficient market, finding profit opportunities has to be more involved than sitting down with Value Line for a half hour.

The exercise also highlights the importance of performing sensitivity analysis when you attempt to value stocks. Your estimates of stock values are no better than your assumptions. Sensitivity analysis will highlight the inputs that need to be most carefully examined. For example, we just found that very small changes in the estimated growth rate for the post-1997 period would result in big changes in intrinsic value. Similarly, small changes in the assumed capitalization rate would change intrinsic value substantially. On the other hand, reasonable changes in the dividends forecast between 1993 and 1997 would have a small impact on intrinsic value.

CONCEPT CHECK

Question 5. Confirm that the intrinsic value of Motorola using $g = 11.8\%$ is \$128.65. (Hint: First calculate the stock price in 1997. Then calculate the present value of all interim dividends plus the present value of the 1997 sales price.)

17.4 PRICE/EARNINGS RATIO

The Price/Earnings Ratio and Growth Opportunities

Much of the real-world discussion of stock market valuation concentrates on the firm's **price/earnings multiple,** the ratio of price per share to earnings per share. Our discussion of growth opportunities shows why stock market analysts focus on this multiple, commonly called the P/E ratio. Both companies considered, Cash Cow and Growth Prospects, had earnings per share (EPS) of \$5, but Growth Prospects reinvested 60% of earnings in prospects with an ROE of 15%, whereas Cash Cow paid out all earnings as dividends. Cash Cow had a price of \$40, giving it a P/E multiple of 40/5 = 8.0, whereas Growth Prospects sold for \$57.14, giving it a multiple of 57.14/5 = 11.4. This observation suggests the P/E ratio might serve as a useful indicator of expectations of growth opportunities. We can see this explicitly by rearranging equation 17.6 to

$$\frac{P_0}{E_1} = \frac{1}{k}\left[1 + \frac{\text{PVGO}}{E/k}\right] \tag{17.7}$$

When PVGO = 0, equation 17.7 shows that $P_0 = E_1/k$. The stock is valued like a nongrowing perpetuity of EPS_1. The P/E ratio is just $1/k$. However, as PVGO becomes an increasingly dominant contributor to price, the P/E ratio can rise dramatically. The ratio of PVGO to E/k has a simple interpretation. It is the ratio of the component of firm value due to growth opportunities to the component of value due to assets already in place (i.e., the no-growth value of the firm, E/k). When future growth opportunities dominate the estimate of total value, the firm will command a high price relative to current earnings. Thus, a high P/E multiple appears to indicate a firm is endowed with ample growth opportunities.

Let's see if this is so. In 1994, Motorola's P/E ratio was 25 while Boston Edison's was 9. These numbers do not necessarily imply Motorola was overpriced compared to

Boston Edison. If investors believed at the time that Motorola would grow sufficiently faster than Boston Edison, the higher P/E multiple would be justified. That is, an investor might well pay a higher price per dollar of *current* earnings if he or she expects that earnings stream to grow rapidly. In fact, Motorola's growth rate has been consistent with its higher P/E multiple. Its earnings per share grew more than eightfold between 1977 and 1994, whereas Boston Edison earnings only increased by a factor of 2.3. Figure 17.4, page 540, shows the EPS history of the two companies.

Clearly, it is differences in expected growth opportunities that justify particular differentials in P/E ratios across firms. The P/E ratio actually is a reflection of the market's optimism concerning a firm's growth prospects. In their use of a P/E ratio, analysts must decide whether they are more or less optimistic than the market. If they are more optimistic, they will recommend buying the stock.

There is a way to make these insights more precise. Look again at the constant growth DDM formula, $P_0 = D_1/(k - g)$. Now recall that dividends equal the earnings that are *not* reinvested in the firm: $D_1 = E_1(1 - b)$. Recall also that $g = \text{ROE} \times b$. Hence, substituting for D_1 and g, we find that

$$P_0 = \frac{E_1(1 - b)}{k - \text{ROE} \times b}$$

implying the P/E ratio is

$$\frac{P_0}{E_1} = \frac{(1 - b)}{k - \text{ROE} \times b} \tag{17.8}$$

It is easy to verify that the P/E ratio increases with ROE. This makes sense, because high ROE projects give the firm good opportunities for growth.[5] We also can verify that the P/E ratio increases for higher b as long as ROE exceeds k. This too makes sense. When a firm has good investment opportunities, the market will reward it with a higher P/E multiple if it exploits those opportunities more aggressively by plowing back more earnings into those opportunities.

Remember we noted, however, that growth is not desirable for its own sake. Examine Table 17.3 where we use equation 17.8 to compute both growth rates and P/E ratios for different combinations of ROE and b. Although growth always increases with the plowback rate (move across the rows in Table 17.3**A**), the P/E ratio does not (move across the rows in Panel **B**). In the top row of Table 17.3**B**, the P/E falls as the plowback rate increases. In the middle row, it is unaffected by plowback. In the third row, it increases.

This pattern has a simple interpretation. When the expected ROE is less than the required return, k, investors prefer that the firm pay out earnings as dividends rather than reinvest earnings in the firm at an inadequate rate of return. That is, for ROE lower than k, the value of the firm falls as plowback increases. Conversely, when ROE exceeds k, the firm offers superior investment opportunities, so the value of the firm is enhanced as those opportunities are more fully exploited by increasing the plowback rate.

[5] Note that equation 17.8 is a simple rearrangement of the DDM formula, with $\text{ROE} \times b = g$. Because that formula requires that $g < k$, equation 17.8 is valid only when $\text{ROE} \times b < k$.

Table 17.3 Effect of ROE and Plowback on Growth and the P/E Ratio

	Plowback Rate (*b*)			
ROE	**0**	**.25**	**.50**	**.75**
A. Growth Rate, *g*				
10%	0	2.5%	5.0%	7.5%
12	0	3.0	6.0	9.0
14	0	3.5	7.0	10.5
B. P/E Ratio				
10%	8.33	7.89	7.14	5.56
12	8.33	8.33	8.33	8.33
14	8.33	8.82	10.00	16.67

Assumption: $k = 12\%$ per year.

Finally, where ROE just equals k, the firm offers "break-even" investment opportunities with a fair rate of return. In this case, investors are indifferent between reinvestment of earnings in the firm or elsewhere at the market capitalization rate, because the rate of return in either case is 12%. Therefore, the stock price is unaffected by the plowback rate.

One way to summarize these relationships is to say the higher the plowback rate, the higher the growth rate, but a higher plowback rate does not necessarily mean a higher P/E ratio. A higher plowback rate increases P/E only if investments undertaken by the firm offer an expected rate of return higher than the market capitalization rate. Otherwise, higher plowback hurts investors because it means more money is sunk into projects with inadequate rates of return.

CONCEPT CHECK

Question 6. ABC stock has an expected ROE of 12% per year, expected earnings per share of $2, and expected dividends of $1.50 per share. Its market capitalization rate is 10% per year.

a. What are its expected growth rate, its price, and its P/E ratio?

b. If the plowback rate were 0.4, what would be the expected dividend per share, the growth rate, price, and the P/E ratio?

Pitfalls in P/E Analysis

No description of P/E analysis is complete without mentioning some of its pitfalls. First, consider that the denominator in the P/E ratio is accounting earnings, which are influenced by somewhat arbitrary accounting rules such as the use of historical cost in depreciation and inventory valuation. In times of high inflation, historic cost depreciation and inventory costs will tend to underrepresent true economic values, because the

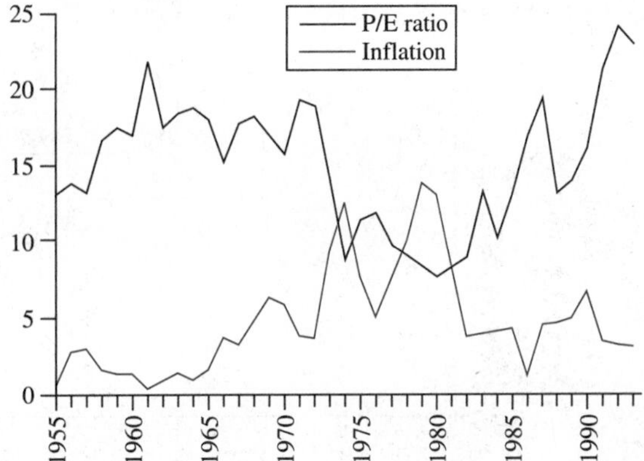

Figure 17.3
P/E ratios and inflation, 1955–1993

replacement cost of both goods and capital equipment will rise with the general level of prices. As Figure 17.3 demonstrates, P/E ratios have tended to be lower when inflation has been higher. This reflects the market's assessment that earnings in these periods are of "lower quality," artificially distorted by inflation, and warranting lower P/E ratios.

Another confounding factor in the use of P/E ratios is related to the business cycle. We were careful in deriving the DDM to define earnings as being net of *economic* depreciation, that is, the maximum flow of income that the firm could pay out without depleting its productive capacity. And reported earnings, as we note above, are computed in accordance with generally accepted accounting principles and need not correspond to economic earnings. Beyond this, however, notions of a normal or justified P/E ratio, as in equations 17.7 or 17.8, assume implicitly that earnings rise at a constant rate, or, put another way, on a smooth trend line. In contrast, reported earnings can fluctuate dramatically around a trend line over the course of the business cycle.

Another way to make this point is to note that the "normal" P/E ratio predicted by equation 17.8 is the ratio of today's price to the trend value of future earnings, E_1. The P/E ratio reported in the financial pages of the newspaper, by contrast, is the ratio of price to the most recent *past* accounting earnings. Current accounting earnings can differ considerably from future economic earnings. Because ownership of stock conveys the right to future as well as current earnings, the ratio of price to most recent earnings can vary substantially over the business cycle, as accounting earnings and the trend value of economic earnings diverge by greater and lesser amounts.

As an example, Figure 17.4 graphs the earnings per share of Motorola and Boston Edison since 1977. Note that Motorola's EPS fluctuate considerably. This reflects the company's relatively high degree of sensitivity to the business cycle. Value Line estimates its beta at 1.20. Boston Edison, by contrast, shows much less variation in earnings per share around a smoother and flatter trend line. Its beta was only 0.75.

Because the market values the entire stream of future dividends generated by the company, when earnings are temporarily depressed, the P/E ratio should tend to be

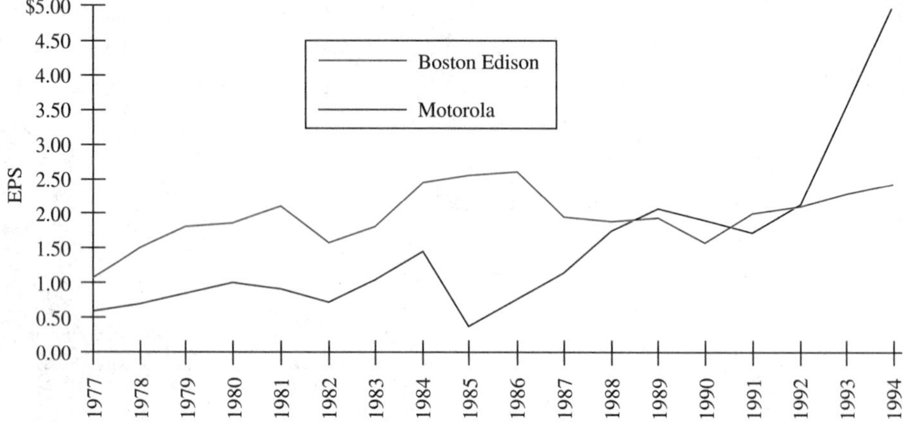

Figure 17.4
Earnings per share, 1977–1994

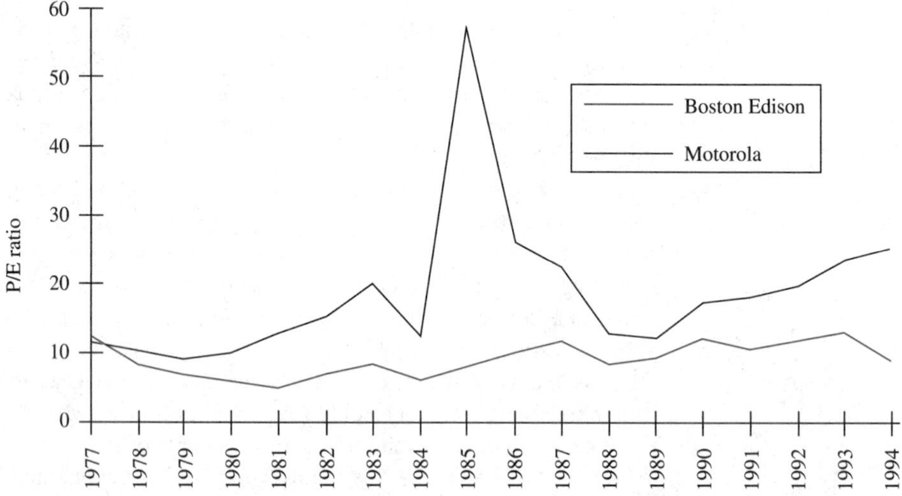

Figure 17.5
Price/earnings ratios, 1977–1994

high—that is, the denominator of the ratio responds more sensitively to the business cycle than the numerator. This pattern is borne out well.

Figure 17.5 graphs the Motorola and Boston Edison P/E ratios. Motorola, with the more volatile earnings profile, also has a more volatile P/E profile. For example, in 1985, when EPS fell to a far-below-trend value of $0.31, the P/E rose to 56.3. The market clearly recognized that earnings were depressed only temporarily.

This example shows why analysts must be careful in using P/E ratios. There is no way to say P/E ratio is overly high or low without referring to the company's long-run growth prospects, as well as to current earnings per share relative to the long-run trend line.

Nevertheless, Figures 17.4 and 17.5 demonstrate a clear relationship between P/E ratios and growth. Despite considerable short-run fluctuations, Motorola's EPS clearly

Figure 17.6 P/E Ratios based on 1992, 1993, and 1994 EPS

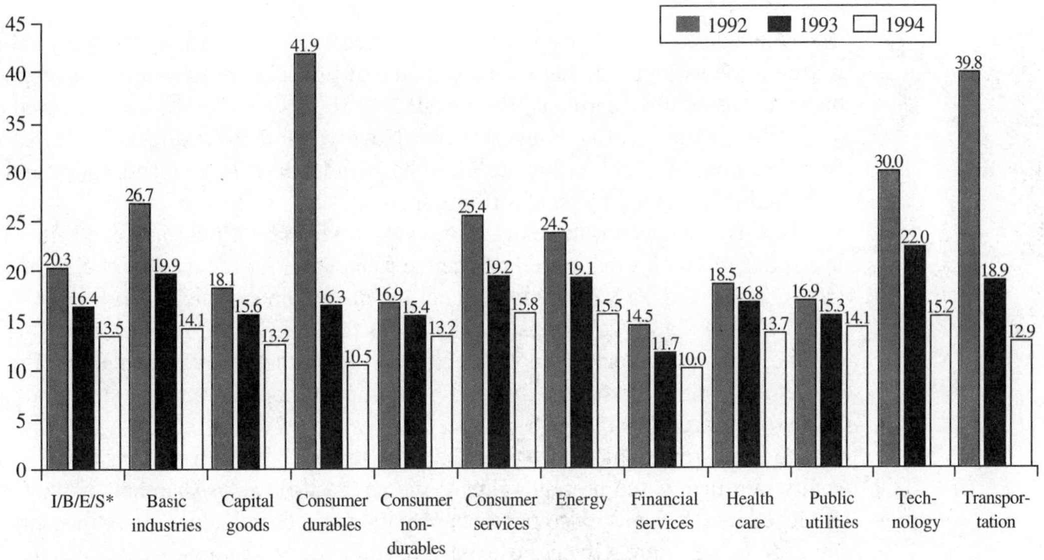

*Data for entire universe.

Source: Institutional Brokers Estimate System (I/B/E/S), *U.S. Comments,* May 28, 1993.

trended upward over the period. Its compound rate of growth between 1977 and 1993 was 13.5%. Boston Edison's earnings grew less rapidly, with an average growth rate of 5.1%. The growth prospects of Motorola are reflected in its consistently higher P/E multiple.

This analysis suggests that P/E ratios should vary across industries, and in fact they do. Figure 17.6 shows P/E ratios in mid-1993 for a sample of industries. P/E ratios for each industry are computed in three ways: by taking the ratio of price to previous year earnings, current year earnings, and projected next-year earnings. Notice that although the ratios based on 1992 or even 1993 earnings appear quite high, the ratios are far more moderate when prices are compared to 1994 earnings. This should not surprise you, because stock market prices are based on firms' future earnings prospects.

Combining P/E Analysis and the DDM

Some analysts use P/E ratios in conjunction with earnings forecasts to estimate the price of a stock at an investor's horizon date. The Motorola analysis in Figure 17.2 shows that Value Line forecasted a P/E ratio for 1997 of 20.0. EPS for 1997 were forecast at \$5.00, implying a price in 1997 of 20 × \$5.00 = \$100. Given an estimate of \$100 for the 1997 sales price, we would compute Motorola's intrinsic value as

$$V_{1993} = \frac{\$.54}{(1.123)} + \frac{\$.66}{(1.123)^2} + \frac{\$.78}{(1.123)^3} + \frac{\$.90 + \$100}{(1.123)^4} = \$65$$

17.5 Corporate Finance and the Free Cash Flow Approach

(10)

In both the discounted dividend and capitalized earnings approaches to equity valuation we made the assumption that the only source of financing of new equity investment in the firm was retained earnings. How would our results be affected if we allowed external equity financing of new investments? How would they be affected if we assumed debt financing of new investments? In other words, how do dividend policy and capital structure affect the value of a firm's shares?

The classic answer to these questions was provided by Modigliani and Miller (MM) in a series of articles that have become the foundation for the modern theory of corporate finance,[6] and we will briefly explain the main points of their theory.[7]

MM claim that if we take as given a firm's future investments, then the value of its existing common stock is not affected by how those investments are financed. Therefore, neither the firm's dividend policy nor its capital structure should affect the value of a share of its equity.

The basic reasoning underlying the MM theory is that the intrinsic value of the equity in a firm is the present value of the net cash flows to shareholders that can be produced by the firm's existing assets plus the net present value of any investments to be made in the future. Given those existing and expected future investments, the firm's dividend and financing decisions will affect only the form in which existing shareholders will receive their future returns, that is, as dividends or capital gains, but not their present value.

As a by-product of their proof of these propositions, MM show the equivalence of three seemingly different approaches to valuing the equity in a firm. The first two are the discounted dividend and capitalized earnings approaches presented in the earlier parts of this chapter. The third is the free cash flow approach.

This third approach starts with an estimate of the value of the firm as a whole and derives the value of the equity by subtracting the market value of all nonequity claims. The estimate of the value of the firm is found as the present value of cash flows, assuming all-equity financing plus the net present value of tax shields created by using debt. This approach is similar to that used by the firm's own management in capital budgeting, or the valuation approach that another firm would use in assessing the firm as a possible acquisition target.

For example, consider the MiMo Corporation. Its cash flow from operations before interest and taxes was $1 million in the year just ended, and it expects that this will grow by 6% per year forever. To make this happen, the firm will have to invest an amount equal to 15% of pretax cash flow each year. The tax rate is 30%. Depreciation was $100,000 in the year just ended and is expected to grow at the same rate as the

[6] The original two papers are M. Miller and F. Modigliani, "Dividend Policy, Growth and the Valuation of Shares," *Journal of Business,* October 1961; and F. Modigliani and M. Miller, "The Cost of Capital, Corporation Finance, and the Theory of Investment," *American Economic Review*, June 1958. Miller has revised his views in "Debt and Taxes," *Journal of Finance,* May 1976, and Modigliani his in "Debt, Dividend Policy, Taxes, Inflation and Market Valuation," *Journal of Finance*, May 1982.

[7] For a more complete treatment see Stephen A. Ross, Randolph W. Westerfield, and Jeffrey F. Jaffe, *Corporate Finance* (Homewood, Ill.: Richard D. Irwin, 1993), Chapters 15 and 16 or Richard A. Brealey and Stewart C. Myers, *Principles of Corporate Finance,* 4th ed. (New York: McGraw-Hill Inc., 1991), Chapters 16 and 17.

operating cash flow. The appropriate market capitalization rate for the unleveraged cash flow is 10% per year, and the firm currently has debt of $2 million outstanding.

MiMo's projected free cash flow for the coming year is

Before-tax cash flow from operations	$1,060,000
Depreciation	106,000
Taxable income	954,000
Taxes (at 30%)	286,200
After-tax unleveraged income	667,800
After-tax cash flow from operations (after-tax unleveraged income plus depreciation)	773,800
New investment (15% of cash flow from operations)	159,000
Free cash flow (after-tax cash flow from operations minus new investment)	614,800

It is important to realize that this projected free cash flow is what the firm's cash flow would be under all-equity financing. It ignores the interest expense on the debt, as well as any tax savings resulting from the deductibility of the interest expense.

The present value of all future free cash flows is

$$V_0 = \frac{C_1}{k - g} = \frac{\$614{,}800}{.10 - .06} = \$15{,}370{,}000$$

Thus, the value of the whole firm, debt plus equity, is $15,370,000. Because the value of the debt is $2 million, the value of the equity is $13,370,000.

If we believe that the use of financial leverage enhances the total value of the firm, then we should add to the $15,370,000 estimate of the firm's unleveraged value the gain from leverage. Thus, if in our example we believe that the tax shield provided by the deductibility of interest payments on the debt increases the firm's total value by $0.5 million, the value of the firm would be $15,870,000 and the value of the equity $13,870,000.

In reconciling this free cash flow approach with either discounted dividend or the capitalized earnings approaches, it is important to realize that the capitalization rate to be used in the present value calculation is different. In the free cash flow approach it is the rate appropriate for unleveraged equity, whereas in the other two approaches, it is the rate appropriate for leveraged equity. Because leverage affects the stock's beta, these two capitalization rates will be different.

The article from *The Wall Street Journal* in the accompanying box discusses the relative merits and shortcomings of some of the indicators of stock market valuation that we have discussed in this chapter: the price-to-book ratio, dividend yield, free cash flow, and the price-earnings ratio. The article points out that the "justifiable" P/E ratio depends on both the level of interest and inflation rates. In fact, the "rule of 20" discussed in the article is consistent with the relationship between P/E ratios and inflation depicted in Figure 17.3.

17.6 INFLATION AND EQUITY VALUATION

NO

What about the effects of inflation on stock prices? We start with an "inflation-neutral" case in which all *real* variables, and therefore the stock price, are unaffected by inflation. We then explore the ways in which reality might differ.

Flaws in Market Gauges Make Stocks Seem Expensive

Even before last week's impressive rally, the stock market was outrageously expensive. At least that's what some key market yardsticks show.

But hold on to your sell orders. Many investment experts reckon the fault lies not with the market, but with the measuring sticks. In particular, these experts see serious shortcomings in three popular stock-market gauges: the price-to-book value ratio, dividend yield and the price-to-earnings multiple.

The three standard measures "are all flawed in some way," says Frazier Evans, senior economist at Colonial Group, the Boston mutual-fund company. "You have to look under the surface. I'd say that the market is not as expensive as it looks."

Dwindling Dividends

Consider, for instance, the market's dividend yield. The companies in the Standard & Poor's 500-stock index are paying annual dividends amounting to 2.8% of their current stock prices. That's well below the historical average dividend yield of 4.7%.

A danger signal? Maybe not. The reason is that corporations seem to be paying out far less of their earnings as dividends these days. Instead, companies are using profits to expand their businesses and buy their own shares—actions designed to boost stock prices.

Effect on Book Value

At first blush, the market's price-to-book value also suggests shares are richly priced. Bargain hunters often look for stocks that are trading below book value, which is the difference between a company's assets and its liabilities expressed on a per-share basis.

But these days, precious few stocks trade below book value. But once again, the measuring gauge may be faulty. Book value has been distorted by share repurchases, special charges due to corporate restructurings and the adoption of a new accounting rule concerning retiree health benefits.

What about price-to-earnings multiples? Right now, the market is trading at about 15 times expected 1995 earnings, a tad above the historical average. "There are fewer problems with P/E ratios than with the other two measures," says Kathleen Crowley, a senior vice president with Chicago's Stratford Advisory Group.

Even so, earnings multiples also can mislead. In recent years, reported earnings have been depressed by special charges. In addition, experts say the market's earnings multiple shouldn't be viewed in isolation, but instead should be considered in the context of items like interest rates and inflation.

Colonial's Mr. Evans thinks the inflation rate is especially important. "When inflation has been high, price-earnings ratios have been low," he says. "And when inflation is low, price-earnings ratios have been high."

The Rule of 20

Mr. Evans says "this relationship can be summed up in the rule of 20," which states that "you take 20, subtract the consumer price index, and you have the P/E for the market."

With inflation expected to run between 3% and 3.5% this year, the rule of 20 indicates the market would be fairly priced at a P/E as high as 17.

But if price-to-earnings, price-to-book value and dividend yield are indeed misleading, what's the alternative? Kenneth Hackel, president of Systematic Financial Management in Fort Lee, N.J., prefers to look at free cash flow, which he defines as the maximum amount of cash that a company could potentially distribute to its shareholders each year. By that measure, he reckons stocks are cheap.

Mr. Hackel looks at the 400 industrial companies in the S&P 500 index. "The S&P industrials currently trade for 22 times their free cash flow," Mr. Hackel says. "The market has traded at between 15 and 34 times free cash flow in the postwar period. It would be difficult, in my opinion, to make a bear case."

Source: Jonathan Clements, *The Wall Street Journal*, February 7, 1995. Reprinted by permission of *The Wall Street Journal*.

Consider the case of Inflatotrend, a firm that in the absence of inflation pays out all earnings as dividends. Earnings and dividends per share are \$1, and there is no growth. We will use asterisked (*) letters to denote variables in the no-inflation case, or what represents the real value of variables. We again consider an equilibrium capitalization rate, k^*, of 10% per year. The price per share of this stock should be \$10:

$$P_0 = \frac{\$1}{.10} = \$10$$

Now imagine that inflation (i) is 6% per year, but that the values of the other economic variables adjust so as to leave their real values unchanged. Specifically, the *nominal* capitalization rate, k, becomes $(1 + k^*)(1 + i) - 1 = 1.10 \times 1.06 - 1 = .166$ or 16.6%, and the expected nominal growth rate of dividends, g, is now 6%, which is necessary to maintain a constant level of real dividends. The *nominal* dividend expected at the end of this year is therefore \$1.06 per share.

If we apply the constant growth DDM to these nominal variables we get the same price as in the no-inflation case:

$$P_0 = \frac{D_1}{k - g} = \frac{\$1.06}{.166 - .060} = \$10$$

Thus, as long as real values are unaffected, the stock's current price is unaffected by inflation.

Note that the expected nominal dividend yield, D_1/P_0, is 10.6% and the expected nominal capital gains rate, $(P_1 - P_0)/P_0$ is 6%. Almost the entire 6.6% increase in nominal HPR comes in the form of expected capital gains. A capital gain is necessary if the real value of the stock is to remain unaffected by inflation.

Let us see how these assumptions affect the other variables: earnings and the plowback ratio. To illuminate what otherwise may be confusing implications, we can explore a simplified story behind the examples above.

Inflatotrend produces a product that requires purchase of inventory at the beginning of each year, and sells the finished product at the end of the year. Last year there was no inflation. The inventory cost \$10 million. Labor, rent, and other processing costs (paid at year-end) were \$1 million, and revenue was \$12 million. Assuming no taxes, earnings were \$1 million.

Revenue	\$12 million
−Labor and rent	1 million
−Cost of goods sold	10 million
Earnings	\$ 1 million

All earnings are distributed as dividends to the 1 million shareholders. Because the only invested capital is the \$10 million in inventory, the ROE is 10%.

This year, inflation of 6% is expected, and all prices are expected to rise at that rate. Because inventory is paid for at the beginning of the year, it will still cost \$10 million. However, revenue will be \$12.72 million instead of \$12 million, and other costs will be \$1.06 million.

Nominal Earnings

Revenue	\$12.72 million
−Labor and rent	1.06 million
−Cost of goods sold	10.00 million
Earnings	\$ 1.66 million
ROE	16.6%

Note that the amount required to *replace* inventory at year's end is \$10.6 million, rather than the beginning *cost* of \$10 million, so the amount of cash available to distribute as dividends is \$1.06 million, not the reported earnings of \$1.66 million.

A dividend of \$1.06 million would be just enough to keep the real value of dividends unchanged and at the same time allow for maintenance of the same real value of inventory. The reported earnings of \$1.66 million overstate true economic earnings, in other words.

We thus have the following set of relationships:

	No Inflation	6% Inflation
Dividends	\$1 million	\$1.06 million
Reported earnings	\$1 million	\$1.66 million
ROE	10%	16.6%
Plowback ratio	0	.36145
Price of a share	\$10	\$10
P/E ratio	10	6.0241

There are some surprising findings in this case of "neutral" inflation, that is, inflation that leaves the real interest rate and real earnings unaffected. Although nominal dividends rise at the rate of inflation, 6%, reported earnings increase initially by 66%. In subsequent years, as long as inflation remains at a constant rate of 6%, earnings will grow at 6%.

Note also that the plowback ratio rises from 0 to .36145. Although plowback in the no-inflation case was zero, positive plowback of reported earnings now becomes necessary to maintain the level of inventory at a constant real value. Inventory must rise from a nominal level of \$10 million to a level of \$10.6 million to maintain its real value. This inventory investment requires reinvested earnings of \$.6 million.

Thus, the proportion of reported income that must be retained and reinvested to keep the real growth rate of earnings at zero is .36145 if inflation is 6% per year. Multiplying this plowback ratio by the nominal ROE of 16.6% produces a nominal growth rate of dividends of 6%, which is equal to the inflation rate:

$$\begin{aligned} g &= b \times \text{ROE} \\ &= .36145 \times 16.6\% = 6\% \text{ per year} \end{aligned}$$

More generally, the relationship between nominal and real variables is:

Variable	Real	Nominal
Growth rate	g^*	$g = (1 + g^*)(1 + i) - 1$
Capitalization rate	k^*	$k = (1 + k^*)(1 + i) - 1$
Return on equity	ROE*	$\text{ROE} = (1 + \text{ROE}^*)(1 + i) - 1$

Expected dividend	D_1^*	$D_1 = (1 + i)D_1^*$
Plowback ratio	b^*	$b = \frac{(1 + b^* \times \text{ROE}^*)(1 + i) - 1}{(1 + \text{ROE}^*)(1 + i) - 1}$

Note that it is not true that $E_1 = (1 + i)E_1^*$. That is, expected reported earnings do not, in general, equal expected real earnings times one plus the inflation rate. The reason, as you have seen, is that stated earnings do not accurately measure the cost of replenishing assets.

For example, cost of goods sold is treated as if it were $10 million, even though it now costs $10.6 million to replace the inventory. Historical cost accounting in this case distorts the measured cost of goods sold, which in turn distorts the reported earnings figures. We will return to this point in Chapter 18.

Note also the effect of inflation on the P/E ratio. In our example the P/E ratio drops from 10 in the no-inflation scenario to 6.0241 in the 6% inflation scenario. This is entirely a result of the fact that the reported earnings figure gets distorted by inflation and overstates true economic earnings.

This is true in the real world too, not just in our simplified example. Look back at Figure 17.3 and you will see that P/E ratios fall dramatically when the inflation rate increases. Many companies show gains in reported earnings during inflationary periods, even though real earnings may be unaffected. This is one reason analysts must interpret data on the past behavior of P/E ratios over time with great care.

CONCEPT CHECK

Question 7. Assume that Inflatotrend has a 4% annual expected constant growth rate of earnings if there is no inflation. $E_1^* = \$1$ per share; ROE* = 10% per year; $b^* = .4$; and $k^* = 10\%$ per year.

a. What is the current price of a share?

b. What are the expected real dividend yield and rate of capital appreciation?

c. If the firm's real revenues and dividends are unaffected by inflation, and expected inflation is 6% per year, what should be the nominal growth rate of dividends, the expected nominal dividend yield, the expected ROE, and the nominal plowback ratio?

For many years financial economists considered stocks to be an inflation-neutral investment in the sense that we have described. They believed, and many of them still believe, that changes in the rate of inflation, whether expected or unexpected, have no effect on the expected real rate of return on common stocks.

Recent empirical research, however, seems to indicate that real rates of return are negatively correlated with inflation. In terms of the simple constant growth rate DDM, this would mean that an increase in inflation is associated with (but is not necessarily caused by) either a decrease in D_1, an increase in k, a decrease in g, or some combination of all three.

One school of thought[8] believes that economic "shocks" such as oil price hikes can cause a simultaneous increase in the inflation rate and decline of expected real earnings (and dividends). This would result in a negative correlation between inflation and real stock returns.

[8] See Eugene F. Fama, "Stock Returns, Real Activity, Inflation, and Money," *American Economic Review*, September 1981.

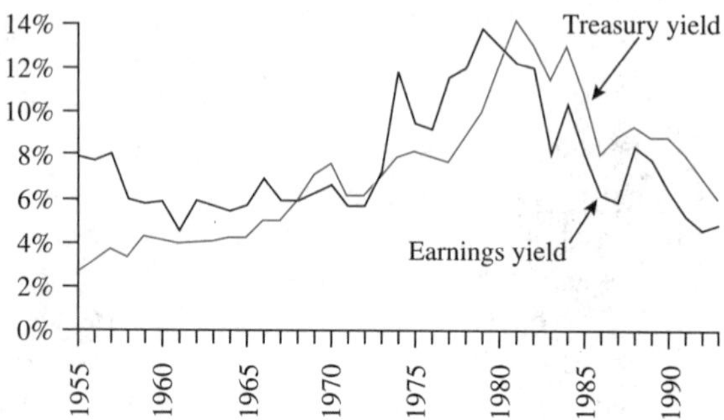

Figure 17.7
Earnings yield of S&P 500 versus Treasury bond yield, 1966–1993

A second view[9] is that the higher the rate of inflation, the riskier real stock returns are perceived to be. The reasoning here is that higher inflation is associated with greater uncertainty about the economy, which tends to induce a higher required rate of return on equity. In addition, a higher k implies a lower level of stock prices.

A third perspective[10] is that higher inflation results in lower real dividends because our tax system causes lower after-tax real earnings as the inflation rate rises.

Finally, there is the view[11] that many investors in the stock market suffer from a form of "money illusion." Investors mistake the rise in nominal rate of interest for a rise in the real rate. As a result, they undervalue stocks in a period of higher inflation.

17.7 Behavior of the Aggregate Stock Market

Explaining Past Behavior

It has been well documented that the stock market is a leading economic indicator.[12] This means that it tends to fall before a recession and to rise before an economic recovery. However, the relationship is far from perfectly reliable.

Most scholars and serious analysts would agree that, although the stock market appears to have a substantial life of its own, responding perhaps to bouts of mass euphoria and then panic, economic events and the anticipation of such events do have a substantial effect on stock prices.[13] Perhaps the two factors with the greatest impact are interest rates and corporate profits.

Figure 17.7 shows the behavior of the earnings-to-price ratio (i.e., the earnings yield) of the S&P 500 stock index versus the yield to maturity on long-term Treasury bonds over a 30-year period. Our discussion of valuation models earlier in this chapter gives us some insights into the relationship between these two yields.

---

9 See Burton Malkiel, *A Random Walk Down Wall Street*, 4th ed. (New York: W.W. Norton, 1985).

10 See Martin Feldstein, "Inflation and the Stock Market," *American Economic Review*, December 1980.

11 See Franco Modigliani and Richard Cohn, "Inflation, Rational Valuation, and the Market," *Financial Analysts Journal*, March–April 1979.

12 See, for example, Stanley Fischer and Robert C. Merton, "Macroeconomics and Finance: The Role of the Stock Market," *Carnegie-Rochester Conference Series on Public Policy* 21 (1984).

13 For a discussion of the current debate on the rationality of the stock market, see the suggested readings at the end of this chapter.

Table 17.4 Effect of Inflation on Stock and Bond Yields

Rate of Inflation	Earnings Yield on Stocks	Yield to Maturity on Bonds
0	9% per year	3% per year
8% per year	9% per year	11% per year

For example, in the special case that (1) inflation equals zero, (2) the expected ROE on future real investments in the corporate sector is equal to the equity capitalization rate, and (3) current earnings per share equal expected future earnings per share, the earnings yield on the S&P 500 equals the expected real rate of return on the stock market. This, in turn, should be equal to the yield to maturity on Treasury bonds plus a risk premium, which may change slowly over time.

Inflation will alter this relationship for several reasons. First, as shown earlier in this chapter, even in the case of neutral inflation, reported earnings tend to rise in a period of high inflation. Thus, at least part of the sharp rise in the S&P earnings yield in Figure 17.7 in the 1970s can be attributed to the sharp rise in the rate of inflation during that period.[14]

However, a more important fact is that the yield to maturity on Treasury bonds is a nominal rate that embodies the inflation expectations of market participants. The earnings yield on common stocks, on the other hand, is a real yield. Thus, if stocks are inflation neutral, the difference between the earnings yield on stocks and the yield to maturity on Treasury bonds will reflect both the risk premium on stocks and the expected long-run inflation rate. This implies that when the expected rate of inflation is low the earnings yield on stocks should exceed the yield to maturity on bonds, and when the expected rate of inflation is high the reverse should be true.

For example, suppose that in the absence of inflation the earnings yield on stocks is 9% per year and the yield to maturity on bonds 3% per year, implying an equity risk premium of 6% per year. As you can see in Figure 17.7, this appeared to be the case in the 1960s. Now suppose the expected rate of inflation is 8% per year. If stocks are inflation neutral, the earnings yield will still be 9% (assuming that reported earnings are not greatly distorted by historical cost accounting practices). But the yield to maturity on bonds, since it is a nominal rate, will jump to 11% per year. Thus, the yield to maturity on bonds will exceed the earnings yield on stocks by 2% per year, the difference between the expected rate of inflation (8% per year) and the equity risk premium (6% per year). These hypothetical relationships are summarized in Table 17.4.

Something like this appears to be what actually happened in the late 1970s and the 1980s. Of course, other things that might have affected stock and bond yields were happening during this period as well. Perhaps the most important were changes in the relative risk of stocks and bonds. Long-term bonds, in particular, became much riskier during this period as a result of changes in Federal Reserve monetary policy and the variability in the inflation rate.

[14] Franco Modigliani and Richard Cohn claim that for the S&P 500 stocks as a whole the reported earnings may not be all that distorted during this period because the upward bias induced by historic cost depreciation and FIFO inventory accounting was offset by the downward bias caused by understatement of the real interest expense on the debt. This is discussed further in Chapter 18. See "Inflation, Rational Valuation, and the Market," *Financial Analysts Journal,* March–April 1979.

Forecasting the Stock Market

What can we learn from all of this about the future rate of return on stocks? First, a note of optimism. Although timing the stock market is a very difficult and risky game, it may not be impossible. For example, we saw in Chapter 12 that some variables such as the market dividend yield seem to predict market returns.

However, if market history teaches us anything at all, it is that the market has great variability. Thus, although we can use a variety of methods to derive a best forecast of the expected holding-period return on the market, the uncertainty surrounding that forecast will always be high.

The most popular approach to forecasting the overall stock market is the earnings multiplier approach applied at the aggregate level. The first step is to forecast corporate profits for the coming period. Then we derive an estimate of the earnings multiplier, the aggregate P/E ratio, based on a forecast of long-term interest rates. The product of the two forecasts is the estimate of the end-of-period level of the market.

The forecast of the P/E ratio of the market is sometimes derived from a graph similar to that in Figure 17.7, which plots the *earnings yield* (earnings per share divided by price per share, the reciprocal of the P/E ratio) of the S&P 500 and the yield to maturity on 10-year Treasury bonds. The figure shows that both yields rose dramatically in the 1970s. In the case of Treasury bonds, this was because of an increase in the inflationary expectations built into interest rates. The earnings yield on the S&P 500, however, probably rose because of inflationary distortions that artificially increased reported earnings. We have already seen that P/E ratios tend to fall when inflation rates increase. For most of the 1980s, the earnings yield ran about one percentage point below the T-bond rate.

One might use this relationship and the current yield on 10-year Treasury bonds to forecast the earnings yield on the S&P 500. Given that earnings yield, a forecast of earnings could be used to predict the level of the S&P in some future period. Let's consider a simple example of this procedure.

The mid-1993 forecast for 1993 earnings per share for the S&P 500 portfolio was about $28.50.[15] The 10-year Treasury bond yield in mid-1993 was about 7%. Because the earnings yield on the S&P 500 has been about one percentage point below the 10-year Treasury yield, a first guess for the earnings yield on the S&P 500 might be 6%. This would imply a P/E ratio of $1/.06 = 16.7$. Our forecast for the P/E of the S&P 500 portfolio would then be $16.7 \times 28.50 = 476$.

Of course, there is uncertainty regarding all three inputs into this analysis: the actual earnings on the S&P 500 stocks, the level of Treasury yields at year end, and the spread between the Treasury yield and the earnings yield. One would wish to perform sensitivity or scenario analysis to examine the impact of changes in all of these variables. To illustrate, consider Table 17.5, which shows a simple scenario analysis treating possible effects of variation in the Treasury bond yield. The scenario analysis shows that the forecasted level of the stock market varies inversely and with dramatic sensitivity to interest rate changes.

---

[15] According to Institutional Brokers Estimate System (I/B/E/S) as of May 1993. I/B/E/S surveys a large sample of stock analysts and reports several analyses of their forecasts for both the economy and individual stocks.

Table 17.5 S&P 500 Price Forecasts under Various Scenarios

	Most Likely Scenario	Pessimistic Scenario	Optimistic Scenario
Treasury bond yield	7%	7.5%	6.5%
Earnings yield	6%	6.5%	5.5%
Resulting P/E ratio	16.7	15.4	18.2
EPS forecast	\$ 28.50	\$ 28.50	\$ 28.50
Forecast for S&P 500	476	439	519

Forecast for the earnings yield on the S&P 500 equals Treasury bond yield minus 1%. The P/E ratio is the reciprocal of the forecasted earnings yield.

Some analysts use an aggregate version of the dividend discount model rather than an earnings multiplier approach. All of these models, however, rely heavily on forecasts of such macroeconomic variables as GDP, interest rates, and the rate of inflation, which are difficult to predict accurately.

Because stock prices reflect expectations of future dividends, which are tied to the economic fortunes of firms, it is not surprising that the performance of a broadbased stock index like the S&P 500 is taken as a leading economic indicator, that is, a predictor of the performance of the aggregate economy. Stock prices are viewed as embodying consensus forecasts of economic activity and are assumed to move up or down in anticipation of movements in the economy. The government's index of leading economic indicators, which is taken to predict the progress of the business cycle, is made up in part of recent stock market performance. However, the predictive value of the market is far from perfect. A well-known joke, often attributed to Paul Samuelson, is that the market has forecast eight of the last five recessions.

SUMMARY

1. One approach to firm valuation is to focus on the firm's book value, either as it appears on the balance sheet or as adjusted to reflect current replacement cost of assets or liquidation value. Another approach is to focus on the present value of expected future dividends.

2. The dividend discount model holds that the price of a share of stock should equal the present value of all future dividends per share, discounted at an interest rate commensurate with the risk of the stock.

3. The constant growth version of the DDM asserts that if dividends are expected to grow at a constant rate forever, then the intrinsic value of the stock is determined by the formula

$$V_0 = \frac{D_1}{k - g}$$

This version of the DDM is simplistic in its assumption of a constant value of g. There are more sophisticated multistage versions of the model for more complex environments. When the constant growth assumption is reasonably satisfied, the formula can be inverted to infer the market capitalization rate for the stock:

$$k = \frac{D_1}{P_0} + g$$

4. Stock market analysts devote considerable attention to a company's price-to-earnings ratio. The P/E ratio is a useful measure of the market's assessment of the firm's growth opportunities. Firms with no growth opportunities should have a P/E ratio that is just the reciprocal of the capitalization rate, k. As growth opportunities become a progressively more important component of the total value of the firm, the P/E ratio will increase.

5. The expected growth rate of earnings is related both to the firm's expected profitability and to its dividend policy. The relationship can be expressed as

$$g = (\text{ROE on new investment}) \times (1 - \text{Dividend payout ratio})$$

6. You can relate any DDM to a simple capitalized earnings model by comparing the expected ROE on future investments to the market capitalization rate, k. If the two rates are equal, then the stock's intrinsic value reduces to expected earnings per share (EPS) divided by k.

7. Many analysts form their estimate of a stock's value by multiplying their forecast of next year's EPS by a P/E multiple derived from some empirical rule. This rule can be consistent with some version of the DDM, although often it is not.

8. The free cash flow approach is the one used most often in corporate finance. The analyst first estimates the value of the entire firm as the present value of expected future free cash flows, assuming all-equity financing, then adds the value of tax shields arising from debt financing, and finally subtracts the value of all claims other than equity. This approach will be consistent with the DDM and capitalized earnings approaches as long as the capitalization rate is adjusted to reflect financial leverage.

9. We explored the effects of inflation on stock prices in the context of the constant growth DDM. Although traditional theory has been that inflation should have a neutral effect on real stock returns, recent historical evidence shows a striking negative correlation between inflation and real stock market returns. There are four different explanations that may account for this negative correlation.

a. Economic "shocks" that simultaneously produce high inflation and lower real earnings.

b. Increased riskiness of stocks in a more inflationary environment.

c. Lower real after-tax earnings and dividends attributable to inflation-induced distortions in the tax system.

d. Money "illusion."

10. The models presented in this chapter can be used to explain and forecast the behavior of the aggregate stock market. The key macroeconomic variables that determine the level of stock prices in the aggregate are interest rates and corporate profits.

Key Terms

Fundamental analysts
Technical analysts
Book value
Liquidation value
Replacement cost
Tobin's q
Intrinsic value
Market capitalization rate
Dividend discount model
Constant growth DDM
Dividend payout ratio
Plowback ratio
Earnings retention ratio
Price/earnings multiple

Selected Readings

For the key issues in the recent debate about the link between fundamentals and stock prices see:

Merton, Robert C. "On the Current State of the Stock Market Rationality Hypothesis." In *Macroeconomics and Finance, Essays in Honor of Franco Modigliani,* eds. Rudiger Dornbusch, Stanley Fischer, and John Bossons. Cambridge, Mass.: MIT Press, 1986.

Cutler, David M.; James M. Poterba; and Lawrence H. Summers. "What Moves Stock Prices?" *Journal of Portfolio Management* 15 (Spring 1989), pp. 4–12.

West, Kenneth D. "Bubbles, Fads, and Stock Price Volatility Tests: A Partial Evaluation." *Journal of Finance* 43 (July 1988), pp. 639–55.

Problems

1. *a.* Computer stocks currently provide an expected rate of return of 16%. MBI, a large computer company, will pay a year-end dividend of \$2 per share. If the stock is selling at \$50 per share, what must be the market's expectation of the growth rate of MBI dividends?
   b. If dividend growth forecasts for MBI are revised downward to 5% per year, what will happen to the price of MBI stock? What (qualitatively) will happen to the company's price-earnings ratio?
2. *a.* MF Corp. has an ROE of 16% and a plowback ratio of 50%. If the coming year's earnings are expected to be \$2 per share, at what price will the stock sell? The market capitalization rate is 12%.
   b. What price do you expect MF shares to sell for in three years?

3. The constant growth dividend discount model can be used both for the valuation of companies and for the estimation of the long- term total return of a stock.*

   Assume: \$20 = the price of a stock today
   8% = the expected growth rate of dividends
   \$0.60 = the annual dividend one year forward

   a. Using *only* the above data, compute the expected long-term total return on the stock using the constant growth dividend discount model. Show your calculations.
   b. Briefly discuss two disadvantages of the constant growth dividend discount model in its application to investment analysis.
   c. Identify two alternative methods to the dividend discount model for the valuation of companies.
4. The market consensus is that Analog Electronic Corporation has an ROE = 9%, a beta of 1.25, and it plans to maintain indefinitely its traditional plowback ratio of 2/3. This year's earnings were \$3 per share. The annual dividend was just paid. The consensus estimate of the coming year's market return is 14%, and T-bills currently offer a 6% return.
   a. Find the price at which Analog stock should sell.
   b. Calculate the P/E ratio.

---

*Reprinted, with permission, from the *CFA Study Guide,* Association for Investment Management and Research, Charlottesville, VA.

c. Calculate the present value of growth opportunities.

d. Suppose your research convinces you Analog will announce momentarily that it will immediately reduce its plowback ratio to 1/3. Find the intrinsic value of the stock. The market is still unaware of this decision. Explain why V_0 no longer equals P_0 and why V_0 is greater or less than P_0.

5. If the expected rate of return of the market portfolio is 15% and a stock with a beta of 1.0 pays a dividend yield of 4%, what must the market believe is the expected rate of price appreciation on that stock?

6. The FI Corporation's dividends per share are expected to grow indefinitely by 5% per year.

a. If this year's year-end dividend is \$8 and the market capitalization rate is 10% per year, what must the current stock price be according to the DDM?

b. If the expected earnings per share are \$12, what is the implied value of the ROE on future investment opportunities?

c. How much is the market paying per share for growth opportunities (i.e., for an ROE on future investments that exceeds the market capitalization rate)?

7. Using the data provided, discuss whether the common stock of United States Tobacco Company is attractively priced based on at least three different valuation approaches. (Hint: Use the asset value, DDM, and earnings multiplier approaches.)*

	U.S. Tobacco	S&P 500
Recent price	\$27.00	\$290
Book value per share	\$ 6.42	
Liquidation value per share	\$ 4.90	
Replacement costs of assets per share	\$ 9.15	
Anticipated next year's dividend	\$ 1.20	\$ 8.75
Estimated annual growth in dividends and earnings	10.0%	7.0%
Required return	13.0%	
Estimated next year's EPS	\$ 2.40	\$16.50
P/E ratio based on next year's earnings	11.3	17.6
Dividend yield	4.4%	3.0%

8. The risk-free rate of return is 10%, the required rate of return on the market is 15%, and High-Flyer stock has a beta coefficient of 1.5. If the dividend per share expected during the coming year, D_1, is \$2.50 and $g = 5\%$, at what price should a share sell?

9. Your preliminary analysis of two stocks has yielded the information set forth below. The market capitalization rate for both Stock A and Stock B is 10% per year.

	Stock A	Stock B
Expected return on equity, ROE	14%	12%
Estimated earnings per share, E_1	\$ 2.00	\$ 1.65
Estimated dividends per share, D_1	\$ 1.00	\$ 1.00
Current market price per share, P_0	\$27.00	\$25.00

a. What are the expected dividend payout ratios for the two stocks?
b. What are the expected dividend growth rates of each?
c. What is the intrinsic value of each stock?
d. In which, if either, of the two stocks would you chose to invest?

10. The Tennant Company, founded in 1870, has evolved into the leading producer of large-sized floor sweepers and scrubbers, which are ridden by their operators. Some of its financial data are presented in the following table:*

Tennant Company
Selected Historic Operating and Balance Sheet Data (000 omitted)
as of December 31

	1980	1986	1992
Net sales	$47,909	$109,333	$166,924
Cost of goods sold	27,395	62,373	95,015
Gross profits	20,514	46,960	71,909
Selling, general, and administrative expenses	11,895	29,649	54,151
Earnings before interest and taxes	8,619	17,311	17,758
Interest on long-term debt	0	53	248
Pretax income	8,619	17,258	17,510
Income taxes	4,190	7,655	7,692
After-tax income	4,429	9,603	9,818
Total assets	$33,848	$ 63,555	$106,098
Total common stockholders' equity	25,722	46,593	69,516
Long-term debt	6	532	2,480
Total common shares outstanding	5,654	5,402	5,320
Earnings per share	$ .78	$ 1.78	$ 1.85
Dividends per share	.28	.72	.96
Book value per share	4.55	8.63	13.07

a. Based on these data, calculate a value for Tennant common stock by applying the constant growth dividend discount model. Assume an investor's required rate of return is a five percentage point premium over the current risk-free rate of return of 7%.

b. To your disappointment, the calculation you completed in Part *a* results in a value below the stock's current market price. Consequently, you apply the constant growth DDM using the same required rate of return as in your calculation for Part *a*, but using the company's stated goal of earning 20% per year on stockholders' equity and maintaining a 35% dividend payout ratio. However, you find you are unable to calculate a meaningful answer. Explain why you cannot calculate a meaningful answer, and identify an alternative DDM that may provide a meaningful answer.

11. You are a portfolio manager considering the purchase of Nucor common stock. Nucor is the preeminent "mini-mill" steel producer in the United States. Mini-mills use scrap steel as their raw material and produce a limited number of products, primarily for the construction market. You are provided with the following information:*

Nucor Corporation	
Stock price (Dec. 30, 1990)	$53.00
1990 Estimated earnings	$ 4.25
1990 Estimated book value	$25.00
Indicated dividend	$ 0.40
Beta	1.10
Risk-free return	7.0%
High grade corporate bond yield	9.0%
Risk premium—stocks over bonds	5.0%

a. Calculate the expected stock market return. Show your calculations.
b. Calculate the implied total return of Nucor stock.
c. Calculate the required return of Nucor stock using the security market line model.
d. Briefly discuss the attractiveness of Nucor based on these data.

12. The stock of Nogro Corporation is currently selling for $10 per share. Earnings per share in the coming year are expected to be $2. The company has a policy of paying out 50% of its earnings each year in dividends. The rest is retained and invested in projects that earn a 20% rate of return per year. This situation is expected to continue indefinitely.
    a. Assuming the current market price of the stock reflects its intrinsic value as computed using the constant growth rate DDM, what rate of return do Nogro's investors require?
    b. By how much does its value exceed what it would be if all earnings were paid as dividends and nothing were reinvested?
    c. If Nogro were to cut its dividend payout ratio to 25%, what would happen to its stock price? What if Nogro eliminated the dividend?
13. Chiptech, Inc. is an established computer chip firm with several profitable existing products as well as some promising new products in development. The company earned $1 a share last year, and just paid out a dividend of $.50 per share. Investors believe the company plans to maintain its dividend payout ratio at 50%. ROE equals 20%. Everyone in the market expects this situation to persist indefinitely.
    a. What is the market price of Chiptech stock? The required return for the computer chip industry is 15%, and the company has just gone ex-dividend (i.e., the next dividend will be paid a year from now, at $t = 1$).
    b. Suppose you discover that Chiptech's competitor has developed a new chip that will eliminate Chiptech's current technological advantage in this market. This new product, which will be ready to come to the market in two years, will force Chiptech to reduce the prices of its chips to remain competitive. This will decrease ROE to 15%, and, because of falling demand for its product, Chiptech will decrease the plowback ratio to .40. The plowback ratio will be decreased at the end of the second year, at $t = 2$: the annual year-end dividend for the second year (paid at $t = 2$) will be 60% of that year's earn-

*Reprinted, with permission, from the Level I 1986 *CFA Study Guide*. The Institute of Chartered Financial Analysts, Charlottesville, VA.

ings. What is your estimate of Chiptech's intrinsic value per share? (Hint: carefully prepare a table of Chiptech's earnings and dividends for each of the next three years. Pay close attention to the change in the payout ratio in $t = 2$.)

c. No one else in the market perceives the threat to Chiptech's market. In fact, you are confident that no one else will become aware of the change in Chiptech's competitive status until the competitor firm publicly announces its discovery near the end of year 2. What will be the rate of return on Chiptech stock in the coming year (i.e., between $t = 0$ and $t = 1$)? In the second year (between $t = 1$ and $t = 2$)? The third year (between $t = 2$ and $t = 3$)? (Hint: Pay attention to when *the market* catches on to the new situation. A table of dividends and market prices over time might help.)

14. The risk-free rate of return is 8%, the expected rate of return on the market portfolio is 15%, and the stock of Xyrong Corporation has a beta coefficient of 1.2. Xyrong pays out 40% of its earnings in dividends, and the latest earnings announced were $10 per share. Dividends were just paid and are expected to be paid annually. You expect that Xyrong will earn an ROE of 20% per year on all reinvested earnings forever.

a. What is the intrinsic value of a share of Xyrong stock?

b. If the market price of a share is currently $100, and you expect the market price to be equal to the intrinsic value one year from now, what is your expected one-year holding-period return on Xyrong stock?

15. The Digital Electronic Quotation System (DEQS) Corporation pays no cash dividends currently and is not expected to for the next five years. Its latest EPS was $10, all of which was reinvested in the company. The firm's expected ROE for the next five years is 20% per year, and during this time it is expected to continue to reinvest all of its earnings. Starting six years from now the firm's ROE on new investments is expected to fall to 15%, and the company is expected to start paying out 40% of its earnings in cash dividends, which it will continue to do forever after. DEQS's market capitalization rate is 15% per year.

a. What is your estimate of DEQS's intrinsic value per share?

b. Assuming its current market price is equal to its intrinsic value, what do you expect to happen to its price over the next year? The year after?

c. What effect would it have on your estimate of DEQS's intrinsic value if you expected DEQS to pay out only 20% of earnings starting in Year 6?

CFA

16. At year-end 1991, the Wall Street consensus was that Philip Morris's earnings and dividends would grow at 20% for five years, after which growth would fall to a marketlike 7%. Analysts also projected a required rate of return of 10% for the U.S. equity market.*

a. Using the data in the accompanying table and the multistage dividend discount model, calculate the intrinsic value of Philip Morris stock at year-end 1991. Assume a similar level of risk for Philip Morris stock as for the typical U.S. stock. Show all your work.

---

*Reprinted, with permission, from the Level I 1993 *CFA Study Guide*. Copyright 1993, Association for Investment Management and Research, Charlottesville, VA.

b. Using the data in the accompanying table, calculate Philip Morris's price-earnings ratio and the price-earnings ratio relative to the S&P 500 Stock Index as of December 31, 1991.

c. Using the data in the accompanying table, calculate Philip Morris's price-book ratio and the price-book ratio relative to the S&P 500 Stock Index as of December 31, 1991.

Philip Morris Corporation
Selected Financial Data
Years Ending December 31
($ millions except per share data)

	1991	1981
Earnings per share	$4.24	$0.66
Dividends per share	$1.91	$0.25
Stockholders' equity	12,512	3,234
Total liabilities and stockholders' equity	$47,384	$9,180
Other Data		
Philip Morris		
Common shares outstanding (millions)	920	1,003
Closing price common stock	$80.250	$6.125
S&P 500 Stock Index:		
Closing price	417.09	122.55
Earnings per share	16.29	15.36
Book value per share	161.08	109.43

17. *a.* State one major advantage and one major disadvantage of each of the three valuation methodologies you used to value Philip Morris in the previous question.*

b. State whether Philip Morris stock is undervalued or overvalued as of December 31, 1991. Support your conclusion using your answers to previous questions and any data provided. (The past 10-year average S&P 500 Stock Index relative price-earnings and price-book ratios for Philip Morris were 0.80 and 1.61, respectively.)*

18. The Duo Growth Company just paid a dividend of $1 per share. The dividend is expected to grow at a rate of 25% per year for the next three years and then to level off to 5% per year forever. You think the appropriate market capitalization rate is 20% per year.

a. What is your estimate of the intrinsic value of a share of the stock?

b. If the market price of a share is equal to this intrinsic value, what is the expected dividend yield?

c. What do you expect its price to be one year from now? Is the implied capital gain consistent with your estimate of the dividend yield and the market capitalization rate?

---

*Reprinted, with permission, from the Level I 1993 *CFA Study Guide*.

19. The Generic Genetic (GG) Corporation pays no cash dividends currently and is not expected to for the next four years. Its latest EPS was \$5, all of which was reinvested in the company. The firm's expected ROE for the next four years is 20% per year, during which time it is expected to continue to reinvest all of its earnings. Starting five years from now, the firm's ROE on new investments is expected to fall to 15% per year. GG's market capitalization rate is 15% per year.

a. What is your estimate of GG's intrinsic value per share?

b. Assuming its current market price is equal to its intrinsic value, what do you expect to happen to its price over the next year?

20. The MoMi Corporation's cash flow from operations before interest and taxes was \$2 million in the year just ended, and it expects that this will grow by 5% per year forever. To make this happen, the firm will have to invest an amount equal to 20% of pretax cash flow each year. The tax rate is 34%. Depreciation was \$200,000 in the year just ended and is expected to grow at the same rate as the operating cash flow. The appropriate market capitalization rate for the underleveraged cash flow is 12% per year, and the firm currently has debt of \$4 million outstanding. Use the free cash flow approach to value the firm's equity.

21. The CPI Corporation is expected to pay a real dividend of \$1 per share this year. Its expected growth rate of real dividends is 4% per year, and its current market price per share is \$20.

a. Assuming the constant growth DDM is applicable, what must be the real market capitalization rate for CPI?

b. If the expected rate of inflation is 6% per year, what must be the nominal capitalization rate, the nominal dividend yield, and the growth rate of nominal dividends?

c. If the expected real earnings per share are \$1.80, what would be your estimate of intrinsic value if you used a simple capitalized earnings model?

U.S. Equities On Floppy Problems and Projects

22. The constant growth version of the dividend discount model predicts that the expected rate of return on a stock may be expressed as the dividend yield plus the growth rate, and that the growth rate may be forecast as the product of return on equity and the plowback ratio. Use U.S. Equities On Floppy to obtain the dividend yield and calculate the growth rate for a sample of firms. Then calculate the actual rate of return on these stocks and see whether the predicted rate of return, $D_1/P_0 + g$, is related to the realized rate of return. (Hint: It probably is best to form 5 to 10 portfolios of firms based on predicted return, and then test to see whether high predicted return portfolios tend to be high actual return portfolios.)

23. Is the predicted return of stocks based on the dividend discount model correlated with the beta of the stock? (Why should it be according to the CAPM?) Use U.S. Equities On Floppy to test this hypothesis.

24. Use U.S. Equities On Floppy to find the growth rate of earnings per share. Use your data from Question 1 to test whether earnings growth is correlated with the predicted growth rate from the dividend discount model, ROE $\times$ b.

Chapter 18
Financial Statement Analysis

IN THE PREVIOUS CHAPTER, WE EXPLORED EQUITY VALUATION TECHNIQUES. These techniques take the firm's dividends and earnings prospects as inputs. Although the valuation analyst is interested in economic earnings streams, only financial accounting data are readily available. What can we learn from a company's accounting data that can help us estimate the intrinsic value of its common stock?

In this chapter, we show how investors can use financial data as inputs into stock valuation analysis. We start by reviewing the basic sources of such data—the income statement, the balance sheet, and the statement of cash flows. We next discuss the difference between economic and accounting earnings. Although economic earnings are more important for issues of valuation, we examine evidence suggesting that, whatever their shortcomings, accounting data still are useful in assessing the economic prospects of the firm. We show how analysts use financial ratios to explore the sources of a firm's profitability and evaluate the "quality" of its earnings in a systematic fashion. We also examine the impact of debt policy on various financial ratios. Finally, we conclude with a discussion of the limitations of financial statement analysis as a tool in uncovering mispriced securities. Some of these limitations are due to differences in firms' accounting procedures. Others arise from inflation-induced distortions in accounting numbers.

18.1 The Major Financial Statements

The Income Statement

The **income statement** is a summary of the profitability of the firm over a period of time, such as a year. It presents revenues generated during the operating period, the

Table 18.1 Consolidated Statement of Income for The Gillette Company for the year ended December 31, 1993 (figures in millions)

Operating Revenues	
Net Sales	$5,411
Operating Expenses	
Cost of sales	$2,044
Selling, general, & administrative expenses	2,061
Depreciation and amortization	218
Other expenses	263
Total operating expenses	$4,586
Operating income	$ 825
Nonoperating income and expenses	109
Earnings before interest and income taxes	716
Net interest expense	33
Earnings before income taxes	683
Income taxes	256
Net income*	$ 427

*Net income is computed without an additional charge reflecting the effect of accounting changes.
Note: Column sums subject to rounding error.
Source: *Moody's Industrial Manual*, 1994.

expenses incurred during that same period, and the company's net earnings or profits, which are simply the difference between revenues and expenses.

It is useful to distinguish four broad classes of expenses: cost of goods sold, which is the direct cost attributable to producing the product sold by the firm; general and administrative expenses, which correspond to overhead expenses, salaries, advertising, and other costs of operating the firm that are not directly attributable to production; interest expense on the firm's debt; and taxes on earnings owed to federal and local governments.

Table 18.1 presents a 1993 income statement for The Gillette Company. At the top are revenues from operations. Next come operating expenses, the costs incurred in the course of generating those revenues, including a depreciation allowance. The difference between operating revenues and operating costs is called *operating income*. Income or expenses from other, primarily nonrecurring, sources are then added or subtracted to obtain earnings before interest and taxes (EBIT), which is what the firm would have earned if not for obligations to its creditors and the tax authorities. EBIT is a measure of the profitability of the firm's operations abstracting from any interest burden attributable to debt financing. The income statement then goes on to subtract net interest expense from EBIT to arrive at taxable income. Finally, the income tax due the government is subtracted to arrive at net income, the "bottom line" of the income statement.

The Balance Sheet

While the income statement provides a measure of profitability over a period of time, the **balance sheet** provides a "snapshot" of the financial condition of the firm at a particular time. The balance sheet is a list of the firm's assets and liabilities at that moment. The difference in assets and liabilities is the net worth of the firm, also called *stockholders' equity*. Like income statements, balance sheets are reasonably standardized in presentation. Table 18.2 is the balance sheet of Gillette for the year-end 1993.

The first section of the balance sheet gives a listing of the assets of the firm. Current assets are presented first. These are cash and other items such as accounts receivable or inventories that will be converted into cash within one year. Next comes a listing of long-term assets, which generally corresponds to the company's property, plant, and equipment. The sum of current and long-term assets is total assets, the last line of the assets section of the balance sheet.

The liability and stockholders' equity section is arranged similarly. First come short-term or "current" liabilities such as accounts payable, accrued taxes, and debts that are due within one year. Following this is long-term debt and other liabilities due in more than one year. The difference between total assets and total liabilities is stockholders' equity. This is the net worth or book value of the firm. Stockholders' equity is divided into par value of stock, additional paid-in capital, and retained earnings, although this division is usually unimportant. Briefly, par value plus additional paid-in capital represent the proceeds realized from the sale of stock to the public, whereas retained earnings represent the buildup of equity from profits plowed back into the firm. Even if the firm issues no new equity, book value will increase each year by the retained earnings of the firm.

The Statement of Cash Flows

The **statement of cash flows** replaces what used to be called the *statement of changes in financial position* or *flow of funds statement*. It is a report of the cash flow generated by the firm's operations, investments, and financial activities. This statement was mandated by the Financial Accounting Standards Board in 1987 and is sometimes called the *FASB Statement No. 95*.

Although the income statement and balance sheets are based on accrual methods of accounting, which means that revenues and expenses are recognized when incurred even if no cash has yet been exchanged, the statement of cash flows recognizes only transactions in which cash changes hands. For example, if goods are sold now, with payment due in 60 days, the income statement will treat the revenue as generated when the sale occurs, and the balance sheet will be immediately augmented by accounts receivable, but the statement of cash flows will not recognize the transaction until the bill is paid and the cash is in hand.

Table 18.3 is the 1993 statement of cash flows for Gillette. The first entry listed under cash flows from operations is net income. The next entries modify that figure by components of income that have been recognized but for which cash has not yet changed hands. Increases in accounts receivable, for example, mean that income has been claimed on the income statement, but cash has not yet been collected. Hence, increases in accounts receivable reduce the cash flows realized from operations in this

Table 18.2 Consolidated Balance Sheet for The Gillette Company as of December 31, 1993 (figures in millions)

Assets	
Current assets	
Cash and cash equivalents	$ 38
Receivables	1,227
Inventories	875
Prepaid taxes and other expenses	388
Total current assets	$2,528
Property, plant and equipment (net of depreciation)	$1,215
Net intangible assets	917
Other assets	443
Total assets	$5,102
Liabilities and Stockholders' Equity	
Current liabilities	
Loans payable	$395
Current portion of long-term debt	46
Accounts payable	1,122
Income taxes due	197
Total current liabilities	$1,760
Long-term debt	$840
Deferred income taxes	166
Other long-term liabilities	857
Total liabilities	$3,623
Stockholders' equity:	
Common stock, par value	$279
Additional paid-in capital	259
Retained earnings	2,357
Cumulative foreign currency adjustments	(415)
Treasury stock	(1,047)
Other	45
Total stockholders' equity	$1,479
Total liabilities and stockholders' equity	$5,102

Note: Column sums subject to rounding error.
Source: *Moody's Industrial Manual,* 1994.

period. Similarly, increases in accounts payable mean that expenses have been incurred, but cash has not yet left the firm. Any payment delay increases the company's net cash flows in this period.

Another major difference between the income statement and the statement of cash flows involves depreciation, which is a major addition to income in the adjustment section of the statement of cash flows in Table 18.3. The income statement attempts to "smooth" large capital expenditures over time to reflect a measure of profitability not distorted by large infrequent expenditures. The depreciation expense on the income

Table 18.3 Consolidated Statement of Cash Flows for The Gillette Company for the year ended December 31, 1993 (figures in millions)

Cash Flows from Operating Activities	
Net income	$427
Adjustments to reconcile net income to net cash provided by operating activities	
Depreciation and amortization	219
Other	216
Changes in operating assets and liabilities:	
Decrease (increase) in accounts receivable	(102)
Decrease (increase) in inventories	(56)
Increase (decrease) in accounts payable	11
Decrease (increase) in other current assets	(31)
Decrease (increase) in noncurrent assets	48
Total adjustments	$305
Net cash provided by operating activities	$732
Cash Flows from Investing Activities	
Cash provided (used) by disposal of (additions to) property, plant, and equipment	$(342)
Acquisitions of businesses	(453)
Other	(40)
Net cash provided (used) in investing activities	$(835)
Cash Flows from Financing Activities	
Proceeds from exercise of stock option and purchase plans	$25
Proceeds from issuance of long-term debt	500
Repayment of long-term debt	(415)
Increase (decrease) in loans payable	178
Dividends paid	(183)
Net cash provided by (used in) financing activities	$105
Net increase (decrease) in cash and cash equivalents	$ 2

Note: Column sums subject to rounding error.
Source: *Moody's Industrial Manual,* 1994.

statement is a way of doing this by recognizing capital expenditures over a period of many years rather than at the specific time of those expenditures.

The statement of cash flows, however, recognizes the cash implication of a capital expenditure when it occurs. It will ignore the depreciation "expense" over time, but will account for the full capital expenditure when it is paid.

Rather than smooth or allocate expenses over time, as in the income statement, the statement of cash flows reports cash flows separately for operations, investing, and financing activities. This way, any large cash flows such as those for big investments can be recognized explicitly as nonrecurring without affecting the measure of cash flow generated by operating activities.

The second section of the statement of cash flows is the accounting of cash flows from investing activities. These entries are investments in the capital stock necessary for the firm to maintain or enhance its productive capacity.

Finally, the last section of the statement lists the cash flows realized from financing activities. Issuance of securities will contribute positive cash flows. For example, Gillette issued $500 of long-term debt in 1993, which was a major source of cash flow. In contrast, payments of dividends and repurchase of stock reduced net cash flow. Notice that although dividends paid are included in the cash flows from financing, interest on debt is included with operating activities, presumably because unlike dividends, interest payments are not discretionary.

The statement of cash flows provides evidence on the well-being of a firm. If a company cannot pay its dividends and maintain the productivity of its capital stock out of cash flow from operations, for example, and it must resort to borrowing to meet these demands, this is a serious warning that the firm cannot maintain the dividend payout at its current level in the long run. The statement of cash flows will reveal this developing problem, when it shows that cash flow from operations is inadequate and that borrowing is being used to maintain dividend payments at unsustainable levels.

18.2 Accounting versus Economic Earnings

We've seen that stock valuation models require a measure of **economic earnings**, i.e., the sustainable cash flow that can be paid out to stockholders without impairing the productive capacity of the firm. In contrast, **accounting earnings** are affected by several conventions regarding the valuation of assets such as inventories (e.g., LIFO versus FIFO treatment), and by the way some expenditures such as capital investments are recognized over time (as depreciation expenses). We will discuss problems with some of these accounting conventions in greater detail later in the chapter. In addition to these accounting issues, as the firm makes its way through the business cycle, its earnings will rise above or fall below the trend line that might more accurately reflect sustainable economic earnings. This introduces an added complication in interpreting net income figures. One might wonder how closely accounting earnings approximate economic earnings and, correspondingly, how useful accounting data might be to investors attempting to value the firm.

In fact, the net income figure on the firm's income statement does convey considerable information concerning a firm's prospects. We see this in the fact that stock prices tend to increase when firms announce earnings greater than market analysts or investors had anticipated. There are several studies to this effect.

One well-known study, Foster, Olsen, and Shevlin[1] used time series of earnings for many firms to forecast the coming quarter's earnings announcement. They estimated an equation for more than 2,000 firms between 1974 and 1981:

[1] George Foster, Chris Olsen, and Terry Shevlin, "Earnings Releases, Anomalies, and the Behavior of Security Returns," *The Accounting Review* 59 (October 1984).

$$E_{i,t} = E_{i,t-4} + a_i(E_{i,t-1} - E_{i,t-5}) + g_i$$

where

$E_{i,t}$ = Earnings of firm i in quarter t
a_i = Adjustment factor for firm i
g_i = Growth factor for firm i

The rationale is that this quarter's earnings, $E_{i,t}$, will equal last year's earnings for the same quarter $E_{i,t-4}$, plus a factor representing recent above-trend earnings performance as measured by the difference between last quarter's earnings and the corresponding quarter's earnings a year earlier, plus another factor that represents steady earnings growth over time. Regression techniques are used to estimate a_i and g_i. Given these estimates, the equation is used together with past earnings to forecast future earnings.

Now it is easy to determine the effect of earnings surprises. Simply take the difference between actual earnings and forecasted or expected earnings, and see whether earnings surprises correlate with stock price movements.

Before doing so, however, these researchers introduced an extra refinement (first suggested by Latane and Jones[2]). Instead of using the earnings forecast error itself as the variable of interest, they first divided the forecast errors for each period by the standard deviation of forecast errors calculated from earlier periods; they effectively deflated the earnings surprise in a particular quarter by a measure of the typical surprise in an average quarter. This discounts forecast errors for firms with historically very unpredictable earnings. A large error for such firms might not be as significant as for a firm with typically very predictable earnings. The resulting "normalized" forecast error commonly is called the "standardized unexpected earnings" (SUE) measure. SUE is the variable that was correlated with stock price movements.

Each earnings announcement was placed in one of 10 deciles ranked by the magnitude of SUE, and the abnormal returns of the stock in each decile were calculated. The abnormal return in a period is the portfolio return after adjusting for both the market return in that period and the portfolio beta. It measures return over and above what would be expected given market conditions in that period. Figure 18.1 is a graph of the cumulative abnormal returns.

The results of this study are dramatic. The correlation between SUE ranking and abnormal returns across deciles is as predicted. There is a large abnormal return (a large increase in cumulative abnormal return) on the earnings announcement day (time 0). The abnormal return is positive for high-SUE and negative for low-SUE (actually negative-SUE) firms.

The more remarkable, and disturbing, result of the study concerns stock price movements *after* the announcement date. The cumulative abnormal returns of high-SUE stocks continue to grow even after the earnings information becomes public, whereas the low-SUE firms continue to suffer negative abnormal returns. The market appears to adjust to the earnings information only gradually, resulting in a sustained period of abnormal returns.

---

[2] H. A. Latane and C. P. Jones, "Standardized Unexpected Earnings—1971–1977," *Journal of Finance*, June 1979.

Figure 18.1 Cumulative abnormal returns in response to earnings announcements

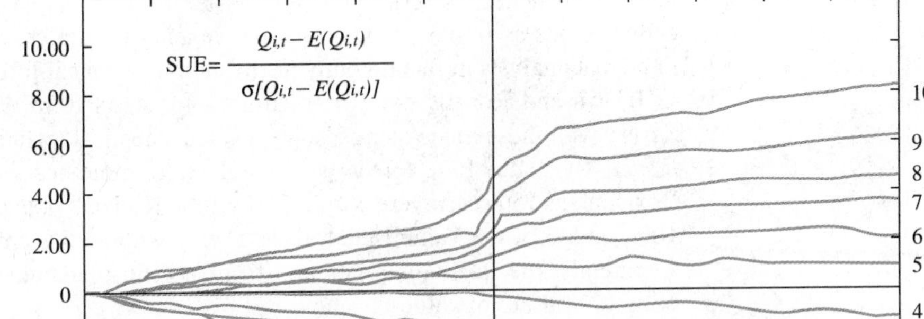

Evidently, one can earn abnormal profits simply by waiting for earnings announcements and purchasing a stock portfolio of high-SUE companies. These are precisely the types of predictable continuing trends that ought to be impossible in an efficient market.

This finding is not unique. Many earnings announcement studies have found similar results. Some research suggests that the post-announcement drift in security prices might be related in part to trading costs. Bernard and Thomas[3] found that post-announcement abnormal returns increase with the magnitude of SUE until the earnings surprise becomes fairly large. Beyond this point, they speculated the change in the perceived value of the firm due to the earnings announcement is so large that transaction costs no longer impede trading. They also pointed out that post-announcement abnormal returns are larger for smaller firms, for which trading costs are higher.

Still, these results do not satisfactorily explain the post-announcement drift anomaly. First, although trading costs may explain the existence of post-announcement drift, they do not explain why the total post-announcement abnormal return is higher for high-SUE firms. Second, Bernard and Thomas showed that firms with positive earnings surprises in one quarter exhibit positive abnormal returns at the earnings announcement in the *following* quarter, suggesting that the market does not fully account for the implications of current earnings announcements when it revises its expectations for future earnings. This suggests informational inefficiency, leaving this phenomenon a topic for future research.

---

[3] Victor L. Bernard and Jacob K. Thomas, "Post-Earnings-Announcement Drift: Delayed Price Response or Risk Premium? *Journal of Accounting Research* 27 (1989), pp. 1–36.

You might wonder whether security analysts can predict earnings more accurately than mechanical time series equations. After all, analysts have access to these statistical equations as well as to other qualitative and quantitative data. The evidence seems to be that analysts in fact do outperform such mechanical forecasts.

Brown and Rozeff[4] compared earnings forecasts from the *Value Line Investment Survey* with those made using a sophisticated statistical technique called a *Box-Jenkins model.* The Value Line forecasts generally were more accurate. Although 54% of the Box-Jenkins forecasts were within 25% of the realized values, and 26.5% were within 10%, 63.5% of the Value Line forecasts were within 25% and 23% were within 10%. Apparently, the qualitative data and firm-specific fundamental analysis that analysts bring to bear are of value.

18.3 Return on Equity

Past versus Future ROE

We noted in Chapter 17 that **return on equity** (ROE) is one of the two basic factors in determining a firm's growth rate of earnings. There are two sides to using ROE. Sometimes it is reasonable to assume that future ROE will approximate its past value, but a high ROE in the past does not necessarily imply a firm's future ROE will be high.

A declining ROE, on the other hand, is evidence that the firm's new investments have offered a lower ROE than its past investments. The best forecast of future ROE in this case may be lower than the most recent ROE. The vital point for an analyst is not to accept historical values as indicators of future values. Data from the recent past may provide information regarding future performance, but the analyst should always keep an eye on the future. It is expectations of future dividends and earnings that determine the intrinsic value of the company's stock.

Financial Leverage and ROE

An analyst interpreting the past behavior of a firm's ROE or forecasting its future value must pay careful attention to the firm's debt-equity mix and to the interest rate on its debt. An example will show why. Suppose Nodett is a firm that is all-equity financed and has total assets of $100 million. Assume it pays corporate taxes at the rate of 40% of taxable earnings.

Table 18.4 shows the behavior of sales, earnings before interest and taxes, and net profits under three scenarios representing phases of the business cycle. It also shows the behavior of two of the most commonly used profitability measures: operating **return on assets** (ROA), which equals EBIT/assets, and ROE, which equals net profits/equity.

Somdett is an otherwise identical firm to Nodett, but $40 million of its $100 million of assets are financed with debt bearing an interest rate of 8%. It pays annual interest expenses of $3.2 million. Table 18.5 shows how Somdett's ROE differs from Nodett's.

[4] Lawrence D. Brown and Michael Rozeff, "The Superiority of Analysts' Forecasts as Measures of Expectations: Evidence from Earnings," *Journal of Finance*, March 1978.

Table 18.4 Nodett's Profitability over the Business Cycle

Scenario	Sales ($ Millions)	EBIT ($ Millions)	ROA (% per Year)	Net Profit ($ Millions)	ROE (% per Year)
Bad year	80	5	5	3	3
Normal year	100	10	10	6	6
Good year	120	15	15	9	9

Table 18.5 Impact of Financial Leverage on ROE

	Nodett			Somdett	
Scenario	EBIT ($ Millions)	Net Profits ($ Millions)	ROE (%)	Net Profits* ($ Millions)	ROE† (%)
Bad year	5	3	3	1.08	1.8
Normal year	10	6	6	4.08	6.8
Good year	15	9	9	7.08	11.8

*Somdett's after-tax profits are given by .6(EBIT—$3.2 million).
†Somdett's equity is only $60 million.

Note that annual sales, EBIT, and therefore ROA for both firms are the same in each of the three scenarios; that is, business risk for the two companies is identical. It is their financial risk that differs. Although Nodett and Somdett have the same ROA in each scenario, Somdett's ROE exceeds that of Nodett in normal and good years and is lower in bad years.

We can summarize the exact relationship among ROE, ROA, and leverage in the following equation:[5]

$$\text{ROE} = (1 - \text{Tax rate})\left[\text{ROA} + (\text{ROA} + \text{Interest rate})\frac{\text{Debt}}{\text{Equity}}\right] \qquad \textbf{(18.1)}$$

The relationship has the following implications. If there is no debt or if the firm's ROA equals the interest rate on its debt, its ROE will simply equal (1 minus the tax rate)

[5] The derivation of equation 18.1 is as follows:

$$\begin{aligned}
\text{ROE} &= \frac{\text{Net profit}}{\text{Equity}} \\
&= \frac{\text{EBIT} - \text{Interest} - \text{Taxes}}{\text{Equity}} \\
&= \frac{(1 - \text{Tax rate})(\text{EBIT} - \text{Interest})}{\text{Equity}} \\
&= (1 - \text{Tax rate})\left[\frac{(\text{ROA} \times \text{Assets} - \text{Interest rate} \times \text{Debt})}{\text{Equity}}\right] \\
&= (1 - \text{Tax rate})\left[\text{ROA} \times \frac{(\text{Equity} + \text{Debt})}{\text{Equity}} - \text{Interest Rate} \times \frac{\text{Debt}}{\text{Equity}}\right] \\
&= (1 - \text{Tax rate})\left[\text{ROA} + (\text{ROA} - \text{Interest rate})\frac{\text{Debt}}{\text{Equity}}\right]
\end{aligned}$$

times ROA. If its ROA exceeds the interest rate, then its ROE will exceed (1 minus the tax rate) times ROA by an amount that will be greater the higher the debt-to-equity ratio.

This result makes intuitive sense: If ROA exceeds the borrowing rate, the firm earns more on its money than it pays out to creditors. The surplus earnings are available to the firm's owners, the equityholders, which raises ROE. If, on the other hand, ROA is less than the interest rate, then ROE will decline by an amount that depends on the debt-to-equity ratio.

To illustrate the application of equation 18.1, we can use the numerical example in Table 18.5. In a normal year, Nodett has an ROE of 6%, which is .6 (1 minus the tax rate) times its ROA of 10%. However, Somdett, which borrows at an interest rate of 8% and maintains a debt/equity ratio of $\frac{2}{3}$, has an ROE of 6.8%. The calculation using equation 18.1 is

$$\begin{aligned} ROE &= .6[10\% + (10\% - 8\%)\tfrac{2}{3}] \\ &= .6[10\% + \tfrac{4}{3}\%] \\ &= 6.8\% \end{aligned}$$

The important point to remember is that increased debt will make a positive contribution to a firm's ROE only if the firm's ROA exceeds the interest rate on the debt.

Note also that financial leverage increases the risk of the equityholder returns. Table 18.5 shows that ROE on Somdett is worse than that of Nodett in bad years. Conversely, in good years, Somdett outperforms Nodett because the excess of ROA over ROE provides additional funds for equityholders. The presence of debt makes Somdett more sensitive to the business cycle than Nodett. Even though the two companies have equal business risk (reflected in their identical EBITs in all three scenarios), Somdett carries greater financial risk than Nodett.

Even if financial leverage increases the expected ROE of Somdett relative to Nodett (as it seems to in Table 18.5), this does not imply that the market value of Somdett's equity will be higher. Financial leverage increases the risk of the firm's equity as surely as it raises the expected ROE.

CONCEPT CHECK Question 1. Mordett is a company with the same assets as Nodett and Somdett but a debt-to-equity ratio of 1.0 and an interest rate of 9%. What would its net profit and ROE be in a bad year, a normal year, and a good year?

18.4 Ratio Analysis

Decomposition of ROE

To understand the factors affecting a firm's ROE, including its trend over time and its performance relative to competitors, analysts often "decompose" ROE into the product of a series of ratios. Each component ratio is in itself meaningful, and the process serves to focus the analyst's attention on the separate factors influencing performance. This kind of decomposition of ROE is often called the **Du Pont system.**

Table 18.6 Ratio Decomposition Analysis for Nodett and Somdett

	ROE	(1) Net Profit/ Pretax Profit	(2) Pretax Profit/EBIT	(3) EBIT/Sales (ROS)	(4) Sales/Assets (ATO)	(5) Assets/ Equity	(6) Compound Leverage Factor (2) × (5)
Bad year							
Nodett	.030	.6	1.000	.0625	0.800	1.000	1.000
Somdett	.018	.6	0.360	.0625	0.800	1.667	0.600
Normal year							
Nodett	.060	.6	1.000	.1000	1.000	1.000	1.000
Somdett	.068	.6	0.680	.1000	1.000	1.667	1.134
Good year							
Nodett	.090	.6	1.000	.1250	1.200	1.000	1.000
Somdett	.118	.6	0.787	.1250	1.200	1.667	1.311

One useful decomposition of ROE is

$$\text{ROE} = \frac{\text{Net profits}}{\text{Pretax profits}} \times \frac{\text{Pretax profits}}{\text{EBIT}} \times \frac{\text{EBIT}}{\text{Sales}} \times \frac{\text{Sales}}{\text{Assets}} \times \frac{\text{Assets}}{\text{Equity}}$$

$$(1) \times (2) \times (3) \times (4) \times (5)$$

Table 18.6 shows all these ratios for Nodett and Somdett Corporations under the three different economic scenarios.

Let us first focus on factors 3 and 4. Notice that their product, EBIT/Assets, gives us the firm's ROA.

Factor 3 is known as the firm's operating **profit margin** or **return on sales** (ROS). ROS shows operating profit per dollar of sales. In an average year, Nodett's ROS is 0.10 or 10%; in a bad year, it is 0.0625, or 6.25%, and in a good year, 0.125, or 12.5%.

Factor 4, the ratio of sales to assets, is known as **asset turnover** (ATO). It indicates the efficiency of the firm's use of assets in the sense that it measures the annual sales generated by each dollar of assets. In a normal year, Nodett's ATO is 1.0 per year, meaning that sales of $1 per year were generated per dollar of assets. In a bad year, this ratio declines to 0.8 per year, and in a good year, it rises to 1.2 per year.

Comparing Nodett and Somdett, we see that factors 3 and 4 do not depend on a firm's financial leverage. The firms' ratios are equal to each other in all three scenarios.

Similarly, factor 1, the ratio of net income after taxes to pretax profit, is the same for both firms. We call this the tax-burden ratio. Its value reflects both the government's tax code and the policies pursued by the firm in trying to minimize its tax burden. In our example it does not change over the business cycle, remaining a constant .6.

Although factors 1, 3, and 4 are not affected by a firm's capital structure, factors 2 and 5 are. Factor 2 is the ratio of pretax profits to EBIT. The firm's pretax profits will be greatest when there are no interest payments to be made to debtholders. In fact, another way to express this ratio is

$$\frac{\text{Pretax profits}}{\text{EBIT}} = \frac{\text{EBIT} - \text{Interest expense}}{\text{EBIT}}$$

We will call this factor the *interest-burden ratio* (IB). It takes on its highest possible value, 1, for Nodett, which has no financial leverage. The higher the degree of financial leverage, the lower the IB ratio. Nodett's IB ratio does not vary over the business cycle. It is fixed at 1.0, reflecting the total absence of interest payments. For Somdett, however, because interest expense is fixed in a dollar amount while EBIT varies, the IB ratio varies from a low of 0.36 in a bad year to a high of 0.787 in a good year.

Factor 5, the ratio of assets to equity, is a measure of the firm's degree of financial leverage. It is called the **leverage ratio** and is equal to 1 plus the debt-to-equity ratio.[6] In our numerical example in Table 18.6, Nodett has a leverage ratio of 1, while Somdett's is 1.667.

From our discussion in Section 18.2, we know that financial leverage helps boost ROE only if ROA is greater than the interest rate on the firm's debt. How is this fact reflected in the ratios of Table 18.6?

The answer is that to measure the full impact of leverage in this framework, the analyst must take the product of the IB and leverage ratios (i.e., factors 2 and 5, shown in Table 18.6 as column 6). For Nodett, factor 6, which we call the *compound leverage factor,* remains a constant 1.0 under all three scenarios. But for Somdett, we see that the compound leverage factor is greater than 1 in normal years (1.134) and in good years (1.311), indicating the positive contribution of financial leverage to ROE. It is less than 1 in bad years, reflecting the fact that when ROA falls below the interest rate, ROE falls with increased use of debt.

We can summarize all of these relationships as follows:

$$\text{ROE} = \text{Tax burden} \times \text{Interest burden} \times \text{Margin} \times \text{Turnover} \times \text{Leverage}$$

Because

$$\text{ROA} = \text{Margin} \times \text{Turnover}$$

and

$$\text{Compound leverage factor} = \text{Interest burden} \times \text{Leverage}$$

we can decompose ROE equivalently as follows:

$$\text{ROE} = \text{Tax burden} \times \text{ROA} \times \text{Compound leverage factor}$$

Table 18.6 compares firms with the same ROS and ATO but different degrees of financial leverage. Comparison of ROS and ATO usually is meaningful only in evaluating firms in the same industry. Cross-industry comparisons of these two ratios are often meaningless and can even be misleading.

For example, let us take two firms with the same ROA of 10% per year. The first is a supermarket chain, the second is a gas and electric utility.

As Table 18.7 shows, the supermarket chain has a "low" ROS of 2% and achieves a 10% ROA by "turning over" its assets five times per year. The capital-intensive utility, on the other hand, has a "low" ATO of only 0.5 times per year and achieves its 10% ROA by having an ROS of 20%. The point here is that a "low" ROS or ATO ratio need not indicate a troubled firm. Each ratio must be interpreted in light of industry norms.

---

[6] $\frac{\text{Assets}}{\text{Equity}} = \frac{\text{Equity} + \text{Debt}}{\text{Equity}} = 1 + \frac{\text{Debt}}{\text{Equity}}$

Table 18.7 Differences between ROS and ATO across Industries

	ROS	×	ATO	=	ROA
Supermarket chain	.02		5.0		.10
Utility	.20		0.5		.10

Even within an industry, ROS and ATO sometimes can differ markedly among firms pursuing different marketing strategies. In the retailing industry, for example, Neiman-Marcus pursues a high-margin, low-ATO policy compared to Wal-Mart, which pursues a low-margin, high-ATO policy.

CONCEPT CHECK Question 2. Do a ratio decomposition analysis for the Mordett corporation of Question 1, preparing a table similar to Table 18.6.

Turnover and Other Asset Utilization Ratios

It is often helpful in understanding a firm's ratio of sales to assets to compute comparable efficiency-of-utilization, or turnover, ratios for subcategories of assets. For example, fixed-asset turnover would be

$$\frac{\text{Sales}}{\text{Fixed assets}}$$

This ratio measures sales per dollar of the firm's money tied up in fixed assets.

To illustrate how you can compute this and other ratios from a firm's financial statements, consider Growth Industries, Inc. (GI). GI's income statement and opening and closing balance sheets for the years 19X1, 19X2, and 19X3 appear in Table 18.8.

GI's total asset turnover in 19X3 was 0.303, which was below the industry average of 0.4. To understand better why GI underperformed, we decide to compute asset utilization ratios separately for fixed assets, inventories, and accounts receivable.

GI's sales in 19X3 were $144 million. Its only fixed assets were plant and equipment, which were $216 million at the beginning of the year and $259.2 million at year's end. Average fixed assets for the year were, therefore, $237.6 million [($216 million + $259.2 million)/2]. GI's fixed-asset turnover for 19X3 was $144 million per year/$237.6 million = 0.606 per year. In other words, for every dollar of fixed assets, there were $.606 in sales during the year 19X3.

Comparable figures for the fixed-asset turnover ratio for 19X1 and 19X2 and the 19X3 industry average are

19X1	19X2	19X3	19X3 Industry average
0.606	0.606	0.606	0.700

GI's fixed asset turnover has been stable over time and below the industry average.

Whenever a financial ratio includes one item from the income statement, which covers a period of time, and another from a balance sheet, which is a "snapshot" at a

Table 18.8 Growth Industries Financial Statements, 19X1–19X3 ($ thousands)

	19X0	19X1	19X2	19X3
Income statements				
Sales revenue		$100,000	$120,000	$144,000
Cost of goods sold (including depreciation)		55,000	66,000	79,200
Depreciation		15,000	18,000	21,600
Selling and administrative expenses		15,000	18,000	21,600
Operating income		30,000	36,000	43,200
Interest expense		10,500	19,095	34,391
Taxable income		19,500	16,905	8,809
Income tax (40% rate)		7,800	6,762	3,524
Net income		11,700	10,143	5,285
Balance sheets (end of year)				
Cash and marketable securities	$ 50,000	60,000	72,000	86,400
Accounts receivable	25,000	30,000	36,000	43,200
Inventories	75,000	90,000	108,000	129,600
Net plant and equipment	150,000	180,000	216,000	259,200
Total assets	$300,000	$360,000	$432,000	$518,400
Accounts payable	$ 30,000	$ 36,000	$ 43,200	$ 51,840
Short-term debt	45,000	87,300	141,957	214,432
Long-term debt (8% bonds maturing in 19X7)	75,000	75,000	75,000	75,000
Total liabilities	$150,000	$198,300	$260,157	341,272
Shareholders' equity (1 million shares outstanding)	$150,000	$161,700	$171,843	$177,128
Other data				
Market price per common share at year-end		$93.60	$61.00	$21.00

particular time, the practice is to take the average of the beginning and end-of-year balance sheet figures. Thus, in computing the fixed-asset turnover ratio you divide sales (from the income statement) by average fixed assets (from the balance sheet).

Another widely followed turnover ratio is the inventory turnover ratio, which is the ratio of cost of goods sold per dollar of inventory. It is usually expressed as cost of goods sold (instead of sales revenue) divided by average inventory. It measures the speed with which inventory is turned over.

In 19X1, GI's cost of goods sold (less depreciation) was $40 million, and its average inventory was $82.5 million [($75 million + $90 million)/2]. Its inventory turnover was 0.485 per year ($40 million/$82.5 million). In 19X2 and 19X3, inventory turnover remained the same and continued below the industry average of 0.5 per year.

Another measure of efficiency is the ratio of accounts receivable to sales. The accounts receivable ratio usually is computed as average accounts receivable/sales × 365. The result is a number called the **average collection period,** or **days receivables,** which equals the total credit extended to customers per dollar of daily sales. It is the number of days' worth of sales tied up in accounts receivable. You can also think of it as the average lag between the date of sale and the date payment is received.

For GI in 19X3 this number was 100.4 days:

$$\frac{(\$36 \text{ million} + \$43.2 \text{ million})/2}{\$144 \text{ million}} \times 365 = 100.4 \text{ days}$$

The industry average was 60 days.

In summary, use of these ratios lets us see that GI's poor total asset turnover relative to the industry is in part caused by lower-than-average fixed-asset turnover and inventory turnover and higher-than-average days receivables. This suggests GI may be having problems with excess plant capacity along with poor inventory and receivables management procedures.

Liquidity and Coverage Ratios

Liquidity and interest coverage ratios are of great importance in evaluating the riskiness of a firm's securities. They aid in assessing the financial strength of the firm. Liquidity ratios include the current ratio, quick ratio, and interest coverage ratio.

1. **Current ratio:** Current assets/current liabilities. This ratio measures the ability of the firm to pay off its current liabilities by liquidating its current assets (i.e., turning them into cash). It indicates the firm's ability to avoid insolvency in the short run. GI's current ratio in 19X1, for example, was (60 + 30 + 90)/(36 + 87.3) = 1.46. In other years, it was

19X1	19X2	19X3	19X3 Industry Average
1.46	1.17	.97	2.0

   This represents an unfavorable time trend and poor standing relative to the industry.
2. **Quick ratio:** (Cash + receivables)/current liabilities. This ratio is also called the **acid test ratio.** It has the same denominator as the current ratio, but its numerator includes only cash, cash equivalents, and receivables. The quick ratio is a better measure of liquidity than the current ratio for firms whose inventory is not readily convertible into cash. GI's quick ratio shows the same disturbing trends as its current ratio:

19X1	19X2	19X3	19X3 Industry Average
.73	.58	.49	1.0

3. **Interest coverage ratio:** EBIT/interest expense. This ratio is often called **times interest earned.** It is closely related to the interest-burden ratio discussed in the previous section. A high coverage ratio tells the firm's shareholders and lenders that the likelihood of bankruptcy is low because annual earnings are significantly greater than annual interest obligations. It is widely used by both lenders and borrowers in determining the firm's debt capacity and is a major determinant of the firm's bond rating. GI's interest coverage ratios are

19X1	19X2	19X3	19X3 Industry Average
2.86	1.89	1.26	5

GI's interest coverage ratio has fallen dramatically over this three-year period, and by 19X3 it is far below the industry average. Probably its credit rating has been declining as well, and no doubt GI is considered a relatively poor credit risk in 19X3.

Market Price Ratios

There are two market price ratios: the market-to-book-value ratio and the price/earnings ratio.

The **market-to-book-value ratio** (P/B) equals the market price of a share of the firm's common stock divided by its *book value,* that is, shareholders' equity per share. Analysts sometimes consider the stock of a firm with a low market-to-book value to be a "safer" investment, seeing the book value as a "floor" supporting the market price.

Analysts presumably view book value as the level below which market price will not fall because the firm always has the option to liquidate, or sell, its assets for their book values. However, this view is questionable. In fact, some firms, such as Digital (see Chapter 17), do sometimes sell for less than book value. Nevertheless, low market-to-book-value ratio is seen by some as providing a "margin of safety," and some analysts will screen out or reject high P/B firms in their stock selection process.

Proponents of the P/B screen would argue that, if all other relevant attributes are the same for two stocks, the one with the lower P/B ratio is safer. Although there may be firms for which this approach has some validity, book value does not necessarily represent liquidation value, which renders the margin of safety notion unreliable.

The theory of equity valuation offers some insight into the significance of the P/B ratio. A high P/B ratio is an indication that investors think a firm has opportunities of earning a rate of return on their investment in excess of the market capitalization rate, *k*.

To illustrate this point, we can return to the numerical example in Chapter 17, Table 17.3. That example assumes the market capitalization rate is 12% per year. Now add the assumptions that the book value per share is \$8.33, and that the coming year's expected EPS is \$1, so that in the case for which the expected ROE on future investments also is 12%, the stock will sell at \$1/.12 = \$8.33, and the P/B ratio will be 1.

Table 18.9 shows the P/B ratio for alternative assumptions about future ROE and plowback ratio. Reading down any column, you can see how the P/B ratio changes with ROE. The numbers reveal that, for a given plowback ratio, the P/B ratio is higher, the higher the expected ROE. This makes sense, because the greater the expected profitability of the firm's future investment opportunities, the greater its market value as an ongoing enterprise compared with the cost of acquiring its assets.

We've noted that the **price/earnings ratio** that is based on the firm's financial statements and reported in newspaper stock listings is not the same as the price/earnings multiple that emerges from a discounted dividend model. The numerator is the same (the market price of the stock), but the denominator is different. The P/E ratio uses the most recent past accountings earnings, whereas the P/E multiple predicted by valuation models uses expected future economic earnings.

Many security analysts pay careful attention to the accounting P/E ratio in the belief that among low P/E stocks they are more likely to find bargains than with high P/E

Table 18.9 Effect of ROE and Plowback Ratio on P/B

	Plowback Ratio (b)			
ROE	**0**	**25%**	**50%**	**75%**
10%	1.00	0.95	0.86	0.67
12%	1.00	1.00	1.00	1.00
14%	1.00	1.06	1.20	2.00

The assumptions and formulas underlying this table are: E_1 = \$1; book value per share = \$8.33; k = 12% per year.

$$g = b \times \text{ROE}$$

$$P_0 = \frac{(1 - b)E}{k - g}$$

$$\text{P/B} = P_0/\$8.33$$

stocks. The idea is that you can acquire a claim on a dollar of earnings more cheaply if the P/E ratio is low. For example, if the P/E ratio is 8, you pay \$8 per share per \$1 of *current* earnings, whereas if P/E is 12, you must pay \$12 for a claim on \$1 of current earnings.

Note, however, that current earnings may differ substantially from future earnings. The higher P/E stock still may be a bargain relative to the low P/E stock if its earnings and dividends are expected to grow at a faster rate. Our point is that ownership of the stock conveys the right to future earnings, as well as to current earnings. An exclusive focus on the commonly reported accounting P/E ratio can be shortsighted, because by its nature it ignores future growth in earnings.

An efficient markets adherent will be skeptical of the notion that a strategy of investing in low P/E stocks would result in an expected rate of return greater than that of investing in high or medium P/E stocks having the same risk. The empirical evidence on this question is mixed, but even if the strategy has worked in the past, it still should not work in the future because too many investors would be following it. This is the lesson of market efficiency.

Before leaving the P/B and P/E ratios, it is worth pointing out the relationship among these ratios and ROE:

$$\begin{aligned} \text{ROE} &= \frac{\text{Earnings}}{\text{Bookvalue}} \\ &= \frac{\text{Market price}}{\text{Book value}} \div \frac{\text{Market price}}{\text{Earnings}} \\ &= \text{P/B ratio} \div \text{P/E ratio} \end{aligned}$$

By rearranging the terms, we find that a firm's **earnings yield,** the ratio of earnings to price, is equal to its ROE divided by the market-book value ratio:

$$\frac{E}{P} = \frac{\text{ROE}}{\text{P/B}}$$

Thus, a company with a high ROE can have a relatively low earnings yield because its P/B ratio is high. This indicates that a high ROE does not in and of itself imply the stock is a good buy: The price of the stock already may be bid up to reflect an attractive ROE. If so, the P/B ratio will be above 1.0, and the earnings yield to stockholders will be below the ROE, as the equation demonstrates. The relationship shows that a strategy of investing in the stock of high ROE firms may produce a lower holding-period return than investing in those with a low ROE.

Clayman[7] found that investing in the stocks of 29 "excellent" companies, with mean reported ROE of 19.05% during the period of 1976 to 1980, produced results much inferior to investing in 39 "unexcellent" companies, those with a mean ROE of 7.09% during the period. An investor putting equal dollar amounts in the stocks of unexcellent companies would have earned a portfolio rate of return over the 1981 to 1985 period that was 11.3% higher per year than the rate of return on a comparable portfolio of excellent company stocks.

CONCEPT CHECK Question 3. What were GI's ROE, P/E, and P/B ratios in the year 19X3? How do they compare to the industry average ratios, which were:
ROE = 8.64%
P/E = 8
P/B = .69
How does GI's earnings yield in 19X3 compare to the industry average?

18.5 An Illustration of Financial Statement Analysis

In her 19X3 annual report to the shareholders of Growth Industries, Inc. the president wrote: "19X3 was another successful year for Growth Industries. As in 19X2, sales, assets, and operating income all continued to grow at a rate of 20%."

Is she right?

We can evaluate her statement by conducting a full-scale ratio analysis of Growth Industries. Our purpose is to assess GI's performance in the recent past, to evaluate its future prospects, and to determine whether its market price reflects its intrinsic value.

Table 18.10 shows the key financial ratios we can compute from Gi's financial statements. The president is certainly right about the growth rate in sales, assets, and operating income. Inspection of GI's key financial ratios, however, contradicts her first sentence: 19X3 was not another successful year for GI—it appears to have been another miserable one.

ROE has been declining steadily from 7.51% in 19X1 to 3.03% in 19X3. A comparison of GI's 19X3 ROE to the 19X3 industry average of 8.64% makes the deteriorating time trend appear especially alarming. The low and falling market-to-book value ratio and the falling price/earnings ratio indicate investors are less and less optimistic about the firm's future profitability.

The fact that ROA has not been declining, however, tells us that the source of the declining time trend in GI'2 ROE must be inappropriate use of financial leverage. And we see that, while GI's leverage ratio climbed from 2.117 in 19X1 to 2.723 in 19X3, its interest-burden ratio fell from 0.650 to 0.204—with the net result that the compound leverage factor fell from 1.376 to 0.556.

---

[7] Michelle Clayman, "In Search of Excellence: The Investor's Viewpoint," *Financial Analysts Journal,* May–June 1987.

Table 18.10 Key Financial Ratios of Growth Industries, Inc.

Year	ROE	(1) Net Profit/ Pretax Profit	(2) Pretax Profit/ EBIT	(3) EBIT/ Sales (ROS)	(4) Sales/ Assets (ATO)	(5) Assets/ Equity	(6) Compound Leverage Factor (2) × (5)	(7) ROA (3) × (4)	P/E	P/B
19X1	7.51%	.6	.650	30%	.303	2.117	1.376	9.09%	8	.58
19X2	6.08	.6	.470	30	.303	2.375	1.116	9.09	6	.35
19X3	3.03	.6	.204	30	.303	2.723	0.556	9.09	4	.12
Industry average	8.64%	.6	.800	30%	.400	1.500	1.200	12.00%	8	.69

The rapid increase in short-term debt from year to year and the concurrent increase in interest expense make it clear that, to finance its 20% growth rate in sales, GI has incurred sizable amounts of short-term debt at high interest rates. The firm is paying rates of interest greater than the ROA it is earning on the investment financed with the new borrowing. As the firm has expanded, its situation has become ever more precarious.

In 19X3, for example, the average interest rate on short-term debt was 20% versus an ROA of 9.09%. (We compute the average interest rate on short-term debt by taking the total interest expense of $34,391,000, subtracting the $6 million in interest on the long-term bonds, and dividing by the beginning-of-year short-term debt of $141,957,000.)

GI's problems become clear when we examine its statement of cash flows in Table 18.11. The statement is derived from the income statement and balance sheet in Table 18.8. GI's cash flow from operations is falling steadily, from $12,700,000 in 19X1 to $6,725,000 in 19X3. The firm's investment in plant and equipment, by contrast, has increased greatly. Net plant and equipment (i.e., net of depreciation) rose from $150,000,000 in 19X0 to $259,200,000 in 19X3. This near doubling of the capital assets makes the decrease in cash flow from operations all the more troubling.

The source of the difficulty is GI's enormous amount of short-term borrowing. In a sense, the company is being run as a pyramid scheme. It borrows more and more each year to maintain its 20% growth rate in assets and income. However, the new assets are not generating enough cash flow to support the extra interest burden of the debt, as the falling cash flow from operations indicates. Eventually, when the firm loses its ability to borrow further, its growth will be at an end.

At this point GI stock might be an attractive investment. Its market price is only 12% of its book value, and with a P/E ratio of 4 its earnings yield is 25% per year. GI is a likely candidate for a takeover by another firm that might replace GI's management and build shareholder value through a radical change in policy.

CONCEPT CHECK

Question 4. You have the following information for IBX Corporation for the years 1995 and 1992 (all figures are in $ millions):

Table 18.11 Growth Industries Statement of Cash Flows ($ thousands)

	19X1	19X2	19X3
Cash Flow from Operating Activities			
Net income	$ 11,700	$ 10,143	$ 5,285
+ Depreciation	15,000	18,000	21,600
+ Decrease (increase) in accounts receivable	(5,000)	(6,000)	(7,200)
+ Decrease (increase) in inventories	(15,000)	(18,000)	(21,600)
+ Increase in accounts payable	6,000	7,200	8,640
	$ 12,700	$ 11,343	$ 6,725
Cash Flow from Investing Activities			
Investment in plant and equipment*	$(45,000)	$(54,000)	$(64,800)
Cash Flow from Financing Activities			
Dividends paid†	$ 0	$ 0	$ 0
Short-term debt issued	$ 42,300	$ 54,657	$ 72,475
Change in cash and marketable securities‡	$ 10,000	$ 12,000	$ 14,400

*Gross investment equals increase in net plant and equipment plus depreciation.
†We can conclude that no dividends are paid because stockholders' equity increases each year by the full amount of net income, implying a plowback ratio of 1.0.
‡Equals cash flow from operations plus cash flow from investment activities plus cash flow from financing activities. Note that this equals the yearly change in cash and marketable securities on the balance sheet.

Concept Check (continued)

	1995	1992
Net income	$ 253.7	$ 239.0
Pretax income	411.9	375.6
EBIT	517.6	403.1
Average assets	4,857.9	3,459.7
Sales	6,679.3	4,537.0
Shareholders' equity	2,233.3	2,347.3

What is the trend in IBX's ROE, and how can you account for it in terms of tax burden, margin, turnover, and financial leverage?

18.6 Comparability Problems

Financial statement analysis gives us a good amount of ammunition for evaluating a company's performance and future prospects. But comparing financial results of different companies is not so simple. There is more than one acceptable way to represent various items of revenue and expense according to generally accepted accounting principles (GAAP). This means two firms may have exactly the same economic income yet very different accounting incomes.

THE MANY WAYS OF FIGURING FINANCIAL RESULTS

An investor in First Boston Corp. might have had a pleasant surprise while reading the investment banking company's 1987 financial statement. Despite taking heavy hits in the volatile bond markets and October's stock crash. First Boston reported earnings of $3.12 per share—down 40 percent from the heights of 1986, but about the same as profits in 1984.

But hold on. Looking through Value Line's *Investment Survey,* the same investor would be dismayed to find that First Boston's earnings for last year were only 59¢ a share. What gives? In this case the explanation is fairly simple. Value Line doesn't take into account the profits First Boston made in selling its Park Avenue headquarters, while the company and other reporting services such as Standard & Poor's do.

This type of discrepancy in reported financial figures is very common (table) and points to a general rule: Where the bottom line falls depends on who's drawing it. S&P's *Stock Report* generally follows the company's accounting in regard to nonrecurring items, but Value Line doesn't. For example, Union Carbide's reserve for Bhopal litigation amounted to 40¢ per share. S&P and Carbide subtracted it from earnings, but Value Line left it in.

The Bottom Line: Take Your Choice

	1987 Earnings per Share	
	S&P	**Value Line**
Alcoa	$2.52	$4.14
Affiliated Publ.	4.08	0.61
First Boston	3.12	0.59
Merrill Lynch	3.58	1.52
Union Carbide	1.76	2.17

Source: Data from Standard & Poor's Corp.,Value Line Inc.

Forecast Tool

With the rash of mergers, acquisitions, and divestitures in recent years, the varying approaches of reporting services can result in enormous differences. In 1985, for example, when Warner-Lambert cut its losses by selling three hospital-supply units, S&P showed the company losing $4.05 per share for the year, while Value Line reported a gain of $3.05 per share.

To try to get a "clear-cut number," Value Line will remove from earnings such items as gains or losses from discontinued operations and other special items, says a senior analyst at the firm. He says such a number is more useful to investors looking at the future earning power of a company. Similarly, *Business Week's* Corporate Scoreboard shows earnings from continuing operations, excluding special, nonrecurring, or extraordinary items. Dan Mayper at S&P says S&P's philosophy is to reflect all the special items in the figures and explain their significance in the narrative of the report.

There are also wide variations when it comes to computing a company's book value. That's basically what's left over when you subtract liabilities from assets. Unlike Value Line, S&P gives no credit to such intangible assets as customer lists, patents, trademarks, or franchises. Companies with many intangibles on their books, such as broadcasters and publishers, are bound to look a lot worse in S&P's calculations. For example, Capital Cities/ABC had a 1986 per-share book value of $120.82, said Value Line, while S&P showed a negative net worth of $24.26 per share.

Value Line analyst Marc Gerstein believes that including the intangibles on the balance sheet gives the best idea of a company's value as an ongoing concern. S&P regards its approach as more conservative, designed to approximate the company's liquidation value.

Furthermore, interpreting a single firm's performance over time is complicated when inflation distorts the dollar measuring rod. Comparability problems are especially acute in this case because the impact of inflation on reported results often depends on the particular method the firm adopts to account for inventories and depreciation. The security analyst must adjust the earnings and the financial ratio figures to a uniform standard before attempting to compare financial results across firms and over time.

Comparability problems can arise out of the flexibility of GAAP guidelines in accounting for inventories and depreciation and in adjusting for the effects of inflation. Other important potential sources of noncomparability include the capitalization of leases and other expenses and the treatment of pension costs, but they are beyond the scope of this book. The box on the previous page illustrates the types of problems an analyst must be aware of in using financial statements to identify bargain stocks.

Inventory Valuation

There are two commonly used ways to value inventories: **LIFO** (last-in first-out) and **FIFO** (first-in first-out). We can explain the difference using a numerical example.

Suppose Generic Products, Inc. (GPI) has a constant inventory of 1 million units of generic goods. The inventory turns over once per year, meaning the ratio of cost of goods sold to inventory is 1.

The LIFO system calls for valuing the million units used up during the year at the current cost of production, so that the last goods produced are considered the first ones to be sold. They are valued at today's cost.

The FIFO system assumes that the units used up or sold are the ones that were added to inventory first, and goods sold should be valued at original cost.

If the price of generic goods has been constant, at the level of $1, say, the book value of inventory and the cost of goods sold would be the same, $1 million under both systems. But suppose the price of generic goods rises by 10 cents per unit during the year as a result of general inflation.

LIFO accounting would result in a cost of goods sold of $1.1 million, whereas the end-of-year balance sheet value of the 1 million units in inventory remains $1 million. The balance sheet value of inventories is given as the cost of the goods still in inventory. Under LIFO the last goods produced are assumed to be sold at the current cost of $1.10; the goods remaining are the previously produced goods, at a cost of only $1. You can see that, although LIFO accounting accurately measures the cost of goods sold today, it understates the current value of the remaining inventory in an inflationary environment.

In contrast, under FIFO accounting, the cost of goods sold would be $1 million, and the end-of-year balance sheet value of the inventory is $1.1 million. The result is that the LIFO firm has both a lower reported profit and a lower balance sheet value of inventories than the FIFO firm.

LIFO is preferred over FIFO in computing economic earnings (i.e., real sustainable cash flow), because it uses up-to-date prices to evaluate the cost of goods sold. A disadvantage is that LIFO accounting induces balance sheet distortions when it values investment in inventories at original cost. This practice results in an upward bias in ROE because the investment base on which return is earned is undervalued.

In computing the gross national product, the U.S. Department of Commerce has to make an inventory valuation adjustment (IVA) to eliminate the effects of FIFO accounting on the cost of goods sold. In effect, it puts all firms in the aggregate onto a LIFO basis.

Depreciation

Another source of problems is the measurement of depreciation, which is a key factor in computing true earnings. The accounting and economic measures of depreciation can differ markedly. According to the *economic* definition, depreciation is the amount of a firm's operating cash flow that must be reinvested in the firm to sustain its real cash flow at the current level.

The *accounting* measurement is quite different. Accounting depreciation is the amount of the original acquisition cost of an asset that is allocated to each accounting period over an arbitrarily specified life of the asset. This is the figure reported in financial statements.

Assume, for example, that a firm buys machines with a useful economic life of 20 years at $100,000 apiece. In its financial statements, however, the firm can depreciate the machines over 10 years using the straight-line method, for $10,000 per year in depreciation. Thus, after 10 years a machine will be fully depreciated on the books, even though it remains a productive asset that will not need replacement for another 10 years.

In computing accounting earnings, this firm will overestimate depreciation in the first 10 years of the machine's economic life and underestimate it in the last 10 years. This will cause reported earnings to be understated compared with economic earnings in the first 10 years and overstated in the last 10 years.

If the management of the firm had a zero plowback policy and distributed as cash dividends only its accounting earnings, it would pay out too little in the first 10 years relative to the sustainable cash flow. Similarly, a security analyst who relied on the (unadjusted) reported earnings figure during the first few years would see understated economic earnings and would underestimate the firm's intrinsic value.

Depreciation comparability problems add one more wrinkle. A firm can use different depreciation methods for tax purposes than for other reporting purposes. Most firms use accelerated depreciation methods for tax purposes and straight-line depreciation in published financial statements. There also are differences across firms in their estimates of the depreciable life of plant, equipment, and other depreciable assets.

The major problem related to depreciation, however, is caused by inflation. Because conventional depreciation is based on historical costs rather than on the current replacement cost of assets, measured depreciation in periods of inflation is understated relative to replacement cost, and *real* economic income (sustainable cash flow) is correspondingly overstated.

The situation is similar to what happens in FIFO inventory accounting. Conventional depreciation and FIFO both result in an inflation-induced overstatement of real income because both use original cost instead of current cost to calculate net income.

For example, suppose Generic Products, Inc., has a machine with a three-year useful life that originally cost $3 million. Annual straight-line depreciation is $1 million, regardless of what happens to the replacement cost of the machine. Suppose inflation in the first year turns out to be 10%. Then the true annual depreciation expense is $1.1 million in current terms, whereas conventionally measured depreciation remains fixed at $1 million per year. Accounting income overstates *real* economic income by the inflation factor, $0.1 million.

As it does in the case of inventory valuation, the Commerce Department in its computation of GNP tries to adjust aggregate depreciation. It does this by applying "capital consumption allowances" (CCA), to account for the distorting effects of conventional depreciation techniques.

Inflation and Interest Expense

Although inflation can cause distortions in the measurement of a firm's inventory and depreciation costs, it has perhaps an even greater effect on calculation of *real* interest expense. Nominal interest rates include an inflation premium that compensates the lender for inflation-induced erosion in the real value of principal. From the perspective of both lender and borrower, therefore, part of what is conventionally measured as interest expense should be treated more properly as repayment of principal.

For example, suppose Generic Products has debt outstanding with a face value of $10 million at an interest rate of 10% per year. Interest expense as conventionally measured is $1 million per year. However, suppose inflation during the year is 6%, so that the real interest rate is 4%. Then $0.6 million of what appears as interest expense on the income statement is really an inflation premium, or compensation for the anticipated reduction in the real value of the $10 million principal; only $0.4 million is *real* interest expense. The $0.6 million reduction in the purchasing power of the oustanding principal may be thought of as repayment of principal, rather than as an interest expense. Real income of the firm is, therefore, understated by $0.6 million.

This mismeasurement of real interest means inflation deflates the statement of real income. The effects of inflation on the reported values of inventories and depreciation that we have discussed work in the opposite direction.

CONCEPT CHECK Question 5. In a period of rapid inflation, companies ABC and XYZ have the same *reported* earnings. ABC uses LIFO inventory accounting, has relatively fewer depreciable assets, and has more debt than XYZ. XYZ uses FIFO inventory accounting. Which company has the higher *real* income, and why?

International Accounting Conventions

The examples cited above illustrate some of the problems that analysts can encounter when attempting to interpret financial data. Even greater problems arise in the interpretation of the financial statements of foreign firms. This is because these firms do not follow GAAP guidelines. Accounting practices in various countries differ to greater or lesser extents from U.S. standards. Here are some of the major issues that you should be aware of when using the financial statements of foreign firms.

Reserving Practices. Many countries allow firms considerably more discretion in setting aside reserves for future contingencies than is typical in the United States. Because additions to reserves result in a charge against income, reported earnings are far more subject to managerial discretion than in the United States.

Germany is a country that allows particularly wide discretion in reserve practice. When Daimler-Benz AG (producer of the Mercedes Benz) decided to issue shares on the New York Stock Exchange in 1993, it had to revise its accounting statements in accordance with U.S. standards. The revisions transformed a small profit for the first half of 1993 using German accounting rules into a *loss* of a $592 million under more stringent U.S. rules. The nearby box discusses Daimler's decision.

Depreciation. In the United States, firms typically maintain separate sets of accounts for tax and reporting purposes. For example, accelerated depreciation is typically used for tax purposes, whereas straight-line depreciation is used for reporting purposes. In contrast, most other countries do not allow dual sets of accounts, and most firms in foreign countries use accelerated depreciation to minimize taxes despite the fact that it results in lower reported earnings. This makes reported earnings of foreign firms lower than they would be if the firms were allowed to use the U.S. practice.

Intangibles. Treatment of intangibles such as goodwill can vary widely. Are they amortized or expensed? If amortized, over what period? Such issues can have a large impact on reported profits.

The effect of different accounting practices can be substantial. A study by Speidell and Bavishi[8] recalculated the financial statements of firms in several countries using common accounting rules. Figure 18.2, from their study, compares P/E ratios as reported and restated on a common basis. The variation is considerable.

Inflation Accounting

In recognition of the need to adjust for the effects of inflation, the Financial Accounting Standards Board in 1980 issued Rule No. 33 (FASB 33). It required large public corporations to supplement their customary financial statements with data pertaining to the effect of inflation.

A survey reported by Norby[9] however, indicated that security analysts, by and large, were ignoring the inflation-adjusted data. One possible reason is that analysts believed FASB 33 just added another element of noncomparability. In other words, analysts may have judged the inflation-adjusted earnings to be poorer estimates of real economic earnings than the original unadjusted figures.

In 1987, after a lengthy evaluation of the effects of FASB 33, the FASB decided to discontinue it. Today, analysts interested in adjusting reported financial statements for inflation are on their own.

---

[8] Lawrence S. Speidell and Vinod Bavishi, "GAAP Arbitrage: Valuation Opportunities in International Accounting Standards," *Financial Analysts Jounal,* November–December 1992, pp. 58–66.

[9] W. C. Norby, "Applications of Inflation-Adjusted Accounting Data," *Financial Analysis Journal,* March–April 1983.

Daimler Plays Ball

Berlin

"They want to play baseball in America, but they want seven strikes, no umpire and a right to cancel the game." So said the chief of America's Securities and Exchange Commission (SEC), Richard Breeden, of German companies that want to list shares in America without disclosing their financial condition as American companies do. Daimler-Benz, one of the chief targets of Mr. Breeden's scorn, has now agreed to play by at least some of his rules.

On March 24th Daimler announced that it would bcome the first German company to list its shares in the New York Stock Exchange, after reaching a compromise with the SEC over its accounting practices. Daimler demonstrated its new candour by revealing DM4 billion ($2.5 billion) of its hidden reserves, which the company will declare as extraordinary profit for 1992.

Just how far this candour will go is unclear. Neither Daimler nor the SEC has revealed details of their agreement: Mr. Breeden is to wrap up the deal with Daimler's chief financial officer next week. If Daimler were to adopt American standards fully, it would abandon the conservatism for which German companies are notorious and would present its accounts to suit shareholders rather than creditors.

Under an American regime, Daimler would disclose its financial results quarterly, by division. It currently makes no quarterly disclosure of earnings and reveals divisional results only yearly. Because the accounting methods it applies to its subsidiaries are not uniform, their combined results differ from those of the group as a whole. That will change. Daimler would also have less scope to hide profits through unidentified provisions. And it might use less-conservative depreciation schedules, which would fatten its reported profits.

Daimler's reward for disrobing will be better access to the capital of American investors.

Daimler's deal with the SEC could be the biggest break so far with Germany's shareholder-unfriendly style of capitalism. German companies have recently faced growing pressure from their owners, especially foreign ones, to disclose more information and to manage in the interests of investors. Daimler now seems prepared to give its shareholders a better deal. If other big companies follow Daimler's lead, German capitalism may never be the same again.

Source: *The Economist,* March 27, 1993.

18.7 Value Investing: The Graham Technique

No presentation of fundamental security analysis would be complete without a discussion of the ideas of Benjamin Graham, the greatest of the investment "gurus." Until the evolution of modern portfolio theory in the latter half of this century, Graham was the single most important thinker, writer, and teacher in the field of investment analysis. His influence on investment professionals remains very strong.

Graham's magnum opus is *Security Analysis,* written with Columbia Professor David Dodd in 1934. Its message is similar to the ideas presented in this chapter. Graham believed careful analysis of a firm's financial statements could turn up bargain stocks. Over the years, he developed many different rules for determining the most important financial ratios and the critical values for judging a stock to be undervalued. Through many editions, his book has had a profound influence on investment profes-

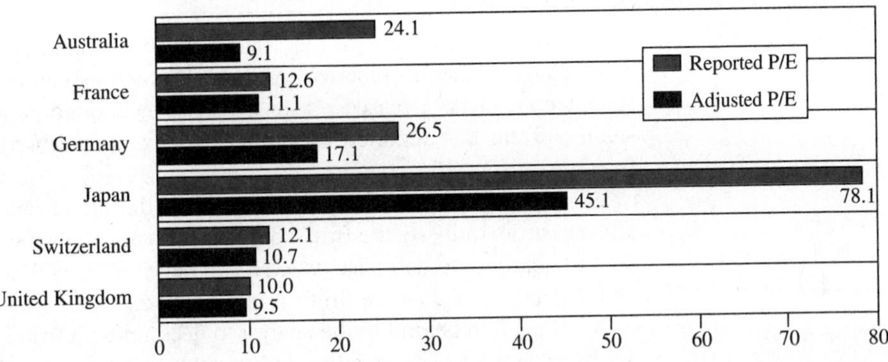

Figure 18.2
Adjusted versus reported price/earnings ratios

sionals. It has been so influential and successful, in fact, that widespread adoption of Graham's techniques has led to elimination of the very bargains they are designed to identify.

In a 1976 seminar Graham said:[10]

> I am no longer an advocate of elaborate techniques of security analysis in order to find superior value opportunities. This was a rewarding activity, say, forty years ago, when our textbook "Graham and Dodd" was first published; but the situation has changed a good deal since then. In the old days any well-trained security analyst could do a good professional job of selecting undervalued issues through detailed studies; but in the light of the enormous amount of research now being carried on, I doubt whether in most cases such extensive efforts will generate sufficiently superior selections to justify their cost. To that very limited extent I'm on the side of the "efficient market" school of thought now generally accepted by the professors.

Nonetheless, in that same seminar, Graham suggested a simplified approach to identify bargain stocks:

> My first, more limited, technique confines itself to the purchase of common stocks at less than their working-capital value, or net current-asset value, giving no weight to the plant and other fixed assets, and deducting all liabilities in full from the current assets. We used this approach extensively in managing investment funds, and over a 30-odd-year period we must have earned an average of some 20 percent per year from this source. For a while, however, after the mid-1950s, this brand of buying opportunity became very scarce because of the pervasive bull market. But it has returned in quantity since the 1973–1974 decline. In January 1976 we counted over 100 such issues in the Standard & Poor's *Stock Guide*—about 10 percent of the total. I consider it a foolproof method of systematic investment—once again, not on the basis of individual results but in terms of the expectable group income.

There are two convenient sources of information for those interested in trying out the Graham technique: Both Standard & Poor's *Outlook* and *The Value Line Investment Survey* carry lists of stocks selling below net working capital value.

---

[10] As cited by John Train in *Money Masters* (New York: Harper & Row, 1987).

SUMMARY

1. The primary focus of the security analyst should be the firm's real economic earnings rather than its reported earnings. Accounting earnings as reported in financial statements can be a biased estimate of real economic earnings, although empirical studies reveal that reported earnings convey considerable information concerning a firm's prospects.

2. A firm's ROE is a key determinant of the growth rate of its earnings. ROE is affected profoundly by the firm's degree of financial leverage. An increase in a firm's debt-to-equity ratio will raise its ROE and hence its growth rate only if the interest rate on the debt is less than the firm's return on assets.

3. It is often helpful to the analyst to decompose a firm's ROE ratio into the product of several accounting ratios and to analyze their separate behavior over time and across companies within an industry. A useful breakdown is

$$\text{ROE} = \frac{\text{Net profits}}{\text{Pretax profits}} \times \frac{\text{Pretax profits}}{\text{EBIT}} \times \frac{\text{EBIT}}{\text{Sales}} \times \frac{\text{Sales}}{\text{Assets}} \times \frac{\text{Assets}}{\text{Equity}}$$

4. Other accounting ratios that have a bearning on a firm's profitability and/or risk are fixed-asset turnover, inventory turnover, days receivables, and the current, quick, and interest coverage ratios.

5. Two ratios that make use of the market price of the firm's common stock in addition to its financial statements are the ratios of market-to-book value and price-to-earnings. Analysts sometimes take low values for these ratios as a margin of safety or a sign that the stock is a bargain.

6. A strategy of investing in stocks with high reported ROE seems to have produced a lower rate of return to the investor than investing in low ROE stocks. This implies that high reported ROE stocks were overpriced compared with low ROE stocks.

7. A major problem in the use of data obtained from a firm's financial statements is comparability. Firms have a great deal of latitude in how they choose to compute various items of revenue and expense. It is, therefore, necessary for the security analyst to adjust accounting earnings and financial ratios to a uniform standard before attempting to compare financial results across firms.

8. Comparability problems can be acute in a period of inflation. Inflation can create distortions in accounting for inventories, depreciation, and interest expense.

Key Terms

Income statement
Balance sheet
Statement of cash flows
Accounting earnings
Economic earnings
Return on equity
Return on assets
Du Pont system
Profit margin
Return on sales
Average collection period
Days receivables
Current ratio
Quick ratio
Acid test ratio
Interest coverage ratio
Times interest earned
Market-to-book-value ratio
Price/earnings ratio
Earnings yield

Asset turnover	LIFO
Leverage ratio	FIFO

Selected Readings

The classic book on the use of financial statements in equity valuation, now in its fifth edition, is:

Cottle, S.; R. Murray; and F. Block, *Graham and Dodd's Security Analysis.* New York: McGraw-Hill, 1988.

Problems

1. The Crusty Pie Co., which specializes in apple turnovers, has a return on sales higher than the industry average, yet its ROA is the same as the industry average. How can you explain this?
2. The ABC Corporation has a profit margin on sales below the industry average, yet its ROA is above the industry average. What does this imply about its asset turnover?
3. Firm A and Firm B have the same ROA, yet Firm A's ROE is higher. How can you explain this?

(Questions 4 through 19 are from past CFA Examinations.)

4. Which of the following *best* explains a ratio of "net sales to average net fixed assets" that *exceeds* the industry average?*
   a. The firm added to its plant and equipment in the past few years.
   b. The firm makes less efficient use of its assets than other firms.
   c. The firm has a lot of old plant and equipment.
   d. The firm uses straight-line depreciation.
5. The rate of return on assets is equivalent to:*
   a. Profit margin × Total asset turnover
   b. Profit margin × Total asset turnover × Leverage ratio/Interest expense
   c. $\dfrac{\text{Net income} + \text{Interest expense net of income tax} + \text{Minority interest in earnings}}{\text{Average total assets}}$
   d. $\dfrac{\text{Net income} + \text{Minority interest in earnings}}{\text{Average total assets}}$
      i. *a* only.
      ii. *a* and *c*.
      iii. *b* only.
      iv. *b* and *d*.
6. The financial statements for Seattle Manufacturing Corporation are to be used to compute the following ratios for 1991 (Tables 18A and 18B).†

---

*Reprinted, with permission, from the Level I 1988 *CFA Study Guide*. Copyright 1988, The Institute of Chartered Financial Analysts, Charlottesville, VA. All rights reserved.

† Reprinted, with permission, from the Level I 1987 *CFA Study Guide*. Copyright 1987, The Institute of Chartered Financial Analysts, Charlottesville, VA. All rights reserved.

Table 18A Seattle Manufacturing Corp. Consolidated Balance Sheet, as of December 31 ($ millions)

	1990	1991
Assets		
Current assets:		
Cash	$ 6.2	$ 6.6
Short-term investment in commercial paper	20.8	15.0
Accounts receivable	77.0	93.2
Inventory	251.2	286.0
Pepaid manufacturing expense	1.4	1.8
Total current assets	356.6	402.6
Leased property under capital leases net of accumulated amortization	181.4	215.6
Other	6.2	9.8
Total assets	$544.2	$628.0
Liabilities		
Current liabilities:		
Accounts payable	$143.2	$161.0
Dividends payable	13.0	14.4
Current portion of long-term debt	12.0	16.6
Current portion of obligations under capital leases	18.8	22.6
Estimated taxes on income	10.8	9.8
Total current liabilities	$197.8	$224.4
Long-term debt	86.4	107.0
Obligations under capital leases	140.8	165.8
Total liabilities	$425.0	$497.2
Shareholders' Equity		
Common stock, $10 par value 4,000,000 shares authorized, 3,000,000 and 2,680,000 outstanding, respectively	26.8	30.0
Cumulative preferred stock, Series A 8%; $25 par value; 1,000,000 authorized; 600,000 oustanding	15.0	15.0
Additional paid-in capital	26.4	27.0
Retained earnings	51.0	58.8
Total shareholders' equity	119.2	130.8
Total liabilities and shareholders' equity	$544.2	$628.0

a. Return on total assets.
b. Earnings per share of common stock.
c. Acid test ratio.
d. Interest coverage ratio.
e. Receivables collection period.
f. Leverage ratio.

Table 18B Seattle Manufacturing Corp. Income Statement, Years Ending December 31 ($ millions)

	1990	1991
Sales	$1,166.6	$1,207.6
Other income, net	12.8	15.6
Total revenues	1,179.4	1,223.2
Cost of sales	$ 912.0	$ 961.2
Amortization of leased property	43.6	48.6
Selling and administrative expense	118.4	128.8
Interest expense	16.2	19.8
Total costs and expenses	1,090.2	1,158.4
Income before income tax	$ 89.2	$ 64.8
Income tax	19.2	10.4
Net income	$ 70.0	$ 54.4

7. The financial statements for Chicago Refrigerator Inc. are to be used to compute the following ratios for 1991 (Tables 18C and 18D).*
   a. Quick ratio.
   b. Return on assets.
   c. Return on common shareholders' equity.
   d. Earnings per share of common stock.
   e. Profit margin.
   f. Times interest earned.
   g. Inventory turnover.
   h. Leverage ratio.
8. The financial statements for Atlas Corporation are to be used to compute the following ratios for 1991 (Tables 18E and 18F).†
   a. Acid-test ratio.
   b. Inventory turnover.
   c. Earnings per share.
   d. Interest coverage.
   e. Leverage.
9. Philip Morris Corporation is a major consumer products company operating worldwide. The company's brand names have immediate recognition in most markets and include Marlboro, Benson & Hedges, Kraft, Kool-Aid, Jell-O, Miller, and Maxwell House. Some of these brands were the result of acquisi-

Table 18C Chicago Refrigerator Inc. Balance Sheet, as of December 31 ($ thousands)

	1990	1991
Assets		
Current assets:		
Cash	$ 683	$ 325
Accounts receivable	1,490	3,599
Inventories	1,415	2,423
Prepaid expenses	15	13
Total current assets	3,603	6,360
Property, plant, equipment, net	1,066	1,541
Other	123	157
Total assets	$4,792	$8,058
Liabilities		
Current liabilities:		
Notes payable to bank	$ —	$ 875
Current portion of long-term debt	38	116
Accounts payable	485	933
Estimated income tax	588	472
Accrued expenses	576	586
Customer advance payment	34	963
Total current liabilities	1,721	3,945
Long-term debt	122	179
Other liabilities	81	131
Total liabilities	$1,924	$4,255
Shareholders' Equity		
Common stock, $1 par value 1,000,000 shares authorized; 550,000 and 829,000 outstanding, respectively	$ 550	$ 829
Preferred stock, Series A 10%; $25.00 par value; 25,000 authorized; 20,000 and 18,000 outstanding, respectively	500	450
Additional paid-in capital	450	575
Retained earnings	1,368	1,949
Total shareholders' equity	$2,868	$3,803
Total liabilities and shareholders' equity	$4,792	$8,058

tions, but many of them have been established through years of marketing effort and advertising expenditures.†

Philip Morris is the world leader in tobacco products, and this line is its primary source of profits. Tobacco product sales are growing slowly, particularly in the United States, for both health and economic reasons. However, cigarette prices have increased much faster than the rate of inflation in the United States

†Reprinted, with permission, from the Level I 1993 *CFA Study Guide*.

Table 18D Chicago Refrigerator Inc. Income Statement, Years Ending December 31 ($ thousands)

	1990	1991
Net sales	$7,570	$12,065
Other income, net	261	345
Total revenues	7,831	12,410
Cost of goods sold	$4,850	$ 8,048
General administrative and marketing expense	1,531	2,025
Interest expense	22	78
Total costs and expenses	6,403	10,151
Net income before tax	$1,428	$ 2,259
Income tax	628	994
Net income	$ 800	$ 1,265

due to a combination of excise tax pressure and aggressive pricing by Philip Morris and other tobacco companies. One justification for this trend put forth by the tobacco industry is that the price increases are necessary to cover the extensive legal fees arising from the large number of negligence and liability suits now pending against tobacco companies.

For many years, Philip Morris has been redeploying the growing excess cash flow from operations (defined as cash over and above that necessary to sustain the intrinsic growth of the basic business). The strategy has been to consistently increase dividends, repurchase common shares, and make acquisitions in consumer nondurable businesses. Dividends have been raised in every year over the past decade, and shares have been steadily repurchased at prices well above book value. Some repurchased stock is held as treasury stock, and the remainder has been retired. Philip Morris has also made many sizable acquisitions (almost all on a purchase basis), which have added substantial goodwill to the balance sheet.

Philip Morris uses the LIFO method for costing all domestic inventories and the straight-line method for recording depreciation. Goodwill and other intangibles are amortized on a straight-line basis over 40 years. The company was an early adopter of FAS 106, "Employers' Accounting for Postretirement Benefits Other than Pensions,"doing so on the immediate recognition basis on January 1, 1991, for all U.S. employee benefit plans. The 1991 year-end accrued postretirement health care cost liability amounted to $1,854 million. Table 18G presents other pertinent information on the firm.

a. Using the DuPont method, identify and calculate Philip Morris's five primary components of return on equity for the years 1981 and 1991. Using these components, calculate and return on equity for both years.

b. Using your answers to Part (*a*), identify the two most significant components contributing to the observed difference in Philip Morris's ROE between 1981 and 1991. Briefly discuss the likely reasons for the changes in those components.

Table 18E Atlas Corporation Consolidated Balance Sheet, as of December 31 ($ millions)

	1990	1991
Assets		
Current assets:		
Cash	$ 3.1	$ 3.3
Short-term investment in commercial paper	2.9	—
Accounts receivable	38.5	46.6
Inventory	125.6	143.0
Prepaid manufacturing expense	.7	.9
Total current assets	$170.8	$193.8
Leased property under capital leases net of accumulated amortization	$ 90.7	$107.8
Other	3.1	4.9
Total assets	$264.6	$306.5
Liabilities		
Current liabilities:		
Accounts payable	$ 71.6	$ 81.7
Dividends payable	6.5	6.0
Current portion of long-term debt	6.0	8.3
Current portion of obligation under capital leases	9.4	11.3
Estimated taxes on income	5.4	4.9
Total current liabilities	$ 98.9	$112.2
Long-term debt	$ 43.2	$ 53.5
Obligations under capital leases	70.4	82.9
Total liabilities	$212.5	248.6
Shareholders' Equity		
Common stock, $10 par value 2,000,000 shares authorized; 1,340,000 and 1,500,000 outstanding respectively	13.4	15.0
Additional paid-in capital	13.2	13.5
Retained earnings	25.5	29.4
Total shareholders' equity	52.1	57.9
Total liabilities and shareholders' equity	$264.6	$306.5

c. Calculate Philip Morris's sustainable growth rate (i.e., ROE $\times$ b) using the 1981 data. The company's actual compound annual growth rate in earnings per share over the 1981–91 period was 20.4%. Discuss why the sustainable growth rate was or was not a good predictor of actual growth over the 1981–91 period.

10. Just before the onset of inflation, a firm switched from FIFO to LIFO. If nothing else changed, the inventory turnover for the next year would be:*

*Reprinted, with permission, from the *CFA Study Guide.* Association for Investment Management and Research, Charlottesville, VA. All rights reserved.

Table 18F Atlas Corporation Income Statement, Years Ending December 31 ($ millions)

	1990	1991
Sales	$583.3	$603.8
Other income, net	6.4	2.8
Main revenues	589.7	606.6
Cost of sales	456.0	475.6
Amortization of leased property	21.8	24.3
Selling and administrative expense	59.2	64.4
Interest expense	8.1	9.9
Total costs and expenses	545.1	574.2
Income before income tax	44.6	32.4
Income tax	9.6	5.2
Net income	$ 35.0	$ 27.2

a. Higher.
b. Lower.
c. Unchanged.
d. Unpredictable from the information given.

11. In an inflationary period, the use of FIFO will make which *one* of the following more realistic than the use of LIFO?*
    a. Balance sheet.
    b. Income statement.
    c. Cash flow statement.
    d. None of the above.
12. A company acquires a machine with an estimated 10-year service life. If the company uses the sum-of-the-years-digits depreciation method instead of the straight-line method:*
    a. Income will be higher in the 10th year.
    b. Total depreciation expense for the 10 years will be lower.
    c. Depreciation expense will be lower in the first year.
    d. Scrapping the machine after eight years will result in a larger loss.
13. Why might a firm's ratio of long-term debt to long-term capital be lower than the industry average, but its ratio of income-before-interest-and-taxes to debt-interest charges be lower than the industry average?*
    a. The firm has a higher profitability than average.
    b. The firm has more short-term debt than average.
    c. The firm has a high ratio of current assets to current liabilities.
    d. The firm has a high ratio of total cash flow to total long-term debt.

*Reprinted, with permission, from the *CFA Study Guide.* Association for Investment Management and Research, Charlottesville, VA.

Table 18G Philip Morris Corporation Selected Financial Statement and Other Data Years Ending December 31 ($ millions except per share data)

	1991	1981
Income Statement		
Operating revenue	$56,458	$10,886
Cost of sales	25,612	5,253
Excise taxes on products	8,394	2,580
Gross profit	$22,452	$3,053
Selling, general, and administrative expenses	13,830	1,741
Operating income	$ 8,622	$ 1,312
Interest expense	1,651	232
Pretax earnings	$ 6,971	$ 1,080
Provision for income taxes	3,044	420
Net earnings	$ 3,927	$ 660
Earnings per share	$4.24	$0.66
Dividends per share	$1.91	$0.25
Balance Sheet		
Current assets	$12,594	$ 3,733
Property, plant, and equipment, net	9,946	3,583
Goodwill	18,624	634
Other assets	6,220	1,230
	$47,384	$ 9,180
Current liabilities	$11,824	$ 1,936
Long-term debt	14,213	3,499
Deferred taxes	1,803	455
Other liabilities	7,032	56
Stockholders' equity	12,512	3,234
Total liabilities and stockholders' equity	$47,384	$ 9,180
Other Data		
Philip Morris:		
Common shares outstanding (millions)	920	1,003
Closing price common stock	$80.250	$6.125
S&P 500 Stock Index:		
Closing price	417.09	122.55
Earnings per share	16.29	15.36
Book value per share	161.08	109.43

14. Assuming continued inflation, a firm that uses LIFO will tend to have a ______ current ratio than a firm using FIFO, and the difference will tend to ______ as time passes.*

*Reprinted, with permission, from the *CFA Study Guide.* Association for Investment Management and Research, Charlottesville, VA.

Table 18H Income Statements and Balance Sheets

	1992	1995
Income statement data		
Revenues	$542	$979
Operating income	38	76
Depreciation and amortization	3	9
Interest expense	3	0
Pretax income	32	67
Income taxes	13	37
Net income after tax	19	30
Balance sheet data		
Fixed assets	$ 41	$ 70
Total assets	245	291
Working capital	123	157
Total debt	16	0
Total shareholders' equity	159	220

a. Higher, increase.
b. Higher, decrease.
c. Lower, decrease.
d. Lower, increase.

15. In a cash flow statement prepared in accordance with FASB 95, cash flow from investing activities *excludes*:*
    a. Cash paid for acquisitions.
    b. Cash received from sale of fixed assets.
    c. Inventory increase due to new (internally developed) product line.
    d. All of the above.
16. Cash flow from operating activities *includes*:*
    a. Inventory increases resulting from acquisitions.
    b. Inventory changes due to changing exchange rates.
    c. Interest paid to stockholders.
    d. Dividends paid to stockholders.
17. All other things being equal, what effect will the payment of a cash dividend have on the following ratios?*

	Times Interest Earned	Debt/Equity Ratio
a.	Increase	Increase
b.	No effect	Increase
c.	No effect	No effect
d.	Decrease	Decrease

*Reprinted, with permission, from the *CFA Study Guide.* Association for Investment Management and Research, Charlottesville, VA.

18. The Du Pont formula defines the net return on shareholders' equity as a function of the following components:*

    - Operating margin.
    - Asset turnover.
    - Interest burden.
    - Financial leverage.
    - Income tax rate.

    Using *only* the data in Table 18H:

    a. Calculate each of the five components listed above for 1992 and 1995, and calculate the return on equity (ROE) for 1992 and 1995, using all of the five components.

    b. Briefly discuss the impact of the changes in asset turnover and financial leverage on the change in ROE from 1992 and 1995.

U.S. Equities On Floppy Problems and Projects

19. Use U.S. Equities On Floppy to find the profit margin, or return on sale s (U.S. Equities On Floppy calls this return on revenues) and the asset turnover of several nonfinancial industry groups. What seems to be the relationship between return on sales and turnover? Is this result expected or unexpected? Why?

20. Choose an industry of interest to you, and compare the return on assets of several firms in that industry to the industry average. Why does the firm do better or worse than the industry average? Use the Du Pont formula to guide your analysis. Compare the debt ratios, asset turnover, and return on sales of your firms to the industry average.

Part VI

Options, Futures, and Other Derivatives

Chapter 19
Options Markets: Introduction

A RELATIVELY RECENT, BUT EXTREMELY IMPORTANT CLASS OF FINANCIAL ASSETS IS DERIVATIVE SECURITIES, OR SIMPLY DERIVATIVES. These are securities whose prices are determined by, or "derive from," the prices of other securities. These assets are also called *contingent claims* because their payoffs are contingent on the prices of other securities.

Options and futures contracts are both derivative securities. We will see that their payoffs depend on the value of other securities. Swaps, which we discussed in Chapter 15, also are derivatives. Because the value of derivatives depends on the value of other securities, they can be powerful tools for both hedging and speculation. We will investigate these applications in the next four chapters, starting in this chapter with options.

Trading of standardized options contracts on a national exchange started in 1973 when the Chicago Board Options Exchange (CBOE) began listing call options. These contracts were almost immediately a great success, crowding out the previously existing over-the-counter trading in stock options.

Option contracts are traded now on several exchanges. They are written on common stock, stock indexes, foreign exchange, agricultural commodities, precious metals, and interest rate futures. In addition, the over-the-counter market also has enjoyed a tremendous resurgence in recent years as trading in custom-tailored options has exploded. Popular and potent tools in modifying portfolio characteristics, options have become essential tools a portfolio manager must understand.

This chapter is an introduction to options markets. It explains how puts and calls work and examines their investment characteristics. Popular option strategies are considered next. Finally, we examine a range of securities with embedded options such as callable or convertible bonds, and take a quick look at so-called exotic options.

19.1 THE OPTION CONTRACT

A **call option** gives its holder the right to purchase an asset for a specified price, called the **exercise or strike price,** on or before some specified expiration date. For example, a July call option on IBM stock with exercise price $70 entitles its owner to purchase IBM stock for a price of $70 at any time up to and including the expiration date in July. The holder of the call is not required to exercise the option. It will pay for the holder to exercise the call only if the market value of the asset to be purchased exceeds the exercise price. When the market price does exceed the exercise price, the optionholder may either sell the option or "call away" the asset for the exercise price and reap a profit. Otherwise, the option may be left unexercised. If it is not exercised before the expiration date of the contract, a call option simply expires and no longer has value.

The purchase price of the option is called the *premium.* It represents the compensation the purchaser of the call must pay for the ability to exercise the option if exercise becomes profitable. Sellers of call options, who are said to *write* calls, receive premium income now as payment against the possibility they will be required at some later date to deliver the asset in return for an exchange price lower than the market value of the asset. If the option is left to expire worthless because the exercise price remains above the market price of the asset, then the writer of the call clears a profit equal to the premium income derived from the sale of the option.

To illustrate, consider a January 1995 maturity call option on a share of IBM stock with an exercise price of $70 per share that sells on December 13, 1994, for $2.375. Exchange-traded options expire on the third Friday of the expiration month, which for this option is January 21, 1995. Until the expiration day, the purchaser of the calls is entitled to buy shares of IBM for $70. On December 13, however, IBM stock sells for $69.625. If it remains below $70, the call will expire worthless, and the investor who buys the call on that day will lose the $2.375 he or she paid for it. If, on the other hand, IBM sells for $75 on January 21, the option will turn out to be a profitable investment, because it will give its holder the right to pay $70 for a stock worth $75. The proceeds from exercise will be

$$\text{Proceeds} = \text{Stock price} - \text{Exercise price} = \$75 - \$70 = \$5$$

and the profit to the investor will be

$$\text{Profit} = \text{Proceeds} - \text{Original investment} = \$5 - \$2.375 = \$2.625$$

This is a holding period return of $2.625/$2.375 = 1.10 or 110% over only 39 days! Obviously, option sellers on December 13 did not consider this outcome very likely.

A **put option** gives its holder the right to *sell* an asset for a specified exercise or strike price on or before some expiration date. A July put on IBM with exercise price $70 entitles its owner to sell IBM stock to the put writer at a price of $70 at any time before expiration in July even if the market price of IBM is less than $70. While profits on call options increase when the asset increases in value, profits on put options increase when the asset value falls. A put will be exercised only if the exercise price is greater than the price of the underlying asset, that is, only if its holder can deliver for the exercise price an asset with market value less than the exercise price. (One doesn't need to own the shares of IBM to exercise the IBM put option. Upon exercise, the investor's broker purchases the necessary shares of IBM at the market price and immediately delivers or "puts them" to an option writer for the exercise price. The owner of the put profits by the difference between the exercise price and market price.)

To illustrate, consider a January 1995 maturity put option on IBM with an exercise price of $70 that sells on December 13, 1994, for $2.25. It entitles its owner to sell a share of IBM for $70 at any time until January 21, 1995. This means that immediate exercise would provide a payoff of $70 − $69.625 = $.375. Obviously, an investor who pays $2.25 for the put has no intention of exercising immediately. If IBM stock rises above $70 by the expiration date, the put will be left to expire worthless. If, on the other hand, IBM sells for $68 at expiration, the put holder will find it optimal to exercise. The payoff from exercising will be

$$\text{Proceeds} = \text{Exercise price} - \text{Stock price} = \$70 - \$68 = \$2.$$

Despite the $2 payoff at maturity, the investor still realizes a loss of $.25 on the put, because it cost $2.25 to purchase. Nevertheless, exercise of the put will be optimal at maturity if the stock price is below the exercise price, because the exercise proceeds will offset at least part of the investment in the option.

An option is described as **in the money** when its exercise would produce profits for its holder. An option is **out of the money** when exercise would be unprofitable. A call option is in the money when the exercise price is below the asset's value because purchase at the exercise price would be profitable. It is out of the money when the exercise price exceeds the asset value; no one would exercise the right to purchase for the strike price an asset worth less than that price. Conversely, put options are in the money when the exercise price exceeds the asset's value, because delivery of the lower-valued asset in exchange for the exercise price is profitable for the holder. Options are **at the money** when the exercise price and asset price are equal.

Options Trading

Some options trade on over-the-counter markets. The OTC market offers the advantage that the terms of the option contract—the exercise price, maturity date, and number of shares committed—can be tailored to the needs of the traders. The costs of establishing an OTC option contract, however, are higher than for exchange-traded options. Today, most option trading occurs on organized exchanges, but the OTC market in customized options is also thriving.

Options contracts traded on exchanges are standardized by allowable maturity dates and exercise prices for each listed option. Each stock option contract provides for the right to buy or sell 100 shares of stock (except when stock splits occur after the contract is listed and the contract is adjusted for the terms of the split).

Standardization of the terms of listed option contracts means all market participants trade in a limited and uniform set of securities. This increases the depth of trading in any particular option, which lowers trading costs and results in a more competitive market. Exchanges, therefore, offer two important benefits: ease of trading, which flows from a central marketplace where buyers and sellers or their representatives congregate; and a liquid secondary market where buyers and sellers of options can transact quickly and cheaply.

Figure 19.1 is a reproduction of listed stock option quotations from *The Wall Street Journal.* The highlighted options are for shares of IBM. The numbers in the column below the company name represent the last recorded price on the New York Stock Exchange for IBM stock, $69 5/8 per share.[1] The first column shows that options are traded on IBM at exercise prices of $45 through $85. These values are also called the *strike prices.*

The exercise or strike prices bracket the stock price. While exercise prices generally are set at five-point intervals for stocks, larger intervals may be set for stocks selling above $100, and intervals of $2½ may be used for stocks selling below $30. If the stock price moves outside the range of exercise prices of the existing set of options, new options with appropriate exercise prices may be offered. Therefore, at any time, both in-the-money and out-of-the-money options will be listed, as in the IBM example.

The next column in Figure 19.1 gives the maturity month of each contract, followed by two pairs of columns showing the number of contracts traded on that day and the closing price for the call and put, respectively. When we compare prices of call options with the same maturity date but different exercise prices in Figure 19.1, we see that the value of call is lower when the exercise price is higher. This makes sense, because the right to purchase a share at a given exercise price is not as valuable when the purchase price is higher. Thus, the January maturity IBM call option with strike price $70 sells for $2.375, whereas the $75 exercise price January call sells for only $11/16. Conversely, put options are worth *more* when the exercise price is higher: You would rather have the right to sell IBM shares for $75 than for $70, and this is reflected in the prices of the puts. The January maturity put options with strike price $75 sells for $5.625, whereas the $70 exercise price January put sells for only $2.25.

Throughout Figure 19.1, you will see that many options may go an entire day without trading. Lack of trading is denoted by three dots in the volume and price columns. Because trading is infrequent, it is not unusual to find option prices that appear out of line with other prices. You might see, for example, two calls with different exercise prices that seem to sell for the same price. This discrepancy arises because the last trades for these options may have occurred at different times during the day. At any moment, the call with the lower exercise price must be worth more than an otherwise-identical call with a higher exercise price.

Figure 19.1 illustrates that the maturities of most exchange-traded options tend to be fairly short, ranging up to only several months. For larger firms and some stock indexes, however, longer-term options are traded with maturities ranging up to three years. These options are called LEAPS (for *l*ong-*t*erm *e*quity *a*ntici*p*ation *s*ecurities).

---

[1] Occasionally, this price may not match the closing price listed for the stock on the stock market page. This is because some NYSE stocks also trade on the Pacific Stock Exchange, which closes after the NYSE, and the stock pages may reflect the more recent Pacific Exchange closing price. The options exchanges, however, close with the NYSE, so the closing NYSE stock price is appropriate for comparison with the closing option price.

Figure 19.1
Stock options

Source: *The Wall Street Journal,* December 14, 1994. Reprinted by permission of *The Wall Street Journal,*

LISTED OPTIONS QUOTATIONS

Option/Strike		Exp.	Call Vol.	Call Last	Put Vol.	Put Last
Epitpe	20	Dec	45	9/16	...	...
20 3/8	20	Jan	45	2	50	1 1/4
20 3/8	22 1/2	Jan	50	3/4	...	...
Exbyte	17 1/2	Dec	54	1 3/8	...	...
Exxon	60	Dec	116	1 1/2	...	...
61	60	Jan	98	2	284	9/16
	60	Jul	75	2 3/4	45	2
[illegible]		...	70	3	[illegible]	...
26 1/8	27 1/2	Dec	15	1/16	260	1 3/8
26 1/8	27 1/2	Jan	214	9/16	88	2
26 1/8	30	Dec	2	1/16	31	3 3/4
26 1/8	30	Jan	158	1/8	19	3 3/4
26 1/8	30	Mar	108	1/2	460	4 3/8
26 1/8	30	Jun	84	1	30	4 3/8
FounHl	40	Dec	...	...	90	9 3/8
FrnkRs	35	Jan	...	...	60	2
FM Cop	20	Jan	30	1 1/8	...	...
20 3/8	20	Jun	40	2 9/16	...	...
20 3/8	22 1/2	Mar	62	11/16	...	...
FrMcRP	17 1/2	Dec	...	...	104	2 13/16
FruitL	22 1/2	Jan	...	...	200	3/8
25	30	Feb	80	3/8	...	...
GP Fnl	17 1/2	Apr	88	2 7/8	...	...
19 3/4	20	Jul	22	2 1/8	20	2
19 3/4	22 1/2	Jan	154	7/16	...	...
19 3/4	25	Jan	425	3/16	300	5 1/2
G T E	30	Dec	29	11/16	...	...
30 5/8	30	Jan	67	1 1/4	50	5/16
30 5/8	30	Jun	32	2 3/16	10	1 5/16
Galoob	5	Dec	30	9/16	...	...
5 1/4	5	Feb	28	1 1/16	...	...
5 1/4	7 1/2	Dec	21	1/16	...	...
Gap	30	Dec	50	2	...	...
32	30	Jan	215	2 3/4	28	7/8
32	35	Dec	30	1/16	91	3 1/4
32	35	Jan	83	5/8	30	3 1/2
32	35	Mar	60	1 1/8	2	4
Gtwy2000	20	Dec	10	2 1/8	125	3/16
21 7/8	22 1/2	Dec	20	1/4	5	7/8
21 7/8	22 1/2	Mar	7	2 1/16	100	2 9/16
GaylCn	10	Jun	550	1 1/8	...	...
Gentch	40	Jan	45	4 7/8	20	5/8
43 1/2	45	Dec	50	5/8	90	2 1/8
43 1/2	45	Jan	28	2	...	...
43 1/2	45	Jul	55	4 1/2	70	4 1/8
43 1/2	50	Dec	100	1/16	...	...
43 1/2	50	Jan	260	5/8	...	...
43 1/2	55	Jan	64	1/4	...	...
GenDyn	40	Dec	20	1 13/16	...	

Option/Strike		Exp.	Call Vol.	Call Last	Put Vol.	Put Last
Honwll	25	Jan	...	...	200	1/4
29 7/8	30	Dec	70	1/4	...	...
29 7/8	30	Jan	50	1 3/8	13	1 1/4
29 7/8	35	Jan	200	3/8	...	...
Houshl	35	Apr	40	3 1/8	...	...
Houstnl	35	Jan	25	1 3/8	...	...
Hum[illegible]	20	Dec	114	15/16		
[illegible]	7 1/2	[illegible]			[illegible]	4 5/8
Intrmag	12 1/2	Apr	50	2 7/16	...	...
13 1/2	12 1/2	Jul	50	2 3/4	...	...
13 1/2	15	Jul	50	1 3/4	...	...
13 1/2	17 1/2	Jul	60	1 1/16	...	...
I B M	45	Jan	25	26 1/4	...	...
69 5/8	60	Jan	18	11 1/4	48	3/16
69 5/8	65	Dec	85	4 7/8	9	1/16
69 5/8	65	Jan	28	6 3/8	260	11/16
69 5/8	65	Apr	1	8 3/8	235	2 1/16
69 5/8	70	Dec	2625	11/16	1863	1
69 5/8	70	Jan	995	2 3/8	702	2 1/4
69 5/8	70	Apr	181	4 3/4	61	3 5/8
69 5/8	70	Jul	38	6 5/8	5	4 5/8
69 5/8	75	Dec	...	...	35	4 3/4
69 5/8	75	Jan	457	11/16	35	5 5/8
69 5/8	75	Apr	171	2 11/16	20	6 1/2
69 5/8	75	Jul	225	4 1/4	...	...
69 5/8	80	Dec	...	...	40	9 1/2
69 5/8	80	Jan	429	3/16	...	...
69 5/8	80	Apr	786	1 7/16	40	10
69 5/8	85	Jan	409	1/16	...	...
69 5/8	85	Apr	169	11/16	...	...
In Flv	45	Dec	52	1 7/8	...	...
47	50	Feb	60	3/8	...	...
IGame	15	Dec	48	3/8	10	1/4
15 1/8	15	Jan	214	1 1/8	4	7/8
15 1/8	15	Apr	85	1 7/8	79	1 3/4
15 1/8	17 1/2	Dec	90	1/16	387	2 1/2
15 1/8	17 1/2	Jan	114	3/16	62	2 1/2
15 1/8	17 1/2	Apr	10	15/16	92	3 1/8
15 1/8	17 1/2	Jul	31	1 3/4	...	...
15 1/8	20	Dec	10	1/16	77	5
15 1/8	20	Jan	49	1/16	10	5
15 1/8	20	Apr	62	1/2	30	4 7/8
15 1/8	20	Jul	21	15/16	...	...
15 1/8	22 1/2	Jan	25	1/16	2	7 3/8
15 1/8	22 1/2	Apr	30	1/4	...	...
In Pap	70	Jan	...	...	30	1
72 1/4	75	Jan	...	...	25	3 5/8
IntRec	20	Dec	25	1 5/8	...	...

Option/Strike		Exp.
Maytag	17 1/2	Jan
Mc Don	25	Dec
28 3/8	25	Jan
28 3/8	27 1/2	Dec
28 3/8	27 1/2	Jan
28 3/8	30	Dec
41 1/4	50	A
Microp	7 1/2	D
9 1/4	10	F
Micsft	55	Ja
62 3/4	55	A
62 3/4	60	D
62 3/4	60	Ja
62 3/4	60	A
62 3/4	65	D
62 3/4	65	Ja
62 3/4	65	A
62 3/4	65	Ju
62 3/4	70	Ja
62 3/4	70	A
MAWste	7 1/2	Ja
M M M	50	Ju
52	55	Ap
MblTel	17 1/2	De
16 5/8	17 1/2	Ja
16 5/8	17 1/2	M
16 5/8	20	M
MltenM	20	Ja
Monsan	75	Ja
72 5/8	75	Ap
72 5/8	80	Ap
MorgSt	60	Ja
Morgan	50	Ja
59 1/8	55	Ma
59 1/8	55	Ju
59 1/8	60	De
59 1/8	60	Ja
59 1/8	60	Ma
59 1/8	65	Ja
Motrla	40	Ja
55 1/4	45	Ja
55 1/4	50	Ja
55 1/4	50	Ap
55 1/4	55	De
55 1/4	55	Jar
55 1/4	55	Ap
55 1/4	55	Jul

Concept Check

Question 1.

a. What will be the proceeds and net profits to an investor who purchases the January maturity IBM calls with exercise price \$75 if the stock price at maturity is \$70? What if the stock price at maturity is \$80?

b. Now answer part (*a*) for an investor who purchases a January maturity IBM put option with exercise price \$75.

American and European Options

An **American option** allows its holder to exercise the right to purchase (if a call) or sell (if a put) the underlying asset on *or before* the expiration date. **European options** allow for exercise of the option only on the expiration date. American options, because they allow more leeway than their European counterparts, generally will be more valuable. Virtually all traded options in this country are American. Foreign currency options and stock index options traded on the Chicago Board Options Exchange are notable exceptions to this rule, however.

Adjustments in Option Contract Terms

Because options convey the right to buy or sell shares at a stated price, stock splits would radically alter their value if the terms of the options contract were not adjusted to account for the stock split. For example, reconsider the IBM call options in Figure 19.1. If IBM were to announce a 10-for-1 split, its share price would fall from $69⅝ to about $7. A call option with exercise price $70 would be just about worthless, with virtually no possibility that the stock would sell at more than $70 before the options expired.

To account for a stock split, the exercise price is reduced by a factor of the split, and the number of options held is increased by that factor. For example, the original IBM call option with exercise price of $70 would be altered after a 10-for-1 split to 10 new options, with each option carrying an exercise price of $7. A similar adjustment is made for stock dividends of more than 10%; the number of shares covered by each option is increased in proportion to the stock dividend, and the exercise price is reduced by that proportion.

In contrast to stock dividends, cash dividends do not affect the terms of an option contract. Because payment of a cash dividend reduces the selling price of the stock without inducing offsetting adjustments in the option contract, the value of the option is affected by dividend policy. Other things being equal, call option values are lower for high-dividend-payout policies, because such policies slow the rate of increase of stock prices; conversely, put values are higher for high-dividend payouts. (Of course, the option values do not necessarily rise or fall on the dividend payment or ex-dividend dates. Dividend payments are anticipated, so the effect of the payment already is built into the original option price.)

CONCEPT CHECK

Question 2. Suppose that IBM's stock price at the exercise date is $80, and the exercise price of the call $70. What is the profit on one option contract? After a 10-for-1 split, the stock price is $8, the exercise price is $7, and the option holder now can purchase 1,000 shares. Show that the split leaves option profits unaffected.

The Option Clearing Corporation

The Option Clearing Corporation (OCC), the clearinghouse for options trading, is jointly owned by the exchanges on which stock options are traded. Buyers and sellers of options who agree on a price will strike a deal. At this point, the OCC steps in. The OCC places itself between the two traders, becoming the effective buyer of the option from the writer and the effective writer of the option to the buyer. All individuals, therefore, deal only with the OCC, which effectively guarantees contract performance.

When an optionholder exercises an option, the OCC arranges for a member firm with clients who have written that option to make good on the option obligation. The member firm selects from its clients who have written that option to fulfill the contract.

The selected client must deliver 100 shares of stock at a price equal to the exercise price for each call option contract written or must purchase 100 shares at the exercise price for each put option contract written.

Because the OCC guarantees contract performance, option writers are required to post margin amounts to guarantee that they can fulfill their contract obligations. The margin required is determined in part by the amount by which the option is in the money, because that value is an indicator of the potential obligation of the option writer upon exercise of the option. When the required margin exceeds the posted margin, the writer will receive a margin call. The holder of the option need not post margin because the holder will exercise the option only if it is profitable to do so. After purchasing the option, no further money is at risk.

Margin requirements are determined in part by the other securities held in the investor's portfolio. For example, a call option writer owning the stock against which the option is written can satisfy the margin requirement simply by allowing a broker to hold that stock in the brokerage account. The stock is then guaranteed to be available for delivery should the call option be exercised. If the underlying security is not owned, however, the margin requirement is determined by the value of the underlying security as well as by the amount by which the option is in or out of the money. Out-of-the-money options require less margin from the writer, for expected payouts are lower.

Other Listed Options

Options on assets other than stocks are also widely traded. These include options on market indexes and industry indexes, on foreign currency, and even on the futures prices of agricultural products, gold, silver, fixed-income securities, and stock indexes. We will discuss these in turn.

Index Options. An index option is a call or put based on a stock market index such as the S&P 500 or the New York Stock Exchange Index. Index options are traded on several broad-based indexes as well as on a few industry-specific indexes and even commodity price indexes. We discussed many of these indexes in Chapter 2.

The construction of the indexes can vary across contracts or exchanges. For example, the S&P 100 index is a value-weighted average of the 100 stocks in the Standard & Poor's 100 stock group. The weights are proportional to the market value of outstanding equity for each stock. The Major Market Index, by contrast, is a price-weighted average of 20 stocks, most of which are in the Dow Jones Industrial Average group, whereas the Value Line Index is an equally weighted average of roughly 1,700 stocks.

Option contracts on many foreign stock indexes also trade. For example, options on the (Japanese) Nikkei 225 stock average trade on the Chicago Mercantile Exchange and options on the Japan Index trade on the American Stock Exchange. The Chicago Board Options Exchange reached agreement with the London Stock Exchange in 1991 to list options on three European stock indexes: the Financial Times Share Exchange (FT-SE) 100 Index, which is the most popular equity benchmark in the United Kingdom; the Eurotrak 100 Index, which includes stocks from 11 European countries excluding the U.K.; and the Eurotrak 200 Index, which combines the stocks in the FT-SE 100 and Eurotrak 100.

Figure 19.2
Index options

Source: *The Wall Street Journal,* December 9, 1994. Reprinted by permission of *The Wall Street Journal,* © 1994 Dow Jones & Company, Inc. All Rights Reserved Worldwide.

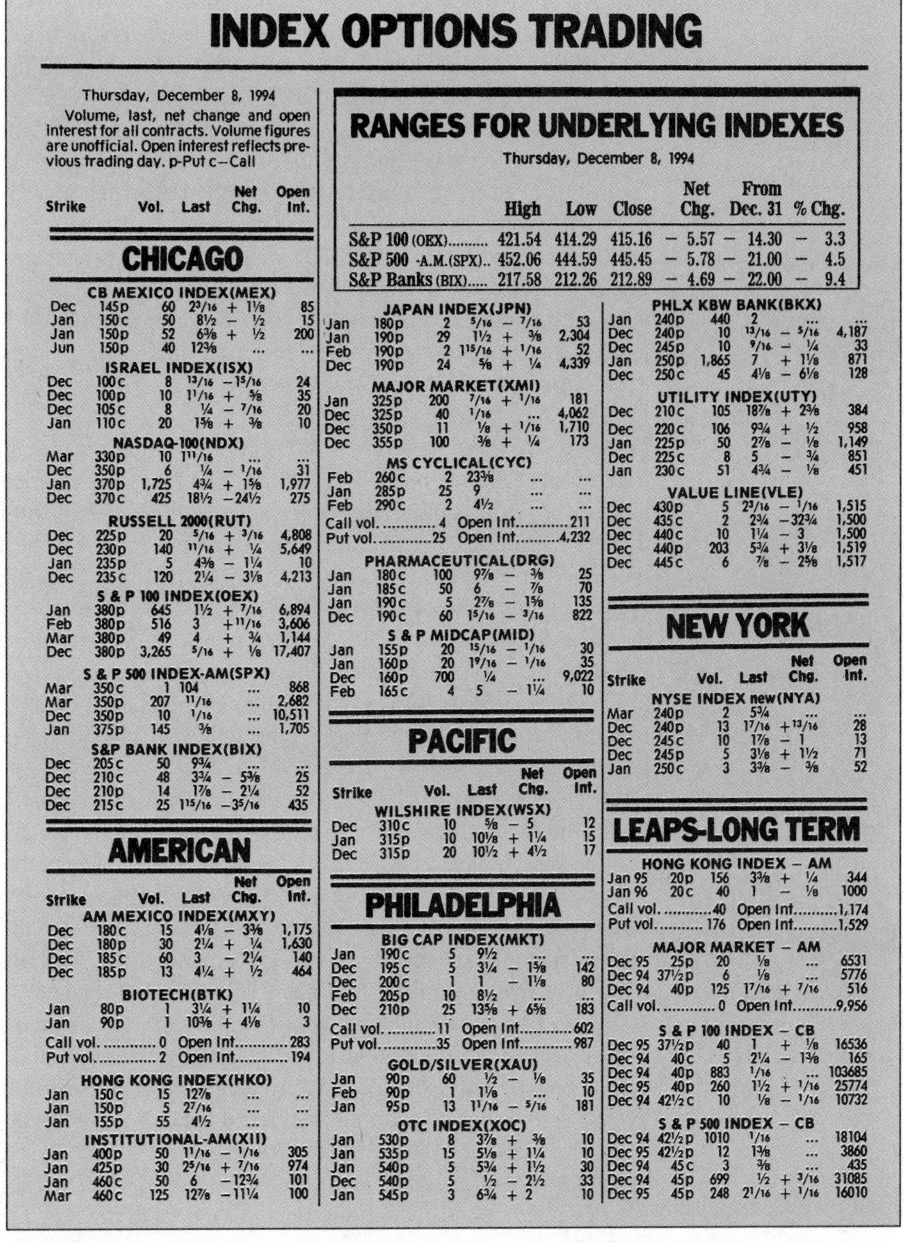

INDEX OPTIONS TRADING

Thursday, December 8, 1994

Volume, last, net change and open interest for all contracts. Volume figures are unofficial. Open interest reflects previous trading day. p-Put c–Call

RANGES FOR UNDERLYING INDEXES

Thursday, December 8, 1994

	High	Low	Close	Net Chg.	From Dec. 31	% Chg.
S&P 100 (OEX)..........	421.54	414.29	415.16	– 5.57	– 14.30	– 3.3
S&P 500 -A.M.(SPX)..	452.06	444.59	445.45	– 5.78	– 21.00	– 4.5
S&P Banks (BIX).....	217.58	212.26	212.89	– 4.69	– 22.00	– 9.4

CHICAGO

	Strike	Vol.	Last	Net Chg.	Open Int.
CB MEXICO INDEX(MEX)					
Dec	145p	60	2 3/16	+ 1 1/8	85
Jan	150c	50	8 1/2	– 1/2	15
Jan	150p	52	6 3/8	+ 1/2	200
Jun	150p	40	12 3/8	...	...
ISRAEL INDEX(ISX)					
Dec	100c	8	13/16	–1 5/16	24
Dec	100p	10	1 1/16	+ 5/8	35
Dec	105c	8	1/4	– 7/16	20
Jan	110c	20	1 5/8	+ 3/8	10
NASDAQ-100(NDX)					
Mar	330p	10	1 11/16	...	...
Dec	350p	6	1/4	– 1/16	31
Jan	370p	1,725	4 3/4	+ 1 5/8	1,977
Dec	370c	425	18 1/2	–24 1/2	275
RUSSELL 2000(RUT)					
Dec	225p	20	5/16	+ 3/16	4,808
Dec	230p	140	11/16	+ 1/4	5,649
Jan	235p	5	4 3/8	– 1 1/4	10
Dec	235c	120	2 1/4	– 3 1/8	4,213
S & P 100 INDEX(OEX)					
Jan	380p	645	1 1/2	+ 7/16	6,894
Feb	380p	516	3	+11/16	3,606
Mar	380p	49	4	+ 3/4	1,144
Dec	380p	3,265	5/16	+ 1/8	17,407
S & P 500 INDEX-AM(SPX)					
Mar	350c	1	104	...	868
Mar	350p	207	11/16	...	2,682
Dec	350p	10	1/16	...	10,511
Jan	375p	145	3/8	...	1,705
S&P BANK INDEX(BIX)					
Dec	205c	50	9 3/4	...	...
Dec	210c	48	3 3/4	– 5 3/8	25
Dec	210p	14	1 7/8	– 2 1/4	52
Dec	215c	25	1 15/16	–3 5/16	435
JAPAN INDEX(JPN)					
Jan	180p	2	5/16	– 7/16	53
Jan	190p	29	1 1/2	+ 3/8	2,304
Feb	190p	2	1 15/16	+ 1/16	52
Dec	190p	24	5/8	+ 1/4	4,339
MAJOR MARKET(XMI)					
Jan	325p	200	7/16	+ 1/16	181
Dec	325p	40	1/16	...	4,062
Dec	350p	11	1/8	+ 1/16	1,710
Dec	355p	100	3/8	+ 1/4	173
MS CYCLICAL(CYC)					
Feb	260c	2	23 3/8	...	...
Jan	285p	25	9	...	...
Feb	290c	2	4 1/2	...	...

Call vol. .... 4 Open Int. 211
Put vol. .... 25 Open Int. 4,232

	Strike	Vol.	Last	Net Chg.	Open Int.
PHARMACEUTICAL(DRG)					
Jan	180c	100	9 7/8	– 3/8	25
Jan	185c	50	6	– 7/8	70
Jan	190c	5	2 7/8	– 1 5/8	135
Dec	190c	60	1 5/16	– 3/16	822
S & P MIDCAP(MID)					
Jan	155p	20	15/16	– 1/16	30
Jan	160p	20	1 9/16	– 1/16	35
Dec	160p	700	1/4	...	9,022
Feb	165c	4	5	– 1 1/4	10

AMERICAN

	Strike	Vol.	Last	Net Chg.	Open Int.
AM MEXICO INDEX(MXY)					
Dec	180c	15	4 1/8	– 3 3/8	1,175
Dec	180p	30	2 1/4	+ 1/4	1,630
Dec	185c	60	3	– 2 1/4	140
Dec	185p	13	4 1/4	+ 1/2	464
BIOTECH(BTK)					
Jan	80p	1	3 1/4	+ 1 1/4	10
Jan	90p	1	10 3/8	+ 4 1/8	3

Call vol. .... 0 Open Int. 283
Put vol. .... 2 Open Int. 194

	Strike	Vol.	Last	Net Chg.	Open Int.
HONG KONG INDEX(HKO)					
Jan	150c	15	12 7/8	...	...
Jan	150p	5	2 7/16	...	...
Jan	155p	55	4 1/2	...	...
INSTITUTIONAL-AM(XII)					
Jan	400p	50	1 1/16	– 1/16	305
Jan	425p	30	2 5/16	+ 7/16	974
Jan	460c	50	6	–12 3/4	101
Mar	460c	125	12 7/8	–11 1/4	100

PACIFIC

	Strike	Vol.	Last	Net Chg.	Open Int.
WILSHIRE INDEX(WSX)					
Dec	310c	10	5/8	– 5	12
Jan	315p	10	10 1/8	+ 1 1/4	15
Dec	315p	20	10 1/2	+ 4 1/2	17

PHILADELPHIA

	Strike	Vol.	Last	Net Chg.	Open Int.
BIG CAP INDEX(MKT)					
Jan	190c	5	9 1/2	...	...
Dec	195c	5	3 1/4	– 1 5/8	142
Dec	200c	1	1	– 1 1/8	80
Feb	205p	10	8 1/2	...	...
Dec	210p	25	13 5/8	+ 6 5/8	183

Call vol. .... 11 Open Int. 602
Put vol. .... 35 Open Int. 987

	Strike	Vol.	Last	Net Chg.	Open Int.
GOLD/SILVER(XAU)					
Jan	90p	60	1/2	– 1/8	35
Feb	90p	1	1 1/8	...	10
Jan	95p	13	1 1/16	– 5/16	181
OTC INDEX(XOC)					
Jan	530p	8	3 7/8	+ 3/8	10
Jan	535p	15	5 1/8	+ 1 1/4	10
Jan	540p	5	5 3/4	+ 1 1/2	30
Dec	540p	5	1/2	– 2 1/2	33
Jan	545p	3	6 3/4	+ 2	10
PHLX KBW BANK(BKX)					
Jan	240p	440	2	...	...
Dec	240p	10	13/16	– 5/16	4,187
Dec	245p	10	9/16	– 1/4	33
Jan	250p	1,865	7	+ 1 1/8	871
Dec	250c	45	4 1/8	– 6 1/8	128
UTILITY INDEX(UTY)					
Dec	210c	105	18 7/8	+ 2 3/8	384
Dec	220c	106	9 3/4	+ 1/2	958
Jan	225p	50	2 7/8	– 1/8	1,149
Dec	225c	8	5	– 3/4	851
Jan	230c	51	4 3/4	– 1/8	451
VALUE LINE(VLE)					
Dec	430p	5	2 3/16	– 1/16	1,515
Dec	435c	2	2 3/4	–32 3/4	1,500
Dec	440c	10	1 1/4	– 3	1,500
Dec	440p	203	5 3/4	+ 3 1/8	1,519
Dec	445c	6	7/8	– 2 5/8	1,517

NEW YORK

	Strike	Vol.	Last	Net Chg.	Open Int.
NYSE INDEX new(NYA)					
Mar	240p	2	5 3/4	...	...
Dec	240p	13	1 7/16	+13/16	28
Dec	245c	10	1 7/8	– 1	13
Dec	245p	5	3 1/8	+ 1 1/2	71
Jan	250c	3	3 3/8	– 3/8	52

LEAPS-LONG TERM

	Strike	Vol.	Last	Net Chg.	Open Int.
HONG KONG INDEX – AM					
Jan 95	20p	156	3 3/8	+ 1/4	344
Jan 96	20c	40	1	– 1/8	1000

Call vol. .... 40 Open Int. 1,174
Put vol. .... 176 Open Int. 1,529

	Strike	Vol.	Last	Net Chg.	Open Int.
MAJOR MARKET – AM					
Dec 95	25p	20	1/8	...	6531
Dec 94	37 1/2p	6	1/8	...	5776
Dec 94	40p	125	1 7/16	+ 7/16	516

Call vol. .... 0 Open Int. 9,956

	Strike	Vol.	Last	Net Chg.	Open Int.
S & P 100 INDEX – CB					
Dec 95	37 1/2p	40	1	+ 1/8	16536
Dec 94	40c	5	2 1/4	– 1 3/8	165
Dec 94	40p	883	1/16	...	103685
Dec 95	40p	260	1 1/2	+ 1/16	25774
Dec 94	42 1/2c	10	1/8	– 1/16	10732
S & P 500 INDEX – CB					
Dec 94	42 1/2p	1010	1/16	...	18104
Dec 95	42 1/2p	12	1 3/8	...	3860
Dec 94	45c	3	3/8	...	435
Dec 94	45p	699	1/2	+ 3/16	31085
Dec 95	45p	248	2 1/16	+ 1/16	16010

Figure 19.2 is a reproduction of the listings of index options from *The Wall Street Journal.* The top of the listing shows recent price ranges for several stock indexes. The listings for index options are similar to those of stock options. However, instead of supplying separate columns for puts and calls, the index options are all listed in one column, and the letters *p* or *c* are used to denote puts or calls. The index options listings

also report the *open interest* for each contract, which is the number of contracts currently outstanding. Notice from the trading volume and open interest columns that the S&P 100 options contract, often called the *OEX* after its ticker symbol, is the most actively traded contract on the CBOE, although volume on S&P 500 index contracts is also quite high. Together, these contracts dominate CBOE volume.

In contrast to stock options, index options do not require that the call writer actually "deliver the index" upon exercise or that the put writer "purchase the index." Instead, a cash settlement procedure is used. The payoff that would accrue upon exercise of the option is calculated, and the option writer simply pays that amount to the option holder. The payoff is equal to the difference between the exercise price of the option and the value of the index. For example, if the S&P index is at $510 when a call option on the index with exercise price $500 is exercised, the holder of the call receives a cash payment of the $10 difference times the contract multiplier of 100, or $1,000 per contract.

Futures Options. Futures options give their holders the right to buy or sell a specified futures contract, using as a futures price the exercise price of the option. Although the delivery process is slightly complicated, the terms of futures options contracts are designed in effect to allow the option to be written on the futures price itself. The optionholder receives upon exercise a net payoff equal to the difference between the current futures price on the specified asset and the exercise price of the option. Thus, if the futures price is, say, $37, and the call has an exercise price of $35, the holder who exercises the call option on the futures gets a payoff of $2. Many of the futures options in Figure 19.3 are foreign exchange futures options; they are written on the futures price of foreign exchange rather than on the actual or spot exchange rate.

Foreign Currency Options. A currency option offers the right to buy or sell a quantity of foreign currency for a specified amount of domestic currency. Foreign currency options have traded on the Philadelphia Stock Exchange since December 1982. Since then, the Chicago Board Options Exchange and the Chicago Mercantile Exchange have listed foreign currency options. Currency option contracts call for purchase or sale of the currency in exchange for a specified number of U.S. dollars. Contracts are quoted in cents or fractions of a cent per unit of foreign currency.

Figure 19.4 shows a listing from *The Wall Street Journal* of some of these contracts. The size of each option contract is specified for each listing. The call option on the British pound on the Philadelphia exchange, for example, entitles its holder to purchase 31,250 pounds for a specified number of cents per pound on or before the expiration date. The March call option with strike price of 155 cents sells for 3.34 cents, which means each contract costs $\$.0334 \times 31{,}250 = \$1043.75$. The current exchange rate is 156 cents per pound. Therefore, the option is in the money by one cent, the difference between the current exchange rate (156 cents) and the exercise price of 155 cents per pound.

There is an important difference between the options traded on the Philadelphia exchange and the futures options traded on the International Monetary Market (IMM). The former provide payoffs that depend on the difference between the exercise price and the exchange rate at maturity. The latter are foreign exchange futures options that provide payoffs that depend on the difference between the exercise price and the

Figure 19.3
Futures options

Source: *The Wall Street Journal*, December 14, 1994. Reprinted by permission of *The Wall Street Journal*,

FUTURES OPTIONS PRICES

Tuesday, December 13, 1994.

AGRICULTURAL

CORN (CBT)
5,000 bu.; cents per bu.

Strike	Calls—Settle			Puts—Settle		
Price	Mar	May	Jly	Mar	May	Jly
210	21	28	32½	⅜	⅜	½
220	11⅞	19	23¾	1⅜	1¼	1⅝
230	5⅛	11¼	16½	4⅜	3¼	4¼
240	1¾	6¼	11	11⅛	8	8½
250	⅝	3¼	7	19¾	....	14⅝
260	¼	1⅝	4¾	29¼	....	....

Est vol 6,500 Mon 3,708 calls 2,000 puts
Op int Mon 80,246 calls 51,244 puts

SOYBEANS (CBT)
5,000 bu.; cents per bu.

Strike	Calls—Settle			Puts—Settle		
Price	Jan	Mar	May	Jan	Mar	May
525	38½	49½	58¼	⅛	1	1⅝
550	14	28	37¼	⅝	3¾	5
575	¾	11½	21	12¼	13	13
600	⅛	4	10	36½	29½	27½
625	⅛	1½	4¾	61½	51½	....
650	⅛	⅝	2½	86½	....	....

Est vol 5,000 Mon 1,148 calls 1,714 puts
Op int Mon 83,959 calls 45,533 puts

SOYBEAN MEAL (CBT)
100 tons; $ per ton

Strike	Calls—Settle			Puts—Settle		
Price	Jan	Mar	May	Jan	Mar	May
150	9.10	....	....	.10	.65	....
155	4.15	....	....	.20	1.30	1.40
160	.40	5.35	9.00	1.40	2.60	2.40
165	.10	2.85	6.00	6.00	5.10	4.25
170	.05	1.50	3.75	11.00	8.75	7.00
175	.05	.75	2.50	16.00	12.95	....

Est vol 650 Mon 305 calls 507 puts
Op int Mon 6,799 calls 9,554 puts

SOYBEAN OIL (CBT)
60,000 lbs.; cents per lb.

Strike	Calls—Settle			Puts—Settle		
Price	Jan	Mar	May	Jan	Mar	May
26	1.490	1.350	1.060	.030	.800	1.260
27	.650	.850	.750	.140	1.280	....
28	.180	.530	.540	.700	1.950	....
29	.050	.350	.370	1.600	....	....
30	.010	.220	....	....	....	....
31	.010	....	....	....	....	....

Est vol 750 Mon 287 calls 104 puts
Op int Mon 9,316 calls 14,571 puts

WHEAT (CBT)
5,000 bu.; cents per bu.

Strike	Calls—Settle			Puts—Settle		
Price	Mar	May	Jly	Mar	May	Jly
370	20¾	15½	7⅝	5	15	....
380	14½	12	6	8¾	21	42½
390	10⅛	8¾	4½	14¼	28	50¾
400	6½	6¾	3¼	20¾	35¾	....
410	4½	5	....	28¼	44	....
420	2⅞	3¾	....	36½	52¾	....

Est vol 4,000 Mon 2,091 calls 2,939 puts
Op int Mon 40,431 calls 28,506 puts

WHEAT (KC)
5,000 bu.; cents per bu.

Strike	Calls—Settle			Puts—Settle		
Price	Mar	May	Jly	Mar	May	Jly
370	21⅞	17⅝	9¾	4	11⅝	28⅛
380	15¾	13⅛	6½	9¼	16⅝	....
390	10½	9⅝	5	13	23½	....
400	7	6¾	3½	19⅝	31	....
410	4¾	4½	2⅛	27	....	....
420	2⅞	3⅜	....	35¼	....	....

Est vol 154 Mon 19 calls 4 puts
Op int Mon 4,179 calls 2,438 puts

COTTON (CTN)
50,000 lbs.; cents per lb.
Strike Calls—Settle Puts—Settle

LIVESTOCK

CATTLE-FEEDER (CME)
50,000 lbs.; cents per lb.

Strike	Calls—Settle			Puts—Settle		
Price	Jan	Mar	Apr	Jan	Mar	Apr
73	2.02	....	....	0.50	....	....
74	1.37	0.90	0.85	0.85	2.70	3.70
75	0.80	....	....	1.35	....	....
76	0.50	0.40	0.45	2.00	....	....
77	....	....	....	....	....	....
78	0.05	0.10	0.30	3.60	....	....

Est vol 382 Mon 25 calls 149 puts
Op int Mon 2,384 calls 4,622 puts

CATTLE-LIVE (CME)
40,000 lbs.; cents per lb.

Strike	Calls—Settle			Puts—Settle		
Price	Feb	Apr	Jun	Feb	Apr	Jun
68	2.55	3.47	1.00	0.85	1.15	3.75
69	1.92	2.87	....	1.20	1.52	....
70	1.37	2.30	0.57	1.65	1.92	....
71	0.95	1.77	....	2.22	2.40	....
72	0.62	1.35	0.22	2.87	2.95	....
73	0.40	1.00	....	....	....	....

Est vol 2,234 Mon 664 calls 901 puts
Op int Mon 15,108 calls 21,910 puts

HOGS–LIVE (CME)
40,000 lbs.; cents per lb.

Strike	Calls—Settle			Puts—Settle		
Price	Feb	Apr	Jun	Feb	Apr	Jun
35	2.62	....	....	0.80	1.10	....
36	1.95	2.77	....	1.10	1.45	0.45
37	1.45	2.25	....	1.60	....	....
38	1.00	1.85	5.57	2.15	2.50	0.77
39	0.67	1.50	....	2.80	....	....
40	0.45	1.20	4.15	3.57	3.80	1.32

Est vol 653 Mon 726 calls 222 puts
Op int Mon 11,465 calls 3,683 puts

METALS

COPPER (CMX)
25,000 lbs.; cents per lb.

Strike	Calls—Settle			Puts—Settle		
Price	Feb	Mar	May	Feb	Mar	May
125	9.70	10.70	8.85	2.55	3.55	6.50
130	6.45	7.85	6.50	4.30	5.70	9.15
135	4.20	5.45	4.70	7.05	8.30	12.35
140	2.60	3.70	3.40	10.95	11.55	16.05
145	1.50	2.55	2.50	14.85	15.40	20.15
150	0.85	1.70	1.80	19.20	19.55	24.40

Est vol 500 Mon 173 calls 280 puts
Op int Mon 5,367 calls 4,757 puts

GOLD (CMX)
100 troy ounces; $ per troy ounce

Strike	Calls—Settle			Puts—Settle		
Price	Feb	Mar	Apr	Feb	Mar	Apr
360	20.40	24.80	24.80	0.30	0.50	0.90
370	11.20	15.60	15.40	1.00	1.30	1.80
380	4.00	7.80	8.80	3.70	3.50	4.60
390	1.30	3.60	4.40	11.20	9.30	10.20
400	0.50	1.50	2.30	20.20	17.20	18.00
410	0.20	0.90	1.20	29.70	26.60	26.50

Est vol 6,500 Mon 2,259 calls 1,804 puts
Op int Mon 87,788 calls 37,165 puts

SILVER (CMX)
5,000 troy ounces; cts per troy ounce

Strike	Calls—Settle			Puts—Settle		
Price	Feb	Mar	May	Feb	Mar	May
425	54.8	57.0	64.8	1.0	3.0	5.8
450	32.4	36.4	45.9	3.4	7.4	11.8
475	15.3	20.7	31.4	11.3	16.7	21.5
500	6.3	11.7	20.1	27.5	32.7	34.7
525	2.5	6.6	13.5	48.4	52.6	53.0
550	1.0	3.5	9.0	71.3	74.5	73.0

Est vol 4,700 Mon 2,713 calls 941 puts
Op int Mon 74,679 calls 23,599 puts

COFFEE (CSCE)
37,500 lbs.; cents per lb.

Strike	Calls—Settle			Puts—Settle		
Price	Feb	Mar	May	Feb	Mar	May
145	11.60	14.35	18.50	3.00	5.75	8.40
150	9.32	11.10	15.75	5.72	7.50	10.60
155	5.64	8.90	13.50	7.50	10.30	13.25
160	5.02	6.00	11.25	11.42	13.30	16.00

CURRENCY

JAPANESE YEN (CME)
12,500,000 yen; cents per 100 yen

Strike	Calls—Settle			Puts—Settle		
Price	Jan	Feb	Mar	Jan	Feb	Mar
10000	1.24	1.70	2.16	0.40	0.87	1.33
10050	0.92	1.42	1.89	0.58	1.08	1.55
10100	0.66	1.17	1.64	0.82	1.33	1.80
10150	0.47	0.96	1.42	1.13	1.62	....
10200	0.32	0.78	1.23	1.48	1.93	2.38
10250	0.22	0.63	1.05	1.87	2.28	....

Est vol 5,795 Mon 4,821 calls 18,289 puts
Op int Mon 35,224 calls 52,642 puts

DEUTSCHEMARK (CME)
125,000 marks; cents per mark

Strike	Calls—Settle			Puts—Settle		
Price	Jan	Feb	Mar	Jan	Feb	Mar
6300	1.01	1.34	1.61	0.23	0.57	0.84
6350	0.68	1.05	1.34	0.40	0.77	1.06
6400	0.43	0.80	1.09	0.65	1.02	1.31
6450	0.27	0.60	0.88	0.99	1.31	....
6500	0.16	0.44	0.71	1.37	1.65	1.92
6550	0.09	0.31	0.55	1.80	....	2.25

Est vol 3,770 Mon 16,284 calls 25,-
016 puts
Op int Mon 43,300 calls 44,204 puts

CANADIAN DOLLAR (CME)
100,000 Can.$, cents per Can.$

Strike	Calls—Settle			Puts—Settle		
Price	Jan	Feb	Mar	Jan	Feb	Mar
7100	....	....	1.26	....	....	0.31
7150	....	....	0.92	....	0.30	0.47
7200	0.32	0.49	0.65	0.36	0.52	0.69
7250	0.13	0.29	0.44	0.67	0.83	0.97
7300	0.06	0.16	0.29	1.10	....	1.32
7350	0.03	....	0.19	1.56	....	1.71

Est vol 494 Mon 869 calls 3,883 puts
Op int Mon 4,516 calls 2,526 puts

BRITISH POUND (CME)
62,500 pounds; cents per pound

Strike	Calls—Settle			Puts—Settle		
Price	Jan	Feb	Mar	Jan	Feb	Mar
1500	6.02	....	6.58	0.04	0.24	0.64
1525	....	....	4.66	0.14	0.64	1.20
1550	1.66	....	3.10	0.66	1.44	2.10
1575	0.50	1.28	1.92	2.00	2.76	3.40
1600	0.16	0.60	1.12	4.14	4.56	5.08
1625	0.06	0.28	0.64	6.54	....	7.06

Est vol 543 Mon 4,726 calls 12,140 puts
Op int Mon 13,774 calls 9,402 puts

SWISS FRANC (CME)
125,000 francs; cents per franc

Strike	Calls—Settle			Puts—Settle		
Price	Jan	Feb	Mar	Jan	Feb	Mar
7450	1.46	1.85	....	0.25	0.65	....
7500	1.10	1.54	1.87	0.39	0.84	1.17
7550	0.80	1.27	1.61	0.59	1.06	1.40
7600	0.56	1.02	1.37	0.85	1.31	1.66
7650	0.38	0.81	1.16	1.17	....	....
7700	0.24	0.65	0.97	1.52	....	2.24

Est vol 4,324 Mon 1,117 calls 9,460 puts
Op int Mon 19,560 calls 12,116 puts

U.S. DOLLAR INDEX (FINEX)

LIBOR – 1 Mo. (CME)
$3 million; pts. of 100%

Strike	Calls—Settle			Puts—Settle		
Price	Dec	Jan	Feb	Dec	Jan	Feb
9325	....	....	....	....	....	....
9350	....	....	0.12	0.00	....	0.28
9375	0.09	0.11	0.05	0.02	0.15	0.46
9400	0.01	0.04	0.02	0.19	0.33	0.68
9425	0.00	0.00	0.01	0.43	0.54	0.91
9450	0.00	0.00	....	....	0.79	....

Est vol 11 Mon 170 calls 0 puts
Op int Mon 2,450 calls 2,253 puts

2 YR. MID-CURVE EURODOLLAR (CME)
$1,000,000 contract units; pts. of 100%

Strike	Calls—Settle			Puts—Settle		
Price	Dec	Mar	....	Dec	Mar	....
9125	....	....	....	0.00	....	....
9150	0.27	....	....	0.01	0.13	....
9175	0.06	0.28	....	0.05	0.20	....
9200	0.01	0.16	....	0.25	0.33	....

Figure 19.4
Foreign currency options

Source: *The Wall Street Journal,* December 14, 1994. Reprinted by permission of *The Wall Street Journal,*

OPTIONS
PHILADELPHIA EXCHANGE

		Calls Vol.	Calls Last	Puts Vol.	Puts Last
DMark					**63.66**
62,500 German Mark EOM-European style.					
62	Dec	...	...	50	0.05
62,500 German Marks EOM-European style.					
60½	Dec	...	...	25	0.01
61½	Dec	...	...	25	0.02
Australian Dollar					**77.49**
50,000 Australian Dollar EOM-cents per unit.					
77	Dec	...	...	4	0.29
50,000 Australian Dollars-cents per unit.					
75	Dec	60	2.58	...	...
75	Jan	120	2.62	...	...
76	Dec	10	1.50	...	...
77	Dec	50	0.65	...	...
77	Mar	...	...	1	0.89
78	Jan	50	0.43	...	...
British Pound					**156.05**
31,250 British Pounds-cents per unit.					
155	Mar	4	3.34	...	...
157½	Dec	...	...	160	1.45
160	Jan	50	0.28	...	...
160	Mar	96	1.32	...	...
British Pound-GMark					**245.12**
31,250 British Pound-German Mark cross.					
248	Mar	3	1.40	3	4.20
250	Dec	...	...	2	4.88
252	Dec	...	...	2	6.90
31,250 British Pound-German mark EOM.					
246	Dec	10	0.72	...	...
Canadian Dollar					**72.14**
50,000 Canadian Dollars-European Style.					
72½	Mar	...	...	20	0.94
73	Dec	...	...	20	0.85
50,000 Canadian Dollars-cents per unit.					
72½	Dec	...	...	10	0.35
72½	Jan	10	0.24	...	...
73	Mar	10	0.37	5	1.33
75½	Dec	...	...	20	3.26
French Franc					**184.80**
250,000 French Francs-10ths of a cent per unit.					
18½	Mar	...	...	28	3.70
GMark-JYen					**63.76**
62,500 GMark-JYen cross EOM.					
64½	Dec	50	0.11	...	...
German Mark					**63.66**
62,500 German Marks EOM-cents per unit.					
63	Dec	21	0.77	1378	0.20
63½	Dec	400	0.32	...	...
64	Dec	28	0.27	28	0.64
65	Dec	30	0.08	...	...
62,500 German Marks-European Style.					
58	Dec	5	5.58	...	...
63½	Dec	...	...	15	0.20
63½	Jan	...	...	30	0.60
62,500 German Marks-cents per unit.					
58½	Dec	4	5.10	...	...
58½	Jan	4	5.11	...	...
61	Dec	8	2.60	...	...
61	Jan	8	2.65	...	...
62	Mar	...	...	2500	0.62
62½	Dec	35	1.10	...	...
63	Dec	81	0.59	38	0.05
63	Mar	...	...	4	0.95
63½	Dec	301	0.39	803	0.12
63½	Jan	45	0.74	...	...
64	Dec	412	0.12	398	0.39
64	Mar	200	1.12	217	1.32
64½	Dec	27	0.03	38	1.00
64½	Jan	3	0.28	100	1.05
65	Dec	...	...	4	1.49
67	Mar	200	0.27	...	...
Japanese Yen					**99.85**
6,250,000 Japanese Yen EOM-100ths of a cent per unit.					
98	Jan	...	...	50	0.33
102	Jan	2	0.47	...	...
6,250,000 Japanese Yen EOM.					
99½	Dec	...	...	5	0.42
6,250,000 Japanese Yen-100ths of a cent per unit.					
97½	Jan	...	...	100	0.12
98	Dec	...	...	50	0.01
98	Jan	...	...	50	0.25
99	Dec	14	0.68	1170	0.07
99	Jan	...	...	50	0.50
99½	Dec	30	0.47	...	...
99½	Jan	...	...	140	0.56
100	Dec	575	0.18	72	0.40
100	Jan	20	0.97	...	...
100	Mar	12	2.11	20	1.63
100½	Dec	25	0.12	...	...
101	Dec	1020	0.05	...	...
101	Jan	10	0.48	...	...
102	Dec	...	...	10	2.20
102	Jan	20	0.27	...	...
103	Mar	50	0.96	...	...
6,250,000 Japanese Yen-European Style.					
99½	Dec	...	...	4	0.13
99½	Jan	...	...	4	0.53
Swiss Franc					**75.29**
62,500 Swiss Franc EOM-cents per unit.					
75	Dec	255	0.70	255	0.50
62,500 Swiss Francs EOM.					
75½	Dec	43	0.60	43	0.54
62,500 Swiss Francs-European Style.					
71	Mar	32	4.59	...	...
72	Dec	32	3.03	...	...
72	Mar	32	3.75	...	...
74	Mar	...	...	32	0.97
62,500 Swiss Francs-cents per unit.					
71	Mar	...	...	15	0.23
74	Dec	...	...	10	0.02
74	Jan	...	...	200	0.36
75	Dec	29	0.44	10	0.25
75	Jan	...	...	60	0.76
75	Mar	...	...	3	1.22
76	Dec	50	0.11	3	0.78
76	Jan	1	0.51	...	...
78	Mar	2	0.69	...	...

Call Vol ...... 4,720 Open Int ... 406,113
Put Vol .... 11,187 Open Int ... 365,717

exchange rate *futures price* at maturity. Because exchange rates and exchange rate futures prices generally are not equal, the options and futures-options contracts will have different values, even with identical expiration dates and exercise prices. For example, in Figure 19.3, the call option on the British pound with strike price 155 cents and March maturity is quoted at 3.10 cents. The corresponding futures option in Figure 19.4 with the same strike price and maturity is quoted at 3.34 cents.

Interest Rate Options. Options on particular U.S. Treasury notes and bonds are listed on the Amex and the CBOE. Options also are traded on Treasury bills, certificates of deposit, GNMA pass-through certificates, and yields on Treasury securities of various maturities. Options on several interest rate futures also trade. Among these are contracts on Treasury bond, Treasury note, municipal bond, LIBOR, Eurodollar, and Euromark futures.

19.2 Values of Options at Expiration

Call Options

Recall that a call option gives the right to purchase a security at the exercise price. If you hold a call option on IBM stock with an exercise price of $70, and IBM is now selling at $80, you can exercise your option to purchase the stock at $70 and simultane-

Figure 19.5
Payoff and profit to call option at expiration

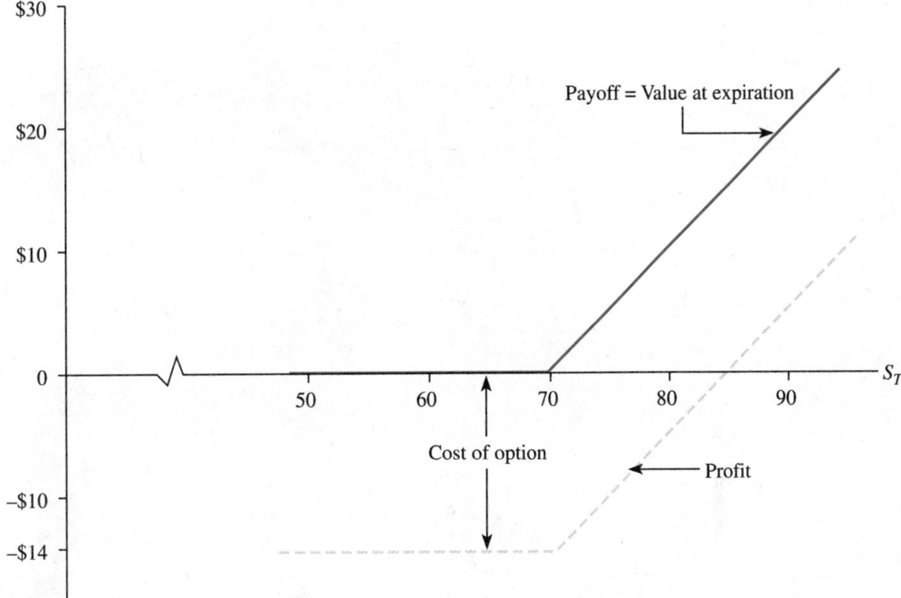

ously sell the shares at the market price of $80, clearing $10 per share. Yet if the shares sell below $70, you can sit on the option and do nothing, realizing no further gain or loss. The value of the call option at expiration equals:

$$\text{Payoff to callholder} = \begin{array}{ll} S_T - X & \text{if } S_T > X \\ 0 & \text{if } S_T \leq X \end{array}$$

where S_T is the value of the stock at expiration, and X is the exercise price. This formula emphasizes the option property because the payoff cannot be negative. That is, the option is exercised only if S_T exceeds X. If S_T is less than X, exercise does not occur, and the option expires with zero value. The loss to the optionholder in this case equals the price originally paid for the right to buy at the exercise price. More generally, the *profit* to the optionholder is the value of the option at expiration minus the original purchase price.

The value at expiration of the call on IBM with exercise price $70 is given by the schedule:

IBM value:	$60	$70	$80	$90	$100
Option value:	0	0	10	20	30

For IBM prices at or below $70, the option is worthless. Above $70, the option is worth the excess of IBM's price over $70. The option's value increases by one dollar for each dollar increase in the IBM stock price. This relationship can be depicted graphically, as in Figure 19.5.

The solid line in Figure 19.5 depicts the value of the call at maturity. The net *profit* to the holder of the call equals the gross payoff less the initial investment in the call.

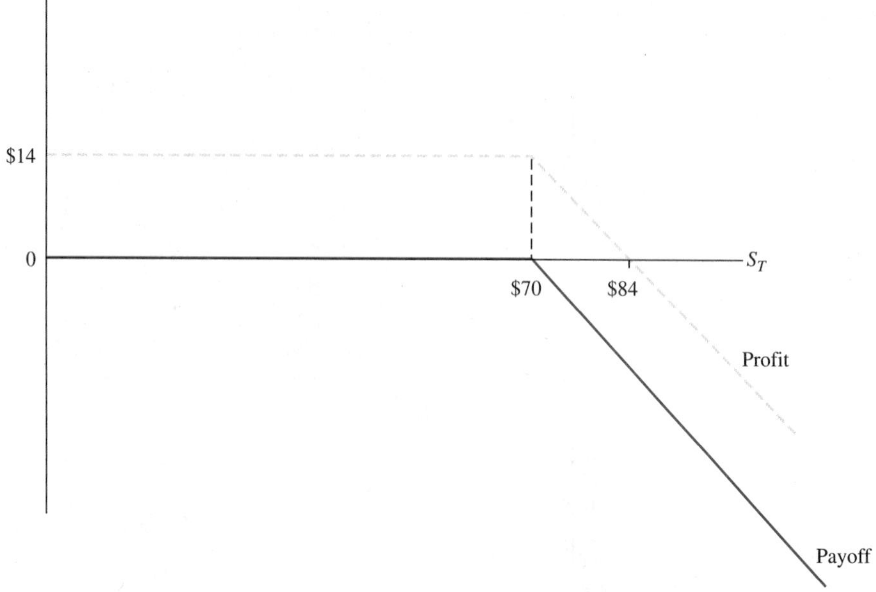

Figure 19.6
Payoff and profit to call writers at expiration

Suppose the call cost $14. Then the profit to the call holder would be as given in the dashed (bottom) line of Figure 19.5. At option expiration, the investor has suffered a loss of $14 if the stock price is less than or equal to $70.

Profits do not become positive unless the stock price at expiration exceeds $84. The break-even point is $84, because at that price the payoff to the call, $S_T - X = \$84 - \$70 = \$14$, equals the cost paid to acquire the call. Hence, the callholder shows a profit only if the stock price is higher.

Conversely, the writer of the call incurs losses if the stock price is high. In that scenario, the writer will receive a call and will be obligated to deliver a stock worth S_T for only X dollars:

$$\text{Payoff to callholder} = \begin{cases} -(S_T - X) & \text{if } S_T > X \\ 0 & \text{if } S_T \leq X \end{cases}$$

The call writer, who is exposed to losses if IBM increases in price, is willing to bear this risk in return for the option premium.

Figure 19.6 depicts the payoff and profit diagrams for the call writer. These are the mirror images of the corresponding diagrams for call holders. The break-even point for the option writer also is $84. The (negative) payoff at that point just offsets the premium originally received when the option was written.

Put Options

A put option conveys the right to sell an asset at the exercise price. In this case, the holder will not exercise the option unless the asset sells for *less* than the exercise price. For example, if IBM shares were to fall to $60, a put option with exercise price $70

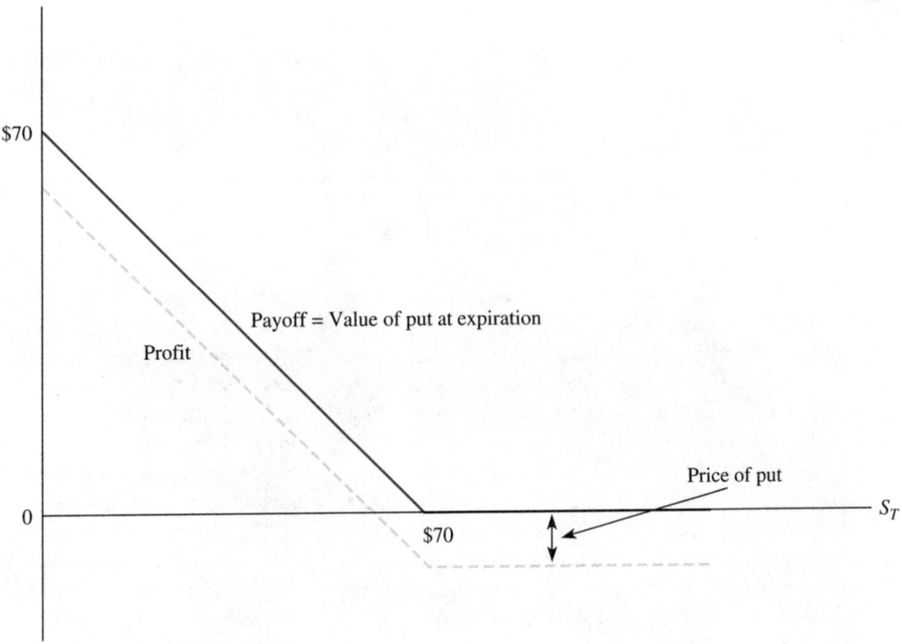

Figure 19.7
Payoff and profit to put option at expiration

could be exercised to give a $10 profit to its holder. The holder would purchase a share of IBM for $60 and simultaneously deliver it to the put option writer for the exercise price of $70.

The value of a put option at expiration is:

$$\text{Payoff to putholder} = \begin{cases} 0 & \text{if } S_T \geq X \\ X - S_T & \text{if } S_T < X \end{cases}$$

The solid line in Figure 19.7 illustrates the payoff at maturity to the holder of a put option on IBM stock with an exercise price of $70. If the stock price at option maturity is above $70, the put has no value, as the right to sell the shares at $70 would not be exercised. Below a price of $70, the put value at expiration increases by one dollar for each dollar the stock price falls. The dashed line in Figure 19.7 is a graph of the put option owner's profit at expiration, net of the initial cost of the put.

Writing puts *naked* (i.e., writing a put without an offsetting short position in the stock for hedging purposes) exposes the writer to losses if the market falls. Writing naked out-of-the-money puts was once considered an attractive way to generate income, as it was believed that as long as the market did not fall sharply before the option expiration, the option premium could be collected without the put holder ever exercising the option against the writer. Because only sharp drops in the market could result in losses to the writer of the put, the strategy was not viewed as overly risky. However, the accompanying box notes that in the wake of the market crash of October 1987, such put writers suffered huge losses. Participants now perceive much greater risk to this strategy.

THE BLACK HOLE: HOW SOME INVESTORS LOST ALL THEIR MONEY IN THE MARKET CRASH

Their Sales of "Naked Puts" Quickly Come to Grief, Damage Suits Are Filed

When Robert O'Connor got involved in stock-index options, he hoped his trading profits would help put his children through college. His broker, Mr. O'Connor explains, "said we would make about $1,000 a month, and if our losses got to $2,000 to $3,000, he would close out the account."

Instead, Mr. O'Connor, the 46-year-old owner of a small medical X-ray printing concern in Grand Rapids, Michigan, got caught in one of the worst investor blowouts in history. In a few minutes on October 19, he lost everything in his account plus an *additional* $91,000—a total loss of 175 percent of his original investment.

Scene of Disaster

For Mr. O'Connor and hundreds of other investors, a little-known corner of the Chicago Board Options Exchange was the "black hole" of Black Monday's market crash. In a strategy marketed by brokers nationwide as a sure thing, these customers had sunk hundreds of millions of dollars into "naked puts"—unhedged, highly leveraged bets that the stock market was in no danger of plunging. Most of these naked puts seem to have been options on the Standard & Poor's 100 stock index, which are traded on the CBOE. When stocks crashed, many traders with unhedged positions got margin calls for several times their original investment.

The 'Put' Strategy

The losses were especially sharp in "naked, out-of-the-money puts." A seller of puts agrees to buy stock or stock-index contracts at a set price before the put expires. These contracts are usually sold "out of the money"—priced at a level below current market prices that makes it unprofitable to exercise the option so long as the market rises or stays flat. The seller pockets a small amount per contract.

But if the market plunges, as it did October 19, the option swings into the money. The seller, in effect, has to pay pre-plunge stock prices to make good on his contract—and he takes a big loss.

"You have to recognize that there is unlimited potential for disaster" in selling naked options, says Peter Thayer, executive vice president of Gateway Investment Advisors Inc., a Cincinnati-based investment firm that trades options to hedge its stock portfolios. Last September, Gateway bought out-of-the-money put options on The S&P 100 stock index on the CBOE at $2 to $3 a contract as "insurance" against a plunging market. By October 20, the day after the crash, the value of those contracts had soared to $130. Although Gateway profited handsomely, the parties on the other side of the trade were clobbered.

Firm Sued

Brokers who were pushing naked options assumed that the stock market wouldn't plunge into uncharted territory. Frank VanderHoff, one of the two main brokers who put 50 to 70 H.B. Shaine clients into stock-index options, says he told clients that the strategy's risk was "moderate barring a nuclear attack or a crash like 1929." It wasn't speculative. The market could go up or down, but not *substantially* up or down. If the crash had only been as bad as '29, he adds, "we would have made it."

Source: Abridged from *The Wall Street Journal,* December 2, 1987. Reprinted by permission of *The Wall Street Journal,*

CONCEPT CHECK

Question 3. Analyze the strategy of put writing.

a. What is the payoff to a put writer as a function of the stock price?
b. What is the profit?
c. Draw the payoff and profit graphs.
d. When do put writers do well? When do they do poorly?

Option versus Stock Investments

Purchasing call options is a bullish strategy; that is, the calls provide profits when stock prices increase. Purchasing puts in contrast, is a bearish strategy. Symmetrically, writing calls is bearish, whereas writing puts is bullish. Because option values depend on the price of the underlying stock, purchase of options may be viewed as a substitute for direct purchase or sale of a stock. Why might an option strategy be preferable to direct stock transactions?

For example, why would you purchase a call option rather than buy IBM stock directly? Maybe you have some information that leads you to believe IBM stock will increase in value from its current level, which in our examples we will take to be $70. You know your analysis could be incorrect, however, and that IBM also could fall in price. Suppose a six-month maturity call option with exercise price $70 currently sells for $7, and the interest rate for the period is 3%. Consider these three strategies for investing a sum of money, say, $7,000. For simplicity, suppose IBM will not pay any dividends until after the six-month period.

Strategy A: Purchase 100 shares of IBM stock.
Strategy B: Purchase 1,000 call options on IBM with exercise price $70. (This would require 10 contracts, each for 100 shares.)
Strategy C: Purchase 100 call options for $700. Invest the remaining $6,300 in six-month T-bills, to earn 3% interest. The bills will grow in value from $6,300 to $6,300(1.03) = $6,489.

Let us trace the possible values of these three portfolios when the options expire in six months as a function of IBM stock price at that time.

	IBM Price				
Portfolio	**$50**	**$60**	**$70**	**$80**	**$90**
Portfolio A: All stock	$5,000	$6,000	$7,000	$ 8,000	$ 9,000
Portfolio B: All options	0	0	0	10,000	20,000
Portfolio C: Call plus bills	6,489	6,489	6,489	7,489	8,489

Portfolio A will be worth 100 times the share value of IBM. Portfolio B is worthless unless IBM sells for more than the exercise price of the call. Once that point is reached, the portfolio is worth 1,000 times the excess of the stock price over the exercise price. Finally, portfolio C is worth $6,489 from the investment in T-bills plus any profits from the 100 call options. Remember that each of these portfolios involves the same $7,000 initial investment. The rates of return on these three portfolios are as follows:

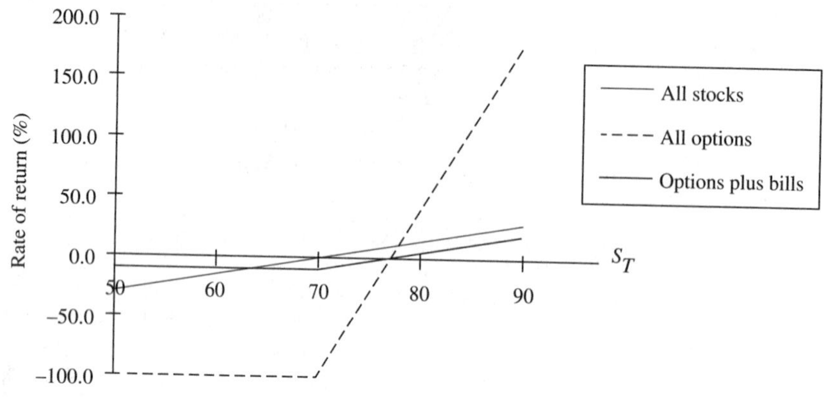

Figure 19.8
Rate of return to three strategies

Portfolio	IBM Price				
	$50	$60	$70	$80	$90
Portfolio A: All stock	− 28.6%	− 14.3%	0.0%	14.3%	28.6%
Portfolio B: All options	−100.0	−100.0	−100.0	43.3	185.7
Portfolio C: Call plus bills	− 7.3	− 7.3	− 7.3	7.0	21.3

These rates of return are graphed in Figure 19.8.

Comparing the returns of Portfolios B and C to those of the simple investment in IBM stock represented by Portfolio A, we see that options offer two interesting features. First, an option offers leverage. Compare the returns of Portfolios B and A. Unless IBM stock increases from its initial value of $70, the value of Portfolio B falls precipitously to zero—a rate of return of negative 100%. Conversely, if the stock price increases by 14%, from $70 to $80, the all-option portfolio jumps in value by a disproportionate 48.3%. In this sense, calls are a levered investment on the stock. Their values respond more than proportionately to changes in the stock value.

Figure 19.8 vividly illustrates this point. The slope of the all-option portfolio is far steeper than that for the all-stock portfolio, reflecting its greater proportional sensitivity to the value of the underlying security. The leverage factor is the reason investors (illegally) exploiting inside information commonly choose options as their investment vehicle.

The potential insurance value of options is the second interesting feature, as Portfolio C shows. The T-bill plus option portfolio cannot be worth less than $6,489 after six months, as the option can always be left to expire worthless. The worst possible rate of return on Portfolio C is −7.3%, compared to a (theoretically) worst possible rate of return of IBM stock of −100% if the company were to go bankrupt. Of course, this insurance comes at a price: When IBM does well, Portfolio C, the option-plus-bills portfolio, does not perform quite as well as Portfolio A, the all-stock portfolio.

This simple example makes an important point. Although options can be used by speculators as effectively leveraged stock positions, as in Portfolio B, they also can be used by investors who desire to tailor their risk exposures in creative ways, as in Portfolio C. For example, the call plus T-bills strategy of Portfolio C provides a rate of return profile quite unlike that of the stock alone. The absolute limitation on downside risk is a novel and attractive feature of this strategy. We will discuss below several option strategies that provide other novel risk profiles that might be attractive to hedgers and other investors.

19.3 Option Strategies

An unlimited variety of payoff patterns can be achieved by combining puts and calls with various exercise prices. Below we explain the motivation and structure of some of the more popular ones.

Protective Put

Imagine you would like to invest in a stock, but you are unwilling to bear potential losses beyond some given level. Investing in the stock alone seems risky to you because in principle you could lose all the money you invest. You might consider instead investing in stock and purchasing a put option on the stock. Table 19.1 shows the total value of your portfolio at option expiration: Whatever happens to the stock price, you are guaranteed a payoff equal to the put option's exercise price because the put gives you the right to sell IBM for the exercise price even if the stock price is below that value.

For example, if the strike price is X = \$65 and IBM is selling at \$62 at option expiration, then the value of your total portfolio is \$65: The stock is worth \$62 and the value of the expiring put option is

$$X - S_T = \$65 - \$62 = \$3$$

Another way to look at it is that you are holding the stock and a put contract giving you the right to sell the stock for \$65. The right to sell locks in a minimum portfolio value of \$65. On the other hand, if the stock price is above \$65, say \$69, then the right to sell a share at \$65 is worthless. You allow the put to expire unexercised, ending up with a share of stock worth S_T = \$69.

Figure 19.9 illustrates the payoff and profit to this **protective put** strategy. The solid line in Figure 19.9C is the total payoff. The dashed line is displaced downward by the cost of establishing the position, $S_0 + P$. Notice that potential losses are limited. See the nearby box for further discussion of this strategy.

It is instructive to compare the profit on the protective put strategy with that of the stock investment. For simplicity, consider an at-the-money protective put, so that $X = S_0$. Figure 19.10 compares the profits for the two strategies. The profit on the stock is zero if the stock price remains unchanged, and $S_T = S_0$. It rises or falls by \$1 for every dollar swing in the ultimate stock price. The profit on the protective put is negative and

Table 19.1 Value of Protective Put Portfolio at Option Expiration

	$S_T \leq X$	$S_T > X$
Stock	S_T	S_T
Put	$X - S_T$	0
TOTAL	X	S_T

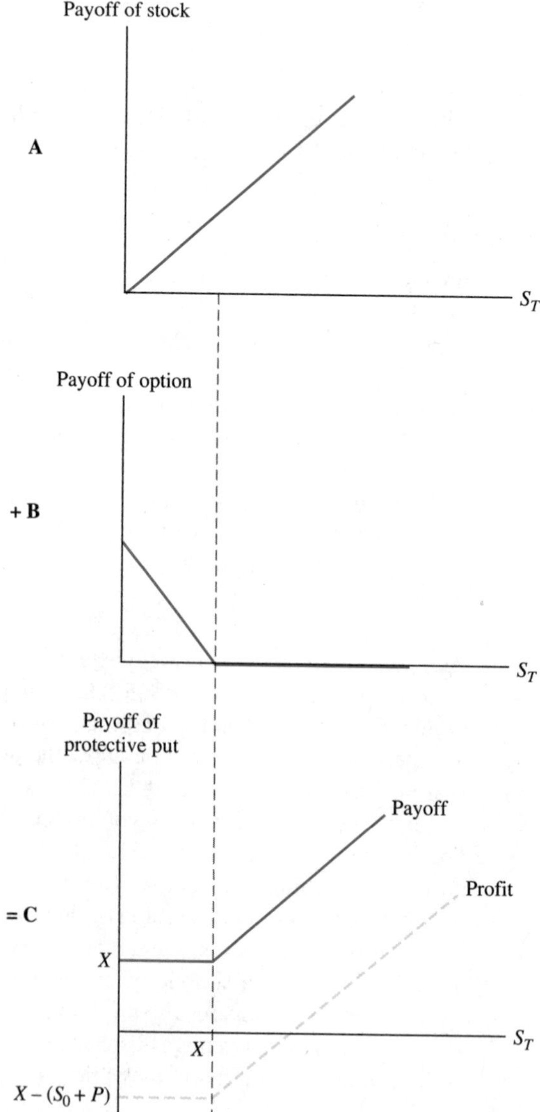

Figure 19.9
Value of a protective put position at option expiration

PROTECTIVE PUTS VERSUS STOP-LOSS ORDERS

We have seen that protective puts guarantee that the end-of-period value of a portfolio will equal or exceed the put's exercise price. As a specific example, consider a share of stock protected by a European put option with one year maturity and an exercise price of $40. Even if the stock at year-end is selling below $40, the put can be exercised and the stock can be sold for the exercise price, locking in a minimum payoff of $40.

Another common tool to protect a portfolio position is the stop-loss order. This is an order to your broker to sell your stock when and if its price falls to some lower boundary such as $40 per share. Thus, should the stock price fall substantially, your shares will be sold before losses mount, so that your proceeds will not fall below $40 per share.

It would seem that the stop-loss order provides the same stock price insurance offered by the protective put. However, the stop-loss order can be executed by your broker for no extra cost. Does this mean that the stop-loss order is effectively a free put option? What does the put offer that the stop-loss order does not?

To resolve this seeming paradox, look at the accompanying figure, which graphs one possible path for the stock price over the course of the year. Notice that, although the stock price falls below $40 at time *t*, it ultimately recovers and ends the year at $60. The protective put position will end the year worth $60—the put will expire worthless, but the stock will be worth $60. The stop-loss order, however, required that the stock be sold at time *t* as soon as its price fell below $40. This strategy will yield by year-end only $40 plus any interest accumulated between time *t* and the end of the year, far less than the payoff on the protective put strategy.

The protective put strategy does offer an advantage over the stop-loss strategy. With a stop-loss order in force, the investor realizes the $40 lower bound if the stock price *ever* reaches that boundary because the stock is sold as soon as the boundary is reached. Even if the stock price rebounds from the $40 limit, the investor using the stop-loss order will not share in the gain. The holder of the put option, on the other hand, need not exercise when the stock hits $40. Instead, the option-holder may wait until the end of the year to exercise the option, knowing that the $40 exercise price is guaranteed regardless of how far the stock falls, but that, should the stock price recover, the stock still will be held and any gain will be captured.*

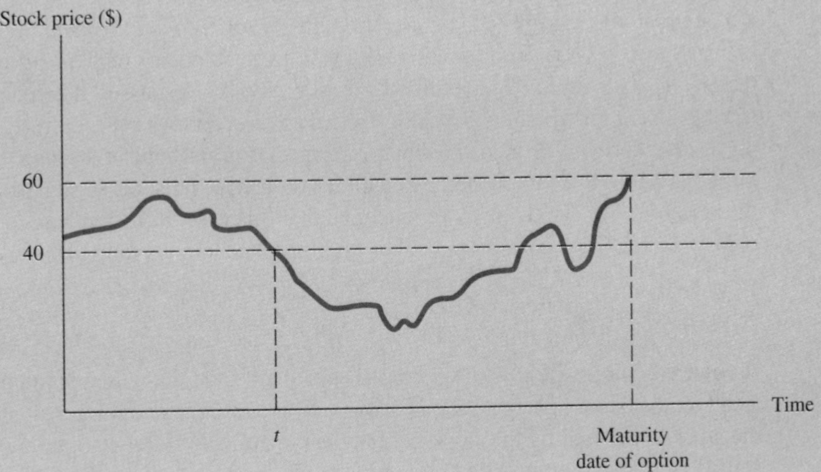

*Another disadvantage of the stop-loss order, which is of a more practical nature, is that the selling price is not guaranteed. Problems in executing trades could lead to a transaction at a price lower than $40.

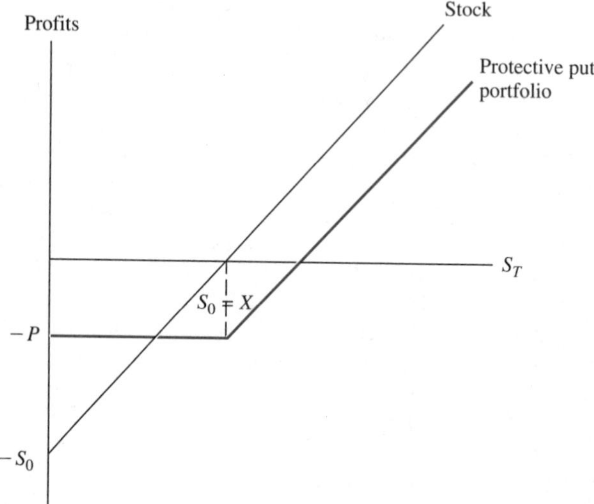

Figure 19.10
Protective put versus stock investment

equal to the cost of the put if S_T is below S_0. The profit on the protective put increases one for one with increases in the stock price once S_T exceeds S_0.

Figure 19.10 makes it clear that the protective put offers some insurance against stock price declines in that it limits losses. Therefore, protective put strategies provide a form of *portfolio insurance*. The cost of the protection is that, in the case of stock price increases, your profit is reduced by the cost of the put, which turned out to be unneeded.

This example also shows that despite the common perception that derivatives mean risk, derivative securities can be used effectively for *risk management*. In fact, such risk management is becoming accepted as part of the fiduciary responsibility of financial managers. The nearby box entitled "Future Shock" discusses the recent court case *Brane* v. *Roth,* in which a company's board of directors was successfully sued for failing to use derivatives to hedge the price risk of grain held in storage. Such hedging might have been accomplished using either protective puts, or, as suggested in the box, futures contracts. Many observers believe that this case will soon lead to a broad legal obligation for firms to use derivatives and other techniques to manage risk.

Covered Calls

A **covered call** position is the purchase of a share of stock with a simultaneous sale of a call on that stock. The position is "covered" because the potential obligation to deliver the stock is covered by the stock held in the portfolio. Writing an option without an offsetting stock position is called by contrast *naked option writing*. The value of a covered call position at the expiration of the call, presented in Table 19.2, equals the stock value minus the value of the call. The call value is *subtracted* because the covered call position involves issuing a call to another investor who can choose to exercise it to profit at your expense.

Future Shock

A company's board of directors is successfully sued by its shareholders for not using derivatives to hedge its risks? It sounds far-fetched. But, after a court decision in America last year, the day when directors have a legal duty to hedge could be coming closer.

The case of *Brane* v. *Roth* involved no Wall Street investment bank or securities house, but a humble grain co-operative in Indiana. America has thousands of agricultural co-ops, which buy and sell produce on behalf of their shareholders (local farmers who entrust their annual harvests to co-ops in the hope of getting the best price). When the manager of the Indiana co-op finished selling his farmers' crops in 1980—a year in which the price of grain collapsed—the co-op had made a gross loss of $424,000.

He might have avoided the loss by using grain futures on the Chicago Board of Trade to hedge against falling prices. The co-op's worried accountant had, in fact, advised the board the previous year that it should be hedging against this risk. The directors authorised the manager to do so. As a result, the manager did hedge—but only a paltry $20,050 of the co-op's $7.3m of grain sales. Losses mounted as the price of grain tumbled.

"Negligence," cried shareholders, and promptly sued the co-op's manager and four directors. After long proceedings, the Indiana courts agreed, citing the failure to hedge as the manager's central sin. As for the directors, they had a duty to understand hedging techniques and should have watched over the manager more carefully. In June 1992 the co-op's directors lost their final appeal.

The case, believed to be the first ruling of its kind, was spotted recently by Philip Johnson, a partner of a New York law firm, Skadden, Arps, Slate, Meagher & Flom (and a former chairman of the Commodities and Futures Trading Commission). He reckons the ruling, though it has no legal force outside Indiana, will prove an irresistible precedent for lawyers elsewhere: ignorance of derivatives is no excuse for not using them. And that applies to ordinary businesses as well as to the financial institutions which most obviously must manage financial risk. If Mr. Johnson is right in his assessment, the next case will not be long in coming.

Source: *The Economist*, March 13, 1993.

The solid line in Figure 19.11**C** illustrates the payoff pattern. You see that the total position is worth S_T when the stock price at time T is below X and rises to a maximum of X when S_T exceeds X. In essence, the sale of the call options means the call writer has sold the claim to any stock value above X in return for the initial premium (the call price). Therefore, at expiration, the position is worth at most X. The dashed line of Figure 19.11**C** is the net profit to the covered call.

Writing covered call options has been a popular investment strategy among institutional investors. Consider the managers of a fund invested largely in stocks. They might find it appealing to write calls on some or all of the stock in order to boost income by the premiums collected. Although they thereby forfeit potential capital gains should the stock price rise above the exercise price, if they view X as the price at which they plan to sell the stock anyway, then the call may be viewed as enforcing a kind of "sell discipline." The written call guarantees the stock sale will occur as planned.

For example, assume a pension fund holds 1,000 shares of IBM stock, with a current price of $70 per share. Suppose management intends to sell all 1,000 shares if the share price hits $80, and a call expiring in 60 days with an exercise price of $80 cur-

Table 19.2 Value of Covered Call Position at Option Expiration

	$S_T \le X$	$S_T > X$
Payoff of stock	S_T	S_T
Payoff of written call	-0	$-(S_T - X)$
TOTAL	S_T	X

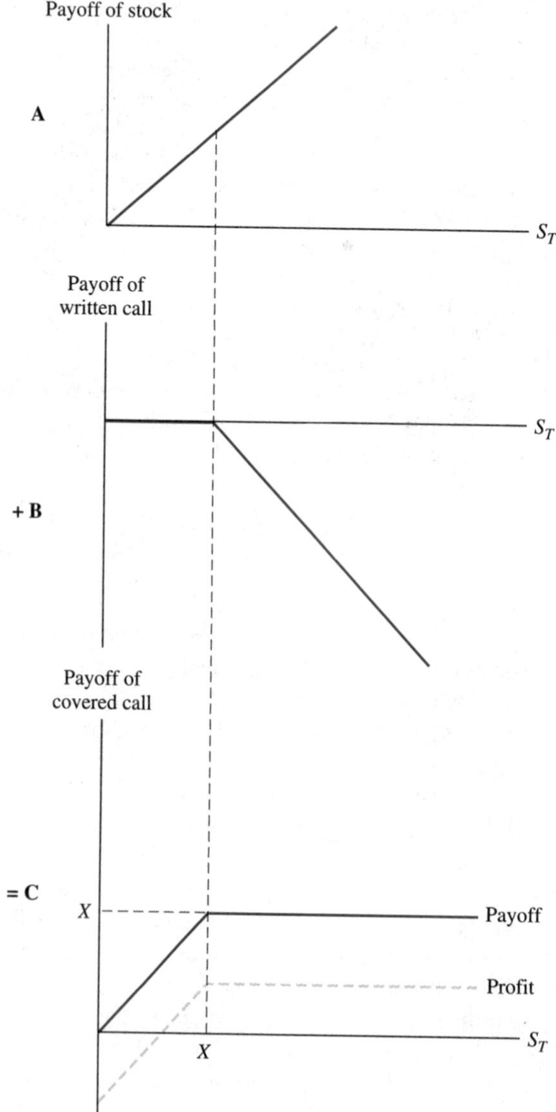

Figure 19.11
Value of a covered call position at expiration

rently sells for $5. By writing 10 IBM call contracts (100 shares each) the fund can pick up $5,000 in extra income. The fund would lose its share of profits from any movement of IBM stock above $80 per share, but given that it would have sold its shares at $80, it would not have realized those profits anyway.

Straddle

A long **straddle** is established by buying both a call and a put on a stock, each with the same exercise price, X, and the same expiration date, T. Straddles are useful strategies for investors who believe a stock will move a lot in price but are uncertain about the direction of the move. For example, suppose you believe an important court case that will make or break a company is about to be settled, and the market is not yet aware of the situation. The stock will either double in value if the case is settled favorably or will drop by half if the settlement goes against the company. The straddle position will do well regardless of the outcome because its value is highest when the stock price makes extreme upward or downward moves from X.

The worst-case scenario for a straddle is no movement in the stock price. If S_T equals X, both the call and the put expire worthless, and the investor's outlay for the purchase of both options is lost. Straddle positions, therefore, are bets on volatility. An investor who establishes a straddle must view the stock as more volatile than the market does. Conversely, investors who *write* straddles—selling both a call and a put—must believe the market is less volatile. They accept the option premiums now, hoping the stock price will not change much before option expiration.

The payoff to a straddle is presented in Table 19.3. The solid line of Figure 19.3**C** illustrates this payoff. Notice the portfolio payoff is always positive, except at the one point where the portfolio has zero value, $S_T = X$. You might wonder why all investors don't pursue such a seemingly "no-lose" strategy. The straddle requires that both the put and call be purchased. The value of the portfolio at expiration, while never negative, still must exceed the initial cash outlay for a straddle investor to clear a profit.

The dashed line of Figure 19.12**C** is the profit to the straddle. The profit line lies below the payoff line by the cost of purchasing the straddle, $P + C$. It is clear from the diagram that the straddle position generates a loss unless the stock price deviates substantially from X. The stock price must depart from X by the total amount expended to purchase the call and the put in order for the purchaser of the straddle to clear a profit.

Strips and *straps* are variations of straddles. A strip is two puts and one call on a security with the same exercise price and maturity date. A strap is two calls and one put.

CONCEPT CHECK Question 4. Graph the profit and payoff diagrams for strips and straps.

Spreads

A **spread** is a combination of two or more call options (or two or more puts) on the same stock with differing exercise prices or times to maturity. Some options are bought, whereas others are sold, or written. A *money spread* involves the purchase of one option

Table 19.3 Value of a Straddle Position at Option Expiration

	$S_T < X$	$S_T \geq X$
Payoff of call	0	$S_T - X$
+ Payoff of put	$+(X - S_T)$	+0
TOTAL	$X - S_T$	$S_T - X$

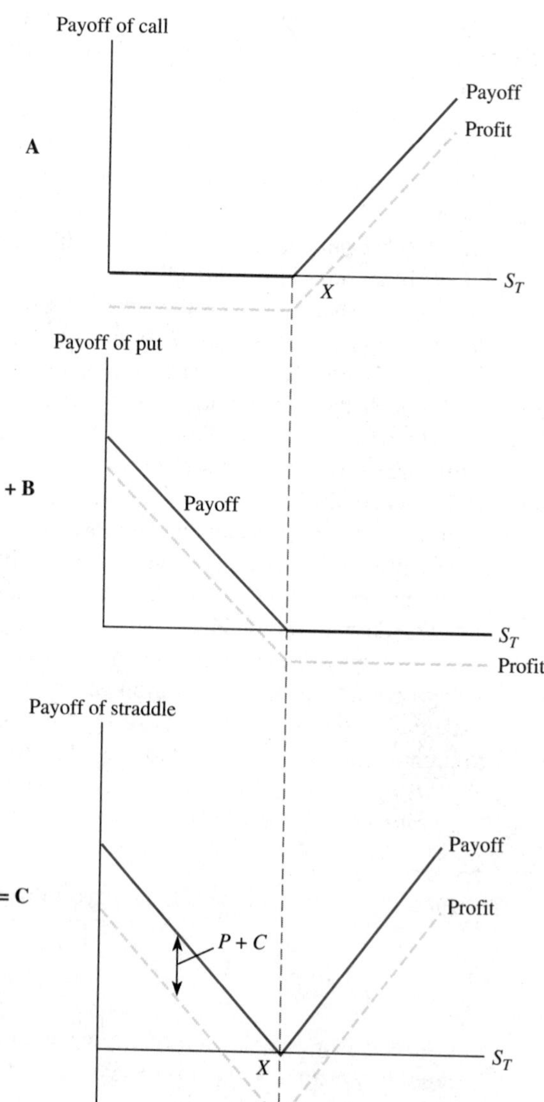

Figure 19.12
Value of a straddle at expiration

and the simultaneous sale of another with a different exercise price. A *time spread* refers to the sale and purchase of options with differing expiration dates.

Consider a money spread in which one call option is bought at an exercise price X_1, whereas another call with identical expiration date, but higher exercise price, X_2, is written. The payoff to this position will be the difference in the value of the call held and the value of the call written, as in Table 19.4.

There are now three instead of two outcomes to distinguish: the lowest-price region where S_T is below both exercise prices, a middle region where S_T is between the two exercise prices, and a high-price region where S_T exceeds both exercise prices. Figure 19.13 illustrates the payoff and profit to this strategy, which is called a *bullish spread* because the payoff either increases or is unaffected by stock price increases. Holders of bullish spreads benefit from stock price increases.

One motivation for a bullish spread might be that the investor thinks one option is overpriced relative to another. For example, an investor who believes an $X = \$135$ call is cheap compared to an $X = \$150$ call might establish the spread, even without a strong desire to take a bullish position in the stock.

A product called CAPS, which mimics European vertical spreads on the S&P 100 and S&P 500 indexes and the Major Market Index, began trading a few years ago. The spread position, which is long one option and short another, is in effect traded as a single security. For example, the exercise price of the long call position is accompanied by a higher exercise price called the *cap price.* The cap price is in effect the exercise price of the call that would be written in an explicit spread position. Similarly, put CAPS accompany the stated exercise price with a lower cap price. The spread between the exercise price and the cap price is 30 points on the S&P contracts, and 20 points on the MMI contract. CAPS differ from actual spread positions in that they are automatically exercised as soon as the index reaches the cap price.

Collars

A **collar** is an options strategy that brackets the value of a portfolio between two bounds. Suppose that an investor currently is holding a large position in IBM, which is currently selling at \$70 per share. A lower bound of \$60 can be placed on the value of the portfolio by buying a protective put with exercise price \$60. This protection, however, requires that the investor pay the put premium. To raise the money to pay for the put, the investor might write a call option, say with exercise price \$80. The call might sell for roughly the same price as the put, meaning that the net outlay for the two options positions is approximately zero. The call limits the portfolio's upside potential. Even if the stock price moves above \$80, the investor will do no better than \$80, because at a higher price the stock will be called away. Thus, the investor obtains the downside protection represented by the exercise price of the put by selling her claim to any upside potential beyond the exercise price of the call.

A collar would be appropriate for an investor who has a target wealth goal in mind but is unwilling to risk losses beyond a certain level. If you are contemplating buying a house for \$150,000, for example, you might set this figure as your goal. Your current wealth may be \$140,000, and you are unwilling to risk losing more than \$10,000. A col-

Table 19.4 Value of a Bullish Vertical Spread Position at Expiration

	$S_T \le X_1$	$X_1 < S_T \le X_2$	$S_T \ge X_2$
Payoff of purchased call, exercise price = X_1	0	$S_T - X_1$	$S_T - X_1$
Payoff of written call, exercise price = X_2	−0	−0	$-(S_T - X_2)$
TOTAL	0	$S_T - X_1$	$X_2 - X_1$

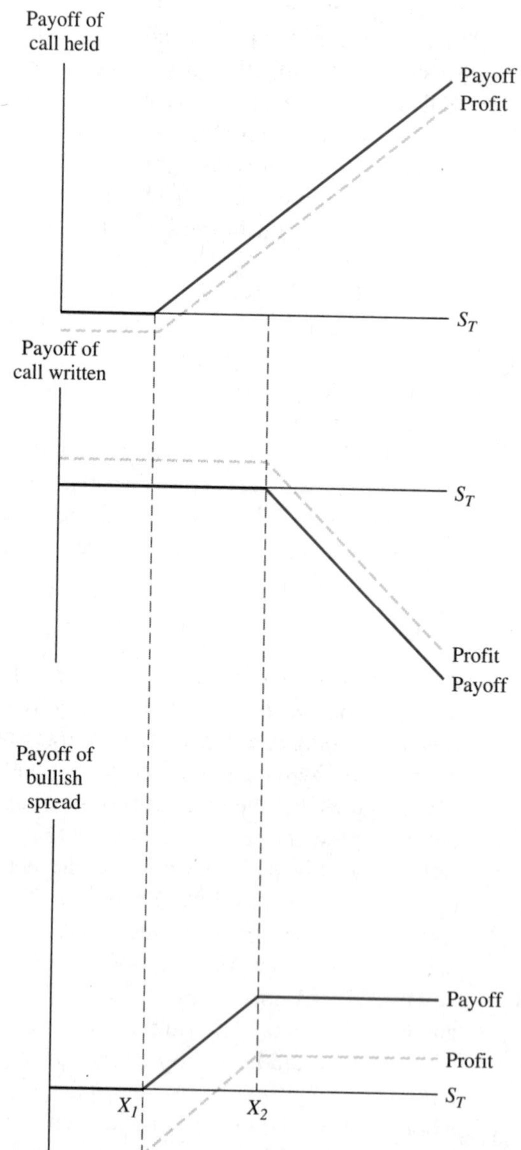

Figure 19.13 Value of a bullish spread position at expiration

lar established by: (1) purchasing 1,000 shares of stock currently selling at $140 per share, (2) purchasing 1,000 put options (10 option contracts) with exercise price $130, and (3) writing 1,000 calls with exercise price $150 would give you a good chance to realize the $10,000 capital gain without risking a loss of more than $10,000.

CONCEPT CHECK Question 5. Graph the payoff diagram for the IBM collar just described with exercise price of the put equal to $60, and exercise price of the call equal to $80.

19.4 THE PUT-CALL PARITY RELATIONSHIP

We saw in the previous section that a protective put portfolio, comprising a stock position and a put option on that position, provides a payoff with a guaranteed minimum value, but with unlimited upside potential. This is not the only way to achieve such protection, however. A call-plus-bills portfolio also can provide limited downside risk with unlimited upsided potential.

Consider the strategy of buying a call option and, in addition, buying Treasury bills with face value equal to the exercise price of the call, and with maturity date equal to the expiration date of the option. For example, if the exercise price of the call option is $100, then each option contract (which is written on 100 shares) would require payment of $10,000 upon exercise. Therefore, you would purchase one T-bill, which also has a maturity value of $10,000. More generally, for each option that you hold with exercise price X, you would purchase a risk-free zero-coupon bond with face value X.

Examine the value of this position at time T, when the options expire and the zero-coupon bond matures.

	$S_T \le X$	$S_T > X$
Value of call option	0	$S_T - X$
Value of riskless bond	X	X
TOTAL	X	S_T

If the stock price is below the exercise price, the call is worthless, but the riskless bond matures to its face value, X. The bond therefore provides a floor value to the portfolio. If the stock price exceeds X, then the payoff to the call, $S_T - X$, is added to the face value of the bond to provide a total payoff of S_T. The payoff to this portfolio is precisely identical to the payoff of the protective put that we derived in Table 19.1.

If two portfolios always provide equal values, then they must cost the same amount to establish. This is the law of one price. Therefore, the call-plus-bond portfolio must cost the same as the stock-plus-put portfolio. Each call costs C. The riskless zero-coupon bond costs $X/(1 + r_f)^T$. Therefore, the call-plus-bond portfolio costs $C + X/(1 + r_f)^T$ to establish. The stock costs S_0 to purchase now (at time zero), while the put costs P. Therefore, we conclude that

$$C + X/(1 + r_f)^T = S_0 + P \qquad (19.1)$$

Equation 19.1 is called the **put-call parity theorem** because it represents the proper relationship between put and call prices. If the parity relation is ever violated, an arbi-

Table 19.5 Arbitrage Strategy

Position	Immediate Cash Flow	Cash Flow in Six Months	
		$S_T < 105$	$S_T \geq 105$
Buy stock	−110	S_T	S_T
Borrow $105/1.1025^{1/2}$ = $100	+100	−105	−105
Sell call	+17	0	$-(S_T - 105)$
Buy put	−5	$105 - S_T$	0
TOTAL	2	0	0

trage opportunity arises. For example, suppose you confront these data for a certain stock:

Stock price	$110
Call price (six-month maturity, X = $105)	$ 17
Put price (six-month maturity, X = $105)	$ 5
Risk-free interest rate	10.25% per year

We can use these data in equation 19.1 to see if parity is violated:

$$C + X/(1 + r_f)^T \stackrel{?}{=} S_0 + P$$

$$17 + \frac{105}{1.1025^{1/2}} \stackrel{?}{=} 110 + 5$$

$$117 \stackrel{?}{=} 115$$

This result, a violation of parity—117 does not equal 115—indicates mispricing. To exploit the mispricing you buy the relatively cheap portfolio (the stock-plus-put position represented on the right-hand side of the equation), and sell the relatively expensive portfolio (the call-plus-bond position corresponding to the left-hand side). Therefore, if you *buy* the stock, *buy* the put, *write* the call, and *borrow* $100 for six months (because borrowing money is the opposite of buying a bond), you should earn arbitrage profits.

Let's examine the payoff to this strategy. In six months, the stock will be worth S_T. The $100 borrowed will be paid back with interest, resulting in a cash flow of $105. The written call will result in a cash outflow of S_T − $105 if S_T exceeds $105. The purchased put pays off $105 − S_T if the stock price is below $105.

Table 19.5 summarizes the outcome. The immediate cash inflow is $2. In six months, the various positions provide exactly offsetting cash flows: The $2 inflow is realized without any offsetting outflows. This is an arbitrage opportunity that investors will pursue on a large scale until buying and selling pressure restores the parity condition expressed in equation 19.1.

Equation 19.1 actually applies only to options on stocks that pay no dividends before the maturity date of the option. The extension of the parity condition for European call options on dividend-paying stocks is, however, straightforward. Problem 5 at the end of the chapter leads you through the extension of the parity relationship. The more general formulation of the put-call parity condition is:

$$\textbf{Put-call parity: } P = C - S_0 + PV(X) + PV(\text{dividends}) \qquad \textbf{(19.2)}$$

where PV(dividends) is the present value of the dividends that will be paid by the stock during the life of the option. If the stock does not pay dividends, equation 19.2 becomes identical to equation 19.1.

Notice that this generalization would apply as well to European options on assets other than stocks. Instead of using dividend income per se in equation 19.2, we would let any income paid out by the underlying asset play the role of the stock dividends. For example, European put and call options on bonds would satisfy the same parity relationship, except that the bond's coupon income would replace the stock's dividend payments in the parity formula.

Even this generalization, however, applies only to European options, as the cash flow streams from the two portfolios represented by the two sides of equation 19.2 will match only if each position is held until maturity. If a call and a put may be optimally exercised at different times before their common expiration date, then the equality of payoffs cannot be assured, or even expected, and the portfolios will have different values.

Let's see how well parity works using real data on the IBM options in Figure 19.1. The January maturity call with exercise price $70 and time to expiration of 39 days cost $2.375, whereas the corresponding put option cost $2.25. IBM was selling for $69.625, and the annualized short-term interest rate on this date was 5.2%. There are no dividends to be paid to a stock purchaser between the date of the listing, December 13, 1994, and the option maturity date, January 21, 1995. According to parity, we should find that

$$\begin{aligned}
P &= C \quad + \quad PV(X) \quad - S_0 + PV(\text{dividends}) \\
2.25 &= 2.375 + \frac{70}{(1.052)^{39/365}} - 69.625 + 0 \\
2.25 &= 2.375 + 69.622 - 69.625 \\
2.25 &= 2.372
\end{aligned}$$

So parity is violated by about $.12 per share. Is this a big enough difference to exploit? Probably not. You have to weigh the potential profit against the trading costs of the call, put, and stock. More important, given the fact that options trade relatively infrequently, this deviation from parity might not be "real," but may instead be attributable to "stale" price quotes at which you cannot actually trade.

19.5 Optionlike Securities

Suppose you never traded an option directly. Why do you need to appreciate the properties of options in formulating an investment plan? Many financial instruments and agreements have features that convey implicit or explicit options to one or more parties. If you are to value and use these securities correctly, you must understand these embedded option attributes.

Figure 19.14
Values of callable bonds compared with straight bonds

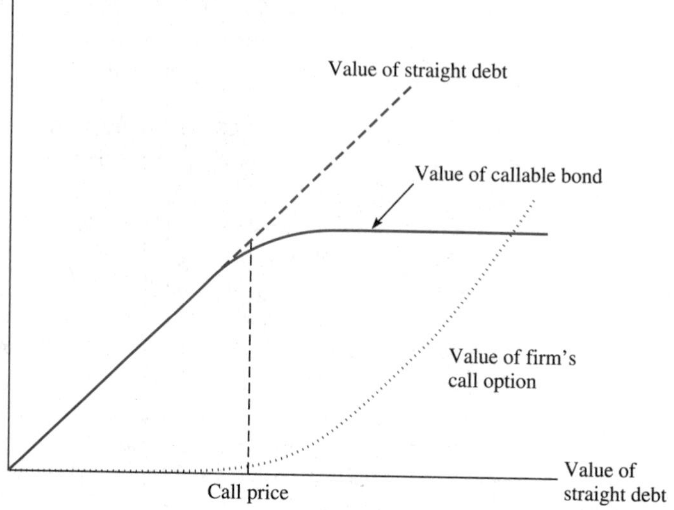

Callable Bonds

You know from Chapter 13 that most corporate bonds are issued with call provisions entitling the issuer to buy bonds back from bondholders at some time in the future at a specified call price. A call provision conveys a call option to the issuer, where the exercise price is equal to the price at which the bond can be repurchased. A callable bond arrangement is essentially a sale of a *straight bond* (a bond with no option features such as callability or convertibility) to the investor and the concurrent issuance of a call option by the investor to the bond-issuing firm.

There must be some compensation for conveying this implicit call option to the firm. If the callable bond were issued with the same coupon rate as a straight bond, we would expect it to sell at a lower price than the straight bond. In fact, we would expect the price difference to equal the value of the call. To sell callable bonds at par, firms must issue them with coupon rates higher than the coupons on straight debt. The higher coupons are the investor's compensation for the call option retained by the issuer. Coupon rates usually are selected so that the newly issued bond will sell at par value.

Figure 19.14 illustrates this optionlike property. The horizontal axis is the value of a straight bond with otherwise identical terms as the callable bond. The dashed 45-degree line represents the value of straight debt. The solid line is the value of the callable bond, and the dotted line is the value of the call option retained by the firm. A callable bond's potential for capital gains is limited by the firm's option to repurchase at the call price.

CONCEPT CHECK Question 6. How is a callable bond similar to a covered call strategy on a straight bond?

The option inherent in callable bonds actually is more complex than an ordinary call option, because usually it may be exercised only after some initial period of call protection. The price at which the bond is callable may change over time also. Unlike exchange-listed options, these features are defined in the initial bond covenants and will depend on the needs of the issuing firm and its perception of the market's tastes.

CONCEPT CHECK

Question 7. Suppose the period of call protection is extended. How will the coupon rate the company needs to offer on its bonds change to enable the issuer to sell the bonds at par value?

Convertible Securities

Convertible bonds and convertible preferred stock convey options to the holder of the security rather than to the issuing firm. A convertible security typically gives its holder the right to exchange each bond or share of preferred stock for a fixed number of shares of common stock, regardless of the market prices of the securities at the time.

CONCEPT CHECK

Question 8. Should a convertible bond issued at par value have a higher or lower coupon rate than a nonconvertible bond at par?

For example, a bond with a *conversion ratio* of 10 allows its holder to convert one bond of par value $1,000 into 10 shares of common stock. Alternatively, we say the *conversion price* in this case is $100: To receive 10 shares of stock, the investor sacrifices bonds with face value $1,000 or, put another way, $100 of face value per share. If the present value of the bond's scheduled payments is less than 10 times the value of one share of stock, it may pay to convert; that is, the conversion option is in the money. A bond worth $950 with a conversion ratio of 10 could be converted profitably if the stock were selling above $95, as the value of the 10 shares received for each bond surrendered would exceed $950. Most convertible bonds are issued "deep out of the money." That is, the issuer sets the conversion ratio so that conversion will not be profitable unless there is a substantial increase in stock prices and/or decrease in bond prices from the time of issue.

A bond's *conversion value* equals the value it would have if you converted it into stock immediately. Clearly, a bond must sell for at least its conversion value. If it did not, you could purchase the bond, convert it, and clear an immediate profit. This condition could never persist, for all investors would pursue such a strategy and ultimately would bid up the price of the bond.

The straight bond value or "bond floor" is the value the bond would have if it were not convertible into stock. The bond must sell for more than its straight bond value because a convertible bond has more value; it is in fact a straight bond plus a valuable call option. Therefore, the convertible bond has two lower bounds on its market price: the conversion value and the straight bond value.

Figure 19.15 illustrates the optionlike properties of the convertible bond. Figure 19.15**A** shows the value of the straight debt as a function of the stock price of the issu-

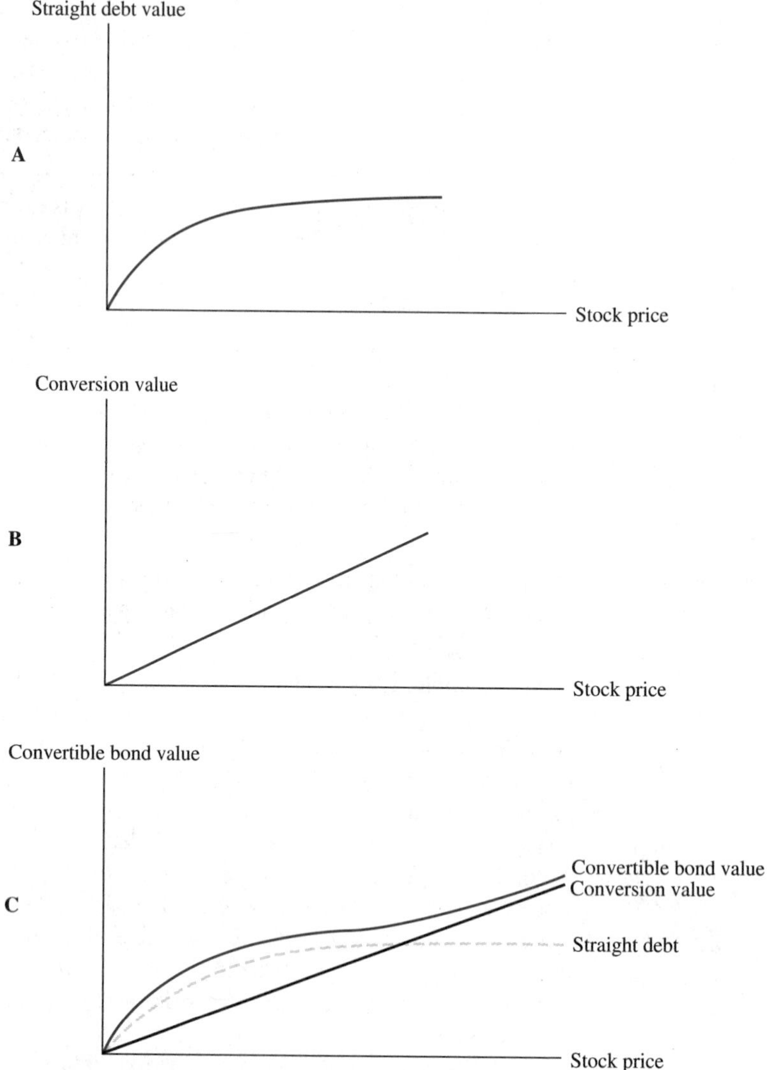

Figure 19.15
Value of a convertible bond as a function of stock price. **A,** Straight debt value, or bond floor. **B,** Conversion value of the bond. **C,** Total value of convertible bond

ing firm. For healthy firms, the straight debt value is almost independent of the value of the stock because default risk is small. However, if the firm is close to bankruptcy (stock prices are low), default risk increases, and the straight bond value falls. Panel **B** shows the conversion value of the bond. Panel **C** compares the value of the convertible bond to these two lower bounds.

When stock prices are low, the straight bond value is the effective lower bound, and the conversion option is nearly irrelevant. The convertible will trade like straight debt. When stock prices are high, the bond's price is determined by its conversion value. With conversion all but guaranteed, the bond is essentially equity in disguise.

We can illustrate with two examples.

	Bond A	Bond B
Annual coupon	$80	$80
Maturity date	10 years	10 years
Quality rating	Baa	Baa
Conversion ratio	20	25
Stock price	$30	$50
Conversion value	$600	$1,250
Market yield on 10-year Baa-rated bonds	8.5%	8.5%
Value as straight debt	$967	$967
Actual bond price	$972	$1,255
Reported yield to maturity	8.42%	4.76%

Bond A has a conversion value of only $600. Its value as straight debt, in contrast, is $967. This is the present value of the coupon and principal payments at a market rate for straight debt of 8.5%. The bond's price is $972, so the premium over straight bond value is only $5, reflecting the low probability of conversion. Its reported yield to maturity based on scheduled coupon payments and the market price of $972 is 8.42 percent, close to that of straight debt.

The conversion option on Bond B is in the money. Conversion value is $1,250, and the bond's price, $1,255, reflects its value as equity (plus $5 for the protection the bond offers against stock price declines). The bond's reported yield is 4.76%, far below the comparable yield on straight debt. The big yield sacrifice is attributable to the far greater value of the conversion option.

In theory, we could value convertible bonds by treating them as straight debt plus call options. In practice, however, this approach is often impractical for several reasons:

1. The conversion price frequently increases over time, which means the exercise price of the option changes.
2. Stocks may pay several dividends over the life of the bond, further complicating the option valuation analysis.
3. Most convertibles also are callable at the discretion of the firm. In essence, both the investor and the issuer hold options on each other. If the issuer exercises its call option to repurchase the bond, the bondholders typically have a month during which they still can convert. When issuers use a call option, knowing bondholders will choose to convert, the issuer is said to have *forced a conversion.* These conditions together mean the actual maturity of the bond is indeterminate.

Warrants

Warrants are essentially call options issued by a firm. One important difference between calls and warrants is that exercise of a warrant requires the firm to issue a new share of stock—the total number of shares outstanding increases. Exercise of a call option requires only that the writer of the call deliver an already-issued share of stock to discharge the obligation. In that case, the number of shares outstanding remains fixed. Also unlike call options, warrants result in a cash flow to the firm when the warrant holder pays the exercise price. These differences mean that warrant values will differ somewhat from the values of call options with identical terms.

Like convertible debt, warrant terms may be tailored to meet the needs of the firm. Also like convertible debt, warrants generally are protected against stock splits and dividends in that the exercise price and the number of warrants held are adjusted to offset the effects of the split.

Warrants are often issued in conjunction with another security. Bonds, for example, may be packaged together with a warrant "sweetener," frequently a warrant that may be sold separately. This is called a *detachable warrant.*

Issue of warrants and convertible securities creates the potential for an increase in outstanding shares of stock if exercise occurs. Exercise obviously would affect financial statistics that are computed on a per share basis, so annual reports must provide earnings per share figures under the assumption that all convertible securities and warrants are exercised. These figures are called *fully diluted earnings per share.*[2]

Collateralized Loans

Many loan arrangements require that the borrower put up collateral to guarantee the loan will be paid back. In the event of default, the lender takes possession of the collateral. A nonrecourse loan gives the lender no recourse beyond the right to the collateral. That is, the lender may not sue the borrower for further payment if the collateral turns out not to be valuable enough to repay the loan.

This arrangement gives an implicit call option to the borrower. Assume the borrower is obligated to pay back L dollars at the maturity of the loan. The collateral will be worth S_T dollars at maturity. (Its value today is S_0.) The borrower has the option to wait until loan maturity and repay the loan only if the collateral is worth more than the L dollars necessary to satisfy the loan. If the collateral is worth less than L, the borrower can default on the loan, discharging the obligation by forfeiting the collateral, which is worth only S_T.

Another way of describing such a loan is to view the borrower as turning over the collateral to the lender but retaining the right to reclaim it by paying off the loan. The transfer of the collateral with the right to reclaim it is equivalent to a payment of S_0 dollars, less a simultaneous recovery of a sum that resembles a call option with exercise price L. Basically, the borrower turns over collateral and keeps an option to "repurchase" it for L dollars at the maturity of the loan if L turns out to be less than S_T. This is a call option.

A third way to look at a collateralized loan is to assume that the borrower will repay the L dollars with certainty but also retain the option to sell the collateral to the lender for L dollars, even if S_T is less than L. In this case, the sale of the collateral would generate the cash necessary to satisfy the loan. The ability to "sell" the collateral for a price of L dollars represents a put option, which guarantees the borrower can raise enough money to satisfy the loan simply by turning over the collateral.

It is perhaps surprising to realize that we can describe the same loan as involving either a put option or a call option, as the payoffs to calls and puts are so different. Yet

[2] We should note that the exercise of a convertible bond need not reduce EPS. Diluted EPS will be less than undiluted EPS only if interest saved (per share) on the convertible bonds is less than the prior EPS.

the equivalence of the two approaches is nothing more than a reflection of the put-call parity relationship. In our call-option description of the loan, the value of the borrower's liability is $S_0 - C$: The borrower turns over the asset, which is a transfer of S_0 dollars, but retains a call worth C dollars. In the put-option description, the borrower is obligated to pay L dollars but retains the put, which is worth P: The present value of this net obligation is $L/(1 + r_f)^T - P$. Because these alternative descriptions are equivalent ways of viewing the same loan, the value of the obligations must be equal:

$$S_0 - C = L/(1 + r_f)^T - P \tag{19.3}$$

Treating L as the exercise price of the option, equation 19.3 is simply the put-call parity relationship.

Figure 19.16 illustrates this fact. Figure 19.16**A** is the value of the payment to be received by the lender, which equals the minimum of S_T or L. Panel **B** shows that this amount can be expressed as S_T minus the payoff of the call implicitly written by the lender and held by the borrower. Panel **C** shows it also can be viewed as a receipt of L dollars minus the proceeds of a put option.

Levered Equity and Risky Debt

Investors holding stock in incorporated firms are protected by limited liability, which means that if the firm cannot pay its debts, the firm's creditors may attach only the firm's assets, not sue the corporation's equityholders for further payment. In effect, any time the corporation borrows money, the maximum possible collateral for the loan is the total of the firm's assets. If the firm declares bankruptcy, we can interpret this as an admission that the assets of the firm are insufficient to satisfy the claims against it. The corporation may discharge its obligations by transferring ownership of the firm's assets to the creditors.

Just as is true for nonrecourse collateralized loans, the required payment to the creditors represents the exercise price of the implicit option, while the value of the firm is the underlying asset. The equityholders have a put option to transfer their ownership claims on the firm to the creditors in return for the face value of the firm's debt.

Alternatively, we may view the equityholders as retaining a call option. They have, in effect, already transferred their ownership claim to the firm to the creditors but have retained the right to reacquire that claim by paying off the loan. Hence, the equityholders have the option to "buy back" the firm for a specified price: They have a call option.

The significance of this observation is that analysts can value corporate bonds using option pricing techniques. The default premium required of risky debt in principle can be estimated using option valuation models. We will consider some of these models in the next chapter.

19.6 Financial Engineering

One of the attractions of options is the ability they provide to create investment positions with payoffs that depend in a variety of ways on the values of other securities. We have seen evidence of this capability in the various options strategies examined in

Figure 19.16
Collateralized loan

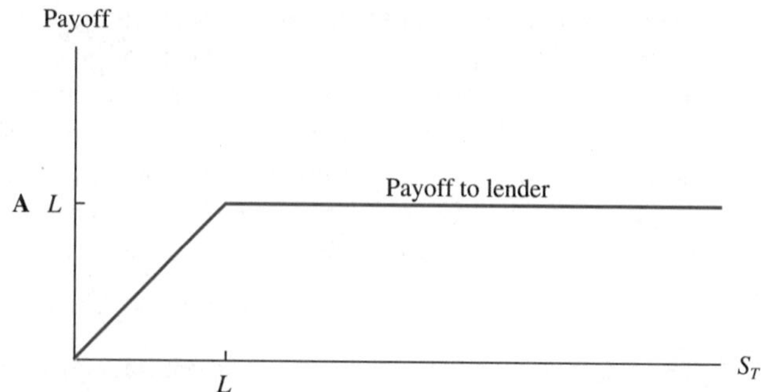

When S_T exceeds L, the loan is repaid and the collateral is reclaimed. Otherwise, the collateral is forfeited and the total loan repayment is worth only S_T.

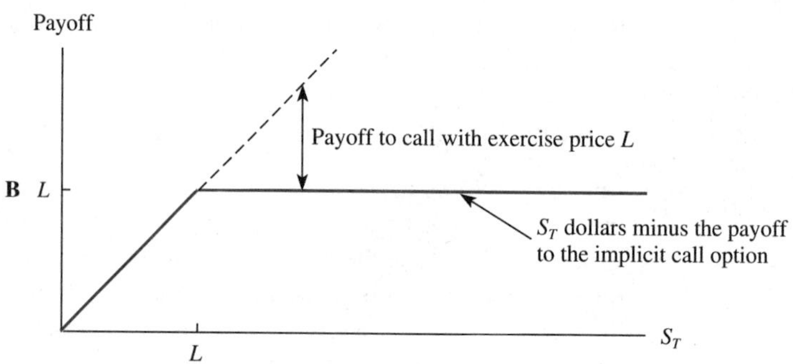

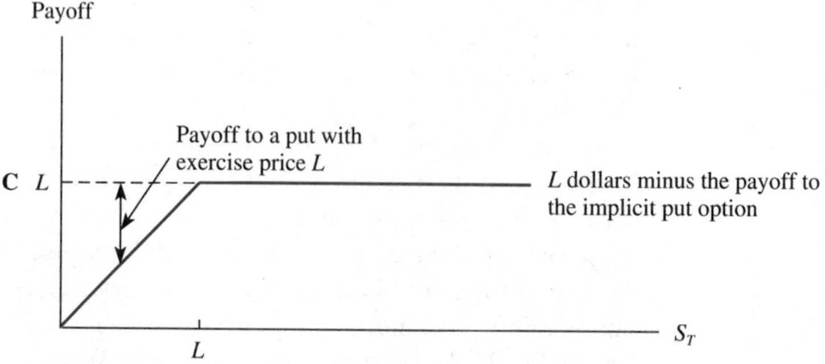

Section 19.4. Options also can be used to custom design new securities or portfolios with desired patterns of exposure to the price of an underlying security. In this sense, options (and futures contracts, to be discussed in Chapters 21 and 22) provide the ability to engage in *financial engineering,* the creation of portfolios with specified payoff patterns. The nearby box discusses the rapid pace of innovation.

Most financial engineering takes place for institutional investors. However, some applications have been designed for the retail market. One highly successful retail product of financial engineering, first introduced by Merrill Lynch in 1985, is the Liquid Yield Option Note, or LYON.[3] A LYON is a *zero-coupon, convertible, callable,* and *puttable* bond. To illustrate how the bond works, consider the first LYON issued, by Waste Management, Inc. The bond paid no coupon income and was priced at $250 in 1985, with a maturity value of $1,000 in 2001. If the security is not called, converted, or redeemed, it provides a yield to maturity of about 9%. However, three options may result in early retirement of the issue.

First, the investor can convert each bond into 4.36 shares of Waste Management stock. Second, the investor can put (sell) the bond back to Waste Management at a predetermined exercise price that rises over time according to a schedule detailed in the bond indenture. Finally, Waste Management can call the bond back from the investor at fixed exercise prices that also increase over time.

This combination of option results in risk-sharing attributes that seem to be attractive to both the issuer and investors. The convertibility feature provides the opportunity to profit from price advances in Waste Management stock. At the same time, the embedded put option provides the LYON holder a protective floor. Finally, the call feature allows Waste Management to call the bonds back for refinancing if interest rates drop considerably. The Waste Management LYON was a big success for Merrill Lynch. Although only 10% of a convertible bond typically is purchased by individual investors, they purchased approximately 40% of the LYON issue. Although other underwriters have since brought LYON competitors to the market, Merrill Lynch remains dominant in the field.

A simpler new product also engineered with options is the "bull" certificate of deposit. Bull CDs are offered in the United States, but seem to be more popular in Europe. They enable retail investors to take small positions in index options. Unlike conventional CDs, which pay a fixed rate of interest, *bull CDs* pay depositors a specified fraction of the rate of return on a market index such as the S&P 500, while guaranteeing a minimum rate of return should the market fall. A bull CD may offer 70% of any market increase, but protect its holder from any market decrease by guaranteeing at least no loss.

This arrangement is clearly a type of call option. If the market rises, the depositor profits according to the *participation rate* or *multiplier,* in this case 70%; if the market falls, the investor is insured against loss. Just as clearly, the bank offering these CDs is in effect writing call options and can hedge its position by buying index calls in the options market. Figure 19.17 shows the nature of the bank's obligation to its depositors.

How might the bank set the appropriate multiplier? To answer this, note various features of the option:

1. The price the depositor is paying for the options is the forgone interest on the conventional CD that could be purchased. Because interest is received at the end of the period, the present value of the interest payment on each dollar invested is $r_f/(1 + r_f)$. Therefore, the depositor trades a sure payment with present value per dollar invested of $r_f/(1 + r_f)$ for a return that depends on the market's per-

---

[3] This discussion is based on a paper by John McConnell and Eduardo Schwartz. See the selected readings at the end of the chapter.

Mathematicians Race to Develop New Kinds of Trading Instruments

From the quiet cubicles at International Business Machines Corp.'s central research facility here to secretive research labs inside brokerage firms, mathematicians are working on Wall Street's computer revolution, part two.

Over the past five years, Wall Street has spent enormously to upgrade its computing horsepower. Now, researchers at IBM and major securities firms are trying to harness that computing muscle with a new generation of "analytics," or sophisticated mathematical computer models that identify hundreds of never-before-imagined trades in stocks, bonds, and currencies.

For example, computers at Algorithms Inc., a Toronto firm, recently created a synthetic option on the benchmark Nikkei Index of 225 Japanese stocks. Produced by the computer out of a combination of Nikkei stock-index futures and exchange-traded stock-index options, the synthetic Nikkei option cost less than the real thing; this allowed traders at a Canadian investment bank to make $500,000 on a single trade.

Myron Scholes, who developed the widely used Black-Scholes option pricing model in 1973 with Fischer Black, says high-powered computers have extended the application of his model greatly. "The people who don't have these [analytics] are going to be relatively obsolete," says Mr. Scholes, who recently joined Salomon Brothers Inc.'s high-tech bond trading department as a managing director. (He is also a professor of finance at Stanford University.)

For years, Wall Street's computers were used for little more than fast accounting programs, known as spreadsheets. Now, some Wall Street firms are using mathematical formulas that imitate how traders think about and look at markets—but several hundred times faster than humans can. The next generation of analytics, in development at IBM and other research labs, seeks to apply elaborate financial theories—such as the "Markowitz mean variance model," for instance—to markets for up-to-the-minute use.

The development of analytics is one of the most closely guarded secrets inside Wall Street firms. Competition for clients has never been more intense; the only monopoly available to Wall Street now may be the proprietary mathematics of analytical systems that ferret out profit opportunities in markets that are ruthlessly efficient.

So closely guarded are the mathematics at O'Connor & Associates, a Chicago futures and options trading firm, that clients and even family members are barred from the trading floor at O'Connor's headquarters. Visitors can observe the firm at work only from a catwalk 20 feet above the trading floor. An O'Connor executive says the firm has about 40 people developing analytical software for trading purposes, and about 100 traders using these systems."

Elsewhere, IBM is working on a mathematical model that will allow investors to assemble hundreds of portfolios in seconds that have various shadings of investment risk and reward.

But no matter how refined the mathematical model Wall Street researchers build, the markets often prove elusive. Unlike physics, Mr. Winograd notes, finance has very few basic laws. "Economics hasn't had its Newton or its Einstein," he says. "Basic statistical behavior is still in question. Human beings are not molecules."

But that's precisely why Wall Street firms seek out mathematicians. Since markets are run by humans, there will always be imperfections that can be turned into profits. Or, in Mr. Winograd's words, "that's why you can make tons of money; or lose tons of money."

Source: Craig Torres, *The Wall Street Journal*, October 18, 1991. Reprinted by permission of *The Wall Street Journal*,

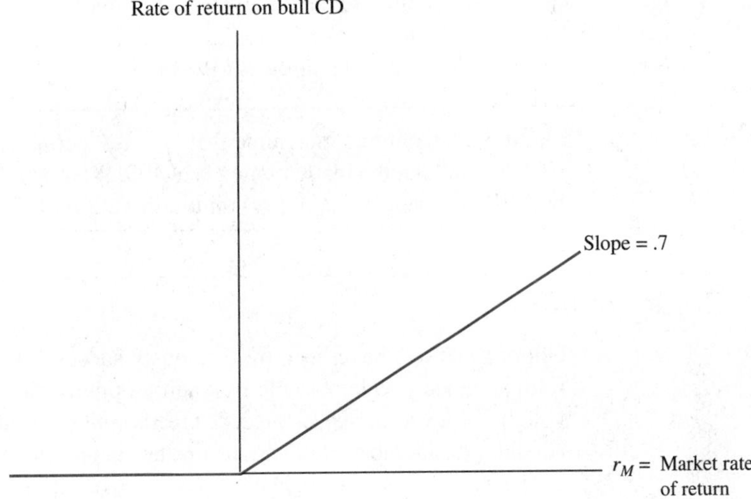

Figure 19.17
Bull CD

formance. Conversely, the bank can fund its obligation using the interest that it would have paid on a conventional CD.

2. The option we have described is an at-the-money option, meaning that the exercise price equals the current value of the stock index. The option goes into the money as soon as the market index increases from its level at the inception of the contract.
3. We can analyze the option on a per-dollar-invested basis. For example, the option costs the depositor $r_f/(1 + r_f)$ dollars per dollar placed in the bull CD. The market price of the option per dollar invested is C/S_0: The at-the-money option costs C dollars and is written on one unit of the market index, currently at S_0.

Now it is easy to determine the multiplier that the bank can offer on its bull CDs. It receives from its depositors a "payment" of $r_f/(1 + r_f)$ per dollar invested. It costs the bank C/S_0 to purchase the call option on a \$1 investment in the market index. Therefore, if $r_f/(1 + r_f)$ is, for example, 70% of C/S_0, the bank can purchase at most 0.7 call options on the \$1 investment and the multiplier will be 0.7. More generally, the multiplier on a bull CD is $r_f/(1 + r_f)$ divided by C/S_0.

As an example, suppose that $r_f = 6\%$ per year, and that six-month maturity at-the-money calls on the market index currently cost \$20. The index is at \$400. Then the option costs \$20/\$400 = \$.05 per dollar of market value. The CD rate is 3% per six months, meaning that $r_f/(1 + r_f) = .03/1.03 = .0291$. Therefore, the multiplier would be $.0291/.05 = .5825$.

This version of the bull CD has several variants. Investors can purchase bull CDs that guarantee a positive minimum return if they are willing to settle for a smaller multiplier. In this case, the option is "purchased" by the depositor for $(r_f - r_{min})/(1 + r_f)$ dollars per dollar invested, where r_{min} is the guaranteed minimum return. Because the purchase price is lower, fewer options can be purchased, which results in a lower multiplier. Another variant is the *bear CD,* which pays depositors a fraction of any *fall* in the market index. For example, a bear CD might offer a rate of return of 0.6 times any percentage decline in the S&P 500.

CONCEPT CHECK

Question 9. Continue to assume that $r_f = 3\%$ per half year, that at-the-money calls sell for $20, and that the market index is at 400. What would be the multiplier for six-month bull CDs offering a guaranteed minimum return of .5% over the term of the CD?

19.7 EXOTIC OPTIONS

Options markets have been tremendously successful. Investors clearly value the portfolio strategies made possible by trading options; this is reflected in the heavy trading volume in these markets. Success breeds imitation, and in recent years we have witnessed considerable innovation in the range of option instruments available to investors. Part of this innovation has occurred in the market for customized options, which now trade in active over-the-counter markets. Many of these options have terms that would have been highly unusual even a few years ago; they are therefore called "exotic options." In this section, we will survey some of the more interesting variants of these new instruments.

Asian Options

You already have been introduced to American and European options. *Asian options* are options with payoffs that depend on the *average* price of the underlying asset during at least some portion of the life of the option. For example, an Asian call option may have a payoff equal to the average stock price over the last 3 months minus the strike price if that value is positive, and zero otherwise. These options may be of interest, for example to firms that wish to hedge a profit stream that depends on the average price of a commodity over some period of time.

Barrier Options

Barrier options have payoffs that depend not only on some asset price at option expiration, but also on whether the underlying asset price has crossed through some "barrier." For example, a down-and-out option is one type of barrier option that automatically expires worthless if and when the stock price falls below some barrier price. Similarly, down-and-in options will not provide a payoff unless the stock price *does* fall below some barrier at least once during the life of the option. These options also are referred to as knock-out and knock-in options.

Lookback Options

Lookback options have payoffs that depend in part on the minimum or maximum price of the underlying asset during the life of the option. For example, a lookback call option might provide a payoff equal to the *maximum* stock price during the life of the option minus the exercise price, instead of the *closing* stock price minus the exercise price.

Such an option provides (for a fee, of course) a form of perfect marketing timing, providing the call holder with a payoff equal to the one that would accrue if the asset were purchased for X dollars and later sold at what turns out to be its high price.

Currency-Translated Options

Currency-translated options have either asset or exercise prices denominated in a foreign currency. A good example of such an option is the *quanto*, which allows an investor to fix in advance the exchange rate at which an investment in a foreign currency can be converted back into dollars. The right to translate a fixed amount of foreign currency into dollars at a given exchange rate is a simple foreign exchange option. Quantos are more interesting, however, because, the amount of currency that will be translated into dollars depends on the investment performance of the foreign security. Therefore, a quanto in effect provides a *random number* of options.

Binary Options

Binary or "bet" options have fixed payoffs that depend on whether a condition is satisfied by the price of the underlying asset. For example, a binary call option might pay off a fixed amount of $100 if the stock price at maturity exceeds the exercise price.

There are many more exotic options that we do not have room to discuss, and new ones are continually being created. For a comprehensive review of these options and their valuation (which is far more complex than the valuation of the simple options emphasized in this chapter), we refer you to the collection of articles compiled by RISK Magazine listed in the Suggested Readings at the end of the chapter.

SUMMARY

1. A call option is the right to buy an asset at an agreed-upon exercise price. A put option is the right to sell an asset at a given exercise price.

2. American options allow exercise on or before the exercise date. European options allow exercise only on the expiration date. Most traded options are American in nature.

3. Options are traded on stocks, stock indexes, foreign currencies, fixed-income securities, and several futures contracts.

4. Options can be used either to lever up an investor's exposure to an asset price or to provide insurance against volatility of asset prices. Popular option strategies include covered calls, protective puts, straddles, spreads, and collars.*

5. The put-call parity theorem relates the prices of put and call options. If the relationship is violated, arbitrage opportunities will result. Specifically, the relationship that must be satisfied is

$$P = C - S_0 + PV(X) + PV(\text{dividends})$$

where X is the exercise price of both the call and the put options, $PV(X)$ is the present value of a claim to X dollars to be paid at the expiration date of the options, and PV(dividends) is the present value of dividends to be paid before option expiration.

6. Many commonly traded securities embody option characteristics. Examples of these securities are callable bonds, convertible bonds, and warrants. Other arrangements such as collateralized loans and limited-liability borrowing can be analyzed as conveying implicit options to one or more parties.

7. Trading in so-called exotic options now takes place in an active over-the-counter market.

Key Terms

Call option
Exercise or strike price
Put option
In the money
Out of the money
At the money
American option
European option
Protective put
Covered call
Straddle
Spread
Collar
Put-call parity
Warrant

Selected Readings

A good treatment of the institutional organization of option markets is in the Chicago Board Options Exchange Reference Manual. *The CBOE also publishes a* Margin Manual *that provides an overview of margin requirements on many option positions.*

An excellent discussion of option trading strategies is:

Black, Fischer, "Fact and Fantasy in the Use of Options." *Financial Analysts Journal,* July–August 1975, pp. 3–20.

The Winter 1992 issue of the Journal of Applied Corporate Finance *highlights financial innovation. The issue contains several articles on the use of futures and options in new security design and risk management. Our discussion of LYONs is based on "The Origins of LYONs: A Case Study in Financial Innovation," by John J. McConnell and Eduardo S. Schwartz, which appeared in this issue.*

RISK Magazine is an excellent source of material on current developments in option pricing, applications of derivative instruments, and new developments in the derivatives markets. It has assembled a collection of articles that have appeared in its previous issues on option pricing generally and exotic options in particular in:

From Black-Scholes to Black Holes: New Frontiers in Options, London: RISK Magazine, 1992.

Problems

1. Suppose you think Wal-Mart stock is going to appreciate substantially in value in the next six months. Say the stock's current price, S_0, is $100, and the call option expiring in six months has an exercise price, X, of $100 and is selling at a price, C, of $10. With $10,000 to invest, you are considering three alternatives.
   a. Invest all $10,000 in the stock, buying 100 shares.
   b. Invest all $10,000 in 1,000 options (10 contracts).

c. Buy 100 options (one contract) for $1,000, and invest the remaining $9,000 in a money market fund paying 4 percent in interest over six months (8% per year).

What is your rate of return for each alternative for the following four stock prices six months from now? Summarize your results in the table and diagram below.

Rate of Return on Investment

	Price of Stock Six Months from Now			
	80	100	110	120
a. All stocks (100 shares)				
b. All options (1,000 shares)				
c. Bills + 100 options				

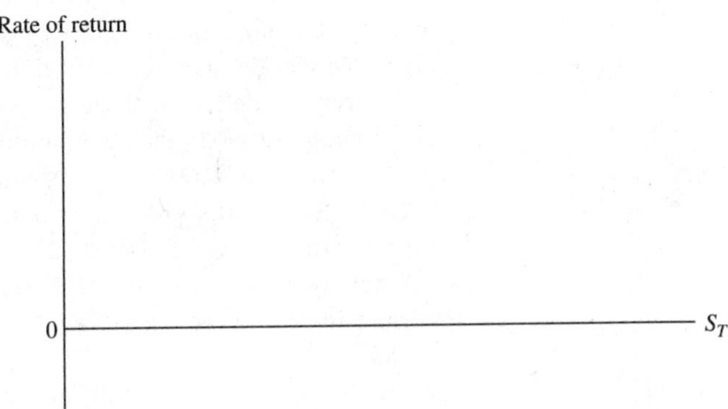

2. The common stock of the P.U.T.T. Corporation has been trading in a narrow price range for the past month, and you are convinced it is going to break far out of that range in the next three months. You do not know whether it will go up or down, however. The current price of the stock is $100 per share, and the price of a three-month call option at an exercise price of $100 is $10.
   a. If the risk-free interest rate is 10% per year, what must be the price of a three-month put option on P.U.T.T. stock at an exercise price of $100? (The stock pays no dividends.)
   b. What would be a simple options strategy to exploit your conviction about the stock price's future movements? How far would it have to move in either direction for you to make a profit on your initial investment?
3. The common stock of the C.A.L.L. Corporation has been trading in a narrow range around $50 per share for months, and you believe it is going to stay in that range for the next three months. The price of a three-month put option with an exercise price of $50 is $4.
   a. If the risk-free interest rate is 10% per year, what must be the price of a three-month call option on C.A.L.L. stock at an exercise price of $50 if it is at the money? (The stock pays no dividends.)

b. What would be a simple options strategy using a put and a call to exploit your conviction about the stock price's future movement? What is the most money you can make on this position? How far can the stock price move in either direction before you lose money?

c. How can you create a position involving a put, a call, and riskless lending that would have the same payoff structure as the stock at expiration? What is the net cost of establishing that position now?

4. On the death of his grandmother several years ago, Bill Melody received as a bequest from her estate 2,000 shares of General Motors common stock. The price of the stock at the time of distribution from the estate was $75 a share, and this became the cost basis of Melody's holding. Late in 1990, Melody agreed to purchase a new condominium for his parents at a total cost of $160,000, payable in full upon its completion in March 1991. Melody planned to sell the General Motors stock in order to raise funds to purchase the condominium.*

   At year-end 1990, GM's market price was around $75 a share, but it looked to be weakening. This concerned Melody, for if the price of the stock were to drop by a significant amount before he sold, the proceeds would not be sufficient to cover the purchase of the condominium in March 1991.

   Melody visited with three investment counseling firms to seek advice in developing a strategy that, at a minimum, would protect the value of his principal at or near $150,000 ($75 a share). Ideally, the strategy would enhance the value to $160,000 so Melody would have the total cost of the condominium. Four alternatives were discussed:

   a. Melody's own opinion was to sell the General Motors stock at $75 a share and invest the proceeds in a 10% certificate of deposit maturing in three months.

   b. Anderson Investment Advisors suggested Melody write a March 1991 call option on his General Motors holding at a strike price of $80. The March 1991 calls were quoted at $2.

   c. Cole Capital Management suggested Melody purchase March 1991 at-the-money put contracts on General Motors, now quoted at $2.

   d. MBA Associates suggested Melody keep the stock, purchase March 1991 at-the-money put contracts on GM, and finance the purchase by writing March calls with a strike price of $80.

   Disregarding transaction costs, dividend income, and margin requirements, rank order the four alternatives in terms of their fulfilling the strategy of at least preserving the value of Melody's principal at $150,000 and preferably increasing the value to $160,000 by March 1991. Support your conclusions by showing the payoff structure of each alternative.

5. In this problem, we derive the put-call parity relationship for European options on stocks that pay dividends before option expiration. For simplicity, assume that the stock makes one dividend payment of $\$D$ per share at the expiration date of the option.

---

*Reprinted, with permission, from the Level III 1984 *CFA Study Guide*.

a. What is the value of a stock-plus-put position on the expiration date of the option?

b. Now consider a portfolio comprising a call option and a zero-coupon bond with the same maturity date as the option and with face value $(X + D)$. What is the value of this portfolio on the option expiration date? You should find that its value equals that of the stock-plus-put portfolio regardless of the stock price.

c. What is the cost of establishing the two portfolios in parts (*a*) and (*b*)? Equate the costs of these portfolios, and you will derive the put-call parity relationship, equation 19.2.

6. *a.* A butterfly spread is the purchase of one call at exercise price X_1, the sale of two calls at exercise price X_2, and the purchase of one call at exercise price X_3. X_1 is less than X_2, and X_2 is less than X_3 by equal amounts, and all calls have the same expiration date. Graph the payoff diagram to this strategy.

b. A vertical combination is the purchase of a call with exercise price X_2 and a put with exercise price X_1, with X_2 greater than X_1. Graph the payoff to this strategy.

7. A bearish spread is the purchase of a call with exercise price X_2 and the sale of a call with exercise price X_1, with X_2 greater than X_1. Graph the payoff to this strategy and compare it to Figure 19.13.

8. You are attempting to formulate an investment strategy. On the one hand, you think there is great upward potential in the stock market and would like to participate in the upward move if it materializes. However, you are not able to afford substantial stock market losses and so cannot run the risk of a stock market collapse, which you also think is a possibility. Your investment advisor suggests a protective put position: buy both shares in a market index stock fund and put options on those shares with three-month maturity and exercise price of $260. The stock index is currently selling for $300. However, your uncle suggests you instead buy a three-month call option on the index fund with exercise price $280 and buy three-month T-bills with face value $280.

a. On the same graph, draw the *payoffs* to each of these strategies as a function of the stock fund value in three months. (Hint: Think of the options as being on one "share" of the stock index fund, with the current price of each share of the index equal to $300.)

b. Which portfolio must require a greater initial outlay to establish? (Hint: Does either portfolio provide a final payoff that is always at least as great as the payoff of the other portfolio?)

c. Suppose the market prices of the securities are as follows:

Stock fund	$300
T-bill (face value 280)	$270
Call (exercise price 280)	$ 40
Put (exercise price 260)	$ 2

Make a table of the profits realized for each portfolio for the following values of the stock price in three months: S_T = $0, $260, $280, $300, $320.

Graph the profits to each portfolio as a function of S_T on a single graph.

d. Which strategy is riskier? Which should have a higher beta?
e. Explain why the data for the securities given in Part (*c*) do *not* violate the put-call parity relationship.

9. The agricultural price support system guarantees farmers a minimum price for their output. Describe the program provisions as an option. What is the asset? The exercise price?
10. In what ways is owning a corporate bond similar to writing a put option? A call option?
11. A executive compensation scheme might provide a manager a bonus of $1,000 for every dollar by which the company's stock price exceeds some cutoff level. In what way is this arrangement equivalent to issuing the manager call options on the firm's stock?
12. Consider the following options portfolio. You write a January maturity call option on IBM with exercise price 75. You write a January IBM put option with exercise price 70.
    a. Graph the payoff of this portfolio at option expiration as a function of IBM's stock price at that time.
    b. What will be the profit/loss on this position if IBM is selling at 72 on the option maturity date? What if IBM is selling at 85? Use *The Wall Street Journal* listing from Figure 19.1 to answer this question.
    c. At what two stock prices will you just break even on your investment?
    d. What kind of "bet" is this investor making: that is, what must this investor believe about IBM's stock price in order to justify this position?
13. Consider the following portfolio. You write a put option with exercise price 90 and buy a put option on the same stock with the same maturity date with exercise price 95.
    a. Plot the value of the portfolio at the maturity date of the options.
    b. On the same graph, plot the profit of the portfolio. Which option must cost more?
14. A Ford put option with strike price 60 trading on the Acme options exchange sells for $2. To your amazement, a Ford put with the same maturity selling on the Apex options exchange but with strike price 62 also sells for $2. If you plan to hold the options positions to maturity, devise a zero-net-investment arbitrage strategy to exploit the pricing anomaly. Draw the profit diagram at maturity for your position.
15. Using the IBM option prices in Figure 19.1, calculate the market price of a riskless zero-coupon bond with face value $70 that matures in January on the same date as the listed options.
16. You buy a share of stock, write a one-year call option with X = $10 and buy a one-year put option with X = $10. Your net outlay to establish the entire portfolio is $9.50. What is the risk-free interest rate? The stock pays no dividends.
17. Demonstrate than an at-the-money call option on a given stock must cost more than an at-the-money put option on that stock with the same maturity. (Hint: Use put-call parity.)

18. You write a put option with $X = 100$ and buy a put with $X = 110$. The puts are on the same stock and have the same maturity date.
    a. Draw the payoff graph for this strategy.
    b. Draw the profit graph for this strategy.
    c. If the underlying stock has positive beta, does this portfolio have positive or negative beta?
19. Joe Finance has just purchased a stock index fund, currently selling at \$400 per share. To protect against losses, Joe also purchased an at-the-money European put option on the fund for \$20, with exercise price \$400, and three-month time to expiration. Sally Calm, Joe's financial advisor, points out that Joe is spending a lot of money on the put. She notes that three-month puts with strike prices of \$390 cost only \$15, and suggests that Joe use the cheaper put.
    a. Analyze Joe's and Sally's strategies by drawing the *profit* diagrams for the stock-plus-put positions for various values of the stock fund in three months.
    b. When does Sally's strategy do better? When does it do worse?
    c. Which strategy entails greater systematic risk?
20. You write a call option with $X = 50$ and buy a call with $X = 60$. The options are on the same stock and have the same maturity date. One of the calls sells for \$3; the other sells for \$9.
    a. Draw the payoff graph for this strategy at the option maturity date.
    b. Draw the profit graph for this strategy.
    c. What is the break-even point for this strategy? Is the investor bullish or bearish on the stock?
21. Devise a portfolio using only call options and shares of stock with the following value (payoff) at the option maturity date. If the stock price is currently 53, what kind of bet is the investor making?

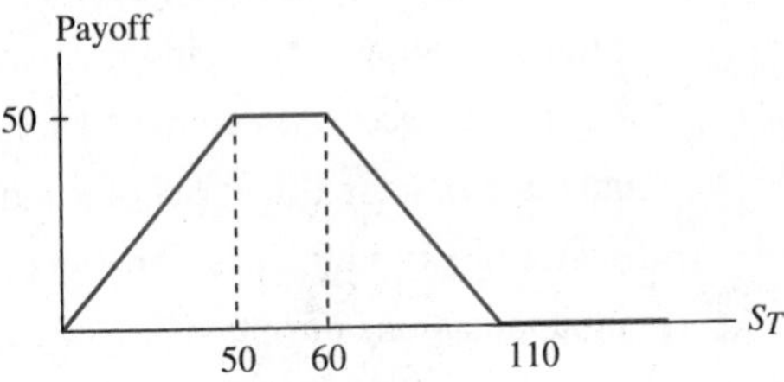

Chapter 20
Option Valuation

IN THE PREVIOUS CHAPTER, WE EXAMINED OPTION MARKETS AND STRATEGIES. We noted that many securities contain embedded options that affect both their values and their risk-return characteristics. In this chapter, we turn our attention to option valuation issues. To understand most option-valuation models requires considerable mathematical and statistical background. Still, many of the ideas and insights of these models can be demonstrated in simple examples, and we will concentrate on these.

We start with a discussion of the factors that ought to affect option prices. After this discussion, we present several bounds within which option prices must lie. Next, we turn to quantitative models, starting with a simple "two-state" option-valuation model, and then showing how this approach can be generalized into a useful and accurate pricing tool. Next, we move on to one particular valuation formula, the famous Black-Scholes model, one of the most significant breakthroughs in finance theory in the past three decades. Finally, we look at some of the more important applications of option-pricing theory in portfolio management and control.

20.1 Option Valuation: Introduction

Intrinsic and Time Values

Consider a call option that is out of the money at the moment, with the stock price below the exercise price. This does not mean the option is valueless. Even though immediate exercise today would be unprofitable, the call retains a positive value because there is always a chance the stock price will increase sufficiently by the expiration date to allow for profitable exercise. If not, the worst that can happen is that the option will expire with zero value.

The value $S_0 - X$ is sometimes called the **intrinsic value** of in-the-money call options because it gives the payoff that could be obtained by immediate exercise. Intrinsic value is set equal to zero for out-of-the-money or at-the-money options. The difference between the actual call price and the intrinsic value is commonly called the *time value* of the option.

"Time value" is an unfortunate choice of terminology, because it may confuse the option's time value with the time value of money. Time value in the options context refers simply to the difference between the option's price and the value the option would have if it were expiring immediately. It is the part of the option's value that may be attributed to the fact that it still has positive time to expiration.

Most of an option's time value typically is a type of "volatility value." As long as the optionholder can choose not to exercise, the payoff cannot be worse than zero. Even if a call option is out of the money now, it still will sell for a positive price because it offers the potential for a profit if the stock price increases, while imposing no risk of additional loss should the stock price fall. The volatility value lies in the value of the right *not* to exercise the option if that action would be unprofitable. The option to exercise, as opposed to the obligation to exercise, provides insurance against poor stock price performance.

As the stock price increases substantially, it becomes more likely that the call option will be exercised by expiration. In this case, with exercise all but assured, the volatility value becomes minimal. As the stock price gets ever larger, the option value approaches the "adjusted" intrinsic value, the stock price minus the present value of the exercise price, $S_0 - PV(X)$.

Why should this be? If you are virtually certain the option will be exercised and the stock purchased for X dollars, it is as though you own the stock already. The stock certificate, with a value today of S_0, might as well be sitting in your safe-deposit box now, as it will be there in only a few months. You just haven't paid for it yet. The present value of your obligation is the present value of X, so the net value of the call option is $S_0 - PV(X)$.[1]

Figure 20.1 illustrates the call option valuation function.The value curve shows that when the stock price is low, the option is nearly worthless, because there is almost no chance that it will be exercised. When the stock price is very high, the option value approaches adjusted intrinsic value. In the midrange case, where the option is approximately at the money, the option curve diverges from the straight lines corresponding to adjusted intrinsic value. This is because although exercise today would have a negligible (or negative) payoff, the volatility value of the option is quite high in this region. The option always increases in value with the stock price. The slope is greatest, however, when the option is deep in the money. In this case, exercise is all but assured, and the option increases in price one for one with the stock price.

[1] This discussion presumes that the stock pays no dividends until after option expiration. If the stock does pay dividends before maturity, then there *is* a reason you would care about getting the stock now rather than at expiration—getting it now entitles you to the interim dividend payments. In this case, the adjusted intrinsic value of the option must subtract the value of the dividends the stock will pay out before the call is exercised. Adjusted intrinsic value would more generally be defined as $S_0 - PV(X) - PV(D)$ where D is the dividend to be paid before option expiration.

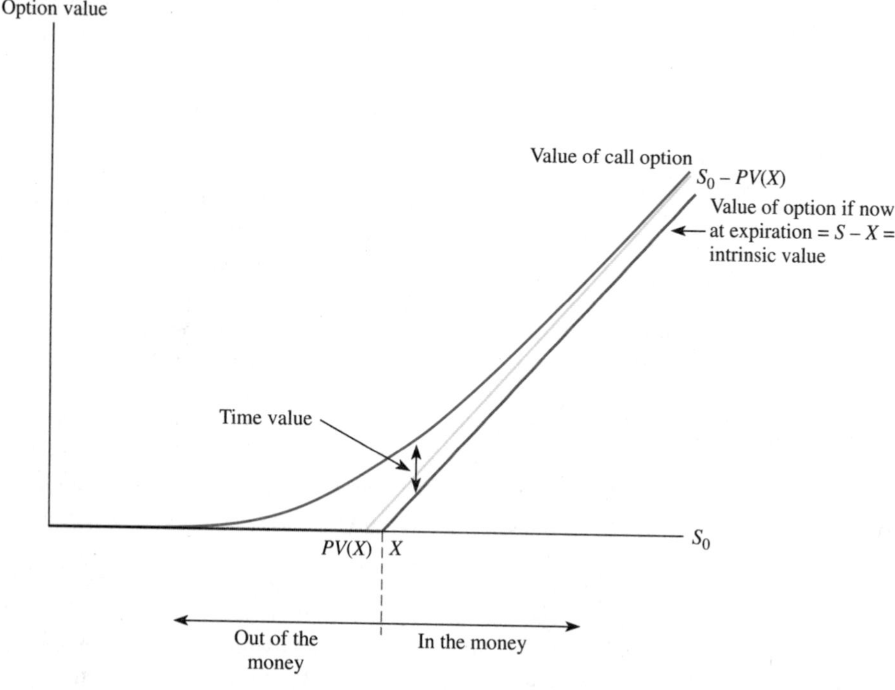

Figure 20.1
Call option value before expiration

Determinants of Option Values

We can identify at least six factors that should affect the value of a call option: the stock price, the exercise price, the volatility of the stock price, the time to expiration, the interest rate, and the dividend rate of the stock. The call option should increase in value with the stock price and decrease in value with the exercise price because the payoff to a call, if exercised, equals $S_T - X$. The magnitude of the expected payoff from the call increases with the difference $S_0 - X$.

Call option values also increase with the volatility of the underlying stock price. To see why, consider circumstances where possible stock prices at expiration may range from \$10 to \$50 compared to a situation where stock prices may range only from \$20 to \$40. In both cases, the expected, or average, stock price will be \$30. Suppose the exercise price on a call option is also \$30. What are the option payoffs?

High-Volatility Scenario

Stock price	\$10	\$20	\$30	\$40	\$50
Option payoff	0	0	0	10	20

Low-Volatility Scenario

Stock price	\$20	\$25	\$30	\$35	\$40
Option payoff	0	0	0	5	10

Table 20.1 Determinants of Call Option Values

If This Variable Increases ...	The Value of a Call Option
Stock price, S	Increases
Exercise price, X	Decreases
Volatility, σ	Increases
Time to expiration, T	Increases
Interest rate, r_f	Increases
Dividend payouts	Decreases

If each outcome is equally likely, with probability .2, the expected payoff to the option under high-volatility conditions will be \$6, but under low-volatility conditions the expected payoff to the call option is half as much, only \$3.

Despite the fact that the average stock price in each scenario is \$30, the average option payoff is greater in the high-volatility scenario. The source of this extra value is the limited loss an optionholder can suffer, or the volatility value of the call. No matter how far below \$30 the stock price drops, the optionholder will get zero. Obviously, extremely poor stock price performance is no worse for the call optionholder than moderately poor performance.

In the case of good stock performance, however, the call option will expire in the money, and it will be more profitable the higher the stock price. Thus, extremely good stock outcomes can improve the option payoff without limit, but extremely poor outcomes cannot worsen the payoff below zero. This asymmetry means that volatility in the underlying stock price increases the expected payoff to the option, thereby enhancing its value.

CONCEPT CHECK Question 1. Should a put option increase in value with the volatility of the stock?

Similarly, longer time to expiration increases the value of a call option. For more distant expiration dates, there is more time for unpredictable future events to affect prices, and the range of likely stock prices increases. This has an effect similar to that of increased volatility. Moreover, as time to expiration lengthens, the present value of the exercise price falls, thereby benefiting the call optionholder and increasing the option value. As a corollary to this issue, call option values are higher when interest rates rise (holding the stock price constant) because higher interest rates also reduce the present value of the exercise price.

Finally, the dividend payout policy of the firm affects option values. A high dividend payout policy puts a drag on the rate of growth of the stock price. For any expected total rate of return on the stock, a higher dividend yield must imply a lower expected rate of capital gain. This drag on stock price appreciation decreases the potential payoff from the call option, thereby lowering the call value. Table 20.1 summarizes these relationships.

CONCEPT CHECK Question 2. Prepare a table like Table 20.1 for the determinants of put option values. How should put values respond to increases in S, X, σ, T, r_f, and dividend payouts?

20.2 RESTRICTIONS ON OPTION VALUES

Several quantitative models of option pricing have been devised, and we will examine some of these in this chapter. All models, however, rely on simplifying assumptions. You might wonder which properties of option values are truly general and which depend on the particular simplifications. To start with, we will consider some of the more important general properties of option prices. Some of these properties have important implications for the effect of stock dividends on option values and the possible profitability of early exercise of an American option.

Restrictions on the Value of a Call Option

The most obvious restriction on the value of a call option is that its value cannot be negative. Because the option need not be exercised, it cannot impose any liability on its holder; moreover, as long as there is any possibility that at some point the option can be exercised profitably, the option will command a positive price. Its payoff must be zero at worst, and possibly positive, so that investors are willing to pay a positive amount to purchase it.

We can place another lower bound on the value of a call option. Suppose that the stock will pay a dividend of D dollars just before the expiration date of the option, denoted by T (where today is time zero). Now compare two portfolios, one consisting of a call option on one share of stock and the other a leveraged equity position consisting of that share and borrowing of $(X + D)/(1 + r_f)^T$ dollars. The loan repayment is $X + D$ dollars, due on the expiration date of the option. For example, for a half-year maturity option with exercise price \$70, dividends to be paid of \$5, and effective annual interest of 10%, you would purchase one share of stock and borrow $\$75/(1.10)^{1/2} =$ \$71.51. In six months, when the loan matures, the payment due is \$75.

At that time, the payoff to the leveraged equity position would be

	In General	Our Numbers
Stock value	$S_T + D$	$S_T + 5$
−Payback of loan	$-(X + D)$	-75
TOTAL	$S_T - X$	$S_T - 70$

where S_T denotes the stock price at the option expiration date. Notice that the payoff to the stock is the ex-dividend stock value plus dividends received. Whether the total payoff to the stock-plus-borrowing position is positive or negative depends on whether S_T exceeds X. The net cash outlay required to establish this leveraged equity position is S_0 − \$71.51, or, more generally, $S_0 - (X + D)/(1 + r_f)^T$, that is, the current price of the purchased stock, S_0, less the initial cash inflow from the borrowing position.

Figure 20.2
Range of possible call option values

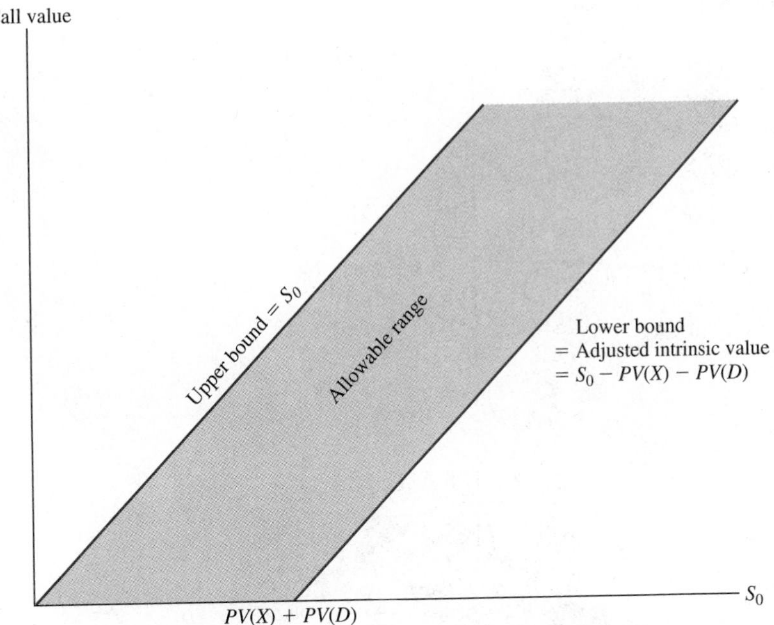

The payoff to the call option will be $S_T - X$ if the option expires in the money and zero otherwise. Thus, the option payoff is equal to the leveraged equity payoff when that payoff is positive and is greater when the leveraged equity position has a negative payoff. Because the option payoff is always greater than or equal to that of the leveraged equity position, the option price must exceed the cost of establishing that position.

Therefore, the value of the call must be greater than $S_0 - (X + D)/(1 + r_f)^T$, or more generally,

$$C \geq S_0 - PV(X) - PV(D).$$

where $PV(X)$ denotes the present value of the exercise and $PV(D)$ is the present value of the dividends the stock will pay at the option's expiration. More generally, we can interpret $PV(D)$ as the present value of any and all dividends to be paid prior to the option expiration date. Because we know already that the value of a call option must be nonnegative, we may conclude that C is greater than the *maximum* of either 0 or $S_0 - PV(X) - PV(D)$.

We also can place an upper bound on the possible value of the call: this bound is simply the stock price. No one would pay more than S_0 dollars for the right to purchase a stock currently worth S_0 dollars. Thus, $C \leq S_0$.

Figure 20.2 demonstrates graphically the range of prices that is ruled out by these upper and lower bounds for the value of a call option. Any option value outside the shaded area is not possible according to the restrictions we have derived. Before expiration, the call option value normally will be *within* the allowable range, touching neither the upper nor lower bounds, as in Figure 20.3.

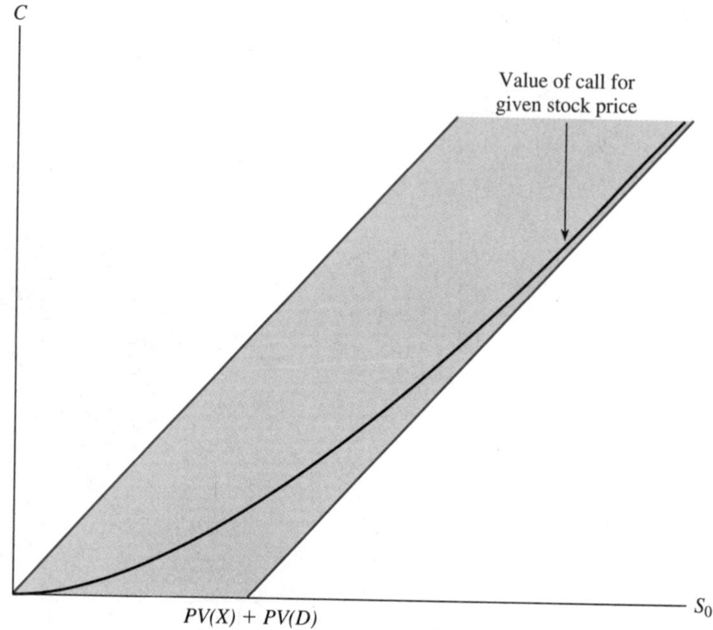

Figure 20.3
Call option value as a function of the current stock price

Early Exercise and Dividends

A call optionholder who wants to close out that position has two choices: exercise the call or sell it. If the holder exercises at time t, the call will provide a profit of $S_t - X$, assuming, of course that the option is in the money. We have just seen that the option can be sold for at least $S_t - PV(X) - PV(D)$. Therefore, for an option on a nondividend paying stock, C is greater than $S_t - PV(X)$. Because the present value of X is less than X itself, it follows that

$$C \geq S_t - PV(X) \geq S_t - X$$

The implication here is that the proceeds from a sale of the option (at price C) must exceed the proceeds from an exercise ($S_t - X$). It is economically more attractive to sell the call, which keeps it alive, than to exercise and thereby end the option. In other words calls on nondividend-paying stocks are "worth more alive than dead."

If it never pays to exercise a call option before maturity, the right to exercise early actually must be valueless. The right of the American callholder to exercise early is irrelevant because it will never pay to exercise early. We therefore conclude that the values of otherwise identical American and European call options on stocks paying no dividends are equal. If we can find the value for the European call, we also will have found the value of the American call. This simplifies matters, because any valuation formula that applies to the conceptually easier European call, for which only one exercise date need be considered, also must apply to an American call.

Figure 20.4
Put option values as a function of the current stock price

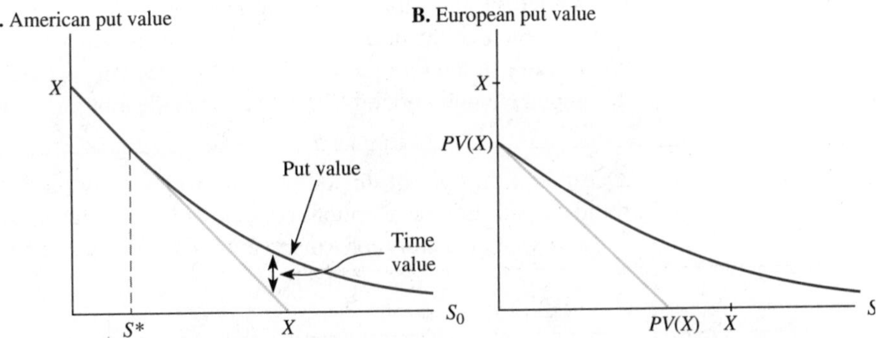

As most stocks do pay dividends, you may wonder whether this result is just a theoretical curiosity. It is not: Reconsider our argument and you will see that all that we really require is that the stock pay no dividends *until the option expires*. This condition will be true for many real-world options.

Early Exercise of American Puts

For American *put options*, the optimality of early exercise is most definitely a possibility. To see why, consider a simple example. Suppose that you purchase a put option on a stock. Soon the firm goes bankrupt, and the stock price falls to zero. Of course you want to exercise now, because the stock price can fall no lower. Immediate exercise gives you immediate receipt of the exercise price which can be invested to start generating income. Delay in exercise means a time-value-of-money cost. The right to exercise a put option before maturity must have value.

Now suppose instead that the firm is only nearly bankrupt, with the stock selling at just a few cents. Immediate exercise may still be optimal. After all, the stock price can fall by only a very small amount, meaning that the proceeds from future exercise cannot be more than a few cents greater than the proceeds from immediate exercise. Against this possibility of a tiny increase in proceeds must be weighed the time-value-of-money cost of deferring exercise. Clearly, there is some stock price below which early exercise is optimal.

This argument also proves that the American put must be worth more than its European counterpart. The American put allows you to exercise anytime before maturity. Because the right to exercise early may be useful in some circumstances, it will command a positive price in the capital market. The American put therefore will sell for a higher price than a European put with otherwise identical terms.

Figure 20.4**A** illustrates the value of an American put option as a function of the current stock price, S_0. Once the stock price drops below a critical value, denoted S^* in the figure, exercise becomes optimal. At that point the option-pricing curve is tangent to the straight line depicting the intrinsic value of the option. If and when the stock price reaches S^*, the put option is exercised and its payoff equals its intrinsic value.

In contrast, the value of the European put, which is graphed in Figure 20.4**B**, does not asymptote to the intrinsic value line. Because early exercise is prohibited, the maximum value of the European put is *PV(X)*, which occurs at the point $S_0 = 0$. Obviously, for a long enough horizon, *PV(X)* can be made arbitrarily small.

CONCEPT CHECK Question 3. In light of this discussion, explain why the put-call parity relationship is valid only for European options on nondividend-paying stocks. If the stock pays no dividends, what *inequality* for American options would correspond to the parity theorem?

20.3 BINOMIAL OPTION PRICING

Two-State Option Pricing

A complete understanding of commonly used option-valuation formulas is difficult without a substantial mathematics background. Nevertheless, we can develop valuable insight into option valuation by considering a simple special case. Assume that a stock price can take only two possible values at option expiration: The stock will either increase to a given higher price or decrease to a given lower price. Although this may seem an extreme simplification, it allows us to come closer to understanding more complicated and realistic models. Moreover, we can extend this approach to describe far more reasonable specifications of stock price behavior. In fact, several major financial firms employ variants of this simple model to value options and securities with option-like features.

Suppose the stock now sells at $100, and the price will either double to $200 or fall in half to $50 by year-end. A call option on the stock might specify an exercise price of $125 and a time to expiration of one year. The interest rate is 8%. At year-end, the payoff to the holder of the call option will be either zero, if the stock falls, or $75, if the stock price goes to $200.

These possibilities are illustrated by the following "trees."

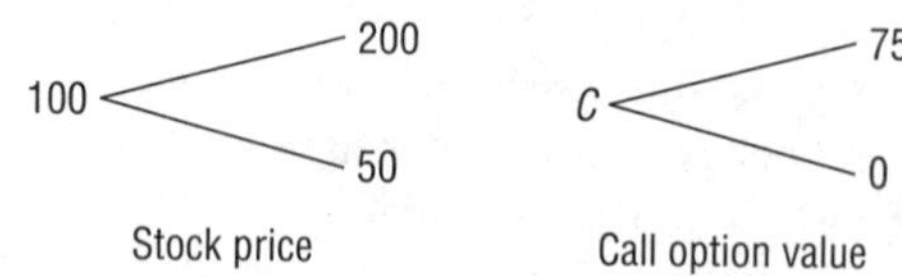

Compare the payoff of the call to that of a portfolio consisting of one share of the stock and borrowing of $46.30 at the interest rate of 8%. The payoff of this portfolio also depends on the stock price at year-end:

Value of stock at year-end	$50	$200
− Repayment of loan with interest	−50	−50
Total	$ 0	$150

We know the cash outlay to establish the portfolio is $53.70: $100 for the stock, less the $46.30 proceeds from borrowing. Therefore the portfolio's value tree is

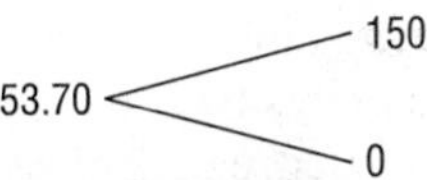

The payoff of this portfolio is exactly twice that of the call option for either value of the stock price. In other words two call options will exactly replicate the payoff to the portfolio; it follows that two call options should have the same price as the cost of establishing the portfolio. Hence, the two calls should sell for the same price as the "replicating portfolio." Therefore,

$$2C = \$53.70$$

or each call should sell at $C = \$26.85$. Thus, given the stock price, exercise price, interest rate, and volatility of the stock price (as represented by the magnitude of the up or down movements), we can derive the fair value for the call option.

This valuation approach relies heavily on the notion of *replication.* With only two possible end-of-year values of the stock, the payoffs to the levered stock portfolio replicate the payoffs to two call options and, therefore, command the same market price. This notion of replication is behind most option-pricing formulas. For more complex price distributions for stocks, the replication technique is correspondingly more complex, but the principles remain the same.

One way to view the role of replication is to note that, using the numbers assumed for this example, a portfolio made up of one share of stock and two call options written is perfectly hedged. Its year-end value is independent of the ultimate stock price:

Stock value	\$50	\$200
− Obligations from 2 calls written	− 0	−150
Net payoff	\$50	\$ 50

The investor has formed a riskless portfolio, with a payout of \$50. Its value must be the present value of \$50 or \$50/1.08 = \$46.30. The value of the portfolio, which equals \$100 from the stock held long, minus $2C$ from the two calls written, should equal \$46.30. Hence, $\$100 - 2C = \$46.30$, or $C = \$26.85$.

The ability to create a perfect hedge is the key to this argument. The hedge locks in the end-of-year payout, which can be discounted using the risk-free interest rate. To find the value of the option in terms of the value of the stock, we do not need to know either the option's or the stock's beta or expected rate of return. The perfect hedging, or replication, approach enables us to express the value of the option in terms of the current value of the stock without this information. With a hedged position, the final stock price does not affect the investor's payoff, so the stock's risk and return parameters have no bearing.

The hedge ratio of this example is one share of stock to two calls, or one half. For every call option written, one-half share of stock must be held in the portfolio to hedge away risk. This ratio has an easy interpretation in this context: It is the ratio of the range of the values of the option to those of the stock across the two possible outcomes. The option is worth either zero or \$75, for a range of \$75. The stock is worth either \$50 or \$200, for a range of \$150. The ratio of ranges, 75/150, is one half, which is the hedge ratio we have established.

The hedge ratio equals the ratio of ranges because the option and stock are perfectly correlated in this two-state example. When the returns of the option and stock are perfectly correlated, a perfect hedge requires that the option and stock be held in a fraction determined only by relative volatility.

We can generalize the hedge ratio for other two-state option problems as

$$H = \frac{C^+ - C^-}{S^+ - S^-}$$

where C^+ or C^- refers to the call option's value when the stock goes up or down, respectively, and S^+ and S^- are the stock prices in the two states. The hedge ratio, H, is the ratio of the swings in the possible end-of-period values of the option and the stock. If the investor writes one option and holds H shares of stock, the value of the portfolio will be unaffected by the stock price. In this case, option pricing is easy: simply set the value of the hedged portfolio equal to the present value of the known payoff.

Using our example, the option-pricing technique would proceed as follows:

1. Given the possible end-of-year stock prices, $S^+ = 200$ and $S^- = 50$, and the exercise price of 125, calculate that $C^+ = 75$ and $C^- = 0$. The stock price range is 150, while the option price range is 75.
2. Find that the hedge ratio of 75/150 = 0.5.
3. Find that a portfolio made up of 0.5 shares with one written option would have an end-of-year value of \$25 with certainty.
4. Show that the present value of \$25 with a one-year interest rate of 8% is \$23.15.
5. Set the value of the hedged position to the present value of the certain payoff:

$$0.5S_0 - C_0 = \$23.15$$
$$\$50 - C_0 = \$23.15$$

6. Solve for the call's value, $C_0 = \$26.85$.

What if the option were overpriced, perhaps selling for \$30? Then you can make arbitrage profits. Here is how:

	Initial Cash Flow	Cash Flow in One Year for Each Possible Stock Price	
		$S = 50$	$S = 200$
1. Write 2 options	\$ 60	\$ 0	\$−150
2. Purchase 1 share	−100	50	200
3. Borrow \$40 at 8% interest Repay in 1 year	40	−43.20	−43.20
Total	\$ 0	\$ 6.80	\$ 6.80

Although the net initial investment is zero, the payoff in one year is positive and riskless. If the option were underpriced, one would simply reverse this arbitrage strategy: buy the option, and sell the stock short to eliminate price risk. Note, by the way, that the present value of the profit to the arbitrage strategy above exactly equals twice the amount by which the option is overpriced. The present value of the risk-free profit of \$6.80 at an 8% interest rate is \$6.30. With two options written in the strategy above, this translates to a profit of \$3.15 per option, exactly the amount by which the option was overpriced: \$30 versus the "fair value" of \$26.85.

CONCEPT CHECK Question 4. Suppose the call option had been underpriced, selling at \$24. Formulate the arbitrage strategy to exploit the mispricing, and show that it provides a riskless cash flow in one year of \$3.08 per option purchased.

Generalizing the Two-State Approach

Although the two-state stock price model seems simplistic, we can generalize it to incorporate more realistic assumptions. To start, suppose we were to break up the year into two six-month segments, and then assert that over each half-year segment the stock price could take on two values. Here we will say it can increase 10% or decrease 5%. A stock initially selling at 100 could follow these possible paths over the course of the year:

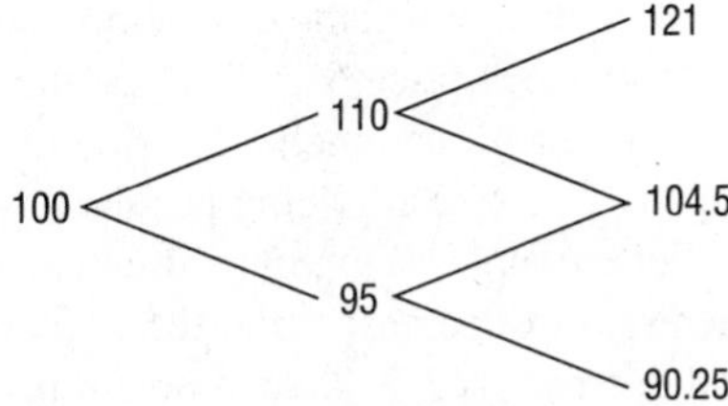

The midrange value of 104.5 can be attained by two paths: an increase of 10% followed by a decrease of 5%, or a decrease of 5% followed by a 10% increase.

There are now three possible end-of-year values for the stock and three for the option.

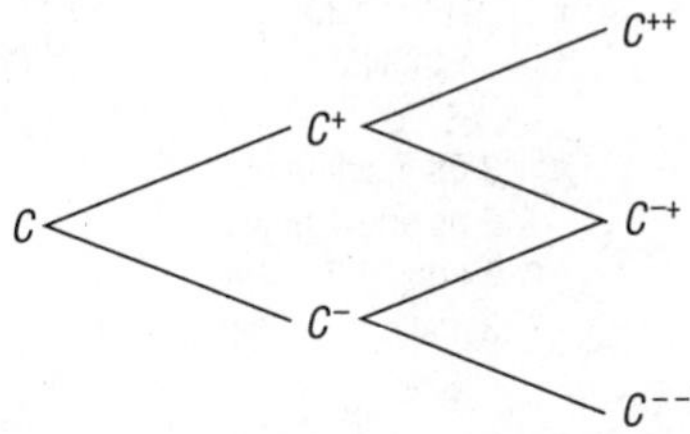

Using methods similar to those we followed above, we could value C^+ from knowledge of C^{++} and C^{+-}, then value C^- from knowledge of C^{-+} and C^{--}, and finally value C from knowledge of C^+ and C^-. And there is no reason to stop at six-month intervals. We could next break the year into four three-month units, or 12 one-month units, or 365 one-day units, each of which would be posited to have a two-state process. Although the calculations become quite numerous and correspondingly tedious, they are easy to program into a computer, and such computer programs are used widely by participants in the options market.

As we break the year into progressively finer subintervals, the range of possible year-end stock prices expands and, in fact, will ultimately take on a familiar bell-shaped distribution. This can be seen from an analysis of the event tree for the stock for a period with three subintervals:

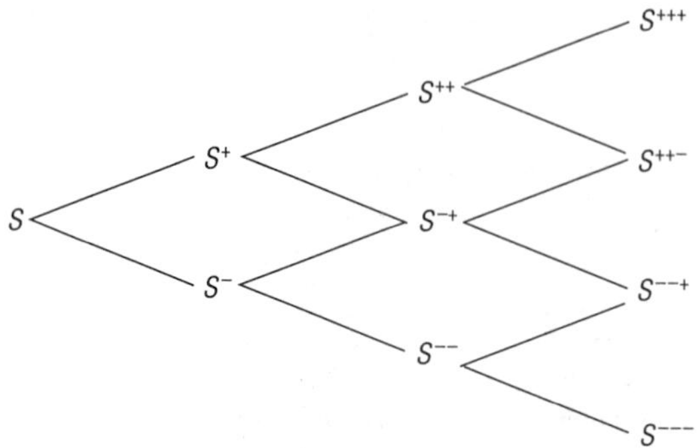

First, notice that as the number of subintervals increases, the number of possible stock prices also increases. Second, notice that extreme events such as S^{+++} or S^{---} are relatively rare, as they require either three consecutive increases or decreases in the three subintervals. More moderate, or midrange, results such as S^{++-} can be arrived at by more than one path—any combination of two price increases and one decrease will result in stock price S^{++-}. Thus, the midrange values will be more likely. The probability of each outcome is described by the binomial distribution, and this multiperiod approach to option pricing is called the **binomial model.**

For example, using our initial stock price of $100, equal probability of stock price increases or decreases, and three intervals for which the possible price increase is 5% and decrease is 3%, we can obtain the probability distribution of stock prices from the calculations following. There are eight possible combinations for the stock price movements in the three periods: $+ + +$, $+ + -$, $+ - +$, $- + +$, $+ - -$, $- + -$, $- - +$, $- - -$. Each has probability of 1/8. Therefore, the probability distribution of stock prices at the end of the last interval would be:

Event	Probability	Stock Price
3 up movements	1/8	$100 \times 1.05^3 = 115.76$
2 up and 1 down	3/8	$100 \times 1.05^2 \times .97 = 106.94$
1 up and 2 down	3/8	$100 \times 1.05 \times .97^2 = 98.79$
3 down movements	1/8	$100 \times .97^3 = 91.27$

The midrange values are three times as likely to occur as the extreme values. Figure 20.5**A** is a graph of the frequency distribution for this example. The graph approaches the appearance of the familiar bell-shaped curve. In fact, as the number of intervals increases, as in Figure 20.5**B**, the frequency distribution progressively approaches the lognormal distribution rather than the normal distribution.[2]

[2] Actually, more complex considerations enter here. The limit of this process is lognormal only if we assume also that stock prices move continuously, by which we mean that over small time intervals only small price movements can occur. This rules out rare events such as sudden, extreme price moves in response to dramatic information (like a takeover attempt). For a treatment of this type of "jump process," see John C. Cox and Stephen A. Ross, "The Valuation of Options for Alternative Stochastic Processes," *Journal of Financial Economics* 3 (January–March 1976), pp. 145–66, or Robert C. Merton, "Option Pricing When Underlying Stock Returns Are Discontinuous," *Journal of Financial Economics* 3 (January–March 1976), pp. 125–44.

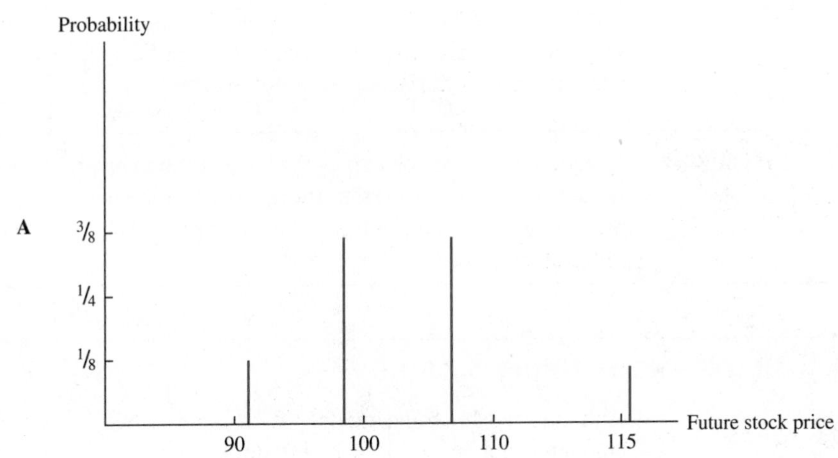

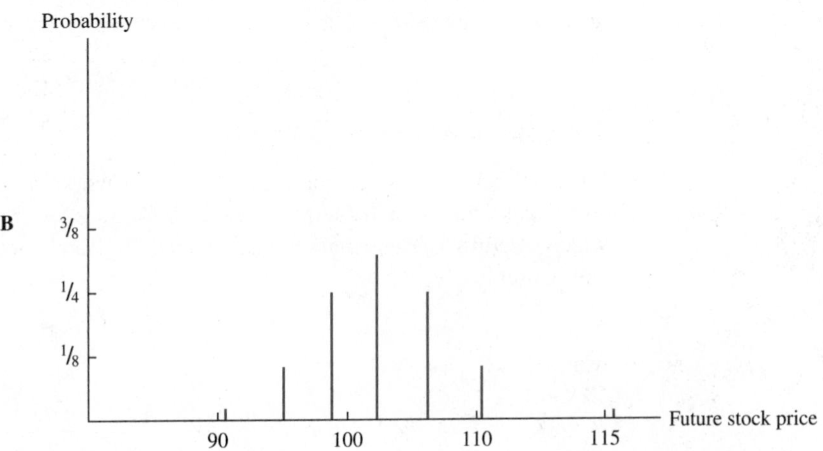

Figure 20.5
Probability distributions.
A, Possible outcomes and associated probabilities for stock prices after three periods. The stock price starts at $100, and in each period it can increase by 5% or decrease by 3%. **B,** Each period is subdivided into two smaller subperiods. Now there are six periods, and in each of these the stock price can increase by 2.5% or fall by 1.5%. As the number of periods increases, the stock price distribution approaches the familiar bell-shaped curve.

Suppose we were to continue subdividing the interval in which stock prices are posited to move up or down. Eventually, each node of the event tree would correspond to an infinitesimally small time interval. The possible stock price movement within that time interval would be correspondingly small. As those many intervals passed, the end-of-period stock price would more and more closely resemble a lognormal distribution. Thus, the apparent oversimplification of the two-state model can be overcome by progressively subdividing any period into many subperiods.

At any node, one still could set up a portfolio that would be perfectly hedged over the next tiny time interval. Then, at the end of that interval, on reaching the next node, a new hedge ratio could be computed and the portfolio composition could be revised to remain hedged over the coming small interval. By continuously revising the hedge position, the portfolio would remain hedged and would earn a riskless rate of return over each interval. This is called *dynamic hedging*, the continued updating of the hedge ratio as time passes. As the dynamic hedge becomes ever finer, the resulting option-valuation procedure becomes more precise.

CONCEPT CHECK Question 5. Would you expect the hedge ratio to be higher or lower when the call option is more in the money? (Hint: Remember that the hedge ratio is the change in the option price divided by the change in the stock price. When is the option price most sensitive to the stock price?)

20.4 BLACK-SCHOLES OPTION VALUATION

Although the binomial model we have described is extremely flexible, it requires a computer to be useful in actual trading. An option-pricing *formula* would be far easier to use than the involved algorithm involved in the binomial model. It turns out that such a formula can be derived if one is willing to make just two more assumptions: that both the risk-free interest rate and stock price volatility are constant over the life of the option.

The Black-Scholes Formula

Financial economists searched for years for a workable option-pricing model before Black and Scholes[3] and Merton[4] derived a formula for the value of a call option. Now widely used by options market participants, the **Black-Scholes pricing formula** for a call option is

$$C_0 = S_0N(d_1) - Xe^{-rT}N(d_2) \tag{20.1}$$

where

$$d_1 = \frac{ln(S_0/X) + (r + \sigma^2/2)T}{\sigma\sqrt{T}}$$

$$d_2 = d_1 - \sigma\sqrt{T}$$

and where

C_0 = Current call option value.
S_0 = Current stock price.
$N(d)$ = The probability that a random draw from a standard normal distribution will be less than d. This equals the area under the normal curve up to d, as in the shaded area of Figure 20.6.
X = Exercise price.
e = 2.71828, the base of the natural log function.

---

[3] Fischer Black and Myron Scholes, "The Pricing of Options and Corporate Liabilities," *Journal of Political Economy* 81 (May/June 1973).

[4] Robert C. Merton, "Theory of Rational Option Pricing," *Bell Journal of Economics and Management Science* 4 (Spring 1973).

Figure 20.6
A standard normal curve

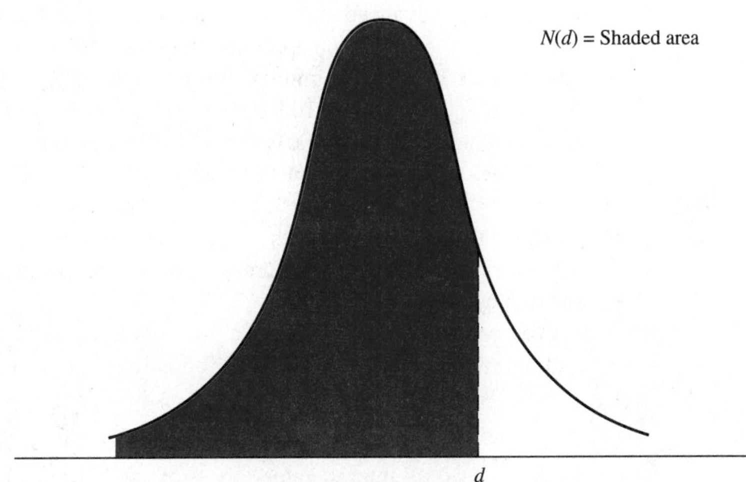

r	=	Risk-free interest rate (the annualized continuously compounded rate on a safe asset with the same maturity as the expiration of the option, which is to be distinguished from r_f, the discrete period interest rate).
T	=	Time to maturity of option, in years.
ln	=	Natural logarithm function.
σ	=	Standard deviation of the annualized continuously compounded rate of return of the stock.

The option value does *not* depend on the expected rate of return on the stock. In a sense, this information is already built into the formula with the inclusion of the stock price, which itself depends on the stock's risk and return characteristics. This version of the Black-Scholes formula is predicated on the assumption that the stock pays no dividends.

Although you may find the Black-Scholes formula intimidating, we can explain it at a somewhat intuitive level. The trick is to view the *N(d)* terms (loosely) as risk-adjusted probabilities that the call option will expire in the money. First, look at equation 20.1 assuming both *N(d)* terms are close to 1.0, that is, when there is a very high probability the option will be exercised. Then the call option value is equal to $S_0 - Xe^{-rT}$, which is what we called earlier the adjusted intrinsic value, $S_0 - PV(X)$. This makes sense; if exercise is certain, we have a claim on a stock with current value S_0, and an obligation with present value *PV(X)*, or, with continuous compounding, Xe^{-rT}.

Now look at equation 20.1 assuming the *N(d)* terms are close to zero, meaning the option almost certainly will not be exercised. Then the equation confirms that the call is worth nothing. For middle-range values of *N(d)* between 0 and 1, equation 20.1 tells us that the call value can be viewed as the present value of the call's potential payoff adjusting for the probability of in-the-money expiration.

How do the $N(d)$ terms serve as risk-adjusted probabilities? This question quickly leads us into advanced statistics. Notice, however, that $ln(S_0/X)$, which appears in the numerator of d_1 and d_2, is approximately the percentage amount by which the option is currently in or out of the money. For example, if $S_0 = 105$ and $X = 100$, the option is 5% in the money, and $ln(105/100) = .049$. Similarly, if $S_0 = 95$, the option is 5% out of the money, and $ln(95/100) = -.051$. The denominator, $\sigma\sqrt{T}$, adjusts the amount by which the option is in or out of the money for the volatility of the stock price over the remaining life of the option. An option in the money by a given percent is more likely to stay in the money if both stock price volatility and time to maturity are small. Therefore $N(d_1)$ and $N(d_2)$ increase with the probability that the option will expire in the money.

You can use the Black-Scholes formula fairly easily. Suppose you want to value a call option under circumstances as following:

Stock Price	S_0	=	100
Exercise price	X	=	95
Interest rate	r	=	.10 (10% per year)
Time to expiration	T	=	.25 (one-quarter of a year)
Standard deviation	σ	=	.50 (50% per year)

First calculate

$$d_1 = \frac{ln(100/95) + (.10 + .5^2/2).25}{.5\sqrt{.25}} = .43$$

$$d_2 = .43 - .5\sqrt{.25} = .18$$

Next find $N(d_1)$ and $N(d_2)$. The values of the normal distribution are tabulated and may be found in many statistics textbooks. A table of $N(d)$ is provided here as Table 20.2. The table reveals (using interpolation for .43) that

$$N(.43) = .6664$$
$$N(.18) = .5714$$

Thus, the value of the call option is

$$C = 100 \times .6664 - 95e^{-.10\times.25} \times .5714$$
$$= 66.64 - 52.94 = \$13.70$$

CONCEPT CHECK Question 6. Calculate the call option value if the standard deviation on the stock were 0.6 instead of 0.5. Confirm that the option is worth more using this higher volatility.

What if the option price in our example were \$15 rather than \$13.70? Is the option mispriced? Maybe, but before betting your fortune on that, you may want to reconsider the valuation analysis. First, like all models, the Black-Scholes formula is based on some simplifying abstractions that make the formula only approximately valid.

Some of the important assumptions underlying the formula are the following:

1. The stock will pay no dividends until after the option expiration date.
2. Both the interest rate, r, and variance rate, σ^2, of the stock are constant (or in slightly more general versions of the formula, both are *known* functions of time—any changes are perfectly predictable).
3. Stock prices are continuous, meaning that sudden extreme jumps such as those in the aftermath of an announcement of a takeover attempt are ruled out.

Variants of the Black-Scholes formula have been developed to deal with some of these limitations.

Second, even within the context of the Black-Scholes model, you must be sure of the accuracy of the parameters used in the formula. Four of these—S_0, X, T, and r—are straightforward. The stock price, exercise price, and time to maturity are readily determined. The interest rate used is the money market rate for a maturity equal to that of the option.

The last input, though, the standard deviation of the stock return, is not directly observable. It must be estimated from historical data, from scenario analysis, or from the prices of other options, as we will describe momentarily.

We saw in Chapter 4 that the historical variance of stock market returns can be calculated from n observations as follows:

$$\sigma^2 = \frac{n}{n-1} \sum_{t=1}^{n} \frac{(r_t - \bar{r})^2}{n}$$

where $\bar{r}$ is the average return over the sample period. The rate of return on day t is defined to be consistent with continuous compounding as $r_t = ln(S_t/S_{t-1})$. [We note again that the natural logarithm of a ratio is approximately the percentage difference between the numerator and denominator so that $ln(S_t/S_{t-1})$ is a measure of the rate of return of the stock from time $t - 1$ to time t.] Historical variance commonly is computed using daily returns over periods of several months. Because the standard deviation of stock returns must be estimated, however, it is always possible that discrepancies between an option price and its Black-Scholes value are simply artifacts of error in the estimation of the stock's volatility.

In fact, market participants often give the option-valuation problem a different twist. Rather than calculating a Black-Scholes option value for a given stock standard deviation, they ask instead: "What standard deviation would be necessary for the option price that I observe to be consistent with the Black-Scholes formula?" This is called the **implied volatility** of the option, the volatility level for the stock that the option price implies. Investors can then judge whether they think the actual stock standard deviation exceeds the implied volatility. If it does, the option is considered a good buy; if actual volatility seems greater than the implied volatility, its fair price would exceed the observed price.

Another variation is to compare two options on the same stock with equal expiration dates but different exercise prices. The option with the higher implied volatility would be considered relatively expensive, because a higher standard deviation is required to justify its price. The analyst might consider buying the option with the lower implied volatility and writing the option with the higher implied volatility.

Table 20.2 Cumulative Normal Distribution

d	*N(d)*	*d*	*N(d)*	*d*	*N(d)*
−3.00	.0013	−1.58	.0571	−0.76	.2236
−2.95	.0016	−1.56	.0594	−0.74	.2297
−2.90	.0019	−1.54	.0618	−0.72	.2358
−2.85	.0022	−1.52	.0643	−0.70	.2420
−2.80	.0026	−1.50	.0668	−0.68	.2483
−2.75	.0030	−1.48	.0694	−0.66	.2546
−2.70	.0035	−1.46	.0721	−0.64	.2611
−2.65	.0040	−1.44	.0749	−0.62	.2676
−2.60	.0047	−1.42	.0778	−0.60	.2743
−2.55	.0054	−1.40	.0808	−0.58	.2810
−2.50	.0062	−1.38	.0838	−0.56	.2877
−2.45	.0071	−1.36	.0869	−0.54	.2946
−2.40	.0082	−1.34	.0901	−0.52	.3015
−2.35	.0094	−1.32	.0934	−0.50	.3085
−2.30	.0107	−1.30	.0968	−0.48	.3156
−2.25	.0122	−1.28	.1003	−0.46	.3228
−2.20	.0139	−1.26	.1038	−0.44	.3300
−2.15	.0158	−1.24	.1075	−0.42	.3373
−2.10	.0179	−1.22	.1112	−0.40	.3446
−2.05	.0202	−1.20	.1151	−0.38	.3520
−2.00	.0228	−1.18	.1190	−0.36	.3594
−1.98	.0239	−1.16	.1230	−0.34	.3669
−1.96	.0250	−1.14	.1271	−0.32	.3745
−1.94	.0262	−1.12	.1314	−0.30	.3821
−1.92	.0274	−1.10	.1357	−0.28	.3897
−1.90	.0287	−1.08	.1401	−0.26	.3974
−1.88	.0301	−1.06	.1446	−0.24	.4052
−1.86	.0314	−1.04	.1492	−0.22	.4129
−1.84	.0329	−1.02	.1539	−0.20	.4207
−1.82	.0344	−1.00	.1587	−0.18	.4286
−1.80	.0359	−0.98	.1635	−0.16	.4365
−1.78	.0375	−0.96	.1685	−0.14	.4443
−1.76	.0392	−0.94	.1736	−0.12	.4523
−1.74	.0409	−0.92	.1788	−0.10	.4602
−1.72	.0427	−0.90	.1841	−0.08	.4681
−1.70	.0446	−0.88	.1894	−0.06	.4761
−1.68	.0465	−0.86	.1949	−0.04	.4841
−1.66	.0485	−0.84	.2005	−0.02	.4920
−1.64	.0505	−0.82	.2061	0.00	.5000
−1.62	.0526	−0.80	.2119	0.02	.5080
−1.60	.0548	−0.78	.2177	0.04	.5160

Figure 20.7 presents plots of the historical and implied standard deviation of the rate of return on the S&P 500 Index. The implied volatility is derived from prices of option contracts traded on the index. Notice that although both series have considerable tendency to move together, there is some slippage between the two estimates of volatility. Notice also that both volatility series vary considerably over time. Therefore, choosing

Table 20.2 *(Concluded)*

d	N(d)	d	N(d)	d	N(d)
0.06	.5239	0.86	.8051	1.66	.9515
0.08	.5319	0.88	.8106	1.68	.9535
0.10	.5398	0.90	.8159	1.70	.9554
0.12	.5478	0.92	.8212	1.72	.9573
0.14	.5557	0.94	.8264	1.74	.9591
0.16	.5636	0.96	.8315	1.76	.9608
0.18	.5714	0.98	.8365	1.78	.9625
0.20	.5793	1.00	.8414	1.80	.9641
0.22	.5871	1.02	.8461	1.82	.9656
0.24	.5948	1.04	.8508	1.84	.9671
0.26	.6026	1.06	.8554	1.86	.9686
0.28	.6103	1.08	.8599	1.88	.9699
0.30	.6179	1.10	.8643	1.90	.9713
0.32	.6255	1.12	.8686	1.92	.9726
0.34	.6331	1.14	.8729	1.94	.9738
0.36	.6406	1.16	.8770	1.96	.9750
0.38	.6480	1.18	.8810	1.98	.9761
0.40	.6554	1.20	.8849	2.00	.9772
0.42	.6628	1.22	.8888	2.05	.9798
0.44	.6700	1.24	.8925	2.10	.9821
0.46	.6773	1.26	.8962	2.15	.9842
0.48	.6844	1.28	.8997	2.20	.9861
0.50	.6915	1.30	.9032	2.25	.9878
0.52	.6985	1.32	.9066	2.30	.9893
0.54	.7054	1.34	.9099	2.35	.9906
0.56	.7123	1.36	.9131	2.40	.9918
0.58	.7191	1.38	.9162	2.45	.9929
0.60	.7258	1.40	.9192	2.50	.9938
0.62	.7324	1.42	.9222	2.55	.9946
0.64	.7389	1.44	.9251	2.60	.9953
0.66	.7454	1.46	.9279	2.65	.9960
0.68	.7518	1.48	.9306	2.70	.9965
0.70	.7580	1.50	.9332	2.75	.9970
0.72	.7642	1.52	.9357	2.80	.9974
0.74	.7704	1.54	.9382	2.85	.9978
0.76	.7764	1.56	.9406	2.90	.9981
0.78	.7823	1.58	.9429	2.95	.9984
0.80	.7882	1.60	.9452	3.00	.9986
0.82	.7939	1.62	.9474	3.05	.9989
0.84	.7996	1.64	.9495		

the proper volatility value to use in any option-pricing model always presents a formidable challenge. A considerable amount of recent research has been devoted to new techniques to predict changes in volatility. These techniques, which go by the name ARCH models, posit that changes in stock volatility are partially predictable, and that by analyzing recent levels and trends in volatility, one can improve predictions of future volatility.

Figure 20.7 S&P 500 implied and historical volatility comparison

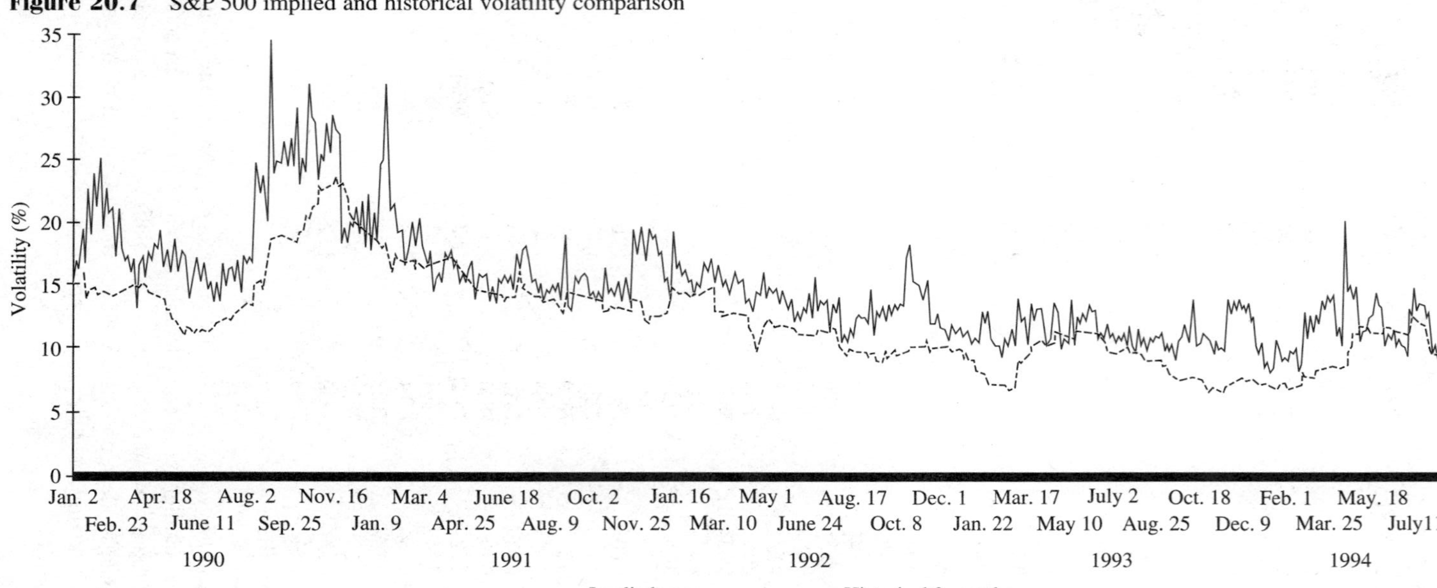

Source: Goldman Sachs, reported in Roger G. Clarke, "Estimating and Using Volatility: Part 2," *Derivatives Quarterly,* Winter 1994, p. 39.

CONCEPT CHECK Question 7. Consider the option in the example selling for \$15 with Black-Scholes value of \$13.70. Is its implied volatility more or less than 50%?

Dividends and Call Option Valuation

We noted earlier that the Black-Scholes call option formula applies to stocks that do not pay dividends. When dividends are to be paid before the option expires, we need to adjust the formula. The payment of dividends raises the possibility of early exercise, and for most realistic dividend payout schemes the valuation formula becomes significantly more complex than the Black-Scholes equation.

We can apply some simple rules of thumb to approximate the option value, however. One popular approach, originally suggested by Black, calls for adjusting the stock price downward by the present value of any dividends that are to be paid before option expiration.[5] Therefore, we would simply replace S_0 with $S_0 - PV(\text{dividends})$ in the Black-Scholes formula. Such an adjustment will take dividends into account by reflecting their eventual impact on the stock price. The option value then may be computed as before, assuming that the option will be held to expiration.

This procedure would yield a very good approximation of option value for European call options that must be held until maturity, but it does not allow for the fact that the holder of an American call option might choose to exercise the option just before a dividend. The current value of a call option, assuming that the option will be exercised just before the ex-dividend date, might be greater than the value of the option assuming it will be held until maturity. Although holding the option until maturity allows greater effective time to expiration, which increases the option value, it also entails more dividend payments, lowering the expected stock price at maturity and thereby lowering the current option value.

For example, suppose that a stock selling at \$20 will pay a \$1 dividend in four months, whereas the call option on the stock does not expire for six months. The effective annual interest rate is 10%, so that the present value of the dividend is $\$1/(1.10)^{1/3} = \$0.97$. Black suggests that we can compute the option value in one of two ways:

1. Apply the Black-Scholes formula assuming early exercise, thus using the actual stock price of \$20 and a time to expiration of four months (the time until the dividend payment).
2. Apply the Black-Scholes formula assuming no early exercise, using the dividend-adjusted stock price of $\$20 - \$0.97 = \$19.03$ and a time to expiration of six months.

The greater of the two values is the estimate of the option value, recognizing that early exercise might be optimal. In other words, the so-called **pseudo-American call option value** is the maximum of the value derived by assuming that the option will be held until expiration and the value derived by assuming that the option will be exercised just before an ex-dividend date. Even this technique is not exact, however, for it

[5] Fischer Black, "Fact and Fantasy in the Use of Options," *Financial Analysts Journal* 31 (July–August 1975).

assumes that the optionholder makes an irrevocable decision now on when to exercise, when in fact the decision is not binding until exercise notice is given.[6]

Put Option Valuation

We have concentrated so far on call option valuation. We can derive Black-Scholes European put option values from call option values using the put-call parity theorem. To value the put option, we simply calculate the value of the corresponding call option in equation 20.1 from the Black-Scholes formula, and solve for the put option value as

$$\begin{aligned} P &= C + PV(X) - S_0 \\ &= C + Xe^{-rT} - S_0 \end{aligned} \tag{20.2}$$

We must calculate the present value of the exercise price using continuous compounding to be consistent with the Black-Scholes formula.

Using data from the Black-Scholes call option example (C = \$13.70, X = \$95, S = \$100, r = .10, and T = .25), we find that a European put option on that stock with identical exercise price and time to maturity is worth

$$P = \$13.70 + \$95e^{-.10\times.25} - \$100 = \$6.35$$

As we noted traders can do, we might then compare this formula value to the actual put price as one step in formulating a trading strategy.

Equation 20.2 is valid for European puts on nondividend-paying stocks. Listed put options are American options that offer the opportunity of early exercise, however, and we have seen that the right to exercise puts early can turn out to be valuable. This means that an American option must be worth more than the corresponding European option. Therefore, equation 20.2 describes only the lower bound on the true value of the American put. However, in many applications the approximation is very accurate.[7]

20.5 Using the Black-Scholes Formula

Hedge Ratios and the Black-Scholes Formula

In the last chapter, we considered two investments in IBM: 1,000 shares of IBM stock or 10,000 call options on IBM. We saw that the call option position was more sensitive to swings in IBM's stock price than was the all-stock position. To analyze the overall exposure to a stock price more precisely, however, it is necessary to quantify these rel-

[6] An exact formula for American call valuation on dividend–paying stocks has been developed in Richard Roll, "An Analytic Valuation Formula for Unprotected American Call Options on Stocks with Known Dividends," *Journal of Financial Economics* 5 (November 1977). The technique has been discussed and revised in Robert Geske, "A Note on an Analytical Formula for Unprotected American Call Options on Stocks with Known Dividends," *Journal of Financial Economics* 7 (December 1979), and Robert E. Whaley, "On the Valuation of American Call Options on Stocks with Known Dividends," *Journal of Financial Economics* 9 (June 1981). These are difficult papers, however.

[7] For a more complete treatment of American put valuation, see R. Geske and H. E. Johnson, "The American Put Valued Analytically," *Journal of Finance* 39 (December 1984), pp. 1511–24.

Figure 20.8
Call option value and hedge ratio

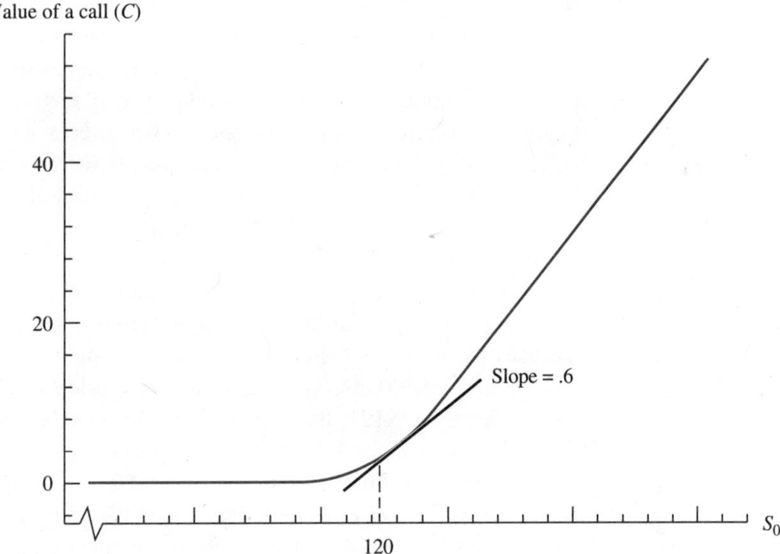

ative sensitivities. A tool that enables us to summarize the overall exposure of portfolios of options with various exercise prices and times to maturity is the hedge ratio. An option's **hedge ratio** is the change in the price of an option for a \$1 increase in the stock price. A call option, therefore, has a positive hedge ratio and a put option a negative hedge ratio. The hedge ratio is commonly called the option's **delta**.

If you were to graph the option value as a function of the stock value as we have done for a call option in Figure 20.8, the hedge ratio is simply the slope of the value function evaluated at the current stock price. For example, suppose the slope of the curve at S_0 = \$120 equals .60. As the stock increases in value by \$1, the option increases by approximately \$0.60, as the figure shows.

For every call option written, 0.60 shares of stock would be needed to hedge the investor's portfolio. For example, if one writes 10 options and holds six shares of stock, according to the hedge ratio of 0.6, a \$1 increase in stock price will result in a gain of \$6 on the stock holdings, whereas the loss on the 10 options written will be 10 × \$0.60, an equivalent \$6. The stock price movement leaves total wealth unaltered, which is what a hedged position is intended to do. The investor holding the stock and an option in proportions dictated by their relative price movements hedges the portfolio.

Black-Scholes hedge ratios are particularly easy to compute. The hedge ratio for a call is $N(d_1)$, whereas the hedge ratio for a put is $N(d_1) - 1$. We defined $N(d_1)$ as part of the Black-Scholes formula in equation 20.1. Recall that $N(d)$ stands for the area under the standard normal curve up to d. Therefore, the call option hedge ratio must be positive and less than 1.0, whereas the put option hedge ratio is negative and of smaller absolute value than 1.0.

Figure 20.8 verifies the insight that the slope of the call option valuation function is less than 1.0, approaching 1.0 only as the stock price becomes extremely large. This tells us that option values change less than one for one with changes in stock prices. Why should this be? Suppose an option is so far in the money that you are absolutely certain it will be exercised. In that case, every dollar increase in the stock price would increase the option value by one dollar. But if there is a reasonable chance the call option will expire out of the money, even after a moderate stock price gain, a $1 increase in the stock price will not necessarily increase the ultimate payoff to the call; therefore, the call price will not respond by a full dollar.

The fact that hedge ratios are less than 1.0 does not contradict our earlier observation that options offer leverage and are sensitive to stock price movements. Although *dollar* movements in option prices are slighter than dollar movements in the stock price, the *rate of return* volatility of options remains greater than stock return volatility because options sell at lower prices. In our example, with the stock selling at $120, and a hedge ratio of 0.6, an option with exercise price $120 may sell for $5. If the stock price increases to $121, the call price would be expected to increase by only $0.60 to $5.60. The percentage increase in the option value is $0.60/$5.00 = 12%, however, whereas the stock price increase is only $1/$120 = 0.83%. The ratio of the percent changes is 12%/0.83% = 14.4. For every 1% increase in the stock price, the option price increases by 14.4%. This ratio, the percent change in option price per percent change in stock price, is called the **option elasticity.**

The hedge ratio is an essential tool in portfolio management and control. An example will show why. Consider two portfolios, one holding 750 IBM calls and 200 shares of IBM and the other holding 800 shares of IBM. Which portfolio has greater dollar exposure to IBM price movements? You can answer this question easily using the hedge ratio.

Each option changes in value by H dollars for each dollar change in stock price, where H stands for the hedge ratio. Thus, if H equals 0.6, the 750 options are equivalent to 450 (0.6×750) shares in terms of the response of their market value to IBM stock price movements. The first portfolio has less dollar sensitivity to stock price change because the 450 share-equivalents of the options plus the 200 shares actually held are less than the 800 shares held in the second portfolio.

This is not to say, however, the first portfolio is less sensitive to the stock's rate of return changes. As we noted in discussing option elasticities, the first portfolio may be of lower total value than the second, so despite its lower sensitivity in terms of total market value, it might have greater rate of return sensitivity. Because a call option has a lower market value than the stock, its price changes more than proportionally with stock price changes, even though its hedge ratio is less than 1.0.

CONCEPT CHECK Question 8. What is the elasticity of a put option currently selling for $4 with exercise price $120, and hedge ratio −0.4 if the stock price is currently $122?

Portfolio Insurance

In Chapter 19, we showed that protective put strategies offer a sort of insurance policy on an asset. The protective put has proved to be extremely popular with investors. Even

Figure 20.9
Return characteristics for a portfolio with a protective put

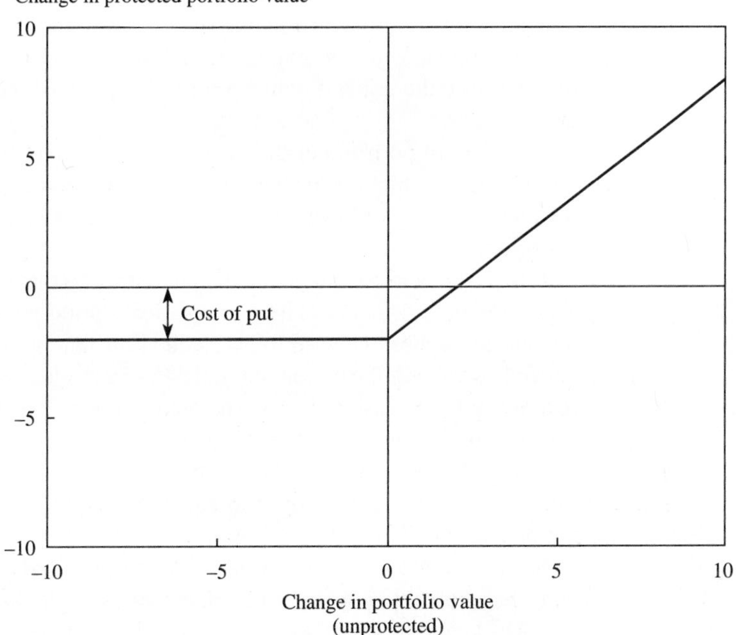

if the asset price falls, the put conveys the right to sell the asset for the exercise price, which is a way to lock in a minimum portfolio value. With an at-the-money put ($X = S_0$), the maximum loss that can be realized is the cost of the put. The asset can be sold for X, which equals its original value, so even if the asset price falls, the investor's net loss over the period is just the cost of the put. If the asset value increases, however, upside potential is unlimited. Figure 20.9 graphs the profit or loss on a protective put position as a function of the change in the value of the underlying asset.

While the protective put is a simple and convenient way to achieve **portfolio insurance,** that is, to limit the worst-case portfolio rate of return, there are practical difficulties in trying to insure a portfolio of stocks. First, unless the investor's portfolio corresponds to a standard market index for which puts are traded, a put option on the portfolio will not be available for purchase. And if index puts are used to protect a nonindexed portfolio, tracking error can result. For example, if the portfolio falls in value while the market index rises, the put will fail to provide the intended protection. Tracking error limits the investor's freedom to pursue active stock selection because such error will be greater as the managed portfolio departs more substantially from the market index.

Moreover, the desired horizon of the insurance program must match the maturity of a traded put option in order to establish the appropriate protective put position. Today long-term options on market indexes and some larger stocks called LEAPS (for *long-term equity anticipation securities*) trade on the CBOE with maturities of several years. However, this market has been active only for a few years. In the mid-1980s, while most investors pursuing insurance programs had horizons of several years, actively traded puts were limited to maturities of less than a year. Rolling over a sequence of short-term puts, which might be viewed as a response to this problem, introduces new risks because the prices at which successive puts will be available in the future are not known today.

Providers of portfolio insurance who had horizons of several years, therefore, could not rely on the simple expedient of purchasing protective puts for their clients' portfolios. Instead, they followed trading strategies to replicate the payoffs to the protective put position.

Here is the general idea. Even if a put option on the desired portfolio with the desired expiration date does not exist, a theoretical option-pricing model (such as the Black-Scholes model) can be used to determine how that option's price would respond to the portfolio's value if the option did trade. For example, if stock prices were to fall, the put option would increase in value. The option model could quantify this relationship. The net exposure of the (hypothetical) protective put portfolio to swings in stock prices is the sum of the exposures of the two components of the portfolio, the stock and the put. The net exposure of the portfolio equals the equity exposure less the (offsetting) put option exposure.

We can create "synthetic" protective put positions by holding a quantity of stocks with the same net exposure to market swings as the hypothetical protective put position. The key to this strategy is the option delta, or hedge ratio, that is, the change in the price of the protective put option per change in the value of the underlying stock portfolio.

An example will clarify the procedure. Suppose a portfolio is currently valued at $100 million. An at-the-money put option on the portfolio might have a hedge ratio or delta of −.6, meaning the option's value swings $0.60 for every dollar change in portfolio value, but in an opposite direction. Suppose the stock portfolio falls in value by 2%. The profit on a hypothetical protective put position (if the put existed) would be as follows (in millions of dollars):

Loss on stocks:	2% of $100	= $2.00
+ Gain on put:	.6 × $2.00	= 1.20
Net loss		= $ .80

We create the synthetic option position by selling a proportion of shares equal to the put option's delta (i.e., selling 60% of the shares) and placing the proceeds in risk-free T-bills. The rationale is that the hypothetical put option would have offset 60% of any change in the stock portfolio's value, so one must reduce portfolio risk directly by selling 60% of the equity and putting the proceeds into a risk-free asset. Total return on a synthetic protective put position with $60 million in risk-free investments such as T-bills and $40 million in equity is

Loss on stocks:	2% of $40	= $.80
+ Loss on bills:		= 0
Net loss		= $.80

The synthetic and actual protective put positions have equal returns. We conclude that if you sell a proportion of shares equal to the put option's delta and place the pro-

Figure 20.10
Hedge ratios change as the stock price fluctuates

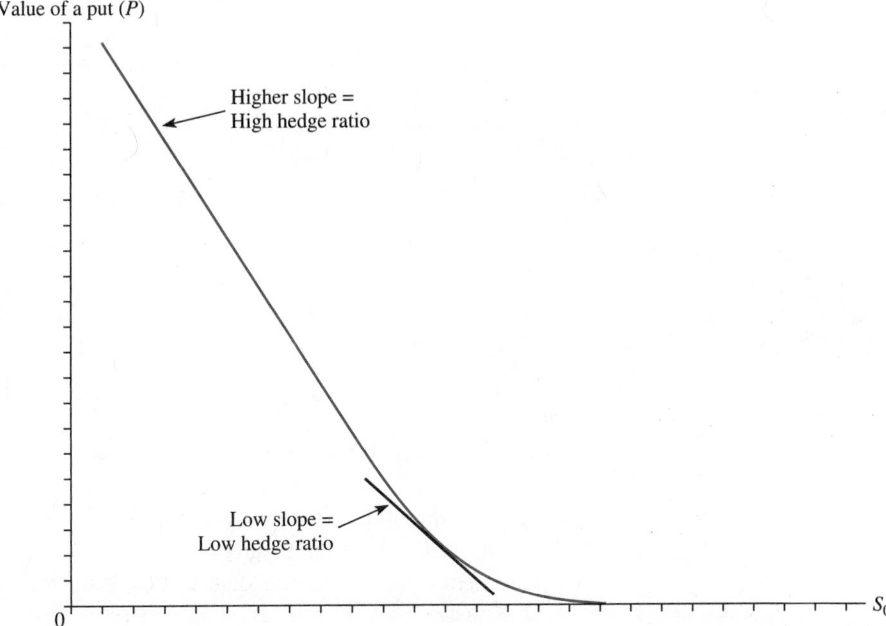

ceeds in cash equivalents, your exposure to the stock market will equal that of the desired protective put position.

The difficulty with this procedure is that deltas constantly change. Figure 20.10 shows that as the stock price falls, the magnitude of the appropriate hedge ratio increases. Therefore, market declines require extra hedging, that is, additional conversion of equity into cash. This constant updating of the hedge ratio is called **dynamic hedging.**

Dynamic hedging is one reason portfolio insurance has been said to contribute to market volatility. Market declines trigger additional sales of stock as portfolio insurers strive to increase their hedging. These additional sales are seen as reinforcing or exaggerating market downturns.

In practice, portfolio insurers do not actually buy or sell stocks directly when they update their hedge positions. Instead, they minimize trading costs by buying or selling stock index futures as a substitute for sale of the stocks themselves. As you will see in the next chapter, stock prices and index futures prices usually are very tightly linked by cross-market arbitrageurs so that futures transactions can be used as reliable proxies for stock transactions. Instead of selling equities based on the put option's delta, insurers will sell an equivalent number of futures contracts.[8]

Several portfolio insurers suffered great setbacks during the market crash of October 19, 1987, when the Dow Jones Industrial Average fell more than 500 points. A description of what happened then should let you appreciate the complexities of applying a seemingly straightforward hedging concept.

[8] Notice, however, that the use of index futures reintroduces the problem of tracking error between the portfolio and the market index.

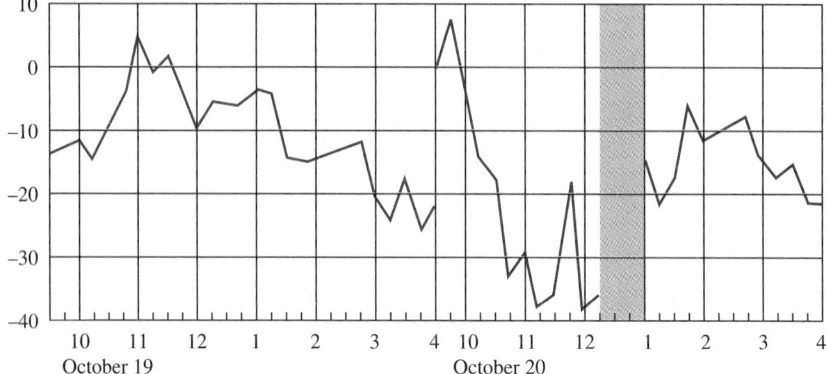

Figure 20.11
S&P 500 cash-to-futures spread in points at 15-minute intervals

Note: Trading in futures contracts halted between 12:15 and 1:05.
Source: *The Wall Street Journal.* Reprinted by permission of *The Wall Street Journal,* © 1987 Dow Jones & Company, Inc. All Rights Reserved Worldwide.

1. Market volatility at the crash was much greater than ever encountered before. Put option deltas based on historical experience were too low; insurers underhedged, held too much equity, and suffered excessive losses.
2. Prices moved so fast that insurers could not keep up with the necessary rebalancing. They were "chasing deltas" that kept getting away from them. The futures market saw a "gap" opening, where the opening price was nearly 10% below the previous day's close. The price dropped before insurers could update their hedge ratios.
3. Execution problems were severe. First, current market prices were unavailable, with trade execution and the price quotation system hours behind, which made computation of correct hedge ratios impossible. Moreover, trading in stocks and stock futures ceased during some periods. The continuous rebalancing capability that is essential for a viable insurance program vanished during the precipitous market collapse.
4. Futures prices traded at steep discounts to their proper levels compared to reported stock prices, thereby making the sale of futures (as a proxy for equity sales) seem expensive. Although you will see in the next chapter that stock index futures prices normally exceed the value of the stock index, Figure 20.11 shows that on October 19, futures sold far below the stock index level. The so-called cash-to-futures spread was negative most of the day. When some insurers gambled that the futures price would recover to its usual premium over the stock index, and chose to defer sales, they remained underhedged. As the market fell farther, their portfolios experienced substantial losses.

Although most observers believe that the portfolio insurance industry will never recover from the market crash, the nearby box points out that delta hedging is still alive and well on Wall Street. Dynamic hedges are widely used by large firms to hedge potential losses from the options they write. The article also points out, however, that these traders are increasingly aware of the practical difficulties in implementing dynamic hedges in very volatile markets.

Delta-Hedging: The New Name in Portfolio Insurance

Portfolio insurance, the high-tech hedging strategy that helped grease the slide in the 1987 stock-market crash, is alive and well.

And just as in 1987, it doesn't always work out as planned, as some financial institutions found out in the recent European bond-market turmoil.

Banks, securities firms and other big traders rely heavily on portfolio insurance to contain their potential losses when they buy and sell options. But since portfolio insurance got a bad name after it backfired on investors in 1987, it goes by an alias these days—the sexier, Star Trek moniker of "delta-hedging."

Whatever you call it, the recent turmoil in European bond markets taught some practitioners—including banks and securities firms that were hedging options sales to hedge funds and other investors—the same painful lessons of earlier portfolio insurers: Delta-hedging can break down in volatile markets, just when it is needed most.

What's more, at such times, it can actually feed volatility. The complexities of hedging certain hot-selling "exotic" options may only compound such glitches.

"The tried-and-true strategies for hedging [these products] work fine when the markets aren't subject to sharp moves or large shocks," says Victor S. Filatov, president of Smith Barney Global Capital Management in London. But turbulent times can start "causing problems for people who normally have these risks under control."

Options are financial arrangements that give buyers the right to buy, or sell, securities or other assets at prearranged prices over some future period. An option can gyrate wildly in value with even modest changes in the underlying security's price; the relationship between the two is known as the option's "delta." Thus, dealers in these instruments need some way to hedge their delta to contain the risk.

How you delta-hedge depends on the bets you're trying to hedge. For instance, delta-hedging would prompt options sellers to sell into falling markets and buy into rallies. It would give the opposite directions to options buyers, such as dealers who might hold big options inventories.

In theory, delta-hedging takes place with computer-timed precision, and there aren't any snags. But in real life, it doesn't always work so smoothly.

"When volatility ends up being much greater than anticipated, you can't get your delta trades off at the right points," says an executive at one big derivatives dealer.

A Scenario in Treasurys

How does this happen? Take the relatively simple case of dealers who sell "call" options on long-term Treasury bonds. Such options give buyers the right to buy bonds at a fixed price over a specific time period. And compared with buying bonds outright, these options are much more sensitive to market moves.

Because selling the calls made those dealers vulnerable to a rally, they delta-hedged by buying bonds. As bond prices turned south [and option deltas fell] the dealers shed their hedges by selling bonds, adding to the selling orgy. The plunging markets forced them to sell at lower prices than expected, causing unexpected losses on their hedges.

To be sure, traders say delta-hedging wasn't the main source of selling in the markets' fall. That dubious honor goes to the huge dumping by speculators of bond and stock holdings that were purchased with borrowed money. While experts may agree that delta-hedging doesn't actually cause crashes, in some cases it can speed the decline once prices slip.

By the same token, delta-hedging also tends to buoy prices once they turn up—which may be one reason why markets correct so suddenly these days.

Source: Abridged from Barbara Donnelly Granito, "Delta-Hedging: The New Name in Portfolio Insurance," *The Wall Street Journal,* March 17, 1994, p. C1.

20.6 Empirical Evidence

There have been an enormous number of empirical tests of the Black-Scholes option-pricing model. For the most part, the results of the studies have been positive in that the Black-Scholes model generates option values fairly close to the actual prices at which options trade. At the same time, some regular empirical failures of the model have been noted. For example the Black-Scholes model tends to undervalue deep in-the-money calls and overvalue deep out-of-the-money calls. Geske and Roll[9] have argued that these empirical results can be attributed to the failure of the Black-Scholes model to account for the possible early exercise of American calls on stocks that pay dividends. They show that the theoretical bias induced by this failure corresponds exactly to the actual "mispricing" observed empirically.

Whaley[10] examines the performance of the Black-Scholes formula relative to that of more complicated option formulas that allow for early exercise. His findings indicate that formulas allowing for the possibility of early exercise do better at pricing than the Black-Scholes formula. The Black-Scholes formula seems to perform worst for options on stocks with high dividend payouts. The true American call option formula, on the other hand, seems to fare equally well in the prediction of option prices on stocks with high or low dividend payouts.

In a recent paper, Rubinstein[11] pointed out that the performance of the Black-Scholes model has deteriorated in recent years in the sense that options on the same stock with the same strike price that *should* have the same implied volatility actually exhibit progressively different implied volatilities. He attributed this to an increasing fear of another market crash like that in 1987, and noted that, consistent with this hypothesis, out-of-the-money put options are priced higher (i.e., with higher implied volatilities) than are other puts. He suggests a method to extend the option valuation framework to allow for these issues.

Summary

1. Option values may be viewed as the sum of intrinsic value plus time or "volatility" value. The volatility value is the right to choose not to exercise if the stock price moves against the holder. Thus, optionholders cannot lose more than the cost of the option regardless of stock price performance.

2. Call options are more valuable when the exercise price is lower, when the stock price is higher, when the interest rate is higher, when the time to maturity is greater, when the stock's volatility is greater, and when dividends are lower.

3. Call options must sell for at least the stock price less the present value of the exercise price and dividends to be paid before maturity. This implies that a call option on a nondividend-paying stock may be sold for more than the proceeds from immedi-

[9] Robert Geske and Richard Roll, "On Valuing American Call Options with the Black–Scholes European Formula," *Jouirnal of Finance* 39 (June 1984).

[10] Robert E. Whaley, "Valuation of American Call Options on Dividend–Paying Stocks: Empirical Tests," *Journal of Financial Economics* 10 (1982).

[11] Mark Rubinstein, "Implied Binomial Trees," *Journal of Finance* 49 (July 1994), 771–818.

ate exercise. Thus, European calls are worth as much as American calls on stocks that pay no dividends, because the right to exercise the American call early has no value.

4. Options may be priced relative to the underlying stock price using a simple two-period, two-state pricing model. As the number of periods increases, the model can approximate more realistic stock price distributions. The Black-Scholes formula may be seen as a limiting case of the binomial option model, as the holding period is divided into progressively smaller subperiods when the interest rate and stock volatility are constant.

5. The Black-Scholes formula is valid for options on stocks that pay no dividends. Dividend adjustments may be adequate to price European calls on dividend-paying stocks, but the proper treatment of American calls on dividend-paying stocks requires more complex formulas.

6. Put options may be exercised early, whether the stock pays dividends or not. Therefore, American puts generally are worth more than are European puts.

7. European put values can be derived from the call value and the put-call parity relationship. This technique cannot be applied to American puts for which early exercise is a possibility.

8. The hedge ratio is the number of shares of stock required to hedge the price risk involved in writing one option. Hedge ratios are near zero for deep out-of-the-money call options and approach 1.0 for deep in-the-money calls.

9. Although hedge ratios are less than 1.0, call options have elasticities greater than 1.0. The rate of return on a call (as opposed to the dollar return) responds more than one for one with stock price movements.

10. Portfolio insurance can be obtained by purchasing a protective put option on an equity position. When the appropriate put is not traded, portfolio insurance entails a dynamic hedge strategy where a fraction of the equity portfolio equal to the desired put option's delta is sold and placed in risk-free securities.

Key Terms

Intrinsic value
Binomial model
Black-Scholes pricing formula
Implied volatility
Pseudo-American call option value
Hedge ratio
Delta
Option elasticity
Portfolio insurance
Dynamic hedging

Selected Readings

The breakthrough articles in option pricing are:

Black, Fischer, and Myron Scholes. "The Pricing of Options and Corporate Liabilities." *Journal of Political Economy* 81 (May-June 1973), pp. 637–59.

Merton, Robert C. "Theory of Rational Option Pricing." *Bell Journal of Economics and Management Science* 4 (Spring 1973), pp. 141–83.

The two-state approach was first suggested in:

Sharpe, William F. *Investments.* Englewood Cliffs, N.J.: Prentice Hall, 1978.

The approach was developed more fully in:

Rendelman, Richard J., Jr.; and Brit J. Bartter. "Two-State Option Pricing." *Journal of Finance* 34 (December 1979), pp. 1093–110.

Cox, John C.; Stephen Ross; and Mark Rubinstein. "Option Pricing: A Simplified Approach." *Journal of Financial Economics* 7 (September 1979), pp. 229–63.

A popular textbook on option valuation models is:

Hull, John C., *Options, Futures, and other Derivative Securities*, 2nd ed., Englewood Cliffs, N.J.: Prentice Hall, 1993.

Problems

1. We showed in the text that the value of a call option increases with the volatility of the stock. Is this also true of put option values? Use the put-call parity theorem as well as a numerical example to prove your answer.
2. In each of the following questions, you are asked to compare two options with parameters as given. The risk-free interest rate for *all* cases should be assumed to be 6%. Assume the stocks on which these options are written pay no dividends.

i.

Put	T	X	σ	Price of Option
A	.5	50	.20	$10
B	.5	50	.25	$10

Which put option is written on the stock with the lower price?

a. A.
b. B.
c. Not enough information.

ii.

Put	T	X	σ	Price of Option
A	.5	50	.2	$10
B	.5	50	.2	$12

Which put option must be written on the stock with the lower price?

a. A.
b. B.
c. Not enough information.

iii.

Call	S	X	σ	Price of Option
A	50	50	.20	$12
B	55	50	.20	$10

Which call option must have the lower time to maturity?

a. A.
b. B.
c. Not enough information.

iv.

Call	T	X	S	Price of Option
A	.5	50	55	$10
B	.5	50	55	$12

Which call option is written on the stock with higher volatility?

a. A.

b. B.

c. Not enough information.

v.

Call	T	X	S	Price of Option
A	.5	50	55	\$10
B	.5	50	55	\$ 7

Which call option is written on the stock with higher volatility?

a. A.

b. B.

c. Not enough information.

3. Reconsider the determination of the hedge ratio in the two-state model (page 658), where we showed that one-half share of stock would hedge one option. What is the hedge ratio at the following exercise prices: 115, 100, 75, 50, 25, 10? What do you conclude about the hedge ratio as the option becomes progressively more in the money?
4. Show that Black-Scholes call option hedge ratios also increase as the stock price increases. Consider a one-year option with exercise price \$50, on a stock with annual standard deviation 20%. The T-bill rate is 8% per year. Find $N(d_1)$ for stock prices \$45, \$50, and \$55.
5. We will derive a two-state put option value in this problem. Data $S_0 = 100$; $X = 110$; $1 + r = 1.1$. The two possibilities for S_T are 130 and 80.
   a. Show that the range of S is 50, whereas that of P is 30 across the two states. What is the hedge ratio of the put?
   b. Form a portfolio of three shares of stock and five puts. What is the (nonrandom) payoff to this portfolio? What is the present value of the portfolio?
   c. Given that the stock currently is selling at 100, solve for the value of the put.
6. Calculate the value of call option on the stock in Question 5 with an exercise price of 110. Verify that the put-call parity theorem is satisfied by your answers to Questions 5 and 6. (Do not use continuous compounding to calculate the present value of X in this example because we are using a two-state model here, not a continuous-time Black-Scholes model.)
7. Use the Black-Scholes formula to find the value of a call option on the following stock:

Time to maturity	=	6 months
Standard deviation	=	50% per year
Exercise price	=	50
Stock price	=	50
Interest rate	=	10%

8. Recalculate the value of the option in Question 7, successively substituting one of the changes below while keeping the other parameters as in Question 7:
   a. Time to maturity = 3 months.

b. Standard deviation = 25% per year.
c. Exercise price = \$55.
d. Stock price = \$55.
e. Interest rate = 15%.

Consider each scenario independently. Confirm that the option value changes in accordance with the prediction of Table 20.1.

9. A call option with X = \$50 on a stock currently priced at S = \$55 is selling for \$10. Using a volatility estimate of $\sigma = .30$, you find that $N(d_1) = .6$ and $N(d_2) = .5$. The risk-free interest rate is zero. Is the implied volatility based on the option price more or less than .30? Explain.
10. Would you expect a \$1 increase in a call option's exercise price to lead to a decrease in the option's value of more or less than \$1?
11. Is a put option on a high-beta stock worth more than one on a low-beta stock? The stocks have identical firm-specific risk.
12. All else equal, is a call option on a stock with a lot of firm-specific risk worth more than one on a stock with little firm-specific risk? The betas of the two stocks are equal.
13. All else equal, will a call option with a high exercise price have a higher or lower hedge ratio than one with a low exercise price?
14. Should the rate of return of a call option on a long-term Treasury bond be more or less sensitive to changes in interest rates than is the rate of return of the underlying bond?
15. If the stock price falls and the call price rises, then what has happened to the call option's implied volatility?
16. If the time to maturity falls and the put price rises, then what has happened to the put option's implied volatility?
17. According to the Black-Scholes formula, what will be the value of the hedge ratio of a call option as the stock price becomes infinitely large? Explain briefly.
18. According to the Black-Scholes formula, what will be the value of the hedge ratio of a put option for a very small exercise price?
19. The hedge ratio of an at-the-money call option on IBM is 0.4. The hedge ratio of an at-the-money put option is −0.6. What is the hedge ratio of an at-the-money straddle position on IBM?
20. A collar is established by buying a share of stock for \$50, buying a 6-month put option with exercise price \$45, and writing a 6-month call option with exercise price \$55. Based on the volatility of the stock, you calculate that for a strike price of \$45 and maturity of six months, $N(d_1) = .60$, whereas for the exercise price of \$55, $N(d_1) = .35$.
    a. What will be the gain or loss on the collar if the stock price increases by \$1?
    b. What happens to the delta of the portfolio if the stock price becomes very large? Very small?
21. These three put options are all written on the same stock. One has a delta of −.9, one a delta of −.5, and one a delta of −.1. Assign deltas to the three puts by filling in this table.

Put	X	Delta
A	10	
B	20	
C	30	

22. You are *very* bullish (optimistic) on stock EFG, much more so than the rest of the market. In each question, choose the portfolio strategy that will give you the biggest dollar profit if your bullish forecast turns out to be correct. Explain your answer.
    a. *Choice A:* \$10,000 invested in calls with $X = 50$.
    Choice B: \$10,000 invested in EFG stock.
    b. *Choice A:* 10 call options contracts (for 100 shares each), with $X = 50$.
    Choice B: 1,000 shares of EFG stock.
23. Imagine you are a provider of portfolio insurance. You are establishing a four-year program. The portfolio you manage is currently worth \$100 million, and you hope to provide a minimum return of 0%. The equity portfolio has a standard deviation of 25% per year, and T-bills pay 5% per year. Assume for simplicity that the portfolio pays no dividends (or that all dividends are reinvested).
    a. What fraction of the portfolio should be placed in bills? What fraction in equity?
    b. What should the manager do if the stock portfolio falls by 3% on the first day of trading?
24. You would like to be holding a protective put position on the stock of XYZ Co. to lock in a guaranteed minimum value of \$100 at year-end. XYZ currently sells for \$100. Over the next year the stock price will increase by 10% or decrease by 10%. The T-bill rate is 5%. Unfortunately, no put options are traded on XYZ Co.
    a. Suppose the desired put option were traded. How much would it cost to purchase?
    b. What would have been the cost of the protective put portfolio?
    c. What portfolio position in stock and T-bills will ensure you a payoff equal to the payoff that would be provided by a protective put with $X = 100$? Show that the payoff to this portfolio and the cost of establishing the portfolio matches that of the desired protective put.
25. Suppose that the risk-free interest rate is zero. Would an American put option ever be exercised early? Explain.
26. Let $p(S,T,X)$ denote the value of a European put on a stock selling at S dollars, with time to maturity T, and with exercise price X, and let $P(S,T,X)$ be the value of an American put.
    a. Evaluate $p(0,T,X)$.
    b. Evaluate $P(0,T,X)$.
    c. Evaluate $p(S,T,0)$.
    d. Evaluate $P(S,T,0)$.

e. What does your answer to (b) tell you about the possibility that American puts may be exercised early?

27. You are considering the sale of a call option with an exercise price of $100 and one year to expiration. The underlying stock pays no dividends, its current price is $100, and you believe it has a 50% chance of increasing to $120 and a 50% change of decreasing to $80. The risk-free rate of interest is 10%.*
    a. Describe the specific steps involved in applying the binomial option-pricing model to calculate the call option's value.
    b. Compare the binomial option-pricing model to the Black-Scholes option-pricing model.
28. Consider an increase in the volatility of the stock in Question 27. Suppose that if the stock increases in price, it will increase to $130, and that if it falls, it will fall to $70. Show that the value of the call option is now higher than the value derived in Question 27.
29. Calculate the value of a put option with exercise price $100 using the data in Question 27. Show that put-call parity is satisfied by your solution.
30. XYZ Corp. will pay a $2 per share dividend in two months. Its stock price currently is $60 per share. A call option on XYZ has an exercise price of $55 and three-month time to maturity. The risk-free interest rate is 0.5% per month, and the stock's volatility (standard deviation) = 7% per month. Find the pseudo-American option value. (Hint: Try defining one "period" as a month, rather than as a year.)
31. "The beta of a call option on General Motors is greater than the beta of a share of General Motors." True or false?
32. "The beta of a call option on the S&P 500 index with an exercise price of 330 is greater than the beta of a call on the index with an exercise price of 340." True or false?
33. What will happen to the hedge ratio of a convertible bond as the stock price becomes very large?

---

*Reprinted, with permission, from the Level III 1987 *CFA Study Guide*. Copyright 1987, The Institute of Chartered Financial Analysts, Charlottesville, VA. All rights reserved.

Chapter 21
Futures Markets

FUTURES AND FORWARD CONTRACTS ARE LIKE OPTIONS IN THAT THEY SPECIFY PURCHASE OR SALE OF SOME UNDERLYING SECURITY AT SOME FUTURE DATE. The key difference is that the holder of an option to buy is not compelled to buy and will not do so if the trade is unprofitable. A futures or forward contract, however, carries the obligation to go through with the agreed-upon transaction.

A forward contract is not an investment in the strict sense that funds are paid for an asset. It is only a commitment today to transact in the future. Forward arrangements are part of our study of investments, however, because they offer powerful means to hedge other investments and generally modify portfolio characteristics.

Forward markets for future delivery of various commodities go back at least to ancient Greece. Organized *futures markets,* though, are a relatively modern development, dating only to the 19th century. Futures markets replace informal forward contracts with highly standardized, exchange-traded securities.

This chapter describes the workings of futures markets and the mechanics of trading in these markets. We show how futures contracts are useful investment vehicles for both hedgers and speculators and how the futures price relates to the spot price of an asset. Chapter 21 deals with general principles of future markets. Chapter 22 describes specific futures markets in greater detail.

21.1 THE FUTURES CONTRACT

To see how futures and forwards work and how they might be useful, consider the portfolio diversification problem facing a farmer growing a single crop, let us say wheat. The entire planting season's revenue depends critically on the highly volatile crop price. The farmer can't easily diversify his position because virtually his entire wealth is tied up in the crop.

The miller who must purchase wheat for processing faces a portfolio problem that is the mirror image of the farmer's. He is subject to profit uncertainty because of the unpredictable future cost of the wheat.

Both parties can reduce this source of risk if they enter into a **forward contract** requiring the farmer to deliver the wheat when harvested at a price agreed upon now, regardless of the market price at harvest time. No money need change hands at this time. A forward contract is simply a deferred-delivery sale of some asset with the sales price agreed on now. All that is required is that each party be willing to lock in the ultimate price to be paid or received for delivery of the commodity. A forward contract protects each party from future price fluctuations.

Futures markets formalize and standardize forward contracting. Buyers and sellers do not have to rely on a chance matching of their interests; they can trade in a centralized futures market. The futures exchange also standardizes the types of contracts that may be traded: it establishes contract size, the acceptable grade of commodity, contract delivery dates, and so forth. Although standardization eliminates much of the flexibility available in informal forward contracting, it has the offsetting advantage of liquidity because many traders will concentrate on the same small set of contracts. Futures contracts also differ from forward contracts in that they call for a daily settling up of any gains or losses on the contract. In the case of forward contracts, no money changes hands until the delivery date.

In a centralized market, buyers and sellers can trade through brokers without personally searching for trading partners. The standardization of contracts and the depth of trading in each contract allows futures positions to be liquidated easily through a broker rather than personally renegotiated with the other party to the contract. Because the exchange guarantees the performance of each party to the contract, costly credit checks on other traders are not necessary. Instead, each trader simply posts a good faith deposit, called the *margin,* in order to guarantee contract performance.

The Basics of Futures Contracts

The futures contract calls for delivery of a commodity at a specified delivery or maturity date, for an agreed-upon price, called the **futures price,** to be paid at contract maturity. The contract specifies precise requirements for the commodity. For agricultural commodities, the exchange sets allowable grades (e.g., No. 2 hard winter wheat or No. 1 soft red wheat). The place or means of delivery of the commodity is specified as well. Delivery of agricultural commodities is made by transfer of warehouse receipts issued by approved warehouses. In the case of financial futures, delivery may be made by wire transfer; in the case of index futures, delivery may be accomplished by a cash settlement procedure such as those for index options. (Although the futures contract technically calls for delivery of an asset, delivery rarely occurs. Instead, parties to the contract much more commonly close out their positions before contract maturity, taking gains or losses in cash.)

Because the futures exchange specifies all the terms of the contract, the traders need bargain only over the futures price. The trader taking the **long position** commits to purchasing the commodity on the delivery date. The trader who takes the **short position** commits to delivering the commodity at contract maturity. The trader in the long position is said to "buy" a contract; the short side trader "sells" a contract. The words *buy* and *sell* are figurative only, because a contract is not really bought or sold like a stock or bond; it is entered into by mutual agreement. At the time the contract is entered into, no money changes hands.

Figure 21.1 shows prices for several agricultural futures contracts as they appear in the *The Wall Street Journal*. The boldface heading lists in each case the commodity, the exchange where the futures contract is traded in parentheses, the contract size, and the pricing unit. The first contract listed is for corn, traded on the Chicago Board of Trade (CBT). Each contract calls for delivery of 5,000 bushels, and prices in the entry are quoted in cents per bushel.

The next several rows detail price data for contracts expiring on various dates. The March 1995 maturity corn contract, for example, opened during the day at a futures price of 227½ cents per bushel. The highest futures price during the day was 228, the lowest was 227, and the settlement price (a representative trading price during the last few minutes of trading) was 227¾. The settlement price decreased by ¼ cent from the previous trading day. The highest futures price over the contract's life to date was 282½, the lowest 220½ cents. Finally, open interest, or the number of outstanding contracts, was 116,889. Similar information is given for each maturity date.

The trader holding the long position, that is, the person who will purchase the good, profits from price increases. Suppose that when the contract matures in July, the price of corn turns out to be 232¾ cents per bushel. The long position trader who entered the contract at the futures price of 227¾ cents earns a profit of 5 cents per bushel: the eventual price is 5 cents higher than the originally agreed-to futures price. As each contract calls for delivery of 5,000 bushels, (ignoring brokerage fees) the profit to the long position equals 5,000 × \$.05 = \$250 per contract. Conversely, the short position loses 5 cents per bushel. The short position's loss equals the long position's gain.

To summarize, at maturity:

$$\text{Profit to long} = \text{Spot price at maturity} - \text{Original futures price}$$
$$\text{Profit to short} = \text{Original futures price} - \text{Spot price at maturity}$$

where the spot price is the actual market price of the commodity at the time of the delivery.

The futures contract is, therefore, a zero sum game, with losses and gains to all positions netting out to zero. Every long position is offset by a short position. The aggregate profits to futures trading, summing over all investors, also must be zero, as is the net exposure to changes in the commodity price. For this reason, the establishment of a futures market in a commodity should not have a major impact on the spot market for that commodity.

CONCEPT CHECK

Question 1. Graph the profit realized by an investor who enters the long side of a futures contract as a function of the price of the asset on the maturity date. Compare this graph to a graph of the profits realized by the purchaser of the asset itself. Next, try the same exercise for a short futures position and a short sale of the asset.

Figure 21.1 Futures listings

FUTURES PRICES

Thursday, December 15, 1994

Open Interest Reflects Previous Trading Day.

GRAINS AND OILSEEDS

CORN (CBT) 5,000 bu.; cents per bu.

	Open	High	Low	Settle	Change	Lifetime High	Lifetime Low	Open Interest
Dec	216½	217	216	216½	....	277	210½	2,946
Mr95	227½	228	227	227¾	− ¼	282½	220½	116,889
May	233¾	235	233¾	234¾	....	285	228	44,682
July	238¼	239½	238	239	+ ½	285½	232½	45,573
Sept	241¾	243	241¾	242½	+ ½	270½	238	5,114
Dec	245¼	246¾	245¼	246¼	+ ¼	263	235½	28,623
Mr96	252	253¼	252	252¾	+ ¼	260¼	249½	1,761
July	259½	260¾	259¼	260½	+ ½	267	254	1,530
Dec	250½	250½	250	250½	+ 1	257	239	486

Est vol 26,500; vol Wed 41,927; open int 247,606, +2,431.

OATS (CBT) 5,000 bu.; cents per bu.

	Open	High	Low	Settle	Change	Lifetime High	Lifetime Low	Open Interest
Dec	112¾	112¾	112½	113½	+ ½	157¼	106	9
Mr95	120¾	122¼	120½	122¼	+ 1½	152¾	116½	8,596
May	126	127½	126	127	+ 1	151	122¼	3,012
July	132½	132½	132½	132½	+ 1½	142½	127½	1,733

Est vol 500; vol Wed 741; open int 13,382, +58.

SOYBEANS (CBT) 5,000 bu.; cents per bu.

	Open	High	Low	Settle	Change	Lifetime High	Lifetime Low	Open Interest
Jan	560	563½	559	562¾	+ 1½	704	537¼	42,468
Mar	570½	574	569½	573¼	+ 2	705	547¼	34,018
May	577½	582½	577½	582	+ 2¼	705½	556	18,613
July	583½	587¾	583	587¼	+ 2¼	706½	563½	25,935
Aug	586	590½	586	590¼	+ 2¾	612	566½	2,293
Sept	588	591½	588	590½	+ 2½	615	571	1,237
Nov	594	598½	593¾	598½	+ 3	645	578¼	12,150
Ja96	604	604½	604	605	+ 3	616	596	123
Nov	601	604	601	604	+ 2	616	589	128

Est vol 23,000; vol Wed 25,235; open int 137,055, +575.

SOYBEAN MEAL (CBT) 100 tons; $ per ton.

	Open	High	Low	Settle	Change	Lifetime High	Lifetime Low	Open Interest
Dec	156.50	156.60	155.90	156.20	− .10	209.00	154.10	2,103
Ja95	157.40	157.80	157.00	157.30	− .10	207.50	155.50	27,677
Mar	161.00	161.50	160.60	160.80	− .10	207.50	159.30	29,686
May	164.90	165.40	164.60	164.90	+ .20	207.00	163.50	14,726
July	169.30	169.80	169.00	169.20	− .10	206.00	168.40	12,430
Aug	175.50	175.50	171.30	171.30	− .10	182.60	170.60	3,184
Sept	173.40	173.70	173.30	173.30	− .10	182.70	172.60	1,489
Oct	175.00	175.50	175.00	174.90	− .20	181.80	174.50	5,488
Dec	177.80	178.10	177.70	177.80	− .20	185.20	176.50	3,394

Est vol 13,000; vol Wed 15,010; open int 100,187, −973.

SOYBEAN OIL (CBT) 60,000 lbs.; cents per lb.

	Open	High	Low	Settle	Change	Lifetime High	Lifetime Low	Open Interest
Dec	28.65	29.12	28.60	29.11	+ .27	29.75	22.00	7,608
Ja95	27.30	27.75	27.30	27.73	+ .19	28.55	22.65	33,878
Mar	26.45	26.84	26.45	26.83	+ .18	28.30	22.91	28,310
May	25.75	26.05	25.75	26.02	+ .12	28.05	22.85	18,580
July	25.31	25.50	25.31	25.47	+ .06	27.85	22.76	10,967
Aug	25.15	25.25	25.15	25.15	+ .05	27.20	22.73	2,256
Sept	25.00	25.00	24.90	24.90	+ .10	25.05	22.75	2,276
Oct	24.80	24.85	24.70	24.71	+ .03	24.85	22.75	4,081
Dec	24.55	24.65	24.50	24.65	+ .05	24.65	22.80	5,232

Est vol 13,700; vol Wed 16,210; open int 113,272, −1,453.

WHEAT (CBT) 5,000 bu.; cents per bu.

	Open	High	Low	Settle	Change	Lifetime High	Lifetime Low	Open Interest
Dec	368½	372¾	368½	372	+ 4¼	418¾	309	892
Mr95	382	387½	382	386	+ 3½	426¾	327	43,940
May	364	370¾	364	369½	+ 4	398½	325	7,083
July	338	341¾	337¾	340¾	+ 3½	363¾	311½	14,116
Sept	344	346¼	344	346¼	+ 3½	365	339	731
Dec	354½	356¾	354½	354¾	+ 1¾	375	331	261

Est vol 15,000; vol Wed 18,616; open int 67,036, +52.

WHEAT (KC) 5,000 bu.; cents per bu.

	Open	High	Low	Settle	Change	Lifetime High	Lifetime Low	Open Interest
Dec	395½	398¾	395½	398½	+ 6¾	423¼	312½	1,689
Mr95	382¼	388	382	387	+ 4¾	427¼	326½	23,313
May	368½	374	368½	373¼	+ 3¾	403	321½	3,172
July	344	348¾	344	347½	+ 3½	368¼	316½	4,778
Sept	350	352½	350	351	+ 4	377	329	115

Est vol 5,417; vol Wed 6,669; open int 33,094, −677.

WHEAT (MPLS) 5,000 bu.; cents per bu.

	Open	High	Low	Settle	Change	Lifetime High	Lifetime Low	Open Interest
Dec	364	367½	364	368½	+ 5½	419½	304	399
Mr95	378	385	378	383¾	+ 4	431	325¼	11,739
May	379	383½	379	382¾	+ 7¼	419¼	332½	1,575
July	....	....	....	365½	+ 3¼	386	324½	267
Sept	352	353	352	353	+ 1	366	346	162

Est vol 3,330; vol Wed 4,224; open int 14,159, +260.

RICE–ROUGH (CBT) 2000 cwt; $ per cwt

	Open	High	Low	Settle	Change	Lifetime High	Lifetime Low	Open Interest
Jan	6.450	6.460	6.370	6.390	− .010	6.950	6.160	683
Mar	6.600	6.670	6.530	6.550	− .030	7.070	6.340	1,596
May	6.800	6.800	6.670	6.670	− .030	7.100	6.500	193

Est vol na; vol Wed 172; open int 2,511, −12.

CANOLA (WPG) 20 metric tons; Can. $ per ton

	Open	High	Low	Settle	Change	Lifetime High	Lifetime Low	Open Interest
Jan	432.00	436.10	432.00	435.80	− .20	443.50	317.50	10,201
Mar	437.70	441.80	437.00	440.70	+ 1.00	447.00	331.00	17,873
June	439.50	445.00	439.50	443.60	+ .20	449.90	346.50	13,964
Aug	420.50	421.00	420.50	421.00	− .50	425.00	362.00	731
Sept	391.50	391.50	391.50	391.50	+ .50	397.00	350.00	833
Nov	390.00	393.20	390.00	392.70	+ 1.50	394.00	331.00	5,910

Est vol 4,410; vol Wed 8,872; open int 49,512, −324.

WHEAT (WPG) 20 metric tons; Can. $ per ton

	Open	High	Low	Settle	Change	Lifetime High	Lifetime Low	Open Interest
Dec		....	....	153.50	+ 1.00	154.70	97.80	482

METALS AND PETROLEUM

COPPER-HIGH (CMX)—25,000 lbs.; cents per lb.

	Open	High	Low	Settle	Change	Lifetime High	Lifetime Low	Open Interest
Dec	138.70	139.70	138.00	138.90	+ 2.40	139.70	75.75	4,146
Ja95	137.50	139.55	137.50	138.85	+ 2.90	139.55	76.90	1,774
Feb	137.70	136.70	136.70	137.50	+ 2.15	136.70	87.85	764
Mar	135.90	137.20	135.65	136.15	+ 1.90	137.20	76.30	28,814
Apr		....	....	132.65	+ 1.40	131.00	90.10	759
May	130.80	131.50	129.70	129.70	+ .95	131.50	76.85	3,894
June		....	....	127.00	+ .65	126.00	106.30	503
July	124.50	124.50	124.00	123.70	+ .35	125.70	78.00	3,360
Aug		....	....	120.20	− 1.15	120.00	111.40	357
Sept	117.70	118.60	117.70	117.70	− .25	121.00	79.10	1,777
Oct		....	....	115.25	− 1.15	115.50	113.00	202
Dec	113.50	113.50	112.00	111.50	− 1.05	115.50	88.00	3,277
Mr96	109.50	109.50	109.50	108.00	− 1.05	112.30	99.20	559
May		....	....	106.50	− 1.05	109.50	107.00	136

Est vol 14,000; vol Wed 11,950; open int 50,516, +524.

GOLD (CMX)—100 troy oz.; $ per troy oz.

	Open	High	Low	Settle	Change	Lifetime High	Lifetime Low	Open Interest
Dec	379.90	380.30	378.90	380.20	+ 1.30	426.50	343.00	163
Fb95	381.80	382.80	381.20	382.70	+ 1.20	411.00	363.50	92,432
Apr	385.50	386.50	385.30	386.70	....	425.00	381.70	13,430
June	389.80	391.00	389.80	390.90	....	430.00	351.00	21,516
Aug	394.80	394.80	394.80	395.40	....	414.50	380.50	12,006
Oct		....	....	399.80	....	419.20	401.00	4,839
Dec	403.20	403.50	403.20	404.40	....	439.50	358.00	9,445
Fb96		....	....	409.00	....	424.50	404.60	2,141
Apr		....	....	413.60	....	430.20	418.30	2,260
June		....	....	418.40	....	447.00	370.90	5,565
Aug		....	....	423.10	....	....	....	314
Dec		....	....	432.80	....	447.50	379.60	4,065
Ju97		....	....	447.40	....	456.00	436.00	1,920
Dec		....	....	462.20	+ 1.10	477.00	402.00	2,444
Ju98		....	....	476.90	+ 1.30	489.50	481.00	1,875
Dec		....	....	491.80	+ 1.50	505.00	468.00	3,263
Ju99		....	....	507.20	+ 1.80	520.00	511.00	2,483

Est vol 20,000; vol Wed 29,534; open int 180,167, +821.

PLATINUM (NYM)—50 troy oz.; $ per troy oz.

	Open	High	Low	Settle	Change	Lifetime High	Lifetime Low	Open Interest
Ja95	409.50	414.00	409.10	411.70	+ 3.10	435.50	374.80	11,912
Apr	na	417.00	412.50	415.40	+ 2.90	439.00	390.00	13,331
July	417.00	417.50	417.00	419.90	+ 2.90	439.00	409.10	2,063
Oct		....	....	424.60	+ 2.90	441.30	413.00	826
Ja96		....	....	428.30	+ 2.90	439.50	420.00	114

Est vol 5,608; vol Wed 4,780; open int 28,246, −205.

PALLADIUM (NYM) 100 troy oz.; $ per troy oz.

	Open	High	Low	Settle	Change	Lifetime High	Lifetime Low	Open Interest
Dec	na	154.00	154.00	153.45	+ .45	164.00	122.50	23
Mr95	154.55	155.50	154.50	155.20	+ .45	164.50	134.00	5,826
June	156.00	156.00	156.00	156.45	+ .45	166.00	151.60	781
Sept	157.10	157.10	157.10	157.70	+ .45	161.25	157.10	129

Est vol 394; vol Wed 267; open int 6,770, −53.

SILVER (CMX)—5,000 troy oz.; cents per troy oz.

	Open	High	Low	Settle	Change	Lifetime High	Lifetime Low	Open Interest
Dec	474.0	477.0	473.0	478.8	+ 3.4	597.0	380.0	100
Fb96		....	....	481.7	+ 3.2	477.0	471.0	2
Mar	480.0	487.0	479.0	484.7	+ 3.2	604.0	416.5	75,602
May	487.0	492.0	485.0	490.7	+ 3.2	606.5	418.0	10,346
July	493.0	499.0	492.0	497.1	+ 3.3	610.0	403.0	7,431
Sept	504.0	504.0	504.0	503.7	+ 3.4	615.0	477.5	9,795
Dec	511.5	515.5	510.0	514.0	+ 3.5	628.0	434.0	16,782
Mr96	524.5	524.5	524.5	524.5	+ 3.5	622.0	498.0	7,494
May	532.0	532.0	532.0	531.7	+ 3.5	599.0	499.0	2,255
July		....	....	538.7	+ 3.5	630.0	520.0	1,336
Dec		....	....	557.0	+ 3.3	670.0	454.0	1,864
Jl97		....	....	585.5	+ 3.3	655.0	588.0	537
Dec		....	....	607.9	+ 3.3	695.0	502.0	310
Dc98		....	....	662.9	+ 3.3	734.0	645.0	109

Est vol 16,000; vol Wed 14,421; open int 134,054, −973.

SILVER (CBT)—1,000 troy oz.; cents per troy oz.

	Open	High	Low	Settle	Change	Lifetime High	Lifetime Low	Open Interest
Dec	465.5	475.0	465.5	475.0	+ 3.5	596.0	414.0	34
Fb95	473.0	477.0	472.0	476.0	+ 3.5	582.0	448.0	1,238
Apr	479.0	484.0	478.5	483.0	+ 3.0	605.0	455.0	733
June	486.0	490.0	486.0	489.5	+ 2.0	605.0	460.0	1,408
Dec	510.0	512.0	508.0	510.0	+ 2.0	614.0	480.0	1,318

Est vol 200; vol Wed 202; open int 4,799, +60.

CRUDE OIL, Light Sweet (NYM) 1,000 bbls.; $ per bbl.

	Open	High	Low	Settle	Change	Lifetime High	Lifetime Low	Open Interest
Jan	16.93	16.99	16.63	16.73	− .26	20.12	15.15	53,999
Feb	16.95	17.05	16.75	16.83	− .23	19.60	15.28	91,096
Mar	na	17.13	16.90	16.96	− .17	20.66	15.42	53,637
Apr	na	17.18	17.04	17.08	− .14	19.68	15.55	20,774
May	na	17.28	17.15	17.17	− .12	19.23	15.69	12,489
June	17.28	17.34	17.25	17.25	− .10	21.21	15.73	28,359
July	na	17.41	17.31	17.33	− .08	18.85	16.28	12,976
Aug	na	17.50	17.39	17.40	− .07	18.85	16.90	10,356
Sept	17.52	17.60	17.48	17.47	− .06	19.84	16.28	13,242
Oct	17.58	17.60	17.53	17.53	− .04	18.88	16.42	8,061
Nov	17.62	17.65	17.61	17.59	− .03	18.87	17.15	6,055
Dec	na	17.70	17.63	17.64	− .02	20.80	16.50	18,396
Ja96	na	17.74	17.69	17.71	....	18.89	17.00	8,562
Feb	17.76	17.76	17.76	17.77	+ .01	18.84	17.53	2,954
Mar	17.80	17.80	17.80	17.82	+ .02	18.80	17.15	6,415
Apr	17.84	17.84	17.84	17.87	+ .03	18.27	17.81	769
May		....	....	17.92	+ .03	18.32	18.32	4,788
June	18.05	18.05	17.95	17.98	+ .03	20.40	17.22	16,501
Sept		....	....	18.14	+ .05	18.47	18.38	1,926
[illegible]				18.22	+ .06	20.40	17.65	15,755

	Open	High	Low	Settle	Change	Lifetime High	Lifetime Low	Open Interest
Oct	157.25	157.50	157.25	156.50	− .75	155.25	154.00	342
Nov		....	....	158.25	− .75	161.50	161.25	220
Dec	160.50	160.75	160.25	160.25	− .25	170.00	156.50	2,244

Est vol 13,448; vol Wed 13,317; open int 92,185, −3,310.

INTEREST RATE

TREASURY BONDS (CBT)—$100,000; pts. 32nds of 100%

	Open	High	Low	Settle	Change	Lifetime High	Lifetime Low	Open Interest
Dec	99-27	100-05	99-21	99-29	....	118-08	91-19	43,283
Mr95	99-10	99-20	99-03	99-11	....	116-20	95-13	357,183
June	98-26	99-05	98-21	98-29	....	113-15	94-27	12,813
Sept	98-22	98-28	98-17	98-21	....	112-15	94-10	887
Dec	....	....	....	98-14	....	111-23	93-27	263

Est vol 350,000; vol Wed 398,792; op int 414,544, +6,074.

TREASURY BONDS (MCE)—$50,000; pts. 32nds of 100%

	Open	High	Low	Settle	Change	Lifetime High	Lifetime Low	Open Interest
Dec	99-29	99-29	99-20	99-27	− 1	114-00	96-01	125
Mr95	99-13	99-20	99-03	99-09	− 1	104-07	95-13	12,701

Est vol 5,000; vol Wed 7,523; open int 12,843, −379.

TREASURY NOTES (CBT)—$100,000; pts. 32nds of 100%

	Open	High	Low	Settle	Change	Lifetime High	Lifetime Low	Open Interest
Dec	100-23	100-30	100-19	100-25	+ 4	114-21	99-02	28,731
Mr95	99-29	100-10	99-27	100-02	+ 3	111-07	98-11	233,911
June	99-14	99-22	99-13	99-17	+ 3	105-22	97-27	2,354
Sept	....	....	....	99-04	+ 3	100-07	97-11	11

Est vol 100,004; vol Wed 120,654; open int 265,029, +3,308.

5 YR TREAS NOTES (CBT)—$100,000; pts. 32nds of 100%

	Open	High	Low	Settle	Change	Lifetime High	Lifetime Low	Open Interest
Dec	100-22	101-03	100-22	100-27	+ 4.0	104-20	100-02	31,892
Mr95	100-08	100-24	00-075	00-135	+ 4.0	103-09	99-15	180,561
June	100-03	100-04	100-03	100-04	+ 4.0	100-08	99-06	281
Sept	....	....	....	99-27	+ 4.0	99-07	99-07	2

Est vol 68,500; vol Wed 79,072; open int 212,736, +1,992.

2 YR TREAS NOTES (CBT)—$200,000, pts. 32nds of 100%

	Open	High	Low	Settle	Change	Lifetime High	Lifetime Low	Open Interest
Dec	100-21	00-265	00-205	00-237	+ 4	102-25	100-12	2,256
Mr95	00-015	00-085	100-01	00-045	+ 3¼	101-02	99-252	38,726

Est vol 8,000; vol Wed 7,985; open int 40,982, +1,439.

30-DAY FEDERAL FUNDS (CBT)-$5 million; pts. of 100%

	Open	High	Low	Settle	Change	Lifetime High	Lifetime Low	Open Interest
Dec	94.33	94.35	94.33	94.34	+ .01	96.00	94.16	4,093
Ja95	94.06	94.10	94.06	94.10	+ .05	94.66	93.93	3,811
Feb	93.61	93.66	93.60	93.66	+ .08	94.56	93.49	4,039
Mar	93.41	93.47	93.41	93.47	+ .09	94.44	93.28	3,074

Est vol 1,999; vol Wed 2,318; open int 15,096, +10.

TREASURY BILLS (CME)—$1 mil.; pts. of 100%

	Open	High	Low	Settle	Chg	Discount Settle	Discount Chg	Open Interest
Mar	93.31	93.43	93.31	93.42	+ .12	6.58	− .12	17,972
June	92.71	92.86	92.70	92.85	+ .15	7.15	− .15	3,739
Sept	92.51	92.55	92.51	92.55	+ .12	7.45	− .12	954

Est vol 1,704; vol Wed 2,524; open int 22,665, −264.

LIBOR-1 MO. (CME)—$3,000,000; points of 100%

	Open	High	Low	Settle	Chg	Settle	Chg	Open Interest
Dec	93.91	93.93	93.89	93.92	+ .03	6.08	− .03	13,265
Ja96	93.78	93.81	93.76	93.81	+ .04	6.19	− .04	16,448
Feb	93.43	93.51	93.41	93.48	+ .07	6.58	− .07	5,187
Mar	93.06	93.17	93.06	93.16	+ .15	6.84	− .15	2,302
Apr	....	....	....	92.87	+ .13	7.17	− .13	394
May	....	....	....	92.64	+ .13	7.36	− .13	362
June	....	....	....	92.42	+ .16	7.58	− .16	87
Oct	....	....	....	92.03	+ .12	7.97	− .12	170

Est vol 9,927; vol Wed 6,714; open int 38,329, +1,647.

MUNI BOND INDEX (CBT)-$1,000; times Bond Buyer MBI

	Open	High	Low	Settle	Chg	High	Low	Open Interest
Dec	85-10	85-10	84-28	84-31	− 9	91-17	80-31	7,297
Mr95	84-30	84-31	84-13	84-15	− 13	88-09	79-28	27,445

Est vol 5,000; vol Wed 8,309; open int 34,742, −225.
The index: Close 84-23; Yield 7.40.

EURODOLLAR (CME)—$1 million; pts of 100%

	Open	High	Low	Settle	Chg	Yield Settle	Yield Chg	Open Interest
Dec	93.65	93.69	93.63	93.68	+ .04	6.32	− .04	297,451
Mr95	92.71	92.84	92.69	92.83	+ .13	7.17	− .13	489,918
June	92.08	92.25	92.06	92.23	+ .16	7.77	− .16	352,406
Sept	91.82	91.99	91.80	91.96	+ .15	8.04	− .15	277,482
Dec	91.67	91.81	91.66	91.78	+ .13	8.22	− .13	194,345
Mr96	91.77	91.86	91.75	91.84	+ .10	8.16	− .10	176,186
June	91.84	91.89	91.82	91.88	+ .07	8.12	− .07	137,498
Sept	91.89	91.96	91.88	91.93	+ .05	8.07	− .05	114,825
Dec	91.89	91.94	91.88	91.91	+ .03	8.09	− .03	99,738
Mr97	91.96	92.00	91.94	91.97	+ .02	8.03	− .02	94,753
June	91.99	92.03	91.97	91.99	+ .01	8.01	− .01	77,042
Sept	92.01	92.05	91.97	92.00	....	8.00	....	59,887
Dec	91.97	92.02	91.92	91.94	− .02	8.06	+ .02	48,615
Mr98	92.01	92.05	91.96	91.97	− .03	8.03	+ .03	49,349
June	92.01	92.05	91.96	91.97	− .03	8.03	+ .03	39,027
Sept	92.00	92.04	91.95	91.95	− .04	8.05	+ .04	31,042
Dec	91.97	91.97	91.87	91.89	− .06	8.11	+ .06	28,331
Mr99	91.98	92.00	91.89	91.92	− .06	8.08	+ .06	28,757
June	91.95	91.97	91.87	91.88	− .07	8.12	+ .07	19,369
Sept	91.92	91.94	91.83	91.85	− .07	8.15	+ .07	12,651
Dec	91.86	91.87	91.76	91.77	− .09	8.23	+ .09	10,737
Mr00	91.89	91.90	91.79	91.80	− .09	8.20	+ .09	8,684
June	91.86	91.87	91.76	91.77	− .09	8.23	+ .09	6,329
Sept	91.83	91.84	91.73	91.73	− .10	8.27	+ .10	6,273
Dec	91.76	91.78	91.64	91.65	− .11	8.35	+ .11	5,797
Mr01	91.81	91.83	91.69	91.70	− .11	8.30	+ .11	6,034

CURRENCY

JAPAN YEN (CME)—12.5 million yen; $ per yen (.00)

	Open	High	Low	Settle	Change	Lifetime High	Lifetime Low	Open Interest
Dec	.9980	.9984	.9963	.9965	− .0002	1.0490	.9525	35,880
Mr95	1.0066	1.0080	1.0053	1.0057	− .0003	1.0560	.9680	65,421
June	1.0190	1.0200	1.0186	1.0183	− .0007	1.0670	.9915	2,256
Sept	....	....	....	1.0312	− .0011	1.0775	1.0200	319
Dec	....	....	....	1.0442	− .0014	1.0760	1.0420	114

Est vol 19,845; vol Wed 21,989; open int 104,022, −456.

DEUTSCHEMARK (CME)—125,000 marks; $ per mark

	Open	High	Low	Settle	Change	Lifetime High	Lifetime Low	Open Interest
Dec	.6363	.6373	.6352	.6366	− .0006	.6731	.5590	52,038
Mr95	.6385	.6389	.6362	.6376	− .0007	.6745	.5798	62,889
June	.6396	.6410	.6393	.6402	− .0008	.6747	.5980	1,665
Sept	....	....	....	.6432	− .0008	.6770	.6290	124

Est vol 24,506; vol Wed 29,201; open int 116,716, +1,359.

CANADIAN DOLLAR (CME)—100,000 dlrs.; $ per Can $

	Open	High	Low	Settle	Change	Lifetime High	Lifetime Low	Open Interest
Dec	.7212	.7218	.7199	.7204	− .0013	.7670	.7038	21,709
Mr95	.7190	.7210	.7189	.7191	− .0013	.7605	.7020	41,544
June	.7184	.7184	.7171	.7171	− .0011	.7600	.6990	1,486
Sept	.7155	.7161	.7155	.7154	− .0007	.7438	.6965	1,172
Dec	.7150	.7150	.7140	.7137	− .0003	.7400	.7025	261

Est vol 6,336; vol Wed 12,614; open int 66,200, −804.

BRITISH POUND (CME)—62,500 pds.; $ per pound

	Open	High	Low	Settle	Change	Lifetime High	Lifetime Low	Open Interest
Dec	1.5610	1.5638	1.5590	1.5628	+ .0014	1.6436	1.4400	29,409
Mr95	1.5620	1.5640	1.5586	1.5626	+ .0012	1.6440	1.4530	43,745
June	1.5618	1.5640	1.5618	1.5624	+ .0012	1.6380	1.5330	160

Est vol 8,060; vol Wed 10,617; open int 73,318, +345.

SWISS FRANC (CME)—125,000 francs; $ per franc

	Open	High	Low	Settle	Change	Lifetime High	Lifetime Low	Open Interest
Dec	.7533	.7546	.7521	.7536	+ .0001	.8108	.6885	33,254
Mr95	.7573	.7581	.7555	.7569	....	.8136	.7287	33,614
June	.7611	.7624	.7610	.7620	....	.8165	.7193	4686

Est vol 11,171; vol Wed 17,312; open int 67,391, +928.

AUSTRALIAN DOLLAR (CME)—100,000 dlrs.; $ per A.$

	Open	High	Low	Settle	Change	Lifetime High	Lifetime Low	Open Interest
Dec	.7778	.7795	.7770	.7774	+ .0017	.7795	.6965	9,120
Mr95	.7737	.7767	.7737	.7748	+ .0017	.7767	.7275	13,007

Est vol 3,900; vol Wed 2,584; open int 22,131, +89.

U.S. DOLLAR INDEX (FINEX)—1,000 times USDX

	Open	High	Low	Settle	Change	Lifetime High	Lifetime Low	Open Interest
Dec	89.44	89.61	89.44	89.50	+ .04	99.00	84.95	1,557
Mr95	89.52	89.80	89.56	89.63	+ .06	96.65	85.28	4,652

Est vol 2,200; vol Wed 748; open int 6,263, −156.
The index: High 89.68; Low 89.44; Close 89.52 +.03

INDEX

S&P 500 INDEX (CME) $500 times index

	Open	High	Low	Settle	Chg	High	Low	Open Interest
Dec	455.00	457.70	454.70	455.40	+ .60	487.10	438.85	88,367
Mr95	458.10	460.85	457.80	458.65	+ .55	484.10	441.45	192,420
June	463.15	464.60	462.70	463.00	+ .55	487.40	449.50	6,674
Sept	467.80	467.80	467.80	467.90	+ .25	487.70	456.55	2,145

Est vol 111,457; vol Wed 142,708; open int 289,606, −1,612.
Indx prelim High 456.84; Low 454.50; Close 455.35 +.38

S&P MIDCAP 400 (CME) $500 times index

	Open	High	Low	Settle	Chg	High	Low	Open Interest
Dec	166.50	167.00	166.30	166.70	+ 1.10	187.05	162.30	3,226
Mr95	167.40	168.75	167.40	168.20	+ 1.20	188.25	163.50	12,604

Est vol 2,072; vol Wed 3,899; open int 15,859, +5.
The index: High 166.69; Low 165.52; Close 166.59 +1.07

NIKKEI 225 STOCK AVERAGE (CME)—$5 times index

	Open	High	Low	Settle	Chg	High	Low	Open Interest
Mar	19250.	19300.	19230.	19270.	+ 125	21950.	18810.	20,414

Est vol 750; vol Wed 1,139; open int 20,426, +202.
The index: High 19177.54; Low 18964.19; Close 19121.12 +189.63

GSCI (CME)—$250 times nearby index

	Open	High	Low	Settle	Chg	High	Low	Open Interest
Feb	174.20	175.30	174.20	174.80	+ 60	181.20	171.40	4,338
Apr	174.30	174.40	174.30	174.80	+ .40	179.90	172.50	385

Est vol 389; vol Wed 466; open int 4,723, −18.
The index: High 174.86; Low 173.64; Close 174.25 −.06

MAJOR MARKET INDEX (CME)—$500 times index

	Open	High	Low	Settle	Chg	High	Low	Open Interest
Dec	391.40	393.60	391.40	392.55	+ 1.55	411.50	361.75	1,598
Ja95	393.00	394.70	393.00	393.70	+ 1.55	410.90	382.00	520

Est vol 2,025; vol Wed 450; open int 2,124, +40.
The index: High 393.59; Low 390.84; Close 395.25 +1.20

NYSE COMPOSITE INDEX (NYFE)—500 times index

	Open	High	Low	Settle	Chg	High	Low	Open Interest
Dec	249.55	249.80	248.30	249.15	+ .70	264.50	242.60	1,957
Mar	250.00	251.40	249.80	250.55	+ .65	264.60	231.25	3,231

Est vol 3,801; vol Wed 4,159; open int 5,319, −628.
The index: High 249.26; Low 248.09; Close 248.96 +.63

KR-CRB INDEX (NYFE)—500 times index

	Open	High	Low	Settle	Chg	High	Low	Open Interest
Mar	230.50	231.30	229.80	231.20	+ .95	242.75	228.05	1,078
May	231.40	231.40	230.90	232.00	+ .90	242.75	228.70	1,148
July	232.30	232.30	231.70	232.90	+ .90	240.10	229.40	571

Est vol 130; vol Wed 203; open int 2,798, +31.
The index: High 230.96; Low 229.50; Close 230.79 +1.15

CAC-40 STOCK INDEX (MATIF)—FFr 200 per index pt.

	Open	High	Low	Settle	Chg	High	Low	Open Interest
Dec	1950.	1954.	1935.	1937.	− 6.0	2195.	1818.	30,619
Ja95	1958.	1962.	1946.	1945.5	− 6.0	2008.5	1905.	4,026
Feb	1965.5	1965.5	1965.5	1955.5	− 6.0	1971.5	1937.	503
Mar	1978.	1980.	1972.	1965.	− 6.0	2044.5	1854.5	10,512
June		....	....	1947.	− 6.0	2042.	1905.	3,348
Sept	1985.5	1985.5	1984.	1974.	− 6.0	2017.	1946.	4,500

Est vol 15,059; vol Wed 25,503; open int 53,508, +4,529.

FT–SE 100 INDEX (LIFFE)—£25 per index point

	Open	High	Low	Settle	Chg	High	Low	Open Interest
Dec	2986.	3000.	2965.	2974.	− 4.0	3292.	2928.	25,246
Mr95	3003.	3019.	2987.5	2996.	....	3173.	2946.	41,980

	Open	High	Low	Settle	Change	Lifetime High	Lifetime Low	Open Interest
Mr95	155.00	156.00	155.00	156.00	+ .50	157.40	100.30	5,283
May	155.30	155.50	155.20	155.50	+ .50	157.20	100.30	2,355
July	154.20	154.20	154.00	154.20	+ .20	155.00	101.00	1,184
Oct	142.00	142.20	141.50	142.20	+ .20	144.40	105.00	1,075
Dec		....	....	141.20	+ .20	145.40	137.00	605

Est vol 390; vol Wed 872; open int 10,984, +239.

LIVESTOCK AND MEAT

CATTLE–FEEDER (CME) 50,000 lbs.; cents per lb.

	Open	High	Low	Settle	Change	Lifetime High	Lifetime Low	Open Interest
Jan	74.80	75.20	74.67	75.12	+ .45	80.95	71.40	3,753
Mar	72.35	72.75	72.25	72.70	+ .40	80.25	70.15	3,095
Apr	71.50	71.90	71.35	71.72	+ .40	76.90	69.95	1,166
May	70.40	70.85	70.40	70.80	+ .37	76.45	69.30	960
Aug	70.85	71.15	70.85	71.05	+ .35	73.10	69.55	234

Est vol 1,305; vol Wed 1,274; open int 9,322, +106.

CATTLE–LIVE (CME) 40,000 lbs.; cents per lb.

	Open	High	Low	Settle	Change	Lifetime High	Lifetime Low	Open Interest
Dec	70.57	70.75	70.32	70.57	....	74.30	66.75	3,984
Fb95	70.30	70.65	70.15	70.50	+ .32	74.25	66.47	30,656
Apr	70.65	70.92	70.50	70.72	+ .17	75.10	67.27	19,970
June	65.42	65.90	65.37	65.77	+ .40	72.50	64.00	6,650
Aug	63.40	63.92	63.35	63.67	+ .37	68.10	62.50	2,965
Oct	64.10	64.50	64.07	64.50	+ .40	67.55	63.10	1,464
Dec	65.00	65.25	64.90	65.15	+ .35	66.55	63.85	205

Est vol 12,653; vol Wed 14,398; open int 65,894, –649.

HOGS (CME) 40,000 lbs.; cents per lb.

	Open	High	Low	Settle	Change	Lifetime High	Lifetime Low	Open Interest
Dec	34.40	35.60	33.50	33.72	– .40	50.50	30.40	1,627
Fb95	37.30	38.42	37.17	38.10	+ 1.17	50.80	34.02	14,436
Apr	37.75	38.90	37.50	38.12	+ .60	48.80	35.05	8,449
June	43.40	44.30	43.30	43.85	+ .52	51.55	40.35	4,522
July	43.35	44.25	43.35	43.85	+ .57	49.00	40.65	950
Aug	43.10	44.20	43.10	43.70	+ .65	47.00	40.60	1,284
Oct	41.40	42.50	41.35	42.07	+ .77	42.50	38.30	1,100
Dec	43.00	44.05	43.00	43.65	+ .65	44.05	39.00	306

Est vol 12,822; vol Wed 6,112; open int 32,741, –480.

PORK BELLIES (CME) 40,000 lbs.; cents per lb.

	Open	High	Low	Settle	Change	Lifetime High	Lifetime Low	Open Interest
Feb	38.30	40.15	38.05	39.30	+ 1.15	60.05	35.15	7,833
Mar	38.80	40.42	38.47	39.60	+ 1.10	60.20	35.50	1,634
May	39.90	41.42	39.70	40.35	+ .75	61.15	36.90	515
July	41.10	42.30	40.70	41.45	+ .80	54.00	37.80	461
Aug	39.95	41.00	39.70	40.02	+ .50	52.25	36.70	215

Est vol 3,821; vol Wed 3,628; open int 10,669, +152.

FOOD AND FIBER

COCOA (CSCE) – 10 metric tons; $ per ton.

	Open	High	Low	Settle	Change	Lifetime High	Lifetime Low	Open Interest
Mar	1,288	1,315	1,286	1,296	+ 30	1,605	1,077	39,443
May	1,295	1,321	1,295	1,303	+ 27	1,612	1,111	12,271
July	1,310	1,333	1,310	1,323	+ 33	1,600	1,225	5,725
Sept	1,348	1,350	1,348	1,348	+ 32	1,611	1,263	2,047
Dec	1,369	1,369	1,369	1,369	+ 34	1,633	1,290	4,811
Mr96		....	....	1,399	+ 34	1,676	1,350	7,005
May		....	....	1,425	+ 34	1,642	1,473	4,377
July		....	....	1,444	+ 34	1,595	1,410	2,016

Est vol 14,855; vol Wed 17,619; open int 77,775, +236.

COFFEE (CSCE) – 37,500 lbs.; cents per lb.

	Open	High	Low	Settle	Change	Lifetime High	Lifetime Low	Open Interest
Dec	144.10	147.65	147.00	147.75	+ 3.50	244.25	77.10	49
Mr95	148.50	150.60	147.50	150.40	+ 3.30	244.00	78.90	16,989
May	151.00	152.50	149.25	152.30	– 3.60	244.40	82.50	6,654
July	152.50	153.25	151.00	153.15	– 4.35	245.10	85.00	2,739
Sept	154.00	154.40	151.80	153.90	– 4.90	238.00	89.00	2,053
Dec	154.25	154.25	151.00	153.15	– 5.70	242.00	151.00	1,658
Mr96	154.00	154.00	151.35	152.25	– 7.25	202.00	151.35	282

Est vol 6,995; vol Wed 9,018; open int 30,450, –430.

SUGAR – WORLD (CSCE) – 112,000 lbs.; cents per lb.

	Open	High	Low	Settle	Change	Lifetime High	Lifetime Low	Open Interest
Mar	14.53	15.03	14.47	15.01	+ .41	15.25	10.56	96,951
May	14.57	15.05	14.53	15.03	+ .37	15.18	10.57	37,816
July	14.21	14.75	14.21	14.70	+ .38	14.75	10.57	23,993
Oct	13.39	13.83	13.39	13.78	+ .27	13.96	10.57	24,942
Mr96	12.76	13.10	12.76	13.10	+ .20	13.28	10.88	6,526
May		....	....	12.91	+ .25	13.00	11.56	1,931
July		....	....	12.66	+ .20	12.72	11.75	1,418
Oct		....	....	12.48	+ .20	12.50	12.00	69

Est vol 28,151; vol Wed 21,,121; open int 193,646, +513.

SUGAR – DOMESTIC (CSCE) – 112,000 lbs.; cents per lb.

	Open	High	Low	Settle	Change	Lifetime High	Lifetime Low	Open Interest
Mar	22.38	22.40	22.37	22.40	+ .01	22.40	21.60	3,802
May	22.48	22.52	22.48	22.52	+ .04	22.52	21.81	3,394
July	22.58	22.60	22.58	22.60	+ .02	22.60	22.00	3,354
Sept	22.58	22.61	22.58	22.60	+ .02	22.61	21.95	2,795
Nov	22.14	22.17	22.14	22.16	+ .03	22.17	21.80	1,516
Ja96		....	....	22.00	....	22.03	21.80	232
Mar		....	....	21.97	....	21.90	21.90	262

Est vol 472; vol Wed 1,145; open int 15,355, +606.

COTTON (CTN) – 50,000 lbs.; cents per lb.

	Open	High	Low	Settle	Change	Lifetime High	Lifetime Low	Open Interest
Mar	83.43	85.00	83.43	84.88	+ 1.65	85.00	64.00	32,099
May	83.75	85.20	83.65	85.13	+ 1.90	85.20	64.00	11,276
July	83.30	84.60	83.10	84.45	+ 1.52	84.97	69.30	6,385
Oct	74.80	75.15	74.70	75.08	+ .53	75.15	66.80	1,281
Dec	72.00	72.50	72.00	72.33	+ .43	72.80	66.25	6,140

Est vol 12,500; vol Wed 7,768; open int 57,269, +778.

ORANGE JUICE (CTN) – 15,000 lbs.; cents per lb.

	Open	High	Low	Settle	Change	Lifetime High	Lifetime Low	Open Interest
Jan	113.95	114.00	111.75	113.35	– .40	132.00	89.00	10,174
Mar	117.00	117.30	115.30	117.15	– .15	124.25	93.00	8,554
May	119.50	120.00	118.25	120.00	....	124.65	97.50	1,646
July		....	....	122.75	+ .05	127.50	100.50	939
Sept	125.75	126.00	125.00	126.00	+ .30	130.25	102.50	2,226
Nov	123.75	123.75	123.50	125.25	– .45	129.00	109.00	1,562
Ja96		....	....	126.75	– .45	129.00	105.50	546

Est vol 2,500; vol Wed 3,082; open int 25,659, +177.

	Open	High	Low	Settle	Change	Lifetime High	Lifetime Low	Open Interest
Dec		....	....	18.32	+ .06	20.40	17.65	15,755
Ju97	18.60	18.65	18.60	18.67	+ .06	19.60	18.30	8,457
Dec		....	....	19.02	+ .06	19.14	18.70	10,621

Est vol 95,191; vol Wed 87,462; open int 406,188, –2,895.

HEATING OIL NO. 2 (NYM) 42,000 gal.; $ per gal.

	Open	High	Low	Settle	Change	Lifetime High	Lifetime Low	Open Interest
Jan	.4925	.4960	.4870	.4878	– .0076	.5850	.4600	33,913
Feb	.4925	.4985	.4900	.4907	– .0068	.5875	.4690	39,397
Mar	na	.4965	.4900	.4905	– .0060	.5750	.4700	21,408
Apr	na	.4900	.4865	.4855	– .0055	.5500	.4525	13,623
May	na	.4845	.4815	.4810	– .0050	.5350	.4700	7,893
June	na	.4815	.4795	.4785	– .0045	.5300	.4679	6,699
July	na	.4810	.4800	.4800	– .0045	.5290	.4730	7,703
Aug	.4880	,4880	.4870	.4845	– .0045	.5390	.4740	3,089
Sept		....	....	.4930	– .0045	.5310	.4845	2,277
Oct	.5040	.5040	.5040	.5020	– .0045	.5355	.5025	1,824
Nov		....	....	.5110	– .0045	.5330	.5120	1,350
Dec	.5225	.5225	.5225	.5200	– .0045	.5550	.5185	5,536
Ja96		....	....	.5250	– .0045	.5525	.5225	891
Feb		....	....	.5245	– .0045	.5930	.5300	814
Mar		....	....	.5185	– .0045	.5490	.5240	320
Apr		....	....	.5115	– .0045	.5450	.5450	225

Est vol 27,840; vol Wed 35,033; open int 146,962, –123.

GASOLINE-NY Unleaded (NYM) 42,000 gal.; $ per gal.

	Open	High	Low	Settle	Change	Lifetime High	Lifetime Low	Open Interest
Jan	.5230	.5310	.5130	.5152	– .0113	.5860	.4750	20,097
Feb	.5155	.5190	.5080	.5095	– .0093	.5825	.4815	17,469
Mar	na	.5220	.5110	.5129	– .0082	.5695	.4900	8,617
Apr	na	.5495	.5385	.5419	– .0091	.6030	.5270	10,176
May	.5360	.5425	.5340	.5364	– .0076	.5870	.5240	5,487
June	na	.5450	.5370	.5374	– .0066	.5800	.5290	1,462
July	.5370	.5370	.5320	.5339	– .0061	.5794	.5160	974
Aug	.5340	.5340	.5340	.5289	– .0061	.5729	.5300	854
Sept		....	....	.5224	– .0061	.5600	.5220	597
Oct		....	....	.5149	– .0061	.5535	.5150	397
Nov		....	....	.5094	– .0061	.5500	.5085	413
Dec		....	....	.5064	– .0061	.5379	.5070	539

Est vol 22,123; vol Wed 22,825; open int 67,082, +585.

NATURAL GAS, (NYM) 10,000 MMBtu.; $ per MMBtu's

	Open	High	Low	Settle	Change	Lifetime High	Lifetime Low	Open Interest
Jan	1.720	1.740	1.680	1.718	+ .004	2.720	1.620	23,684
Feb	1.728	1.740	1.700	1.721	– .007	2.460	1.660	21,950
Mar	1.720	1.735	1.700	1.720	+ .005	2.360	1.670	16,347
Apr	1.685	1.700	1.675	1.690	+ .005	2.310	1.640	9,689
May	1.685	1.705	1.675	1.690	+ .005	2.275	1.650	9,462
June	1.695	1.710	1.695	1.700	+ .005	2.245	1.665	7,142
July	1.705	1.730	1.700	1.710	+ .005	2.214	1.685	7,397
Aug	1.715	1.735	1.710	1.718	+ .005	2.244	1.695	6,603
Sept	1.720	1.740	1.720	1.725	+ .005	2.267	1.710	6,798
Oct	1.783	1.790	1.770	1.778	+ .005	2.280	1.760	5,204
Nov	1.865	1.890	1.865	1.870	+ .005	2.360	1.860	4,692
Dec	1.957	1.980	1.955	1.962	+ .005	2.444	1.944	7,088
Ja96	1.970	1.990	1.970	1.977	+ .007	2.416	1.965	6,609
Feb	1.910	1.920	1.905	1.907	+ .007	2.295	1.901	1,985
Mar	1.855	1.860	1.850	1.847	+ .007	2.290	1.830	2,216
Apr	1.787	1.807	1.787	1.794	+ .007	2.100	1.785	1,682
May	1.790	1.807	1.790	1.794	+ .007	2.055	1.790	1,201
June	1.790	1.810	1.790	1.794	+ .007	1.865	1.790	1,537

Est vol 24,307; vol Wed 39,887; open int 141,286, +269.

BRENT CRUDE (IPE) 1,000 net bbls.; $ per bbl.

	Open	High	Low	Settle	Change	Lifetime High	Lifetime Low	Open Interest
Jan	16.05	16.05	15.82	15.87	– .10	18.35	14.60	49,862
Feb	16.00	16.00	15.78	15.78	– .18	18.25	15.50	82,207
Mar	15.94	15.95	15.81	15.81	– .14	18.10	15.60	20,927
Apr	15.94	16.12	15.84	15.87	– .09	17.97	15.68	10,954
May	15.95	15.95	15.87	15.89	– .09	17.90	15.05	7,144
June	15.98	15.98	15.90	15.92	– .12	18.00	15.73	7,003
July	15.97	15.98	15.97	15.92	– .13	17.84	15.85	4,324
Aug	16.05	16.05	16.05	16.05	– .06	17.80	15.83	1,809
Sept		....	....	16.08	– .09	17.20	15.89	1,445
Oct	16.10	16.10	16.10	16.10	– .13	17.20	16.15	1,096
Nov		....	....	16.15	– .14	16.76	16.13	1,110
Dec	16.23	16.26	16.23	16.21	– .14	16.84	16.07	2,215

Est vol 54,783; vol Wed 65,343; open int 190,099, –8,424.

GAS OIL (IPE) 100 metric tons; $ per ton

	Open	High	Low	Settle	Change	Lifetime High	Lifetime Low	Open Interest
Jan	143.50	144.00	142.75	143.00	– .50	176.75	139.50	40,500
Feb	145.50	146.25	145.25	145.25	– .50	175.25	142.00	22,092
Mar	148.00	148.00	147.00	147.50	– .50	174.00	143.75	12,245
Apr	148.25	148.25	147.50	147.50	– .75	171.00	144.00	4,521
May	148.25	148.25	148.25	148.25	– .50	167.00	145.00	1,665
June	149.25	149.50	148.50	148.50	– 1.00	168.75	145.75	6,623
July	151.00	151.00	150.25	150.25	– 1.00	163.00	148.00	796
Aug		....	....	152.50	– .75	162.00	150.00	118
Sept	155.00	155.00	155.00	154.25	– .75	164.00	152.00	819

EXCHANGE ABBREVIATIONS
(for commodity futures and futures options)

CBT-Chicago Board of Trade; CME-Chicago Mercantile Exchange; CSCE-Coffee, Sugar & Cocoa Exchange, New York; CMX-Commodity Exchange, New York; IPE-International Petroleum Exchange; KC-Kansas City Board of Trade; LIFFE-London International Financial Futures Exchange; MATIF-Marche A Terme International De France; ME-Montreal Exchange; MCE-MidAmerica Commodity Exchange; MPLS-Minneapolis Grain Exchange; CTN-New York Cotton Exchange; NYM-New York Mercantile Exchange; SFE-Sydney Futures Exchange; TFE-Toronto Futures Exchange; WPG-Winnipeg Commodity Exchange.

Mr01	91.81	91.83	91.69	91.70	– .11	8.30	+ .11	6,034
June	91.79	91.81	91.66	91.67	– .12	8.33	+ .12	4,909
Sept	91.77	91.79	91.64	91.65	– .12	8.35	+ .12	5,362
Dec	91.73	91.73	91.60	91.61	– .12	8.39	+ .12	4,749
Mr02	91.73	91.73	91.65	91.66	– .12	8.34	+ .12	3,005
June	91.73	91.73	91.64	91.65	– .12	8.35	+ .12	2,617
Sept	91.67	91.70	91.62	91.63	– .12	8.37	+ .12	2,069
Dec	91.66	91.66	91.57	91.58	– .12	8.42	+ .12	1,341
Mr03	91.70	91.70	91.61	91.62	– .12	8.38	+ .12	1,918
June	91.67	91.67	91.58	91.59	– .12	8.41	+ .12	1,747
Sept	91.62	91.62	91.54	91.55	– .12	8.45	+ .12	1,537
Dec	91.46	91.48	91.46	91.48	– .12	8.52	+ .12	1,006
Mr04	91.57	91.57	91.50	91.51	– .12	8.49	+ .12	1,598
June	91.50	91.50	91.48	91.49	– .12	8.51	+ .12	367
Sept	....	....	....	91.46	– .12	8.54	+ .12	293

Est vol 599,288; vol Wed 848,202; open int 2,705,044, –1,537.

STERLING (LIFFE) – £500,000; pts of 100%

	Open	High	Low	Settle	Change	Lifetime High	Lifetime Low	Open Interest
Dec	93.51	93.56	93.51	93.54	+ .03	95.23	90.10	99,729
Mr95	92.55	92.64	92.55	92.60	+ .05	95.10	90.70	93,704
June	91.92	91.99	91.92	91.96	+ .05	94.23	91.42	63,831
Sept	91.51	91.55	91.51	91.52	+ .05	94.81	91.01	62,652
Dec	91.30	91.33	91.27	91.29	+ .02	94.66	90.71	44,720
Mr96	91.20	91.21	91.15	91.16	....	94.61	90.50	38,381
June	91.12	91.14	91.07	91.07	– .03	94.25	90.39	33,130
Sept	91.09	91.11	91.04	91.04	– .03	93.64	90.30	17,648
Dec	91.07	91.08	91.07	91.02	– .02	93.50	90.20	12,429
Mr97	91.02	91.02	91.01	90.98	....	93.33	90.05	14,078
June	90.96	90.96	90.92	90.92	+ .01	90.96	89.92	9,364
Sept	90.92	90.92	90.88	90.88	+ .01	90.92	90.17	8,213

Est vol 50,761; vol Wed 59,992; open int 497,879, –3,706.

LONG GILT (LIFFE) – £50,000; 32nds of 100%

	Open	High	Low	Settle	Change	Lifetime High	Lifetime Low	Open Interest
Dec	102-19	102-30	102-19	102-28	+ 0-08	103-18	97-14	18,394
Mr95	101-28	102-13	101-15	102-06	+ 0-08	102-28	100-13	108,493

Est vol 30,104; vol Wed 52,139; open int 126,887, +275.

EUROMARK (LIFFE) – DM 1,000,000; pts of 100%

	Open	High	Low	Settle	Change	Lifetime High	Lifetime Low	Open Interest
Dec	94.45	94.50	94.45	94.50	+ .05	95.73	91.81	117,636
Mr95	94.29	94.38	94.29	94.36	+ .06	95.83	92.45	210,750
June	94.00	94.08	94.00	94.05	+ .06	95.91	93.15	141,343
Sept	93.68	93.76	93.68	93.73	+ .07	95.83	93.35	83,574
Dec	93.39	93.42	93.39	93.39	+ .05	95.74	93.05	63,371
Mr96	93.10	93.15	93.10	93.11	+ .04	95.62	92.84	50,171
June	92.84	92.87	92.83	92.84	+ .03	95.45	92.64	31,596
Sept	92.66	92.66	92.63	92.62	....	94.26	92.48	26,292
Dec	92.48	92.48	92.38	92.41	– .04	94.10	92.22	25,955
Mr97	92.39	92.39	92.36	92.37	....	93.99	92.20	15,487
June	92.30	92.30	92.26	92.28	....	93.10	92.06	13,716
Sept	92.27	92.27	92.22	92.22	– .03	92.40	91.97	7,009

Est vol 112,634; vol Wed 163,259; open int 786,900, +10,130.

EUROSWISS (LIFFE) – SFr 1,000,000; pts of 100%

	Open	High	Low	Settle	Change	Lifetime High	Lifetime Low	Open Interest
Dec	95.70	95.73	95.70	95.72	+ .03	96.80	95.14	10,654
Mr95	95.38	95.44	95.38	95.41	+ .03	96.15	94.80	16,351
June	95.10	95.13	95.10	95.13	+ .06	95.48	94.42	7,856
Sept	94.89	94.91	94.88	94.91	+ .08	95.13	94.41	3,710

Est vol 6,061; vol Wed 8,615; open int 38,571, –1,181.

3-MONTH EURO LIRA (LIFFE) – ItI 1,000,000; pts of 100%

	Open	High	Low	Settle	Change	Lifetime High	Lifetime Low	Open Interest
Dec	90.63	90.83	90.60	90.80	+ .13	91.81	88.80	20,472
Mr95	89.74	89.97	89.69	89.93	+ .16	90.77	88.41	30,711
June	89.36	89.59	89.36	89.56	+ .12	90.24	88.05	18,092
Sept	89.17	89.37	89.16	89.35	+ .15	89.85	87.83	21,183
Dec	89.95	89.14	88.95	89.13	+ .18	89.69	87.59	15,925
Mr96	88.73	88.93	88.73	88.91	+ .18	89.27	88.16	10,096

Est vol 16,171; vol Wed 21,878; open int 116,479, –2,954.

GERMAN GOVT. BOND (LIFFE)
250,000 marks; pts of 100%

	Open	High	Low	Settle	Change	Lifetime High	Lifetime Low	Open Interest
Mar	89.62	89.89	89.59	89.74	+ .01	99.30	87.09	174,859
June	....	....	....	89.12	+ .01	90.04	89.55	785

Est vol 56,703; vol Wed 76,844; open int 175,644, +1,636.

ITALIAN GOVT. BOND (LIFFE)
ITL 200,000,000; pts of 100%

	Open	High	Low	Settle	Change	Lifetime High	Lifetime Low	Open Interest
Mar	98.58	99.56	98.53	99.47	+ .79	101.22	95.46	44,373

Est vol 27,124; vol Wed 25,143; open int 44,393, +134.

CANADIAN BANKERS ACCEPTANCE (ME) – C$1,000,000

	Open	High	Low	Settle	Change	Lifetime High	Lifetime Low	Open Interest
Dec	92.94	93.02	92.91	93.01	+ .17	95.76	90.85	33,046
Mr95	91.57	91.79	91.55	91.75	+ .31	95.56	90.86	45,821
June	91.20	91.24	91.10	91.21	+ .25	95.33	90.47	23,238
Sept	91.10	91.10	90.99	91.04	+ .16	95.11	90.42	12,257
Dec	90.91	90.98	90.89	90.94	+ .11	94.79	90.15	7,316
Mr96	90.88	90.88	90.85	90.89	+ .09	92.27	89.95	5,367
June	90.86	90.86	90.85	90.83	+ .05	91.19	89.92	9,594
Sept	90.78	90.80	90.75	90.76	+ .06	90.80	90.42	3,910

Est vol 14,280; vol Wed 19,966; open int 140,549, +6,765.

10 YR. CANADIAN GOVT. BONDS (ME) – C$100,000

	Open	High	Low	Settle	Change	Lifetime High	Lifetime Low	Open Interest
Dec	....	....	....	99.29	+ .25	102.60	95.60	5,342
Mr95	98.63	98.80	98.45	98.57	+ .25	99.37	97.59	22,421

Est vol 2,888; vol Wed 6,500; open int 27,763, –3,089.

10 YR. FRENCH GOVT. BONDS (MATIF)
FFr 500,000; 100ths of 100%

	Open	High	Low	Settle	Change	Lifetime High	Lifetime Low	Open Interest
Dec	111.87	111.96	111.78	111.80	– .14	118.44	108.98	35,555
Mr95	111.12	111.24	111.08	111.10	– .14	115.90	108.22	113,310
June	110.50	110.50	110.44	110.42	– .12	111.94	107.66	2,810
Sept	109.92	109.92	109.92	109.84	– .12	111.32	109.44	800

Est vol 165,026; vol Wed 200,802; open int 218,505, +1,762.

3 YR. COMMONWEALTH T-BONDS (SFE) – A$100,000

	Open	High	Low	Settle	Change	Lifetime High	Lifetime Low	Open Interest
Dec	89.73	89.78	89.66	89.77	+ .06	91.46	89.66	89,361
Mr95	89.53	89.59	89.41	89.58	+ .14	90.70	89.41	89,134

Est vol 49,587; vol Wed 80,341; open int 178,495, –82,905.

	Open	High	Low	Settle	Change	Lifetime High	Lifetime Low	Open Interest
Mr95	[illegible]	[illegible]	[illegible]	[illegible]	....	[illegible]	[illegible]	[illegible]
June	3019.	3021.	3000.	3005.	....	3163.5	2997.	2,488

Est vol 28,154; vol Wed 31,198; open int 69,714, –815.

ALL ORDINARIES SHARE PRICE INDEX (SFE)
A$25 times index

	Open	High	Low	Settle	Change	Lifetime High	Lifetime Low	Open Interest
Dec	1895.	1910.	1886.	1909.	+ 40.0	2300.	1793.	81,398
Mr95	1910.	1931.	1904.	1927.	+ 41.0	2242.	1803.	20,460
June	1928.	1935.	1928.	1947.	+ 41.0	2200.	1861.	4,983
Sept	1954.	1954.	1954.	1969.	+ 41.0	2080.	1925.	1,245

Est vol 12,237; vol Wed 10,026; open int 108,136, +1,952.
The index: High 1900.3; Low 1863.8; Close 1895.0 +31.2

OTHER FUTURES

Settlement prices of selected contracts. Actual volume (from previous session) and open interest of all contract months.

	Vol.	High	Low	Close	Net Change	Lifetime High	Lifetime Low	Open Interest
BARLEY (WPG) 20 metric tons; Can. $ per ton								
Feb	347	123.00	121.90	122.70	+ .40	126.40	90.80	9,177
BRITISH POUND (MCE) 12,500 pounds; $ per pound								
Mar	373	1.5638	1.5592	1.5626	+ .0006	1.6366	.9412	485
CANADIAN GOVT. BONDS (CBT) C$100,000; $ per C$								
Mar	0	....	....	98.57	+ .25	97.90	97.85	0
CATTLE-LIVE (MCE) 20,000 lb.; ¢ per lb.								
Feb	72	70.50	70.20	70.50	+ .33	73.80	66.85	192
CORN (MCE) 1,000 bu.; cents per bu.								
Mar	713	228	227	227¾	– ¼	282	220½	3,916
DEUTSCHEMARK (MCE) 62,500 marks; $ per mark								
Mar	144	.6382	.6363	.6377	– .0007	.6723	.6316	572
DEUTSCHEMARK FORWARD (CME) 250,000 U.S. $; mark per $								
Mar	978	....	....	156837	+ 17.0	157035	154030	7,970
DEUTSCHEMARK–FR. FRANC CROSSRATE (FINEX) 500,000 Dmarks; FFr per DM								
Mar	63	3.4503	3.4488	3.4460	– .0030	3.4511	3.4133	1,429
DEUTSCHEMARK–JAP. YEN CROSSRATE (FINEX) 125,000 marks; yen per mark								
Mar	29	63.83	63.75	63.88	– .03	64.99	62.66	2,665
DM ROLLING SPOT (CME) $250,000; DM per U.S. $								
Mar	1,345	1.5743	1.5693	1.5711	+ .0017	1.5743	1.4865	5,708
DIAMMONIUM PHOSPHATE (CBT) 100 tons; $ per ton								
Mar	183	170.00	170.00	170.00	....	171.00	156.00	329
EURODOLLAR (MCE) $500,000; pts. of 100%								
Mar	22	92.92	92.75	92.83	+ .13	95.58	92.57	325
EUROMARK (CME) DM 1,000,000; pts. of 100%								
Mar	0	....	....	94.36	+ .06	95.89	94.01	10
EUROTOP 100 INDEX (CMX) – $100 times index								
Mar	237	1175.8	1175.0	1175.5	+ 7.5	1320.0	1159.0	1,285
The index: High 1167.5; Low 1163.3; Close 1163.5 +5.6								
FLAXSEED (WPG) 20 metric tons; Can. $ per ton								
Mar	206	310.40	307.60	309.20	– .80	325.00	267.20	5,017
FRENCH FRANC (CME) 500,000 FF; $ per franc								
Mar	596	.18480	.18428	.18480	– .0006	.19640	.17496	1,548
GOLD-NY (MCE) 33.2 fine troy oz.; cents per troy oz.								
Feb	11	382.40	381.40	382.70	+ 1.20	405.20	378.40	1,090
GOLD-KILO (CBT) 32.15 troy oz.; $ per troy oz.								
Fec	41	382.80	381.50	382.80	+ 1.50	405.50	377.50	382
HOGS (MCE) 20,000 lb.; ¢ per lb.								
Feb	70	38.40	37.20	38.10	+ 1.18	50.50	34.05	584
JAPANESE YEN (MCE) 6.25 million yen; $ per yen (.00)								
Mar	169	1.0074	1.0055	1.0057	....	1.0538	.9800	336
KC MINI VALUE LINE (KC) – 100 times index								
Mar	333	447.40	443.40	447.00	+ 3.90	478.10	434.30	1,146
KC VALUE LINE INDEX (KC) – 500 times index								
Mar	479	447.40	443.40	447.00	+ 4.00	478.10	434.30	1,440
The index: High 442.49; Low 438.19; Close 442.49 +4.24								
LUMBER (CME) 160,000 bd .ft., $ per 1,000 bd.ft.								
Jan	593	299.50	287.00	290.00	– 8.50	465.00	294.00	1,882
OATS (MCE) 1,000 bu.; ¢ per bu.								
Mar	7	122¼	121	122¼	+ 1½	145	116¾	101
PLATINUM (MCE) 25 troy oz.; cents per troy oz.								
Jan	554	410.00	410.00	411.70	+ 3.10	431.50	391.20	627
PROPANE (NYM) 42,000 gal.; ¢ per gal.								
Jan	268	34.80	34.60	34.70	+ .25	36.05	29.90	3,125
RUSSELL 2000 INDEX (CME) $500 times index								
Mar	350	243.50	240.25	243.50	+ 4.00	277.50	236.80	3,833
SILVER (MCE) 1,000 troy oz.; cents per troy oz.								
Mar	10	485.0	485.0	484.7	+ 3.2	592.0	459.0	2,327
SILVER (CBT) 5,000 troy oz.; cents per troy oz.								
Feb	0	476.0	473.0	476.0	+ 3.5	573.0	464.0	6,337
SOYBEANS (MCE) 1,000 bu.; cents per bu.								
Jan	2,142	563¾	559	562¾	+ 1½	701	537¼	8,915
SOYBEAN MEAL (MCE) 20 tons; cents per ton								
Jan	6	157.80	157.80	157.30	– .10	198.50	155.60	191
STERLING-MARK CROSSRATE (FINEX) 125,000 B. Pds; B. Pd per DM								
Mar	15	2.4551	2.4530	2.4546	+ .0042	2.4677	2.3855	1,041
SWISS FRANC (MCE) 62,500 francs; $ per franc								
Mar	111	.7579	.7556	.7570	+ .0002	.8120	.7375	987
10 – YEAR T.NOTES (MCE) 50,000; pts. 32nds of 100%								
Mar	112	100-02	99-31	100-02	+ 5	103-03	98-14	1,356
TORONTO 35 INDEX (TFE) $500 x index								
Mar	1,113	220.50	219.00	220.36	+ 1.76	229.00	212.60	4,609
The index: High 218.62; Low 216.59; Close 218.18 +1.59								
WHEAT (MCE) 1,000 bu.; cents per bu.								
Mar	641	387½	382	386	+ 3½	426½	330½	4,181
WHITE WHEAT (MPLS) 5,000 bu.; cents per bu.								
Mar	212	453	450	453	+ 4	487	355	1,684

Source: *The Wall Street Journal*, December 16, 1994. Reprinted by permission of *The Wall Street Journal*,

Figure 21.2
Trading volume in futures contracts
Source: Chicago Board of Trade *Annual Report*, 1994.

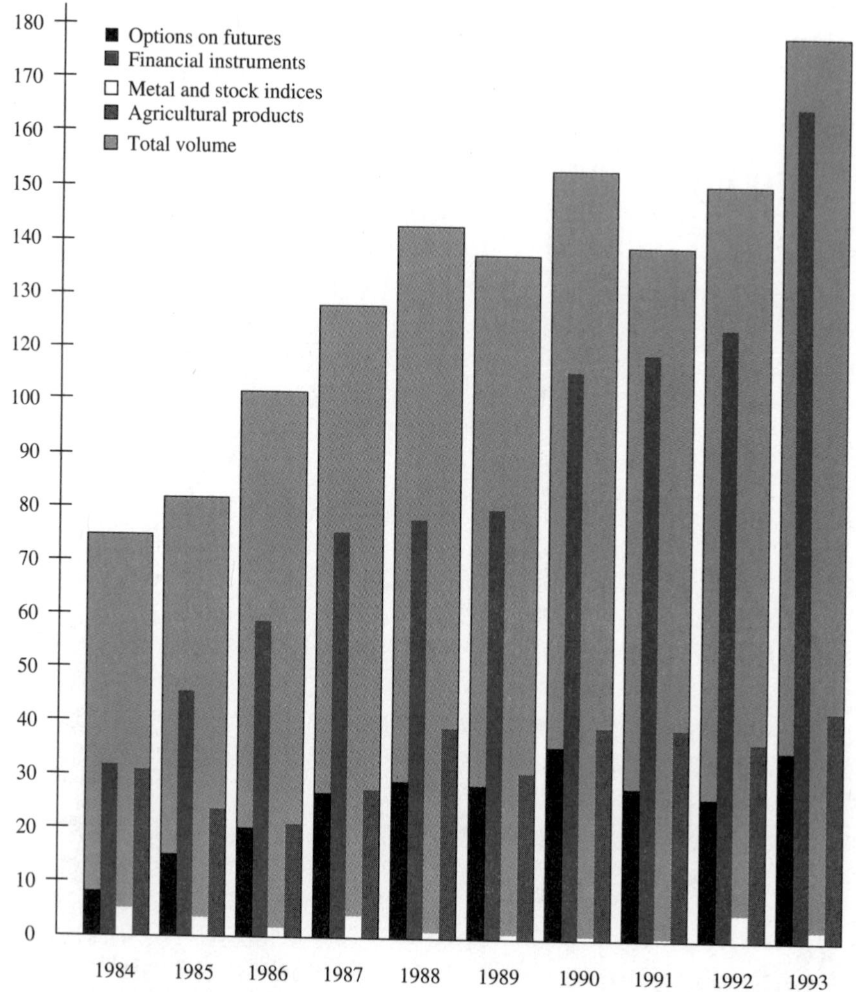

Existing Contracts

Futures and forward contracts are traded on a wide variety of goods in four broad categories: agricultural commodities, metals and minerals (including energy commodities), foreign currencies, and financial futures (fixed-income securities and stock market indexes). The financial futures contracts are a relatively recent innovation, for which trading was introduced in 1975. Innovation in financial futures has been rapid and is ongoing. Figure 21.2 illustrates both the tremendous growth in futures trading in the last decade, and the preeminent role of financial futures. Table 21.1 enumerates some of the various contracts trading in the United States in 1995.

Outside the futures markets, a well-developed network of banks and brokers has established a forward market in foreign exchange. This forward market is not a formal

Table 21.1 Sample of Futures Contracts

Foreign Currencies	Agricultural	Metals and Energy	Interest Rate Futures	Equity Indexes
British pound	Corn	Copper	Eurodollars	S&P 500
Canadian dollar	Oats	Aluminum	Euromark	S&P midcap 400
Japanese yen	Soybeans	Gold	Eurolira	NYSE index
Swiss franc	Soybean meal	Platinum	Euroswiss	Value Line index
French franc	Soybean oil	Palladium	Treasury bonds	Major market index
Deutschemark	Wheat	Silver	Treasury bills	OTC
U.S. dollar index	Barley	Crude oil	Treasury notes	Russell 2000
European currency unit	Flaxseed	Heating oil	Municipal bond index	Nikkei 225
Australian dollar	Canola	Gas oil	LIBOR	Eurotop 100
Mark/Yen cross rate	Rye	Natural gas	Short gilt†	FT-SE index
Sterling/Mark cross rate	Cattle (feeder)	Gasoline	Long gilt†	CAC-40
	Cattle (live)	Propane	Australian government bond	Australia ordinary share
	Hogs	CRB index*	German government bond	Toronto 35
	Pork bellies		Canadian government bond	
	Cocoa		Italian government bond	
	Coffee		Federal funds rate	
	Cotton			
	Orange juice			
	Sugar			
	Lumber			
	Rice			

*The Commodity Research Bureau's index of futures prices of agricultural as well as metal and energy prices.
†Gilts are British government bonds.

exchange in the sense that the exchange specifies the terms of the traded contract. Instead, participants in a forward contract may negotiate for delivery of any quantity of goods, whereas in the formal futures markets contract size is set by the exchange. In forward arrangements, banks and brokers simply negotiate contract for clients (or themselves) as needed.

21.2 Mechanics of Trading in Futures Markets

The Clearinghouse and Open Interest

Trading in futures contracts is more complex than making ordinary stock transactions. If you want to make a stock purchase, your broker simply acts as an intermediary to enable you to buy shares from or sell to another individual through the stock exchange. In futures trading, however, the clearinghouse plays a more active role.

When an investor contacts a broker to establish a futures position, the brokerage firm wires the order to the firm's trader on the floor of the futures exchange. In contrast to stock trading, which involves specialists or market makers in each security, most futures trades in the United States occur among floor traders in the "trading pit" for each contract. Traders use voice or hand signals to signify their desire to buy or sell.

Figure 21.3
A, Trading without the Clearinghouse.
B, Trading with a Clearinghouse

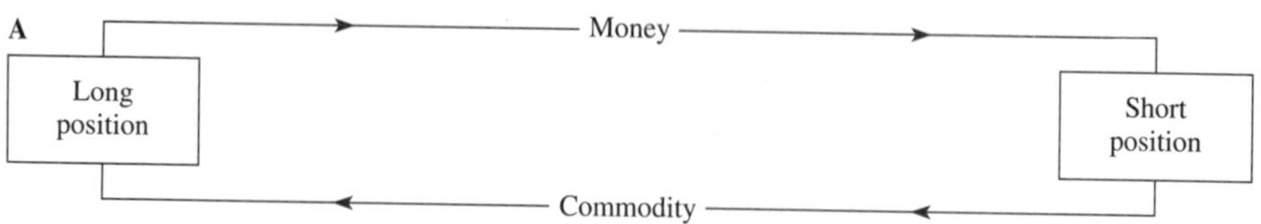

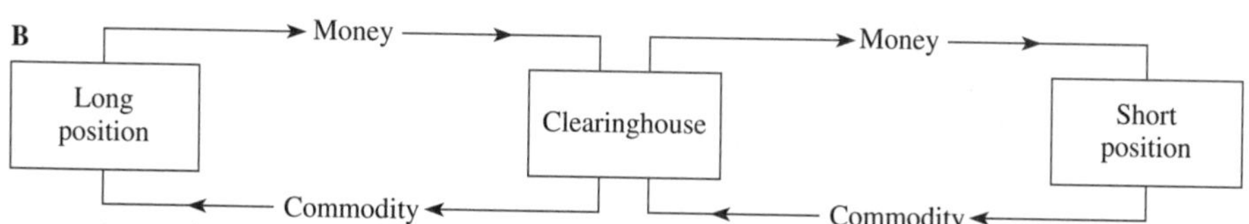

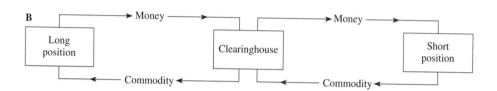

Once a trader willing to accept the opposite side of a trade is located, the trade is recorded and the investor is notified.

At this point, just as is true for options contracts, the **clearinghouse** enters the picture. Rather than having the long and short traders hold contracts with each other, the clearinghouse becomes the seller of the contract for the long position and the buyer of the contract for the short position. The clearinghouse is obligated to deliver the commodity to the long position and to pay for delivery from the short; consequently, the clearinghouse's position nets to zero. This arrangement makes the clearinghouse the trading partner of each trader, both long and short. The clearinghouse, bound to perform on its side of each contract, is the only party that can be hurt by the failure of any trader to observe the obligations of the futures contract. This arrangement is necessary because a futures contract calls for future performance, which cannot be as easily guaranteed as an immediate stock transaction.

Figure 21.3 illustrates the role of the clearinghouse. Panel **A** shows what would happen in the absence of the clearinghouse. The trader in the long position would be obligated to pay the futures price to the short position trader, and the trader in the short position would be obligated to deliver the commodity. Panel **B** shows how the clearinghouse becomes an intermediary, acting as the trading partner for each side of the contract. The clearinghouse's position is neutral, as it takes a long and a short position for each transaction.

The clearinghouse makes it possible for traders to liquidate positions easily. If you are currently long in a contract and want to undo your position, you simply instruct your broker to enter the short side of a contract to close out your position. This is called a *reversing trade*. The exchange nets out your long and short positions, reducing your net position to zero. Your zero net position with the clearinghouse eliminates the need to fulfill at maturity either the original long or reversing short position.

The **open interest** on the contract is the number of contracts outstanding. (Long and short positions are not counted separately, meaning that open interest can be defined as either the number of long or short contracts outstanding.) The clearinghouse's position nets out to zero, and so is not counted in the computation of open interest. When contracts begin trading, open interest is zero. As time passes, open interest increases as progressively more contracts are entered. Almost all traders, however, liquidate their positions before the contract maturity date.

Instead of actually taking or making delivery of the commodity, market participants, virtually all enter reversing trades to cancel their original positions, thereby realizing the profits or losses on the contract. Actual deliveries and purchases of commodities are then made via regular channels of supply, usually via warehouse receipts. The fraction of contracts that result in actual delivery is estimated to range from less than 1% to 3%, depending on the commodity and the activity in the contract. The image of a trader awakening one delivery date with a mountain of wheat in the front yard is amusing, but unlikely.

You can see the typical pattern of open interest in Figure 21.1. In the corn contract, for example, the December delivery contract is close to maturity, and open interest is relatively small; most contracts have been reversed already. The next few maturities have significant open interest. Finally, the most distant maturity contracts have little open interest, as they have been available only recently, and few participants have yet traded. For other contracts, where January or February is the nearest maturity, open interest is typically highest in the nearest contract.

Marking to Market and the Margin Account

Anyone who saw the film *Trading Places* knows that Eddie Murphy as a trader in orange juice futures had no intention of purchasing or delivering orange juice. Traders simply bet on the futures price of juice. The total profit or loss realized by the long trader who buys a contract at time 0 and closes, or reverses, it at time t is just the change in the futures price over the period, $F_t - F_0$. Symmetrically, the short trader earns $F_0 - F_t$.

The process by which profits or losses accrue to traders is called *marking to market.* At initial execution of a trade, each trader establishes a margin account. The margin is a security account consisting of cash or near-cash securities, such as Treasury bills, that ensures the trader is able to satisfy the obligations of the futures contract. Because both parties to a futures contract are exposed to losses, both must post margin. If the initial margin on corn, for example, is 10%, then the trader must post $1,138.75 per contract of the margin account. This is 10% of the value of the contract (2.2775 per bushel × 5,000 bushels per contract).

Because the initial margin may be satisfied by posting interest-earning securities, the requirement does not impose a significant opportunity cost of funds on the trader. The initial margin is usually set between 5% and 15% of the total value of the contract. Contracts written on assets with more volatile prices require higher margins.

On any day that futures contracts trade, futures prices may rise or may fall. Instead of waiting until the maturity date for traders to realize all gains and losses, the clearinghouse requires all positions to recognize profits as they accrue daily. If the futures price of corn rises from 227¾ to 229¾ cents per bushel, the clearinghouse credits the margin account of the long position for 5,000 bushels times 2 cents per bushel, or $100 per contract. Conversely, for the short position, the clearinghouse takes this amount from the margin account for each contract held. Although the price of corn has changed by only 0.88% (2/227.75), the percentage return on the long corn position on that day is 10 times greater: 8.8% ($100/$1,138.75). The 10-to-1 ratio of percentage changes reflects the leverage inherent in the futures position, since the corn contract was established with an initial margin of 1/10th the value of the underlying asset.

This daily settling is called **marking to market.** It means the maturity date of the contract does not govern realization of profit or loss. Marking to market ensures that, as futures prices change, the proceeds accrue to the trader's margin account immediately. We will provide a more detailed example of this process shortly.

CONCEPT CHECK Question 2. What must be the net inflow or outlay from marking to market for the clearinghouse?

If a trader accrues sustained losses from daily marking to market, the margin account may fall below a critical value called the **maintenance, or variation, margin.** Once the value of the account falls below this value, the trader receives a margin call. For example, if the maintenance margin on corn is 5%, then the margin call will go out when the 10% margin initially posted has fallen about in half, to $569 per contract. (This requires that the futures price fall only about 12 cents, as each 1-cent drop in the futures price results in a loss of $50 to the long position.) Either new funds must be transferred into the margin account, or the broker will close out enough of the trader's position to meet the required margin for that position. This procedure safeguards the position of the clearinghouse. Positions are closed out before the margin account is exhausted—the trader's losses are covered, and the clearinghouse is not affected.

Marking to market is the major way in which futures and forward contracts differ, besides contract standardization. Futures follow this pay- (or receive-) as-you-go method. Forward contracts are simply held until maturity, and no funds are transferred until that date, although the contracts may be traded.

It is important to note that the futures price on the delivery date will equal the spot price of the commodity on that date. As a maturing contract calls for immediate delivery, the futures price on that day must equal the spot price—the cost of the commodity from the two competing sources is equalized in a competitive market.[1] You may obtain delivery of the commodity either by purchasing it directly in the spot market or by entering the long side of a futures contract.

A commodity available from two sources (spot or futures market) must be priced identically, or else investors will rush to purchase it from the cheap source in order to sell it in the high-priced market. Such arbitrage activity could not persist without prices

[1] Small differences between the spot and futures price at maturity may persist because of transportation costs, but this is a minor factor.

adjusting to eliminate the arbitrage opportunity. Therefore, the futures price and the spot price must converge at maturity. This is called the **convergence property.**

For an investor who establishes a long position in a contract now (time 0) and holds that position until maturity (time T), the sum of all daily settlements will equal $F_T - F_0$, where F_T stands for the futures price at contract maturity. Because of convergence, however, the futures price at maturity, F_T, equals the spot price, P_T, so total futures profits also may be expressed as $P_T - F_0$. Thus, we see that profits on a futures contract held to maturity perfectly track changes in the value of the underlying asset.

A concrete example can illustrate the time profile of returns to a futures contract. Assume the current futures price for silver for delivery five days from today is $5.10 per ounce. Suppose that over the next five days, the futures price evolves as follows:

Day	Futures Price
0 (today)	$5.10
1	5.20
2	5.25
3	5.18
4	5.18
5 (delivery)	5.21

The spot price of silver on the delivery date is $5.21: the convergence property implies that the price of silver in the spot market must equal the futures price on the delivery day.

The daily mark-to-market settlements for each contract held by the long position will be as follows:

Day	Profit (Loss) per Ounce	× 5,000 Ounces/Contract = Daily Proceeds
1	5.20 − 5.10 = .10	$500
2	5.25 − 5.20 = .05	250
3	5.18 − 5.25 = −.07	−350
4	5.18 − 5.18 = 0	0
5	5.21 − 5.18 = .03	150
		Sum = $550

The profit on Day 1 is the increase in the futures price from the previous day, or ($5.20 − $5.10) per ounce. Because each silver contract on the Commodity Exchange (CMX) calls for purchase and delivery of 5,000 ounces, the total profit per contract is 5,000 times $0.10, or $500. On Day 3, when the futures price falls, the long position's margin account will be debited by $350. By Day 5, the sum of all daily proceeds is $550. This is exactly equal to 5,000 times the difference between the final futures price of $5.21 and original futures price of $5.10. Thus, the sum of all the daily proceeds (per ounce of silver held long) equals $P_T - F_0$.

Cash versus Actual Delivery

Most futures markets call for delivery of an actual commodity such as a particular grade of wheat or a specified amount of foreign currency if the contract is not reversed before maturity. For agricultural commodities, where quality of the delivered good may vary, the exchange sets quality standards as part of the futures contract. In some cases, contracts may be settled with higher- or lower-grade commodities. In these cases, a premium or discount is applied to the delivered commodity to adjust for the quality difference.

Some futures contracts call for **cash delivery.** An example is a stock index futures contract where the underlying asset is an index such as the Standard & Poor's 500 or the New York Stock Exchange Index. Delivery of every stock in the index clearly would be impractical. Hence, the contract calls for "delivery" of a cash amount equal to the value that the index attains on the maturity date of the contract. The sum of all the daily settlements from marking to market results in the long position realizing total profits or losses of $S_T - F_0$, where S_T is the value of the stock index on the maturity date T, and F_0 is the original futures price. Cash settlement closely mimics actual delivery, except the cash value of the asset rather than the asset itself is delivered by the short position in exchange for the futures price.

More concretely, the S&P 500 index contract calls for delivery of \$500 times the value of the index. At maturity, the index might list at 475, the market-value-weighted index of the prices of all 500 stocks in the index. The cash settlement contract calls for delivery of \$500 × 475, or \$237,500 cash in return for 500 times the futures price. This yields exactly the same profit as would result from directly purchasing 500 units of the index for \$237,500 and then delivering it for 500 times the original futures price.

Regulations

Futures markets are regulated by the Commodities Futures Trading Commission, a federal agency. The CFTC sets capital requirements for member firms of the futures exchanges, authorizes trading in new contracts, and oversees maintenance of daily trading records.

The futures exchange may set limits on the amount by which futures prices may change from one day to the next. For example, the price limit on silver contracts traded on the Chicago Board of Trade is \$1, which means that if silver futures close today at \$5.10 per ounce, trades in silver tomorrow may vary only between \$6.10 and \$4.10 per ounce. The exchanges may increase or reduce these price limits in response to perceived changes in price volatility of the contract. Price limits are often eliminated as contracts approach maturity, usually in the last month of trading.

Price limits traditionally are viewed as a means to limit violent price fluctuations. This reasoning seems dubious. Suppose an international monetary crisis overnight drives up the spot price of silver to \$8.00. No one would sell silver futures at prices for future delivery as low as \$5.10. Instead, the futures price would rise each day by the \$1 limit, although the quoted price would represent only an unfilled bid order—no contracts would trade at the low quoted price. After several days of limit moves of \$1 per day, the futures price would finally reach its equilibrium level, and trading would occur again. This process means no one could unload a position until the price reached its equilibrium level. This example shows that price limits offer no real protection against fluctuations in equilibrium prices.

Taxation

Because of the mark-to-market procedure, investors do not have control over the tax year in which they realize gains or losses. Instead, price changes are realized gradually, with each daily settlement. Therefore, taxes are paid at year-end on cumulated profits or losses regardless of whether the position has been closed out.

21.3 Futures Markets Strategies

Hedging and Speculation

Hedging and speculating are two polar uses of futures markets. A speculator uses a futures contract to profit from movements in futures prices, a hedger to protect against price movement.

If speculators believe prices will increase, they will take a long position for expected profits. Conversely, they exploit expected price declines by taking a short position. As an example of a speculative strategy, let's consider the use of the T-bond futures contract, the listing for which appear in Figure 21.1. Each T-bond contract on the Chicago Board of Trade (CBT) calls for delivery of $100,000 par value of bonds. The listed futures price of 99–29 (i.e., 99 and 29/32) means the market price of the underlying bonds is 99.90625% of par, or $99,906.25. Therefore, for every increase of one point in the T-bond futures price (e.g., to 100–29), the long position gains $1,000, and the short loses that amount. Therefore, if you are bullish on bond prices, you might speculate by buying T-bond futures contracts.

If the T-bond futures price increases by one point to 100–29, then you profit by your speculation by $1,000 per contract. If the forecast is incorrect, and T-bond futures prices decline, you lose $1,000 times the decrease in the futures price for each contract purchased. Speculators bet on the direction of futures price movements.

Why does a speculator buy a T-bond futures contract? Why not buy T-bonds directly? One reason lies in transaction costs, which are far smaller in futures markets.

Another reason is the leverage futures trading provides. Recall that each T-bond contract calls for delivery of $100,000 par value, worth about $99,906 in our example. The initial margin required for this account might be only $10,000. The $1,000 per contract gain translates into a 10% ($1,000/$10,000) return on the money put up, despite the fact that the T-bond futures price increases only 1% (1/99.906). Futures margins, therefore, allow speculators to achieve much greater leverage than is available from direct trading in a commodity.

Hedgers by contrast use futures markets to insulate themselves against price movements. An investor holding a T-bond portfolio, for example, might anticipate a period of interest rate volatility and want to protect the value of the portfolio against price fluctuations. In this case, the investor has no desire to bet on price movements in either direction. To achieve such protection, a hedger takes short position in T-bond futures, which obligates the hedger to deliver T-bonds at the contract maturity date for the current futures price. This locks in the sales price for the bonds and guarantees that the total value of the bond-plus-futures position at the maturity date is the futures price.[2]

For illustration, suppose as in Figure 21.1 that the futures price for December delivery is $99.91 per $100 par value (rounded off to the nearest penny), and that the only three possible T-bond prices in December are $98.91, $99.91, and $100.91. If investors currently hold 200 bonds, each with par value $1,000, they would take short positions in two contracts, each for $100,000 par value. Protecting the value of a portfolio with short futures positions is called *short hedging*. Taking the futures position requires no current investment. (The initial margin requirement is small relative to the size of the contract, and because it may be posted in interest-bearing securities, it does not represent a time-value or opportunity cost to the hedger.)

The profits in December from each of the two short futures contracts will be 1,000 times any decrease in the futures price. At maturity, the convergence property ensures that the final futures price will equal the spot price of the T-bonds. Hence, the futures profit will be 2,000 times $(F_0 - P_T)$, where P_T is the price of the bonds on the delivery date, and F_0 is the original futures price, $99.91.

Now consider the hedged portfolio consisting of the bonds and the short futures positions. The portfolio value as a function of the bond price in December can be computed as follows:

	T-Bond Price in December		
	$98.91	**$99.91**	**$100.91**
Bond holdings (value = 2,000 P_T)	$197,820	$199,820	$201,820
Futures profits or losses	2,000	0	− 2,000
TOTAL	$199,820	$199,820	$199,820

The total portfolio value is unaffected by the eventual bond price, which is what the hedger wants. The gains or losses on the bond holdings are exactly offset by those on the two contracts held short.

For example, if bond prices fall to $98.91, the losses on the bond portfolio are offset by the $2,000 gain on the futures contracts. That profit equals the difference between the futures price on the maturity date (which equals the spot price on that date of $98.91) and the originally contracted futures price of $99.91. For short contracts, a profit of $1 per $100 par value is realized from the fall in the spot price. Because two contracts call for delivery of $200,000 par value, this results in a $2,000 gain that offsets the decline in the value of the bonds held in portfolio. In contrast to a speculator, a hedger is indifferent to the ultimate price of the asset. The short hedger who has in essence arranged to sell the asset for an agreed-upon price need not be concerned about further developments in the market price.

[2] To keep things simple, we will assume that the T-bond futures contract calls for delivery of a bond with the same coupon and maturity as that in the investor's portfolio. In practice, a variety of bonds may be delivered to satisfy the contract, and a "conversion factor" is used to adjust for the relative values of the eligible delivery bonds. We will ignore this complication.

To generalize this numerical example, you can note that the bond will be worth P_T at maturity, whereas the profit on the futures contract is $F_0 - P_T$. The sum of the two positions is F_0 dollars, which is independent of the eventual bond price.

A *long hedge* is the analogue to a short hedge for a purchaser of an asset. Consider, for example, a pension fund manager who anticipates a cash inflow in two months that will be invested in fixed-income securities. The manager views T-bonds as very attractively priced now and would like to lock in current prices and yields until the investment actually can be made two months hence. The manager can lock in the effective cost of the purchase by entering the long side of a contract, which commits her to purchasing at the current futures price.

CONCEPT CHECK Question 3. Suppose, as in our example, that T-bonds will be priced at $98.91, $99.91, or $100.91 in two months. Show that the cost in December of purchasing $200,000 par value of T-bonds net of the profit/loss on two long T-bond contracts will be $199,820 regardless of the eventual bond price.

Exact futures hedging may be impossible for some goods because the necessary futures contract is not traded. For example, miners of bauxite, the ore from which aluminum is made, might like to trade in bauxite futures, but they cannot because such contracts are not listed. Because bauxite and aluminum prices are highly correlated, however, a close hedge may be established by shorting aluminum futures. Hedging a position using futures on another commodity is called *cross-hedging*.

CONCEPT CHECK Question 4. What are the sources of risk to an investor who uses aluminum futures to hedge an inventory of bauxite?

Futures contracts may be used also as general portfolio hedges. Bodie and Rosansky[3] found that commodity futures returns have had a negative correlation with the stock market. Investors therefore may add a diversified portfolio of futures contracts to a diversified stock portfolio to lower the standard deviation of the overall rate of return. Moreover, the average rate of increase in commodity futures prices has been roughly the same as for common stock as these futures show:

	1950 to 1976	
	Average Annual Return	**Annual Standard Deviation**
Portfolio of T-bills and 23 commodity futures	13.85%	22.43%
S&P 500 index	13.05%	18.95%

The correlation coefficient between the two portfolios during the estimation period was −.24. This implies that long positions in commodity futures would add substantial diversification benefits to a stock portfolio.

[3] Zvi Bodie and Victor Rosansky, "Risk and Return in Commodity Futures," *Financial Analysts Journal,* May/June 1980.

To illustrate, suppose that you invest a fraction of your total wealth in stocks and use the remainder to invest in commodity futures contracts, posting 100% margin with T-bills. The stock-futures-bills portfolio presents you with substantial reduction in risk and no sacrifice in expected return. Bodie and Rosansky found that a portfolio composed of 60% stock and 40% T-bills with futures would have had a return of 13.36% and standard deviation of only 12.68%: virtually an unchanged average return from either portfolio taken alone, but with roughly a one-third reduction in standard deviation.

Commodity futures are also inflation hedges. When commodity prices increase because of unanticipated inflation, returns from long futures positions will increase because the contracts call for delivery of goods for the price agreed on before the high inflation rate became a reality.

Basis Risk and Hedging

The **basis** is the difference between the futures price and the spot price.[4] As we have noted, on the maturity date of a contract, the basis must be zero: The convergence property implies that $F_T - P_T = 0$. Before maturity, however, the futures price for later delivery may differ substantially from the current spot price.

We discussed the case of a short hedger who holds an asset (T-bonds, in our example) and a short position to deliver that asset in the future. If the asset and futures contract are held until maturity, the hedger bears no risk, as the ultimate value of the portfolio on the delivery date is determined by the current futures price. Risk is eliminated because the futures price and spot price at contract maturity must be equal: gains and losses on the futures and the commodity position will exactly cancel. If the contract and asset are to be liquidated early, before contract maturity, however, the hedger bears **basis risk,** because the futures price and spot price need not move in perfect lockstep at all times before the delivery date. In this case, gains and losses on the contract and the asset need not exactly offset each other.

Some speculators try to profit from movements in the basis. Rather than betting on the direction of the futures or spot prices per se, they bet on the changes in the difference between the two. A long spot-short futures position will profit when the basis narrows. For example, consider an investor holding 100 ounces of gold, who is short one gold-futures contract. Suppose that gold today sells for $391 an ounce; and the futures price for June delivery is $396 an ounce. Therefore, the basis is currently $5. Tomorrow, the spot price might increase to $394, while the futures price increases to $398.50, so the basis narrows to $4.50. The investor gains $3 per ounce on the gold holdings, but loses $2.50 an ounce on the short futures position. The net gain is the decrease in the basis, or $.50 an ounce.

A related strategy is a **spread** position, where the investor takes a long position in a futures contract of one maturity and a short position in a contract on the same commodity, but with a different maturity. Profits accrue if the difference in futures prices

[4] Usage of the word *basis* is somewhat loose. It sometimes is used to refer to the futures-spot difference $F - P$, and sometimes to the spot-futures difference $P - F$. We will consistently call the basis $F - P$.

between the two contracts changes in the hoped-for direction; that is, if the futures price on the contract held long increases by more (or decreases by less) than the futures price on the contract held short.

Consider an investor who holds a September maturity contract long and a June contract short. If the September futures price increases by 5 cents while the June futures price increases by 4 cents, the net gain will be 5 cents − 4 cents, or 1 cent. Like basis strategies, spread positions aim to exploit movements in relative price structures rather than to profit from movements in the general level of prices.

21.4 The Determination of Futures Prices

The Spot-Futures Parity Theorem

We have seen that a futures contract can be used to hedge changes in the value of the underlying asset. If the hedge is perfect, meaning that the asset-plus-futures portfolio has no risk, then the hedged position must provide a rate of return equal to the rate on other risk-free investments. Otherwise, there will be arbitrage opportunities that investors will exploit until prices are brought back into line. This insight can be used to derive the theoretical relationship between a futures price and the price of its underlying asset.

Suppose, for example, that the S&P 500 index currently is at 460 and an investor who holds $460 in a mutual fund indexed to the S&P 500 wishes to temporarily hedge her exposure to market risk. Assume that the indexed portfolio pays dividends totaling $8 over the course of the year, and for simplicity, that all dividends are paid at year-end. Finally, assume that the futures price for year-end delivery of the S&P 500 contract is $475.[5] Let's examine the end-of-year proceeds for various values of the stock index if the investor hedges her portfolio by entering the short side of the futures contract.

Value of stock portfolio	$440	$450	$460	$470	$480	$490
Payoff from short futures position (equals $F_0 - F_T = \$475 - S_T$)	35	25	15	5	−5	−15
Dividend income	8	8	8	8	8	8
TOTAL	$483	$483	$483	$483	$483	$483

The payoff from the short futures position equals the difference between the original futures price, $475, and the year-end stock price. This is because of convergence: The futures price at contract maturity will equal the stock price at that time.

Notice that the overall position is perfectly hedged. Any increase in the value of the indexed stock portfolio is offset by an equal decrease in the payoff of the short futures position, resulting in a final value independent of the stock price. The $483 payoff is the sum of the current futures price, $F_0 = \$475$, and the $8 dividend. It is as though the

[5] Actually, the futures contract calls for delivery of $500 times the value of the S&P 500 index, so that each contract would be settled for $500 times the index. We will simplify by assuming that you can buy a contract for one unit rather than 500 units of the index. In practice, one contract would hedge about $500 × 460 = $230,000 worth of stock. Of course, institutional investors would consider a stock portfolio of this size to be quite small.

investor arranged to sell the stock at year-end for the current futures price, thereby eliminating price risk and locking in total proceeds equal to the sales price plus dividends paid before the sale.

What rate of return is earned on this riskless position? The stock investment requires an initial outlay of \$460, whereas the futures position is established without an initial cash outflow. Therefore, the \$460 portfolio grows to a year-end value of \$483, providing a rate of return of 5%. More generally, a total investment of S_0, the current stock price, grows to a final value of $F_0 + D$, where D is the dividend payout on the portfolio. The rate of return is therefore:

$$\text{Rate of return on perfectly hedged stock portfolio} = \frac{(F_0 + D) - S_0}{S_0}$$

This return is essentially riskless. We observe F_0 at the beginning of the period when we enter the futures contract. While dividend payouts are not perfectly riskless, they are highly predictable over short periods, especially for diversified portfolios. Any uncertainty is *extremely* small compared to the uncertainty in stock prices.

Presumably, 5% must be the rate of return available on other riskless investments. If not, then investors would face two competing risk-free strategies with different rates of return, a situation that could not last. Therefore, we conclude that

$$\frac{(F_0 + D) - S_0}{S_0} = r_f$$

Rearranging, we find that the futures price must be

$$F_0 = S_0(1 + r_f) - D = S_0(1 + r_f - d) \tag{21.1}$$

where d is the dividend yield on the stock portfolio, defined as D/S_0. This result is called the **spot-futures parity theorem.** It gives the normal or theoretically correct relationship between spot and futures prices.

Suppose that parity were violated. For example, suppose the risk-free interest rate in the economy were only 4% so that according to parity, the futures price should be \$460(1.04) − 8 = \$470.40. The actual futures price, F_0 = \$475, is \$4.60 higher than its "appropriate" value. This implies that an investor can make arbitrage profits by shorting the relatively overpriced futures contract and buying the relatively underpriced stock portfolio using money borrowed at the 4% market interest rate. The proceeds from this strategy would be as follows:

Action	Initial Cash Flow	Cash Flow in One Year
Borrow \$460, repay with interest in one year	+\$460	−460(1.04) = −\$478.40
Buy stock for \$460	−\$460	S_T + \$8 dividend
Enter short futures position (F_0 = \$475)	0	\$475 − S_T
TOTAL	0	\$4.60

The net initial investment of the strategy is zero. But its cash flow in one year is positive and riskless. The payoff is \$4.60 regardless of the stock price. This payoff is precisely equal to the mispricing of the futures contract relative to its parity value.

When parity is violated, the strategy to exploit the mispricing produces an arbitrage profit—a riskless profit requiring no initial net investment. If such an opportunity existed, all market participants would rush to take advantage of it. The results? The stock price would be bid up, and/or the futures price offered down until equation 21.1 is satisfied. A similar analysis applies to the possibility that F_0 is less than \$470.40. In this case, you simply reverse the strategy above to earn riskless profits. We conclude, therefore, that in a well-functioning market in which arbitrage opportunities are competed away, $F_0 = S_0(1 + r_f) - D$.

CONCEPT CHECK Question 5. Return to the arbitrage strategy just laid out. What would be the three steps of the strategy if F_0 were too low, say \$465? Work out the cash flows of the strategy now and in one year in a table like the one in the text.

The arbitrage strategy can be represented more generally as follows:

Action	Initial Cash Flow	Cash Flow in One Year
1. Borrow S_0	S_0	$-S_0(1 + r_f)$
2. Buy stock for S_0	$-S_0$	$S_T + D$
3. Enter short futures position	0	$F_0 - S_T$
TOTAL	0	$F_0 - S_0(1 + r_f) + D$

The initial cash flow is zero by construction: The money necessary to purchase the stock in Step 1 is borrowed in Step 2, and the futures position in Step 3, which is used to hedge the value of the stock position, does not require an initial outlay. Moreover, the total cash flow to the strategy at year-end is riskless because it involves only terms that are already known when the contract is entered. This situation could not persist, as all investors would try to cash in on the arbitrage opportunity. Ultimately prices would change until the year-end cash flow is reduced to zero, at which point F_0 would once again equal $S_0(1 + r_f) - D$.

The parity relationship also is called the **cost-of-carry relationship** because it asserts that the futures price is determined by the relative costs of buying a stock with deferred delivery in the futures market versus buying it in the spot market with immediate delivery and "carrying" it in inventory. If you buy stock now, you tie up your funds and incur a time-value-of-money cost of r_f per period. On the other hand, you receive dividend payments with a current yield of d. The net carrying-cost advantage of deferring delivery of the stock is therefore $r_f - d$ per period. This advantage must be offset by a differential between the futures price and the spot price. The price differential just offsets the cost-of-carry advantage when $F_0 = S_0(1 + r_f - d)$.

The parity relationship is easily generalized to multiperiod applications. We simply recognize that the difference between the futures and spot price will be larger as the maturity of the contract is longer. This reflects the longer period to which we apply the net cost of carry. For contract maturity of T periods, the parity relationship is

$$F_0 = S_0(1 + r_f - d)^T \qquad \textbf{(21.2)}$$

Although we have described parity in terms of stocks and stock index futures, it should be clear that the logic applies as well to any financial futures contract. For gold futures, for example, we would simply set the dividend yield to zero. For bond contracts, we would let the coupon income on the bond play the role of dividend payments. In both cases, the parity relationship would be essentially the same as equation 21.2.

The arbitrage strategy described above should convince you that these parity relationships are more than just theoretical results. Any violations of the parity relationship give rise to arbitrage opportunities that can provide large profits to traders. We will see in the next chapter that index arbitrage in the stock market is a tool to exploit violations of the parity relationship for stock index futures contracts.

Spreads

Just as we can predict the relationship between spot and futures prices, there are similar ways to determine the proper relationships among futures prices for contracts of different maturity dates. Equation 21.2 shows that the futures price is in part determined by time to maturity. If $r_f > d$, as typically is the case for stock index futures, then the futures price will be higher on longer-maturity contracts. For futures on assets like gold, which pay no "dividend yield" we can set $d = 0$ and conclude that F must increase as time to maturity increases.

To be more precise about spread pricing, call $F(T_1)$ the current futures price for delivery at date T_1, and $F(T_2)$ the futures price for delivery at T_2. Let d be the dividend yield of the stock. We know from the parity equation 21.2 that

$$F(T_1) = S_0(1 + r_f - d)^{T_1}$$
$$F(T_1) = S_0(1 + r_f - d)^{T_2}$$

As a result,

$$F(T_2)/F(T_1) = (1 + r_f - d)^{(T_2 - T_1)}$$

Therefore, the basic parity relationship for spreads is

$$F(T_2) = F(T_1)(1 + r_f - d)^{(T_2 - T_1)} \qquad \textbf{(21.3)}$$

Note that equation 21.3 is quite similar to the spot-futures parity relationship. The major difference is in the substitution of $F(T_1)$ for the current spot price. The intuition is also similar. Delaying delivery from T_1 to T_2 provides the long position the knowledge that the stock will be purchased for $F(T_2)$ dollars at T_2 but does not require that money be tied up in the stock until T_2. The savings realized are the net cost of carry between T_1 and T_2. Delaying delivery from T_1 until T_2 frees up $F(T_1)$ dollars, which earn risk-free interest at r_f. The delayed delivery of the stock also results in the lost dividend yield between T_1 and T_2. The net cost of carry saved by delaying the delivery is thus $r_f - d$. This gives the proportional increase in the futures price that is required to compensate market participants for the delayed delivery of the stock and postponement of the payment of the futures price. If the parity condition for spreads is violated, arbitrage opportunities will arise. (Problem 19 at the end of the chapter explores this possibility.)

To see how to use equation 21.3, consider the following data for a hypothetical contract:

Figure 21.4
Gold futures prices, October 1994

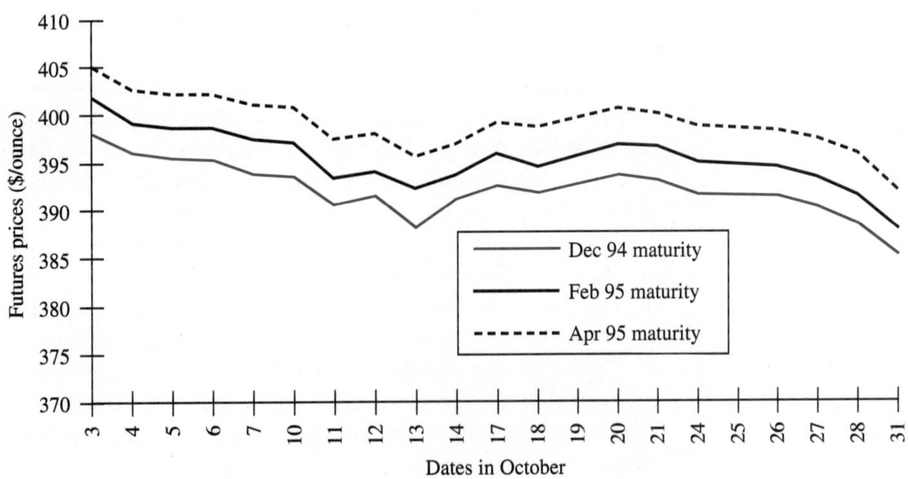

Contract Maturity Data	Futures Price
January 15	105.00
March 15	105.10

Suppose that the effective annual T-bill rate is expected to persist at 5% and that the dividend yield is 4% per year. The "correct" March futures price relative to the January price is, according to equation 21.3,

$$105(1 + .05 - .04)^{1/6} = 105.174$$

The actual March futures price is 105.10, meaning that the March futures price is slightly underpriced compared to the January futures, and that, aside from transaction costs, an arbitrage opportunity seems to be present.

Equation 21.3 shows that futures prices should all move together. Actually, it is not surprising that futures prices for different maturity dates move in unison, because all are linked to the same spot price through the parity relationship. Figure 21.4 plots futures prices on gold for three maturity dates. It is apparent that the prices move in virtual lockstep and that the more distant delivery dates require higher futures prices, as equation 21.3 predicts.

Forward versus Futures Pricing

Until now we have paid little attention to the differing time profile of returns of futures and forward contracts. Instead, we have taken the sum of daily mark-to-market proceeds to the long position as $P_T - F_0$ and assumed for convenience that the entire profit to the futures contract accrues on the delivery date. The parity theorems we have derived apply strictly to forward pricing because they are predicted on the assumption that contract proceeds are realized only on delivery. Although this treatment is appropriate for a forward contract, the actual timing of cash flows influences the determination of the futures price.

Futures prices will deviate from parity values when marking to market gives a systematic advantage to either the long or short position. If marking to market tends to favor the long position, for example, the futures price should exceed the forward price, since the long position will be willing to pay a premium for the advantage of marking to market.

When will marking to market favor either a long or short trader? A trader will benefit if daily settlements are received when the interest rate is high and are paid when the interest rate is low. Receiving payments when the interest rate is high allows investment of proceeds at a high rate; traders therefore prefer a high correlation between the level of the interest rate and the payments received from marking to market. The long position will benefit if futures prices tend to rise when interest rates are high. In such circumstances the long trader will be willing to accept a higher futures price. Whenever there is a positive correlation between interest rates and changes in futures prices, the "fair" futures price will exceed the forward price. Conversely, a negative correlation means that marking to market favors the short position and implies that the equilibrium futures price should be below the forward price.

In practice, however, it appears that the covariance between prices and interest rates is so low that futures prices and forward prices differ by negligible amounts. In estimating the theoretically appropriate difference in futures and forward prices on foreign exchange contracts, Cornell and Reinganum[6] found that the mark-to-market premium is so small that contracts as quoted do not carry enough decimal points to reflect the predicted difference in the two prices.

21.5 Futures Prices versus Expected Spot Prices

So far we have considered the relationship between futures prices and the current spot price. One of the oldest controversies in the theory of futures pricing concerns the relationship between futures price and the expected value of the spot price of the commodity at some *future* date. Three traditional theories have been put forth: the expectations hypothesis, normal backwardation, and contango. Today's consensus is that all of these traditional hypotheses are subsumed by the insights provided by modern portfolio theory. Figure 21.5 show the expected path of futures under the three traditional hypotheses.

Expectations Hypothesis

The *expectations hypothesis* is the simplest theory of futures pricing. It states that the futures price equals the expected value of the future spot price of the asset: $F_0 = E(P_T)$. Under this theory the expected profit to either position of a futures contract would equal

[6] Bradford Cornell and Marc R. Reinganum, "Forward and Futures Prices: Evidence from the Foreign Exchange Markets," *Journal of Finance* 36 (December 1981).

Figure 21.5
Futures price over time, in the special case that the expected spot price remains unchanged

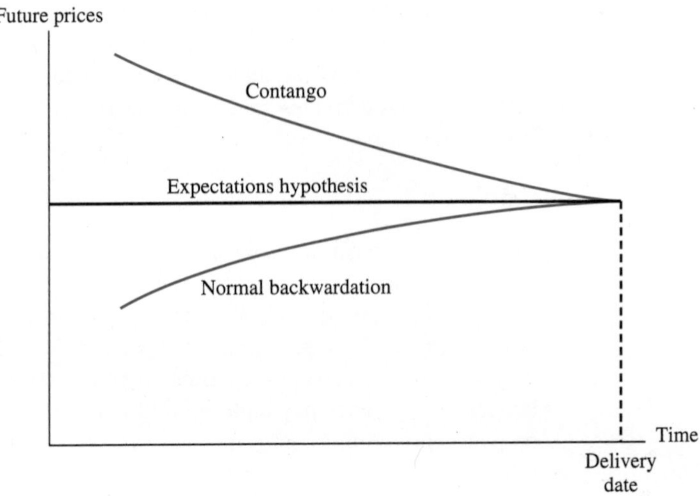

zero: The short position's expected profit is $F_0 - E(P_T)$, whereas the long's is $E(P_T) - F_0$. With $F_0 = E(P_T)$, the expected profit to either side is zero. This hypothesis relies on a notion of risk neutrality. If all market participants are risk neutral, they should agree on a futures price that provides an expected profit of zero to all parties.

The expectations hypothesis bears a resemblance to market equilibrium in a world with no uncertainty; that is, if prices of goods at all future dates are currently known, then the futures price for delivery at any particular date would equal the currently known future spot price for that date. It is a tempting but incorrect leap to assert next that under uncertainty the futures price should equal the currently expected spot price. This view ignores the risk premiums that must be built into futures prices when ultimate spot prices are uncertain.

Normal Backwardation

This theory is associated with the famous British economists John Maynard Keynes and John Hicks. They argued that for most commodities there are natural hedgers who desire to shed risk. For example, wheat farmers will desire to shed the risk of uncertain wheat prices. These farmers will take short positions to deliver wheat in the future at a guaranteed price; they will short hedge. In order to induce speculators to take the corresponding long positions, the farmers need to offer speculators an expectation of profit. Speculators will enter the long side of the contract only if the futures price is below the expected spot price of wheat, for an expected profit of $E(P_T) - F_0$. The speculator's expected profit is the farmers' expected loss, but farmers are willing to bear the expected loss on the contract in order to shed the risk of uncertain wheat prices. The theory of *normal backwardation* thus suggests that the futures price will be bid down to a level below the expected spot price, and will rise over the life of the contract until the maturity date, at which point $F_T = P_T$.

Although this theory recognizes the important role of risk premiums in futures markets, it is based on total variability rather than on systematic risk. (This is not surprising, as Keynes wrote almost 40 years before the development of modern portfolio theory.) The modern view refines the measure of risk used to determine appropriate risk premiums.

Contango

The polar hypothesis to backwardation holds that the natural hedgers are the purchasers of a commodity, rather than the suppliers. In the case of wheat, for example, we would view grain processors as willing to pay a premium to lock in the price that they must pay for wheat. These processors hedge by taking a long position in the futures market; they are long hedgers, as opposed to farmers who are short hedgers. Because long hedgers will agree to pay high futures prices to shed risk, and because speculators must be paid a premium to enter into the short position, the *contango* theory holds that F_0 must exceed $E(P_T)$.

It is clear that any commodity will have both natural long hedgers and short hedgers. The compromise traditional view, called the "net hedging hypothesis," is that F_0 will be less than $E(P_T)$ when short hedgers outnumber long hedgers and vice versa. The strong side of the market will be the side (short or long) that has more natural hedgers. The strong side must pay a premium to induce speculators to enter into enough contracts to balance the "natural" supply of long and short hedgers.

Modern Portfolio Theory

The three traditional hypotheses all envision a mass of speculators willing to enter either side of the futures market if they are sufficiently compensated for the risk they incur. Modern portfolio theory fine-tunes this approach by refining the notion of risk used in the determination of risk premiums. Simply put, if commodity prices pose positive systematic risk, futures prices must be lower than expected spot prices.

As an example of the use of modern portfolio theory to determine the equilibrium futures price, consider once again a stock paying no dividends. If $E(P_T)$ denotes today's expectation of the time T price of the stock, and k denotes the required rate of return on the stock, then the price of the stock today must equal the present value of its expected future payoff as follows:

$$P_0 = \frac{E(P_T)}{(1 + k)^T} \tag{21.4}$$

We also know from the spot-futures parity relationship that

$$P_0 = \frac{F_0}{(1 + r_f)^T} \tag{21.5}$$

Therefore, the right-hand sides of equations 21.4 and 21.5 must be equal. Equating these terms allows us to solve for F_0:

$$F_0 = E(P_T)\left(\frac{1 + r_f}{1 + k}\right)^T \tag{21.6}$$

You can see immediately from equation 21.6 that F_0 will be less than the expectation of P_T whenever k is greater than r_f, which will be the case for any positive-beta asset. This means that the long side of the contract will make an expected profit [F_0 will be lower than $E(P_T)$] when the commodity exhibits positive systematic risk (k is greater than r_f).

Why should this be? A long futures position will provide a profit (or loss) of $P_T - F_0$. If the ultimate realization of P_T involves positive systematic risk, the profit to the long position also involves such risk. Speculators with well-diversified portfolios will be willing to enter long futures positions only if they receive compensation for bearing that risk in the form of positive expected profits. Their expected profits will be positive only if $E(P_T)$ is greater than F_0. The converse is that the short position's profit is the negative of the long's and will have negative systematic risk. Diversified investors in the short position will be willing to suffer an expected loss in order to lower portfolio risk and will be willing to enter the contract even when F_0 is less than $E(P_T)$. Therefore, if P_T has positive beta, F_0 must be less than the expectation of P_T. The analysis is reversed for negative-beta commodities.

CONCEPT CHECK

Question 6. What must be true of the risk of the spot price of an asset if the futures price is an unbiased estimate of the ultimate spot price?

SUMMARY

1. Forward contracts are arrangements that call for future delivery of an asset at a currently agreed-on price. The long trader is obligated to purchase the good, and the short trader is obligated to deliver it. If the price of the asset at the maturity of the contract exceeds the forward price, the long side benefits by virtue of acquiring the good at the contract price.

2. A futures contract is similar to a forward contract, differing most importantly in the aspects of standardization and marking to market, which is the process by which gains and losses on futures contract positions are settled daily. In contrast, forward contracts call for no cash transfers until contract maturity.

3. Futures contracts are traded on organized exchanges that standardize the size of the contract, the grade of the deliverable asset, the delivery date, and the delivery location. Traders negotiate only over the contract price. This standardization creates increased liquidity in the marketplace and means that buyers and sellers can easily find many traders for a desired purchase or sales.

4. The clearinghouse acts as an intermediary between each pair of traders, acting as the short position for each long, and as the long position for each short. In this way traders need not be concerned about the performance of the trader on the opposite side of the contract. In turn, traders post margins to guarantee their own performance on the contracts.

5. The gain or loss to the long side for the futures contract held between time 0 and t is $F_t - F_0$. Because $F_T = P_T$, the long's profit if the contract is held until maturity is $P_T - F_0$, where P_T is the spot price at time T and F_0 is the original futures price. The gain or loss to the short position is $F_0 - P_T$.

6. Futures contracts may be used for hedging or speculating. Speculators use the contracts to take a stand on the ultimate price of an asset. Short hedgers take short positions in contracts to offset any gains or losses on the value of an asset already held in inventory. Long hedgers take long positions to offset gains or losses in the purchase price of a good.

7. The spot-futures parity relationship states that the equilibrium futures price on an asset providing no service or payments (such as dividends) is $F_0 = P_0(1 + r_f)^T$. If the futures price deviates from this value, then market participants can earn arbitrage profits.

8. If the asset provides services or payments with yield d, the parity relationship becomes $F_0 = P_0(1 + r_f - d)^T$. This model is also called the cost-of-carry model, because it states that futures price must exceed the spot price by the net cost of carrying the asset until maturity date T.

9. The equilibrium futures price will be less than the currently expected time T spot price if the spot price exhibits systematic risk. This provides an expected profit for the long position who bears the risk and imposes an expected loss on the short position who is willing to accept that expected loss as a means to shed risk.

Key Terms

Forward contract
Futures price
Long position
Short position
Clearinghouse
Open interest
Marking to market
Maintenance margin
Variation margin
Convergence property
Cash delivery
Basis
Basis risk
Spread
Spot-futures parity theorem
Cost-of-carry relationship

Selected Readings

An extensive treatment of the institutional background of several futures markets is provided in:

Siegel, Daniel R.; and Diane F. Siegel, *Futures Markets.* Chicago: Dryden Press, 1990.

Excellent, although challenging, treatments of the differences between futures and forward markets and the pricing of each type of contract are in:

Jarrow, Robert; and George Oldfield. "Forward Contracts and Futures Contracts." *Journal of Financial Economics* 9 (December 1981).

Cox, John; Jonathan Ingersoll; and Stephen A. Ross. "The Relation between Forward Prices and Futures Prices." *Journal of Financial Economics* 9 (December 1981).

Black, Fischer. "The Pricing of Commodity Contracts." *Journal of Financial Economics* 3 (January–March 1976).

For a treatment of backwardation/contango debate, see:

Cootner, Paul H. "Speculation and Hedging." Food Research Institute Studies, Supplement, Stanford, Calif., 1967.

Keynes, John Maynard. *Treatise on Money*. 2nd ed. London: Macmillan, 1930.

Working, Holbrook. "The Theory of Price of Storage." *American Economic Review* 39 (December 1949).

Hicks, J.R. *Value and Capital.* 2nd ed. London: Oxford University Press, 1946.

The use of futures contracts in risk management is treated extensively in:

Smith, Clifford W., Jr; Charles W. Smithson; with D. Sykes Wilford. *Managing Financial Risk,* Burr Ridge, Ill.: Irwin Professional Publishing, 1995.

The magazine Futures *provides ongoing analysis of futures and options markets and strategies.*

Problems

1. *a.* Using Figure 21.1, compute the dollar value of the stocks traded on one contract on the Standard & Poor's 500 index. The closing spot price of the S&P 500 index is given in the last line of the listing. If the margin requirement is 10% of the futures price times the multiplier of 500, how much must you deposit with your broker to trade the December contract?
   b. If the December futures price were to increase to $460, what percentage return would you earn on your net investment if you entered the long side of the contract at the price shown in the figure?
   c. If the December futures price falls by 1%, what is your percentage return?
2. Why is there no futures market in cement?
3. Why might individuals purchase futures contracts rather than the underlying asset?
4. What is the difference in cash flow between short-selling an asset and entering a short futures position?
5. Are the following statements true or false? Why?
   a. All else equal, the futures price on a stock index with a high dividend yield should be higher than the futures price on an index with a low dividend yield.
   b. All else equal, the futures price on a high-beta stock would be higher than the futures price on a low-beta stock.
   c. The beta of a short position in the S&P 500 futures contract is negative.
6. *a.* A hypothetical futures contract on a nondividend-paying stock with current price $150 has a maturity of one year. If the T-bill rate is 8%, what should the futures price be?
   b. What should the futures price be if the maturity of the contract is three years?
   c. What if the interest rate is 12% and the maturity of the contract is three years?
7. Your analysis leads you to believe the stock market is about to rise substantially. The market is unaware of this situation. What should you do?
8. CFA In each of the following cases, discuss how you, as a portfolio manager, could use financial futures to protect a portfolio.*
   a. You own a large position in a relatively illiquid bond that you want to sell.
   b. You have a large gain on one of your long Treasuries and want to sell it, but you would like to defer the gain until the next accounting period, which begins in four weeks.
   c. You will receive a large contribution next month that you hope to invest in long-term corporate bonds on a yield basis as favorable as is now available.

---

*Reprinted, with permission, from the Level III 1982 *CFA Study Guide.*

9. Suppose the value of the S&P 500 stock index is currently 510. If the one-year T-bill rate is 6% and the expected dividend yield on the S&P 500 is 2%, what should the one-year maturity futures price be?
10. Consider a stock that pays no dividends on which a futures contract, a call option, and a put option trade. The maturity date for all three contracts is T, the exercise price of the put and the call are both X, and the futures price is F. Show that if $X = F$, then the call price equals the put price. Use parity conditions to guide your demonstration.
11. It is now January. The current interest rate is 8%. The June futures price for gold is $346.30, whereas the December futures price is $360.00. Is there an arbitrage opportunity here? If so, how would you exploit it?
12. The Chicago Board of Trade has just introduced a new futures contract on Brandex stock, a company that currently pays no dividends. Each contract calls for delivery of 1,000 shares of stock in one year. The T-bill rate is 6% per year.
    a. If Brandex stock now sells at $120 per share, what should the futures price be?
    b. If the Brandex price drops by 3%, what will be the change in the futures price and the change in the investor's margin account?
    c. If the margin on the contract is $12,000, what is the percentage return on the investor's position?
13. The multiplier for a futures contract on the stock market index is 500. The maturity of the contract is one year, the current level of the index is 400, and the risk-free interest rate is 0.5% per month. The dividend yield on the index is .2% per month. Suppose that after one month, the stock index is at 410.
    a. Find the cash flow from the mark-to-market proceeds on the contract. Assume that the parity condition always holds exactly.
    b. Find the holding period return if the initial margin on the contract is $15,000.
14. CFA Your client, for whom you are underwriting a $400 million bond issue, is concerned that market conditions will change before the issue is brought to market. He has heard it may be possible to reduce the risk exposure by hedging in the Government National Mortgage Association (GNMA) futures market. Specifically, he asks you to:*
    a. Briefly explain how the hedge works.
    b. Describe *four* practical problems that would limit the effectiveness of the hedge.
15. You are a corporate treasurer who will purchase $1 million of bonds for the sinking fund in three months. You believe rates will soon fall, and would like to repurchase the company's sinking fund bonds (which currently are selling below par) in advance of requirements. Unfortunately, you must obtain approval from the board of directors for such a purchase, and this can take up to two months. What action can you take in the futures market to hedge any adverse

---

movements in bond yields and prices until you can actually buy the bonds? Will you be long or short? Why? A qualitative answer is fine.

16. Futures contracts and options on a futures contract can be used to modify risk. Identify the fundamental distinction between a futures contract and an option on a futures contract, and briefly explain the difference in the manner that futures and options modify portfolio risk.*

17. The S&P portfolio pays a dividend yield of 2% annually. Its current value is 510. The T-bill rate is 5%. Suppose the S&P futures price for delivery in one year is 530. Construct an arbitrage strategy to exploit the mispricing and show that your profits one year hence will equal the mispricing in the futures market.

18. *a.* How should the parity condition (equation 21.2) for stocks be modified for futures contracts on Treasury bonds? What should play the role of the dividend yield in that equation?

b. In an environment with an upward-sloping yield curve, should T-bond futures prices on more distant contracts be higher or lower than those on near-term contracts?

c. Confirm your intuition by examining Figure 21.1.

19. Consider this arbitrage strategy to derive the parity relationship for spreads: (1) enter a long futures position with maturity date T_1 and futures price $F(T_1)$; (2) enter a short position with maturity T_2 and futures price $F(T_2)$; (3) at T_1, when the first contract expires, buy the asset and borrow $F(T_1)$ dollars at rate r_f; (4) pay back the loan with interest at time T_2.

a. What are the total cash flows to this strategy at times 0, T_1, and T_2?

b. Why must profits at time T_2 be zero if no arbitrage opportunities are present?

c. What must the relationship between $F(T_1)$ and $F(T_2)$ be for the profits at T_2 to be equal to zero? This relationship is the parity relationship for spreads.

20. What is the difference between the futures price and the value of the futures contract?

21. Evaluate the criticism that futures markets siphon off capital from more productive uses.

*Reprinted, with permission, from the Level III 1986 *CFA Study Guide*.

Chapter 22
Futures and Swaps: A Closer Look

THE PREVIOUS CHAPTER PROVIDED A BASIC INTRODUCTION TO THE OPERATION OF FUTURES MARKETS AND THE PRINCIPLES OF FUTURES PRICING. This chapter explores selected futures markets in more depth. Most of the growth has been in financial futures, which now dominate trading, so we emphasize these contracts.

We begin by discussing stock index futures, where we focus on program trading and index arbitrage. That is followed by a treatment of foreign exchange futures. Next, we move on to the most actively traded markets, those for interest rate futures. Finally, we turn to the swap markets in foreign exchange and fixed-income securities. We will see that swaps can be interpreted as portfolios of forward contracts and valued accordingly.

22.1 Stock Index Futures

The Contracts

In contrast to most futures contracts, which call for delivery of a specified commodity, stock index contracts are settled by a cash amount equal to the value of the stock index in question on the contract maturity date times a multiplier that scales the size of the contract. The total profit to the long position is $S_T - F_0$, where S_T is the value of the stock index on the maturity date. Cash settlement avoids the costs that would be incurred if the short trader had to purchase the stocks in the index and deliver them to the long position, and if the long position then had to sell the stocks for cash. Instead, the long trader's profit is $S_T - F_0$ dollars, and the short trader's is $F_0 - S_T$ dollars. These profits duplicate those that would arise with actual delivery.

There are several stock index futures contracts currently traded. Table 22.1 lists some of the major ones, showing under contract size the multiplier used to calculate contract settlements. An S&P 500 contract, for example, with a futures price of 450 and

Table 22.1 Stock Index Futures

Contract	Underlying Market Index	Contract Size	Exchange
S&P 500	Standard & Poor's 500 index. A value-weighted arithmetic average of 500 stocks.	$500 times the S&P 500 index	Chicago Mercantile Exchange
Value Line	Value Line Composite Average. An equally weighted average of about 1,700 firms.	$500 times the Value Line Index	Kansas City Board of Trade
NYSE	NYSE Composite Index. Value-weighted arithmetic average of all stocks listed on the NYSE.	$500 times the NYSE index	New York Futures Exchange
Major Market Index	Price-weighted arithmetic average of 20 blue-chip stocks. Index is designed to track the Dow Jones Industrial Average.	$500 times the Major Market Index	Chicago Mercantile Exchange
S&P Mid-Cap	Index of 400 firms of midrange market value.	$500 times index	Chicago Mercantile Exchange
National Over-the-Counter	Value-weighted arithmetic average of 100 of the largest over-the-counter stocks.	$500 times the OTC index	Philadelphia Board of Trade
Nikkei	Nikkei 225 stock average.	$5 times the Nikkei Index	Chicago Mercantile Exchange
FT-SE 100	Financial Times–Share Exchange Index of 100 U.K. firms.	£25 times the FT-SE Index	London International Financial Futures Exchange
FT-SE Eurotrack 100	Index of 100 non-U.K. European firms.	50 deutschemarks times the index	London International Financial Futures Exchange

a final index value of 455 would result in a profit for the long side of $500 \times (455 - 450) = \$2,500$. The S&P contract by far dominates the market in stock index futures.

Most futures contracts such as the S&P 500 or NYSE are written explicitly on a particular stock index. This gives investors the ability to hedge against or speculate on the performance of the given index. The Major Market Index is a bit of an exception. Because the Chicago Board of Trade was not given permission by Dow Jones to create a contract explicitly tied to the Dow Jones Industrial Average, it was forced instead to create its own index designed to track the DJIA as closely as possible. Figure 21.1 from the previous chapter is a reproduction of the futures contracts listed in *The Wall Street Journal,* and includes several stock-index futures.

The broad-based stock market indexes are all highly correlated. Table 22.2 presents a correlation matrix for five indexes. The only index whose correlation with the others is below .90 is the Value Line Index. This index uses an equally weighted geometric average of 1,700 firms, as opposed to the NYSE or S&P indexes, which use market weights. (See Chapter 2, Section 2.4, for a review of geometric averages.) This means

Table 22.2 Correlations among Major U.S. Stock Market Indexes

Index	DJIA	MMI	S&P 500	Value Line	NYSE
DJIA	1.0000	.9779	.9774	.8880	.9750
MMI		1.0000	.9497	.8104	.9403
S&P 500			1.0000	.9137	.9972
Value Line				1.0000	.9337
NYSE					1.0000

Note: Correlations were computed from weekly percentage rates of price appreciation during calendar year 1989.
Source: Hans R. Stoll and Robert E. Whaley, *Futures and Options: Theory and Applications* (Cincinnati: South-Western Publishing, 1993).

that the Value Line contract overweights small firms compared to the other indexes, which may explain the lower observed correlation.

Creating Synthetic Stock Positions: An Asset Allocation Tool

One reason stock index futures are so popular is that they substitute for holdings in the underlying stocks themselves. Index futures let investors participate in broad market movements without actually buying or selling large numbers of stocks.

Because of this, we say futures represent "synthetic" holdings of the market portfolio. Instead of holding the market directly, the investor takes a long futures position in the index. Such a strategy is attractive because the transaction costs involved in establishing and liquidating futures positions are much lower than taking actual spot positions. Investors who wish to frequently buy and sell market positions find it much less costly to play the futures market rather than the underlying spot market. "Market timers," who speculate on broad market moves rather than on individual securities, are large players in stock index futures for this reason.

One means to market time, for example, is to shift between Treasury bills and broad-based stock market holdings. Timers attempt to shift from bills into the market before market upturns, and to shift back into bills to avoid market downturns, thereby profiting from broad market movements. Market timing of this sort, however, can result in huge brokerage fees with the frequent purchase and sale of many stocks. An attractive alternative is to invest in Treasury bills and hold varying amounts of market index futures contracts.

The strategy works like this. When timers are bullish, they will establish many long futures positions that they can liquidate quickly and cheaply when expectations turn bearish. Rather than shifting back and forth between T-bills and stocks, they buy and hold T-bills, and adjust only the futures position. This minimizes transaction costs. An advantage of this technique for timing is that investors can implicitly buy or sell the market index in its entirety, whereas market timing in the spot market would require the simultaneous purchase or sale of all the stocks in the index. This is technically difficult to coordinate and can lead to slippage in execution of a timing strategy.

You can construct a T-bill plus index futures position that duplicates the payoff to holding the stock index itself. Here is how:

1. Hold as many market index futures contracts long as you need to purchase your desired stock position. A desired holding of $1,000 multiplied by the S&P 500 index, for example, would require the purchase of two contracts because each contract calls for delivery of $500 multiplied by the index.
2. Invest enough money in T-bills to cover the payment of the futures price at the contract's maturity date. The necessary investment will equal the present value of the futures price that will be paid to satisfy the contracts. The T-bill holdings will grow by the maturity date to a level equal to the futures price.

For example, suppose that an institutional investor wants to invest $40 million in the market for one month and, to minimize trading costs, chooses to buy the S&P 500 futures contracts as a substitute for actual stock holdings. If the index is now at 400, the one-month delivery futures price is 404, and the T-bill rate is 1% per month, it would buy 200 contracts. (Each contract controls $500 × 400 = $200,000 worth of stock, and $40 million/$200,000 = 200.) The institution thus has a long position on 100,000 times the S&P 500 index (200 contracts times the contract multiplier of 500). To cover payment of the futures price, it must invest 100,000 times the present value of the futures price in T-bills. This equals 100,000 × (404/1.01) = $40 million market value of bills. Notice that the $40 million outlay in bills is precisely equal to the amount that would have been needed to buy the stock directly.

This is an artificial, or synthetic, stock position. What is the value of this portfolio at the maturity date? Call S_T the value of the stock index on the maturity date T, and as usual, let F_0 be the original futures price:

	In General (Per Unit of the Index)	Our Numbers
1. Profits from contract	$S_T - F_0$	$100{,}000(S_T - 404)$
2. Value of T-bills	F_0	40,400,000
TOTAL	S_T	$100{,}000S_T$

The total payoff on the contract maturity date is exactly proportional to the value of the stock index. In other words, adopting this portfolio strategy is equivalent to holding the stock index itself, aside from the issue of interim dividend distributions and tax treatment.

This bills-plus-futures contracts strategy may be viewed as a 100% stock strategy. At the other extreme, investing in zero futures results in a 100% bills position. Moreover, a short futures position will result in a portfolio equivalent to that obtained by short selling the stock market index, because in both cases the investor gains from decreases in the stock price. Bills-plus-futures mixtures clearly allow for a flexible and low-transaction-cost approach to market timing. The futures positions may be established or reversed quickly and cheaply. Also, since the short futures position allows the investor to earn interest on T-bills, it is superior to a conventional short sale of the stock, where the investor may earn little or no interest on the proceeds of the short sale.

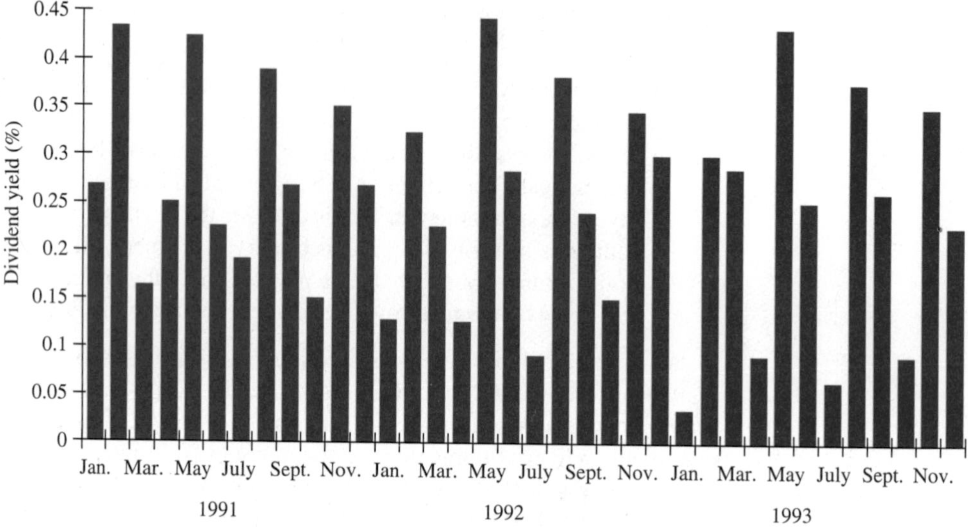

Figure 22.1 Monthly dividend yield of the S&P 500

The nearby box illustrates that it is now commonplace for money managers to use futures contracts to create synthetic equity positions in stock markets. The article notes that futures positions can be particularly helpful in establishing synthetic positions in foreign equities, where trading costs tend to be greater and markets tend to be less liquid.

CONCEPT CHECK Question 1. As the payoffs of the synthetic and actual stock positions are identical, so should be their costs. What does this say about the spot-futures parity relationship?

Empirical Evidence on Pricing of Stock Index Futures

Recall the spot-futures parity relationship between the futures and spot stock price:

$$F_0 = S_0(1 + r_f - d)^T \tag{22.1}$$

Several investigators have tested this relationship empirically. The general procedure has been to calculate the theoretically appropriate futures price using the current value of the stock index and equation 22.1. The dividend yield of the index in question is approximated using historical data. Although dividends of individual securities may fluctuate unpredictably, the annualized dividend yield of a broad-based index such as the S&P 500 is fairly stable, usually in the neighborhood of 3% per year. The yield is seasonal with regular and predictable peaks and troughs however, so the dividend yield for the relevant months must be the one used. Figure 22.1 illustrates the dividend yield of the S&P 500 index from 1991 to 1993. Notice that some months, such as July, have consistently low yields. Others, such as May, have consistently high yields.

If the actual futures price deviates from the value dictated by the parity relationship, then (aside from transaction costs), an arbitrage opportunity arises. Given an estimate

Got a Bundle to Invest Fast? Think Stock-Index Futures

As investors go increasingly global and market turbulence grows, stock-index futures are emerging as the favorite way for nimble money managers to deploy their funds.

Indeed, research from Goldman, Sachs & Co. shows that, in most major markets, trading in stock futures now exceeds the buying and selling of actual shares. In the U.S., for instance, average daily trading volume of futures based on the Standard & Poor's 500 stock-index was a whopping $16.8 billion in 1994. By contrast, New York Stock Exchange trading averaged only $10.56 billion a day.

What's the big appeal? Speed, ease and cheapness. For most major markets, stock futures not only boast greater liquidity but also lower transaction costs than traditional trading methods.

Portfolio managers stress that in today's fast-moving markets, it's critical to implement decisions quickly. For giant mutual and pension funds eager to keep assets fully invested, shifting billions around through stock-index futures is much easier than trying to identify individual stocks to buy and sell.

"When I decide it's time to move into France, Germany or Britain, I don't necessarily want to wait around until I find exactly the right stocks," says Fabrizio Pierallini, manager of New York-based Vontobel Ltd.'s Euro Pacific Fund.

Mr. Pierallini, who has $120 million invested in stocks in Europe, Asia and Latin America, says he later fine-tunes his market picks by gradually shifting out of futures into favorite stocks. To the extent Mr. Pierallini's stocks outperform the market, futures provide a means to preserve those gains, even while hedging against market declines.

For instance, by selling futures equal to the value of the underlying portfolio, a manager can almost completely insulate a portfolio from market moves. Say a manager succeeds in outperforming the market, but still loses 3% while the market as a whole falls 10%. Hedging with futures would capture that margin of outperformance, transforming the loss into a profit of roughly 7%. Demand for such protection helped account for stock futures' surging popularity in last year's difficult markets, Goldman said in its report.

"You can get all the value your managers are going to add" relative to the market, "and you don't need to worry about the costs of trading" actual securities, said David Leinweber, director of research at First Quadrant Corp., a Pasadena, Calif., investment firm that traded some $59 billion of futures in 1994.

Among First Quadrant's futures-intensive strategies is "global tactical asset allocation," which involves trading whole markets worldwide as traditional managers might trade stocks. The growing popularity of such asset-allocation strategies has given futures a big boost in recent years.

To capitalize on global market swings, "futures do the job for us better than stocks, and they're cheaper," said Jarrod Wilcox, director of global investments at PanAgora Asset Management, a Boston-based asset allocator. Even when PanAgora does take positions in individual stocks, it often employs futures to modify its position, such as by hedging part of its exposure to that particular stock market.

When it comes to investing overseas, Mr. Wilcox noted, futures are often the only vehicle that makes sense from a cost standpoint. Abroad, transaction taxes and sky-high commissions can wipe out more than 1% of the money deployed on each trade. By contrast, a comparable trade in futures costs as little as 0.05%.

"Futures allow us to convert [even] modest opportunities into profits for our clients," Mr. Wilcox said. If trading actual stocks "costs 1% in fees to get in and another 1% to get out, it's too costly to do."

Source: Suzanne McGee, *The Wall Street Journal*, February 21, 1995.

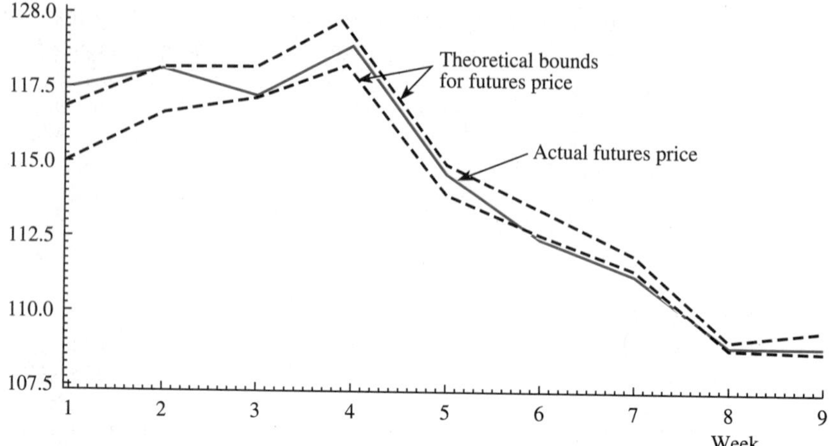

Figure 22.2
Prices of S&P 500 contract maturing June 1982. Data plotted for April 21–June 16, 1982

Source: David Modest and Mahadevan Sundaresan, "The Relationship Between Spot and Futures Prices in Stock Index Futures Markets: Some Preliminary Evidence," *Journal of Futures Markets* 3 (Spring 1983). © John Wiley & Sons, Inc., 1983.

of transaction costs, we can bracket the theoretically correct futures price within a band. If the actual futures price lies within that band, the discrepancy between the actual and the proper futures price is too small to exploit because of the transaction costs; if the actual price lies outside the no-arbitrage band, profit opportunities are worth exploiting.

Modest and Sundaresan[1] constructed such a test. Figure 22.2 replicates an example of their results. The figure shows that the futures prices generally did lie in the theoretically determined no-arbitrage band, but that profit opportunities occasionally were possible for low-cost transactors.

Modest and Sundaresan pointed out that much of the cost of short selling shares is attributable to the investor's inability to invest the entire proceeds from the short sale. Proceeds must be left on margin account, where they do not earn interest. Arbitrage opportunities, or the width of the no-arbitrage band, therefore depend on assumptions regarding the use of short-sale proceeds. Figure 22.2 assumes that one-half of the proceeds are available to the short seller.

CONCEPT CHECK

Question 2. What (if anything) would happen to the top of the no-arbitrage band if short sellers could obtain full use of the proceeds from the short sale? What would happen to the low end of the band? (Hint: When do violations of parity call for a long futures–short stock position versus short futures–long stock?)

Index Arbitrage and the Triple-Witching Hour

Whenever the actual futures price falls outside the no-arbitrage band, there is an opportunity for profit. This is why the parity relationships are so important. Far from being theoretical academic constructs, they are in fact a guide to trading rules that can generate large profits. One of the most notable developments in trading activity has been the

[1] David Modest and Mahadevan Sundaresan, "The Relationship Between Spot and Futures Prices in Stock Index Futures Markets: Some Preliminary Evidence," *Journal of Futures Markets* 3 (Spring 1983).

advent of **index arbitrage,** an investment strategy that exploits divergences between the actual futures price and its theoretically correct parity value.

In theory, index arbitrage is simple. If the futures price is too high, short the futures contract and buy the stocks in the index. If it is too low, go long in futures and short the stocks. You can perfectly hedge your position and should earn arbitrage profits equal to the mispricing of the contract.

In practice, however, index arbitrage is difficult to implement. The problem lies in buying "the stocks in the index." Selling or purchasing shares in all 500 stocks in the S&P 500 is impractical for two reasons. The first is transaction costs, which may outweigh any profits to be made from the arbitrage. Second, it is extremely difficult to buy or sell stock of 500 different firms simultaneously, and any lags in the execution of such a strategy can destroy the effectiveness of a plan to exploit temporary price discrepancies.

Arbitrageurs need to trade an entire portfolio of stocks quickly and simultaneously if they hope to exploit disparities between the futures price and its corresponding stock index. For this they need a coordinated trading program; hence the term **program trading,** which refers to coordinated purchases or sales of entire portfolios of stocks. The response has been the designated order turnaround (DOT) system, which enables traders to send coordinated buy or sell programs to the floor of the stock exchange via computer.

In each year, there are four maturing S&P 500 futures contracts. These four Fridays, which occur simultaneously with the expiration of S&P index options and options on some individual stocks, have been dubbed the **triple-witching hour** because of the volatility believed to be associated with the expirations in the three types of contracts.

Expiration-day volatility can be explained by program trading to exploit arbitrage opportunities. Suppose that some time before a stock index future contract matures, the futures price is a little above its parity value. Arbitrageurs will attempt to lock in superior profits by buying the stocks in the index (the program trading buy order) and taking an offsetting short futures position. If and when the pricing disparity reverses, the position can be unwound at a profit. Alternatively, arbitrageurs can wait until contract maturity day and realize a profit by simultaneously closing out the offsetting stock and futures positions. By waiting until contract maturity, arbitrageurs can be assured that the futures price and stock index price will be aligned—they rely on the convergence property.

Obviously, when many program traders follow such a strategy at contract expiration, a wave of program selling passes over the market. The result? Prices go down. This is the expiration-day effect. If execution of the arbitrage strategy calls for an initial sale (or short sale) of stocks, unwinding on expiration day requires repurchase of the stocks, with the opposite effect: Prices will increase.

The success of these arbitrage positions and associated program trades depends on only two things: the relative levels of spot and futures prices and synchronized trading in the two markets. Because arbitrageurs exploit disparities in futures and spot prices, absolute price levels are unimportant. This means that large buy or sell programs can hit the floor even if stock prices are at "fair" levels, that is, at levels consistent with fundamental information. The markets in individual stocks may not be sufficiently deep to absorb the arbitrage-based program trades without significant price movements despite the fact that those trades are not informationally motivated.

In an investigation of expiration-day effects on stock prices Stoll and Whaley[2] found that the market is in fact somewhat more volatile at contract expirations. For example, in their study, the standard deviation of the last-hour return on the S&P 500 index is .641% on expirations of the S&P 500 futures contract, compared to only .211% on non-expiration days. Interestingly, the last-hour volatility of non-S&P 500 stocks appears unaffected by expiration days, consistent with the hypothesis that the effect is related to program trading of the stocks in the index.

If these price swings are based only on temporary market pressure coming from simultaneous program trades, we should expect price declines or advances to reverse after the trades are executed, when profit seekers attempt to buy or sell stocks that are subsequently mispriced according to fundamental information. For this reason, reversals might be the best measure of the price impact of expiration-day trading. To the extent that Monday returns tend to be positive following negative Friday returns, or negative following positive Friday returns, we have evidence that prices were pushed beyond their equilibrium or intrinsic values by program traders, and returned to their equilibrium values on the next trading day. In fact, Stoll and Whaley found some tendency for large price swings to be reversed on the day following the expiration activity.

In an attempt to mitigate expiration-day effects, expiring futures contracts on the S&P 500, S&P 100, and NYSE indexes now cease trading on Thursday afternoon rather than Friday. The contracts are marked to market for the last time on Friday using the stock index value at market *opening*. Because the final futures price is based on market opening prices, arbitrageurs must use market-on-open orders (instead of market-on-close orders) to ensure convergence and lock in a profit from earlier futures mispricing. Futures and options on the Major Market Index and the Value Line Index still settle as they always have at the Friday closing price.

The purported advantage of the morning settlement is that supply-demand imbalances can be more easily rectified when they occur before market opening. Arbitrageurs must submit their market-on-open unwinding orders before 9 A.M. on the expiration day, while the market is closed. When buy-sell imbalances emerge, other participants will be aware of them, and can take the opposite side of the trade for only slight price concessions if they are convinced the imbalance is due only to index arbitrage and not to changes in intrinsic values.

Stoll and Whaley[3] later updated their original study to measure expiration-day effects before and after the change in the contract settlement procedures. Table 22.3 presents some of their results on average reversals following quarterly expirations. The table shows that before settlement procedures changed in June 1987, average reversals of price movements at market close on expiration days were greater than either typical reversals at market open or reversals experienced on nonexpiration days. This confirms

[2] Hans R. Stoll and Robert E. Whaley, "Program Trading and Expiration-Day Effect," *Financial Analysts Journal*, March–April 1987.

[3] Hans R. Stoll and Robert E. Whaley, "Expiration-Day Effects: What Has Changed?" *Financial Analysts Journal*, January–February 1991.

Table 22.3 Portfolio Reversals on Quarterly Expirations

Index	Type of Day	Reversal at Close	Reversal at Open
Pre-June 1987			
MMI	Expiration day	.506	.095
	Nonexpiration day	.020	.024
S&P 100	Expiration day	.493	.011
	Nonexpiration day	.074	−.070
S&P 500	Expiration day	.364	.011
	Nonexpiration day	.074	−.080
Post-June 1987			
MMI	Expiration day	.171	.224
	Nonexpiration day	−.075	.021
S&P 100	Expiration day	.178	.282
	Nonexpiration day	−.061	−.095
S&P 500	Expiration day	.255	.208
	Nonexpiration day	−.034	−.096

Source: Hans R. Stoll and Robert E. Whaley, "Expiration-Day Effects: What Has Changed?" *Financial Analysts Journal,* January–February 1991.

that expiration-day trading seems to have had some influence on stock prices. After June 1987, reversals at closing have been smaller than their pre-June levels. However, reversals at market opening are now larger, signifying that the expiration-day price pressure simply shifted to the earlier settlement time.

Stoll and Whaley noted, however, that any expiration-day effects detected in their sample are quite mild. A reversal of 0.3%, for example, corresponds to a price movement of only 12 cents on a $40 stock, less than the bid-ask spread. They conclude that expiration-day effects are small, and that the market seems to handle expirations of index futures contracts reasonably well. Index arbitrage probably does not have a major impact on stock prices, and any impact it does have appears to be extremely short-lived.

The program trading activity associated with index arbitrage commonly accounts for 5% to 10% of NYSE daily volume. *The Wall Street Journal* regularly reports on program trading, both in aggregate and for the largest traders. Figure 22.3 is a reproduction of one such report.

22.2 Foreign Exchange Futures

The Markets

Exchange rates between currencies vary continually and often substantially. This variability can be a source of concern for anyone involved in international business. A U.S.

Figure 22.3

Program trading activity

Source: *The Wall Street Journal*, December 16, 1994. Reprinted by permission of *The Wall Street Journal*, © 1994 Dow Jones & Company, Inc. All Rights Reserved Worldwide.

PROGRAM TRADING

NEW YORK – Program trading in the week ended Dec. 9 accounted for 9%, or an average 27.7 million daily shares, of New York Stock Exchange volume.

Brokerage firms executed an additional 12 million daily shares of program trading away from the Big Board, mostly on foreign markets. Program trading is the simultaneous purchase or sale of at least 15 different stocks with a total value of $1 million or more.

Of the program total on the Big Board, 41.9% involved stock-index arbitrage, up from 38% the prior week. In this strategy, traders dart between stocks and stock-index options and futures to capture fleeting price differences.

Some 57.4% of program trading was executed by firms for their own accounts, or principal trading, and 41.9% was for their customers. Another 0.7% was customer facilitation, in which firms use principal positions to facilitate customer trades.

Of the five most-active firms, Nomura Securities, UBS Securities, First Boston and Cooper Neff executed all or most of their program trading for their own accounts, while Morgan Stanley did most of its trading for its customers.

NYSE PROGRAM TRADING

Volume (in millions of shares) for the week ending Dec. 9, 1994

Top 15 Firms	Index Arbitrage	Derivative-Related*	Other Strategies	Total
Morgan Stanley	1.7	...	13.0	14.7
Cooper Neff	...	13.5	0.2	13.7
Nomura Securities	12.0	...	0.7	12.7
UBS Securities	8.6	...	0.3	8.9
First Boston	5.7	...	3.1	8.8
Daiwa Securities	3.1	...	4.7	7.8
Bear Stearns	...	...	7.7	7.7
Lehman Brothers	2.1	0.3	3.9	6.3
J.P. Morgan	4.8	0.6	...	5.4
WG Trading	3.9	0.8	0.7	5.4
Thomas Williams	4.2	...	0.8	5.0
Spear Leeds	4.0	...	1.0	5.0
LIT America	3.6	...	0.5	4.1
PaineWebber	...	...	3.8	3.8
Interactive Brokers	...	...	3.7	3.7
OVERALL TOTAL	58.0	15.3	65.3	138.6

*Other derivative-related strategies besides index arbitrage

Source: New York Stock Exchange

exporter who sells goods in England, for example, will be paid in British pounds, and the dollar value of those pounds depends on the exchange rate at the time payment is made. Until that date, the U.S. exporter is exposed to foreign exchange rate risk. This risk can be hedged through currency futures or forward markets. For example, if you know you will receive £100,000 in 90 days, you can sell those pounds forward today in the forward market and lock in an exchange rate equal to today's forward price.

The forward market in foreign exchange is fairly informal. It is simply a network of banks and brokers that allows customers to enter forward contracts to purchase or sell currency in the future at a currently agreed-upon rate of exchange. The bank market in currencies is among the largest in the world, and most large traders with sufficient creditworthiness execute their trades here rather than in futures markets. Unlike those in futures markets, contracts in forward markets are not standardized in a formal market setting. Instead, each is negotiated separately. Moreover, there is no marking to market as would occur in futures markets. Currency forward contracts call for execution only at the maturity date.

Figure 22.4
Spot and forward prices in foreign exchange

Source: *The Wall Street Journal*, December 21, 1994. Reprinted by permission of *The Wall Street Journal*,

CURRENCY TRADING

EXCHANGE RATES

Tuesday, December 20, 1994

The New York foreign exchange selling rates below apply to trading among banks in amounts of $1 million and more, as quoted at 3 p.m. Eastern time by Bankers Trust Co., Dow Jones Telerate Inc. and other sources. Retail transactions provide fewer units of foreign currency per dollar.

Country	U.S. $ equiv. Tues.	U.S. $ equiv. Mon.	Currency per U.S. $ Tues.	Currency per U.S. $ Mon.
Argentina (Peso)	1.01	1.00	.99	1.00
Australia (Dollar)	.7755	.7761	1.2895	1.2886
Austria (Schilling)	.09052	.09024	11.05	11.08
Bahrain (Dinar)	2.6413	2.6524	.3786	.3770
Belgium (Franc)	.03099	.03090	32.27	32.36
Brazil (Real)	1.0893246	1.1792453	.92	.85
Britain (Pound)	1.5600	1.5605	.6410	.6408
30-Day Forward	1.5604	1.5608	.6409	.6407
90-Day Forward	1.5601	1.5606	.6410	.6408
180-Day Forward	1.5601	1.5602	.6410	.6410
Canada (Dollar)	.7176	.7173	1.3935	1.3942
30-Day Forward	.7180	.7174	1.3929	1.3939
90-Day Forward	.7180	.7164	1.3927	1.3958
180-Day Forward	.7177	.7146	1.3934	1.3993
Czech. Rep. (Koruna)				
Commercial rate	.0356239	.0354057	28.0710	28.2440
Chile (Peso)	.002564	.002476	390.01	403.85
China (Renminbi)	.115221	.117923	8.6790	8.4801
Colombia (Peso)	.001204	.001203	830.43	831.15
Denmark (Krone)	.1623	.1618	6.1626	6.1790
Ecuador (Sucre)				
Floating rate	.000438	.000434	2281.02	2306.54
Finland (Markka)	.20576	.20500	4.8599	4.8781
France (Franc)	.18476	.18440	5.4125	5.4230
30-Day Forward	.18488	.18447	5.4089	5.4209
90-Day Forward	.18512	.18455	5.4020	5.4185
180-Day Forward	.18570	.18482	5.3851	5.4105
Germany (Mark)	.6369	.6352	1.5700	1.5743
30-Day Forward	.6374	.6354	1.5689	1.5738
90-Day Forward	.6385	.6365	1.5661	1.5712
180-Day Forward	.6414	.6391	1.5590	1.5648
Greece (Drachma)	.004124	.004109	242.50	243.35
Hong Kong (Dollar)	.12924	.12924	7.7375	7.7375
Hungary (Forint)	.0089582	.0089485	111.4900	111.4900
India (Rupee)	.03211	.03184	31.14	31.40
Indonesia (Rupiah)	.0004589	.0004573	2179.03	2186.62
Ireland (Punt)	.6490	.6506	1.5408	1.5372
Israel (Shekel)	.3298	.3315	3.0320	3.0162
Italy (Lira)	.0006074	.0006074	1646.31	1646.46
Japan (Yen)	.009986	.009984	100.14	100.17
30-Day Forward	.010020	.010017	99.80	99.83
90-Day Forward	.010085	.010084	99.16	99.16
180-Day Forward	.010205	.010204	97.99	98.00
Jordan (Dinar)	1.4516	1.4205	.6889	.7040
Kuwait (Dinar)	3.3361	3.3319	.2998	.3001
Lebanon (Pound)	.000604	.000607	1656.00	1648.00
Malaysia (Ringgit)	.3910	.3897	2.5575	2.5661
Malta (Lira)	.3680	.3718	2.7174	2.6896
Mexico (Peso)				
Floating rate	.2906977	.2886253	3.4535	3.4535
Netherland (Guilder)	.5690	.5674	1.7574	1.7623
New Zealand (Dollar)	.6382	.6399	1.5669	1.5629
Norway (Krone)	.1459	.1455	6.8554	6.8705
Pakistan (Rupee)	.0326	.0325	30.63	30.73
Peru (New Sol)	.4692	.4632	2.13	2.16
Philippines (Peso)	.04167	.04153	24.00	24.08
Poland (Zloty)	.00002639	.00004110	24323.00	24323.00
Portugal (Escudo)	.006203	.006186	161.21	161.65
Saudi Arabia (Riyal)	.26662	.26663	3.7506	3.7506
Singapore (Dollar)	.6838	.6819	1.4625	1.4665
Slovak Rep. (Koruna)	.0316857	.0316857	31.5600	31.5600
South Africa (Rand)				
Commercial rate	.2813	.2813	3.5662	3.5662
Financial rate	.2500	.2488	4.0000	4.0200
South Korea (Won)	.0012579	.0012620	795.00	792.40
Spain (Peseta)	.007564	.007556	132.21	132.35
Sweden (Krona)	.1327	.1327	7.5351	7.5351
Switzerland (Franc)	.7533	.7508	1.3275	1.3320
30-Day Forward	.7547	.7522	1.3251	1.3295
90-Day Forward	.7574	.7545	1.3203	1.3255
180-Day Forward	.7621	.7593	1.3121	1.3169
Taiwan (Dollar)	.037965	.037840	26.34	26.43
Thailand (Baht)	.03984	.03980	25.10	25.13
Turkey (Lira)	.0000264	.0000264	37753.00	37753.00
United Arab (Dirham)	.2724	.2723	3.6715	3.6728
Uruguay (New Peso)				
Financial	.182482	.178891	5.48	5.59
Venezuela (Bolivar)	.00587	.00589	170.28	169.87

SDR	1.45139	1.45040	.68899	.68946
ECU	1.21360	1.21100	....	....

Special Drawing Rights (SDR) are based on exchange rates for the U.S., German, British, French and Japanese currencies. Source: International Monetary Fund.

European Currency Unit (ECU) is based on a basket of community currencies.

z-Not quoted.

For currency *futures,* however, there are formal markets established by the Chicago Mercantile Exchange (International Monetary Market), the London International Financial Futures Exchange, and the MidAmerica Commodity Exchange. Here, contracts are standardized by size, and daily marking to market is observed. Moreover, there are standard clearing arrangements that allow traders to enter or reverse positions easily.

Figure 22.4 reproduces *The Wall Street Journal* listing of foreign exchange spot and forward rates. The listing gives the number of U.S. dollars required to purchase some unit of foreign currency and then the amount of foreign currency needed to purchase $1. Figure 22.5 reproduces futures listings, which show the number of dollars needed to purchase a given unit of foreign currency. In Figure 22.4, both spot and forward exchange rates are listed for various delivery dates.

Figure 22.5
Foreign exchange futures

Source: *The Wall Street Journal*, December 21, 1994. Reprinted by permission of *The Wall Street Journal*, © 1994 Dow Jones & Company, Inc. All Rights Reserved Worldwide.

CURRENCY

	Open	High	Low	Settle	Change	Lifetime High	Lifetime Low	Open Interest
JAPAN YEN (CME)–12.5 million yen; \$ per yen (.00)								
Mar	1.0076	1.0082	1.0057	1.0069	– .0008	1.0560	.9680	71,005
June	1.0200	1.0207	1.0189	1.0194	– .0009	1.0670	.9915	2,325
Sept	....	....	....	1.0322	– .0009	1.0775	1.0200	327
Dec	1.0462	1.0462	1.0450	1.0452	– .0009	1.0760	1.0420	117
Est vol 11,045; vol Mon 13,797; open int 99,931, –2,880.								
DEUTSCHEMARK (CME)–125,000 marks; \$ per mark								
Mar	.6371	.6383	.6366	.6377	+ .0013	.6744	.5798	69,696
June	.6404	.6408	.6404	.6402	+ .0011	.6747	.5980	1,719
Sept	....	....	....	.6432	+ .0013	.6770	.6290	138
Est vol 10,989; vol Mon 15,437; open int 110,643, –5,323.								
CANADIAN DOLLAR (CME)–100,000 dlrs.; \$ per Can \$								
Dec	.7185	.7185	.7177	.7177	+ .0006	.7670	.7038	17,708
Mar	.7154	.7176	.7154	.7172	+ .0009	.7605	.7020	46,067
June	.7151	.7153	.7145	.7154	+ .0009	.7600	.6990	1,521
Sept	.7135	.7143	.7135	.7139	+ .0009	.7438	.6965	1,183
Dec	....	....	....	.7122	+ .0009	.7400	.7025	250
Est vol 2,848; vol Mon 6,241; open int 66,775, +375.								
BRITISH POUND (CME)–62,500 pds.; \$ per pound								
Mar	1.5622	1.5622	1.5590	1.5598	– .0008	1.6440	1.4530	49,301
June		....	....	1.5592	– .0010	1.6380	1.5330	184
Est vol 3,290; vol Mon 5,062; open int 73,994, –489.								
SWISS FRANC (CME)–125,000 francs; \$ per franc								
Mar	.7547	.7567	.7541	.7556	+ .0014	.8136	.7287	36,924
June	.7600	.7610	.7600	.7607	+ .0014	.8165	.7193	505
Est vol 5,317; vol Mon 8,699; open int 64,439, –1,941.								
AUSTRALIAN DOLLAR (CME)–100,000 dlrs.; \$ per A.\$								
Mar	.7731	.7748	.7723	.7729	+ .0001	.7767	.7275	14,965
Est vol 179; vol Mon 743; open int 22,470, –102.								
U.S. DOLLAR INDEX (FINEX)–1,000 times USDX								
Dec	89.62	89.63	89.57	89.59	– .14	99.00	84.95	1,247
Mr95	89.77	89.77	89.62	89.67	– .16	96.65	85.28	5,129
Est vol 1,600; vol Mon 440; open int 5,433, +1,287.								
The index: High 89.74; Low 89.58; Close 89.62 –.07								

The forward quotations always apply to rolling delivery in 30, 90, or 180 days. Thus, tomorrow's forward listings will apply to a maturity date one day later than today's listing. In contrast, the futures contracts mature at specified dates in March, June, September, and December; these four maturity days are the only dates each year when futures contracts settle.

Interest Rate Parity

As is true of stocks and stock futures, there is a spot-futures exchange rate relationship that will prevail in well-functioning markets. Should this so-called interest rate parity relationship be violated, arbitrageurs will be able to make risk-free profits in foreign exchange markets with zero net investment. Their actions will force futures and spot exchange rate back into alignment.

We can illustrate the **interest rate parity theorem** by using two currencies, the U.S. dollar and the British (U.K.) pound. Call E_0 the current exchange rate between the two currencies, that is, E_0 dollars are required to purchase one pound. F_0, the forward price, is the number of dollars that is agreed to today for purchase of one pound at time T in the future. Call the risk-free interest rates in the United States and United Kingdom r_{US} and r_{UK}, respectively.

The interest rate parity theorem then states that the proper relationship between E_0 and F_0 is given as

$$F_0 = E_0\left(\frac{1 + r_{US}}{1 + r_{UK}}\right)^T \tag{22.2}$$

For example, if $r_{US} = .06$ and $r_{UK} = .05$ annually, while $E_0 = \$1.80$ per pound, then the proper futures price for a one-year contract would be

$$\$1.80\left(\frac{1.06}{1.05}\right) = \$1.817 \text{ per pound}$$

Consider the intuition behind this result. If r_{US} is greater than r_{UK}, money invested in the United States will grow at a faster rate than money invested in the United Kingdom. If this is so, why wouldn't all investors decide to invest their money in the United States? One important reason why not is that the dollar may be depreciating relative to the pound. Although dollar investments in the United States grow faster than pound investments in the United Kingdom, each dollar is worth progressively fewer pounds as time passes. Such an effect will exactly offset the advantage of the higher U.S. interest rate.

To complete the argument, we need only determine how a depreciating dollar will show up in equation 22.2. If the dollar is depreciating, meaning that progressively more dollars are required to purchase each pound, then the forward exchange rate F_0 (which equals the dollars required to purchase one pound for delivery in one year) must exceed E_0, the current exchange rate. This is exactly what equation 22.2 tells us: When r_{US} exceeds r_{UK}, F_0 must exceed E_0. The depreciation of the dollar embodied in the ratio of F_0 to E_0 exactly compensates for the difference in interest rates available in the two countries. Of course, the argument also works in reverse: If r_{US} is less than r_{UK}, then F_0 is less than E_0.

What if the interest rate parity relationship is violated? For example, suppose the futures price is \$1.81 instead of \$1.817. You could adopt the following strategy to reap arbitrage profits. In this example let E_1 denote the exchange rate that will prevail in one year. E_1 is, of course, a random variable from the perspective of today's investors.

Action	Initial Cash Flow (\$)	CF in 1 Year (\$)
1. Borrow 1 U.K. pound in London. Convert to dollars.	1.80	$-E_1(1.05)$
2. Lend \$1.80 in the United States.	−1.80	1.80(1.06)
3. Enter a contract to purchase 1.05 pounds at a (futures) price of $F_0 = \$1.81$.	0	$1.05(E_1 - 1.81)$
TOTAL	0	\$.0075

In Step 1, you exchange the one pound borrowed in the United Kingdom for \$1.80 at the current exchange rate. After one year you must repay the pound borrowed with interest. Because the loan is made in the United Kingdom at the U.K. interest rate, you would repay 1.05 pounds, which would be worth $E_1(1.05)$ dollars. The U.S. loan in Step 2 is made at the U.S. interest rate of 6%. The futures position in Step 3 results in receipt of 1.05 pounds, for which you would first pay F_0 dollars each, and then trade into dollars at rate E_1.

Note that the exchange rate risk here is exactly offset between the pound obligation in Step 1 and the futures position in Step 3. The profit from the strategy is therefore risk-free and requires no net investment.

To generalize this strategy:

Action	Initial CF ($)	CF in 1 Year ($)
1. Borrow 1 U.K. pound in London. Convert to dollars.	$\$E_0$	$-\$E_1(1 + r_{UK})$
2. Use proceeds of borrowing in London to lend in the U.S.	$-\$E_0$	$\$E_0(1 + r_{US})$
3. Enter $(1 + r_{UK})$ futures positions to purchase 1 pound for F_0 dollars.	0	$(1 + r_{UK})(E_1 - F_0)$
TOTAL	0	$E_0(1 + r_{US}) - F_0(1 + r_{UK})$

Let us again review the stages of the arbitrage operation. The first step requires borrowing one pound in the United Kingdom. With a current exchange rate of E_0, the one pound is converted into E_0 dollars, which is a cash inflow. In one year the British loan must be paid off with interest, requiring a payment in pounds of $(1 + r_{UK})$, or in dollars of $E_1(1 + r_{UK})$. In the second step the proceeds of the British loan are invested in the United States. This involves an initial cash outflow of $\$E_0$, and a cash inflow of $\$E_0(1 + r_{US})$ in one year. Finally, the exchange risk involved in the British borrowing is hedged in Step 3. Here, the $(1 + r_{UK})$ pounds that will need to be delivered to satisfy the British loan are purchased ahead in the futures contract.

The net proceeds to the arbitrage portfolio are risk-free and given by $E_0(1 + r_{US}) - F_0(1 + r_{UK})$. If this value is positive, borrow in the United Kingdom, lend in the United States, and enter a long futures position to eliminate foreign exchange risk. If the value is negative, borrow in the United States, lend in the United Kingdom, and take a short position in pound futures. When prices are aligned properly to preclude arbitrage opportunities, the expression must equal zero. If it were positive, investors would pursue the arbitrage portfolio. If it were negative, they would pursue the reverse positions.

Rearranging this expression gives us the relationship

$$F_0 = \frac{1 + r_{US}}{1 + r_{UK}} E_0 \tag{22.3}$$

which is the interest rate parity theorem for a one-year horizon, known also as the **covered interest arbitrage relationship.**

CONCEPT CHECK Question 3. What are the arbitrage strategy and associated profits if the initial futures price is $F_0 = \$1.83$/pound?

Ample empirical evidence bears out this relationship. For example, on May 18, 1994, the interest rate on U.S. Treasury securities with maturity of one-half year was 4.85%, whereas the comparable rate in the United Kingdom was 5.19%. The spot exchange rate was \$1.5095/£. Using these values, we find that interest rate parity implies that the forward exchange rate for delivery in one-half year should have been $1.5095 \times (1.0485/1.0519)^{1/2} = \$1.5071$/£. The actual forward rate was \$1.5073/£, which was so close to the parity value that transaction costs would have prevented arbitrageurs from profiting from the discrepancy.

22.3 Interest Rate Futures

The late 1970s and 1980s saw a dramatic increase in the volatility of interest rates, leading to investor desire to hedge returns on fixed-income securities against changes in interest rates. As one example, thrift institutions that had loaned money on home mortgages before 1975 suffered substantial capital losses on those loans when interest rates later increased. An interest rate futures contract could have protected banks against such large swings in yields. The significance of these losses has spurred trading in interest rate futures.

The major U.S. interest rate contracts currently traded are on Treasury bills, Treasury notes, Treasury bonds, and a municipal bond index. The range of these securities provides an opportunity to hedge against a wide spectrum of maturities from very short (T-bills) to long term (T-bonds). In addition, futures contracts tied to Eurodollar rates and interest rates in Germany and the United Kingdom trade on the London International Financial Futures Exchange (LIFFE) and are listed in *The Wall Street Journal*. Figure 21.1 from Chapter 21 includes listings of some of these contracts.

The Treasury contracts call for delivery of a Treasury bond, bill, or note. Should interest rates rise, the market value of the security at delivery will be less than the original futures price, and the deliverer will profit. Hence, the short position in the interest rate futures contract gains when interest rates rise.

Similarly, Treasury bond futures can be useful hedging vehicles for bond dealers or underwriters. We saw earlier, for example, how the T-bond contract could be used by an investor to hedge the value of a T-bond portfolio or by a pension fund manager who anticipates the purchase of a Treasury bond. The newer contract on the municipal bond index allows for more direct hedging of long-term bonds other than Treasury issues.

An episode that occurred in October 1979 illustrates the potential hedging value offered by T-bond contracts. Salomon Brothers, Merrill Lynch, and other underwriters brought out a $1 billion issue of IBM bonds. As is typical, the underwriting syndicate quoted an interest rate at which it guaranteed the bonds could be sold. (In essence, the syndicate buys the company's bonds at an agreed-upon price and then takes the responsibility of reselling them in the open market. If interest rates increase before the bonds can be sold to the public, the syndicate, not the issuer, bears the capital loss from the fall in the value of the bonds.)

In this case, the syndicate led by Salomon Brothers and Merrill Lynch brought out the IBM debt to sell at yields of 9.62% for $500 million of 7-year notes and 9.41% for $500 million of 25-year bonds. These yields were only about four basis points above comparable maturity U.S. government bond yields, reflecting IBM's excellent credit rating. The debt issue was brought to market on Thursday, October 4, when the underwriters began placing the bonds with customers. Interest rates, however, rose slightly that Thursday, making the IBM yields less attractive, and only about 70% of the issue had been placed by Friday afternoon, leaving the syndicate still holding between $250 million and $300 million of bonds.

Then on Saturday, October 6, the Federal Reserve Board announced a major credit-tightening policy. Interest rates jumped by almost a full percentage point. The underwriting syndicate realized the balance of the IBM bonds could not be placed to its regular customers at the original offering price and decided to sell them in the open bond market. By that time, the bonds had fallen nearly 5% in value, so that the underwriter's loss was about $12 million on the unsold bonds. The net loss on the underwriting operation came to about $7 million, after the profit of $5 million that had been realized on the bonds that were placed.

As the major underwriter with the lion's share of the bonds, Salomon lost about $3.5 million on the bond issue. Yet, although most of the other underwriters were vulnerable to the interest rate movement, Salomon had hedged its bond holdings by shorting about $100 million in GNMA and Treasury bond futures. Holding a short position, Salomon Brothers realized profits on the contracts when interest rates increased. The profits on the short futures position resulted because the value of the bonds required to be delivered to satisfy the contracts decreased when interest rates rose. Salomon Brothers probably about broke even on the entire transaction, making estimated gains on the futures position of about $3.5 million, which largely offset the capital loss on the bonds it was holding.

How could Salomon Brothers have constructed the proper hedge ratio, that is, the proper number of futures contracts per bond held in its inventory? The T-bond futures contract nominally calls for delivery of an 8% coupon, 20-year maturity government bond in return for the futures price. (In practice, other bonds may be substituted for this standard bond to settle the contract, but we will use the 8% bond for illustration.) Suppose the market interest rate is 10% and Salomon is holding $100 million worth of bonds, with a coupon rate of 10% and 20 years to maturity. The bonds currently sell at 100% of par value. If the interest rate were to jump to 11% the bonds would fall in value to a market value of $91.98 per $100 of par value, a loss of $8.02 million. (We use semi-annual compounding in this calculation.)

To hedge this risk, Salomon would need to short enough futures so that the profits on the futures position would offset the loss on the bonds. The 8%, 20-year bond of the futures contract would sell for $82.84 at an interest rate of 10%. If the interest rate were to jump to 11%, the bond price would fall to $75.93, and the fall in the price of the 8% bond, $6.91, would approximately equal the profit on the short futures position per $100 par value.[4] Because each contract calls for delivery of $100,000 par value of bonds, the gain on each short position would equal $6,910. Thus, to offset the $8.02 million loss on the value of the bonds, Salomon theoretically would need to hold $8.02 million/$6,910 = 1,161 contracts short. The total gain on the contracts would offset the loss on the bonds and leave Salomon unaffected by interest rate swings.

The actual hedging problem is more difficult for several reasons: (1) Salomon probably would hold more than one issue of bonds in its inventory; (2) interest rates on government and corporate bonds will not be equal and need not move in lockstep; (3) the

[4] We say approximately because the exact figure depends on the time to maturity of the contract. We assume here that the maturity date is less than a month away so that the futures price and the bond price move in virtual lockstep.

T-bond contract may be settled with any of several bonds instead of the 8% benchmark bond; and (4) taxes could complicate the picture. Nevertheless, the principles illustrated here underlie all hedging activity.

22.4 Commodity Futures Pricing

Commodity futures prices are governed by the same general considerations as stock futures. One difference, however, is that the cost of carrying commodities, especially those subject to spoilage, is greater than the cost of carrying financial assets. Moreover, spot prices for some commodities demonstrate marked seasonal patterns that can affect futures pricing.

Pricing with Storage Costs

The cost of carrying commodities includes, in addition to interest costs, storage costs, insurance costs, and an allowance for spoilage of goods in storage. To price commodity futures, let us reconsider the earlier arbitrage strategy that calls for holding both the asset and a short position in the futures contract on the asset. In this case we will denote the price of the commodity at time T as P_T, and assume for simplicity that all noninterest carrying costs (C) are paid in one lump sum at time T, the contract maturity. Carrying costs appear in the final cash flow.

Action	Initial Cash Flow	CF at Time T
Buy asset; pay carrying costs at T	$-P_0$	$P_T - C$
Borrow P_0; repay with interest at time T	P_0	$-P_0(1 + r_f)$
Short futures position	0	$F_0 - P_T$
TOTAL	0	$F_0 - P_0(1 + r_f) - C$

Because market prices should not allow for arbitrage opportunities, the terminal cash flow of this zero net investment, risk-free strategy should be zero.

If the cash flow were positive, this strategy would yield guaranteed profits for no investment. If the cash flow were negative, the reverse of this strategy also would yield profits. In practice, the reverse strategy would involve a short sale of the commodity. This is unusual but may be done as long as the short sale contract appropriately accounts for storage costs.[5] Thus, we conclude that

$$F_0 = P_0(1 + r_f) + C$$

Finally, if we call $c = C/P_0$, and interpret c as the percentage "rate" of carrying costs, we may write

[5] Robert A. Jarrow and George S. Oldfield, "Forward Contracts and Futures Contracts," *Journal of Financial Economics* 9 (1981).

$$F_0 = P_0(1 + r_f + c) \tag{22.4}$$

which is a (one-year) parity relationship for futures involving storage costs. Compare equation 22.4 to the first parity relation for stocks, equation 22.1, and you will see that they are extremely similar. In fact, if we think of carrying costs as a "negative dividend," the equations are identical. This treatment makes intuitive sense because, instead of receiving a dividend yield of d, the storer of the commodity must pay a storage cost of c. Obviously, this parity relationship is simply an extension of those we have seen already.

Actually, although we have called c the carrying cost of the commodity, we may interpret it more generally as the *net* carrying cost, that is, the carrying cost net of the benefits derived from holding the commodity in inventory. For example, part of the "convenience yield" of goods held in inventory is the protection against stocking out, which may result in lost production or sales.

It is vital to note that we derive equation 22.4 assuming that the asset will be bought and stored; it therefore applies only to goods that currently *are* being stored. Two kinds of commodities cannot be expected to be stored. The first is highly perishable goods, such as fresh strawberries, for which storage is technologically not feasible. The second includes goods that are not stored for economic reasons. For example, it would be foolish to buy wheat now, planning to store it for ultimate use in three years. Instead, it is clearly preferable to delay the purchase of the wheat until after the harvest of the third year. The wheat is then obtained without incurring the storage costs. Moreover, if the wheat harvest in the third year is comparable to this year's, you could obtain it at roughly the same price as you would pay this year. By waiting to purchase, you avoid both interest and storage costs.

In fact, it is generally not reasonable to hold large quantities of agricultural goods across a harvesting period. Why pay to store this year's wheat, when you can purchase next year's wheat when it is harvested? Maintaining large wheat inventories across harvests makes sense only if such a small wheat crop is forecast that wheat prices will not fall when the new supply is harvested.

CONCEPT CHECK

Question 4. People are willing to buy and "store" shares of stock despite the fact that their purchase ties up capital. Most people, however, are not willing to buy and store wheat. What is the difference in the properties of the expected evolution of stock prices versus wheat prices that accounts for this result?

Because storage across harvests is costly, equation 22.4 should not be expected to apply for holding periods that span harvest times, nor should it apply to perishable goods that are available only "in season." You can see that this is so if you look at the futures markets page of the newspaper. Figure 22.6, for example, gives futures prices for several times to maturity for corn and for gold. Whereas the futures price for gold, which is a stored commodity, increases steadily with the maturity of the contract, the futures price for corn is seasonal; it rises within a harvest period as equation 22.4 would predict, but the price then falls across harvests as new supplies become available.

Figure 22.6

Futures prices for corn and gold

Source: *The Wall Street Journal*, December 21, 1994. Reprinted by permission of *The Wall Street Journal*,

Tuesday, December 20, 1994

Open Interest Reflects Previous Trading Day.

	Open	High	Low	Settle	Change	Lifetime High	Lifetime Low	Open Interest
GRAINS AND OILSEEDS								
CORN (CBT) 5,000 bu.; cents per bu.								
Dec	215¾	219¼	215¼	219	+ 3	277	210½	1,158
Mr95	226½	229¾	226¼	228¾	+ 2	282½	220½	115,575
May	234	237	233½	236	+ 1¾	285	228	45,590
July	238¼	241	238	240¼	+ 1¾	285½	232½	45,240
Sept	241¾	244¼	241¾	243¾	+ 1½	270½	238	5,117
Dec	245¾	248¼	245½	247¾	+ 1¼	263	235½	29,032
Mr96	252	255	252	254½	+ 1½	260¼	249½	1,903
July	259	261¾	259	261¾	+ 1¼	267	254	1,568
Dec	250	251½	250	251½	+ 1	257	239	494
Est vol 36,000; vol Mon 28,520; open Int 245,677, +1,345.								
OATS (CBT) 5,000 bu.; cents per bu.								
Est vol 10,000; vol Mon 11,463; open int 50,439, −989.								
GOLD (CMX) – 100 troy oz.; $ per troy oz.								
Dec	381.80	382.30	381.40	381.80	+ 2.60	426.50	343.00	116
Fb95	382.50	385.20	382.50	384.20	+ 2.50	411.00	363.50	88,808
Apr	386.30	389.10	386.30	388.20	+ 2.50	425.00	381.70	13,551
June	390.50	393.30	390.50	392.40	+ 2.50	430.00	351.00	21,491
Aug		....	....	396.80	+ 2.50	414.50	380.50	12,225
Oct		....	....	401.30	+ 2.60	419.20	401.00	4,839
Dec	405.00	406.00	405.00	406.00	+ 2.60	439.50	358.00	9,526
Fb96		....	....	410.70	+ 2.70	424.50	404.60	2,140
Apr		....	....	415.40	+ 2.80	430.20	418.30	2,260
June		....	....	420.20	+ 2.80	447.00	370.90	5,556
Aug		....	....	424.90	+ 2.80	....	....	314
Dec		....	....	434.60	+ 2.80	447.50	379.60	4,071
Ju97		....	....	449.20	+ 2.80	456.00	436.00	1,951
Dec		....	....	464.00	+ 2.80	477.00	402.00	2,696
Ju98		....	....	478.70	+ 2.80	489.50	481.00	1,875
Dec		....	....	493.60	+ 2.80	505.00	468.00	3,263
Ju99		....	....	509.00	+ 2.80	520.00	511.00	2,613
Est vol 20,000; vol Mon 7,674; open Int 177,311, +117.								

Compare, for example, the corn futures price for delivery in July 1996 versus December 1996.

Futures pricing across seasons requires a different approach that is not based on storage across harvest periods. In place of general no-arbitrage restrictions we rely instead on risk premium theory and discounted cash flow (DCF) analysis.

Discounted Cash Flow Analysis for Commodity Futures

We have said that most agricultural commodities follow seasonal price patterns; prices rise before a harvest and then fall at the harvest when the new crop becomes available for consumption. Figure 22.7 graphs this pattern. The price of the commodity following the harvest must rise at the rate of the total cost of carry (interest plus noninterest carrying costs) to induce holders of the commodity to store it willingly for future sale instead of selling it immediately. Inventories will be run down to near zero just before the next harvest.

Clearly, this pattern differs sharply from financial assets such as stocks or gold, for which there is no seasonal price movement. For financial assets, the current price is set in market equilibrium at a level that promises an expected rate of capital gains plus dividends equal to the required rate of return on the asset. Financial assets are stored only if their economic rate of return compensates for the cost of carry. In other words,

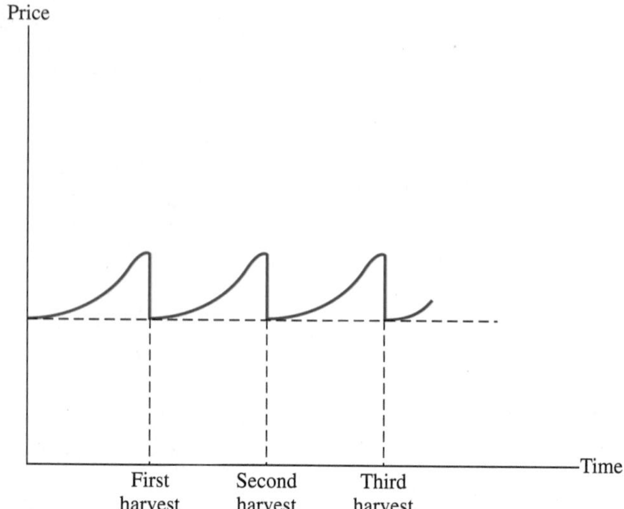

Figure 22.7
Typical commodity price pattern over the season. Prices adjusted for inflation.

financial assets are priced so that storing them produces a fair return. Agricultural prices, by contrast, are subject to steep periodic drops as each crop is harvested, which makes storage across harvests consequently unprofitable.

Of course, neither the exact size of the harvest nor the demand for the good is known in advance, so the spot price of the commodity cannot be perfectly predicted. As weather forecasts change, for example, the expected size of the crop and the expected future spot price of the commodity are updated continually.

Given the current expectation of the spot price of the commodity at some future date and a measure of the risk characteristics of that price, we can measure the present value of a claim to receive the commodity at that future date. We simply calculate the appropriate risk premium from a model such as the CAPM or APT and discount the expected spot price at the appropriate risk-adjusted interest rate.

Table 22.4, which presents betas on a variety of commodities, shows that the beta of orange juice, for example, was estimated to be .117 over the period. If the T-bill rate is currently 4.5% and the historical market risk premium has been about 8.5%, the appropriate discount rate for orange juice would be given by the CAPM as

$$4.5\% + .117(8.5\%) = 5.49\%$$

If the expected spot price for orange juice six months from now is \$1.45 per pound, the present value of a six-month deferred claim to a pound of orange juice is simply

$$\$1.45/(1.0549)^{1/2} = \$1.41$$

What would the proper futures price for orange juice be? The contract calls for the ultimate exchange of orange juice for the futures price. We have just shown that the present value of the juice is \$1.41. This should equal the present value of the futures price that will be paid for the juice. A commitment to a payment of F_0 dollars in six months has a present value of $F_0/(1.045)^{1/2} = .978 \times F_0$. (Note that the discount rate

Table 22.4 Commodity Betas

Commodity	Beta
Wheat	−0.370
Corn	−0.429
Oats	0.000
Soybeans	−0.266
Soybean oil	−0.650
Soybean meal	0.239
Broilers	−1.692
Plywood	0.660
Potatoes	−0.610
Platinum	0.221
Wool	0.307
Cotton	−0.015
Orange juice	0.117
Propane	−3.851
Cocoa	−0.291
Silver	−0.272
Copper	0.005
Cattle	0.365
Hogs	−0.148
Pork bellies	−0.062
Egg	−0.293
Lumber	−0.131
Sugar	−2.403

Source: Zvi Bodie and Victor Rosansky, "Risk and Return in Commodity Futures," *Financial Analysts Journal* 36 (May–June 1980).

is the risk-free rate of 4.5%, because the promised payment is fixed and therefore independent of market conditions.)

To equate the present values of the promised payment of F_0 and the promised receipt of orange juice, we would set

$$.978F_0 = \$1.41$$

or $F_0 = \$1.44$.

The general rule, then, to determine the appropriate futures price is to equate the present value of the future payment of F_0 and the present value of the commodity to be received. This gives us

$$\frac{F_0}{(1 + r_f)^T} = \frac{E(P_T)}{(1 + k)^T}$$

or (22.5)

$$F_0 = E(P_T)\left(\frac{1 + r_f}{1 + k}\right)^T$$

where k is the required rate of return on the commodity, which may be obtained from a model of asset market equilibrium such as the CAPM.

Note that equation 22.5 is perfectly consistent with the spot-futures parity relationship. For example, apply equation 22.5 to the futures price for a stock paying no dividends. Because the entire return on the stock is in the form of capital gains, the expected rate of capital gains must equal k, the required rate of return on the stock. Consequently, the expected price of the stock will be its current price times $(1 + k)^T$, or $E(P_T) = P_0(1 + k)^T$. Substituting this expression into equation 22.5 results in $F_0 = P_0(1 + r_f)^T$, which is exactly the parity relationship. This equilibrium derivation of the parity relationship simply reinforces the no-arbitrage restrictions we derived earlier. The spot-futures parity relationship may be obtained from the equilibrium condition that all portfolios earn fair expected rates of return.

The advantage of the arbitrage proofs that we have explored is that they do not rely on the validity of any particular model of security market equilibrium. The absence of arbitrage opportunities is a much more robust basis for argument than the CAPM, for example. Moreover, arbitrage proofs clearly demonstrate how an investor can exploit any misalignment in the spot-futures relationship. To their disadvantage, arbitrage restrictions may be less precise than desirable in the face of storage costs or costs of short selling.

We can summarize by saying that the actions of arbitrageurs force the futures prices of financial assets to maintain a precise relationship with the price of the underlying financial asset. This relationship is described by the spot-futures parity formula. Opportunities for arbitrage are more limited in the case of commodity futures because such commodities often are not stored. Hence, to make a precise prediction for the correct relationship between futures and spot prices, we must rely on a model of security market equilibrium such as the CAPM or APT and estimate the unobservables, the expected spot price, and the appropriate interest rate. Such models will be perfectly consistent with the parity relationships in the benchmark case where investors willingly store the commodity.

CONCEPT CHECK

Question 5. Suppose that the systematic risk of orange juice were to increase, holding the expected time T price of juice constant. If the expected spot price is unchanged, would the futures price change? In what direction? What is the intuition behind your answer?

22.5 SWAPS

We noted in Chapter 15 that interest rate swaps have become common tools for interest rate risk management. Since their inception in 1981, swaps have grown to a market of well over $6 trillion in notional principal. A large and active market also exists for foreign exchange swaps. Recall that a swap arrangement obligates two counterparties to exchange cash flows at one or more future dates. To illustrate, a **foreign exchange swap** might call for one party to exchange $1.6 million for 1 million British pounds in each of the next five years. An **interest rate swap** with notional principal of $1 million might call for one party to exchange a variable cash flow equal to $1 million times the

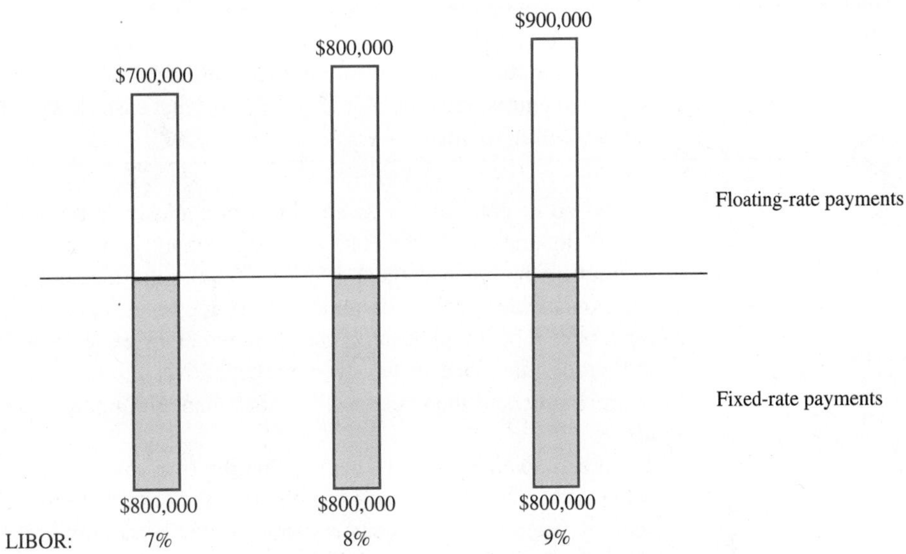

Figure 22.8
Three-year interest rate swap

LIBOR rate for $1 million times a fixed rate of 8%. In this way the two parties exchange the cash flows corresponding to interest payments on a fixed-rate 8% coupon bond for those corresponding to payments on a floating-rate bond paying LIBOR.

Swaps offer participants easy ways to restructure their balance sheets. Consider, for example, a firm that has issued long-term bonds with total par value of $10 million at a fixed interest rate of 8%. The firm is obligated to make interest payments of $800,000 per year. However, it can change the nature of its interest obligations from fixed rate to floating rate by entering a swap agreement to pay a floating rate of interest and receive a fixed rate.

A swap with notional principal of $10 million that exchanges LIBOR for an 8% fixed rate will bring the firm fixed cash inflows of $800,000 per year and obligate it to pay instead $10 million × r_{LIBOR}. The receipt of the fixed payments from the swap agreement offsets the firm's interest obligations on the outstanding bond issue, leaving it with a net obligation to make floating-rate payments. The swap, therefore, is a way for the firm to effectively convert its outstanding fixed-rate debt into synthetic floating-rate debt.

To illustrate the mechanics of the swap agreement, suppose that the swap is for three years and the LIBOR rates turns out to be 7%, 8%, and 9% in the next three years. The cash flow streams called for by the swap would be as illustrated in Figure 22.8. In the first year, when LIBOR is 7%, the fixed-rate payer would be owed a cash flow equal to 0.07 × $10 million = $700,000, and would owe the 8% fixed rate on the notional principal, or $800,000. Actually, instead of two cash payments, the parties would simply exchange one payment equal to the difference in required payments. Here, the fixed-rate payer would pay $100,000 to the fixed-rate receiver. In the second year, when LIBOR equals 8%, no net payments would be exchanged. In the third year, the fixed-rate payer would receive a net cash flow of $100,000.

CONCEPT CHECK Question 6. Suppose that two parties enter a three-year swap agreement to exchange the LIBOR rate for a 7% fixed rate on \$20 million of notional principal. If LIBOR in the three years turns out to be 8%, 7%, and 9%, what cash flows will be exchanged between the two counterparties?

Instead of entering the swap, the firm could have retired its outstanding debt and issued floating-rate notes. The swap agreement is a far cheaper and quicker way to restructure the balance sheet, however. The swap does not entail trading costs to buy back outstanding bonds or underwriting fees and lengthy registration procedures to issue new debt. In addition, if the firm perceives price advantages in either the fixed- or floating-rate markets, the swap market allows it to issue its debt in the cheaper of the two markets, and then "convert" to the financing mode it feels best suits its business needs.

Foreign exchange swaps also enable the firm to quickly and cheaply restructure its balance sheet. Suppose, for example, that the firm that issued the \$10 million in debt actually preferred that its interest obligations be denominated in British pounds. For example, the issuing firm might have been a British corporation that perceived advantageous financing opportunities in the United States but prefers pound-denominated liabilities. Then the firm, whose debt currently obliges it to make dollar-denominated payments of \$800,000, can agree to swap a given number of pounds each year for \$800,000. By so doing, it effectively covers its dollar obligation and replaces it with a new pound-denominated obligation.

How can the fair swap rate be determined? For example, do we know that an exchange of LIBOR is a fair trade for a fixed rate of 8%? Or, what is the fair swap rate between dollars and pounds for the foreign exchange swap we considered? To answer these questions we can exploit the analogy between a swap agreement and forward or futures contract.

Consider a swap agreement to exchange dollars for pounds for one period only. Next year, for example, one might exchange \$1 million for £0.6 million. This is no more than a simple forward contract in foreign exchange. The dollar-paying party is contracting to buy British pounds in one year for a number of dollars agreed to today. The forward exchange rate for one-year delivery is $F_1 = \$1.67$/pound. We know from the interest rate parity relationship that this forward price should be related to the spot exchange rate, E_0, by the formula $F_1 = E_0(1 + r_{US})/(1 + r_{UK})$. Because a one-period swap is in fact a forward contract, the fair swap rate is also given by the parity relationship.

Now consider an agreement to trade foreign exchange for two periods. This agreement could be structured as a portfolio of two separate forward contracts. If so, the forward price for the exchange of currencies in one year would be $F_1 = E_0(1 + r_{US})/(1 + r_{UK})$, while the forward price for the exchange in the second year would be $F_2 = E_0[(1 + r_{US})/(1 + r_{UK})]^2$. As an example, suppose that $E_0 = \$1.70$/pound, $r_{US} = 4$ percent, and $r_{UK} = 7\%$. Then, using the parity relationship, we would have prices for forward delivery of $F_1 = \$1.70/£ \times (1.05/1.07) = \$1.668/£$ and $F_2 = \$1.70/£ \times (1.05/1.07)^2 = \$1.637/£$. Figure 22.9**A,** illustrates this sequence of cash exchanges assuming that the swap calls for delivery of one pound in each year. Although the dollars to be paid in each of the two years are known today, they vary from year to year.

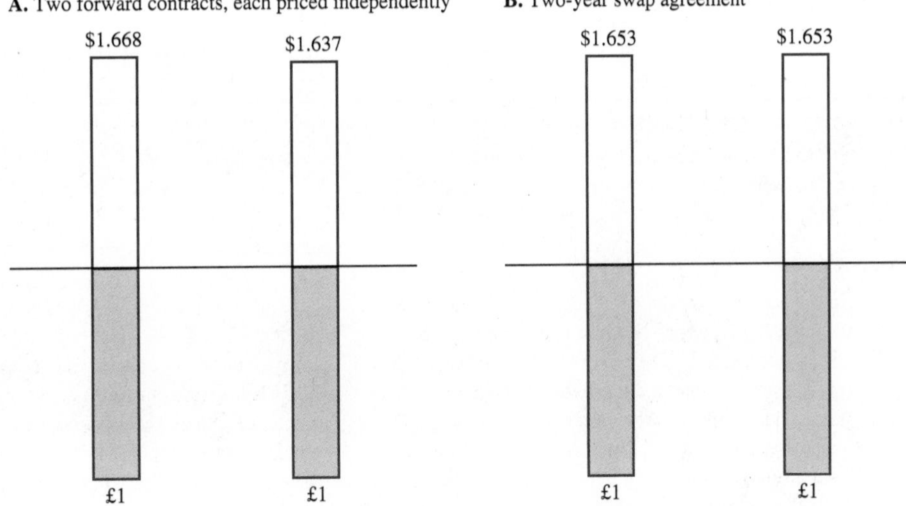

Figure 22.9
Forward contracts versus swaps

In contrast, a swap agreement to exchange currency for two years would call for a fixed exchange rate to be used for the duration of the swap. This means that the same number of dollars would be paid per pound in each year, as illustrated in Figure 22.9 **B.** Because the forward prices for delivery in each of the next two years are $1.668/£ and $1.637/£, the fixed exchange rate that makes the two-period swap a fair deal must be between these two values. Therefore, the dollar payer underpays for the pound in the first year (compared to the forward exchange rate) and overpays in the second year. Thus, the swap can be viewed as a portfolio of forward transactions, but instead of each transaction being priced independently, one forward price is applied to all of the transactions.

Given this insight, it is easy to determine the fair swap price. If we were to purchase one pound per year for two years using two independent forward rate agreements, we would pay F_1 dollars in a one year and F_2 dollars in two years. If instead we enter a swap, we pay a constant rate of F^* dollars per pound. Because both strategies must be equally costly, we conclude that

$$\frac{F_1}{1+y_1} + \frac{F_2}{(1+y_2)^2} = \frac{F^*}{1+y_1} + \frac{F^*}{(1+y_2)^2}$$

where y_1 and y_2 are the appropriate yields from the yield curve for discounting dollar cash flows of one- and two-years maturity, respectively. In our example, where we have assumed a flat U.S. yield curve at 5%, we would solve

$$\frac{1.668}{1.05} + \frac{1.637}{1.05^2} = \frac{F^*}{1.05} + \frac{F^*}{1.05^2}$$

which implies that $F^* = 1.653$. The same principle would apply to a foreign exchange swap of any other maturity. In essence, we need to find the level annuity, F^*, with the same present value as the stream of annual cash flows that would be incurred in a sequence of forward rate agreements.

CBOT, Chicago Merc Plan to Better Monitor Swaps

Both the Chicago Mercantile Exchange and the Chicago Board of Trade are working to attract business from the privately traded derivatives market by setting up systems that would improve monitoring of these "over-the-counter" transactions.

In the latest move, the Merc announced last week that it was creating an agency to manage collateral for interest-rate swap dealers. The CBOT, meanwhile, would go a step further to create a clearinghouse to actually guarantee swaps and other derivatives transactions. Exchange officials say such efforts could reduce the risk of unpleasant surprises in the $6.5 trillion swap market, such as those that caused heavy losses for Procter & Gamble Cos. and Gibson Greetings Inc. earlier this year.

Swaps are agreements to exchange streams of payments over time. In a simple interest-rate swap, a dealer or large institution will commit to pay a fixed interest rate, in return for receiving payments based on a short-term floating rate. Because these contracts are privately traded between two consenting parties, they carry the risk that one of the participants won't keep its promise. To guard against that possibility, participants increasingly desire that swap partners post collateral against their obligations.

Among its new services, the Merc plans to value swap positions and collateral daily at current market prices. By providing up-to-the-minute data on changes in the accounts, it could help swappers avert nasty surprises. The Merc system isn't a clearinghouse, or middleman that actually guarantees transactions if one participant defaults. But regulators and dealers see it as a positive step in curbing risks in the market.

"It's useful to have transactions and collateral valued on a daily basis so exposures can be monitored a little more closely," said Mary Schapiro, chairman of the Commodity Futures Trading Commission, which regulates the futures industry.

Guaranteed Transactions

The CBOT system, by contrast, would not only provide collateral services, but also guarantee transactions through the Board of Trade Clearing Corp. Ms. Schapiro called the CBOT effort "a wonderful development," but noted that it faces greater obstacles because it is more ambitious.

"Given the size of the over-the-counter [derivatives] market and some of the volatility we've seen in the last couple months, anything like a collateral management

Interest rate swaps can be subjected to precisely the same analysis. Here, the forward contract is on an interest rate. For example, if you swap LIBOR for an 8% fixed rate with notional principal of $100, then you have entered a forward contract for delivery of $100 times r_{LIBOR} for a fixed "forward" price of $8. If the swap agreement is for many periods, the fair spread will be determined by the entire sequence of interest rate forward prices over the life of the swap.

Credit Risk in the Swap Market

The rapid growth of the swap market, which now exceeds $6 trillion in notional principal for interest rate swaps alone, has given rise to increasing concern about credit risk in these markets and the possibility of a default by a major swap trader. The nearby box discusses plans by the Chicago Board of Trade and the Chicago Mercantile Exchange to offer collateral management systems, marking-to-market services, and possibly even exchange guarantees to the swap market to help swap traders manage credit risk.

facility or a clearing system is going to provide market users some greater comfort about the integrity" of their transactions, Ms. Schapiro said.

The Merc already manages more than $9 billion in collateral against futures trades, and some swaps dealers question whether a new collateral facility is really needed. But one advantage with the new depositor is that swaps participants wouldn't have to trade futures to have access to it.

Lower Cost

The Merc's depository would also provide a lower-cost way to manage collateral by consolidating dealers' payments. As interest-rate moves alter the value of swap positions, collateral requirements likewise change. Thus, a dealer with many swaps outstanding would typically have to make many payments to meet all its collateral demands. By contrast, with the Merc system, "if you owe money to 50 swaps dealers, you would just write one check and we net it out," said Todd Petzel, a Merc executive vice president.

The exchange stresses it wants to attract business from the private derivatives market in a way that doesn't directly compete with swaps dealers. "This is not intended as a competitive wedge to get into the swaps market," said Merton H. Miller, a Nobel laureate and finance professor at the University of Chicago who sits on the Merc's board of directors.

CBOT, by contrast, is taking a more aggressive tack by challenging the large banks and financial-services firms that currently act as clearers. "Here's a vehicle to trade swaps on a screen and have the added advantage of marking to market, clearing and transparent pricing," said David Prosperi, CBOT spokesman.

Booming Swaps Market

Privately traded interest rate swaps have grown at a torrid pace, attracting the interest of Chicago futures exchanges (outstanding national value, roughly equivalent to open interest in trillions of dollars)

Source: International Swaps and Derivatives Association

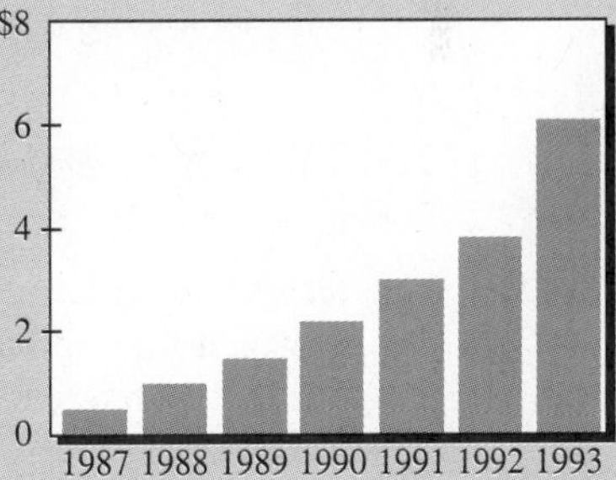

Source: Steven E. Levingston, *The Wall Street Journal*, December 15, 1994. Reprinted by permission of *The Wall Street Journal*,

Actually, although credit risk in the swap market certainly is not trivial, it is not nearly as large as the magnitude of notional principal would suggest. To see why, consider a simple interest-rate swap of LIBOR for a fixed rate. At the time the transaction is initiated, it has zero net present value to both parties for the same reason that a futures contract has zero value at inception: Both are simply contracts to exchange cash in the future at terms established today that make both parties willing to enter into the deal. Even if one party were to back out of the deal at this moment, it would not cost the counterparty anything, because another trader could be found to take its place.

Once interest rates change, however, the situation is not as simple. Suppose, for example, that interest rates increase shortly after the swap agreement has begun. The floating-rate payer therefore suffers a loss, while the fixed-rate payer enjoys a gain. If the floating-rate payer reneges on its commitment at this point, the fixed-rate payer suffers a loss. However, that loss is not as large as the notional principal of the swap, for the default of the floating-rate payer relieves the fixed-rate payer from its obligation as well. The loss is only the *difference* between the values of the fixed-rate and floating-rate obligations, not the *total* value of the payments that the floating-rate payer was obligated to make.

Let's illustrate with an example. Consider a swap written on $1 million of notional principal that calls for exchange of LIBOR for a fixed rate of 8% for five years. Suppose, for simplicity, that the yield curve is currently flat at 8%. With LIBOR thus equal to 8%, no cash flows will be exchanged unless interest rates change. But now suppose that the yield curve immediately shifts up to 9%. The floating-rate payer now is obligated to pay a cash flow of (.09 − .08) × $1 million = $10,000 each year to the fixed rate payer (as long as rates remain at 9%). If the floating-rate payer defaults on the swap, the fixed-rate payer loses the prospect of that five-year annuity. The present value of that annuity is $10,000 × PA(9%, 5 years) = $38,897. This loss may not be trivial, but it is less than 4% of notional principal. We conclude that the credit risk of the swap is far less than notional principal. Again, this is because the default by the floating-rate payer costs the counterparty only the net difference between the LIBOR rate and the fixed rate.

Swap Variations

Swaps have given rise to a wide range of spinoff products. Many of these add option features to the basic swap agreement. For example, an *interest rate cap* is an agreement in which the cap buyer makes a payment today in exchange for possible future payments if a "reference" interest rate (usually LIBOR) exceeds a "limit rate" on a series of settlement dates. For example, if the limit rate is 7%, then the cap holder receives (r_{LIBOR} − 0.07) for each dollar of notional principal if the LIBOR rate exceeds 7%. The purchaser of the cap in effect has entered a swap agreement to exchange the LIBOR rate for a fixed rate of 7% with an option not to do the swap in any period that the transaction is unprofitable. The payoff to the holder of the cap is

(Reference rate − Limit rate) × Notional principal *if* this value is positive

and zero otherwise. This, of course, is the payoff of an option to purchase a cash flow proportional to the LIBOR rate for an exercise price proportional to the limit rate.

Analogously to caps, an *interest rate floor* pays its holder in any period that the reference interest rate falls *below* some limit. This is analogous to a sequence of options to sell the reference rate for a stipulated "strike rate."

A *collar* combines interest rate caps and floors. A collar entails the purchase of a cap with one limit rate, and the sale of a floor with a lower limit rate. If a firm starts with a floating-rate liability and buys the cap, it achieves protection against rates rising. If rates do rise, the cap provides a cash flow equal to the reference interest rate for a payment equal to the limit rate. Therefore, the cap places an upper bound equal to the limit rate on the firm's interest rate expense. The written floor places a limit on how much the firm can benefit from rate declines. Even if interest rates fall dramatically, the firm's savings on its floating-rate obligation will be offset by its obligation to pay the difference between the reference rate and the limit rate. Therefore, the collar limits the firm's net cost of funds to a value between the limit rate on the cap and the limit rate on the floor.

Other option-based variations on the basic swap arrangement are *swaptions*. A swaption is an option on a swap. The buyer of the swaption has the right to enter an interest rate swap on some reference interest rate at a prespecified fixed interest rate on or before some expiration date. A call swaption (often called a *payer swaption*) is the right to pay the fixed rate in a swap and receive the floating rate. A put swaption is the right to receive the fixed rate and pay the floating rate. An exit option is the right to walk away from a swap without penalty. Swaptions can be European or American.

There also are futures and forward variations on swaps. A forward swap, for example, obligates both traders to enter a swap at some date in the future with terms agreed to today.

SUMMARY

1. Futures contracts calling for cash settlement are traded on various stock market indexes. The contracts may be mixed with Treasury bills to construct artificial equity positions, which makes them potentially valuable tools for market timers. Market index contracts are used also by arbitrageurs who attempt to profit from violations of the parity relationship.

2. Foreign exchange futures trade on several foreign currencies, as well as on a European currency index. The interest rate parity relationship for foreign exchange futures is

$$F_0 = E_0\left(\frac{1 + r_{\text{US}}}{1 + r_{\text{foreign}}}\right)^T$$

Deviations of the futures price from this value imply arbitrage opportunity. Empirical evidence, however, suggests that generally the parity relationship is satisfied.

3. Interest rate futures allow for hedging against interest rate fluctuations in several different markets. The most actively traded contract is for Treasury bonds.

4. Commodity futures pricing is complicated by costs for storage of the underlying commodity. When the asset is willingly stored by investors, then the storage costs enter the futures pricing equation as follows:

$$F_0 = P_0(1 + r_f + c)$$

The noninterest carrying costs, c, play the role of a "negative dividend" in this context.

5. When commodities are not stored for investment purposes, the correct futures price must be determined using general risk-return principles. In this event.

$$F_0 = E(P_T)\left(\frac{1 + r_f}{1 + k}\right)^T$$

The equilibrium (risk-return) and the no-arbitrage predictions of the proper futures price are consistent with one another.

6. Swaps, which call for the exchange of a series of cash flows, may be viewed as portfolios of forward contracts. Each transaction may be viewed as a separate forward agreement. However, instead of pricing each exchange independently, the swap sets one "forward price" that applies to all of the transactions. Therefore, the swap price will be an average of the forward prices that would prevail if each exchange were priced separately.

Key Terms

Index arbitrage
Program trading
Triple-witching hour
Interest rate parity theorem
Covered interest arbitrage relationship
Foreign exchange swap
Interest rate swap

Selected Readings

A good textbook on futures markets is:

Siegel, Daniel R.; and Diane F. Siegel. *Futures Markets.* Chicago: Dryden Press, 1990.

Evidence on the effects of index arbitrage on stock market prices and volatility is given in:

Stoll, Hans R.; and Robert E. Whaley. "Expiration-Day Effects: What Has Changed?" *Financial Analysts Journal,* January–February 1991.

A useful introduction to foreign exchange markets may be found in:

Chrystal, K. Alex. "A Guide to Foreign Exchange Markets." *Federal Reserve Bank of St. Louis,* March 1984.

The use of futures contracts in the management of interest rate risk is explored in several articles in:

Fabozzi, Frank J.; T. Dessa Fabozzi; and Irving M. Pollack, eds. *The Handbook of Fixed Income Securities,* 3rd ed. Homewood Ill.: Business One Irwin, 1991.

A good introduction to swaps is:

Brown, Keith C.; and Donald J. Smith. *Interest Rate and Currency Swaps: A Tutorial.* Charlottesville, Va.: Institute of Chartered Financial Analysts, 1995.

Problems

1. Consider the futures contract written on the S&P 500 index, and maturing in six months. The interest rate is 5% per six-month period, and the future value of dividends expected to be paid over the next six months is $8. The current index level is 427.5. Assume that you can short sell the S&P index.
   a. Suppose the expected rate of return on the market is 10% per six-month period. What is the expected level of the index in six months?
   b. What is the theoretical no-arbitrage price for a six-month futures contract on the S&P 500 stock index?
   c. Suppose the futures price is 424. Is there an arbitrage opportunity here? If so, how would you exploit it?
2. Suppose that the value of the S&P 500 stock index is 450.
   a. If each futures contract costs $25 to trade with a discount broker, how much is the transaction cost per dollar of stock controlled by the futures contract?
   b. If the average price of a share on the NYSE is about $40, how much is the transaction cost per "typical share" controlled by one futures contract?
   c. For small investors, the typical transaction cost per share in trading stocks directly is about 30 cents per share. How many times the transactions costs in futures markets is this?
3. The one-year futures price on a stock-index portfolio is 406, the stock index currently is 400, the one-year risk-free interest rate is 3%, and the year-end dividend that will be paid on a $400 investment in the market index portfolio is $5.

a. By how much is the contract mispriced?
b. Formulate a zero-net-investment arbitrage portfolio and show that you can lock in riskless profits equal to the futures mispricing.
c. Now assume (as is true for small investors) that if you short sell the stocks in the market index, the proceeds of the short sale are kept with the broker, and you do not receive any interest income on the funds. Is there still an arbitrage opportunity (assuming that you don't already own the shares in the index)? Explain.
d. Given the short-sale rules, what is the no-arbitrage *band* for the stock-futures price relationship? That is, given a stock index of 400, how high and how low can the futures price be without giving rise to arbitrage opportunities?

4. Consider these futures market data for the June delivery S&P 500 contract, exactly six months hence. The S&P 500 index is at 400, and the June maturity contract is at $F_0 = 401$.
a. If the current interest rate is 2.2% semiannually, and the average dividend rate of the stocks in the index is 1.2% semiannually, what fraction of the proceeds of stock short sales would need to be available to you to earn arbitrage profits?
b. Suppose that you in fact have access to 90% of the proceeds from a short sale. What is the lower bound on the futures price that rules out arbitrage opportunities? By how much does the actual futures price fall below the no-arbitrage bound? Formulate the appropriate arbitrage strategy, and calculate the profits to that strategy.

5. You manage a $4 million portfolio, currently all invested in equities, and believe that you have extraordinary market-timing skills. You believe that the market is on the verge of a big but short-lived downturn; you would move your portfolio temporarily into T-bills, but you do not want to incur the transaction costs of liquidating and reestablishing your equity position. Instead, you decide to temporarily hedge your equity holdings with S&P 500 index futures contracts.
a. Should you be long or short the contracts? Why?
b. If your equity holdings are invested in a market-index fund, into how many contracts should you enter? The S&P 500 index is now at 400 and the contract multiplier is 500.
c. How does your answer to (*b*) change if the beta of your portfolio is .6?

CFA®

6. Michelle Industries issued a Swiss franc-denominated five-year discount note for SFr 200 million. The proceeds were converted to U.S. dollars to purchase capital equipment in the U.S. The company wants to hedge this currency exposure and is considering the following alternatives:*
a. At-the-money Swiss franc call options.
b. Swiss franc forwards.
c. Swiss franc futures.
Contrast the essential characteristics of each of these three derivative instruments.

---

7. Suppose that the spot price of the Swiss franc is currently 40 cents. The one-year futures price is 44 cents. Is the interest rate higher in the United States or Switzerland?
8. *a.* The spot price of the British pound is currently \$1.60. If the risk-free interest rate on one-year government bonds is 4% in the United States and 8% in the United Kingdom, what must the forward price of the pound be for delivery one year from now?

   b. How could an investor make risk-free arbitrage profits if the forward price were higher than the price you gave in answer to (*a*)? Give a numerical example.
9. Consider the following information:

$$r_{US} = 4\% \qquad r_{UK} = 8\%$$
$$E_0 = 1.60 \text{ dollars per pound}$$
$$F_0 = 1.58 \text{ (one-year delivery)}$$

where the interest rates are annual yields on U.S. or U.K. bills. Given this information:

   a. Where would you lend?

   b. Where would you borrow?

   c. How could you arbitrage?

10. René Michaels, CFA, plans to invest \$1 million in U.S. government cash equivalents for the next 90 days. Michaels's client has authorized her to use non-U.S. government cash equivalents, but only if the currency risk is hedged to U.S. dollars by using forward currency contracts.*

   a. Calculate the U.S. dollar value of the hedged investment at the end of 90 days for each of the two cash equivalents in the table below. Show all calculations.

   b. Briefly explain the theory that best accounts for your results.

   c. Based on this theory, estimate the implied interest rate for a 90-day U.S. government cash equivalent.

Interest Rates
90-Day Cash Equivalents

Japanese government	7.6%
German government	8.6%

Exchange Rates
Currency Units per U.S. Dollar

	Spot	90-Day Forward
Japanese yen	133.05	133.47
German deutschemark	1.5260	1.5348

11. You believe that the spread between municipal bond yields and U.S. Treasury bond yields is going to narrow in the coming month. How can you profit from such a change using the municipal bond and T-bond futures contracts?

*Reprinted, with permission, from the Level III 1991 *CFA Study Guide*.

12. Salomon Brothers is underwriting an issue of a 30-year zero-coupon corporate bonds with a face value of $100 million and a current market value of $5.354 million (a yield of 5% per six-month period). The firm must hold the bonds for a few days before issuing them to the public, which exposes it to interest rate risk. Salomon wishes to hedge its position by using T-bond futures contracts. The current T-bond futures price is $90.80 per $100 par value, and the T-bond contract will be settled using a 20-year, 8% coupon bond paying interest semi-annually. The contract is due to expire in a few days, so the T-bond price and the T-bond futures price are virtually identical. The yield implied on the bond is therefore 4.5% per six-month period. (Confirm this as a first step.) Assume that the yield curve is flat and that the corporate bond will continue to yield 0.5% more than T-bonds per six-month period, even if the general level of interest rates should change. What hedge ratio should Salomon Brothers use to hedge its bond holdings against possible interest rate fluctuations over the next few days?
13. If the spot price of gold is $350 per troy ounce, the risk-free interest rate is 10%, and storage and insurance costs are zero, what should the forward price of gold be for delivery in one year? Use an arbitrage argument to prove your answer. Include a numerical example showing how you could make risk-free arbitrage profits if the forward price exceeded its upper bound value.
14. If the corn harvest today is poor, would you expect this fact to have any effect on today's futures prices for corn to be delivered (postharvest) two years from today? Under what circumstances will there be no effect?
15. Suppose that the price of corn is risky, with a beta of .5. The monthly storage cost is $0.03, and the current spot price is $2.75, with an expected spot price in three months of $2.94. If the expected rate of return on the market is 1.8% per month, with a risk-free rate of 1% per month, would you store corn for three months?

16. You are provided the information outlined as follows to be used in answering this question.*

Issue	Price	Yield to Maturity	Modified Duration*
U.S. Treasury bond 11¾% maturing Nov. 15, 2014	100	11.75%	7.6 years
U.S. Treasury long bond futures contract (contract expiration date December 1986)	63.33	11.85%	8.0 years
XYZ Corporation bond 12½% maturing June 1, 2005 (sinking fund debenture, rated AAA)	93	13.50%	7.2 years
Volatility of AAA corporate bond yields relative to U.S. Treasury bond yields = 1.25 to 1.0 (1.25 times)			

Assume no commission and no margin requirements on U.S. Treasury long bond futures contracts. Assume no taxes.

One U.S. Treasury long bond futures contract is a claim on $100,000 par value long-term U.S. Treasury bonds.

*Modified duration = Duration/(1 + r).

*Reprinted, with permission, from the Level III 1985 *CFA Study Guide*.

Situation A. A fixed-income manager holding a $20 million market value position of U.S. Treasury 11¾% bonds maturing November 15, 2014, expects the economic growth rate and the inflation rate to be above market expectations in the near future. Institutional rigidities prevent any existing bonds in the portfolio from being sold in the cash market.

Situation B. The treasurer of XYZ Corporation has recently become convinced that interest rates will decline in the near future. He believes it is an opportune time to purchase his company's sinking fund bonds in advance of requirements since these bonds are trading at a discount from par value. He is preparing to purchase in the open market $20 million par value XYZ Corporation 12½% bonds maturing June 1, 2005. A $20 million par value position of these bonds is currently offered in the open market at 93. Unfortunately, the treasurer must obtain approval from the board of directors for such a purchase, and this approval process can take up to two months. The board of directors' approval in this instance is only a formality.

For each of these two situations, outline and calculate how the interest rate risk can be hedged using the Treasury long bond futures. Show all calculations, including the total number of futures contracts used.

17. The U.S. yield curve is flat at 5% and the German yield curve is flat at 8%. The current exchange rate is $0.65 per mark. What will be the swap rate on an agreement to exchange currency over a three-year period? The swap will call for the exchange of 1 million deutschemarks for a given number of dollars in each year.
18. Firm ABC enters a five-year swap with firm XYZ to pay LIBOR in return for a fixed 8% rate on notional principal of $10 million. Two years from now, the market rate on three-year swaps is LIBOR for 7%; at this time, firm XYZ goes bankrupt and defaults on its swap obligation.
    a. Why is firm ABC harmed by the default?
    b. What is the market value of the loss incurred by ABC as a result of the default?
    c. Suppose instead that ABC had gone bankrupt. How do you think the swap would be treated in the reorganization of the firm?
19. At the present time, one can enter five-year swaps that exchange LIBOR for 8%. Five-year caps with limit rates of 8% sell for $0.30 per dollar of notional principal. What must be the price of five-year floors with a limit rate of 8%?
20. At the present time, one can enter five-year swaps that exchange LIBOR for 8%. An *off-market swap* would then be defined as a swap of LIBOR for a fixed rate other than 8%. For example, a firm with 10% coupon debt outstanding might like to convert to synthetic floating-rate debt by entering a swap in which it pays LIBOR and receives a fixed rate of 10%. What up-front payment will be required to induce a counterparty to take the other side of this swap? Assume notional principal is $10 million.

Part VII

Active Portfolio Management

Chapter 23

The Theory of Active Portfolio Management

THUS FAR WE HAVE ALLUDED TO ACTIVE PORTFOLIO MANAGEMENT IN ONLY THREE INSTANCES: THE MARKOWITZ METHODOLOGY OF GENERATING THE OPTIMAL RISKY PORTFOLIO (CHAPTER 7); SECURITY ANALYSIS THAT GENERATES FORECASTS TO USE AS INPUTS WITH THE MARKOWITZ PROCEDURE (CHAPTERS 16 THROUGH 18); AND FIXED-INCOME PORTFOLIO MANAGEMENT (CHAPTER 15). These brief analyses are not adequate to guide investment managers in a comprehensive enterprise of active portfolio management. Probably, you wonder about the seeming contradiction between our equilibrium analysis in Part III—in particular, the theory of efficient markets—and the real-world environment where profit-seeking investment managers use active management to exploit perceived market inefficiencies.

Despite the efficient market hypothesis, there are reasons to believe that active management can have effective results, and we discuss these at the outset. Next we consider the objectives of active portfolio management. We analyze two forms of active management: market timing, which is based solely on macroeconomic factors; and security selection, which includes microeconomic forecasting. At the end of the chapter we show the use of multifactor models in active portfolio management.

23.1 The Lure of Active Management

How can a theory of active portfolio management be reconciled with the notion that markets are in equilibrium? You may want to look back at the analysis in Chapter 12, but we can interpret our conclusions as follows.

Market efficiency prevails when many investors are willing to depart from maximum diversification, or a passive strategy, by adding mispriced securities to their portfolios in the hope of realizing abnormal returns. The competition for such returns ensures that prices will be near their "fair" values. Most managers will not beat the passive strategy on a risk-adjusted basis. However, in the competition for rewards to investing, exceptional managers might beat the average forecasts built into market prices.

There is both economic logic and some empirical evidence to indicate that exceptional portfolio managers can beat the average forecast. Let us discuss economic logic first. We must assume that, if no analyst can beat the passive strategy, investors will be smart enough to divert their funds from strategies entailing expensive analysis to less expensive passive strategies. In that case funds under active management will dry up, and prices will no longer reflect sophisticated forecasts. The consequent profit opportunities will lure back active managers who once again will become successful.[1] Of course, the critical assumption is that investors allocate management funds wisely. Direct evidence on that has yet to be produced.

As for empirical evidence, consider the following: (1) Some portfolio managers have produced streaks of abnormal returns that are hard to label as lucky outcomes; (2) the "noise" in realized rates is enough to prevent us from rejecting outright the hypothesis that some money managers have beaten the passive strategy by a statistically small, yet economically significant, margin; and (3) some anomalies in realized returns have been sufficiently persistent to suggest that portfolio managers who identified them in a timely fashion could have beaten the passive strategy over prolonged periods.

These conclusions persuade us that there is a role for a theory of active portfolio management. Active management has an inevitable lure even if investors agree that security markets are nearly efficient.

Suppose that capital markets are perfectly efficient, that an easily accessible market index portfolio is available, and that this portfolio is for all practical purposes the efficient risky portfolio. Clearly, in this case security selection would be a futile endeavor. You would be better off with a passive strategy of allocating funds to a money market fund (the safe asset) and the market index portfolio. Under these simplifying assumptions the optimal investment strategy seems to require no effort or know-how.

Such a conclusion, however, is too hasty. Recall that the proper allocation of investment funds to the risk-free and risky portfolios requires some analysis because the fraction, y, to be invested in the risky market portfolio, M, is given by

$$y = \frac{E(r_M) - r_f}{.01\, A\sigma_M^2} \tag{23.1}$$

where $E(r_M) - r_f$ is the risk premium on M, σ_M^2 its variance, and A is the investor's coefficient of risk aversion. Any rational allocation therefore requires an estimate of σ_M and $E(r_M)$. Even a passive investor needs to do some forecasting, in other words.

Forecasting $E(r_M)$ and σ_M is further complicated by the existence of security classes that are affected by different environmental factors. Long-term bond returns, for example, are driven largely by changes in the term structure of interest rates, whereas

---

[1] This point is worked out fully in Sanford J. Grossman and Joseph E. Stiglitz, "On the Impossibility of Informationally Efficient Markets," *American Economic Review* 70 (June 1980).

equity returns depend on changes in the broader economic environment, including macroeconomic factors beyond interest rates. Once our investor determines relevant forecasts for separate sorts of investments, she might as well use an optimization program to determine the proper mix for the portfolio. It is easy to see how the investor may be lured away from a purely passive strategy, and we have not even considered temptations such as international stock and bond portfolios or sector portfolios.

In fact, even the definition of a "purely passive strategy" is problematic, because simple strategies involving only the market index portfolio and risk-free assets now seem to call for market analysis. For our purposes we define purely passive strategies as those that use only index funds *and* weight those funds by fixed proportions that do not vary in response to perceived market conditions. For example, a portfolio strategy that always places 60% in a stock market index fund, 30% in a bond index fund, and 10% in a money market fund is a purely passive strategy.

More important, the lure into active management may be extremely strong because the potential profit from active strategies is enormous. At the same time, competition among the multitude of active managers creates the force driving market prices to near efficiency levels. Although enormous profits may be increasingly difficult to earn, decent profits to diligent analysts must always be the rule rather than the exception. For prices to remain efficient to some degree, some analysts must be able to eke out a reasonable profit. Absence of profits would decimate the active investment management industry, eventually allowing prices to stray from informationally efficient levels. The theory of managing active portfolios is the concern of this chapter.

23.2 Objectives of Active Portfolios

What does an investor expect from a professional portfolio manager, and how does this expectation affect the operation of the manager? If the client were risk-neutral, that is, indifferent to risk, the answer would be straightforward. The investor would expect the portfolio manager to construct a portfolio with the highest possible expected rate of return. The portfolio manager follows this dictum and is judged by the realized average rate of return.

When the client is risk averse, the answer is more difficult. Without a normative theory of portfolio management, the manager would have to consult each client before making any portfolio decision in order to ascertain that reward (average return) is commensurate with risk. Massive and constant input would be needed from the client-investors, and the economic value of professional management would be questionable.

Fortunately, the theory of mean-variance efficient portfolio management allows us to separate the "product decision," which is how to construct a mean-variance efficient risky portfolio, and the "consumption decision," or the investor's allocation of funds between the efficient risky portfolio and the safe asset. We have seen that construction of the optimal risky portfolio is purely a technical problem, resulting in a single optimal risky portfolio appropriate for all investors. Investors will differ only in how they apportion investment to that risky portfolio and the safe asset. For evidence that the theory of efficient frontiers is seeping through to the practitioner community, see the nearby box, which presents an advertisement by J.P. Morgan.

Another feature of the mean-variance theory that affects portfolio management decisions is the criterion for choosing the optimal risky portfolio. In Chapter 7 we established that the optimal risky portfolio for any investor is the one that maximizes the reward-to-variability ratio, or the expected excess rate of return (over the risk-free rate) divided by the standard deviation. A manager who uses this Markowitz methodology to construct the optimal risky portfolio will satisfy all clients regardless of risk aversion. Clients, for their part, can evaluate managers using statistical methods to draw inferences from realized rates of return to prospective, or ex-ante, reward-to-variability ratios.

William Sharpe's assessment of mutual fund performance[2] is the seminal work in the area of portfolio performance evaluation (see Chapter 24). The reward-to-variability ratio has come to be known as **Sharpe's measure:**

$$S = \frac{E(r_P) - r_f}{\sigma_P}$$

It is now a common criterion for tracking performance of professionally managed portfolios.

Briefly, mean-variance portfolio theory implies that the objective of professional portfolio managers is to maximize the (ex-ante) Sharpe measure, which entails maximizing the slope of the CAL (capital allocation line). A "good" manager is one whose CAL is steeper than the CAL representing the passive strategy of holding a market index portfolio. Clients can observe rates of return and compute the realized Sharpe measure (the ex-post CAL) to evaluate the relative performance of their manager.

Ideally, clients would like to invest their funds with the most able manager, one who consistently obtains the highest Sharpe measure and presumably has real forecasting ability. This is true for all clients regardless of their degree of risk aversion. At the same time, each client must decide what fraction of investment funds to allocate to this manager, placing the remainder in a safe fund. If the manager's Sharpe measure is constant over time (and can be estimated by clients), the investor can compute the optimal fraction to be invested with the manager from equation 23.1, based on the portfolio long-term average return and variance. The remainder will be invested in a money market fund.

The manager's ex-ante Sharpe measure from updated forecasts will be constantly varying. Clients would have liked to increase their allocation to the risky portfolio when the forecasts are optimistic, and vice versa. However, it would be impractical to constantly communicate updated forecasts to clients and for them to constantly revise their allocation between the risky portfolios and risk-free asset.

Allowing managers to shift funds between their optimal risky portfolio and a safe asset according to their forecasts alleviates the problem. Indeed, many stock funds allow the managers reasonable flexibility to do just that.

---

[2] William F. Sharpe, "Mutual Fund Performance," *Journal of Business, Supplement on Security Prices* 39 (January 1966).

How J. P. Morgan Investment sponsors in international

International fixed income securities account for nearly half the world's $5.4 trillion bond market—and offer plan sponsors increasingly attractive opportunities. J.P. Morgan Investment, the leader in this field, manages more than $3 billion of international fixed income securities. We believe you should consider including international bonds in your pension portfolio.

Estimated market value $5.4 trillion (publicly issued securities)

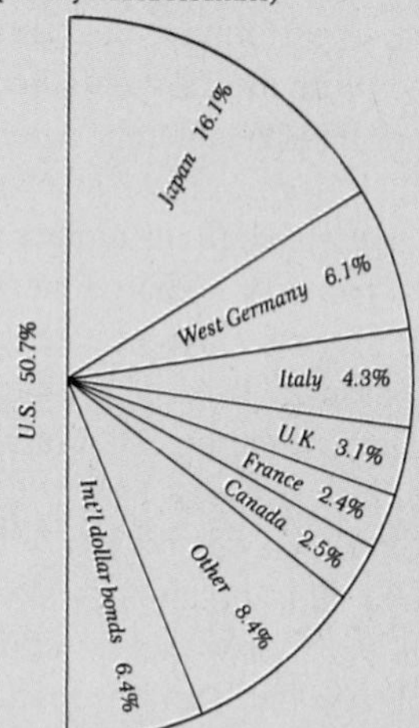

Shown at J.P. Morgan Investment's London headquarters are international fixed income team members (left to right) Anthony G. Bird, Hans K.-E. Danielsson, Bernard A. Wagenmann, and Adrian F. Lee.

finds opportunities for plan fixed income markets

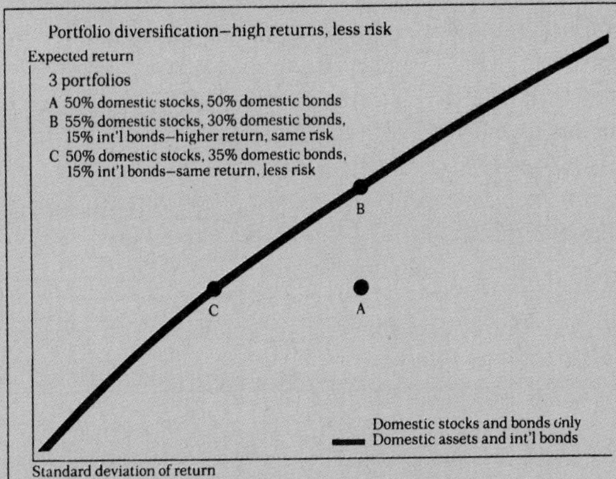

The graph above shows that international fixed income investments can reduce your portfolio's risk and improve its return. Even if your pension plan already includes international equities, bonds will provide an effective way to further diversify your portfolio at lower levels of risk. In addition, the immediate outlook for international bonds is particularly favorable due to government fiscal and monetary policies now taking effect in many non-U.S. economies.

Managing markets and currencies

At J.P. Morgan Investment we seek to maximize long-term benefits for our clients, as well as to capitalize on short-term market movements. We select the markets most likely to offer the best return. At the same time we ensure maximum control of currency risk through active hedging.

Using this approach, J.P. Morgan Investment has outperformed return indexes in both rising and falling markets.

Active management, global strength

Our strength in international fixed income management is our global network of portfolio managers, analysts, and traders, and the worldwide resources of The Morgan Bank. Professionals in New York, London, Singapore, and Tokyo continuously monitor and assess market developments to find the opportunities that will produce the best returns for our clients.

To learn more about our ideas and strengths in international fixed income management, write or call: Adrian F. Lee, Vice President, J.P. Morgan Investment Management Inc., 83 Pall Mall, London SW1Y 5ES; telephone 01-930 9444. Or Anthony P. Wilson, Vice President, 522 Fifth Avenue, New York, NY 10036; telephone (212) 837-2300.

J.P. Morgan Investment—An active investor in world capital markets. J.P. Morgan Investment has managed international bonds since 1977. We participate actively in both U.S. and international fixed income markets. Our International Investment Group, headquartered in London since 1974, serves clients all over the world, and specializes in managing single and multicurrency portfolios for corporations and governments diversifying into other markets.

J.P. Morgan Investment

23.3 Market Timing

Consider the results of the following two different investment strategies:

1. An investor who put $1,000 in 30-day commercial paper on January 1, 1927, and rolled over all proceeds into 30-day paper (or into 30-day T-bills after they were introduced) would have ended on December 31, 1978, 52 years later, with $3,600.
2. An investor who put $1,000 in the NYSE index on January 1, 1927, and reinvested all dividends in that portfolio would have ended on December 31, 1978, with $67,500.

Suppose we defined perfect **market timing** as the ability to tell (with certainty) at the beginning of each month whether the NYSE portfolio will out-perform the 30-day paper portfolio. Accordingly, at the beginning of each month, the market timer shifts all funds into either cash equivalents (30-day paper) or equities (the NYSE portfolio), whichever is predicted to do better. Beginning with $1,000 on the same date, how would the perfect timer have ended up 52 years later?

This is how Professor Robert Merton began a seminar with finance professors several years ago. As he collected responses, the boldest guess was a few million dollars. The correct answer: $5.36 *billion.*

Concept Check

Question 1. What was the monthly and annual compounded rate of return for the three strategies over the period 1926 to 1978?

These numbers have some lessons for us. The first has to do with the power of compounding. Its effect is particularly important because more and more of the funds under management represent pension savings. The horizons of such investments may not be as long as 52 years, but by and large they are measured in decades, making compounding a significant factor.

Another result that may seem surprising at first is the huge difference between the end-of-period value of all-safe asset strategy ($3,600) and that of the all-equity strategy ($67,500). Why would anyone invest in safe assets given this historical record? If you have internalized the lessons of previous chapters, you know the reason: risk. The average rates of return and the standard deviations on the all-bills and all-equity strategies are:

	Arithmetic Mean	Standard Deviation
Bills	2.55	2.10
Equities	10.70	22.14

The significantly higher standard deviation of the rate of return on the equity portfolio is commensurate with its significantly higher average return.

Can we also view the rate-of-return premium on the perfect-timing fund as a risk premium? The answer must be "no," because the perfect timer never does worse than either bills or the market. The extra return is not compensation for the possibility of poor returns but is attributable to superior analysis. It is the value of superior information that is reflected in the tremendous end-of-period value of the portfolio.

The monthly rate-of-return statistics for the all-equity portfolio and the timing portfolio are

Per Month	All Equities (%)	Perfect Timer No Charge (%)	Perfect Timer Fair Charge (%)
Average rate of return	0.85	2.58	0.55
Average excess return over return on safe asset	0.64	2.37	0.34
Standard deviation	5.89	3.82	3.55
Highest return	38.55	38.55	30.14
Lowest return	−29.12	0.06	−7.06
Coefficient of skewness	0.42	4.28	2.84

Ignore for the moment the fourth column ("Perfect Timer—Fair Charge"). The results of rows one and two are self-explanatory. The third item, standard deviation, requires some discussion. The standard deviation of the rate of return earned by the perfect market timer was 3.82%, far greater than the volatility of T-bill returns over the same period. Does this imply that (perfect) timing is a riskier strategy than investing in bills? No. For this analysis standard deviation is a misleading measure of risk.

To see why, consider how you might choose between two hypothetical strategies: the first offers a sure rate of return of 5%; the second strategy offers an uncertain return that is given by 5% *plus* a random number that is zero with probability .5 and 5% with probability .5. The characteristics of each strategy are

	Strategy 1 (%)	Strategy 2 (%)
Expected return	5	7.5
Standard deviation	0	2.5
Highest return	5	10.0
Lowest return	5	5.0

Clearly, Strategy 2 dominates Strategy 1 because its rate of return is *at least* equal to that of Strategy 1 and sometimes greater. No matter how risk averse you are, you will always prefer Strategy 2 to Strategy 1, despite the significant standard deviation of Strategy 2. Compared to Strategy 1, Strategy 2 provides only "good surprises," so the standard deviation in this case cannot be a measure of risk.

These results are analogous to the case of the perfect timer compared with an all-equity or all-bills strategy. In every period the perfect timer obtains at least as good a return, in some cases a better one. Therefore the timer's standard deviation is a misleading measure of risk compared to an all-equity or all-bills strategy.

Returning to the empirical results, you can see that the highest rate of return is identical for the all-equity and the timing strategies, whereas the lowest rate of return is positive for the perfect timer and disastrous for all the all-equity portfolio. Another reflection of this is seen in the coefficient of skewness, which measures the asymmetry of the distribution of returns. Because the equity portfolio is almost (but not exactly) normally distributed, its coefficient of skewness is very low at 0.42. In contrast, the perfect timing strategy effectively eliminates the negative tail of the distribution of portfolio returns (the part below the risk-free rate). Its returns are "skewed to the right," and its coefficient of skewness is therefore quite large, 4.28.

Now for the fourth column, "Perfect Timer—Fair Charge," which is perhaps the most interesting of the three results columns. Most assuredly, the perfect timer will charge clients for such a valuable service. (The perfect timer may have other-worldly predictive powers, but saintly benevolence is unlikely.)

Subtracting a fair fee (discussed later) from the monthly rate of return of the timer's portfolio gives us an average rate of return lower than that of the passive, all-equity strategy. However, because the fee is *assumed* to be fair, the two portfolios (the all-equity strategy and the market timing with fee strategy) must be equally attractive after risk adjustment. In this case, again, the standard deviation of the market timing strategy (with fee) is of no help in adjusting for risk because the coefficient of skewness remains high, 2.84. In other words, standard mean-variance analysis is quite complicated for valuing market timing. We need an alternative approach.

Valuing Market Timing as an Option

The key to analyzing the pattern of returns to the perfect market timer is to recognize that perfect foresight is equivalent to holding a call option on the equity portfolio. The perfect timer invests 100% in either the safe asset or the equity portfolio, whichever will yield the higher return. This is shown in Figure 23.1. The rate of return is bounded from below by r_f.

To see the value of information as an option, suppose that the market index currently is at S_0, and that a call option on the index has an exercise price of $X = S_0(1 + r_f)$. If the market outperforms bills over the coming period, S_T will exceed X, whereas it will be less than X otherwise. Now look at the payoff to a portfolio consisting of this option and S_0 dollars invested in bills.

Payoff to Portfolio

	$S_T < X$	$S_T \geq X$
Bills:	$S_0(1 + r_f)$	$S_0(1 + r_f)$
Option:	0	$S_T - X$
TOTAL	$S_0(1 + r_f)$	S_T

The portfolio pays the risk-free return when the market is bearish (i.e., the market return is less than the risk-free rate), and pays the market return when the market is bullish and beats bills. Such a portfolio is a perfect market timer. Consequently, we can

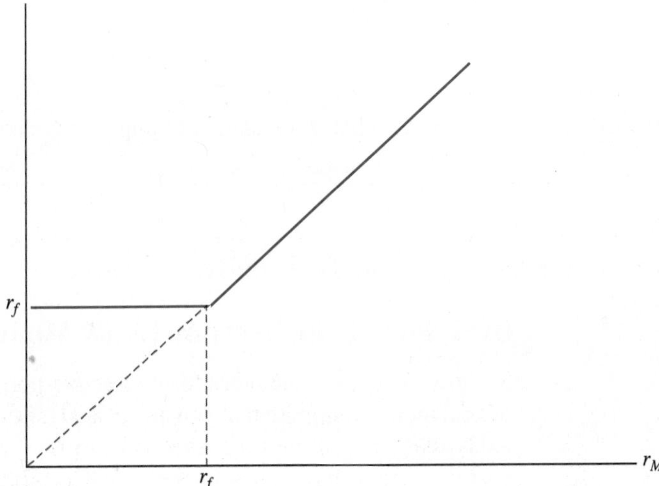

Figure 23.1
Rate of return of a perfect market timer

measure the value of perfect ability as the value of the call option, because a call enables the investor to earn the market return only when it exceeds r_f.

This insight lets Merton[3] value timing ability using the theory of option of valuation, and from this we calculate our fair charge for timing.

The Value of Imperfect Forecasting

Unfortunately, managers are not perfect forecasters, as you and Merton know. It seems pretty obvious that if managers are right most of the time they are doing very well. However, when we say right "most of the time," we cannot mean merely the percentage of the time a manager is right. The weather forecaster in Tucson, Arizona, who *always* predicts no rain, may be right 90% of the time. But a high success rate for a "stopped-clock" strategy clearly is not evidence of forecasting ability.

Similarly, the appropriate measure of market forecasting ability is not the overall proportion of correct forecasts. If the market is up two days out of three and a forecaster always predicts market advance, the two-thirds success rate is not a measure of forecasting ability. We need to examine the proportion of bull markets ($r_M > r_f$) correctly forecast *and* the proportion of bear markets ($r_M < r_f$) correctly forecast.

If we call P_1 the proportion of the correct forecasts of bull markets and P_2 the proportion for bear markets, then $P_1 + P_2 - 1$ is the correct measure of timing ability. For example, a forecaster who always guesses correctly will have $P_1 = P_2 = 1$, and will show ability of 1 (100%). An analyst who always bets on a bear market will mispredict all bull markets ($P_1 = 0$), will correctly "predict" all bear markets ($P_2 = 1$), and will end up with timing ability of $P_1 + P_2 - 1 = 0$. If C denotes the (call option) value of a

[3] Robert C. Merton, "On Market Timing and Investment Performance: An Equilibrium Theory of Value for Market Forecasts," *Journal of Business,* July 1981.

perfect market timer, then $(P_1 + P_2 - 1)C$ measures the value of imperfect forecasting ability.

CONCEPT CHECK Question 2. What is the market timing score of someone who flips a fair coin to predict the market?

23.4 SECURITY SELECTION: THE TREYNOR-BLACK MODEL

Overview of the Treynor-Black Model

Security analysis is the other form of active portfolio management besides timing the overall market. Suppose that you are an analyst studying individual securities. It is quite likely that you will turn up several securities that appear to be mispriced. They offer positive anticipated alphas to the investor. But how do you exploit your analysis? Concentrating a portfolio on these securities entails a cost, namely, the firm-specific risk that you could shed by more fully diversifying. As an active manager you must strike a balance between aggressive exploitation of perceived security mispricing and diversification motives that dictate that a few stocks should not dominate the portfolio.

Treynor and Black[4] developed an optimizing model for portfolio managers who use security analysis. It represents a portfolio management theory that assumes security markets are *nearly* efficient. The essence of the model is this:

1. Security analysts in an active investment management organization can analyze in depth only a relatively small number of stocks out of the entire universe of securities. The securities not analyzed are assumed to be fairly priced.
2. For the purpose of efficient diversification, the market index portfolio is the baseline portfolio, which the model treats as the passive portfolio.
3. The macro forecasting unit of the investment management firm provides forecasts of the expected rate of return and variance of the passive (market index) portfolio.
4. The objective of security analysis is to form an active portfolio of a necessarily limited number of securities. Perceived mispricing of the analyzed securities is what guides the composition of this active portfolio.
5. Analysts follow several steps to make up the active portfolio and evaluate its expected performance:
   a. Estimate the beta of each analyzed security and its residual risk. From the beta and the macro forecast, $E(r_M) - r_f$, determine the *required* rate of return of the security.
   b. Given the degree of mispricing of each security, determine its expected return and expected *abnormal* return (alpha).

---

[4] Jack Treynor and Fischer Black, "How to Use Security Analysis to Improve Portfolio Selection," *Journal of Business*, January 1973.

   c. The cost of less than full diversification comes from the nonsystematic risk of the mispriced stock, the variance of the stock's residual, which offsets the benefit (alpha) of specializing in an underpriced security.
   d. Use the estimates for the values of alpha, beta, and residual risk to determine the optimal weight of each security in the active portfolio.
   e. Estimate the alpha, beta, and residual risk for the active portfolio according to the weights of the securities in the portfolio.
6. The macroeconomic forecasts for the passive index portfolio and the composite forecasts for the active portfolio are used to determine the optimal risky portfolio, which will be a combination of the passive and active portfolios.

Treynor and Black's model did not take the industry by storm. This is unfortunate for several reasons:

1. Just as even imperfect market timing ability has enormous value, security analysis of the sort Treynor and Black proposed has similar potential value. Even with far from perfect security analysis, proper active management can add value.
2. The Treynor-Black model is conceptually easy to implement. Moreover, it is useful even when some of its simplifying assumptions are relaxed.
3. The model lends itself to use in decentralized organizations. This property is essential to efficiency in complex organizations.

Portfolio Construction

Assuming that all securities are fairly priced, and using the index model as a guideline for the rate of return on fairly priced securities, the rate of return on the ith security is given by

$$r_i = r_f + \beta_i(r_M - r_f) + e_i \tag{23.2}$$

where e_i is the zero mean, firm-specific disturbance.

Absent security analysis, Treynor and Black (TB) took equation 23.2 to represent the rate of return on all securities and assumed that the market portfolio, M, is the efficient portfolio. For simplicity, they also assumed that the nonsystematic components of returns, e_i, are independent across securities. As for market timing, TB assumed that the forecast for the **passive portfolio** already has been made, so that the expected return on the market index, r_M, as well as the variance, σ_M^2, has been assessed.

Now a portfolio manager unleashes a team of security analysts to investigate a subset of the universe of available securities. The objective is to form an active portfolio of positions in the analyzed securities to be mixed with the index portfolio. For each security, k, that is researched, we write the rate of return as

$$r_k = r_f + \beta_k(r_M - r_f) + e_k + \alpha_k \tag{23.3}$$

where α_k represents the extra expected return (called the *abnormal return*) attributable to any perceived mispricing of the security. Thus, for each security analyzed the research team estimates the parameters

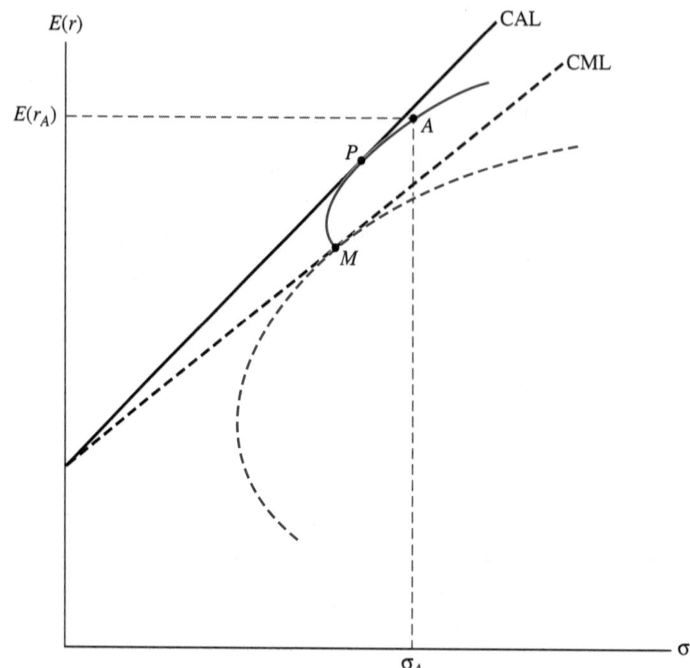

Figure 23.2
The optimization process with active and passive portfolios

$$\alpha_k, \beta_k, \sigma^2(e_k)$$

If all the α_k turn out to be zero, there would be no reason to depart from the passive strategy and the index portfolio *M* would remain the manager's choice. However, this is a remote possibility. In general, there will be a significant number of nonzero alpha values, some positive and some negative.

One way to get an overview of the TB methodology is to examine what we should do with the active portfolio once we get it. Suppose that the **active portfolio** (*A*) has been constructed somehow and has the parameters

$$\alpha_A, \beta_A, \sigma^2(e_A)$$

Its total variance is the sum of its systematic variance, $\beta_A^2\,\sigma_M^2$, plus the nonsystematic variance $\sigma^2(e_A)$. Its covariance with the market index portfolio, *M*, is

$$\text{Cov}(r_A, r_M) = \beta_A\sigma_M^2$$

Figure 23.2 shows the optimization process with the active and passive portfolios. The dashed efficient frontier represents the universe of all securities assuming that they are all fairly priced, that is, that all alphas are zero. By definition, the market index, *M*, is on this efficient frontier and is tangent to the (dashed) capital market line (CML). In practice the analysts do not need to know this frontier. They need only to observe the market index portfolio and construct a portfolio resulting in a capital allocation line that lies above the CML. Given their perceived superior analysis, they will view the market index portfolio as inefficient: the active portfolio, *A*, constructed from mispriced securities must lie, by design, above the CML.

To locate the active portfolio *A* in Figure 23.2, we need its expected return and standard deviation. The standard deviation is

$$\sigma_A = [\beta_A^2\sigma_M^2 + \sigma^2(e_A)]^{1/2}$$

Because of the positive alpha value that is forecast for *A*, it plots above the (dashed) CML with expected return

$$E(r_A) = \alpha_A + r_f + \beta_A[E(r_M) - r_f]$$

The optimal combination of the active portfolio, *A*, with the passive portfolio, *M*, is a simple application of the construction of optimal risky portfolios from two component assets that we first encountered in Chapter 7. Because the active portfolio is not perfectly correlated with the market index portfolio, we need to account for their mutual correlation in the determination of the optimal allocation between the two portfolios. This is evident from the solid blue efficient frontier that passes through *M* and *A*. It supports the optimal capital allocation line (CAL) and identifies the optimal risky portfolio, *P*, which combines portfolios *A* and *M*, and is the tangency point of the CAL to the efficient frontier. The active portfolio *A* in this example is not the ultimate efficient portfolio, because we need to mix *A* with the passive market portfolio to achieve greater diversification.

Let us now outline the algebraic approach to this optimization problem. If we invest a proportion, *w*, in the active portfolio and $1 - w$ in the market index, the portfolio return will be

$$r_p(w) = w\, r_A + (1 - w)r_M$$

We can use this equation to calculate Sharpe's measure (dividing the mean excess return by the standard deviation of the return) as a function of the weight, *w*, then find the optimal weight, w^*, that maximizes the measure. This is the value of *w* that makes *P* the optimal tangency portfolio in Figure 23.2. This maximization ultimately leads to the solution

$$w^* = \frac{w_0}{1 + (1 - \beta_A)w_0} \qquad (23.4)$$

where

$$w_0 = \frac{\alpha_A/\sigma^2(e_A)}{[E(r_M) - r_f]/\sigma_M^2}$$

Equation 23.4 is actually a restatement of the formula for determining the optimal weights to invest in two risky assets that you first encountered in Chapter 7. Here we state the equation in terms of portfolio alphas relative to the CAPM, but the approach is identical.

First look at w_0. This would be the optimal weight in the active portfolio *if* its beta (β_A) were 1.0. This weight is a ratio of two measures. In the numerator is the reward from the active portfolio, α_A, reflecting its mispricing, against the nonsystematic risk, $\sigma^2(e_A)$, incurred in holding it. This ratio is divided by an analogous measure for the index portfolio

$$\frac{E(r_M) - r_f}{\sigma_M^2}$$

which is the ratio of the reward from holding the index $E(r_M) - r_f$ to its risk, σ_M^2.

The intuition here is straightforward. We mix the active portfolio with the index for the benefit of diversification. The position to take in the active portfolio relative to the market portfolio depends on the ratio of the active portfolio's abnormal return, α_A, to its potentially diversifiable risk, $\sigma^2(e_A)$. The optimal weights also will depend on the opportunities for diversification, which in turn depend on the correlation between the two portfolios and can be measured by β_A. To adjust the optimal weight for the fact that the beta of the active portfolio may not be 1.0, we compute w^* in equation 23.4.

What is the reward-to-variability ratio of the optimal risky portfolio once we find the best mix, w^*, of the active and passive index portfolios? It turns out that if we compute the square of Sharpe's measure of the risky portfolio, we can separate the contributions of the index and active portfolios as follows:

$$\begin{aligned} S_P^2 &= S_M^2 + \frac{\alpha_A^2}{\sigma^2(e_A)} \\ &= \left[\frac{E(r_M) - r_f}{\sigma_M}\right]^2 + \left[\frac{\alpha_A}{\sigma(e_A)}\right]^2 \end{aligned} \tag{23.5}$$

This decomposition of the Sharpe measure of the optimal risky portfolio, which by the way is valid *only* for the optimal portfolio, tells us how to construct the active portfolio. Look at the last equality in equation 23.5. It shows that the highest Sharpe measure for the risky portfolio will be attained when we construct an active portfolio that maximizes the value of $\alpha_A/\sigma(e_A)$. The ratio of alpha to residual standard deviation of the active portfolio will be maximized when we choose a weight for the kth analyzed security as follows:

$$w_k = \frac{\alpha_k/\sigma^2(e_k)}{\sum_{i=1}^{n} \alpha_i/\sigma^2(e_i)} \tag{23.6}$$

This makes sense: The weight of a security in the active portfolio depends on the ratio of the degree of mispricing, α_k, to the nonsystematic risk, $\sigma^2(e_k)$, of the security. The denominator, the sum of the ratio across securities, is a scale factor to guarantee that the weights sum to one.

Note from equation 23.5 that the square of Sharpe's measure of the optimal risky portfolio is increased over the square of the Sharpe measure of the passive (market-index) portfolio by the amount

$$\left[\frac{\alpha_A}{\sigma(e_A)}\right]^2$$

The ratio of the degree of mispricing, α_A, to the nonsystematic standard deviation, $\sigma(e_A)$, becomes a natural performance measure of the active component of the risky portfolio. Sometimes this is called the **appraisal ratio.**

We can calculate the contribution of a single security in the active portfolio to the portfolio's overall performance. When the active portfolio contains n analyzed securities, the total improvement in the squared Sharpe measure equals the sum of the squared appraisal ratios of the analyzed securities,

$$\left[\frac{\alpha_A}{\sigma(e_A)}\right]^2 = \sum_{i=1}^{n}\left[\frac{\alpha_i}{\sigma(e_i)}\right]^2$$

The appraisal ratio for each security, $\alpha_i/\sigma(e_i)$, is a measure of the contribution of that security to the performance of the active portfolio.

The best way to illustrate the Treynor-Black process is through an example. Suppose that the macroforecasting unit of Drex Portfolio Inc. (DPF) issues a forecast for a 15% market return. The forecast's standard error is 20%. The risk-free is 7%. The macro data can be summarized as follows:

$$E(r_M) - r_f = 8\%;\ \sigma_M = 20\%$$

At the same time the security analysis division submits to the portfolio manager the following forecast of annual returns for the three securities that it covers:

Stock	α	β	$\sigma(e)$
1	7%	1.6	45%
2	−5	1.0	32
3	3	.5	26

Note that the alpha estimates appear reasonably moderate. The estimates of the residual standard deviations are correlated with the betas, just as they are in reality. The magnitudes also reflect typical values for NYSE stocks.

First, let us construct the optimal active portfolio implied by the security analyst input list. To do so we compute the appraisal ratios as follows (remember to use decimal representations of returns in the formulas):

Stock	$\alpha/\sigma^2(e)$	$\dfrac{\alpha_i}{\sigma^2(e_i)}\Big/\sum_{i=1}^{3}\dfrac{\alpha_i}{\sigma^2(e_i)}$
1	$.07/.45^2 =$ .3457	.3457/.3012 = 1.1477
2	$-.05/.32^2 =$ −.4883	−.4883/.3012 = −1.6212
3	$.03/.26^2 =$ .4438	.4438/.3012 = 1.4735
TOTAL	.3012	1.0000

The last column presents the optimal positions of each of the three securities in the active portfolio. Obviously, Stock 2 has a negative weight. The magnitudes of the individual positions in the active portfolio (e.g., 114.77% in Stock 1) seem quite extreme. However, this should not concern us because the active portfolio will later be mixed with the well-diversified market index portfolio, resulting in much more moderate positions, as we shall see shortly.

The forecasts for the stocks, together with the proposed composition of the active portfolio, lead to the following parameter estimates (in decimal form) for the active portfolio:

$$\begin{aligned}\alpha_A &= 1.1477 \times .07 + (-1.6212) \times (-.05) + 1.4735 \times .03 \\ &= .2056 = 20.56\% \\ \beta_A &= 1.1477 \times 1.6 + (-1.6212) \times 1.0 + 1.4735 \times .5 = .9519 \\ \sigma(e_A) &= [1.1477^2 \times .45^2 + (-1.6212)^2 \times .32^2 + 1.4735^2 \times .26^2]^{1/2} \\ &= .8262 = 82.62\%\end{aligned}$$

Note that the negative weight (short position) on the negative alpha stock results in a positive contribution to the alpha of the active portfolio. Note also that because of the assumption that the stock residuals are uncorrelated, the active portfolio's residual variance is simply the weighted sum of the individual stock residual variances, with the squared portfolio proportions as weights.

The parameters of the active portfolio are now used to determine its proportion in the overall risky portfolio.

$$\begin{aligned}w_0 &= \frac{\alpha_A/\sigma^2(e_A)}{[E(r_M) - r_f]/\sigma_M^2} \\ &= \frac{.2056/.6826}{.08/.04} \\ &= .1506\end{aligned}$$

$$\begin{aligned}w^* &= \frac{w_0}{1 + (1 - \beta_A)w_0} \\ &= \frac{.1506}{1 + (1 - .9519) \times .1506} \\ &= .1495\end{aligned}$$

Although the active portfolio's alpha is impressive (20.56%), its proportion in the overall risky portfolio, before adjustment for beta, is only 15.06%, because of its large nonsystematic risk (82.62%). Such is the importance of diversification. As it happens, the beta of the active portfolio is almost 1.0, and hence the correction for beta (from w_0 to w^*) is small, from 15.06% to 14.95%. The direction of the change makes sense. If the beta of the active portfolio is low (less than 1.0) there are more potential gains from diversification. Hence, a smaller position in the active portfolio is called for. If the beta of the active portfolio were significantly greater than 1.0, a larger correction in the opposite direction would be called for.

The proportions of the individual stocks in the active portfolio, together with the proportion of the active portfolio in the overall risky portfolio, determine the proportions of each individual stock in the overall risky portfolio.

Stock	Final Position				
1	.1495	×	1.1477	=	.1716
2	.1495	×	(−1.6212)	=	−.2424
3	.1495	×	1.4735	=	.2202
Active portfolio					.1495
Market portfolio					.8505
					1.0000

The parameters of the active portfolio and market-index portfolio are now used to forecast the performance of the optimal, overall risky portfolio. When optimized, a property of the risky portfolio is that its squared Sharpe measure increases by the square of the active portfolio's appraisal ratio:

$$S_P^2 = \left[\frac{E(r_M) - r_f}{\sigma_M}\right]^2 + \left[\frac{\alpha_A}{\sigma^2(e_A)}\right]^2$$
$$= .16 + .0619 = .2219$$

and hence the Sharpe measure of the active portfolio is $\sqrt{.2219} = .47$, compared with .40 for the passive portfolio.

Concept Check

Question 3.

a. When short positions are prohibited, the manager simply discards stocks with negative alphas. Using the preceding example, what would be the composition of the active portfolio if short sales were disallowed? Find the cost of the short-sale restriction in terms of the decline in performance of the new overall risky portfolio.

b. How would your answer change if the macro forecast is adjusted upwards, for example, to $E(r_M) - r_f = 12\%$, and short sales are again allowed?

23.5 Multifactor Models and Active Portfolio Management

Perhaps in the foreseeable future a multifactor structure of security returns will be developed and accepted as conventional wisdom. So far our analytical framework for active portfolio management seems to rest on the validity of the index model, that is, on a single-factor security model. Despite this appearance, a multifactor structure will not affect the construction of the active portfolio because the entire TB analysis focuses on the residuals of the index model. If we were to replace the one-factor model with a multifactor model, we would continue to form the active portfolio by calculating each security's alpha relative to its fair return (given its betas on *all* factors), and again would combine the active portfolio with the portfolio that would be formed in the absence of security analysis. The multifactor framework, however, does raise several new issues in portfolio management.

You saw in Chapter 9 how the index model simplifies the construction of the input list necessary for portfolio optimization programs. If

$$r_i - r_f = \alpha_i + \beta_i(r_M - r_f) + e_i$$

adequately describes the security market, then the variance of any asset is the sum of systematic and nonsystematic risk: $\sigma^2(r_i) = \beta_i^2 \sigma_M^2 + \sigma^2(e_i)$, and the covariance between any two assets is $\beta_i \beta_j \sigma_M^2$.

How do we generalize this rule to use in a multifactor model? To simplify, let us consider a two-factor world, and let us call the two factor portfolios M and H. Then we generalize the index model to

$$\begin{aligned} r_i - r_f &= \beta_{iM}(r_M - r_f) + \beta_{iH}(r_H - r_f) + \alpha_i + e_i \\ &= r_\beta + \alpha_i e_i \end{aligned} \quad (23.7)$$

β_M and β_H are the betas of the security relative to portfolios M and H. Given the rates of return on the factor portfolios, r_M and r_H, the fair excess rate of return over r_f on a security is denoted r_β and its expected abnormal return is α_i.

How can we use equation 23.7 to form optimal portfolios? Suppose that investors wish to maximize the Sharpe measures of their portfolios. The factor structure of equation 23.7 can be used to generate the inputs for the Markowitz portfolio selection algorithm. The variance and covariance estimates are now more complex, however:

$$\sigma^2(r_i) = \beta_{iM}^2 \sigma_M^2 + \beta_{iH}^2 \sigma_H^2 + 2\beta_{iM}\beta_{iH}\text{Cov}(r_M, r_H) + \sigma^2(e_i)$$

$$\text{Cov}(r_i, r_j) = \beta_{iM}\beta_{jM}\sigma_M^2 + \beta_{iH}\beta_{jH}\sigma_H^2 + (\beta_{iM}\beta_{jH} + \beta_{jM}\beta_{iH})\text{Cov}(r_M, r_H)$$

Nevertheless, the informational economy of the factor model still is valuable, because we can estimate a covariance matrix for an n-security portfolio from:

n estimates of β_{iM}
n estimates of β_{iH}
n estimates of $\sigma^2(e_i)$
1 estimate of σ_M^2
1 estimate of σ_H^2

rather than $n(n + 1)/2$ separate variance and covariance estimates. Thus, the factor structure continues to simplify portfolio construction issues.

The factor structure also suggests an efficient method to allocate research effort. Analysts can specialize in forecasting means and variances of different factor portfolios. Having established factor betas, they can form a covariance matrix to be used together with expected security returns generated by they CAPM or APT to construct an optimal passive risky portfolio. If active analysis of individual stocks also is attempted, the procedure of constructing the optimal active portfolio and its optimal combination with the passive portfolio is identical to that followed in the single-factor case.

It is likely, however, that the factor structure of the market has hedging implications. As we discuss in Chapter 25, this means that clients will be willing to accept an inferior Sharpe measure to maintain a risky portfolio that has the desired hedge qualities. Portfolio optimization for these investors obviously is more complicated, requiring specific information on client preferences. The portfolio manager will not be able to satisfy diverse clients with one portfolio.

In the case of the multifactor market even passive investors (meaning those who accept market prices as "fair") need to do a considerable amount of work. They need forecasts of the expected return and volatility of each factor return, *and* need to determine the appropriate weights on each factor portfolio to maximize their expected utility. Such a process is straightforward in principle, but quickly becomes computationally demanding.

SUMMARY

1. A truly passive portfolio strategy entails holding the market index portfolio and a money market fund. Determining the optimal allocation to the market portfolio requires an estimate of its expected return and variance, which in turn suggests delegating some analysis to professionals.

2. Active portfolio managers attempt to construct a risky portfolio that maximizes the reward-to-variability (Sharpe) ratio.

3. The value of perfect market timing ability is considerable. The rate of return to a perfect market timer will be uncertain. However, its risk characteristics are not measurable by standard measures of portfolio risk, because perfect timing dominates a passive strategy, providing "good" surprises only.

4. Perfect timing ability is equivalent to the possession of a call option on the market portfolio, whose value can be determined using option valuation techniques such as the Black-Scholes formula.

5. With imperfect timing, the value of a timer who attempts to forecast whether stocks will outperform bills is given by the conditional probabilities of the true outcome given the forecasts $P_1 + P_2 - 1$. Thus, if the value of perfect timing is given by the option value, C, then imperfect timing has the value $(P_1 + P_2 - 1)C$.

6. The Treynor-Black security selection model envisions that a macroeconomic forecast for market performance is available and that security analysts estimate abnormal expected rates of return, α, for various securities. Alpha is the expected rate of return on a security beyond that explained by its beta and the security market line.

7. In the Treynor-Black model the weight of each analyzed security is proportional to the ratio of its alpha to its nonsystematic risk, $\sigma^2(e)$.

8. Once the active portfolio is constructed, its alpha value, nonsystematic risk, and beta can be determined from the properties of the component securities. The optimal risky portfolio, P, is then constructed by holding a position in the active portfolio according to the ratio of α_P to $\sigma^2(e_P)$, divided by the analogous ratio for the market index portfolio. Finally, this position is adjusted by the beta of the active portfolio.

9. When the overall risky portfolio is constructed using the optimal proportions of the active portfolio and passive portfolio, its performance, as measured by the square of Sharpe's measure, is improved (over that of the passive, market index portfolio) by the amount $[\alpha_A/\sigma(e_A)]^2$.

10. The contribution of each security to the overall improvement in the performance of the active portfolio is determined by its degree of mispricing and nonsystematic risk. The contribution of each security to portfolio performance equals $[\alpha_i/\sigma(e_i)]^2$, so that for the optimal risky portfolio,

$$S_P^2 = \left[\frac{E(r_M) - r_f}{\sigma_M}\right]^2 + \sum_{i=1}^{n}\left[\frac{\alpha_i}{\sigma(e_i)}\right]^2$$

Key Terms

Sharpe's measure
Market timing
Passive portfolio
Active portfolio
Appraisal ratio

Selected Readings

The valuation of market timing ability using the option-pricing framework was developed in:

Merton, Robert C. "On Market Timing and Investment Performance: An Equilibrium Theory of Value for Market Forecasts," *Journal of Business,* July 1981.

The Treynor-Black model was laid out in:

Treynor, Jack; and Fischer Black. "How to Use Security Analysis to Improve Portfolio Selection," *Journal of Business,* January 1973.

Problems

1. The five-year history of annual rates of return in excess of the T-bill rate for two competing stock funds is

The Bull Fund	The Unicorn Fund
−21.7%	−1.3%
28.7	15.5
17.0	14.4
2.9	−11.9
28.9	25.4

   a. How would these funds compare in the eye of a risk-neutral potential client?
   b. How would these funds compare by Sharpe's measure?
   c. If a risk-averse investor (with a coefficient of risk aversion $A = 3$) had to choose one of these funds to mix with T-bills, which fund should he choose, and how much should be invested in that fund on the basis of the available data?

2. Historical data suggest that the standard deviation of an all-equity strategy is about 5.5% per month. Suppose that the risk-free rate is now 1% per month and that market volatility is at its historical level. What would be a fair monthly fee to a perfect market timer, based on the Black-Scholes formula?

3. In scrutinizing the record of two market timers a fund manager comes up with the following table:

Number of months that $r_M > r_f$	135	
Correctly predicted by timer *A*		78
Correctly predicted by timer *B*		86
Number of months that $r_M < r_f$	92	
Correctly predicted by timer *A*		57
Correctly predicted by timer *B*		50

a. What are the conditional probabilities, P_1 and P_2, and the total ability parameters for timers *A* and *B*?

b. Using the historical data of Question 2, what is a fair monthly fee for the two timers?

4. A portfolio manager summarizes the input from the macro and micro forecasters in the following table:

Micro Forecasts

Asset	Expected Return (%)	Beta	Residual Standard Deviation (%)
Stock A	20	1.3	58
Stock B	18	1.8	71
Stock C	17	0.7	60
Stock D	12	1.0	55

Macro Forecasts

Asset	Expected Return (%)	Standard Deviation (%)
T-bills	8	0
Passive equity portfolio	16	23

a. Calculate expected excess returns, alpha values, and residual variances for these stocks.

b. Construct the optimal risky portfolio.

c. What is Sharpe's measure for the optimal portfolio and how much of it is contributed by the active portfolio?

d. What should be the exact makeup of the complete portfolio for an investor with a coefficient of risk aversion of 2.8?

5. Recalculate Problem 4 for a portfolio manager who is not allowed to short-sell securities.

a. What is the cost in terms of Sharpe's measure of the restriction?

b. What is the utility loss to the investor ($A = 2.8$) given his new complete portfolio?

6. A portfolio management house approximates the return-generating process by a two-factor model and uses two-factor portfolios to construct its passive portfolio. The input table that is constructed by the house analysts looks as follows:

Micro Forecasts

Asset	Expected Return (%)	Beta on *M*	Beta on *H*	Residual Standard Deviation (%)
Stock A	20	1.2	1.8	58
Stock B	18	1.4	1.1	71
Stock C	17	0.5	1.5	60
Stock D	12	1.0	0.2	55

Macro Forecasts

Asset	**Expected Return (%)**	**Standard Deviation (%)**
T-bills	8	0
Factor *M* portfolio	16	23
Factor *H* portfolio	10	18

The correlation coefficient between the two-factor portfolios is .6.

a. What is the optimal passive portfolio?

b. By how much is the optimal passive portfolio superior to the single-factor passive portfolio, *M*, in terms of Sharpe's measure?

c. Analyze the utility improvement to the $A = 2.8$ investor relative to holding portfolio *M* as the sole risky asset that arises from the expanded macro model of the portfolio manager.

7. Construct the optimal active and overall risky portfolio with the data of Problem 6 with no restrictions on short sales.

   a. What is the Sharpe measure of the optimal risky portfolio and what is the contribution of the active portfolio to that measure?

   b. Compare the risky portfolio to that from Problem 4.

   c. Analyze the utility value of the optimal risky portfolio for the $A = 2.8$ investor. Compare to that of Problem 4.

8. Recalculate Problem 7 with a short-sale restriction. Compare the results to those from Problems 5 and 7.

Chapter 24
Portfolio Performance Evaluation

In CHAPTER 23 WE SURVEYED INVESTMENT STRATEGIES THAT ACTIVE MANAGERS MIGHT PURSUE. In this chapter we ask how we can evaluate the performance of a portfolio manager. It turns out that even measuring average portfolio returns is not as straightforward as it might seem. In addition, difficulties lie in adjusting average returns for risk, which presents a host of other problems.

We begin with issues on measurement of portfolio returns. From there, we move on to conventional approaches to risk adjustment. We show the problems with these approaches when they are applied in a real and complex world. Finally, we discuss some promising developments in the theory of performance evaluation and examine evaluation procedures used in the field.

24.1 MEASURING INVESTMENT RETURNS

The rate of return of an investment is a simple concept in the case of a one-period investment. It is simply the total proceeds derived from the investment per dollar initially invested. Proceeds must be defined broadly to include both cash distributions and capital gains. For stocks, total returns are dividends plus capital gains. For bonds, total returns are coupon or interest paid plus capital gains.

To set the stage for discussing the more subtle issues that follow, let us start with a trivial example. Consider a stock paying a dividend of $2 annually that currently sells for $50. You purchase the stock today and collect the $2 dividend, and then you sell the stock for $53 at year-end. Your rate of return is

$$\frac{\text{Total proceeds}}{\text{Initial investment}} = \frac{\text{Income} + \text{Capital gain}}{50}$$
$$= \frac{2 + 3}{50}$$
$$= .10$$
$$= 10\%$$

Another way to derive the rate of return that is useful in the more difficult multiperiod case is to set up the investment as a discounted cash flow problem. Call r the rate of return that equates the present value of all cash flows from the investment with the initial outlay. In our example the stock is purchased for \$50 and generates cash flows at year-end of \$2 (dividend) plus \$53 (sale of stock). Therefore we solve $50 = (2 + 53)/(1 + r)$ to find again that $r = 10\%$.

Time-Weighted Returns versus Dollar-Weighted Returns

When we consider investments over a period during which cash was added to or withdrawn from the portfolio, measuring the rate of return becomes more difficult. To continue our example, suppose that you were to purchase a second share of the same stock at the end of the first year, and hold both shares until the end of Year 2, at which point you sell each share for \$54.

Total cash outlays are

Time	Outlay
0	\$50 to purchase first share
1	\$53 to purchase second share a year later
	Proceeds
1	\$2 dividend from initially purchased share
2	\$4 dividend from the 2 shares held in the second year, plus \$108 received from selling both shares at \$54 each

Using the discounted cash flow (DCF) approach, we can solve for the average return over the two years by equating the present values of the cash inflows and outflows:

$$50 + \frac{53}{1 + r} = \frac{2}{1 + r} + \frac{112}{(1 + r)^2}$$

resulting in $r = 7.117\%$.

This value is called the internal rate of return or the **dollar-weighted rate of return** on the investment. It is "dollar weighted" because the stock's performance in the second year, when two shares of stock are held, has a greater influence on the average overall return than the first-year return, when only one share is held.

An alternative to the internal or dollar-weighted return is the **time-weighted return.** This method ignores the number of shares of stock held in each period. The stock return in the first year was 10%. (A \$50 purchase provided \$2 in dividends and \$3 in capital gains.) In the second year the stock had a starting value of $53 and sold at year-end for $54, for a total one-period rate of return of $3 ($2 dividend plus $1 capital gain) divided by $53 (the stock price at the start of the second year), or 5.66%. The time-weighted return is the average of 10% and 5.66%, which is 7.83%. This average return considers only the period-by-period returns without regard to the amounts invested in the stock in each period.

Note that the dollar-weighted return is less than the time-weighted return in this example. The reason is that the stock fared relatively poorly in the second year, when the investor was holding more shares. The greater weight that the dollar-weighted average places on the second-year return results in a lower measure of investment performance. In general, dollar- and time-weighted returns will differ, and the difference can be positive or negative depending on the configuration of period returns and portfolio composition.

Which measure of performance is superior? At first, it appears that the dollar-weighted return must be more relevant. After all, the more money you invest in a stock when its performance is superior, the more money you end up with. Certainly your performance measure should reflect this fact.

Time-weighted returns have their own use, however, especially in the money management industry. This is so because in some important applications a portfolio manager may not directly control the timing or the amount of money invested in securities. Pension fund management is a good example. A pension fund manager faces cash inflows into the fund when pension contributions are made, and cash outflows when pension benefits are paid. Obviously, the amount of money invested at any time can vary for reasons beyond the manager's control. Because dollars invested do not depend on the manager's choice, it is inappropriate to weight returns by dollars invested when measuring the investment ability of the manager. Consequently, the money management industry normally uses time-weighted returns for performance evaluation.

CONCEPT CHECK

Question 1. Shares of XYZ Corp. pay a $2 dividend at the end of every year on December 31. An investor buys two shares of the stock on January 1 at a price of $20 each, sells one of those shares for $22 a year later on the next January 1, and sells the second share an additional year later for $19. Find the time- and dollar-weighted rates of return on the two-year investment.

Arithmetic versus Geometric Averages

Our example takes the arithmetic average of the two annual returns, 10% and 5.66%, as the time-weighted average, 7.83%. Another approach is to take a geometric average, denoted r_G.

The motivation for this calculation comes from the principle of compounding. If dividend proceeds are reinvested, the accumulated value of an investment in the stock will grow by a factor of 1.10 in the first year and by an additional factor of 1.0566 in the second year. The compound average growth rate, r_G, is then calculated as the solution to the following equation.

Table 24.1 Average Annual Returns by Investment Class, 1926–1994

	Arithmetic Average	Geometric Average	Difference	Standard Deviation
Common stocks of small firms*	17.4	12.2	5.2	34.6
Common stocks of large firms	12.2	10.2	2.0	20.3
Long-term Treasury bonds	5.2	4.8	0.4	8.8
U.S. Treasury bills	3.7	3.7	0.0	3.3

*These are firms with relatively low market values of equity. Market capitalization is computed as price per share times shares outstanding.

Source: *Stocks, Bonds, Bills, and Inflation, 1995 Yearbook*™, Ibbotson Associates, Chicago (annually updates work by Roger G. Ibbotson and Rex A. Sinquefield). Used with permission.

$$(1 + r_G)^2 = (1.10)(1.0566).$$

This approach would entail computing

$$1 + r_G = [(1.10)(1.0566)]^{1/2}] = 1.0781$$

or $r_G = 7.81\%$.

More generally for an n-period investment, the geometric average rate of return is given by:

$$1 + r_G = [(1 + r_1)(1 + r_2) \ldots (1 + r_n)]^{1/n}$$

where r_t is the return in each time period.

The geometric average return in this example, 7.81%, is slightly less than the arithmetic average return, 7.83%. This is a general property: Geometric averages never exceed arithmetic ones. To see the intuition for this result, consider a stock that doubles in price in period 1 ($r_1 = 100\%$ and halves in price in period 2 ($r_2 = -50\%$). The arithmetic average is $r_A = [100 + (-50)]/2 = 25\%$, whereas the geometric average is $r_G = [(1 + 1)(1 - .5)]^{1/2} - 1 = 0$. The effect of the -50% return in period 2 fully offsets the 100% return in period 1 in the calculation of the geometric average, resulting in an average return of zero. This is not true of the arithmetic average. In general, the bad returns have a greater influence on the averaging process in the geometric technique. Therefore, geometric averages are lower.

Moreover, the difference in the two averaging techniques will be greater the greater is the variability of period-by-period returns. The general rule when returns are expressed as decimals (rather than percentages) is as follows:

$$r_G \approx r_A - {}^1\!/_2\sigma^2 \tag{24.1}$$

where σ^2 is the variance of returns. Equation 24.1 is exact when returns are normally distributed.

For example, consider Table 24.1, which presents arithmetic and geometric returns over the 1926–1994 period for a variety of investments. The arithmetic averages all exceed the geometric ones, with the difference greatest in the case of stocks of small firms, where annual returns exhibit the greatest standard deviation. The difference between the two averages falls to zero only when there is no variation in yearly returns. The table indicates that when the standard deviation falls to a level characteristic of T-bills, the difference is quite small.

To illustrate equation 24.1, consider the average returns for large stocks. According to the equation,

$$.102 \approx .122 - \tfrac{1}{2}(.203)^2$$
$$.102 \approx .1014$$

As predicted, the arithmetic mean (.122) exceeded the geometric mean (.102) by approximately one-half the variance in returns. Clearly, when comparing returns, one never should mix and match the two averaging techniques.

This last point leads to another question. Which is the superior measure of investment performance, the arithmetic average or the geometric average? The geometric average has considerable appeal because it represents exactly the constant rate of return we would have needed to earn in each year to match actual performance over some past investment period. It is an excellent measure of *past* performance. However, if our focus is on future performance, then the arithmetic average is the statistic of interest because it is an unbiased estimate of the portfolio's expected future return (assuming of course, that the expected return does not change over time). In contrast, because the geometric return over a sample period is always less than the arithmetic mean, it constitutes a downward-biased estimator of the stock's expected return in any future year.

To illustrate this concept, consider again a stock that will either double in value ($r =$ 100%) with probability of .5, or halve in value ($r = -50\%$) with probability .5. The following table illustrates these outcomes:

Investment Outcome	Final Value of Each Dollar Invested	One-Year Rate of Return
Double	$2.00	100%
Halve	$0.50	−50

Suppose that the stock's performance over a two-year period is characteristic of the probability distribution, doubling in one year, and halving in the other. The stock's price ends up exactly where it started, and the geometric average annual return is zero:

$$\begin{aligned} 1 + r_G &= [(1 + r_1)(1 + r_2)]^{1/2} \\ &= [(1 + 1)(1 - .50)]^{1/2} \\ &= 1 \end{aligned}$$

so that

$$r_G = 0$$

which confirms that a zero year-by-year return would have replicated the total return earned on the stock.

The expected annual future rate of return on the stock, however, is *not* zero: it is the arithmetic average of 100% and −50%: (100 − 50)/2 = 25%. To confirm this, note that there are two equally likely outcomes for each dollar invested: either a gain of

\$1 (when r = 100%) or a loss of \$.50 (when r = −50%). The expected profit is (\$1 − \$.50)/2 = \$.25, for a 25% expected rate of return. The profit in the good year more than offsets the loss in the bad year, despite the fact that the geometric return is zero. The arithmetic average return thus provides the best guide to expected future returns from an investment.

This argument carries forward into multiperiod investments. Consider, for example, all the possible outcomes over a two-year period:

Investment Outcome	Final Value of Each Dollar Invested	Total Return over Two Years
Double, double	\$4.00	300%
Double, halve	\$1.00	0
Halve, double	\$1.00	0
Halve, halve	\$.025	−75%

The expected final value of each dollar invested is (4 + 1 + 1 + .25)/4 = \$1.5625 for two years, again indicating an average rate of return of 25% per year, equal to the arithmetic average. Note that an investment yielding 25% per year with certainty will yield the same final compounded value as the expected final value of this investment, as $1.25^2 = 1.5625$. The arithmetic average return on the stock is [300 + 0 + 0 + (−75)]/4 = 56.25% per two years, for an effective annual return of 25%, that is, $1.5625^{1/2} - 1$. In contrast, the geometric mean return is zero:

$$[(1 + 3)(1 + 0)(1 + 0)(1 - .75)]^{1/4} = 1.0$$

Again, the arithmetic average is the better guide to *future* performance.

CONCEPT CHECK Question 2. Suppose that a stock now selling for \$100 will either increase in value by 15% by year-end with probability .5, or fall in value by 5% with probability .5. The stock pays no dividends.

a. What are the geometric and arithmetic mean returns on the stock?
b. What is the expected end-of-year value of the share?
c. Which measure of expected return is superior?

24.2 THE CONVENTIONAL THEORY OF PERFORMANCE EVALUATION

Calculating average portfolio returns does not mean the task is done. Returns must be adjusted for risk before they can be compared meaningfully. The simplest and most popular way to adjust returns for portfolio risk is to compare rates of return with those of other investment funds with similar risk characteristics. For example, high-yield bond portfolios are grouped into one "universe," growth stock equity funds are grouped into another universe, and so on. Then the (usually time-weighted) average returns of each fund within the universe are ordered, and each portfolio manager receives a percentile ranking depending on relative performance with the **comparison universe.** For

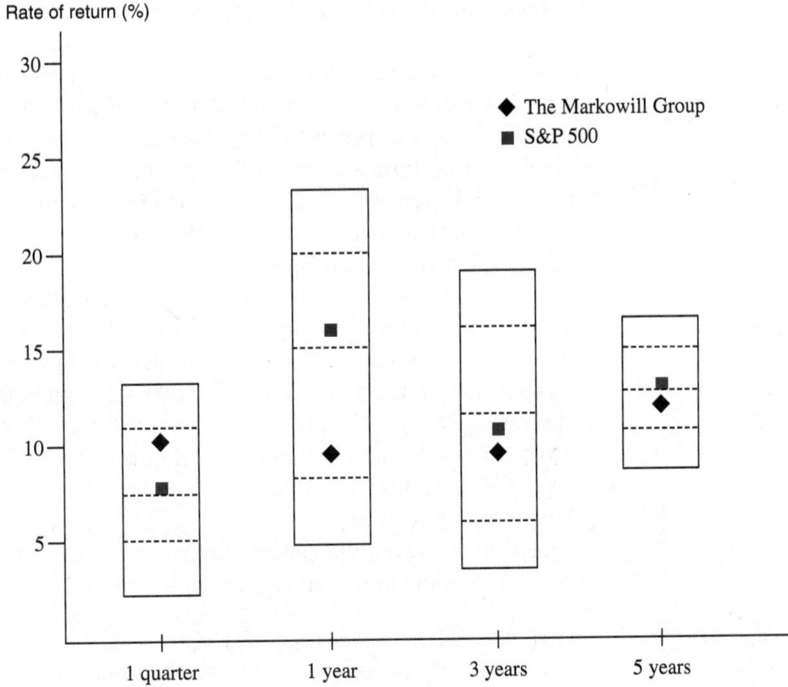

Figure 24.1
Universe comparison. Periods ending December 31, 1995

example, the manager with the ninth-best performance in a universe of 100 funds would be the 90th percentile manager: Her performance was better than 90% of all competing funds over the evaluation period.

These relative rankings are usually displayed in a chart such as that in Figure 24.1. The chart summarizes performance rankings over four periods: 1 quarter, 1 year, 3 years, and 5 years. The top and bottom lines of each box are drawn at the rate of return of the 95th and 5th percentile managers. The three dotted lines correspond to the rates of return of the 75th, 50th (median), and 25th percentile managers. The diamond is drawn at the average return of a particular fund and the square is drawn at the return of a benchmark index such as the S&P 500. The placement of the diamond within the box is an easy-to-read representation of the performance of the fund relative to the comparison universe.

This comparison of performance with other managers of similar investment style is a useful first step in evaluating performance. However, such rankings can be misleading. For example, within a particular universe, some managers may concentrate on particular subgroups, so that portfolio characteristics are not truly comparable. For example, within the equity universe, one manager may concentrate on high-beta stocks. Similarly, within fixed income universes, durations can vary across managers. These considerations suggest that a more precise means for risk adjustment is desirable.

Methods of risk-adjusted performance evaluation using mean-variance criteria came on stage simultaneously with the capital asset pricing model. Jack Treynor,[1] William Sharpe,[2] and Michael Jensen[3] recognized immediately the implications of the CAPM for rating the performance of managers. Within a short time, academicians were in command of a battery of performance measures, and a bounty of scholarly investigation of mutual fund performance was pouring from ivory towers. Shortly thereafter, agents emerged who were willing to supply rating services to portfolio managers eager for regular feedback. This trend has since lost some of its steam.

One explanation for the lagging popularity of risk-adjusted performance measures is the generally negative cast to the performance statistics. In nearly efficient markets it is extremely difficult for analysts to perform well enough to offset costs of research and transaction costs. Indeed, we have seen that the most professionally managed equity funds generally underperform the S&P 500 index on both risk-adjusted and raw return measures.

Another reason mean-variance criteria may have suffered relates to intrinsic problems in the measures. We will explore these problems, as well as some innovations suggested to overcome them.

For now, however, we can catalog some possible risk-adjusted performance measures and examine the circumstances in which each measure might be most relevant.

1. *Sharpe's measure:* $(\bar{r}_P - \bar{r}_f)/\sigma_P$
   Sharpe's measure divides average portfolio excess return over the sample period by the standard deviation of returns over that period. It measures the reward to (total) volatility trade-off.[4]
2. *Treynor's measure:* $(\bar{r}_P - \bar{r}_f)/\beta_P$
   Like Sharpe's, **Treynor's measure** gives excess return per unit of risk, but uses systematic risk instead of total risk.
3. *Jensen's measure:* $\alpha_P = \bar{r}_P - [\bar{r}_f + \beta_P(r_M - \bar{r}_f)]$
   Jensen's measure is the average return on the portfolio over and above that predicted by the CAPM, given the portfolio's beta and the average market return. Jensen's measure is the portfolio's alpha value.
4. *Appraisal ratio:* $\alpha_P/\sigma(e_P)$
   The **appraisal ratio** divides the alpha of the portfolio by the nonsystematic risk of the portfolio. It measures abnormal return per unit of risk that in principle could be diversified away from holding a market index portfolio.

Each measure has some appeal. But each does not necessarily provide consistent assessments of performance, since the risk measures used to adjust returns differ substantially.

---

[1] Jack L. Treynor, "How to Rate Management Investment Funds," *Harvard Business Review* 43 (January–February 1966).

[2] William F. Sharpe, "Mutual Fund Performance," *Journal of Business* 39 (January 1966).

[3] Michael C. Jensen, "The Performance of Mutual Funds in the Period 1945–1964," *Journal of Finance,* May 1968; and "Risk, the Pricing of Capital Assets, and the Evaluation of Investment Portfolios," *Journal of Business,* April 1969.

[4] We place bars over r_f as well as r_P to denote the fact that since the risk-free rate may not be constant over the measurement period, we are taking a sample average, just as we do for r_P.

CONCEPT CHECK

Question 3. Consider the following data for a particular sample period:

	Portfolio *P*	Market *M*
Average return	35%	28%
Beta	1.20	1.00
Standard deviation	42%	30%
Nonsystematic risk, $\sigma(e)$	18%	0

Calculate the following performance measures for portfolio *P* and the market: Sharpe, Jensen (alpha), Treynor, appraisal ratio. The T-bill rate during the period was 6%. By which measures did portfolio *P* outperform the market?

Sharpe's Measure as the Criterion for Overall Portfolios

Suppose that Jane Close constructs a portfolio and holds it for a considerable period of time. She makes no changes in portfolio composition during the period. In addition, suppose that the daily rates of return on all securities have constant means, variances, and covariances. This assures that the portfolio rate of return also has a constant mean and variance. These assumptions are unrealistic, but they make it easier to highlight the important issues. They are also crucial to understanding the shortcoming of conventional applications of performance measurement.

Now we want to evaluate the performance of Jane's portfolio. Has she made a good choice of securities? This is really a three-pronged question. First, "good choice" compared with what alternatives? Second, in choosing between two distinct alternatives, what are the appropriate criteria to use to evaluate performance? Finally, having identified the alternatives and the performance criteria, is there a rule that will separate basic ability from the random luck of the draw?

Fortunately, earlier chapters of this text help to determine portfolio choice criteria. If investor preferences can be summarized by a mean-variance utility function such as that introduced in Chapter 5, we can arrive at a relatively simple criterion. The particular utility function that we have used in this text is

$$U = E(r_P) - .005A\sigma_P^2$$

where *A* is the coefficient of risk aversion. With mean-variance preferences, we have seen that Jane will want to maximize her Sharpe measure (i.e., the ratio $[E(r_P) - r_f]/\sigma_P$ of her *complete* portfolio of assets). Recall that this is the criterion that led to the selection of the tangency portfolio in Chapter 7. Jane's problem reduces to that of whether her overall portfolio is the one with the highest possible Sharpe ratio.

Appropriate Performance Measures in Three Scenarios

To evaluate Jane's portfolio choice, we first ask whether she intends this portfolio to be her exclusive investment vehicle. If the answer is no, we need to know what her "complementary" portfolio is, the portfolio to which she is adding the one in question. The appropriate measure of portfolio performance depends critically on whether the portfolio is the entire investment fund or only a portion of the investor's overall wealth.

Jane's Choice Portfolio Represents Her Entire Risky Investment Fund. In this simplest case we need to ascertain only whether Jane's portfolio has the highest possible (ex ante) Sharpe measure. But how can this be done? In principle we can follow these four steps:

1. Assume that past security performance is representative of expected future performance, meaning that security returns over Jane's holding period exhibit averages and sample covariances that Jane might have anticipated.
2. Estimate the entire efficient frontier of risky assets from return data over Jane's holding period.
3. Using the risk-free rate at the time of decision, find the portfolio with the highest Sharpe measure.
4. Compare Jane's Sharpe measure to that of the best alternative.

This comprehensive approach, however, is problematic. It requires not only an extensive database and optimization techniques, but also exacerbates the problem of inference from sample data. We have to rely on a limited sample to estimate the means and covariances of a very large set of securities. The verdict on Jane's choice will be subject to estimation errors. The very complexity of the procedure makes it hard to assess the reliability and significance of the verdict. Is there a second-best alternative?

In fact, it makes sense to compare Jane's choice to a restricted set of alternative portfolios that were easy for her to assess and invest in at the time of her decision. An obvious first candidate for this restricted set is the passive strategy, the market index portfolio. Other candidates are professionally managed active funds. The method to use to compare Jane's portfolio to any specific alternative is the same: compare their Sharpe measures.

In essence, when Jane's portfolio represents her entire investment fund for the holding period in question, the benchmark alternative is the market index or another specific portfolio. The performance criterion is the Sharpe measure of the actual portfolio versus the benchmark portfolios.

Jane's Portfolio Is an Active Portfolio and Is Mixed with the Passive Market Index Portfolio. How do we evaluate the optimal mix in this case? Call Jane's portfolio *P,* and denote the market portfolio by *M*. when the two portfolios are mixed optimally, we have seen (in Chapter 23) that the square of the Sharpe measure of the composite portfolio, *C*, is given by

$$S_C^2 = S_M^2 + \left[\frac{\alpha_P}{\sigma(e_P)}\right]^2$$

where α_P is the abnormal return of the active portfolio, relative to the passive market portfolio, and $\sigma(e_P)$ is the diversifiable risk. The ratio $\alpha_P/\sigma(e_P)$ is thus the correct performance measure for *P* for this case, since it gives the improvement in the Sharpe measure of the overall portfolio attributable to the inclusion of *P*.

To see the intuition of this result, recall the single-index model:

$$r_P - r_f = \alpha_P + \beta_P(r_M - r_f) + e_P$$

Table 24.2 Portfolio Performance

	Portfolio *P*	Portfolio *Q*	Market
Beta	.90	1.60	1.0
Excess return ($\bar{r} - \bar{r}_f$)	11%	19%	10%
Alpha*	2%	3%	0

*Alpha = Excess return − (Beta × Market excess return)
$= (\bar{r} - \bar{r}_f) - \beta(\bar{r}_M - \bar{r}_f)$
$= \bar{r} - [\bar{r}_f + \beta(\bar{r}_M - \bar{r}_f)]$

If P is fairly priced, then $\alpha_P = 0$, and e_P is just diversifiable risk that can be avoided. If P is mispriced, however, α_P no longer equals zero. Instead, it represents the expected abnormal return. Holding P in addition to the market portfolio thus brings a reward of α_P against the nonsystematic risk voluntarily incurred, $\sigma(e_P)$. Therefore, the ratio of $\alpha_P/\sigma(e_P)$ is the natural benefit-to-cost ratio for portfolio P. This performance measurement is sometimes called the *appraisal ratio*:

$$AR_P = \frac{\alpha_P}{\sigma(e_P)}$$

Jane's Choice Portfolio Is One of Many Portfolios Combined into a Large Investment Fund. This third case might describe the situation where Jane, as a corporate financial officer, manages the corporate pension fund. She parcels out the entire fund to a number of portfolio managers. Then she evaluates the performance of individual managers to reallocate parts of the fund to improve future performance. What is the correct performance measure?

We could continue to use the appraisal ratio if it were reasonable to assume that the complementary portfolio to P is approximately equal to the market index portfolio by virtue of being spread among many managers and thus well diversified. The appraisal ratio is adequate in these circumstances. But you can imagine that the portfolio managers would take offense at this assumption. Jane, too, is likely to respond, "Do you think I am exerting all this effort just to end up with a passive portfolio?"

If we cannot treat this form of management as the same as investing in the index portfolio, we could make the following approximation. The benefit of portfolio P to the entire diversified fund is measured by P's alpha value. Although α_P is not a full measure of portfolio P's performance value, it will give Jane some indication of P's potential contribution to the overall portfolio. An even better solution, however, is to use Treynor's measure.

Suppose you determine that portfolio P exhibits an alpha value of 2%. "Not bad," you tell Jane. But she pulls out of her desk a report and informs you that another portfolio, Q, has an alpha of 3%. "One hundred basis points is significant," says Jane. "Should I transfer some of my funds from P's manager to Q's?"

You tabulate the relevant data, as in Table 24.2, and graph the results as in Figure 24.2. Note that we plot P and Q in the mean return–beta (rather than the mean–standard

Figure 24.2
Treynor measure

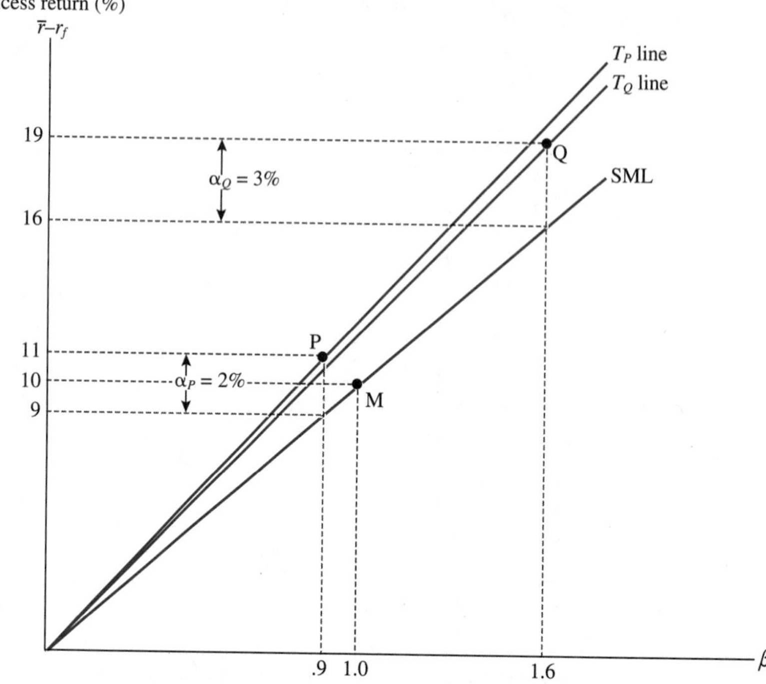

deviation) plane, because we assume that P and Q are two of many subportfolios in the fund, and thus that nonsystematic risk will be largely diversified away, leaving beta as the appropriate risk measure. The security market line (SML) shows the value of α_P and α_Q as the distance of P and Q above this line.

Suppose that portfolio Q can be mixed with T-bills. Specifically, if we invest w_Q in Q and $w_F = 1 - w_Q$ in T-bills, the resulting portfolio, Q^*, will have alpha and beta values proportional to Q's alpha and beta and to w_Q:

$$\alpha_{Q*} = w_Q\alpha_Q$$
$$\beta_{Q*} = w_Q\beta_Q$$

Thus all portfolios Q^* generated from mixes of Q and T-bills plot on a straight line from the origin through Q. We call it the T-line for the Treynor measure, which is the slope of this line.

Figure 24.2 shows the T-line for portfolio P as well. You can see immediately that P has a steeper T-line; despite its lower alpha, P is a better portfolio in this case after all. For any *given* beta, a mixture of P with T-bills will give a better alpha than a mixture of Q with T-bills.

To see this, suppose that we choose to mix Q with T-bills to create a portfolio Q^* with a beta equal to that of P. We find the necessary proportion by solving for w_Q:

$$\beta_{Q*} = w_Q\beta_Q = 1.6w_Q = \beta_P = .9$$
$$w_Q = 9/16$$

Portfolio Q^* therefore has an alpha of

$$\alpha_{Q^*} = 9/16 \times 3 = 1.69\%$$

which in fact is less than that of P.

In other words, the slope of the T-line is the appropriate performance criterion for the third case. The slope of the T-line for P, denoted by T_P, is given by

$$T_P = \frac{\bar{r}_P - \bar{r}_f}{\beta_P}$$

Treynor's performance measure is appealing in the sense that it shows that when an asset is part of a large investment portfolio, you should weigh its mean excess return, $\bar{r}_P - \bar{r}_f$ against its *systematic* risk (as measured by beta) rather than against total diversifiable risk (as measured by its standard deviation) to evaluate its contribution to performance.

Relationships among the Various Performance Measures

We have shown that under various scenarios one of four different performance measures is appropriate:

Sharpe: $\dfrac{E(r_P) - r_f}{\sigma_P}$

Treynor: $\dfrac{E(r_P) - r_f}{\beta_P}$

Jensen, or Alpha: α_P

Appraisal ratio: $\dfrac{\alpha_P}{\sigma(e_P)}$

It is interesting to see how these measures are related to one another. Beginning with Treynor's measure, note that as the market index beta is 1.0 Treynor's measure for the market index is

$$T_M = \bar{r}_M - \bar{r}_f$$

The mean excess return of portfolio P is

$$\bar{r}_P - \bar{r}_f = \alpha_P + \beta_P(\bar{r}_M - \bar{r}_f)$$

and thus its Treynor measure is

$$\begin{aligned} T_P &= \frac{\alpha_P + \beta_P(\bar{r}_M - \bar{r}_f)}{\beta_P} \\ &= \frac{\alpha_P}{\beta_P} + \bar{r}_M - \bar{r}_f \\ &= \frac{\alpha_P}{\beta_P} + T_M \end{aligned} \tag{24.2}$$

Treynor's measure compares portfolios on the basis of the alpha-to-beta ratio.[5] Note that this is very different in numerical value *and spirit* from the appraisal ratio, which is the ratio of alpha to residual risk.

The Sharpe measure for the market index portfolio is

$$S_M = \frac{\bar{r}_M - \bar{r}_f}{\sigma_M}$$

For portfolio P we have

$$S_P = \frac{\bar{r}_P - \bar{r}_f}{\sigma_P} = \frac{\alpha_P + \beta_P(\bar{r}_M - \bar{r}_f)}{\sigma_P}$$

With some algebra that relies on the fact that ρ^2 between P and M is

$$\rho^2 = \frac{\beta^2\sigma_M^2}{\beta^2\sigma_M^2 + \sigma^2(e)} = \frac{\beta^2\sigma_M^2}{\sigma_P^2}$$

we find that

$$S_P = \frac{\alpha_P}{\sigma_P} + \frac{\beta_P(\bar{r}_M - \bar{r}_f)}{\sigma_P}$$

$$= \frac{\alpha_P}{\sigma_P} + \rho S_M$$

This expression yields some insight into the process of generating valuable performance with active management. It is obvious that one needs to find significant-alpha stocks to establish potential value. A higher portfolio alpha, however, has to be tempered by the increase in standard deviation that arises when one departs from full diversification. The more we tilt toward high alpha stocks, the lower the correlation with the market index, ρ, and the greater the potential loss of performance value.

We conclude that it is important to use the performance measure that fits the relevant scenario. Evaluating portfolios by different performance measures may yield quite different results.

Actual Performance Measurement: An Example

Now that we have examined possible criteria for performance evaluation, we need to deal with a statistical issue: how can we derive an appropriate performance measure for ex ante decisions using ex post data? Before we plunge into a discussion of this problem, let us look at the rate of return on Jane's portfolio over the last 12 months. Table 24.3 shows the excess return recorded each month for Jane's portfolio P, one of her alternative portfolios Q, and the benchmark index portfolio M. The last rows in Table 24.3 give sample average and standard deviations. From these, and regressions of P and Q on M, we obtain the necessary performance statistics.

[5] Interestingly, although our definition of the Treynor measure is conventional, Treynor himself initially worked with the alpha-to-beta ratio. In this form the measure is independent of the market. Either measure will rank-order portfolio performance identically, because they differ by a constant (the market's Treynor value). Some call the ratio of alpha to beta "modified alpha" or "modified Jensen's measure," not realizing that this is really Treynor's measure.

Table 24.3 Excess Returns for Portfolios *P* and *Q* and the Benchmark *M* over 12 Months

Month	Jane's Portfolio *P*	Alternative *Q*	Benchmark *M*
1	3.58%	2.81%	2.20%
2	−4.91	−1.15	−8.41
3	6.51	2.53	3.27
4	11.13	37.09	14.41
5	8.78	12.88	7.71
6	9.38	39.08	14.36
7	−3.66	−8.84	−6.15
8	5.56	0.83	2.74
9	−7.72	0.85	−15.27
10	7.76	12.09	6.49
11	−4.01	−5.68	−3.13
12	0.78	−1.77	1.41
Year's average	2.76	7.56	1.63
Standard deviation	6.17	14.89	8.48

Table 24.4 Performance Statistics

	Portfolio *P*	Portfolio *Q*	Portfolio *M*
Sharpe's Measure	0.45	0.51	0.19
SCL Regression Statistics			
Alpha	1.63	5.28	0.00
Beta	0.69	1.40	1.00
Treynor	4.00	3.77	1.63
$\sigma(e)$	1.95	8.98	0.00
Appraisal ratio	0.84	0.59	0.00
R-SQR	0.91	0.64	1.00

The performance statistics in Table 24.4 show that portfolio *Q* is more aggressive than *P*, in the sense that its beta is significantly higher (1.40 versus 0.69). On the other hand, from its residual standard deviation *P* appears better diversified (1.95% versus 8.98%). Both portfolios have outperformed the benchmark market index portfolio, as is evident from their larger Sharpe measures and positive alphas.

Which portfolio is more attractive, based on reported performance? If *P* or *Q* represents the entire investment fund, *Q* would be preferable on the basis of its higher Sharpe measure (.51 versus .45). On the other hand, as an active portfolio to be mixed with the market index, *P* is preferable to *Q*, as is evident from its appraisal ratio (.84 versus .59). For the third scenario, where *P* and *Q* are competing for a role as one of a number of subportfolios, the inadequacy of alpha as a performance measure is evident. Whereas

Q's alpha is larger (5.28% versus 1.63%), P's beta is low enough to give it a better Treynor measure (4.00 versus 3.77), suggesting that it is superior to Q as one portfolio to be mixed with many others.

This analysis is based on 12 months of data only, a period too short to lend statistical significance to the conclusions. Even longer observation intervals may not be enough to make the decision clear-cut, which represents a further problem.

Realized Returns versus Expected Returns

When evaluating a portfolio, the evaluator knows neither the portfolio manager's original expectations nor whether those expectations made sense. One can only observe performance after the fact and hope that random results are not taken for, or do not hide, true underlying ability. But risky asset returns are "noisy," which complicates the inference problem. To avoid making mistakes, we have to determine the "significance level" of a statistic to know whether a portfolio performance measure reliably indicates ability. Quite frequently, however, we can make no significant distinction about performance.

Consider Joe Dart, a portfolio manager. Suppose that his ability is such that his portfolio has an alpha value of 20 basis points per month. (This makes for a hefty 2.4% per year before compounding.) Let us assume that the return distribution of Joe's portfolio has a constant mean, beta, and alpha, a heroic assumption, but one that is in line with the usual treatment of performance measurement. Suppose that for the measurement period Joe's portfolio beta is 1.2 and the monthly standard deviation of the residual (nonsystematic risk) is .02 (2%). With the market portfolio standard deviation of 6.5% per month (22.5% per year), Joe's portfolio systematic variance is

$$\beta^2\sigma_M^2 = 1.2^2 \times 6.5^2 = 60.84$$

and hence the correlation coefficient between his portfolio and the market index is

$$\begin{aligned}\rho &= \left[\frac{\beta^2\sigma_M^2}{\beta^2\sigma_M^2 + \sigma^2(e)}\right]^{1/2} \\ &= \left[\frac{60.84}{60.84 + 4}\right]^{1/2} \\ &= .97\end{aligned}$$

which shows that his portfolio appears to be quite well diversified. We calculate these statistics only to show that there is nothing unusual about Joe's portfolio.

To estimate Joe's portfolio alpha, we would estimate the portfolio security characteristic line (SCL), regressing the portfolio excess returns against those of the market index. Suppose that we are in luck in the sense that over the measurement period, the regression estimates yield the true parameters. That means that our SCL estimates for the N months are:

$$\alpha = .2\%, \qquad \beta = 1.2, \qquad \sigma(e) = 2\%$$

The evaluators who run such a regression, however, do not know the true values, and hence they must compute the t-statistic of the estimated alpha value to determine whether they can reject the hypothesis that Joe's alpha is zero, that is, that he has no ability.

The standard error of the alpha estimate in the SCL regression is approximately

$$\sigma(\alpha) = \frac{\sigma(e)}{\sqrt{N}}$$

where N is the number of observations and $\sigma(e)$ is the sample estimate of nonsystematic risk. The t-statistic for the alpha estimate is then

$$t(\alpha) = \frac{\alpha}{\sigma(\alpha)} = \frac{\alpha\sqrt{N}}{\sigma(e)} \tag{24.3}$$

Suppose that we require a significance level of 5%. This requires a $t(\alpha)$ value of 1.96 if N is large. With $\alpha = .2$ and $\sigma(e) = 2$ we solve equation 24.3 for N and find that

$$1.96 = \frac{.2\sqrt{N}}{2}$$
$$N = 384 \text{ months}$$

or 32 years!

What have we shown? Here is an analyst who has very substantial ability. The example is biased in his favor in the sense that we have assumed away statistical problems. Nothing changes in the parameters over a long period of time. Furthermore, the sample period "behaves" perfectly. Regression estimates are all perfect. Still, it will take Joe's entire working career to get to the point where statistics will confirm his true ability. We have to conclude that the problem of statistical inference makes performance evaluation extremely difficult in practice.

CONCEPT CHECK Question 4. Suppose an analyst has a measured alpha of 0.2% with a standard error of 2%, as in our example. What is the probability that the positive alpha is due to luck of the draw and that true ability is zero?

24.3 PERFORMANCE MEASUREMENT WITH CHANGING PORTFOLIO COMPOSITION

We have seen already that the high variance of stock returns requires a very long observation period to determine performance levels with any statistical significance, even if portfolio returns are distributed with constant mean and variance. Imagine how this problem is compounded when portfolio return distributions are constantly changing.

It is acceptable to assume that the return distributions of passive strategies have constant mean and variance when the measurement interval is not too long. However, under an active strategy return distributions change by design, as the portfolio manager updates the portfolio in accordance with the dictates of financial analysis. In such a case estimating various statistics from a sample period assuming a constant mean and variance may lead to substantial errors. Let us look at an example.

Suppose that the Sharpe measure of the passive strategy is .4. A portfolio manager is in search of a better, active strategy. Over an initial period of 52 weeks he executes a low-risk strategy with an annualized mean excess return of 1% and standard deviation

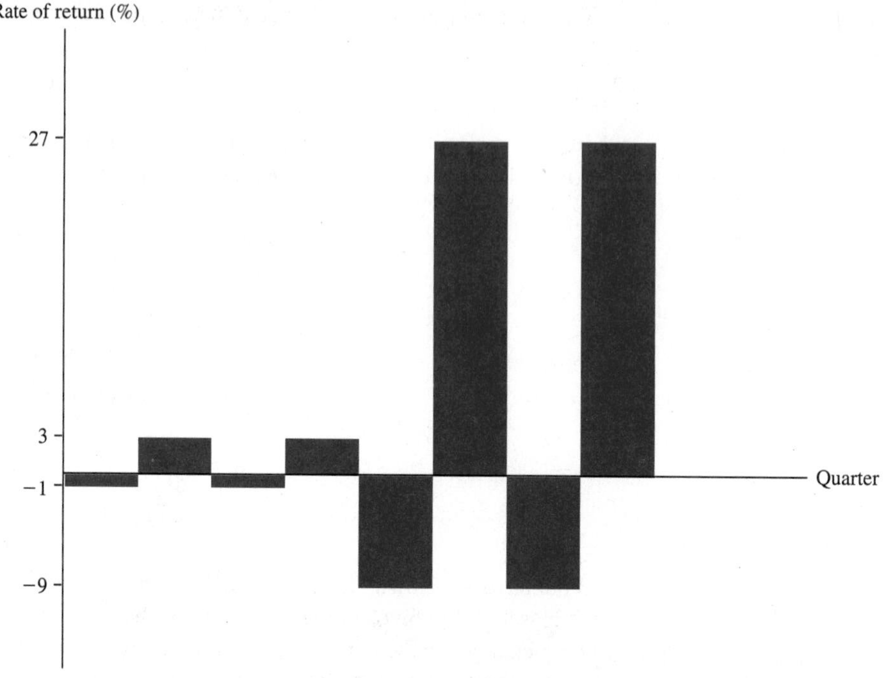

Figure 24.3
Portfolio returns

of 2%. This makes for a Sharpe measure of .5, which beats the passive strategy. Over the next period of another 52 weeks this manager finds that a *high*-risk strategy is optimal, with an annual mean excess return of 9% and standard deviation of 18%. Here, again, the Sharpe measure is .5. Over the two-year period our manager maintains a better-than-passive Sharpe measure.

Figure 24.3 shows a pattern of (annualized) quarterly returns that are consistent with our description of the manager's strategy of two years. In the first four quarters the excess returns are −1%, 3%, −1%, and 3%, making for an average of 1% and standard deviation of 2%. In the next four quarters the returns are: −9%, 27%, −9%, 27%, making for an average of 9% and a standard deviation of 18%. Thus *both* years exhibit a Sharpe measure of .5. However, if we take the eight-quarter sequence as a single measurement period, and measure the portfolio's mean and standard deviation over that full period, we will obtain an average excess return of 5% and standard deviation of 13.42%, making for a Sharpe measure of only .37, apparently inferior to the passive strategy!

What happened? The shift in the mean from the first four quarters to the next was not recognized as a shift in strategy. Instead, the difference in mean returns in the two years added to the *appearance* of volatility in portfolio returns. The active strategy with shifting means appears riskier than it really is and biases the estimate of the Sharpe measure downward. We conclude that for actively managed portfolios it is crucial to keep track of portfolio composition and changes in portfolio mean and risk. We will see another example of this problem in the next section, which deals with market timing.

Figure 24.4 Characteristic lines. **A,** No market timing, beta is constant. **B,** Market timing, beta increases with expected market excess return. **C,** Market timing with only two values of beta

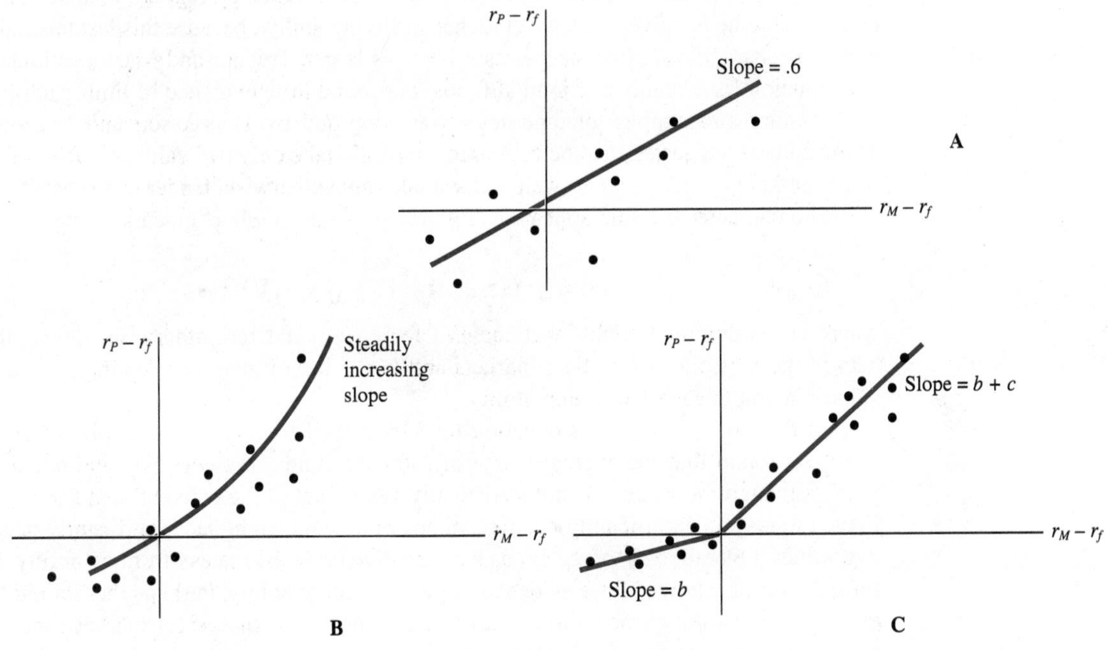

24.4 Market Timing

In its pure form, market timing involves shifting funds between a market index portfolio and a safe asset, such as T-bills or a money market fund, depending on whether the market as a whole is expected to outperform the safe asset. In practice, of course, most managers do not shift fully between T-bills and the market. How might we measure partial shifts into the market when it is expected to perform well?

To simplify, suppose that the investor holds only the market index portfolio and T-bills. If the weight of the market were constant, for example, .6, then the portfolio beta would also be constant, and the portfolio characteristic line would plot as a straight line with slope .6, as in Figure 24.4**A**. If, however, the investor could correctly time the market, and shift funds into it in periods when the market does well, the characteristic line would plot as in Figure 24.4**B**. The idea is that if the timer can predict bull and bear markets the investor will shift more into the market when the market is about to go up. The portfolio beta and the slope of the characteristic line will be higher when r_M is higher, resulting in the curved line that appears in Figure 24.4**B**.

Treynor and Mazuy[6] were the first to propose that such a line can be estimated by adding a squared term to the usual linear index model:

[6] Jack L. Treynor and Kay Mazuy, "Can Mutual Funds Outguess the Market," *Harvard Business Review* 43 (July–August 1966).

$$r_P - r_f = a + b(r_M - r_f) + c(r_M - r_f)^2 + e_P$$

where r_P is the portfolio return, and *a, b,* and *c* are estimated by regression analysis. If *c* turns out to be positive, we have evidence of timing ability, because this last term will make the characteristic line steeper as $r_M - r_f$ is larger. Treynor and Mazuy estimated this equation for a number of mutual funds, but found little evidence of timing ability.

A similar and simpler methodology was proposed by Henriksson and Merton.[7] These authors suggested that the beta of the portfolio take only two values: a large value if the market is expected to do well and a small value otherwise. Under this scheme the portfolio characteristic line appears as Figure 24.4**C**. such a line appears in regression form as

$$r_P - r_f = a + b(r_M - r_f) + c(r_M - r_f)D + e_P$$

where D is a dummy variable that equals 1 for $r_M > r_f$ and zero otherwise. Hence, the beta of the portfolio is b in bear markets and $b + c$ in bull markets. Again, a positive value of c implies market timing ability.

Henriksson[8] estimated this equation for 116 mutual funds over the period 1968 to 1980. He found that the average value of *c* for the funds was *negative*, and equal to −.07, although the value was not statistically significant at the conventional 5% level. Eleven funds had significantly positive values of *c*, while eight had significantly negative values. Overall, 62% of the funds had negative point estimates of timing ability. In sum, the results showed little evidence of market timing ability. Perhaps this should be expected; given the tremendous values to be reaped by a successful market timer, it would be surprising in nearly efficient markets to uncover clear-cut evidence of such skills.

To illustrate a test for market timing, return to Table 24.3. Regressing the excess returns of portfolios *P* and *Q* on the excess returns on *M* and the square of these returns,

$$r_P - r_f = a_P + b_P(r_M - r_f) + c_P(r_M - r_f)^2 + e_P$$
$$r_Q - r_f = a_Q + b_Q(r_M - r_f) + c_Q(r_M - r_f)^2 + e_Q$$

we derive the following statistics:

	Portfolio	
Estimate	***P***	***Q***
Alpha (*a*)	1.77 (1.63)	−2.29 (5.28)
Beta (*b*)	.70 (0.69)	1.10 (1.40)
Timing (*c*)	0.00	0.10
R-SQR	0.91 (0.91)	0.98 (0.64)

The numbers in parentheses are the regression estimates from the single variable regression reported in Table 24.4. The results reveal that portfolio *P* shows no timing.

[7] Roy D. Henriksson and R. C. Merton, "On Market Timing and Investment Performance. II. Statistical Procedures for Evaluating Forecast Skills," *Journal of Business* 54 (October 1981).

[8] Roy D. Henriksson, "Market Timing and Mutual Fund Performance: An Empirical Investigation," *Journal of Business* 57 (January 1984).

It is not clear whether this is a result of Jane's making no attempt at timing or that the effort to time was in vain and served only to increase portfolio variance unnecessarily.

The results for portfolio Q, however, reveal that timing has, in all likelihood, successfully been attempted. The timing coefficient, c, is estimated at .10. This describes a successful timing effort that was offset by unsuccessful stock selection. Note that the alpha estimate, a, is now -2.29% as opposed to the 5.28% estimate derived from the regression equation that did not allow for the possibility of timing activity.

Indeed, this is an example of the inadequacy of conventional performance evaluation techniques that assume constant mean returns and constant risk. The market timer constantly shifts beta and mean return, moving into and out of the market. Whereas the expanded regression captures this phenomenon, the simple SCL does not. The relative desirability of portfolios P and Q remains unclear in the sense that the value of the timing success and selectivity failure of Q compared with P has yet to be evaluated. The important point for performance evaluation, however, is that expanded regressions can capture many of the effects of portfolio composition change that would confound the more conventional mean-variance measures.

24.5 Performance Attribution Procedures

Rather than focus on risk-adjusted returns, practitioners often want simply to ascertain which decisions resulted in superior or inferior performance. Superior investment performance depends on an ability to be in the "right" securities at the right time. Such timing and selection ability may be considered broadly, such as being in equities as opposed to fixed-income securities when the stock market is performing well. Or it may be defined at a more detailed level, such as choosing the relatively better-performing stocks within a particular industry.

Portfolio managers constantly make both broad-brush asset market allocation decisions as well as more detailed sector and security allocation decisions within markets. Performance attribution studies attempt to decompose overall performance into discrete components that may be identified with a particular level of the portfolio selection process.

Attribution studies start from the broadest asset allocation choices and progressively focus on ever-finer details of portfolio choice. The difference between a managed portfolio's performance and that of a benchmark portfolio then may be expressed as the sum of the contributions to performance of a series of decisions made at the various levels of the portfolio construction process. For example, one common attribution system decomposes performance into three components: (1) broad asset market allocation choices across equity, fixed-income, and money markets; (2) industry (sector) choice within each market; and (3) security choice within each sector.

To illustrate this method, consider the attribution results for a hypothetical portfolio. The portfolio invests in stocks, bonds, and money market securities. An attribution analysis appears in Tables 24.5 through 24.8. The portfolio return over the month is 5.34%.

Table 24.5 Performance of the Managed Portfolio

Bogey Performance and Excess Return		
Component	Benchmark Weight	Return of Index during Month (percent)
Equity (S&P 500)	.60	5.81
Bonds (Lehman Brothers Index)	.30	1.45
Cash (money market)	.10	0.48

Bogey = (.60 × 5.81) + (.30 × 1.45) + (.10 × 0.48) = 3.97%

Return of managed portfolio	5.34%
− Return of bogey portfolio	3.97
Excess return of managed portfolio	1.37%

The first step is to establish a benchmark level of performance against which performance ought to be compared. This benchmark is called the **bogey.** It is designed to measure the returns the portfolio manager would earn if he or she were to follow a completely passive strategy. "Passive" in this context has two attributes. First, it means that the allocation of funds across broad asset classes is set in accord with a notion of "usual" or neutral allocation across sectors. This would be considered a passive asset market allocation. Second, it means that within each asset class, the portfolio manager holds an indexed portfolio such as the S&P 500 index for the equity sector. In such a manner, the passive strategy used as a performance benchmark rules out both asset allocation as well as security selection decisions. Any departure of the manager's return from the passive benchmark must be due to either asset allocation bets (departures from the neutral allocation across markets) or security selection bets (departures from the passive index within asset classes.)

While we have already discussed in earlier chapters the justification for indexing within sectors, it is worth briefly explaining the determination of the neutral allocation of funds across the broad asset classes. Weights that are designated as "neutral" will depend on the risk tolerance of the investor and must be determined in consultation with the client. For example, risk-tolerant clients may place a large fraction of their portfolio in the equity market, perhaps directing the fund manager to set neutral weights of 75% equity, 15% bonds and 10% cash equivalents. Any deviation from these weights must be justified by a belief that one or another market will either over- or underperform its usual risk-return profile. In contrast, more risk-averse clients may set neutral weights of 45%/35%/20% for the three markets. Therefore, their portfolios in normal circumstances will be exposed to less risk than that of the risk-tolerant client. Only intentional bets on market performance will result in departures from this profile.

In Table 24.5, the neutral weights have been set at 60% equity, 30% fixed-income, and 10% cash (money market securities). The bogey portfolio, comprised of investments in each index with the 60/30/10 weights, returned 3.97%. The managed portfolio's measure of performance is positive and equal to its actual return less the return of the bogey: 5.34 − 3.97 = 1.37%. The next step is to allocate the 1.37% excess return to the separate decisions that contributed to it.

Asset Allocation Decisions

Our hypothetical managed portfolio is invested in the equity, fixed-income, and money markets with weights of 70%, 7%, and 23%, respectively. The portfolio's performance could have to do with the departure of this weighting scheme from the benchmark 60/30/10 weights and/or to superior or inferior results *within* each of the three broad markets.

To isolate the effect of the manager's asset allocation choice, we measure the performance of a hypothetical portfolio that would have been invested in the indexes for each market with weights 70/7/23. This return measures the effect of the shift away from the benchmark 60/30/10 weights without allowing for any effects attributable to active management of the securities selected within each market.

Superior performance relative to the bogey is achieved by overweighting investments in markets that turn out to perform better than the bogey and by underweighting those in poorly performing markets. The contribution of asset allocation to superior performance equals the sum over all markets of the excess weight in each market times the return of the market index in excess of the bogey.

Table 24.6**A** demonstrates that asset allocation contributed 31 basis points to the portfolio's overall excess return of 137 basis points. The major factor contributing to superior performance in this month is the heavy weighting of the equity market in a month when the equity market has an excellent return of 5.81%.

Sector and Security Selection Decisions

If 0.31% of the excess performance can be attributed to advantageous asset allocation across markets, the remaining 1.06% then must be attributable to sector selection and security selection within each market. Table 24.6**B** details the contribution of the managed portfolio's sector and security selection to total performance.

Panel **B** shows that the equity component of the managed portfolio has a return of 7.28% versus a return of 5.81% for the S&P 500. The fixed-income return is 1.89% versus 1.45% for the Lehman Brothers Index. The superior performance in both equity and fixed-income markets weighted by the portfolio proportions invested in each market sums to the 1.06% contribution to performance attributable to sector and security selection.

Table 24.7 documents the sources of the equity market performance by each sector within the market. The first three columns detail the allocation of funds within the equity market compared to their representation in the S&P 500. Column (4) shows the rate of return of each sector, and Column (5) documents the performance of each sector relative to the return of the S&P 500. The contribution of each sector's allocation presented in Column (6) equals the product of the difference in the sector weight and the sector's relative performance.

Table 24.6 Performance Attribution

A. Contribution of Asset Allocation to Performance					
Market	(1) Actual Weight in Market	(2) Benchmark Weight in Market	(3) Excess Weight	(4) Market Return Minus Bogey (percent)	(5) = (3) × (4) Contribution to Performance (percent)
Equity	.70	.60	.10	1.84	.1840
Fixed-income	.07	.30	−.23	−2.52	.5796
Cash	.23	.10	.13	−3.49	−.4537
Contribution of asset allocation					.3099

B. Contribution of Selection to Total Performance					
Market	(1) Portfolio Performance (percent)	(2) Index Performance (percent)	(3) Excess Performance (percent)	(4) Portfolio Weight	(5) = (3) × (4) Contribution (percent)
Equity	7.28	5.81	1.47	.70	1.03
Fixed-income	1.89	1.45	0.44	.07	0.03
Contribution of selection within markets					1.06

Table 24.7 Sector Selection within the Equity Market

Sector	(1) (2) Beginning of Month Weights (percent) Portfolio	S&P 500	(3) Difference in Weights	(4) Sector Return	(5) Sector Over/Under Performance*	(6) = (3) × (5) Sector Allocation Contribution
Basic materials	1.96	8.3	−6.34	6.4	0.9	−5.7
Business services	7.84	4.1	3.74	6.5	1.0	3.7
Capital goods	1.87	7.8	−5.93	3.7	−1.8	10.7
Consumer cyclical	8.47	12.5	−4.03	8.4	2.9	−11.7
Consumer noncyclical	40.37	20.4	19.97	9.4	3.9	77.9
Credit sensitive	24.01	21.8	2.21	4.6	0.9	2.0
Energy	13.53	14.2	−0.67	2.1	−3.4	2.3
Technology	1.95	10.9	−8.95	−0.1	−5.6	50.1
Total						129.3

* S&P 500 performance net of dividends was 5.5%. Returns were compared net of dividends.

Note that good performance (a positive contribution) derives from overweighting well-performing sectors such as consumer nondurables, as well as underweighting poorly performing sectors such as capital goods. The excess return of the equity com-

Table 24.8 Portfolio Attribution: Summary

		Contribution (basis points)
1. Asset allocation		31
2. Selection		
a. Equity excess return		
i. Sector allocation	129	
ii. Security allocation	18	
	147 × .70 (portfolio weight) =	102.9
b. Fixed-income excess return	44 × .07 (portfolio weight) =	3.1
Total excess return of portfolio		137.0

ponent of the portfolio attributable to sector allocation alone is 1.29%. Table 24.6**B**, Column (3) shows that the equity component of the portfolio outperformed the S&P 500 by 1.47%. We conclude that the effect of security selection *within* sectors must have contributed an additional 1.47 − 1.29 or 0.18% to the performance of the equity component of the portfolio.

A similar sector analysis can be applied to the fixed-income portion of the portfolio, but we do not show those results here.

Summing Up Component Contributions

In this particular month, all facets of the portfolio selection process were successful. Table 24.8 details the contribution of each aspect of performance. Asset allocation across the major security markets contributes 31 basis points. Sector and security allocation within those markets contributes 106 basis points, for total excess portfolio performance of 137 basis points.

The sector and security allocation of 106 basis points can be partitioned further. Sector allocation within the equity market results in excess performance of 129 basis points, and security selection within sectors contributes 18 basis points. (The total equity excess performance of 147 basis points is multiplied by the 70% weight in equity to obtain contribution to portfolio performance.) Similar partitioning could be done for the fixed-income sector.

CONCEPT CHECK

Question 5.

a. Suppose the benchmark weights had been set at 70% equity, 25% fixed-income, and 5% cash equivalents. What then are the contributions of the manager's asset allocation choices?

b. Suppose the S&P 500 return is 5%. Compute the new value of the manager's security selection choices.

24.6 Evaluating Performance Evaluation

Performance evaluation has two very basic problems:

1. Many observations are needed for significant results even when portfolio mean and variance are constant.
2. Shifting parameters when portfolios are actively managed make accurate performance evaluation all the more elusive.

Although these objective difficulties cannot be overcome completely, it is clear that to obtain reasonably reliable performance measures we need to do the following:

1. Maximize the number of observations by taking more frequent return readings.
2. Specify the exact makeup of the portfolio to obtain better estimates of the risk parameters at each observation period.

Suppose an evaluator knows the exact portfolio composition at the opening of each day. Because the daily return on each security is available, the total daily return on the portfolio can be calculated. Furthermore, the exact portfolio composition allows the evaluator to estimate the risk characteristics (variance, beta, residual variance) for each day. Thus, daily risk-adjusted rates of return can be obtained. Although a performance measure for one day is statistically unreliable, the number of days with such rich data accumulates quickly. Performance evaluation that accounts for frequent revision in portfolio composition is superior by far to evaluation that assumes constant risk characteristics over the entire measurement period.

What sort of evaluation takes place in practice? Performance reports for portfolio managers traditionally have been based on quarterly data over 5 to 10 years. Currently, managers of mutual funds are required to disclose the exact composition of their portfolios only quarterly. Trading activity that immediately precedes the reporting date is known as "window dressing." Rumor has it that window dressing involves changes in portfolio composition to make it look as if the manager chose successful stocks. If IBM performed well over the quarter, for example, a portfolio manager will make sure that his or her portfolio includes a lot of IBM on the reporting date whether or not it did during the quarter and whether or not IBM is expected to perform as well over the next quarter. Of course, portfolio managers deny such activity, and we know of no published evidence to substantiate the allegation. However, if window dressing is quantitatively significant, even the reported quarterly composition data can be misleading. Mutual funds publish portfolio values on a daily basis, which means the rate of return for each day is publicly available, but portfolio composition is not.

Moreover, mutual fund managers have had considerable leeway in the presentation of both past investment performance and fees charged for management services. The resultant noncomparability of net-of-expense performance numbers has made it difficult to meaningfully compare funds.

This situation may be changing, however. The money management industry is beginning to respond to demands for more complete and easily interpretable data on historical performance. For example, the Association of Investment Management and Research (AIMR) recently published an extensive set of *Performance Presentation*

Highlights of Performance Presentation Standards of the Association for Investment Management and Research (AIMR)

- Returns must be total returns, including income and capital appreciation. Income should include accrued interest on securities.
- Annual returns should be reported for all years individually, as well as for longer periods. Firms should present time-weighted average rates of return (with portfolios valued at least quarterly, but preferably monthly or more frequently where feasible) and present geometric average linked returns (compound annualized returns) to summarize average performance. Portfolios should be revalued whenever large cash flows (e.g., more than 10% of the portfolio's value) might affect performance.
- Performance should be reported before fees, except where SEC advertising requirements mandate after-fee performance (because fees are often a function of size of assets). Fee schedules should be clearly presented.
- Composite results should reflect the record of the firm, not of individual managers. A portfolio's return should be included in the firm's composite performance as of the first full reporting period for which the portfolio is under management. Asset weighting within a composite should use beginning-of-period weights based on market value. Composite returns may not be biased by excluding selected portfolios. For example, portfolios no longer under management must be included in historical composites. Composite results may not be adjusted because of changes in the firm's organization or personnel.
- Composite returns should be reported for at least a 10-year period; 20 years is preferable if the company has been in existence for that period. Firms may not link simulated (or model) portfolio returns based on some trading strategy with actual performance.
- Performance results must be presented, including positions in cash and cash equivalents. Cash positions must be assigned to various portfolios at the beginning of each reporting period.
- The total return of multiple-asset portfolios (e.g., balanced accounts) must be included in composite results. If segment returns (i.e., individual asset class returns) from multiple-asset composite portfolios are included in the performance of a single asset class composite, a cash allocation to each segment must be made at the beginning of each reporting period.
- Risk measures such as beta, duration, or standard deviation are encouraged. In addition, benchmarks for performance evaluation such as returns on market indexes or normal portfolios should be chosen to reflect the expected risk or investment style of the client portfolio. Rebalancing of the benchmark asset allocation of multiple-asset portfolios should be agreed to by managers and clients in advance.
- In addition to actual results, performance for accounts utilizing leverage should be restated to an all-cash (no leverage) basis.

Standards (see the selected readings). The above box briefly summarizes some of the highlights of these recommendations. The thrust of these recommendations is that firms are not allowed to "cherry pick" when presenting their performance history: A complete record of performance is required. For example, firms must present returns for all years, as opposed to strategically choosing a starting date that makes subsequent performance look best. They also should provide the investment performance of an index against which their performance may reasonably be compared. Similarly, composite results for the firm must include returns of all of its managers, even those who have since left the firm. The firm, therefore, may not ignore the results of its unsuccessful managers who have since been replaced. The firm, not the individual manager, has the responsibility for performance. Finally, the firm is encouraged to supply risk measures such as beta or duration to make risk-return trade-offs easier to evaluate. Although the AIMR guidelines do not have the force of law, it nevertheless is expected that they will form the basis for industry performance presentation practices.

Traditional academic research uses monthly, weekly, and more recently even daily data. But such research makes no use of changes in portfolio composition because the data usually are unavailable. Therefore, performance evaluation is unsatisfactory in both the academic and practitioner communities.

Portfolio managers reveal their portfolio composition only when they have to, which so far is quarterly. This is not nearly sufficient for adequate evaluation. However, current computer and communication technology makes it easy to use daily composition data for evaluation purposes. If the technology required for meaningful evaluation is in place, implementation of more accurate performance measurement techniques could improve welfare by enabling the public to identify the truly talented investment managers.

SUMMARY

1. The appropriate performance measure depends on the role of the portfolio to be evaluated. Appropriate performance measures are as follows:

   a. Sharpe: when the portfolio represents the entire investment fund.
   b. Appraisal ratio: when the portfolio represents the active portfolio to be optimally mixed with the passive portfolio.
   c. Treynor: when the portfolio represents one subportfolio of many.

2. Many observations are required to eliminate the effect of the "luck of the draw" from the evaluation process because portfolio returns commonly are very "noisy."

3. The shifting mean and variance of actively managed portfolios make it even harder to assess performance. A typical example is the attempt of portfolio managers to time the market, resulting in ever-changing portfolio betas.

4. A simple way to measure timing and selection success simultaneously is to estimate an expanded SCL, with a quadratic term added to the usual index model.

5. Common attribution procedures partition performance improvements to asset allocation, sector selection, and security selection. Performance is assessed by calculating departures of portfolio composition from a benchmark or neutral portfolio.

Key Terms

Dollar-weighted rate of return
Time-weighted return
Comparison universe
Sharpe's measure
Treynor's measure
Jensen's measure
Appraisal ratio
Bogey

Selected Readings

The mean-variance-based performance evaluation literature is based on early papers by:

Sharpe, William. "Mutual Fund Performance." *Journal of Business* 39 (January 1966).

Treynor, Jack L. "How to Rate Management Investment Funds." *Harvard Business Review* 43 (January–February 1966).

Jensen, Michael C. "The Performance of Mutual Funds in the Period 1945–1964." *Journal of Finance*, May 1968.

Jensen, Michael C. "Risk, the Pricing of Capital Assets, and the Evaluation of Investment Portfolios." *Journal of Business*, April 1969.

The problems that arise when conventional mean-variance measures are calculated in the presence of a shifting-return distribution are treated in:

Dybvig, Philip H.; and Stephen A. Ross. "Differential Information and Performance Measurement Using a Security Market Line." *Journal of Finance* 40 (June 1985).

The separation of investment ability into timing versus selection activity derives from:

Fama, Eugene. "Components of Investment Performance." *Journal of Finance* 25 (June 1970).

The Association for Investment Management and Research, the parent of the ICFA, has proposed a set of standards for reporting investment performance. See:

Performance Presentation Standards. AIMR, 1993.

Problems

1. Consider the rate of return of stocks ABC and XYZ.

Year	r_{ABC}	r_{XYZ}
1	20%	30%
2	10	10
3	14	18
4	5	0
5	1	−8

a. Calculate the arithmetic average return on these stocks over the sample period.

b. Which stock has greater dispersion around the mean?

c. Calculate the geometric average returns of each stock. What do you conclude?

d. If you were equally likely to earn a return of 20%, 10%, 14%, 5%, or 1%, in each of the five annual returns for stock ABC, what would be your expected rate of return? What if the five outcomes were those of stock XYZ?

2. XYZ stock price and dividend history are as follows:

Year	Beginning of Year Price	Dividend Paid at Year-End
1991	$100	$4
1992	$110	$4
1993	$ 90	$4
1994	$ 95	$4

An investor buys three shares of XYZ at the beginning of 1991, buys another two shares at the beginning of 1992, sells one share at the beginning of 1993, and sells all four remaining shares at the beginning of 1994.

a. What are the arithmetic and geometric average time-weighted rates of return for the investor?

b. What is the dollar-weighted rate of return? (Hint: Carefully prepare a chart of cash flows for the *four* dates corresponding to the turns of the year for January 1, 1991 to January 1, 1994. If your calculator cannot calculate internal rate of return you will have to use trial and error.)

3. A manager buys three shares of stock today, and then sells one of those shares each year for the next three years. His actions and the price history of the stock are summarized below. The stock pays no dividends.

Time	Price	Action
0	90	Buy 3 shares
1	100	Sell 1 share
2	100	Sell 1 share
3	100	Sell 1 share

a. Calculate the time-weighted geometric average return on this "portfolio."

b. Calculate the time-weighted arithmetic average return on this portfolio.

c. Calculate the dollar-weighted average return on this portfolio.

4. Based on current dividend yields and expected capital gains, the expected rates of return on portfolios A and B are 11% and 14%, respectively. The beta of A is 0.8, while that of B is 1.5. The T-bill rate is currently 6%, whereas the expected rate of return of the S&P 500 index is 12%. The standard deviation of portfolio A is 10% annually, that of B is 31%, and that of the S&P 500 index is 20%.

a. If you currently hold a market-index portfolio, would you choose to add either of these portfolios to your holdings? Explain.

b. If instead you could invest *only* in T-bills and *one* of these portfolios, which would you choose?

5. Consider the two (excess return) index-model regression results for Stocks A and B. The risk-free rate over the period was 6%, and the market's average return was 14%.

i. $r_A - r_f = 1\% + 1.2(r_M - r_f)$
R-SQR = .576
Residual standard deviation, $\sigma(e_A) = 10.3\%$
Standard deviation of $r_A - r_f = 26.1\%$

ii. $r_B - r_f = 2\% + .8(r_M - r_f)$
R-SQR = .436
Residual standard deviation, $\sigma(e_B) = 19.1\%$
Standard deviation of $r_B - r_f = 24.9\%$

a. Calculate the following statistics for each stock:

i. Alpha.

ii. Appraisal ratio.

  iii. Sharpe measure.
  iv. Treynor measure.

b. Which stock is the best choice under the following circumstances?
  i. This is the only risky asset to be held by the investor.
  ii. This stock will be mixed with the rest of the investor's portfolio, currently composed solely of holdings in the market index fund.
  iii. This is one of many stocks that the investor is analyzing to form an actively managed stock portfolio.

6. Evaluate the timing and selection abilities of four managers whose performances are plotted in the following diagrams.

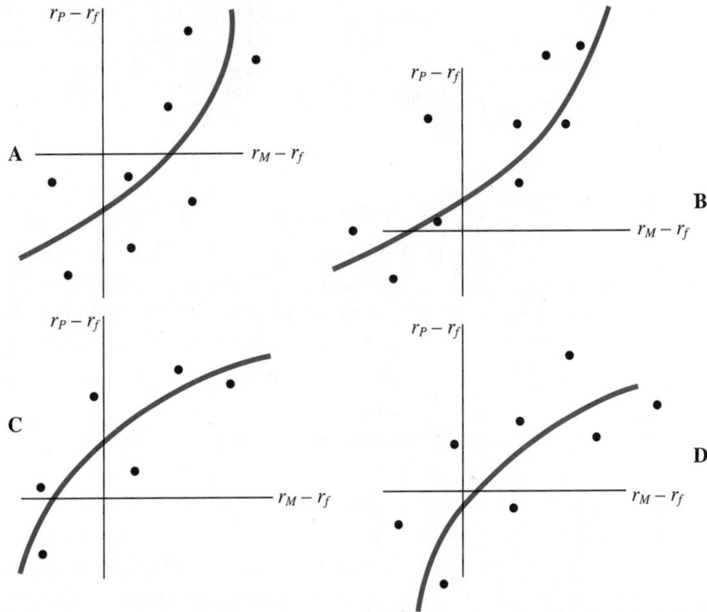

7. Consider the following information regarding the performance of a money manager in a recent month. The table represents the actual return of each sector of the manager's portfolio in Column 1, the fraction of the portfolio allocated to each sector in Column 2, the benchmark or neutral sector allocations in Column 3, and the returns of sector indices in Column 4.

	Actual Return	Actual Weight	Benchmark Weight	Index Return
Equity	2%	.70	.60	2.5% (S&P 500)
Bonds	1	.20	.30	1.2 (Salomon Brothers Index)
Cash	0.5	.10	.10	0.5

a. What was the manager's return in the month? What was her overperformance or underperformance?

b. What was the contribution of security selection to relative performance?
c. What was the contribution of asset allocation to relative performance? Confirm that the sum of selection and allocation contributions equals her total "excess" return relative to the bogey.

8. A global equity manager is assigned to select stocks from a universe of large stocks throughout the world. The manager will be evaluated by comparing her returns to the return on the MSCI World Market Portfolio, but she is free to hold stocks from various countries in whatever proportions she finds desirable. Results for a given month are contained in the following table.

Country	Weight in MSCI Index	Manager's Weight	Manager's Return in Country	Return of Stock Index for That Country
U.K.	.15	.30	20%	12%
Japan	.30	.10	15	15
U.S.	.45	.40	10	14
Germany	.10	.20	5	12

a. Calculate the total value added of all the manager's decisions this period.
b. Calculate the value added (or subtracted) by her *country* allocation decisions.
c. Calculate the value added from her stock selection ability within countries. Confirm that the sum of the contributions to value added from her country allocation plus security selection decisions equals total over- or underperformance.

9. Conventional wisdom says that one should measure a manager's investment performance over an entire market cycle. What arguments support this convention? What arguments contradict it?

10. Does the use of universes of managers with similar investment styles to evaluate relative investment performance overcome the statistical problems associated with instability of beta or total variability?

11. During a particular year, the T-bill rate was 6%, the market return was 14%, and a portfolio manager with beta of 0.5 realized a return of 10%.
a. Evaluate the manager based on the portfolio alpha.
b. Reconsider your answer to Part (*a*) in view of the Black-Jensen-Scholes finding that the security market line is too flat. Now how do you assess the manager's performance?

12. The chairman provides you with the following data, covering one year, concerning the portfolios of two of the fund's equity managers (Firm A and Firm B). Although the portfolios consist primarily of common stocks, cash reserves are included in the calculation of both portfolio betas and performance. By way of perspective, selected data for the financial markets are included in the following table:*

	Total Return	Beta
Firm A	24.0%	1.0
Firm B	30.0	1.5
S&P 500	21.0	
Lehman, Kuhn Loeb Total Bond Index	31.0	
91-day Treasury bills	12.0	

a. Calculate and compare the risk adjusted performance of the two firms relative to each other and to the S&P 500.

b. Explain *two* reasons the conclusions drawn from this calculation may be misleading.

13. Carl Karl, a portfolio manager for the Alpine Trust Company, has been responsible since 1990 for the City of Alpine's Employee Retirement Plan, a municipal pension fund. Alpine is a growing community, and city services and employee payrolls have expanded in each of the past 10 years. Contributions to the plan in fiscal 1995 exceeded benefit payments by a three-to-one ratio.

The plan board of trustees directed Karl five years ago to invest for total return over the long term. However, as trustees of this highly visible public fund, they cautioned him that volatile or erratic results could cause them embarrassment. They also noted a state statute that mandated that not more than 25% of the plan's assets (at cost) be invested in common stocks.

At the annual meeting of the Trustees in November 1995, Karl presented the following portfolio and performance report to the Board:*

Alpine Employee Retirement Plan

Asset Mix as of 9/30/95	At Cost (millions)		At Market (millions)	
Fixed-income assets:				
Short-term securities	$ 4.5	11.0%	$ 4.5	11.4%
Long-term bonds and mortgages	26.5	64.7	23.5	59.5
Common stocks	10.0	24.3	11.5	29.1
	$41.0	100.0%	$39.5	100.0%

Investment Performance

	Annual Rates of Return For Periods Ending 9/30/95	
	5 Years	1 Year
Total Alpine Fund:		
Time-weighted	8.2%	5.2%
Dollar-weighted (internal)	7.7%	4.8%
Assumed actuarial return	6.0%	6.0%
U.S. Treasury bills	7.5%	11.3%

*Reprinted, with permission, from the Level III 1981 *CFA Study Guide*.

Large sample of pension funds (average 60% equities, 40% fixed income)	10.1%	14.3%
Common stocks—Alpine Fund	13.3%	14.3%
Average portfolio beta coefficient	0.90	0.89
Standard & Poor's 500 Stock Index	13.8%	21.1%
Fixed-income securities—Alpine Fund	6.7%	1.0%
Salomon Brothers' Bond Index	4.0%	−11.4%

Karl was proud of his performance and was chagrined when a trustee made the following critical observations:

a. "Our one-year results were terrible, and it's what you've done for us lately that counts most."

b. "Our total fund performance was clearly inferior compared to the large sample of other pension funds for the last five years. What else could this reflect except poor management judgment?"

c. "Our common stock performance was especially poor for the five-year period."

d. Why bother to compare your returns to the return from Treasury bills and the actuarial assumption rate? What your competition could have earned for us or how we would have fared if invested in a passive index (which doesn't charge a fee) are the only relevant measures of performance."

e. "Who cares about time-weighted return? If it can't pay pensions, what good is it!"

Appraise the merits of each of these statements and give counterarguments that Mr. Karl can use.

14. The Retired Fund is an open-ended mutual fund composed of $500 million in U.S. bonds and U.S. Treasury bills. This fund has had a portfolio duration (including T-bills) of between three and nine years. Retired has shown first-quartile performance over the past five years, as measured by an independent fixed-income measurement service. However, the directors of the fund would like to measure the market timing skill of the fund's sole bond investor manager. An external consulting firm has suggested the following three methods:*

I. Method I examines the value of the bond portfolio at the beginning of every year, then calculates the return that would have been achieved had that same portfolio been held throughout the year. This return would then be compared with the return actually obtained by the fund.

II. Method II calculates the average weighting of the portfolio in bonds and T-bills for each year. Instead of using the actual bond portfolio, the return on a long-bond market index and T-bill index would be used. For example, if the portfolio on average was 65% in bonds and 35% in T-bills, the annual return on a portfolio invested 65% in a long-bond index and 35% in T-bills would be calculated. This return is compared with the annual return that would have been generated using the indexes and the manager's actual bond/T-bill weighting for each quarter of the year.

---

*Reprinted, with permission, from the *CFA Study Guide,* Association for Investment Management and Research, Charlottesville, VA.

III. Method III examines the net bond purchase activity (market value of purchases less sales) for each quarter of the year. If net purchases were positive (negative) in any quarter, the performance of the bonds would be evaluated until the net purchase activity became negative (positive). Positive (negative) net purchases would be viewed as a bullish (bearish) view taken by the manager. The correctness of this view would be measured.

Critique *each* method with regard to market timing measurement problems.

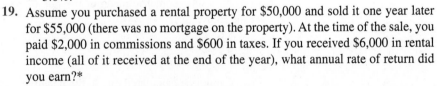

15. A plan sponsor with a portfolio manager who invests in small-capitalization, high-growth stocks should have the plan sponsor's performance measured against which *one* of the following?*
    a. S&P 500 index.
    b. Wilshire 5000 index.
    c. Dow Jones Industrial Average.
    d. S&P 400 index.

16. In measuring the comparative performance of different fund managers, the preferred method of calculating rate of return is:*
    a. Internal.
    b. Time-weighted.
    c. Dollar-weighted.
    d. Income.

17. Which *one* of the following is a valid benchmark against which a portfolio's performance can be measured over a given time period?*
    a. The portfolio's dollar-weighted rate of return.
    b. The portfolio's time-weighted rate of return.
    c. The portfolio manager's "normal" portfolio.
    d. The average beta of the portfolio.

18. Assume you invested in an asset for two years. The first year you earned a 15% return, and the second year you earned a *negative* 10% return. What was your annual geometric return?*
    a. 1.7%.
    b. 2.5%.
    c. 3.5%.
    d. 5.0%.

19. Assume you purchased a rental property for $50,000 and sold it one year later for $55,000 (there was no mortgage on the property). At the time of the sale, you paid $2,000 in commissions and $600 in taxes. If you received $6,000 in rental income (all of it received at the end of the year), what annual rate of return did you earn?*
    a. 15.3%.
    b. 15.9%.
    c. 16.8%.
    d. 17.1%.

---

*Reprinted, with permission, from the *CFA Study Guide,* Association for Investment Management and Research, Charlottesville, VA.

20. A portfolio of stocks generates a −9% return in 1990, a 23% return in 1991, and a 17% return in 1992. The annualized return (geometric mean) for the entire period is:*
    a. 7.2%.
    b. 9.4%.
    c. 10.3%.
    d. None of the above.

21. A two-year investment of $2,000 results in a return of $150 at the end of the first year and a return of $150 at the end of the second year, in addition to the return of the original investment. The internal rate of return on the investment is:*
    a. 6.4%.
    b. 7.5%.
    c. 15.0%.
    d. None of the above.

22. In measuring the performance of a portfolio, the time-weighted rate of return is superior to the dollar-weighted rate of return because:*
    a. When the rate of return varies, the time-weighted return is higher.
    b. The dollar-weighted return assumes all portfolio deposits are made on Day 1.
    c. The dollar-weighted return can only be estimated.
    d. The time-weighted return is unaffected by the timing of portfolio contributions and withdrawals.

23. The annual rate of return for JSI's common stock has been:†

	1989	1990	1991	1992
Return	14%	19%	−10%	14%

a. What is the arithmetic mean of the rate of return for JSI's common stock over the four years?
   i. 8.62%.
   ii. 9.25%.
   iii. 14.25%.
   iv. None of the above.

b. What is the geometric mean of the rate of return for JSI's common stock over the four years?
   i. 8.62%.
   ii. 9.25%.
   iii. 14.21%.
   iv. Cannot be calculated due to the negative return in 1991.

24. A pension fund portfolio begins with $500,000 and earns 15% the first year and 10% the second year. At the beginning of the second year, the sponsor con-

*Reprinted, with permission, from the *CFA Study Guide,* Association for Investment Management and Research, Charlottesville, VA. All rights reserved.

† Reprinted, with permission, from the Level I 1993 *CFA Study Guide.* Association for Investment Management and Research, Charlottesville, VA. All rights reserved.

tributes another $500,000. The dollar-weighted and time-weighted rates of return were:*

a. 12.5% and 11.7%.
b. 8.7% and 11.7%.
c. 12.5% and 15.0%.
d. 15.0% and 11.7%.

25. Strict market timers attempt to maintain a __________ portfolio beta and a __________ portfolio alpha.†

a. Constant; shifting.
b. Shifting; zero.
c. Shifting; shifting.
d. Zero; zero.

26. Which *one* of the following methods measures the reward to volatility trade-off by dividing the average portfolio excess return over the standard deviation of returns?‡

a. Sharpe's measure.
b. Treynor's measure.
c. Jensen's measure.
d. Appraisal ratio.

Chapter 25
Hedging

YOU MIGHT WONDER WHAT POSSIBLY COULD BE LEFT TO SAY ABOUT RISK MANAGEMENT AFTER OUR EXTENSIVE DISCUSSION OF PORTFOLIO THEORY. This chapter, however, treats risk in a very different manner than portfolio theory does. Portfolio theory deals with the big picture—the risk and return attributes of the investor's overall portfolio of assets. Here, we will focus much more narrowly on how investors can eliminate their vulnerability to one particular source of risk. For example, an exporter may want to offset a large exposure to foreign exchange fluctuations, or a farmer may want to reduce his dependence on the price of wheat. **Hedging** is understood as a technique to offset particular sources of risk rather than as a more ambitious search for the optimal risk-return profile for the entire portfolio.

In the next section we examine basic hedging strategies. We start with a discussion of the general principles of hedging, illustrating with an example of an exporting firm that seeks to manage its exposure to exchange rate fluctuations. Then we turn to specific applications. We demonstrate how stock index futures can be used to hedge against market risk and allow portfolio managers to separate bets on firm-specific versus marketwide performance. We turn next to hedging tools in the fixed-income market, and see how interest rate futures contracts can be used to offset interest rate risk. Finally, we show how the hedge ratios that emerge from option-pricing models like the Black-Scholes formula can be used to allow options traders to speculate on perceived option mispricing without inadvertently taking a position on the performance of the underlying stock.

In the last section, we explore the ramifications of hedging demands on capital market equilibrium. We will see that when many individuals hedge particular risks to their consumption or investment opportunities, these demands can affect equilibrium rates of return. Thus, these hedging demands provide a link between the CAPM and the multifactor APT.

25.1 Hedging Techniques

General Principles

Consider a U.S. firm that exports most of its product to Great Britain. The firm is vulnerable to fluctuations in the dollar/pound exchange rate for several reasons. First, the dollar value of the pound-denominated revenue derived from its customers will fluctuate with the exchange rate. Second, the pound price that the firm can charge its customers in the U.K. will itself be affected by the exchange rate. For example, if the pound depreciates by 10% relative to the dollar, the firm would need to increase the pound price of its goods by 10% in order to maintain the dollar-equivalent price. However, the firm might not be able to raise the price by 10% if it faces competition from British producers, or if it believes the higher pound-denominated price would reduce demand for its product.

To offset its foreign exchange exposure, the firm might engage in transactions that bring it profits when the pound depreciates. The lost profits from business operations resulting from a depreciation will then be offset by gains on its financial transactions. Suppose, for example, that the firm enters a futures contract to deliver pounds for dollars at an exchange rate agreed to today. As the deliverer of the currency, the firm enters the short side of the pound futures contract. Therefore, if the pound depreciates, the futures position will yield a profit.

For example, suppose that the futures price is currently $1.70 per pound for delivery in three months. If the firm enters a futures contract with a futures price of $1.70 per pound, and the exchange rate in three months is $1.60 per pound, then the profit on the transaction is $0.10 per pound. The futures price converges at the maturity date to the spot exchange rate of $1.60 and the profit to the short position is therefore $F_0 - F_T =$ $1.70 − $1.60 = $0.10 per pound.

How many pounds should be sold in the futures market to most fully offset the exposure to exchange rate fluctuations? Suppose the dollar value of profits in the next quarter will fall by $200,000 for every $0.10 depreciation of the pound. Given this information, the proper hedge position is easy to calculate. We need to find the number of pounds we should commit to delivering in order to provide a $200,000 profit for every $0.10 that the pound depreciates. Therefore, we need a futures position to deliver 2,000,000 pounds. As we have just seen, the profit per pound on the futures contract equals the difference in the current futures price and the ultimate exchange rate; therefore, the foreign exchange profits resulting from a $0.10 depreciation[1] will equal $0.10 × 2,000,000 = $200,000.

[1] Actually, the profit on the contract depends on the change in the futures price, not the spot exchange rate. For simplicity, we call the decline in the futures price the depreciation in the pound.

The proper hedge position in pound futures is independent of the actual depreciation in the pound as long as the relationship between profits and exchange rates is approximately linear. For example, if the pound depreciates by only half as much, \$0.05, the firm would lose only \$100,000 in operating profits. The futures position would also return half the profits: \$0.05 × 2,000,000 = \$100,000, again just offsetting the operating exposure. If the pound *appreciates,* the hedge position still (unfortunately in this case) offsets the operating exposure. If the pound appreciates by \$0.05, the firm might gain \$100,000 from the enhanced value of the pound; however, it will lose that amount on its obligation to deliver the pounds for the original futures price.

The hedge ratio is the number of futures positions necessary to hedge the risk of the unprotected portfolio, in this case the firm's export business. In general, we can think of the **hedge ratio** as the number of hedging vehicles (e.g., futures contracts) one would establish to offset the risk of a particular unprotected position. The hedge ratio, H, in this case is:

$$H = \frac{\text{Change in value of unprotected position for a given change in exchange rate}}{\text{Profit derived from one futures position for the same change in exchange rate}}$$

$$= \frac{\$200{,}000 \text{ per } \$0.10 \text{ change in \$/£ exchange rate}}{\$0.10 \text{ profit } \textit{per pound} \text{ delivered per } \$0.10 \text{ change in \$/£ exchange rate}}$$

$$= 2{,}000{,}000 \text{ pounds to be delivered}$$

Because each pound-futures contract on the International Monetary Market (a division of the Chicago Mercantile Exchange) calls for delivery of 62,500 pounds, you would need to short 2,000,000/62,500 per contract = 32 contracts.

One interpretation of the hedge ratio is as a ratio of sensitivities to the underlying source of uncertainty. The sensitivity of operating profits is \$200,000 per swing of \$0.10 in the exchange rate. The sensitivity of futures profits is \$0.10 per pound to be delivered per swing of \$0.10 in the exchange rate. Therefore, the hedge ratio is 200,000/.10 = 2,000,000 pounds.

We could just as easily have defined the hedge ratio in terms of futures contracts rather than in terms of pounds. Because each contract calls for delivery of 62,500 pounds, the profit on each contract per swing of \$0.10 in the exchange rate is \$6,250. Therefore, the hedge ratio defined in units of futures contracts is \$200,000/\$6,250 = 32 contracts, as derived above.

CONCEPT CHECK

Question 1. Suppose a multinational firm is harmed when the *dollar* depreciates. Specifically, suppose that its profits decrease by \$200,000 for every \$0.05 rise in the dollar/pound exchange rate. How many contracts should the firm enter? Should it take the long side or the short side of the contracts?

Once you know the sensitivity of the unhedged position to changes in the exchange rate, calculating the risk-minimizing hedge position is easy. Far more difficult is the determination of that sensitivity. For the exporting firm, for example, a naive view

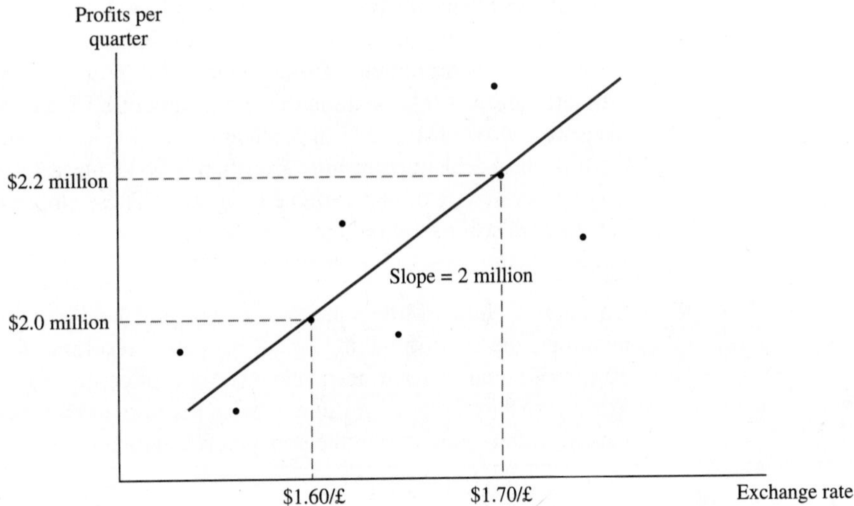

Figure 25.1
Profits as a function of the exchange rate

might hold that one need only estimate the expected pound-denominated revenue, and then contract to deliver that number of pounds in the futures or forward market. This approach, however, fails to recognize that pound revenue is itself a function of the exchange rate by virtue of the fact that the U.S. firm's competitive position in the U.K. is determined in part by the exchange rate. In fact, estimating the sensitivity of business exposure to the exchange rate requires considerable judgment.

One approach relies, in part, on historical relationships. Suppose, for example, that the firm prepares a scatter diagram as in Figure 25.1 that relates its business profits (measured in dollars) in each of the last 40 quarters to the dollar/pound exchange rate in that quarter. The general tendency is that profits are lower when the exchange rate is lower, that is, when the pound depreciates. To quantify that sensitivity, we might draw a line to represent the average tendency through the scatter diagram, or even better, estimate the following regression equation:

$$\text{Profits} = a + b\,(\$/£ \text{ exchange rate})$$

The slope of the regression, the estimate of b, is the sensitivity of quarterly profits to the exchange rate. For example, if the estimate of b turns out to be 2,000,000 as in Figure 25.1, then the regression equation is interpreted as stating that on average, the relationship between profits and the exchange rate is that a one-dollar *increase* in the value of the pound results in a $2,000,000 *increase* in quarterly profits. This, of course, is the sensitivity we posited when we asserted that a $0.10 drop in the dollar/pound exchange rate would decrease profits by $200,000.

Of course, one must interpret regression output with care. For example, one would not want to extrapolate the historical relationship between profitability and exchange rates exhibited in a period when the exchange rate hovered between $1.60 and $1.90 per pound to scenarios in which the exchange rate might be forecast at below $1.20 per pound or above $2.50 per pound.

In addition, one always must use care when extrapolating past relationships into the future. We saw in Chapter 9 that regression betas from the index model tend to vary across time; such problems are not unique to the index model. Moreover, regression estimates are just that—estimates. Parameters of a regression equation are sometimes measured with considerable imprecision.

Still, historical relationships are often a good place to start when looking for the average sensitivity of one variable to another. These slope coefficients are not perfect, but they are still useful indicators of hedge ratios.

CONCEPT CHECK Question 2. United Millers purchases corn to make cornflakes. When the price of corn increases, the cost of making cereal increases, resulting in lower profits. Historically, profits per quarter have been related to the price of corn according to the equation: Profits = \$8 million − 1 million × price per bushel. How many bushels of corn should United Millers purchase in the corn futures market to hedge its corn-price risk?

Hedging Systematic Risk

We saw in Chapter 21 that pure market timers might use a combination of money market securities and stock index futures contracts to adjust market exposure in response to changing forecasts about stock market performance. When the outlook is bullish, more contracts would be added to the fixed position in cash equivalents.

This form of timing is a bit restrictive, however, in that it allows for equity positions in only the stock index. How might a manager of a more actively constructed portfolio hedge market exposure? Suppose, for example, that you manage a \$30 million portfolio with a beta of .8. You are bullish on the market over the long term, but are afraid that over the next two months, the market is vulnerable to a sharp downturn. If trading were costless, you could sell your portfolio, place the proceeds in T-bills for two months, and then reestablish your position after you perceive that the risk of the downturn has passed. In practice, however, this strategy would result in unacceptable trading costs, not to mention tax problems resulting from the realization of capital gains or losses on the portfolio. An alternative approach would be to use stock index futures to hedge your market exposure.

For example, suppose that the S&P 500 index currently is at 400. A decrease in the index to 390 would represent a drop of 2.5%. Given the beta of your portfolio, you would expect a loss of .8 × 2.5% = 2%, or in dollar terms, 0.02 × \$30 million = \$600,000. Therefore, the sensitivity of your portfolio value to market movements is \$600,000 per 10-point movement in the S&P 500 index.

To hedge this risk, you could sell stock index futures. When your portfolio falls in value along with declines in the broad market, the futures contract will provide an offsetting profit.

The sensitivity of a futures contract to market movements is easy to determine. With its contract multiplier of 500, the profit on the S&P 500 futures contract varies by \$5,000 for every 10-point swing in the index. Therefore, to hedge your market exposure for two months, you could calculate the hedge ratio as follows:

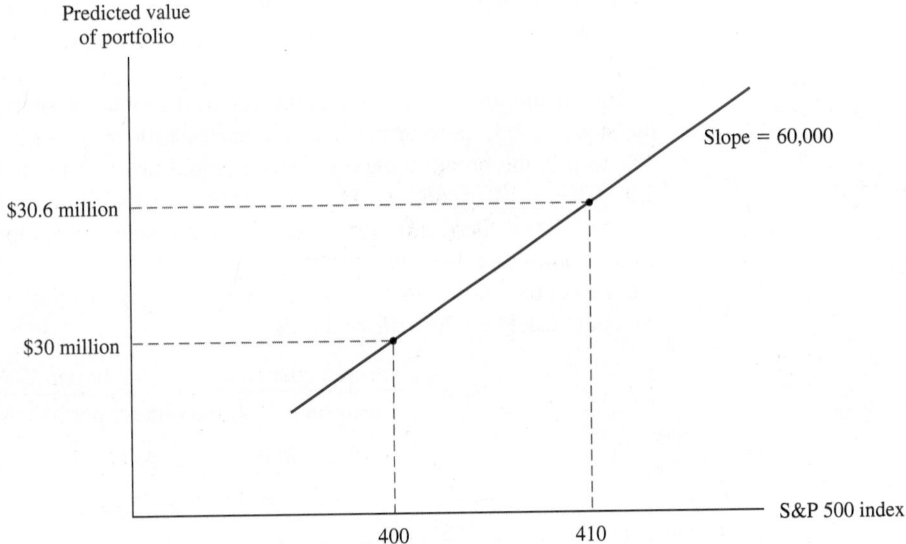

Figure 25.2
Predicted value of the portfolio as a function of the market index

$$H = \frac{\text{Change in portfolio value}}{\text{Profit on one futures contract}} = \frac{\$600{,}000}{\$5{,}000} = 120 \text{ contracts (short)}$$

You would enter the short side of the contracts, because you want profits from the contract to offset the exposure of your portfolio to the market. Because your portfolio does poorly when the market falls, you need a position that will do well when the market falls.

We also could approach the hedging problem using the regression procedure illustrated above. The predicted value of the portfolio is graphed in Figure 25.2 as a function of the value of the S&P 500 index. With a beta of .8, the slope of the relationship is 60,000: A 2.5% increase in the index, from 400 to 410, results in a capital gain of 2% of $30 million, or $600,000. Therefore, your portfolio will increase in value by $60,000 for each increase of one point in the index. As a result, you should enter a short position on 60,000 units of the S&P 500 index to fully offset your exposure to marketwide movements. Because the contract multiplier is 500 units of the index, you need to sell 60,000/500 = 120 contracts.

Notice that when the slope of the regression line relating your unprotected position to the value of an asset is positive, your hedge strategy calls for a *short* position in that asset. The hedge ratio is the negative of the regression slope. This is because the hedge position should offset your initial exposure. If you do poorly when the asset value falls, you need a hedge vehicle that will do well when the asset value falls. This calls for a short position in the asset.

Active managers sometimes face the following problem. They might believe that a particular asset is underpriced, but that the market as a whole is about to fall. Even if the asset is a good buy relative to other stocks in the market, it still might perform poorly in a broad market downturn. The manager would like to separate the bet on the firm from the bet on the market. To do so, the bet on the company must be offset with a hedge against the market exposure that normally would accompany a purchase of the stock.

Here again, the stock's beta is the key to the hedging strategy. Suppose the beta of the stock is 2/3, and the manager purchases $300,000 worth of the stock. For every 3% drop in the broad market, the stock would be expected to respond with a drop of $2/3 \times 3\% = 2\%$, or $6,000. The S&P 500 contract will fall by 12 points from a current value of 400 if the market drops 3%. With the contract multiplier of $500, this would entail a profit to a short futures position of $12 \times \$500 = \$6,000$ per contract. Therefore, the market risk of the stock can be offset by shorting one S&P contract. More formally, we could calculate the hedge ratio as

$$H = \frac{\text{Expected change in stock value per 3\% market drop}}{\text{Profit on one short contract per 3\% market drop}}$$

$$= \frac{\text{\$6,000 swing in unprotected position}}{\text{\$6,000 profit per contract}}$$

$$= 1 \text{ contract}$$

Now that market risk is hedged, the only source of variability in the performance of the stock-plus-futures portfolio will be the firm-specific performance of the stock.

By allowing investors to bet on market performance, the futures contract allows the portfolio manager to make stock picks without concern for the market exposure of the stocks chosen. After the stocks are chosen, the resulting systematic risk of the portfolio can be modulated to any degree using the stock futures contracts.

Portfolio managers actually do use futures to separate firm-specific bets from bets on overall market performance. The article from *The Wall Street Journal* reproduced in Chapter 22 (page 719) cited a Goldman Sachs study on stock futures' trading that cited such motives as responsible in part for the rapid increase in stock futures' trading volume. The article noted that

> For instance, by selling futures equal to the value of the underlying portfolio, a manager can almost completely insulate a portfolio from market moves. Say a manager succeeds in outperforming the market, but still loses 3% while the market as a whole falls 10%. Hedging with futures would capture that margin of outperformance, translating the loss into a profit of roughly 7%.

Hedging Interest Rate Risk

Like equity managers, fixed-income managers also desire to separate security-specific decisions from bets on movements in the entire structure of interest rates. Consider, for example, these problems:

1. A fixed-income manager holds a bond portfolio on which considerable capital gains have been earned. She foresees an increase in interest rates, but is reluctant to sell her portfolio and replace it with a lower-duration mix of bonds because such rebalancing would result in large trading costs as well as realiza-

tion of capital gains for tax purposes. Still, she would like to hedge her exposure to interest rate increases.

2. A corporation plans to issue bonds to the public. It believes that now is a good time to act, but it cannot issue the bonds for another three months because of the lags inherent in SEC registration. It would like to hedge the uncertainty surrounding the yield at which it eventually will be able to sell the bonds.
3. A pension fund will receive a large cash inflow next month that it plans to invest in long-term bonds. It is concerned that interest rates may fall by the time it can make the investment, and would like to lock in the yield currently available on long-term issues.

In each of these cases, the investment manager wishes to hedge interest rate uncertainty. To illustrate the procedures that might be followed, we will focus on the first example, and suppose that the portfolio manager has a $10 million bond portfolio with a modified duration of nine years.[2] If, as feared, market interest rates increase and the bond portfolio's yield also rises, say by 10 basis points (0.1%), the fund will suffer a capital loss. Recall from Chapter 15 that the capital loss in percentage terms will be the product of modified duration, D^*, and the change in the portfolio yield. Therefore, the loss will be

$$D^* \times \Delta y = 9 \times 0.1\% = 0.9\%$$

or $90,000. This establishes that the sensitivity of the value of the unprotected portfolio to changes in market yields is $9,000 per one basis point change in the yield. Market practitioners call this ratio the **price value of a basis point,** or PVBP. The PVBP represents the sensitivity of the dollar value of the portfolio to changes in interest rates. Here, we've shown that

$$\text{PVBP} = \frac{\text{Change in portfolio value}}{\text{Predicted change in yield}} = \frac{\$90{,}000}{10 \text{ basis points}} = \$9{,}000 \text{ per basis point}$$

One way to hedge this risk is to take an offsetting position in an interest rate futures contract. The Treasury bond contract is the most widely traded contract. The bond nominally calls for delivery of $100,000 par value T-bonds with 8% coupons and 20-year maturity. In practice, the contract delivery terms are fairly complicated because many bonds with different coupon rates and maturities may be substituted to settle the contract. However, we will assume that the bond to be delivered on the contract already is known and has a modified duration of 10 years. Finally, suppose that the futures price currently is $90 per $100 par value. Because the contract requires delivery of $100,000 par value of bonds, the contract multiplier is $1,000.

Given these data, we can calculate the PVBP for the futures contract. If the yield on the delivery bond increases by 10 basis points, the bond value will fall by $D^* \times 0.1\% = 10 \times 0.1\% = 1\%$. The futures price also will decline 1% from 90 to 89.10.[3] Because

---

[2] Recall that modified duration, D^*, is related to duration, D, by the formula $D^* = D/(1 + y)$, where y is the bond's yield to maturity. If the bond pays coupons semiannually, then y should be measured as a semiannual yield. For simplicity, we will assume annual coupon payments, and treat y as the effective annual yield to maturity.

[3] This assumes the futures price will be exactly proportional to the bond price, which ought to be nearly true.

Figure 25.3
Yield spread between long-term government and Aaa-rated corporate bonds

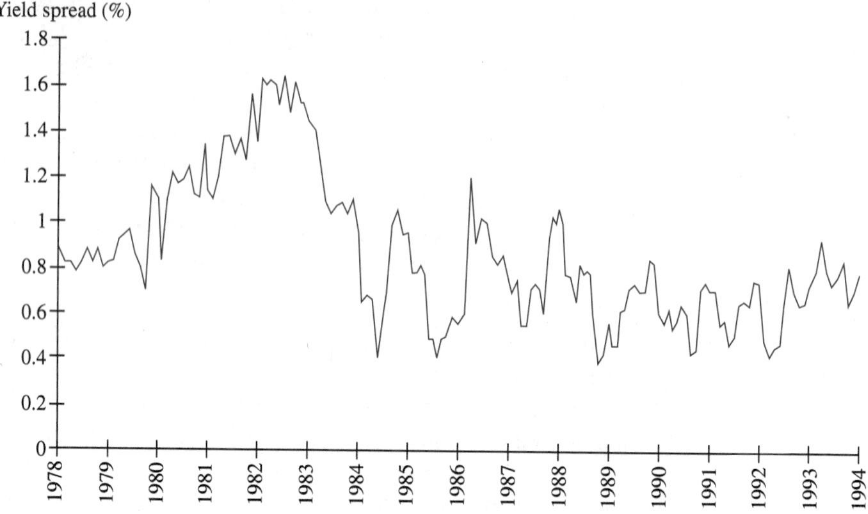

the contract multiplier is \$1,000, the gain on each short contract will be \$1,000 × .90 = \$900. Therefore, the PVBP for one futures contract is \$900/10-basis-point change, or \$90 for a change in yield of one basis point.

Now we can easily calculate the hedge ratio as follows:

$$H = \frac{\text{PVBP of portfolio}}{\text{PVBP of hedge vehicle}} = \frac{\$9{,}000}{\$90 \text{ per contract}} = 100 \text{ contracts}$$

Therefore, 100 T-bond futures contracts will serve to offset the portfolio's exposure to interest rate fluctuations.

CONCEPT CHECK

Question 3. Suppose the bond portfolio is twice as large, \$20 million, but that its modified duration is only 4.5 years. Show that the proper hedge position in T-bond futures is the same as the value just calculated, 100 contracts.

Although the hedge ratio is easy to compute, the hedging problem in practice is more difficult. We assumed in our example that the yields on the T-bond contract and the bond portfolio would move perfectly in unison. Although interest rates on various fixed-income instruments do tend to vary in tandem, there is considerable slippage across sectors of the fixed-income market. For example, Figure 25.3 shows that the spread between long-term corporate and Treasury bond yields has fluctuated considerably over time. Our hedging strategy would be fully effective only if the yield spread across the two sectors of the fixed-income market were constant (or at least perfectly predictable) so that yield changes in both sectors were equal.

This problem highlights the fact that most hedging activity is in fact **cross-hedging,** meaning that the hedge vehicle is a different asset than the one to be hedged. To the extent that there is slippage between prices or yields of the two assets, the hedge will not be perfect. Nevertheless, even cross-hedges can eliminate a large fraction of the total risk of the unprotected portfolio.

Hedging Bets on Mispriced Options

Suppose you believe that the standard deviation of IBM stock returns will be 35% over the next few weeks, but IBM put options are selling at a price consistent with a volatility of 33%. Because the put's implied volatility is less than your forecast of the stock volatility, you believe the option is underpriced. Using your assessment of volatility in an option-pricing model like the Black-Scholes formula, you would estimate that the fair price for the puts exceeds the actual price.

Does this mean that you ought to buy put options? Perhaps it does, but by doing so, you risk great losses if IBM stock performs well, *even if* you are correct about the volatility. You would like to separate your bet on volatility from the "attached" bet inherent in purchasing a put that IBM's stock price will fall. In other words, you would like to speculate on the option mispricing by purchasing the put option, but hedge the resulting exposure to the performance of IBM stock.

We saw in Chapter 20 that the option *delta* is in fact a hedge ratio that can be used for this purpose. The delta was defined as

$$\text{Delta} = \frac{\text{Change in value of option}}{\text{Change in value of stock}}$$

Therefore, delta is the slope of the option-pricing curve.

This ratio tells us precisely how many shares of stock we must hold to offset our exposure to IBM. For example, if the delta is $-.6$, then the put will fall by \$0.60 in value for every one-point increase in IBM stock, and we need to hold 0.6 shares of stock to hedge each put. If we purchase 10 option contracts, each for 100 shares, we would need to buy 600 shares of stock. If the stock price rises by \$1, each put option will decrease in value by \$0.60, resulting in a loss of \$600. However, the loss on the puts will be offset by a gain on the stock holdings of \$1 per share × 600 shares.

To see how the profits on this strategy might develop, let's use the following example:

Option maturity, *T*	60 days
Put price, *P*	\$4.495
Exercise price, *X*	\$90
Stock price, *S*	\$90
Risk-free rate, *r*	4%

We assume that the stock will not pay a dividend in the next 60 days. Given these data, the implied volatility on the option is 33%, as we posited. However, you believe the true volatility is 35%, implying that the fair put price is \$4.785. Therefore, if the market assessment of volatility is revised to the value you believe is correct, your profit will be \$0.29 per put purchased.

Recall from chapter 20 that the hedge ratio, or delta, of a put option equals $N(d_1) - 1$, where N(•) is the cumulative normal distribution function and

Table 25.1 Profit on Hedged Put Portfolio

A. Cost to Establish Hedged Position

1,000 put options @ $4.495/option	$ 4,495
453 shares @ $90/share	40,770
Total outlay	$45,265

B. Value of Put Option as a Function of the Stock Price at Implied Volatility of 35%

Stock price:	89	90	91
Put price	$5.254	$4.785	$4.347
Profit (loss) on each put	0.759	0.290	(0.148)

C. Value of and Profit on Hedged Put Portfolio

Stock price:	89	90	91
Value of 1,000 put options	$ 5,254	$ 4,785	$ 4,347
Value of 453 shares	40,317	40,770	41,223
TOTAL	$45,571	$45,555	$45,570
Profit (= Value − Cost from Panel A)	306	290	305

$$d_1 = \frac{ln(S/X) + (r + \sigma^2/2)T}{\sigma\sqrt{T}}$$

Using your estimate of $\sigma = .35$, you find that the hedge ratio, $N(d_1) - 1 = -.453$.

Suppose, therefore, that you purchase 10 option contracts (1,000 puts) and purchase 453 shares of stock. Once the market "catches up" to your presumably better volatility estimate, the put options purchased will increase in value. If the market assessment of volatility changes as soon as you purchase the options, your profits should equal 1,000 × $0.29 = $290. The option price will be affected as well by any change in the stock price, but this part of your exposure will be eliminated if the hedge ratio is chosen properly. Your profit should be based solely on the effect of the change in the implied volatility of the put, with the impact of the stock price hedged away.

Table 25.1 illustrates your profits as a function of the stock price assuming that the put price changes to reflect *your* estimate of volatility. Panel B shows that the put option alone can provide profits or losses depending on whether the stock price falls or rises. We see in Panel C, however, that each *hedged* put option provides profits nearly equal to the original mispricing, regardless of the change in the stock price.[4]

[4] The profit is not exactly independent of the stock price. This is because as the stock price changes, so do the deltas used to calculate the hedge ratio. The hedge ratio in principle would need to be continually adjusted as deltas evolve. The sensitivity of the delta to the stock price is called the *gamma* of the option. Option gammas are analogous to bond convexity. In both cases, the curvature of the value function means that hedge ratios or durations change with market conditions, making rebalancing a necessary part of hedging strategies.

This hedging strategy is similar in spirit to the strategy used by the active equity manager who wishes to make a firm-specific bet without taking a position on the direction of the broad market. The equity manager buys the stock perceived to be underpriced and uses stock-index futures to hedge the stock's market exposure. Here, the options manager buys the option perceived to be underpriced and uses the stock to hedge the exposure of the option to changes in the price of the stock.

CONCEPT CHECK Question 4. Suppose you bet on volatility by purchasing calls instead of puts. How would you hedge your exposure to stock-price fluctuations? What is the hedge ratio?

A variant of this strategy involves cross-option speculation. Suppose you observe a 45-day maturity call option on IBM with strike price 95 selling at a price consistent with a volatility of $\sigma = 33\%$ while another 45-day call with strike price 90 has an implied volatility of only 27%. Because the underlying asset and maturity date are identical, you conclude that the call with the higher implied volatility is relatively overpriced. To exploit the mispricing, you might buy the cheap calls (with strike price 90 and implied volatility of 27%) and write the expensive calls (with strike price 95 and implied volatility of 33%). If the risk-free rate is 4% and IBM is selling at $90 per share, the calls purchased will be priced at $3.6202 and the calls written will be priced at $2.3735.

Despite the fact that you are long one call and short another, your exposure to IBM stock-price uncertainty will not be hedged using this strategy. This is because calls with different strike prices have different sensitivities to the price of the underlying asset. The lower-strike-price call has a higher delta and, therefore, greater exposure to the price of IBM. If you take an equal number of positions in these two options, you will inadvertently establish a bullish position in IBM, as the calls you purchase have higher deltas than the calls you write. In fact, you may recall from Chapter 19 that this portfolio (long call with low exercise price and short call with high exercise price) is called a *bullish spread.*

To establish a hedged position, we can use the hedge ratio approach as follows. Consider the 95-strike-price options you write as the asset that hedges your exposure to the 90-strike-price options you purchase. Then the hedge ratio is

$$H = \frac{\text{Change in value of 90-strike-price call for \$1 change in IBM}}{\text{Change in value of 95-strike-price call for \$1 change in IBM}}$$

$$= \frac{\text{Delta of 90-strike-price call}}{\text{Delta of 95-strike-price call}} > 1$$

You need to write *more* than one call with the higher strike price to hedge the purchase of each call with the lower strike price. Because the prices of higher-strike-price calls are less sensitive to IBM prices, more of them are required to offset the exposure.

Suppose the true annual volatility of the stock is midway between the two implied volatilities, so $\sigma = 30\%$. We know from Chapter 20 that the delta of a call option is $N(d_1)$. Therefore, the deltas of the two options and the hedge ratio are computed as follows:

Table 25.2 Profits on Delta-Neutral Options Portfolio

A. Cash Flow When Portfolio Is Established

Purchase 1,000 calls (X = 90) @ \$3.6202 (Option priced at implied volatility of 27%)	\$3,620.20 cash outflow
Write 1,589 calls (X = 95) @ \$2.3735 (Option priced at implied volatility of 33%)	3,771.50 cash inflow
TOTAL	\$ 151.30 net cash inflow

B. Option Prices at Implied Volatility of 30%

Stock price:	89	90	91
90-strike-price calls	\$3.478	\$3.997	\$4.557
95-strike-price calls	1.703	2.023	2.382

C. Value of Portfolio After Implied Volatilities Coverge to 30%

Stock price:	89	90	91
Value of 1,000 calls held	\$3,478	\$3,997	\$4,557
– Value of 1,589 calls written	2,705	3,214	3,785
TOTAL	\$ 773	\$ 782	\$ 772

Option with strike price 90:

$$d_1 = \frac{ln(90/90) + (.04 + .30^2/2) \times 45/365}{.30\sqrt{45/365}} = .0995$$

$$N(d_1) = .5396$$

Option with strike price 95:

$$d_1 = \frac{ln(90/95) + (.04 + .30^2/2) \times 45/365}{.30\sqrt{45/365}} = -.4138$$

$$N(d_1) = .3395$$

Hedge ratio:

$$\frac{.5396}{.3395} = 1.589$$

Therefore, for every 1,000 call options purchased with strike price 90, we need to write 1,589 call options with strike price 95. Following this strategy enables us to bet on the relative mispricing of the two options without taking a position on IBM. Panel A of Table 25.2 shows that the position will result in a cash inflow of \$151.30. The premium income on the calls written exceeds the cost of the calls purchased.

When you establish a position in stocks and options that is hedged with respect to fluctuations in the price of the underlying asset, your portfolio is said to be **delta neutral,** meaning that the portfolio has no tendency to either increase or decrease in value when the stock price fluctuates.

Let's check that our options position is in fact delta neutral. Suppose that the implied volatilities of the two options come back into alignment just after you establish your position, so that both options are priced at implied volatilities of 30%. You expect to profit from the increase in the value of the call purchased as well as from the decrease in the value of the call written. The option prices at 30% volatility are given in Panel B of Table 25.2 and the values of your position for various stock prices are presented in Panel C. Although the profit or loss on each option is affected by the stock price, the value of the delta-neutral option portfolio is positive and essentially independent of the price of IBM. Moreover, we saw in Panel A that the portfolio would have been established without ever requiring a cash outlay. You would have cash inflows both when you establish the portfolio *and* when you liquidate it after the implied volatilities converge to 30%.

This unusual profit opportunity arises because you have identified prices out of alignment. Such opportunities could not arise if prices were at equilibrium levels. By exploiting the pricing discrepancy using a delta-neutral strategy, you lock in profits regardless of the price movement in IBM stock.

Delta-neutral hedging strategies are also subject to practical problems, the most important of which is the difficulty in assessing the proper volatility for the coming period. If the volatility estimate is incorrect, so will be the deltas, and the overall position will not truly be hedged. Moreover, option or option-plus-stock positions generally will not be neutral with respect to changes in volatility. For example, a put option hedged by a stock might be delta neutral, but it is not volatility neutral. Changes in the market assessments of volatility will affect the option price even if the stock price is unchanged.

These problems can be serious, because volatility estimates are never fully reliable. First, volatility cannot be observed directly, and must be estimated from past data, which imparts measurement error to the forecast. Second, we've seen that both historical and implied volatilities fluctuate over time. Therefore, we are always shooting at a moving target. Although delta-neutral positions are hedged against changes in the price of the underlying asset, they still are subject to **volatility risk,** the risk incurred from unpredictable changes in volatility. Thus, although delta-neutral option hedges might eliminate exposure to risk from fluctuations in the value of the underlying asset, they do not eliminate volatility risk.

25.2 Effects of Hedging Demands on Capital Market Equilibrium

One implication of the capital asset pricing model was that all investors would decide that the same portfolio of risky assets, the market portfolio, provides the best risk-to-reward ratio. The CAPM, however, assumes that investors face only one source of risk—namely, uncertainty about future values of securities—and that the dollar value of wealth is the only determinant of economic welfare.

In reality, of course, investors must deal with many other sources of risk. Among these are:

1. Uncertain labor income.

2. Uncertain prices of consumption goods, for example, oil or housing price uncertainty.
3. Uncertain life expectancy.
4. Uncertainty about future investment opportunities, for example, uncertainty in future interest rates.

Naturally, investors will attempt to hedge these risks to the greatest extent possible. For example, life insurance policies may be viewed as hedging vehicles for the uncertainty in life expectancy. Extra hedging demands against various sources of risk mean that our earlier treatment of portfolio demands must be modified. We can illustrate with an example.

The dramatic fluctuations in oil prices in the 1970s and 1980s illustrated the vulnerability of the economy to oil price shocks. In addition to the direct effect of oil prices on stock market values, consumers and investors found that oil prices had substantial effects on unemployment and inflation rates as well as on the cost of heating their homes and commuting to work. The important effect of oil price uncertainty for most investors had more to do with their activities as consumers and employees than with the impact of oil prices on the value of energy stocks such as Exxon.

It would not be surprising for individuals to search for investment vehicles to offset, or hedge, the risk they face from oil price uncertainty. A natural hedge security would be shares of energy sector stocks that should do well when the rest of the economy is harmed by an oil price shock. Investors would thus form hedge portfolios of stocks like Exxon to offset their oil price exposure. Therefore, the optimal risky portfolio would no longer be just the market portfolio. Investors would add to the market portfolio an additional position in the hedge portfolio.

But if many investors tilt their portfolios away from the market portfolio toward a specific sector such as energy stocks, the relative prices of those securities will change to reflect this extra hedging demand. For example, the prices of energy stocks will be bid up by the hedging demand, and their rates of return driven down. Investors will be willing to hold these stocks even with an expected rate of return lower than that dictated by the expected return–beta relationship of the CAPM because of the hedging value of the securities. The simple expected return–beta relationship therefore needs to be generalized to account for the effects of extramarket hedging demands on equilibrium rates of return.

Merton[5] has shown that these hedging demands will result in an expanded or "multifactor" version of the CAPM that recognizes the multidimensional nature of risk. The focal point of Merton's model is not dollar returns per se but the consumption and investment made possible by the investor's wealth. Each source of risk to consumption or investment opportunities may in principle command its own risk premium.

In the case of oil price risk, for example, Merton's model would imply that the expected return–beta relationship of the single-factor CAPM would be generalized to the following two-factor relationship

$$E(r_i) - r_f = \beta_{iM}[E(r_M) - r_f] + \beta_{io}[E(r_o) - r_f]$$

[5] Robert C. Merton, "An Intertemporal Capital Asset Pricing Model," *Econometrica* 41 (1973).

where β_{iM} is the beta of security i with respect to the market portfolio and β_{io} is the beta with respect to oil price risk. Just as we measure the beta in the traditional index model using simple regression analysis, we can measure the multiple betas in this extended model in a multiple regression that allows for several explanatory or systematic factors. Similarly, $[E(r_o) - r_f]$ is the risk premium associated with exposure to oil price uncertainty. The rate of return on the portfolio that best hedges the oil price uncertainty is r_o. This equation, therefore, is a two-factor CAPM. More generally, we will have a beta and a risk premium for every significant source of risk that consumers try to hedge.

Notice that this expanded version of the CAPM provides a prediction for security returns identical to that of the multifactor APT. Therefore, there is no contradiction between these two theories of risk premiums. They provide complementary but consistent ways of deriving determinants of risk premiums. The CAPM approach does offer one notable advantage, however. In contrast to the APT, which takes the systematic factors in the economy as given, the CAPM provides guidance as to where to look for those factors. The important factors will be those sources of risk that large groups of investors try to offset by establishing extramarket hedge portfolios. By specifying the likely sources of risk against which dominant groups of investors attempt to hedge, we identify the dimensions along which the CAPM needs to be generalized. Therefore, we might specify that some important sources of extramarket risk are uncertainty in interest rates, inflation rates, and prices of goods in major sectors of the economy such as energy or housing.

CONCEPT CHECK

Question 5. Consider the following regression results for Stock *X*.

$$r_X = 2\% + 1.2 \text{ (percentage change in oil prices)}$$

a. If I live in Louisiana, where the local economy is heavily dependent on oil industry profits, does stock *X* represent a useful asset to hedge my overall economic well-being?

b. What if I live in Massachusetts, where most individuals and firms are energy *consumers?*

c. If energy consumers are far more numerous than energy producers, will high oil-beta stocks have higher or lower expected rates of return in market equilibrium than low oil-beta stocks?

SUMMARY

1. Hedging requires investors to purchase assets that will offset the sensitivity of their portfolios to particular sources of risk. A hedged position requires that the hedging vehicle provide profits that vary inversely with the value of the position to be protected.

2. The hedge ratio is the number of hedging vehicles such as futures contracts required to offset the risk of the unprotected position.

3. The hedge ratio for systematic market risk is proportional to the size and beta of the underlying stock portfolio. The hedge ratio for fixed-income portfolios is

proportional to the price value of a basis point, which in turn is proportional to modified duration and the size of the portfolio.

4. The option delta is used to determine the hedge ratio for options positions. Delta-neutral portfolios are independent of price changes in the underlying asset. Even delta-neutral option portfolios are subject to volatility risk, however.

5. Investors are concerned with a host of extramarket sources of uncertainty pertaining to future consumption and investment opportunities. These concerns give rise to demands for securities that hedge these risks. Hedge portfolios with high correlation with one of the relevant sources of uncertainty will be sought to offset those sources of risk.

6. With the extra hedging demands, equilibrium security returns will satisfy a multifactor generalization of the expected return–beta relationship. This relationship is identical to the one predicted by the multifactor APT. A risk premium will arise if there is an aggregate desire to hedge an extramarket risk.

Key Terms

Hedging
Hedge ratio
Price value of a basis point
Cross-hedging
Delta neutral
Volatility risk

Selected Reading

A good book devoted to risk management is:

Smithson, Charles H.; Clifford W Smith; with D. Sykes Wilford. *Managing Financial Risk.* Burr Ridge, Ill.: Irwin Professional Publishing, 1995.

Problems

1. A manager is holding a $1 million stock portfolio with a beta of 1.25. She would like to hedge the risk of the portfolio using the S&P 500 stock index futures contract. How many dollars' worth of the index should she sell in the futures market to minimize the volatility of her position?
2. A manager is holding a $1 million bond portfolio with a modified duration of eight years. She would like to hedge the risk of the portfolio by short-selling Treasury bonds. The modified duration of T-bonds is 10 years. How many dollars' worth of T-bonds should she sell to minimize the variance of her position?
3. Farmer Brown grows Number 1 red corn, and would like to hedge the value of the coming harvest. However, the futures contract is traded on the Number 2 yellow grade of corn. Suppose that yellow corn typically sells for 90% of the price of red corn. If he grows 100,000 bushels, and each futures contract calls for delivery of 5,000 bushels, how many contracts should Farmer Brown buy or sell to hedge his position?
4. Yields on short-term bonds tend to be more volatile than yields on long-term bonds. Suppose that you have estimated that the yield on 20-year bonds changes

by 10 basis points for every 15-basis-point move in the yield on five-year bonds. You hold a $1 million portfolio of five-year maturity bonds with modified duration four years and desire to hedge your interest rate exposure with T-bond futures, which currently have modified duration nine years and sell at F_0 = $95. How many futures contracts should you sell?

5. A corporation plans to issue $10 million of 10-year bonds in three months. At current yields the bonds would have modified duration of eight years. The T-note futures contract is selling at $F_0 = 100$, and has modified duration of six years. How can the firm use this futures contract to hedge the risk surrounding the yield at which it will be able to sell its bonds?
6. You hold a $8 million stock portfolio with a beta of 1.0. You believe that the risk-adjusted abnormal return on the portfolio (the alpha) over the next three months is 2%. The S&P 500 index currently is at 400 and the risk-free rate is 1% per quarter.
   a. What will be the futures price on the three-month maturity S&P 500 futures contract?
   b. How many S&P 500 futures contracts are needed to hedge the stock portfolio?
   c. What will be the profit on that futures position in three months as a function of the value of the S&P 500 index on the maturity date?
   d. If the alpha of the portfolio is 2%, show that the expected rate of return (in decimal form) on the portfolio as a function of the market return is $r_P = .03 + 1.0 \times (r_M - .01)$.
   e. Call S_T the value of the index in three months. Then $S_T/S_0 = S_T/400 = 1 + r_M$. (We are ignoring dividends here to keep things simple.) Substitute this expression in the equation for the portfolio return, r_P, and calculate the expected value of the hedged stock-plus-futures portfolio in three months as a function of the value of the index.
   f. Show that the hedged portfolio provides an expected rate of return of 3% over the next three months.
   g. What is the beta of the hedged portfolio? What is the alpha of the hedged portfolio?
7. Suppose that the relationship between the rate of return on IBM stock, the market index, and a computer industry index can be described by the following regression equation: $r_{IBM} = .5r_M + .75r_{Industry}$. If a futures contract on the computer industry is traded, how would you hedge the exposure to the systematic and industry factors affecting the performance of IBM stock? How many dollars' worth of the market and industry index contracts would you buy or sell for each dollar held in IBM?
8. Salomon Brothers believes that market volatility will be 20% annually for the next 3 years. Three-year at-the-money call and put options on the market index sell at an implied volatility of 22%. What options portfolio can Salomon Brothers establish to speculate on its volatility belief without taking a bullish or bearish position on the market? Using Salomon's estimate of volatility, three-year at-the-money options have $N(d_1) = .6$.

9. Suppose that call options on Exxon stock with time to maturity three months and strike price $60 are selling at an implied volatility of 30%. Exxon stock currently is $60 per share, and the risk-free rate is 4%. If you believe the true volatility of the stock is 32%, how can you trade on your belief without taking on exposure to the performance of Exxon? How many shares of stock will you hold for each option contract purchased or sold?
10. Using the same data in Question 9, suppose that three-month put options with a strike price of $60 are selling at an implied volatility of 34%. Construct a delta-neutral portfolio comprising positions in calls and puts that will profit when the option prices come back into alignment.
11. Suppose that Salomon Brothers sells call options on $1 million worth of a stock portfolio with beta = 1.5. The option delta is .8. It wishes to hedge out its resultant exposure to a market advance by buying market index futures contracts.
    a. If the current value of the market index is 400 and the contract multiplier is 500, how many contracts should it buy?
    b. What if Salomon instead uses market index puts to hedge its exposure? Should it buy or sell puts? Each put option is on 100 units of the index, and the index at current prices represents $400 worth of stock.
12. You are holding call options on a stock. The stock's beta is .75, and you are concerned that the stock market is about to fall. The stock is currently selling for $5 and you hold 1 million options on the stock (i.e., you hold 10,000 contracts for 100 shares each). The option delta is .8. How many market index futures contracts must you buy or sell to hedge your market exposure if the current value of the market index is 400 and the contract multiplier is 500?
13. Suppose that everyone agrees that uncertainty in the relative price of coal energy versus oil energy is an important factor to hedge, but that because energy-supply companies are diversified, no securities have returns correlated with the ratio of oil to coal prices. Would the multifactor CAPM in this case predict any departures from the simple CAPM?
14. Consider the following regression results for stock X:

$$R_X = .01 + 1.7 \times \text{Inflation rate}$$

    a. If I am retired and live on my pension, which provides a fixed number of dollars each month, does stock X represent a useful asset to hedge my overall economic well-being? Why or why not?
    b. What if I am a gold producer, and I am aware that gold prices increase when inflation accelerates?
    c. If retirees are far more numerous than gold producers in this economy, will high inflation–beta stocks have higher or lower expected rates of return in market equilibrium than low inflation–beta stocks?
15. An example of a factor that might be identified as explaining stock returns, but not appear in the multifactor CAPM, is the return on a particular industry group such as machine tools.
    a. Why might this industry factor seem to be a useful explanatory variable in describing security returns, yet still not appear in the multifactor CAPM?

Table 25A Bonds

Name	Coupon	Maturity	Price	Yield	Duration (years)	Price Value of a Basis Point
Procter & Gamble	8⅝%	4/1/16	86.36	10.10%	10.08	0.08286
U.S. Treasury bond	9⅛%	5/15/13	99.125	9.21%	9.25	0.08766

Table 25B Futures (contract size = $100,000)

Contract	Expiration	Settlement Price	Yield	Price Value of a Basis Point	Converstion Factor
U.S. Treasury bond future	Dec. 1989	86.3125	9.51%	0.0902	1.1257

b. Would you expect this factor to command a significant risk premium? More generally, what types of factors will not command such premiums?

16. On June 1, 1989, Byron Henry was examining a new fixed income account that his firm, Hawaiian Advisors, had accepted. Included in the new portfolio was a $10 million par value position in Procter & Gamble (PG) 8⅝% bonds due April 1, 2016.*

CFA

Henry was concerned about this position for three reasons: (1) There was an unrealized loss on the PG bonds due to a widening in the yield spread between U.S. Treasuries and high-grade corporate bonds; (2) he felt that the PG bonds represented too large a portion of the $100 million portfolio; and (3) he feared that interest rates would move higher over the short term.

Hawaiian Advisors has the capability to do short sales and to use financial futures as well as options on futures. With this in mind, Henry collected some information on the PG bonds and on some alternative vehicles, shown in Tables 25A and 25B.

Henry recalled that the formula for calculating a hedge ratio is as follows:

$$\text{Hedge ratio} = \text{Yield beta} \times \frac{PVBP\ (y)}{PVBP\ (x)}$$

Where

$PVBP\ (y)$ = the price change for a one-basis-point change ($PVBP$) in the target vehicle (the PG bond)

$PVBP\ (x)$ = the price change for a one-basis-point change ($PVBP$) in the hedge vehicle (the U.S. Treasury bond or the U.S. Treasury bond future)

*Reprinted, with permission, from the *CFA Study Guide.* Association for Investment Management and Research, Charlottesville, VA.

Henry did a regression using Y (the dependent variable) as the yield of the PG bonds, and X (the independent variable) as the yield of the U.S. Treasury bonds. The result was the following equation:

$$Y = 1.75 + 0.89X \text{ } (R\text{-squared} = 0.81)$$

Henry did a second regression using Y (the dependent variable) as the yield of the PG bonds, and X (the independent variable) as the yield on the futures contract. The result was the following equation:

$$Y = 5.25 + 0.47X \text{ } (R\text{-squared} = 0.49)$$

For tax reasons, Henry does not want to sell the PG bonds now but would like to protect the portfolio from any further price decline. Formulate two hedging strategies, using only the investment vehicles cited in Tables 25A and 25B that would protect against any further decline in the price of the PG bonds. Calculate the relevant hedge ratio for each strategy. Comment on the appropriateness of each of these strategies for this portfolio.

Chapter 26
International Diversification

ALTHOUGH WE IN THE UNITED STATES CUSTOMARILY TREAT THE S&P 500 AS THE MARKET INDEX PORTFOLIO, THE PRACTICE IS INCREASINGLY INAPPROPRIATE. Equities represent less than 25% of total U.S. wealth and a much smaller proportion than that of world wealth. In this chapter, we look beyond domestic markets to survey issues of international and extended diversification.

In one sense, international investing may be viewed as no more than a straightforward generalization of our earlier treatment of portfolio selection with a larger menu of assets from which to construct a portfolio. One faces similar issues of diversification, security analysis, security selection, and asset allocation. On the other hand, international investments pose some problems not encountered in domestic markets. Among these are the presence of exchange rate risk, restrictions on capital flows across national boundaries, an added dimension of political risk and country-specific regulations, and differing accounting practices in different countries.

Therefore, in this chapter we will review the major topics covered in the rest of the book with a view toward what is special in the international context. We start with the central concept of portfolio theory—diversification. We will see that global diversification offers dramatic opportunities for improving portfolio risk-return trade-offs, and that investors are beginning to take advantage of these opportunities. We also will see how exchange rate fluctuations affect the risk of international investments. We next turn to passive and active investment styles in the international context. We will consider some of the special problems involved in the interpretation of passive index portfolios, and will show how active asset allocation can be generalized to incorporate country and currency choices in addition to traditional domestic asset-class choices.

Figure 26.1
Wealth of the world, 1993

Source: Copyright 1994 Ibbotson Associates' EnCorr.

All values are in billions of U.S. dollars

Equity

$11,765 / 40.3%
A. U.S. and Canada
$5,621 / 19.2%
B. Europe, Mideast, Africa
$2,498 / 8.6%
C. Latin America
$337 / 1.2%
D. Japan
$2,271 / 7.8%
E. Other Asia & Pacific
$1,038 / 3.6%

Bonds

$15,666 / 53.6%
Government
F. U.S.
$4,733 / 16.3%
G. Japan
$1,552 / 5.3%
H. Europe and Other
$2,938 / 10.1%
*Corporate & Misc.**
I. U.S.
$2,104 / 7.2%
J. Japan
$1,474 / 5.0%
K. Europe and Other
$2,826 / 9.7%

Cash

$1,780 / 6.1%
L. U.S.
$1,245 / 4.3%
M. Japan
$210 / 0.7%
N. Europe and Other
$325 / 1.1%

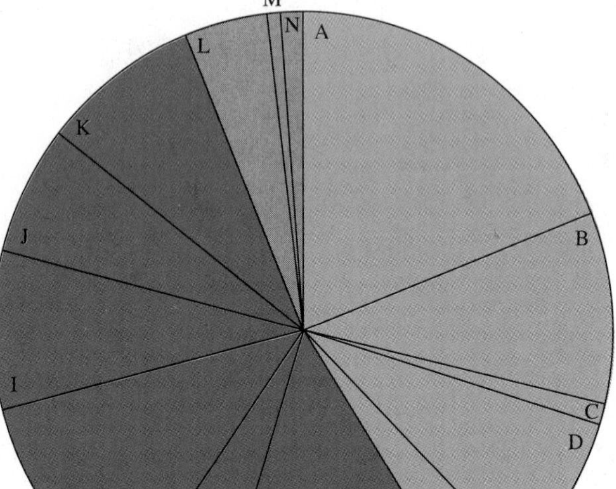

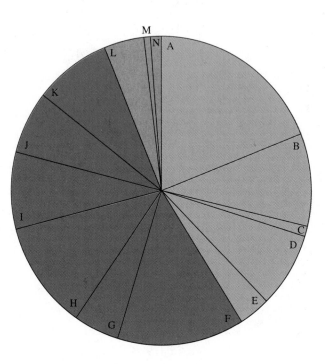

*Miscellaneous bonds include domestic public and private issues, foreign bonds and Eurobonds.

26.1 INTERNATIONAL INVESTMENTS

The World Market Portfolio

To appreciate the folly of an exclusive investment focus on U.S. stocks and bonds, consider in Figure 26.1 the components of **world investable wealth.** The pie chart shows the investable part of world wealth, that is, the part of world wealth that is traded and therefore accessible to investors. According to these estimates, U.S. equity makes up less than 20% of the world portfolio, whereas U.S. stocks and bonds together comprise less than 35% of the world capital market. The figure excludes direct investment in durables and foreign real estate.

Figure 26.2 shows another view of the relative share of the United States in the world economy. Here, the breakdown is by gross domestic product rather than the size

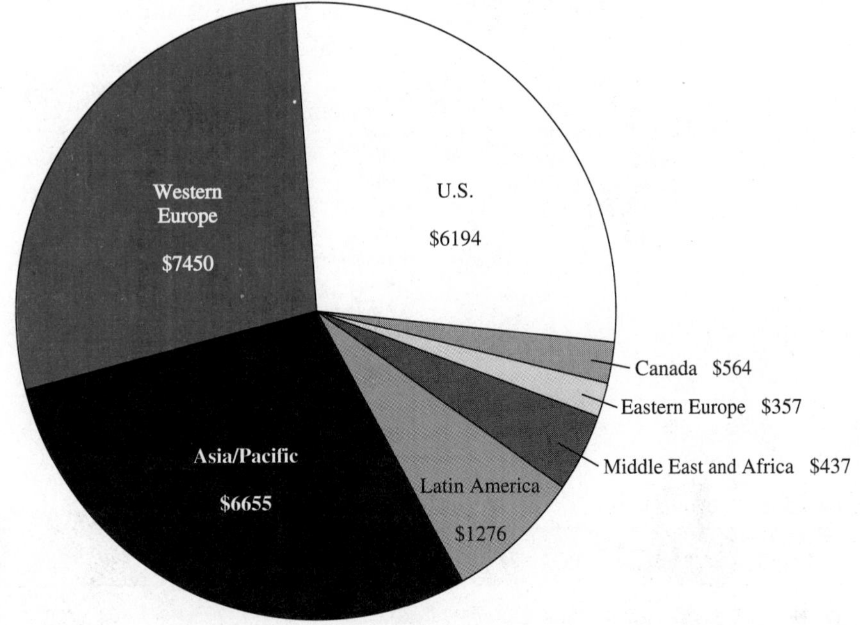

Figure 26.2
Estimates of the gross domestic product of major economies, 1993 (data in billions of dollars)
Source: *Global Outlook,* March 1993.

of the capital market, but the message is the same: The United States does not comprise the majority of the world economy. International diversification is worth exploring.

This is clear evidence that "traditional" U.S. assets—stocks, bonds, and bills—are but a small fraction of the potential universe of investments. Table 26.1 further highlights the potential of international diversification per se, even ignoring diversification into real assets such as metals or real estate. The table shows that U.S. equities in 1994 represented only a 43.2% share of some of the world's major equity markets. If you confine a portfolio exclusively to U.S. asset classes, you will pass up important opportunities for diversification.

International Diversification

From the discussion of diversification in Chapter 7, you know that adding to a portfolio assets that are not perfectly correlated will enhance the reward-to-volatility ratio. Increasing globalization lets us take advantage of foreign securities as a feasible way to extend diversification.

The evidence in Figure 26.3 is clear. The figure presents the standard deviation of equally weighted portfolios of various sizes as a percentage of the average standard deviation of a one-stock portfolio. For example, a value of 20 means the diversified portfolio has only 20% the standard deviation of a typical stock.

There is a marked reduction in risk for a portfolio that includes foreign as well as U.S. stocks, so rational investors should invest across borders. Adding international to

Table 26.1 Major Equity Markets, 1994

	Percentage of Global Equity Market
United States	43.2%
Japan	25.0
United Kingdom	9.8
France	3.6
Germany	3.5
Canada	2.4
Switzerland	2.1
Other	10.5
TOTAL	100

Source: *Worth*, March 1994.

Table 26.2 Correlations of Country Equity Returns

Portfolio	Aa	Au	Be	Ca	De	Fr	Ge	HK	It	Ja	Ne	No	Sp	Sw	Sz	U.K.	U.S.
World	.57	.29	.62	.75	.47	.61	.54	.41	.42	.63	.74	.50	.41	.50	.68	.67	.86
Australia	—	.16	.32	.59	.28	.37	.28	.36	.24	.28	.40	.41	.32	.36	.42	.46	.47
Austria		—	.46	.18	.30	.43	.55	.21	.24	.25	.43	.28	.29	.27	.49	.23	.12
Belgium			—	.38	.45	.64	.63	.32	.42	.46	.65	.53	.40	.44	.67	.50	.41
Canada				—	.30	.44	.30	.29	.27	.28	.55	.45	.28	.35	.48	.52	.72
Denmark					—	.35	.39	.31	.26	.39	.45	.33	.30	.30	.44	.35	.33
France						—	.57	.24	.44	.41	.58	.47	.36	.33	.62	.52	.42
Germany							—	.28	.34	.42	.66	.37	.34	.39	.74	.38	.33
Hong Kong								—	.22	.32	.42	.29	.24	.27	.34	.35	.29
Italy									—	.38	.36	.25	.35	.30	.38	.34	.22
Japan										—	.45	.17	.35	.33	.43	.35	.27
Netherlands											—	.52	.38	.43	.73	.62	.56
Norway												—	.25	.38.	.48	.40	.44
Spain													—	.31	.33	.30	.25
Sweden														—	.47	.39	.38
Switzerland															—	.55	.49
United Kingdom																—	.49
United States																	—

Note: The correlations are based on monthly data from 1970:2–1989:5 (232 observations). The country returns are calculated in U.S. dollars in excess of the holding-period return on the Treasury bill that is closest to 30 days maturity.
Source: Campbell R. Harvey, "The World Price of Covariance Risk," *Journal of Finance* 46 (March 1991), pp. 111–58.

national investments enhances the power of portfolio diversification. Indeed, the figure indicates that the risk of an internationally diversified portfolio can be reduced to less than one half the level of a diversified U.S. portfolio.

Table 26.2 presents results from a study of equity returns showing that although the correlation coefficients between the U.S. stock index and stock index portfolios of other

Figure 26.3
International diversification

Source: Modified from B. Solnik, "Why Not Diversify Internationally Rather Than Domestically," *Financial Analysts Journal*, July–August 1974.

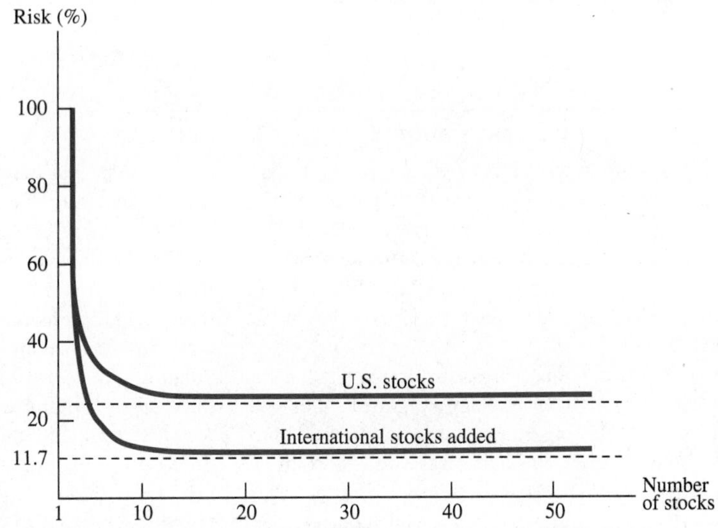

large industrialized economies are typically positive, they are much smaller than 1.0. Most correlations are below .5. In contrast, correlation coefficients between diversified U.S. portfolios, say, with 40 to 50 securities, typically exceed .9. This imperfect correlation across national boundaries allows for the improvement in diversification potential that shows up in Figure 26.3. The nearby box highlights one explanation for the low correlation across countries, namely, industrial structure across countries.

CONCEPT CHECK Question 1. What would Figure 26.3 look like if we allowed the possibility of diversifying into real estate investments in addition to foreign equity?

Figure 26.4 gives yet a different perspective on opportunities for international diversification. It shows risk-return opportunities offered by equity indexes of several countries, alone and combined into portfolios. (All returns here are calculated in terms of U.S. dollars.) The efficient frontiers generated from the full set of assets offers the best possible risk-return pairs; they are far superior to the risk-return profile of U.S. stocks alone.

Lest you think that mean-variance analysis is too "academic," consider Figure 26.5, which is reproduced from a paper in the *Journal of Portfolio Management* and was written by a portfolio manager at Batterymarch Financial Management.[1] It is from an article devoted to the management of "risk for international portfolios." The entire analysis of risk management is performed in terms of efficient frontiers that exploit international diversification. In this exhibit, the author examines the efficiency of one index of non-U.S. stocks, the EAFE index (which we will describe in detail below).

[1]Jarrod W. Wilcox, "EAFE Is for Wimps," *Journal of Portfolio Management*, Spring 1994.

No Place Like Abroad

American investors rushed into foreign securities last year. Most people expect them to keep doing so. The rationale is simple: they have relatively little of their money invested abroad; investing in foreign securities will diversify their portfolios and thus should lower risks. But might they do better to diversify at home instead?

The question for American investors is whether the diversification benefits of buying foreign securities outweigh the extra dealing costs involved. After all, they could diversify simply by buying a varied collection of, say, Silicon Valley shares. The factors that affect each firm's performance will partly balance each other out, so eliminating "firm-specific" risk. Investing in companies that operate in disparate industries (say, a collection of S&P-500 stocks), would reduce that risk still further.

Many financial economists have argued that the differences among countries' stockmarkets stem mostly from their disparate industry mixes. Thus an index of Swiss firms will be weighted towards finance; an index of British firms towards utilities. For the would-be foreign diversifier this is just industry diversification by another—more expensive—means. International diversification will generate real risk reduction only if the returns on foreign stocks vary for reasons beyond their industries and unique circumstances, such as government policies, demographics or weather.

A recent study* suggests that diversifying abroad does indeed pay off. The authors examined the monthly returns between 1978 and 1992 from shares of over 800 companies, operating in seven different industry groups and 12 European countries. They constructed a dozen country indexes. They then examined the differences in the volatility of their returns. Lower volatility is the main gain to be had from diversification. To see whether borders mattered, the authors broke down this volatility to see what was due to the industry composition and what was due to the country itself.

They found that the differences in a country's industrial mix accounted for less than 1% of the variation in returns. Indeed, as the chart shows, diversifying across countries, but staying within a single industry, reduces volatility by more than diversifying across industries in a single country, even though both portfolios carry the same average return. If the returns from shares in a dozen well-integrated European countries can differ so markedly, a more far-flung portfolio could yield even bigger risk reduction. More American money is on its way to foreign climes.

HOME AND AWAY

(portfolio volatility as % of average stock volatility)

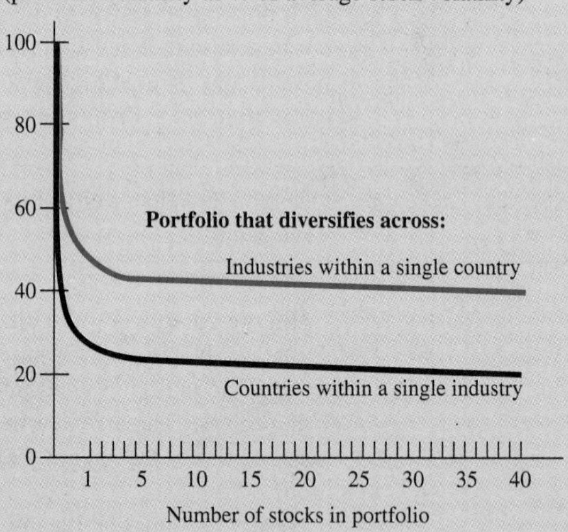

Source: *Journal of Financial Economics.*

*"Does Industrial Structure Explain the Benefits of International Diversification?" By S. Heston and G. Rouwenhorst, *Journal of Financial Economics*, August 1994.

Source: *The Economist,* December 17, 1994, p. 83.

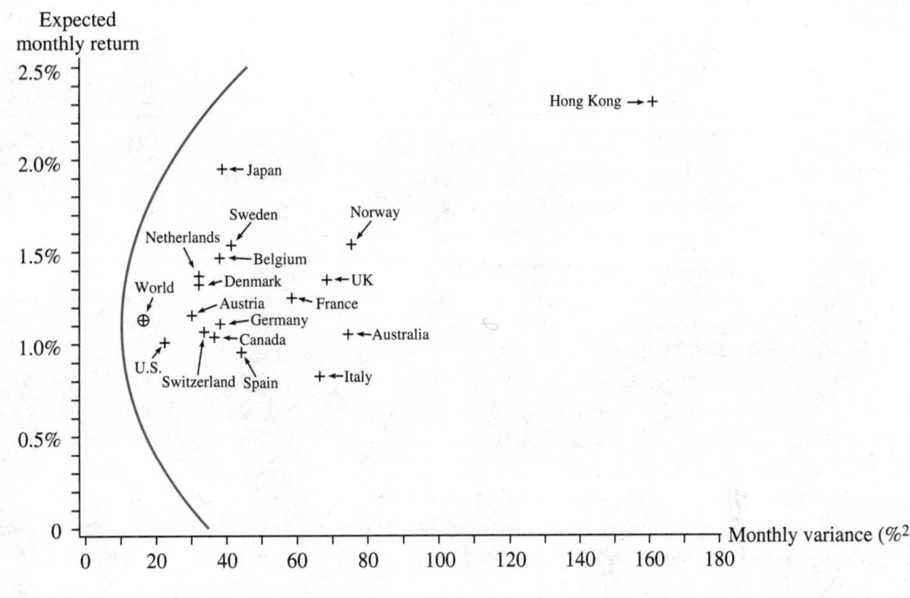

Figure 26.4

The minimum variance frontier. The minimum variance frontier is calculated from the unconditional means, variances, and convariances of 17 country returns. The returns are in U.S. dollars and are from Morgan Stanley Capital International. The data are from 1970:2–1989:5 (232 observations)

Source: Campbell R. Harvey, "The World Price of Covariance Risk," *Journal of Finance* 46 (March 1991) pp. 111–58.

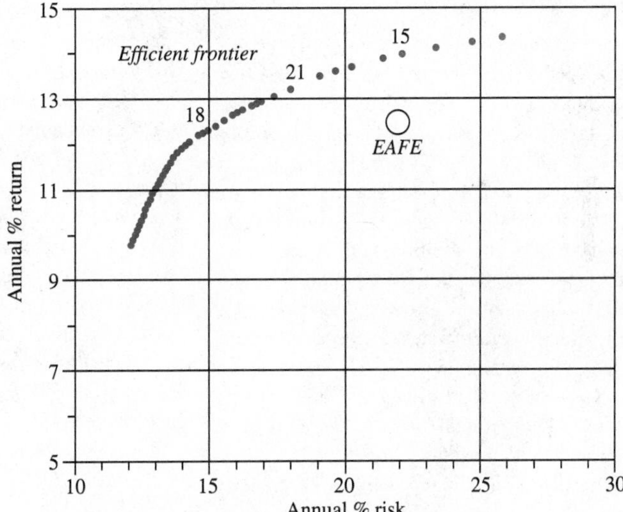

Figure 26.5

Passive efficient frontier versus EAFE (return based on country risk)

Techniques for Investing Internationally

U.S. investors have several avenues through which they can invest internationally. The most obvious method, which is available in practice primarily to larger institutional investors, is to purchase securities directly in the capital markets of other countries. However, even small investors now may take advantage of several investment vehicles with an international focus.

FOR THE LATEST LINE ON ADRs, GET ON-LINE

Used to be, your broker had the edge. He had immediate access to the stock quotes, the research, the news. "On-line" meant that he would return your phone calls.

That was especially true if you wanted the word on companies abroad. But no longer. Such consumer on-line services as America Online Inc. and Prodigy Services Co. offer at least rudimentary financial data—including prices of listed American depositary receipts—usually at no premium over their basic monthly fees. Even more is available on a pay-as-you-go basis. And some services offer quotes and information on "pink sheet" ADRs traded over the counter. "It turns out that these thinly traded stocks are exactly what small investors are looking for," says Chris Hill, who heads up personal investor products for IDD Information Services.

Hefty Fees

For listed ADRs, the premier information service remains Dow Jones News/Retrieval. "Without question, it is the best and most exhaustive service for the individual investor," says Robert Schwabach, author of *The Business Week Guide to Global Investments Using Electronic Tools,* published by Osborne/McGraw-Hill. Dow's Market Monitor service costs $29.95 for eight hours of access a month, and additional hours are $3.60. The catch? You can't use it before 7:01 p.m. weekdays, and it puts some limits on the information you can download. Stock price and performance histories, for example, go back only two years.

Still, there's a wealth of information available. You can get Dow Jones International News for foreign news and search through a database of hundreds of publications, including *The Wall Street Journal* and *Barrons,* for news on foreign companies. If you need more or need to use DJ during the day, you can venture into the full Dow Jones News/Retrieval service at regular rates—a hefty $1.50 for 1,000 characters of information, about two-thirds of your computer screen.

Another extensive source is CompuServe Inc. But count on spending at least $9.60 an hour for "extended" services and probably much more if you're serious about foreign stocks. Global Report, a collection of news wires including Britain's Financial Times, France's AFP, and Japan's Kyodo, costs $30 an hour extra after 7 p.m. and twice that during the day.

The up-and-comer is Reuters Money Network, a product of Reuters Holdings PLC, Dow's British rival. If you don't like spending hours browsing on-line, this is for you. You specify the companies and industries you're interested in, and your computer calls Reuters and fetches quotes, tables, reports, and news in batches. Everything is then displayed in a clever newspaper format. The basic service is $12.95 per month. News and fundamental analysis is $9.95 a month more.

Money Network is still thin on foreign news. But by yearend, it will offer the full Reuters international news and quote feed. You'll be able to click your mouse on major global exchanges, type in a stock symbol, and download the goods on overseas companies.

It's easy to sample services before you sign up. With the exception of Dow Jones, most of them offer trial runs, usually for the cost of the start-up software. So set aside a weekend or two to go global on the Infopike, and see how much you can unearth. You'll be surprised at how far you can expand your horizons—not to mention your portfolio.

Source: Larry Armstrong, "For the Latest Line on ADR, Get On-Line," *Business Week,* September 19, 1994, p. 104.

Shares of several foreign firms are traded in U.S. markets in the form of **American Depository Receipts,** or ADRs. A U.S. financial institution like a bank will purchase shares of a foreign firm in that firm's country, then issue claims to those shares in the United States. Each ADR is then a claim on a given number of the shares of stock held by the bank. In this way, the stock of foreign companies can be traded on U.S. stock

Table 26.3 Sampling of Emerging Country Mutual Funds, 1994

Closed-End Funds		
Fund Name	**Symbol**	**Assets (millions)**
Europe/Middle East		
First Israel	ISL	$73.6
Portugal	PGF	52.8
Turkish Inv.	TKF	58.5
Latin America		
Argentina	AF	$59.1
Brazil	BZF	222.7
Brazilian Eqty.	BZL	69.6
Chile	CH	180.5
Emerging Mexico	MEF	105.4
Latin Amer. Eqty.	LAQ	95.7
Latin Amer. Inv.	LAM	112.8
Latin Amer. Disc.	LDF	103.5
Mexico Equity & Income	MXF	110.9
Pacific/Asia		
Asia Pacific	APB	$143.9
China	CHN	119.9
First Philippine	FPF	133.5
Greater China	GCH	103.2
India Growth	IGF	62.9
Indonesia	IF	43.1
Jakarta Growth	JGF	98.9
Jardine Fleming China	JFC	114.4
Korea	KF	257.6
Korean Inv.	KIF	44.5
Malaysia	MF	133.4
R.O.C. Taiwan	ROC	242.1
Scudder New Asia	SAF	127.3
Taiwan	TWN	150.8
Thai	TTF	206.7
Thai Capital	TC	75.5

Closed-End Funds		
Fund Name	**Symbol**	**Assets (millions)**
Global		
Emerging Markets Tele.	ETF	$133.6
Morgan Stanley EM	MSF	260.5
Templeton Emerging	EMF	263.1
Income		
Alliance World	AWG	$133.6
Emerging Markets Income	EMD	57.9
Latin Amer. Dollar	LBF	87.8

Open-End Funds	
Fund Name	**Assets (millions)**
Fidelity Emerging Markets	$168.10
G. T. global Emerging Market A	119.55
G. T. Latin Amer. Growth A	99.48
Govett Emerging Markets	33.72
Lexington Worldwide EM	37.19
Merrill Develop Cap. Market	142.15
Merrill Latin Amer. A	37.92
Merrill Latin Amer. B	152.70
Montgomery Emerging Mkt.	204.32
Morgan Stanley EM	240.18
Scudder Latin America	101.41
Templeton Dev. Mkts.	419.40

exchanges. Trading foreign stocks with ADRs has become increasingly easy, as the nearby box shows.

There are also a wide array of mutual funds with an international focus. **Single-country funds** are mutual funds that invest in the shares of only one country. These tend to be closed-end funds, as the listing of these funds in Table 26.3 indicates. In addition to single-country funds, there are several open-end mutual funds with an international focus. For example, Fidelity offers funds with investments concentrated overseas, generally in Europe, in the Pacific basin, and in developing economies in an emerging opportunities fund. Vanguard, consistent with its indexing philosophy, offers

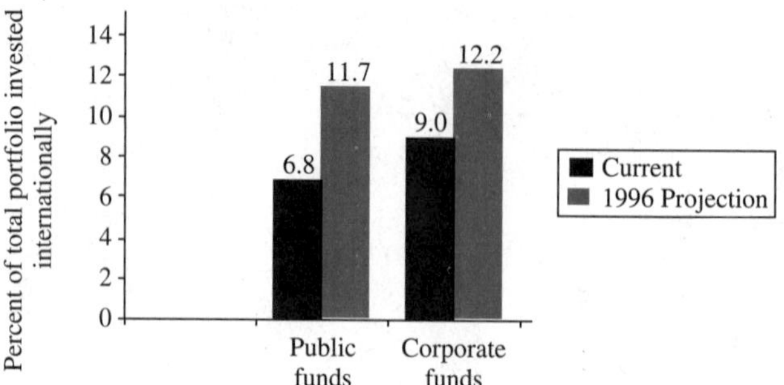

Figure 26.6
Percent of assets invested abroad by private and public pension funds

Source: Leslie Scism, "Pension Funds Venture Abroad in Search of Big Returns," *The Wall Street Journal*, January 19, 1994.

separate index funds for Europe and the Pacific basin. The nearby box shows that investors are increasingly taking advantage of opportunities to invest internationally.

U.S. investors also can trade derivative securities based on prices in foreign security markets. For example, they can trade options and futures on the Nikkei stock index of 225 stocks traded on the Tokyo stock exchange, or on FTSE (Financial Times Share Exchange) indexes of U.K. and European stocks.

Investors seem increasingly aware of the importance of international diversification. For example, Figure 26.6 shows that pension plans are devoting a large fraction of their investment budgets to the international sector.

Many corporations now issue securities geared toward the increased interest in international investments. For example, many U.S. and foreign corporations now issue bonds denominated in the European Currency Unit (ECU), a market-weighted index of 12 European currencies. ECU bonds provide a simple way to achieve currency diversification. An example of an ECU-dominated bond appeared in Chapter 1, Figure 1.2.

Exchange Rate Risk

International investing poses unique challenges and a variety of new risks for U.S. investors. Information in foreign markets may be less timely and more difficult to come by. In smaller economies with correspondingly smaller securities markets, there may be higher transaction costs and liquidity problems. Table 26.4 shows that trading costs abroad are substantially higher than in the United States. Investment advisors need special expertise concerning **political risk,** by which we mean the possibility of the expropriation of assets, changes in tax policy, the institution of restrictions on the exchange of foreign currency for domestic currency, or other changes in the business climate of a country. A good example of political risk surrounds the Gulf War in early 1991, when investors in Kuwait saw their investments destroyed by the war.

Beyond these risks, international investing entails **exchange rate risk.** The dollar return from a foreign investment depends not only on the returns in the foreign currency, but also on the exchange rate between the dollar and that currency.

To see this, consider an investment in England in risk-free British government bills paying 10% annual interest in British pounds. Although these U.K. bills would be the

Americans Snap Up Securities Overseas at Record Pace

Pulled by booming overseas stock markets and pushed by low U.S. interest rates, Americans are gobbling up foreign securities at a record pace.

In the second quarter of this year, U.S. investors purchased a record net $13.2 billion of foreign stocks, according to the Securities Industry Association, or SIA. It marked the 20th consecutive quarter that Americans have added shares to their portfolios in companies such as British drug giant Glaxo Holdings PLC, Mexican telephone concern Telefonos de Mexico SA and NV Royal Dutch Petroleum Co. During that period, U.S. investors have bought $109 billion of foreign stocks, lifting total overseas equity holdings to $210 billion.

U.S. investors also purchased $27.3 billion of foreign bonds in the first half, surpassing the record $21.9 billion they bought in all of 1990.

Noting that U.S. pension funds currently hold roughly 6% to 7% of their total assets in international stocks and bonds, Bob Michaelson, chief global investment officer for Citibank Global Asset Management here, said that "most are targeting 10%, and some of the most sophisticated are up to 20%."

Americans' non-U.S. stock portfolios have nearly doubled during the past two and a half years, pointed out David Strongin, director of international finance at the SIA in New York.

Accelerating the move into foreign securities is the combination of slow U.S. growth, low U.S. interest rates and the expectation that falling interest rates in Europe will fire up stock and bond markets there. In addition, Mr. Strongin of the SIA said the actual and planned selloff of government-owned industries in many countries, relaxation of restrictions of foreign investment and rapid economic growth in the Third World is "serving as a powerful attraction for U.S. capital."

During the first half of this year, U.S. investors purchased a net $21.7 billion of foreign stocks, nearly double the amount they bought in the first six months of 1992 and 67% of the total they bought in all of last year. A little more than half of the $21.7 billion went into European stock markets, with British shares accounting for $5.2 billion. Americans' next-favorite major foreign market was Canada, followed by Japan, Hong Kong, Italy, Spain and Germany. American investors also purchased a net $2.3 billion of Latin American shares in the first half, including $980 million in Mexico.

The $1.8 billion of Hong Kong stocks they added to their portfolios is astounding, given that the Hong Kong stock market is one-fourteenth the size of Japan's, in which Americans invested a net $2.3 billion. Because so many Hong Kong companies do business in China and have manufacturing facilities there, the colony's stock market is considered a play on the mainland's fast-growing economy.

THE GROWING APPETITE FOR FOREIGN SECURITIES:
U.S. INVESTORS' NET PURCHASES OF FOREIGN SECURITIES (in billions of dollars)

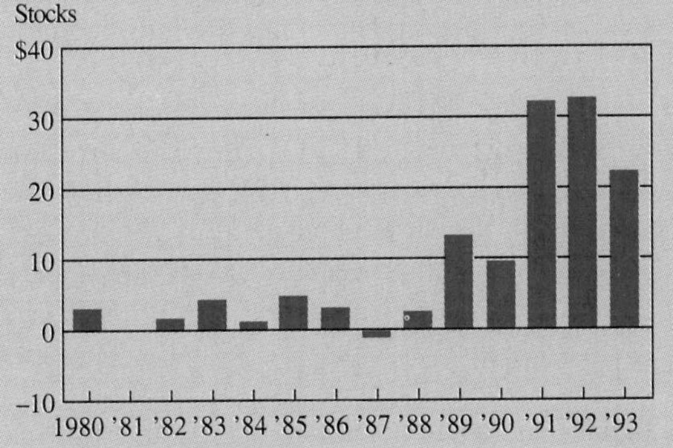

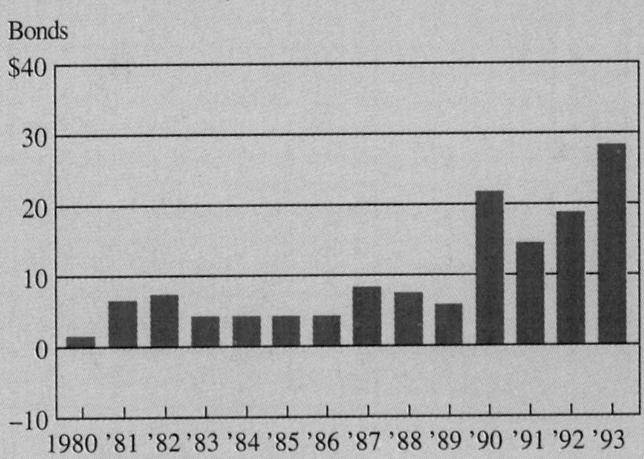

Source: Securities Industry Association.

Source: Michael R. Sesit, "Americans Snap Up Securities Overseas At Record Pace," *The Wall Street Journal*, October 19, 1993. Reprinted by permission of The Wall Street Journal,

Table 26.4 Effective Transactions Costs in Non-U.S. Markets in Basis Points (trade size $500,000)

Market	Buy	Sell	Average
Australia	80	80	80
Belgium	70	70	70
Canada	50	50	50
France	58	58	58
Germany	58	58	58
Hong Kong	80	80	80
Italy	72	72	72
Japan	40	95	68
Netherlands	40	40	40
Singapore	100	100	100
Spain	85	85	85
Sweden	130	130	130
Switzerland	54	54	54
U.K.	70	20	45
Weighted non-U.S. average	50	78	64
U.S.	20	20	20

Source: Anthony W. Robinson, "Comparison of Fundamental Issues in International and Domestic Equity Investing," in *International Investing for U.S. Pension Funds,* Institute for Fiduciary Education, May 1989.

risk-free asset to a British investor, this is not the case for a U.S. investor. Suppose, for example, the current exchange rate is $2 per pound, and the U.S. investor starts with $20,000. That amount can be exchanged for £10,000 and invested at a riskless 10% rate in the United Kingdom to provide £11,000 in one year.

What happens if the dollar–pound exchange rate varies over the year? Say that during the year, the pound depreciates relative to the dollar, so that by year-end only $1.80 is required to purchase £1. The £11,000 can be exchanged at the year-end exchange rate for only $19,800 (£11,000 × $1.80/£), resulting in a loss of $200 relative to the initial $20,000 investment. Despite the positive 10% pound-denominated return, the dollar-denominated return is a negative 1%.

We can generalize from these results. The $20,000 is exchanged for $20,000/E_0$ pounds, where E_0 denotes the original exchange rate ($2/£). The U.K. investment grows to $(20{,}000/E_0)[1 + r_f(\text{UK})]$ British pounds, where $r_f(\text{UK})$ is the risk-free rate in the United Kingdom. The pound proceeds ultimately are converted back to dollars at the subsequent exchange rate E_1, for total dollar proceeds of $20{,}000(E_1/E_0)[1 + r_f(\text{UK})]$. The dollar-denominated return on the investment in British bills, therefore, is

$$1 + r(\text{US}) = [1 + r_f(\text{UK})]E_1/E_0 \qquad \textbf{(26.1)}$$

We see in equation 26.1 that the dollar-denominated return for a U.S. investor equals the pound-denominated return times the exchange rate "return." For a U.S. investor, the investment in the British bill is a combination of a safe investment in the United Kingdom and a risky investment in the performance of the pound relative to the dollar.

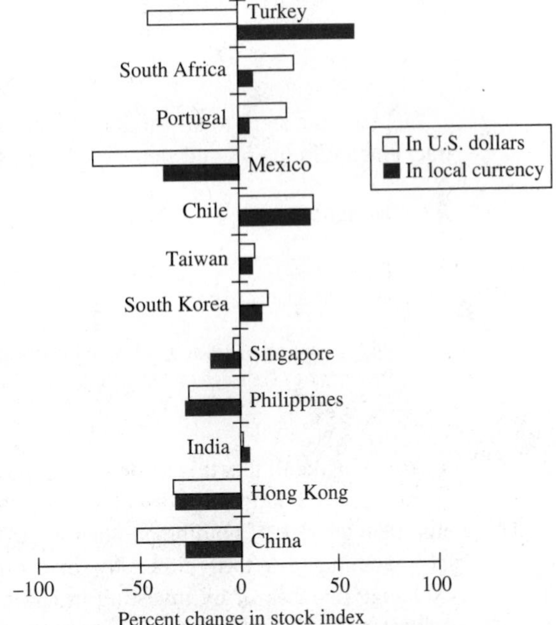

Figure 26.7
Change in stock market indexes in larger emerging stock markets (15 months, ending in March 1995)
Source: *The Economist,* March 18, 1995.

Here, the pound fared poorly, falling from a value of $2.00 to only $1.80. The loss on the pound more than offsets the earnings on the British bill.

Figure 26.7 illustrates this point. It presents returns on stock market indexes in some of the larger emerging stock markets for a 15-month period ending in March 1995. The dark boxes depict returns in local currencies, whereas the light boxes depict returns in dollars, adjusting for exchange rate movements. It is clear that exchange rate fluctuations over this period had large effects on dollar-denominated returns. For example, Turkey showed a 59% gain in local currency, but a 44% loss in dollars!

CONCEPT CHECK Question 2. Calculate the rate of return in dollars to a U.S. investor holding the British bill if the year-end exchange rate is: (*a*) E_1 = $2.00/£; (*b*) E_1 = $2.20/£.

The investor in our example could have hedged the exchange rate risk using a forward or futures contract in foreign exchange. Recall that a forward or futures contract on foreign exchange calls for delivery or acceptance of one currency for another at a stipulated exchange rate. Here, the U.S. investor would agree to deliver pounds for dollars at a fixed exchange rate, thereby eliminating the future risk involved with conversion of the pound investment back into dollars.

If the futures exchange rate had been F_0 = $1.93/£ when the investment was made, the U.S. investor could have assured a riskless dollar-denominated return by locking in the year-end exchange rate at $1.93/£. In this case, the riskless U.S. return would have been 6.15%:

$$\begin{aligned} &[1 + r_f(\text{UK})]F_0/E_0 \\ &= (1.10)\ 1.93/2.00 \\ &= 1.0615 \end{aligned}$$

Here are the steps to take to lock in the dollar-denominated returns. The futures contract entered in the second step exactly offsets the exchange rate risk incurred in Step 1.

Initial Transaction	End-of-Year Proceeds in Dollars
Exchange \$20,000 for £10,000 and invest at 10% in the United Kingdom	£11,000 × E_1
Enter a contract to deliver £11,000 for dollars at the (forward) exchange rate \$1.93/£	£11,000(1.93 − E_1)
TOTAL	£11,000 × \$1.93/£ = \$21,320

You may recall that this is the same type of hedging strategy at the heart of the interest rate parity relationship discussed in Chapter 22, where futures markets are used to eliminate the risk of holding another asset. The U.S. investor can lock in a riskless dollar-denominated return either by investing in the United Kingdom and hedging exchange rate risk or by investing in riskless U.S. assets. Because the returns on two riskless strategies must provide equal returns, we conclude

$$[1 + r_f(\text{UK})]\frac{F_0}{E_0} = 1 + r_f(\text{US})$$

Rearranging,

$$\frac{F_0}{E_0} = \frac{1 + r_f(\text{US})}{1 + r_f(\text{UK})} \qquad \textbf{(26.2)}$$

This is the **interest rate parity relationship** or **covered interest arbitrage relationship** presented in Chapter 22.

Unfortunately, such perfect exchange rate hedging is usually not so easy. In our example, we knew exactly how many pounds to sell in the forward or futures market because the pound-denominated proceeds in the United Kingdom were riskless. If the U.K. investment had not been in bills, but instead had been in risky U.K. equity, we would know neither the ultimate value in pounds of our U.K. investment nor how many pounds to sell forward. That is, the hedging opportunity offered by foreign exchange forward contracts would be imperfect.

To summarize, the generalization of equation 26.1 is that

$$1 + r(\text{US}) = [1 + r(\text{foreign})]\ E_1/E_0 \qquad \textbf{(26.3)}$$

where r(foreign) is the possibly risky return earned in the currency of the foreign investment. You can set up a perfect hedge only in the special case that r(foreign) is itself a known number. In that case, you know you must sell in the forward or futures market an amount of foreign currency equal to $[1 + r(\text{foreign})]$ for each unit of that currency you purchase today.

CONCEPT CHECK Question 3. How many pounds would need to be sold forward to hedge exchange rate risk in the above example if: (*a*) *r*(UK) = 20%, (*b*) *r*(UK) = 30%?

Passive and Active International Investing

Passive Benchmarks. When we discussed investment strategies in the purely domestic context, we used a market index portfolio like the S&P 500 as a benchmark passive equity investment. This suggests a world market index might be a useful starting point for a passive international strategy.

One widely used index of non-U.S. stocks is the **Europe, Australia, Far East (EAFE) index** computed by Morgan Stanley. Table 2.5 (Chapter 2) presented a sample of the extensive set of Morgan Stanley Capital International indexes. Additional indexes of world equity performance are published by Salomon Brothers, First Boston, and Goldman, Sachs. Portfolios designed to mirror or even replicate the country, currency, and company representation of these indexes would be the obvious generalization of the purely domestic passive equity strategy.

An issue that sometimes arises in the international context is the appropriateness of market-capitalization weighting schemes in the construction of international indexes. Capitalization weighting is far and away the most common approach. However, some argue that it might not be the best weighting scheme in an international context. This is in part because different countries have differing proportions of their corporate sector organized as publicly traded firms. For example, in 1993 U.K. firms received a total weighting of 16.7% of the EAFE index in terms of market value of equity, but accounted for only 8% of the gross domestic product (GDP) of the EAFE countries. In contrast, French firms represented 5.8% of the market-value weighted index despite that fact that France accounted for fully 11.4% of EAFE GDP.

Some argue that it is more appropriate to weight international indexes by GDP rather than market capitalization because an internationally diversified portfolio should purchase shares in proportion to the broad asset base of each country, and GDP might be a better measure of the importance of a country in the international economy than the value of its outstanding stocks. Others have even suggested weights proportional to the import share of various countries. The argument is that investors who wish to hedge the price of imported goods might choose to hold securities in foreign firms in proportion to the goods imported from those countries.

Another problem with market capitalization weights arises from the practice of **cross-holdings** that tend to overstate the aggregate value of outstanding equity. Cross-holdings refer to equity investments that firms make in other firms. These purchases can increase the sum of the market values of outstanding equity. To see how, consider the following example.

Firms A and B each have $10 million in plant and equipment and no debt outstanding; therefore, each has $10 million in equity. This situation is illustrated in panel A of Table 26.5. Now suppose that Firm A issues $5 million of new equity to buy shares in Firm B. The new balance sheets of the two firms are illustrated in panel B. Although the market value of Firm B is unchanged, Firm A now has a market value of

Table 26.5 The Effect of Cross-Holding on Market Value of Equity (all dollar values in millions)

A. Before the Cross-Holding

Firm A				Firm B			
Assets		**Liabilities and NW**		**Assets**		**Liabilities and NW**	
Plant, equipment, other assets	$10	Equity	$10	Plant, equipment, other assets	$10	Equity	$10

B. After the Cross-Holding

Firm A				Firm B			
Assets		**Liabilities and NW**		**Assets**		**Liabilities and NW**	
Plant, equipment, other assets	$10	Equity	$15	Plant, equipment, other assets	$10	Equity	$10
Shares in Firm B	$5						

$15 million. One of its assets is a claim on Firm B, however, meaning that half the physical assets of Firm B are now counted in the computation of the values of *both* Firm A and Firm B. What has not changed is the value of equity held by the noncorporate sector. Private shareholders still have a total claim of $20 million: $15 million in Firm A and $5 million in Firm B. (The other $5 million of Firm B is held by Firm A.) To measure the aggregate value of the productive assets of the two firms, we must net out the intercorporate shareholdings that result in the double counting and measure only the value of noncorporate equity holdings. This number is unaffected by cross-holdings.

French and Poterba[2] calculated the effect of cross-holdings on the U.S. and Japanese equity markets. They found that in mid-1990, the value of the Japanese equity market fell from $3,266 billion to $1,623 billion when cross-holdings were netted out. In contrast, in the United States, where cross-holdings are minimal, the value of equity fell only slightly, from $3,044 billion to $3,006 billion.

Table 26.6 uses data from 1993 to illustrate the different weightings that would emerge for the EAFE countries using market capitalization and GDP. The differing methodologies result in substantially different weights for some countries. In particular, Japan had a market-value weight of 48.3% despite that fact that its GDP was only 33.4% of the EAFE total. This disproportionate weight was due primarily to much

[2] Kenneth R. French and James M. Poterba, "Were Japanese Stock Prices Too High?" *Journal of Financial Economics* 29 (October 1991), pp. 337–63.

Table 26.6 Weighting Schemes for EAFE Countries

Country	Market Capitalization	Gross Domestic Product (GDP)
Australia	2.4%	2.4%
Austria	0.4	1.6
Belgium	1.1	1.9
Denmark	0.6	1.2
Finland	0.3	0.8
France	5.8	11.4
Germany	6.7	15.4
Hong Kong	3.3	0.9
Italy	1.9	9.2
Ireland	0.2	0.4
Japan	48.3	33.4
Malaysia	1.6	0.5
New Zealand	0.3	0.3
Netherlands	2.9	2.8
Norway	0.3	0.9
Singapore	0.9	1.4
Spain	1.8	4.6
Sweden	1.3	1.8
Switzerland	4.2	2.1
U.K.	16.7	8.0

Source: Bruce Clarke and Anthony W. Ryan, "Proper Overseas Benchmark a Critical Choice," *Pensions and Investments*, May 30, 1994, p. 28.

higher price earnings ratios in Japan in 1993 and the more common practice of cross-holdings in Japan.

Asset Allocation. Active portfolio management in an international context may be viewed similarly as an extension of active domestic management. In principle, one would form an efficient frontier from the full menu of world securities and determine the optimal risky portfolio. We saw in Chapter 7 that even in the domestic context, the need for specialization in various asset classes usually calls for a two-step procedure in which asset allocation is fixed initially, and then security selection within each asset class in determined. The complexities of the international market argue even more strongly for the primacy of asset allocation, and this is the perspective often taken in the evaluation of active portfolio management. Performance attribution of international managers focuses on these potential sources of abnormal returns: currency selection, country selection, stock selection within countries, and cash-bond selection within countries.

We can measure the contribution of each of these factors following a manner similar to the performance attribution techniques introduced in Chapter 24.

1. *Currency selection* measures the contribution to total portfolio performance attributable to exchange rate fluctuations relative to the investor's benchmark

Table 26.7 Example of Performance Attribution: International

	EAFE Weight	Return on Equity Index	Currency Application $E_1/E_0 - 1$	Manager's Weight	Manager's Return
Europe	.30	10%	10%	.35	8%
Australia	.10	5	−10	.10	7
Far East	.60	15	30	.55	18

Currency Selection

EAFE: (.30 × 10%) + (.10 × −10%) + (.60 × 30%) = 20% appreciation
Manager: (.35 × 10%) + (.10 × −10%) + (.55 × 30%) = 19% appreciation
Loss of 1% relative to EAFE

Country Selection

EAFE: (.30 × 10%) + (.10 × 5%) + (.60 × 15%) = 12.5%
Manager: (.35 × 10%) + (.10 × 5%) + (.55 × 15%) = 12.25%
Loss of .25% relative to EAFE

Stock Selection

(8% − 10%).35 + (7% − 5%).10 + (18% − 15%).55 = 1.15%
Contribution of 1.15% relative to EAFE

currency, which we will take to be the U.S. dollar. We might use a benchmark like the EAFE index to compare a portfolio's currency selection for a particular period to a passive benchmark. EAFE currency selection would be computed as the weighted average of the currency appreciation of the currencies represented in the EAFE portfolio using as weights the fraction of the EAFE portfolio invested in each currency.

2. *Country selection* measures the contribution to performance attributable to investing in the better-performing stock markets of the world. It can be measured as the weighted average of the equity *index* returns of each country using as weights the share of the manager's portfolio in each country. We use index returns to abstract from the effect of security selection within countries. To measure a manager's contribution relative to a passive strategy, we might compare country selection to the weighted average across countries of equity index returns using as weights the share of the EAFE portfolio in each country.
3. *Stock selection* ability may, as in Chapter 24, be measured as the weighted average of equity returns *in excess of the equity index* in each country. Here, we would use local currency returns and use as weights the investments in each country.
4. *Cash/bond selection* may be measured as the excess return derived from weighting bonds and bills differently from some benchmark weights.

Table 26.7 gives an example of how to measure the contribution of the decisions an international portfolio manager might make.

CONCEPT CHECK Question 4. Using the data in Table 26.7, compute the manager's country and currency selection if portfolio weights had been 40% in Europe, 20% in Australia, and 40% in the Far East.

Security Analysis. Security analysis of non-U.S. companies is complicated by noncomparabilities in accounting data. Security analysts must attempt to place accounting statements on an equal footing before comparing companies. Some of the major issues are:

1. *Depreciation:* The United States allows firms to use different financial reports for tax and reporting purposes. As a result, even firms that use accelerated depreciation for tax purposes in the United States tend to use straight-line depreciation for reporting purposes. This use of dual statements is uncommon elsewhere. Non-U.S. firms tend to use accelerated depreciation for reporting as well as taxes, which affects both earnings and book values of assets.
2. *Reserves:* U.S. standards generally allow lower discretionary reserves for possible losses resulting in higher reported earnings than in other countries. There are also big differences in how firms reserve for pension liabilities.
3. *Consolidation:* Accounting practice in some countries does not call for all subsidiaries to be consolidated in the corporation's income statement.
4. *Taxes:* Taxes may be reported either as paid or accrued.
5. *P/E ratios:* There may be different practices for calculating the number of shares used to calculate P/E ratios. Firms may use end-of-year shares, year-average shares, or even beginning-of-year shares.

Factor Models and International Investing

International investing presents a good opportunity to demonstrate an application of multifactor models of security returns such as those considered in connection with the arbitrage pricing model. Natural factors might include:

1. A world stock index.
2. A national (domestic) stock index.
3. Industrial-sector indexes.
4. Currency movements.

Solnik and de Freitas[3] used such a framework, and Table 26.8 shows some of their results for several countries. The first four columns of numbers present the *R*-square of various one-factor regressions. Recall that the *R*-square, or R^2, measures the percentage of return volatility of a company's stock that can be explained by the particular factor treated as the independent or explanatory variable. Solnik and de Freitas estimated the factor regressions for many firms in a given country and reported the average *R*-square across the firms in that country.

[3] Bruno Solnik and A. de Freitas, "International Factors of Stock Price Behavior," in S. Khoury and A. Ghosh (eds.), *Recent Developments in International Finance and Banking* (Lexington, Mass.: Lexington Books, 1988). Cited in Bruno Solnik, *International Investments*, 2nd ed. (Reading, Mass.: Addison-Wesley, 1991).

Table 26.8 Relative Importance of World, Industrial, Currency, and Domestic Factors in Explaining Return of a Stock

	Average R-SQR of Regression on Factors				
	Single-Factor Tests				
Locality	World	Industrial	Currency	Domestic	Joint Test All Four Factors
Switzerland	0.18	0.17	0.00	0.38	0.39
West Germany	0.08	0.10	0.00	0.41	0.42
Australia	0.24	0.26	0.01	0.72	0.72
Belgium	0.07	0.08	0.00	0.42	0.43
Canada	0.27	0.24	0.07	0.45	0.48
Spain	0.22	0.03	0.00	0.45	0.45
United States	0.26	0.47	0.01	0.35	0.55
France	0.13	0.08	0.01	0.45	0.60
United Kingdom	0.20	0.17	0.01	0.53	0.55
Hong Kong	0.06	0.25	0.17	0.79	0.81
Italy	0.05	0.03	0.00	0.35	0.35
Japan	0.09	0.16	0.01	0.26	0.33
Norway	0.17	0.28	0.00	0.84	0.85
Netherlands	0.12	0.07	0.01	0.34	0.31
Singapore	0.16	0.15	0.02	0.32	0.33
Sweden	0.19	0.06	0.01	0.42	0.43
All countries	0.18	0.23	0.01	0.42	0.46

Source: Modified from Bruno Solnik, *International Investments*, 2nd ed. © 1991, Addison-Wesley Publishing Co., Inc., Reading, Mass. Exhibit 5.6. Reprinted with permission.

In this case, the table reveals that the domestic factor seems to be the dominant influence on stock returns. While the domestic index alone generates an average R-square of 0.42 across all countries, adding the three additional factors (in the last column of the table) increases average R-square only to 0.46. This is consistent with the low cross-country correlation coefficients in Table 26.2, reiterating the value of international diversification.

At the same time, there is clear evidence of a world market factor in results of the market crash of October 1987. Even though we have said equity returns across borders show only moderate correlation, a study by Richard Roll[4] showed negative October 1987 equity index returns in all 23 countries considered. Figure 26.8, reproduced from Roll's study, shows the values he found for regional equity indexes during that month. The obvious correlation among returns suggests some underlying world factor common to all economies. Roll found that the beta of a country's equity index on a world index (estimated through September 1987) was the best predictor of that index's response to the October 1987 crash, which lends further support to the presence of a world factor.

[4] Richard Roll, "The International Crash of October 1987," *Financial Analysts Journal*, September/October 1988.

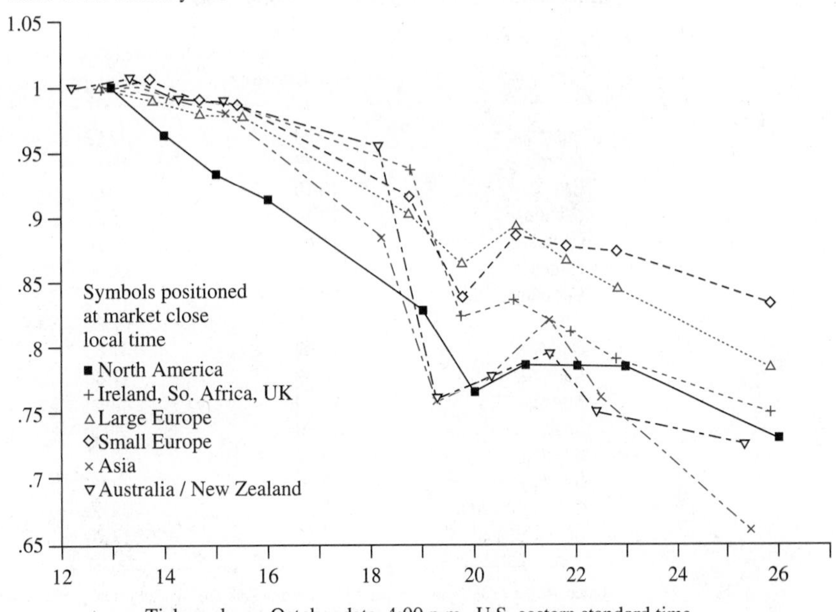

Figure 26.8 Regional indexes around the crash, October 14–October 26, 1987

Source: Richard Roll, "The International Crash of October 1987," *Financial Analysts Journal,* September–October 1988.

Equilibrium in International Capital Markets

We can use the CAPM or the APT to predict expected rates of return in an international capital market equilibrium, just as we can for domestic assets. The models need some adaptation for international use, however.

For example, one might expect that a world CAPM would result simply by replacing a narrow domestic market portfolio with a broad world market portfolio and measuring betas relative to the world portfolio. This approach was pursued in part of a paper by Ibbotson, Carr, and Robinson,[5] who calculated betas of equity indexes of several countries against a world equity index. Their results appear in Table 26.9. The betas for different countries show surprising variability.

Although such a straightforward generalization of the simple CAPM seems like a reasonable first step, it is subject to some problems:

1. Taxes, transaction costs, and capital barriers across countries make it difficult and not always attractive for investors to hold a world index portfolio. Some assets are simply unavailable to foreign investors.
2. Investors in different countries view exchange rate risk from the perspective of their different domestic currencies. Thus, they will not agree on the risk

[5] Roger G. Ibbotson, Richard C. Carr, and Anthony W. Robinson, "International Equity and Bond Returns," *Financial Analysts Journal,* July/August 1982.

Table 26.9 Equity Returns, 1960–1980

	Average Return	Standard Deviation of Return	Beta	Alpha
Australia	12.20	22.80	1.02	1.52
Austria	10.30	16.90	0.01	4.86
Belgium	10.10	13.80	0.45	2.44
Canada	12.10	17.50	0.77	2.75
Denmark	11.40	24.20	0.60	2.91
France	8.10	21.40	0.50	0.17
Germany	10.10	19.90	0.45	2.41
Italy	5.60	27.20	0.41	−1.92
Japan	19.00	31.40	0.81	9.49
Netherlands	10.70	17.80	0.90	0.65
Norway	17.40	49.00	−.27	13.39
Spain	10.40	19.80	0.04	4.73
Sweden	9.70	16.70	0.51	1.69
Switzerland	12.50	22.90	0.87	2.66
United Kingdom	14.70	33.60	1.47	1.76
United States	10.20	17.70	1.08	−0.69

Source: Roger G. Ibbotson, Richard C. Carr, and Anthony W. Robinson, "International Equity and Bond Returns," *Financial Analysts Journal,* July/August 1982.

characteristics of various securities and, therefore, will not derive identical efficient frontiers.

3. Investors in different countries tend to consume different baskets of goods, either because of differing tastes or because of tariffs, transportation costs, or taxes. If relative prices of goods vary over time, the inflation risk perceived by investors in different countries will also differ.

These problems suggest that the simple CAPM will not work as well in an international context as it would if all markets were fully integrated. Some evidence suggests that assets that are less accessible to foreign investors carry higher risk premiums than a simple CAPM would predict.[6]

The APT seems better designed for use in an international context than the CAPM, as the special risk factors that arise in international investing can be treated much like any other risk factor. World economic activity and currency movements might simply be included in a list of factors already used in a domestic APT model.

SUMMARY

1. U.S. assets are only a small fraction of the world wealth portfolio. International capital markets offer important opportunities for portfolio diversification with enhanced risk-return characteristics.

[6] Vihang Errunza and Etienne Losq, "International Asset Pricing Under Mild Segmentation: Theory and Test," *Journal of Finance* 40 (March 1985), pp. 105–24.

2. Exchange rate risk imparts an extra source of uncertainty to investments denominated in foreign currencies. Much of that risk can be hedged in foreign exchange futures or forward markets, but a perfect hedge is not feasible unless the foreign currency rate of return is known.

3. Several world market indexes can form a basis for passive international investing. Active international management can be partitioned into currency selection, country selection, stock selection, and cash/bond selection.

4. A factor model applied to international investing would include a world factor as well as the usual domestic factors. Although some evidence suggests domestic factors dominate stock returns, effects of the October 1987 crash demonstrate existence of an important international factor.

Key Terms

World investable wealth
American Depository Receipts
Single-country funds
Political risk
Exchange rate risk
Interest rate parity relationship
Covered interest arbitrage relationship
Europe, Australia, Far East (EAFE) index
Cross-holdings
Currency selection
Country selection

Selected Readings

Two textbooks on international investing and capital markets are:

Giddy, Ian H. *Global Financial Markets.* Lexington, Mass.: D.C. Heath, 1993.

Solnik, Bruno. *International Investments,* 2nd edition. Reading, Mass.: Addison-Wesley, 1991.

Problems

1. Suppose a U.S. investor wishes to invest in a British firm currently selling for £40 per share. The investor has $10,000 to invest, and the current exchange rate is $2/£

   a. How many shares can the investor purchase?

   b. Fill in the table below for rates of return after one year in each of the nine scenarios (three possible prices per share in pounds times three possible exchange rates).

		Dollar-Denominated Return for Year-End Exchange Rate		
Price per Share (£)	**Pound-Denominated Return (%)**	**$1.80/£**	**$2/£**	**$2.20/£**
£35				
£40				
£45				

c. When is the dollar-denominated return equal to the pound-denominated return?

2. If each of the nine outcomes in Question 1 is equally likely, find the standard deviation of both the pound- and dollar-denominated rates of return.
3. Now suppose that the investor in Question 1 also sells forward £5,000 at a forward exchange rate of $2.10/£.
   a. Recalculate the dollar-denominated returns for each scenario.
   b. What happens to the standard deviation of the dollar-denominated return? Compare it both to its old value and the standard deviation of the pound-denominated return.
4. Calculate the contribution to total performance from currency, country, and stock selection for the manager in the example below:

	EAFE Weight	Return on Equity Index	$E_1/E_0 - 1$	Manager's Weight	Manager's Return
Europe	.30	20%	−10%	.35	18%
Australia	.10	15	0	.15	20
Far East	.60	25	+10	.50	20

5. If the current exchange rate is $1.75/£, the one-year forward exchange rate is $1.85/£, and the interest rate on British government bills is 8% per year, what risk-free dollar-denominated return can be locked in by investing in the British bills?
6. If you were to invest $10,000 in the British bills of Question 5, how would you lock in the dollar-denominated return?

7. John Irish, CFA, is an independent investment advisor who is assisting Alfred Darwin, the head of the Investment Committee of General Technology Corporation, to establish a new pension fund. Darwin asks Irish about international equities and whether the Investment Committee should consider them as an additional asset for the pension fund.*
   a. Explain the rationale for including international equities in General's equity portfolio. Identify and describe three relevant considerations in formulating your answer.
   b. List three possible arguments against international equity investment and briefly discuss the significance of each.
   c. To illustrate several aspects of the performance of international securities over time, Irish shows Darwin the graph at the top of the following page of investment results experienced by a U.S. pension fund in the 1970–83 period. Compare the performance of the U.S. dollar and non-U.S. dollar equity and fixed-income asset categories, and explain the significance of the result of the Account Performance Index relative to the results of the four individual asset class indexes.

*Reprinted, with permission, from the Level III 1986 *CFA Study Guide*.

8. A global manager plans to invest $1 million in U.S. government cash equivalents for the next 90 days. However, she is also authorized to use non-U.S. government cash equivalents, as long as the currency risk is hedged to U.S. dollars using forward currency contracts.*

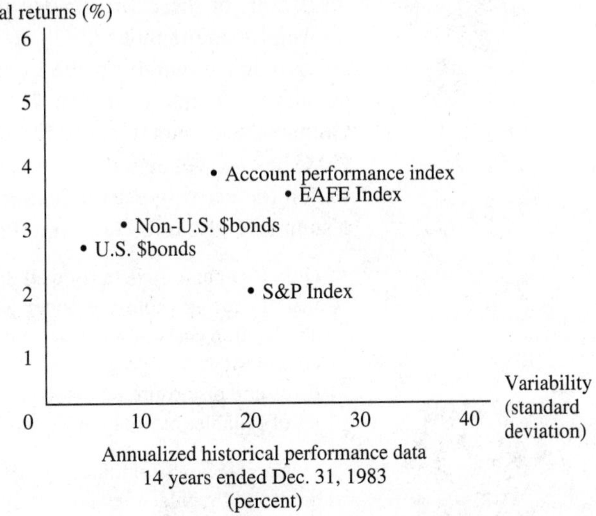

a. What rate of return will the manager earn if she invests in money market instruments in either Canada or Japan and hedges the dollar value of her investment? Use the data in the following tables.

b. What must be the approximate value of the 90-day interest rate available on U.S. government securities?

Interest Rates (APR)
90-Day Cash Equivalents

Japanese government	2.52%
Canadian government	6.74%

Exchange Rates
Dollars per Unit of Foreign Currency

	Spot	90-Day Forward
Japanese yen	.0119	.0120
Canadian dollar	.7284	.7269

9. Suppose two all-equity-financed firms, ABC and XYZ, both have $100 million of equity outstanding. Each firm now issues $10 million of new stock and uses the proceeds to purchase the other's shares.

a. What happens to the sum of the value of outstanding equity of the two firms?

*Reprinted, with permission, from the Level III 1986 *CFA Study Guide.*

b. What happens to the value of the equity in these firms held by the noncorporate sector of the economy?

c. Prepare the balance sheet for these two firms before and after the stock issues.

d. If both of these firms were in the S&P 500, what would happen to their weights in the index?

10. After much research on the developing economy and capital markets of the country of Otunia, your firm, GAC, has decided to include an investment in the Otunia stock market in its Emerging Markets Commingled Fund. However, GAC has not yet decided whether to invest actively or by indexing. Your opinion on the active versus indexing decision has been solicited. The following is a summary of the research findings:*

> Otunia's economy is fairly well diversified across agricultural and natural resources, manufacturing (both consumer and durable goods), and a growing finance sector. Transaction costs in securities markets are relatively large in Otunia because of high commissions and government "stamp taxes" on securities trades. Accounting standards and disclosure regulations are quite detailed, resulting in wide public availability of reliable information about companies' financial performance.
>
> Capital flows into and out of Otunia, and foreign ownership of Otunia securities are strictly regulated by an agency of the national government. The settlement procedures under these ownership rules often cause long delays in settling trades made by nonresidents. Senior finance officials in the government are working to deregulate capital flows and foreign ownership, but GAC's political consultant believes that isolationist sentiment may prevent much real progress in the short run.

a. Briefly discuss aspects of the Otunia environment that favor investing actively, and aspects that favor indexing.

b. Recommend whether GAC should invest in Otunia actively or by indexing. Justify your recommendation based on the factors identified in Part (*a*).

---

*Reprinted, with permission, from the Level III 1992 *CFA Study Guide*.

Part VIII

Players and Strategies

Chapter 27
Managing Client Portfolios

THE INVESTMENT PROCESS IS A CHAIN OF CONSIDERATIONS AND ACTIONS FOR AN INDIVIDUAL, FROM THINKING ABOUT INVESTING TO PLACING BUY/SELL ORDERS FOR INVESTMENT ASSETS SUCH AS STOCKS AND BONDS. Likewise, for institutions such as insurance companies and pension funds, the investment process starts with a mission and a budget and ends with a detailed investment portfolio.

Establishing a clear hierarchy of the investment process is useful. The first step is to determine the investor's objectives. The second step is to identify all the constraints, that is, the qualifications and requirements of the resultant portfolio. Finally, the objectives and constraints must be translated into investment policies. These steps are necessary for both individual and institutional investors.

Individuals' objectives and constraints are greatly affected by their stage in the life cycle. A young father's goals are very different from a retired widow's. Institutional investors do the lion's share of investing. However, their constraints are often compounded by legal restrictions and regulations.

27.1 Making Investment Decisions

Translating the aspirations and circumstances of diverse households into desirable investment decisions is a daunting task. Accomplishing the same task for institutions with many stakeholders, which are regulated by various authorities, is equally perplexing. Put simply, the investment process is not easily programmable into an efficient procedure.

A natural place to look for quality investment procedures is in the offices of professional investors. Better yet, we choose to examine the approach of the Association for Investment Management and Research (AIMR), which was established by a merger of

Table 27.1 Determination of Portfolio Policies

Objectives	Constraints	Policies
Return requirements	Liquidity	Asset allocation
Risk tolerance	Horizon	Diversification
	Regulations	Risk positioning
	Taxes	Tax positioning
	Unique needs	Income generation

the Financial Analysts Federation (FAF) with the Institute of Chartered Financial Analysts (ICFA).

The AIMR administers three examinations for those who wish to be certified as chartered financial analysts (CFAs). To become a CFA, a candidate must pass exams at Levels I, II, and III, and show a satisfactory record of experience. The AIMR helps CFA candidates by organizing classes and compiling reading materials. Our analysis in this chapter is compiled along the lines of the AIMR model.

The basic idea is to subdivide the major steps (objectives, constraints, and policies) into concrete considerations of the various aspects, making the task of organization more tractable. The standard format appears in Table 27.1. In the next sections, we elaborate briefly (there is a lot more to be said than this text will allow) on the construction of the three parts of the investment process, along the lines of Table 27.1.

Objectives

Portfolio objectives center on the **risk-return trade-off** between the expected return the investors want (*return requirements* in the first column of Table 27.1) and how much risk they are willing to assume (*risk tolerance*). Investment managers must know the level of risk that can be tolerated in the pursuit of a better expected rate of return. Table 27.2 lists factors governing return requirements and risk attitudes for each of the seven major investor categories discussed.

Individual Investors

The basic factors affecting individual investor return requirements and risk tolerance are life-cycle stage and individual preferences (see box). We will have much more to say about individual investor objectives in Chapter 28.

Personal Trusts

Personal trusts are established when an individual confers legal title to property to another person or institution (the trustee) to manage that property for one or more beneficiaries. Beneficiaries customarily are divided into **income beneficiaries,** who receive the interest and dividend income from the trust during their lifetimes, and

MERRILL LYNCH ASKS: HOW MUCH RISK CAN YOU TAKE?

When it comes to investing how much risk can you stomach?

Merrill Lynch & Co. wants to know.

In coming weeks, the nation's biggest brokerage firm will begin asking the individual investors behind its 7.2 million retail accounts to decide for themselves just how aggressive they're really willing to be in buying stocks, bonds, and other investments.

With the new setup, individual investors will, be asked to put themselves in one of four risk categories: "conservative for income," "conservative for growth," "moderate risk," and "aggressive risk." Each category will have its own recommended asset allocation, or investment mix.

Merrill Lynch isn't the only securities firm that wants investors to state more explicitly how willing they are to risk losing money in the pursuit of profit. Earlier this year, Kidder, Peabody & Co., General Electric Co.'s brokerage unit, adopted a five-category asset-allocation model. Some other brokerage firms say they're looking at such setups, too.

Getting investors to pigeonhole themselves in this way can be a good thing because it forces them to come to grips with their feelings about risk. And it gives their stockbrokers formal written notice about these desires. The customer's choice "goes into the record," says George Grune, managing director of Kidder Peabody's asset management group.

At the same time, getting investors on record about their risk tolerances is likely to make it easier for a brokerage firm to defend itself if it gets hit with lawsuits or arbitration claims by investors who don't like what their brokers are doing.

An investor who picks the "aggressive risk" category, for example, is agreeing to "move aggressively among asset classes" and deal in "speculative and high-risk issues," according to guidelines distributed to Merrill Lynch brokers last week. Such an investor might have a difficult time claiming that his or her broker was *too* aggressive.

Legal issues like that are a growing concern on Wall Street. Over the past year, brokerage firms have been forced to pay increasingly stiff punitive-damage awards in arbitration cases brought by disgruntled investors.

Brokers are required by securities law to make sure customers are put into "suitable" investments. Unsuitability lawsuits are brought when it's alleged that a broker knew, or should have known, that an investment wasn't consistent with a client's investment objectives.

Merrill Lynch officials stress that such legal concerns aren't the main reason for the new system, although they don't deny they are a factor. The officials say they mainly wanted to be more "flexible" with the firm's asset-allocation recommendations, tailoring the research department's advice on the markets to an investor's general profile.

Avoiding customer disputes is "one of the side benefits, but that's not why it was created in the first place," says John Steffens, president of Merrill Lynch's individual-investor operations. " 'The Street,' in my view, in general has dealt with this whole asset-allocation subject a little bit too simplistically," he says.

Sam Scott Miller, a New York securities lawyer, says getting investors to segment themselves according to risk preferences is a "sound and prudent

(Continued)

remaindermen, who receive the principal of the trust when the income beneficiary dies and the trust is dissolved. The trustee is usually a bank, a savings and loan association, a lawyer, or an investment professional. Investment of a trust is subject to trust laws, as well as "prudent man" rules that limit the types of allowable trust investment to those that a prudent man would select.

Objectives in the case of personal trusts normally are more limited in scope than those of the individual investor. Because of their fiduciary responsibility, personal trust approach" to heading off legal disputes, providing the firms monitor the systems well. Not only should it protect the firm in disputes with customers, it might also be an early warning to a securities firm if one of its brokers is pushing customers into unsuitable investments. If a certain broker "brings in all 'aggressive' accounts, they're going to want to take a look at it," he says.

Some of Merrill Lynch's competitors have less-formal ways of tailoring asset-allocation recommendations. Firms including St. Louis–based A. G. Edwards & Sons Inc. and Raymond James & Associates Inc., St. Petersburg, Fla., already have more than one asset-allocation model for different investor profiles. But they don't ask investors to commit formally to one or the other.

"There is a temptation with asset allocation to put the retail client into a profile," says Raymond Worseck, investment strategy coordinator at A. G. Edwards, which has decided not to institute a formal system like Merrill Lynch's. Such a system has "compliance pluses" for brokerage firms, "because it protects them legally from a risk standpoint." But the investor can sometimes be better served with a more personalized approach, he says.

Merrill Lynch emphasizes that getting investors to specify their risk tolerance is only a beginning for grooming an investor's portfolio. Once an investor picks a risk category, the broker uses computer models and other tools to build a portfolio of appropriate stocks and bonds. Investors can switch risk categories, but frequent switching isn't encouraged, Merrill Lynch officials say.

Charles Clough, Merrill Lynch's chief investment strategist, says he realizes there are critics of his firm's plan. "You could say a multitude of asset guidelines just adds to the confusion of the issue," he says. But Mr. Clough adds that having the set categories helps to organize investors whose risk profiles otherwise would be "all over the map."

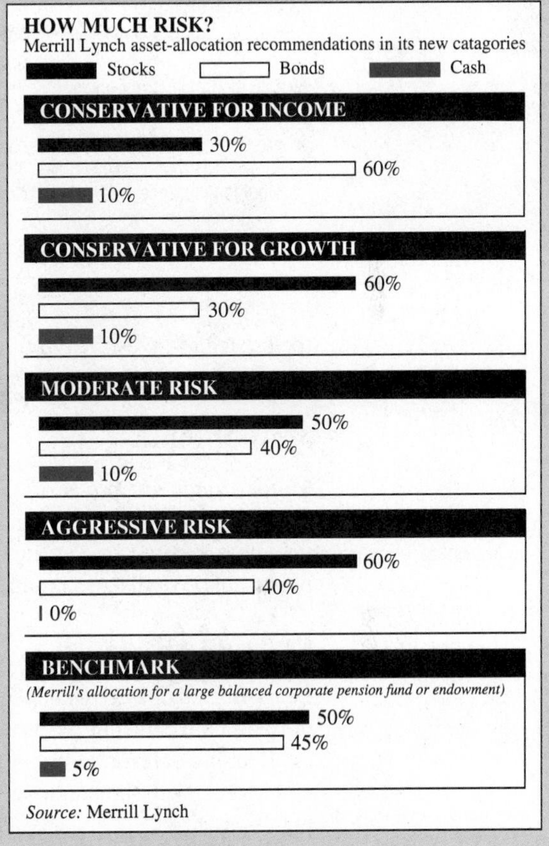

Source: William Power, "Merrill Lynch Asks: How Much Risk Can You Take?" *The Wall Street Journal*, July 2, 1990. Reprinted by permission of *The Wall Street Journal*,

managers typically are more risk averse than are individual investors. Certain asset classes such as options and futures contracts, for example, and strategies such as short-selling or buying on margin are ruled out.

When there are both income beneficiaries and remaindermen, the trustee faces a built-in conflict between the interests of the two sets of beneficiaries because greater current income inherently entails a sacrifice of future capital gain. For the typical case where the life beneficiary has substantial income requirements, there is pressure on

Table 27.2 Matrix of Objectives

Type of Investor	Return Requirement	Risk Tolerance
Individual and personal trusts	Life cycle (education, children, retirement)	Life cycle (younger are more risk tolerant)
Mutual funds	Variable	Variable
Pension funds	Assumed actuarial rate	Depends on proximity of payouts
Endowment funds	Determined by current income needs and need for asset growth to maintain real value	Generally conservative
Life insurance companies	Should exceed new money rate by sufficient margin to meet expenses and profit objectives; also actuarial rates important	Conservative
Nonlife insurance companies	No minimum	Conservative
Banks	Interest spread	Variable

the trustee to invest heavily in fixed-income securities or high-dividend-yielding common stocks.

Mutual Funds

Mutual funds are pools of investors' money. They invest in ways specified in their prospectuses and issue shares to investors entitling them to a pro rata portion of the income generated by the funds. The objectives of a mutual fund are spelled out in its prospectus. We discuss mutual funds in detail in Chapter 3.

Pension Funds

Pension fund objectives depend on the type of pension plan. There are two basic types: **defined contribution plans** and **defined benefit plans.** Defined contribution plans are in effect tax-deferred retirement savings accounts established by the firm in trust for its employees, with the employee bearing all the risk and receiving all the return from the plan's assets.

The largest pension funds, however, are defined benefit plans. In these plans the assets serve as collateral for the liabilities that the firm sponsoring the plan owes to plan beneficiaries. The liabilities are life annuities, earned during the employee's working years, that start at the plan participant's retirement. Thus, it is the sponsoring firm's shareholders who bear the risk in a defined benefit pension plan. We discuss pension plans more fully in Chapter 28.

Endowment Funds

Endowment funds are organizations chartered to use their money for specific nonprofit purposes. They are financed by gifts from one or more sponsors and are typically managed by educational, cultural, and charitable organizations or by independent foundations established solely to carry out the fund's specific purposes. Generally, the investment objectives of an endowment fund are to produce a steady flow of income subject to only a moderate degree of risk. Trustees of an endowment fund, however, can specify other objectives as dictated by the circumstances of the particular endowment fund.

Life Insurance Companies

Life insurance companies generally try to invest so as to hedge their liabilities, which are defined by the policies they write. Thus, there are as many objectives as there are distinct types of policies. Until a decade or so ago there were only two types of life insurance policies available for individuals: whole-life and term.

A **whole-life insurance policy** combines a death benefit with a kind of savings plan that provides for a gradual buildup of cash value that the policyholder can withdraw at a later point in life, usually at age 65. **Term insurance,** on the other hand, provides death benefits only, with no buildup of cash value.

The interest rate that is imbedded in the schedule of cash value accumulation promised under a whole-life policy is a fixed rate, and life insurance companies try to hedge this liability by investing in long-term bonds. Often the insured individual has the right to borrow at a prespecified fixed interest rate against the cash value of the policy.

During the inflationary years of the 1970s and early 1980s, when many older whole-life policies carried contractual borrowing rates as low as 4% or 5% per year, policyholders borrowed heavily against the cash value to invest in money market mutual funds paying double-digit yields. Other actual and potential policyholders abandoned whole-life policies and took out term insurance, investing the difference in the premiums on their own. By 1981, term insurance accounted for more than half the volume of new sales of individual life policies.

In response to these developments the insurance industry came up with two new policy types: **variable life** and **universal life.** Under a variable life policy the insured's premium buys a fixed death benefit plus a cash value that can be invested in a variety of mutual funds from which the policyholder can choose. With a universal life policy, policyholders can increase or reduce the premium or death benefit according to their needs. Furthermore, the interest rate on the cash value component changes with market interest rates.

The great advantage of variable and universal life insurance policies is that earnings on the cash value are not taxed until the money is withdrawn. Since the Tax Reform Act of 1986 these policies are one of the few tax-advantaged investments left.

The life insurance industry also provides products for pension plans. The two major products are insured defined benefit pensions and **guaranteed insurance contracts (GICs).**

In the case of insured defined benefit pensions, the firm sponsoring the pension plan enters into a contractual agreement by which the life insurance company assumes all liability for the benefits accrued under the plan. The insurance company provides this service in return for an annual premium based on the benefit formula, and the number and characteristics of the employees covered by the plan. In the case of GICs the insurance company sells to a pension plan a contract promising a stated nominal interest rate over some specified period of time, usually several years. A GIC is in effect a zero-coupon bond issued by an insurance company. With respect to both types of product the insurance company usually pursues an investment policy designed to hedge the associated risk.

Life insurance companies may be organized as either mutual companies or stock companies. In principle, the organizational form should affect the investment objectives of the company. Mutual companies are supposed to be run solely for the benefit of their policyholders, whereas stock companies have as their objective the maximization of shareholder value.

In actuality, it is hard to discern from its investment policies which organizational form a particular insurance company has. Some examples of mutual insurance companies are Prudential and Mutual of Omaha. Examples of stock companies are Travelers and Aetna.

Nonlife Insurance Companies

Nonlife insurance companies such as property and casualty insurers have investable funds primarily because they pay claims *after* they collect policy premiums. Typically, they are conservative in their attitude toward risk. As with life insurers, nonlife insurance companies can be either stock companies or mutual companies.

Banks

The defining characteristic of banks is that most of their investments are loans to businesses and consumers and most of their liabilities are accounts of depositors. As investors, the objective of banks is to try to match the risk of assets to liabilities while earning a profitable spread between the lending and borrowing rates.

27.2 Constraints

Both individuals and institutional investors restrict their choice of investment assets. These restrictions arise from their specific circumstances. Identifying these restrictions/constraints will affect the choice of investment policy. Five common types of constraints are described below. Table 27.3 presents a matrix summarizing the main constraints in each category for each of the seven types of investors.

Liquidity

Liquidity is the ease (speed) at which an asset can be sold and still fetch a fair price. It is a relationship between the time dimension (how long will it take to dispose) and the price dimension (any discount from fair market price) of an investment asset.

When an actual concrete measure of liquidity is necessary, one thinks of the discount when an immediate sale is unavoidable. Cash and money market instruments such as

Table 27.3 Matrix of Constraints

Type of Investor	Liquidity	Horizon	Regulatory	Taxes
Individuals and personal trusts	Variable	Life cycle	None	Variable
Mutual funds	High	Variable	Little	None
Pension funds	Young, low; mature, high	Long	ERISA	None
Endowment funds	Low	Long	Little	None
Life insurance companies	Low	Long	Complex	Yes
Nonlife insurance companies	High	Short	Little	Yes
Banks	High	Short	Changing	Yes

Treasury bills and commercial paper, where the bid-ask spread is a fraction of 1%, are the most liquid assets, and real estate is among the least liquid[1]. Office buildings and manufacturing structures can easily experience a 50% liquidity discount.

Both individual and institutional investors must consider how likely they are to dispose of assets at short notice. From this likelihood, they establish the minimum level of liquid assets they want in the investment portfolio.

Investment Horizon

This is the *planned* liquidation date of the investment or part of it. Examples of an individual **investment horizon** could be the time to fund college education or the retirement date for a wage earner. For a university endowment, an investment horizon could relate to the time to fund a major campus construction project. Horizon needs to be considered when investors choose between assets of various maturities, such as bonds, which pay off at specified future dates.

Regulations

Only professional and institutional investors are constrained by regulations. First and foremost is the **prudent man law.** That is, professional investors who manage other people's money have a fiduciary responsibility to restrict investment to assets that would have been approved by a prudent investor. The law is purposefully nonspecific. Every professional investor must stand ready to defend an investment policy in a court of law, and interpretation may differ according to the standards of the times.

Also, specific regulations apply to various institutional investors. For instance, U.S. mutual funds (institutions that pool individual investor money under professional management) may not hold more than 5% of the shares of any publicly traded corporation. This regulation keeps professional investors from getting involved in the actual management of corporations.

[1] In most cases it is impossible to know the liquidity of an asset with certainty, before it is put up for sale. In dealer markets (described in Chapter 4), however, the liquidity of the traded assets can be observed from the bid-ask spread that is quoted by the dealers, that is, the difference between the "bid" quote (the lower price the dealer will pay the owner), and the "ask" quote (the higher price a buyer would have to pay the dealer).

Tax Considerations

Tax consequences are central to investment decisions. The performance of any investment strategy is measured by how much it yields (jargon for what its rate of return is expected to be) after taxes. For household and institutional investors who face significant tax rates, tax sheltering and deferral of tax obligations may be pivotal in their investment strategy.

Unique Needs

Virtually every investor faces special circumstances. Imagine husband-and-wife aeronautical engineers holding high-paying jobs in the same aerospace corporation. The entire human capital of that household is tied to a single player in a rather cyclical industry. This couple would need to hedge the risk (find investment assets that yield more when the risk materializes, thus partly offsetting the risk) of a deterioration of the economic well-being of the aerospace industry.

An example of a unique need for an institutional investor is a university whose trustees let the administration use only cash income from the endowment fund. This constraint would translate into a preference for high-dividend-paying assets.

27.3 Asset Allocation

Consideration of their objectives and constraints leads investors to a set of investment policies. The policies column in Table 27.1 lists the various dimensions of portfolio management policymaking—asset allocation, diversification, risk and tax positioning, and income generation. By far the most important part of policy determination is asset allocation, that is, deciding how much of the portfolio to invest in each major asset category.

We can view the process of asset allocation as consisting of the following steps:

1. Specify asset classes to be included in the portfolio. The major classes usually considered are the following:
   a. Money market instruments (usually called *cash*).
   b. Fixed-income securities (usually called *bonds*).
   c. Stocks.
   d. Real estate.
   e. Precious metals.
   f. Other.

   Institutional investors will rarely invest in more than the first four categories, whereas individual investors frequently will include precious metals and other more exotic types of investments in their portfolios.
2. Specify capital market expectations. This step consists of using both historical data and economic analysis to determine your expectations of future rates of return over the relevant holding period on the assets to be considered for inclusion in the portfolio.
3. Derive the efficient portfolio frontier. This step consists of finding portfolios that achieve the maximum expected return for any given degree of risk.

Table 27.4 Probability Distribution of HPR on Stocks, Bonds, and Cash

		Holding-Period Return (%)		
State of Economy	**Probability**	**Stocks**	**Bonds**	**Cash**
Boom with low inflation	.1	74	4	6
Boom with high inflation	.2	20	−10	6
Normal growth	.4	14	9	6
Recession with low inflation	.2	0	35	6
Recession with high inflation	.1	−30	0	6
Expected return	$E(r)$	14.0	9.0	6
Standard deviation	σ	24.5	14.8	0

Correlation coefficient between stocks and bonds is −.2372.

4. Find the optimal asset mix. This step consists of selecting the efficient portfolio that best meets your risk and return objectives while satisfying the constraints you face.

Let us illustrate how the process works by considering a simple example. We start the process by initially restricting our portfolio to cash, bonds, and stocks. Later we will consider how much of an improvement we can achieve by adding real estate and other asset classes.

Specifying Capital Market Expectations

Having decided to restrict ourselves to cash, bonds, and stocks, we must specify our expectations of the holding-period returns on these asset classes over the period until our next planned revision in the asset mix. Although professional investors usually revise their asset mix every three months when they receive new information about the state of the economy, market developments may cause us to revise more frequently.[2] In our example we will express all rates of return in annualized terms, but the holding period should be thought of as three months.

The set of capital market expectations must be in a form that allows assessment of both expected rates of return and risk. Sometimes investors will make only point forecasts of holding-period returns on assets. These may serve as measures of expected rates of return, but they do not allow assessment of risks.

There are two sources of information relevant to forming capital market expectations: historical data on capital market rates and economic forecasts. The investment professional must exercise considerable judgment when deciding how much to rely on each of these two sources.

For example, suppose that based entirely on economic forecasts derived from careful analysis of all the information we can assemble, we have determined the probability distribution of holding-period returns exhibited in Table 27.4.

[2] The Department of Commerce, for example, releases its figures on the Gross National Product quarterly.

Our assessment of the HPR on bonds comes from a consideration of a 30-year U.S. Treasury bond with a 9% coupon. If there is normal growth, then we expect interest rates to remain at their current level and we will experience neither capital gains nor losses on the bond. Our HPR will simply equal the coupon rate of 9%.

If there is a boom, then we think interest rates will rise and the price of the bond will fall. The amount by which interest rates will rise depends on whether there is a low or a high rate of inflation. With low inflation interest rates will rise a little bit, causing a capital loss of only 5% on bonds, for a net HPR of 4%. However, if inflation is high, interest rates will rise a lot, causing a capital loss of 19%, for a net HPR of −10% on bonds.

If there is a recession, then we think that the direction of interest rates will depend on inflation. If there is low inflation interest rates will fall, but if there is high inflation they will rise despite the recession. In the low inflation recessionary scenario bonds will do very well, with an HPR of 35%. But in the high inflation recessionary scenario, the bond price will fall by 9%, leaving an HPR of zero.

The assessment of the rates of return on stocks for each scenario is evident from Table 27.4. Stocks are expected to do best in a noninflationary boom and worst in an inflationary recession.

To the extent that these parameter estimates—either the means, the standard deviations, or the correlation coefficient—differ from what they have been in the past, we may want to adjust their values so that they conform more to historical experience. In the rest of our example, however, we will use the unadjusted numbers calculated in Table 27.4

CONCEPT CHECK

Question 1. Suppose that you revised your assessment of the probabilities of each of the five economic scenarios in Table 27.4 as follows:

		Holding-Period Return (%)		
State of Economy	**Probability**	**Stocks**	**Bonds**	**Cash**
Boom with low inflation	.05	74	4	6
Boom with high inflation	.20	20	−10	6
Normal growth	.50	14	9	6
Recession with low inflation	.20	0	35	6
Recession with high inflation	.05	−30	0	6

What are your new estimates of expected returns, standard deviations, and correlations?

Deriving the Efficient Portfolio Frontier

Given the probability distribution of holding-period returns in Table 27.4, what is the efficient portfolio frontier? Because we are considering only two risky assets for inclusion in the portfolio, we can use the formula presented in Chapter 7 to find the optimal combination of stocks and bonds to be combined with the risk-free asset.

The formula is reproduced here as equation 27.1.

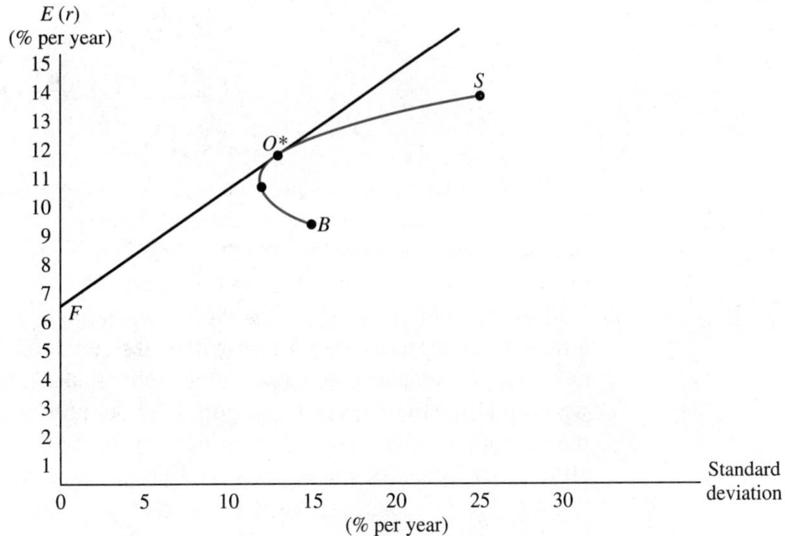

Figure 27.1
The risk-reward trade-off for portfolios of stocks, bonds, and cash

$$w^* = \frac{[E(r_s) - r_f]\sigma_b^2 - [E(r_b) - r_f]\text{cov}(r_s,r_b)}{[E(r_s) - r_f]\sigma_b^2 + [E(r_b) - r_f]\sigma_s^2 - [E(r_s) - r_f + E(r_b) - r_f]\text{cov}(r_s,r_b)} \quad \textbf{(27.1)}$$

where w^* is the proportion of stocks and $1 - w^*$ is the proportion of bonds.

Substituting in this equation we find that $w^* = .45$:

$$w^* = \frac{(14 - 6) \times 218 - (9 - 6) \times (-86)}{8 \times 218 + 3 \times 600 - (8 + 3)(-86)} = .45$$

Thus, the optimal stock-bond portfolio to be combined with cash is 45% stocks and 55% bonds.

Its expected HPR, $E(r^*)$, and standard deviation, σ^*, are

$$\begin{aligned} E(r^*) &= w^*E(r_s) + (1 - w^*)E(r_b) \\ &= .45 \times 14\% + .55 \times 9\% \\ &= 11.25\% \\ \sigma^{*2} &= w^{*2}\sigma_s^2 + (1 - w^*)^2\sigma_b^2 + 2\,w^*(1 - w^*)\text{cov}(r_s,r_b) \\ &= .45^2 \times 600 + .55^2 \times 218 + 2 \times .45 \times .55 \times (-86) \\ &= 144.875 \\ \sigma^* &= 12.0\% \end{aligned}$$

Figure 27.1 displays the efficient portfolio frontier.

Point F represents 100% invested in cash, Point B 100% of bonds, and Point S 100% in stocks. Point O^* is the optimal combination of stocks and bonds (45% stocks and 55% bonds) to be combined with cash to form the investor's final portfolio. All efficient portfolios lie along the straight line connecting Points F and O^*. The slope of this efficient frontier, the reward to variability ratio, is:

$$S^* = \frac{E(r^*) - r_f}{\sigma^*}$$
$$= \frac{11.25\% - 6\%}{12.0}$$
$$= .4375$$

The fact that we have drawn the segment of the efficient frontier to the right of O^* with the same slope as to the left reflects the assumption that we can borrow at a risk-free rate of 6% per year to buy the O^* portfolio on margin. If the borrowing rate is higher than 6% per year, then the slope to the right of Point O^* will be lower than to the left.

If we rule out buying the O^* portfolio on margin altogether, then the segment of the efficient frontier to the right of O^* will be the curve linking points O^* and S. This indicates that, to achieve an expected HPR higher than $E(r^*)$ in the absence of borrowing, we would have to increase the proportion of our portfolio invested in stocks and reduce the proportion in bonds relative to their proportions in O^*. The maximum expected HPR under these circumstances would be the expected HPR on stocks, achieved by investing 100% in stocks.

CONCEPT CHECK Question 2. What is the O^* portfolio for the set of revised capital market parameters you derived in Question 1?

The Optimal Mix

Our choice of where to be on the efficient frontier will depend on our degree of risk aversion, as shown in Chapters 5 through 7. We reproduce here as equation 27.2 the formula for the optimal proportion to invest in Portfolio O^*:

$$y^* = \frac{E(r^*) - r_f}{.01\, A\sigma^{*2}} \tag{27.2}$$

where A is our coefficient of risk aversion.

For example, we might wonder how risk averse we need to be to want to hold the portfolio O^* itself, with nothing invested in cash. To find the answer, we set y^* equal to 1 and solve for A. The answer is $A = 3.65$.

Diversifying into Different Asset Classes

Diversification is a good thing in asset allocation. But can there be too much of a good thing? After all, there are many different asset categories. Should you have some of each in your portfolio: stocks, bonds, real estate, precious metals, art, collectibles, and so on? And if so, how much?

The basic principle of efficient diversification suggests that you can never be made worse off by broadening the set of assets included in your portfolio. However, when we quantify the improvement in portfolio efficiency resulting from including additional assets, we often find that it is not large enough to justify the additional time, trouble, and other transaction costs associated with implementing it.

Table 27.5 Capital Market Expectations: Stocks, Bonds, and Real Estate

	Stocks	Bonds	Real Estate	Cash
Expected HPR $E(r)$	14.0%	9.0%	10.0%	6%
Standard deviation σ	24.5%	14.8%	20.0%	0
Correlation Coefficients				
Stocks	1.00	−.24	0	
Bonds		1.00	0	
Real estate			1.00	

For example, let us consider whether we should add real estate to our portfolio in the example above. The first thing we need is the mean, standard deviation, and the correlations of the HPR on real estate with the returns on stocks and bonds. One way to derive them is from an expansion of the scenario analysis presented earlier in this chapter. Another way is by looking at past data.

Data on real estate holding-period returns is not as readily available as data on stock and bond returns. One feasible approach, however, is to gather data on a few publicly traded REITs[3] and treat them as representative of real estate as a whole. The advantage of doing so is that we can then invest in the shares of those same REITs when it comes time to implement our investment policy.

Let us assume that we have used one or more of these methods to derive the following set of capital market parameters for real estate:

$$E(r_{\text{RE}}) = 10\% \text{ per year}$$
$$\sigma_{\text{RE}} = 20\%$$
$$\rho_{\text{RE},s} = 0 \text{ (correlation between real estate and stock returns)}$$
$$\rho_{\text{RE},b} = 0 \text{ (correlation between real estate and bond returns)}$$

In addition, let us use the parameters for stocks, bonds, and cash as we did in Table 27.4:

$$r_f = 6\%$$
$$E(r_s) = 14\% \quad \sigma_s = 24.5\%$$
$$E(r_b) = 9\% \quad \sigma_b = 14.8\%$$
$$\rho_{sb} = -.24 \text{ (correlation between stock and bond returns)}$$

Table 27.5 presents a convenient summary of these capital market assumptions.

We use a computer-based optimization program to find the optimal combination of risky assets to combine with cash.[4] Table 27.6 shows the new O^* portfolio composition and characteristics, as well as the old.

Thus the reward-to-variability ratio that we face is .480, compared with .438 in the case without real estate. The optimal portfolio for an investor whose coefficient of risk

[3] REITs (real estate investment trusts) are discussed in Chapter 3. They are investment companies that invest either directly in real estate or in debt instruments secured by real estate.

[4] The software diskette provided with this text contains such a program.

Table 27.6 The Optimal Combination of Risky Assets (O^*) with and without Real Estate

	New	Old
Portfolio Proportions		
Stocks	35%	45%
Bonds	43%	55%
Real estate	22%	
Parameters of O^* Portfolio		
Expected HPR $E(r^*)$	11.0%	11.25%
Standard deviation σ^*	10.4%	12.0%
Reward-to-variability ratio S^*	.480	.438

aversion is 3.65 and who previously would have chosen to hold the old O^* portfolio with no cash would be:

$$\begin{aligned} y^* &= \frac{E(r^*) - r_f}{.01A\sigma^2} \\ &= \frac{11 - 6}{.01 \times 3.65 \times 108} \\ &= 1.27 \end{aligned}$$

Thus, if this were you and if you had \$100,000 of your own money to invest, you should invest \$127,000 in the O^* mutual fund, borrowing the other \$27,000 at an interest rate of 6% per year.

The mean and standard deviation of your optimal portfolio would be

$$\begin{aligned} E(r) &= r_f + 1.27[E(r^*) - r_f] \\ &= 6\% + 1.27(11\% - 6\%) \\ &= 12.35\% \\ \sigma &= 1.27\sigma^* \\ &= 1.27 \times 10.4\% \\ &= 13.21\% \end{aligned}$$

And your certainty-equivalent HPR would be

$$\begin{aligned} U &= E(r) - .005A\sigma^2 \\ &= 12.35 - .005 \times 3.65 \times 175 \\ &= 9.2\% \text{ per year} \end{aligned}$$

This is 0.6% per year higher than the comparable certainty-equivalent HPR of 8.6% per year that you have if you excluded real estate from your portfolio.

What can we conclude from all of this about the value of adding real estate to stocks, bonds, and cash in creating your investment portfolio? Is it worth the effort?

The first thing to point out is that the specific results we got are very sensitive to the specific assumptions that we made about the parameters of the probability distribution of the HPR on real estate. In our example the reward-to-variability ratio goes up from

Table 27.7 Capital Market Expectations: Stocks, Bonds, Real Estate, and Gold

	Stocks	Bonds	Real Estate	Gold	Cash
Expected HPR $E(r)$	14.0%	9.0%	10.0%	7.0%	6%
Standard deviation σ	24.5%	14.8%	20.0%	20.0%	0
Correlation Coefficients					
Stocks	1.0	−.24	0	0	
Bonds		1.00	0	0	
Real estate			1.0	0	
Gold				1.0	

.438 to .480, but had we assumed different numbers for the means, standard deviations, and correlation coefficients, the results could have been very different.

For example, had we assumed a higher value for the expected HPR on real estate, the optimization program would have indicated that we should invest much more heavily in it. The resultant increase in the reward-to-variability ratio would have been higher too. By experimenting with the optimization program that accompanies this text, you can gain a feel for the contribution that real estate would make to improving the efficiency of your portfolio under a variety of assumptions about the relevant parameter values.

Whenever we add an asset class, the process is identical to the one described for real estate. We first must specify the mean and standard deviation of the HPR and its correlation with the other asset classes. Our optimization program then tells us what the optimal proportions of all risky assets are in the O^* portfolio. We then can compute $E(r^*)$, σ^*, and S^*, and decide which combination of the risk-free asset and the new, expanded O^* mutual fund is optimal for us.

For example, suppose we are thinking of adding gold to our portfolio. Suppose that we think that its $E(r)$ is 7%, its σ is 20%, and its correlation with the other three risky assets is zero. Table 27.7 summarizes our capital market assumptions. What is the composition of the new O^* portfolio, and how much do we gain by diversifying into gold?

Our portfolio optimization program tells us that the new O^* has the following portfolio proportions:

Stocks	33%
Bonds	41%
Real estate	21%
Gold	5%

The expected return and risk of this new O^* portfolio are

$$E(r^*) = 10.76\%$$
$$\sigma^* = 9.87\%$$

and the new reward-to-variability ratio is

$$S^* = .482$$

This compares with a reward-to-variability ratio of .480 for the previous case without gold. It would appear that the gain from adding gold to the portfolio is slight.

Doing the Asset-Manager Tango: Don't Try Dancing in the Dark

This year, mutual-fund marketers aren't letting a bad market get in the way of a hot fund concept.

It's a maddening year to be diversified. Stocks have disappointed. Bonds have languished even though they are widely deemed safer than stocks. A lot of foreign markets have slumped, too. And the asset-allocation mutual funds, which hope to profit by carving up their bets among far-flung assets such as stocks, bonds and cash, are showing a nine-month average loss of 1.7%.

But that isn't stopping mutual-fund companies from pushing these funds as a form of one-stop shopping. They know that novice investors—especially in pension plans—are confused by the proliferation of mutual funds today.

'Pretty Daunting' Task

"We really see a need for a one-decision fund," said Robert Leo, a senior vice president at Massachusetts Financial Services, which introduced such a fund this year. "It's a convenient way to invest."

Newcomers to mutual-fund investing face two risks. If they stick to low-yielding, stable investments such as money-market funds, inflation will erode their nest egg. But if they take bigger risks they may eventually panic, bailing out of stock funds at a loss. So, by holding a bunch of different asset classes including U.S. and foreign stocks, bonds and cash, the one-stop funds try to minimize portfolio swings that might scare away novice investors. And they keep enough in growth investments such as stocks to beat inflation.

The inspiration for today's boom in asset-allocation funds is the $11 billion Fidelity Asset Manager. Introduced in 1988, Asset Manager, and some associated Fidelity funds and variable annuities, have grown to $17.4 billion in assets. Standing separately, they would constitute the 25th-largest fund family in America, says Lipper Analytical Services Inc. Merrill Lynch was early in the game, too, and its Global Allocation fund has grown to about $8 billion since 1989.

Yet this has been a bad year for Fidelity Asset Manager, which was down about 3.5% in the nine months. In the first part of the year, "No matter what I invested in, [it] went down," said Robert Beckwitt, who runs the fund. He was particularly hard hit by big positions in emerging-market bonds.

Aiming Lower

Nevertheless, Asset Manager and other funds like it have done much better in recent years than the first wave of asset-allocation funds. They've succeeded largely because they aim lower. The asset-allocation funds of yore were so-called market-timing funds, aiming to nim-

(Continued)

In general it seems to be true that, unless you can identify an additional asset that has a high expected HPR, the gain from further diversification will be slight. You can explore the gains from additional diversification, using your own capital market assumptions, with the aid of the portfolio optimization program provided with this book.

If you are willing to rely on the judgment of others regarding both capital market expectations and your risk-return preferences, then, as the nearby box describes, you can select a mutual fund that will do asset allocation for you.

Hedging against Inflation

An inflation hedge is an asset that enables households and other investors to reduce the risk of loss of purchasing power stemming from uncertainty about the prices of consumer goods. The people considered most vulnerable to such losses are retirees whose bly avoid losses in down markets but pick up the gains of rising markets.

Other such funds were created, predictably, after the stock-market crashes of the early 1970s and 1987. "These funds were initially crafted by market technicians to say, 'I have a way of keeping out of every dangerous period in the market.' It's really an impossible feat," says Fidelity's Mr. Beckwitt.

The newer breed sets floors and ceilings on the proportion of stocks, bonds and money-market instruments the funds can hold. For instance, Asset Manager can put 10% to 60% in stocks, 20% to 60% in bonds, and zero to 70% in money-market or other short-term instruments. (The mix recently: 37% stocks, 34% bonds and 29% cash.) Often a good proportion of the assets is invested overseas. Asset Manager has 28% abroad.

Some of the funds invest in other mutual funds. Many financial consultants caution, however, against investing in funds that unnecessarily charge two layers of fees, one layer for the asset-allocation fund and another for the underlying funds. Dreyfus Omni Fund, for instance, plans to invest mostly in non-Dreyfus mutual funds. It will levy an annual advisory fee of 0.75% of assets, in addition to the expenses of the underlying funds. The T. Rowe Price Spectrum and Vanguard Star funds avoid double-dipping.

Like Asset Manager, many of the new funds come in small "families" of three or more asset-allocation funds, running from conservative to daring. The "Growth Portfolio" of Putnam's Asset Allocation funds can be invested 65% to 95% in stocks; the "Conservative Portfolio" holds 25% to 45% stocks.

The pitch from the fund marketers: The longer your goal, the riskier ("more aggressive") the fund you should pick. A 45-year-old investor might choose an aggressive fund in saving for retirement, but a conservative fund in saving for college for a 15-year-old child.

Adding risky or unusual investments to the tamer ones can spice up a portfolio's returns with little extra risk. For instance, investing in Japan, a volatile market, has helped funds this year, said Jeffrey Shames, chief equity officer at Massachusetts Financial. "The beauty of asset allocation is, you're in all categories. Even if some asset types do poorly you're also in the one that's outperforming."

But many of the new crop of allocation funds, while they may dabble in riskier market sectors, say they won't swing for the fences. Massachusetts Financial's Global Asset Allocation Fund, Mr. Shames says, is "not a high-performance fund. Our main goal is to give solid, consistent returns with a lot less volatility."

Robert McGough, *The Wall Street Journal,* October 5, 1994. Reprinted by permission of *The Wall Street Journal,*

only asset is a pension annuity of a fixed sum of money per month. Such individuals face inflation risk, and if they are risk averse, they will want to hedge at least some of it. This section of the chapter analyzes the effectiveness and the cost of various types of inflation hedges, including index-linked bonds, floating-rate bonds, common stocks, and commodities. Although the analysis focuses on the U.S. and U.K. capital markets, most of the observations apply equally to the rest of the world.

Index-Linked Financial Instruments. For pensioners, the perfect inflation hedge is an annuity denominated in terms of a basket of consumption goods. Indeed, the retirement annuities promised by the U.S. government under social security are intended to be so denominated, and therefore the payments are linked to the consumer price index (CPI). Government-sponsored mandatory retirement schemes throughout the world generally follow this practice.

In 1980, the U.K. government began issuing bonds whose principal and interest are linked to that country's official retail price index (RPI) with a lag of six months. Initially, these index-linked bonds could be purchased only by U.K. pension funds. Since 1981, however, anyone can buy or resell them, and consequently an active secondary market for them has developed. Except for the six-month lag, these bonds offer a guaranteed real rate of interest. Their nominal rate therefore equals the promised real rate plus the actual rate of inflation.

Index-linked U.K. Treasury bonds are a perfect inflation hedge for anyone interested in securing a constant amount of purchasing power as measured by the RPI in the U.K. Marketable index-linked bonds are also available in Israel and several other countries. In all cases, however, they are indexed to the domestic price level and payable in the local currency. They would therefore be appropriate as inflation hedges for the residents of other countries only if the relevant exchange rates maintained purchasing power parity. Although the U.S. government has never issued index-linked bonds, some federally insured private savings institutions have done so.[5]

Index-linked bonds are not the only perfect inflation hedge. A forward or a futures contract on the consumer price index (CPI) can serve as well. Let us illustrate with a forward contract on the CPI. A buyer of a CPI forward contract receives compensation for inflation only if the CPI at the contract maturity date exceeds the forward price at the time the contract is entered into. Thus, for a one-year contract, the forward price might be 5% higher than the current CPI. If the CPI rises by more than 5% during the year, the buyer of the forward contract receives the difference from the seller. But if the CPI rises by less than 5%, the buyer must pay the seller the difference.

By combining such a CPI forward contract with a conventional Treasury bond, an investor can synthesize an index-linked bond. The guaranteed real rate of interest on a synthetic index-linked bond is the difference between the interest rate on the Treasury bill and the inflation rate embodied in the forward price. Thus, in our example, if the one-year Treasury bill rate is 8% and the inflation rate implied by the CPI forward contract is 5%, the real rate on the synthetic index-linked bond is 3%. A CPI futures contract works essentially the same way as a CPI forward contract. The Coffee, Sugar, and Cocoa Exchange in New York created a market for CPI futures contracts in 1985, but eventually abandoned the effort due to lack of trading volume.

CPI forward and futures contracts are symmetric in their treatment of inflation: The buyer receives money if the rate of inflation exceeds the forward rate or pays money if the rate of inflation is less than the forward rate. By contrast, an inflation insurance policy allows people to eliminate only downside inflation risk. The insured party receives money if the rate of inflation exceeds some specified rate but pays nothing otherwise. An inflation insurance policy is equivalent to a call option on the CPI.[6]

The rate of interest on U.K. index-linked bonds (the risk-free real rate) has averaged about 3% per year since they began trading in 1981. The interest rate on conventional U.K. Treasury bonds of comparable maturity (the risk-free nominal rate) has been con-

---

[5] See Zvi Bodie, "Inflation, Index-Linked Bonds, and Asset Allocation," *Journal of Portfolio Management,* Winter 1990.

[6] For a full development of this subject, see Zvi Bodie, "Inflation Insurance," *Journal of Risk and Insurance,* December 1990.

siderably greater. Although the spread between the risk-free nominal and real rates reflects a variety of tax and other features that are different for the two types of bonds, part of the spread is certainly due to inflation expectations. Finance theory suggests that for any given maturity, the spread between the nominal interest rate on a default-free nominal bond and the real rate on a default-free real bond will equal the sum of the expected rate of inflation and a risk premium. According to the capital asset pricing model, the size of this risk premium depends on the correlation between the rate of inflation and the real rate of return on the market portfolio.

Floating-Rate Bonds. Where index-linked bonds or CPI futures contracts do not exist, it is natural to consider alternatives that are imperfect inflation hedges. In contrast to CPI-linked bonds, floating-rate bonds tie interest payments to the current level of interest rates as measured by some reference rate. The reference rate of interest might be the rate on U.S. Treasury obligations of a specified maturity, LIBOR, or some other indicator of current interest rates.

If the reference rate of interest changes only because of changes in the rate of inflation, then floating-rate bonds are an effective inflation hedge. More formally, if interest rates are perfectly correlated with inflation, then floating-rate bonds are a perfect inflation hedge. Although economic theory offers some reason to believe that nominal interest rates adjust to reflect changes in expected inflation (the "Fisher effect"), that reasoning does not directly carry over to the connection between nominal interest rates and actual inflation. Empirical studies show that interest rates in many countries have been positively correlated with inflation in the past, but the correlation is far from perfect.

Common Stocks as an Inflation Hedge. When some people suggest that common stocks are a good inflation hedge, they have in mind a definition different from ours. Often what they mean is that the real rate of return on common stocks is unaffected by the rate of inflation. The reasoning behind this view is that stocks are an ownership claim over real physical capital. Real profits are either unaffected or enhanced when there is inflation, so owners of real capital should not be hurt by it. Thus, in a regression of nominal stock returns against the rate of inflation, the slope coefficient should be 1.

Even if this proposition is true, however, it does not imply that stocks can be used effectively to hedge inflation risk in our earlier sense. The slope coefficient merely determines the proportion of an inflation hedger's portfolio that should be devoted to the proposed hedge asset. Its effectiveness in reducing inflation risk is determined by its degree of correlation with inflation—the R^2 in the regression. Empirical studies show that stock returns in the United States have been negatively correlated with inflation in the past, and the degree of correlation is small.[7]

There is yet another sense in which common stocks have been said to be a good inflation hedge. Some investment advisers, in comparing stocks to bonds and other fixed-income securities, state that stocks are a good long-term inflation hedge. They claim that over a long holding period—say 20 years—stocks are very likely to offer a

[7] See Zvi Bodie, "Common Stocks as a Hedge against Inflation." *Journal of Finance,* May 1976.

higher rate of return than fixed-income securities, and are therefore especially suitable as an investment for retirement funds. Upon analysis, this proposition turns out to mean no more than that common stocks have a significantly higher expected rate of return than fixed-income securities. In investment portfolio selection, however, risk as well as expected return must be considered. Unfortunately, some of these advisers tend to understate the long-term risk of common stocks. No matter how attractive they may be in terms of expected returns, common stocks are not a completely safe asset even in the long run.

Gold, Commodities, and Real Estate. It has sometimes been suggested that investors can use gold or commodities to hedge against inflation risk. The empirical evidence, however, indicates that although price changes of gold and commodities traded on futures markets are positively correlated with consumer price changes, the degree of correlation is not very great.[8] The same is true of real estate. Thus, although they may be desirable investments because of their high expected rates of return in certain periods, they are not very effective inflation hedges in the conventional finance sense of being useful in eliminating inflation risk.

Taxes and Asset Allocation

Until this point we have completely ignored the issue of income taxes in discussing asset allocation. Of course, to the extent that you are a tax-exempt investor such as a pension fund, or if all of your investment portfolio is in a tax-sheltered account such as an individual retirement account (IRA), then taxes are irrelevant to your portfolio decisions.

But let us say that at least some of your investment income is subject to income taxes at a rate of 38.5%, the highest rate under current U.S. law. You are interested in the after-tax HPR on your portfolio. At first glance it might appear to be a simple matter to figure out what the after-tax HPRs on stocks, bonds, and cash are if you know what they are before taxes. However, there are several complicating factors.

The first is the fact that you can choose between tax-exempt and taxable bonds. We discussed this issue in Chapter 2 and concluded there that you will choose to invest in tax-exempt bonds (i.e., munis) if your personal tax rate is such that the after-tax rate of interest on taxable bonds is less than the interest rate on munis.

Because we are assuming that you are in the highest tax bracket, it is fair to assume that you will prefer to invest in munis for both the short maturities (cash) and the long maturities (bonds). As a practical matter, this means that cash for you will probably be a tax-exempt money market fund.

The second complication is not quite so easy to deal with. It arises from the fact that part of your HPR is in the form of a capital gain or loss. Under the current tax system you pay income taxes on a capital gain only if you *realize* it by selling the asset during the holding period. This applies to bonds, as well as stocks, and makes the after-tax HPR a function of whether the security will actually be sold at the end of the holding

[8] See Zvi Bodie, "Commodity Futures as an Inflation Hedge," *Journal of Portfolio Management,* Spring 1983.

period. Sophisticated investors time the realization of their sales of securities to maximize their tax advantage. This often calls for selling securities that are losing money at the end of the tax year and holding on to those that are making money.

Furthermore, because cash dividends on stocks are fully taxable and capital gains taxes can be deferred by not selling stocks that appreciate in value, the after-tax HPR on stocks will depend on the dividend payout policies of the corporations that issued the stock.

These tax complications make the process of portfolio selection for a taxable investor a lot harder than for the tax-exempt investor. There is a whole branch of the money management industry that deals with ways to defer or avoid paying taxes through special investment strategies. Unfortunately, many of these strategies contradict the principles of efficient diversification.

We will discuss these and related issues in greater detail in Chapter 28.

SUMMARY

1. When discussing the principles of portfolio management, it is useful to distinguish among seven classes of investors:

a. Individual investors and personal trusts.
b. Mutual funds.
c. Pension funds.
d. Endowment funds.
e. Life insurance companies.
f. Nonlife insurance companies.
g. Banks.

In general, these groups have somewhat different investment objectives, constraints, and portfolio policies.

2. To some extent, most institutional investors seek to match the risk-and-return characteristics of their investment portfolios to the characteristics of their liabilities.

3. The process of asset allocation consists of the following steps:

a. Specification of the asset classes to be included.
b. Specification of capital market expectations.
c. Finding the efficient portfolio frontier.
d. Determining the optimal mix.

4. People living on money-fixed incomes are vulnerable to inflation risk and may want to hedge against it. The effectiveness of an asset as an inflation hedge is related to its correlation with unanticipated inflation. Thus, a forward or futures contract on the consumer price index would be a perfect inflation hedge.

5. For investors who must pay taxes on their investment income, the process of asset allocation is complicated by the fact that they pay income taxes only on certain kinds of investment income. Interest income on munis is exempt from tax, and high-tax-bracket investors will prefer to hold them rather than short- and long-term taxable bonds. However, the really difficult part of the tax effect to deal with is the fact that capital gains are taxable only if realized through the sale of an asset during the holding period. Investment strategies designed to avoid taxes may contradict the principles of efficient diversification.

Key Terms

Risk-return trade-off
Personal trusts
Income beneficiaries
Remaindermen
Defined contribution plans
Defined benefit plans
Endowment funds
Whole-life insurance policy
Term insurance
Variable life
Universal life
Guaranteed insurance contracts
Liquidity
Investment horizon
Prudent man law

Selected Readings

For a collection of essays presenting the Institute of Chartered Financial Analysts approach to portfolio management see:

Maginn, John L.; and Donald L. Tuttle, eds. *Managing Investment Portfolios*. 2nd ed. New York: Warren, Gorham, & Lamont, 1990.

A good discussion of asset allocation in practice is:

Brinson, G. P.; J. J. Diermeier; and G. G. Schlarbaum. "A Composite Portfolio Benchmark for Pension Plans." *Financial Analysts Journal,* March–April 1986.

Problems

1. Several discussion meetings have provided the following information about one of your firm's new advisory clients, a charitable endowment fund recently created by means of a one-time $10,000,000 gift:*

Objectives

Return requirement. Planning is based on a minimum total return of 8% per year, including an initial current income component of $500,000 (5% of beginning capital). Realizing this current income target is the endowment fund's primary return goal. (See "Unique needs" following.)

Constraints

Time horizon. Perpetuity, except for requirement to make an $8,500,000 cash distribution on June 30, 1998. (See "Unique needs.")
Liquidity needs. None of a day-to-day nature until 1998. Income is distributed annually after year-end. (See "Unique needs" below.)
Tax considerations. None; this endowment fund is exempt from taxes.
Legal and regulatory considerations. Minimal, but the prudent man rule applies to all investment actions.
Unique needs, circumstances, and preferences. The endowment fund must pay out to another tax-exempt entity the sum of $8,500,000 in cash on June 30, 1998. The assets remaining after this distribution will be retained by the fund in

*Reprinted, with permission, from the Level I 1988 *CFA Study Guide*. Copyright 1988, The Institute of Chartered Financial Analysts, Charlottesville, VA. All rights reserved.

perpetuity. The endowment fund has adopted a "spending rule" requiring a first year current income payout of $500,000; thereafter the annual payout is to rise by 3% in real terms. Until 1998, annual income in excess of that required by the spending rule is to be reinvested. After 1998, the spending rate will be reset at 5% of the then-existing capital.

With this information and information found in this chapter, do the following:

a. Formulate an appropriate investment policy statement for the endowment fund.

b. Identify and briefly explain three major ways in which your firm's initial asset allocation decisions for the endowment fund will be affected by the circumstances of the account.

2. Your client says, "With the unrealized gains in my portfolio, I have almost saved enough money for my daughter to go to college in eight years, but educational costs keep going up." Based on this statement alone, which one of the following appears to be least important to your client's investment policy?*
   a. Time horizon.
   b. Purchasing power risk.
   c. Liquidity.
   d. Taxes.

3. The common stock investments of the defined contribution plan of a corporation are being managed by the trust department of a national bank. The risk of investment loss is borne by the *
   a. Pension Benefit Guarantee Corporation.
   b. Employees.
   c. Corporation.
   d. Federal Deposit Insurance Corporation.

4. The aspect least likely to be included in the portfolio management process is*
   a. Identifying an investor's objectives, constraints, and preferences.
   b. Organizing the management process itself.
   c. Implementing strategies regarding the choice of assets to be used.
   d. Monitoring market conditions, relative values, and investor circumstances.

5. Investors in high marginal tax brackets probably would be least interested in a*
   a. Portfolio of diversified stocks.
   b. Tax-free bond fund.
   c. Commodity pool.
   d. High-income bond fund.

6. Sam Short, CFA, has recently joined the investment management firm of Green, Spence, and Smith (GSS).† For several years, GSS has worked for a broad array of clients, including employee benefit plans, wealthy individuals, and charitable organizations. Also, the firm expresses expertise in managing stocks, bonds, cash reserves, real estate, venture capital, and international securities. To date,

---

*Reprinted, with permission, from the Level I 1988 *CFA Study Guide.* Copyright 1988, The Institute of Chartered Financial Analysts, Charlottesville, VA. All rights reserved.

†Reprinted, with permission, from the Level II 1988 *CFA Study Guide.* Copyright 1988, The Institute of Chartered Financial Analysts, Charlottesville, VA. All rights reserved.

the firm has not utilized a formal asset allocation process but instead has relied on the individual wishes of clients or the particular preferences of its portfolio managers. Short recommends to GSS management that a formal asset allocation process would be beneficial and emphasizes that a large part of a portfolio's ultimate return depends on asset allocation. He is asked to take his conviction an additional step by making a proposal to executive management.

a. Recommend and justify an approach to asset allocation that could be used by GSS.

b. Apply the approach to a middle-aged, wealthy individual characterized as a fairly conservative investor (sometimes referred to as a "guardian investor").

7. You are a portfolio manager and senior executive vice president of Advisory Securities Selection, Inc. Your firm has been invited to meet with the trustees of the Wood Museum Endowment Funds. Wood Museum is a privately endowed charitable institution that is dependent on the investment return from a $25 million endowment fund to balance the budget. The treasurer of the museum has recently completed the budget that indicates a need for cash flow of $3 million in 1992, $3.2 million in 1993, and $3.5 million in 1994 from the endowment fund to balance the budget in those years. At the present time the entire endowment portfolio is invested in Treasury bills and money market funds because the trustees fear a financial crisis. The trustees do not anticipate any further capital contributions to the fund.*

The trustees are all successful businesspeople, and they have been critical of the fund's previous investment advisors because they did not follow a logical decision-making process. In fact, several previous managers have been dismissed because of their inability to communicate with the trustees and the preoccupation with the fund's relative performance rather than the cash flow needs.

Advisory Securities Selection, Inc., has been contacted by the trustees because of its reputation for understanding and relating to their client's needs. The trustees have asked you, as a prospective portfolio manager for the Wood Museum Endowment Fund, to prepare a written report in response to the following questions. Your report will be circulated to the trustees before the initial interview on June 15, 1991.

Explain in detail how each of the following relates to the determination of either investor objectives or investor constraints that can be used to determine the portfolio policies for this three-year period for the Wood Museum Endowment Fund.

a. Liquidity requirements.

b. Return requirements.

c. Risk tolerance.

d. Time horizon.

e. Tax considerations.

---

*Reprinted, with permission, from the Level II 1981 *CFA Study Guide.*

f. Regulatory and legal considerations.
g. Unique needs and circumstances.

8. Mrs. Mary Atkins, age 66, has been your firm's client for five years, since the death of her husband, Dr. Charles Atkins.* Dr. Atkins had built a successful newspaper business that he sold two years before his death to Merit Enterprises, a publishing and broadcasting conglomerate, in exchange for Merit common stock. The Atkinses had no children, and their wills provide that upon their deaths the remaining assets shall be used to create a fund for the benefit of Good Samaritan Hospital, to be called the Atkins Endowment Fund.

   Good Samaritan is a 180-bed, not-for-profit hospital with an annual operating budget of $12.5 million. In the past the hospital's operating revenues have often been sufficient to meet operating expenses and occasionally even generate a small surplus. In recent years, however, rising costs and declining occupancy rates have caused Good Samaritan to run a deficit. The operating deficit has averaged $300,000 to $400,000 annually over the last several years. Existing endowment assets (i.e., excluding the Atkins' estate) of $7.5 million currently generate approximately $375,000 of annual income, up from less than $200,000 five years ago. This increased income has been the result of somewhat higher interest rates, as well as a shift in asset mix toward more bonds. To offset operating deficits, the Good Samaritan Board of Governors has determined that the endowment's current income should be increased to approximately 6% of total assets (up from 5% currently). The hospital has not received any significant additions to its endowment assets in the past five years.

   Identify and describe an appropriate set of investment objectives and constraints for the Atkins Endowment Fund to be created after Mrs. Atkins's death.

9. You have been named as investment advisor to a foundation established by Dr. Walter Jones with an original contribution consisting entirely of the common stock of Jomedco, Inc. Founded by Dr. Jones, Jomedco manufactures and markets medical devices invented by the doctor and collects royalties on other patented innovations.†

   All of the shares that made up the initial contribution to the foundation were sold at a public offering of Jomedco common stock, and the $5 million proceeds will be delivered within the next week. At the same time, Mrs. Jones will receive $5 million in proceeds from the sale of her stock in Jomedco. Dr. Jones's purpose in establishing the Jones Foundation was to "offset the effect of inflation on medical school tuition for the maximum number of worthy students."

   You are preparing for a meeting with the foundation trustees to discuss investment policy and asset allocation.

   a. Define and give examples that show the differences among an investment objective, an investment constraint, and investment policy.

---

*Reprinted, with permission, from the Level III 1985 *CFA Study Guide*. Copyright 1985, The Institute of Chartered Financial Analysts, Charlottesville, VA. All rights reserved.

†Reprinted, with permission, from the Level III 1982 *CFA Study Guide*. Copyright 1982, The Institute of Chartered Financial Analysts, Charlottesville, VA. All rights reserved.

Table 27A Capital Market Expectations: Stocks, Bonds, and Real Estate

	Stocks	Bonds	Real Estate	Cash
Expected HPR $E(r)$	14.0%	9.0%	11.0%	6%
Standard deviation σ	24.5%	14.8%	20.0%	0
Correlation Coefficients				
Stocks	1.0	−.24	0	
Bonds		1.00	0	
Real estate			1.0	

b. Identify and describe an appropriate set of investment objectives and investment constraints for the Jones Foundation.

c. Based on the investment objectives and investment constraints identified in Part (*b*), prepare a comprehensive investment policy statement for the Jones Foundation to be recommended for adoption by the trustees.

10. (Use the computer-based portfolio optimization program to do this problem.)

    Assume the set of capital market expectations regarding stocks, bonds, real estate, and cash given in Table 27A. What is the composition of the O^* portfolio, its mean, standard deviation, and the reward-to-variability ratio?*

11. John Franklin is a recent widower with some experience in investing for his own account. Following his wife's recent death and settlement of the estate, Mr. Franklin owns a controlling interest in a successful privately held manufacturing company in which Mrs. Franklin was formerly active, a recently completed warehouse property, the family residence, and his personal holdings of stocks and bonds. He has decided to retain the warehouse property as a diversifying investment but intends to sell the private company interest, giving half of the proceeds to a medical research foundation in memory of his deceased wife. Actual transfer of this gift is expected to take place about three months from now. You have been engaged to assist him with the valuations, planning, and portfolio building required to structure his investment program appropriately.

    Mr. Franklin has introduced you to the finance committee of the medical research foundation that is to receive his \$45 million cash gift three months hence (and will eventually receive the assets of his estate). This gift will greatly increase the size of the foundation's endowment (from \$10 million to \$55 million) as well as enable it to make larger grants to researchers. The foundation's grant-making (spending) policy has been to pay out virtually all of its annual net investment income. As its investment approach has been very conservative, the endowment portfolio now consists almost entirely of fixed-income assets. The finance committee understands that these actions are causing the real value

*Reprinted, with permission, from the Level III 1993 *CFA Study Guide*. Copyright 1993, Association for Investment Management and Research, Charlottesville, VA. All rights reserved.

Table 27B Capital Markets Annualized Return Data

	1926–1992 Averages	1993–2000 Consensus Forecast
U.S. Treasury bills	3.7%	4.2%
Intermediate-term U.S. T-bonds	5.2	5.8
Long-term U.S. T-bonds	4.8	7.7
U.S. corporate bonds (AAA)	5.5	8.8
Non-U.S. bonds (AAA)	N/A	8.4
U.S. common stocks (all)	10.3	9.0
U.S. common stocks (small-cap)	12.2	12.0
Non-U.S. common stocks (all)	N/A	10.1
U.S. inflation	3.1	3.5

of foundation assets and the real value of future grants to decline due to the effects of inflation. Until now, the finance committee has believed that it had no alternative to these actions, given the large immediate cash needs of the research programs being funded and the small size of the foundation's capital base. The foundation's annual grants must at least equal 5% of its assets' market value to maintain its U.S. tax-exempt status, a requirement that is expected to continue indefinitely. No additional gifts or fund-raising activities are expected over the foreseeable future.

Given the change in circumstances that Mr. Franklin's gift will make, the finance committee wishes to develop new grant-making and investment policies. Annual spending must at least meet the level of 5% of market value that is required to maintain the foundation's tax-exempt status, but the committee is unsure about how much higher than 5% it can or should be. The committee wants to pay out as much as possible because of the critical nature of the research being funded; however, it understands that preserving the real value of the foundation's assets is equally important in order to preserve its future grant-making capabilities. You have been asked to assist the committee in developing appropriate policies.

a. Identify and briefly discuss the three key elements that should determine the foundation's grant-making (spending) policy.

b. Formulate and justify an investment policy statement for the foundation, taking into account the increased size of its assets arising from Mr. Franklin's gift. Your policy statement must encompass all relevant objectives, constraints, and the key elements identified in your answer to Part (*a*) above.

c. Recommend and justify a long-term asset allocation that is consistent with the investment policy statement you created in Part (*b*) above. Explain how your allocation's expected return meets the requirements of a feasible grant-making (spending) policy for the foundation. (Your allocation must sum to 100%, and should use the economic/market data presented in Table 27B and your knowledge of historical asset-class characteristics.)

12. The foundation's grant-making and investment policy issues have been finalized. Receipt of the expected $45 million Franklin cash gift will not occur for 90 days, yet the committee believes current stock and bond prices are unusually attractive and wishes to take advantage of this perceived opportunity.*
    a. Briefly describe two strategies that utilize derivative financial instruments and could be implemented to take advantage of the committee's market expectations.
    b. Evaluate whether or not it is appropriate for the foundation to undertake a derivatives-based hedge to bridge the expected 90-day time gap, considering both positive and negative factors.

APPENDIX

Why Stocks Are Not Less Risky in the Long Run†

The conventional "wisdom" in the professional investment community seems to be that investors with a long time horizon should invest more heavily in stocks than investors with a short time horizon. The idea is that the riskiness of stocks diminishes with the length of one's time horizon, so that the risk-reward trade-off faced, for example, by a young person saving for retirement is more favorable to stocks than that faced by an older person who is already retired.[9]

The following excerpt from the Spring 1990 issue of *In The Vanguard,* a publication of The Vanguard Group (of mutual funds), is typical of the proposition and the reasoning behind it:

> Over the past six decades, stocks have achieved an average annual rate of return of 9.7%—far exceeding the 5.2% average return on corporate bonds and the 3.6% average return on U.S. Treasury bills. Yet it's no secret that the stock market is subject to wide and unpredictable price swings in any given year. Consider, however, that *the volatility of stock market returns diminishes markedly over time . . .*
>
> During any one-year period between 1960 and 1989, the maximum spread in annual returns of stocks (as measured by the unmanaged Standard and Poor's 500 Composite Stock Price Index) was 64% (from a high of 37.2% to a low of −26.5%). Over ten-year holding periods, the difference in annual rates of return decreased to 16% (17.5% to 1.2%) and, over 25 years, less than 2% (10.2% to 8.4%). Note that for ten-year periods and beyond, the returns were all positive. *Clearly, over time, stock market risk hardly seems excessive—even for the most cautious long-term investor.* So, take stock of time when investing in stocks.[10]

---

* Reprinted, with permission, from the Level III 1993 *CFA Study Guide.* Copyright 1993, Association for Investment Management and Research, Charlottesville, VA. All rights reserve

† This appendix is adapted from Z. Bodie, "On the Risk of Stocks in the Long Run," *Financial Analysts Journal,* May/June 1995.

[9] For example, a popular proposed rule is to set the portfolio proportion invested in stocks equal to 100% less one's age. Thus, a 40-year-old should invest 60% in stocks, and a 60-year-old should invest 40% in stocks.

[10] B. G. Malkiel makes virtually the same statement in *A Random Walk Down Wall Street* (New York: Norton, paperback edition 1991); p. 343. For a similar view presented in the recent academic literature, see J. F. Marshall, "The Role of the Investment Horizon in Optimal Portfolio Sequencing," *The Financial Review,* November 1994, pp. 557–76.

Robert C. Merton and Paul A. Samuelson have written numerous articles over the years showing the fallacy in such statements.[11] The proofs and counterarguments presented by Merton and Samuelson rely on the theory of expected utility maximization. In this appendix, we use option pricing theory to demonstrate the fallacy. Taking as a measure of the riskiness of an investment the cost of insuring it against earning less than the risk-free rate of return over the investor's time horizon, the appendix shows that the riskiness of stocks *increases* rather than *decreases* with the length of that horizon. This is so both under the assumption of a "random-walk" process for stock returns and for the kinds of "mean-reverting" processes that have been reported in the economics and finance literature.[12]

The appendix then briefly discusses the investment implications of this finding for individuals and for guarantors of money-fixed annuities. It shows that the case for young people investing more heavily in stocks than old people cannot rest solely on the long-run properties of stock returns. For guarantors of money-fixed annuities, the proposition that stocks in their portfolio are a better hedge the longer the maturity of their obligations is unambiguously wrong.

Measuring the Risk of Stocks

In discussions of the performance of stocks over various time horizons, a widely used concept of risk is that of a "shortfall." A shortfall occurs when the value of a stock portfolio at the horizon date is less than some value determined by a specified "target" rate of return.[13] A natural choice for this target rate of return is the rate of interest on default-free zero-coupon bonds maturing on the horizon date. Because such bonds are free of risk over the relevant time horizon, they represent a logical benchmark against which to measure the risk of stocks.

The basis for the proposition that stocks are less risky in the long run appears to be the observation that the longer the time horizon, the smaller the *probability* of a shortfall. If the *ex ante* mean rate of return on stocks exceeds the risk-free rate of interest, it is indeed true that the probability of a shortfall declines with the length of the investment time horizon. For example, suppose the rate of return on stocks is lognormally distributed with a risk premium of 8% per year and an annualized standard deviation of 20%. With a time horizon of only one year, the probability of a shortfall is 34%, whereas at 20 years that probability is only 4%.

[11] See R. C. Merton and P. A. Samuelson, "Fallacy of the Log-Normal Approximation to Portfolio Decision-Making Over Many Periods," *Journal of Financial Economics,* March 1974, pp. 67–94; and P. A. Samuelson, "Risk and Uncertainty: A Fallacy of Large Numbers," *Scientia,* April–May 1963, pp. 1–6; "The Fallacy of Maximizing the Geometric Mean in Long Sequences of Investing or Gambling," *Proceedings of the National Academy of Science,* 1971, pp. 207–11; "The Judgment of Economic Science on Rational Portfolio Management: Timing and Long-Horizon Effects," *Journal of Portfolio Management,* Fall 1989, pp. 4–12; and "The Long-Term Case for Equities and How It Can Be Oversold," *Journal of Portfolio Management,* Fall 1994, pp. 15–24.

[12] For example, see A. Lo and C. MacKinlay, "Stock Market Prices Do Not Follow Random Walks: Evidence from a Simple Specification Test," *Review of Financial Studies,* 1988, pp. 41–66.

[13] See, for example, M. L. Leibowitz and W. S. Krasker, "The Persistence of Risk: Shortfall Probabilities Over the Long Term," *Financial Analysts Journal,* November/December 1988.

But as has been shown in the literature, the probability of a shortfall is a flawed measure of risk because it completely ignores how large the potential shortfall might be.[14] It is easiest to see this point if we assume that in any one-year period, the rate of return on stocks can take only one of two values. For example, assume that the rate of return will either be +20% or −20%. Consider the worst possible outcome for time horizons of increasing length. For a one-year horizon one can lose 20% of the initial investment, for a two-year period 36%, and for a 20-year period as much as 99%. Using the probability of a shortfall as the measure of risk, no distinction is made between a loss of 20% or a loss of 99%.

The Cost of Insuring against a Shortfall

If it were true that stocks are less risky in the long run, then the cost of insuring against earning less than the risk-free rate of interest should decline as the length of the investment horizon increases. But the opposite is true.

To see this, define the cost of shortfall insurance, P, as the additional amount of money one has to add at the investment starting date to ensure that at the horizon date the portfolio will have a value at least as great as it would have earning the risk-free interest rate. Thus, for each dollar insured against a shortfall, the total amount actually invested at the starting date is $1 + P.

To find P, we use modern option pricing methodology.[15] Insurance against shortfall risk is effectively a *put* option. The put is of the European type (i.e., it can only be exercised at the expiration date), and it matures in T years. The put's exercise price is the insured value of the portfolio. If at the expiration date T years from now the portfolio's value exceeds its insured value, then the put expires worthless. If, however, there is a shortfall, then the put's payoff is equal to the shortfall.

Because we are insuring against earning less than the risk-free interest rate, the exercise price of the put equals the future value of the underlying stock portfolio compounded at the risk-free T-year interest rate. Therefore, the *put-call parity theorem* tells us that the price of the put equals the price of the corresponding call.[16]

To show that the value of the put increases with T, we could use any option pricing model based on the condition that the financial markets do not allow anyone to earn risk-free arbitrage profits.[17] Because it is so compact and so widely used in practice, we

---

[14]See W. V. Harlow, "Asset Allocation in a Downside Risk Framework," *Financial Analysts Journal,* September/October 1991, pp. 28–40.

[15] The reference here is to the option-pricing theory presented in Chapter 20 of this text.

[16] The put-call parity theorem for European options says that:

$$P + S = C + Ee^{-rT}$$

where P is the price of the put, S is the price of the underlying stock, C is the price of the corresponding call, E is the exercise price, and r is the risk-free interest rate. In our case:

$$E = Se^{rT}$$

By substituting into the put-call parity relation we get:

$$P = C$$

[17] The option price is derived by considering a dynamic investment strategy involving only the underlying stock and the risk-free asset, which has as its objective to produce at the horizon date a payoff equal to that of the put. The strategy is self-financing, that is, no additional infusions of money beyond the original P are required. As is well known in the literature, an option's price can also be expressed using a "risk-neutral" valuation method. This method makes explicit that the cost of shortfall insurance reflects a weighting of the possible shortfall magnitudes.

Table 27A.1 Cost of Shortfall Insurance as a Function of Time Horizon

Length of Time Horizon in Years	Cost per Dollar Insured (in cents)
0	0
1	7.98
5	17.72
10	24.84
20	34.54
30	41.63
50	52.08
75	61.35
100	68.27
200	84.27

Notes: The table was derived using the simplified Black-Scholes formula with $\sigma = .2$ per year. The cost of the insurance is independent of the risk-free rate.

will use the Black-Scholes formula. In our special case a simplified form of the formula can be used to compute P. Moreover, with no loss of generality, we can express the price of the put as a fraction of the price of the stock:

$$\frac{P}{S} = N(d_1) - N(d_2)$$

$$d_1 = \frac{\sigma\sqrt{T}}{2}$$

$$d_2 = \frac{-\sigma\sqrt{T}}{2}$$

where:

S = price of the stock
T = time to maturity of the option in years
σ = standard deviation of the annualized continuously compounded rate of return on the stock
$N(d)$ = the probability that a random draw from a standard normal distribution will be less than d.

Note that P/S is independent of the risk-free interest rate; it depends only on σ and T. Table 27A.1 and Figure 27A.1 show the result of applying the formula to compute P/S assuming the annualized standard deviation of stock returns (σ) is .2.[18]

The cost of the insurance rises with T. For a one-year horizon, the cost is 8% of the investment, for a 10-year horizon, it is 25%, and for a 50-year horizon it is 52%. As the length of the horizon grows without limit, the cost of the insurance approaches 100% of the investment. In other words, it can never cost more than \$1 to insure that a dollar invested in stocks will earn the risk-free rate. This is because one can always invest the \$1 insurance premium in risk-free bonds maturing in T years, so that even if the value of stocks falls to zero, the investor still will have the guaranteed minimum.

[18] An alternative procedure would be to deduct the cost of insurance from the initial investment. In that case, the insured value of the portfolio at the horizon date becomes (\$1 − P) e^{rT} instead of e^{rT}.

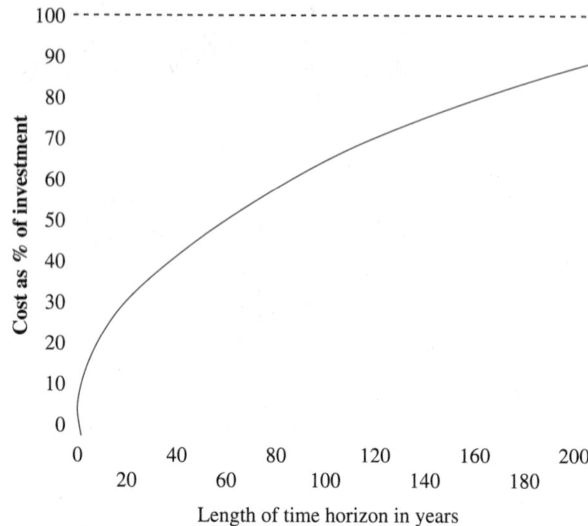

Figure 27A.1
Cost of shortfall insurance as a function of time horizon

Mean Reversion in Stock Returns Does Not Matter

Some financial economists and other observers of the stock market have claimed that stock returns do not follow a random walk in the long run. Rather, they argue, the behavior of stock returns is best characterized as a mean-reverting process.[19] It is mean reversion in stock returns, some say, that is the reason stocks are less risky for investors with a long time horizon.[20]

But our result is valid for mean-reverting processes as well. The reason is that arbitrage-based option pricing models, such as the Black-Scholes or binomial models are valid regardless of the process for the mean. They are based on the law of one price and the condition of no-arbitrage profits. Investors who disagree about the mean rate of return on stocks, but agree about the variance, will therefore agree about the option price. This is a feature of these models that may at first seem counterintuitive, but is nonetheless true.[21]

For the relation depicted in Figure 27A.1 to be invalid, mean reversion is not enough. Stock prices would have to behave just like the price of a T-period zero-coupon bond that converges toward the bond's face value as the horizon data approaches. In other words, stocks would have to be indistinguishable from the risk-free asset for a T-period horizon.

[19] See, for example, J. M. Poterba and L. Summers, "Mean Reversion in Stock Returns: Evidence and Implications," *Journal of Financial Economics,* 1988, pp. 27–60.

[20] See, for example, the footnote on page 344 of B. Malkiel, *A Random Walk Down Wall Street* (New York: Norton, 1990).

[21] Although mean reversion does not affect the Black-Scholes formula, it does affect the measured variance over the observation period. See A. Lo and J. Wang, "Implementing Option Pricing Models When Asset Returns Are Predictable," (National Bureau of Economic Research Working Paper No. 4720, 1994), for a discussion of this effect.

Investment Implications for Individuals

We have seen that despite the fact that the probability that stocks will earn less than the risk-free rate of interest *decreases* with the length of the time horizon, the cost of insuring against this eventuality *increases*. What are the investment implications of this finding? In particular, what about the popular notion that because of their longer time horizon, the young should invest more in stocks than the old?

Finance theory indicates that there is no such simple rule that applies in all cases. If investors act so as to rationally maximize the expected utility of consumption over their lifetimes, then an investor's age per se has no predictable effect on the optimal proportion to invest in stocks.[22] Asset allocation for individuals should be viewed in the broader context of deciding on an allocation of total wealth between risk-free and risky assets.

A critical determinant of optimal asset allocation for individuals is the time and risk profile of their human capital. A person faces an expected stream of labor income over the working years, and human capital is the present value of that stream. One's human capital is a large proportion of total wealth (human capital + other assets) when one is young, and eventually decreases as one ages. From this perspective, it may be optimal to start out in the early years with a higher proportion of one's investment portfolio in stocks and decrease it over time as suggested by the conventional wisdom. However, the conventional wisdom may not apply to broad classes of individuals who face substantial human-capital risk early in their careers. For such individuals, the *opposite* policy may be optimal, that is, to start out with a relatively low fraction of the investment portfolio in stocks and increase it over time.[23]

Another critical determinant of the optimal investment in stocks is how close people are to some minimum "subsistence" level of consumption. People should be expected to insure against falling below such a level through their asset allocation policy.[24]

Implications for Guarantors of Annuities

What does our finding imply about investment policy for a guarantor of money-fixed annuities, such as the Pension Benefit Guaranty Corporation (PBGC)? The pension annuities that are guaranteed by the PBGC are annuities fixed in dollar amount, and their present value is extremely sensitive to changes in long-term interest rates. At the same time, the pension fund assets securing the promised benefits are heavily invested in stocks. As guarantor of the promised pension benefits, the PBGC bears the risk of a shortfall between the value of insured benefits and the assets securing those benefits.

[22] For example, for constant relative risk aversion utility functions, the proportion of total wealth to invest is stocks in independent of the investor's age. See R. C. Merton, "Lifetime Portfolio Selection by Dynamic Stochastic Programming: The Continuous Time Case," *Review of Economics and Statistics,* August 1969; and P. A. Samuelson, "Lifetime Portfolio Selection by Dynamic Stochastic Programming," *Review of Economics and Statistics,* August 1969.

[23] For example, see Z. Bodie, R. C. Merton, and W. Samuelson, "Labor Supply Flexibility and Portfolio Choice in a Life-Cycle Model," *Journal of Economic Dynamics and Control,* 1992, pp. 427–49.

[24] For a discussion of dynamic investment strategies designed to guarantee a minimum level of consumption while preserving the upside potential of the portfolio, see F. Black and A. Perold, "Theory of Constant Proportion Portfolio Insurance," *Journal of Economic Dynamics and Control,* 1992, pp. 403–26.

Thus, the PBGC is exposed to two types of risk—interest-rate risk and stock-market risk.[25]

The magnitude of the PBGC's exposure to shortfall risk because of the mismatch between pension fund assets and liabilities appears to be not well understood.[26] It is apparently a widespread belief among policymakers that a well-diversified pension portfolio of stocks provides an effective long-run hedge against liabilities of defined-benefit pension plans, so that there is no mismatch problem.

As we have seen, this belief is mistaken. Stocks are not a hedge against fixed-income liabilities, even in the long run. Exactly the opposite is the case: When a pension plan sponsor invests the pension assets in stocks, the actuarial present value cost to the PBGC of providing a guarantee against a shortfall increases rather than decreases with the length of the time horizon, even for plans that might start out fully funded.

Stocks as a Long-Run Inflation Hedge

It is often pointed out that investing in bonds exposes the investor to inflation risk—the risk of depreciation in the purchasing power of the currency in which the bond payments are denominated. One straightforward way to address this problem is to denominate the bonds in terms of a unit of *constant* purchasing power. Indeed, the governments of the United Kingdom and more recently Australia and Canada have issued long-term bonds linked to an index of consumer prices with precisely this purpose in mind, that is, to offer investors a safe way to eliminate both interest rate risk and inflation risk over a long horizon.[27]

One sometimes gets the impression from reading popular articles on stocks as an inflation hedge that their authors view stocks as if they were long-term real bonds. But there is a very big difference between stocks and long-term real bonds. With real bonds, the investor knows that regardless of what happens to the price of the bond *prior* to its maturity date, *at* maturity it will pay its holder a known number of units of purchasing power. With stocks there is no certainty of value—real or nominal—at any date in the future.

In the academic finance literature, researchers investigating whether stocks are an inflation hedge in the long run usually hypothesize that real stock returns are unaffected by inflation in the long run. By this they mean that the real return on stocks is uncorrelated with inflation.[28] They do not mean that stocks offer a risk-free real rate of return, even in the long run.

---

[25] Under certain assumptions, it is also exposed to the risk of a rise in wages.

[26] In this respect, there are some important lessons that the PBGC can learn from the experience of the Federal Savings and Loan Insurance Corporation (FSLIC). FSLIC was the government agency that insured deposits at savings and loan associations until it was replaced in 1989, leaving a massive deficit to be financed by taxpayers. For greater detail, see Z. Bodie, "What the Pension Benefit Guaranty Corporation Can Learn from the Federal Savings and Loan Insurance Corporation" *Journal of Financial Services Research,* 10, no. 1, January 1996.

[27] For a discussion of these bonds and their use in retirement portfolios, see Z. Bodie, "Inflation, Index-Linked Bonds, and Asset Allocation," *Journal of Portfolio Management,* Winter 1990.

[28] See J. Boudoukh and M. P. Richardson, "Stock Returns and Inflation: A Long-Horizon Perspective," *American Economic Review,* December 1993.

Chapter 28

Managing Retirement Assets and Pension Funds

THE OVERRIDING CONSIDERATION IN INDIVIDUAL INVESTOR GOAL-SETTING IS ONE'S STAGE IN THE LIFE CYCLE. Most young people start their adult lives with only one asset—their earning power. In this early stage of the life cycle an individual may not have much interest in investing in stocks and bonds. The needs for liquidity and preserving safety of principal dictate a conservative policy of putting savings in a bank or a money market fund. If and when a person gets married, the purchase of life and disability insurance will be required to protect the value of human capital.

When a married couple's labor income grows to the point at which insurance and housing needs are met, the couple may start to save for their children's college education and their own retirement, especially if the government provides tax incentives for retirement savings. Retirement savings typically constitute a family's first pool of investable funds. This is money that can be invested in stocks, bonds, and real estate (other than the primary home).

This chapter focuses primarily on the institutional forms that private retirement savings can take, and how they should be invested. By far the most important institution in the retirement income system is the employer-sponsored pension plan. These plans vary in form and complexity, but they all share certain common elements in every country. In general, investment strategy depends on the type of plan.

28.1 The Life Cycle and the Risk-Return Trade-Off

Human Capital and Insurance

The first significant investment decision for most individuals concerns education, building up their human capital. The major asset most people have during their early

Table 28.1 Amount of Risk Investors Said They Were Willing to Take by Age

	Under 35	35–54	55 and Over
No risk	54%	57%	71%
A little risk	30	30	21
Some risk	14	18	8
A lot of risk	2	1	1

Source: Market Facts, Inc., Chicago, Ill.

working years is the earning power that draws on their human capital. In these circumstances, the risk of illness or injury is far greater than the risk associated with their financial wealth.

The most direct way of hedging human capital risk is to purchase insurance. Viewing the combination of your labor income and a disability insurance policy as a portfolio, the rate of return on this portfolio is less risky than the labor income by itself. Life insurance is a hedge against the complete loss of income as a result of death of any of the family's income earners.

Investment in Residence

The first major economic asset many people acquire is their own house. Deciding to buy rather than rent a residence qualifies as an investment decision.

An important consideration in assessing the risk and return aspects of this investment is the value of a house as a hedge against two kinds of risk. The first kind is the risk of increases in rental rates. If you own a house, any increase in rental rates will increase the return on your investment.

The second kind of risk is that the particular house or apartment where you live may not always be available to you. By buying, you guarantee its availability.

Saving for Retirement and the Assumption of Risk

People save and invest money to provide for future consumption and leave an estate. The primary aim of lifetime savings is to allow maintenance of the customary standard of living after retirement. Life expectancy, when one makes it to retirement at age 65, approaches 85 years, so the average retiree needs to prepare a 20-year nest egg and sufficient savings to cover unexpected health-care costs. Investment income may also increase the welfare of one's heirs, favorite charity, or both.

The leisure that investment income can be expected to produce depends on the degree of risk the household is willing to take with its investment portfolio. Empirical observation summarized in Table 28.1 indicates a person's age and stage in the life cycle affect attitude toward risk.

The evidence in Table 28.1 supports the life-cycle view of investment behavior. Questionnaires suggest that attitudes shift away from risk tolerance and toward risk aversion as investors near retirement age. With age, individuals lose the potential to recover from a disastrous investment performance. When they are young, investors can respond to a loss by working harder and saving more of their income. But as retirement approaches, investors realize there will be less time to recover. Hence the shift to safe assets.

The "right" portfolio for an individual also depends on unique circumstances. The accompanying box discusses some of these.

CONCEPT CHECK Question 1.

a. Think about the financial circumstances of your closest relative in your parents' generation (preferably your parents' household if you are fortunate enough to have them around). Write down the objectives and constraints for their investment decisions.

b. Now consider the financial situation of your closest relative who is in his or her 30s. Write down the objectives and constraints that would fit his or her investment decision.

c. How much of the difference between the two statements is due to the age of the investors?

28.2 MANAGE YOUR OWN PORTFOLIO OR RELY ON OTHERS?

Lots of people have assets such as social security benefits, pension and group insurance plans, and savings components of life insurance policies. Yet they exercise limited control, if any, on the investment decisions of these plans. The funds that secure pension and life insurance plans are managed by institutional investors.

Outside of the "forced savings" plans, however, individuals can manage their own investment portfolios. As the population grows richer, more and more people face this decision.

Managing your own portfolio *appears* to be the lowest-cost solution. Conceptually, there is little difference between managing one's own investments and professional financial planning/investment management.

Against the fees and charges that financial planners and professional investment managers impose, you will want to offset the value of your time and energy expended on diligent portfolio management. People with a suitable background may even look at investment as recreation. Most of all, you must recognize the *potential* difference in investment results.

Besides the need to deliver better-performing investments, professional managers face two added difficulties. First, getting clients to communicate their objectives and constraints requires considerable skill. This is not a one-time task because objectives and constraints are forever changing. Second, the professional needs to articulate the financial plan and keep the client abreast of outcomes. Professional management of large portfolios is complicated further by the need to set up an efficient organization where decisions can be decentralized and information properly disseminated.

The task of life-cycle financial planning is a formidable one for most people. It is not surprising that a whole industry has sprung up to provide personal financial advice.

Diversity Is More Than Stocks and Bonds

Every investor has heard about how crucial it is to diversify, but many people—even some with varied stock and bond holdings—probably don't realize how *un*diversified they really are.

"Individuals rarely take an overall view" when it comes to diversification, says Michael Lipper, who heads Lipper Analytical Services. "They think of it in terms of different chunks of money" they have invested in stocks, bonds, cash, and other assets. In reality, "securities are only one part of the total [diversification] picture—and not even the most important one at that."

Take the case of a young Wall Street executive with a mortgaged cooperative apartment in lower Manhattan. A diversified stock portfolio would actually compound, not lessen, such an individual's risk because all those "assets"—job, home, and savings—are heavily exposed to the vagaries of the stock market.

The way the professionals see it, diversification for individuals isn't driven by fancy theories about market volatility. Instead, they say, it starts with a basic grasp of personal economic risk.

At different points in an individual's investing lifetime, diversification has two roles to play, the pros say. Initially, its function is to protect the individual from being hit hard by losses in basic "assets," such as job, home, and purchasing power.

"Most people don't think of their job as their No. 1 investment," says Mr. Lipper. "But over their lifetime, it's salary, insurance, and pension benefits that will wind up setting their whole investment picture."

The second purpose of diversification is to protect against the long-term risk of "outliving one's capital" once the job ends, says Mr. Lipper. In this context, says Owen Quattlebaum, head of personal financial services at Brown Brothers Harriman & Co., diversification means "branching out into other, risky assets" such as stocks and bonds. In other words, it becomes "something genuinely defined as a way to make money," he says.

What strategies should the individual use to hedge these risks? The pros offer some advice:

Job Risk

At the end of a long economic expansion, especially in this age of corporate restructurings and increasing foreign competition, job risk—unemployment and other factors that threaten income and benefits—is relatively high. In such a hazardous environment, individuals should safeguard their option of seeking new opportunity elsewhere.

Depending on how marketable a person's skills are and how vulnerable his or her industry is, everyone should hold between three months' and a year's worth of after-tax salary in short-term cash investments, such as bank deposits and money market funds, the specialists say.

Additionally, says Mr. Lipper, an individual should hedge against the loss of 3 to 12 months of pension and other benefits—a sum usually equal to about a third of pretax salary. That money should be invested in risky assets, such as stocks and long-term bonds.

House Risk

A mortgaged home is probably the individual's major exposure to "the factors in the local area that will vibrate with the job risk and, in effect, double up the job risk," says Mr. Quattlebaum of Brown Brothers.

The risk of having to meet house payments while searching for a new job would probably be covered by the cash reserves mentioned above. However, says Mr. Lipper, people who think they might have to sell their home and move to find employment in another area should consider protecting themselves against potential losses.

Today's "short-term weakness in housing prices might entail a 10 percent to 20 percent hit to the equity in your house," compared with what it would cost to buy a comparable home in a more-vibrant area, he says. He recommends setting aside money to cover that potential shortage and buying "intermediate bonds of one to five years' maturity and roll them over—so that you get a reasonable interest rate."

Source: Barbara Donnelly, *The Wall Street Journal,* September 14, 1989.

28.3 TAX SHELTERING

In this section we explain three important tax sheltering options that can radically affect optimal asset allocation for individual investors. The first is the tax-deferral option, which arises from the fact that you do not have to pay tax on a capital gain until you choose to realize the gain. The second is tax-deferred retirement plans such as Individual Retirement Accounts, and the third is tax-deferred annuities offered by life insurance companies. Not treated here at all is the possibility of investing in the tax-exempt instruments discussed in Chapter 2.

The Tax-Deferral Option

A fundamental feature of the U.S. Internal Revenue Code is that tax on a capital gain on an asset is payable only when the asset is sold[1]; this is its **tax-deferral option.** The investor therefore can control the timing of the tax payment. From a tax perspective this option makes stocks in general preferable to fixed-income securities.

To see this, compare IBM stock with an IBM bond. Suppose both offer an expected total return of 15% this year. The stock has a dividend yield of 5% and an expected appreciation in price of 10%, whereas the bond has an interest rate of 15%. The bond investor must pay tax on the bond's interest in the year it is earned, whereas the IBM stockholder pays tax only on the dividend and defers paying tax on the capital gain until the stock is sold.

Suppose the investor is investing \$2,000 for five years and is in a 28% tax bracket. An investment in the bond will earn an after-tax return of 10.8% per year (.72 × 15%). The amount of money available after taxes at the end of five years is:

$$\$1,000 \times 1.108^5 = \$1,669.93$$

For the stock, dividend yield after taxes will be 3.6% per year (.72 × 5%). Because no taxes are paid on the capital gain until Year 5, the return before paying the capital gains tax is

$$\begin{aligned} \$1,000 \times (1 + .036 + .10)^5 &= 1,000(1.136)^5 \\ &= \$1,891.87 \end{aligned}$$

In Year 5 the capital gain is

$$\begin{aligned} \$1,891.87 - \$1,000(1.036)^5 &= 1,891.87 - 1,193.44 \\ &= \$698.43 \end{aligned}$$

Taxes due are \$195.56, leaving \$1,696.31, which is \$26.38 more than the bond investment yields. Deferral of the capital gains tax allows the investment to compound at a faster rate until the tax is actually paid.

Note that the more of one's total return that is in the form of price appreciation, the greater the value of the tax-deferral option.

[1] The only exception to this rule occurs in futures investing, where the IRS treats a gain as taxable in the year it occurs regardless of whether the investor closes his or her position.

Tax-Deferred Retirement Plans

Recent years have seen establishment of **tax-deferred retirement plans** in which investors can choose how to allocate assets. Such plans would include IRAs, Keogh plans, and employer-sponsored "tax-qualified" defined contribution plans. A feature they all have in common is that contributions and earnings are not subject to federal income tax until the individual withdraws them as benefits.

Typically, an individual may have some investment in the form of such qualified retirement accounts and some in the form of ordinary taxable accounts. The basic investment principle that applies is to hold whatever bonds you want to hold in the retirement account while holding equities in the ordinary account. You maximize the tax advantage of the retirement account by holding it in the security that is the least tax advantaged.

To see this point, consider the following example. Suppose Eloise has $200,000 of wealth, $100,000 of it in a tax-qualified retirement account. She has decided to invest half of her wealth in bonds and half in stocks, so she allocates half of her retirement account and half of her nonretirement funds to each. By doing this, Eloise is not maximizing her after-tax returns. She could reduce her tax bill with no change in before-tax returns by simply shifting her bonds into the retirement account and holding all her stocks outside the retirement account.

CONCEPT CHECK Question 2. Suppose Eloise earns a 10% per year rate of interest on bonds and 15% per year on stocks, all in the form of price appreciation. In five years she will withdraw all her funds and spend them. By how much will she increase her final accumulation if she shifts all bonds into the retirement account and holds all stocks outside the retirement account? She is in a 28% tax bracket.

Deferred Annuities

Deferred annuities are essentially tax-sheltered accounts offered by life insurance companies. They combine the same kind of deferral of taxes available on IRAs with the option of withdrawing one's funds in the form of a life annuity. Variable annuity contracts offer the additional advantage of mutual fund investing. One major difference between an IRA and a variable annuity contract is that whereas the amount one can contribute to an IRA is tax-deductible and extremely limited as to maximum amount, the amount one can contribute to a deferred annuity is unlimited, but not tax-deductible.

The defining characteristic of a life annuity is that its payments continue as long as the recipient is alive, although virtually all deferred annuity contracts have several withdrawal options, including a lump sum of cash paid out at any time. You need not worry about running out of money before you die. Like social security, therefore, life annuities offer longevity insurance and thus would seem to be an ideal asset for someone in the retirement years. Indeed, theory suggests that where there are no bequest motives, it would be optimal for people to invest heavily in actuarially fair life annuities.[2]

[2] For an elaboration of this point see Laurence J. Kotlikoff and Avia Spivak, "The Family as an Incomplete Annuities Market," *Journal of Political Economy* 89 (April 1981).

There are two types of life annuities, **fixed annuities** and **variable annuities.** A fixed annuity pays a fixed nominal sum of money per period (usually each month), whereas a variable annuity pays a periodic amount linked to the investment performance of some underlying portfolio.

In pricing annuities, insurance companies use **mortality tables** that show the probabilities that individuals of various ages will die within a year. These tables enable the insurer to compute with reasonable accuracy how many of a large number of people in a given age group will die in each future year. If it sells life annuities to a large group, the insurance company can estimate fairly accurately the amount of money it will have to pay in each future year to meet its obligations.

Variable annuities are structured so that the investment risk of the underlying asset portfolio is passed through to the recipient, much as shareholders bear the risk of a mutual fund. There are two stages in a variable annuity contract: an accumulation phase and a payout phase. During the *accumulation* phase, the investor contributes money periodically to one or more open-end mutual funds and accumulates shares. The second, or *payout,* stage usually starts at retirement, when the investor typically has several options, including the following:

1. Taking the market value of the shares in a lump sum payment.
2. Receiving a fixed annuity until death.
3. Receiving a variable amount of money each period that is computed according to a certain procedure.

This procedure is best explained by the following example. Assume that at retirement John Shortlife has $100,000 accumulated in a variable annuity contract. The initial annuity payment is determined by setting an assumed investment return (AIR), 4% per year in this example, and an assumption about mortality probabilities. In Shortlife's case we assume he will live for only three years after retirement and will receive three annual payments starting one year from now.

The benefit payment in each year, B_t, is given by the recursive formula:

$$B_t = B_{t-1} \frac{1 + R_t}{1 + \text{AIR}} \tag{28.1}$$

where R_t is the actual holding-period return on the underlying portfolio in year t. In other words, each year the amount Shortlife receives equals the previous year's benefit multiplied by a factor that reflects the actual investment return compared with the assumed investment return. In our example, if the actual return equals 4%, the factor will be one, and this year's benefits will equal last year's. If R_t is greater than 4%, the benefit will increase, and if R_t is less than 4%, the benefit will decrease.

The starting benefit is found by computing a hypothetical constant payment with a present value of $100,000 using the 4% AIR to discount future values and multiplying it by the first year's performance factor. In our example the hypothetical constant payment is $36,035.

The nearby box on page 900 summarizes the computation and shows what the payment will be in each of three years if R_t is 6%, then 2% and 4%. The last column shows the balance in the fund after each payment.

ILLUSTRATION OF A VARIABLE ANNUITY

Starting accumulation = \$100,000

R_t = Rate of return on underlying portfolio in year t

Assumed investment return (AIR) = 4% per year

B_t = Benefit received at end of year t = $B_{t-1}\,\dfrac{1 + R_t}{1 + \text{AIR}}$

B_0 = \$36,035; this is the hypothetical constant payment, which has a present value of \$100,000, using a discount rate of 4% per year

A_t = Remaining balance after B_t is withdrawn

t	R_t	B_t	Remaining balance = $A_t = A_{t-1} \times (1 + R_t) - B_t$
0			\$100,000
1	6%	\$36,728	69,272
2	2	36,022	34,635
3	4	36,022	0

This method guarantees that the initial \$100,000 will be sufficient to pay all benefits due regardless of what actual holding-period returns turn out to be. In this way the variable annuity contract passes all portfolio risk through to the annuitant.

By selecting an appropriate mix of underlying assets, such as stocks, bonds, and cash, an investor can create a stream of variable annuity payments with a wide variety of risk-return combinations. Naturally, the investor wants to select a combination on the efficient frontier, that is, a combination that offers the highest expected level of payments for any specified level of risk.[3]

CONCEPT CHECK

Question 3. Assume Victor is now 75 years old and is expected to live until age 80. He has \$100,000 in a variable annuity account. If the assumed investment return is 4% per year, what is the initial annuity payment? Suppose the annuity's asset base is the S&P 500 equity portfolio and its holding-period return for the next five years is each of the following: 4%, 10%, −8%, 25%, and 0. How much would Victor receive each year? Verify that the insurance company would wind up using exactly \$100,000 to fund Victor's benefits.

[3] For an elaboration on possible combinations see Zvi Bodie, "An Innovation for Stable Real Retirement Income," *Journal of Portfolio Management,* Fall 1980; and Zvi Bodie and James E. Pesando, "Retirement Annuity Design in an Inflationary Climate," Chap. 11 in Zvi Bodie and J. B. Shoven, *Financial Aspects of The United States Pension System* (Chicago: University of Chicago Press, 1983).

Variable and Universal Life Insurance

Variable life insurance is another tax-deferred investment vehicle offered by the life insurance industry. A variable life insurance policy combines life insurance with the tax-deferred annuities described earlier.

To invest in this product, you pay either a single premium or a series of premiums. In each case there is a stated death benefit, and the policyholder can allocate the money invested to several portfolios, which generally include a money market fund, a bond fund, and at least one common stock fund. The allocation can be changed at any time.

A variable life policy has a cash surrender value equal to the investment base minus any surrender charges. Typically, there is a surrender charge (about 6% of the purchase payments) if you surrender the policy during the first several years, but not thereafter. At policy surrender income taxes become due on all investment gains.

Variable life insurance policies offer a death benefit that is the greater of the stated face value or the market value of the investment base. In other words, the death benefit may rise with favorable investment performance, but it will not go below the guaranteed face value. Furthermore, the surviving beneficiary is not subject to income tax on the death benefit.

The policyholder can choose from a number of income options to convert the policy into a stream of income, either on surrender of the contract or as a partial withdrawal. In all cases income taxes are payable on the part of any distribution representing investment gains.

The insured can gain access to the investment without having to pay income tax by borrowing against the cash surrender value. Policy loans of up to 90% of the cash value are available at any time at a contractually specified interest rate.

A universal life insurance policy is similar to a variable life policy except that, instead of having a choice of portfolios to invest in, the policyholder earns a rate of interest that is set by the insurance company and changed periodically as market conditions change. The disadvantage of universal life insurance is that the company controls the rate of return to the policyholder, and, although companies may change the rate in response to competitive pressures, changes are not automatic. Different companies offer different rates, so it often pays to shop around for the best.

Since the passage of the Tax Reform Act of 1986, the investment products offered by the life insurance industry—tax-deferred annuities and variable and universal life insurance—are among the most attractive of the remaining tax-advantaged opportunities.

Growth versus Income

There is a strong tendency in the popular investments literature to talk as if the investor must use only dividend and interest income for current consumption spending and reserve appreciation in security prices (i.e., growth) for future spending. The only sensible justification behind such a policy would be the existence of significant transaction costs for selling securities, because in fact expenses can be met by selling securities just as easily as by collecting and dispensing the cash from dividends or interest.

For example, suppose you have $100,000 in assets and expect to spend $8,000 this year. You are trying to decide between two mutual funds that have the same expected return and risk. Income Fund offers an expected dividend yield of 8% and zero expected capital gains, while Growth Fund offers a dividend yield of 5% and expected capital gains of 3%. You can meet your planned $8,000 current expenditure in two ways:

	Invest in Income Fund	Invest in Growth Fund
Expected rate of return	8%	8%
Dividends	$8,000	$5,000
Sale of shares	0	$3,000
TOTAL	$8,000	$8,000
Portfolio Value		
Before sale of shares	$100,000	$103,000
Sale of shares	0	−$3,000
End-of-year value	$100,000	$100,000

Note that in both cases the $8,000 for current spending is derived from portfolio returns and the end-of-year portfolio is worth the same $100,000. Whether the $8,000 comes from dividends or capital gains is irrelevant.

The classification of stocks into income versus growth stocks really represents an implicit assessment about risk. Mutual funds termed "income funds" tend to have lower risk and lower expected returns than so-called growth funds. The choice between income and growth funds really should be viewed in terms of the risk-return trade-off. The purpose to which investment returns will be applied is irrelevant.

28.4 Pension Funds

Pension plans are defined by the terms specifying the "who," "when," and "how much," for both the plan benefits and the plan contributions used to pay for those benefits. The *pension fund* of the plan is the cumulation of assets created from contributions and the investment earnings on those contributions, less any payments of benefits from the fund. In the United States, contributions to the fund by either employer or employee are tax-deductible, and investment income of the fund is not taxed. Distributions from the fund, whether to the employer or the employee, are taxed as ordinary income. There are two "pure" types of pension plans: *defined contribution* and *defined benefit.*

Defined-Contribution Plans

In a defined-contribution plan, a formula specifies contributions but not benefit payments. Contribution rules usually are specified as a predetermined fraction of salary (e.g., the employer contributes 15% of the employee's annual wages to the plan), although that fraction need not be constant over the course of an employee's career. The pension fund consists of a set of individual investment accounts, one for each employee. Pension benefits are not specified, other than that at retirement the employee applies that total accumulated value of contributions and earnings on those contributions to purchase an annuity. The employee often has some choice over both the level of contributions and the way the account is invested.

In principle, contributions could be invested in any security, although in practice most plans limit investment choices to bond, stock, and money market funds. The employee bears all the investment risk; the retirement account is, by definition, fully funded by the contributions, and the employer has no legal obligation beyond making its periodic contributions.

For defined-contribution plans, investment policy is essentially the same as for a tax-qualified individual retirement account. Indeed, the main providers of investment products for these plans are the same institutions such as mutual funds and insurance companies that serve the general investment needs of individuals. Therefore, in a defined-contribution plan much of the task of setting and achieving the income-replacement goal falls on the employee.

Defined-Benefit Plans

In a defined-benefit plan, a formula specifies benefits, but not the manner, including contributions, in which these benefits are funded. The benefit formula typically takes into account years of service for the employer and level of wages or salary (e.g., the employer pays the employee for life, beginning at age 65, a yearly amount equal to 1% of his final annual wage for each year of service.) The employer (called the "plan sponsor") or an insurance company hired by the sponsor guarantees the benefits and thus absorbs the investment risk. The obligation of the plan sponsor to pay the promised benefits is like a long-term debt liability of the employer.

As measured both by number of plan participants and the value of total pension liabilities, the defined-benefit form dominates in most countries around the world. This is so in the United States, although the trend since the mid-1970s is for sponsors to choose the defined-contribution form when starting new plans. But the two plan types are not mutually exclusive. Many sponsors adopt defined-benefit plans as their primary plan, in which participation is mandatory, and supplement them with voluntary defined-contribution plans.

With defined-benefit plans, there is an important distinction between the pension *plan* and the pension *fund*. The plan is the contractual arrangement setting out the rights and obligations of all parties; the fund is a separate pool of assets set aside to provide collateral for the promised benefits. In defined-contribution plans, by definition, the value of the benefits equals that of the assets, so the plan is always fully funded. But in defined-benefit plans, there is a continuum of possibilities. There may be no separate fund, in which case the plan is said to be unfunded. When there is a separate fund with assets worth less than the present value of the promised benefits, the plan is underfunded. And if the plan's assets have a market value that exceeds the present value of the plan's liabilities, it is said to be overfunded.

Alternative Perspectives on Defined-Benefit Pension Obligations

As previously described, in a defined-benefit plan, the pension benefit is determined by a formula that takes into account the employee's history of service and wages or salary. The plan sponsor provides this benefit regardless of the investment performance of the pension fund assets. The annuity promised to the employee is therefore the employer's liability. What is the nature of this liability?

Private-sector defined-benefit pension plans in the United States offer an *explicit* benefit determined by the plan's benefit formula. However, many plan sponsors have from time to time provided voluntary increases in benefits to their retired employees, depending on the financial condition of the sponsor and the increase in the living costs of retirees. Some observers have interpreted such increases as evidence of *implicit* cost-of-living indexation. These voluntary ad hoc benefit increases, however, are very different from a formal COLA (cost-of-living adjustment). It is unambiguous that under current laws in the United States, the plan sponsor is under no legal obligation to pay more than the amount promised explicitly under the plan's benefit formula.

There is a widespread belief that in final-pay formula plans, pension benefits are protected against inflation at least up to the date of retirement. But this is a misperception. Unlike social security benefits, whose starting value is indexed to a general index of wages, pension benefits even in final-pay private-sector plans are "indexed" only to the extent that (1) the employee continues to work for the same employer, (2) the employee's own wage or salary keeps pace with the general index, and (3) the employer continues to maintain the same plan. Very few private corporations in the United States offer pension benefits that are automatically indexed for inflation. This lack of inflation indexation gives rise to the portability problem. Workers who change jobs wind up with lower pension benefits at retirement than otherwise identical workers who stay with the same employer, even if the employers have defined-benefit plans with the same final-pay benefit formula.

Both the rule-making body of the accounting profession (the Financial Accounting Standards Board) and Congress have adopted the present value of the nominal benefits as the appropriate measure of a sponsor's pension liability. FASB Statement 87 specifies that the measure of corporate pension liabilities to be used on the corporate balance sheet in external reports is the accumulated benefit obligation (ABO)—that is, the present value of pension benefits owed to employees under the plan's benefit formula absent any salary projections and discounted at a nominal rate of interest. Similarly, in its Omnibus Budget Reconciliation Act (OBRA) of 1987, Congress defined the current liability as the measure of a corporation's pension liability and set limits on the amount of tax-qualified contributions a corporation could make as a proportion of the current liability. OBRA's definition of the current liability is essentially the same as FASB Statement 87's definition of the ABO.

The ABO is thus a key element in a pension fund's investment strategy. It not only affects a corporation's reported balance sheet liabilities, it also reflects economic reality.

Statement 87, however, recognizes an additional measure of a defined-benefit plan's liability: the projected benefit obligation (PBO). The PBO is a measure of the sponsor's pension liability that includes projected increases in salary up to the expected age of retirement. Statement 87 requires corporations to use the PBO in computing pension expense reported in their income statements. This is perhaps useful for financial analysts, in that the amount may help them to derive an appropriate estimate of expected future labor costs for discounted cash flow valuation models of the firm as a going concern. The PBO is not, however, an appropriate measure of the benefits that the employer has explicitly guaranteed. The difference between the PBO and the ABO should not be treated as a liability of the firm, because these additional pension costs will only be realized if the employees continue to work in the future. If these future contingent labor costs are to be treated as a liability of the firm, then why not book the entire future wage bill as a liability? If this is done, then shouldn't one add as an asset the present value of future revenues generated by these labor activities? It is indeed difficult to see either the accounting or economic logic for using the PBO as a measure of pension liabilities.

The PBO would be the correct number to use for the firm's liability if benefits were tied to some index of wages up to the age of retirement, independently of whether the employee stays with the employer. Because private plans in the United States do not offer such automatic indexation, however, it is a mistake to use the PBO as the measure of what the sponsor is contractually obliged to pay to employees.[4] Hence, it may not be an appropriate target for the pension fund to hedge in its investment strategy.

CONCEPT CHECK

Question 4. An employee is 40 years old and has been working for the firm for 15 years. If normal retirement age is 65, the interest rate is 8%, and the employee's life expectancy is 80, what is the present value of the accrued pension benefit?

Pension Investment Strategies

The special tax status of pension funds creates the same incentive for both defined-contribution and defined-benefit plans to tilt their asset mix towards assets with the largest spread between pretax and after-tax rates of return. In a defined-contribution plan, because the participant bears all of the investment risk, the optimal asset mix also depends on the risk tolerance of the participant.

In defined-benefit plans, optimal investment policy may be different because the sponsor absorbs the investment risk. If the sponsor has to share some of the upside potential of the pension assets with plan participants, there is an incentive to eliminate all investment risk by investing in securities that match the promised benefits. If, for example, the plan sponsor has to pay $100 per year for the next five years, it can provide this stream of benefit payments by buying a set of five zero-coupon bonds each with a face value of $100 and maturing sequentially. By so doing, the sponsor eliminates the risk of a shortfall. This is called **immunization** of the pension liability.

If a corporate pension fund has an ABO that exceeds the market value of its assets, FASB Statement 87 requires that the corporation recognize the unfunded liability on its

[4] In contrast to the situation in the United States, current law in the United Kingdom requires pension sponsors to index accrued pension benefits for inflation to the age of retirement, subject to a cap of 5% per year. Thus, even a terminated employee has indexation for general inflation up to retirement age, as long as the benefit is vested. Therefore, under the UK system, the PBO is the appropriate measure of the sponsor's liability.

balance sheet. If, however, the pension assets exceed the ABO, the corporation cannot include the surplus on its balance sheet. This asymmetric accounting treatment expresses a deeply held view about defined-benefit pension funds. Representatives of organized labor, some politicians, and even a few pension professionals believe that, as guarantor of the accumulated pension benefits, the sponsoring corporation is liable for pension asset shortfalls but does not have a clear right to the entire surplus in case of pension overfunding.

If the pension fund is overfunded, then a 100% fixed-income portfolio is no longer required to minimize the cost of the corporate pension guarantee. Management can invest surplus pension assets in equities, provided it reduces the proportion so invested when the market value of pension assets comes close to the value of the ABO. Such an investment strategy is a type of portfolio insurance known as *contingent immunization.*

To understand how contingent immunization works, consider a simple version of it that makes use of a stop-loss order. Imagine that the ABO is $100 and that the fund has $120 of assets entirely invested in equities. The fund can protect itself against downside risk by maintaining a stop-loss order on all its equities at a price of $100. This means that should the price of the stocks fall to $100, the fund manager would liquidate all the stocks and immunize the ABO. A stop-loss order at $100 is not a perfect hedge because there is no guarantee that the sell order can be executed at a price of $100. The result of a series of stop-loss orders at prices starting well above $100 is even better protection against downside risk.

Investing in Equities. If the only goal guiding corporate pension policy were shareholder wealth maximization, it is hard to understand why a financially sound pension sponsor would invest in equities at all. A policy of 100% bond investment would minimize the cost of guaranteeing the defined benefits.

In addition to the reasons given for a fully funded pension plan to invest only in fixed-income securities, there is a tax reason for doing so too. The tax advantage of a pension fund stems from the ability of the sponsor to earn the pretax interest rate on pension investments. To maximize the value of this tax shelter, it is necessary to invest entirely in assets offering the highest pretax interest rate. Because capital gains on stocks can be deferred and dividends are taxed at a much lower rate than interest on bonds, corporate pension funds should invest entirely in taxable bonds and other fixed-income investments.

Yet we know that in general pension funds invest from 40% to 60% of their portfolios in equity securities. Even a casual perusal of the practitioner literature suggests that they do so for a variety of reasons—some right and some wrong. There are three possible correct reasons.

The first is that corporate management views the pension plan as a trust for the employees and manages fund assets as if it were a defined contribution plan. It believes that a successful policy of investment in equities might allow it to pay extra benefits to employees and is therefore worth taking the risk. As explained before, if the plan is overfunded, then the sponsor can invest in stocks and still minimize the cost of providing the benefit guarantee by pursuing a contingent immunization strategy.

The second possible correct reason is that management believes that through superior market timing and security selection it is possible to create value in excess of management fees and expenses. Many executives in nonfinancial corporations are used to creating value in excess of cost in their businesses. They assume that it can also be done in the area of portfolio management. Of course, if that is true then one must ask why they do not do it on their corporate account rather than in the pension fund. That way they could have their tax shelter "cake" and eat it too. It is important to realize, however, that to accomplish this feat, the plan must beat the market, not merely match it.

Note that a very weak form of the efficient markets hypothesis would imply that management cannot create shareholder value simply by shifting the pension portfolio out of bonds and into stocks. Even when the entire pension surplus belongs to the shareholders, investing in stocks just moves the shareholders along the capital market line (the market trade-off between risk and return for passive investors) and does not create value. When the net cost of providing plan beneficiaries with shortfall risk insurance is taken into account, increasing the pension fund equity exposure reduces shareholder value unless the equity investment can put the firm above the capital market line. This implies that it only makes sense for a pension fund to invest in equities *if* it intends to pursue an active strategy of beating the market either through superior timing or security selection. A completely passive strategy will add no value to shareholders.

For an underfunded plan of a corporation in financial distress there is another possible reason for investing in stocks and other risky assets—federal pension insurance. Firms in financial distress have an incentive to invest pension fund money in the riskiest assets, just as troubled thrift institutions insured by the Federal Savings and Loan Insurance Corporation (FSLIC) had similar motivation with respect to their loan portfolios.

Wrong Reasons to Invest in Equities. The wrong reasons for a pension fund to invest in equities stem from several interrelated fallacies. The first is the notion that stocks are not risky in the long run. This fallacy was discussed at length in an appendix to Chapter 27. Another related fallacy is the notion that stocks are a hedge against inflation. The reasoning behind this fallacy is that stocks are an ownership claim over real physical capital. Real profits are either unaffected or enhanced when there is unanticipated inflation, so owners of real capital should not be hurt by it.

Let us assume that this proposition is true, and that the real rate of return on stocks is uncorrelated or slightly positively correlated with inflation. If stocks are to be a good hedge against inflation risk in the conventional sense, however, the nominal return on stocks has to be *highly* positively correlated with inflation.

To see this, suppose that the benefit the sponsor is obliged to pay is indexed for inflation. The way to immunize an inflation-protected pension obligation is with zero-coupon bonds linked to the price index, not by investing in an equity portfolio. Although stocks may be free of inflation risk, they are not free of stock market risk.

Alternatively, suppose that you are a pensioner living on a money-fixed pension and therefore concerned about inflation risk. You could eliminate this risk to your real income stream by hedging with CPI-linked bonds. You might want to invest some of your money in stocks to increase your expected return, but by doing so you increase your exposure to market risk. There is no way to use stocks to reduce your risk in any significant way.

To have any valid economic content, the proposition that stocks are a good inflation hedge can mean only that nominal stock returns tend to rise and fall in proportion to changes in the rate of inflation. Even if this were true, the explanatory power of the relation (R^2) would have to be high for stocks to be useful as a vehicle for hedging against inflation risk. Empirical studies show that stock returns have been negatively correlated with inflation in the past with a low R^2. Thus, even in the best of circumstances, stocks can offer only a limited hedge against inflation risk.

SUMMARY

1. The life-cycle approach to the management of an individual's investment portfolio views the individual as passing through a series of stages, becoming more risk averse in later years. The rationale underlying this approach is that as we age, we use up our human capital and have less time remaining to recoup possible portfolio losses through increased labor supply.

2. People buy life and disability insurance during their prime earning years to hedge against the risk associated with loss of their human capital, that is, their future earning power.

3. There are three ways to shelter investment income from federal income taxes besides investing in tax-exempt bonds. The first is by investing in assets whose returns take the form of appreciation in value, such as common stocks or real estate. As long as capital gains taxes are not paid until the asset is sold, the tax can be deferred indefinitely.

The second way of tax sheltering is through investing in tax-deferred retirement plans such as IRAs. The general investment rule is to hold the least tax-advantaged assets in the plan and the most tax-advantaged assets outside of it.

The third way of sheltering is to invest in the tax-advantaged products offered by the life insurance industry—tax-deferred annuities and variable and universal life insurance. They combine the flexibility of mutual fund investing with the tax advantages of tax deferral.

4. Distinguishing between income and growth in investment returns is justified only to the extent that transaction costs of selling assets are significant.

5. Pension plans are either defined-contribution plans or defined-benefit plans. Defined-contribution plans are in effect retirement funds held in trust for the employee by the employer. The employees in such plans bear all the risk of the plan's assets and often have some choice in the allocation of those assets. Defined-benefit plans give the employees a claim to a money-fixed annuity at retirement. The annuity level is determined by a formula that takes into account years of service and the employee's wage or salary history.

6. If the only goal guiding corporate pension policy were shareholder wealth maximization, it is hard to understand why a financially sound pension sponsor would invest in equities at all. A policy of 100% bond investment would both maximize the tax advantage of funding the pension plan and minimize the costs of guaranteeing the defined benefits.

7. If sponsors viewed their pension liabilities as indexed for inflation, then the appropriate way for them to minimize the cost of providing benefit guarantees would be to hedge using securities whose returns are highly correlated with inflation.

Common stocks would not be an appropriate hedge because they have a low correlation with inflation.

Key Terms

Tax-deferred option
Tax-deferred retirement plans
Deferred annuities
Fixed annuities
Variable annuities
Mortality tables
Immunization

Selected Readings

For a further discussion of the theory and evidence regarding the investment policies of corporate defined-benefit pension plans see:

Bodie, Z.; J. Light; R. Morck; and R. A. Taggart. "Corporate Pension Policy: An Empirical Investigation." *Financial Analysts Journal* 41, no. 5 (September/October 1985).

Bodie, Z. "Managing Pension and Retirement Assets: An International Perspective." *Journal of Financial Services Research,* December 1990.

Problems

1. Your neighbor has heard that you have just successfully completed a course in investments and has come to seek your advice. She and her husband are both 50 years old. They have just finished making their last payments for their condominium and their children's college education and are planning for retirement. What advice on investing their retirement savings would you give them? If they are very risk averse, what would you advise?

2. C. B. Snow, deceased president of Highway Cartage Company, left a net estate of $300,000 in the late 1970s. Under his will, a trust of $300,000 was created for his surviving spouse, with Peninsular Trust Company named trustee. A daughter is the remainderman of her mother's trust. The widow's trust is composed of the following assets:*

	Proportion of Portfolio	Amount at Market	Current Yield (%)
Money market fund	25%	$ 75,000	14.7
Tax-exempt municipal bonds	35%	105,000	8.0*
Highway Cartage Co. common stock	40%	120,000	7.9
	100%	$300,000	

*Yield to maturity equals 12.0%

As a portfolio manager with Peninsular, you have just attended a meeting with the widow and learned the following:

She is 65 and in good health (mortality tables indicate an expected life span of 18 years). As a retirement benefit, she is eligible for Highway's generous group medical insurance plan for the remainder of her life.

Her estimated household and other expenses last year, adjusted to allow for inflation this year, are $19,600. In the absence of her husband's salary, her tax bracket will decline substantially to 30%. Next week she will be eligible to receive social security payments of $600 per month. (See the note at the end of this question on the taxation of social security benefits.)

She plans to purchase a $60,000 condominium as a vacation residence within the next six months, using $15,000 in deferred compensation (after taxes) due her husband as a down payment. Conventional mortgage financing is available for 75% of the cost at 17.5% for 30 years. She anticipates that any tax savings from the credit for mortgage interest payments will be consumed by maintenance fees charged to the owner. She also intends to join an adjacent golf club where the dues are $125 per month.

She wishes to retain all of the Highway common stock because, "It's the only stock C.B. ever owned and he had such great confidence in the company's future. Also, the yield is very generous, I think, despite the dividend reduction last year when the economy sagged."

At the conclusion of the meeting, Mrs. Snow requested that the assets in her trust be left intact, if possible. Mrs. Snow is cotrustee of her trust and can veto any of your recommendations.

a. Calculate Mrs. Snow's income sources and expenses, assuming her request is honored, and state whether her income requirements can be met.

b. Identify and discuss the investment objectives and constraints that appear applicable to Mrs. Snow's situation.

c. Recommend and justify changes in her present trust portfolio that are consistent with the objectives and constraints in Part (*b*). (Use the information in Table 28A.)

Note on the taxation of social security benefits:

If the sum of all income (including interest on municipal bonds) plus one-half of social security benefits is greater than $32,000 (for the couple filing jointly; $25,000 for an individual) then either one-half of the social security benefit or the excess of total income over $32,000 is taxable as ordinary income.

3. George More is a participant in a defined-contribution pension plan that offers a fixed-income fund and a common stock fund as investment choices. He is 40 years old and has an accumulation of $100,000 in each of the funds. He currently contributes $1,500 per year to each. He plans to retire at age 65, and his life expectancy is age 80.

   a. Assuming a 3% per year real earnings rate for the fixed-income fund and 6% per year for common stocks, what will be George's expected accumulation in each account at age 65?

   b. What will be the expected real retirement annuity from each account, assuming these same real earnings rates?

   c. If George wanted a retirement annuity of $30,000 per year from the fixed-income fund, by how much would he have to increase his annual contributions?

4. A firm has a defined-benefit pension plan that pays an annual retirement benefit of 1.5% of final salary per year of service. Joe Loyal is 60 years old and has

Table 28A Market Data

Category	Beta Coefficient	Implied Total Return	Current Yield
Fixed-Income Securities			
Money market funds			14.7%
Government bonds:			
Intermediate term			14.4
Long term			14.0
Corporate bonds (A-rated):			
Intermediate term			15.1
Long term			16.0
Tax-exempt municipals:			
Intermediate term			10.2
Long term			11.1
Common Stocks			
Industrials	1.0	17.0%	5.2%
Trucking	1.1	14.8	4.0
Highway Cartage Co.	1.3	14.8	7.9
Consumer Price Index (Average Annual Index)			
8.9% projected current year	8.0% projected next year	5%–15% range next 5 years	7%–10% most probable next 5 years

been working for the firm for the last 35 years. His current salary is $40,000 per year.

a. If normal retirement age is 65, the interest rate is 8%, and Joe's life expectancy is 80, what is the present value of his accrued pension benefit?

b. If Joe wanted to retire now, what would be an actuarially fair annual pension benefit? (Assume the first payment would be made one year from now.)

5. John Oliver, formerly a senior partner of a large management consulting firm, has been elected president of Mid-South Trucking Company.* He has contacted you, a portfolio manager for a large investment advisory firm, to discuss the company's defined-benefit pension plan. Upon assuming his duties, Oliver learned that Mid-South's pension plan was 100% in bonds, with a maximum maturity of 10 years. He believes that "a pension plan should be managed so as to maximize return within well-defined risk parameters," and "anyone can buy bonds and sit on them." Mr. Oliver has suggested that he meet with you, as an objective advisor, and the plan's actuary to discuss possible changes in plan asset mix. To aid you in preparing for the meeting, Mr. Oliver has provided the current portfolio (Table 28B). He also has provided the following information about the company and its pension plan.

*Reprinted, with permission, from the Level II 1987 *CFA Study Guide*.

Table 28B Current Portfolio

	Cost	Market Value	Current Yield	Yield to Maturity
Short-term reserves	$10,000,000	$ 10,000,000	5.8%	5.8%
Notes, 90 days to 1 year	25,000,000	25,500,000	6.5	6.4
Notes, 1 to 5 years	110,000,000	115,000,000	8.0	7.8
Bonds, 5 to 10 years	115,000,000	127,500,000	8.8	8.5
TOTAL	$260,000,000	$278,000,000	8.1%	7.9%

Company. Mid-South is the eighth largest domestic trucking company, with annual revenues of $500 million. Revenues have grown about 8% per year over the past five years, with one down year. The company employs about 7,000 people, compared with 6,500 five years ago. The annual payroll is about $300 million. The average age of the work force is 43 years. Company profits last year were $20 million, compared with $12 million five years ago.

Pension Plan. Mid-South's pension plan is a defined-benefit plan that was established in 1965. The company annually contributes 7% of payroll to fund the plan. During the past five years portfolio income has been used to meet payments for retirees, while company contributions have been available for investment. Although the plan is adequately funded on a current basis, unfunded past service liabilities are equal to 40% of plan assets. The liability is to be funded over the next 35 years. Plan assets are valued annually on a rolling four-year average for actuarial purposes.

Whereas FASB No. 87 requires an annual reassessment of the assumed rate of return, for purposes of this analysis Mid-South's management, in consultation with the actuary, has decided to use an assumed annual rate of 7%. This compares with actual plan results that have averaged 10% per year over the past 20 years. Wages and salaries are assumed to increase 5% per year, identical with past company experience.

Before the meeting, you review your firm's investment projections, dated March 31, 1987. Your firm believes that continued prosperity is the most likely outlook for the next three to five years but has allowed for two alternatives: first, a return to high inflation; or second, a move into deflation/depression. The details of the projections are shown in Table 28C.

a. Based on this information, create an investment policy statement for the Mid-South Trucking Company's pension plan. Based on your policy statement and the expectations shown recommend an appropriate asset allocation strategy for Mid-South Trucking Company's pension plan limited to the same asset classes shown. Justify your changes, if any, from the current portfolio. Your allocation must sum to 100%.

b. At the meeting the actuary suggests that Mid-South consider terminating the defined-benefit plan, purchasing annuities for retirees and vested employees

Table 28C Investment Projections

Scenarios	Expected Annual Total Return (%)
Continued Prosperity (60% probability)	
Short-term reserves (Treasury bills)	6.0
Stocks (S&P 500 index)	12.0
Bonds (S&P high-grade bond index)	8.0
High-Inflation Scenario (25% Probability)	
Short-term reserves (Treasury bills)	10.0
Stocks (S&P 500 index)	15.0
Bonds (S&P high-grade bond index)	3.0
Deflation/Depression Scenario (15% Probability)	
Short-term reserves (Treasury bills)	2.0
Stocks (S&P 500 index)	−6.0
Bonds (S&P high-grade bond index)	12.0

with the proceeds, and establishing a defined-contribution plan. The company would continue to contribute 7% of payroll to the defined-contribution plan.

Compare the key features of a defined-benefit plan and a defined-contribution plan. Assuming Mid-South were to adopt and retain responsibility for a defined-contribution plan, briefly explain any revisions to your asset allocation strategy developed in Part (*a*) above. Again, your allocation must sum to 100% and be limited to the same asset classes shown.

6. You are Mr. R. J. Certain, a retired C.F.A., who formerly was the chief investment officer of a major investment management organization. Although you have over 30 years of experience in the investment business, you have kept up with the literature and developed a reputation for your knowledge and ability to blend modern portfolio theory and traditional portfolio methods.*

The chairman of the board of Morgan Industries has asked you to serve as a consultant to him and the other members of the board of trustees of the company's pension fund. Because you are interested in developing a consulting practice and in keeping actively involved in the investment management business, you welcome the opportunity to develop a portfolio management decision-making process for Morgan Industries that you could apply to all types of investment portfolios.

Morgan Industries is a company in transition. Its long-established business, dating back to the early years of the century, is the production of steel. Since the 1960s, however, Morgan has gradually built a highly profitable stake in the domestic production of oil and gas.

*Reprinted, with permission, from the Level III 1983 *CFA Study Guide*.

Most of the company's 1982 sales of $4 billion were still derived from steel operations. Because Morgan occupies a relatively stable niche in a specialized segment of the steel industry, its losses on steel during the 1982 recession were moderate compared to industry experience. At the same time, profit margins for Morgan's oil and gas business remained satisfactory despite all the problems in the world oil market. This segment of the company's operations accounted for the entire 1982 net profit of $150 million. Even when steel operations recover, oil and gas operations are expected to contribute, on average, over half of Morgan's annual profits.

Based on the combination of the two segments of the company's operations, the overall cyclicality of company earnings appears to be approximately the same as that of the S&P 500. Several sell-regarded security analysts, citing the outlook for recovery in steel operations, as well as further gains in the oil and gas production, project earnings progress for Morgan over the next five years at about the same rate as for the S&P 500. Debt comprises about 35% of the long-term capital structure, and the beta (market risk) for the company's common stock is also about the same as for the S&P 500.

Morgan's defined-benefit pension plan covers 25,000 active employees, vested and unvested, and 15,000 retired employees, with the latter projected to exceed 20,000 in five years. The burden of pension liabilities is large because the steel industry has long been labor intensive and the company's current labor force in this area of operations is not as large as it was some years ago. The oil and gas operations, although growing at a significant rate, account for only 10% of the active plan participants and for even less of the retired beneficiaries.

Pension assets amounted to $1 billion of market value at the end of 1982. For the purpose of planning investment policy, the present value of the unfunded pension liability is calculated at $500 million. Although the company's outstanding debt is $600 million, it is clear that the unfunded pension liability adds significantly to the leverage in the capital structure.

Pension expenses charged to company income—and reflected in company contributions to the pension trust—were $80 million in 1982. The level of expenses, which are projected to rise with payroll, reflects current assumptions concerning inflation, the rate of return on pension assets, wage and salary increases, and benefits changes. If these assumptions were to prove completely correct, the current method of funding would amortize the unfunded pension liability over 20 years. Because assumptions are subject to change in the light of new information, they must be reviewed periodically. Revision by one percentage point in the assumed rate of investment return, for example, would require a current change in the level of pension expenses by $15 million before taxes, or about $7 million after taxes. The current actuarially assumed rate of return is 8.5%.

Pension investment policy, through its influence on pension expenses, unfunded pension liability, and the company's earnings progress, is a critical issue of Morgan management. The chairman is strongly committed to the corporate goal of achieving a total investment return for shareholders superior to that of other large industrial companies. He recognizes that a more aggressive pension investment policy—if successful—would facilitate attainment of the corporate goal through a significant reduction in pension expenses and unfunded pension liability. He also worries, however that a significant drop in the market value of the company's pension fund—now $1 billion—could result in a major setback in the company's growth strategy. Current pension investment policy is based on an asset mix of approximately 50% common stocks and 50% fixed-income securities.

The chairman is concerned about the overall investment management and direction of the pension fund and is very interested in your informed and objective evaluation.

What recommendations would you make to the chairman, and why?

CFA

7. You are Faye Trotter, assistant treasurer of Ednam Products Company, a firm that recently terminated its defined-benefit (pension) retirement plan in favor of a new defined-contribution (profit-sharing) retirement plan. Termination proceeds were used to purchase an annuity for each employee, with normal retirement age at 65. Before termination, Ednam had also sponsored a generous savings plan under which many employees have accumulated sizable participations. These accumulations have been incorporated into the employees' individual accounts as an integral part of the new plan, which is fully qualified under ERISA and meets all requirements for protecting employee tax benefits that are part of this arrangement.*

Each employee is now responsible for investment decisions in his or her own personal plan account. This includes selection of the vehicles of implementation, current disposition of the accumulated monies now awaiting investment, and ongoing monitoring and adjustment of account exposure, as well as disposition of future company profit-sharing contributions. This decision-making requirement is a totally new experience for most employees and is one about which many concerns have been expressed to Ednam management.

Responding to these concerns, the company has made five investment alternatives available under the plan and has designated you as a resource person for interested employees.

Your role is to provide information about the plan and its investment alternatives, about the no-load mutual funds selected by the company as investment vehicles, about consensus capital market expectations, and about the fundamentals of investing. Although Ednam management realizes that this response falls short of being a complete counseling program, they believe that the combination of a wide range of investment vehicles and continuing access to an objective and experienced person should enable employees to make intelligent investment choices. Moreover, the plan provides that allocations to any or all of the five investment vehicles may be changed at six-month intervals. Employees have been told that investing is a process that requires their continuing participation, with particular attention to adjustment of market exposures as personal and external conditions change through time. Overall, employee reactions

*Reprinted, with permission, from the Level II 1985 *CFA Study Guide*.

have been enthusiastic and three individuals already have requested appointments with you. The following background information on the three individuals has been made available to you:

- Tom David, sales manager, age 58; he intends to retire at age 62; married; no children; wife employed. Owns $150,000 house (no mortgage) and $100,000 portfolio of growth stocks. No family health problems; no major indebtedness. Accumulated in plan investment account: $160,000.
- Margaret Custer, assistant director of Market Research, age 30, single; excellent health; buying condominium (heavily mortgaged) and car. Accumulated in plan investment account: $40,000.
- Glen Abbott, plant supervisor, age 42, widower, two children, ages 14 and 10; buying $130,000 house ($80,000 mortgage). No other indebtedness except regular heavy use of credit cards. Accumulated in plan investment account: $110,000.

You expect that each of these individuals will want to discuss allocation of their account accumulations, as well as details of the plan and the no-load mutual fund investment vehicles described here:

- Money market fund. Average maturity typically is 30 days.
- High-grade bond fund. Average duration maintained at 15 years.
- Index stock fund. An S&P 500 proxy. Beta of 1.00.
- Growth stock fund. Portfolio beta maintained at 1.30.
- Real estate equity fund. Owns diversified portfolio of commercial properties. Holds no mortgages; not a tax-shelter fund.

As part of your preparation, you have determined that consensus risk-and-return expectations for the various asset classes over the next several years are in line with average historical experience, accompanied by modest inflation levels.

Utilizing this information and your own assessment of the risk-bearing capacities of Tom, Margaret, and Glen, do the following:

a. Identify and discuss the differences in investor life cycle position and in investment objectives and constraints that exist among the three individuals. Frame the identification part of your answer in the matrix format shown below:

Investment Considerations	Tom	Margaret	Glen

Figure 28A

Planet Trade Company defined-benefit pension plan, Investment Policy Statement (6/1/92)

The plan should emphasize production of adequate levels of real return as its primary return objective, giving special attention to the inflation-related aspects of the plan. To the extent consistent with appropriate control of portfolio risk, investment action should seek to maintain or increase the surplus of plan assets relative to benefit liabilities over time. Five-year periods, updated annually, shall be employed in planning for investment decision making; the plan's actuary shall update the benefit liabilities breakdown by country every three years.

The orientation of investment planning shall be long term in nature. In addition, minimal liquidity reserves shall be maintained so long as annual company funding contributions and investment income exceed annual benefit payments to retirees and the operating expenses of the plan. The plan's actuary shall update plan cash flow projections annually. Plan administration shall ensure compliance with all laws and regulations related to maintenance of the plan's tax-exempt status and with all requirements of the Employee Retirement Income Security Act (ERISA).

b. Prepare a normal, long-term allocation of the accumulated monies in each of the three individual accounts and justify the resulting asset mix. Your allocations should sum to 100% in each case and be based on your Part (*a*) conclusions. Do not base your answer on any qualitative considerations related to current or expected market considerations as you perceive them.

The following information pertains to Problems 8–10.

Planet Trade Company (PTC) is a major U.S.-based import/export firm. Headquartered in New York City, PTC also has offices and employees in Tokyo, Sydney, Madrid, Bangkok, and several other non-U.S. locations. Permanent employees in all locations are covered by a defined-benefit pension plan whose liabilities reflect the following background facts:

- Wages are inflation adjusted, and retirement benefits (which are based on final pay levels) provide for automatic postretirement inflation adjustment.
- Because the average age of the work force is relatively young, company contributions into the fund are expected to exceed annual plan operating expenses and benefit payments for at least the next 10 years.
- An estimated 30% of benefit payments will be non-U.S. dollar based for an extended period of time. The current non-U.S. liabilities breakdown by country is as follows:

  7% Australia.
  6% Japan.
  6% Singapore.
  4% Thailand.
  4% Spain.
  3% Malaysia.

PTC's internal Investment Committee is assisted in administration of the company's employee benefits program by Benefits Advisory Group (BAG), a well-known pension consulting organization. To provide guidance to its Investment Committee and to its investment managers, PTC's board has adopted the Investment Policy Statement shown in Figure 28A for its pension plan.

8. PTC's Investment Committee intends to adopt a set of long-term asset allocation ranges for the firm's defined benefit pension plan that takes into consideration the plan's liability structure as set forth in the introduction. In addition, the committee requires a set of short-term asset allocation targets that will position the fund's current exposure within the long-term setting. As a principal of BAG, this strategic and tactical goal-setting assignment has been given to you. You intend to preface your recommendations to the committee with a brief review of three alternative methods that may be used for determining appropriate asset allocations, including:*

- Extrapolation and adjustment of long-term historical asset class data.
- Multiple-scenario forecasting.
- Asset/liability forecasting.

a. Briefly describe the three alternatives listed above. In your discussion, cite one strength and one weakness of each method relative to the purpose of determining long-term pension portfolio asset allocation ranges.

b. Based on the information provided in the introduction and Figure 28A, and your general knowledge of asset class characteristics, create a set of long-term asset allocation ranges for the PTC pension portfolio using the format presented below, and justify your range selection for each asset class.

	Range	Midpoint
U.S. equities	______ – ______%	______%
Non-U.S. equities	______ – ______%	______%
Equity real estate	______ – ______%	______%
U.S. bonds	______ – ______%	______%
Non-U.S. bonds	______ – ______%	______%
Cash equivalents	______ – ______%	______%
		100%

c. i. Table 28D provides expected return data for six asset classes under three alternative economic scenarios. Identify two other asset-class statistics not shown in Table 28D that are essential for making effective asset allocation decisions, and explain the importance of each of these two statistics in the asset allocation process.

ii. Based solely on the data contained in Table 28D, calculate the expected return for each asset class using the multiple scenario forecasting method. Show all your calculations.

iii. Considering the scenario weightings in Table 28D, the expected returns calculated in Part (*ii*), and your general knowledge about the two missing asset class statistics, create and justify a short-term asset allocation for the PTC pension portfolio. Your allocation must sum to 100%.

d. Explain how you could use derivative securities to make short-term asset allocation adjustments away from long-term targets, and cite one reason for and one reason against using derivative securities to do so.

*Reprinted, with permission, from the Level III 1992 *CFA Study Guide*.

Table 28D Expected Annual Asset Class Returns over the Next Three Years under Different Global Economic Scenarios (in U.S. dollar terms)

	Scenario I: Recession/ Deflation	Scenario II: Slow Growth/ Low Inflation	Senario III: Rapid Growth/ High Inflation
Probability of occurrence	30%	50%	20%
Asset Class Expected Annual Returns			
U.S. equities	7%	12%	8%
Non-U.S. equities	4	10	9
Equity real estate	0	9	14
U.S. bonds	15	8	3
Non-U.S. bonds	10	9	2
Cash equivalents	3	5	9

9. As PTC's new Chief Financial Officer, you have recently assumed responsibility for internal administration of the firm's pension plan. In this capacity, you have completed a detailed review of the portfolio assets and the minutes of the Investment Committee meetings at which the policies determining the broad outline for plan investment actions were discussed and adopted. You note that the Investment Committee's decision to accept equity real estate investments for the portfolio followed a discussion in which two assertions were offered as key favorable considerations:*

   - Equity real estate provides its owners with a prime means for offsetting inflation's erosive effects on both investment value and the income stream.
   - Inclusion of an equity real estate component in a portfolio significantly reduces total portfolio risk as a result of the low standard deviation of real estate returns.

   a. Evaluate these assertions, including in your response two observations that support them and two observations that dispute them.

   Among the holdings of the PTC pension portfolio's equity real estate component, which is well diversified geographically and across property types, is a 12-story Class A office building situated in the downtown center of a major U.S. city. Built in 1983, the building is 95% leased at an average of $23 per square foot. All leases call for rent escalation at a rate matching the U.S. Consumer Price Index (CPI). The key tenant in the building, occupying 45% of rentable space, has given notice that it will vacate the space at the end of its current lease in December 1993.

   The area's economy, highly sensitive to conditions in the energy industry in the past, has benefited recently from the arrival of new businesses that have diversified the city's industrial base. Demographic projections indicate a

*Reprinted, with permission, from the Level III 1992 *CFA Study Guide.*

500,000-person increase in metropolitan-area population by the year 2010, with job growth gaining proportionally at approximately 2.5% per year.

The downtown center vacancy rate in the city is currently 22%; in the suburban area, it approaches 30%. New leases in Class A buildings are being written at $12 per square foot, with some inducement concessions being offered as well. No new office buildings have been completed in the immediate area since 1987. This lack of new construction, and the arrival of new businesses, has permitted about 10% of previously available space to be absorbed within the past 12 months.

b. Evaluate the above-described property in terms of its ability to provide the inflation protection and diversification benefits stated in Part (*a*). Segment your discussion into 5-year and 20-year time frames.

10. In the 1970s, when PTC was a much smaller company and all employees were U.S.-based, its retirement plan consisted solely of a tax-exempt defined-contribution (profit-sharing) arrangement. Annual contributions to employees' accounts under this plan ceased some years ago, when the company's present tax-exempt defined-benefit (pension) program was adopted. As a result, all participants in the profit-sharing plan are older U.S. employees who are also covered by PTC's newer pension plan. Their profit sharing interests are "frozen" in the sense that withdrawals are permitted only on their retirement or an earlier termination of PTC employment, and then only in lump-sum form.

On review, BAG has discovered that the original Investment Policy Statement for the profit-sharing plan has not been updated since inception, despite the passage of time and changes in the company's retirement program. The Investment Committee intends to adopt a new statement to recognize current circumstances and obligations and has requested your recommendations. It has been suggested that you use an objectives/constraints approach in your presentation.*

a. Prepare and justify an appropriate Investment Policy Statement for the PTC profit-sharing plan.

b. Compare the elements in your Part (*a*) profit-sharing policy statement to those of the PTC pension plan statement presented in Figure 28A and briefly comment on any major differences between the two.

The chairman of the Investment Committee has proposed that an international securities component be added to the present U.S.-only securities portfolio in which the interests of the profit-sharing plan's participants are invested. However, another member of the committee is strongly opposed to doing so, basing his objection on the fact that the profit-sharing plan has only U.S.-dollar liabilities and all participants are U.S.-based.

c. Critique the opposing committee member's position on this issue, including in your response specific reference to the grounds he has cited for his objection.

---

*Reprinted, with permission, from the Level III 1992 *CFA Study Guide.* Copyright 1992, Association for Investment Management and Research, Charlottesville, VA. All rights reserved.

Chapter 29 Some Recent Developments in Investment Research

THE MATERIAL IN THE PRECEDING CHAPTERS OF *INVESTMENTS* COMPRISES THE UNDERLYING FOUNDATION OF CONTEMPORARY INVESTMENT MANAGEMENT. Although the history of science teaches us to expect many further revisions, this material represents our current understanding. On the important issues of the empirical support for asset pricing models (Chapter 11) and the broader question of market efficiency (Chapter 12), we have reported on gaps in our present knowledge, and identified pricing anomalies (such as the January effect) that are yet to be explained.

Obviously, the quest for better understanding of capital markets and for better investment techniques is ongoing. A few thousand scholars and investment professionals regularly publish reports of their research efforts in the area of investments. The purpose of this chapter is to interpret the findings of a small set of these reports. We restrict our scope to acquired knowledge that, in our view, may already be valuable to practitioners in the investment field. We expect that future editions of this text will incorporate this material into the preceding chapters, leaving this chapter for even newer findings. We welcome your comments on our choices in the present exposition, and would appreciate suggestions for developments to be included in the next edition of *Investments*.

In this edition, our choices include time-varying volatility in asset returns, the current assessment of the validity of asset pricing models, and extensions of option pricing theory.

29.1 Stochastic Volatility and Asset Returns

The price of a stock may change for two reasons: First, the arrival of new information may lead investors to change their assessment of intrinsic value; second, even in the absence of new information, unexpected changes in investor liquidity needs combined with trading frictions may create temporary buying or selling pressures that cause the price to fluctuate around its intrinsic value. Except for the least liquid assets, however, new information should account for the lion's share of price changes, at least when we examine returns for horizons longer than a few weeks. Therefore, we may associate the variance of the rate of return on the stock with the rate of arrival of new information. As a casual survey of the media would indicate, the rate of revision in predictions of business cycles, industry ascents or descents, and the fortunes of individual enterprises fluctuates regularly; in other words, the rate of arrival of new information is time varying. Consequently, we should expect the variances of the rates of return on stocks (as well as the covariances among them) to be time varying.

In an exploratory study of the volatility of NYSE stocks over more than 150 years (using monthly returns over 1835–1987), Pagan and Schwert[1] compute estimates of the variance of monthly returns. Their results, depicted in Figure 29.1, show just how important it may be to consider time variation in stock variance. The centrality of the risk–return trade-off suggests that once we make sufficient progress in the modeling, estimation, and prediction of the time variation in return variances and covariances, we should expect a significant refinement in understanding expected returns as well.

When we consider a time-varying return distribution, we must refer to the *conditional* mean, variance, and covariance, that is, the mean, variance, or covariance conditional on currently available information. The "conditions" that vary over time are the values of variables that determine the level of these parameters. In contrast, the usual estimate of return variance, the average of squared deviations over the sample period, provides an *unconditional* estimate, because it treats the variance as constant over time.

The most widely used model to estimate the conditional (hence, time varying) variance of stocks and stock index returns is the Generalized Auto-Regressive Conditional Heteroskedasticity (GARCH) model, pioneered by Robert F. Engle.[2] Bollerslev, Chou, and Kroner[3] provide an extensive survey of the contribution of this technique to empirical work in finance. The work we present here is illustrative of the issues examined in current lines of research, but is far from exhaustive.

The GARCH model uses rate of return history as the information set that conditions our estimates of variance. The model posits that the forecast of market volatility evolves relatively smoothly each period in response to new observations on market returns. The updated estimate of market-return variance in each period depends on both the previous estimate and the most recent squared residual return on the market. The squared residual is an unbiased estimate of variance, so this technique essentially mixes in a statistically efficient manner the previous volatility estimate with an unbiased estimate based on the new observation of market return. The updating formula is:

---

[1] Adrian Pagan and G. William Schwert, "Alternative Models for Conditional Stock Volatility," *Journal of Econometrics* 45 (1990), pp. 267–90.

[2] Robert F. Engle, "Autoregressive Conditional Heteroskedasticity with Estimates of the Variance of the U.K. Inflation," *Econometrica* 50 (1982), pp. 987–1008.

[3] Tim Bollerslev, Ray Chou, and Kenneth Kroner, "ARCH Modeling in Finance: A Review of the Theory and Empirical Evidence," *Journal of Econometrics* 52 (1992), pp. 5–59.

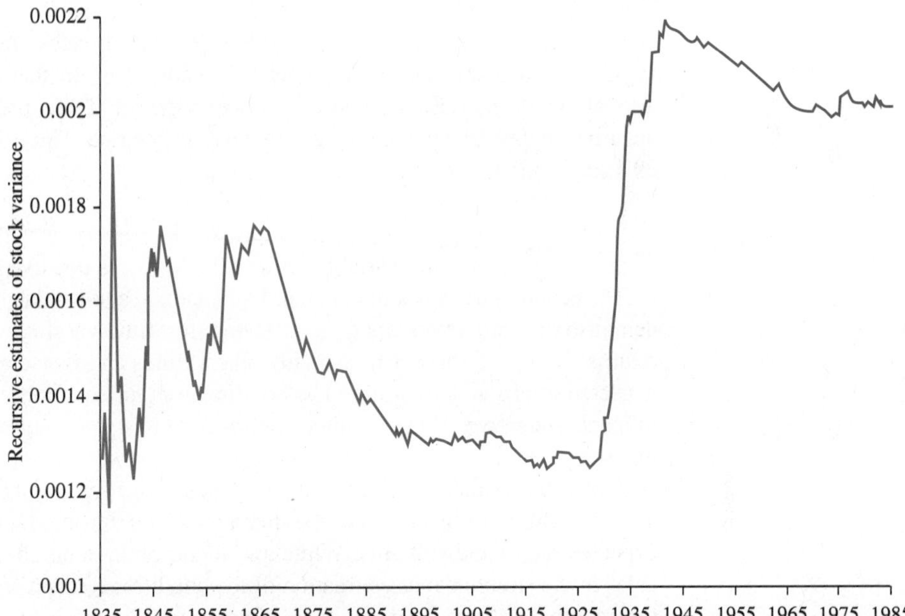

Figure 29.1
Estimates of the monthly stock return variance, 1835–1987

Source: Adrian R. Pagan and G. William Schwert, "Alternative Models for Conditional Stock Volatility," *Journal of Econometrics* 45 (1990), pp. 267–90.

$$\sigma_t^2 = a_0 + a_1\epsilon_{t-1}^2 + a_2\sigma_{t-1}^2 \tag{29.1}$$

As noted, equation 29.1 asserts that the updated forecast of variance is a function of the most recent variance forecast σ_{t-1}^2, and the most recent squared prediction error in market return, ϵ_{t-1}^2. The parameters a_0, a_1, and a_2 are estimated from past data.

To estimate the return surprise, ϵ_t, we require an equation for the expected return. One of the extensions of the model, GARCH-Mean, estimates two simultaneous equations for the expected excess return and variance. The first equation is 29.1; the second is an equation for the market excess return:

$$r_t - r_{ft} = b_0 + b_1\sigma_t^2 + \epsilon_t \tag{29.2}$$

Equation 29.2 asserts that the expected market excess return is an increasing function of predicted variance, with slope coefficient b_1. Therefore, the expected excess return on the stock index is linear in the predicted variance from equation (29.1).

In testing this model with monthly NYSE data for April 1951 through December 1989, Glosten, Jagannathan, and Runkle[4] find that the model more closely fits the data when the residual (i.e., unexpected) excess return is described by

$$\epsilon_t = \eta_t(1 + \lambda_1\text{OCT} + \lambda_2\text{JAN}) \tag{29.2a}$$

[4] Lawrence R. Glosten, Ravi Jagannathan, and David E. Runkle, "On the Relation between the Expected Value and the Volatility of the Nominal Excess Return on Stocks," *Journal of Finance* 48 (1993), pp. 1779–1802.

The dummy variables, OCT and JAN are set to 1.0 in October or January, respectively, and zero otherwise, allowing for different expected excess returns in those months. In addition to using the better specified residual, η_t, in the variance equation, they also allow the variance prediction to be different if the previous excess return is negative, and to respond to changes in the risk-free rate. Thus, they generalize equation 29.1 to:

$$\sigma_t^2 = a_0 + a_1\eta_{t-1}^2 + a_2\sigma_{t-1}^2 + a_3 r_{ft} + a_4 I_{t-1} \tag{29.1a}$$

where I_{t-1} is a dummy variable set to 1.0 if η_{t-1} is positive and zero otherwise.

The econometric work of Glosten, Jagannathan, and Runkle (as well as many others) demonstrates the importance of allowing for time-varying volatility and expected returns. However, this study, as many others, finds an inverse relationship between the expected return and volatility: The coefficient b_1 in equation 29.2 turns out to be significantly negative. This troubling result is hard to square with the notion of risk averse investors.

A possible explanation for the apparent negative correlation between expected return and volatility originates with the impact of the business cycle on predictions of expected return and volatility. Whitelaw[5] incorporates a number of business cycle variables in the simultaneous estimation of the conditional mean and standard deviation of the monthly returns on the CRSP (Center for Research in Security Prices) value-weighted stock index over the period April 1954 through April 1989. Table 29.1 illustrates the role of these variables in the determination of the moments of the return distribution.

The time series of the estimated conditional means and standard deviations of stock returns reveal a nonsynchronous cyclical pattern, as illustrated in Figure 29.2. The correlation patterns implied by these offset cycles differ from those implied by coincident cycles. Because the cycles for expected return and volatility are not synchronous, the correlation between mean return and risk may appear positive in some periods and negative in others. This may explain the puzzling results of earlier studies.

Whitelaw further investigates the relationship between the estimates from month $t - 1$ to month t of the expected excess return ($m_{t-1,t}$) and volatility ($v_{t-1,t}$) by estimating simultaneously the equations

$$m_{t-1,t} = b_0 + b_1 m_{t-2,t-1} + b_2 v_{t-2,t-1} + \epsilon_{mt} \tag{29.3a}$$

$$v_{t-1,t} = a_0 + a_1 m_{t-2,t-1} + a_2 v_{t-2,t-1} + \epsilon_{vt} \tag{29.3b}$$

The estimates from these equations, which allow for feedback between the levels of the forecasts, are presented in Table 29.2. The table reports coefficient estimates of: $b_1 = .977$ and $a_2 = .824$ in equations 29.3a and 29.3b, confirming that the variables are highly autocorrelated.

Whitelaw finds that the coefficient of volatility in the mean equation (equation 29.3a) is positive ($b_2 = .118$) and statistically significant, a finding that is consistent

[5] Robert F. Whitelaw, "Time Variations and Covariations in the Expectation and Volatility of Stock Returns," *Journal of Finance* 49 (1994), pp. 515-42.

Table 29.1 Estimation of Conditional First and Second Moments of Returns

Regressions of monthly, quarterly, and annual, continuously compounded, excess stock returns and volatilities for the CRSP value-weighted index on lagged explanatory variables for the periods May 1953 to April 1989, July 1953 to April 1989, and April 1954 to April 1989, respectively. The conditioning variables are the Baa-Aaa spread (DEF), the commercial paper-Treasury spread (CP), the one-year Treasury yield (1YR), and the dividend yield (DIV). Heteroscedasticity-consistent standard errors are in parentheses. DW is the Durbin-Watson statistic. The $\chi^2(4)$ statistic tests the hypothesis that all the coefficients except the constant are zero. The number in brackets is the probability that a $\chi^2(4)$ will exceed the value of the statistic.

	Explanatory Variables							
Constant	DEF	CP	1YR	DIV	Adj. R^2	R^2	DW	$\chi^2(4)$
				Mean				
				Monthly				
−1.820	2.295**	−0.313	−0.469**	0.794**	0.074	0.082	1.991	39
(1.003)	(0.618)	(0.720)	(0.086)	(0.269)				[0.00]
				Quarterly				
−5.991*	5.817**	−0.242	−1.270*	2.430**	0.176	0.184	0.764	34
(2.863)	(1.777)	(1.921)	(0.256)	(0.821)				[0.00]
				Annual				
−28.037**	9.806	3.970	−3.410**	10.546**	0.412	0.417	0.249	26
(10.537)	(5.974)	(3.928)	(0.933)	(2.908)				[0.00]
				Volatility				
				Monthly				
1.884**	−0.044	2.070**	0.104	−0.029	0. 099	0.107	2.071	34
(0.734)	(0.500)	(0.476)	(0.067)	(0.217)				[0.00]
				Quarterly				
4.979**	−0.364	2.466**	0.274*	−0.378	0 .059	0.067	1.263	19
(1.777)	(1.007)	(0.793)	(0.136)	(0.579)				[0.00]
				Annual				
16.197**	−1.559	0.277	0.822**	−1.830	0 .053	0.062	0.635	8.6
(3.340)	(2.435)	(1.548)	(0.332)	(1.110)				[0.07]

*Significant at the 5% level.
**Significant at the 1% level.
Source: Robert F. Whitelaw, "Time Variations and Covariations in the Expectation and Volatility of Stock Returns," *Journal of Finance* 49 (1994), pp 515–42.

with risk aversion. We also see that the mean has a significantly negative coefficient in the volatility equation, suggesting that volatility decreases when means are high.

Understanding the forces that drive the risk premium on stocks over time is also important to understanding co-movements of expected returns. Evans[6] allows for time varying risk premia and betas, where the latter are identified from the dynamics of the conditional covariances of returns. He estimates a two-factor CAPM using CRSP monthly stock and bond returns over the period 1963–1990. Evans concludes that

[6] Martin D. Evans, "Expected Returns, Time Varying Risk, and Risk Premia," *Journal of Finance* 49 (1994), pp. 655–79.

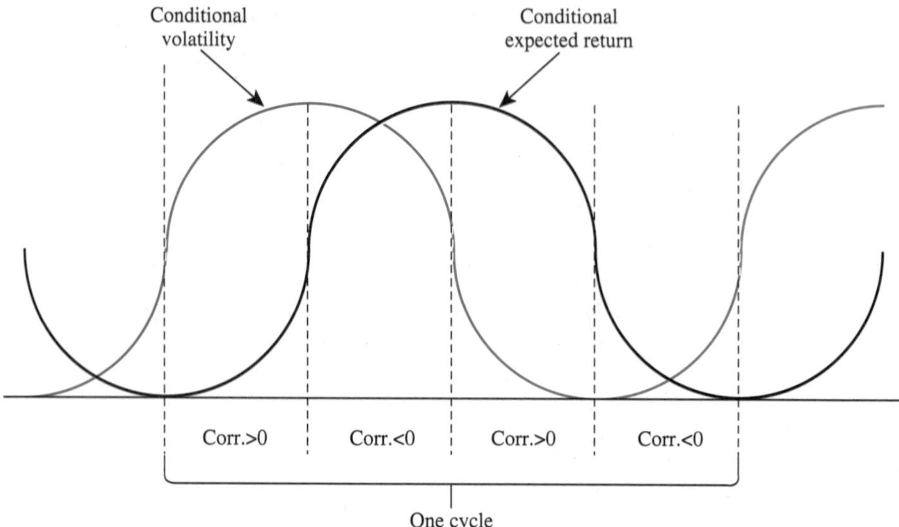

Figure 29.2

A schematic representation of the cyclical variation in the conditional mean and the conditional volatility of returns and the implied contemporaneous correlations between the moments.

Source: Robert F. Whitelaw, "Time Variations and Covariations in the Expectation and Volatility of Stock Returns," *Journal of Finance* 49 (1994), pp 515–42.

changes in the risk premiums on the stock and bond factors dominate the effects of changes in beta on the prediction of portfolio returns.

The sum total of applications of time-series techniques to accommodate the time-varying nature of rates of return is still tentative. However, the gathering momentum suggests to us that these techniques will soon find their way into the standard tool kit of practitioners. As we shall see, the ideas discussed so far are relevant to the developments we discuss next.

29.2 The Empirical Content of Asset Pricing Models

As Chapter 11 indicated, the search for empirical support for the CAPM and the APT has been frustrating. Study after study has concluded that asset returns do not line up around the hypothesized security market line predicted by the CAPM and APT. Several researchers surmise that even if a positive expected return-beta relationship is valid, a full-blown asset pricing model cannot currently be empirically validated because of a host of statistical problems that, perhaps, can never be fully overcome.

It is not surprising that a study by Fama and French,[7] briefly discussed in Chapter 12, received great attention when it reported that:

"Two easily measured variables, size and book-to-market equity, combine to capture the cross-sectional variation in average stock returns associated with market β, size, leverage, book-to-market equity, and earnings-price ratios. Moreover, when the tests allow for variation in β that is unrelated to size, the relation between market β and average returns is flat, even when β is the only explanatory variable."

[7] Eugene F. Fama and Kenneth R. French, "The Cross-Section of Expected Stock Returns," Journal of Finance 47 (1992), pp. 427–466.

Table 29.2 VAR(1) Estimation of the Fitted Conditional Expectation and Volatility of Returns

A VAR(1) estimation of the conditional moments of monthly, continuously compounded, excess returns for the CRSP value-weighted index for the period June 1953 to April 1989. $m_{t-1,t}$ and $v_{t-1,t}$ are the fitted mean and volatility from the estimation of equations 29.3a and 29.3b. Heteroscedasticity-consistent standard errors are in parentheses.

	Explanatory Variables				
	Constant	$m_{t-2,t-1}$	$v_{t-2,t-1}$	Adj. R^2	R^2
$m_{t-1,t}$	0.459	0.977**	0.118*	0.895	0.895
	(0.239)	(0.038)	(0.058)		
$v_{t-1,t}$	0.743**	−0.107*	0.824**	0.759	0.760
	(0.258)	(0.045)	(0.067)		

*Significant at the 5% level.
**Significant at the 1% level.
Source: Robert F. Whitelaw, "Time Variations and Covariations in the Expectation and Volatility of Stock Returns," *Journal of Finance* 49 (1994), pp 515–42.

This is a highly disturbing conclusion. If the empirical evidence suggests that systematic risk is unrelated to expected returns, we must relinquish one of the cornerstones of the theory of finance. Indeed, in Fama and French's words: "In short, our tests do not support the central prediction of the [CAPM and APT], that average stock returns are positively related to β." This conclusion captured the attention of the practitioner as well as academic communities, and was reported in the *New York Times* and *The Economist* (see the nearby box).

The most damning evidence that Fama and French (FF) provide is of the lack of a positive relation between average returns and beta. Table 29.3 best illustrates this point. FF find that both size and beta are positively correlated with average returns. But because these explanatory variables are highly (negatively) correlated, they seek to isolate the effect of beta. They accomplish this by forming 10 portfolios of different betas *within* each of the 10 size groups.

The top line in Panel B of Table 29.3 shows that the portfolio beta of each beta group, averaged across the ten size portfolios steadily increases from .76 to 1.69. The top line in Panel C shows that the average portfolio size within each beta group is almost identical, ranging from 4.34 to 4.40. This allows us to interpret Panel A as a test of the net effect of beta on average returns holding size fixed.

Panel A of the table clearly shows that, for the period 1941–1990, average returns are not positively related to beta. The two highest beta portfolios have the two lowest average returns, and the highest average returns occur in the fourth and fifth beta portfolios. The response to these results has been of three strands: utilizing better econometrics in the test procedures; improving estimates of asset betas; and reconsidering the theoretical sources and implications of the results in the FF and similar studies.

Beta Beaten

A battle between some of the top names in financial economics is attracting attention on Wall Street. Under attack is the famous capital-asset pricing model (CAPM), widely used to assess risk and return. A new paper by two Chicago economists, Eugene Fama and Kenneth French, explodes that model by showing that its key analytical tool does not explain why returns on shares differ.*

According to the CAPM, returns reflect risk. The model uses a measure called beta—shorthand for relative volatility—to compare the riskiness of one share with that of the whole market, on the basis of past price changes. A share with a beta of one is just as risky as the market; one with a beta of 0.5 is less risky. Because investors need to earn more on riskier investments, share prices will reflect the requirement for higher-than-average returns on shares with higher betas.

Whether beta does predict returns has long been debated. Studies have found that market capitalization, price/earnings ratios, leverage and book-to-market ratios do just as well. Messrs. Fama and French are clear: Beta is not a good guide.

The two economists look at all non-financial shares traded on the NYSE, AMEX and NASDAQ between 1963 and 1990. The shares were grouped into portfolios. When grouped solely on the basis of size (i.e., market capitalization), the CAPM worked—but each portfolio contained a wide range of betas. So the authors grouped shares of similar beta and size. Betas now were a bad guide to returns.

Instead of beta, say Messrs. Fama and French, differences in firm size and in the ratio of book value to market value explain differences in returns—especially the latter. When shares were grouped by book-to-market ratios, the gap in returns between the portfolio with the lowest ratio and that with the highest was far wider than when shares were grouped by size.

So should analysts stop using the CAPM? Probably not. Although Mr. Fama and Mr. French have produced intriguing results, they lack a theory to explain them. Their best hope is that size and book-to-market ratios are proxies for other fundamentals. For instance, a high book-to-market ratio may indicate a firm in trouble; its earnings prospects might thus be especially sensitive to economic conditions, so its shares would need to earn a higher return than its beta suggested.

Advocates of CAPM—including Fischer Black, of Goldman Sachs, an investment bank, and William Sharpe of Stanford University, who won the Nobel prize for economics in 1990—reckon the results of the new study can be explained without discarding beta. Investors may irrationally favor big firms. Or they may lack the cash to buy enough shares to spread risk completely, so that risk and return are not perfectly matched in the market.

Those looking for a theoretical alternative to CAPM will find little satisfaction, however. Voguish rivals, such as the "arbitrage-pricing theory," are no better than CAPM and betas at explaining actual share returns. Which leaves Wall Street with an awkward choice: believe the Fama–French evidence, despite its theoretical vacuum, and use size and the book-to-market ratios as a guide to returns; or stick with a theory that, despite the data, is built on impeccable logic.

*Eugene Fama and Kenneth French, "The Cross-Section of Expected Stock Returns," *Journal of Finance* 47 (1992), pp. 427-466.
Source: From *The Economist*, March 7, 1992, p. 87

Improving the econometric procedures employed in tests of asset returns seems the most direct response to the FF results. Amihud, Bent, and Mendelson[8] improve on the FF test procedures, using Generalized Least Squares (GLS) and pooling the time-

[8] Yakov Amihud, Jesper C. Bent, and Haim Mendelson, "Further Evidence on the Risk–Return Relationship," Working Paper, Graduate School of Business, Standard University (1992).

Table 29.3 Properties of Portfolios Formed on Size and Pre-Ranking β: NYSE Stocks Sorted by ME (Down) then Pre-Ranking β (Across): 1941–1990

At the end of year $t-1$, the NYSE stocks on CRSP are assigned to 10 size (ME) portfolios. Each size decile is subdivided into 10 β portfolios using preranking βs of individual stocks, estimated with 24 to 60 monthly returns (as available) ending in December of year $t-1$. The equal-weighted monthly returns on the resulting 100 portfolios are then calculated for year t. The average returns are the time-series averages of the monthly returns, in percent. The postranking βs use the full 1941–1990 sample of postranking returns for each portfolio. The pre- and postranking βs are the sum of the slopes from a regression of monthly returns on the current and prior month's NYSE value-weighted market return. The average size for a portfolio is the time-series average of each month's average value of ln(ME) for stocks in the portfolio. ME is denominated in millions of dollars. There are, on average, about 10 stocks in each size-β portfolio each month. The All column shows parameter values for equal-weighted size-decile (ME) portfolios. The All rows show parameter values for equal-weighted portfolios of the stocks in each β group.

	All	Low-β	β-2	β-3	β-4	β-5	β-6	β-7	β-8	β-9	High-β
Panel A: Average Monthly Return (in percent)											
All		1.22	1.30	1.32	1.35	1.36	1.34	1.29	1.34	1.14	1.10
Small-ME	1.78	1.74	1.76	2.08	1.91	1.92	1.72	1.77	1.91	1.56	1.46
ME-2	1.44	1.41	1.35	1.33	1.61	1.72	1.59	1.40	1.62	1.24	1.11
ME-3	1.36	1.21	1.40	1.22	1.47	1.34	1.51	1.33	1.57	1.33	1.21
ME-4	1.28	1.26	1.29	1.19	1.27	1.51	1.30	1.19	1.56	1.18	1.00
ME-5	1.24	1.22	1.30	1.28	1.33	1.21	1.37	1.41	1.31	0.92	1.06
ME-6	1.23	1.21	1.32	1.37	1.09	1.34	1.10	1.40	1.21	1.22	1.08
ME-7	1.17	1.08	1.23	1.37	1.27	1.19	1.34	1.10	1.11	0.87	1.17
ME-8	1.15	1.06	1.18	1.26	1.25	1.26	1.17	1.16	1.05	1.08	1.04
ME-9	1.13	0.99	1.13	1.00	1.24	1.28	1.31	1.15	1.11	1.09	1.05
Large-ME	0.95	0.99	1.01	1.12	1.01	0.89	0.95	0.95	1.00	0.90	0.68
Panel B: Post-Ranking β											
All		0.76	0.95	1.05	1.14	1.22	1.26	1.34	1.38	1.49	1.69
Small-ME	1.52	1.17	1.40	1.31	1.50	1.46	1.50	1.69	1.60	1.75	1.92
ME-2	1.37	0.86	1.09	1.12	1.24	1.39	1.42	1.48	1.60	1.69	1.91
ME-3	1.32	0.88	0.96	1.18	1.19	1.33	1.40	1.43	1.56	1.64	1.74
ME-4	1.26	0.69	0.95	1.06	1.15	1.24	1.29	1.46	1.43	1.64	1.83
ME-5	1.23	0.70	0.95	1.04	1.10	1.22	1.32	1.34	1.41	1.56	1.72
ME-6	1.19	0.68	0.86	1.04	1.13	1.20	1.20	1.35	1.36	1.48	1.70
ME-7	1.17	0.67	0.88	0.95	1.14	1.18	1.26	1.27	1.32	1.44	1.68
ME-8	1.12	0.64	0.83	0.99	1.06	1.14	1.14	1.21	1.26	1.39	1.58
ME-9	1.06	0.68	0.81	0.94	0.96	1.06	1.11	1.18	1.22	1.25	1.46
Large-ME	0.97	0.65	0.73	0.90	0.91	0.97	1.01	1.01	1.07	1.12	1.38
Panel C: Average Size (ln(ME))											
All		4.39	4.39	4.40	4.40	4.39	4.40	4.38	4.37	4.37	4.34
Small-ME	1.93	2.04	1.99	2.00	1.96	1.92	1.92	1.91	1.90	1.87	1.80
ME-2	2.80	2.81	2.79	2.81	2.83	2.80	2.79	2.80	2.80	2.79	2.79
ME-3	3.27	3.28	3.27	3.28	3.27	3.27	3.28	3.29	3.27	3.27	3.26
ME-4	3.67	3.67	3.67	3.67	3.68	3.68	3.67	3.68	3.66	3.67	3.67
ME-5	4.06	4.07	4.06	4.05	4.06	4.07	4.06	4.05	4.05	4.06	4.06
ME-6	4.45	4.45	4.44	4.46	4.45	4.45	4.45	4.45	4.44	4.45	4.45
ME-7	4.87	4.86	4.87	4.86	4.87	4.87	4.88	4.87	4.87	4.85	4.87
ME-8	5.36	5.38	5.38	5.38	5.35	5.36	5.37	5.37	5.36	5.35	5.34
ME-9	5.98	5.96	5.98	5.99	6.00	5.98	5.98	5.97	5.95	5.96	5.96
Large-ME	7.12	7.10	7.12	7.16	7.17	7.20	7.29	7.14	7.09	7.04	6.83

Source: Eugene F. Fama and Kenneth R. French, "The Cross-Section of Expected Stock Returns," *Journal of Finance* 47 (1992), pp. 427–66.

series and cross-section rates of return. For the entire period analyzed by FF, 1941–1990, Amihud, Bent, and Mendelson find a significantly positive relation between average returns and beta, even when controlling for size and book-to-market ratio. The expected return-beta relationship is still not statistically significant for the most recent subperiod 1972–1990. However, in light of the considerable variability of stock returns, it is perhaps not surprising that it is difficult to obtain statistically significant results over shorter sample periods.

Kothari, Shanken, and Sloan[9] concentrate on the measurement of stock betas. They choose annual intervals for the estimation of stock betas to sidestep problems caused by trading frictions, nonsynchronous trading, and seasonality in monthly returns. As it turns out, this procedure generates results that are more favorable to the expected return-beta hypothesis. Thus, they conclude that there has been substantial compensation for beta risk over the 1941–1990 period, and even more over the 1927–1990 period. Table 29.4 shows the coefficient estimates for the average return-beta relationship with and without the presence of the size variable, for five different ways of grouping portfolios and for two periods.

A different approach is taken by Roll and Ross[10] and Kandel and Stambaugh[11]. Their work expands on the well-known "Roll's Critique" (see Chapter 11 for a review). Essentially, the argument is that tests that reject a positive relationship between average return and beta point to inefficiency of the market proxy used in those tests, rather than a refutation of the theoretical expected return-beta relationship. Put another way, there always exists a portfolio that, if used as market proxy, will produce an exact linear relationship between average return and beta. That portfolio lies on the efficient frontier derived from the realized returns. The FF results imply only that the value-weighted market proxy that they use does not lie on the ex post efficient frontier.

The new wrinkle in the Roll and Ross and Kandel and Stambaugh studies is a demonstration that it is plausible that even well-diversified portfolios (such as the value- or equally weighted portfolios of all stocks in the sample) will fail to produce a significant average return-beta relationship.

Roll and Ross (RR) derive an analytical characterization of indices (proxies for the market portfolio) that produce an *arbitrary* cross-sectional slope coefficient in the regression of asset returns on beta. Their derivation applies to any universe of assets and requires only that the market proxy be constructed from that universe or one of its subsets. They show that the set of indices that produce a zero cross-sectional slope lie within a parabola that is tangent to the efficient frontier at the point corresponding to the global minimum variance portfolio.

One of the properties of the efficient frontier is that the covariance of any asset with the global minimum variance portfolio (G) is the same, and equal to the variance of

---

[9] S.P. Kothari, J. Shanken, and Richard G. Sloan, "Another Look at the Cross-Section of Stock Returns," *Journal of Finance* 49 (1994), pp. 101–21.

[10] Richard Roll and Stephen A. Ross, "On the Cross-Sectional Relation between Expected Return and Betas," *Journal of Finance* 50 (1995), pp. 185–224.

[11] Schmuel Kandel and Robert F. Stambaugh, "Portfolio Inefficiency and the Cross-Section of Expected Returns," *Journal of Finance* 50 (1995), pp. 185–224; "A Mean-Variance Framework for Tests of Asset Pricing Models," *Review of Financial Studies* 2 (1989), pp. 125-56; "On Correlations and Inferences About Mean-Variance Efficiency," *Journal of Financial Economics* 18 (1987), pp. 61-90.

Table 29.4 Cross-Sectional Regressions of Monthly Returns on Beta and Firm Size: Equally-weighted Market Index

Time-series averages of estimated coefficients from the following monthly cross-sectional regressions from 1927 to 1990 (Panel A) and from 1941 to 1990 (Panel B), associated *t*-statistics, and adjusted R^2s are reported (with and without Size being included in the regressions).

$$R_{pt} = \gamma_{0t} + \gamma_{1t}\beta_p + \gamma_{2t}\, Size_{pt-1} + \epsilon_{pt}$$

where R_{pt} is the buy-and-hold return on portfolio *p* for one month during the year beginning from July 1 of the year *t* to June 30 of year *t* + 1; β_p is the full-period postranking beta of portfolio *p* and is the slope coefficient from a time-series regression of annual buy-and-hold postranking portfolio returns on the returns on a equally-weighted portfolio of all the beta-size portfolios; $Size_{pt-1}$ is the natural log of the average market capitalization in millions of dollars on June 30 of year *t* of the stocks in portfolio *p*; γ_{0t}, γ_{1t}, and γ_{2t} are regression parameters; and ϵ_{pt} is the regression error. Portfolios are formed in five different ways: (i) 20 portfolios by grouping on beta alone; (ii) 20 portfolios by grouping on size alone; (iii) taking intersections of 10 independent beta or size groupings to obtain 100 portfolios; (iv) ranking stocks first on beta into 10 portfolios and then on size within each beta group into 10 portfolios; and (v) ranking stocks first on size into 10 portfolios and then on beta within each size group into 10 portfolios. When ranking on beta, the beta for an individual stock is estimated by regressing 24 to 60 monthly portfolio returns ending in June of each year on the CRSP equally-weighted portfolio. The *t*-statistic below the average γ_0 value is for the difference between the average γ_0 and the average risk-free rate of return over the 1927–1990 or 1941–1990 period. The *t*-statistics below γ_1 and γ_2 are for their average values from zero.

Portfolios	γ_0 *t*-statistic	γ_1 *t*-statistic	γ_2 *t*-statistic	Adj. R^2
	Panel A. 1927 to 1990			
20, beta ranked	0.76	0.54		0.32
	3.25	1.94		
	1.76		−0.16	0.27
	2.48		−2.03	
	1.68	0.09	−0.14	0.35
	3.82	0.41	−2.57	
20, size ranked	0.30	1.02		0.32
	−0.18	3.91		
	1.73		−0.18	0.33
	3.70		−3.50	
	−0.05	1.15	0.03	0.40
	−0.85	4.61	0.76	
100, beta and size ranked independently	0.63	0.66		0.07
	1.67	3.65		
	1.72		−0.17	0.09
	3.92		−3.17	
	1.21	0.04	−0.11	0.12
	3.74	2.63	−2.83	
100, first beta, then size ranked	0.57	0.73		0.12
	1.43	3.49		
	1.73		−0.18	0.12
	3.70		−3.48	
	1.12	0.45	−0.10	0.16
	3.43	2.83	−2.65	
100, first size, then beta ranked	0.58	0.71		0.12
	1.54	3.39		
	1.72		−0.18	0.12
	3.66		−3.43	
	1.14	0.43	−0.10	0.16
	3.78	2.58	−2.87	

Table 29.4 (Continued)

Portfolios	γ_0 *t*-statistic	γ_1 *t*-statistic	γ_2 *t*-statistic	Adj. R^2
	Panel B. 1941 to 1990			
20, beta ranked	0.95	0.36		0.33
	4.69	1.63		
	1.61		−0.10	0.28
	2.31		−1.49	
	1.70	−0.03	−0.10	0.36
	3.49	−0.18	−2.00	
20, size ranked	0.54	0.76		0.32
	0.82	3.69		
	1.73		−0.14	0.34
	4.03		−3.28	
	0.32	0.85	0.02	0.44
	−0.15	4.35	0.56	
100, beta and size ranked independently	0.87	0.42		0.07
	2.95	3.33		
	1.70		−0.13	0.10
	4.29		−3.40	
	1.43	0.20	−0.10	0.13
	4.63	2.12	−2.89	
100, first beta, then size ranked	0.82	0.49		0.12
	2.76	3.07		
	1.73		−0.14	0.13
	3.99		−3.22	
	1.35	0.26	−0.09	0.17
	4.35	2.20	−2.78	
100, first size then beta ranked	0.81	0.49		0.12
	2.75	3.12		
	1.71		−0.13	0.13
	3.96		−3.17	
	1.32	0.27	−0.09	0.17
	4.39	2.38	−2.77	

Source: Eugene F. Fama and Kenneth R. French, "The Cross-Section of Expected Stock Returns," *Journal of Finance* 47 (1992), pp. 427–66.

portfolio *G*. Hence, the beta of any asset with respect to Portfolio *G* is equal to 1.0. Thus, if *G* were to be used as the market proxy, the covariance of asset returns with their betas would be zero (because all stocks would have an identical beta of 1.0), and so would be the slope coefficient of average return as a function of beta. But, as RR show, *G* is the only efficient portfolio with this property. All other portfolios that produce a zero slope coefficient must lie inside the efficient frontier.

Figure 29.3 shows one such configuration. In this "plausible" universe (where plausible is taken to mean that the return distribution is not extraordinary), the set of portfolios with zero slope coefficient of the return-beta regression lies near the efficient

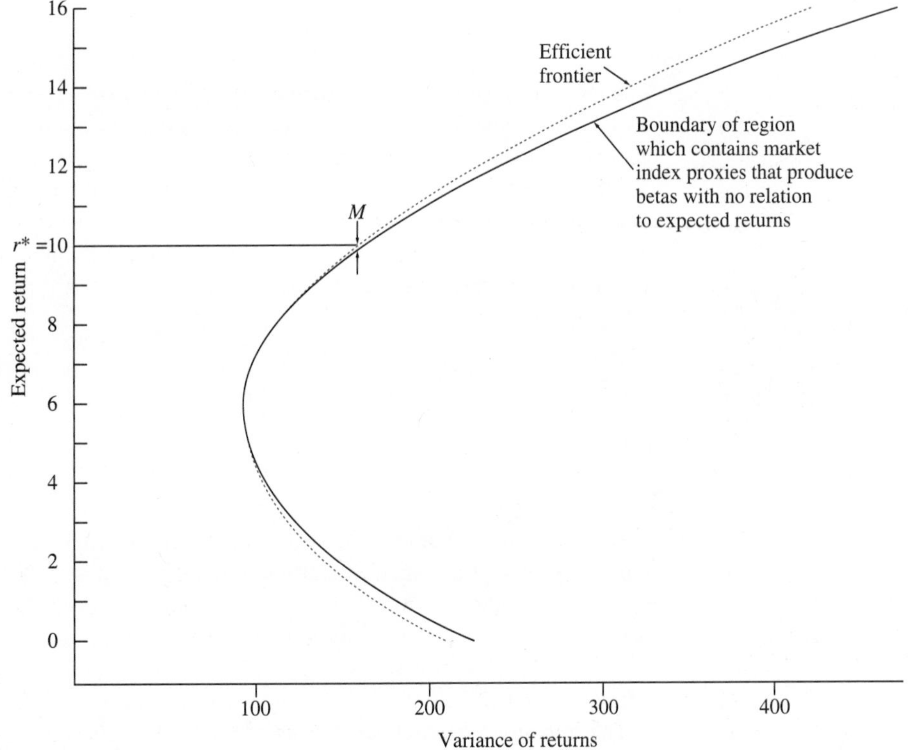

Figure 29.3

Market index proxies that produce betas having no relation to expected returns.

These proxies are located within a restricted region of the mean-variance space, a region bounded by a parabola that lies inside the efficient frontier except for a tangency at the global minimum variance point. The market proxy is located on the boundary at a distance of $M = 22$ basis points below the efficient frontier. While betas against this market proxy have zero cross-sectional correlation with expected returns, a market proxy on the efficient frontier just 22 basis points above it would produce betas that are perfectly positively collinear with expected returns.

Source: Richard Roll and Stephen A. Ross, "On the Cross-Sectional Relation between Expected Return and Betas," *Journal of Finance* 49 (1994), pp. 101–21.

frontier. Thus, even portfolios that are "nearly efficient" do not necessarily support the expected return-beta relationship.

RR make the point that the slope coefficient in the average return-beta regression cannot be relied on to reject the theoretical expected return-beta relationship. It can only indicate that the market proxy that produces this result is inefficient. But their results are valid only for tests that use Ordinary Least Squares (OLS) regressions, such as those of FF, Kothari et al., and many others. Their result does not apply to results that use Generalized Least Squares (GLS) regressions, such as Amihud et al.

Kandel and Stambaugh (KS) proceed with similar insight to derive a more constructive theory of the relation between the efficiency of a portfolio and the expected return-beta relationship it produces. In doing so, they extend Roll and Ross's conclusions and go further in interpreting the practical implications of "Roll's Critique."

KS derive a measure of *relative efficiency* for any portfolio (P). This measure is based on the expected return of Portfolio P (m_P), and the expected returns of two unique portfolios: (i) The global minimum variance portfolio (G) with mean return m_G; and (ii) the efficient frontier portfolio (X) with the same variance as P, with mean return m_X.

Because P and X are equally risky, the relative efficiency of Portfolio P (denoted RE_P) is defined in terms of risk premiums over the minimum-variance portfolio G as follows:

$$RE_P = \frac{m_P - m_G}{m_X - m_G}$$

This measure results in values between -1.0 and 1.0. When P is efficient, so that $m_P = m_X$, $RE_P = 1.0$. The value -1.0 occurs when P lies on the discarded part of the efficient frontier directly below X.

When average asset returns are regressed against their betas on P using GLS, the procedure makes use of the entire covariance matrix of the asset asset-returns, unlike OLS which uses only the betas and returns. This results in an intercept (a_0) and slope (a_1) coefficient that have the properties:

$$a_0 = m_{X0} + (1 - RE_P)(m_X - m_{X0}) \tag{29.4a}$$

$$a_1 = RE_P(m_X - m_{X0}) \tag{29.4b}$$

and the square correlation coefficient of the regression is:

$$R^2_{GLS} = RE^2_P$$

where $X0$ is the (unique) zero beta portfolio of X with mean return m_{X0}. Note that equation 24.4 implies that when P is efficient (so that $RE_P = 1.0$), the CAPM will hold. In this case, the intercept in (29.4a) will be equal to the zero-beta mean return, and the slope coefficient in (29.4b) will equal the risk premium on portfolio X which is identical to that of P. Moreover, when, as we expect in practice, Portfolio P is inefficient, the correlation coefficient of the GLS regression reveals the relative efficiency of P, RE_P.

The RR and KS studies teach us a practical lesson about the implications of the CAPM. We saw in Chapter 8 that the CAPM implies both that: (i) the market portfolio is mean-variance efficient, and (ii) the relation between expected return and beta is linear. Now we know that when the CAPM provides, at best, an approximate description of reality, one of these implications can hold approximately while the other can fail completely. Thus, it is useful to think about each implication separately and concentrate on that which is relevant to the issue at hand.

In the context of performance evaluation, when an index fund is pitted against an alternative portfolio strategy with similar risk, the mean-variance efficiency of the index is the relevant implication. However, we now know that the degree of efficiency of the index has little bearing on the properties of the expected return-beta relationship. In this context, KS caution that using the expected return-beta relationship for capital budgeting purposes may be misleading when the expected return-beta relationship is not exact.

29.3 Option Pricing

Research involving contingent claims analysis is probably the most active in the area of finance. The scope and economic importance of applications of contingent claims analysis has spawned a quite distinct professional expertise, usually referred to as financial engineering, which is really a separate field in investment management, investment

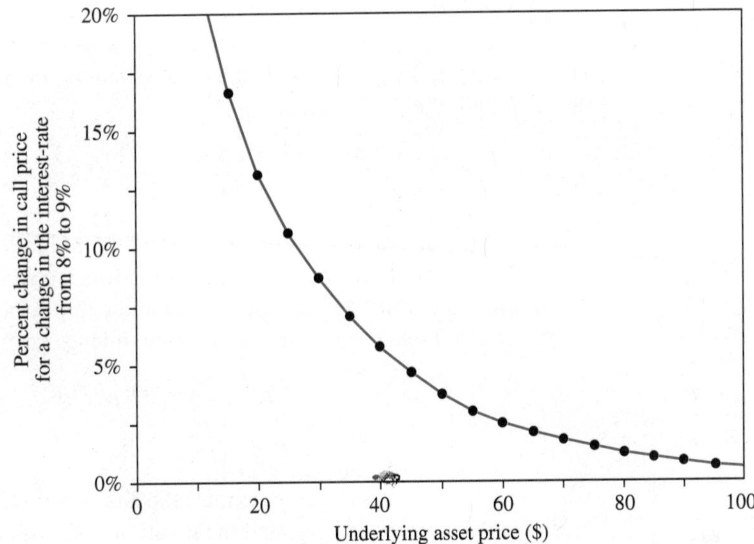

Figure 29.4
The percent change in a call price (with $60 exercise price and half a year to expiration, on an underlying asset with price variability of 0.3%/year) for a change in the annual interest rate from 8% to 9%, as a function of the underlying asset price

banking, and corporate finance. Several journals (for example, *Derivatives Quarterly* and *The Journal of Derivatives*) are dedicated to research in this area, while a significant part of the space in other finance journals contains articles in this area. Recent advances in this field tend to be highly technical, however, and, for the large part, the marginal contribution of this work to the *conceptual* framework of investments relative to its technical difficulty would put it outside standard courses in investments and the scope of this text. We briefly describe one exception, an article by Bergman[12] that extends option pricing to incorporate differential borrowing and lending rates. This article is a significant departure from other work because it shows that the no-arbitrage option pricing relationships (such as the pricing models based on replication that we developed in Chapter 20) are not necessarily independent across each asset and its derivative securities. In fact, Bergman shows that no-arbitrage bands will depend on the number of securities that are traded.

The Black-Scholes option pricing model assumes a complete market without trading friction and with a uniform borrowing and lending rate. Almost no attention in the literature has been given to the potential implications for option pricing of differences in the borrowing and lending rates. Bergman suggests that the reason is that prices of equity options appear insensitive to changes in interest rates. To motivate his attempt to incorporate differential interest rates into the model, Bergman first demonstrates that for a range of underlying prices and interest rates, call prices will in fact change by a large *proportional* amount when interest rates change. See Figure 29.4 for an example of this analysis.

12 Yaacov Z. Bergman, "Option Pricing with Differential Interest Rates," *Review of Financial Studies* 8 (1995).

Suppose that at time $t = 0$ a European put and a call written on the same stock, with identical exercise price, X, and maturity T, are selling for P and C, respectively. Then if the borrowing rate, r_B exceeds the lending rate r_L, the familiar put-call parity must be replaced with the double inequality,

$$e^{r_L T} \leq \frac{X}{S + P - C} \leq e^{r_B T} \tag{29.5}$$

It can be seen that when $r_L = r_B$, equation 29.5 reduces to the familiar put-call parity condition. When all other assumptions of the Black-Scholes (BS) model hold, equation 29.5 implies an arbitrage band on the put and call prices, bounded by the BS prices of the put and call evaluated at the appropriate interest rate:

$$C_{BS}(r_L) \leq C \leq C_{BS}(r_B) \tag{26.6a}$$

$$P_{BS}(r_B) \leq P \leq P_{BS}(r_L) \tag{26.6b}$$

where $C_{BS}(r_L)$ in equation 26.6 denotes the Black-Scholes value of a call option evaluated using the interest rate r_L, and the notation is similar for put options and borrowing rates.

Now consider two call options on the same stock with the same maturity date but with different exercise prices, $X_1 < X_2$. We can find all price combinations that rule out arbitrage opportunities based on any option position that is long one contract of C_1 (the call with X_1) and short μ contracts of C_2 (the call with X_2). If we repeat this exercise for different values of μ, and combine all the no-arbitrage bands implied by all possible values of μ, we will produce a no-arbitrage oval (i.e., an oval-shaped region of price combinations in which arbitrage opportunities are not present), as depicted in Figure 29.5. This oval links the prices of options with different exercise prices.

Bergman extends this analysis in two ways. First, when short sales are costly, contingent claim pricing is analogous to the case of differential interest rates. Second, the existence of contingent claims on other underlying assets generates no-arbitrage bands on spreads with pairs of contingent claims on two assets, and so on. Thus, no-arbitrage ovals can be constructed for the entire set of contingent claims on a universe of underlying assets. The important conclusion is that trade frictions imply that the option prices that are consistent with the absence of arbitrage opportunities are not unique. The frictions result in entire regions—Bergman's arbitrage ovals—that link the prices of all contingent claims. Moreover, an increase in the number of claims mitigates the cost of the friction (i.e., shrinks the arbitrage ovals).

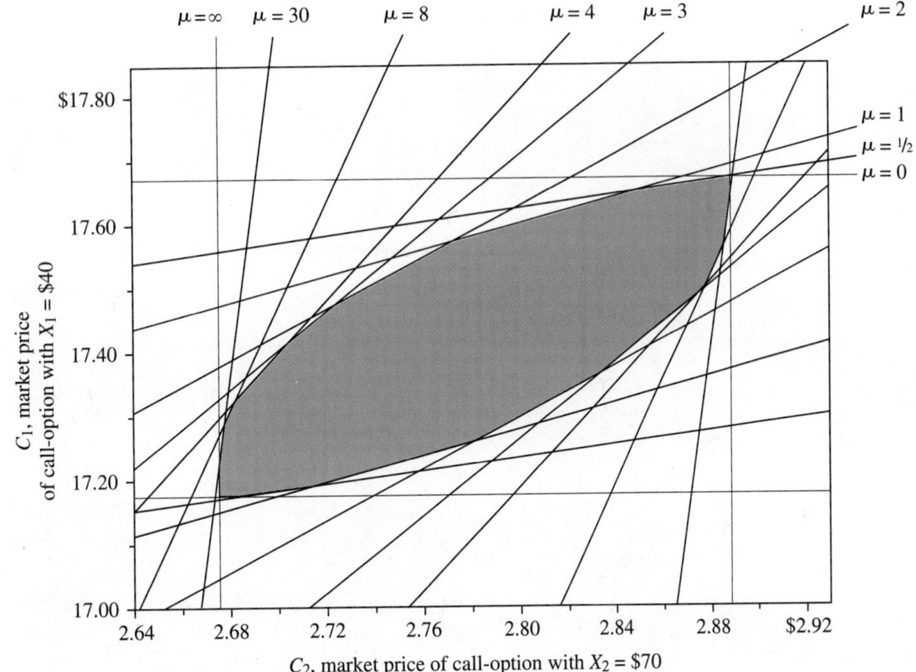

Figure 29.5
The arbitrage oval. Any pair of call prices that lies outside the arbitrage oval represents an arbitrage opportunity

Appendix

A Quantitative Review

B Solutions to Concept Checks

Appendix A
Quantitative Review

STUDENTS IN MANAGEMENT AND INVESTMENT COURSES TYPICALLY COME FROM A VARIETY OF BACKGROUNDS. Some, who have had strong quantitative training, may feel perfectly comfortable with formal mathematical presentation of material. Others, who have had less technical training, may easily be overwhelmed by mathematical formalism.

Most students, however, will benefit from some coaching to make the study of investment easier and more efficient. If you had a good introductory quantitative methods course, and like the text that was used, you may want to refer to it whenever you feel in need of a refresher. If you feel uncomfortable with standard quantitative texts, this reference is for you. Our aim is to present the essential quantitative concepts and methods in a self-contained, nontechnical, and intuitive way. Our approach is structured in line with requirements for the CFA program. The material included is relevant to investment management by the ICFA, the Institute of Chartered Financial Analysts. We hope you find this appendix helpful. Use it to make your venture into investments more enjoyable.

Note: If you do not already have a financial calculator, we strongly advise you get one. Many financial calculators have a statistical mode that allows you to compute expected values, standard deviations, and regressions with ease. Actually, working through the user manual is a helpful exercise by itself. If you are interested in investments, you should look at a financial calculator as a good initial investment.

A.1 PROBABILITY DISTRIBUTIONS

Statisticians talk about "experiments," or "trials," and refer to possible outcomes as "events." In a roll of a die, for example, the "elementary events" are the numbers

1 through 6. Turning up one side represents the most disaggregate *mutually exclusive* outcome. Other events are *compound,* that is, they consist of more than one elementary event, such as the result "odd number" or "less than 4." In this case "odd" and "less than 4" are not mutually exclusive. Compound events can be mutually exclusive outcomes, however, such as "less than 4" and "equal to or greater than 4."

In decision making, "experiments" are circumstances in which you contemplate a decision that will affect the set of possible event (outcomes) and their likelihood (probabilities). Decision theory calls for you to identify optimal decisions under various sets of circumstances (experiments), which you may do by determining losses from departures from optimal decisions.

When the outcomes of a decision (experiment) can be quantified, that is, when a numerical value can be assigned to each elementary event, the decision outcome is called a *random variable.* In the context of investment decision making, the random variable (the payoff to the investment decision), is denominated either in dollars or as a percentage rate of return.

The set or list of all possible values of a random variable, *with* their associated probabilities, is called the *probability distribution* of the random variable. Values that are impossible for the random variable to take on are sometimes listed with probabilities of zero. All possible elementary events are assigned values and probabilities, and thus the probabilities have to sum to 1.0.

Sometimes the values of a random variable are *uncountable,* meaning that you cannot make a list of all possible values. For example, suppose you roll a ball on a line and report the distance it rolls before it comes to a rest. Any distance is possible, and the precision of the report will depend on the need of the roller and/or the quality of the measuring device. Another uncountable random variable is one that describes the weight of a newborn baby. Any positive weight (with some upper bound) is possible.

We call uncountable probability distributions "continuous," for the obvious reason that, at least within a range, the possible outcomes (those with positive probabilities) lie anywhere on a continuum of values. Because there is an infinite number of possible values for the random variable in any continuous distribution, such a probability distribution has to be described by a formula that relates the values of the random variable and their associated probabilities, instead of by a simple list of outcomes and probabilities. We discuss continuous distributions later in this section.

Even countable probability distributions can be complicated. For example, on the New York Stock Exchange stock prices are quoted in eighths. This means the price of a stock at some future date is a *countable* random variable. Probability distributions of countable random variables are called *discrete distributions.* Although a stock price cannot dip below zero, it has no upper bound. Therefore a stock price is a random variable that can take on infinitely many values, even though they are countable, and its discrete probability distribution will have to be given by a formula just like a continuous distribution.

There are random variables that are both discrete and finite. When the probability distribution of the relevant random variable is countable and finite, decision making is tractable and relatively easy to analyze. One example is the decision to call a coin toss "heads" or "tails," with a payoff of zero for guessing wrong and 1 for guessing right.

Table A.1 Anheuser-Busch Companies, Inc., Dispersion of Potential Returns

Outcome	Probability	Expected Return*
Number 1	.20	20%
Number 2	.50	30
Number 3	.30	50

*Assume for the moment that the expected return in each scenario will be realized with certainty. This is the way returns were expressed in the original question.

The random variable of the decision to guess "heads" has a discrete, finite probability distribution. It can be written as

Event	Value	Probability
Heads	1	.5
Tails	0	.5

This type of analysis usually is referred to as "scenario analysis." Because scenario analysis is relatively simple, it is used sometimes even when the actual random variable is infinite and uncountable. You can do this by specifying values and probabilities for a set of compound, yet exhaustive and mutually exclusive, events. Because it is simple and has important uses, we handle this case first.

Here is a problem from the 1988 CFA examination.

Mr. Arnold, an Investment Committee member, has confidence in the forecasting ability of the analysts in the firm's research department. However, he is concerned that analysts may not appreciate risk as an important investment consideration. This is especially true in an increasingly volatile investment environment. In addition, he is conservative and risk averse. He asks for your risk analysis for Anheuser-Busch stock.

1. Using Table A.1, calculate the following measures of dispersion of returns for Anheuser-Busch stock under each of the three outcomes displayed. Show calculations.
   a. Range.
   b. Variance: $\Sigma \Pr(i)[r_i - E(r)]^2$.
   c. Standard deviation.
   d. Coefficient of variation: $CV = \dfrac{\sigma}{E(r)}$.
2. Discuss the usefulness of each of the four measures listed in quantifying risk.

The examination questions require very specific answers. We use the questions as a framework for exposition of scenario analysis.

Table A.1 specifies a three-scenario decision problem. The random variable is the rate of return on investing in Anheuser-Busch stock. However, the third column that specifies the value of the random variable does not say simply "Return"—it says "Expected Return." This tells us that the scenario description is a compound event consisting of many elementary events, as is almost always the case. We streamline or simplify reality in order to gain tractability.

Analysts who prepare input lists must decide on the number of scenarios with which to describe the entire probability distribution, as well as the rates of return to allocate to each one. This process calls for determining the probability of occurrence of each scenario, *and* the expected rate of return *within* (conditional on) each scenario, which governs the outcome of each scenario. Once you become familiar with scenario analysis, you will be able to build a simple scenario description from any probability distribution.

Expected Returns. The expected value of a random variable is the answer to the question, "What would be the average value of the variable if the 'experiment' (the circumstances and the decision) were repeated infinitely?" In the case of an investment decision, your answer is meant to describe the reward from making the decision.

Note that the question is hypothetical and abstract. It is hypothetical because, practically, the exact circumstances of a decision (the "experiment") often cannot be repeated even once, much less infinitely. It is abstract because, even if the experiment were to be repeated many times (short of infinitely), the *average* rate of return may not be one of the possible outcomes. To demonstrate, suppose that the probability distribution of the rate of return on a proposed investment project is +20% or −20%, with equal probabilities of .5. Intuition indicates that repeating this investment decision will get us ever closer to an average rate of return of zero. But a one-time investment cannot produce a rate of return of zero. Is the "expected" return still a useful concept when the proposed investment represents a one-time decision?

One argument for using expected return to measure the reward from making investment decisions is that, although a specific investment decision may be made only once, the decision maker will be making many (although different) investment decisions over time. Over time, then, the average rate of return will come close to the average of the expected values of all the individual decisions. Another reason for using the expected value is that admittedly we lack a better measure.[1]

The probabilities of the scenarios in Table A.1 predict the relative frequencies of the outcomes. If the current investment in Anheuser-Busch could be replicated many times, a 20% return would occur 20% of the time, a 30% return would occur 50% of the time, and 50% return would occur the remaining 30% of the time. This notion of probabilities and the definition of the expected return tells us how to calculate the expected return.[2]

$$E(r) = .20 \times .20 + .50 \times .30 + .30 \times .50 = .34 \text{ (or 34\%)}$$

Labeling each scenario $i = 1,2,3$, and using the summation sign, Σ, we can write the formula for the expected return:

$$\begin{aligned} E(r) &= \Pr(1)r_1 + \Pr(2)r_2 + \Pr(3)r_3 \\ &= \sum_{i=1}^{3} \Pr(i)r_i \end{aligned} \tag{A.1}$$

[1] Another case where we use a less-than-ideal measure is the case of yield to maturity on a bond. The YTM measures the rate of return from investing a bond *if* it is held to maturity and *if* the coupons can be reinvested at the same yield to maturity over the life of the bond.

[2] We will consistently perform calculations in decimal fractions to avoid confusion.

The definition of the expectation in equation A.1 reveals two important properties of random variables. First, if you add a constant to a random variable, its expectation is also increased by the same constant. If, for example, the return in each scenario in Table A.1 were increased by 5%, the expectation would increase to 39%. Try this, using equation A.1. If a random variable is multiplied by a constant, its expectation will change by that same proportion. If you multiply the return in each scenario by 1.5, $E(r)$ would change to $1.5 \times .34 = .51$ (or 51%).

Second, the deviation of a random variable from its expected value is itself a random variable. Take any rate of return r_1 in Table A.1 and define its deviation from the expected value by

$$d_i = r_i - E(r)$$

What is the expected value of d? $E(d)$ is the expected deviation from the expected value, and by equation A.1 it is necessarily zero because

$$\begin{aligned} E(d) &= \Sigma \Pr(i)d_i = \Sigma \Pr(i)[r_i - E(r)] \\ &= \Sigma \Pr(i)r_i - E(r)\Sigma \Pr(i) \\ &= E(r) - E(r) = 0 \end{aligned}$$

Measures of Dispersion: The Range. Assume for a moment that the expected return for each scenario in Table A.1 will be realized with certainty in the event that scenario occurs. Then the set of possible return outcomes is unambiguously 20%, 30%, and 50%. The *range* is the difference between the maximum and the minimum values of the random variable, 50% − 20% = 30% in this case. Range is clearly a crude measure of dispersion. Here it is particularly inappropriate because the scenario returns themselves are given as expected values, and therefore the true range is unknown. There is a variant of the range, the *interquartile range,* that we explain in the discussion of descriptive statistics.

Measures of Dispersion: The Variance. One interpretation of variance is that it measures the "expected surprises." Although that may sound like a contradiction in terms, it really is not. First, think of a surprise as a deviation from expectation. The surprise is not in the *fact* that expectation has not been realized, but rather in the *direction* and *magnitude* of the deviation.

The example in Table A.1 leads us to *expect* a rate of return of 34% from investing in Anheuser-Busch stock. A second look at the scenario returns, however, tells us that we should stand ready to be surprised because the probability of earning exactly 34% is zero. Being sure that our expectation will not be realized does not mean that we can be sure what the realization is going to be. The element of surprise lies in the direction and magnitude of the deviation of the actual return from expectation, and that is the relevant random variable for the measurement of uncertainty. Its probability distribution adds to our understanding of the nature of the uncertainty that we are facing.

We measure the reward by the expected return. Intuition suggests that we measure uncertainty by the expected *deviation* of the rate of return from expectation. We showed in the previous section, however, that the expected deviation from expectation must be zero. Positive deviations, when weighted by probabilities, are exactly offset by negative deviations. To get around this problem, we replace the random variable "deviation from expectations" (denoted earlier by d) with its square, which must be positive even if d itself is negative.

We define the *variance,* our measure of surprise or dispersion, by the *expected squared deviation of the rate of return from its expectation.* With the Greek letter sigma square denoting variance, the formal definition is

$$\sigma^2(r) = E(d^2) = E[r_i - E(r)]^2 = \Sigma\ \Pr(i)[r_i - E(r)]^2 \qquad \text{(A.2)}$$

Squaring each deviation eliminates the sign, which eliminates the offsetting effects of positive and negative deviations.

In the case of Anheuser-Busch, the variance of the rate of return on the stock is

$$\sigma^2(r) = .2(.20 - .34)^2 + .5(.30 - .34)^2 + .3(.50 - .34)^2 = .0124$$

Remember that if you add a constant to a random variable, the variance does not change at all. This is because the expectation also changes by the same constant, and hence deviations from expectation remain unchanged. You can test this by using the data from Table A.1.

Multiplying the random variable by a constant, however, *will* change the variance. Suppose that each return is multiplied by the factor k. The new random variable, kr, has expectation of $E(kr) = kE(r)$. Therefore the deviation of kr from its expectation is

$$d(kr) = kr - E(kr) = kr - kE(r) = k[r - E(r)] = kd(r)$$

If each deviation is multiplied by k, the squared deviations are multiplied by the square of k:

$$\sigma^2(kr) = k^2\sigma^2(r)$$

To summarize, adding a constant to a random variable does not affect the variance. Multiplying a random variable by a constant, though, will cause the variance to be multiplied by the square of that constant.

Measures of Dispersion: The Standard Deviation. A closer look at the variance will reveal that its dimension is different from that of the expected return. Recall that we squared deviations from the expected return in order to make all values positive. This alters the *dimension* (units of measure) of the variance to "square percents." To transform the variance into terms of percentage return, we simply take the square root of the variance. This measure is the *standard deviation.* In the case of Anheuser-Busch's stock return, the standard deviation is

$$\sigma = (\sigma^2)^{1/2} = \sqrt{.0124} = .1114 \text{ (or } 11.14\%) \qquad \text{(A.3)}$$

Note that you always need to calculate the variance first before you can get the standard deviation. The standard deviation conveys the same information as the variance but in a different form.

We know already that adding a constant to r will not affect its variance, and it will not affect the standard deviation either. We also know that multiplying a random variable by a constant multiplies the variance by the square of that constant. From the definition of the standard deviation in equation A.3, it should be clear that multiplying a random variable by a constant will multiply the standard deviation by the (absolute value of this) constant. The absolute value is needed because the sign of the constant is lost through squaring the deviations in the computation of the variance. Formally,

$$\sigma(kr) = \text{Abs}(k)\,\sigma(r)$$

Try a transformation of your choice using the data in Table A.1.

Measures of Dispersion: The Coefficient of Variation. To evaluate the magnitude of dispersion of a random variable, it is useful to compare it to the expected value. The ratio of the standard deviation to the expectation is called the *coefficient of variation.* In the case of returns on Anheuser-Busch stock, it is

$$\text{CV} = \frac{\sigma}{E(r)} = \frac{.1114}{.3400} = .3285 \tag{A.4}$$

The standard deviation of the Anheuser-Busch return is about one-third of the expected return (reward). Whether this value for the coefficient of variation represents a big risk depends on what can be obtained with alternative investments.

The coefficient of variation is far from an ideal measure of dispersion. Suppose that a plausible expected value for a random variable is zero. In this case, regardless of the magnitude of the standard deviation, the coefficient of variation will be infinite. Clearly, this measure is not applicable in all cases. Generally, the analyst must choose a measure of dispersion that fits the particular decision at hand. In finance, the standard deviation is the measure of choice in most cases where overall risk is concerned. (For individual assets, the measure β, explained in the text, is the measure used.)

Skewness. So far, we have described the measures of dispersion as indicating the size of the average surprise, loosely speaking. The standard deviation is not exactly equal to the average surprise though, because squaring deviations, and then taking the square root of the average square deviation, results in greater weight (emphasis) placed on larger deviations. Other than that, it is simply a measure that tells us how big a deviation from expectation can be expected.

Most decision makers agree that the expected value and standard deviation of a random variable are the most important statistics. However, once we calculate them another question about risk (the nature of the random variable describing deviations from expectations) is pertinent: Are the larger deviations (surprises) more likely to be positive? Risk-averse decision makers worry about bad surprises, and the standard deviation does not distinguish good from bad ones. Most risk avoiders are believed to prefer random variables with likely *small negative surprises* and *less* likely *large positive surprises,* to the reverse, likely *small good surprises* and *less* likely *large bad surprises.* More than anything, risk is really defined by the possibility of disaster (large bad surprises).

One measure that distinguishes between the likelihood of large good-vs.-bad surprises is the "third moment." It builds on the behavior of deviations from the expectation, the random variable we have denoted by *d*. Denoting the *third moment* by M_3, we define it:

$$M_3 = E(d^3) = E[r_i - E(r)]^3 = \Sigma \Pr(i)[r_i - E(r)]^3 \tag{A.5}$$

Cubing each value of d (taking it to the third power) magnifies larger deviations more than smaller ones. Raising values to an odd power causes them to retain their sign. Recall that the sum of all deviations multiplied by their probabilities is zero because positive deviations weighted by their probabilities exactly offset the negative. When *cubed* deviations are multiplied by their probabilities and then added up, however, large deviations will dominate. The sign will tell us in this case whether *large positive* deviations dominate (positive M_3) or whether *large negative* deviations dominate (negative M_3).

Incidentally, it is obvious why this measure of skewness is called the third moment; it refers to cubing. Similarly, the variance is often referred to as the second moment, because it requires squaring.

Returning to the investment decision described in Table A.1, with the expected value of 34%, the third moment is

$$M_3 = .2(.20 - .34)^3 + .5(.30 - .34)^3 + .3(.50 - .34)^3 = .000648$$

The sign of the third moment tells us that larger *positive* surprises dominate in this case. You might have guessed this by looking at the deviations from expectation and their probabilities; that is, the most likely event is a return of 30%, which makes for a small negative surprise. The other negative surprise (20% − 34% = −14%) is smaller in magnitude than the positive surprise (50% − 34% = 16%) *and* is also *less* likely (probability .20) relative to the positive surprise, 30% (probability .30). The difference appears small, however, and we do not know whether the third moment may be an important issue for the decision to invest in Anheuser-Busch.

It is difficult to judge the importance of the third moment, here .000648, without a benchmark. Following the same reasoning we applied to the standard deviation, we can take the *third root* of M_3 (which we denote m_3) and compare it to the standard deviation. This yields $m_3 = .0865 = 8.65\%$, which is not trivial compared with the standard deviation (11.14%).

Another Example: Options on Anheuser-Busch Stock. Suppose that the current price of Anheuser-Busch stock is $30. A call option on the stock is selling for 60 cents, and a put is selling for $4. Both have an exercise price of $42 and maturity date to match the scenarios in Table A.1.

The call option allows you to buy the stock at the exercise price. You will choose to do so if the call ends up "in the money," that is, the stock price is above the exercise price. The profit in this case is the difference between the stock price and the exercise price, less cost of the call. Even if you exercise the call, your profit may still be negative if the cash flow from the exercise of the call does not cover the initial cost of the call. If the call ends up "out of the money," that is, the stock price is below the exercise price, you will let the call expire worthless and suffer a loss equal to the cost of the call.

The put option allows you to sell the stock at the exercise price. You will choose to do so if the put ends up "in the money," that is, the stock price is below the exercise price. Your profit is then the difference between the exercise price and the stock price, less the initial cost of the put. Here again, if the cash flow is not sufficient to cover the

Table A.2 Scenario Analysis for Investment in Options on Anheuser-Busch Stock

	Scenario 1	Scenario 2	Scenario 3
Probability	.20	.50	.30
Event			
1. Return on stock	20%	30%	50%
Stock price (initial price = $30)	$36.00	$39.00	$45.00
2. Cash flow from call (exercise price = $42)	0	0	$3.00
Call profit (initial price = $.60)	−$.60	−$.60	$2.40
Call rate of return	−100%	−100%	400%
3. Cash flow from put (exercise price = $42)	$6.00	$3.00	0
Put profit (initial price = $4)	$2.00	−$1.00	−$4.00
Put rate of return	50%	−25%	−100%

cost of the put, the investment will show a loss. If the put ends up "out of the money," you again let it expire worthless, taking a loss equal to the initial cost of the put.

The scenario analysis of these alternative investments is described in Table A.2.

The expected rates of return on the call and put are

$$E(r_{\text{call}}) = .2(-1) + .5(-1) + .3(4) = .5 \text{ (or 50\%)}$$
$$E(r_{\text{put}}) = .2(.5) + .5(-.25) + .3(-1) = -.325 \text{ (or } -32.5\%)$$

The negative expected return on the put may be justified by the fact that it is a hedge asset, in this case an insurance policy against losses from holding Anheuser-Busch stock. The variance and standard deviation of the two investments are

$$\sigma^2_{\text{call}} = .2(-1 - .5)^2 + .5(-1 - .5)^2 + .3(4 - .5)^2 = 5.25$$
$$\sigma^2_{\text{put}} = .2[.5 - (-.325)]^2 + .5[-.25 - (-.325)]^2 + .3[-1 - (-.325)]^2 = .2756$$
$$\sigma_{\text{call}} = \sqrt{5.25} = 2.2913 \text{ (or 229.13\%)}$$
$$\sigma_{\text{put}} = \sqrt{.2756} = .525 \text{ (or 52.5\%)}$$

These are very large standard deviations. Comparing the standard deviation of the call's return to its expected value, we get the coefficient of variation:

$$\text{CV}_{\text{call}} = \frac{2.2913}{.5} = 4.5826$$

Refer back to the coefficient of variation for the stock itself, .3275, and it is clear that these instruments have high standard deviations. This is quite common for stock options. The negative expected return of the put illustrates again the problem in interpreting the magnitude of the "surprise" indicated by the coefficient of variation.

Moving to the third moments of the two probability distributions:

$$M_3(\text{call}) = .2(-1 - .5)^3 + .5(-1 - .5)^3 + .3(4 - .5)^3 = 10.5$$
$$M_3(\text{put}) = .2[.5 - (-.325)]^3 + .5[-.25 - (-.325)]^3 + .3[-1 - (-.325)]^3$$
$$= .02025$$

Both instruments are positively skewed, which is typical of options and one part of their attractiveness. In this particular circumstance the call is more skewed than the put. To establish this fact, note the third root of the third moment:

$$m_3(\text{call}) = M_3(\text{call})^{1/3} = 2.1898 \text{ (or } 218.98\%)$$
$$m_3(\text{put}) = .02^{1/3} = .2725 \text{ (or } 27.25\%)$$

Compare these figures to the standard deviations, 229.13% for the call and 52.5% for the put, and you can see that a large part of the standard deviation of the option is driven by the possibility of large good surprises instead of by the more likely, yet smaller, bad surprises.[3]

So far we have described discrete probability distributions using scenario analysis. We shall come back to decision making in a scenario analysis framework in Section A.3 on multivariate statistics.

Continuous Distributions: Normal and Lognormal Distributions

When a compact scenario analysis is possible and acceptable, decisions may be quite simple. Often, however, so many relevant scenarios must be specified that scenario analysis is impossible for practical reasons. Even in the case of Anheuser-Busch, as we were careful to specify, the individual scenarios considered actually represented compound events.

When many possible values of rate of return have to be considered, we must use a formula that describes the probability distribution (relates values to probabilities). As we noted earlier, there are two types of probability distributions: discrete and continuous. Scenario analysis involves a discrete distribution. However, the two most useful distributions in investments, the normal and lognormal, are continuous. At the same time they are often used to approximate variables with distributions that are known to be discrete, such as stock prices. The probability distribution of future prices and returns is discrete—prices are quoted in eighths. Yet the industry norm is to approximate these distributions by the normal or lognormal distribution.

Standard Normal Distribution. The normal distribution, also known as Gaussian (after the mathematician Gauss) or bell-shaped, describes random variables with the following properties and is shown in Figure A.1:

- The expected value is the mode (the most frequent elementary event) and also the median (the middle value in the sense that half the elementary events are greater and half smaller). Note that the expected value, unlike the median or mode, requires weighting by probabilities to produce the concept of central value.
- The normal probability distribution is symmetric around the expected value. In other words, the likelihood of equal absolute-positive and negative deviations from expec-

[3] Note that the expected return of the put is −32.5%; hence, the worst surprise is −67.5%, and the best is 82.5%. The middle scenario is also a positive deviation of 7.5% (with a high probability of .50). These two elements explain the positive skewness of the put.

Figure A.1
Probabilities under the normal density

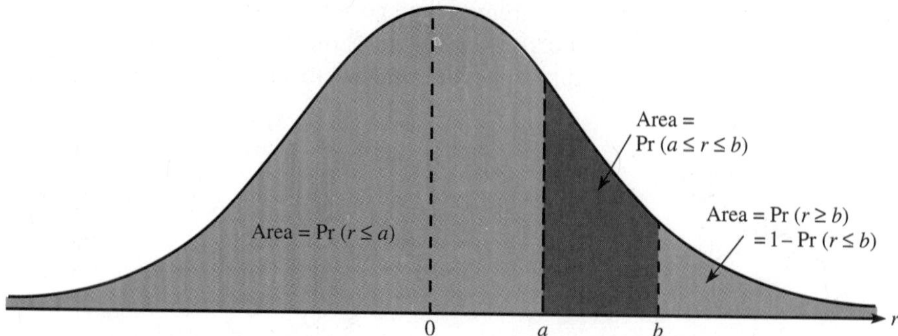

tation is equal. Larger deviations from the expected value are less likely than are smaller deviations. In fact, the essence of the normal distribution is that the probability of deviations decreases exponentially with the magnitude of the deviation (positive and negative alike).

- A normal distribution is identified completely by two parameters, the expected value and the standard deviation. The property of the normal distribution that makes it most convenient for portfolio analysis is that any weighted sum or normally distributed random variables produce a random variable that also is normally distributed. This property is called *stability.* It is also true that if you add a constant to a "normal" random variable (meaning a random variable with a normal probability distribution) or multiply it by a constant, then the transformed random variable also will be normally distributed.

Suppose that n is any random variable (not necessarily normal), with expectation μ and standard deviation σ. As we showed earlier, if you add a constant c to n, the standard deviation is not affected at all, but the mean will change to $\mu + c$. If you multiply n by a constant b, its mean and standard deviation will change by the same proportion to $b\mu$ and $b\sigma$. If n is normal, the transformed variable also will be normal.

Stability, together with the property that a normal variable is completely characterized by its expectation and standard deviation, implies that if we know one normal probability distribution with a given expectation and standard deviation, we know them all.

Subtracting the expected value from each observation and then dividing by the standard deviation we obtain the *standard normal distribution* which has an expectation of zero, and both variance and standard deviation equal to 1.0. Formally, the relationship between the value of the standard normal random variable, z, and its probability, f, is given by

$$f(z) = \frac{1}{\sqrt{2\pi}} \exp\left(\frac{-z^2}{2}\right) \tag{A.6}$$

where "exp" is the quantity e to the power of the expression in the brackets. The quantity e is an important number just like the well-known π that also appears in the function. It is important enough to earn a place on the keyboard of your financial calculator, mostly because it is used also in continuous compounding.

Probability functions of continuous distributions are called *densities* and denoted by f, rather than by the "Pr" of scenario analysis. The reason is that the probability of any of the infinitely many possible values of z is infinitesimally small. Density is a function that allows us to obtain the probability of a *range of values* by integrating it over a desired range. In other words, whenever we want the probability that a standard normal variate (a random variable) will fall in the range from $z = a$ to $z = b$, we have to add up the density values, $f(z)$ for all zs from a to b. There are infinitely many zs in that range, regardless how close a is to b. *Integration* is the mathematical operation that achieves this task.

Consider first the probability that a standard normal variate will take on a value less than or equal to a, that is, z is in the range $[-\infty, a]$. We have to integrate the density from ∞ to a. The result is called the *cumulative (normal) distribution,* and denoted by $N(a)$. When a approaches infinity, any value is allowed for z; hence, the probability that z will end up in that range approaches 1.0. It is a property of any density that when it is integrated over the entire range of the random variable, the cumulative distribution is 1.0.

In the same way, the probability that a standard normal variate will take on a value less than or equal to b is $N(b)$. The probability that a standard normal variate will take on a value in the range $[a,b]$ is just the difference between $N(b)$ and $N(a)$. Formally.

$$\Pr(a \leqq z \leqq b) = N(b) - N(a)$$

These concepts are illustrated in Figure A.1. The graph shows the normal density. It demonstrates the symmetry of the normal density around the expected value (zero form the standard normal variate, which is also the mode and the median), and the smaller likelihood of larger deviations from expectation. As is true for any density, the entire area under the density graph adds up to 1.0. The values a and b are chosen to be positive, so they are to the right of the expected value. The left-most blue shaded area is the proportion of the area under the density for which the value of z is less than or equal to a. Thus this area yields the cumulative distribution for a, the probability that z will be smaller than or equal to a. The gray shaded area is the area under the density graph between a and b. If we add that area to the cumulative distribution of a, we get the entire area up to b, that is, the probability that z will be anywhere to the left of b. Thus, the area between a and b has to be the probability that z will fall between a and b.

Applying the same logic, we find the probability that z will take on a value greater than b. We know already that the probability that z will be smaller than or equal to b is $N(b)$. The compound events "smaller than or equal to b" and "greater than b" are mutually exclusive *and* "exhaustive," meaning that they include all possible outcomes. Thus their probabilities sum to 1.0, and the probability that z is greater than b is simply equal to one minus the probability that z is less than or equal to b. Formally, $\Pr(z > b) = 1 - N(b)$.

Look again at Figure A.1. The area under the density graph between b and infinity is just the difference between the entire area under the graph (equal to 1.0), and the area between minus infinity and b, that is, $N(b)$.

The normal density is sufficiently complex that its cumulative distribution, its integral, does not have an exact formulaic closed-form solution. It must be obtained by numerical (approximation) methods. These values are produced in tables that give the value $N(z)$ for any z, such as Table 20.2 of this text.

Figure A.2
Probabilities and the cumulative normal distribution

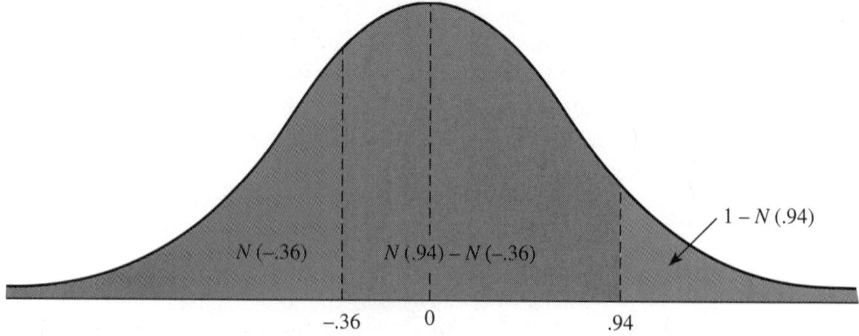

To illustrate, let us find the following probabilities for a standard normal variate:

$$\Pr(z \leqq -.36) = N(-.36) = \text{Probability that } z \text{ is less than or equal to } -.36$$
$$\Pr(z \leqq .94) = N(.94) = \text{Probability that } z \text{ is less than or equal to } .94$$
$$\Pr(-.36 \leqq z \leqq .94) = N(.94) - N(-.36) = \text{Probability that } z \text{ will be in the range } [-.36, .94]$$
$$\Pr(z > .94) = 1 - N(.94) = \text{Probability that } z \text{ is greater than } .94$$

Use Table 20.2 of the cumulative standard normal (sometimes called the area under the normal density) and Figure A.2. The table shows that

$$N(-.36) = .3594$$
$$N(.94) = .8264$$

In Figure A.2 the area under the graph between $-.36$ and $.94$ is the probability that z will fall between $-.36$ and $.94$. Hence,

$$\Pr(-.36 \leqq z \leqq .94) = N(.94) - N(-.36) = .8264 - .3594 = .4670$$

The probability that z is greater than .94 is the area under the graph in Figure A.2, between .94 and infinity. Thus, it is equal to the entire area (1.0) less the area from minus infinity to .94. Hence,

$$\Pr(z > .94) = 1 - N(.94) = 1 - .8264 = .1736$$

Finally, one can ask, "What is the value, a, so that z will be smaller than or equal to a with probability P?" The notation for the function that yields the desired value of a is $\Phi(P)$ so that

$$\text{If } \Phi(P) = a, \text{ then } P = N(a) \qquad \textbf{(A.7)}$$

For instance, suppose the question is, "Which value has a cumulative density of .50?" A glance at Figure A.2 reminds us that the area between minus infinity and zero (the expected value) is .5. Thus, we can write

$$\Phi(.5) = 0, \text{ because } N(0) = .5$$

Similarly,

$$\Phi(.8264) = .94 \text{ because } N(.94) = .8264$$

and

$$\Phi(.3594) = -.36$$

For practice, confirm with Table 20.2 that $\Phi(.6554) = .40$, meaning that the value of z with a cumulative distribution of .6554 is $z = .40$.

Nonstandard Normal Distributions. Suppose that the monthly rate of return on a stock is closely approximated by a normal distribution with a mean of .015 (1.5% per month), and standard deviation of .127 (12.7% per month). What is the probability that the rate of return will fall below zero in a given month? Recall that because the rate is a normal variate, its cumulative density has to be computed by numerical methods. The standard normal table can be used for any normal variate.

Any random variable, x, may be transformed into a new standardized variable, x^*, by the following rule:

$$x^* = \frac{x - E(x)}{\sigma(x)} \tag{A.8}$$

Note that all that we have done to x was (1) *subtract* its expectation and (2) *multiply* by one over its standard deviation, $1/[\sigma(x)]$. According to our earlier discussion, the effect of transforming a random variable by adding and multiplying by a constant is such that the expectation and standard deviation of the transformed variable are

$$E(x^*) = \frac{E(x) - E(x)}{\sigma(x)} = 0; \; \sigma(x^*) = \frac{\sigma(x)}{\sigma(x)} = 1 \tag{A.9}$$

From the stability property of the normal distribution we also know that if x is normal, so is x^*. A normal variate is characterized completely by two parameters: its expectation and standard deviation. For x^*, these are zero and 1.0, respectively. When we subtract the expectation and then divide a normal variate by its standard deviation, we standardize it; that is, we transform it to a standard normal variate. This trick is used extensively in working with normal (and approximately normal) random variables.

Returning to our stock, we have learned that if we subtract .015 and then divide the monthly returns by .127, the resultant random variable will be standard normal. We can now determine the probability that the rate of return will be zero or less in a given month. We know that

$$z = \frac{r - .015}{.127}$$

where z is standard normal and r the return on our stock. Thus, if r is zero, z has to be

$$z(r = 0) = \frac{0 - .015}{.127} = -.1181$$

For r to be zero, the corresponding standard normal has to be -11.81%, a negative number. The event "r will be zero or less" is identical to the event "z will be $-.1181$ or less." Calculating the probability of the latter will solve our problem. That probability is simply $N(-.1181)$. Visit the standard normal table and find that

$$\Pr(r \leqq 0) = N(-.1181) = .5 - .047 = .453$$

The answer makes sense. Recall that the expectation of r is 1.5%. Thus, whereas the probability that r will be 1.5% or less is .5, the probability that it will be *zero* or less has to be close, but somewhat lower.

Confidence Intervals. Given the large standard deviation of our stock, it is logical to be concerned about the likelihood of extreme values for the monthly rate of return. One way to quantify this concern is to ask: "What is the interval (range) within which the stock return will fall in a given month, with a probability of .95?" Such an interval is called the *95% confidence interval.*

Logic dictates that this interval be centered on the expected value, .015, because r is a normal variate (has a normal distribution), which is symmetric around the expectation. Denote the desired interval by

$$[E(r) - a, E(r) + a] = [.015 - a, .015 + a]$$

which has a length of $2a$. The probability that r will fall within this interval is described by the following expression:

$$\Pr(.015 - a \leqq r \leqq .015 + a) = .95$$

To find this probability, we start with a simpler problem, involving the standard normal variate, that is, a normal with expectation of zero and standard deviation of 1.0.

What is the 95% confidence interval for the standard normal variate, z? The variable will be centered on zero, so the expression is

$$\Pr(-a^* \leqq z \leqq a^*) = N(a^*) - N(-a^*) = .95$$

You might best understand the substitution of the difference of the appropriate cumulative distributions for the probability with the aid of Figure A.3. The probability of falling outside of the interval is $1 - .95 = .05$. By the symmetry of the normal distribution, z will be equal to or less than $-a^*$ with probability of .025, and with probability .025, z will be greater than a^*. Thus, we solve for a^* using

$$-a^* = \Phi(.025) \text{ which is equivalent to } N(-a^*) = .025$$

We can summarize the chain that we have pursued so far as follows. If we seek a $P = .95$ level confidence interval, we define α as the probability that r will fall outside the confidence interval. Because of the symmetry, α will be split so that half of it is the probability of falling to the right of the confidence interval, while the other half is the probability of falling to the left of the confidence interval. Therefore, the relation between α and P is

$$\alpha = 1 - P = .05; \frac{\alpha}{2} = \frac{1 - P}{2} = .025$$

We use $\alpha/2$ to indicate that the area that is excluded for r is equally divided between the tails of the distributions. Each tail that is excluded for r has an area of $\alpha/2$. The value, $\alpha = 1 - P$, represents the entire value that is excluded for r.

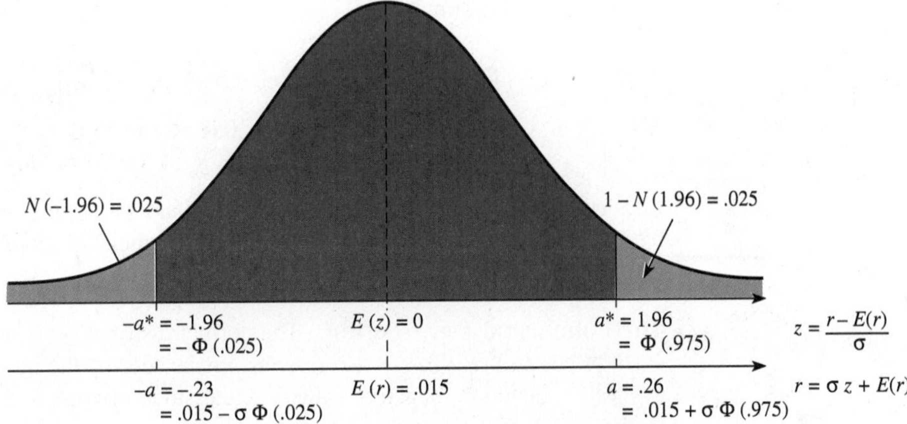

Figure A.3
Confidence intervals and the standard normal density

To find $z = \Phi(\alpha/2)$, which is the lower boundary of the confidence interval for the standard normal variate, we have to locate the z value for which the standard normal cumulative distribution is .025, finding $z = -1.96$. Thus, we conclude that $-a^* = -1.96$ and $a^* = 1.96$. The confidence interval for z is

$$\begin{aligned}[E(z) - \Phi(\alpha/2), E(z) + \Phi(\alpha/2)] &= [-\Phi(.025), \Phi(.025)] \\ &= [-1.96, 1.96]\end{aligned}$$

To get the interval boundaries for the nonstandard normal variate r, we transform the boundaries for z by the usual relationship, $r = z\sigma(r) + E(r) = \Phi(\alpha/2)\sigma(r) + E(r)$. Note that all we are doing is setting the expectation at the center of the confidence interval and extending it by a number of standard deviations. The number of standard deviations is determined by the probability that we allow for falling outside the confidence interval (α), or equivalently, the probability of falling in it (P). Using minus and plus 1.96 for $z = \pm\,\Phi(0.25)$, the distance on each side of the expectation is $\pm 1.96 \times .127 = .249$. Thus we obtain the confidence interval

$$\begin{aligned}[E(r) - \sigma(r)\Phi(\alpha/2), E(r) + \sigma(r)\Phi(\alpha/2)] &= [E(r) - .249, E(r) + .249] \\ &= [-.234, .264]\end{aligned}$$

so that

$$P = 1 - \alpha = \Pr[E(r) - \sigma(r)\Phi(\alpha/2) \leqq r \leqq E(r) + \sigma(r)\Phi(\alpha/2)]$$

which, for our stock (with expectation .015 and standard deviation .127) amounts to

$$\Pr[-.234 \leqq r \leqq .264] = .95$$

Note that, because of the large standard deviation of the rate of return on the stock, the 95% confidence interval is 49% wide.

To reiterate with a variation on this example, suppose we seek a 90% confidence interval for the annual rate of return on a portfolio, r_p, with a monthly expected return of 1.2% and standard deviation of 5.2%.

The solution is simply

$$\Pr\left[E(r) - \sigma(r)\,\Phi\left(\frac{1-P}{2}\right) \leqq r_p \leqq E(r) + \sigma(r)\,\Phi\left(\frac{1-P}{2}\right)\right]$$
$$= \Pr[.012 - .052 \times 1.645) \leqq r_p \leqq .012 + .052 \times 1.645)]$$
$$= \Pr[-.0735 \leqq r_p \leqq .0975] = .90$$

Because the portfolio is of low risk this time (and we require only a 90% rather than a 95% probability of falling within the interval), the 90% confidence interval is only 2.4% wide.

The Lognormal Distribution. The normal distribution is not adequate to describe stock prices and returns for two reasons. First, whereas the normal distribution admits any value, including negative values, actual stock prices cannot be negative. Second, the normal distribution does not account for compounding. The lognormal distribution addresses these two problems.

The lognormal distribution describes a random variable that grows, *every instant,* by a rate that is a normal random variable. Thus, the progression of a lognormal random variable reflects continuous compounding.

Suppose that the *annual continuously compounded* (ACC) rate of return on a stock is normally distributed with expectation $\mu = .12$ and standard deviation $\sigma = .42$. The stock price at the beginning of the year is $P_0 = \$10$. With continuous compounding (see appendix to Chapter 4), if the ACC rate of return, r_C, turns out to be .23, then the end-of-year price will be

$$P_1 = P_0\exp(r_C) = 10e^{.23} = \$12.586$$

representing an effective annual rate of return of

$$r = \frac{P_1 - P_0}{P_0} = e^{r_C} - 1 = .2586 \text{ (or } 25.86\%)$$

This is the practical meaning of r, the annual rate on the stock, being lognormally distributed. Note that however negative the ACC rate of return (r_C) is, the price, P_1, cannot become negative.

Two properties of lognormally distributed financial assets are important: their expected return and the allowance for changes in measurement period.

Expected Return of a Lognormally Distributed Asset. The expected annual rate of return of a lognormally distributed stock (as in our example) is

$$E(r) = \exp(\mu + \tfrac{1}{2}\sigma^2) - 1 = \exp(.12 + \tfrac{1}{2} \times .42^2) - 1 = e^{.2082} - 1$$
$$= .2315 \text{ (or } 23.15\%)$$

This is just a statistical property of the distribution. For this reason, a useful statistic is

$$\mu^* = \mu + \tfrac{1}{2}\sigma^2 = .2082$$

Often, when analysts refer to the expected ACC return on a lognormal asset, they are really referring to μ^*. Often, the asset is said to have a normal distribution of the ACC return with expectation μ^* and standard deviation σ.

Change of Frequency of Measured Returns. The lognormal distribution allows for easy change of the holding period of returns. Suppose that we want to calculate returns monthly instead of annually. We use the parameter t to indicate the fraction of the year that is desired, in the case of monthly periods $t = 1/12$. To transform the annual distribution to a t-period (monthly) distribution, it is necessary merely to multiply the expectation and variance of the ACC return by t (in this case, 1/12).

The monthly continuously compounded return on the stock in our example has the expectation and standard deviation of

$$\begin{aligned} \mu(\text{monthly}) &= .12/12 = .01 \text{ (1\% per month)} \\ \sigma(\text{monthly}) &= .42/\sqrt{12} = .1212 \text{ (or 12.12\% per month)} \\ \mu^*(\text{monthly}) &= .2082/12 = .01735 \text{ (or 1.735\% per month)} \end{aligned}$$

Note that we divide variance by 12 when changing from annual to monthly frequency; the standard deviation therefore is divided by the square root of 12.

Similarly, we can convert a nonannual distribution to an annual distribution by following the same routine. For example, suppose that the weekly continuously compounded rate of return on a stock is normally distributed with $\mu^* = .003$ and $\sigma = .07$. Then the ACC return is distributed with

$$\begin{aligned} \mu^* &= 52 \times .003 = .156 \text{ (or 15.6\% per year)} \\ \sigma &= \sqrt{52} \times .07 = .5048 \text{ (or 50.48\% per year)} \end{aligned}$$

In practice, to obtain normally distributed, continuously compounded returns, R, we take the log of 1.0 plus the raw returns:

$$R = \log(1 + r)$$

For short intervals, raw returns are small, and the continuously compounded returns, R, will be practically identical to the raw returns, r. The rule of thumb is that this conversion is not necessary for periods of 1 month or less. That is, approximating stock returns as normal will be accurate enough. For longer intervals, however, the transformation may be necessary.

A.2 Descriptive Statistics

Our analysis so far has been forward looking, or, as economists like to say, ex ante. We have been concerned with probabilities, expected values, and surprises. We made our analysis more tractable by assuming that decision outcomes are distributed according to relatively simple formulas, and that we know the parameters of these distributions.

Investment managers must satisfy themselves that these assumptions are reasonable, which they do by constantly analyzing observations from relevant random variables that accumulate over time. Distribution of past rates of return on a stock is one element they need to know in order to make optimal decisions. True, the distribution of the rate of return itself changes over time. However, a sample that is not too old does yield information relevant to the next period probability distribution and its parameters. In this section we explain descriptive statistics, or the organization and analysis of such historic samples.

Table A.3 Excess Return (Risk Premiums) on Stocks and Long-Term Treasury Bonds (Maturity Premiums)

Year	Equity Risk Premium	Maturity Premium	Year	Equity Risk Premium	Maturity Premium
1926	8.35	4.50	1963	19.68	−1.91
1927	34.37	5.81	1964	12.94	−0.03
1928	40.37	−3.14	1965	8.52	−3.22
1929	−13.17	−1.33	1966	−14.82	−1.11
1930	−27.31	2.25	1967	19.77	−13.40
1931	−44.41	−6.38	1968	5.85	−5.47
1932	−9.15	15.88	1969	−15.08	−11.66
1933	53.69	−0.38	1970	−2.52	5.57
1934	−1.60	9.86	1971	9.92	8.84
1935	47.50	4.81	1972	15.14	1.84
1936	33.74	7.33	1973	−21.59	−8.04
1937	−35.34	−0.08	1974	−34.47	−3.65
1938	31.14	5.55	1975	31.40	3.39
1939	−0.43	5.92	1976	18.76	11.67
1940	−9.78	6.09	1977	−12.30	−5.79
1941	−11.65	0.87	1978	−0.62	−8.34
1942	20.07	2.95	1979	8.06	−11.60
1943	25.55	1.73	1980	21.18	−15.19
1944	19.42	2.48	1981	−19.62	−12.86
1945	36.11	10.40	1982	10.87	29.81
1946	−8.42	−0.45	1983	13.71	−8.12
1947	5.21	−3.13	1984	−3.58	5.58
1948	4.69	2.59	1985	24.44	23.25
1949	17.69	5.35	1986	12.31	18.28
1950	30.51	−1.14	1987	−0.24	−8.16
1951	22.53	−5.43	1988	10.46	3.32
1952	16.71	−0.50	1989	23.12	9.74
1953	−2.81	1.81	1990	−10.98	−1.63
1954	51.76	6.33	1991	24.95	13.70
1955	29.99	−2.87	1992	4.16	4.54
1956	4.10	−8.05	1993	7.09	15.34
1957	−13.92	4.31			
1958	41.82	−7.64	Average	8.57	1.62
1959	9.01	−5.21	Standard deviation	20.90	8.50
1960	−3.13	11.12	Minimum	−44.41	−15.19
1961	24.76	−1.16	Maximum	53.69	29.81
1962	−11.46	4.16			

Source: Data from the Center for Research of Security Prices, University of Chicago.

Histograms, Boxplots, and Time Series Plots

Table A.3 shows the annual excess returns (over the T-bill rate) for two major classes of assets, the S&P 500 index and a portfolio of long-term government bonds, for the period 1926 to 1993.

One way to understand the data is to present it graphically, commonly in a *histogram* or frequency distribution. Histograms of the 68 observations in Table A.3 are shown in Figure A.4. We construct a histogram according to the following principles:

A

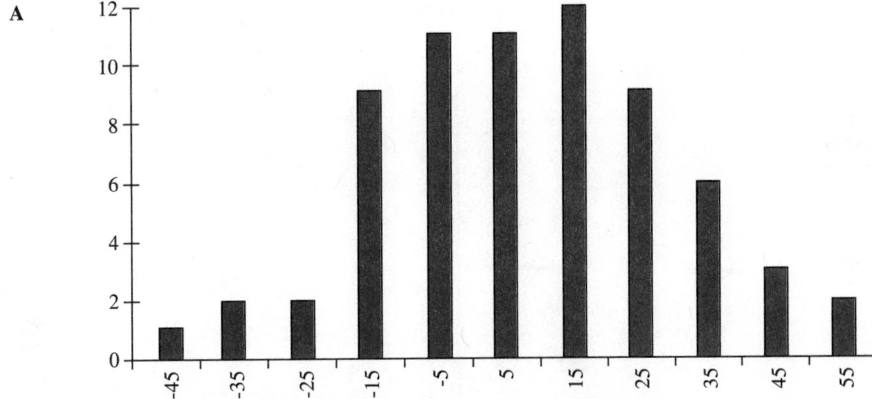

B

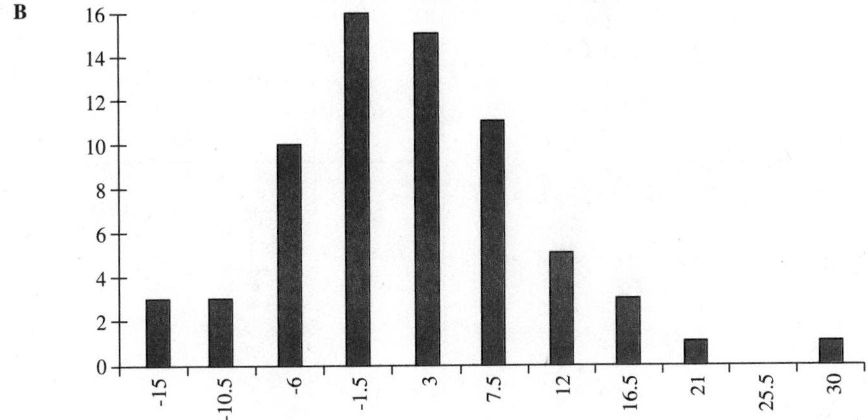

Figure A4
A, Histogram of the equity risk premium.
B, Histogram of the bond maturity premium

- The range (of values) of the random variable is divided into a relatively small number of equal-sized intervals. The number of intervals that makes sense depends on the number of available observations. The data in Table A.3 provide 68 observations, and thus deciles (10 intervals) seem adequate.
- A rectangle is drawn over each interval. The height of the rectangle represents the frequency of observations for each interval.
- If the observations are concentrated in one part of the range, the range may be divided to unequal intervals. In that case the rectangles are scaled so that their *area* represents the frequency of the observations for each interval. (This is not the case in our samples, however.)
- If the sample is representative, the shape of the histogram will reveal the probability distribution of the random variable. In our case 68 observations are not a large sample, but a look at the histogram does suggest that the returns may be reasonably approximated by a normal or lognormal distribution.

Another way to represent sample information graphically is by *boxplots.* Figure A.5 is an example that uses the same data as in Table A.3. Boxplots are most useful to show

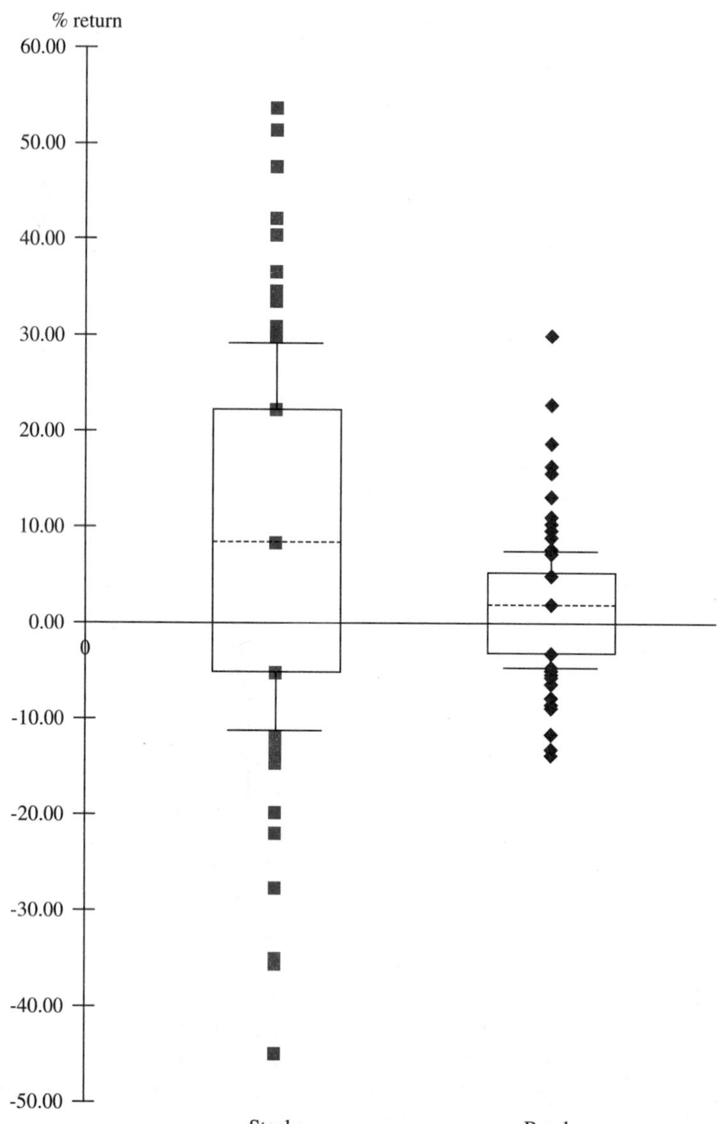

Figure A.5
Boxplots of annual equity risk premium and long-term bond (maturity) risk premium (1926–1993)

the dispersion of the sample distribution. A commonly used measure of dispersion is the *interquartile range.* Recall that the range, a crude measure of dispersion, is defined as the distance between the largest and smallest observations. By its nature, this measure is unreliable because it will be determined by the two most extreme outliers of the sample.

The interquartile range, a more satisfactory variant of the simple range, is defined as the difference between the lower and upper quartiles. Below the *lower* quartile lies 25%

of the sample; similarly, above the *upper* quartile lies 25% of the sample. The interquartile range therefore is confined to the central 50% of the sample. The greater the dispersion of a sample, the greater the distance between these two values.

In the boxplot the horizontal broken line represents the median, the box the interquartile range, and the vertical lines extending from the box the range. The vertical lines representing the range often are restricted (if necessary) to extend only to 1.5 times the interquartile range, so that the more extreme observations can be shown separately (by points) as outliers.

As a concept check, verify from Table A.3 that the points on the boxplot of Figure A.5 correspond to the following list:

	Equity Risk Premium	Bond Maturity Premium
Lowest extreme points	−44.41	−15.19
	−35.34	−13.40
	−34.47	−12.86
	−27.31	−11.66
	−21.59	−11.60
	−19.62	−8.34
	−15.08	−8.16
	−14.82	−8.12
	−13.92	−8.05
	−13.17	−8.04
	−12.30	−7.64
		−6.38
		−5.79
		−5.47
		−5.43
		−5.21
Lowest quartile	−4.79	−3.33
Median	8.77	1.77
Highest quartile	22.68	5.64
Highest extreme points	29.99	8.84
	30.51	9.74
	31.14	9.86
	31.40	10.40
	33.74	11.12
	34.37	11.67
	36.11	13.70
	40.37	15.34
	41.82	15.88
	47.50	18.28
	51.76	23.25
	53.69	29.81
Interquartile range	27.47	8.97
1.5 times the interquartile range	41.20	13.45
From:	−11.84	−4.95
To:	29.37	8.49

Figure A.6
A, Equity risk premium, 1926–1993
B, Bond maturity premium, 1926–1993

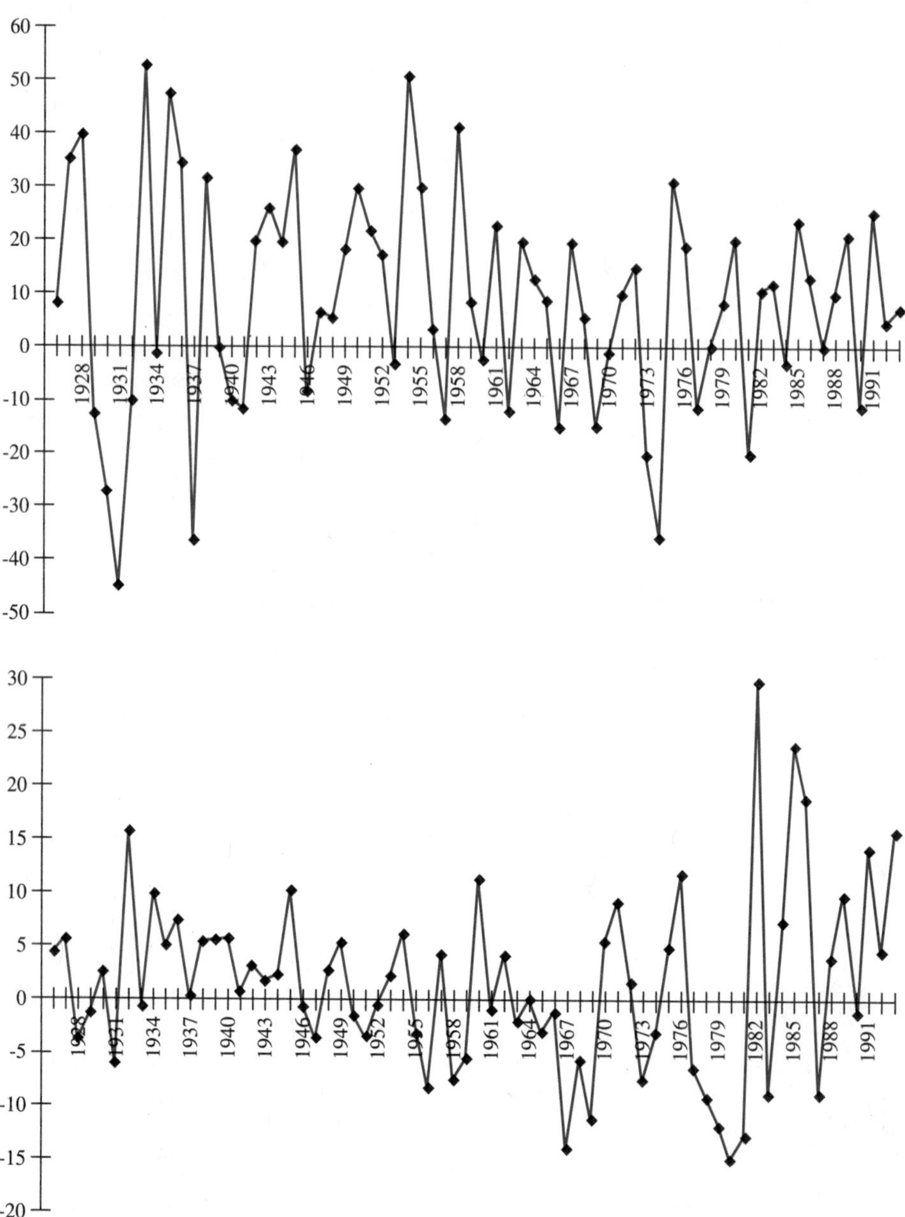

Finally, a third form of graphing is time series plots, which are used to convey the behavior of economic variables over time. Figure A.6 shows a time series plot of the excess returns on stocks and bonds from Table A.3. Even though the human eye is apt to see patterns in randomly generated time series, examining time series evolution over a long period does yield some information. Sometimes, such examination can be as revealing as that provided by formal statistical analysis.

Sample Statistics

Suppose we can assume that the probability distribution of stock returns has not changed over the past 68 years. We wish to draw inferences about the probability distribution of stock returns from the sample of 68 observations of annual stock excess returns in Table A.3.

A central question is whether given observations represent independent observations from the underlying distribution. If they do, statistical analysis is quite straightforward. Our analysis assumes that this is indeed the case. Empiricism in financial markets tends to confirm this assumption in most cases.

Estimating Expected Returns from the Sample Average. The definition of expected returns suggests that the sample average be used as an estimate of the expected value. Indeed, one definition of the expected return is the average of a sample when the number of observations tends to infinity.

Denoting the sample returns in Table A.3 by R_t, $t = 1, \ldots, T = 68$, the estimate of the annual expected excess rate of return is

$$\bar{R} = \frac{1}{T}\,\Sigma R_t = 8.57\%$$

The bar over the R is a common notation for an estimate of the expectation. Intuition suggests that the larger the sample the greater the reliability of the sample average, and the larger the standard deviation of the measured random variable, the less reliable the average. We discuss this property more fully later.

Estimating Higher Moments. The principle of estimating expected values from sample averages applies to higher moments as well. Recall that higher moments are defined as expectations of some power of the deviation from expectation. For example, the variance (second moment) is the expectation of the squared deviation from expectation. Accordingly, the sample average of the squared deviation from the average will serve as the estimate of the variance, denoted by s^2:

$$s^2 = \frac{1}{T-1}\Sigma(R_t - \bar{R})^2 = \frac{1}{67}\,\Sigma(R_t - .0857)^2 = .04368 \ (s = 20.90\%)$$

where $\bar{R}$ is the estimate of the sample average. The average of the squared deviation is taken over $T - 1 = 67$ observations for a technical reason. If we were to divide by T, the estimate of the variance will be downward-biased by the factor $(T - 1)/T$. Here too, the estimate is more reliable the larger the sample and the smaller the true standard deviation.

A.3 Multivariate Statistics

Building portfolios requires combining random variables. The rate of return on a portfolio is the weighted average of the individual returns. Hence, understanding and quantifying the interdependence of random variables is essential to portfolio analysis. In the

Table A.4 Probability Distribution of Anheuser-Busch Stock and Options

	Scenario 1	Scenario 2	Scenario 3
Probability	.20	.50	.30
Rates of Return(%)			
Stock	20	30	50
Call option	−100	−100	400
Put option	50	−25	−100
	$E(r)$	σ	σ^2
Stock	.340	.1114	0.0124
Call option	.500	2.2913	5.2500
Put option	−.325	.5250	0.2756

first part of this section we return to scenario analysis. Later we return to making inferences from samples.

The Basic Measure of Association: Covariance

Table A.4 summarizes what we have developed so far for the scenario returns on Anheuser-Busch stock and options. We know already what happens when we add a constant to one of these return variables, or multiply by a constant. But what if we combine any two of them? Suppose that we add the return on the stock to the return on the call. We create a new random variable that we denote by $r(s + c) = r(s) + r(c)$, where $r(s)$ is the return on the stock and $r(c)$ is the return on the call.

From the definition, the expected value of the combination variable is

$$E[r(s + c)] = \Sigma \Pr(i) r_i(s + c) \tag{A.10}$$

Substituting the definition of $r(s + c)$ into equation A.10 we have

$$\begin{aligned} E[r(s + c)] &= \Sigma \Pr(i)[r_i(s) + r_i(c)] = \Sigma \Pr(i) r_i(s) + \Sigma \Pr(i) r_i(c) \\ &= E[r(s)] + E[r(c)] \end{aligned} \tag{A.11}$$

In words, the expectation of the sum of two random variables is just the sum of the expectations of the component random variables. Can the same be true about the variance? The answer is "no," which is, perhaps, the most important fact in portfolio theory. The reason lies in the statistical association between the combined random variables.

As a first step, we introduce the *covariance,* the basic measure of association. Although the expressions that follow may look intimidating, they are merely squares of sums; that is, $(a + b)^2 = a^2 + b^2 + 2ab$, and $(a - b)^2 = a^2 + b^2 - 2ab$, where the *a*s and *b*s might stand for random variables, their expectations, or their deviations from expectations. From the definition of the variance

$$\sigma^2_{s+c} = E[r_{s+c} - E(r_{s+c})]^2 \tag{A.12}$$

To make equations A.12 through A.20 easier to read, we will identify the variables by subscripts s and c and drop the subscript i for scenarios. Substitute the definition of $r(s + c)$ and its expectation into equation A.12:

$$\sigma^2_{s+c} = E[r_s + r_c - E(r_s) - E(r_c)]^2 \qquad \textbf{(A.13)}$$

Changing the order of variables within the brackets in equation A.13,

$$\sigma^2_{s+c} = E[r_s - E(r_s) + r_c - E(r_c)]^2$$

Within the square brackets we have the sum of the deviations from expectations of the two variables, which we denote by d. Writing this out,

$$\sigma^2_{s+c} = E[(d_s + d_c)^2] \qquad \textbf{(A.14)}$$

Equation A.14 is the expectation of a complete square. Taking the square we find

$$\sigma^2_{s+c} = E(d_s^2 + d_c^2 + 2d_s d_c) \qquad \textbf{(A.15)}$$

The term in the brackets in equation A.15 is the summation of three random variables. Because the expectation of a sum is the sum of the expectations, we can write equation A.15 as

$$\sigma^2_{s+c} = E(d_s^2) + E(d_c^2) + 2E(d_s d_c) \qquad \textbf{(A.16)}$$

In equation A.16 the first two terms are the variance of the stock (the expectation of its squared deviation from expectation) plus the variance of the call. The third term is twice the expression that is the definition of the covariance discussed in equation A.17. (Note that the expectation is multiplied by 2 because expectation of twice a variable is twice the variable's expectation.)

In other words, the variance of a sum of random variables is the sum of the variances, *plus* twice the covariance, which we denote by $\text{Cov}(r_s, r_c)$, or the covariance between the return on s and the return on c. Specifically,

$$\text{Cov}(r_s, r_c) = E(d_s d_c) = E\{[r_s - E(r_s)][r_c - E(r_c)]\} \qquad \textbf{(A.17)}$$

The sequence of the variables in the expression for the covariance is of no consequence. Because the order of multiplication makes no difference, the definition of the covariance in equation A.17 shows that it will not affect the covariance either.

We use the data in Table A.4 to set up the input table for the calculation of the covariance, as shown in Table A.5.

First, we analyze the covariance between the stock and the call. In Scenarios 1 and 2, both assets show *negative* deviations from expectation. This is an indication of *positive co-movement.* When these two negative deviations are multiplied, the product, which eventually contributes to the covariance between the returns, is positive. Multiplying deviations leads to positive covariance when the variables move in the same direction, and negative covariance when they move in the opposite direction. In Scenario 3 both assets show *positive* deviations, reinforcing the inference that the co-movement is positive. The magnitude of the products of the deviations, weighted by the probability of each scenario, when added up, results in a covariance that shows not only the direction of the co-movement (by its sign) but also the degree of the co-movement.

Table A.5 Deviations, Squared Deviations, and Weighted Products of Deviations from Expectations of Anheuser-Busch Stock and Options

	Scenario 1	Scenario 2	Scenario 3	Probability-Weighted Sum
Probability	.20	.50	.30	
Deviation of stock	−.14	−.04	.16	
Squared deviation	.0196	.0016	.0256	.0124
Deviation of call	−1.50	−1.50	3.50	
Squared deviation	2.25	2.25	12.25	5.25
Deviation of put	.825	0.75	−.675	
Squared deviation	.680625	.005625	.455635	.275628
Product of deviations (d_sd_c)	.21	.06	.56	.24
Product of deviations (d_sd_p)	−.1155	−.003	−.108	−.057
Product of deviations (d_cd_p)	−1.2375	−.1125	−2.3625	−1.0125

The covariance is a variancelike statistic. Whereas the variance shows the degree of the movement of a random variable about its expectation, the covariance shows the degree of the co-movement of two variables about their expectations. It is important for portfolio analysis that the covariance of a variable with itself is equal to its variance. You can see this by substituting the appropriate deviations in equation A.17; the result is the expectation of the variable's squared deviation from expectation.

The first three values in the last column of Table A.5 are the familiar variances of the three assets, the stock, the call, and the put. The last three are the covariances; two of them are negative. Examine the covariance between the stock and the put, for example. In the first two scenarios the stock realizes negative deviations, while the put realizes positive deviations. When we multiply such deviations, the sign becomes negative. The same happens in the third scenario, except that the stock realizes a positive deviation and the put a negative one. Again, the product is negative, adding to the inference of negative co-movement.

With other assets and scenarios the product of the deviations can be negative in some scenarios, positive in others. The *magnitude* of the products, when *weighted* by the probabilities, determines which co-movements dominate. However, whenever the sign of the products varies from scenario to scenario, the results will offset one another, contributing to a small, close-to-zero covariance. In such cases we may conclude that the returns have either a small, or no, average co-movement.

Covariance between Transformed Variables. Because the covariance is the expectation of the product of deviations from expectation of two variables, analyzing the effect of transformations on deviations from expectation will show the effect of the transformation on the covariance.

Suppose that we add a constant to one of the variables. We know already that the expectation of the variable increases by that constant; so deviations from expectation will remain unchanged. Just as adding a constant to a random variable does not affect its variance, it also will not affect its covariance with other variables.

Multiplying a random variable by a constant also multiplies its expectation, as well as its deviation from expectation. Therefore, the covariance with any other variable will also be multiplied by that constant. Using the definition of the covariance, check that this summation of the foregoing discussion is true:

$$\text{Cov}[a_1 + b_1 r_s, a_2 + b_2 r_c] = b_1 b_2 \text{Cov}(r_s, r_c) \tag{A.18}$$

The covariance allows us to calculate the variance of sums of random variables, and eventually the variance of portfolio returns.

A Pure Measure of Association: The Correlation Coefficient

If we tell you that the covariance between the rates of return of the stock and the call is .24 (see Table A.5), what have you learned? Because the sign is positive, you know that the returns generally move in the same direction. However, the number .24 adds nothing to your knowledge of the closeness of co-movement of the stock and the call.

To obtain a measure of association that conveys the degree of intensity of the co-movement, we relate the covariance to the standard deviations of the two variables. Each standard deviation is the square root of the variance. Thus, the product of the standard deviations has the dimensions of the variance that is also shared by the covariance. Therefore, we can define the correlation coefficient, denoted by ρ, as

$$\rho_{sc} = \frac{\text{Cov}(r_s, r_c)}{\sigma_s \sigma_c} \tag{A.19}$$

where the subscripts on ρ identify the two variables involved. Because the order of the variables in the expression of the covariance is of no consequence, equation A.19 shows that the order does not affect the correlation coefficient either.

We use the covariances from Table A.5 to show the *correlation matrix* for the three variables:

	Stock	Call	Put
Stock	1.00	.94	−.97
Call	.94	1.00	−.84
Put	−.97	−.84	1.00

The highest (in absolute value) correlation coefficient is between the stock and the put, −.97, although the absolute value of the covariance between them is the lowest by far. The reason is attributable to the effect of the standard deviations. The following properties of the correlation coefficient are important:

- Because the correlation coefficient, just as the covariance, measures only the degree of association, it tells us nothing about causality. The direction of causality has to come from theory and be supported by specialized tests.
- The correlation coefficient is determined completely by deviations from expectations, as are the components in equation A.19. We expect, therefore, that it is not affected by adding constants to the associated random variables. However, the correlation coefficient is invariant also to multiplying the variables by constants. You

can verify this property by referring to the effect of multiplication by a constant on the covariance and standard deviation.

- The correlation coefficient can vary from −1.0, perfect negative correlation, to 1.0, perfect positive correlation. This can be seen by calculating the correlation coefficient of a variable with itself. You expect it to be 1.0. Recalling that the covariance of a variable with itself is its own variance, you can verify this using equation A.19. The more ambitious can verify that the correlation between a variable and the negative of itself is equal to −1.0. First, find from equation A.17 that the covariance between a variable and its negative equals the negative of the variance. Then check equation A.19.

Because the correlation between x and y is the same as the correlation between y and x, the *correlation matrix is symmetric about the diagonal.* The diagonal entries are all 1.0 because they represent the correlations of returns with themselves. Therefore, it is customary to present only the lower triangle of the correlation matrix.

Reexamine equation A.16. You can invert it so that the covariance is presented in terms of the correlation coefficient and the standard deviations as in equation A.20:

$$\text{Cov}(r_s r_c) = \rho_{sc}\sigma_s\sigma_c \tag{A.20}$$

This formulation can be useful, because many think in terms of correlations rather than covariances.

Estimating Correlation Coefficients from Sample Returns. Assuming that a sample consists of independent observations, we assign equal weights to all observations and use simple averages to estimate expectations. When estimating variances and covariances, we get an average by dividing by the number of observations minus one.

Suppose that you are interested in estimating the correlation between stock and long-term default-free government bonds. Assume that the sample of 68 annual excess returns for the period 1926 to 1993 in Table A.3 is representative.

Using the definition for the correlation coefficient in equation A.19, you estimate the following statistics (using the subscripts s for stocks, b for bonds, and t for time):

$$\bar{R}_s = \frac{1}{68}\sum_{t=1}^{68} R_{s,t} = .0857; \quad \bar{R}_b = \frac{1}{68}\sum R_{b,t} = .0162$$

$$\sigma_s = \left[\frac{1}{67}\sum (R_{s,t} - \bar{R}_s)^2\right]^{1/2} = .2090$$

$$\sigma_b = \left[\frac{1}{67}\sum (R_{b,t} - \bar{R}_b)^2\right]^{1/2} = .0850$$

$$\text{Cov}(R_s,R_b) = \frac{1}{67}\sum [(R_{s,t} - \bar{R}_s)(R_{b,t} - \bar{R}_b)] = .00314$$

$$\rho_{sb} = \frac{\text{Cov}(R_s,R_b)}{\sigma_s\sigma_b} = .17916$$

Here is one example of how problematic estimation can be. Recall that we predicate our use of the sample on the assumption that the probability distributions have not changed over the sample period. To see the problem with this assumption, suppose that we reestimate the correlation between stocks and bonds over a more recent period—for example, beginning in 1965, about the time of onset of government debt financing of both the war in Vietnam and the Great Society programs.

Repeating the previous calculations for the period 1965 to 1987, we find:

$$\bar{R}_s = .0312;\ \bar{R}_b = -.00317$$
$$\sigma_s = .15565;\ \sigma_b = .11217$$
$$\text{Cov}(R_s, R_b) = .0057;\ \rho_{sb} = .32647$$

A comparison of the two sets of numbers suggests that it is likely, but by no means certain, that the underlying probability distributions have changed. The variance in the rates of return and the size of the samples are why we cannot be sure. We shall return to the issue of testing the sample statistics shortly.

Regression Analysis

We will use a problem from the CFA examination (Level I, 1986) to represent the degree of understanding of regression analysis that is required for the ground level. However, first let us develop some background.

In analyzing measures of association so far, we have ignored the question of causality, identifying simply *independent* and *dependent* variables. Suppose that theory (in its most basic form) tells us that all asset excess returns are driven by the same economic force, whose movements are captured by a broad-based market index, such as excess return on the S&P 500 stock index.

Suppose further that our theory predicts a simple, linear relationship between the excess return of any asset and the market index. A linear relationship, one that can be described by a straight line, takes on this form:

$$R_{j,t} = a_j + b_j R_{M,t} + e_{j,t} \qquad \textbf{(A.21)}$$

where the subscript j represents any asset, M represents the market index (the S&P 500), and t represents variables that change over time. (In the following discussion we omit subscripts when possible.) On the left-hand side of equation A.21 is the dependent variable, the excess return on asset j. The right-hand side has two parts, the explained and unexplained (by the relationship) components of the dependent variable.

The explained component of R_j is the $a + bR_M$ part. It is plotted in Figure A.7. The quantity a, also called the intercept, gives the value of R_j when the *independent* variable is zero. This relationship assumes that it is a constant. The second term in the explained part of the return represents the driving force, R_M, times the sensitivity coefficient, b, that transmits movements in R_M to movements in R_j. The term b is also assumed to be constant. Figure A.7 shows that b is the slope of the regression line.

The unexplained component of R_j is represented by the *disturbance* term, e_j. The disturbance is assumed to be uncorrelated with the explanatory variable, R_M, and of zero expectation. Such a variable is also called a noise variable, because it contributes to the variance but not to the expectation of the dependent variable, R_j.

A relationship such as that shown in equation A.21 applied to data, with coefficients estimated, is called a *regression equation.* A relationship including only one explana-

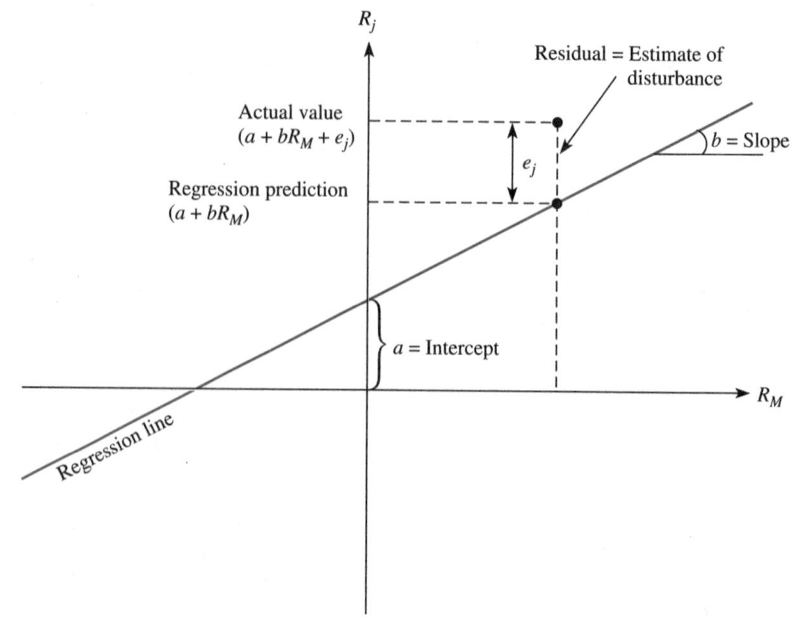

Figure A.7
Simple regression estimates and residuals. The intercept and slope are chosen so as to minimize the sum of the squared deviations from the regression line

tory variable is called *simple regression.* The parameters a and b are called (simple) *regression coefficients.* Because every value of R_j is explained by the regression, the expectation and variance of R_j are also determined by it. Using the expectation of the expression in equation A.21 we get:

$$E(R_j) = a + bE(R_M) \tag{A.22}$$

The constant a has no effect on the variance of R_j. Because the variables r_M and e_j are uncorrelated, the variance of the sum, $bR_m + e$, is the sum of the variances. Accounting for the parameter b multiplying R_M, the variance of R_j will be

$$\sigma_j^2 = b^2\sigma_M^2 + \sigma_e^2 \tag{A.23}$$

Equation A.23 tells us that the contribution of the variance of R_M to that of R_j depends on the regression (slope) coefficient b. The term $(b\sigma_M)^2$ is called the *explained variance.* The variance of the disturbance makes up the *unexplained* variance.

The covariance between R_j and R_M is also given by the regression equation. Setting up the expression, we have

$$\begin{aligned} \text{Cov}(R_j,R_M) &= \text{Cov}(a + bR_M + e, R_M) \\ &= \text{Cov}(bR_M,R_M) = b\text{Cov}(R_M,R_M) = b\sigma_M^2 \end{aligned} \tag{A.24}$$

The intercept, a, is dropped because a constant added to a random variable does not affect the covariance with any other variable. The disturbance term e is dropped because it is, by assumption, uncorrelated with the market return.

Equation A.24 shows that the slope coefficient of the regression, b, is equal to

$$b = \frac{\text{Cov}(R_j, R_M)}{\sigma_M^2}$$

The slope thereby measures the co-movement of j and M as a fraction of the movement of the driving force, the explanatory variable M.

One way to measure the explanatory power of the regression is by the fraction of the variance of R_j that it explains. This fraction is called the *coefficient of determination,* and denoted by ρ^2.

$$\rho_{jM}^2 = \frac{b^2\sigma_M^2}{\sigma_j^2} = \frac{b^2\sigma_M^2}{b_M^2\sigma_M^2 + \sigma_e^2} \quad \text{(A.25)}$$

Note that the unexplained variance, σ_e^2, has to make up the difference between the coefficient of determination and 1.0. Therefore another way to represent the coefficient of determination is by

$$\rho_{jM}^2 = 1 - \frac{\sigma_e^2}{\sigma_j^2}$$

Some algebra shows that the coefficient of determination is the square of the correlation coefficient. Finally, squaring the correlation coefficient tells us what proportion of the variance of the dependent variable is explained by the independent (the explanatory) variable.

Estimation of the regression coefficients a and b is based on minimizing the sum of the square deviation of the observations from the estimated regression line (see Figure A.7). Your calculator, as well as any spreadsheet program, can compute regression estimates.

The CFA 1986 examination for Level I included this question:

Question.

Pension plan sponsors place a great deal of emphasis on universe rankings when evaluating money managers. In fact, it appears that sponsors assume implicitly that managers who rank in the top quartile of a representative sample of peer managers are more likely to generate superior relative performance in the future than managers who rank in the bottom quartile.

The validity of this assumption can be tested by regressing percentile rankings of managers in one period on their percentile rankings from the prior period.

1. Given that the implicit assumption of plan sponsors is true to the extent that there is perfect correlation in percentile rankings from one period to the next, list the numerical values you would expect to observe for the slope of the regression, and the R-squared of the regression.
2. Given that there is no correlation in percentile rankings from period to period, list the numerical values you would expect to observe for the intercept of the regression, the slope of the regression, and the R-squared of the regression.

3. Upon performing such a regression, you observe an intercept of .51, a slope of −.05, and an R-squared of .01. Based on this regression, state your best estimate of a manager's percentile ranking next period if his percentile ranking this period were .15.
4. Some pension plan sponsors have agreed that a good practice is to terminate managers who are in the top quartile and to hire those who are in the bottom quartile. State what those who advocate such a practice expect implicitly about the correlation and slope from a regression of the managers' subsequent ranking on their current ranking.

Answer.

1. Intercept = 0
   Slope = 1
   R-squared = 1
2. Intercept = .50
   Slope = 0.0
   R-squared = 0.0
3. 50th percentile, derived as follows:
   $y = a + bx$
   $= .51 - 0.05(.15)$
   $= .51 - .0075$
   $= .5025$
   Given the very low R-squared, is would be difficult to estimate what the manager's rank would be.
4. Sponsors who advocate firing top-performing managers and hiring the poorest implicitly expect that both the correlation and slope would be significantly negative.

Multiple Regression Analysis

In many cases, theory suggests that a number of independent, explanatory variables drive a dependent variable. This concept becomes clear enough when demonstrated by a two-variable case. A real estate analyst offers the following regression equation to explain the return on a nationally diversified real estate portfolio:

$$RE_t = a + b_1 RE_{t-1} + b_2 NVR_t + e_t \tag{A.26}$$

The dependent variable is the period t real estate portfolio return, RE_t. The model specifies that the explained part of that return is driven by two independent variables. The first is the previous period return, RE_{t-1} representing persistence of momentum. The second explanatory variable is the current national vacancy rate (NVR_t).

As in the simple regression, a is the intercept, representing the value that RE is expected to take when the explanatory variables are zero. The (slope) regression coefficients, b_1 and b_2, represent the *marginal* effect of the explanatory variables.

The coefficient of determination is defined exactly as before. The ratio of the variance of the disturbance, e, to the total variance of RE is 1.0 *minus* the coefficient of determination. The regression coefficients are estimated here, too, by finding coefficients that minimize the sum of squared deviations of the observations from the prediction of the regression.

A.4 Hypothesis Testing

The central hypothesis of investment theory is that nondiversifiable (systematic) risk is rewarded by a higher *expected* return. But do the data support the theory? Consider the data on the excess return on stocks in Table A.3. The estimate of the expected excess return (the sample average) is 8.57%. This appears to be a hefty risk premium, but so is the risk—the estimate of the standard deviation for the same sample is 20.9%. Could it be that the positive average is just the luck of the draw? Hypothesis testing supplies probabilistic answers to such concerns.

The first step in hypothesis testing is to state the claim that is to be tested. This is called the *null hypothesis* (or the null for short), denoted by H_0. Against the null, an alternative claim (hypothesis) is stated, which is denoted by H_1. The objective of hypothesis testing is to decide whether to reject the null in favor of the alternative, while identifying the probabilities of the possible errors in the determination.

A hypothesis is *specified* if it assigns a value to a variable. A claim that the risk premium on stocks is zero is one example of a specified hypothesis. Often, however, a hypothesis is general. A claim that the risk premium on stocks is not zero would be a completely general alternative against the specified hypothesis that the risk premium is zero. It amounts to "anything but the null." The alternative that the risk premium is *positive,* although not completely general, is still unspecified. Although it is sometimes desirable to test two unspecified hypotheses (e.g., the claim that the risk premium is zero or negative, against the claim that it is positive), unspecified hypotheses complicate the task of determining the probabilities of errors in judgment.

What are the possible errors? There are two, called Type I and Type II errors. Type I is the event that we will *reject* the null when it is *true.* The probability of Type I error is called the *significance level.* Type II is the event that we will *accept* the null when it is *false.*

Suppose we set a criterion for acceptance of H_0 that is so lax that we know for certain we will accept the null. In doing so we will drive the significance level to zero (which is good). If we will never reject the null, we will also never reject it when it is true. At the same time the probability of Type II error will become 1 (which is bad). If we will accept the null for certain, we must also do so when it is false.

The reverse is to set a criterion for acceptance of the null that is so stringent that we know for certain that we will reject it. This drives the probability of Type II error to zero (which is good). By never accepting the null, we avoid accepting it when it is false. Now, however, the significance level will go to 1 (which is bad). If we always reject the null, we will reject it even when it is true.

To compromise between the two evils, hypothesis testing fixes the significance level; that is, it limits the probability of Type I error. Then, subject to this present constraint, the ideal test will minimize the probability of Type II error. If we *avoid* Type II error (accepting the null when it is false) we actually *reject* the null when it is indeed *false.* The probability of doing so is *one minus the probability of Type II error,* which is called the *power of the test.* Minimizing the probability of Type II error maximizes the power of the test.

Testing the claim that stocks earn a risk premium, we set the hypotheses as

$$H_0: E(R) = 0 \text{ The expected excess return is zero}$$
$$H_1: E(R) > 0 \text{ The expected excess return is positive}$$

H_1 is an *unspecified alternative.* When a null is tested against a completely general alternative, it is called a *two-tailed test* because you may reject the null in favor of both greater or smaller values.

When both hypotheses are unspecified, the test is difficult because the calculation of the probabilities of Type I and II errors is complicated. Usually, at least one hypothesis is simple (specified) and set as the null. In that case it is relatively easy to calculate the significance level of the test. Calculating the power of the test that assumes the *unspecified* alternative is true remains complicated; often it is left unsolved.

As we will show, setting the hypothesis that we wish to reject, $E(R) = 0$ as the null (the "straw man"), makes it harder to accept the alternative that we favor, our theoretical bias, which is appropriate.

In testing $E(R) = 0$, suppose we fix the significance level at 5%. This means that we will reject the null (and accept that there is a positive premium) *only* when the data suggest that the probability the null is true is 5% or less. To do so, we must find a critical value, denoted z_α (or critical values in the case of two-tailed tests) that corresponds to $\alpha = .05$, which will create two regions, an acceptance region and a rejection region. Look at Figure A.8 as an illustration.

If the sample average is to the right of the critical value (in the rejection region), the null is rejected; otherwise, it is accepted. In the latter case it is too likely (i.e., the probability is greater than 5%) that the sample average is positive simply because of sampling error. If the sample average is greater than the critical value, we will reject the null in favor of the alternative. The probability that the positive value of the sample average results from sampling error is 5% or less.

If the alternative is one-sided (one-tailed), as in our case, the acceptance region covers the entire area from minus infinity to a positive value, above which lies 5% of the distribution (see Figure A.8). The critical value is z_α in Figure A.8. When the alternative is two-tailed, the area of 5% lies at both extremes of the distribution and is equally divided between them, 2.5% on each side. A two-tailed test is more stringent (it is harder to reject the null). In a one-tailed test the fact that our theory predicts the direction in which the average will deviate from the value under the null is weighted in favor of the alternative. The upshot is that for a significance level of 5%, with a one-tailed test, we use a confidence interval of $\alpha = .05$, instead of $\alpha/2 = .025$ as with a two-tailed test.

Hypothesis testing requires assessment of the probabilities of the test statistics, such as the sample average and variance. Therefore, it calls for some assumption about the probability distribution of the underlying variable. Such an assumption becomes an integral part of the null hypothesis, often an implicit one.

In this case we assume that the stock portfolio excess return is normally distributed. The distribution of the test statistic is derived from its mathematical definition and the assumption of the underlying distribution for the random variable. In our case the test statistic is the sample average.

The sample average is obtained by summing all observations ($T = 68$), and then multiplying by $1/T = 1/68$. Each observation is a random variable, drawn indepen-

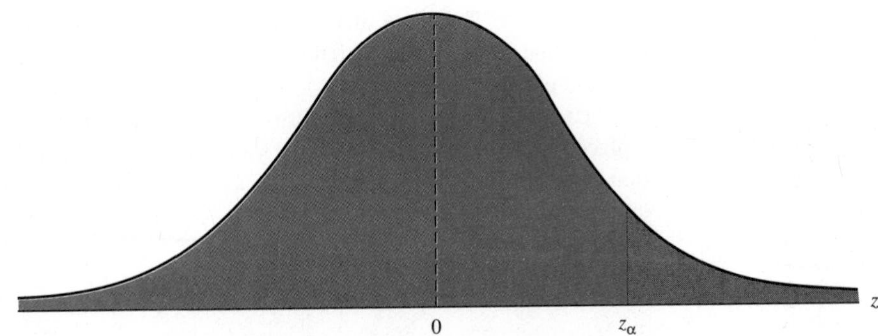

Figure A.8
Under the null hypothesis, the sample average excess return should be distributed around zero. If the actual average exceeds z_α, we conclude that the null hypothesis is false.

dently from the same underlying distribution, with an unknown expectation μ, and standard deviation σ. The expectation of the sum of all observations is the sum of the T expectations (all equal to μ) divided by T, therefore equal to the population expectation. The result is 8.57%, which is equal to the true expectation *plus* sampling errors. Under the null hypothesis, the expectation is zero, and the entire 8.57% constitutes sampling errors.

To calculate the variance of the sample average, recall that we assumed that all observations were independent, or uncorrelated. Hence, the variance of the sum is the sum of the variances, that is, T times the population variance. However, we also transform the sum, multiplying it by $1/T$; therefore, we have to divide the variance of the sum $T\sigma^2$ by T^2. We end up with the variance of the sample average as the population variance divided by T. The standard deviation of the sample average, which is called the *standard error,* is

$$\sigma(\text{average}) = \left(\frac{1}{T^2}\Sigma\sigma^2\right)^{1/2} = \left(\frac{1}{T^2}T\sigma^2\right)^{1/2} = \frac{\sigma}{\sqrt{T}} = \frac{.2090}{\sqrt{68}} = .0253 \tag{A.27}$$

Our test statistic has a standard error of 2.53%. It makes sense that the larger the number of observations, the *smaller* the *standard error* of the estimate of the expectation. However, note that it is the variance that goes down by the proportion $T = 68$. The standard error goes down by a much smaller proportion, $\sqrt{T} = 8.25$.

Now that we have the sample mean, 8.57%, its standard deviation, 2.53%, and know that the distribution under the null is normal, we are ready to perform the test. We want to determine whether 8.57% is significantly positive. We achieve this by standardizing our statistic, which means that we subtract from it its expected value under the null hypothesis and divide by its standard deviation. This standardized statistic can now be compared to z values from the standard normal tables. We ask whether

$$\frac{\overline{R} - E(R)}{\sigma} > z_\alpha$$

We would be finished except for another caveat. The assumption of normality is all right in that the test statistic is a weighted sum of normals (according to our assumption about returns). Therefore, it is also normally distributed. However, the analysis also requires that we *know* the variance. Here we are using a sample variance that is only an *estimate* of the true variance.

The solution to this problem turns out to be quite simple. The normal distribution is replaced with the *student-t* (or t, for short) *distribution.* Like the normal, the t distribution is symmetric. It depends on degrees of freedom, that is, the number of observations less one. Thus, here we replace z_α with $t_{\alpha,T-1}$.

The test is then

$$\frac{\overline{R} - E(R)}{\sigma} > t_{\alpha,T-1}$$

When we substitute in sample results, the left-hand side is a standardized statistic and the right-hand side is a t-value derived from t tables for $\alpha = .05$ and $T - 1 = 68 - 1 = 67$. We ask whether the inequality holds. If it does, we *reject* the null hypothesis with a 5% significance level; if it does not we *cannot reject* the null hypothesis. (In this example, $t_{.05,67} = 1.67$.) Proceeding, we find that

$$\frac{.0857 - 0}{.0253} = 3.39 > 1.67$$

In our sample the inequality holds, and we reject the null hypothesis in favor of the alternative that the risk premium is positive.

A repeat of the test of this hypothesis for the 1965-to-1987 period may make a skeptic out of you. For that period the sample average is 3.12%, the sample standard deviation is 15.57%, and there are $23 - 1 = 22$ degrees of freedom. Does that give you second thoughts?

The t-Test of Regression Coefficients

Suppose that we apply the simple regression model (equation A.21), to the relationship between the long-term government bond portfolio and the stock market index, using the sample in Table A.3. The estimation result (% per year) is

$$a = .9913,\ b = .0729,\ R\text{-squared} = .0321$$

We interpret these coefficients as follows. For periods when the excess return on the market index is zero, we expect the bonds to earn an excess return of 99.13 basis points. This is the role of the intercept. As for the slope, for each percentage return of the stock portfolio in any year, the bond portfolio is expected to earn, *additionally,* 7.29 basis points. With the average equity risk premium for the sample period of 8.57%, the sample average for bonds is $.9913 + .0729 \times 8.57 = 1.62\%$. From the squared correlation coefficient you know that the variation in stocks explains 3.21% of the variation in bonds.

Can we rely on these statistics? One way to find out is to set up a hypothesis test, presented here for the regression coefficient b.

H_0: $b = 0$ The regression slope coefficient is zero, meaning that changes in the independent variable do not explain changes in the dependent variable

H_1: $b > 0$ The dependent variable is sensitive to changes in the independent variable (with a *positive* covariance)

Any decent regression software supplies the statistics to test this hypothesis. The regression customarily assumes that the dependent variable and the disturbance are normally distributed, with an unknown variance that is estimated from the sample. Thus, the regression coefficient b is normally distributed. Because once again the null is that $b = 0$, all we need is an estimate of the standard error of this statistic.

The estimated standard error of the regression coefficient is computed from the estimated standard deviation of the disturbance and the standard deviation of the explanatory variable. For the regression at hand, that estimate is, $s(b) = .0493$. Just as in the previous exercise, the critical value of the test is

$$s(b)t_{\alpha,T-1}$$

Compare this value to the value of the estimated coefficient b. We will reject the null in favor of $b > 0$ if

$$b > s(b)t_{\alpha,T-1}$$

which, because the standard deviation $s(b)$ is positive, is equivalent to the following condition:

$$\frac{b}{s(b)} > t_{\alpha,T-1}$$

The t-test reports the ratio of the estimated coefficient to its estimated standard deviation. Armed with this *t-ratio,* the number of observations, T, and a table of the student-t distribution, you can perform the test at the desired significance level.

The t-ratio for our example is $.0729/.0493 = 1.4787$. The t-table for 68 degrees of freedom shows we cannot reject the null at a significance level of 5%, for which the critical value is 1.67.

A question from the CFA 1987 level exam calls for understanding of regression analysis and hypothesis testing.

Question.

An academic suggests to you that the returns on common stocks differ based on a company's market capitalization, its historical earnings growth, the stock's current yield, and whether or not the company's employees are unionized. You are skeptical that there are any attributes other than market exposure as measured by beta that explain differences in returns across a sample of securities.

Nonetheless, you decide to test whether or not these other attributes account for the differences in returns. You select the S&P 500 stocks as your sample, and regress their returns each month for the past five years against the company's market capitalization at the beginning of each month, the company's growth in earnings throughout the previous 12 months, the prior year's dividend divided by the stock price at the beginning of each month, and a dummy variable that has a value of 1 if employees are unionized and 0 if not.

1. The average R-squared from the regressions is .15, and it varies very little from month to month. Discuss the significance of this result.
2. You note that all of the coefficients of the attributes have t-statistics greater than 2 in most of the months in which the regressions were run. Discuss the significance of these attributes in terms of explaining differences in common stock returns.
3. You observe in most of the regressions that the coefficient of the dummy variable is $-.14$, and that the t-statistic is -4.74. Discuss the implication of the coefficient regarding the relationship between unionization and the return on a company's common stock.

Answer.

1. Differences in the attributes' values together explain about 15% of the differences in return among the stocks in the S&P 500 index. The remaining unexplained differences in return may be attributable to omitted attributes, industry affiliations, or stock-specific factors. This information by itself is not sufficient to form any qualitative conclusions. The fact that the R-squared varied little from month to month implies that the relationship is stable and the observed results are not sample specific.
2. Given a t-statistic greater than 2 in most of the months, one would regard the attribute coefficients as statistically significant. If the attribute coefficients were not significantly different from zero, one would expect t-statistics greater than 2 in fewer than 5% of the regressions for each attribute coefficient. Because the t-statistics are greater than 2 much more frequently, one should conclude that they are definitely significant in terms of explaining differences in stock returns.
3. Because the coefficient for the dummy variable representing unionization has persistently been negative and since it persistently has been statistically significant, one would conclude that disregarding all other factors, unionization lowers a company's common stock return. That is, everything else being equal, nonunionized companies will have higher returns than companies whose employees are unionized. Of course, one would want to test the model further to see if there are omitted variables of other problems that might account for this apparent relationship.

Appendix B

Solutions to Concept Checks

Chapter 1

1. The real assets are patents, customer relations, and the college education. These assets enable individuals or firms to produce goods or services that yield profits or income. Lease obligations are simply claims to pay or receive income and do not in themselves create new wealth. Similarly, the $5 bill is only a paper claim on the government and does not produce wealth.
2. The car loan is a primitive security. Payments on the loan depend only on the solvency of the borrower.
3. The borrower has a financial liability, the loan owed to the bank. The bank treats the loan as a financial asset.
4. *a.* Used cars trade in direct search markets when individuals advertise in local newspapers, and in dealer markets at used-car lots or automobile dealers.
   b. Paintings trade in broker markets when clients commission brokers to buy or sell art for them, in dealer markets at art galleries, and in auction markets.
   c. Rare coins trade mostly in dealer markets in coin shops, but they also trade in auctions and in direct search markets when individuals advertise they want to buy or sell coins.
5. Creative unbundling can separate interest or dividend from capital gains income. Dual funds do just this. In tax regimes where capital gains are taxed at lower rates than other income, or where gains can be deferred, such unbundling may be a way to attract different tax clienteles to a security.

Chapter 2

1. The discount yield at bid is 5.03. Therefore

$$P = 10{,}000\,[1 - .0503 \times (85/360)] = \$9{,}881.24$$

2. If the bond is selling below par, it is unlikely that the government will find it optimal to call the bond at par, when it can instead buy the bond in the sec-

ondary market for less than par. Therefore, it makes sense to assume that the bond will remain alive until its maturity date. In contrast, premium bonds are vulnerable to call because the government can acquire them by paying only par value. Hence, it is likely that the bonds will repay principal at the first call date, and the yield to first call is the statistic of interest.

3. A 6% taxable return is equivalent to an after-tax return of $6(1 - .28) = 4.32\%$. Therefore, you would be better off in the taxable bond. The equivalent taxable yield of the tax-free bond is $4/(1 - .28) = 5.55\%$. So a taxable bond would have to pay a 5.55% yield to provide the same after-tax return as a tax-free bond offering a 4% yield.
4. *a.* You are entitled to a prorated share of IBM's dividend payments and to vote in any of IBM's stockholder meetings.

   b. Your potential gain is unlimited because IBM's stock price has no upper bound.

   c. Your outlay was $\$50 \times 100 = \$5,000$. Because of limited liability, this is the most you can lose.
5. The price-weighted index increases from 62.5 [(100 + 25)/2] to 65 [(110 + 20)/2], a gain of 4%. An investment of one share in each company requires an outlay of \$125 that would increase in value to \$130, for a return of 4% (5/125), which equals the return to the price-weighted index.
6. The market value–weighted index return is calculated by computing the increase in value of the stock portfolio. The portfolio of the two stocks starts with an initial value of \$100 million + \$500 million = \$600 million and falls in value to \$110 million + \$400 million = \$510 million, a loss of 90/600 = .15 or 15%. The index portfolio return is a weighted average of the returns on each stock with weights of $^1/_6$ on XYZ and $^5/_6$ on ABC, (weights proportional to relative investments). Because the return on XYZ is 10%, while that on ABC is −20%, the index portfolio return is $^1/_6 \times 10\% + {^5/_6} \times (-20\%) = -15\%$, equal to the return on the market value–weighted index.
7. The payoff to the option is \$8 per share at maturity. The option cost is \$4.75 per share. The dollar profit is therefore \$3.25. The put option expires worthless. Therefore, the investor's loss is the cost of the put, or \$.25.

Chapter 3

1. $$\frac{100P - \$4,000}{100P} = .4$$

   $$100P - \$4,000 = 40P$$

   $$60P = \$4,000$$

   $$P = \$66.67 \text{ per share}$$

2. The investor will purchase 150 shares, with a rate of return as follows:

Year-End Change in Price	Year-End Value of Shares	Repayment of Principal and Interest	Investor's Rate of Return
30%	19,500	$5,450	40.5%
No change	15,000	5,450	−4.5
−30%	10,500	5,450	−49.5

3. $$\frac{\$150{,}000 - 1{,}000P}{1{,}000P} = .4$$
$$\$150{,}000 - 1{,}000P = 400P$$
$$1{,}400P = \$150{,}000$$
$$P = \$107.14 \text{ per share}$$

Chapter 4

1. *a.* Solving:

$$1 + R = (1 + r)(1 + i) = (1.03)(1.08) = 1.1124$$
$$R = 11.24\%$$

b. Solving:

$$1 + R = (1.03)(1.10) = 1.133$$
$$R = 13.3\%$$

2. The mean excess return for the period 1926–1934 is 4.5 percent (below the historical average), and the standard deviation (dividing by $n - 1$) is 30.79 (above the historical average). These results reflect the severe downturn of the great crash and the unusually high volatility of stock returns in this period.
3. $r = (.12 - .13)/1.13 = -.00885$ or $-.885\%$.
When the inflation rate exceeds the nominal interest rate, the real rate of return is negative.

Chapter 5

1. The expected rate of return on the risky portfolio is $22,000/$100,000 = .22, or 22%. The T-bill rate is 5%. The risk premium therefore is 22% − 5% = 17%.
2. The investor is taking on exchange rate risk by investing in a pound-denominated asset. If the exchange rate moves in the investor's favor, the investor will benefit and will earn more from the U.K. bill than the U.S. bill. For example, if both the U.S. and U.K. interest rates are 5 percent, and the current exchange rate is $1.50 per pound, a $1.50 investment today can buy one pound, which can be invested in England at a certain rate of 5 percent, for a year-end value of 1.05 pounds. If the year-end exchange rate is $1.60 per pound, the 1.05 pounds can be exchanged for 1.05 × $1.60 = $1.68 for a rate of return in

dollars of $1 + r = \$1.68/\$1.50 = 1.12$, or 12%, more than is available from U.S. bills. Therefore, if the investor expects favorable exchange rate movements, the U.K. bill is a speculative investment. Otherwise, it is a gamble.

3. For the $A = 4$ investor the utility of the risky portfolio is

$$\begin{aligned} U &= 20 - .005 \times 4 \times 20^2 \\ &= 12 \end{aligned}$$

while the utility of bills is

$$\begin{aligned} U &= 7 - .005 \times 4 \times 0 \\ &= 7 \end{aligned}$$

The investor will prefer the risky portfolio to bills. (Of course, a mixture of bills and the portfolio might be even better, but that is not a choice here.)

For the $A = 8$ investor, the utility of the risky portfolio is

$$\begin{aligned} U &= 20 - .005 \times 8 \times 20^2 \\ &= 4 \end{aligned}$$

while the utility of bills is again 7. The more risk-averse investor therefore prefers the risk-free alternative.

4. The less risk-averse investor has a shallower indifference curve. An increase in risk requires less increase in expected return to restore utility to the original level.

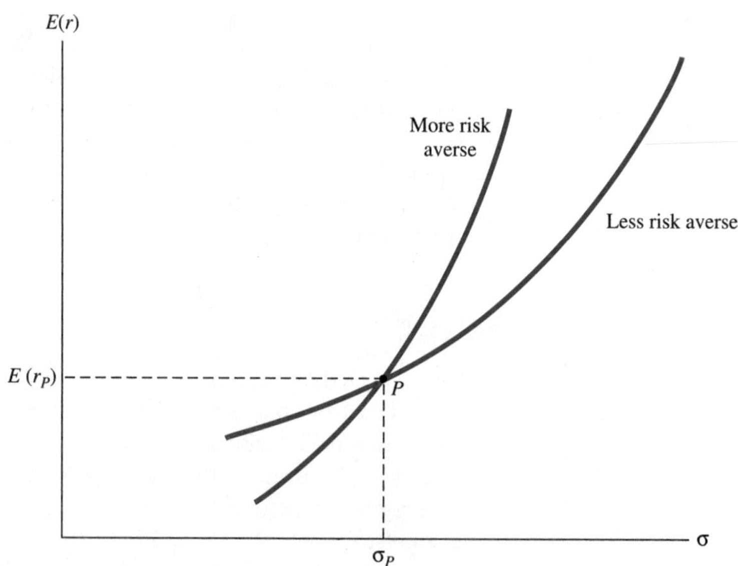

5. Despite the fact that gold investments *in isolation* seem dominated by the stock market, gold still might play a useful role in a diversified portfolio. Because

gold and stock market returns have very low correlation, stock investors can reduce their portfolio risk by placing part of their portfolios in gold.

6. *a.* With the given distribution for SugarKane, the scenario analysis looks as follows:

	Normal Year for Sugar		Abnormal Year
	Bullish Stock Market	Bearish Stock Market	Sugar Crisis
Probability	.5	.3	.2
		Rate of Return (%)	
Best Candy	25	10	−25
SugarKane	7	−5	20
T-bills	5	5	5

The expected return and standard deviation of SugarKane is now

$$E(r_{\text{SugarKane}}) = .5 \times 7 + .3(-5) + .2 \times 20 = 6$$

$$\sigma_{\text{SugarKane}} = [.5(7-6)^2 + .3(-5-6)^2 + .2(20-6)^2]^{1/2} = 8.72$$

The covariance between the returns of Best and SugarKane is

$$\text{Cov(SugarKane, Best)} = .5(7-6)(25-10.5) + .3(-5-6)(10-10.5) + .2(20-6)(-25-10.5) = -90.5$$

and the correlation coefficient is

$$\rho_{(\text{SugarKane, Best})} = \frac{\text{Cov(SugarKane, Best)}}{\sigma_{\text{SugarKane}}\sigma_{\text{Best}}} = \frac{-90.5}{8.72 \times 18.90} = -.55$$

The correlation is negative, but less than before (−.55 instead of −.86) so we expect that SugarKane will now be a less powerful hedge than before. Investing 50% in SugarKane and 50% in Best will result in a portfolio probability distribution of

Probability	.5	.3	.2
Portfolio return	16	2.5	−2.5

resulting in a mean and standard deviation of

$$E(r_{\text{Hedged portfolio}}) = .5 \times 16 + .3 \times 2.5 + .2(-2.5) = 8.25$$

$$\sigma_{\text{Hedged portfolio}} = [.5(16 - 8.25)^2 + .3(2.5 - 8.25)^2 + .2(-2.5 - 8.25)^2]^{1/2} = 7.94$$

b. It is obvious that even under these circumstances the hedging strategy dominates the risk-reducing strategy that uses T-bills (which results in $E(r) = 7.75\%$, $\sigma = 9.45\%$). At the same time, the standard deviation of the hedged position (7.94%) is not as low as it was using the original data.

c, *d*. Using Rule 5 for portfolio variance, we wound find that

$$\begin{aligned}\sigma^2 &= .5^2 \times \sigma^2_{\text{Best}} + .5^2 \times \sigma^2_{\text{Kane}} + 2 \times .5 \times .5 \times \text{Cov(SugarKane, Best)} \\ &= .5^2 \times 18.9^2 + .5^2 \times 8.72^2 + 2 \times .5 \times .5 \times (-90.5) \\ &= 63.06\end{aligned}$$

which implies that $\sigma = 7.94$, precisely the same result that we obtained by analyzing the scenarios directly.

A.1. Investors appear to be more sensitive to extreme outcomes relative to moderate outcomes than variance and higher *even* moments can explain. Casual evidence suggests that investors are eager to insure extreme losses and express great enthusiasm for highly, positively skewed lotteries. This hypothesis is, however, extremely difficult to prove with properly controlled experiments.

A.2. The better diversified the portfolio, the smaller is its standard deviation, as the sample standard deviations of Table 5A.1 confirm. When we draw from distributions with smaller standard deviations, the probability of extreme values shrinks. Thus the expected smallest and largest values from a sample get closer to the expected value as the standard deviation gets smaller. This expectation is confirmed by the samples of Table 1 for both the sample maximum and minimum annual rate.

B.1. *a*.

$$\begin{aligned}U(W) &= \sqrt{W} \\ U(50{,}000) &= \sqrt{50{,}000} \\ &= 223.61 \\ U(150{,}000) &= 387.30\end{aligned}$$

b.

$$\begin{aligned}E(U) &= .5 \times 223.61 + .5 \times 387.30 \\ &= 305.45\end{aligned}$$

c. We must find W_{CE} that has utility level 305.45. Therefore

$$\begin{aligned}\sqrt{W_{CE}} &= 305.45 \\ W_{CE} &= 305.45^2 \\ &= \$93{,}301\end{aligned}$$

d. Yes. The certainty equivalent of the risky venture is less than the expected outcome of $100,000.

e. The certainty equivalent of the risky venture to this investor is greater than it was for the log utility investor considered in the text. Hence this utility function displays less risk aversion.

Chapter 6

1. Holding 50% of your invested capital in Ready Assets means that your investment proportion in the risky portfolio is reduced from 70% to 50%.

Your risky portfolio is constructed to invest 54% in IBM and 46% in GM. Thus the proportion of IBM in your overall portfolio is .5 × 54 = 27%, and the dollar value of your position in IBM is $300,000 × .27 = $81,000.

2. In the expected return–standard deviation plane all portfolios that are constructed from the same risky and risk-free funds (with various proportions) lie on a line from the risk-free rate through the risky fund. The slope of the CAL (capital allocation line) is the same everywhere; hence the reward-to-variability ratio is the same for all of these portfolios. Formally, if you invest a proportion, y, in a risky fund with expected return, $E(r_P)$, and standard deviation, σ_P, and the remainder, $1 - y$, in a risk-free asset with a sure rate, r_f, then the portfolio's expected return and standard deviation are

$$E(r_C) = r_f + y[E(r_P) - r_f]$$
$$\sigma_C = y\sigma_P$$

and therefore the reward-to-variability ratio of this portfolio is

$$S_C = \frac{E(r_C) - r_f}{\sigma_C} = \frac{y[E(r_P) - r_f]}{y\sigma_P} = \frac{E(r_P) - r_f}{\sigma_P}$$

which is independent of the proportion, y.

3. The lending and borrowing rates are unchanged at: $r_f = 7\%$, $r_f^B = 9\%$. The standard deviation of the risky portfolio is still 22%, but its expected rate of return shifts from 15% to 17%.

The slope of the two-part CAL is

$$\frac{E(r_P) - r_f}{\sigma_P} \text{ for the lending range}$$

$$\frac{E(r_P) - r_f^B}{\sigma_P} \text{ for the borrowing range}$$

Thus, in both cases the slope increases: from 8/22 to 10/22 for the lending range, and from 6/22 to 8/22 for the borrowing range.

4. *a.* The parameters are: $r_f = 7$, $E(r_P) = 15$, $\sigma_P = 22$. With these parameters an investor with a degree of risk aversion, A, will choose a proportion, y, in the risky portfolio of

$$y = \frac{E(r_P) - r_f}{.01 \times A\sigma_P^2}$$

With $A = 3$ we find that

$$y = \frac{15 - 7}{.01 \times 3 \times 484} = .55$$

When the degree of risk aversion decreases from the original value of four to the new value of three, investment in the risky portfolio increases from 41% to 55%. Accordingly, the expected return and standard deviation of the optimal portfolio increase.

$$E(r_C) = 7 + .55 \times 8 = 11.4 \text{ (before: 10.28)}$$
$$\sigma_C = .55 \times 22 = 12.1 \text{ (before: 9.02)}$$

b. All investors whose degree of risk aversion is such that they would hold the risky portfolio in a proportion equal to 100% or less ($y < 1.00$) are lending rather than borrowing, and so are unaffected by the borrowing rate. The least risk-averse of these investors hold 100% in the risky portfolio ($y = 1$). We can solve for the degree of risk aversion of these "cut off" investors from the parameters of the investment opportunities:

$$y = 1 = \frac{E(r_P) - r_f}{.01 \times A\sigma_P^2} = \frac{8}{4.84A}$$

which implies

$$A = \frac{8}{4.84} = 1.65$$

Any investor who is more risk tolerant (that is, with A less than 1.65) would borrow if the borrowing rate were 7%. For borrowers,

$$y = \frac{E(r_P) - r_f^B}{.01 \times A\sigma_P^2}$$

Suppose, for example, an investor has an A of 1.1. When $r_f = r_f^B = 7\%$, this investor chooses to invest in the risky portfolio.

$$y = \frac{8}{.01 \times 1.1 \times 4.84} = 1.50$$

which means that the investor will borrow 50% of the total investment capital. Raise the borrowing rate, in this case to $r_f^B = 9\%$, and the investor will invest less in the risky asset. In that case,

$$y = \frac{6}{.01 \times 1.1 \times 4.84} = 1.13$$

and "only" 13% of his or her investment capital will be borrowed. Graphically, the line from r_f to the risky portfolio shows the CAL for lenders. The dashed part *would* be relevant if the borrowing rate equaled the lending rate. When the borrowing rate exceeds the lending rate, the CAL is kinked at the point corresponding to the risky portfolio.

The following figure shows indifference curves of two investors. The steeper indifference curve portrays the more risk-averse investor, who chooses portfolio C_0, which involves lending. This investor's choice is unaffected by the borrowing rate.

The more risk-tolerant investor is portrayed by the shallower-sloped indifference curves. If the lending rate equaled the borrowing rate, this investor would choose portfolio C_1 on the dashed part of the CAL. When the borrowing rate goes up, this investor chooses portfolio C_2 (in the borrowing range of the kinked CAL), which involves less borrowing than before. This investor is hurt by the increase in the borrowing rate.

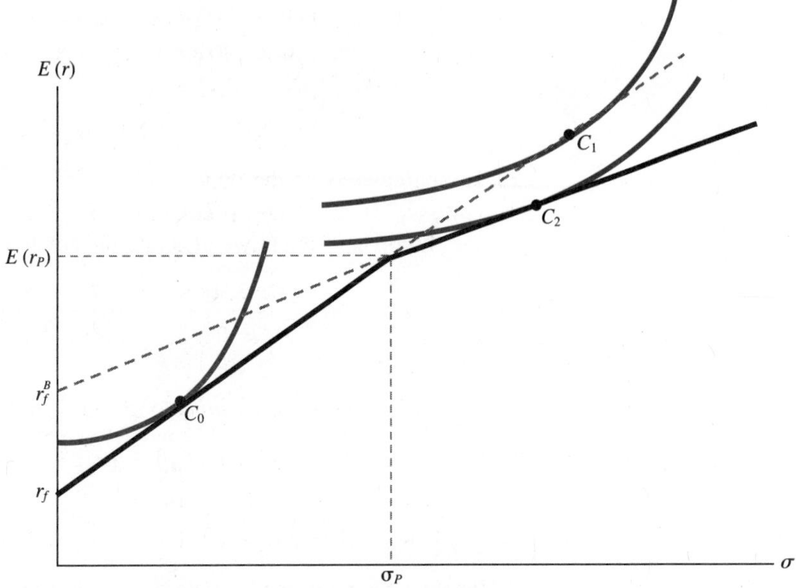

5. If all the investment parameters remain unchanged, the only reason for an investor to decrease the investment proportion in the risky asset is an increase in the degree of risk aversion. If you think that this is unlikely, then you have to reconsider your faith in your assumptions. Perhaps the S&P 500 is not a good proxy for the optimal risky portfolio. Perhaps investors expect a higher real rate of T-bills (inflation is ignored in this model).

Chapter 7

1. *a.* The first term will be $w_D \times w_D \times \sigma_D^2$, since this is the element in the top corner of the matrix (σ_D^2) times the term on the column border (w_D) times the term on the row border (w_D). Applying this rule to each term of the covariance matrix results in the sum $w_D^2\sigma_D^2 + w_D w_E \text{Cov}(r_E, r_D) + w_E w_D \text{Cov}(r_D, r_E) + w_E^2\sigma_E^2$, which is the same as equation 7.2, since $\text{Cov}(r_E, r_D) = \text{Cov}(r_D, r_E)$.

   b. The bordered covariance matrix is

	W_X	W_Y	W_Z
W_X	σ_X^2	$\text{Cov}(r_X, r_Y)$	$\text{Cov}(r_X, r_Z)$
W_Y	$\text{Cov}(r_Y, r_X)$	σ_Y^2	$\text{Cov}(r_Y, r_Z)$
W_Z	$\text{Cov}(r_Z, r_X)$	$\text{Cov}(r_Z, r_Y)$	σ_Z^2

   There are nine terms in the covariance matrix. Portfolio variance is calculated, from these nine terms:

$$\begin{aligned}\sigma_P^2 &= w_X^2\sigma_X^2 + w_Y^2\sigma_Y^2 + w_Z^2\sigma_Z^2\\ &\quad + w_Xw_Y\text{Cov}(r_X,r_Y) + w_Yw_X\text{Cov}(r_Y,r_X)\\ &\quad + w_Xw_Z\text{Cov}(r_X,r_Z) + w_Zw_X\text{Cov}(r_Z,r_X)\\ &\quad + w_Yw_Z\text{Cov}(r_Y,r_Z) + w_Zw_Y\text{Cov}(r_Z,r_Y)\\ &= w_X^2\sigma_X^2 + w_Y^2\sigma_Y^2 + w_Z^2\sigma_Z^2\\ &\quad + 2w_Xw_Y\text{Cov}(r_X,r_Y) + 2w_Xw_Z\text{Cov}(r_X,r_Z) + 2w_Yw_Z\text{Cov}(r_Y,r_Z)\end{aligned}$$

2. The parameters of the opportunity set are $E(r_D) = 8\%$, $E(r_E) = 13\%$, $\sigma_D = 12\%$, $\sigma_E = 20\%$, and $\rho(D,E) = .25$. From the standard deviations and the correlation coefficient we generate the covariance matrix:

Stock	D	E
D	144	60
E	60	400

The *global minimum-variance* portfolio is constructed so that

$$\begin{aligned}w_D &= [\sigma_E^2 - \text{Cov}(r_D,r_E)] \div [\sigma_D^2 + \sigma_E^2 - 2\,\text{Cov}(r_D,r_E)]\\ &= (400 - 60) \div (144 + 400 - 2 \times 60) = .8019\\ w_E &= 1 - w_D = .1981\end{aligned}$$

Its expected return and standard deviation are

$$\begin{aligned}E(r_P) &= .8019 \times 8 + .1981 \times 13 = 8.99\%\\ \sigma_P &= [w_D^2\sigma_D^2 + w_E^2\sigma_E^2 + 2w_Dw_E\text{Cov}(r_D,r_E)]^{1/2}\\ &= [.8019^2 \times 144 + .1981^2 \times 400 + 2 \times .8019 \times .1981 \times 60]^{1/2}\\ &= 11.29\%\end{aligned}$$

For the other points we simply increase w_D from .10 to .90 in increments of .10; accordingly, w_E ranges from .90 to .10 in the same increments. We substitute these portfolio proportions in the formulas for expected return and standard deviation. Note that for w_D or w_E equal to 1.0, the portfolio parameters equal those of the stock.

We then generate the following table:

w_E	w_D	$E(r)$	σ
0.0	1.0	8.0	12.00
0.1	0.9	8.5	11.46
0.2	0.8	9.0	11.29
0.3	0.7	9.5	11.48
0.4	0.6	10.0	12.03
0.5	0.5	10.5	12.88
0.6	0.4	11.0	13.99
0.7	0.3	11.5	15.30
0.8	0.2	12.0	16.76
0.9	0.1	12.5	18.34
1.0	0.0	13.0	20.00
0.1981	.8019	8.99	11.29 minimum variance portfolio

You can now draw your graph.

3. *a.* The computations of the opportunity set of the stock and risky bond funds are like those of question 2 and will not be shown here. You should perform these computations, however, in order to give a graphical solution to part *a*. Note that the covariance between the funds is

$$\begin{aligned} \text{Cov}(r_A, r_B) &= \rho(A,B) \times \sigma_A \times \sigma_B \\ &= -.2 \times 20 \times 60 = -240 \end{aligned}$$

b. The proportions in the optimal risky portfolio are given by

$$\begin{aligned} w_A &= \frac{(10-5)60^2 - (30-5)(-240)}{(10-5)60^2 + (30-5)20^2 - 30(-240)} \\ &= .6818 \\ w_B &= 1 - w_A = .3182 \end{aligned}$$

The expected return and standard deviation of the optimal risky portfolio are

$$\begin{aligned} E(r_P) &= .6818 \times 10 + .3128 \times 30 = 16.36\% \\ \sigma_P &= [.6818^2 \times 20^2 + .3182^2 \times 60^2 + 2 \times .6818 \times .3182(-240)]^{1/2} \\ &= 21.13\% \end{aligned}$$

Note that in this case the standard deviation of the optimal risky portfolio is smaller than the standard deviation of stock *A*. Note also that portfolio *P* is not the global minimum-variance portfolio. The proportions of the latter are given by

$$\begin{aligned} w_A &= [60^2 - (-240)] \div [60^2 + 20^2 - 2(-240)] = .8571 \\ w_B &= 1 - w_A = .1429 \end{aligned}$$

With these proportions, the standard deviation of the minimum-variance portfolio is

$$\begin{aligned} \sigma(\text{min}) &= [.8571^2 \times 20^2 + .1429^2 \times 60^2 + 2 \times .8571 \times .1429 \times (-240)]^{1/2} \\ &= 17.57\% \end{aligned}$$

which is smaller than that of the optimal risky portfolio.

c. The CAL is the line from the risk-free rate through the optimal risky portfolio. This line represents all efficient portfolios that combine T-bills with the optimal risky portfolio. The slope of the CAL is

$$\begin{aligned} S &= [E(r_P) - r_f]/\sigma_P \\ &= (16.36 - 5)/21.13 = .5376 \end{aligned}$$

d. Given a degree of risk aversion, *A*, an investor will choose a proportion, *y*, in the optimal risky portfolio of

$$\begin{aligned} y &= [E(r_P) - r_f]/(.01 \times A\sigma_P^2) \\ &= (16.36 - 5)/(.01 \times 5 \times 21.13^2) = .5089 \end{aligned}$$

This means that the optimal risky portfolio, with the given data, is attractive enough for an investor with $A = 5$ to invest 50.89% of his or her wealth in it. Since stock A makes up 68.18% of the risky portfolio and stock B 31.82%, the investment proportions for this investor are

Stock *A*:	.5089 × 68.18 =	34.70%
Stock *B*:	.5089 × 31.82 =	16.19%
	TOTAL	50.89%

4. Efficient frontiers derived by portfolio managers depend on forecasts of the rates of return on various securities and estimates of risk, that is, the covariance matrix. The forecasts themselves do not control outcomes. Thus preferring managers with rosier forecasts (northwesterly frontiers) is tantamount to rewarding the bearers of good news and punishing the bearers of bad news. What we should do is reward bearers of *accurate* news. Thus, if you get a glimpse of the frontiers (forecasts) of portfolio managers on a regular basis, what you want to do is develop the track record of their forecasting accuracy and steer your advisees toward the more accurate forecaster. Their portfolio choices will, in the long run, outperform the field.
5. *a.* Portfolios that lie on the CAL are combinations of the tangency (risky) portfolio and the risk-free asset. Hence they are just as dependent on the accuracy of the efficient frontier as portfolios that are on the frontier itself. If we judge forecasting accuracy by the accuracy of the reward-to-volatility ratio, then all portfolios on a CAL will be exactly as accurate as the tangency portfolio.

   b. All portfolios on CAL_1 are combinations of portfolio P_1 with lending (long bonds). This combination of one risky asset with a risk-free asset leads to a linear relationship between the portfolio expected return and its standard deviation:

$$\bar{r}_P = \bar{r}_f + \frac{r_{P1} - r_f}{\sigma_{P1}} \sigma_P \qquad \textbf{(5.b)}$$

The same applies to all portfolios on CAL_2; just replace $\bar{r}_{P_1},\sigma_{P_1}$ in equation 5.b with $\bar{r}_{P_2},\sigma_{P_2}$.

An investor who wishes to have an expected return between $\bar{r}_{P_1}$ and $\bar{r}_{P_2}$ must find the appropriate portfolio on the efficient frontier of risky assets between P_1 and P_2 in the correct proportions.

A.1. The parameters are $E(r) = 15$, $\sigma = 60$, and the correlation between any pair of stocks is $\rho = .5$.

a. The portfolio expected return is invariant to the size of the portfolio because all stocks have identical expected returns. The standard deviation of a portfolio with $n = 25$ stocks is

$$\begin{aligned}\sigma_P &= [\sigma^2(1/n) + \rho \times \sigma^2(n - 1)/n]^{1/2} \\ &= [60^2/25 + .5 \times 60^2 \times 24/25]^{1/2} = 43.27\end{aligned}$$

b. Because the stocks are identical, efficient portfolios are equally weighted. To obtain a standard deviation of 43%, we need to solve for n:

$$43^2 = 60^2/n + .5 \times 60^2(n - 1)/n$$
$$1849n = 3600 + 1800n - 1800$$
$$n = \frac{1800}{49} = 36.73$$

Thus we need 37 stocks and will come in slightly under the target.

c. As n gets very large, the variance of an efficient (equally weighted) portfolio diminishes, leaving only the variance that comes from the covariances among stocks, that is

$$\sigma_P = \sqrt{\rho \times \sigma^2} = \sqrt{.5 \times 60^2} = 42.43$$

Note that with 25 stocks we came within 84 basis points of the systematic risk, that is, the nonsystematic risk of portfolio of 25 stocks is 84 basis points. With 37 stocks the standard deviation is 43%, of which nonsystematic risk is 57 basis points.

d. If the risk-free is 10%, then the risk premium on any size portfolio is 15 − 10 = 5%. The standard deviation of a well-diversified portfolio is (practically) 42.43%, hence the slope of the CAL is

$$S = 5/42.43 = .1178$$

Chapter 8

1. We can characterize the entire population by two representative investors. One is the "uninformed" investor, who does not engage in security analysis and holds the market portfolio, whereas the other optimizes using the Markowitz algorithm with input from security analysis. The uninformed investor does not know what input the informed investor uses to make portfolio purchases. The uninformed investor knows, however, that if the other investor is informed the market portfolio proportions will be optimal. Therefore to depart from these proportions would constitute an uninformed bet, which will, on average, reduce the efficiency of diversification with no compensating improvement in expected returns.

2. *a.* Substituting the historical mean and standard deviation in equation 8.2 yields a coefficient of risk aversion of

$$\overline{A} = \frac{E(r_M) - r_f}{.01 \times \sigma_M^2} = \frac{8.6}{.01 \times 20.5^2} = 2.05$$

b. This relationship also tells us that for the historical standard deviation and a coefficient of risk aversion of 3.5 the risk premium would be

$$E(r_M) - r_f = .01 \times \overline{A}\sigma_M^2 = .01 \times 3.5 \times 20.5^2 = 14.7\%$$

3. For these investment proportions, w_{Ford}, w_{GM}, the portfolio β is

$$\beta_P = w_{\text{Ford}}\beta_{\text{Ford}} + w_{\text{GM}}\beta_{\text{GM}}$$
$$= .75 \times 1.25 + .25 \times 1.10 = 1.2125$$

As the market risk premium, $E(r_M) - r_f$, is 8%, the portfolio risk premium will be

$$E(r_P) - r_f = \beta_P[E(r_M) - r_f]$$
$$= 1.2125 \times 8 = 9.7\%$$

4. The alpha of a stock is its expected return in excess of that required by the CAPM.

$$\alpha = E(r) - [r_f + \beta[E(r_M) - r_f]]$$
$$\alpha_{XYZ} = .12 - [.05 + 1.0(.11 - .05)] = .01 = 1\%$$
$$\alpha_{ABC} = .13 - [.05 + 1.5(.11 - .05)] = -.01 = -1\%$$

ABC plots below the SML, while *XYZ* plots above.

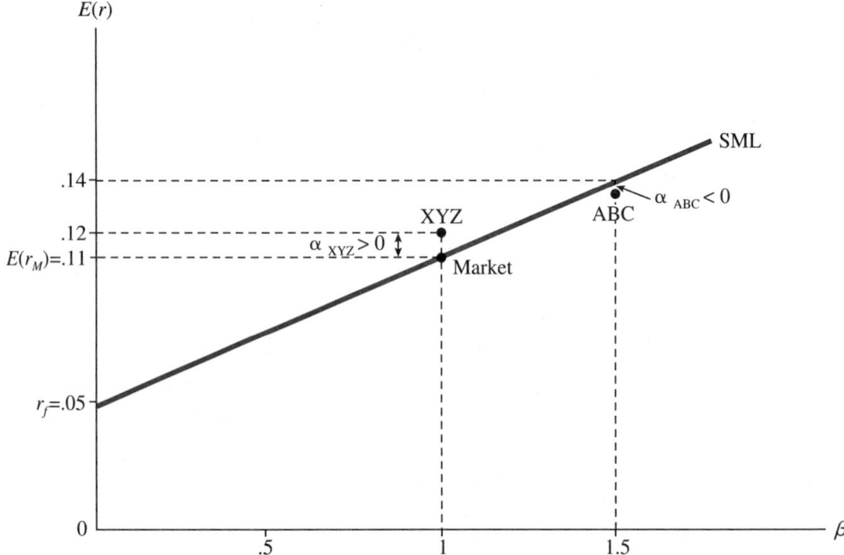

5. The project-specific required expected return is determined by the project beta coupled with the market risk premium and the risk-free rate. The CAPM tells us that an acceptable expected rate of return for the project is

$$r_f + \beta[E(r_M) - r_f] = 8 + 1.3(16 - 8) = 18.4\%$$

which becomes the project's hurdle rate. If the IRR of the project is 19%, then it is desirable. Any project with an IRR equal to or less than 18.4% should be rejected.

6. If the basic CAPM holds, any zero-beta asset must be expected to earn on average the risk-free rate. Hence the posited performance of the zero-beta portfolio violates the simple CAPM. It does not, however, violate the zero-beta CAPM. Since we know that borrowing restrictions do exist, we expect the zero-beta version of the model is more likely to hold, with the zero-beta rate differing from the virtually risk-free T-bill rate.

Chapter 9

1. The variance of each stock is $\beta^2\sigma_M^2 + \sigma^2(e)$.
   For stock A, we obtain

$$\sigma_A^2 = .9^2(20)^2 + 30^2 = 1224$$
$$\sigma_A = 35$$

   For stock B,

$$\sigma_B^2 = 1.1^2(20)^2 + 10^2 = 584$$
$$\sigma_B = 24$$

   The covariance is

$$\beta_A\beta_B\sigma_M^2 = .9 \times 1.1 \times 20^2 = 396$$

2. $\sigma^2(e_P) = (1/2)^2[\sigma^2(e_A) + \sigma^2(e_B)]$
   $= (1/4)(30^2 + 10^2)$
   $= 250$

   Therefore
   $\sigma(e_P) = 15.8$

3. *a*. Total market capitalization is 3,000 + 1,940 + 1,360 = 6,300. Therefore, the mean excess return of the index portfolio is

$$\frac{3{,}000}{6{,}300} \times 10 + \frac{1{,}940}{6{,}300} \times 2 + \frac{1{,}360}{6{,}300} \times 17 = 10$$

   b. The covariance between stock A and the index portfolio equals

$$\text{Cov}(R_A, R_M) = \beta_A\sigma_M^2 = .2 \times 25^2 = 125$$

   c. The variance of B equals

$$\sigma_B^2 = \text{Var}(\beta_B R_M + e_B) = \beta_B^2\sigma_M^2 + \sigma^2(e_B)$$

   Thus, the firm-specific variance of B equals

$$\sigma^2(e_B) = \sigma_B^2 - \beta_B^2\sigma_M^2 = 30^2 - .2^2 \times 25^2 = 875$$

4. The CAPM is a model that relates expected rates of return to risk. It results in the expected return-beta relationship where the expected excess return on any asset is proportional to the expected excess return on the market portfolio with beta as the proportionality constant. As such the model is impractical for two reasons: (i) expectations are unobservable, and (ii) the theoretical market portfolio includes every risky asset and is in practice unobservable. The next three models incorporate assumptions that overcome these problems.

   The single-factor model assumes that one economic factor, denoted F, exerts the only common influence on security returns. Beyond it, security returns are driven by independent, firm-specific factors. Thus, for any security i,

$$r_i = a_i + b_i F + e_i$$

The single-index model assumes that in the single-factor model, the factor, F, is perfectly correlated with and therefore can be replaced by a broad-based index of securities that can proxy for the CAPM's theoretical market portfolio.

At this point it should be said that many interchange the meaning of the index and market models. The concept of the market model is that rate of return *surprises* on a stock are proportional to corresponding surprises on the market index portfolio, again with proportionality constant β.

5. Merrill Lynch's alpha is related to the CAPM alpha by

$$\alpha_{\text{Merrill}} = \alpha_{\text{CAPM}} + (1 - \beta)r_f$$

For GM, $\alpha_{\text{Merrill}} = 0.12\%$, $\beta = .83$, and we are told that r_f was 0.6%. Thus

$$\begin{aligned}\alpha_{\text{CAPM}} &= .12\% - (1 - .83).6\% \\ &= .018\%\end{aligned}$$

GM still performed well relative to the market and the index model. It beat its "benchmark" return by an average of 0.018% per month.

6. The industries with positive adjustment factors are most sensitive to the economy. Their betas would be expected to be higher because the business risk of the firms is higher. In contrast, the industries with negative adjustment factors are in business fields with a lower sensitivity to the economy. Therefore, for any given financial profile, their betas are lower.

Chapter 10

1. The least profitable scenario currently yields a profit of \$10,000 and gross proceeds from the equally weighted portfolio of \$700,000. As the price of Dreck falls, less of the equally weighted portfolio can be purchased from the proceeds of the short sale. When Dreck's price falls by more than a factor of 10,000/700,000, arbitrage no longer will be feasible, because the profits in the worst state will be driven below zero.

To see this, suppose that Dreck's price falls to \$10 × (1 − 1/70). The short sale of 300,000 shares now yields \$2,957,142, which allows dollar investments of only \$985,714 in each of the other shares. In the high real interest rate-low inflation scenario, profits will be driven to zero:

Stock	Dollar Investment	Rate of Return	Dollar Return
Apex	\$ 985,714	.20	\$197,143
Bull	985,714	.70	690,000
Crush	985,714	−.20	−197,143
Dreck	−2,957,142	.23	−690,000
TOTAL	0		0

At any price for Dreck stock *below* \$10 × (1 − 1/70) = \$9.857, profits are negative, which means this arbitrage opportunity is eliminated. *Note:* \$9.857 is not the equilibrium price of Dreck. It is simply the upper bound on Dreck's price that rules out the simple arbitrage opportunity.

2. $\sigma(e_P) = = \sigma^2(e_i)/n$

   a. $\sqrt{30/10} = 1.732\%$

   b. $\sqrt{30/100} = .548\%$

   c. $\sqrt{30/1,000} = .173\%$

   d. $\sqrt{30/10,000} = .055\%$

   We conclude that nonsystematic volatility can be driven to arbitrarily low levels in well-diversified portfolios.

3. A portfolio consisting of two thirds of portfolio *A* and one third of the risk-free asset will have the same beta as portfolio *E*, but an expected return of $(\frac{1}{3} \times 4 + \frac{2}{3} \times 10) = 8$ percent, less than that of portfolio *E*. Therefore one can earn arbitrage profits by shorting the combination of portfolio *A* and the safe asset, and buying portfolio *E*.

4. *a.* For portfolio *P*,

$$K = \frac{E(r_P) - r_f}{\beta_P} = \frac{.10 - .05}{.5} = .10$$

   For portfolio *Q*,

$$K = \frac{.15 - .05}{1} = .10$$

   b. The equally weighted portfolio has an expected return of 12.5% and a beta of .75. $K = (.125 - .05)/.75 = .10$.

5. Using equation 10.5, the expected return is

$$4 + .2(6) + 1.4(8) = 16.4\%$$

Chapter 11

1. The SCL is estimated for each stock; hence we need to estimate 100 equations. Our sample consists of 60 monthly rates of return for each of the 100 stocks and for the market index. Thus each regression is estimated with 60 observations. Equation 11.1 in the text shows that when stated in excess return form, the SCL should pass through the origin, that is, have a zero intercept.
2. When the SML has a positive intercept and its slope is less than the mean excess return on the market portfolio, it is flatter than predicted by the CAPM. Low-beta stocks therefore have yielded returns that, on average, were more than they should have been on the basis of their beta. Conversely, high-beta stocks were found to have yielded, on average, less than they should have on the basis of their betas.
3. The intercept of the SML was .359 (36 basis points) instead of zero as it should have been according to the simple CAPM. Equation 11.5 in the text shows that if the zero-beta version of the CAPM is valid because of restrictions on borrowing, and the SCL and SML are estimated from excess returns over the risk-free rate (rather than over the zero-beta rate), then the intercept will be the difference between the zero-beta rate and the risk-free rate. Thus, if BJS had

found that the average risk premium of the zero-beta portfolio was 36 basis points (per month), the zero-beta version of the CAPM would have been supported. Similarly, the slope of the estimated SML should equal the difference between the market mean return and that of the zero-beta portfolio. The market index risk premium averaged 1.42% per month, and the slope of the SML was estimated as 1.08%. Here, a risk premium of 34 basis points would have supported the zero-beta version of the CAPM.

4. A positive coefficient on beta-squared would indicate that the relationship between risk and return is nonlinear. High beta securities would provide expected returns more than proportional to risk. A positive coefficient on $\sigma(e)$ would indicate that firm-specific risk affects expected return, a direct contradiction of the CAPM and APT.
5. It is very difficult to identify the portfolios that serve to hedge systematic sources of risk to future consumption opportunities. Both lines of research explore the data in search of such portfolios. Factor analysis techniques indicate the portfolios that may be providing hedge services. Researchers can then try to figure out what the source of risk is and show how important it is. The second line of attack attempts to use theoretical arguments to guess at the identity of economic variables that may be correlated with consumption risk and then determines whether these variables do indeed explain rates of return.

Chapter 12

1. The information sets that pertain to the weak, semistrong, and strong form of the EMH can be described by the following illustration:

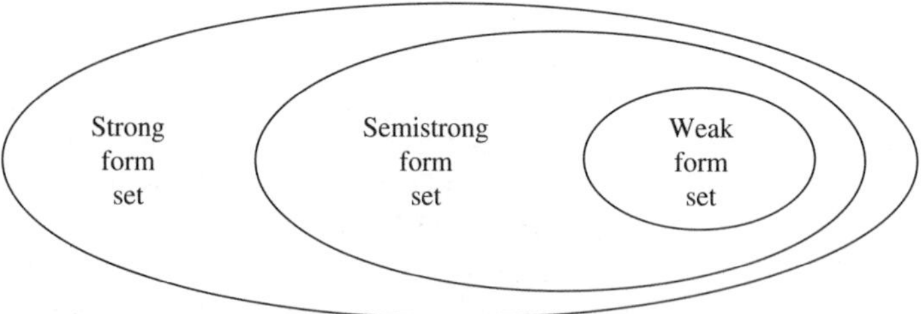

The weak-form information set includes only the history of prices and volumes. The semistrong-form set includes the weak form set *plus* all publicly available information. In turn, the strong-form set includes the semistrong set *plus* insiders' information. It is illegal to act on the incremental information (insiders' private information). The direction of *valid* implication is

$$\text{Strong-form EMH} \Rightarrow \text{Semistrong-form EMH} \Rightarrow \text{Weak-form EMH}$$

The reverse direction implication is *not* valid. For example, stock prices may reflect all past price data (weak-form efficiency) but may not reflect relevant fundamental data (semistrong-form inefficiency).

2. The point we made in the preceding discussion is that the very fact that we observe stock prices near so-called resistance levels belies the assumption that the price can be a resistance level. If a stock is observed to sell *at any price*, then

investors must believe that a fair rate of return can be earned if the stock is purchased at that price. It is logically impossible for a stock to have a resistance level *and* offer a fair rate of return at prices just below the resistance level. If we accept that prices are appropriate, we must reject any presumption concerning resistance levels.

3. If *everyone* follows a passive strategy, sooner or later prices will fail to reflect new information. At this point there are profit opportunities for active investors who uncover mispriced securities. As they buy and sell these assets, prices again will be driven to fair levels.
4. Predictably declining CARs do violate the EMH. If one can predict such a phenomenon, a profit opportunity emerges: sell (or short sell) the affected stocks on an event date just before their prices are predicted to fall.
5. The answer depends on your prior beliefs about market efficiency. Magellan's record was incredibly strong. On the other hand, with so many funds in existence, it is less surprising that *some* fund would appear to be consistently superior after the fact. Still, Magellan's record was so good that even accounting for its selection as the "winner" of an investment "contest," it still appears to be too good to be attributed to chance.
6. If profits can be made, one would expect mutual funds specializing in small stocks to spring into existence. Moreover, one wonders why buyers of small stocks do not compete for those stocks in December and bid up their prices before the January rise.
7. Concern over the deficit was an ongoing issue in 1987. No significant *new* information concerning the deficit was released on October 19. Hence this explanation for the crash is not consistent with the EMH.

Chapter 13

1. The callable bond will sell at the *lower* price. Investors will not be willing to pay as much if they know that the firm retains a valuable option to reclaim the bond for the call price if interest rates fall.
2. It should receive a negative coefficient. A high ratio of liabilities to assets is a poor omen for a firm that should lower its credit rating.
3. At a semiannual interest rate of 3%, the bond is worth $40 × PA(3%, 60) + $1,000 × PF(3%, 60) = $1,276.75, which results in a capital gain of $276.75. This exceeds the capital loss of $189.29 ($1,000 − $810.71) when the interest rate increased to 5%.
4. Yield to maturity exceeds current yield, which exceeds coupon rate. Take as an example the 8% coupon bond with a yield to maturity of 10% per year (5% per half year). Its price is $810.71, and therefore its current yield is 80/810.71 = .0987, or 9.87%, which is higher than the coupon rate but lower than the yield to maturity.
5. The bond with the 6% coupon rate currently sells for 30 × PA(3.5%, 20) + 1,000 × PF(3.5%, 20) = $928.94. If the interest rate immediately drops to 6% (3% per half year), the bond price will rise to $1,000, for a capital gain of $71.06, or 7.65%. The 8% coupon bond currently sells for $1,071.06. If the

interest rate falls to 6%, the present value of the *scheduled* payments increases to $1,148.77. However, the bond will be called at $1,100, for a capital gain of only $28.94, or 2.70%.

6. The current price of the bond can be derived from the yield to maturity. Using your calculator, set: n = 40 (semiannual periods); payment = $45 per period; Future value = $1,000; interest rate = 4% per semiannual period. Calculate present value as $1,098.96. Now we can calculate yield to call. The time to call is five years, or 10 semiannual periods. The price at which the bond will be called is $1,050. To find yield to call, we set: n = 10 (semiannual periods); payment = $45 per period; future value = $1,050; present value = $1,098.96. Calculate yield to call as 3.72%.
7. The coupon payment is $45. There are 20 semiannual periods. The final payment is assumed to be $600. The present value of expected cash flows is $750. The yield to maturity is 5.42% semiannual or 10.8%.
8. Price = $70 × PA(8%, 1) + $1,000 × PF(8%, 1) = $990.74

$$\text{Rate of return to investor} = \frac{\$70 + (\$990.74 - \$982.17)}{\$982.17} = .080$$
$$= 8\%$$

9. At the lower yield, the bond price will be $631.67 [n = 29, i = 7%, FV = $1000, PMT = $40]. Therefore, total after-tax income is

Coupon	$40 × (1 − .36) =	$25.60
Imputed interest	($553.66 − $549.69) × (1 − .36) =	2.54
Capital gains	($631.67 − $553.66) × (1 − .28) =	56.17
Total income after taxes		$84.31

Rate of return = 84.31/549.69 = .153 = 15.3%

Chapter 14

1. The bond sells today for $683.18 (from Table 14.2). Next year, it will sell for $1,000 ÷ [(1.10)(1.11)(1.11)] = $737.84, for a return 1 + r = 737.84/683.18 = 1.08, or r = 8%.
2. The data pertaining to the T-bill imply that the six-month interest rate is $300/$9,700 = .03093, or 3.093%. To obtain the forward rate, we look at the 1-year T-bond: The pricing formula

$$1{,}000 = \frac{40}{1.03093} + \frac{1040}{(1.03093)(1 + f)}$$

implies that f = .04952, or 4.952%.
3. 9%.
4. The risk premium will be zero.
5. If issuers wish to issue long-term bonds, they will be willing to accept higher expected interest costs on long bonds over short bonds. This willingness combines with investors' demands for higher rates on long-term bonds to reinforce the tendency toward a positive liquidity premium.

6. If r_4 equaled 9.66%, then the four-year bond would sell for \$1,000/[(1.08)(1.10)(1.11)(1.0966)] = \$691.53. The yield to maturity would satisfy the equation $691.53(1 + y_4)^4 = 1{,}000$, or $y_4 = 9.66\%$. At a lower value of r_4, the bond would sell for a higher price and offer a lower yield. At a higher value of r_4, the yield would be greater.

Chapter 15

1. *a.*

(1) Time until Payment	(2) Payment	(3) Payment Discounted at 10%	(4) Weight	(5) Column (1) × Column (4)
1	\$ 90	\$ 81.8182	.0833	.0833
2	1,090	900.8264	.9167	1.8334
		\$982.6446	1.0	1.9167

Duration is 1.1967 years. Price is \$982.6446.

b. At an interest rate of 10.05%, the bond's price is

$$90 \times PA(10.05\%, 2) + 1{,}000\ PF(10.05\%, 2) = 981.7891$$

The percentage change in price is −.087%.

c. The duration formula would predict a price change of

$$-\frac{1.9167}{1.10} \times .0005 = -.00087 = -.087\%$$

which is the same answer that we obtained from direct computation in (*b*).

2. The duration of a level perpetuity is $(1 + y)/y$ or $1 + 1/y$, which clearly falls as y increases. Tabulating duration as a function of y we get

y	*D*
.01	101 years
.02	51
.05	21
.10	11
.20	6
.25	5
.40	3.5

3. Potential gains and losses are proportional to both duration *and* portfolio size. The dollar loss on a fixed-income portfolio resulting from an increase in the portfolio's yield to maturity is, from equation 15.2, $D \times P \times \Delta y/(1 + y)$, where P is the initial market value of the portfolio. Hence $D \times P$ must be equated for immunization.

4. The perpetuity's duration now would be 1.08/.08 = 13.5. We need to solve the following equation for w:

$$w \times 2 + (1 - w) \times 13.5 = 6$$

Therefore $w = .6522$

5. Dedication would be more attractive. Cash flow matching eliminates the need for rebalancing and thus saves transaction costs.

6. The 30-year 8% coupon bond will provide a stream of coupons of $40 per half-year, which invested at the assumed rate of 4% per half-year will accumulate to $480.24. The bond will sell in five years at a price equal to $40 × PA(4.25%, 50) + $1,000 × PF(4.25%, 50), or $948.52, for a capital gain of $51.71. The total five-year income is $51.71 + $480.24 = $531.95, for a five-year return of $531.95/$896.81 = .5932, or 59.32%. Based on this scenario, the 20-year 10% coupon bond offers a higher return for a five-year horizon.
7. The trigger point is $10*M*/(1.12)^3 = $7.118*M*.
8. The manager would like to hold on to the money market securities because of the relative pricing compared to other short-term assets. However, there is an expectation that rates will fall. The manager can hold this *particular* portfolio of short-term assets and still benefit from the drop in interest rates by entering a swap to pay a short-term interest rate and receive a fixed interest rate. The resulting synthetic fixed-rate portfolio will increase in value if rates do fall.

Chapter 16

1. The downturn in the auto industry will reduce the demand for the product of this economy. The economy will, at least in the short term, enter a recession. This would suggest that:
   a. GDP will fall.
   b. The unemployment rate will rise.
   c. The government deficit will increase. Income tax receipts will fall, and government expenditures on social welfare programs probably will increase.
   d. Interest rates should fall. The contraction in the economy will reduce the demand for credit. Moreover, the lower inflation rate will reduce nominal interest rates.
2. Expansionary fiscal policy coupled with expansionary monetary policy will stimulate the economy, with the loose monetary policy keeping down interest rates.
3. A traditional demand-side interpretation of the tax cuts is that the resulting increase in after-tax income increased consumption demand and stimulated the economy. A supply-side interpretation is that the reduction in marginal tax rates made it more attractive for businesses to invest and for individuals to work, thereby increasing economic output.
4. Firm C has the lowest fixed cost and highest variable costs. It should be least sensitive to the business cycle. In fact, it is. Its profits are highest of the three firms in recessions but lowest in expansions.

	Recession	Normal	Expansion
Revenue	$10	$12	$14
Fixed cost	2	2	2
Variable cost	7.5	9	10.5
Profits	$ 0.5	$ 1	$ 1.5

Chapter 17

1. *a.* Dividend yield = \$2.15/\$50 = 4.3%
   Capital gains yield = (59.77 − 50)/50 = 19.54%
   Total return = 4.3% + 19.54% = 23.84%
   b. k = 6% + 1.15(14% − 6%) = 15.2%
   c. V_0 = (\$2.15 + \$59.77)/1.152 = \$53.75, which exceeds the market price. This would indicate a "buy" opportunity.
2. *a.* $D_1/(k - g)$ = \$2.15/(.152 − .112) − \$53.75
   b. $P_1 = P_0(1 + g)$ = \$53.75(1.112) = \$59.77
   c. The expected capital gain equals \$59.77 − \$53.75 = \$6.02, for a percentage gain of 11.2%. The dividend yield is D_1/P_0 = 2.15/53.75 = 4%, for a holding-period return of 4% + 11.2% = 15.2%.
3. $g = \text{ROE} \times b = .20 \times .60 = .12$
   $D_1 = .4 \times E_1 = .4 \times \$5 = \$2$
   $P_0 = 2/(.125 - .12) = 400$
   $\text{PVGO} = P_0 - E_1/k = 400 - 5/.125 = 360$
   PVGO represents an extremely high fraction of the total value of the firm. This is because the assumed dividend growth rate, 12%, is nearly as high as the discount rate, 12.5%. The assumption that the growth rate can remain so close to the discount rate for an indefinitely long period represents an extremely optimistic (and probably unrealistic) view of the long-term growth prospects of the firm.
4. Given current management's investment policy, the dividend growth rate will be

$$g = \text{ROE} \times b = 10\% \times .6 = 6\%$$

and the stock price should be

$$P_0 = \frac{\$2}{.15 - .06} = \$22.22$$

The present value of growth opportunities is

$$\begin{aligned}\text{PVGO} &= \text{Price per share} - \text{No-growth value per share} \\ &= \$22.22 - E_1/k \\ &= \$22.22 - \$5/.15 \\ &= -\ \$11.11\end{aligned}$$

PVGO is *negative*. This is because the net present value of the firm's projects is negative: The rate of return on those assets is less than the opportunity cost of capital.

Such a firm would be subject to takeover, because another firm could buy the firm for the market price of \$22.22 per share and increase the value of the firm by changing its investment policy. For example, if the new management simply paid out all earnings as dividends, the value of the firm would increase to its no-growth value, E_1/k = \$5/.15 = \$33.33.

5. $V_{1993} = \frac{.54}{(1.123)} + \frac{.66}{(1.123)^2} + \frac{.78}{(1.123)^3} + \frac{.90 + P_{1997}}{(1.123)^4}$

Now compute the sales price in 1997 using the constant growth dividend discount model.

$$P_{1997} = \frac{.90 \times (1 + g)}{k - g} = \frac{\$90 \times 1.118}{.123 - .118} = \$201.24$$

Therefore, $V_{1993} = \$128.65$

6. *a.* ROE = 12%
$b = \$.50/\$2.00 = .25$
$g = \text{ROE} \times b = 12\% \times .25 = 3\%$
$P_0 = D_1/(k - g) = \$1.50/(.10 - .03) = \$21.43$
$P_0/E_1 = \$21.43/\$2.00 = 10.71$

b. If $b = .4$, then $.4 \times \$2 = \$0.80$ would be reinvested and the remainder of earnings, or \$1.20, would be paid as dividends
$g = 12\% \times .4 = 4.8\%$
$P_0 = D_1/(k - g) = \$1.20/(.10 - .048) = \$23.08$
$P_0/E_1 = \$23.08/\$2.00 = 11.54$

7. *a.* $P_0 = \frac{(1 - b)E_1}{k - g} = \frac{.6 \times \$1}{.10 - .04} = \$10$

b. $\frac{E(D_1^*)}{P_0} = \frac{(1 - b)E_1^*}{P_0} = \frac{(1 - .4) \times \$1}{\$10} = .06$, or 6% per year

The rate of price appreciation $= g^* = b^* \times \text{ROE}^* = 4\%$ per year

c. *i.* $g = (1.04)(1.06) - 1 = .1024$, or 10.24%

ii. $\frac{E(D_1)}{P_0} = \frac{E(D_1^*)(1 + i)}{P_0} = .06 \times 1.06 = .0636$, or 6.36%

iii. ROE = 16.6%

iv. $b = \frac{g}{\text{ROE}} = \frac{.1024}{.166} = .6169$

Chapter 18

1. A debt/equity ratio of 1 implies that Mordett will have \$50 million of debt and \$50 million of equity. Interest expense will be $.09 \times \$50$ million, or \$4.5 million per year. Mordett's net profits and ROE over the business cycle will therefore be

		Nodett		Mordett	
Scenario	**EBIT**	**Net profits**	**ROE**	**Net Profits**[a]	**ROE**[b]
Bad year	\$ 5M	\$3 million	3%	\$ .3 million	.6%
Normal year	10M	6	6	3.3	6.6
Good year	15M	9	9	6.3	12.6

[a]Mordett's after-tax profits are given by: .6(EBIT − \$4.5 million).
[b]Mordett's equity is only \$50 million.

2.

Ratio Decomposition Analysis for Mordett Corporation

		ROE	(1) Net Profit / Pretax Profit	(2) Pretax Profit / EBIT	(3) EBIT / Sales (ROS)	(4) Sales / Assets (ATO)	(5) Assets / Equity	(6) Combined Leverage Factor (2) × (5)
a.	*Bad year*							
	Nodett	.030	.6	1.000	.0625	.800	1.000	1.000
	Somdett	.018	.6	.360	.0625	.800	1.667	.600
	Mordett	.006	.6	.100	.0625	.800	2.000	.200
b.	*Normal year*							
	Nodett	.060	.6	1.000	.100	1.000	1.000	1.000
	Somdett	.068	.6	.680	.100	1.000	1.667	1.134
	Mordett	.066	.6	.550	.100	1.000	2.000	1.100
c.	*Good year*							
	Nodett	.090	.6	1.000	.125	1.200	1.000	1.000
	Somdett	.118	.6	.787	.125	1.200	1.667	1.311
	Mordett	.126	.6	.700	.125	1.200	2.000	1.400

3. GI's ROE in 19X3 was 3.03 percent computed as follows:

$$\text{ROE} = \frac{\$5{,}285}{.5(\$171{,}843 + \$177{,}128)} = .303\text{, or } 3.03\%$$

Its P/E ratio was $4 = \dfrac{\$21}{\$5.285}$

and its P/B ratio was $.12 = \dfrac{\$21}{\$177}$

Its earnings yield was 25% compared with an industry average of 12.5%.

Note that in our calculations the earnings yields will not equal ROE/(*P*/*B*) because we have computed ROE with average shareholders' equity in the denominator and *P*/*B* with end-of-year shareholders' equity in the denominator.

4.

IBX Ratio Analysis

Year	ROE	(1) Net Profit / Pretax Profit	(2) Pretax Profit / EBIT	(3) EBIT / Sales (ROS)	(4) Sales / Assets (ATO)	(5) Assets / Equity	(6) Combined Leverage Factor (2) × (5)	(7) ROA (3) × (4)
1995	11.4%	.616	.796	7.75%	1.375	2.175	1.731	10.65%
1992	10.2	.636	.932	8.88	1.311	1.474	1.374	11.65

ROE went up despite a decline in operating margin and a decline in the tax burden ratio because of increased leverage and turnover. Note that ROA declined from 11.65% in 1992 to 10.65% in 1995.

5. LIFO accounting results in lower reported earnings than does FIFO. Fewer assets to depreciate results in lower reported earnings because there is less bias associated with the use of historic cost. More debt results in lower reported earnings because the inflation premium in the interest rate is treated as part of

interest expense and not as repayment of principal. If ABC has the same reported earnings as XYZ despite these three sources of downward bias, its real earnings must be greater.

Chapter 19

1. *a.* Proceeds $= S_T - X = S_T -$ \$75 if this value is positive; otherwise the call expires worthless

   Profit $=$ Proceeds $-$ price of option

   $=$ Proceeds $-$ \$11/16 $=$ Proceeds $-$ \$.6875

	$S_T = \$70$	$S_T = \$80$
Proceeds	\$ 0	\$5
Profits	$-$\$.6875	\$4.3125

   a. Proceeds $= X - S_T =$ \$75 $- S_T$ if this value is positive; otherwise the put expires worthless

   Profit $=$ Proceeds $-$ price of option $=$ Proceeds $-$ \$5⅝.

	$S_T = \$70$	$S_T = \$80$
Proceeds	\$5	\$0
Profits	$-$\$.625	$-$\$5.625

2. Before the split, profits would have been 100 × (\$100 − \$90) = \$1,000. After the split, profits are 1,000 × (\$10 − \$9) = \$1,000. Profits are unaffected.

3. *a.* Payoff to put writer $= 0$ if $S_T \geq X$

   $-(X - S_T)$ if $S_T < X$

   b. Profit $=$ Initial premium realized $+$ Ultimate payoff

   $= P$ if $S_T \geq X$

   $P - (X - S_T)$ if $S_T < X$

   c.

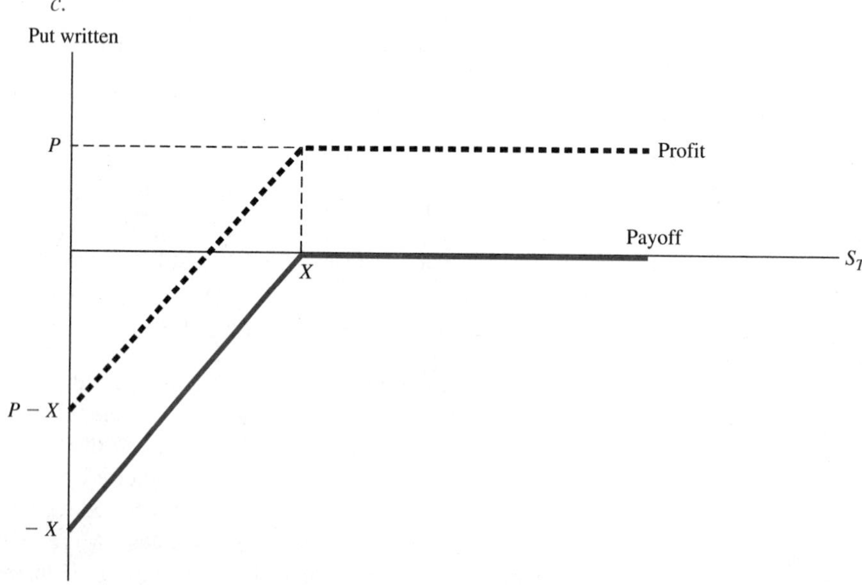

d. Put writers do well when the stock price increases and poorly when it falls.

4.

Payoff to a Strip

	$S_T \leq X$	$S_T > X$
2 Puts	$2(X - S_T)$	0
1 Call	0	$S_T - X$

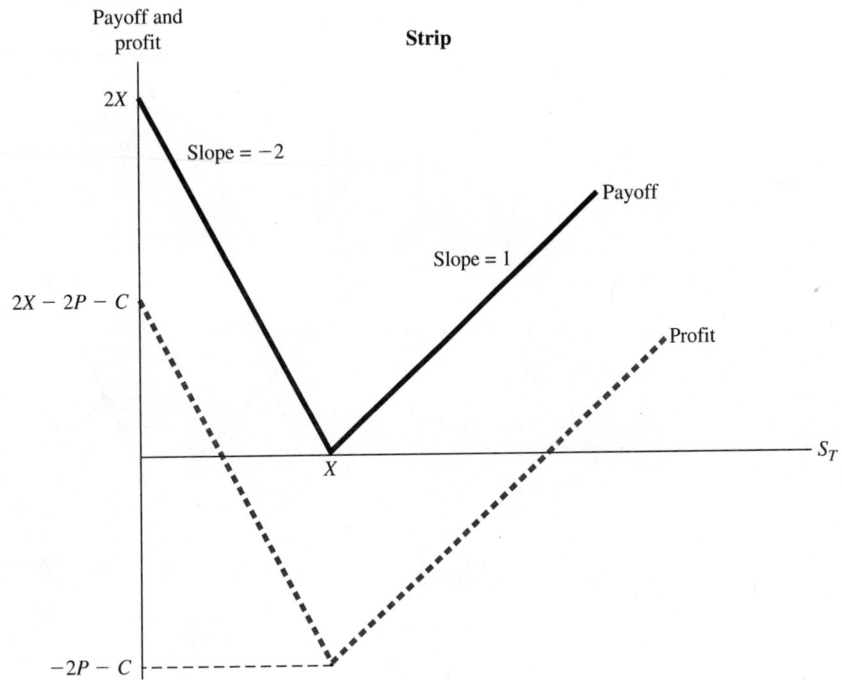

Payoff to a Strap

	$S_T \leq X$	$S_T > X$
1 Put	$X - S_T$	0
2 Calls	0	$2(S_T - X)$

Strap

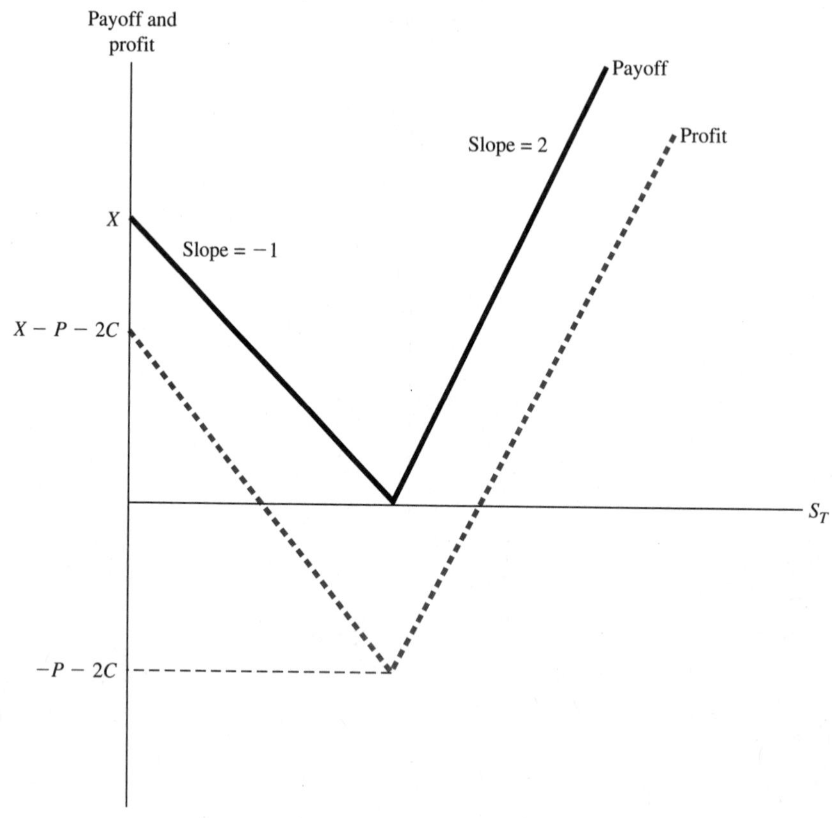

5.

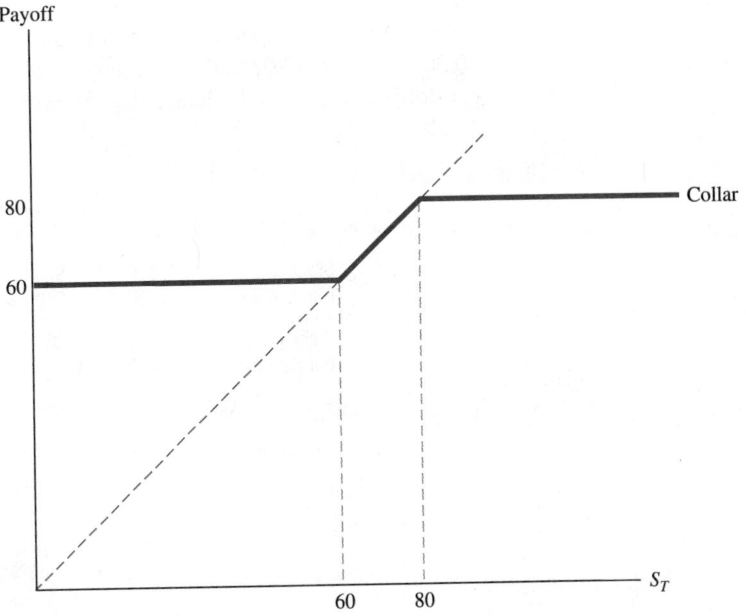

6. The covered call strategy would consist of a straight bond with a call written on the bond. The value of the strategy at option expiration as a function of the value of the straight bond is given in the figure following, which is virtually identical to Figure 19.14.

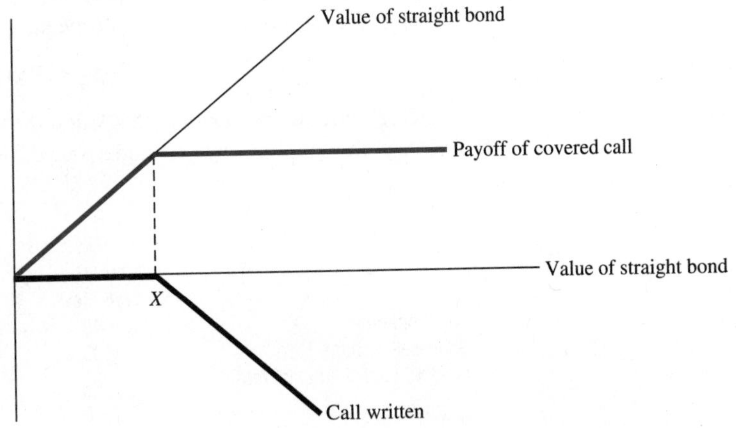

7. The call option is worth less as call protection is expanded. Therefore, the coupon rate need not be as high.

8. Lower. Investors will accept a lower coupon rate in return for the conversion option.
9. The depositor's implicit cost per dollar invested is now only ($0.03 − $0.005)/1.03 = $0.02427 per six-month period. Calls cost $20/$400 = $0.05 per dollar invested in the index. The multipler falls to .02427/.05 = .4854.

Chapter 20

1. Yes. Consider the same scenarios as for the call

Stock price	$10	$20	$30	$40	$50
Put payoff	$20	$10	$ 0	$ 0	$ 0

Stock price	$20	$25	$30	$35	$40
Put payoff	$10	$ 5	$ 0	$ 0	$ 0

The low volatility scenario yields a lower expected payoff.

2.

If this Variable Increases	The Value of a Put Option
S	Decreases
X	Increases
σ	Increases
T	Increases
r_f	Decreases
Dividends	Increases

3. The parity relationship assumes that all options are held until expiration and that there are no cash flows until expiration. These assumptions are valid only in the special case of European options on nondividend-paying stocks. If the stock pays no dividends, the American and European calls are equally valuable, whereas the American put is worth more than the European put. Therefore, although the parity theorem for European options states that

$$P = C + S_0 - \text{PV}(X)$$

in fact, P will be *greater* than this value if the put is American.

4. Because the option now is underpriced, we want to reverse our previous strategy.

	Initial Cash Flow	Cash Flow in 1 Year for Each Possible Stock Price: S = 50	S = 200
Buy 2 options	−48	0	150
Short-sell 1 share	100	−50	−200
Lend $52 at 8% interest rate	52	56.16	56.16
TOTAL	0	6.16	6.16

5. Higher. For deep out-of-the-money options, an increase in the stock price still leaves the option unlikely to be exercised. Its value increases only fractionally. For deep in-the-money options, exercise is likely, and option holders benefit by a full dollar for each dollar increase in the stock, as though they already own the stock.

6. Because $\sigma = .6$, $\sigma^2 = .36$.

$$d_1 = \frac{ln(100/95) + (.10 + .36/2)\,.25}{.6\sqrt{.25}} = .4043$$

$$d_2 = d_1 - .6\sqrt{.25} = .1043$$

Using Table 20.2 and interpolation,

$$N(d_1) = .6570$$
$$N(d_2) = .5415$$
$$C = 100 \times .6570 - 95\, e^{-.10 \times .25} \times .5415$$
$$= 15.53$$

7. Implied volatility exceeds 0.5. Given a standard deviation of 0.5, the option value is \$13.70. A higher volatility is needed to justify the actual \$15 price.
8. A \$1 increase in stock price is a percentage increase of 1/122 = .82%. The put option will fall by (.4 × \$1) = \$0.40, a percentage decrease of \$0.40/\$4 = 10%. Elasticity is − 10/.82 = − 12.2.

Chapter 21

1.

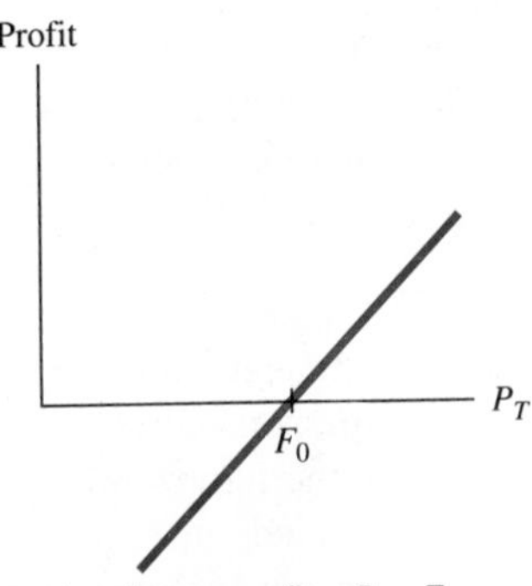

Long futures profit = $P_T - F_0$

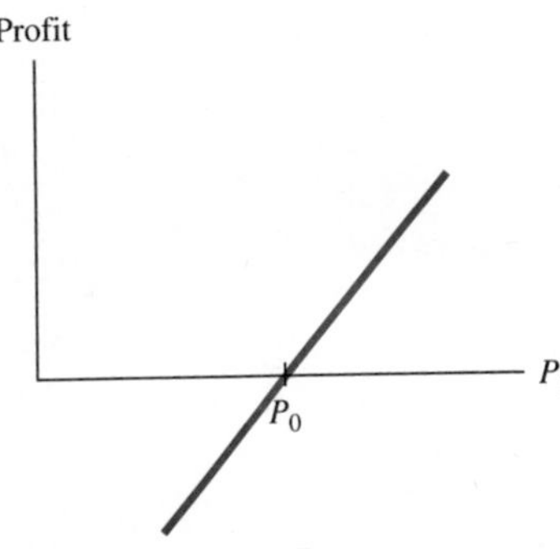

Asset profit = $P_T - P_0$

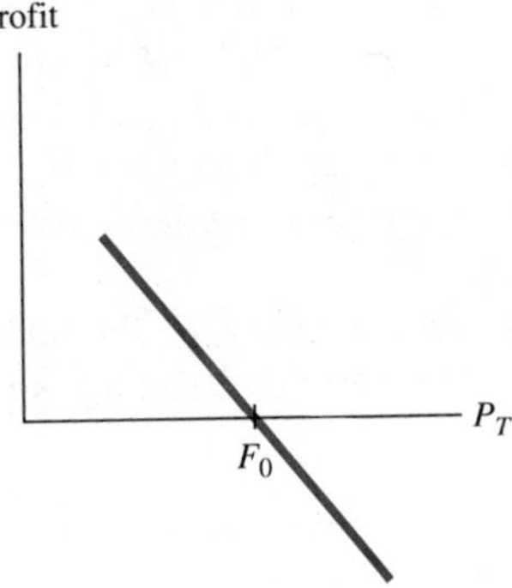

Short futures profit = $F_0 - P_T$

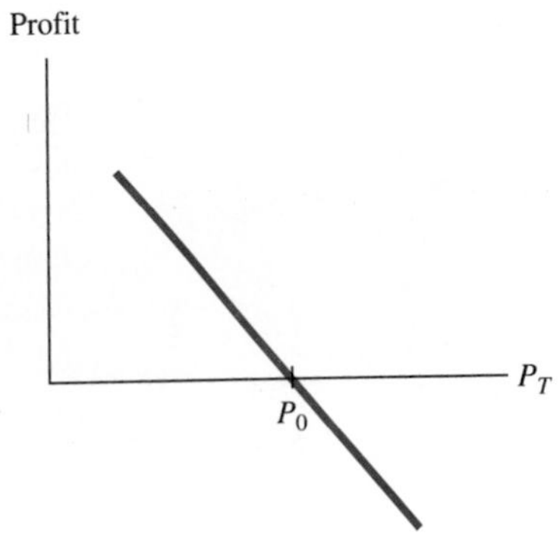

Profit

P_T

P_0

Short sale profit = $P_0 - P_T$

2. The clearinghouse has a zero net position in all contracts. Its long and short positions are offsetting, so that net cash flow from marking to market must be zero.

3.

	T-Bond Price in December		
	$98.91	$99.91	$100.91
Cash flow to purchase bonds (= $-2{,}000\ P_T$)	−$197,820	−$199,820	−$201,820
Profits on long futures position	−2,000	0	2,000
Total cash flow	−$199,820	−$199,820	−$199,820

4. The risk would be that aluminum and bauxite prices do not move perfectly together. Thus, basis risk involving the spread between the futures price and bauxite spot prices could persist even if the aluminum futures price were set perfectly relative to aluminum itself.

5.

Action	Initial Cash Flow	Cash Flow in One Year
Lend S_0	−460	460(1.04) = 478.40
Short stock	+460	$-S_T - 8$
Long futures	0	$S_T - 465$
TOTAL	0	$5.40 risklessly

6. It must have zero beta. If the futures price is an unbiased estimator, then we infer that it has a zero risk premium, which means that beta must be zero.

Chapter 22

1. As the payoffs to the two strategies are identical, so should be the costs of establishing them. The synthetic stock strategy costs $F_0/(1 + r_f)^T$ to establish, this being the present value of the futures price. The stock index purchased directly costs S_0. Therefore we conclude that $S_0 = F_0/(1 + r_f)^T$, or, $F_0 = S_0(1 + r_f)^T$, which is the parity relationship in the case of no dividends.
2. If the futures price is above the parity level, investors would sell futures and buy stocks. Short selling would not be necessary. Therefore the top of the no-arbitrage band would be unaffected by the use of the proceeds. If the futures price is too low, investors would want to short sell stocks and buy futures. Now the costs of short selling are important. If proceeds from the short sale become available, short selling becomes less costly and the bottom of the band will move up.
3. According to interest rate parity, F_0 should be $1.817. Since the futures price is too high, we should reverse the arbitrage strategy just considered.

	CF Now ($)	CF in 1 Year
1. Borrow $1.80 in the U.S. Convert to one pound.	+1.80	−1.80(1.06)
2. Lend the one pound in the U.K.	−1.80	$1.05E_1$
3. Enter a contract to sell 1.05 pounds at a futures price of 1.83.	0	$(1.05)(1.83 - E_1)$
TOTAL	0	.0135

4. Stocks offer a total return (capital gain plus dividends) large enough to compensate investors for the time value of the money tied up in the the stock. Wheat prices do not necessarily increase over time. In fact, across a harvest, wheat prices will fall. The returns necessary to make storage economically attractive are lacking.
5. If systematic risk were higher, the appropriate discount rate, k, would increase. Referring to equation 22.5, we conclude that F_0 would fall. Intuitively, the claim to 1 pound of orange juice is worth less today if its expected price is unchanged, but the risk associated with the value of the claim increases. Therefore, the amount investors are willing to pay today for future delivery is lower.
6. Year 1. LIBOR − 7% = .01. Therefore, fixed-rate payer receives .01 × $20 million = $200,000 from counterparty.
   Year 2. LIBOR = 7%. No payments are exchanged.
   Year 3. Fixed-rate payer receives .02 × 20 million = $400,000.

Chapter 23

1. We show the answer for the annual compounded rate of return for each strategy and leave you to compute the monthly rate.
   Beginning-of-period fund:

$$F_0 = \$1{,}000$$

End-of-period fund for each strategy:

$$F_1 = \begin{cases} 3{,}600 & \text{Strategy} = \text{Bills only} \\ 67{,}500 & \text{Strategy} = \text{Market only} \\ 5{,}360{,}000{,}000 & \text{Strategy} = \text{Perfect timing} \end{cases}$$

Number of periods: $N = 52$ years
Annual compounded rate:

$$[1 + r_A]^N = \frac{F_1}{F_0}$$

$$r_A = \left(\frac{F_1}{F_0}\right)^{1/N} - 1$$

$$r_A = \begin{cases} 2.49\% & \text{Strategy} = \text{Bills only} \\ 8.44\% & \text{Strategy} = \text{Market only} \\ 34.71\% & \text{Strategy} = \text{Perfect timing} \end{cases}$$

2. The timer will guess bear or bull markets completely randomly. One half of all bull markets will be preceded by a correct forecast, and similarly for bear markets. Hence, $P_1 + P_2 - 1 = \frac{1}{2} + \frac{1}{2} - 1 = 0$.
3. *a.* When short positions are prohibited, the analysis is identical except that negative alpha stocks are dropped from the list. In that case the sum of the ratios of alpha to residual variance for the remaining two stocks is .7895. This leads to the new composition of the active portfolio:

$$x_1 = .3457/.7895 = .4379$$
$$x_2 = .4438/.7895 = .5621$$

The alpha, beta, and residual standard deviation of the active portfolio are now:

$$\alpha_A = .4379 \times .07 + .5621 \times .03 = .0475$$
$$\beta_A = .4379 \times 1.6 + .5621 \times .5 = .9817$$
$$\sigma(e_A) = [.4379^2 \times .45^2 + .5621^2 \times .26^2]^{1/2} = .2453$$

The cost of the short sale restriction is already apparent. The alpha has shrunk from 20.56% to 4.75%, while the reduction in the residual risk is more moderate, from 82.62% to 24.53%. In fact, a negative alpha stock is potentially more attractive than a positive alpha one: since most stocks are positively correlated, the negative position that is required for the negative alpha stock creates a better diversified active portfolio.

The optimal allocation of the new active portfolio is:

$$w_0 = \frac{.0475/.6019}{.08/.04} = .3946$$

$$w^* = \frac{.3946}{1 + (1 - .9817) \times .3946} = .3918$$

Here, too, the beta correction is essentially irrelevant because the portfolio beta is so close to 1.0.

Finally, the performance of the overall risky portfolio is estimated at

$$S_P^2 = .16 + \left[\frac{.0475}{.2453}\right]^2 = .1975; \; S_P = .44$$

It is clear that in this case we have lost about half of the original improvement in the Sharpe measure. Note, however, that this is an artifact of the limited coverage of the security analysis division. When more stocks are covered, then a good number of positive alpha stocks will keep the residual risk of the active portfolio low. This is the key to extracting large gains from the active strategy.

b. When the forecast for the market index portfolio is more optimistic, the position in the active portfolio will be smaller and the contribution of the active portfolio to the Sharpe measure of the risky portfolio will be of a smaller magnitude. In the original example the allocation to the active portfolio would be

$$w_0 = \frac{.2056/.6826}{.12/.04} = .1004$$

$$w^* = \frac{.1004}{1 + (1 - .9519) \times .1004} = .0999$$

Although the Sharpe measure of the market is now better, the improvement derived from security analysis is smaller:

$$S_P^2 = \left(\frac{.12}{.20}\right)^2 + \left(\frac{.2056}{.8262}\right)^2 = .4219$$
$$S_P = .65;\ S_M = .60$$

Chapter 24

1.

Time	Action	Cash Flow
0	Buy two shares	−40
1	Collect dividends; then sell one of the shares	4 + 22
2	Collect dividend on remaining share, then sell it	2 + 19

a. Dollar-weighted return:

$$-40 + \frac{26}{1+r} + \frac{21}{(1+r)^2} = 0$$
$$r = .1191 = 11.91\%$$

b. Time-weighted return:

The rates of return on the stock in the 2 years were:

$$r_1 = \frac{2 + (22 - 20)}{22} = .20$$
$$r_2 = \frac{2 + (19 - 22)}{22} = -.045$$
$$(r_1 + r_2)/2 = .077, \text{ or } 7.7\%$$

2. *a.* $E(r_A) = [.15 + (-.05)]/2 = .05$

$E(r_G) = [(1.15)(.95)]^{1/2} - 1 = .045$

b. The expected stock price is (115 + 95)/2 = 105.

c. The expected rate of return on the stock is 5%, equal to r_A.

3. Sharpe: $(\bar{r} - \bar{r}_f)/\sigma$

$S_P = (35 - 6)/42 = .69$

$S_M = (28 - 6)/30 = .733$

Alpha: $\bar{r} - [\bar{r}_f + \beta(\bar{r}_M - \bar{r}_f)]$

$\alpha_P = 35 - [6 + 1.2(28 - 6)] = 2.6$

$\alpha_M = 0$

Treynor: $(\bar{r} - \bar{r}_f)/\beta$

$T_P = (35 - 6)/1.2 = 24.2$

$T_M = (28 - 6)/1.0 = 22$

Appraisal ratio: $\alpha/\sigma(e)$

$A_P = 2.6/18 = .144$

$A_M = 0$

4. The t-statistic on α is $.2/2 = .1$. The probability that a manager with a true alpha of zero could obtain a sample period alpha with a t-statistic of .1 or better by pure luck can be calculated approximately from a table of the normal distribution. The probability is 46%.
5. Performance Attribution

First compute the new bogey performance as $(.70 \times 5.81) + (.25 \times 1.45) + (.05 \times .48) = 4.45$.

a. Contribution of asset allocation to performance

Market	(1) Actual Weight in Market	(2) Benchmark Weight in Market	(3) Excess Weight	(4) Market Return Minus Bogey (Percent)	(5) = (3) × (4) Contribution to Performance (Percent)
Equity	.70	.70	.00	1.36	.00
Fixed-income	.07	.25	−.18	−3.00	.54
Cash	.23	.05	.18	−3.97	−.71
Contribution of asset allocation					−.17

b. Contribution of selection to total performance

Market	(1) Portfolio Performance (Percent)	(2) Index Performance (Percent)	(3) Excess Performance (Percent)	(4) Portfolio Weight	(5) = (3) × (4) Contribution (Percent)
Equity	7.28	5.00	2.28	.70	1.60
Fixed-income	1.89	1.45	0.44	.07	.03
Contribution of selection within markets					1.63

Chapter 25

1. Because the firm does poorly when the dollar depreciates, it hedges with a futures contract that will provide profits in that scenario. It needs to enter a *long* position in pound futures, which means that it will earn profits on the contract when the futures price increases, that is, when more dollars are required to purchase one pound. The specific hedge ratio is determined by noting that if the number of dollars required to buy one pound rises by \$0.05, profits decrease by \$200,000 at the same time that the profit on a long future contract would be $\$0.05 \times 62{,}500 = \$3{,}125$. The hedge ratio is

$$\frac{\$200{,}000 \text{ per } \$0.05 \text{ depreciation in the dollar}}{\$3{,}125 \text{ per contract per } \$0.05 \text{ depreciation}} = 64 \text{ contracts long}$$

2. Each \$1 increase in the price of corn reduces profits by \$1 million. Therefore, the firm needs to enter futures contracts to purchase 1 million bushels at a price stipulated today. The futures position will profit by \$1 million for each increase of \$1 in the price of corn. The profit on the contract will offset the lost profits on operations.

3. The price value of a basis point is still $900,000, as a one-basis-point change in the interest rate reduces the value of the $20 million portfolio by .01% × 4.5 = .0045%. Therefore, the number of futures needed to hedge the interest rate risk is the same as for a portfolio half the size with double the modified duration.
4. The delta for a call option is $N(d_1)$, which is positive, and in this case, is .547. Therefore, for every 10 option contracts, you would need to *short* 547 shares of stock.
5. *a.* For Louisiana residents, the stock is not a hedge. When their economy does poorly (low oil prices) the stock also does poorly, thereby aggravating their problems.
   b. For Massachusetts residents, the stock is a hedge. When energy prices increase, the stock will provide greater wealth with which to purchase energy.
   c. If energy consumers (who are willing to bid up the price of the stock for its hedge value) dominate the economy, then high oil-beta stocks will have lower expected rates of return than would be predicted by the simple CAPM.

Chapter 26

1. The graph would asymptote to a lower level, as shown in the figure below, reflecting the improved opportunities for diversification. There still would be a positive level of nondiversifiable risk.
2. $1 + r(\text{US}) = [(1 + r_f(\text{UK})] \times (E_1/E_0)$
   a. $1 + r(\text{US}) = 1.1 \times 1.0 = 1.10$. Therefore, $r(\text{US}) = 10\%$
   b. $1 + r(\text{US}) = 1.1 \times 1.1 = 1.21$. Therefore, $r(\text{US}) = 21\%$
3. You must sell forward the number of pounds you will end up with at the end of the year. This value cannot be known with certainty, however, unless the rate of return of the pound-denominated investment is known.
   a. 10,000 × 1.20 = 12,000 pounds.
   b. 10,000 × 1.30 = 13,000 pounds.
4. *Country selection:*

$$(.40 \times .10) + (.20 \times .05) + (.40 \times .15) = .11$$

This is a loss of .015 (1.5%) relative to the EAFE passive benchmark.
Currency selection:

$$(.40 \times 1.10) + (.20 \times .9) + (.40 \times 1.30) = 1.14$$

This is a loss of 6% relative to the EAFE benchmark.

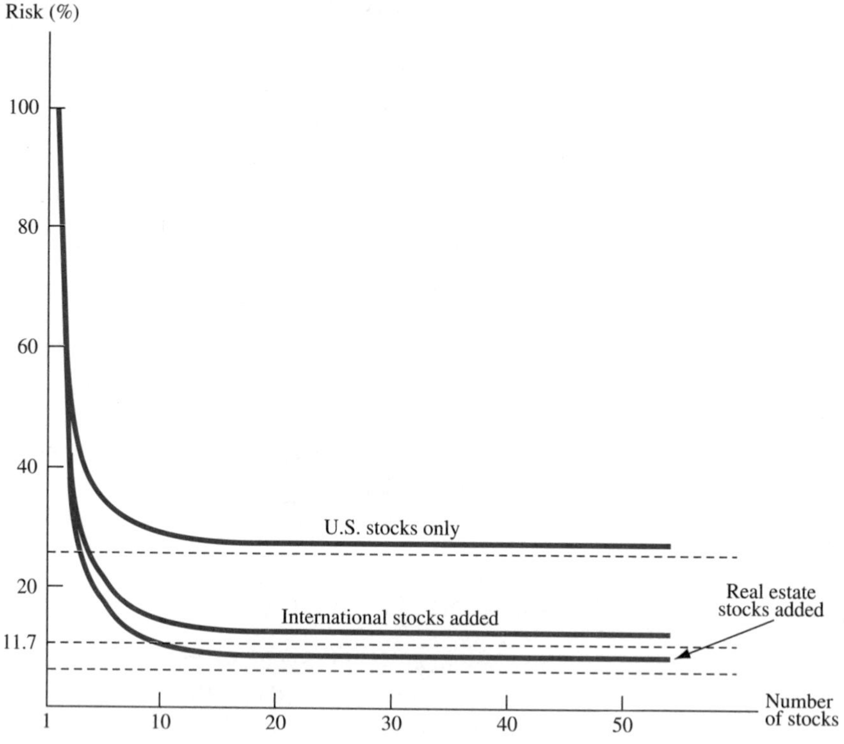

Chapter 27

1. The new estimates are as follows:

		Holding-Period Return		
State of Economy	**Probability**	**Stock**	**Bonds**	**Cash**
Boom with low inflation	.05	74%	4%	6%
Boom with high inflation	.2	20%	−10%	6%
Normal growth	.5	14%	9%	6%
Recession with low inflation	.2	0	35%	6%
Recession with high inflation	.05	−30%	0	6%
Expected return	$E(r)$	13.2%	9.7%	6%
Standard deviation	σ	17.96%	14.57%	0

Correlation coefficient between stocks and bonds is −.3449.

2. To find the composition of the optimal combination of stocks and bonds to be combined with cash we use the following formula:

$$w^* = \frac{[E(r_s) - r_f]\sigma_b^2 - [E(r_b) - r_f]\mathrm{Cov}(r_b, r_s)}{[E(r_s) - r_f]\sigma_b^2 + [E(r_b) - r_f]\sigma_s^2 - [E(r_s) - r_f + E(r_b) - r_f]\mathrm{Cov}(r_b, r_s)}$$

where w^* is the proportion of stocks in portfolio O^* and $1 - w^*$ is the proportion of bonds. Substituting in the formula we get

$$w^* = \frac{(13.2 - 6)212.2849 - (9.7 - 6)(90.2525)}{7.2 \times 212.2849 + 3.7 \times 322.5616 + (7.2 + 3.7)90.2525}$$

$$= \frac{1194.5}{1738.2} = .687$$

So the proportion of stocks in the O^* portfolio changes from 45% to 69%.

Chapter 28

1. Identify the elements that are life-cycle driven in the two schemes of objectives and constraints.
2. If Eloise keeps her present asset allocation, she will have the following amounts to spend after taxes five years from now:

   Tax-qualified account:

Banks: $50,000(1.1)^5 × .72	= $ 57,978.36
Stocks: $50,000(1.15)^5 × .72	= $ 72,408.86
Subtotal	**$130,387.22**

   Nonretirement account:

Bonds: $50,000(1.072)^5	= $ 70,785.44
Stocks: $50,000(1.15)^5 − .28 × [50,000(1.15)^5 − 50,000]	= $ 86,408.86
Subtotal	**$157,194.30**
TOTAL	**$287,581.52**

   If Eloise shifts all of the bonds into the retirement account and all of the stock into the nonretirement account, she will have the following amounts to spend after taxes five years from now:

   Tax-qualified account:

Bonds: $100,000(1.1)^5 × .72	= $115,956.72
Nonretirement account:	
Stocks: $100,000(1.15)^5 − .28 × [100,000(1.15)^5 − 100,000]	= $172,817.72
TOTAL	= **$288,774.44**

   Her spending budget will increase by $1,192.92.
3. $B_0 \times PA$ (4%, 5 years) = 100,000 implies that B_0 = $22,462.71.

t	R_t	B_t	A_t
0			$100,000.00
1	4%	$22,462.71	$ 81,537.29
2	10%	$23,758.64	$ 65,923.38
3	−8%	$21,017.26	$ 39,640.53
4	25%	$25,261.12	$ 24,289.54
5	0	$24,289.54	0

4. He has accrued an annuity of $.01 \times 15 \times 15{,}000 = \$2{,}250$ per year for 15 years, starting in 25 years. The present value of this annuity is $2,812.13:

$$PV = 2{,}250\ PA\ (8\%, 15) \times PF\ (8\%, 25) = 2812.13$$

Glossary

Abnormal return. Return on a stock beyond what would be predicted by market movements alone. Cumulative abnormal return (CAR) is the total abnormal return for the period surrounding an announcement or the release of information.

Accounting earnings. Earnings of a firm as reported on its income statement.

Acid test ratio. See quick ratio.

Active management. Attempts to achieve portfolio returns more than commensurate with risk, either by forecasting broad market trends or by identifying particular mispriced sectors of a market or securities in a market.

Active portfolio. In the context of the Treynor-Black model, the portfolio formed by mixing analyzed stocks of perceived nonzero alpha values. This portfolio is ultimately mixed with the passive market index portfolio.

Adjustable-rate mortgage. A mortgage whose interest rate varies according to some specified measure of the current market interest rate.

Adjusted forecast. A (micro or macro) forecast that has been adjusted for the imprecision of the forecast.

Agency problem. Conflicts of interest among stockholders, bondholders, and managers.

Alpha. The abnormal rate of return on a security in excess of what would be predicted by an equilibrium model like CAPM or APT.

American depository receipts (ADRs). Domestically traded securities representing claims to shares of foreign stocks.

American option, European option. An American option can be exercised before and up to its expiration date. Compare with a *European option,* which can be exercised only on the expiration date.

Announcement date. Date on which particular news concerning a given company is announced to the public. Used in *event studies,* which researchers use to evaluate the economic impact of events of interest.

Appraisal ratio. The signal-to-noise ratio of an analyst's forecasts. The ratio of alpha to residual standard deviation.

Arbitrage. A zero-risk, zero-net investment strategy that still generates profits.

Arbitrage pricing theory. An asset pricing theory that is derived from a factor model, using diversification and arbitrage arguments. The theory describes the relationship between expected returns on securities, given that there are no opportunities to create wealth through risk-free arbitrage investments.

Asked price. The price at which a dealer will sell a security.

Asset allocation decision. Choosing among broad asset classes such as stocks versus bonds.

Asset turnover (ATO). The annual sales generated by each dollar of assets (sales/assets).

Auction market. A market where all traders in a good meet at one place to buy or sell an asset. The NYSE is an example.

Average collection period, or days' receivables. The ratio of accounts receivable to sales, or the total amount of credit extended per dollar of daily sales (average AR/sales × 365).

Balance sheet. An accounting statement of a firm's financial position at a specified time.

Bank discount yield. An annualized interest rate assuming simple interest, a 360-day year, and using the face value of the security rather than purchase price to compute return per dollar invested.

Banker's acceptance. A money market asset consisting of an order to a bank by a customer to pay a sum of money at a future date.

Basis. The difference between the futures price and the spot price.

Basis risk. Risk attributable to uncertain movements in the spread between a futures price and a spot price.

Benchmark error. Use of an inappropriate proxy for the true market portfolio.

Beta. The measure of the systematic risk of a security. The tendency of a security's returns to respond to swings in the broad market.

Bid price. The price at which a dealer is willing to purchase a security.

Bid-asked spread. The difference between a dealer's bid and asked price.

Binomial model. An option valuation model predicated on the assumption that stock prices can move to only two values over any short time period.

Black-Scholes formula. An equation to value a call option that uses the stock price, the exercise price, the risk-free interest rate, the time to maturity, and the standard deviation of the stock return.

Block house. Brokerage firms that help to find potential buyers or sellers of large block trades.

Block sale. A transaction of more than 10,000 shares of stock.

Block transactions. Large transactions in which at least 10,000 shares of stock are bought or sold. Brokers or "block houses" often search directly for other large traders rather than bringing the trade to the stock exchange.

Bogey. The return an investment manager is compared to for performance evaluation.

Bond. A security issued by a borrower that obligates the issuer to make specified payments to the holder over a specific period. A *coupon bond* obligates the issuer to make interest payments called coupon payments over the life of the bond, then to repay the *face value* at maturity.

Bond equivalent yield. Bond yield calculated on an annual percentage rate method. Differs from effective annual yield.

Book value. An accounting measure describing the net worth of common equity according to a firm's balance sheet.

Brokered market. A market where an intermediary (a broker) offers search services to buyers and sellers.

Budget deficit. The amount by which government spending exceeds government revenues.

Bull CD, bear CD. A *bull CD* pays its holder a specified percentage of the increase in return on a specified market index while guaranteeing a minimum rate of return. A *bear CD* pays the holder a fraction of any fall in a given market index.

Bullish, bearish. Words used to describe investor attitudes. *Bullish* means optimistic; *bearish* means pessimistic. Also used in bull market and bear market.

Bundling, unbundling. A trend allowing creation of securities either by combining primitive and derivative securities into one composite hybrid or by separating returns on an asset into classes.

Business cycle. Repetitive cycles of recession and recovery.

Call option. The right to buy an asset at a specified exercise price on or before a specified expiration date.

Call protection. An initial period during which a callable bond may not be called.

Callable bond. A bond that the issuer may repurchase at a given price in some specified period.

Capital allocation decision. Allocation of invested funds between risk-free assets versus the risky portfolio.

Capital allocation line (CAL). A graph showing all feasible risk-return combinations of a risky and risk-free asset.

Capital gains. The amount by which the sale price of a security exceeds the purchase price.

Capital market line (CML). A capital allocation line provided by the market index portfolio.

Capital markets. Includes longer-term, relatively riskier securities.

Cash delivery. The provision of some futures contracts that requires not delivery of the underlying assets (as in agricultural futures) but settlement according to the cash value of the asset.

Cash equivalents. Short-term money-market securities.

Cash flow matching. A form of immunization, matching cash flows from a bond portfolio with an obligation.

Cash/bond selection. Asset allocation in which the choice is between short-term cash equivalents and longer-term bonds.

Certainty equivalent. The certain return providing the same utility as a risky portfolio.

Certificate of deposit. A bank time deposit.

Clearinghouse. Established by exchanges to facilitate transfer of securities resulting from trades. For options and futures contracts, the clearinghouse may interpose itself as a middleman between two traders.

Closed-end (mutual) fund. A fund whose shares are traded through brokers at market prices; the fund will not redeem shares at their net asset value. The market price of the fund can differ from the net asset value.

Collateral. A specific asset pledged against possible default on a bond. *Mortgage* bonds are backed by claims on property. *Collateral trust bonds* are backed by claims on other securities. *Equipment obligation bonds* are backed by claims on equipment.

Collateralized mortgage obligation (CMO). A mortgage pass-through security that partitions cash flows from underlying mortgages into classes called *tranches,* that receive principal payments according to stipulated rules.

Commercial paper. Short-term unsecured debt issued by large corporations.

Commission broker. A broker on the floor of the exchange who executes orders for other members.

Common stock. Equities, or equity securities, issued as ownership shares in a publicly held corporation. Shareholders have voting rights and may receive dividends based on their proportionate ownership.

Comparison universe. The collection of money managers of similar investment style used for assessing relative performance of a portfolio manager.

Complete portfolio. The entire portfolio, including risky and risk-free assets.

Constant growth model. A form of the dividend discount model that assumes dividends will grow at a constant rate.

Contango theory. Holds that the futures price must exceed the expected future spot price.

Contingent claim. Claim whose value is directly dependent on or is contingent on the value of some underlying assets.

Contingent immunization. A mixed passive-active strategy that immunizes a portfolio if necessary to guarantee a minimum acceptable return but otherwise allows active management.

Convergence property. The convergence of futures prices and spot prices at the maturity of the futures contract.

Convertible bond. A bond with an option allowing the bondholder to exchange the bond for a specified number of shares of common stock in the firm. A *conversion ratio* specifies the number of shares. The *market conversion price* is the current value of the shares for which the bond may be exchanged. The *conversion premium* is the excess of the bond's value over the conversion price.

Corporate bonds. Long-term debt issued by private corporations typically paying semiannual coupons and returning the face value of the bond at maturity.

Correlation coefficient. A statistic in which the covariance is scaled to a value between minus one (perfect negative correlation) and plus one (perfect positive correlation).

Cost-of-carry relationship. See spot-futures parity theorem.

Country selection. A type of active international management that measures the contribution to performance attributable to investing in the better-performing stock markets of the world.

Coupon rate. A bond's interest payments per dollar of par value.

Covariance. A measure of the degree to which returns on two risky assets move in tandem. A positive covariance means that asset returns move together. A negative covariance means they vary inversely.

Covered call. A combination of selling a call on a stock together with buying the stock.

Covered interest arbitrage relationship. See interest rate parity theorem.

Credit enhancement. Purchase of the financial guarantee of a large insurance company to raise funds.

Cross hedge. Hedging a position in one asset using futures on another commodity.

Cross holdings. One corporation holds shares in another firm.

Cumulative abnormal return. See abnormal returns.

Currency selection. Asset allocation in which the investor chooses among investments denominated in different currencies.

Current account. The difference between imports and exports, including merchandise, services, and transfers such as foreign aid.

Current ratio. A ratio representing the ability of the firm to pay off its current liabilities by liquidating current assets (current assets/current liabilities).

Current yield. A bond's annual coupon payment divided by its price. Differs from yield to maturity.

Day order. A buy order or a sell order expiring at the close of the trading day.

Days' receivables. See average collection period.

Dealer market. A market where traders specializing in particular commodities buy and sell assets for their own accounts. The OTC market is an example.

Debenture or unsecured bond. A bond not backed by specific collateral.

Dedication strategy. Refers to multiperiod cash flow matching.

Default premium. A differential in promised yield that compensates the investor for the risk inherent in purchasing a corporate bond that entails some risk of default.

Deferred-annuities. Tax-advantaged life insurance product. Deferred annuities offer deferral of taxes with the option of withdrawing one's funds in the form of a life annuity.

Defined-benefit plans. Pension plans in which retirement benefits are set according to a fixed formula.

Defined contribution plans. Pension plans in which the employer is committed to making contributions according to a fixed formula.

Delta (of option). See hedge ratio.

Delta neutral. The value of the portfolio is not affected by changes in the value of the asset on which the options are written.

Derivative asset/contingent claim. Securities providing payoffs that depend on or are contingent on the values of other assets such as commodity prices, bond and stock prices, or market index values. Examples are futures and options.

Derivative security. See primitive security.

Demand shock. An event that affects the demand for goods and services in the economy.

Detachable warrant. A warrant entitles the holder to buy a given number of shares of stock at a stipulated price. A detachable warrant is one that may be sold separately from the package it may have originally been issued with (usually a bond).

Direct search market. Buyers and sellers seek each other directly and transact directly.

Discount function. The discounted value of $1 as a function of time until payment.

Discounted dividend model (DDM). A formula to estimate the intrinsic value of a firm by figuring the present value of all expected future dividends.

Discretionary account. An account of a customer who gives a broker the authority to make buy and sell decisions on the customer's behalf.

Diversifiable risk. Risk attributable to firm-specific risk, or nonmarket risk. *Nondiversifiable* risk refers to systematic or market risk.

Diversification. Spreading a portfolio over many investments to avoid excessive exposure to any one source of risk.

Dividend payout ratio. Percentage of earnings paid out as dividends.

Dollar-weighted return. The internal rate of return on an investment.

Doubling option. A sinking fund provision that may allow repurchase of twice the required number of bonds at the sinking fund call price.

Dow theory. A technique that attempts to discern long- and short-term trends in stock market prices.

Dual funds. Funds in which income and capital shares on a portfolio of stocks are sold separately.

Duration. A measure of the average life of a bond, defined as the weighted average of the times until each payment is made, with weights proportional to the present value of the payment.

Dynamic hedging. Constant updating of hedge positions as market conditions change.

EAFE index. The European, Australian, Far East index, computed by Morgan Stanley, is a widely used index of non-U.S. stocks.

Earnings retention ratio. Plowback ratio.

Earnings yield. The ratio of earnings to price, E/P.

Economic earnings. The real flow of cash that a firm could pay out forever in the absence of any change in the firm's productive capacity.

Effective annual yield. Annualized interest rate on a security computed using compound interest techniques.

Efficient diversification. The organizing principle of modern portfolio theory, which maintains that any risk-averse investor will search for the highest expected return for any level of portfolio risk.

Efficient frontier. Graph representing a set of portfolios that maximize expected return at each level of portfolio risk.

Efficient market hypothesis. The prices of securities fully reflect available information. Investors buying securities in an efficient market should expect to obtain an equilibrium rate of return. Weak-form EMH asserts that stock prices already reflect all information contained in the history of past prices. The semistrong-form hypothesis asserts that stock prices already reflect all publicly available information. The strong-form hypothesis asserts that stock prices reflect all relevant information including insider information.

Elasticity (of an option). Percentage change in the value of an option accompanying a 1 percent change in the value of a stock.

Endowment funds. Organizations chartered to invest money for specific purposes.

Equivalent taxable yield. The pretax yield on a taxable bond providing an after-tax yield equal to the rate on a tax-exempt municipal bond.

Eurodollars. Dollar-denominated deposits at foreign banks or foreign branches of American banks.

European, Australian, Far East (EAFE) index. A widely used index of non-U.S. stocks computed by Morgan Stanley.

European option. A European option can be exercised only on the expiration date. Compare with an American option, which can be exercised before, up to, and including its expiration date.

Event study. Research methodology designed to measure the impact of an event of interest on stock returns.

Excess return. Rate of return in excess of the risk-free rate.

Exchange rate. Price of a unit of one country's currency in terms of another country's currency.

Exchange rate risk. The uncertainty in asset returns due to movements in the exchange rates between the dollar and foreign currencies.

Exchanges. National or regional auction markets providing a facility for members to trade securities. A seat is a membership on an exchange.

Exercise or strike price. Price set for calling (buying) an asset or putting (selling) an asset.

Expectations hypothesis (of interest rates). Theory that forward interest rates are unbiased estimates of expected future interest rates.

Expected return. The probability-weighted average of the possible outcomes.

Expected return–beta relationship. Implication of the CAPM that security risk premiums (expected excess returns) will be proportional to beta.

Face value. The maturity value of a bond.

Factor model. A way of decomposing the factors that influence a security's rate of return into common and firm-specific influences.

Factor portfolio. A well-diversified portfolio constructed to have a beta of 1.0 on one factor and a beta of zero on any other factor.

Fair game. An investment prospect that has a zero risk premium.

FIFO. The first-in first-out accounting method of inventory valuation.

Filter rule. A technical analysis technique stated as a rule for buying or selling stock according to past price movements.

Financial assets. Financial assets such as stocks and bonds are claims to the income generated by real assets or claims on income from the government.

Financial intermediary. An institution such as a bank, mutual fund, investment company, or insurance company that serves to connect the household and business sectors so households can invest and businesses can finance production.

Firm-specific risk. See diversifiable risk.

First-pass regression. A time series regression to estimate the betas of securities or portfolios.

Fiscal policy. The use of government spending and taxing for the specific purpose of stabilizing the economy.

Fixed annuities. Annuity contracts in which the insurance company pays a fixed dollar amount of money per period.

Fixed-charge coverage ratio. Ratio of earnings to all fixed cash obligations, including lease payments and sinking fund payments.

Fixed-income security. A security such as a bond that pays a specified cash flow over a specific period.

Flight to quality. Describes the tendency of investors to require larger default premiums on investments under uncertain economic conditions.

Floating-rate bond. A bond whose interest rate is reset periodically according to a specified market rate.

Floor broker. A member of the exchange who can execute orders for commission brokers.

Flower bond. Special Treasury bond (no longer issued) that may be used to settle federal estate taxes at par value under certain conditions.

Forced conversion. Use of a firm's call option on a callable convertible bond when the firm knows that bondholders will exercise their option to convert.

Foreign exchange market. An informal network of banks and brokers that allows customers to enter forward contracts to purchase or sell currencies in the future at a rate of exchange agreed upon now.

Foreign exchange swap. An agreement to exchange stipulated amounts of one currency for another at one or more future dates.

Forward contract. An agreement calling for future delivery of an asset at an agreed-upon price. Also see futures contract.

Forward interest rate. Rate of interest for a future period that would equate the total return of a long-term bond with that of a strategy of rolling over shorter-term bonds. The forward rate is inferred from the term structure.

Fourth market. Direct trading in exchange-listed securities between one investor and another without the benefit of a broker.

Fully diluted earnings per share. Earnings per share expressed as if all outstanding convertible securities and warrants have been exercised.

Fundamental analysis. Research to predict stock value that focuses on such determinants as earnings and dividends prospects, expectations for future interest rates, and risk evaluation of the firm.

Futures contract. Obliges traders to purchase or sell an asset at an agreed-upon price on a specified future date. The long position is held by the trader who commits to purchase. The short position is held by the trader who commits to sell. Futures differ from forward contracts in their standardization, exchange trading, margin requirements, and daily settling (marking to market).

Futures option. The right to enter a specified futures contract at a futures price equal to the stipulated exercise price.

Futures price. The price at which a futures trader commits to make or take delivery of the underlying asset.

Geometric average. The nth root of the product of n numbers. It is used to measure the compound rate of return over time.

Globalization. Tendency toward a worldwide investment environment, and the integration of national capital markets.

Gross domestic product (GDP). The market value of goods and services produced over time including the income of foreign corporations and foreign residents working in the United States, but excluding the income of U.S. residents and corporations overseas.

Guaranteed insurance contract. A contract promising a stated nominal rate of interest over some specific time period, usually several years.

Hedge ratio (for an option). The number of stocks required to hedge against the price risk of holding one option. Also called the option's delta.

Hedging. Investing in an asset to reduce the overall risk of a portfolio.

Hedging demands. Demands for securities to hedge particular sources of consumption risk, beyond the usual mean-variance diversification motivation.

Holding period return. The rate of return over a given period.

Homogenous expectations. The assumption that all investors use the same expected returns and covariance matrix of security returns as inputs in security analysis.

Horizon analysis. Interest rate forecasting that uses a forecast yield curve to predict bond prices.

Immunization. A strategy that matches durations of assets and liabilities so as to make net worth unaffected by interest rate movements.

Implied volatility. The standard deviation of stock returns that is consistent with an option's market value.

In the money. In the money describes an option whose exercise would produce profits. Out of the money describes an option where exercise would not be profitable.

Income beneficiary. One who receives income from a trust.

Income fund. A mutual fund providing for liberal current income from investments.

Income statement. A financial statement showing a firm's revenues and expenses during a specified period.

Indenture. The document defining the contract between the bond issuer and the bondholder.

Index arbitrage. An investment strategy that exploits divergences between actual futures prices and their theoretically correct parity values to make a profit.

Index fund. A mutual fund holding shares in proportion to their representation in a market index such as the S&P 500.

Index model. A model of stock returns using a market index such as the S&P 500 to represent common or systematic risk factors.

Index option. A call or put option based on a stock market index.

Indifference curve. A curve connecting all portfolios with the same utility according to their means and standard deviations.

Inflation. The rate at which the general level of prices for goods and services is rising.

Initial public offering. Stock issued to the public for the first time by a formerly privately owned company.

Input list. List of parameters such as expected returns, variances, and covariances necessary to determine the optimal risky portfolio.

Inside information. Nonpublic knowledge about a corporation possessed by corporate officers, major owners, or other individuals with privileged access to information about a firm.

Insider trading. Trading by officers, directors, major stockholders, or others who hold private inside information allowing them to benefit from buying or selling stock.

Insurance principle. The law of averages. The average outcome for many independent trials of an experiment will approach the expected value of the experiment.

Interest coverage ratio, or times interest earned. A financial leverage measure (EBIT divided by interest expense).

Interest rate. The number of dollars earned per dollar invested per period.

Interest rate parity theorem. The spot-futures exchange rate relationship that prevails in well-functioning markets.

Interest rate swaps. A method to manage interest rate risk where parties trade the cash flows corresponding to different securities without actually exchanging securities directly.

Intermarket spread swap. Switching from one segment of the bond market to another (from Treasuries to corporates, for example).

Intrinsic value (of a firm). The present value of a firm's expected future net cash flows discounted by the required rate of return.

Intrinsic value of an option. Stock price minus exercise price, or the profit that could be attained by immediate exercise of an in-the-money option.

Investment bankers. Firms specializing in the sale of new securities to the public, typically by underwriting the issue.

Investment company. Firm managing funds for investors. An investment company may manage several mutual funds.

Investment portfolio. Set of securities chosen by an investor.

Investment-grade bond. Bond rated BBB and above or Baa and above. Lower-rated bonds are classified as speculative-grade or junk bonds.

Jensen's measure. The alpha of an investment.

Junk bond. See speculative-grade bond.

Law of one price. The rule stipulating that equivalent securities or bundles of securities must sell at equal prices to preclude arbitrage opportunities.

Leading economic indicators. Economic series that tend to risk or fall in advance of the rest of the economy.

Leakage. Release of information to some persons before official public announcement.

Leverage ratio. Ratio of debt to total capitalization of a firm.

LIFO. The last-in first-out accounting method of valuing inventories.

Limit order. An order specifying a price at which an investor is willing to buy or sell a security.

Limited liability. The fact that shareholders have no personal liability to the creditors of the corporation in the event of bankruptcy.

Liquidation value. Net amount that could be realized by selling the assets of a firm after paying the debt.

Liquidity. Liquidity refers to the speed and ease with which an asset can be converted to cash.

Liquidity preference theory. Theory that the forward rate exceeds expected future interest rates.

Liquidity premium. Forward rate minus expected future short interest rate.

Load fund. A mutual fund with a sales commission, or load.

London Interbank Offered Rate (LIBOR). Rate that most creditworthy banks charge one another for large loans of Eurodollars in the London market.

Long hedge. Protecting the future cost of a purchase by taking a long futures position to protect against changes in the price of the asset.

Maintenance, or variation, margin. An established value below which a trader's margin cannot fall. Reaching the maintenance margin triggers a margin call.

Margin. Describes securities purchased with money borrowed from a broker. Current maximum margin is 50 percent.

Market capitalization rate. The market-consensus estimate of the appropriate discount rate for a firm's cash flows.

Market model. Another version of the index model that breaks down return uncertainty into systematic and nonsystematic components.

Market or systematic risk, firm-specific risk. Market risk is risk attributable to common macroeconomic factors. Firm-specific risk reflects risk peculiar to an individual firm that is independent of market risk.

Market order. A buy or sell order to be executed immediately at current market prices.

Market portfolio. The portfolio for which each security is held in proportion to its market value.

Market price of risk. A measure of the extra return, or risk premium, that investors demand to bear risk. The reward-to-risk ratio of the market portfolio.

Market segmentation or preferred habitat theory. The theory that long- and short-maturity bonds are traded in essentially distinct or segmented markets and that prices in one market do not affect those in the other.

Market timer. An investor who speculates on broad market moves rather than on specific securities.

Market timing. Asset allocation in which the investment in the market is increased if one forecasts that the market will outperform T-bills.

Market value–weighted index. An index of a group of securities computed by calculating a weighted average of the returns of each security in the index, with weights proportional to outstanding market value.

Market-book ratio. Market price of a share divided by book value per share.

Marking to market. Describes the daily settlement of obligations on futures positions.

Mean-variance analysis. Evaluation of risky prospects based on the expected value and variance of possible outcomes.

Mean-variance criterion. The selection of portfolios based on the means and variances of their returns. The choice of the higher expected return portfolio for a given level of variance or the lower variance portfolio for a given expected return.

Measurement error. Errors in measuring an explanatory variable in a regression that leads to biases in estimated parameters.

Membership or seat on an exchange. A limited number of exchange positions that enable the holder to trade for the holder's own accounts and charge clients for the execution of trades for their accounts.

Minimum-variance frontier. Graph of the lowest possible portfolio variance that is attainable for a given portfolio expected return.

Minimum-variance portfolio. The portfolio of risky assets with lowest variance.

Modern portfolio theory (MPT). Principles underlying analysis and evaluation of rational portfolio choices based on risk-return trade-offs and efficient diversification.

Monetary policy. Actions taken by the Board of Governors of the Federal Reserve System to influence the money supply or interest rates.

Money market. Includes short-term, highly liquid, and relatively low-risk debt instruments.

Mortality tables. Tables of probability that individuals of various ages will die within a year.

Mortgage-backed security. Ownership claim in a pool of mortgages or an obligation that is secured by such a pool. Also called a *pass-through,* because payments are passed along from the mortgage originator to the purchaser of the mortgage-backed security.

Multifactor CAPM. Generalization of the basic CAPM that accounts for extra-market hedging demands.

Municipal bonds. Tax-exempt bonds issued by state and local governments, generally to finance capital improvement projects. General obligation bonds are backed by the general taxing power of the issuer. Revenue bonds are backed by the proceeds from the project or agency they are issued to finance.

Mutual fund. A firm pooling and managing funds of investors.

Mutual fund theorem. A result associated with the CAPM, asserting that investors will choose to invest their entire risky portfolio in a market-index mutual fund.

Naked option writing. Writing an option without an offsetting stock position.

Nasdaq. The automated quotation system for the OTC market, showing current bid-asked prices for thousands of stocks.

Neglected-firm effect. That investments in stock of less well-known firms have generated abnormal returns.

Nominal interest rate. The interest rate in terms of nominal (not adjusted for purchasing power) dollars.

Nonsystematic risk. Nonmarket or firm-specific risk factors that can be eliminated by diversification. Also called unique risk or diversifiable risk. Systematic risk refers to risk factors common to the entire economy.

Normal backwardation theory. Holds that the futures price will be bid down to a level below the expected spot price.

Open (good-till-canceled) order. A buy or sell order remaining in force for up to six months unless canceled.

Open interest. The number of futures contracts outstanding.

Open-end (mutual) fund. A fund that issues or redeems its own shares at their net asset value (NAV).

Optimal risky portfolio. An investor's best combination of risky assets to be mixed with safe assets to form the complete portfolio.

Option elasticity. The percentage increase in an option's value given a 1 percent change in the value of the underlying security.

Original issue discount bond. A bond issued with a low coupon rate that sells at a discount from par value.

Out of the money. Out of the money describes an option where exercise would not be profitable. In the money describes an option where exercise would produce profits.

Over-the-counter market. An informal network of brokers and dealers who negotiate sales of securities (not a formal exchange).

Par value. The face value of the bond.

Pass-through security. Pools of loans (such as home mortgage loans) sold in one package. Owners of pass-throughs receive all principal and interest payments made by the borrowers.

Passive investment strategy. See passive management.

Passive management. Buying a well-diversified portfolio to represent a broad-based market index without attempting to search out mispriced securities.

Passive portfolio. A market index portfolio.

Passive strategy. See passive management.

P/E effect. That portfolios of low P/E stocks have exhibited higher average risk-adjusted returns than high P/E stocks.

Peak. The transition from the end of an expansion to the start of a contraction.

Personal trust. An interest in an asset held by a trustee for the benefit of another person.

Plowback ratio. The proportion of the firm's earnings that is reinvested in the business (and not paid out as dividends). The plowback ratio equals 1 minus the dividend payout ratio.

Political risk. Possibility of the expropriation of assets, changes in tax policy, restrictions on the exchange of foreign currency for domestic currency, or other changes in the business climate of a country.

Portfolio insurance. The practice of using options or dynamic hedge strategies to provide protection against investment losses while maintaining upside potential.

Portfolio management. Process of combining securities in a portfolio tailored to the investor's preferences and needs, monitoring that portfolio, and evaluating its performance.

Portfolio opportunity set. The expected return– standard deviation pairs of all portfolios that can be constructed from a given set of assets.

Preferred habitat theory. Holds that investors prefer specific maturity ranges but can be induced to switch if risk premiums are sufficient.

Preferred stock. Nonvoting shares in a corporation, paying a fixed or variable stream of dividends.

Premium. The purchase price of an option.

Price value of a basis point. The change in the value of a fixed-income asset resulting from a one basis point change in the asset's yield to maturity.

Price-earnings multiple. See price-earnings ratio.

Price-earnings ratio. The ratio of a stock's price to its earnings per share. Also referred to as the P/E multiple.

Primary market. New issues of securities are offered to the public here.

Primitive security, derivative security. A *primitive security* is an instrument such as a stock or bond for which payments depend only on the financial status of its issuer. A *derivative security* is created from the set of primitive securities to yield returns that depend on factors beyond the characteristics of the issuer and that may be related to prices of other assets.

Principal. The outstanding balance on a loan.

Profit margin. See return on sales.

Program trading. Coordinated buy orders and sell orders of entire portfolios, usually with the aid of computers, often to achieve index arbitrage objectives.

Prospectus. A final and approved registration statement including the price at which the security issue is offered.

Protective covenant. A provision specifying requirements of collateral, sinking fund, dividend policy, etc., designed to protect the interests of bondholders.

Protective put. Purchase of stock combined with a put option that guarantees minimum proceeds equal to the put's exercise price.

Proxy. An instrument empowering an agent to vote in the name of the shareholder.

Public offering, private placement. A *public offering* consists of bonds sold in the primary market to the general public; a *private placement* is sold directly to a limited number of institutional investors.

Pure yield pickup swap. Moving to higher yield bonds.

Put bond. A bond that the holder may choose either to exchange for par value at some date or to extend for a given number of years.

Put option. The right to sell an asset at a specified exercise price on or before a specified expiration date.

Put-call parity theorem. An equation representing the proper relationship between put and call prices. Violation of parity allows arbitrage opportunities.

Quick ratio. A measure of liquidity similar to the current ratio except for exclusion of inventories (cash plus receivables divided by current liabilities).

Random walk. Describes the notion that stock price changes are random and unpredictable.

Rate anticipation swap. A switch made in response to forecasts of interest rates.

Real assets, financial assets. *Real assets* are land, buildings, and equipment that are used to produce goods and services. *Financial assets* are claims such as securities to the income generated by real assets.

Real interest rate. The excess of the interest rate over the inflation rate. The growth rate of purchasing power derived from an investment.

Realized compound yield. Yield assuming that coupon payments are invested at the going market interest rate at the time of their receipt and rolled over until the bond matures.

Rebalancing. Realigning the proportions of assets in a portfolio as needed.

Registered bond. A bond whose issuer records ownership and interest payments. Differs from a bearer bond, which is traded without record of ownership and whose possession is its only evidence of ownership.

Registered trader. A member of the exchange who executes frequent trades for his or her own account.

Registration statement. Required to be filed with the SEC to describe the issue of a new security.

Regression equation. An equation that describes the average relationship between a dependent variable and a set of explanatory variables.

REIT. Real estate investment trust, which is similar to a closed-end mutual fund. REITs invest in real estate or loans secured by real estate and issue shares in such investments.

Remainderman. One who receives the principal of a trust when it is dissolved.

Replacement cost. Cost to replace a firm's assets. "Reproduction" cost.

Repurchase agreements (repos). Short-term, often overnight, sales of government securities with an agreement to repurchase the securities at a slightly higher price. A *reverse repo* is a purchase with an agreement to resell at a specified price on a future date.

Residual claim. Refers to the fact that shareholders are at the bottom of the list of claimants to assets of a corporation in the event of failure or bankruptcy.

Residuals. Parts of stock returns not explained by the explanatory variable (the market-index return). They measure the impact of firm-specific events during a particular period.

Resistance level. A price level above which it is supposedly difficult for a stock or stock index to rise.

Return on assets (ROA). A profitability ratio; earnings before interest and taxes divided by total assets.

Return on equity (ROE). An accounting ratio of net profits divided by equity.

Return on sales (ROS), or profit margin. The ratio of operating profits per dollar of sales (EBIT divided by sales).

Reversing trade. Entering the opposite side of a currently held futures position to close out the position.

Reward-to-volatility ratio. Ratio of excess return to portfolio standard deviation.

Riding the yield curve. Buying long-term bonds in anticipation of capital gains as yields fall with the declining maturity of the bonds.

Risk arbitrage. Speculation on perceived mispriced securities, usually in connection with merger and acquisition targets.

Risk-averse, risk-neutral, risk lover. A *risk-averse* investor will consider risky portfolios only if they provide compensation for risk via a risk premium. A *risk-neutral* investor finds the level of risk irrelevant and considers only the expected return of risk prospects. A *risk lover* is willing to accept lower expected returns on prospects with higher amounts of risk.

Risk-free asset. An asset with a certain rate of return; often taken to be short-term T-bills.

Risk-free rate. The interest rate that can be earned with certainty.

Risk lover. See risk-averse.

Risk neutral. See risk-averse.

Risk premium. An expected return in excess of that on risk-free securities. The premium provides compensation for the risk of an investment.

Risk-return trade-off. If an investor is willing to take on risk, there is the reward of higher expected returns.

Risky asset. An asset with an uncertain rate of return.

Seasoned new issue. Stock issued by companies that already have stock on the market.

Second-pass regression. A cross-sectional regression of portfolio returns on betas. The estimated slope is the measurement of the reward for bearing systematic risk during the period.

Secondary market. Already-existing securities are bought and sold on the exchanges or in the OTC market.

Securitization. Pooling loans for various purposes into standardized securities backed by those loans, which can then be traded like any other security.

Security market line. Graphical representation of the expected return–beta relationship of the CAPM.

Security analysis. Determining correct value of a security in the marketplace.

Security characteristic line. A plot of the excess return on a security over the risk-free rate as a function of the excess return on the market.

Security selection. See security selection decision.

Security selection decision. Choosing the particular securities to include in a portfolio.

Semistrong-form EMH. See efficient market hypothesis.

Separation property. The property that portfolio choice can be separated into two independent tasks: (1) determination of the optimal risky portfolio, which is a purely technical problem, and (2) the personal choice of the best mix of the risky portfolio and the risk-free asset.

Serial bond issue. An issue of bonds with staggered maturity dates that spreads out the principal repayment burden over time.

Sharpe's measure. Reward-to-volatility ratio; ratio of portfolio excess return to standard deviation.

Shelf registration. Advance registration of securities with the SEC for sale up to two years following initial registration.

Short interest rate. A one-period interest rate.

Short position or hedge. Protecting the value of an asset held by taking a short position in a futures contract.

Short sale. The sale of shares not owned by the investor but borrowed through a broker and later repurchased to replace the loan. Profit is earned if the initial sale is at a higher price than the repurchase price.

Simple prospect. An investment opportunity where a certain initial wealth is placed at risk and only two outcomes are possible.

Single-country funds. Mutual funds that invest in securities of only one country.

Single-factor model. A model of security returns that acknowledges only one common factor. See factor model.

Single index model. A model of stock returns that decomposes influences on returns into a systematic factor, as measured by the return on a broad market index, and firm-specific factors.

Sinking fund. A procedure that allows for the repayment of principal at maturity by calling for the bond issuer to repurchase some proportion of the outstanding bonds either in the open market or at a special call price associated with the sinking fund provision.

Skip-day settlement. A convention for calculating yield that assumes a T-bill sale is not settled until two days after quotation of the T-bill price.

Small-firm effect. That investments in stocks of small firms appear to have earned abnormal returns.

Soft dollars. The value of research services that brokerage houses supply to investment managers "free of charge" in exchange for the investment managers' business.

Specialist. A trader who makes a market in the shares of one or more firms and who maintains a "fair and orderly market" by dealing personally in the stock.

Speculation. Undertaking a risky investment with the objective of earning a greater profit than an investment in a risk-free alternative (a risk premium).

Speculative-grade bond. Bond rated Ba or lower by Moody's, or BB or lower by Standard & Poor's, or an unrated bond.

Spot rate. The current interest rate appropriate for discounting a cash flow of some given maturity.

Spot-futures parity theorem, or cost-of-carry relationship. Describes the theoretically correct relationship between spot and futures prices. Violation of the parity relationship gives rise to arbitrage opportunities.

Spread (futures). Taking a long position in a futures contract of one maturity and a short position in a contract of different maturity, both on the same commodity.

Spread (options). A combination of two or more call options or put options on the same stock with differing exercise prices or times to expiration. A money spread refers to a spread with different exercise price; a time spread refers to differing expiration date.

Squeeze. The possibility that enough long positions hold their contracts to maturity that supplies of the commodity are not adequate to cover all contracts. A *short squeeze* describes the reverse: short positions threaten to deliver an expensive-to-store commodity.

Standard deviation. Square root of the variance.

Statement of cash flows. A financial statement showing a firm's cash receipts and cash payments during a specified period.

Stock exchanges. Secondary markets where already-issued securities are bought and sold by members.

Stock selection. An active portfolio management technique that focuses on advantageous selection of particular stocks rather than on broad asset allocation choices.

Stock split. Issue by a corporation of a given number of shares in exchange for the current number of shares held by stockholders. Splits may go in either direction, either increasing or decreasing the number of shares outstanding. A *reverse split* decreases the number outstanding.

Stop-loss order. A sell order to be executed if the price of the stock falls below a stipulated level.

Straddle. A combination of buying both a call and a put on the same asset, each with the same exercise price and expiration date. The purpose is to profit from expected volatility.

Straight bond. A bond with no option features such as callability or convertibility.

Street name. Describes securities held by a broker on behalf of a client but registered in the name of the firm.

Strike price. See exercise price.

Strip, strap. Variants of a straddle. A *strip* is two puts and one call on a stock; a *strap* is two calls and one put, both with the same exercise price and expiration date.

Stripped of coupons. Describes the practice of some investment banks that sell "synthetic" zero coupon bonds by marketing the rights to a single payment backed by a coupon-paying Treasury bond.

Strong-form EMH. See efficient market hypothesis.

Subordination clause. A provision in a bond indenture that restricts the issuer's future borrowing by subordinating the new leaders' claims on the firm to those of the existing bond holders. Claims of *subordinated* or *junior* debtholders are not paid until the prior debt is paid.

Substitution swap. Exchange of one bond for a bond with similar attributes but more attractively priced.

Supply shock. An event that influences production capacity and costs in the economy.

Support level. A price level below which it is supposedly difficult for a stock or stock index to fall.

Swaption. An option on a swap.

Systematic risk. Risk factors common to the whole economy, for example, nondiversifiable risk; see market risk.

Tax anticipation notes. Short-term municipal debt to raise funds to pay for expenses before actual collection of taxes.

Tax swap. Swapping two similar bonds to receive a tax benefit.

Tax deferral option. The feature of the U.S. Internal Revenue Code that the capital gains tax on an asset is payable only when the gain is realized by selling the asset.

Tax-deferred retirement plans. Employer-sponsored and other plans that allow contributions and earnings to be made and accumulate tax free until they are paid out as benefits.

Tax-timing option. Describes the investor's ability to shift the realization of investment gains or losses and their tax implications from one period to another.

Technical analysis. Research to identify mispriced securities that focuses on recurrent and predictable stock price patterns and on proxies for buy or sell pressure in the market.

Tender offer. An offer from an outside investor to shareholders of a company to purchase their shares at a stipulated price, usually substantially above the market price, so that the investor may amass enough shares to obtain control of the company.

Term insurance. Provides a death benefit only, no build-up of cash value.

Term premiums. Excess of the yields to maturity on long-term bonds over those of short-term bonds.

Term structure of interest rates. The pattern of interest rates appropriate for discounting cash flows of various maturities.

Third market. Trading of exchange-listed securities on the OTC market.

Time value (of an option). The part of the value of an option that is due to its positive time to expiration. Not to be confused with present value or the time value of money.

Time-weighted return. An average of the period-by-period holding-period returns of an investment.

Times interest earned. See interest coverage ratio.

Tobin's *q*. Ratio of market value of the firm to replacement cost.

Tranche. See collateralized mortgage obligation.

Treasury bill. Short-term, highly liquid government securities issued at a discount from the face value and returning the face amount at maturity.

Treasury bond or note. Debt obligations of the federal government that make semiannual coupon payments and are issued at or near par value.

Treynor's measure. Ratio of excess return to beta.

Triple-witching hour. The four times a year that the S&P 500 futures contract expires at the same time as the S&P 100 index option contract and option contracts on individual stocks.

Trough. The transition point between recession and recovery.

Unbundling. See bundling.

Underwriting, underwriting syndicate. Underwriters (investment bankers) purchase securities from the issuing company and resell them. Usually a syndicate of investment bankers is organized behind a lead firm.

Unemployment rate. The ratio of the number of people classified as unemployed to the total labor force.

Unique risk. See diversifiable risk.

Unit investment trust. Money invested in a portfolio whose composition is fixed for the life of the fund. Shares in a unit trust are called redeemable trust certificates, and they are sold at a premium above net asset value.

Universal life policy. An insurance policy that allows for a varying death benefit and premium level over the term of the policy, with an interest rate on the cash value that changes with market interest rates.

Uptick, or zero-plus tick. A trade resulting in a positive change in a stock price, or a trade at a constant price following a preceding price increase.

Utility. The measure of the welfare or satisfaction of an investor.

Utility value. The welfare a given investor assigns to an investment with a particular return and risk.

Variable annuities. Annuity contracts in which the insurance company pays a periodic amount linked to the investment performance of an underlying portfolio.

Variable life policy. An insurance policy that provides a fixed death benefit plus a cash value that can be invested in a variety of funds from which the policyholder can choose.

Variance. A measure of the dispersion of a random variable. Equals the expected value of the squared deviation from the mean.

Variation margin. See maintenance margin.

Volatility risk. The risk in the value of options portfolios due to unpredictable changes in the volatility of the underlying asset.

Warrant. An option issued by the firm to purchase shares of the firm's stock.

Weak-form EMH. See efficient market hypothesis.

Weekend effect. The common recurrent negative average return from Friday to Monday in the stock market.

Well-diversified portfolio. A portfolio spread out over many securities in such a way that the weight in any security is close to zero.

Whole-life insurance policy. Provides a death benefit and a kind of savings plan that builds up cash value for possible future withdrawal.

Workout period. Realignment period of a temporary misaligned yield relationship.

World investable wealth. The part of world wealth that is traded and is therefore accessible to investors.

Writing a call. Selling a call option.

Yield curve. A graph of yield to maturity as a function of time to maturity.

Yield to maturity. A measure of the average rate of return that will be earned on a bond if held to maturity.

Zero-beta portfolio. The minimum-variance portfolio uncorrelated with a chosen efficient portfolio.

Zero coupon bond. A bond paying no coupons that sells at a discount and provides payment of face value only at maturity.

Zero-investment portfolio. A portfolio of zero net value, established by buying and shorting component securities, usually in the context of an arbitrage strategy.

Name Index

Subject Index

J

K

L

Q

R

S